HISTORY OF
THE SECOND WORLD WAR
UNITED KINGDOM MEDICAL SERIES

Editor-in-Chief:

SIR ARTHUR S. MACNALTY, K.C.B., M.A., M.D., F.R.C.P., F.R.C.S., F.S.A.

Burma; one of the leogryphs that guard the southern face of the Buddhist temple area on Mandalay Hill.

THE ARMY MEDICAL SERVICES

BY
F. A. E. CREW, F.R.S.

Campaigns

VOLUME V

BURMA

The Naval & Military Press Ltd

Published by

The Naval & Military Press Ltd
Unit 5 Riverside, Brambleside
Bellbrook Industrial Estate
Uckfield, East Sussex
TN22 1QQ England

Tel: +44 (0)1825 749494

www.naval-military-press.com
www.nmarchive.com

In reprinting in facsimile from the original, any imperfections are inevitably reproduced and the quality may fall short of modern type and cartographic standards.

EDITORIAL BOARD

Sir WELDON DALRYMPLE-CHAMPNEYS, Bart., C.B., M.A., D.M., B.Ch., F.R.C.P. } *Ministry of Health*

J. H. F. BROTHERSTON, Q.H.P., M.D., F.R.C.P. Ed., F.R.S.E.
A. K. BOWMAN, M.B., Ch.B., F.R.F.P.S. } *Department of Health for Scotland*

F. F. MAIN, M.B., Ch.B., F.R.C.P. Ed. { *Government of Northern Ireland*

Sir HAROLD HIMSWORTH, K.C.B., M.D., F.R.C.P., F.R.S.
Dame JANET VAUGHAN, D.B.E., D.M., F.R.C.P. } *Medical Research Council*

Surgeon Vice-Admiral Sir Derek STEELE-PERKINS, K.C.B., K.C.V.O., Q.H.S., F.R.C.S.(Eng.), F.R.A.C.S., D.L.O. } *Admiralty*

Major-General Sir ROBERT DREW, K.C.B., C.B.E., Q.H.P., M.B., F.R.C.P.
Major-General A. SACHS, C.B., C.B.E., Q.H.P., M.Sc., M.D., M.R.C.P. } *War Office*

Air Marshal Sir RICHARD NELSON, K.C.B., O.B.E., Q.H.P., M.D. } *Air Ministry*

Brigadier H. B. LATHAM *Cabinet Office*

Editor-in-Chief: Sir ARTHUR S. MACNALTY, K.C.B., M.A., M.D., F.R.C.P., F.R.C.S., F.S.A.

Secretary: W. FRANKLIN MELLOR

The following persons served on the Editorial Board for varying periods:

The Rt. Hon. Lord Butler of Saffron Walden, P.C.; Sir Cyril Flower, C.B., F.S.A. (*Chairmen*); Brigadier General Sir James E. Edmonds, C.B., C.M.G., D.Litt. (*Committee of Imperial Defence*); Surgeon Vice Admiral Sir Sheldon F. Dudley, K.C.B., O.B.E., M.D., F.R.C.P., F.R.C.S. Ed., F.R.S.; Surgeon Vice Admiral Sir Henry St. Clair Colson, K.C.B., C.B.E., F.R.C.P.; Surgeon Vice Admiral Sir Edward Greeson, K.B.E., C.B., M.D., Ch.B.; Surgeon Vice Admiral Sir Alexander Ingleby-MacKenzie, K.B.E., C.B., Q.H.P., B.M., B.Ch.; Surgeon Vice Admiral Sir Cyril May, K.B.E., C.B., M.C., Q.H.S., F.R.C.S.; Surgeon Vice Admiral W. R. S. Panckridge, C.B., Q.H.P. (*Admiralty*); Lt. General Sir William P. MacArthur, K.C.B., D.S.O., O.B.E., M.D., B.Ch., D.Sc., F.R.C.P.; Lt. General Sir Alexander Hood, G.B.E., K.C.B., M.D., F.R.C.P., LL.D.; Lt. General Sir Neil Cantlie, K.C.B., K.B.E., C.B., M.C., M.B., F.R.C.S.; Lt. General Sir Frederick Harris, K.B.E., C.B., M.C., Q.H.S., M.B., LL.D.; Lt. General Sir Alexander Drummond, K.B.E., C.B., Q.H.S., F.R.C.S., D.L.O.; Lt. General Sir Harold Knott,

K.C.B., O.B.E., Q.H.P., M.A., M.D., LL.D.; Major-General H. M. J. Perry, C.B., O.B.E., F.R.C.P.; Major-General L. T. Poole, C.B., D.S.O., M.C., M.B., Ch.B.; Brigadier Sir John Boyd, O.B.E., M.D., F.R.S.; Brigadier H. T. Findlay, M.B., Ch.B. (*War Office*); Air Marshal Sir Harold E. Whittingham, K.C.B., K.B.E., M.B., Ch.B., F.R.C.P., F.R.C.S., LL.D.; Air Marshal Sir Andrew Grant, K.B.E., C.B., M.B., Ch.B.; Air Marshal Sir Philip C. Livingston, K.B.E., C.B., A.F.C., F.R.C.S.; Air Marshal Sir James M. Kilpatrick, K.B.E., C.B., Q.H.P., M.B., B.Ch.; Air Marshal Sir Patrick Lee Potter, K.B.E., Q.H.S., M.D., D.T.M. & H. (*Air Ministry*); Sir Edward Mellanby, G.B.E., K.C.B., M.D., F.R.C.P., F.R.S. (*Medical Research Council*); Professor J. M. Mackintosh, M.A., M.D., F.R.C.P.; Sir Andrew Davidson, M.D., F.R.C.P. Ed., F.R.C.S. Ed.; Sir Kenneth Cowan, M.D. (*Department of Health for Scotland*); J. Boyd, C.B.E., M.D., F.R.C.P.I. (*Government of Northern Ireland*); Lt. Colonel J. S. Yule, O.B.E., Philip Allen, Esq., G. Godfrey Phillips, Esq., M. T. Flett, Esq., A. M. R. Topham, Esq., D. F. Hubback, Esq., A. B. Acheson, Esq., C.M.G., C.B.E. (*Cabinet Office*); Sir Francis R. Fraser, M.D., F.R.C.P. (*Ministry of Health*).

EDITORIAL COMMITTEE

Sir ARTHUR S. MACNALTY, K.C.B., M.A., M.D., F.R.C.P., F.R.C.S., F.S.A.
(*Chairman*)

Surgeon Captain J. L. S. COULTER, D.S.C., F.R.C.S. (Barrister-at-Law)	} *Admiralty*
Professor F. A. E. CREW, D.Sc., M.D., F.R.C.P. Ed., LL.D., F.R.S.	} *War Office*
Wing Commander S. C. REXFORD-WELCH, M.A., M.R.C.S., L.R.C.P.	} *Air Ministry*
A. K. BOWMAN, M.B., Ch.B., F.R.F.P.S.	{ *Department of Health for Scotland*
F. F. MAIN, M.B., Ch.B., F.R.C.P. Ed.	{ *Government of Northern Ireland*
F. H. K. GREEN, C.B.E., M.D., F.R.C.P.	*Medical Research Council*
A. SANDISON, O.B.E., M.D.	*Ministry of Pensions*
Sir ZACHARY COPE, B.A., M.D., M.S., F.R.C.S.	*Ministry of Health*

Secretary: W. FRANKLIN MELLOR

The following persons served on the Editorial Committee for varying periods:

Surgeon Commander J. J. Keevil, D.S.O., M.D.; Surgeon Lieutenant L. D. de Launay, M.B., B.S.; Surgeon Lieutenant Commander N. M. McArthur, M.D.; Surgeon Commander A. D. Sinclair, M.B., Ch.B. (*Admiralty*); Colonel S. Lyle Cummins, C.B., C.M.G., LL.D., M.D. (*War Office*); Wing Commander R. Oddie, M.B., B.Ch.; Wing Commander E. B. Davies, M.B., B.Ch.; Squadron Leader R. Mortimer, M.B., B.S.; Squadron Leader H. N. H. Genese, M.R.C.S., L.R.C.P. (*Air Ministry*); J. Boyd, C.B.E., M.D., F.R.C.P.I. (*Government of Northern Ireland*); Charles E. Newman, C.B.E., M.D., F.R.C.P.; N. G. Horner, M.D., F.R.C.P., F.R.C.S.; Lt. Colonel C. L. Dunn, C.I.E., I.M.S. (ret.) (*Ministry of Health*); J. Alison Glover, C.B.E., M.D., F.R.C.P. (*Ministry of Education*).

FOREWORD

BY THE EDITOR-IN-CHIEF

This Medical History of the Burma Campaign is the concluding volume (Volume V) of the Army Medical Services Campaigns series. Professor F. A. E. Crew, in addition to drawing on War Diaries, official despatches, books on the campaigns, personal narratives and other sources, has also in the course of prolonged visits to India and Burma studied the terrain of the campaigns on the spot and obtained additional information for the History. I must express my appreciation of his sedulous and ungrudging labours in the preparation and writing of this volume.

On three previous occasions the British Serviceman has been called upon to fight in Burma. Of the first (1824–1826) Captain Marryat, the novelist who commanded the naval forces, recorded the ravages inflicted by disease—cholera, dysentery, scurvy and malaria, while Fortescue, in his *History of the British Army*, wrote 'Never has the British Officer been subjected to more long-continued hardships, privations and discomforts than in this campaign'.

The Second Burmese War, which lasted from 1852 to 1853, arose from interference with the rights of British merchants trading in Burmese ports that had been guaranteed by the Treaty of Yandalu. Disease in the British forces was less serious owing to the shorter period of the campaign. Lower Burma was annexed to Great Britain.

The Third Burmese War arose in 1885 through King Thibaw Min's arbitrary exaction of monopolies from English traders. There was little fighting. On New Year's Day, 1886, Upper Burma was annexed to Great Britain. Lower and Upper Burma as part of India were united under a Chief Commissioner, the military authority being vested in the Commander in Chief, India.

In 1937 Burma ceased to be a province of India and became politically independent.

Privations, disease and discomforts had to be endured again in the Burma campaign—one of the most arduous of the Second World War. The climate was hostile, roads were practically non-existent and much depended upon the air. The contributions of the R.A.F. and the U.S.A.A.F. were of astonishing magnitude. The evacuation of casualties was a herculean task and improvisation rose to heights hitherto unimagined. The wounded and sick had to be transported by native bearers through trackless jungle, down precipitous heights, conveyed on mules across country, in sampans, rafts and boats, in jeeps and ambulances to airstrips, whence they were conveyed by air to hospitals. Enterprises such as Wingate's incursions entailed special difficulties of this kind for the Medical Services. Heroic measures saved countless lives. The record of them is full of lessons for warfare of this description.

The havoc wrought by malaria among the enemy had no counterpart among the Allied troops owing to the preventive measures taken. *In this campaign the responsibility for its control was placed squarely upon the shoulders of the Combatant Officer.* The daily suppressive dose was not a matter of choice but of discipline.

In an environment such as the jungle the troops entered a new ecological system containing many varieties of disease-evoking organisms new to them. Here, for instance, they met scrub typhus, the dread of the beastly and unseen, the leech and its foul habits.

In this epic story is shown how the differences in respect of the efficiency and attitudes of the British-Indian and Japanese Medical Services accounted largely for the Allied victory and the Japanese defeat.

Both in retreat and advance the Medical Services coped magnificently, in appalling conditions, with their many problems, and some of their members died in the performance of their duty.

This volume of the Official Medical History of the Second World War has been prepared under the direction of an Editorial Board appointed by Her Majesty's Government, but the author alone is responsible for the method of presentation of the facts and the opinions expressed.

ARTHUR S. MACNALTY

CONTENTS

	Page
FOREWORD BY THE EDITOR-IN-CHIEF	ix
PREFACE	xli
Précis. THE CAMPAIGN IN BURMA	1
CHAPTER 1. PREPARATION FOR WAR	4
The Physical Features of Burma	15
The Climate	16
Communications	17
Population	20
The Political Climate	20
Medical Intelligence	20
Appendices I and II	26
CHAPTER 2. THE JAPANESE INVADE BURMA . . .	29
The Action near the Kawkareik Pass	29
Medical Cover	30
Medical Arrangements	31
The Loss of Moulmein	32
Medical Cover	33
The Action on the Bilin River and the Disaster on the Sittang River	33
Medical Cover	39
The Withdrawal from Rangoon	41
Medical Cover during the Withdrawal	47
The Loss of Toungoo and Prome	50
The Loss of the Oilfields	53
Medical Cover	61
Medical Arrangements	65
Appendices III and IV	69
CHAPTER 3. THE WITHDRAWAL ACROSS THE INDO-BURMA FRONTIER	72
Medical Cover	80
Medical Arrangements	85
Medical Arrangements in India	92
The Withdrawal from Arakan	93
Reflections upon the Work of the Army Medical Services during this phase of the Campaign	94
Appendices V and VI	96

	Page
CHAPTER 4. THE ABORTIVE OFFENSIVE IN ARAKAN. SEPTEMBER 1942	100
Medical Cover	108
The Assaults upon the Japanese Positions at Donbaik and Rathedaung and the Japanese Counter-Offensive	110
Medical Cover	113
Medical Arrangements	119
The Health of the Troops	123
Appendices VII, VIII and IX	125
CHAPTER 5. THE FIRST CHINDIT EXPEDITION. FEBRUARY 1943	129
Medical Aspects	133
CHAPTER 6. THE OVERLAND ADVANCE OF XV CORPS IN ARAKAN. NOVEMBER 1943	139
Medical Cover	141
XV Corps' Assault upon the Maungdaw-Buthidaung Line	146
Indian 5th Division. Medical Cover	147
The Japanese Counter-Offensive	148
Medical Cover during these Events.	
Indian 7th Division	153
Indian 5th Division	157
36th Division	159
81st W.A. Division	161
Indian 26th Division	166
Medical Arrangements	171
Appendices X, XI and XII	172
CHAPTER 7. SPECIAL FORCE (INDIAN 3RD DIVISION) OPERATION 'THURSDAY'. FEBRUARY 1944	177
Medical Cover	188
The Health of the Troops	195
The Principal Diseases affecting the Troops	195
Medical Examination of a Sample of returning Chindits	201
Psychiatric Examination of a Sample of returning Chindits	202
An Analysis of Chindit Admissions. Panitola Military Hospital	206
Observations by the Senior Medical Officer, 111th Brigade	216
Medical Supplies	231
The Tactical Policy as this affected the Work of the Medical Services of Special Force	232
Appendices XIII and XIV	239

CONTENTS

	Page
CHAPTER 8. THE JAPANESE INCURSION INTO INDIA	243

Medical Cover.
    Indian 17th Division 253
    Indian 20th Division 258
    Indian 23rd Division 260
    Indian 50th Para. Brigade 264
The Siege of Kohima 264
    Medical Aspects of the Siege of Kohima 269
The Advance of 2nd Division from Dimapur to Kohima . 273
Medical Cover. 2nd Division 276
The Advance from Kohima and the Link-up with IV Corps . 277
Medical Cover during the Advance down the Kohima–Imphal road 280
    2nd Division and Indian 7th Division 280
    23rd L.R.P. Brigade 282
Medical Arrangements XXXIII Corps 282
XXXIII Corps. Medical Order of Battle. April 1944 . . 286
XXXIII Corps. Casualties. The Battle of Kohima . . 286
XXXIII Corps. The Principal Diseases affecting the Troops . 288
2nd Division. Casualties 290
2nd Division. The Army Transfusion Service . . . 295
2nd Division. The Army Psychiatric Service . . . 296
2nd Division. The Army Dental Service 298
2nd Division. The Army Hygiene Service 298
Reflections upon the Work of the Medical Services during the Operations around Kohima 299

CHAPTER 9. THE SIEGE OF IMPHAL.	301

Medical Cover.
    Indian 5th Division 306
    Indian 17th Division 307
    Indian 20th Division 311
    Indian 23rd Division 313
Medical Arrangements IV Corps 315
The Health of the Troops 320
The Principal Diseases affecting the Troops . . . 321
Fourteenth Army. Medical Planning 324
Appendices XV, XVI and XVII 333

CHAPTER 10. THE RETURN TO BURMA	341

The Capture of Ukhrul 342
Medical Cover 347
The Capture of Tamu 348
Medical Cover 350
The Advance to Tiddim and Kalemyo 351
The Advance of Indian 5th Division 354

CONTENTS

	Page
Medical Cover.	
Indian 17th Division	357
Indian 5th Division	358
The Operations of Lushai Brigade	364
Medical Cover	365
Casualties	369
The Advance of 11th East African Division	371
Medical Cover	373
Medical Arrangements	376
Appendices XVIII and XIX	382

CHAPTER 11. FROM THE CHINDWIN TO THE IRRAWADDY   389

XXXIII Corps	396
2nd Division	396
Medical Cover	398
Indian 19th Division	400
Medical Cover	400
Indian 20th Division	402
Medical Cover	404
XXXIII Corps Medical Arrangements	406
IV Corps	409
Indian 7th Division. Medical Cover	412
Indian 17th Division. Medical Cover	413
IV Corps Medical Arrangements	413
L. of C. Command. Medical Arrangements	414
The Medical Advisory Division. S.A.C.S.E.A.	416
Appendices XX, XXI and XXII	419

CHAPTER 12. THE CROSSING OF THE IRRAWADDY. THE CAPTURE OF MEIKTILA BY IV CORPS. THE CAPTURE OF MANDALAY BY XXXIII CORPS   426

Indian 19th Division	427
Indian 20th Division	428
Indian 7th Division	430
2nd Division	432
The Capture of Meiktila by IV Corps	436
The Capture of Mandalay by XXXIII Corps	439
Indian 20th Division	441
2nd Division	442
Indian 268th Brigade	442
Medical Cover.	
Indian 7th Division	442
Indian 17th Division	443
Indian 19th Division	444
Indian 20th Division	446
2nd Division	447

	Page
IV Corps. Medical Arrangements	449
XXXIII Corps. Medical Arrangements	450

CHAPTER 13. COMPLEMENTARY OPERATIONS IN NORTHERN COMBAT AREA COMMAND AND IN ARAKAN . . 453

I

The Southward Advance of 36th Division, Mars Brigade and Chinese First and Sixth Armies   454

36th Division	455
Medical Cover	461

II

XV Corps' Limited Advance in Arakan   473

Indian 25th Division	474
Medical Cover	478
Indian 26th Division	499
4th and 71st Brigades. The Assault Landing at Kyaukpyu	500
Medical Cover	500
4th Brigade. The Assault Landing at Letpan	503
Medical Cover	503
81st W.A. Division	503
Medical Cover	504
82nd W.A. Division	509
Medical Cover	513
22nd E.A. Brigade	520
Medical Arrangements	521
XV Corps. Casualty Rates. October 1944–April 1945	523
A.L.F.S.E.A. Medical Arrangements	524
Appendix XXIII	526

CHAPTER 14. THE DRIVE TO THE SOUTH. THE CAPTURE OF RANGOON. THE CLOSING PHASE. THE RE-OCCUPATION OF JAPANESE-HELD TERRITORIES. . 530

XXXIII Corps on the River Axis	533
IV Corps on the Road and Railway Axis	535
Operation 'Dracula'. XV Corps	539
The Closing Phase	543
Medical Cover.	
Indian 5th Division	550
Indian 20th Division	553
Indian 26th Division (Operation 'Dracula')	556

CONTENTS

	Page
Medical Arrangements.	558
XXXIII Corps	561
IV Corps	563
The Re-occupation of Japanese-held Territories	566
Appendices XXIV, XXV, XXVI, XXVII, XXVIII and XXIX	572

CHAPTER 15. THE HEALTH OF THE TROOPS . . . 602

India 1941–45	604
A.L.F.S.E.A. 1943–45	606
Fourteenth Army	614
The Principal Causes of Morbidity	617
Twelfth Army	627
36th Division	628
Indian 20th Division	632

CHAPTER 16. A REVIEW OF THE WORK OF THE ARMY MEDICAL SERVICES 638

1. The Army Nursing Service	638
2. The Army Hygiene Service	639
3. The Army Dental Service	648
4. The Army Transfusion Service	650
5. The Army Psychiatric Service	676
6. The Supply of Medical Stores	685
7. The Army Medical Service	687
8. The Army Surgical Service	688
Evacuation Policy	697
Appendices XXX, XXXI, XXXII, XXXIII, XXXIV, XXXV, XXXVI and XXXVII	712

APPENDICES

Chapter 1

		Page
I.	Order of Battle at the Commencement of Hostilities	26
II.	Hospital Beds available in January 1942	28

Chapter 2

| III. | The Army-in-Burma. Order of Battle. April 1, 1942 | 69 |
| IV. | The Army-in-Burma. Medical Order of Battle. April 1, 1942 | 70 |

Chapter 3

| V. | Total Sick Wastage of Indian 17th Division. May 24–June 1, 1942 | 96 |
| VI. | Notes on Certain Indian and Other Medical Units | 97 |

Chapter 4

VII.	Eastern Army. Order of Battle. January 1943	125
VIII.	Indian 26th Division. Medical Order of Battle. April 1943	127
IX.	Indian 14th Division. Medical Order of Battle. April 1943	128

Chapter 6

X.	XV Corps. Order of Battle as at December 17, 1943	172
XI.	81st West African Division. Order of Battle	174
XII.	Eastern Command and Fourteenth Army. Location of General Hospitals and Casualty Clearing Stations in Eastern India. October 1943	175

Chapter 7

| XIII. | Excerpt from *The Wild Green Earth* by Bernard Fergusson | 239 |
| XIV. | Indian 3rd Division. Order of Battle. March 1, 1944 | 242 |

Chapter 9

XV.	Location Statement. Hospitals and Malaria Forward Treatment Units. Fourteenth Army. March and July 1944	333
XVI.	The Arming of the Personnel of Medical Units	337
XVII.	Excerpt from the Despatch of Sir George Giffard, C. in C. 11 Army Group	338

APPENDICES

Chapter 10

		Page
XVIII.	XXXIII Corps' Order of Battle. July 10, 1944 and October 10, 1944	382
XIX.	Location Statement. General Hospitals, Casualty Clearing Stations, Malaria Forward Treatment Units, Field Hospitals. Eastern Command and Fourteenth Army. October 1944	386

Chapter 11

XX.	Allied Land Forces, South-East Asia. Order of Battle. Mid-November 1944	419
XXI.	The Medical Build-up. 1943–1944	421
XXII.	From the Crossing of the Chindwin to Rangoon. Fourteenth Army. Calculation of Bed-cover required . . .	424

Chapter 13

XXIII.	Location Statement. General Hospitals, Casualty Clearing Stations, Malaria Forward Treatment Units, Field Hospitals and Beach Medical Units. Eastern Command and A.L.F.S.E.A. March 1945	526

Chapter 14

XXIV.	Allied Land Forces, South-East Asia. Order of Battle. May 8, 1945	572
XXV.	11th East African Division. Order of Battle. May 1945	578
	Indian 25th Division. Order of Battle. May 1945 .	578
	36th Division. Order of Battle. May 1945 . .	579
	Indian 23rd Division. Order of Battle. May 1945 .	579
	81st West African Division. Order of Battle. May 1945 .	580
XXVI.	Fourteenth Army. Medical Units. Location Statement. May 17, 1945	580
XXVII.	202 L. of C. Area. Medical Order of Battle. May 1945 .	584
	404 L. of C. Area. Medical Order of Battle. May 1945 .	586
XXVIII.	Twelfth Army. Medical Order of Battle. July 6, 1945 .	588
XXIX.	Twelfth Army. Medical Order of Battle. August 17, 1945.	595

Chapter 16

XXX.	Composition of the Medical Directorate G.H.Q. (India) 1945	712
	Medical Branches of H.Qs. of Commands, Armies, Districts and Areas	712
XXXI.	Indian Medical Units raised 1939–45 . . .	714
XXXII.	Non-Divisional Medical Units in an Indian Corps as in August 1944	715

APPENDICES

		Page
XXXIII.	The Army Medical Services in India. Strength as on December 31, 1944	716
XXXIV.	Ratio of Medical Services, Medical Officers, Nurses and Dental Officers to Troops. 1939–45	717
XXXV.	The Establishment of Specialists in Indian Medical Units	718
XXXVI.	The Civil Affairs Service (Burma) Organisation	720
XXXVII.	Excerpt from Field Marshal Sir William Slim's *Defeat into Victory*	721

ILLUSTRATIONS
SKETCH MAPS AND DIAGRAMS

Chapter 1

Fig.		Page
1.	The Malarious Areas of Burma	21

Chapter 2

2.	Burma. Victoria Point–Rangoon	30
3.	The Action on the Bilin River	34
4.	The Approach to the Sittang Bridge	36
5.	The Withdrawal from Rangoon	46
6.	Burma. Insein–Mandalay	50
7.	The Prome Area	53
8.	The Yenangyaung Area	55
9.	Prome–Yenangyaung	58

Chapter 3

10.	The Ye-U–Tamu Area	75
11.	Burma. Mandalay–Fort Hertz and Ledo	78
12.	The Kabaw Valley	88

Chapter 4

13.	The Indo-Burma Frontier	102
14.	Arakan. Chiringa–Nhila	104
15.	Arakan. Nhila–Rathedaung	105
16.	Arakan. The Valley of the Kaladan	107
17.	Arakan. Rathedaung–Akyab	111

Chapter 6

18.	Indian 7th Division's Administrative Box, Sinzweya	150
19.	The Boxes of Indian 5th and 7th Divisions	151
20.	Dohazari–Chiringa and Ruma	162
21.	Ruma–Mowdok and Satpaung	164

Chapter 7

22.	Ledo–Indawgyi Lake	178
23.	Operation 'Thursday'	182
24.	'Special Force'. Principal Diseases affecting the Troops. Average Monthly Incidence	196
25.	'Special Force'. Average Monthly Sickness. All Causes. By Brigades	208

ILLUSTRATIONS

Chapter 8

Fig.		Page
26.	The Tiddim–Kalewa–Falam–Haka Area	244
27.	The Imphal Plain	248
28.	Withdrawal of Indian 17th Division from Tiddim area to Imphal	249
29.	The Japanese Incursion into India	251
30.	Imphal–Tamu	259
31.	The Dimapur–Kohima road	266
32.	Kohima. Panorama from Punjab Ridge looking eastwards	267
33.	2nd Division's Advance on Kohima. Medical Cover	275
34.	Kohima–Jessami	278
35.	The Movements of the Main Dressing Stations of 2nd Division during the Battle of Kohima and the Advance down the Kohima–Imphal road	279

Chapter 9

36.	The Roads to Imphal	302

Chapter 10

37.	Indian 7th Division's Advance on Ukhrul. June 27–July 8, 1944	343
38.	Indian 20th Division. The Re-opening of the Imphal–Ukhrul road. July 1–16, 1944	344
39.	Maram–Humine	346
40.	Wangjing–Tamu	351
41.	The Advance to Tiddim and Kalemyo	353
42.	The Outflanking March of 123rd Brigade *via* Imphal and Shuganu. August 30–September 14, 1944	355
43.	Lushai Brigade. Medical Cover	366
44.	Lushai Brigade. 77 (Burma) Field Ambulance. Admissions on account of Malaria. May 1944–January 1945	371
45.	Fourteenth Army. Air Evacuation Arrangements. December 1944–February 1945	379

Chapter 11

46.	Kalewa–Yenangyaung	394
47.	2nd Division. Yazagyo–Sadaung	397
48.	Wuntho–Mandalay	399
49.	Indian 20th Division. The Movements of the Field Ambulances during the Advance into Burma. Inbaung–Kume	403
50.	The Advance of IV Corps to the Irrawaddy at Pakokku by way of the Kalewa–Gangaw–Tilin–Pauk road	411
51.	Fourteenth Army. Air Evacuation Arrangements. February–March 1945	414

ILLUSTRATIONS

Chapter 12

Fig.		Page
52.	The Assault Crossings of the Irrawaddy	429
53.	2nd Division. The Assault Crossing of the Irrawaddy. February 24, 1945	433
54.	The Mandalay–Meiktila Area	435
55.	XXXIII Corps. Casualty Air Evacuation at the Time of the Capture of Mandalay	445

Chapter 13

56.	Northern Combat Area Command. The Southward Advance of 36th Division, Mars Brigade and of Chinese First and Sixth Armies. August 1944–March 1945	453
57.	Mohnyin–Mogok	456
58.	Taunggon–Mong Mit	457
59.	36th Division. The Action at Myitson	458
60.	36th Division. Mong Mit–Mandalay and Kalaw Area	460
61.	36th Division. The Movements of the Divisional Field Ambulances during the Advance down the Railway Corridor	466
62.	Arakan. Myohaung–Gwa	476
63.	Arakan. Akyab Island	480
64.	Arakan. Ramree Island	501
65.	81st West African Division. Evacuation Scheme. Chittagong–Paletwa	506
66.	81st West African Division. Evacuation Scheme. Daletme–Myohaung	509
67.	82nd West African Division. Buthidaung–Minbya	512
68.	82nd West African Division. Hpontha–Taungmaw	515
69.	XV Corps. Arakan. The conquest of Malaria	524
70.	Eastern India	529

Chapter 14

71.	Mandalay–Rangoon	531
72.	The Battle of the Break-Out	549
73.	Indian 20th Division. The Movements of the Divisional Field Ambulances during the Advance into Burma. Meiktila–Hmawbi	553
74.	Fourteenth Army. Air Evacuation Arrangements. End of March 1945 onwards	560

Chapter 15

75.	India 1939. Total Admissions to Hospital. All Causes	603
76.	India 1941–45. Total Admissions to Hospital, British Other Ranks. All Causes	604
77.	A.L.F.S.E.A. 1943–45. Admissions to Hospital. All Ethnic Groups. All Causes	605

ILLUSTRATIONS

Fig.		Page
78.	A.L.F.S.E.A. 1943–45. Admissions to Hospital on account of Malaria and N.Y.D.(F.). All Ethnic Groups	606
79.	British, Indian and African Formations in Burma. December 1942–August 1945. Hospital Admissions on account of Wounds and Sickness	613
80.	The Incidence of Tsutsugamushi Fever (Mite Typhus) in Burma and Assam 1943–45	623
81.	36th Division. 15 (Indian) Malaria Forward Treatment Unit. Weekly Admissions on account of Malaria	629
82.	36th Division. The Incidence of Dysentery and Diarrhoea and of Infective Hepatitis. July 1, 1944–April 28, 1945 . . .	631

Chapter 16

83.	The Army Transfusion Service. Distribution Scheme. 1944 .	664
84.	The Army Transfusion Service. Supply Chain. 1945 .	673

ILLUSTRATIONS

PLATES

Frontispiece   Burma; leogryph on Mandalay Hill

Chapter 4

Between Pages

I. Jungle
II. A track newly hewn through virgin country. March 1943

114-115

Chapter 6

III. Typical Arakan hill country
IV. A Patrol wading through a jungle stream
V. Casualties being evacuated on mules
VI. A stretcher case being carried aboard a hospital sampan. Arakan front
VII. Arakan. Ambulance raft on a chaung
VIII. Jeep evacuating casualty to Medical Staging Point
IX. Arakan. Ambulance convoy bringing wounded from Indian 7th Division after their relief
X. Evacuation of wounded by aircraft. Arakan front

162-163

Chapter 7

XI. Chindit casualties awaiting evacuation by air
XII. Casualty being emplaned into a Stinson Light Aircraft. Mayu Range
XIII. Interior of a Dakota equipped for casualty evacuation

194-195

Chapter 9

XIV. Nagas clearing a road
XV. Convoy of jeep-ambulances on the Imphal-Kohima Road
XVI. 2nd Division. Motor cycle stretcher attachment
XVII. 2nd Division. Motor cycle stretcher attachment
XVIII. 2nd Division. One wheeled folding stretcher-carrier
XIX. 2nd Division. One wheeled folding stretcher-carrier

322-323

Chapter 10

XX. Transport plane dropping supplies. Tiddim Road
XXI. Tiddim Front. Chin Hills. A Forward Psychiatric Unit
XXII. Jungle. Lushai Brigade in Action. November 1944
XXIII. Chin tribesmen bringing in wounded of Lushai Brigade. November 1944
XXIV. Lushai Brigade casualty being carried on improvised stretcher
XXV. Lushai Brigade casualty
XXVI. Lushai Brigade casualty being attended by medical officer
XXVII. Evacuation of wounded from front line by glider

354-355

ILLUSTRATIONS

Chapter 11

		Between Pages
XXVIII.	Kalewa. A forward airstrip	
XXIX.	Kalewa. L.5 taking off wounded from a forward airstrip	
XXX.	L.5s. landing at a forward airstrip	
XXXI.	Ywathitgyi. Battle casualty receiving treatment at hurriedly constructed first-aid post	418–419
XXXII.	A 'Field Hospital' near Ondaw, 1½ miles from front line	
XXXIII.	Jungle Casualty Clearing Station	

Chapter 13

XXXIV.	Wading through a chaung	
XXXV.	Pinbaw, December 1944. Foot care after crossing the Nansan Chaung	
XXXVI.	Typical Mobile Bath Unit for forward troops	
XXXVII.	Hopin to Mawlu. November 1944	
XXXVIII.	A Regimental Aid Post. February 1945	
XXXIX.	Myitson. February 1945. A front line Regimental Aid Post	
XL.	Myitson. February 1945. Stretcher bearers of the Buffs	
XLI.	Kumi ration carriers in the Arakan. November 1944	
XLII.	Supplies dropped to 81st West African Division in the Kaladan Valley	498–499
XLIII.	Buthidaung embarkation point. January 1945	
XLIV.	Arakan. November 1944. West African wounded being evacuated by native raft	
XLV.	R.I.N. Landing Craft, Mechanised at the Zani Chaung Supply Head	
XLVI.	Evacuating casualties by D.U.K.W. Kyaukpyu	
XLVII.	Ru-Ywa. An Indian Dental Mechanical Unit in the Beachhead	
XLVIII.	A Main Dressing Station, Kangaw	
XLIX.	A Field Transfusion Unit in the Arakan	
L.	A post-operative unit of a 'Field Hospital'	

Chapter 14

LI.	Rangoon Jail. An I.M.S. Officer examines the stump of a patient whose leg he amputated	
LII.	Rangoon Jail. A group of Prisoners-of-War at the time of their liberation	546–547
LIII.	Men wounded in the battle for Pyinbongyi being tended on the battlefield	
LIV.	Member of the American Field Service tending a wounded Gurkha. Sittang. August 1945	

NOTE. *Most of the photographs are Crown copyright and were supplied by the Imperial War Museum; others were made available by the Combined Historical Section of the Ministry of Defence, India. To these acknowledgement is made.*

TABLES

		Page
	Chapter 3	
1.	Burcorps. Casualties	79
	Chapter 4	
2.	Indian 14th Division. Admissions to Hospital on account of Malaria. April–December 1942	123
	Chapter 6	
3.	Indian 7th Division. Casualties among Medical Personnel in the Administrative Box, Sinzweya	156
	Chapter 7	
4.	Special Force. Operation 'Thursday'. Casualties . . .	195
5.	Special Force. Fortnightly Incidence of the Principal Diseases affecting the Troops	207
6.	Special Force. Total Admissions to Hospital on account of Sickness and of Wounds. By Brigade	209
7.	Special Force. Average Monthly Admissions to Hospital on account of the Principal Diseases	210
8.	Special Force. 77th Brigade. Casualties	212
9.	Special Force. Admissions to Hospital on account of Sickness and Wounds. Rank and Ethnic Group	213
10.	Special Force. Admissions to Hospital on account of the Principal Diseases. Rank and Ethnic Group	215
	Chapter 8	
11.	The Battle of Kohima. XXXIII Corps. Casualties . . .	287
12.	XXXIII Corps. Principal Causes of Sickness. April–June 1944 .	287
13.	XXXIII Corps. Incidence of Malaria. By Formation. May 1944 .	288
14.	2nd Division. Total Admissions to the Field Ambulances. April–July 1944	290
15.	2nd Division. Battle Casualties. April–June 1944 . . .	291
16.	2nd Division. Ratio of Battle Casualties to Sick . . .	291
17.	2nd Division. Wounds. By Missile	291
18.	2nd Division. Admissions to Main Dressing Stations on account of Sickness. April–July 1944	292
19.	14 (Indian) Mobile Surgical Unit. Operations performed during the Period May 1–June 7, 1944	293
20.	14 (Indian) Mobile Surgical Unit. Operations performed during the Advance from Kohima to Imphal	294

		Page
21.	2nd Division. Wounds treated in 6 Field Ambulance. By Missile. April 26–June 16, 1944	294
22.	2nd Division. Time between Wounding and Operation. 6 Field Ambulance. April 26–June 16, 1944	294
23.	2nd Division. Distribution of Wounds by Site. 6 Field Ambulance. April 26–June 16, 1944	295
24.	2nd Division. Quantities of Transfusion Fluids used during the Battle of Kohima	296
25.	2nd Division. Disposal of Psychiatric Casualties	297
26.	2nd Division. Distribution of Psychiatric Casualties within the Division	297
27.	2nd Division. Dental Work performed during the Period April–July 1944	298

Chapter 9

28.	2 Field Transfusion Unit. Record of Work performed during the Siege of Imphal	320
29.	IV Corps. The Incidence of Malaria. By Formation	321
30.	41 Indian General Hospital. Imphal. Admissions on account of Dysentery and Diarrhoea during the Month of May 1944	323

Chapter 10

31.	Lushai Brigade. 77 (Burma) Field Ambulance. Admissions, Discharges, Transfers and Deaths	370
32.	Lushai Brigade. 77 (Burma) Field Ambulance. Principal Causes of Admission	370
33.	XXXIII Corps. Casualties. June 22–December 16, 1944	380
34.	XXXIII Corps. Battle Casualties. June 22–December 16, 1944	381

Chapter 12

| 35. | XXXIII Corps. Casualties. February 20–March 31, 1945 | 451 |
| 36. | XXXIII Corps. Numbers evacuated and Amounts of Medical Supplies and Ordnance Stores delivered by 164th Liaision Squadron. February 20–March 31, 1945 | 452 |

Chapter 13

37.	13 (Indian) Mobile Surgical Unit. Operations performed while with 36th Division	472
38.	Indian 25th Division. Admissions to Medical Units. By Cause. January–March 1945	498
39.	81st West African Division. Weekly Medical Situation Reports. September 1944–January 1945	508
40.	81st West African Division. Numbers evacuated each Week by Air. By Cause. November 1944–January 1945	508

		Page
41.	82nd West African Division. 2 (W.A.) Field Ambulance. Admissions to the Main Dressing Station. October 15, 1944–May 17, 1945	519
42.	XV Corps. Battle Casualties. Arakan. September 1, 1944–May 17, 1945	522

Chapter 14

43.	Indian 5th Division. Admissions to Medical Units. April–June 1945	552
44.	XXXIII Corps Casualties. March 17–May 12, 1945	562
45.	IV Corps. Total Sick-rates per 1,000 per Diem. May 5–September 15, 1945	564
46.	IV Corps. Total Sick-rates. Average Daily Admission-rates per 1,000 per Diem. By Cause. May 5–September 15, 1945	565
47.	Medical Units allotted to the Task Forces for the Re-occupation of Japanese-held Territories	568

Chapter 15

48.	India 1939. Total Admissions to Hospital. All Causes. Rate per 1,000 per Month	603
49.	Allied Land Forces, South-East Asia. 1943, 1944 and 1945. Admissions to Hospital. All Causes and on account of Malaria and N.Y.D.(F.). Rate per 1,000 per Diem	607
50.	Eastern Army. 11 Army Group and Allied Land Forces, South-East Asia. 1943–45. Numbers of Casualties (Disease, Wounds and Injuries)	608
51.	Indo-Burma Front and South-East Asia Command (excluding Ceylon). 1942–45. Admissions to Hospital. British and Indian Troops. Rate per 1,000. By Cause	609
52.	Indo-Burma Front and South-East Asia Command (excluding Ceylon). Non-Battle and Battle Casualties	611
53.	Indo-Burma Front and South-East Asia Command (excluding Ceylon). The Relationship between Casualties caused by Enemy Action and not so caused. British and Indian Troops compared	611
54.	Indo-Burma Front and South-East Asia Command (excluding Ceylon). Average Daily Number of Patients under Treatment in Hospitals and Rate per 1,000. Indian Troops	612
55.	IV Corps, XXXIII Corps and Army Troops. Strengths. November 12, 1944–May 19, 1945	614
56.	Fourteenth Army. Numbers evacuated beyond the Regimental Aid Post. November 12, 1944–May 19, 1945	615
57.	Fourteenth Army. Casualties. November 12, 1944–May 19, 1945	616
58.	Fourteenth Army. Admissions to Hospital on account of Malaria. November 12, 1944–May 19, 1945	618
59.	Indo-Burma Front. 1942–45. Admissions to Medical Units on account of Dysentery and Diarrhoea	619

		Page
60.	Fourteenth Army and its Component Formations. Admissions to Hospital on account of Dysentery and Diarrhoea. November 12, 1944–May 19, 1945	619
61.	Indo-Burma Front. Incidence of Venereal Diseases. Rate per 1,000	620
62.	Fourteenth Army and its Component Formations. Incidence of Venereal Diseases. November 12, 1944–May 19, 1945	620
63.	Fourteenth Army. Admissions to Hospital on account of Special Diseases and Conditions. November 12, 1944–May 19, 1945	621
64.	Burma and South-East Asia Command (excluding Ceylon). Incidence of Cholera 1942–45	625
65.	Fourteenth Army. Admissions on account of 'All Other Causes'. November 12, 1944–May 19, 1945	626
66.	Twelfth Army. Admissions to Medical Units (excluding Battle Casualties). July–August 1945. Rate per 1,000 per Diem	627
67.	Twelfth Army. Admissions to Medical Units. By Ethnic Group. Rate per 1,000 per Diem. July–August 1945	627
68.	Twelfth Army. Admissions to Medical Units. By Cause. July–August 1945	628
69.	36th Division. 15 (Indian) Malaria Forward Treatment Unit. Number of Cases of Benign, Malignant and Cerebral Malaria admitted. October–December 1944	629
70.	36th Division. 15 (Indian) Malaria Forward Treatment Unit. Admissions on account of Malaria. January–March 1945	630
71.	36th Division. 15 (Indian) Malaria Forward Treatment Unit. Fresh Cases and Relapses admitted. January–March 1945	630
72.	Indian 20th Division. Admissions to Divisional Medical Units and Disposal. December 1–May 31, 1943–44 and 1944–45	632
73.	Indian 20th Division. Analysis of Admissions to Divisional Medical Units. By Cause. December 1, 1944–May 31, 1945	632
74.	Indian 20th Division. Admissions to Divisional Medical Units. By Cause and by Ethnic Group. December 1, 1944–May 31, 1945	634
75.	Indian 20th Division. Admissions and Disposals. June 1–August 31, 1945	635
76.	Indian 20th Division. Admissions to Divisional Medical Units. June 1–August 31, 1945	636
77.	Indian 20th Division. Admissions to Divisional Medical Units. By Cause and by Ethnic Group. June 1–August 31, 1945	637
78.	The Army Transfusion Service. Base Transfusion Unit Production. May 1943–August 1945	675
79.	Incidence of Mental Disorders in India Command. 1939–45	676
80.	XV Corps. Psychiatric Casualties. 1943–44. Arakan	679
81.	Examples of Disposal of Psychiatric Casualties	684
82.	Allied Land Forces, South-East Asia. Battle Casualties. January–August 1945	688
83.	Indian 20th Division. Operations performed by 10 (Indian) M.S.U.; 5 (Indian) B.M.U.; 15 (Indian) M.S.U.; and an Improvised Surgical Team. December 1, 1944–May 31, 1945	690

ABBREVIATIONS

A.	The Adjutant General's Department
A.A.	Anti-aircraft
A.A.P.C.	The African Auxiliary Pioneer Corps
A.A.T.O.	Army Air Transport Organisation
A.B.D.A.	American, British, Dutch, Australian (The South-West Pacific Command)
A.B.R.O.(M.)	Army-in-Burma Reserve of Officers (Medical)
A.B.S.D.	Army Blood Supply Depot
A.C.C.	Ambulance Car Company, R.A.S.C.
A.D.D.S.	Assistant Director of (the Army) Dental Service
A.D.H.	Assistant Director of Hygiene
A.D.M.S.	Assistant Director of Medical Services
A.D.P.(T.)	Assistant Director of Pathology (Transfusion)
A.D.S.	Advanced Dressing Station
Adv.	Advanced
Adv. B.T.U.	Advanced Base Transfusion Unit
Adv. Depot Med. Stores	Advanced Depot of Medical Stores
A.E.C.	Air Evacuation Centre
A.F.S.	The American Field Service
A.I.R.O.(M.)	Army-in-India, Reserve of Officers (Medical)
A.L.F.F.I.C.	Allied Land Forces, French Indo-China
A.L.F.S.E.A.	Allied Land Forces, South-East Asia
Amb. Train	Ambulance Train
A.M.U.	Anti-Malaria Unit
A.O.R.(s)	African Other Rank(s)
Armd.	Armoured
A.S.C.	Advanced Surgical Centre
A.T.	Animal Transport
A/Tk	Anti-Tank
A.V.G.	The American Volunteer Group
Aux.	Auxiliary
B.A.F.	The Burmese Auxiliary Force
Baluch	The Baluch Regiment
B.C.	Battle Casualties or Belgian Congo
Bde.	Brigade
B.D.S.	Beach Dressing Station
Bedfs. Herts.	The Bedfordshire and Hertfordshire Regiment
B.F.F.	The Burmese Frontier Force
B.G.H.	British General Hospital
B.L.A.	The British Liberation Army
B.M.H.	British Military Hospital

ABBREVIATIONS

B.M.U.	Beach Medical Unit
Bn.	Battalion
B.O.R.(s)	British Other Rank(s)
Border	The Border Regiment
Br.	British
Br.S.S.	British Staging Section
B.T.	British Troops or Benign Tertian (Malaria)
B.T.U.	Base Transfusion Unit
Bty.	Battery
Buffs	The Royal East Kent Regiment
Bur.	Burma or Burmese
Burcorps.	I Burma Corps
Burdiv.	1st Burma Division
Buregt.	The Burma Regiment
Bur.G.H.	Burmese General Hospital
Bur.H.C.	The Burma Hospital Corps
Burif.	The Burma Rifles
Bur.M.H.	Burmese Military Hospital
Bur.S.S.	Burmese Staging Section
B.W.	The Black Watch (Royal Highland Regiment)
(C.)	Combined (A medical unit accepting both British and Indian patients)
C.A.A.T.O.	Combined Army Air Transport Organisation
C.A.E.U.	Casualty Air Evacuation Unit (R.A.F.)
Cameronians	The Cameronians (Scottish Rifles)
Camerons	The Queen's Own Cameron Highlanders
C.A.S.(B.)	Civil Affairs Service (Burma)
C.C.P.	Casualty Collecting Post
C.C.S.	Casualty Clearing Station
C.D.H.	Combined Detention Hospital
Cdo.	Commando
C.G.H.	Combined General Hospital
C. in C.	Commander-in-Chief
C.M.F.	Central Mediterranean Force
C.M.H.	Combined Military Hospital
Con. Depot	Convalescent Depot
Coy.	Company
C.P.	Car Post
C.R.E.	Commanding Royal Engineers
C.R.S.	Camp Reception Station
D.A.D.D.S.	Deputy Assistant Director of (the Army) Dental Service
D.A.D.H.	Deputy Assistant Director of Hygiene
D.A.D.M.	Deputy Assistant Director, Malaria
D.A.D.M.S.	Deputy Assistant Director of Medical Services
D.A.D.P.	Deputy Assistant Director of Pathology

ABBREVIATIONS

D.C.	Deputy Commissioner (Indian Civil Service)
D.D.G.(Ops.)	Deputy Director General (Operations)
D.D.M.S.	Deputy Director of Medical Services
D.D.T.	Dichloro-diphenyl-trichlorethane
Dent.	Dental
Detach.	Detachment
Devon.	The Devonshire Regiment
D.G.(3rd)	Prince of Wales's Dragoon Guards (3rd Carabiniers)
DGNS	Dragoons
D.I.S.	Detail Issue Store
Div.	Division or Divisional
D.L.I.	The Durham Light Infantry
D.M.P.	Di-methyl Phthalate
D.M.S.	Director of Medical Services
D. of P.	Director of Pathology
Dogra	The Dogra Regiment
Dorset	The Dorsetshire Regiment
D.S.	Dressing Station
D.U.K.W.	An American amphibious truck designed to carry 1½ tons load in smooth water
D.W.R.	The Duke of Wellington's Regiment (West Riding)
E.A.	East African or Caused by Enemy Action
E.A.G.H.	East African General Hospital
E.H.	Entamœba histolytica
E.Lan.R.	The East Lancashire Regiment
E.N.T.	Ear, Nose and Throat
E.P.I.P.	European Privates, Indian Pattern (Tent)
Essex	The Essex Regiment
E. Yorks.	The East Yorkshire Regiment (The Duke of York's Own)
F.A.M.O.	Forward Airfield Maintenance Organisation
F.A.U.	Friends Ambulance Unit
Fd.	Field
Fd. Amb.	Field Ambulance
Fd. Coy.	Field Company (Engineers)
Fd. Hyg. Sec.	Field Hygiene Section
Fd. Lab.	Field Laboratory
F.D.S.	Field Dressing Station
F.F.R.	The Frontier Force Regiment
F.F.Rif.	The Frontier Force Rifles
F.M.A.	Field Maintenance Area
F.M.T.C.	Forward Malaria Treatment Centre
F.S.D.	Field Supply Depot
F.S.U.	Field Surgical Unit
F.T.U.	Field Transfusion Unit

ABBREVIATIONS

G.	General Staff or Gram
G.C.O.	Governor's Commissioned Officer (Burma)
G.C.R.	The Gold Coast Regiment
G.D.O.	General Duty Officer or Orderly
G.E.	Garrison Engineer
G.H.Q.	General Headquarters
Glosters	The Gloucestershire Regiment
G.O.C.	General Officer Commanding
G.O.R.(s)	Gurkha Other Rank(s)
Gp.	Group
G.P.T.	General Purpose Transport
G.R.	The Gurkha Rifles
Green Howards	Alexandra, Princess of Wales's Own Yorkshire Regiment
G.S.W.	Gunshot wound
G.1098	Mobilisation Equipment Scale
H.A.A.	Heavy Anti-Aircraft
H.C.	Hospital Carrier
H.E.	High Explosive
H.M.I.S.	His (Her) Majesty's Indian Ship
H.M.S.	His (Her) Majesty's Ship
H.Q.	Headquarters
H.S.	Hospital Ship
Hussars	7th Queen's Own Hussars
Hybad.	Hyderabad
I.	India
I.A.M.C.	The Indian Army Medical Corps
I.A.T.	Inflammation of the Areolar Tissue
I.B.G.H.	Indian Base General Hospital
i/c	in charge of, in command of
I.C.D.	Indian Convalescent Depot
I.C.S.	The Indian Civil Service
I.E.M.E.	The Indian Electrical and Mechanical Engineers
I.G.H.	Indian General Hospital
I.G.H.(B.T.)	Indian General Hospital for British Troops
I.G.H.(C.)	Indian General Hospital (Combined)
I.G.H.(I.T.)	Indian General Hospital for Indian Troops
I.H.C.	The Indian Hospital Corps
I.M.H.	Indian Military Hospital
I.M.S.	The Indian Medical Service
I.N.A.	The Indian National Army (serving with the Japanese)
Ind.	Indian
(Ind.) S.S.	Indian Staging Section
Inf.	Infantry
I.M.D.	The Indian Medical Department

ABBREVIATIONS

Innisks.	The Royal Inniskilling Fusiliers
I.O.R.(s)	Indian Other Rank(s)
I.P.C.	The Indian Pioneer Corps
I.S.F.	Indian State Forces
I.T.A.	Indian Tea Association
I.T.F.(M.)	The Indian Territorial Force (Medical)
I.W.T.	Inland Water Transport
I.1248	Scale of Medical Mobilisation Equipment, Apparatus and Drugs
Jat	The Jat Regiment
J. & K.	Jammu and Kashmir
K.A.R.	The King's African Rifles
King's Own	The King's Own Royal Regiment (Lancaster)
Kings	The King's Regiment (Liverpool)
K.O.S.B.	The King's Own Scottish Borderers
K.O.Y.L.I.	The King's Own Yorkshire Light Infantry
Lancers	19th King George V's Own Lancers
L.A.D.	Light Aid Detachment
L.C.A.	Landing Craft, Assault
L.C.I.	Landing Craft, Infantry
L.C.I.(D.)	Landing Craft, Infantry (Depot Ship)
L.C.M.	Landing Craft, Mechanised
L.C.T.	Landing Craft, Tank
Leicesters	The Leicestershire Regiment
L.F. or Lan. Fus.	The Lancashire Fusiliers
L.I.	Light Infantry
Lincolns	The Lincolnshire Regiment
L.M.G.	Light Machine Gun
L. of C.	Lines of Communication
L.R.P.	Long Range Penetration
L.R.P.Gp.	Long Range Penetration Group
Lt.	Light
Lt.A.A.	Light Anti-Aircraft
M.A.C.	Motor Ambulance Convoy (R.A.M.C.)
M.A.D.	Medical Advisory Division (S.E.A.C.)
Mahratta	The Mahratta Light Infantry
Mal.	Malaria
Manch.	The Manchester Regiment
M.A.S.	Motor Ambulance Section (R.I.A.S.C.)
M.B., B.S.	Bachelor of Medicine, Bachelor of Surgery
M.C.U.	Malaria Control Unit
M.D.S.	Main Dressing Station
M.E.F.	Middle East Force
M.F.S.U.	Maxillo-facial Surgical Unit

ABBREVIATIONS

M.F.T.U.	Malaria Forward Treatment Unit
M.G.	Machine-gun
M.G.A.	Major-General i/c Administration
M.I. Room	Medical Inspection Room
M.N.O.	Mental Nursing Orderly
M.N.S.U.	Mobile Neuro-surgical Unit
Mob.	Mobile
Mob. X-ray Unit	Mobile X-ray Unit
M.O.U.	Mobile Ophthalmic Unit
M.S.	Milestone
M.S.U.	Mobile Surgical Unit
M.T.	Mechanical Transport or Malignant Tertian (Malaria)
N.	Nigeria
N.C.A.C.	The Northern Combat Area Command
N.C.(E.)	Non-combatant, enrolled
N.C.O.	Non-commissioned Officer
N.E.A.	Not (caused by) Enemy Action
N.O.	Nursing Orderly
Norfolk	The Royal Norfolk Regiment
N.R.	The Nigeria Regiment
Northamptons	The Northamptonshire Regiment
N.R.R.	The Northern Rhodesia Regiment
N.Staffs	The North Staffordshire Regiment (The Prince of Wales's)
Ny.	Nyasaland
N.Y.D.(F.)	Not Yet Diagnosed (Fever)
N.Y.D.(P.)	Not Yet Diagnosed (Psychiatric)
O.C.	Officer Commanding
Offrs.	Officers
O.R.(s)	Other Rank(s)
O.R.A.	Operating Room Assistant (R.A.M.C.)
Orbat	Order of Battle
Ord.	Ordnance
Oxf. Bucks.	The Oxfordshire and Buckinghamshire Light Infantry
Para.	Parachute
Pln.	Platoon
P.O.L.	Petrol, Oil, Lubricants
P.o.W.	Prisoner(s)-of-War
Pr.	Pounder (gun)
Pro.	Provost
P.T.	Physical Training
Punjab	The Punjab Regiment
P.U.O.	Pyrexia of Unknown Origin

ABBREVIATIONS

Q.	Quartan (Malaria)
Q.A.I.M.N.S.	Queen Alexandra's Imperial Military Nursing Service
Queens	The Queen's Royal Regiment (West Surrey)
R.A.	The Royal Regiment of Artillery
R.A.A.F.	The Royal Australian Air Force
R.A.F.	The Royal Air Force
Rajput	The Rajput Regiment
Raj.Rif.(Rajrif.)	The Rajputana Rifles
R.A.M.C.	The Royal Army Medical Corps
R.A.P.	Regimental Aid Post
R.A.P.W.I.(s)	Recovered Allied Prisoners-of-War and Internees
R.A.R.	The Rhodesian African Rifles
R.A.S.C.	The Royal Army Service Corps
R. Berks.	The Royal Berkshire Regiment (Princess Charlotte of Wales's)
R.C.L.	Ramped Craft, Landing
R.E.	The Corps of Royal Engineers
Recce.	Reconnaissance
Regt.	Regiment
R.Garh.Rif.	The Royal Garhwal Rifles
R.G.R.	The Royal Gurkha Rifles
R.H.	Railhead
R.H.A.	The Royal Horse Artillery
R.I.A.F.	The Royal Indian Air Force
R.I.A.S.C.	The Royal Indian Army Service Corps
R.I.N.	The Royal Indian Navy
R.Jat	The Royal Battalion, The Jat Regiment
R.M.O.	Regimental Medical Officer
R.S.	The Royal Scots (The Royal Regiment)
R.S.Fus.	The Royal Scots Fusiliers
R.Sussex	The Royal Sussex Regiment
R.Tks.	The Royal Tank Regiment
R.T.U.	Returned to Unit
R.W.F.	The Royal Welch Fusiliers
R.W.K.	The Queen's Own Royal West Kent Regiment
S.A.C.S.E.A.	Supreme Allied Commander, South-East Asia
Sa.L.R.	The Sierra Leone Regiment
S. and M.	The Indian Sappers and Miners
S. and T.	Supply and Transport
S.B.	Stretcher bearer
S.E.A.C.	The South-East Asia Command
Seaforth	The Seaforth Highlanders (Ross-shire Buffs, The Duke of Albany's)
Sec.	Section
S.E.M.O.	Senior Executive Medical Officer

ABBREVIATIONS

Sigs.(R.Sigs.)	The Royal Corps of Signals
S.I.W.	Self-inflicted Wound
S.Lan.R.	The South Lancashire Regiment (The Prince of Wales's Volunteers)
S.M.O.	Senior Medical Officer
Som.L.I. or Somersets	The Somerset Light Infantry (Prince Albert's)
S.P.	Staging Post
S.S.	Staging Section
S.Staffords	The South Staffordshire Regiment
Sub-sec.	Sub-section
S.W.B.	The South Wales Borderers
Tk.	Tank
Tp.(s)	Troop(s)
T.T.	Tanganyika Territory
U.	Uganda
u/c	under command of
U.S. or U.S.A.	The United States of America
U.S.A.A.F.	The United States Army Air Force
V.A.D.	Voluntary Aid Detachment (British Red Cross Society)
V.C.O.	Viceroy's Commissioned Officer
V.D.	Venereal Disease
V.D.T.C.	Venereal Diseases Treatment Centre
Vet.	The Veterinary Service
V.S.	Venereal Sore
W.A.	West African
W.A.C.(I.)	The Women's Army Corps (India)
W.A.G.H.	West African General Hospital
W.A.O.R.(s)	West African Other Rank(s)
Warwick	The Royal Warwickshire Regiment
W.E.	War Establishment
w/e	week ending
Welch	The Welch Regiment
West Kents	*See* R.W.K.
W.E.T.	War Establishment Table
Wilts.	The Wiltshire Regiment (The Duke of Edinburgh's)
Worc. R.	The Worcestershire Regiment
W.W.C.P.	Walking Wounded Collecting Post
W.Yorks	The West Yorkshire Regiment (The Prince of Wales's Own)
Y. and L.	The York and Lancaster Regiment
Z.	Zanzibar

BIBLIOGRAPHY

PUBLISHED SOURCES

Despatches

AUCHINLECK, Field Marshal Sir CLAUDE. *Operations in the Indo-Burma Theatre based on India from 21st June, 1943 to 15th November, 1943.* The London Gazette. 27th April, 1948. H.M.S.O.

GIFFARD, General Sir GEORGE J., C. in C. 11 Army Group, S.E.A.C. *Operations in Burma and North-East India from 16th November, 1943 to 22nd June, 1944.* The London Gazette. 6th April, 1951. H.M.S.O.

LEESE, Lieut.-General Sir OLIVER, C. in C. Allied Land Forces, South-East Asia. *Operations in Burma from 12th November, 1944 to 15th August, 1945.* The London Gazette. 6th April, 1951. H.M.S.O.

MOUNTBATTEN of Burma, Vice-Admiral the Earl of. *Report to the Combined Chiefs of Staff by the Supreme Commander, South-East Asia.* 1951. H.M.S.O.

WAVELL, General Sir ARCHIBALD P., C. in C. India. *Operations in Burma from 15th December, 1941 to 20th May, 1942.* The London Gazette. 5th March, 1948. H.M.S.O.

    This Despatch covers the reports by Lieut.-General Hutton and General the Honourable Sir Harold Alexander. *Operations in Burma from 27th December, 1941 to 20th May, 1942.*

—— Field Marshal The Viscount. *Operations in the India Command from 1st January, 1943 to 20th June, 1943.* The London Gazette. 20th April, 1948. H.M.S.O.

—— *Operations in the Eastern Theatre, based on India, from March 1942 to December 31, 1942.* The London Gazette. 17th September, 1946. H.M.S.O.

Books

AHRENFELDT, R. H. *Psychiatry in the British Army in the Second World War.* 1958. Routledge and Kegan Paul.
BELDEN, JACK. *Retreat with Stilwell.* 1943. Cassell.
BELL, Lieut.-Commander A. C. *The Manchester Regiment. Regular Battalions. 1922-48.* 1954. Sherrak, Altringham.
BRYANT, Sir ARTHUR. *The Turn of the Tide.* 1957. Collins.
—— *Triumph in the West.* 1959. Collins.
BURCHETT, W. G. *Wingate's Phantom Army.* 1946. Frederick Muller.
CALVERT, MICHAEL. *Prisoners of Hope.* 1952. Jonathan Cape.
CAMPBELL, ARTHUR. *The Siege. A Story from Kohima.* 1956. Allen and Unwin.
CHURCHILL, WINSTON S. *The Second World War.* Vol. VI. 1954. Cassell.

BIBLIOGRAPHY

COLE, Lieut.-Colonel H. N. *On Wings of Healing. The Story of the Airborne Medical Services, 1940–60.* 1963. William Blackwood and Sons Ltd.
COLLIS, M. *Last and First in Burma.* 1956. Faber and Faber.
DONNISON, F. S. V. *British Military Administration in the Far East, 1943–46.* 1956. H.M.S.O.
EVANS, Lieut.-General Sir GEOFFREY and BRETT-JAMES, ANTHONY. *Imphal. A Flower on Lofty Heights.* 1962. Macmillan.
FERGUSSON, BERNARD. *Beyond the Chindwin.* 1945. Collins.
—— *The Wild Green Earth.* 1946. Collins.
—— *The Black Watch and the King's Enemies.* 1950. Collins.
—— *The Watery Maze.* 1961. Collins.
—— *Return to Burma.* 1962. Collins.
FOSTER, GEOFFRY. *36th Division. North Burma 1944–45.* Printers. Edson Ltd. Watford.
HALL, D. G. E. *Burma.* 1950. Hutchison.
HALLEY, DAVID. *With Wingate in Burma.* 1945. Hodge and Co.
HOWARTH, PATRICK. Editor. *Special Operations.* 1955. Routledge.
JEFFREY, W. F. *Sunbeams into Swords.* 1950. Hodder and Stoughton.
JONES, E. C. *Japan's New Order in East Asia. Its Rise and Fall. 1937–45.* 1954. O.U.P.
KIRBY, Major-General S. W. et al. *The War against Japan.* Vol. II. 1958. H.M.S.O.
MASTERS, JOHN. *The Road past Mandalay.* 1961. Michael Joseph.
MCKELVIE, ROY. *The War in Burma.* 1948. Methuen and Co.
MACKENZIE, Colonel K. P. *Operation Rangoon Jail.* 1954. Christopher Johnson.
MORRISON, IAN. *This War against Japan.* 1943. Faber and Faber.
OGBURN, CHARLTON. *The Marauders.* 1959. Harpers.
OWEN, Lieut.-Colonel F. *The Campaign in Burma.* Prepared for S.E.A.C. by the Central Office of Information. 1946. H.M.S.O.
PRASAD, Dr. BISHESHWAR. Editor. *Official History of the Indian Armed Forces in the Second World War, 1939–45. Retreat from Burma 1941–42.* 1953. *Arakan Operations 1942–45.* 1954. *Reconquest of Burma. 1942–45.* Two volumes. Orient Longmans.
RAINA, Lieut.-Colonel B. L., I.A.M.C. Editor. *Official History of the Indian Armed Forces in the Second World War. Medical Services, Administration.* 1953. *Medicine, Surgery and Pathology.* 1955.
REXFORD-WELCH, Squadron-Leader S. C. *The Royal Air Force Medical Services.* Vol. III. 1958. H.M.S.O.
ROBERTS, Brigadier M. R. *The Golden Arrow.* 1952. Gale and Polden. (Indian 7th Division).
SAUNDERS, HILARY ST. G. *Royal Air Force 1939–45.* Vol. III. 1954. H.M.S.O.
SEAGRAVE, Dr. GORDON S. *Burma Surgeon.* 1943. Norton.
SHAW, J. *The March Out.* 1955. Hart Davies. (12th Nigerian Battalion. Second Chindit Incursion).
SLIM, Field Marshal Sir WILLIAM. *Defeat into Victory.* 1956. Cassell.
SMYTH, Sir JOHN, V.C. *Before the Dawn.* 1957. Cassell.
—— *The Only Enemy.* 1959. Hutchinson.

SYKES, CHRISTOPHER. *Orde Wingate.* 1959. Collins.
TYSON, GEOFFREY. *Forgotten Frontier.* 1945. W. H. Targett & Co. Ltd., Calcutta.
WILCOX, W. A. *Chindit Column 76.* 1945. Longmans Green and Co.
WILSON, Professor H. H., F.R.S. *Narrative of the Burmese War in 1824–26.* 1852. W. H. Allen and Co.
WILLIAMS, Lieut.-Colonel J. H. *Elephant Bill.* 1950. Hart Davies.
The History of Fourteenth General Hospital, 1939–45. The Birmingham Printers, Ltd.

Papers published in the Medical and Lay Journals

UNPUBLISHED SOURCES

War Diaries, Quarterly Reports and other similar official documents.
Letters from officers of the Army Medical Services.
Provisional narratives prepared by the members of the Historical Section, Ministry of Defence, New Delhi.
Japanese Monograph No. 134
  Burma Operations Record. 15th Army Operations in Imphal Area and Withdrawal to Northern Burma. (Revised Edition 1957). Prepared by Headquarters United States Army, Japan.

PREFACE

At one time it seemed that it might not be necessary to include in the Army Medical Services series of the United Kingdom Official Medical History of the Second World War a volume dealing with the campaign in Burma.

While the war was still being fought the Government of (pre-partition) India decided to produce an official record of the part played therein by the Indian Armed Forces. An officer was appointed to the C.G.S. Branch of A.H.Q.(I) charged with the duty of collecting the relevant records and collating them. By the end of the war this small beginning had become expanded into the War Department Historical Section. In 1947 Great Britain handed over the control of their own affairs to the two new Sovereign States that resulted from the separation of India and Pakistan. The governments of these two countries agreed that the project of producing this official history should proceed and the Historical Section was re-organised and renamed the Combined Inter-Services Historical Section, India and Pakistan. Accommodation for it was provided within the Ministry of Defence, New Delhi. From it since the end of the war there has been appearing a succession of volumes of two series, one dealing with the operational and the other with the medical aspects of (pre-partition) India's participation in the Second World War. In the medical series a volume dealing with the Burma campaign is to appear.

The great majority of those who fought against the Japanese in Burma and Assam and also of those who served these were Indians (Indians and Pakistanis). In his *Report to the Combined Chiefs of Staff* the Supreme Commander, South-East Asia observes that 'over 90 per cent. of the medical units in South-East Asia were raised and equipped in India and all of these were maintained from India throughout the campaign. Sixty per cent. of the medical officers and 88 per cent. of the medical other ranks belonged to the Indian Services'.

Since the Indian component of the medical services of the Army-in-Burma, of Burcorps, of Eastern Army, of 11 Army Group, of Allied Land Forces, South-East Asia, of XV Corps and of Fourteenth Army was relatively so very large it was thought that the account of the affairs of this Indian component might well serve as an account of the whole of the Army Medical Services.

Those engaged in the writing of the Australian, Canadian, Indian, New Zealand and United Kingdom volumes of the official medical histories have distributed copies of their provisional narratives among their colleagues. Each of them has enjoyed the liberty of making the fullest possible use of the material provided by the others. When the provisional narrative of the Burma campaign, prepared by Lieut.-Colonel B. L. Raina, I.A.M.C., was studied it became clear that he, quite rightly, was focusing his attention upon those aspects of policy, planning and events which were of direct and special interest and importance to India and Pakistan. The conclusion was then reached that it was necessary to attempt to produce a volume that would more easily fit into the Army Medical Services series. Since there were British, Burmese, East and West African medical personnel and units involved, as well as Indian, there was an 'imperial' as well as an Indian story to be told. At this time the Armed Forces of India were instruments that were used by Britain in the pursuit of her aims. Almost without exception the higher posts within them were held by British officers. The Historical Section of the Cabinet Office is producing an official history of the war against Japan although the Combined Inter-Services Historical Section is engaged upon a similar task.

To produce such a volume, it was clearly recognised, would be far from easy. During the war years and immediately afterwards there came into the Army Medical Directorate of the War Office half-a-dozen documents of various kinds from the Burma theatre and of interest to the historian, no more,—a copy of a comprehensive account of the Army Transfusion Service in India and Burma, a full account of the activities of the medical services of 2nd Division during the battle of Kohima and the advance down the Kohima–Imphal road, an incomplete run of the quarterly reports of A.D.M.S. Indian 20th Division, a report of the psychiatrist attached to H.Q. IV Corps, a brief report of the medical arrangements in XXXIII Corps and a single quarterly report of D.M.S. A.L.F.S.E.A. A few war diaries, quarterly reports and other official documents of the same general kind reached the War Office but remained unknown to the Army Medical Directorate until long after the end of the war when they had gravitated into the archives of the Historical Section of the Cabinet Office. Since such documents are the bricks with which the chronicler builds the 'hall of memory' in which the wisdom that is distilled from experience is stored, it was obvious that unless this scant store could be greatly augmented an adequate account of the affairs of the Army Medical Services in the campaign in Burma could not be written.

Fortunately it was possible to make full use of the very considerable stock of source material in the possession of the Combined Inter-Services Historical Section in New Dehli. Mr. W. Franklin Mellor, Secretary of the Editorial Board of the United Kingdom Official Medical History of the War, had initiated a mechanism—the Commonwealth Official Medical Historians Liaison Committee—which met in Ottawa, Oxford, Canberra and New Delhi, and which facilitated the constant flow of information from the one who had it to the one who needed it. The more important documents were sent to me through Mr. Mellor, the Secretary of the Liaison Committee. In several successive years I have also been able to spend many days in the Historical Section in New Delhi where I was given full and free access to the files. Dr. Bisheshwar Prasad and Lieut.-Colonel Raina did everything within their power to help. Their kindness and generosity enabled me to attempt that which at one time I thought was far beyond my powers. To thank them at all adequately is impossible.

As was to be expected, the medical source material in New Delhi is far from complete. During the retreat in 1941–42 the conditions were such as to preclude all possibility of maintaining war diaries and the like. The conditions in Arakan and around Imphal were by no means conducive to the compilation of official reports. The final advance of XV Corps and of Fourteenth Army was so swift and so pregnant with the promise of an early and complete victory that it must have been difficult indeed for those concerned to consider at all seriously the needs of the administrator and of the even more remote historian. It is surprising that so many reports and the like did congregate in New Delhi and Simla. This stock became depleted by loss at the time of the take-over and again during the period of partition.

Among the documents available for study there is very great variation in respect of usefulness. Only a small proportion of them were compiled or written by such as held Regular Commissions. The bulk of them would appear to have been produced by such as had received no advice or instruction concerning the techniques of preparing official documents of this kind. In most instances, it would seem, these routine reports required by regulation had been elaborated reluctantly and painfully by such as had found the task dull, difficult, distasteful and meaningless. Only rarely was a report encountered that suggested that its author had appreciated its purpose and importance and had found satisfaction in writing it.

It has been found possible to fill in a number of the gaps caused by these deficiencies in respect of source material. Several of those who took part in this campaign wrote books about it. Many of those who during the campaign held senior administrative medical posts kept copies of the reports which they had submitted to higher authority and these, in response to requests, were readily lent to me. Many others were very willing, when approached, to unlock the cupboards of their memory and to allow me to take from the contents anything I wanted.

Because of the great differences in the magnitude of the two undertakings this volume may appear before all the operational volumes dealing with the campaign in Burma are completed by the Historical Section of the Cabinet Office. When the latter are published it may be found that the operational sections of this volume differ more or less markedly from the official version. It is submitted that this is a matter of no great importance in so far as the Medical History is concerned. Medical tactical planning and all that emerges therefrom is shaped by the military situation as this is understood to be at the time and not as later it is shown to have been after fuller information has become available and deeper study has been made. In very large measure the operational sections of this volume are derivatives of Despatches and of the accounts given in the books listed in the bibliography. Field Marshal Sir William Slim, Brigadier Bernard Fergusson, Brigadier Michael Calvert, Captain W. J. Jeffrey, W. G. Burchett and Brigadier John Masters especially command my gratitude for the permission they gave for the inclusion in this volume of excerpts of medical interest from their books.

A book and two booklets written by members of the Army Medical Services were very helpful. Colonel K. P. Mackenzie (A.D.M.S. Indian 17th Division), who was taken prisoner during the action at the Sittang Bridge, describes in his book *Operation Rangoon Jail* his experiences during this action and while a prisoner-of-war. He quietly records the inhumanity and sadistic cruelty of the jailors and with equal calm depicts the indestructible dignity of their victims. This book provides strong reinforcement for the view that the medicine that was practised by members of the Army Medical Services in the P.o.W. camps of the Far East must be regarded as an unusual form of military medicine and should be studied as such. Colonel Geoffry Foster (A.D.M.S. 36th Division) produced a booklet of considerable interest that tells the story of this division, first in Arakan and later in its advance down the railway corridor from Mogaung to Katha and beyond. The staff of 14 British General Hospital placed on record in an unambitious booklet the history of this unit in France in 1939–40 and then in the Burma theatre where it occupied a key position in the medical evacuation-treatment system. This narrative is of peculiar interest for the reason that it enables the reader to see events and their consequences through the composite eye of a general hospital that was in close and constant contact with the forward zone and also with the base. The story of its hurried withdrawal from the vicinity of Imphal to Dimapur clearly reveals the uncertainty and confusion that were encountered on all sides and at every level during this critical period.

Among the books that eased my task was one that was never published. It so happened that the urge to explore the significance of events by describing in writing his reactions to them stimulated the one man in the Army Medical Services who was in the best position throughout the campaign to witness and critically to describe happenings in their sequence and to determine their relative importance. At different times

D.D.M.S. Army-in-Burma, D.D.M.S. Eastern Army, D.M.S. 11 Army Group, D.M.S., A.L.F.S.E.A., D.M.S. G.H.Q.(I) and a member of the Medical Advisory Division at H.Q., S.A.C.S.E.A., Lieut.-General Sir Treffry Thompson prepared a lively account of the medical aspects of the war as seen by him and also persuaded a number of those who served under him to produce accounts of particular episodes with which they were familiar. It was his intention to fashion a book out of this material. Instead of doing so, however, he handed this uniquely valuable store of information and of professional judgment to me and it is this that forms the very core of the volume that now appears. To him especially and to those whose help he enlisted—Colonel C. V. F. Foucar, Lieut.-Colonel W. W. Coppinger, Lieut.-Colonel J. R. Jarvie, all of the I.M.S., Lieut.-General Sir Frederick Harris (as he later became when D.G.A.M.S.), Colonel A. Sachs, Lieut.-Colonel R. J. Rosie, Lieut.-Colonel H. Ellis (as they were then) of the R.A.M.C.—my indebtedness is beyond all possible assessment. Sir Treffrey has been good enough to scrutinise my manuscript, has corrected many errors and made many suggestions for its improvement. For whatever faults this narrative now displays he certainly is in no way blameworthy; for whatever merits it possesses he is very largely responsible.

For placing at my disposal material in their possession I am deeply indebted to Major-General G. E. MacAlevey (O.C. 8 (Indian) Casualty Clearing Station, A.D.M.S. Indian 17th Division, D.D.M.S. Fourteenth Army) who lent me a copy of the *Medical History of Fourteenth Army* that he had compiled as an official document and also to Colonel W. H. Wolstenholme (D.A.D.M.S. 11th East African Division and A.D.M.S. Fourteenth Army) for his copy of the same document; to Brigadier G. J. V. Crosby (D.D.M.S. XXXIII Corps) who produced for me a copy of the very comprehensive official narrative of this formation and of its medical services; to Colonel G. B. Jackson (A.D.M.S. Indian 20th Division) who found for me a well-filled file dealing with the affairs of the medical services of this division and to Lieut.-Colonel Saw Marcus Paw of the Army-in-Burma Reserve of Officers (Medical) without whose copy of a report on the activities of 77 (Burma) Field Ambulance which he had commanded nothing could have been told of the medical cover provided for the Lushai Brigade during the six eventful months of 1944 when it was so successfully harassing the Japanese along the length of the Imphal–Tiddim road and around Falam and Haka and in the valley of the Myittha.

Of those who have responded generously to my appeals for help either by reviving their memories of past events or by scrutinising and modifying that which I had written the following have been particularly helpful. Major-General A. N. T. Meneces (D.D.M.S. XV Corps, Arakan) who played a notable part in the laying of the foundations of the success that was gained in this theatre in the fight against malaria—General Meneces put himself to very considerable trouble to read, to correct and to amplify the very imperfect account of the affairs of the medical services of this corps that I had managed to compile; Major-General W. J. Officer (O.C. 57 (Indian) Field Ambulance, A.D.M.S. 2nd Division, D.D.M.S. Special Force) whose help was particularly valuable when it became necessary to examine the opinions and attitudes of that strange 'man of genius who might have become a man of destiny', Major-General Orde Wingate; Brigadier E. C. Lang (D.M.S. Army-in-Burma) from whom I obtained much information concerning the build-up of the medical services immediately prior to the outbreak of war; Colonel F. T. Harrington who commanded 43 Indian General Hospital at the time of the fighting around Kohima and in the Imphal Plain and who was able to give me a graphic description of the conditions in Dimapur at this time; Dr. H. B. T. Holland, now of Oversea Service, who in 1941-42 served as surgeon and adjutant with 8 (Indian) Casualty Clearing Station and who was therefore able to fill in many of the blanks in my knowledge of the affairs of this unit and Major-General F. J. Loftus-Tottenham in command of 81st West African Division, who kindly looked through my account of the division's activities in the Arakan.

I am also indebted to Dr. Desmond Whyte, D.S.O., Senior Medical Officer, 111 Brigade, for an illuminating account of the medical problems of columns of a Long Range Penetration Group and for his helpful comments on the sections dealing with the Chindit operations in general.

The first draft of this narrative was constructed in Rangoon. During its preparation therefore many appeals for help had to be addressed to Mr. W. Franklin Mellor and to Miss F. E. E. Harney of the Central Office of the Official Medical History. These invariably met with a ready and fruitful response and so it is that to Miss Harney, who did much research work and proof-reading on my behalf and to Mr. Franklin Mellor, who guided this volume in its various phases very expertly towards completion, my thanks are due.

It is quite certain that this narrative will be found to be faulty, especially by those who served in this theatre. For these faults, when they are not the direct and unavoidable consequence of deficiencies in the source material, I regretfully and solely am responsible.

F. A. E. C.

PRÉCIS

THE CAMPAIGN IN BURMA
December 11, 1941 — September 2, 1945

IN 1941 Burma was defenceless against a land attack by a modern power. Her garrison consisted of two understrength divisions supported by a handful of R.A.F. and R.I.A.F. planes and by the American Volunteer Group. There were no strategic roads or railways towards her threatened eastern frontier. Neither the United Kingdom nor India could hope to provide adequate reinforcements or supplies at all speedily, for their resources were already being stretched to the limit by the demands of the other theatres of war.

The Japanese invaded Burma during the third week of January 1942, using specially trained and veteran troops. The invasion began with two thrusts into Tenasserim, the more northerly being through the Kawkareik Pass debouching into the Moulmein Plain, the more southerly being from Victoria Point towards Mergui. The Army-in-Burma made its first stand on the line of the River Salween but was quickly driven westwards along the coast road through Thaton and Kyaikto and across the Sittang River to Pegu. A second defeat here led to the evacuation of Rangoon and to a withdrawal to Prome. Failing to hold its positions here the Army-in-Burma withdrew up the line of the Irrawaddy.

Chinese Fifth and Sixth Armies now moved south to the aid of the Army-in-Burma. An attempt was made to hold a line running across the country between Pyinmana and Allanmyo but the Japanese quickly succeeded in piercing this with the result that the Chinese and Burcorps, compounded out of Indian 17th and 1st Burma Divisions, fell back, the Chinese into the Northern Shan States, Burcorps up the valley of the Chindwin. The Japanese severely defeated the Chinese, some of whom, under the command of General Stilwell, succeeded in reaching India *via* Homalin on the Chindwin but the bulk of the Chinese formations disintegrated. Burcorps made its way to Kalewa across the Chindwin and moved through the dreaded Kabaw Valley to Tamu and over the Naga Hills to Imphal. The Japanese had conquered Burma in the space of four months with four divisions supported by an air force that enjoyed complete control of the air.

In the campaigning season of 1942–43 an attempt was made by IV Corps to seize northern Arakan but it ended in failure. Early in 1943 a co-ordinated plan having for its object the beginning of the reoccupation of Burma emerged. General Stilwell's formations were to drive from

Ledo to Myitkyina, IV Corps was to thrust across the Chindwin from Manipur, and 77th Bde., specially trained in long range penetration work by Brigadier Wingate, was to march from Tonhe on the Chindwin to operate behind the Japanese lines without any communications save by air. The Chindits' orgy of sabotage and destruction lost much of its purpose and meaning when the complementary operations had to be cancelled.

In November 1943 South-East Asia Command, with Vice-Admiral Lord Louis Mountbatten as Supreme Commander and with General Stilwell as his deputy, was formed and a comprehensive plan for the recovery of Burma was prepared.

At the end of 1943 a second attempt on northern Arakan was made by XV Corps but it was checked by a strong Japanese counter-offensive early in 1944. In order to forestall any offensive the Allies might launch on the northern front the Japanese had been preparing to seize the Imphal Plain in early 1944. This operation was to be preceded by an offensive in Arakan the purpose of which was to attract and to hold S.E.A.C. reserves.

When the Arakan offensive was launched it was sternly repulsed by XV Corps but when this corps, in its turn, advanced it was checked short of its final objectives.

The attack towards Dimapur began early in March 1944 while General Stilwell was moving towards the Hukawng Valley and just as General Wingate had launched his 'Special Force', mainly airborne, which sought to paralyse Japanese resistance to General Stilwell's advance. For some months the situation around Imphal remained critical but by the end of June the issue had been decided for the Japanese were firmly held and the road from Kohima to Imphal had been reopened. The garrison of the Imphal Plain had been reinforced and supplied by air throughout the long siege. Fourteenth Army now turned to the offensive. The Japanese were soon retreating in disorder from the Imphal front and General Stilwell, with the aid of the Chindits, was relentlessly pressing on towards Myitkyina which fell at the end of August. The cold season of 1944 saw a resumption of operations in Arakan and the Japanese were cleared from the valley of the Kaladan and from the Mayu Peninsula. In January 1945 assault landings were made from the sea at Akyab and at other points along the coast so that airfields might be made ready for the imminent advance of Fourteenth Army southwards into lower Burma.

Fourteenth Army crossed the Chindwin and advanced on Mandalay and on Meiktila. The latter town was captured at the beginning of March by a swift thrust of armour and lorried infantry and the Japanese communications with Rangoon were cut. They threw in all their available reserves in strenuous and long continued attempts to restore the situation but by the end of the month they were obliged to acknowledge defeat, complete and overwhelming. Meanwhile Mandalay had been captured and the Japanese defending the city disorganised and driven into the Shan Hills. Fourteenth Army, racing southwards towards Rangoon down the axes of the Mandalay–Rangoon railway in the east and the Irrawaddy in the west, compelled the Japanese in Arakan to withdraw hurriedly towards the An and Taungup Passes into Lower Burma.

At this point the Burma National Army changed sides and began to make escape for the disintegrating Japanese formations even more difficult. Fourteenth Army reached Prome in time to block the escape routes of the Japanese in Arakan and Toungoo on the railway in the east was taken by IV Corps on 22nd April while the Japanese moving towards it were checked by the Karens who had now risen. Pegu was reached on May 1st. Then the rains came to prevent Fourteenth Army reaching Rangoon before XV Corps which had mounted a combined seaborne and airborne operation against the capital from Akyab and Kyaukpyu in the Arakan. But the Japanese had already withdrawn from Rangoon and the city was entered without opposition.

Fourteenth Army now began its preparations for the assault upon Malaya while a new formation, Twelfth Army, took over from it the task of mopping up such Japanese forces as remained in Burma. There was one final battle, the battle of the break-through to and across the Sittang. These Japanese troops were in a most distressful condition, starved and for the most part sick. They were ill-equipped for the task yet without thought of surrender they made their attempt. A proportion of them got away but for the majority this was the end.

Then a completely new force was unleashed; a whole city—Hiroshima—was destroyed in an instant as though by the foul breath of a malevolent god and awe spread across the world. The Japanese Government, impotent in the face of such terrifying power, promptly surrendered and in this unexpected fashion the campaign in Burma and the Second World War ended.

CHAPTER 1

PREPARATION FOR WAR

UNTIL 1937 Burma, politically, had been part of India and its defence therefore had been the concern of the Indian Government. In 1937 the Government of Burma Act came into force, Burma became separated politically from India and was given a measure of self-government. The defence of the country became a responsibility of the British Governor. The Finance Department was headed by a Burmese Minister. At this time nothing seemed less likely than that Burma would become involved in a war. She was protected by two peaceful states, Thailand and Indo-China and by her mountain ranges and vast forests that seemed to form an impenetrable barrier to large armed forces. The great naval base at Singapore guarded her from seaward. And so it was that attention was not given to matters relating to the defence of the country.

In September 1939 on the outbreak of war with Germany, the Burmese armed forces, such as they were, were placed under the British Chiefs of Staff for operational purposes but remained for administrative and financial purposes under the Government of Burma. In November 1940, when the Far Eastern Command with its headquarters at Singapore was created, the operational control was passed thereto while the administrative responsibility was divided between the Government of Burma and the War Office in London which was now contributing substantially to Burma's defence budget. The Burma War Committee included Burmese Ministers as well as the two British Counsellors and the British G.O.C. The Governor was the president and the Premier of Burma the vice-president of this body. In peace-time Army H.Q. was in Maymyo all the year round. Shortly after the outbreak of war in 1939 H.Q. moved to Rangoon so as to be in closer contact with the departments of government which, though previously spending the hot weather in Maymyo and the winter months in Rangoon, now were in Rangoon permanently. H.Q. Army-in-Burma first opened in the premises of Whiteaway and Laidlaw in Phayre Street but soon moved into more suitable accommodation in a building on the campus of the University of Rangoon on the Prome Road.

On December 8, 1941 Japan, without warning, entered the war. From the air she struck at Hong Kong, Singapore, at the airfields in Malaya and at the U.S. Pacific Fleet at Pearl Harbour, Hawaii. Her troops landed in force at Singora and Patani in the Kra Isthmus, in Thailand and at Kota Bharu on the east coast of north Malaya. In Thailand, the Government, after a slight show of resistance, made peace with the Japanese and declared war upon the Allies. The Japanese spread quickly throughout the country, taking over and developing the airfields. In July 1941 Japanese troops had entered Indo-China which shared a common border with Burma. Now her land forces could approach the Thailand–Burma border at any point in its 800 miles length and the most populous and strategically the most important areas of Burma were within the range of Japanese aircraft based on Thailand airfields.

On December 10, H.M.S. *Prince of Wales* and H.M.S. *Repulse* were sunk by Japanese bombers off the coast of Kuantan in southern Malaya. As a consequence of the destruction of the U.S. Pacific Fleet and of these two British capital ships the command of the sea around the coast of Burma passed into Japanese hands. On December 11 and 12 Japanese Thailand-based aircraft raided Tavoy and Victoria Point, at the north and at the extreme south ends of the Tenasserim strip, nowhere much more than 40 miles wide, which stretches some 400 miles, along with an equally narrow strip of Thai territory, to the Malayan border. *Indian 11th Division in northern Malaya was fighting the first of those actions which punctuated its painful retreat down the Malayan mainland into Johore.* On the 13th Victoria Point was evacuated and on the following day the Japanese occupied it, the first piece of Burmese soil to pass into their possession. On December 23 and again on Christmas Day Japanese aircraft raided Rangoon. Little damage to military installations was caused but civilian casualties were heavy (1,850 were killed or died of their injuries from the first raid) and a panic exodus commenced. This departure of so large a proportion of the labour force of Rangoon and its docks very seriously impeded the working of the essential services and of the docks and greatly disrupted the life of the city. *It was on Christmas Day that the end of resistance came in Hong Kong and by this time the northern half of the Malayan mainland had been lost to the invaders.*

In Burma there were several reactions to these events. On December 12 the operational control of the Burmese forces was passed back to India. Then on the 30th of that month it was transferred again, this time to the newly created South-West Pacific Command with its H.Q. in Java. Administrative responsibility remained with India. With the rapid dissolution of this South-West Pacific Command (A.B.D.A. Com.; American, British, Dutch and Australian) following the Japanese invasion of the Netherland East Indies, all responsibilities for the defence of Burma were passed to India.

Though, as is clear from the many changes that were made in the distribution of responsibility for Burma's defence, great difficulty was at all times encountered in the making of adequate arrangements, at no time was the importance of Burma to the Allies under-estimated. Very strenuous efforts were made by the British Government to give Japan no cause to enter the war. To the Allies the possession of Burma was of the greatest importance. It was a land link between the Western Allies and China. The Burma Road, running from Mandalay through Lashio to the Chinese border near Wanting, crossing the only bridge over the Salween, on through Paoshan and Kunming to reach Chungking, had been finished only in 1939 and along it was passing much material aid to China for use in her long-continued war with Japan. So long as Burma was held, Calcutta and the great industrial centres of north-east India were immune against Japanese air attack. The high mountain ranges and the vast malarious jungles of the north-west of Burma formed an impenetrable shield for India's eastern frontier.

To the Japanese the possession of Burma would mean much. The country formed a natural strategic protective shield for her conquests; it would complete the defensive perimeter which they were rapidly forming around the Japanese mainland. Its occupation would be the obvious prelude to an assault upon India in an attempt to disrupt the flow of the very considerable contributions which India was making to the Allied war effort. The rich resources of Burma—rice, oil, wolfram—could be exploited by Japan to her very great advantage.

It was because of the importance of Burma to the Allied cause and because of her unpreparedness for war that caused General Wavell, C. in C., India, to fly at Christmas-time 1941 to Chungking to discuss the war with Japan with Marshal Chiang Kai-shek. The latter offered to send to Burma two Chinese armies, the Fifth and Sixth. General Wavell at once accepted two of the divisions of the Sixth Army, Chinese 93rd Division, part of which was already approaching the China–Burma border from Puerh and Chinese 49th Division to serve as a reserve on the northern frontier of Burma at Wanting. The third division of this army, Chinese 55th Division, was at that time very widely dispersed and its concentration would take some time. General Wavell asked that the Chinese Fifth Army, which was then concentrating around Kunming, should be held in reserve in this area for the time being. A serious difficulty prevented General Wavell immediately accepting all the help which Marshal Chiang Kai-shek so generously offered. The Marshal insisted that at no time should his troops become intermixed with the British and that a separate L. of C. should be maintained for them especially. It was impossible for General Wavell at that time to undertake to comply with these conditions.

At the time of the political separation of Burma from India the Burma garrison consisted of two battalions of British infantry, four battalions of the Burma Rifles (Burif), an Indian mountain battery, a company of

Indian Sappers and Miners, a small number of Indian Auxiliary Force and of Indian Territorial Force units and a few other small administrative units, all belonging to the Indian Army. In addition there were nine battalions of the Burma Military Police, a quasi-military body.

It was intended to withdraw all the Indian units following the separation. But this was not immediately feasible. The former small Burma District Headquarters had to transform itself into the headquarters of an army, the new Burma Army. This transformation took time and encountered much difficulty but when it was achieved the battalions of the Burma Rifles were transferred to the Burma Army and to this the Indian mountain battery and a company of Indian Sappers and Miners were loaned until they could be replaced by their Burmese equivalents. The two British battalions (1st Glosters, 2nd K.O.Y.L.I.) remained in Burma for internal security reasons. A Burmese Auxiliary Force composed of European, Anglo-Indian and Anglo-Burmese volunteers, and a Burmese Territorial Force, after the Indian pattern, were brought into being and the existing Auxiliary and Territorial units embodied therein. Six of the battalions of the Burma Military Police, largely Indian in composition, became the Burma Frontier Force. The Burma Frontier Force was commanded by an Inspector General and officered by seconded officers, mostly from India, together with a few British Service officers. The force was largely composed of Punjabi Mussalmans, Sikhs and Gurkhas and consisted of a reserve battalion in Pyawbwe near Meiktila and five other battalions stationed throughout the outlying parts of Burma. Each battalion returned to its headquarters station for the monsoon season and spent the rest of the year on tour. The system of administration was very simple and elastic. A lump sum was allotted annually to cover all costs and the Force made its own arrangements for pay, rations, clothing, accommodation, medical services, etc. This system worked satisfactorily in peace-time but had obvious disadvantages under active service conditions.

The medical arrangements were as follows: Each unit engaged a civil assistant surgeon as the R.M.O. and any patient requiring hospitalisation was admitted to the nearest civil hospital to pass under the care of the civil surgeon. When war broke out the B.F.F. provided one battalion, 8th Burif, and four mobile columns, known as F.F.1, F.F.2, F.F.3 and F.F.4 respectively for service in front of the main defence line. The F.F. unit consisted of headquarters, two troops of mounted infantry and three infantry columns each of about one hundred men. In addition to pack transport it had a few lorries and F.F.2 had some motor-driven native river craft. It was later decided that 8th Burif and the four F.F. columns should come directly under Army. This at once caused much disturbance as the civil assistant surgeons, serving as R.M.Os., declined to accept G.C.O. commissions (the equivalent of the V.C.O. commission) demanding full commissioned rank, which could not be given since at that time only such as held the degree of M.B., B.S. or its equivalent were eligible for commissions in the Army-in-Burma Reserve of Officers (Medical). It was not until 1943 that this regulation was altered.

With the outbreak of war in Europe the Burma Army began to expand, this expansion being speeded up as, with the passing of time, the aggressive intentions of the Japanese became increasingly clear. Early in 1941 from India there came to Burma Indian 13th Infantry Brigade (5/1st Punjab Regt.; 2/7th Rajput Regt.; 1/18th Royal Garhwal Rifles) with supporting units. Later in the same year came Indian 16th Infantry Brigade (1 R./9th Jat. Regt.; 4/12th Frontier Force Regt.; 1/7th Gurkha Rifles) with supporting units. As part of the expansion of the Burma armed forces a number of field medical units had to be raised. The immediate requirements were held to be two field ambulances, two casualty clearing stations, two general hospitals, two field hygiene sections, two ambulance trains, and two motor ambulance sections. The raising of these units was to prove to be a very tardy and difficult affair. In Burma at this time there were a Burma Hospital Company in Rangoon, a detention hospital and a depot of medical stores also in Rangoon, a British military hospital with a Burmese wing at Mingaladon, the military cantonment near Rangoon, a B.M.H. and a district laboratory in Maymyo, a Burmese military hospital also in Maymyo, a Bur.M.H. with a British wing in Mandalay and a Bur.M.H. in Meiktila.

In addition to the Director of Medical Services, Deputy Assistant Director of Hygiene and Deputy Assistant Director of Pathology at Burma Army H.Q. there were serving in Burma with the Army a total of 47 medical officers, 12 Royal Army Medical Corps, 12 Indian Medical Service in military employment, 11 assistant surgeons, British cadre and 12 assistant surgeons, Indian cadre. There were nursing sisters, Queen Alexandra's Imperial Military Nursing Service, in the British military hospitals in Mingaladon and Maymyo.

The United Kingdom and India could offer but little help in the matter of providing medical officers from their own resources for they too were hard pressed to meet the needs of their own swiftly expanding armed forces. A recruiting drive in Burma met with very limited success. After prolonged discussion the Prime Minister gave his consent to the conscription of civilian medical practitioners for military service. But events moved too rapidly for much of value to emerge from this scheme.

The shortage of nursing staff was partly made good by the enrolment of civilian nurses, mostly Anglo-Indian, Anglo-Burman and Karen. An Anglo-Burman section of the R.A.M.C. was formed, similar to the Anglo-Indian section in India, and sent to Maymyo for training. The Burma Hospital Company was expanded tenfold to become the Burma

Hospital Corps and a system of intensive training instituted. The existing military hospitals were expanded by the construction of hutted wards built of local materials. New Burma military hospitals were formed and opened in school buildings and hutted expansions in Taunggyi and Toungoo. The siting of these new hospitals was determined not solely by the defensive plan and by the availability of road and rail communications but also by the siting of new Royal Air Force stations then being constructed to meet tactical needs. It falls to be recorded that many of these sites were deep in highly malarious areas. However they were never used by the R.A.F., though they were by the Japanese. It had been decided to place a hospital in each of these sites rather than a small mobile field medical unit because it was understood that theirs would be a static rôle and because the hospital was so much more liberally equipped than was the small mobile field medical unit.

The civil hospitals in Lashio, Kengtung, Tavoy and Mergui were likewise expanded so that each of them could admit military patients. The civil surgeon in charge of the hospital was to become officer commanding the military hospital when he was recalled to military employment. The depot of medical stores in Rangoon was responsible for supplying not only the military hospitals but the civil hospitals also. Subsidiary depots were established in Insein and Mandalay and placed in charge of retired assistant surgeons, British cadre. Plans for the building of a new and much enlarged depot in Rangoon were prepared.

Two field ambulances were raised, 1 (Burma) and 2 (Burma) Field Ambulances. 2 (Bur.) Fd. Amb. was posted to Taunggyi where it remained until it moved to its operational site east of the Salween River. 1 (Bur.) Fd. Amb. was sent to Moulmein where it was engaged partly in training and partly in running a small hospital to serve the local sick. A Burma field hygiene section was formed and a specialist malariologist (major) appointed. The latter carried out anti-malaria work, using local civilian labour pending the formation of an army anti-malaria unit. Plans were made for the raising of pony companies with Chinese civilian grooms for use in forward evacuation, the two general hospitals, the two ambulance trains, the two M.A.Ss., a convalescent depot and for the provision of a hospital ship.

With Indian 13th Infantry Brigade to Burma had come

60 Indian General Hospital, H.Q. and two sections.
4 (Indian) Casualty Clearing Station.
57 (Ind.) Fd. Amb.
and 'B' detachment of an Indian field hygiene section.

The brigade was stationed initially in Fort Dufferin, Mandalay. 60 I.G.H. opened in a nearby school.

With Indian 16th Infantry Brigade had come
'G' and 'Q' sections of an I.G.H.
'C' sub-section of an Indian field hygiene section.
37 (Ind.) Fd. Amb.

This brigade was likewise stationed in Mandalay.

In July 1941 1st Burma Division was formed. It consisted of 1st and 2nd Burma Infantry Brigades and Indian 13th Infantry Brigade. Its divisional headquarters were in Toungoo. Its A.D.M.S. was an officer of the I.M.S. and its field ambulances 1 (Bur.), 2 (Bur.) and 57 (Ind.).

Burma Army Intelligence had been considering the probable weight and direction of an attack, should the Japanese decide to invade Burma. There were but two possible routes, it was decided, both bad but one slightly better than the other. This was in the Shan States where a motor road ran from Kengtung, east of the Salween, for 300 miles to Thazi on the main road and rail communication between Mandalay and Rangoon. It was considered that this would be the path the main Japanese thrust would take. So two brigades of 1st Burma Division, 1st Burma and Indian 13th Bdes., were moved into the Southern Shan States to cover this road. They were to fight a delaying action east of the Salween along the frontier and fall back to the line of Salween itself. This main defensive position along the river was indeed a formidable one; the river in this area is some two hundred yards wide with a current of about ten knots and it runs between steeply shelving banks of soft mud.

But the only road leading to and from this was the one already mentioned, the one from Meiktila through Thazi and Loilem to Kengtung. This road was narrow and tortuous. Forward of the Salween one-way traffic had to be the rule. The Salween itself had to be crossed by means of a wire-rope ferry operated by the strength of the current and capable of taking but one vehicle at a time. It follows that the evacuation of casualties from the forward area was not likely to be a simple matter. It was arranged that the Burma military hospital in Taunggyi would serve as a base hospital. 2 (Bur.) C.C.S. was sent to Nammawngun, 4 (Ind.) C.C.S. was moved up to Loilem and the two field ambulances with the brigades, (2 (Bur.) and 57 (Ind.)), were disposed in the forward area between Kengtung and the Salween; 60 I.G.H. remained in Mandalay. The L. of C. stretched some two hundred miles between the forward area and Taunggyi, the base. From Taunggyi to the railhead at Shwenyaung was about twelve miles. Thence the journey by rail was to Thazi junction. Staging posts were established on both banks of the Salween at Takaw East and Takaw West and also between Takaw and the forward line. In Kengtung itself a small hospital unit was established under the civil surgeon there to serve the local sick. Since no M.A.S. cars were yet available, field ambulance vehicles had to be used for evacuation right back to railhead.

The third brigade of 1st Burma Division, 2nd Burma Infantry Brigade, was stationed in the south with its headquarters in Moulmein and its forward battalions in Tavoy and Mergui in the Tenasserim strip. Evacuation from these battalions and from Moulmein itself was made difficult by the absence of roads linking them up with each other and with Rangoon. There was no road communication between Rangoon and Moulmein. The journey was either by sea or else by rail from Rangoon to Martaban across the Sittang River and then by river to Moulmein. From Moulmein to Tavoy was by train to Ye, across a small river by boat and then by road for a hundred miles to Tavoy. There was a road between Tavoy and Mergui but during the monsoon this was commonly unusable and then the journey was by launch down the Tavoy River to the sea.

1 (Bur.) Fd. Amb. opened in a small hospital in Moulmein. Evacuation therefrom was by train to Rangoon and thence by motor ambulance to the hospital at Mingaladon. In Tavoy and Mergui the local civil surgeons opened military wings in their civil hospitals.

By the beginning of December 1941 the raising of the field medical units was completed in so far as equipment was concerned but they remained woefully deficient in respect of medical officers. No less than 116 medical officers and 174 assistant and sub-assistant surgeons were required to complete their establishments. More than 20 Regular I.M.S. officers out of a total of 32 occupying civil posts in Burma were recalled to military service.

Each of the ambulance trains carried one hundred lying or two hundred sitting patients and had kitchen cars and quarters for the medical and nursing staff. They were stocked with fourteen days' rations and with plenty of medical comforts. They were composed of converted first and second class coaches of Burma Railways. Since the line was only a metre gauge the coaches were without corridors and so for the serving of meals or for the passage from coach to coach the train had to halt. The patient in his stretcher had to be passed through a window. When active operations started the imperfection or lack of the means of intercommunication between train and those concerned with evacuation matters prevented any firm and constant control over the running of these trains.

By December 1941 the strength of Burma Army, including R.A.F. personnel, was around 45,000. For them there were 3,339 hospital beds, a coverage of about 7·4 per cent. A further 1,250 beds were expected to become available during the next two months but at the same time the army was to continue its expansion to become about 60,000 strong. The hospital bed coverage would therefore remain as before. It was recommended that there should be a 10 per cent. coverage and so India was asked to provide further medical units. 41, 58 and 59 I.G.Hs., another C.C.S., three convalescent depots and certain ancillary units were promised. The number and distribution of hospital beds available in early January 1942 are shown in Appendix II.

Medical planning in Burma, as elsewhere and as is inevitable, was made difficult by the frequent and somewhat violent fluctuations in the estimate of the strength of the force to be served. At one time it was expected that one or more of the Australian divisions returning home from the Middle East (Operation 'Stepsister') would be disembarked at Rangoon and take part in the defence of Burma. But the Australian Government of the day found itself unable to consent to this suggestion for the reason that such a diversion would expose Australia itself to great risk. In late December 1941 it was understood that there was every likelihood that Burma Army would be built up to a final strength of 170,000. This would demand a further 10,000 beds, a target that seemed to those on the spot as being far beyond the range of attainment.

The number of hospital beds was linked up, of course, with the possibility or otherwise of evacuating casualties out of Burma altogether. There was no road communication between Burma and India, though a beginning had been made on the Indian end of such a road, the Tamu road. There was no rail communication between these two countries. So long as the port of Rangoon continued to function so long would it remain possible to consider evacuation by hospital ship. Arrangements would need to be made whereby parties of 450 or so casualties for evacuation were collected and held in or near Rangoon so that the actual time spent by the hospital ship in dock would be minimal. But should this port become unusable for any reason, the only possible method of evacuation out of Burma would be by air. Requests for the provision of air ambulances had been addressed to the proper quarters.

MEDICAL LOCATION STATEMENT. DECEMBER 1, 1941

1 Bur. General Hospital H.Q. and one section	Toungoo
B.M.H.	Maymyo
Bur.M.H.	,,
Bur.M.H. with British wing	Mandalay
Bur.M.H.	Meiktila
B.M.H. with Burmese wing	Mingaladon nr. Rangoon
Detention Hospital	Rangoon
Burma Hospital Company H.Q. and Depot	,,
Depot medical stores	,,
District Laboratory	Maymyo

Indian 16th Inf. Bde. Group
   3 (Ind.) Fd. Amb. Troop R.I.A.S.C.
   37 (Ind.) Fd. Amb.
   I.G.H. 'G' and 'Q' sections
   'C' Sub-section of (Ind.) Fd. Hyg. Sec.
	Mandalay

Ind. 13th Inf. Bde. Gp.
    8 M.A.S. detachment — East Taunggyi
    57 (Ind.) Fd. Amb. — ,,
    1 (Ind.) Fd. Amb. Troop R.I.A.S.C. — ,,
    'B' detach. of an Indian Fd. Hyg. Sec. — Loilem
    4 (Ind.) C.C.S. — ,,
    60 I.G.H. — Mandalay

Southern Shan States Area
    Bur.M.H. with British wing — Taunggyi
    2 (Bur.) Fd. Amb. one company leaving for — Taunggyi
    2 (Bur.) Fd. Amb. one company — Loimwe (near the Chinese border and due east of Taunggyi)
    2 (Bur.) C.C.S. less one section — Nammawngun
    2 (Bur.) Fd. Amb. less two coys. — Panghkam (south-east of Laihka and near Namhkam)
    2 (Bur.) Fd. Hyg. Sec. — Taunggyi

Tenasserim Area
    1 (Bur.) Fd. Amb. — Moulmein
    1 (Bur.) C.C.S. — ,,
    1 (Bur.) Fd. Hyg. Sec. — ,,
    Bur.M.H. — Mergui
    Bur.M.H. — Tavoy

At the end of December the troops were so disposed that they could guard the airfields and keep watch upon the most likely invasion routes.

2nd Burma Brigade. H.Q. Moulmein
    Mergui. 2nd Burma Rifles; 3rd Burma Rifles, two companies; Burma Frontier Force, detach.
    Tavoy. 6th Burma Rifles; Tavoy Company of Tenasserim Battalion of the Burma Auxiliary Force (B.A.F.).
    Moulmein. 1/7th Gurkha Rifles; 8th Burma Rifles; Tenasserim Battalion, B.A.F. less Tavoy Company; one Indian mountain battery (12th).
    nr. Kawkareik. 4th Burma Rifles.
    Rangoon. H.Q. Rangoon Area: 1st Glosters; 3rd Burma Rifles (less two companies).
    Southern Shan States. H.Q. 1st Burma Division; Indian 2nd Mountain Battery, a 4-gun 18 pdr. Battery B.A.F.; Indian 13th Inf. Bde.; 1st Burma Bde. (2nd K.O.Y.L.I., 1st and 5th Burma Rifles); Burma Frontier Force, detachments.
    Mandalay Area. Indian 16th Inf. Bde. less one battalion. 7th Burma Rifles in reserve.

On January 5, 1942 the first flight of Indian 17th Division arrived. An advanced headquarters was established in Moulmein. This division originally consisted of 44th, 45th and 46th Brigades. To Burma with the headquarters of the division came 46th Bde. (7/10th Baluch Regt.; 3/7th Gurkha Rifles and 5/17th Dogra Regt.) The other two brigades were diverted to Malaya and were destroyed there. To Indian 17th Division were added 48th Bde. (1/3rd Queen Alexandra's Own Gurkha Rifles, 1/4th Prince of Wales's Own Gurkha Rifles, 2/5th Royal Gurkha Rifles (F.F.)) from Indian 19th Division, withdrawn from the northwest frontier of India and 63rd Bde. (1/11th King George V's Own Sikh Regt.; 2/13th Frontier Force Rifles; 1/10th Gurkha Rifles) which reached Rangoon from India just before this capital city was finally evacuated.

To Burma were sent three unallotted British battalions, 2nd Duke of Wellington's Regt., 1st West Yorkshire Regt. and 1st Cameronians. Early in March, after the sea communications between India and Burma were cut, 1st Royal Inniskilling Fusiliers were flown in to Magwe airfield.

7th Armoured Brigade, (7th Queen's Own Hussars, 2nd Royal Tank Regt., 414th Bty., R.H.A. and 'A' Bty. 95th A/Tk. Regt.) on its way from the Middle East to Malaya, was diverted to Rangoon on the orders of General Wavell.

One regiment of Chinese 93rd Division was moving towards the Southern Shan States with the object of taking over the defence of the Mekong River line. Its headquarters was to be in Mong Yawng, east of Kengtung and near the frontier. The rest of the division was around Puerh, east of the Mekong, but it was agreed that it should be moved to the Kengtung area. Chinese 49th and 55th Divisions were near Paoshan on the Burma-China Road, 49th Division being about to move up to Wanting, in reserve. Later this division was to move into the Southern Shan States to take over the area of the Salween about Takaw when 55th Division would move to Wanting to complete its training.

It was then decided to move Indian 16th Bde. from the Mandalay area to that of Moulmein. At this time this brigade consisted of 1/7th G.R. and 4th Burif. 4/12th F.F.R. was with 2nd Burma Bde. (u/c Indian 17th Division) and 1 R./9th Jat was already in Moulmein along with H.Q. Indian 17th Division. In Mergui were 2nd Burif. and two companies of the third battalion; in Tavoy were 6th Burif. On January 14 the units in the vicinity of Moulmein were distributed as follows:

    Kawkareik. 1/7th G.R. less one company; 4th Burif.; 1 R./9th Jat; and an Indian mountain battery.

    Kyungyaung. 1/7th G.R., one company watching the Three Pagodas Pass.

Moulmein. 4/12th F.F.R. charged with the task of keeping open the road from Ye to Tavoy. 7th Burif.

The turn of the year brought a new G.O.C. and a new D.D.M.S. to Burma. The latter at once obtained sanction for an enlargement of the number of medical officers and clerks on the establishment of the Medical Branch at Army H.Q. He then proceeded to transform the peace-time civil hospitals into Burma General Hospitals. By a stroke of the pen twelve such hospitals were brought into existence, long in advance of the final sanction of the Defence Department being obtained. In order to economise on motor ambulance cars he took steps to have provided a third ambulance train. He also, with the co-operation of the Irrawaddy Flotilla Company, made arrangements for the conversion of a number of their river steamers into hospital river steamers. These were a most useful addition to the medical facilities for in many of the areas in which troops were likely to be engaged there was no railway available for evacuation purposes. The steamers, with their two or three tiers of open decks, were admirably suited for their new function. They were clearly marked with the Red Cross and staffed by 4 (Ind.) C.C.S.

THE PHYSICAL FEATURES OF BURMA

Burma, roughly three times the size of the United Kingdom, lies between the 28th and the 10th degrees of latitude and between the 93rd and 103rd degrees of longtitude. It forms the western portion of the sub-continent of Indo-China and is surrounded on three sides by great mountain ranges and on the fourth by the sea. On the east it is bounded by Thailand, French-Indo-China (now Laos) and China; on the north by Tibet and India; on the west by India (and now also East Pakistan) and the Bay of Bengal; and on the south by the Andaman Sea and the Gulf of Martaban.

Physically the country falls naturally into three well-marked geomorphological divisions; the Western Hills, the Central Belt and the Shan Plateau with its southward continuation in the Tenasserim. The Western Hills stem from the vast mountain knot in the Tibeto-Chinese borderlands and swing southwards through the Naga and the Chin Hills and the Arakan Yomas (Yomas in Burmese means mountain range) in a grand arc of some 700 miles along the sea to Cape Negrais, just west of the Irrawaddy Delta. In the north the Kachin Hills form a semi-circular arc capping the northern tip of the country. The Central Belt consists of the valleys of the Irrawaddy, Chindwin and Sittang Rivers and forms a great trough between the Shan Plateau and the Arakan Yomas to end within the Irrawaddy Delta. The Shan Plateau is a vast tableland with an average height of 3,000 ft. and is deeply scarred with the gorges of the Salween River. A southern continuation of this plateau forms the Tenasserim Yomas, a series of parallel ridges running down the narrow strip of Burma which stretches southwards to the Malayan border.

The mountain system of Burma consists of north-south offshoots of the Tibetan mountains and is shaped like a vast horseshoe which borders Burma's land frontiers in the west, north and east. In the west, mountain ranges 700 miles long and 150 miles broad stretch from the Naga Hills and the Chin Hills in the north to the Arakan Yomas in the south. On the Burma-Tibet border the passes over the mountains are well over 10,000 ft. up. In the east the Kachin Hills, the Shan Plateau, the Karenni Hills and the Tenasserim Yomas range from 3,000 to 5,000 ft. in height. In central Burma the Pegu Yomas, sharply marked off from the surrounding plains, form one of the leading teak areas in the country.

Just as the mountains of Burma run from north to south, so also do the rivers and their valleys. The valley of the Irrawaddy constitutes Burma proper. The river, over 1,000 miles long, rises near Fort Hertz, courses throughout the whole length of Burma and enters the sea near Rangoon. It is navigable for about 900 miles and is Burma's main highway. Below Prome, the Irrawaddy fans out to form the vast Delta of some 10,000 sq. miles, one of the great rice-bowls of the East. The Chindwin, to the west of the Irrawaddy, is the main tributary of this river which it joins near Pakokku. It is navigable for about 300 miles of its length. Near Mandalay the Irrawaddy suddenly bears westwards and then turns southwards again to be joined by the Chindwin. South of this Mandalay twist of the Irrawaddy the Sittang River now runs in the channel which the Irrawaddy formerly occupied. The two rivers are separated by the Pegu Yomas. After a course of about 300 miles the Sittang opens out into a wide estuary and empties into the Gulf of Martaban. The wild Salween River, to the east of the Irrawaddy, rising in Tibet, cuts through the Shan Plateau. It is an angry torrent walled on either side by high banks.

West of the Arakan Yomas the coastland along the Bay of Bengal is deeply intersected by bays, gulfs and islands.

THE CLIMATE

The greater part of Burma lies within the Tropics and the climate throughout the country at low to moderate altitudes is tropical with a well-defined rainy season. This rainy season, due to the south-west monsoon, stretches from mid-May to mid-October. The coastal regions of Arakan and Tenasserim and the mountains in the extreme north of the country have a rainfall of about two hundred inches annually. The Irrawaddy Delta has an average rainfall of about one hundred inches

PREPARATION FOR WAR

and the hills of the east average about eighty inches. The Arakan Yomas cut off central Burma from the monsoon and so this Dry Zone, which includes Mandalay has an annual rainfall of only some 25 to 45 inches.

The hot season precedes the rains and lasts from February to April and follows them in October. Shade temperatures of 100 degrees Fahrenheit (38°C.) are then to be expected in the Delta and in the Dry Zone.

The cold season runs from November to January when the temperature in south Burma can fall to about 60 degrees Fahrenheit (16°C.) while in the Dry Zone and in the mountainous north the cold may become intense.

The Delta and the coastlands are humid at all times throughout the year. In Upper Burma the hill stations provide a cool and very pleasant climate.

In this narrative it is so often necessary to refer to the intense heat and to the torrential rain that by one who does not know the country it might be thought that of Burma's climate nothing good could be said. This is not so. There are periods when, even in the regions with the worst of reputations, the weather is excellent in every way. But when it is bad, it is very bad indeed and so from the military point of view it is the bad weather and not the good that claims importance. When military operations are conducted in monsoon weather, that army which is the better protected against the elements and against the concomitants of bad weather is greatly advantaged. As this story unfolds it will be seen that in this respect the advantage lay with the Allies.

COMMUNICATIONS

From Rangoon, the capital, on the Hlaing River, 20 miles from the sea, radiate all the lines of communication through the country. The Burma Railway, running north to Mandalay, a distance of 386 miles, was double-tracked only for the first 176 miles. The rest and all the branch lines, all metre gauge, were single tracked. From Pegu, 47 miles north of Rangoon, ran two branch lines, one to Thongwa in the south and the other across the Sittang bridge to Martaban, to the east, where a ferry linked it up with Moulmein and the railway that ran south therefrom to Ye. From Pyinmana, 226 miles north of Rangoon, a branch line ran north-west to Taungdwingyi and Kyaukpadaung, the nearest rail point to the oil fields at Yenangyaung and Chauk. At Thazi junction, 306 miles north of Rangoon, two branch lines originated. The Southern Shan States branch ran eastwards to end at Shwenyaung, just west of Taunggyi, the capital of these States. The other branch line was a loop to Meiktila and Myingyan on the Irrawaddy. It rejoined the main line at Paleik, 12 miles south of Mandalay.

From Rangoon a second line ran north-west *via* Tharrawaddy on the Irrawaddy to Prome, 161 miles away. From this line a branch at Letpadan was connected by ferry with Henzada on the right bank of the Irrawaddy and from Henzada one branch ran north to Kyangin and another south to Bassein to serve the western part of the Delta.

From Mandalay, the second city of Burma and the capital of Thibaw, the last of the Burmese kings, one line ran through the Northern Shan States *via* Maymyo to Lashio, another connected Mandalay with Madaya, 17 miles away and a third branch ran to the Irrawaddy a few miles south of the city opposite Sagaing to cross the Ava bridge and to turn north to Shwebo and Myitkyina. From Sagaing there was a branch line which ran through Monywa and Alon on the Chindwin to end at Ye-U. At the end of 1941 only a few miles of the Burma–China railway, which was to link up the Burmese railway at Lashio with the Chinese system, had been laid.

There were several bridges of military importance on this railway system, the one over the Pazundaung creek just outside Rangoon, the one over the Myitnge River and the Ava bridge over the Irrawaddy, both just south of Mandalay, one over the Sittang at Mokpalin and one over the Bilin at Hninpale. In the Northern Shan States there was the Gokteik viaduct over the gorge of this name.

The great thoroughfares of Burma were her rivers. Her road system was very poor and had not been developed. There was no good overland communication between Arakan and the rest of the country. A single track, totally unsuitable for motor traffic, ran from the right bank of the Irrawaddy near Prome westwards across the Arakan Yomas to Taungup, a village on the coast. Intercommunication was mostly by sea or by air. Of the main roads, the all-weather one from Rangoon to Mandalay was the most important. From Pegu it followed the railway fairly closely. Twenty miles north of Rangoon at Taukkyan the road forked, one arm going to Tharrawaddy, Prome, Allanmyo and Taungdwingyi and the oilfields, turning east near Kyaukpadaung to rejoin the main trunk road at Meiktila. This road was metalled and bridged in parts of its length only. Many water courses (chaungs) were unbridged and some were distinctly treacherous, e.g. the Pin Chaung just north of Yenangyaung. As has been already stated, there was no road communication between Rangoon and Moulmein and the bridge over the Sittang was not a road bridge. The Tenasserim strip was wellnigh roadless. From Moulmein a road ran south to Amherst through Thanbyuzayat and thence a short branch went to Pangna. South of this there was no road to Ye. Beyond the Ye River a road led to Tavoy and Mergui though this was cut by many wide streams and small rivers where primitive ferries were in use. Beyond Mergui communication with Victoria Point was by sea. An all-weather road connecting Rangoon with Mergui, begun in 1941, was an item in the defence programme. There were no road links between Moulmein, Tavoy or Mergui with Thailand though there were three recognised routes. The easiest way into Thailand from Moulmein was by the Gyaing River to Kyondo and thence by road to Kawkareik. In 1941 the track between Kawkareik and the frontier village of Myawadi had been improved. At Myawadi the Thaungyin River, a tributary of the Salween, formed the boundary between Burma and Thailand. A good cart track linked Mesoht with Raheng in Thailand and another entered Burma from Thailand by way of the Three Pagodas Pass,* south-east of Moulmein, and joined up with the Kawkareik–Kyondo road. The third route was from Tavoy whence a road ran east to Myitta, quite near the border and from Myitta a track continued into Thailand.

From Toungoo, on the Rangoon–Mandalay trunk road, a road had been built to connect this town with Mawchi and Kemapyu on the Salween. It crossed the Sittang over a bridge and then turned north to Bawlake and Taunggyi. From Meiktila a road passed through the Southern Shan States to Taunggyi, Loilem and Takaw on the Salween and from the east bank of this river to Kengtung and the frontier village of Tachilek, where it linked up with the Thai road system. The crossing of the Salween was by ferry. It had several feeder roads running north and south. Some of these linked up with the Mandalay–Lashio–Wanting road through the Northern Shan States. This Mandalay–Lashio–Wanting road had been considerably improved between Maymyo and Lashio and had been extended from Lashio to the Chinese frontier at Wanting where it linked up with the new Burma Road to Kunming and Chungking. Since the Hankow–Canton railway had been cut by the Japanese in 1938 this road formed the main line of intercommunication between China and the outside world and it was carrying an immense amount of traffic.

The Mandalay–Lashio–Wanting road had several feeders running to the north. The most important of them went to Bhamo and thence continued as a track to Myitkyina. From Mandalay a road led to Sagaing beyond the Irrawaddy and crossed the river by means of the Ava bridge to continue northwards to Shwebo and Kin-U and thence to Ye-U on the Mu River, a tributary of the Irrawaddy. At Ye-U it turned south to Alon and Monywa on the Chindwin and then eastwards to Myinmu on the Irrawaddy. West of Monywa and Ye-U there were no roads. There were tracks of sorts and at times some of these were motorable. In the rainy season they were useless.

In 1941 there were airfields at Mingaladon, Lashio and at Akyab. An air service was operating between Chungking and Rangoon. There were

---

* The Three Pagodas Pass is due east of Ye. It was through this pass that the infamous 'Railway of Death' was later to be built.

airstrips at Moulmein, Tavoy and Mergui and, as has been told, other airfields were being prepared as part of the defence scheme.

POPULATION

In 1941 the total population of Burma numbered about 16,800,000 and included a number of different ethnic groups, e.g. Burmans, Karens, Shans, Chins, Kachins and Nagas in addition to a considerable number of nationals of other countries, particularly Indians and Chinese. Of Indians there were about a million, of Chinese about a quarter of a million. The Kachin country was in the great hills of the north as was that of the Nagas in the north-east. The Chins in the western part and the Shans in the eastern part spread across the central belt of the country. The Burmans were concentrated in the Delta and the Karens along the Thai border but they were also intermingled with the Burmans throughout the southern part of the country. The Indians provided very much of the labour in Rangoon and were concentrated in clerical positions and in trade. In Rangoon there was a large Chinese quarter of which the inhabitants were industriously engaged in trade and crafts.

THE POLITICAL CLIMATE

In Burma, as also in India, there was considerable unrest during the years immediately preceding the war. A nationalist group grew in numbers and strength to demand independence from foreign domination. As the threat of invasion increased in intensity it was found necessary to place the nationalist leaders under arrest. Thirty of them, however, slipped away to Japan where they underwent military training. They returned to Burma with the Japanese troops who captured Tavoy and formed the Burma Independence Army to be used against the British in the liberation of the country. It was estimated that about 5 per cent. of the population of Burma sided with this nationalist party, a small proportion of the whole but enough to add considerably to the difficulties and dangers that beset the British and Indian troops during the disastrous first phase of the campaign in Burma.

MEDICAL INTELLIGENCE

Burma was not an unknown country to the British and the Indian Armies. Their medical services were well acquainted with the principal diseases of military importance that were certainly to be encountered should fighting break out. Malaria was the most widely prevalent disease in the country and was responsible for the greater proportion of the morbidity and of the mortality. In 1939, for example, 39·82 per cent. of the total recorded mortality in Burma was ascribed to 'fevers'. It is certain that more than half of these 'fevers' were in fact instances of malaria. Undoubtedly this was the disease which the military authorities had reason to fear most. In 1941, it must be remembered, thoroughly reliable techniques of malaria control had not yet become standardised, the weapons of precision that were then being forged were not yet ready. The map showing the malarious areas of Burma clearly indicates the gravity of the danger that the troops of both sides would have to face should the Japanese decide to invade the country.

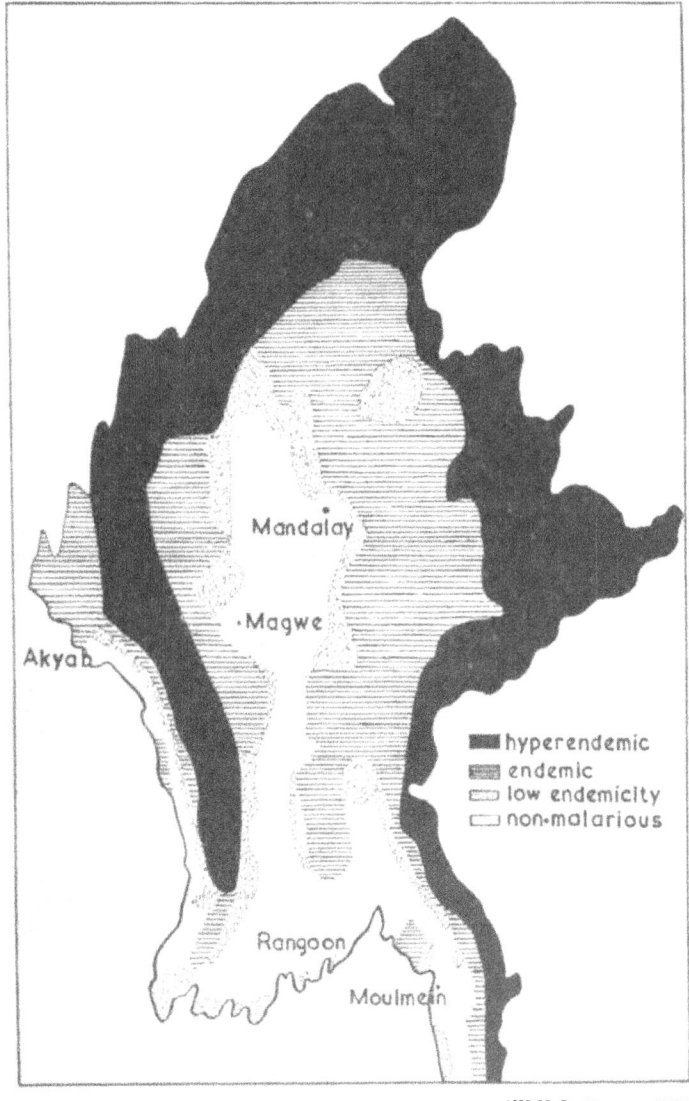

(*W.H.O. Surveys 1958*)

FIG. 1. The Malarious Areas of Burma

Cholera, plague, smallpox, the enteric group of fevers, dysentery and cerebro-spinal fever were known to have caused 1,468, 3,266, 125, 383, 6,531 and 34 deaths respectively in the year 1939 and were surely to be encountered as an army moved through the country. It was known too that no less than 84,208 people had been treated for venereal disease in 1939 and that syphilis and gonorrhoea were very widespread, especially among the hill peoples. Scrub typhus was known to be endemic in the Chin Hills, in parts of the Shan States and in the jungle in the central Mandalay–Thazi area.

Only a very few of the major towns had a piped water supply, the water usually came from upland streams or from deep wells. In the rural areas the main sources of supply were rainwater ponds and surface wells. Rivers, streams and irrigation canals were also much used. Rangoon was the only city which had sewers and these did not serve the whole of the citizens. Most of the towns had a pit privy system of excreta disposal, sometimes as a supplementary measure to the bucket latrine system. The conservancy labourers were exclusively Indian. In the rural areas surface latrines or secluded jungle areas were in common use. There was no system of refuse disposal in the rural areas. In the towns there was no adequate supervision of the labourers who dealt with the refuse. Fly-breeding grounds abounded everywhere.

From the very beginning it was abundantly clear that should there be a campaign in Burma, its medical aspects were likely to assume very great importance. There were very few other theatres on earth in which an army would encounter so many and such violent hazards. In Burma all the dread agents of fell disease and foul death lay in wait. The Army Medical Services would be tested more thoroughly in Burma than anywhere else where armies were likely to fight in the war that was soon to become global in its extent.

It is suggested that it will be found profitable as well as interesting when considering the medical aspects of this campaign, to bear in mind the observations concerning matters medical made by the official historian of the First Burmese War, 1824–26, Professor H. H. Wilson, F.R.S. The following extracts from his book will serve to illustrate the rôle that disease played in determining the outcome of that conflict:

> page 85. 'The vicinity of Rangoon, except about the town or along the main road, was covered with swamp or jungle, through which the men were obliged to wade knee-deep in water, or force their way through harassing and wearisome entanglements. The rains had set in, and the effects of a burning sun were only relieved by the torrents that fell from the accumulated clouds, and which brought disease along with their coolness. Constantly exposed to the vicissitudes of a tropical climate, and exhausted by the necessity of uninterrupted exertion, it need not be a matter of surprise that sickness now began to thin the ranks and impair the energies of the

invaders. No rank was exempt from the operation of these causes, and many officers, amongst whom were the senior naval officer..., the political commissioner... and the commander-in-chief, himself, were attacked with fever during the month of June. Amongst the privates, the Europeans especially, the sickness incident to fatigue and exposure was aggravated by the defective quantity and quality of the provisions which had been supplied for their use. Relying upon the reported facility of obtaining cattle and vegetables at Rangoon, it had not been thought necessary to embark stores for protracted consumption on board the transports from Calcutta and the Madras troops landed with a still more limited stock. As soon as the deficiency was ascertained, arrangements were made to remedy it, but in the meantime, before supplies could reach Rangoon, the troops were dependent upon salt meat, much of which was in a state of putrescence, and biscuit in an equally repulsive condition, under the decomposing influence of heat and moisture. The want of sufficient and wholesome food enhanced the evil effects of the damp soil and atmosphere, and of the malaria from the decaying vegetable matter of the surrounding forests, and the hospitals were rapidly filled with sick beyond the means available of medical treatment; fever and dysentery were the principal maladies, and were no more than the ordinary consequences of local causes; but the scurvy and hospital gangrene, which also made their appearance, were ascribable as much to depraved habits and inadequate nourishment, as to fatigue and exposure. They were also latterly, in some degree, the consequences of extreme exhaustion, forming a peculiar feature of the prevailing fever, which bore an epidemic type, and which had been felt with equal severity in Bengal. The fatal operation of these causes was enhanced by their continuance, and towards the end of the rainy season, scarcely three thousand men were fit for active duty. The arrival of adequate supplies, and more especially, the change of the monsoon, restored the force to a more healthy condition.

'Although, however, the proportion of the sick was a serious deduction from the available force, it was not such as to render it unequal to offensive operations altogether, nor inadequate to repel, in the most decisive manner, the collected assault of the Burman force that had been some time assembling in its vicinity.'

page 105. 'The rains which had intermitted in October, returned with unusual violence in the beginning of November, and prevented the continuance of active operations as well as retarded the convalescence of the sick; scarcely thirteen hundred Europeans were fit for duty, and although the native regiments suffered less severely, they were also greatly enfeebled; the prospect of improved weather and more wholesome supplies kept up the spirits of the men, and they looked forward with impatience to the resumption of hostilities.'

page 285. Note II (referring to the above) 'A correct notion of the extent of the prevailing sickness, may be formed from the following statement of a competent observer. "During June, July, August, September, and October, the average monthly admissions into hospital from the artillery, was sixty-five Europeans and sixty-two natives, being nearly one-third of the greatest numerical strength of the former, and one-fourth of the latter; and large as was this number, I am assured, that it was considerably less, in proportion, than that which was exhibited by any European regiment, in either division of the army. The aggregate number in hospital, during the whole fourteen months, to which this account is limited, was six hundred and five Europeans, and six hundred and eighty-seven natives, a large proportion being made up of re-admission for dysentery. Of the former, forty-nine died, including twelve who had died in the field hospitals of Rangoon and Mergui, or a fraction less than one in twelve and a half. Amongst the latter, thirty-four deaths occurred, or something less than one in twenty. On the setting in of the cold season, the general sickness began to decline, and from January to July 1825, it was comparatively moderate."

page 110. 'The British force, reduced by sickness and by the casualties of the service was far from adequate to the defence of the position they occupied . . .'

page 162. 'The season also brought with it, its usual pestiferous influence, in the midst of a low country over-run with jungle, and intersected by numerous shallow and muddy rivers. Notwithstanding the precautions that had been taken in the timely cantonment of the troops at Arakan, fever and dysentery broke out among them to an alarming extent, and with the most disastrous results. That the unavoidable privations of troops on service tended to aggravate the severity of the complaints, was a necessary occurrence; but all ranks were equally affected, and a large proportion of officers fell victims to the climate, Brigadier-General Morrison himself (*commanding the force*) after struggling through the campaign against it, was obliged to quit the country, and died on his way to Europe. The maladies were so universal, and the chance of subduing them so hopeless, that the Government of Bengal was at last impelled to the necessity of recalling the troops altogether, leaving divisions of them on the islands of Cheduba and Ramree, and the opposite coast of Sandoway, where the climate appeared to be not unfavourable to their health.'

page 184. '. . . in the commencement of May, the periodical change of seasons took place and obliged the force to establish itself in cantonments at Prome. Previous to the setting in of the rains, the thermometer had risen in the shade to 110°, but the nights remained cool, and the climate was not found unhealthy. The monsoon brought with it its ordinary effects upon the condition of the troops, especially the Europeans who, although they suffered less heavily than at Rangoon, lost nearly one-seventh of their number between June and October. The native troops were much more exempt, although not wholly free from disease; . . . it seems probable, therefore, that much of the disease that still prevailed was the consequence of previous exposure and exhaustion, although ascribable in some measure to the effects of climate, and of ill-selected quarters for the troops.'

page 262. 'The cost of the war . . . probably did not exceed five or six crores of rupees, or five millions sterling. The loss of life was a more serious consideration. The mortality amongst the native troops in Ava and Arakan is illustrated in the notes annexed to these page (*Note 14 below*).

For that of His Majesty's regiments, we have the authentic documents of the army medical department, presented to Parliament in 1841. From these it appears that, within the first eleven months after landing at Rangoon, nearly one-half the Europeans died; and that a similar rate of loss occurred in the subsequent operations at Prome and to the northwards. In like manner, in Arakan, at least three-fourths of the European force perished, and of those who survived few were again fit for service. Altogether the deaths nearly equalled the number of British troops originally employed; so that, but for the reinforcements which from time to time arrived, the whole would have been annihilated.'

'Of the loss thus sustained the casualties in action although numerically small, yet bear a very large ratio to the invading force, being nearly equal to that suffered in the peninsular war; the latter being about four, the former about three-and-a-half per cent. The proportionate loss by disease was infinitely greater. In Arakan the mortality was attributable entirely to climate, for there the campaign was short, the supplies were sufficient, and the troops but little exposed. In Burma the climate was comparatively innocuous, for all prior and subsequent experience have established the superior salubrity of Rangoon and the Tenasserim provinces to other parts of India within the tropics. At the same time the season of the year is to be taken into account, and the severity of the exposure which the troops underwent. Their being repeatedly in their field during tropical rain, their daily marching through inundated fields, and their bivouacking unsheltered amidst mud and water, were trials to which no European constitutions could be subjected with impunity, and when to this cause of sickness was added unwholesome and insufficient food, it need not be a matter of surprise that fevers and disorders of the digestive organs should have remorselessly mowed down the ranks of the British force in Ava. . . . a useful lesson may at least be learnt in the event of future warfare in the Burman country as to the necessity for commencing operations at the season best fitted for taking the field, and of being provided with the means of proceeding rapidly through the delta of the Irrawaddi, to the vicinity of the capital, where military operations can be carried out by Europeans without that injury to health and constitution which for a time paralyses their efforts in the lower division of the empire. With these precautions and a due attention to the troops being made independent of local resources for their supplies, it may be anticipated that a very moderate force of Europeans would be able to accomplish what on this occasion employed at Rangoon and Arakan the combined efforts of twenty-thousand men; of whom not more than a tenth part could ultimately be brought into the field in the actions which decided the fate of the empire.'

page 288. Note 14 (referring to the above) 'The whole number of British troops that landed at Rangoon . . . was exclusive of officers, 3,586; the number of reinforcements does not appear but that of the deaths was 3,115, of which not more than 150 occurred in action, or from wounds. Of about 150 officers sixteen were killed in action or in consequence of their wounds, and forty-five died of disease. In Arakan the loss in action was none but of the average strength of the two regiments, amounting to

1,004 men, 595 died in the country in the course of eight months and of those who quitted it not more than a half were alive at the end of twelve months.'

APPENDIX I

ORDER OF BATTLE AT THE COMMENCEMENT OF HOSTILITIES

(1) 1st Burma Division.
    Maymyo Brigade
      2nd K.O.Y.L.I.
      1st Burif.
      6th ,,
      7th ,,
      Indian 12th Mountain Battery
      56th Fd. Coy. Sappers and Miners
    Tenasserim Brigade
      2nd Burif.
      4th ,,
      5th ,,
      8th ,,
      Indian 2nd Mountain Battery
      Fd. Coy. section
    Indian 13th Inf. Bde.
      5/1st Punjab
      2/7th Rajput
      1/18th R. Garh. Rif.
      Indian 23rd Mountain Battery
      5th Fd. Battery R.A., B.A.F.

(2) Rangoon Brigade
    1st Glosters
    3rd Burif.
    Coast Defence Battery

(3) Indian 16th Inf. Bde.
      1 R./9th Jat.
      4/12th F.F.R.
      1/7th G.R.
      Indian 5th Mountain Battery
      Indian 27th Mountain Regt. H.Q.
      50th Fd. Coy. Sappers and Miners

PREPARATION FOR WAR

(4) Burma Frontier Force
    Bhamo   Battalion
    Chin Hills   ,,
    Myitkyina   ,,
    Northern Shan States ,,
    Southern Shan States ,,
    Kokine   ,,
    Reserve   ,,

(5) Garrison Companies. 1st, 2nd, 3rd, 4th and 5th.

(6) Burma Rifles (Territorials)
    11th   Battalion
    12th   ,,
    13th (Southern Shan States) ,,
    14th   ,,   (forming)

(7) Burma Auxiliary Force (B.A.F.)
    Rangoon   Battalion
    Upper Burma   ,,
    Burma Railways   ,,
    Tenasserim   ,,
    An A.A. Regt.   (forming)

(8) Burma Rifles
    9th and 10th battalions (forming)
    Six anti-tank troops
    One field battery

(9) Field Company, forming

(10) Armed Police. Three battalions

Summary
    Infantry
        British   2 battalions
        Indian   6
        Burma Rifles (Regulars)   8 (4 of them just formed)
                   (Territorials)   4
        Garrison Companies   5
        Burma Auxiliary Force   4
        Burma Frontier Force   6
            and in reserve   1
                                                ―
                                          36
    Artillery
        Indian Mountain Batteries   3
        Burma Auxiliary Force   1 field battery of 18 pdrs.
        Burma Frontier Force   5 mobile detachments

(*Operations in the Far East from 17th October, 1940 to 27th December, 1941*
Air Chief Marshal Sir Robert Brooke-Popham, G.C.V.O., K.C.B., C.B., C.M.G., D.S.O., A.F.C. The London Gazette, 22 January, 1948. H.M.S.O.)

APPENDIX II
HOSPITAL BEDS AVAILABLE IN JANUARY 1942

Area	Hospital	British	Indian/Burmese	Totals
Rangoon Area	C.D.H. Rangoon	4	4	8
	B.M.H. with Burmese wing Mingaladon	110	90	200
	59 I.G.H. with British wing from Moulmein	41	140	181
Toungoo Area	1 Bur.G.H. H.Q. and 4 sections Toungoo	—	400	400
Taunggyi Area	Bur.M.H. with British wing	110	390	500
Meiktila Area	Bur.M.H.	4	102	106
Mandalay Area	'G' Sec. I.G.H.	—	100	100
	'Q' Sec. I.G.H.	—	100	100
	60 I.G.H. H.Q. and 2 sections	—	200	200
	Bur.M.H. with British wing	15	325	340
Maymyo Area	B.M.H.	57	—	57
	41 I.G.H. H.Q. and 10 sections	—	1,000	1,000
	Bur.M.H.	—	230	230
Lashio	R.A.F. Hospital	48	—	48
Namsang(Assam)	R.A.F. Hospital	42	—	42
Thayetmyo	Garrison Company Hospital	—	22	22
Indian 17th Division	1 (Bur.) C.C.S.	—	100	100
	2 (Bur.) C.C.S.	—	100	100
	4 (Ind.) C.C.S.	—	200	200
	1 Bur. S.S.	—	25	25
	2 Bur. S.S.	—	25	25
R.A.F. Sections	7 'Sick-bays' 8 beds each	56	—	56
		487	3,553	4,040

CHAPTER 2

THE JAPANESE INVADE BURMA

DURING the early days of January 1942 many reports were received indicating that the Japanese were concentrating in some strength near the Burma–Thai border between Raheng and Myawadi. On the 3rd it was reported that the Japanese were intending to advance on Tavoy in about three weeks' time. On the 16th two companies of 6th Burma Rifles from Tavoy bumped into a party of Japanese about a hundred strong on the track leading from the north of Tavoy to the border. They withdrew but on the following day, being reinforced by a company of 3rd Burma Rifles, recently transferred from Rangoon, they went out again. They ran into trouble, lost their transport and disintegrated. Most of them, taking to the jungle, managed to find their way back to Moulmein there to spread despondency and gloom. On the morning of the 19th the Japanese attacked and gained the Tavoy airfield and got astride the road from Tavoy to Ye. The Tavoy garrison promptly disintegrated. From Victoria Point Japanese patrols were probing towards Mergui. It had been decided that the Mergui garrison should be withdrawn to Tavoy but now that Tavoy had gone it was withdrawn by sea to Rangoon.

THE ACTION NEAR THE KAWKAREIK PASS

On January 20 the Japanese crossed the frontier at points north of the confluence of the Mepale and Thaungyin Rivers, at Myawadi and at Palu south-east of Myawadi on the River Thaungyin and attacked the positions held by Indian 16th Brigade in the woods a few hundred yards from the Thai border in the area of Myawadi. They first came up against the forward posts held by 1/7th G.R. and then on the 21st began to press hard against the main defensive position of the brigade about Kawkareik held by 1 R./9th Jat. Orders had been issued to the effect that the brigade was not to become so involved that withdrawal became impossible and so on the 22nd the brigade withdrew. It meant to proceed to Kyondo from Kawkareik and thence travel by boat down the Gyaing River to Moulmein. Its vehicles had to cross the river by river ferry seven miles south-west of Kawkareik. An overloaded ammunition truck sank this ferry and so the rest of the transport moved with the brigade to Kyondo where the vehicles and most of their contents were destroyed. The brigade then moved down the east bank of the Gyaing until picked up by river steamers and conveyed to Martaban.

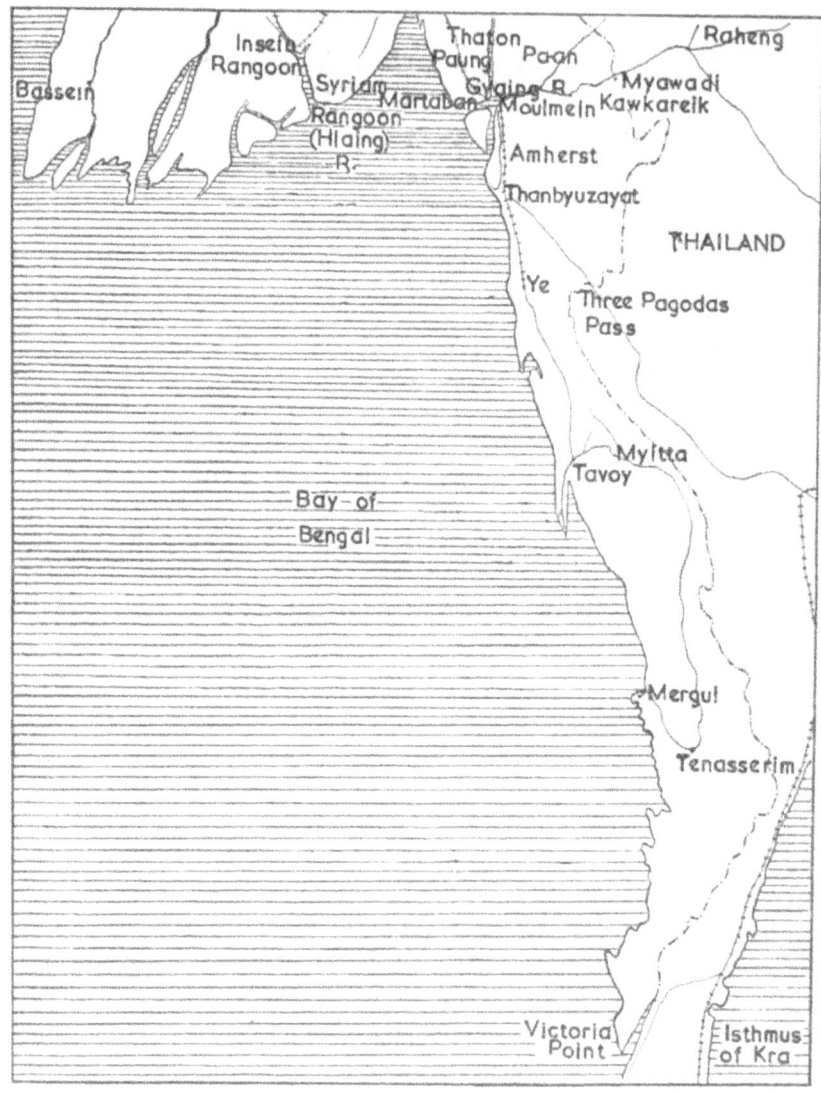

Fig. 2. Burma. Victoria Point–Rangoon

MEDICAL COVER

Providing cover in this area at this time was 1 (Bur.) Fd. Amb., its commanding officer acting as S.M.O. Tenasserim Area. The field ambulance, less one company was in Kawkareik and the company in a house half-way between Kawkareik and the border. With the forward posts of the brigade first-aid parties composed of regimental S.Bs. with ambulance ponies were placed. Malaria was rife. In one company 113 strong there were eighty 'fresh' cases in a month. In order to conserve the strength of the brigade by preventing unnecessary evacuation out of the brigade area a bungalow in Kawkareik was used as a small field hospital.

As the tension mounted a medical officer of the field ambulance was attached to brigade headquarters to serve as liaison officer. During the course of the action all the personnel of the first-aid parties, with the exception of one groom, were lost, presumably taken prisoner. The wounded were sent by river to Moulmein in the only two boats available and the field ambulance moved with the brigade down the left bank of the river for two days until picked up by steamers and conveyed to Martaban.

MEDICAL ARRANGEMENTS

At this time the distribution of the larger medical units was as follows:

General Hospitals

1 Bur. G.H. (H.Q. and 4 sections)	Toungoo
Bur.M.H. with British wing	Mandalay
60 I.G.H. (H.Q. and 2 sections)	,,
'G' and 'Q' Sections of an I.G.H.	,,
41 I.G.H. (H.Q. and 10 sections)	Maymyo
B.M.H.	,,
Bur.M.H.	,,
Bur.M.H.	Meiktila
Bur.M.H. with British wing	Taunggyi
B.M.H. with Burmese wing	Mingaladon
Detention Hospital	Rangoon
Bur.M.H. with British wing	Moulmein
Garrison Hospital	Thayetmyo
R.A.F. Hospitals	Lashio and Namsang

C.C.Ss.

1 (Bur.) C.C.S.	Moulmein
2 (Bur.) C.C.S.	Loilem
4 (Ind.) C.C.S.	,,
Depot of Medical Stores	Rangoon
Branches	Gyogon, Insein and Mandalay, in reserve
13 (Ind.) Depot of Medical Stores	
Laboratories	
District Laboratory	Maymyo
Brigade Laboratory	Mingaladon
Small Laboratories	Taunggyi and Toungoo

Also available at this time were:

M.A.Ss. 22 (Ind.) M.A.S. and 1 (Bur.) M.A.S. detachment
    Staging Sections   1 and 2 (Bur.) S.Ss.
    Ambulance trains   1 and 2 (Bur.) Amb. Trains
    s.s. *Heinrich Jensen*, a requisitioned Danish ship which had escaped from Hong Kong and from Singapore and which was to be the last ship to leave Rangoon. It was used as an ambulance transport.

THE LOSS OF MOULMEIN

Moulmein nestles on the east bank of the Salween Estuary just below the confluence of this river with the Gyaing and the Ataran. It is pressed against the river's edge by the pagoda-crowned Ridge. Its garrison consisted of 2nd Burma Brigade Group, 3rd (less two coys.), 7th and 8th Burif., Ind. 12th Mountain Bty., Ind. 3rd Lt. A.A. Bty., with 4/12th F.F.R. (less one company) in reserve. To the south-east of the town was the airfield guarded by the Kokine Battalion of the Burma Frontier Force. The defensive perimeter around the town was some 11½ miles in extent. Across the Salween in Martaban was Indian 16th Bde. with 1/7th G.R., 4th Burif. and 1 R./9th Jat. It was by no means complete, however, for certain of its component units were still missing after the Kawkareik affair. Indian 46th Bde. of Indian 17th Division was ordered to move up to the area about Bilin. This brigade had reached Rangoon as recently as the 16th without its transport which was not to arrive until the 30th. H.Q. Indian 17th Division had moved back to Kyaikto on the 23rd.

Early on January 30 the Japanese attacked the airfield and by midnight had forced its defenders to withdraw to Moulmein. Four captured lorries of Indian 16th Bde. swiftly approached a road-block on the southern face of the perimeter. Their occupants suddenly opened fire upon its defenders but these had not been deceived and the ruse failed. A heavy general attack upon the perimeter from the south and the east then developed. On the east the Japanese made some progress until checked by 4/12th F.F.R. It became necessary to shorten the perimeter and so its southern face was withdrawn about one thousand yards. Early on the 31st Japanese troops landed at the northern end of the town and heavy pressure was now exerted upon three sides of the defensive 'box'. It was decided that it was necessary to withdraw across the Salween. Fighting their way through the town to the jetties the troops were embarked in launches and under machine-gun fire crossed the Salween to Martaban. About three-quarters of the garrison got away. The general plan now was to hold Martaban and the line of the Salween to the north of Pa-an in order to delay the Japanese advance and to gain time for reinforcements to reach Rangoon.

MEDICAL COVER

From Moulmein casualties were evacuated by launch, boat and sampan across the river to Martaban and thence by ambulance train to one or other of the larger medical installations. During this action 1 (Bur.) Fd. Amb. of 2nd Burma Bde. lost much of its equipment and many of its personnel disappeared. The unit became reduced to about sixty O.Rs. and was sent back to Rangoon to refit.

Moulmein had been heavily bombed on several occasions between January 14 and 24 and as a consequence of this the Burmese clerks and storekeeper of the Burma Military Hospital in the town had deserted. The officer commanding this hospital did an excellent job in getting away all its stores, equipment and nursing staff, in setting up in the Government High School and the American Mission Building in Pegu and in being ready to admit patients within five days. When this hospital moved out of Moulmein 1 (Bur.) C.C.S. opened a small hospital of 100 beds on the Ridge for a short time, sending such cases as required immediate surgical intervention to the civil hospital.

THE ACTION ON THE BILIN RIVER AND THE DISASTER ON THE SITTANG RIVER

Following the withdrawal across the Salween, 3/7th G.R. of Ind. 46th Bde. were in Martaban and 1/7th G.R. of Ind. 16th Bde. in Kuzeik opposite Pa-an, the Karen capital, on the Salween to the north of Martaban. On February 3, Ind. 48th Bde., newly arrived in Rangoon and still lacking its transport, moved up to Bilin to join Indian 17th Division.

Martaban was being subjected to much shelling and bombing and parties of Japanese troops were getting across the Salween and vanishing into the jungle. On February 5, 7/10th Baluch of Ind. 46th Bde. relieved 1/7th G.R. at Kuzeik and the Gurkhas moved back to Bilin. 2nd K.O.Y.L.I. from 1st Burma Brigade in the Southern Shan States came down to Thaton and 8th Burif. and 1 R./9th Jat. of Ind. 16th Bde. moved into reserve in the area of Bilin.

On February 9 the Japanese established a strong road-block on the Martaban–Thaton–Bilin road a few miles south of Paung, not far north of Martaban itself. On the 10th Martaban was heavily shelled and on the 11th the attack upon it opened. 3/7th G.R. were soon compelled to withdraw from the town to Thaton there to join their brigade and 7/10th Baluch in Kuzeik were surrounded. 5/17th Dogra of Ind. 46th Bde. counter-attacked from the direction of Duyinzeik but the general situation progressively deteriorated and on the 15th, the remaining units of Ind. 46th Bde. began to withdraw to the line of the River Bilin. *It was on this day that Singapore capitulated.*

On February 17, H.Q. 2nd Burma Bde. with 7th Burif. moved to Nyaunglebin, north of Pegu and on the railway line, to undertake active patrolling of the line of the Sittang River, 3rd Burif. were in Mokpalin and 1st Burif., from Mergui *via* Rangoon, were sent to Papun to the east of Nyaunglebin to cover the left flank of the Bilin line. Detachments of this battalion were placed to watch likely crossings over the Salween between Papun and Pa-an. 2nd Burma Bde. thus rejoined its own division, 1st Burma.

Ind. 46th Bde. withdrew from Thaton to Kyaikto on the 16th when Indian 17th Division took up a defensive position behind the Bilin. Ind. 16th Bde. held a seven mile sector along the river from Leikkon in the south through Bilin and Danyingon to Yinon in the north. Ind. 48th Bde. was in divisional reserve athwart the main road near the Thebyu Chaung.

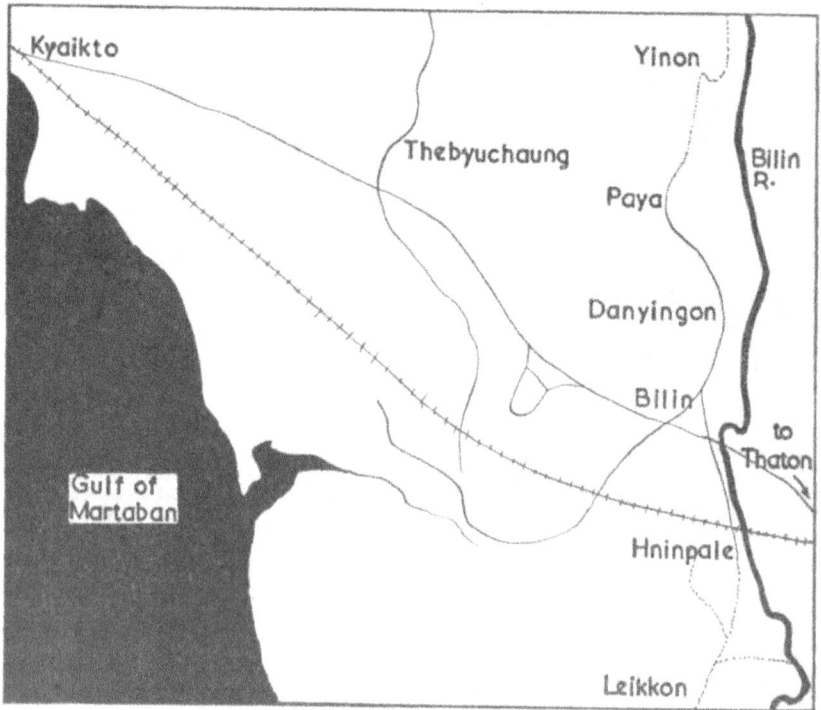

FIG. 3. The Action on the Bilin River.

The River Bilin was not a serious obstacle for it was fordable in many places and ran through a countryside that was hilly and covered with rubber and jungle. The Japanese attack on the Bilin position opened on the 16th. On the 17th a road-block was established by the Japanese half a mile south of Paya and all attempts to clear the road were unsuccessful. Japanese troops landed behind the southern flank of Indian 17th Division to the west of the Bilin Estuary. It became clear that Japanese 55th Division was attempting to pin Indian 17th Division down in the Bilin line while Japanese 33rd Division moved round the north flank of the position and headed for the Sittang and its bridge. It was decided that Indian 17th Division must pull back to the much stronger line of the Sittang and so on the night of the 19th orders for a general withdrawal were issued. With difficulty, Indian 17th Division managed to disengage and to begin to make its way towards the Sittang, 25 miles to the west. Before dawn on the 21st Kyaikto, where H.Q. 17th Division was at the time, was attacked. The Japanese were beaten off but the affair did indicate in the clearest possible fashion that they were moving fast and that there was no time to lose. It was recognised that this withdrawal to the west bank of the Sittang was bound to be a difficult and hazardous operation. The bridge across the river, painted the colour of stale blood, was a railway bridge, yet across it the guns and transport of the division must pass. Above the bridge there was a steamer ferry with three power-driven boats. Several hundreds of sampans were being collected. On the west side of the bridge there was a road as well as a railway line. The road ran to Waw, 10 miles away and thence to Pegu. But on the east side of the bridge the road leading toward it stopped at Kyaikto 16 miles away. From Kyaikto to the bridge there ran a track, it was nothing more. This had been widened and the cut brushwood had been piled high on either side of it. Save in the clearing in which the village of Mokpalin stood, about a mile and a half away from the eastern end of the bridge, the track inches deep in dust, ran through the jungle. At Kyaikto the railway line and the track diverged to come together again at Mokpalin. Thereafter for a mile or so the two ran together until the track turned sharply north-east and then west while the railway continued due west through a cutting in a bluff in Pagoda Hill with an immense stone image of the Buddha on its eastern face. The sweep of the track enclosed this bluff, 'Pagoda Hill' and 'Buddha Hill' to the south of this. To the south of the railway cutting there was another small elevation, 'Bungalow Hill'. At the bridge the river, tidal and fast flowing, was about five hundred yards wide. To enable the bridge to be used as a road bridge it was floored with timber planks.

It was planned that 48th Bde. should move back first through 46th Bde. at Kyaikto, going into divisional reserve on the west bank of the river. The defence of the bridgehead on the east bank was to be undertaken by 4/12th F.F.R. of Ind. 16th Bde., 3rd Burif. and a company of 2nd D.W.R. 46th Bde. was to act as the rearguard. On the 21st its leading battalion would move back to the quarries about two miles to

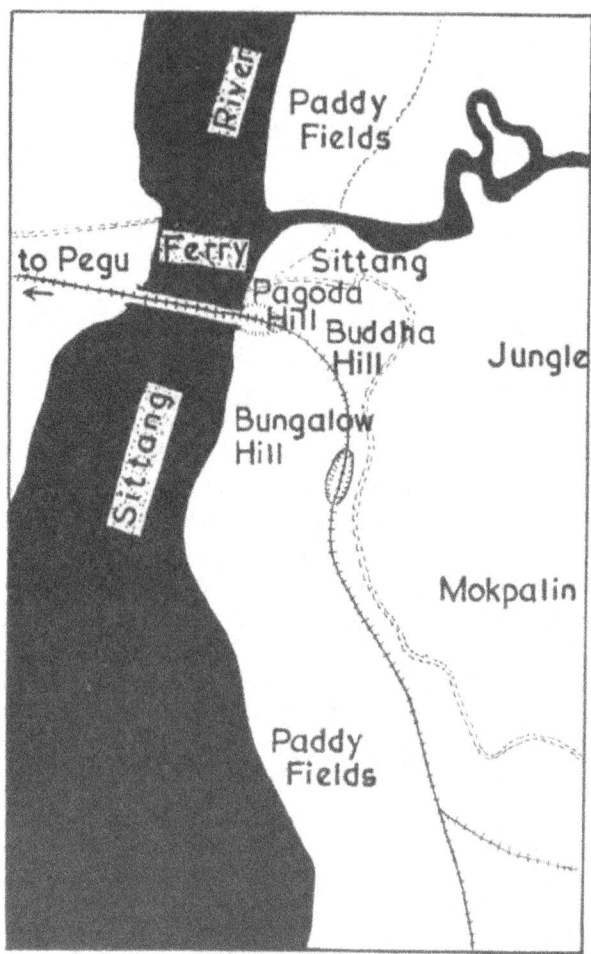

FIG. 4. The Approach to the Sittang Bridge

the east of Mokpalin and the other battalions of the brigade would take up positions some four to seven miles further to the east for the night.

By dawn on February 22 H.Q. Indian 17th Division, H.Q. Ind. 48th Bde. and 1/4th G.R. were across the bridge and on the west bank of the Sittang. Then grave misfortune befell. A 3-ton lorry slipped off the plank roadway on the bridge and caused a complete blockage for about three hours during which the withdrawing columns were held up and the transport clotted in Mokpalin and along the road and track. Then suddenly out of the jungle the Japanese burst to attack the north-east sector of the perimeter. Much disorganisation was caused by this attack and by the counter-attacks that followed and such confusion developed that it was decided to destroy the ferry boats and sampans to prevent them falling into Japanese hands. Other Japanese attacks developed, one on Mokpalin with its densely packed stationary transport and another on 46th Bde. about five miles to the east of this village. The general situation became so confused that the commander of 48th Bde. found it necessary to report to the divisional commander in Waw and to seek consent for the blowing of the bridge. The divisional commander was called upon to make a most difficult decision. He had to decide whether to risk the bridge falling into the hands of the Japanese or to blow it while the bulk of his division was still on the far side in order to preserve the great obstacle of the river between the Japanese and Rangoon. The bridge was blown at 0530 hours on the morning of February 23.

On the east side of the river there were two brigades, 16th and 46th, and two battalions of the third brigade (48th) of the division in a most precarious position. It was quickly decided that the only possible course of action was to get across the river before the disorganisation that was already rapidly increasing became complete. The river, 500 yards wide, had to be crossed, either by swimming or by means of improvised rafts, and under fire. There were wounded to be got across. Transport, guns, heavy automatics, ammunition, equipment that would constitute a handicap, these things would have to be left behind, preferably after having been rendered useless. So, bamboos, empty petrol tins and anything else that would float were used for the making of rafts and improvised 'lifebelts'. On the rafts the wounded were loaded and so evacuated. The Japanese, for the most part, following the destruction of the bridge, had veered off northwards. It became possible for an officer and two N.C.Os. of the D.W.R. by means of ropes to rig up a lifeline across the gap between the piers of the bridge. By means of this some three hundred sepoys and Gurkhas crossed to safety. Some of the troops moved up the river bank and managed to find sampans and the like and so to cross. But the river exacted its toll. Many of those who attempted to make this perilous passage failed to reach the opposite bank, being shot or drowned.

On February 24, Indian 17th Division numbered only 149 officers and 3,335 O.Rs. Its arms consisted of 1,420 rifles, 56 Brens and 68 Thompson sub-machine carbines. Many of the men were without boots and parts of their uniform. They were exhausted and dispirited. It became necessary to disband 46th Bde. and many other units had to be amalgamated or their personnel redistributed. After reorganisation its composition was as follows:

16th Bde.
    'A' Battalion   2nd K.O.Y.L.I. and 2nd D.W.R.
    'B'   „   1 R./9th Jat.
    'C'   „   7/10th Baluch, 5/17th Dogra, and 4/12th F.F.R., 3rd, 4th, and 8th Burifs.

48th Bde.
   'A' Battalion   1/4th G.R.
   'B'   „   5/3rd G.R. (2/5th R.G.R., 1/3rd G.R.)
   'C'   „   7th G.R. (1/7th G.R. and 3/7th G.R.)

The division moved to the Pegu–Waw area to refit. 7th Armd. Bde., landing in Rangoon on February 21, was sent forward to join Indian 17th Division. To this brigade 1st W. Yorks and 1st Cameronians were added. For the time being the division was out of touch with the Japanese. But on the 26th there was much fighting around Waw and in it the Burma Independence Army took an active part. On March 3 and 4 the Japanese, crossing the Sittang to the north of the bridge, occupied Kyaikhla, south-west of Waw, and Payagyi, 12 miles north of Pegu on the Toungoo road. On the 5th they cut the Pegu road and large numbers of them infiltrated into the Pegu Yomas in this area.

It was at this point that General Alexander arrived to take over command in Burma. He found that Indian 17th Division was holding the Pegu–Hlegu area, with 48th Bde. and 7th Armd. Bde. about Pegu and 16th Bde. about Hlegu. Ind. 63rd Inf. Bde., having just reached Rangoon, was about Hlawga, 16 miles north of the capital. 1st Burma Division, having handed over the defence of the Southern Shan States to Chinese Sixth Army, was distributed as follows: Ind. 13th Inf. Bde. about Mawchi, east of Toungoo; 1st Burma Bde. in Pyu between Pegu and Toungoo, and 2nd Burma Bde. around Nyaunglebin. Between the two divisions there was a gap of about forty miles.

General Alexander decided that the most urgent need was to close this gap in order to prevent any further Japanese infiltration into the Pegu Yomas. 48th Bde. of Indian 17th Division was therefore ordered to attack the Japanese in the area of Waw while 2nd Burma Bde. of 1st Burma Division thrust southwards from Nyaunglebin to join up with Indian 17th Division.

Indian 17th Division and 7th Armd. Bde. attacked on March 5 but during the operation the Japanese attacked in their turn from the wooded country bordering Pegu on the west and captured part of the town. Attempts on the part of Indian 17th Division on the 6th to eject the Japanese from Pegu were unsuccessful. The Japanese cut the Pegu–Rangoon road and so isolated the force in Pegu from that in Rangoon. Attempts by Ind. 63rd Bde. to open the road failed. It was known that strong Japanese columns had passed through Paunggyi, about thirty miles north of Hlegu and were moving in a south-westerly direction. It was understood that Japanese–Burmese parties had landed at the mouth of the Hlaing River (Rangoon river) and were threatening the Burma Oil Company's refineries at Syriam where there was only a small garrison.

THE JAPANESE INVADE BURMA

General Alexander decided that Rangoon must be given up, the Syriam refineries destroyed and the troops regrouped north of Rangoon in the Irrawaddy valley.

MEDICAL COVER

As would be expected, the records of the affairs of the Army Medical Services during these events remain very imperfect and fragmentary. The medical units participated fully in the confusion and the disorganisation that were born of disaster. The loss of the transport of the field ambulances began at Kawkareik; it continued during the withdrawal from Moulmein and the fighting in the Bilin line and it became almost complete during the action at the Sittang bridge. This meant that during the later actions there was much hand-carriage of casualties through paddy field and jungle.

During the fighting in and around Martaban and Kuzeik 39 (Ind.) Fd. Amb. (L. of C. unit) had its M.D.S. in a school in Thaton and one of its companies ran an A.D.S. to serve 7/10th Baluch in Kuzeik. A section of another company of the field ambulance formed a C.C.P. to serve 5/17th Dogra during their counter-attack from the direction of Duyinzeik. Casualties were evacuated from M.D.S. to 1 (Bur.) C.C.S. which was now in Kyaikto.

D.D.M.S. found that the two ambulance trains were working right up to Thaton and even up to Martaban itself at one time. Being of the firm opinion that it was much too risky to have these most valuable instruments of evacuation working in front of so vulnerable a structure as the Sittang bridge, when a chance hit destroying but a single culvert could mean the complete loss of these trains at the very beginning of the campaign, he issued instructions that this practice of using an ambulance train to clear a M.D.S. must cease forthwith.

In the action at Kuzeik the regimental medical officer of 7/10th Baluch and several of the staff of his R.A.P. were lost. When Thaton was evacuated on February 16, 39 (Ind.) Fd. Amb. moved to Mokpalin and established a M.D.S. there. While the division was in the Bilin line 1 (Bur.) C.C.S. remained in Kyaikto until February 14 when it was relieved by 23 (Ind.) Fd. Amb. The C.C.S. then moved to Pegu where it opened. The M.D.S. of 23 (Ind.) Fd. Amb. in Kyaikto remained opened between February 15-20. The Bur. M.H. in Pegu was receiving from the field ambulances functioning first in the Martaban area, then in the Pa-an and Thaton area and in the Bilin area. Evacuation from the hospital was by ambulance train to Toungoo and Mandalay.

When Mokpalin village was bombed, attacked and isolated there were many casualties. Several of the ambulance drivers disappeared, taking their ignition keys with them. The officer commanding 37 (Ind.)

Fd. Amb. attempted to get one of the loaded and deserted ambulance cars away but was machine-gunned from the air and all his patients were killed.

39 (Ind.) Fd. Amb. established an A.D.S. in the bridgehead southeast of the railway station at Mokpalin on the 21st. It was overrun during the confused fighting on the 22nd and the A.D.M.S. and D.A.D.M.S. of Indian 17th Division as well as several officers of the field ambulance and the officer commanding 37 (Ind.) Fd. Amb. were captured. The last of these, about to be executed ceremoniously, escaped from his captors when a counter-attack suddenly developed. He got across the river.

Most of the personnel of 37 (Ind.) Fd. Amb. got across the bridge over the Sittang and together with a number of O.Rs. of 39 (Ind.) Fd. Amb., who had also crossed, set up an A.D.S. in Nyaungkashe village about a mile to the west of the bridge.

23 (Ind.) Fd. Amb. came out of the battle practically complete. 37 (Ind.) Fd. Amb. had lost one medical officer, ten O.R.s, most of its transport and nearly all its ordnance equipment. 39 (Ind.) Fd. Amb. lost four of its medical officers, many of its men and all its equipment. 37 and 39 were therefore amalgamated and sent to Yenangyaung, on the Irrawaddy in the oil fields area, to reorganise and refit. All the regimental medical equipment and most of the divisional ambulance cars were lost.

When Indian 17th Division was concentrated in the Pegu-Waw area and during its attempts to link up with 1st Burma Division the medical units were distributed as follows:

A.D.M.S.	Hlegu. Milestone 27·2
13 Lt. Fd. Amb. (7th Armd. Bde.)	M.D.S. open Winkwin. A.D.S. open Hlegu. Milestone 26·5 on the Rangoon–Prome road. A.D.S. open with H.Q. 7th Armd. Bde.
1 (Bur.) Fd. Amb.	M.D.S. open at Milestone 24 on the Rangoon–Prome road.
23 (Ind.) Fd. Amb. less an A.D.S.	Closed Taukkyan. Milestone 21·7 on the Rangoon–Prome road. A.D.S. open Pegu with 48th Bde.
50 (Ind.) Fd. Amb. less an A.D.S.	Closed Hlawga. A.D.S. open Pegu with 63rd Bde.
37/39 (Ind.) Fd. Amb.	Closed Yenangyaung.
22 (Ind.) Fd. Hyg. Sec.	,,
'C' Sub. sec. of an Ind. Fd. Hyg. Sec.	,,

THE WITHDRAWAL FROM RANGOON

It has been related that, following the air raids of December 23 and 25, 1941, there was a general exodus from Rangoon. This had a very serious and adverse effect upon military affairs for the reasons that ships bringing urgently needed stores remained unloaded and Lend-Lease material for China accumulated in vast quantities. For a time in January 1941 while the airmen of fortune—the American Volunteer Group—and the R.A.F. were able to provide protection to the city the situation temporarily improved and about 50 per cent. of the labour force returned. But as the news worsened the exodus began again. The Burmans distributed themselves among the villages of the Delta; the Chinese stayed where they were; for the Indians, a million and more whose sense of insecurity became intensified as the hostility of the Burmans towards them became expressed, there seemed to be no safe place save beyond the frontiers of India. The terrible story of their flight, the magnitude of their sufferings and of the steps that were taken by the Government of India and by voluntary bodies to mitigate these is one that is told in Appendix VIII of the Official Indian Medical History in which the following figures are given:

Numbers of refugees reaching India
By land routes into
East Bengal	200,000
Assam	218,000
By sea, Rangoon and Akyab	70,000
By air	12,000
	500,000
Number dying *en route*	12,500

Here it must suffice to make the point that their flight into the Manipur valley and along the Tamu road into Assam threatened to impede the construction of that road and the passage along it of essential military traffic. Steps had to be taken to prevent this and in these arrangements the Army Medical Services became involved. As the retreat to the north continued the efficiency of very many of those who were involved in the affairs of Indian 17th and 1st Burma Divisions was profoundly and deleteriously affected by their awareness of the dangers to which their families, living in Burma and now attempting to get away, were exposed.

From sporadic air raids military installations in Rangoon suffered but slight damage. The B.M.H. Mingaladon, now 2 Bur.G.H., had a narrow escape. Because it was sited next to the airfield itself and thus was in a legitimate target area, D.D.M.S. strove to obtain for it an alternative site. He was given the loan of a wing of the civil mental hospital at Tadagale and to this the military hospital was transferred. The

Detention Hospital remained behind and the officer in charge of it became increasingly impressed by the extent of the danger to which the patients were being exposed by remaining in the hospital building and, acting on his own responsibility, moved them and his section to the M.I. Room in the infantry lines nearby. That very night the airfield was bombed, the hospital buildings hit and several of the wards completely wrecked.

The third ambulance train was received from the railway shops in Mandalay and came to Rangoon to be equipped and staffed. The services of two volunteer European engine drivers were enlisted and a search among R.A.M.C. units unearthed a peace-time driver and a fireman. These four men drove the train on the Rangoon–Prome line until Prome was lost. Because the train was liable to attack by dacoits and looters, D.D.M.S. arranged for the issue of small arms to its staff. The sister-in-charge of the train always carried a revolver and so was given, by the very many who had reason to be grateful to her, the sobriquet 'Pistol Mary'. The train had no sooner come into use than it ran into danger. By some error it was sent from Rangoon not to Prome but to Pegu which at the time was the centre of much fighting. Messages were sent out by every possible route and fortunately the train was stopped just south of Pegu. During one week it evacuated 1,050 patients from Rangoon to Prome. Just before the final evacuation of Rangoon a fourth train was obtained and a staff collected for it, but the train was never used and the staff was put aboard an improvised steamer which plied between Prome and Mandalay.

As Moulmein, Martaban and the Bilin line were evacuated and following the capitulation of Singapore it became increasingly apparent that Rangoon could not much longer serve as a secure base and so the heads of services began to make plans for the removal to the north of their installations and stores. The principal medical units in Rangoon were the Depot of Medical Stores in the centre of the city and with a branch in Insein, the Depot of the Burma Hospital Corps and 2 Bur. G.H. at Tadagale. It was arranged that the Depot of Medical Stores Rangoon and its branch should be moved to Mandalay. The branch depot in Insein got away with great difficulty. Over a thousand tons of stores had to be packed and loaded. The staff of this depot did an excellent job under the most difficult conditions. For transport they made use of Rangoon Corporation refuse carts and dust carts and other miscellaneous vehicles. A small labour force was collected by means of threats and bribery. Not only were the contents of the depot cleared but a considerable quantity of stores and equipment was salvaged from the abandoned civil hospitals, from business premises and from the docks. Only some four or five loaded waggons which the railway staff were unable to move were lost.

The Burma Hospital Corps Depot was moved to Sagaing near Mandalay but only with difficulty for there were administrative muddles and many desertions. The records of the Depot were left behind.

The small medical embarkation staff encountered difficulties during this period. For example, when H.S. *Neuralia* unexpectedly arrived towards the end of February, intending to stay for a few hours only, the embarkation staff managed to get some three hundred patients aboard At this time it was thought that the Japanese might soon be in Rangoon and so the nursing staff of 2 Bur. G.H. (7 Q.A.I.M.N.S. and 14 V.A.D.) was sent away in this ship. The lack of these nurses was keenly felt by this hospital during the rest of this phase of the campaign.

2 Bur. G.H. went by rail to Prome to open in a school and 8 (Ind.) C.C.S. took over the accommodation at Tadagale. It was intended that this unit, raised in Quetta, should go to Singapore but, not being ready in time to take part in the Malayan disaster, it was sent to Rangoon *via* Madras. It reached the Burmese capital just before the arrival of 7th Armoured Brigade and was at once sent to the mental hospital at Tadagale, just outside Rangoon, where it opened to admit fighter pilots (A.V.G. and R.A.F.) shot down during the fighting over the capital and looters shot by the police. The unit took over such patients as remained in the mental hospital. It falls to be recorded that when the civil hospitals were closed down, suddenly and completely, the staffs being ordered to leave, the patients in the mental hospital at Tadagale were released into a world in which for them there was no place.

The official evacuation plan was set in motion on February 20 and within a few days Rangoon became a deserted city, inhabited only by hungry dogs and furtive looters. In the suburbs, built mainly of wood, fires broke out to destroy whole areas. On the 21st, Rear Headquarters Army-in-Burma closed down and set out by train for Maymyo. D.D.M.S., A.D.H. and one staff captain of the Medical Branch remained behind with the Advanced Headquarters in Rangoon. Remaining in Rangoon also were the medical embarkation staff and the staff of the depot of medical stores, for their tasks were not yet completed. When the decision to evacuate Rangoon was reached, 8 (Ind.) C.C.S. embarked on the Irrawaddy Flotilla Company's paddle steamer *Mysore*. Two roofed lighters were roped to the sides and connected with the steamer by gangplanks and a large Red Cross emblem was painted on the roof. A considerable quantity of surgical equipment was taken from the deserted civil hospital and the ship's engineer, by screening off and by providing lighting for the platforms above the paddles, created two operating theatres, one for 'clean' and the other for 'dirty' surgery. The unit's tentage and ordnance stores were stowed away in the hold and lots of straw for the filling of the mattresses was obtained. Small arms were issued to the personnel of the unit.

The *Mysore* quickly filled with casualties from Indian 17th Division and set off for Mandalay which was reached after seven days. The patients were disembarked for Maymyo. The entire engine-room staff with the exception of the foreman (tindal) deserted. Volunteer replacements were found among unit personnel and the steamer turned about and set off for Prome. After the railway had been put out of action by Japanese bombing, railway-engine stokers were added to the crew of the *Mysore*. A light section of this C.C.S. went by road to Tharrawaddy there to open to serve Indian 17th Division during its withdrawal from the Pegu area.

The medical installations in Pegu were likewise moved northwards. The Burma Military Hospital in Moulmein had moved to Pegu on January 24. It was joined there by personnel of the Burma Military Hospital, Tavoy. All its Burmese clerks and storekeepers had deserted. It opened in Pegu to function as a C.C.S. of 400 beds in the High School. Three officers from an I.G.H., an assistant surgeon and a storekeeper from 4 (Ind.) C.C.S. in Loilem now joined the unit which began to receive casualties from 23, 37 and 39 (Ind.) Fd. Ambs. Evacuation was by train to Toungoo and Mandalay. On February 16, 1 (Bur) C.C.S. arrived in Pegu and took over the Burma Military Hospital. By the 22nd, the conditions in Pegu had become chaotic and it became necessary to evacuate the town. The matron, nurses and 120 patients were sent by train to Maymyo on February 26. One patient was left in the care of 23 (Ind.) Fd. Amb. *En route* the trains carrying the hospital and the Burma Hospital Corps collided near Toungoo, and the engine pulling the train carrying the military hospital broke down. The officer commanding the Hospital Corps gave up the engine of his train to the hospital which proceeded to Maymyo there to open as 3 Bur. G.H. in the English College.

Later, 1 (Bur.) C.C.S. in Pegu was relieved in its turn by 23 (Ind.) Fd. Amb. and went to Meiktila. On the 20th there remained in Pegu the entire equipment of 59 I.G.H. in charge of a small party. This advance party had been sent to Pegu after landing in Rangoon at the beginning of February and was awaiting orders. No orders were received by the officer in charge of the party. (The rest of the unit never left India.) Orders for the complete evacuation of Pegu were now issued. The officer in charge of the party, 12 I.O.Rs. strong, managed, somehow or other, to get hold of fifty railway waggons and 'flats'. He rounded up a labour gang from neighbouring villages complete with bullock carts. He disarmed and took prisoner seven hostile Burmans who strayed into his camp. He collected thirty patients and, with his waggons hitched on to a train, set out for Mandalay. He assumed the position of officer commanding the train and fed its human freight with rations from his stocks. When the train was attacked by hostile Burmans he assumed the offensive and captured eighteen of them and took them with his train to Mandalay. A story such as this does much to balance the impression left on the mind by the accounts of faint-heartedness, indecision and desertion that are to be encountered in plenty.

D.D.M.S., leaving a medical liaison officer and a staff captain (medical) behind with Adv. H.Q., set out for the north to visit the medical units in their new locations. In Prome he arranged with the Irrawaddy Flotilla Company that two more of their steamers should be converted into hospital river steamers, the *Kalaw*, a large one and the *Fano*, a smaller one. From Meiktila, where Rear Headquarters, Army-in-Burma was now established, he sent A.D.M.S. L. of C. to Mandalay where the control of evacuation could be better exercised. He then proceeded to expand all military hospitals. In Maymyo 41 I.G.H. opened all of its 1,000 beds, 3 Bur. G.H. from Pegu, opened in a school and 8 Bur. G.H. was encouraged to expand so as to make available 200 British beds. In Mandalay 60 I.G.H. was given the 'G' and 'Q' sections which lacked an H.Q. and was instructed to expand first to 400 and then to 600 beds.

In Rangoon, a strangely silent city, only Adv. H.Q. now remained. The embarkation staffs had been sent away and everybody was under orders to leave at one hour's notice. Then suddenly it was decided that Rangoon must be held until Indian 63rd Infantry Brigade, then expected, had arrived and disembarked from its nine ships. The embarkation staffs were recalled. The medical embarkation staff had gone to Prome but now returned. In this convoy was 50 (Ind.) Fd. Amb. but its transport could not be unloaded until the following day. In the last of the ships to be unloaded there were hospital stores and also ambulance cars. These last were indeed valuable for they permitted 21 M.A.S. to function, even though on a small scale.

On the morning of March 7, Adv. H.Q. Army-in-Burma, leaving behind a few who were concerned in the demolition of installations of military importance, moved out of Rangoon. The head of the column ran into a road-block near Taukkyan, 21 miles to the north of the capital, at 1100 hours and was held up. Attempts throughout the rest of the day to clear the road by 1st Glosters, 2/13th F.F. Rifles and a number of tanks of 7th Hussars failed. On March 7 the force in Pegu (7th Hussars, Ind. 48th Bde., 1st W. Yorks and 1st Cameronians) finally succeeded in cutting its way through the encircling Japanese and Ind. 63rd Bde., which had unsuccessfully tried to relieve this force on the 6th and which was now near Hlegu, was ordered to attack the road-block near Taukkyan early on the 8th. This attack was unsuccessful like those that had gone before. Ind. 16th Bde. from Hlegu, supported by armour, made a further attack later in the morning and this was surprisingly successful for the road-block was no longer there. It was learnt later

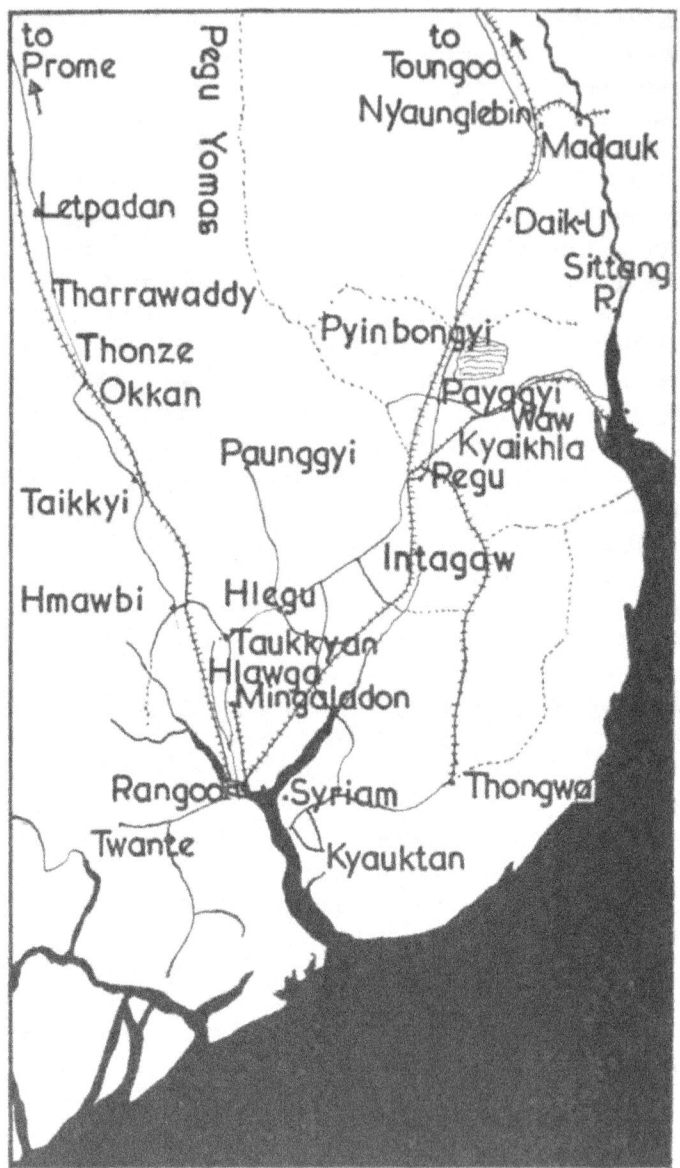

Fig. 5. The Withdrawal from Rangoon

that what happened was as follows: Japanese 33rd Division, heading for Rangoon, had been instructed to cross the Prome road north of Rangoon and then swing to the south to attack the city from the west. The road-block had been constructed not to prevent the Rangoon garrison from escaping to the north but to protect the flank of Japanese 33rd Division as it by-passed the capital. When the division had crossed the Prome road safely the road-block was withdrawn. And so Adv. H.Q. Army-in-Burma, and General Alexander himself, got out of a situation that was rapidly becoming increasingly hopeless.

To the south a great black cloud rose in the sky as the refineries at Syriam were blown up and a series of explosions shook Rangoon as government buildings, the power station and a number of industrial installations were dynamited.

All through March 8 and 9 the column moved northwards along the Prome road under heavy air attack. Adv. H.Q. went on to Maymyo. Meanwhile Indian 17th Division marched from Pegu and Hlegu to the area of Tharrawaddy where intensive reorganisation and re-equipment were carried out.

The loss of Rangoon was an exceedingly serious blow to Allied hopes. It was the only point of entry into Burma through which men and material in large quantity could be moved. The Army-in-Burma was now without a base. There was no L. of C. for at this time there was no land link with India though there was to be one later. The Army-in-Burma was isolated from the outside world save by air.

However, this withdrawal to the north did mean that the army still blocked the path to India and it did give time for the Chinese divisions to move to the south to the aid of the Army-in-Burma. On the other hand, with Rangoon in their hands, the port being repaired, the Japanese would be able to reinforce and supply their divisions in Burma by sea instead of by way of difficult mountain tracks.

MEDICAL COVER DURING THE WITHDRAWAL

Serving Pegu Force during its attempts to clear the road to the south was 23 (Ind.) Fd. Amb. Its commanding officer had been wounded during an air raid on Pegu and he was being evacuated in an ambulance car which was held up, like everything else, by the road-block. Suddenly Japanese troops burst out of the jungle and charged the stationary transport. Such of the wounded as could do so jumped out of the ambulance and scattered into the jungle there to hide. The officer commanding 23 (Ind.) Fd. Amb. and another officer could not do this. The ambulance was sprayed with automatic fire and the two officers, unhit, shammed dead. Japanese troops climbed on to the roof of the ambulance and mounted a machine-gun on it. There they remained for a whole hour until dislodged by Gurkhas when the officers were evacuated in carriers.

When the column from Rangoon was checked by the road-block near Taukkyan the ambulances of 50 (Ind.) and 1 (Bur.) Fd. Ambs. accompanying it sheltered in the rubber plantations that bordered the road. They were holding large numbers of casualties, many of them serious. During that night the column leaguered in these plantations.

When the column resumed its journey to the north a medical convoy of all available ambulance cars was improvised and a large number of casualties evacuated to the light section of 8 (Ind.) C.C.S. in Tharrawaddy. Forty sitting cases were loaded on to passing lorries. Following the loss of Moulmein 1 (Bur.) Fd. Amb. had been withdrawn to Mingaladon, Rangoon. During the withdrawal from the capital its A.D.S. replaced 1 (Bur.) C.C.S. in the mental hospital at Tadagale on February 27 and its M.D.S. was opened at Milestone 24 on the Rangoon–Prome road where it admitted casualties from the fighting at the Taukkyan road-block. Thence the unit moved to Tharrawaddy where it opened its M.D.S. to admit some 150 patients On March 10 these were evacuated to Prome, along with 21 M.A.S. 23 (Ind.) Fd. Amb. and 50 (Ind.) Fd. Amb., joining up, pooled their transport in an attempt to get their personnel and equipment away when Indian 17th Division moved that evening to Taikkyi but unfortunately the cars were unable to return against the stream of traffic for the personnel of 50 Fd. Amb. who marched all through the night in the rear of the division.

It remains difficult to form an opinion concerning the numbers of casualties incurred during these opening months of the campaign. That they were heavy is certain but no accurate and regular returns were made. The proportion of injuries not due to enemy action was undoubtedly high, as in other theatres, road accidents exacting a heavy toll. Evacuation from the Delta was mainly by river to Mandalay. The ambulance trains were used in Upper Burma. As a consequence of the saving and salvaging of medical stores in Rangoon there was no shortage.

The field ambulances of Indian 17th Division had become habituated to the conditions of the fighting in Burma. In place of the full A.D.S. of a whole company of a field ambulance, it had become the practice to make use of a light A.D.S. with one medical officer, one orderly R.A.M.C., eight ambulance sepoys, a cook and a sweeper. If this were not enough then two such light A.D.Ss. were combined. When the division was on the move a light A.D.S. with one 30-cwt lorry and two ambulance cars was attached to each brigade. The light A.D.S. was equipped with medical pannier, six surgical haversacks packed with dressings, a set of Thomas' splints and a number of stretchers and blankets.

It was found that the equipment was too heavy for the work it had to do and so much of the tentage and other heavy ordnance items had to be abandoned quite early in the campaign. The regimental medical pannier was thought to be rather unsuitable for the job and it was suggested that field surgical haversacks and medical panniers which could be carried by the regimental stretcher-bearers would be adequate equipment for a R.A.P. and would not get lost so easily and so frequently.

At all times there was a shortage of transport. In Indian 17th Division, 37 (Ind.) Fd. Amb., at the end of this phase, had 1 ambulance car, 1

30-cwt. truck and 1 motor cycle. 23 and 50 (Ind.) Fd. Ambs. had between them 12 ambulance cars, 19 30-cwt. trucks, 2 3-ton lorries, 1 15-cwt. truck and 4 motor cycles, much in excess of the authorised allotment on the lower scale establishment, but still insufficient. All the vehicles were pooled to form a transport company under the M.T. officer of 39 (Ind.) Fd. Amb. This transport company moved one of the field ambulances to its new site and returned, if possible, to lift the other field ambulance that was marching towards its new site. But frequently, the transport could not make its way back against the stream of traffic. The unit that had been transported had to open and function immediately on arrival; the other one was on the march and so neither got any rest.

In 1st Burma Division the situation was even worse than this. Each of the two field ambulances had 6 ambulances and 3 30-cwt. trucks. 1 (Bur.) Fd. Amb. had lost all these at Moulmein and had picked up in Rangoon a miscellaneous assortment of vehicles in their place. 2 (Bur.) Fd. Amb. had lost several of its ambulances in accidents. 57 (Ind.) Fd. Amb., at the end of this phase, had only one car on the road, the rest had all broken down. Experience suggested that the minimal number of cars per ambulance was ten, for it was usual to place two cars with each brigade and one with the divisional recce. regiment, leaving the M.D.S. with only three for evacuation rearward to railhead.

The use of mules for evacuation work was not successful; the mixture of M.T. and animal transport was not a practical one.

At the end of this phase there were ten general hospitals functioning, four in Maymyo, two in Mandalay, one at Meiktila, two in the Shan States and one in Prome. There were four C.C.Ss., two Indian and two Burmese. The two Indian units were staffing the floating hospitals, *Mysore* and *Siam*. 1 (Bur.) C.C.S. was with the Chinese in Meiktila. A section of 4 (Bur.) G.H. in Taunggyi was placed at the disposal of the Chinese. 2 (Bur.) S.S. was moving to Myingyan. There was no convalescent depot. The Vaccine and Sera Laboratory of the Pasteur Institute, Rangoon, had been moved to Meiktila, where it continued production.

The standard of accommodation of the larger medical units and the nursing in the hospitals was definitely good. D.D.M.S. had enlisted every trained or partially trained nurse in Burma, British, Anglo-Indian, Anglo-Burman, Karen or any other category and the hospitals were nearly up to establishment. The major deficiences were among the cooks, bhistis, sweepers and the like.

There was an epidemic of cholera around Prome and so the whole Indian 17th Division had to be inoculated. In fact the whole of the Army was inoculated save for a Burma Frontier Force unit which was inaccessible at the time; later in it there were 100 cases. It is to be noted that the threat of cholera was a very real one for it was raging among the Indian refugees as they trekked northwards.

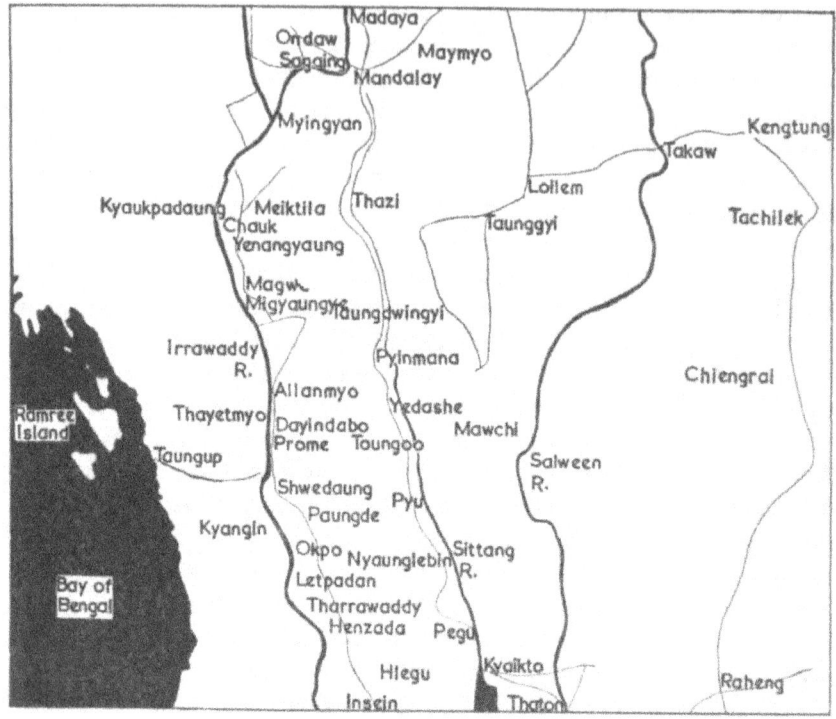

Fig. 6. Burma. Insein–Mandalay

THE LOSS OF TOUNGOO AND PROME

A brief period of comparative quiet followed the withdrawal from Rangoon and during it there was much re-grouping. Indian 17th Division was in the Thonze–Tharrawaddy–Letpadan area. On March 11, to divert attention away from Indian 17th Division, 1st Burma Division had successfully attacked the villages of Shwegyin and Madauk and had thereafter withdrawn to the area north of Kanyutkwin, on the railway just south of Pyu. It was now arranged that Chinese Fifth Army should relieve 1st Burma Division on the Toungoo front and that the Burma division should be brought across into the Irrawaddy valley alongside Indian 17th Division. During January Chinese Sixth Army (49th, 55th, 98th and 200th Divisions) was moving further to the south. It would not go beyond Toungoo however. This meant that when 1st Burma Division was transferred to the Irrawaddy valley a large stretch of the lower Sittang valley, including one of the best rice-producing areas, would be abandoned. As 1st Burma Division pulled back from this area, prior to leaving for the Irrawaddy valley, the Japanese followed up closely and there were many rearguard actions which left the division considerably exhausted by the time Toungoo was reached. Indian 17th

Division, conforming with this movement of 1st Burma Division, moved back towards the Prome area. Mobile columns of the Burma Frontier Force patrolled the Pegu Yomas to prevent Japanese infiltration and other detachments were stationed to the west of the Irrawaddy. Tanks and lorried infantry operated southwards along the Prome-Rangoon road to impede any Japanese movement northwards. Henzada and Letpadan were raided and losses inflicted on bodies of Japanese troops.

On March 19 General Slim arrived to assume command of the corps that was about to be formed—Burcorps—compounded out of 7th Armd. Bde., Indian 17th Division and 1st Burma Division. Corps H.Q. was in Prome.

On March 14 General Stilwell of the U.S. Army had assumed command of the Chinese armies in Burma. On the 24th General Alexander went to Chungking to see Marshal Chiang Kai-shek who, in the course of their discussions, asked him to accept command of all the Allied troops in China. The system of command was, and remained, distinctly peculiar. General Alexander was commander of all the Allied troops; General Stilwell commanded the two Chinese Armies which were component formations of the troops in Burma but he had to issue his orders through a Chinese general. Moreover no order of any major kind affecting Chinese troops could be issued by anybody until it had been endorsed by Marshal Chiang Kai-shek himself.

Prome at this time was being regularly though not heavily bombed by the Japanese. Fires were continually breaking out, usually due to the enterprise of hostile Burmans. Along its streets and about its wharves were bivouacking thousands of Indian refugees from Rangoon waiting to get across the Irrawaddy in order to make their way to Taungup on the Arakan coast. Among them smallpox and cholera had made their appearance. The municipal conservancy services had disintegrated and the cleansing of the streets had to be undertaken by the convicts from the local jail.

During the 21st-24th and on the 27th the Japanese attacked the Magwe and Akyab airfields and as a consequence of the great havoc they caused, the R.A.F. was driven from Burma. From this time onwards the Japanese had practically undisputed command of the sky above Burma and they systematically began to bomb the centres of communications, Prome, Meiktila, Mandalay, Thazi, Pyinmana, Maymyo, Lashio and Taunggyi, and to cause great fires and such panic among the civilian population that these fled into the jungle and so brought all the public utility services to an abrupt halt. Police forces disintegrated, railway and flotilla crews disappeared, post office services and power supplies broke down to embarrass military plans and impede military operations.

On the night of March 21/22, Chinese 200th Division of Chinese Fifth Army relieved 1st Burma Division which then moved by road and rail *via* Pyinmana and Taungdwingyi to the Irrawaddy front. On the 25th Burcorps issued orders for the concentration of the corps in the area Allanmyo–Prome, with 1st Burma Division in the area Dayindabo–Kyaukpadaung–Allanmyo–Thayetmyo; Indian 17th Division in the area Wettigan–Prome–Shwedaung–Sinde and 7th Armd. Bde. in reserve in the area of Tamagauk. The defence of the area was based upon the two brigade groups in Allanmyo and Prome respectively, the rest of the corps being mobile. On the Irrawaddy detachments of Royal Marines, those that had destroyed the Syriam refineries, provided crews for a river patrol.

On the Toungoo front the concentration of Chinese Fifth Army was impeded by the movements of Chinese Sixth Army and by the disintegration of the railway system as a consequence of Japanese bombing attacks. However, on March 24, 200th Division was in a position in and around Toungoo. 22nd Division was arriving in Lashio and 96th Division was nearing the frontier. The Japanese suddenly attacked the airfield north of Toungoo and in so doing got behind and cut off 200th Division. In this action the rear echelon of 1st Burma Division, to which a company of 2 (Bur.) Fd. Amb. was attached, became involved. By the evening of the 26th, 22nd Division had reached Pyinmana–Yedashe on the road to Toungoo from the north but was unable to respond to General Stilwell's order to attack the Japanese and relieve the beleaguered 200th Division. On April 1, 200th Division by its own exertions broke out from Toungoo but had to abandon all its transport and guns and most of its equipment; it suffered over 3,000 casualties. A general withdrawal of the Chinese formations towards Pyinmana followed. The Japanese crossed over the bridge over the Sittang in Toungoo and pressed on to the west.

With Toungoo lost it became doubtful if Prome could be held. The town, surrounded by scrub jungle, could be defended only with difficulty and could easily be cut off. The Japanese had already occupied parts of the west bank of the Irrawaddy and the conditions in the town itself were rapidly worsening. It had been almost completely burnt and cholera was spreading among the refugees and was beginning to attack the troops. The main reason for holding on to it at this time was that on its quays were vast dumps of stores, mainly rice. There was no railway out of Prome and so the river was used to get as large a quantity as possible of stores away to the north but there were many difficulties in the way, a shortage of labour, an abnormally low level of water in the river and the frequent air raids.

On March 26 the Japanese began to probe the positions held by Burcorps. On the 27th four to five thousand of them were reported to be on the west bank of the Irrawaddy in the vicinity of Tonbo. To relieve the pressure being exerted on Chinese Fifth Army, Burcorps was required to launch a local offensive operation south of Prome. On March 28 1st Glosters attacked and took Paungde, a large village 30 miles south of Prome on the trunk road and had thereafter withdrawn. Now that a local offensive was ordered, an improvised striking force from Indian 17th Division, consisting of 414 Bty. R.H.A., 7th Hussars, one company of 1st W. Yorks, 2nd D.W.R., 1st Cameronians and 1st

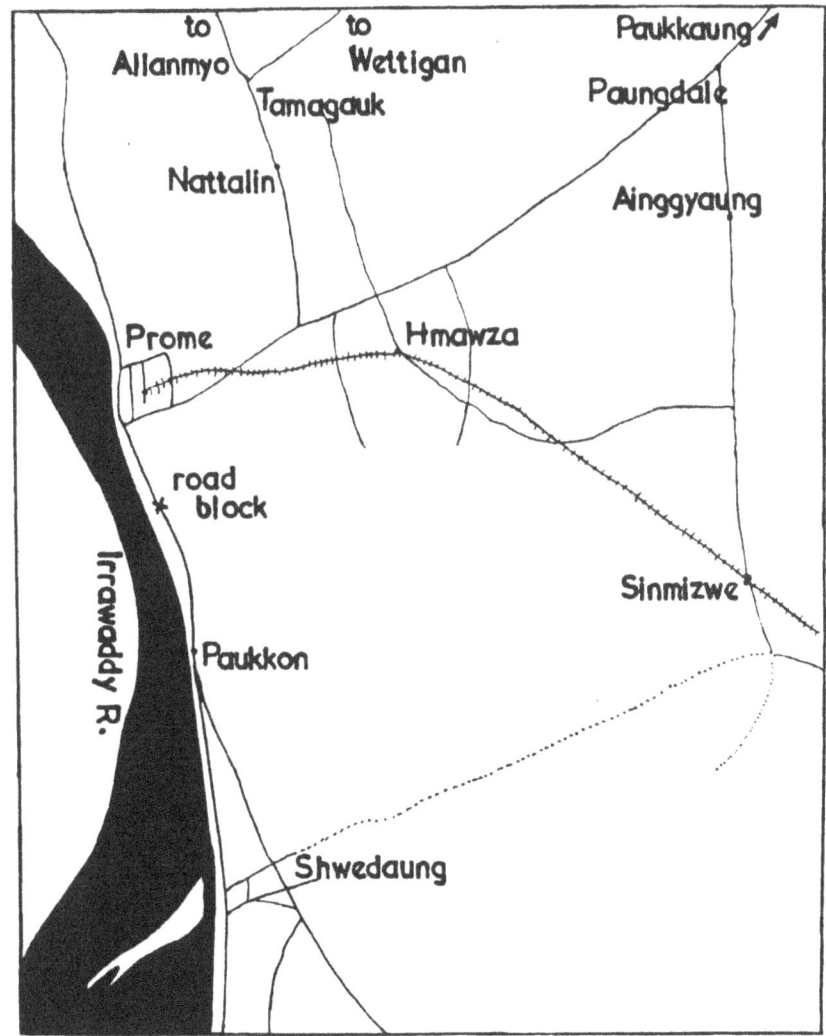

FIG. 7. The Prome Area

Glosters, was sent out to reoccupy this village, and then to move on to Okpo, just north of Tharrawaddy. It found that Paungde was strongly held. The striking force, after much confused fighting, captured part of the village but was driven out again. It was learnt from a liaison officer returning to the divisional headquarters from the striking force that Shwedaung 10 miles south of Prome on the trunk road, and therefore between Paungde and Prome, was full of Japanese troops who apparently had entered the town from the south-west. The striking force in Paungde was ordered to withdraw and to help it two Indian battalions (4/12th F.F.R. and 2/13th F.F.Rif.) were sent from Prome to eject the Japanese from Shwedaung.

The striking force found its way back obstructed by a road-block at the southern end of the town. This was attacked while the relieving column attacked the northern approaches to the town. Both these attacks were checked by heavy fire. A second attack by the striking force made progress but was checked by a second road-block in the town itself. Next morning this was attacked and the force ultimately burst through to be halted once more by a road-block at the north end of the town. Shwedaung was now burning fiercely and the columns were being machine-gunned from the air. The striking force attacked once more while the relieving force again attacked from the north and finally the armour of the striking force crashed through the obstacle to shepherd the trucks and ambulances loaded with wounded to safety. More than three hundred were killed or wounded during this engagement.

THE LOSS OF THE OILFIELDS

The headquarters of 1 Burma Corps now moved to Allanmyo, thirty-five miles to the north where on April 1, Generals Wavell and Alexander, having reviewed the situation, decided that a further withdrawal had become necessary. Burcorps was to concentrate in the area Allanmyo–Kyaukpadaung–Thayetmyo to defend the oilfields around Yenangyaung and also to safeguard Upper Burma. That very evening the Japanese attacked Indian 17th Division which at this time was disposed in three brigade groups, 63rd in Prome and to the south of it, 48th Bde. in Hmawza, four miles to the east of Prome, and 16th Bde. to the east of Prome on the line of the Prome–Paukkaung road. 7th Armd. Bde. was in Tamagauk. The sector held by 63rd Bde. was pierced and through the gap the Japanese poured into Prome. 63rd Bde. was forced to withdraw towards Tamagauk. 48th Bde. was also attacked but stubbornly held on to its positions. It was pulled out of Hmawza and placed astride the main road to prevent the Japanese advancing on Hmawza from Prome. 7th Armd. Bde. was sent forward from Tamagauk to the assistance of 63rd Bde. Reports were received to the effect that a strong Japanese force was moving on Dayindabo, sixteen miles to the north, round the flank of the Prome position. If this were so there was no alternative to a withdrawal to Allanmyo. 1st Burma Bde. of 1st Burma Division was sent to Dayindabo to hold it if threatened and to safeguard the passage through it of Indian 17th Division. On April 3 this division, passing through 1st Burma Division in the area Dayindabo–Pyalo, half-way between Prome and Allanmyo, reached its new position in the area Ywataung–Kyaukpadaung (east of Thayetmyo)–Bwetgyi Chaung and 7th Armd. Bde. and 48th Bde. then proceeded to Satthwa.

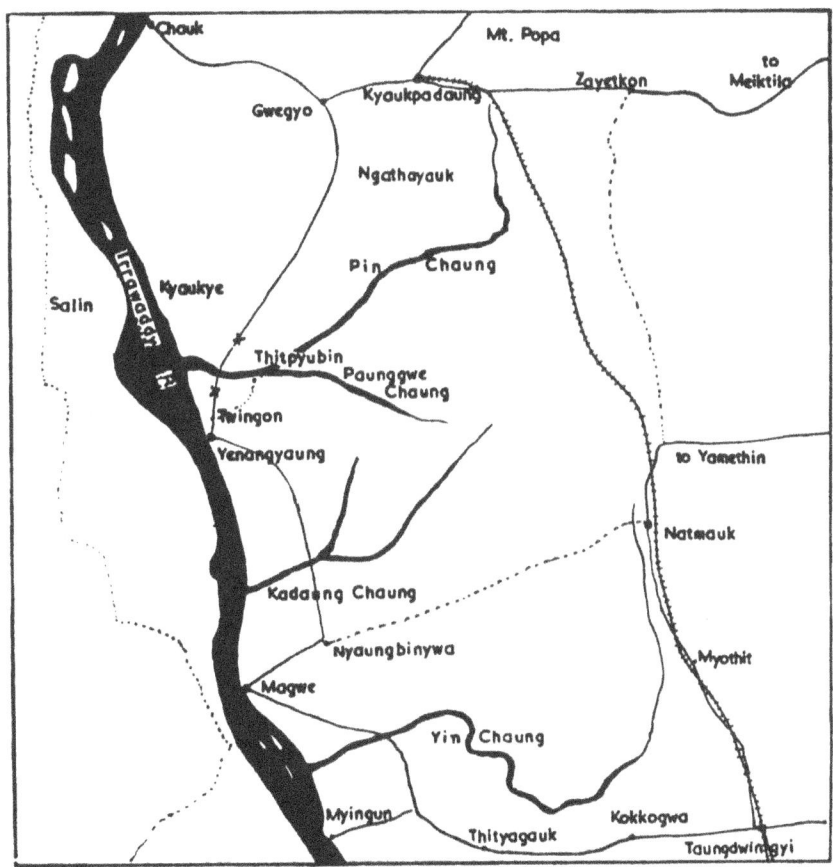

FIG. 8. The Yenangyaung Area

General Slim decided to hold the line just to the south of the Magwe–Taungdwingyi lateral road. It was arranged that a Chinese battalion would take over the eastern end of the line in the Taungdwingyi area. Allanymo was evacuated on April 8, Corps H.Q. moving to Magwe. 1 Burma Corps was now in the Dry Belt of Burma. The lush green of the Delta and its humid air had given place to a bare brown stony earth scarred with water courses, 'chaungs'. It having been arranged that the Chinese would take over the defence of Taungdwingyi,

General Slim planned to collect a striking force for use in counter-attack, consisting of Ind. 13th Bde. of 1st Burma Division, 48th Bde. of Indian 17th Division and 7th Armd. Bde. He proposed to place the last two of these in Kokkogwa, ten miles to the west of Taungdwingyi and 13th Bde. in Thityagauk, eight miles further to the west. Unfortunately the Chinese could not take over the defence of Taungdwingyi and so Indian 17th Division had to remain in this town and turn it into a strong point. General Slim did manage to collect a striking force, however, consisting of two of the three brigades, 7th Armoured and 48th. 2nd Burma Bde. of 1st Burma Division, moving on to the west bank of the Irrawaddy, reached Minhla on April 8/9. The oilfields were now being prepared for destruction. On the 10th, the Japanese attack opened. It grew in intensity throughout that day and on the 11th when 13th Bde. in Thityagauk and 48th Bde. in Kokkogwa were both heavily involved. During the night of April 11/12 a fierce assault was launched upon the Gurkha brigade in Kokkogwa and on 1st Burma Bde. in Migyaungye but both held their ground. The fighting at Kokkogwa was particularly fierce, thrice the Japanese pierced the Gurkhas' line and thrice they were flung back. But large numbers of Japanese succeeded in infiltrating between the defended localities and these established themselves in positions from which they could dominate the Taungdwingyi–Magwe lateral road. During the night of the 12/13th the Japanese attacks upon 1st Burma and 48th Bdes. were resumed. The Gurkhas again repulsed the Japanese but in the sector of 1st Burma Bde. there was much infiltration by strong Japanese forces and ultimately this brigade was forced to give ground. In so doing it exposed the whole right flank and opened the way to Magwe.

By the morning of April 14 it was apparent that there was a wide gap between 1st Burma Division on the right and Indian 17th Division on the left and that the Japanese were astride the lateral road between Kokkogwa and Thityagauk. This being the situation, it had become impossible, without the aid of the Chinese, to continue to hold Taungdwingyi and at the same time to cover the direct approach to the oilfields. To abandon Taungdwingyi would lay bare the flank of Chinese Fifth Army, the leading elements of which were still around Pyinmana. It was decided that Taungdwingyi should be held at all costs and to reinforce its garrison 48th Bde. was moved thereto from Kokkogwa.

1st Burma Division, covered by 7th Armd. Bde., withdrew to the line of the Yin Chaung that runs a meandering course from the Irrawaddy at Magwe in a south-easterly direction towards Thityagauk and then turns north to reach Natmauk. On April 15 the oilfields in the Yenangyaung and Chauk areas were destroyed. On the night of April 16/17 the Japanese attacked 1st Burma Bde. in its new position in the

Yin Chaung and broke through. 1st Burma Division was left with no alternative to withdrawing further to the north along the Magwe-Yenangyaung road to the line of the Pin Chaung which runs from the Irrawaddy just north of Yenangyaung in a north-easterly direction. Part of Corps H.Q. and the corps administrative units had left Magwe for Yenangyaung and now the rest of Corps H.Q. followed.

Crossing the Pin Chaung near the village of Twingon just to the north of Yenangyaung was a ford guarded by a section of 8th H.A.A. Bty. R.A. For vehicular traffic this was the only way across the chaung to the north and it was therefore of the greatest importance to Burcorps. On April 16 Rear H.Q. 1st Burma Division crossed the Pin Chaung and established itself in Gwegyo. 7th Armd. Bde. also passed northwards through the flaming desolation of Yenangyaung. About two miles to the north of the Pin Chaung 2nd R.Tks. was fired on during the night of April 16/17. Japanese troops suddenly appeared at the ford, seized it and took most of its defenders prisoner and thereafter moved on towards Yenangyaung. Other parties of Japanese established road-blocks to the north and to the south of the ford. Apparently these Japanese had reached the Pin Chaung by way of one of its tributaries, the Paunggwe Chaung. In Yenangyaung a small garrison consisting of H.Q. and one company of 1st Glosters had been left to guard the power-house, which was still being used, and to watch the roads. This small force, having covered the destruction of the power-house, opposed the advance of the Japanese moving down the Twingon–Yenangyaung road.

On April 17 from north of the ford a company of 1st W. Yorks and a half-squadron of 2nd R.Tks. with H.Q. 7th Armd. Bde. thrust southwards towards the Pin Chaung while Frontier Force units, supported by armour, struck northwards from the south side of the road-block. The road-block was cleared and the road opened to traffic but during the night of the 17th/18th the Japanese succeeded in cutting the road once more.

Chinese 38th Division moved from Mandalay to Kyaukpadaung to pass u/c Burcorps. It was decided to employ two of its regiments, supported by 414th Bty. R.H.A. and a squadron of 2nd R.Tks., to attack the line of the Pin Chaung from the north on the morning of the 18th. Throughout the 17th the fatigued units of 1st Burma Division had been marching along the Magwe-Yenangyaung road towards the ford across the Pin Chaung from the south-east. The heat was intense and the road shadeless and deep in dust. Japanese aircraft frequently bombed and machine-gunned the marching columns. The leading elements of the division—1st Glosters, a company of Sappers and Miners and the divisional Employment Platoon—reaching the southern outskirts of Yenangyaung, clung precariously to their positions therein. At the end of the day the division had reached a point just to the south of Yenangyaung and near the Pin Chaung. Plans were made by wireless with Burcorps to co-ordinate an attack by 1st Burma Division from the south with an attack by Chinese 38th Division from the north.

At 0630 hours on April 18 the attack by 1st Burma Division opened. It is to be noted that the exceedingly tired troops of this division were to fight throughout the next two days in this arid, shadeless region in the intense April heat. Many of them were already without water. To begin with good progress was made by the Cameronians, 1/18th R. Garh. Rif. and 5/1st Punjab. But around Twingon village the Japanese had gathered in considerable strength and the road-block south of the ford could not be cleared. The division, exhausted and much thinned, formed a perimeter to the south of the village. On the 19th the Japanese closed in on 1st Burma Division and with the coming of dawn began to attack its positions. The division was informed that it must fight its way out, abandoning its transport if necessary. The Chinese attack from the north had not yet been launched; it had been postponed several times. A squadron of 2nd R.Tks. and 'D' Coy, 1st W. Yorks actually made their way to and across the Pin Chaung from the north and made contact with 2nd K.O.Y.L.I. only to be recalled to deal with a Japanese column that was reported to be in Kyaukpadaung.

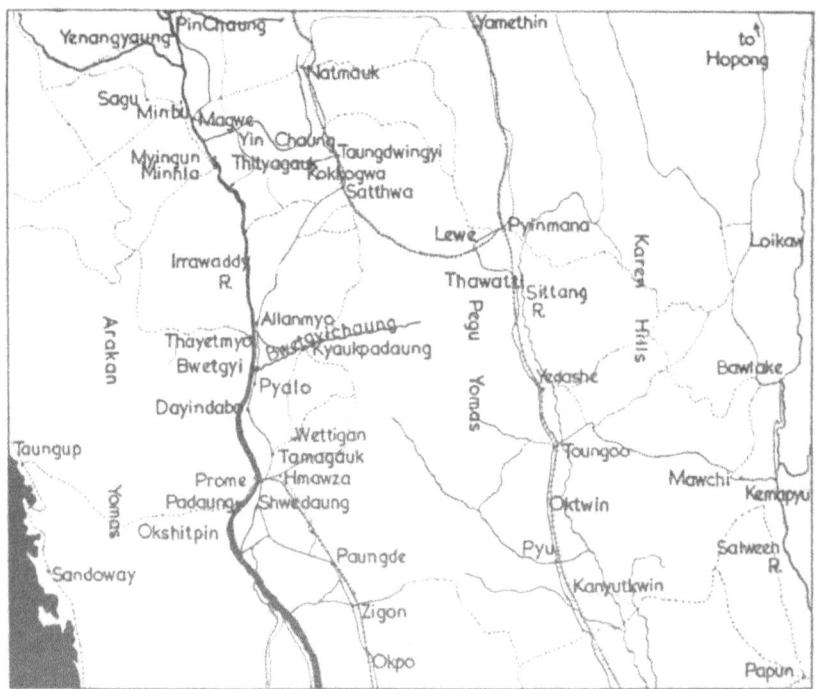

FIG. 9. Prome–Yenangyaung

THE JAPANESE INVADE BURMA 59

These Japanese turned out to be Chinese and so a good chance of forcing the Japanese away from the ford was lost.

In the divisional box the situation was rapidly becoming serious. The commander of 1st Burma Bde. reported that his men were so exhausted that he could not rely upon them to resist very much longer. A similar report was received from Ind. 13th Bde. It was then learnt that there was another track to and across the chaung away to the east. So the transport was formed up with the guns in front followed by the wounded in ambulances and lorries and behind a screen of infantry and tanks the division moved off after having rendered all non-essential vehicles useless. It was now 1400 hours and the Chinese attack from the north had not yet been opened. Very soon, however, loose sand brought the transport to a grinding halt and it had to be abandoned, the wounded being piled on to the tanks. At last the Pin Chaung was reached about two miles to the north-east of Twingon village and was there crossed. The division reassembled in the area of Milestones 372–374 on the Yenangyaung-Kyaukpadaung road near that strange mountain Mount Popa which rises to 5,000 ft. abruptly from the plain. Its losses in men and material were very heavy. Chinese 38th Division attacked at 1500 hours and captured Twingon, releasing some two hundred men of 1st Burma Division from captivity. This attack came too late to be of any help to 1st Burma Division.

While the battle of the oilfields was proceeding the Japanese were attacking Chinese Sixth Army in the Shan States. When Chinese Fifth Army had been driven out of Toungoo northwards towards Pyinmana, Chinese Sixth Army was occupying the hills between the Sittang and the Mandalay-Rangoon line. In this area there are but two roads, one running east to west from Toungoo to Mawchi and the other running north-south from Mawchi through Bawlake to Loikaw. Chinese 55th Division was disposed in depth along the road from Loikaw. Chinese 49th Division was further to the north and Chinese 93rd Division was about Kengtung. Japanese 56th Division troops in strength amounting to a brigade group began to thrust eastwards towards Mawchi in April and overcoming such resistance as was offered by British-led Karen Levies and the Chinese, occupied Mawchi and so gained possession of its wolfram mines. Chinese 55th Division fell back to Bawlake. On April 17 the Japanese cut the road beyond Bawlake and so isolated a large part of Chinese 55th Division which was overwhelmed on the 18th. The Chinese then hurriedly evacuated Loikaw. The Japanese next cut the Thazi-Loilem-Kengtung road in the rear of Chinese Sixth Army which scattered and fell back to a position 12 miles east of Hopong, 80 miles north of Loikaw. By April 21 Chinese Sixth Army had practically ceased to exist. On the 22nd the Japanese occupied both Hopong and Taunggyi and on the following day entered Loilem. The Chinese withdrew across the Burma-China border. Kengtung was occupied by Thai troops under Japanese command. The road north to Lashio was open. The immediate result of this débâcle was that Chinese 200th Division, which had reached Kyaukpadaung to bring aid to Burcorps, was recalled for employment by General Stilwell in an attempt to recapture Taunggyi and so secure the rear of Chinese Fifth Army. Taunggyi was retaken on April 24. On the following day the Japanese were driven out of Hopong and Loilem. But at this point General Stilwell was obliged to return to his headquarters and in his absence the momentum of the Chinese attacks greatly and progressively diminished. 200th Division moved to the north of the Loilem-Lashio road. At this time Chinese 28th and 29th Divisions of Chinese Sixty-sixth Army were entering Burma and were sent to hold the Lashio area. On April 29 the Japanese attacked and took Lashio and the Chinese withdrew into China while the Japanese pressed on towards Bhamo which they entered on May 4. On the 8th they were in Myitkyina. Chinese 200th Division reached Hsipaw, on the Mandalay-Lashio road, from Taunggyi but, finding that Lashio had been occupied by the Japanese, returned to Maymyo and thence proceeded to Mogok there to join part of Chinese 28th Division which had been left behind, and with this to move into China. The only Chinese troops now left in Burma were 38th Division with Burcorps and 22nd and 96th Divisions of Fifth Army. Chinese 22nd and 96th Divisions had been forced out of Pyinmana on April 19 and by the 25th had ceased to be effective fighting formations, their troops were streaming back through Thazi to Mandalay.

The Japanese were now in a position either to threaten the rear of Burcorps through Bhamo and Myitkyina or else to sweep down upon Mandalay. It had become clear that there could be no counter-offensive against Yenangyaung and so General Alexander issued orders for a general withdrawal north of Mandalay. General Slim issued instructions for Chinese 38th Division to cover Kyaukpadaung, for 1st Burma Division, less its brigade (2nd Burma) on the west bank of the Irrawaddy, to complete its reorganisation and to be prepared to move on Taungtha, and for Indian 17th Division to leave Taungdwingyi, move rapidly to the area Mahlaing-Meiktila-Zayetkon and, with 7th Armd. Bde., cover the withdrawal of Chinese Fifth Army. But the complete defeat of the Chinese armies had made impossible any prolonged stand on the Mandalay-Irrawaddy line and all that could now be done was to withdraw to the Indian border. On April 28 orders were issued for a withdrawal to Kalewa. Troops and stores in Maymyo were to be evacuated and Burcorps was to provide a rearguard on the axis Meiktila-Mandalay to cover the withdrawal of the Chinese forces.

On April 25, 7th Armd. Bde. interposed itself between the Chinese and the pursuing Japanese east of Meiktila. Burcorps was now on the

THE JAPANESE INVADE BURMA

general line Seikpyu, on the west bank of the Irrawaddy, –Chauk–Kyaukpadaung–Zayetkon–Meiktila. Indian 17th Division was firmly established in the Meiktila–Zayetkon area supporting 7th Armd. Bde. in its attempts to check the advance of Japanese columns along the main road and the railway. As the retreating Chinese were now clear of Meiktila, General Slim ordered Indian 17th Division to fall back on Wundwin, to hold this place until 1600 hours on the 24th and then to withdraw through Kyaukse. 63rd Bde. remained in Wundwin until midnight on April 26/27 and then fell back through 48th Bde. in Kyaukse to take up positions covering the Ava bridge over the Irrawaddy River just south of Mandalay.

MEDICAL COVER

1 (Bur.) Fd. Amb. with 21 M.A.S. moved from Prome to Allanmyo where on March 18 the civil hospital was taken over. On the 25th the first case of cholera, a civilian, was admitted and promptly died. On the following day one B.O.R. and ten I.O.Rs., all suffering from this disease, were admitted from the Prome area. One of the I.O.Rs. was dead on arrival. On the 28th the hospital was bombed, one orderly and one patient being killed. The unit then moved to a nearby *phongyi kyaung*, a Buddhist temple, 38 patients being evacuated to 8 (Ind.) C.C.S. on the hospital steamer *Mysore*. The numbers of those admitted now increased rapidly, there being 112 from 13 Lt. Fd. Amb. and 50 (Ind.) Fd. Amb. on March 30; 201 from 13 Lt. Fd. Amb. and 50 (Ind.) Fd. Amb. on the 31st; 40 from 13 Lt. Fd. Amb. and 23 (Ind.) Fd. Amb. on April 1, and 46 from 13 Lt. Fd. Amb. on the 2nd. Evacuation was to 8 (Ind.) C.C.S. which quickly became filled with lying cases and therefore found it necessary to erect tentage on the river bank for the walking wounded. While the ship was moored at a point where the road made an S-bend to come quite close to the river, Japanese bombers passed overhead. One of them broke formation and headed straight for the steamer. Just as he began his dive the pilot suddenly flattened out and made off. It was reasonably assumed that he had seen the Red Cross emblem on the roof and that for this reason had spared the ship. The *Mysore* was at once moved away from this particular spot.

An awkward incident now occurred. 2 Bur.G.H., on the authority of a medical staff captain, loaded itself on to the *Mysore* with instructions to displace the C.C.S. The withdrawal of a hospital to the rear was undoubtedly the correct action for at this time Prome was getting dangerously near the front line. But it so happened that this action, taken without reference to higher authority, wrecked the plans of D.D.M.S. who was intending to leave this particular hospital to serve the defended area that was to be organised in the Prome area. When the *Mysore* with 2 Bur.G.H. reached Mandalay, D.D.M.S. promptly ordered the unit to proceed forthwith to Yenangyaung and to stay there until specifically told by him to move. The *Mysore* then reverted to 8 (Ind.) C.C.S. and was taken to a point below Yenangyaung to pick up a load of casualties. The steamer then sailed for Mandalay where its patients were disembarked to proceed by train to Myitkyina.

2 (Bur.) Fd. Amb. reached Allanmyo with 1st Burma Division at the end of March and served 2nd Burma Bde. which was operating on the right bank of the Irrawaddy.

On April 2, 1 (Bur.) Fd. Amb. moved to Taungdwingyi, handing over to 37 (Ind.) Fd. Amb. in Allanmyo. Its 179 patients were evacuated to 8 (Ind.) C.C.S. It then handed over the civil hospital in Taungdwingyi to 23 (Ind.) Fd. Amb. on April 5 and moved to Kokkogwa and thence to a *phongyi kyaung* just to the north of Magwe airfield.

During the action at Shwedaung on March 29-31 four ambulance cars from 13 Lt. Fd. Amb. were allotted to H.Q. 7th Armd. Bde. and in addition one ambulance car from 50 (Ind.) Fd. Amb. was attached to each of the three battalions of this brigade. An A.D.S. was attached to each of the three brigades of Indian 17th Division, 50 (Ind.) Fd. Amb. supplying those with 16th and 63rd Bdes. and 23 (Ind.) Fd. Amb. the one with 48th Bde. 13 Lt. Fd. Amb., which had accompanied the striking force had established its M.D.S. in Shwedaung by 0600 hours on March 29 to receive British casualties. 50 (Ind.) Fd. Amb., accompanying the relieving force, established its M.D.S. a mile east of Prome to receive Indian casualties. When the Japanese began to infiltrate into Shwedaung the M.D.S. of 13 Lt. Fd. Amb. came under small-arms fire and so withdrew to its earlier site at Milestone 183/4 on the Prome road, leaving a forward A.D.S. with four ambulance cars in Shwedaung.

During the morning of the 29th no casualties from south of the road-block at the north end of the town reached the A.D.S., although many were received from the fighting north of this road-block. In the afternoon casualties from south of the block began to arrive on tanks and in armoured vehicles. With the help of six 3-ton lorries the A.D.S. was cleared, the casualties being taken back to the M.D.S. When it became evident that there was but little prospect of soft-skinned vehicles getting through Shwedaung, orders were issued for their abandonment. The wounded were transferred to armoured vehicles. The medical officer of 414th Battery, R.H.A. found that he, his R.A.P. staff, his patients and a handful of R.A.S.C. drivers had been left behind in the southern outskirts of the town. He commandeered vehicles, loaded his wounded into them, had a burning truck shifted out of the way and under machine-gun fire made his way smartly to the north.

By the evening of the 30th some 200 casualties had been admitted to the two M.D.Ss. which were cleared by 21 and 22 M.A.Ss. to Allanmyo.

THE JAPANESE INVADE BURMA

When Indian 17th Division was defending the Prome–Hmawza line with its 63rd Bde. in and around Prome, its 48th Bde. in Hmawza, its 16th Bde. in reserve between these two along the Prome–Hmawza road and when 7th Armd. Bde. was in Tamagauk, their medical units were distributed as follows:

A.D.S. 50 (Ind.) Fd. Amb.	In Prome serving 63rd Bde.
A.D.S. "	On the Prome–Allanmyo road about 3 miles north of Prome, serving 16th Bde.
M.D.S. "	Near Milestone 183 on the Prome–Allanmyo road.
A.D.S. 23 (Ind.) Fd. Amb.	In Hmawza, serving 48th Bde.
M.D.S. "	In Dayindabo.
A.D.S. 13 Lt. Fd. Amb.	In Tamagauk near Milestone 183 on the Prome–Allanmyo road.
M.D.S. "	In Dayindabo
22 M.A.S.	Between Milestone 183 and 184 on the Prome–Allanmyo road.
22 (Ind.) Fd. Hyg. Sec.	In Dayindabo.
37 (Ind.) Fd. Amb.	On the move to Allanmyo.

During the withdrawal to the area of Allanmyo on April 3, 23 and 13 Lt. Fd. Ambs. were in Allanmyo itself. At the beginning of this withdrawal 50 (Ind.) Fd. Amb., now with animal transport only and with bullock carts and riding mules, had its M.D.S. in a wood on the outskirts of Prome. It came under mortar fire; the bullocks bolted and all its carts save four were smashed. Leaving much of its equipment behind the unit set off for the north.

A few miles south of Dayindabo three lorries loaded with troops had closed up while crossing a bridge. They were bombed. About a hundred casualties were admitted to 23 (Ind.) Fd. Amb. the medical staff of which was helped by that of divisional headquarters. Next morning the casualties were evacuated to Allanmyo.

During the withdrawal 13 Lt. and 50 Fd. Ambs. were ferried in M.T. The mules and the bullocks of the latter unit were despatched with a marching column. During this march two more of the bullock carts broke down and had to be abandoned, their loads being transferred to M.T. 23 (Ind.) Fd. Amb., with a little transport for its equipment, brought up the rear. 37 (Ind.) Fd. Amb., which now rejoined the division, opened its M.D.S. in Allanmyo.

During the Japanese attack upon the oilfields when 1st Burma Bde. was so heavily involved, 2 (Bur.) Fd. Amb. established its M.D.S. on a river steamer and picked up casualties from the bank of the river. In the confused fighting about the Pin Chaung 57 (Ind.) Fd. Amb. was overrun and captured. Its second-in-command got clear in a 15-cwt. truck but all the rest were locked in a building which began to burn; it was either hit or else was set on fire deliberately. Many of the inmates were shot when trying to get out. Only 35 out of the 170 who were locked in survived.

1 (Bur.) Fd. Amb. moved from Magwe to Yenangyaung on April 13 and there took over the Burma Oil Company's most admirably equipped hospital from 4 (Ind.) C.C.S. which then embarked on a river steamer. The field ambulance soon received orders to move to the north and so, evacuating 30 patients by M.A.S. to Meiktila, it set out for the Pin Chaung. After overcoming much difficulty caused by traffic jams the unit reached Kyaukpadaung on April 15 and opened in a *phongyi kyaung* in a nearby village. A light section of the unit was sent to Milestone 390 near the Chauk–Kyaukpadaung road junction at the request of A.D.M.S. 1st Burma Division to care for casualties from the fighting around the Twingon road-block.

On April 18 the unit, less its light section, moved to Milestone 27·2 on the Meiktila–Kyaukpadaung road with H.Q. Burcorps, carrying with it a number of seriously ill patients, two British officers, one of them a cholera case, four I.O.Rs., one of them suffering from cholera, and two Chinese soldiers. The cholera cases were from the Bombay Pioneers, a unit which somehow had managed to miss inoculation. On April 21 the light section moved to the vicinity of Mount Popa and there admitted five more cholera cases, all from the Bombay Pioneers.

On April 23, 1 (Bur.) Fd. Amb., less its light section, moved to Milestone 352·2 near Myingyan. On the following day the light section moved to Kyaukpadaung there to serve a mountain battery. On the 26th the field ambulance moved to Ondaw where it was joined by the light section. Evacuation was now to Sagaing. For its next move the unit had to travel *via* Kyaukse for the reason that the road to the Ava bridge *via* Myotha was under repair. On the 27th the unit moved to Milestone 39 on the Mandalay–Shwebo road and on the 29th to Monywa.

During this battle all the field ambulances were very hard pressed, they were very short of transport, were constantly on the move and under fire and the water shortage was acute. When Indian 17th Division was in the vicinity of Taungdwingyi, 23 (Ind.) Fd. Amb. opened its M.D.S. in the local hospital while 37 (Ind.) Fd. Amb. established itself in a nearby *phongyi kyaung*. Both of these units endured much bombardment from the air, the transport lines of 23 being hit, and both were kept extremely busy. When it became necessary for the division to withdraw to the north, owing to the defeat of Chinese Sixth Army in the Shan States, 23 (Ind.) Fd. Amb. accompanied 16th and 63rd Bdes. and 37 (Ind.) Fd. Amb. served 48th Bde., the rearguard. The march to Myothit, half way to Natmauk from Taungdwingyi, had nightmarish qualities. The night was moonless. The troops moved in single file on either side of the road which was deep-rutted and ankle-deep in dust. The transport consisted of slow-moving bullock carts. When Myothit was reached it was found to be empty save for one old Burmese man who, apparently, was past caring about his terrestrial future. The next halt was in Natmauk where 37 (Ind.) Fd. Amb. opened its M.D.S. 50 (Ind.) Fd. Amb. moved on into Meiktila to provide cover for the troops supporting 7th Armd. Bde. in the Meiktila-Zayetkon area. It opened to receive casualties from both 23 and 37 (Ind.) Fd. Ambs. With 50 (Ind.) Fd. Amb. was 22 (Ind.) Fd. Hyg. Sec. 23 (Ind.) Fd. Amb. was ferried forward from Natmauk to Myinthi, south-west of Sagaing, by the divisional M.T. in two parties. 50 (Ind.) Fd. Amb., the only divisional medical unit with transport of its own, then moved from Meiktila into Mahlaing and 37 (Ind.) Fd. Amb., moving with 48th Bde., proceeded to Kyaukse. Evacuation was from 37 to 23 by returning supply lorries and from 23 to 50 by 22 M.A.S. Some of the casualties were sent by 21 M.A.S. and ambulance train to Myingyan.

MEDICAL ARRANGEMENTS

When the withdrawal to the area of Prome began there was great activity in this town on the part of the medical services in attempts to clear the many casualties that had accumulated there as a result of the fighting at Taukkyan and Pegu. When all the available hospital river steamers had been despatched, other steamers were requisitioned, staffed, rationed, equipped, loaded and sent off to Mandalay. Though these steamers had not been converted for the accommodation of the wounded and the sick, they were not at all unsuitable for this purpose; they had tiered open decks and the journey was in itself peaceful and health-restoring.

D.D.M.S., taking advantage of the arrival of transport aircraft at Magwe, bringing reinforcements and supplies, arranged for the evacuation of casualties by air. 2 (Br.) S.S. was posted to the airfield to act as an air evacuation unit. A steady stream of casualties was sent to India from Magwe up to the time when this town was bombed and the airfield wrecked. 2 (Br.) S.S. thereupon proceeded by river steamer to Mandalay.

In Prome 2 Bur. G.H. from Tadagale, Rangoon, was open in a school. In Prome also was the Depot of Medical Stores that had been brought from Rangoon in its own transport—the Rangoon Corporation refuse and dust carts.

At this time intercommunication had become exceedingly difficult and most unreliable. The Post Office and Telegraph system had broken down completely as a consequence of the widespread Japanese bombardment of the chief centres of communication and the few military wireless links were required for messages of the highest priority. An officer courier system between the larger towns was organised. A daily service of fast cars was provided but breakdowns were not uncommon. Twice at the request of A.D.M.S. Burcorps an ambulance train was despatched to Taunggyi and twice it came back to Prome empty owing to failure of intercommunication. On the second occasion it was sent away from Taunggyi by a staff officer of 1st Burma Division who did not know why it had come or who had asked for it.

The time taken by one of the hospital steamers to reach Mandalay depended very largely upon the quantity and quality of the fuel it managed to collect *en route*. Moreover, it so happened at this time that the level of the water was abnormally low so that the danger of grounding became magnified. If a steamer did run on to one of the ever-shifting sand bars, the time required to get her off might be anything from a few hours to several days. When a steamer arrived at Mandalay it became increasingly likely, as the general situation worsened, that the crew would refuse to take her down river again. Several of these steamers were in fact immobilised because their crews walked off them in Mandalay docks.

After the fall of Toungoo, when it was decided to withdraw to the north, a new three-pronged L. of C. was prepared leading to India and to China. To India there were two routes, to China one. The routes to India were

(i) by the River Chindwin from Monywa to Kalewa and thence by road to Tamu and Imphal.

(ii) by rail from Shwebo to Myitkyina and thence by track through the Hukawng valley to Digboi in North Assam.

The route to China was the Maymo–Lashio–Kunming road, the 'Burma Road'.

This plan entailed a complete redistribution of the medical units. This was to be as follows and was to be completed by April 15:

To the North-west	2 Bur. G.H. from Yenangyaung to Monywa.
	2 Bur. Depot Medical Stores (200 tons) from Yenangyaung to Monywa.
	2 (Bur.) C.C.S. from Myingyan to Monywa and Kalewa.
	16 (Ind.) S.S. to Kalewa and thence to Tamu.
To the North	1 Bur. G.H. from Kalaw to Shwebo (the air evacuation centre).
	13 Depot Medical Stores (200 tons) from Mandalay to Shwebo.
	4 Bur.G.H. from Taunggyi to Myitkyina.
	41 I.G.H. from Maymyo to Katha.

	5 and 8 Bur.G.Hs. from Maymyo to Mohnyin, 100 miles south of Myitkyina.
	59 I.G.H. from Myingyan to Katha.
	400 tons of medical stores from Mandalay to Myitkyina.
To the North-east	7 Bur.G.H. (with 3 Field Laboratory and the Depot of Medical Stores) from Maymyo to Bhamo.
	H.Q. Burma Hospital Corps and Training Wing from Sagaing to Bhamo.
	3 Bur.G.H. from Maymyo to Lashio.
	200 tons of medical stores from Mandalay to Lashio.
Other Moves	6 Bur.G.H. from Meiktila to Sagaing
	2 British Staging Section to Mandalay.

Almost every hospital except those in Mandalay was to move. The officer in charge of the Depot of Medical Stores distinguished himself again. Getting transport from sources apparently known only to himself, he sent 200 tons of stores to Lashio, to Shwebo and to Monywa and put the rest on rail for Myitkyina. He found facilities for the Vaccine and Sera Laboratory in Namtu. He even acquired a herd of cattle from the Agriculture College in Mandalay and sent it to Mohnyin in the far north to function as a source of the milk that the hospitals in the north would require.

Movement by rail at this time was exceedingly difficult. There was much bombing and much sabotage. To maintain a degree of close control over the running of the ambulance trains was impossible. The problem facing the medical services was that of providing adequate bed-cover for the troops while the wholesale movement of the hospitals proceeded. There was a shortage of British beds. There was no convalescent depot. Casualties were pouring into Mandalay by train and steamer from the fighting in the oilfields.

The first general hospital to move was 6 Bur.G.H. which had been in the midst of the heavy bombing raids in Meiktila. In Sagaing it functioned as a V.D. hospital expanding to 600 beds. Next 2 (Br.) S.S., moving to Mandalay, was meant to function as an improvised convalescent depot but was forced by circumstances to become a small general hospital holding over a hundred patients. 1 Bur.G.H., from Kalaw reached Shwebo and opened there in school buildings.

To the airfield at Shwebo transport planes were coming, without previous notice and usually just before dark. They remained on the ground for as short a time as possible. A detachment from 1 Bur.G.H. in Shwebo established itself near the airfield to serve as an improvised air evacuation unit. A sentry watched for the approach of a transport plane.

When one was sighted, patients for evacuation by air were hastily sent out from the hospital to the airfield.

4 Bur.G.H. encountered difficulty in getting rail transport for its move from Taunggyi to Myitkyina. When a train was made available not only the patients, the staff and the equipment were put aboard but so also were rations for one month, a very wise instance of intelligent anticipation as it turned out.

While about half the hospitals were closed, the other half, together with a miscellaneous collection of medical units, managed to cope with the demands made upon them. As has been mentioned, 2 (Br.) S.S. in Mandalay was functioning as a small hospital holding 130 assorted patients, 4 (Ind.) C.C.S. on the steamer *Siam* had nearly 500, 60 I.G.H. in Mandalay, nominally a V.D. hospital of 600 beds, was accommodating nearly 700 patients of all varieties. 8 Bur.G.H. in Maymyo, nominally of 77 beds at one time was holding 284 patients, 52 of them officers and 41 I.G.H., also in Maymyo, had over 1,000. A number of convalescent officers opened their own convalescent depot in Maymyo and the chaplain in Maymyo established a convalescent depot for O.Rs.

When the situation was at its most critical on April 3, Mandalay was very heavily bombed. The railway station, the bazaar area, and the southern part of the town received particular attention and soon the thick black smoke of burning buildings filled the air. Fanned by a strong south wind the flames from the dozens of fires merged to sweep through the town. Its wooden houses burned so fiercely that within a few hours there was nothing left to burn. The residential district of the city had vanished completely. Of all the air raids on the Burmese towns this was surely the worst.

No bombs had been dropped in Fort Dufferin nor on areas marked with the Red Cross. Sparks from the burning city, however, leapt across the moat, about 75 yards wide, and over the wall of the fort to fall on the roofs of 5 Bur.G.H. within. Its wooden oiled shingled roof blazed almost like cordite and soon the whole of the hospital was in flames. The patients were moved to the Governor's Lodge on the far side of the fort.

60 I.G.H. was in stone buildings in the west quarter of the city and was not hit. But as the fire spread the hospital became endangered and so the evacuation scheme prepared against such an eventuality was put into operation. Its 600 patients, its equipment, tentage and staff were moved in six and a half hours to a site north of the fort under Mandalay Hill.

The Chinese military hospital and also the civil hospital were hit and burnt out. 2 (Bur.) C.C.S., newly arrived, rendered such help as it could and the two hospitals, under orders to proceed to the north, were moved into temporary accommodation and carried on as best they could.

APPENDIX III

THE ARMY-IN-BURMA
ORDER OF BATTLE. APRIL 1, 1942
(much abbreviated)

Burcorps.
  Corps troops
    7th Armoured Brigade
      7th Queen's Own Hussars
      2nd R. Tks.
      414th Bty. R.H.A.
      'A' Bty. 95th A/Tk. Regt. R.A.
      1st W. Yorks.

  1st Burma Division (Burdiv.)
    1st Burma Bde.
      2/7th Rajput
      1st Burma Rifles (Burif.)
      2nd Burif.
      5th Burif.
    2nd Burma Bde.
      5/1st Punjab
      7th Burif.
    Ind. 13th Bde.
      1/18th R. Garh. Rif.

  Indian 17th Division
    Ind. 16th Bde.
      2nd D.W.R.
      1 R./9th Jat.
      7/10th Baluch.
      4/12th F.F.R.
    Ind. 48th Bde.
      1st Cameronians
      1/3rd G.R.
      2/5th R.G.R.
      1/4th G.R.
      1/7th G.R.
      3/7th G.R.
    Ind. 63rd Bde.
      1st Innisks.
      1/11th Sikh
      2/13th F.F. Rif.
      1/10th G.R.

Divisional troops
(Infantry)
    1st Glosters
    5/17th Dogra
    8th Burif.
    1st, 2nd, 3rd Detachments, B.F.F.
    Royal Marine River Patrol (Force Viper)
    Rangoon Bn. Burma Military Police
    Special Service Detachment (Commando)

Army Tps.
(Infantry)
    9th and 10th Burif.
    Bhamo Bn. B.F.F.
    Chin Hills Bn. B.F.F. (less detach.)
    Myitkyina Bn. B.F.F.
    Northern Shan States Bn. B.F.F.
    Southern Shan States Bn. B.F.F.
    Reserve Bn. B.F.F.
    Kokine Bn. B.F.F. (less detachs.)
    Karen Levies

L. of C. Units and Tps.
(Infantry)
    2nd K.O.Y.L.I.
    3rd, 4th and 6th Burif.
    11th, 12th, 13th and 14th Bns. Burif. (Territorials)

APPENDIX IV

THE ARMY-IN-BURMA MEDICAL ORDER OF BATTLE. APRIL 1, 1942

1 Burma Corps
    13 Lt. Fd. Amb. (7th Armd. Bde.)
    1 (Bur.) Fd. Amb.
    1 (Bur.) Fd. Hyg. Sec.
    7 (Ind.) Anti-malaria Unit
    2 (Bur.) Depot Medical Stores
  S. and T.
    4 Fd. Amb. Tp. R.I.A.S.C.
    22 M.A.S. R.I.A.S.C.

1st Burma Division (1st and 2nd Burma Bdes. Indian 13th Bde.)
    2 (Bur.) Fd. Amb.
    57 (Ind.) Fd. Amb.
    2 (Bur.) Fd. Hyg. Sec.
  S. and T.
    8 M.A.S. section, R.I.A.S.C.
    1 Fd. Amb. Troop. R.I.A.S.C.

Indian 17th Division (16th, 48th and 63rd Bdes.)
  23, 37 and 50 (Ind.) Fd. Ambs.
  22 (Ind.) Fd. Hyg. Sec.
 S. and T.
  5 Fd. Amb. Tp. R.I.A.S.C.

Army Troops
  1 (Bur.) C.C.S. (lent to Chinese)
  4 Bur. G.H.   ,,
  3 (Ind.) Fd. Lab.   ,,
  2 (Bur.) S.S.   ,,
  41 I.G.H. one section ,,
  Depot Indian Hospital Corps
  Depot Burma Hospital Corps
  H.Q. Detachment, R.A.M.C.

L. of C. Troops
  21 M.A.S., R.I.A.S.C.
  3 Fd. Amb. Troop, R.I.A.S.C. personnel only
  1, 2, 3, 5, 6, 7, 8 Bur.G.Hs.
  41, 59 and 60 I.G.Hs. less one section of 41
  1, 2, and 3 (Bur.) Fd. Labs.
  2 (Bur.) C.C.S., 4 (Ind.) C.C.S.
  1 and 2 Ambulance trains
  Hospital Ships
    Mysore and *Kalaw* staffed by 8 (Ind.) C.C.S.
    Fano staffed by 31 (Ind.) S.S.
    Ebro staffed by 3 Ambulance train
    Lady Innes
    39 (Ind.) Fd. Amb.
    3 (Ind.) Fd. Hyg. Sec.
    1 (Bur.) S.S.
    2 (Br.) S.S.
    16 (Ind.) S.S.
    Convalescent Depot (British)
    10 (Ind.) X-ray Unit (did not reach Burma till the end of the year)
    2 (Ind.) E.N.T. Unit
    Burma Base Depot Medical Stores
    13 (Ind.) Depot Medical Stores
    Burma District Laboratory
    Burma Dental Centre
    2 (Ind.) Ophthal. Unit

CHAPTER 3

THE WITHDRAWAL ACROSS THE INDO—BURMA FRONTIER

ON APRIL 28 orders for the withdrawal of Burcorps into India were issued.

  i. 1st Burma Division, less 2nd Burma Bde., was to cross the Sameikkon ferry and move to Monywa where 13th Bde. would cross to the west bank of the Chindwin to secure Monywa from the south and south-west.
  ii. 1st Burma Bde. was to move from Monywa to Kalewa by boat.
  iii. 2nd Burma Bde., which had been moving on the west bank of the Irrawaddy, was to withdraw *via* Pauk and Tilin into the Myittha valley to deny this route to the Japanese and eventually link up with the rest of 1st Burma Division west of Kalewa.
  iv. Indian 17th Division, less 63rd Bde., was to cross and hold the north bank of the Irrawaddy from Myinmu to Allagappa.
  v. 63rd Bde. was to cover the road from Allagappa to Monywa.
  vi. Chinese 38th Division and 7th Armd. Bde. were to hold the line of the Irrawaddy from Sagaing to Ondaw.

Indian 17th Division was instructed to hold Kyaukse until Chinese Fifth Army was north of the Myitnge River, then follow with 7th Armd. Bde., cross the Ava bridge over the Irrawaddy and then blow it.

48th Bde., now only about 1,700 strong and composed of 1/4th G.R.; 7th G.R. compounded out of 1/7th and 3/7th G.R.; 2/5th R.G.R. and 1/3rd G.R., together with 7th Hussars, a company of 1st W. Yorks., a few guns and a demolition party of Bengal Sappers and Miners, covered the southern approaches to Kyaukse on the trunk road south of Mandalay. Through this rearguard passed 63rd Bde. and the last elements of Chinese Fifth Army. A number of Japanese attacks during the night of April 28/29 and during the following day were sternly repulsed. Choosing its own time the brigade withdrew according to plan and the road and rail bridges over the Zawgyi River were blown. 48th Bde. withdrew through 63rd Bde. in its position along the Myitnge. Then 63rd Bde. blew the road and rail bridges over the Myitnge River and fell back to cover the Ava bridge over the Irrawaddy. During April 30 the brigade remained on the east bank of the river and when the last of the Indian and Chinese troops had passed across the bridge, the brigade followed and at 2359 hours on the last day of April this great bridge was blown.

The route that Burcorps was to follow ran from Ye-U to Kaduma, 20 miles to the north-west and then plunged into a vast teak forest to reach the Chindwin 120 miles away at Shwegyin. The track was nothing more than a bullock-cart route and 40 miles of it were completely waterless. It had many sharp bends and many steep gradients and narrow cuttings and crossed several stream beds of soft sand. It had been improved but the work on it was far from finished. Unmetalled and unsurfaced, it would not last a week when the rains began. From Shwegyin to Kalewa, 6 miles away, the journey was by river steamer, shallow-draft stern-wheelers. These few vessels were to be required to ferry the entire Army-in-Burma across the Chindwin. From Kalewa to Tamu (107 miles or six marches) was the next stage of the journey. It was through Kabaw valley, known as 'Death Valley' for the reason that it was so highly malarious. A road from Imphal in northern Assam to Tamu was being built. It had been agreed that India should widen the existing metalled road between Dimapur and Imphal (135 miles) and construct a new road between Imphal and Tamu (65 miles) while Burma built an all-weather road from Ye-U through Kalewa to Tamu (250 miles). The Indian section was finished just in time for the final stages of the withdrawal of Burma Army from Burma. But so little had been done on the Burmese section that India took over the task of completing it. Steps were now taken to stock this route with supplies and where necessary with water. In retrospect it seemed that it would have been wise to have included in these dumps stocks of 'hygiene' chemicals and appliances and the like, for during the final stages of the withdrawal it was not possible to make use of the depots of medical stores.

Now that the fighting troops knew that they were heading for India their morale improved but among L. of C. and base units there was much desertion and large parties of these deserters, heading for the Indian border ahead of the combatant formations, were living on the country, plundering, looting and not infrequently murdering. The Army therefore found itself moving amid a hostile population. Burmese irregulars and dacoits hung around the trail of the retreating army and waylaid stragglers and small detachments, displaying the utmost cruelty. Parties of the bewildered Indian civilians who had fled from Rangoon preceded and followed the troops along this route which promised them security. These too suffered grievously at the hands of the Burmese irregulars.

On April 30, Corps H.Q. had moved through Monywa and had established itself some sixteen miles to the north of this town in Songon. In Monywa itself was a weak detachment of 1st Glosters, a river patrol of Marines and a few Sappers. H.Q. 1st Burma Division was about four miles south-east of the town in Ma-U.

1st Burma Division was ordered to concentrate at Chaung-U, 48th and 63rd Bdes. being placed under its command. Ind. 16th Bde., then moving from Indaw to Ma-U, was instructed to move with all possible speed to Ye-U. A squadron of 7th Armd. Bde. was despatched to Monywa *via* Ye-U and a second squadron was sent to Chaung-U to support 1st Burma Division. Early on May 1 the Japanese attacked the divisional H.Q. at Ma-U and scattered the platoon of raw Burmese troops guarding it. However, the divisional commander and his staff managed to make a fighting withdrawal along the railway line and to reach Chaung-U. Soon after this disruptive event several hundred Japanese crossed the river in launches and landed on the east bank in Monywa, the small garrison of this town being forced to withdraw to the north.

At this moment 1st Burma and Ind. 13th Bdes. were moving along the Sagaing-Monywa road about twenty miles to the south of the latter town and 2nd Burma Bde., on the west bank of the river, was moving from Pakokku to Gangaw and Kalemyo and was about to set out for Myittha. 63rd Bde. was moving by train from the Ava bridge area to Kyehmon, eight miles south-east of Monywa. East of Ma-U 1/10th G.R. and 2/13th F.F.Rif. of 63rd Bde., that afternoon, made contact with the Japanese. The advance of these two battalions was halted and 1/11th Sikh passed through them to take up an outpost line. Ind. 13th Bde. reached Ma-U late that night and was ordered to attack the Japanese positions at dawn. 1st Burma Bde., reaching Chaung-U was instructed to continue its march towards Monywa and to take part in the projected attack upon the town.

The Japanese occupation of Monywa threatened to deny the use of the Chindwin River to the Army-in-Burma and provided the Japanese an opportunity to cut the line of withdrawal through Kalewa. On May 2 Monywa was attacked on a two brigade front, 63rd Bde. advancing astride the railway and 13th Bde. moving on the town from the vicinity of Zalok. Later in the day 1st Burma Bde. joined in the attack. The fighting was very bitter and the Japanese defence exceedingly stubborn. Before the issue could be decided a message was received to the effect that Ind. 13th Bde. was to break off the engagement at once and withdraw to Alon. The impetus of the attack was thus destroyed and 1st Burma and 63rd Bdes. were obliged to abandon the attack and to withdraw towards Ma-U. The origin of this strange message remained mysterious.

During the night of May 2/3, 16th Bde. was rushed to Shwegyin, Kalewa and Kalemyo to forestall any attempt on the part of the Japanese to occupy them. 1st Burma Division held a rearguard position, an arc south of Ye-U, while Indian 17th Division moved off to provide defensive positions at Kaduma, at the entrance to the jungle track, at Pyingaing, half-way along it and at Shwegyin on the Chindwin. Corps H.Q., which had moved back to Ye-U, withdrew on May 5 to

Pyingaing. 1st Burma Bde. was sent, without transport, across country to strike the Chindwin at Pantha 70 miles north of Kalewa, to cross the river there and to make for Tamu following the line of the Yu River.

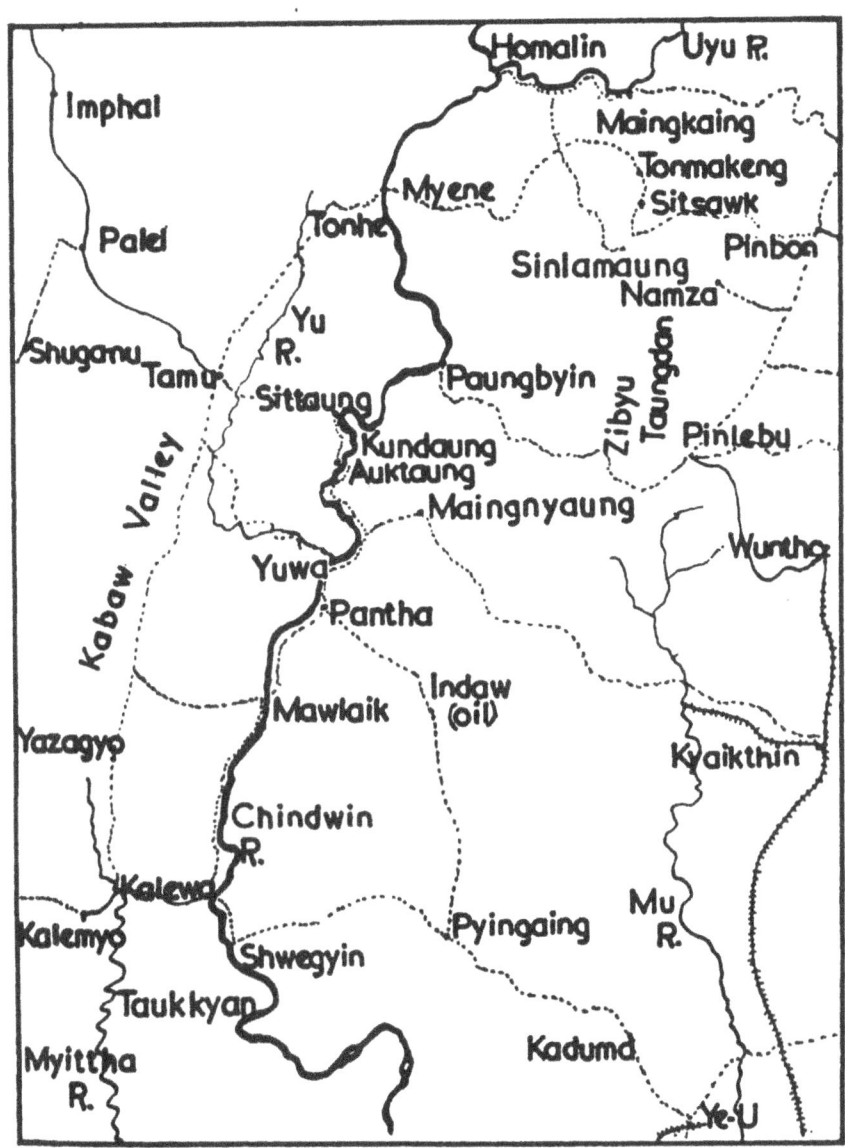

FIG. 10. The Ye-U–Tamu Area

During these days there were three main causes for anxiety. From what was known about the habits of the Japanese it seemed highly probable that they would attempt to insert themselves between the retreating army and the Indian border. There was a danger that if much delay occurred a shortage of food and of supplies generally might develop. Rations were therefore reduced. Thirdly, there was the monsoon that could not be forgotten. The rains were due to start in about the middle of May and when they came the track would quickly become unusable. Speed was necessary and to achieve it most difficult.

To begin with all went smoothly and fairly swiftly. 63rd Bde. was ferried forward in lorries. 1st Burma Division, which by this time had shed most of its Burmese personnel, crossed the Chindwin safely. The first echelon of 7th Armd. Bde. reached Shwegyin, passed the bulk of its wheeled vehicles and men over the river and harboured its tanks along the track while awaiting embarkation. 48th Bde., the rearguard of Indian 17th Division, and the rest of 7th Armd. Bde. were in Pyingaing.

But with the passing of the days there inevitably developed an undesirable accumulation of troops and transport on the east bank of the Chindwin. The loading of the six river steamers each carrying 600 men but only two lorries and two jeeps, was a slow business for there was but one small pier and this ricketty until the engineers built a more serviceable one on May 9. The round trip from Shwegyin to Kalewa took several hours. The approaches to the ferry were blocked with abandoned civilian cars and choked with masses of refugees waiting for a passage. The track to the pier ran for the last 1,500 yards through the 'Basin', a horseshoe-shaped flat space about a half a mile long and some 400 yards broad at its widest point and surrounded on three sides by an escarpment about 200 ft. high and covered with scrub. This 'Basin' soon became close-packed with troops, an agglomeration of animals and vehicles, tanks and refugees. A Gurkha commando unit was watching the most likely approach from the river to the 'Basin'. A floating boom had been constructed about two miles down river from Shwegyin and this was covered by 5/17th Dogra and the detachment of Marines on the banks. 1 R./9th Jat was given the task of guarding the 'Basin' itself.

On May 7 and 9 the 'Basin' was attacked from the air and as a consequence of this the steamer crews deserted in large numbers. The number of the vessels in use became fewer and the time of the turn-round longer. 48th Bde., the rearguard, reached the area of Shwegyin on the evening of May 8 and halted two miles down the track. On the 9th, 7th G.R. of this brigade was sent into the 'Basin' to take part in its defence. The Japanese land forces now arrived. A strong force had come up the river in naval launches and had landed on the eastern bank about eight miles below Shwegyin and another, even stronger, force had been put ashore on the west bank about six miles further to the south. The party on the east bank had moved inland to avoid the battalion guarding the boom and had bumped into the Gurkha commando unit which failed to get any message back to Shwegyin. The Japanese now attacked the 'Basin' and began to mortar it. They got to the edge of the escarpment dominating the eastern side of the 'Basin'. 1 R./9th Jat and 7th Gurkhas drove them back. While the steamers were being loaded with wounded, with administrative troops, refugees and guns, a third attack was launched and was repelled. But a strong body of Japanese troops on a knoll that commanded the 'Basin' could not be dislodged and all embarkation had to be stopped. It was decided that all that could have been done had been done and that the troops in the 'Basin' should be withdrawn across the river before further Japanese reinforcements arrived.

Having destroyed the guns, tanks and vehicles still remaining in the 'Basin' the rearguard set out along a narrow, precipitous track along the river's edge by Kongyi for Kaing, opposite Kalewa. The Japanese did not interfere with this movement. 48th Bde. was then taken from Kalewa to Sittaung by steamer and thence it marched to Tamu through the hills after the steamers were sunk. The bulk of Burcorps marched from Kalewa through 'Death Valley' to Tamu. 2nd Burma Bde. withdrew up the western bank of the Irrawaddy and then turned north-west to follow the Myittha valley towards Kalewa and Tamu. It had several skirmishes with parties of Burmese but met no Japanese. It carried its wounded in bullock carts as far as the Manipur River but the bridge over it had been blown and so the carts had to be abandoned. It joined up with 1st Burma Division in Kalemyo having marched a total distance of 450 miles. At the end of the journey only about eighty members of the brigade had to be hospitalised.

For the rest of the journey Burcorps had only about 50 lorries and 30 jeeps and these were used mainly for ferrying troops forward. Boots had worn out, uniforms were in tatters but the morale of the troops was excellent. As the rearguard of Burcorps left Kalewa on May 12 the rains started and from that moment the trek was utterly and absolutely miserable. However, if the monsoon threatened to maroon all that was left of the Army in Burma, it certainly halted the Japanese so that only Nature remained as the enemy of an army that the Japanese had failed to destroy. Two marches from Tamu mechanical transport from India met the leading elements of the retreating army.

Meanwhile, Chinese Fifth Army, covered by Chinese 38th Division, fell back from Shwebo to the north. General Stilwell, with the American portion of his headquarters, moved to Wuntho on May 1, intending to make for Myitkyina whence he could fly out of Burma. But since this was no longer possible he struck westwards by car and then on foot with pack transport to the Chindwin about Homalin and thence through the hills to Imphal. He reached Assam safely on May 15. Chinese 38th Division followed Chinese Fifth Army to Naba, 50 miles north of Wuntho and on the Myitkyina railway. Learning that it could not hope

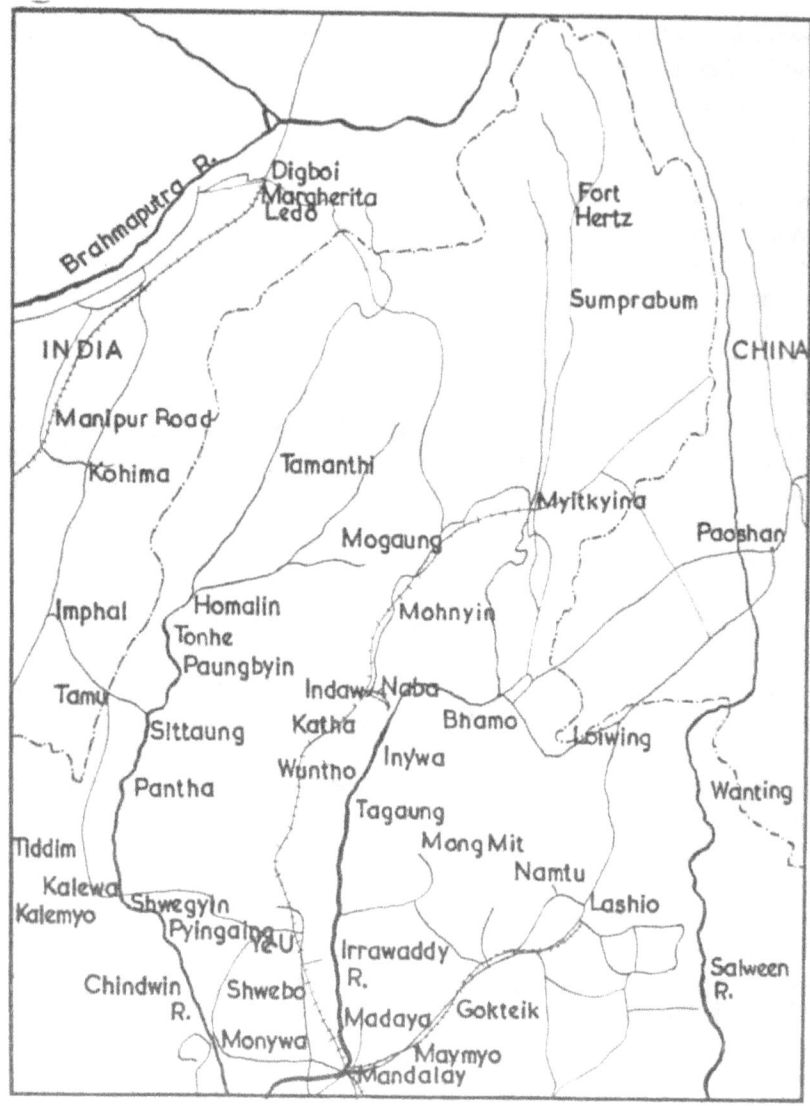

Fig. 11. Burma. Mandalay–Fort Hertz and Ledo

to reach Myitkyina before the Japanese, the division returned to Wuntho and thence struck across the hills to the Chindwin at Paungbyin and from there to Imphal which was reached on May 24.

Arrangements had been made whereby Burma Army would withdraw into India through IV Corps. As the formations reached the border they passed under command of this corps. The rearguard did so at 1800 hours on May 18. It was reasonably expected that when the troops had passed through the lines of a strong force covering the Indo-Burma frontier they would be able to relax and to regain their strength. There were very many among them who needed hospitalisation and many more who, when once the strain was eased, would fall sick since only their resolution and determination had kept them on their feet. But what happened was very different from what had been expected. The welcome they received was sometimes less than warm for, as has been stated, they had been preceded by hordes of deserters and by undisciplined bands by whose behaviour the reputation of Burma Army had suffered. The men of Burcorps found that they themselves were to participate in the defence of the frontier and that their billets were bivouacs on the rain-drenched hill-sides. It is not surprising therefore to learn that among them the incidence of disease rose steeply.

Indian 17th Division, much reduced in numbers, was still a fighting formation and retained its identity. But 1st Burma Division was not. It had sent its Burmese troops—Kachins, Chins, Karens—to their homes before crossing into India, giving each man his rifle, 50 rounds of ammunition, three months' pay and an instruction to be prepared for the return of Burma Army to Burma. The remnants of the division were ultimately reformed as Indian 39th Division. (*See* page 99.)

For the time being fighting ceased for the armies were separated by the mountain-mass of the Indo-Burma frontier which during the next five months of the rainy season remained impassable. The Japanese proceeded to digest their latest and their last conquest; their antagonists at once began to prepare for the resumption of the struggle.

Burcorps' casualties in this opening phase of the campaign in Burma had been very numerous; of the 25,000 officers and men of Burcorps 4,033 were killed or wounded and 9,430 were missing. To these must be added the numbers of sick who were evacuated. The figures given in the following table were taken from the Official Indian Medical History, Appendix III.

TABLE 1

Burcorps. Casualties.

	Killed	Died of Wounds and Disease	Wounded or Missing	Wounded	Missing	P.o.W.	Presumed Dead	Totals
OFFICERS	63	70	—	163	115	—	—	411
OTHER RANKS								
British Units	273	75	49	556	647	—	—	1,600
Indian Army Units								
V.C.Os.	60	—	—	60	80	3	3	206
I.O.Rs.	649	—	—	1,678	5,291	181	57	7,856
Burma Army Units	239	10	12	114	3,052	—	—	3,427
	1,284	155	61	2,571	9,185	184	60	13,500

MEDICAL COVER

During the fighting in and around Monywa when H.Q. 1st Burma Division was partly overrun and when the field ambulances of the division were hard pressed, A.D.M.S. Indian 17th Division sent his D.A.D.M.S. to enquire whether any help was required in the matter of casualty evacuation. At this time 50 (Ind.) Fd. Amb. was in Chaung-U and H.Q. 1st Burma Division some five miles west of this place. The evacuation of casualties through Monywa had become impossible and the only available route was *via* Ondaw to Shwebo along a very poor road. It was arranged with A.D.M.S. 1st Burma Division, who had narrowly escaped capture and had got temporarily out of touch with his divisional medical units, that 50 (Ind.) Fd. Amb. should move back to Myinmu there to open its M.D.S. while 23 (Ind.) Fd. Amb. which had been ordered to move forward to Monywa, should remain in Ondaw to stage casualties on their way back to Shwebo. 37 (Ind.) Fd. Amb. was moved by the pooled transport to Ye-U as was also 13 Lt. Fd. Amb. which had been functioning two miles to the north of Ondaw.

But no sooner had these arrangements been made than 16th Bde. in Sagaing was ordered to withdraw to Ye-U and H.Q. Indian 17th Division promptly expressed the view that it would be impossible for the division to accept responsibility for the protection of 23 (Ind.) Fd. Amb. in Ondaw and suggested that this unit should pass u/c 1st Burma Division. This was done, the second-in-command of the ambulance being attached to H.Q. 1st Burma Division to act as liaison officer between the division and the medical unit which was dangerously isolated and protected only by a small force of Chinese troops in Sagaing.

Many of the casualties admitted to 23 (Ind.) Fd. Amb. from the Monywa fighting were in very poor condition; they were for the most part such as had been in the fighting in the oilfield area and who, in their extremity, had drunk water wherever it was found. Among them there was much persistent diarrhoea. When Burcorps withdrew from the Monywa area there were 150 casualties in this field ambulance. These were loaded into twenty-three ambulance cars and lorries and despatched for Ye-U. Two ambulance cars which had been borrowed from 13 Lt. Fd. Amb. had been sent off with casualties but had not returned. When its M.D.S. had been cleared, 23 (Ind.) Fd. Amb. was ferried to Ye-U in the transport which had been used to move 37 (Ind.) Fd. Amb. thereto. 37 had opened its M.D.S. in Ye-U in a *phongyi kyaung* and was soon holding some 200 casualties. 50 (Ind.) Fd. Amb. from Chaung-U was *en route* for Ye-U, carrying its patients. All available ambulance cars had been sent to help clear the casualties of 1st Burma Division. When this division withdrew 2 (Bur.) Fd. Amb. was called upon to make a most strenuous night march, carrying its patients and equipment in bullock carts.

When 1 (Bur.) Fd. Amb. moved to Monywa *via* Myinmu it found 2 (Bur.) Fd. Amb. established in a school situated just to the west of the village. On April 30 D.D.M.S. Burcorps ordered 1 (Bur.) Fd. Amb., which had halted in a mango grove about a mile to the north of Monywa, to move to Budalin. On May 1 the unit proceeded to a point five miles north of Ye-U and was then ordered to move on to Shwegyin, using M.T. as far as possible. Shwegyin was reached on the 3rd, the M.T. was abandoned about two miles short of this village and the unit crossed the Chindwin to reach Kalewa where it rejoined H.Q. Burcorps and opened its A.D.S. in the local civil hospital.

On May 6 a M.D.S. was established in a *phongyi kyaung* at Milestone 1 on the Kalewa-Tamu road, the unit taking over from a F.A.U. It was fully occupied between May 6 and 11 and at the end of this period was holding some 600 patients. Transport for evacuation, as for all other purposes, had by this time become utterly insufficient. However, the situation was saved by the arrival of lorries from India bringing rations and these vehicles were used on their return journey for the conveyance of casualties.

On May 8 the A.D.S. in Kalewa was handed over to 37 (Ind.) Fd. Amb. as was also the M.D.S. site on the following day. The journey towards Tamu was then resumed and on May 11 the field ambulance reached Milestone 11 north of Yazagyo. Thence it was ferried by M.T. to Tamu on May 12. Thereafter the unit proceeded to Kanglatongbi Camp to rest and reorganise. It opened its A.D.S. in the camp, evacuating its patients to Dimapur. Later it replaced 50 (Ind.) Fd. Amb. with 1st Burma Division and in July moved with this division to Shillong.

On May 3, 23 (Ind.) Fd. Amb. received orders to proceed from Ye-U to Pyingaing and, taking over 37 (Ind.) Fd. Amb's. casualties, get them across the Chindwin. Picking up some 150 casualties from 37 (Ind.) Fd. Amb. in Ye-U, 23 (Ind.) Fd. Amb. set out for Pyingaing. The night march was exceedingly trying for the air was hot and laden with dust and the track wound its way through dense forest and across dry river beds. Many of the vehicles broke down as they struggled with the sand in these chaungs and the casualties in them, especially such as were suffering from burns or cholera suffered greatly in spite of all the care they received. On its way the unit passed 2 (Br.) S.S. in its position in the chain of medical units along the track 14 miles beyond Ye-U. This small unit, which had moved from Sagaing, was attempting to cope with a number of patients far in excess of its capacity and so a medical officer was left with the unit and arrangements were made for the evacuation of its patients. D.D.M.S. commended this staging section for staying in its appointed place and getting on with its job, even though its resources were being too greatly extended. It was impossible at this time for any senior administrative medical officer to exercise any degree of continuous control over the widely dispersed medical units and much had to be left to the discretion of officers commanding units. Too many of these closed and moved on far too soon and in so doing threw far too much work on the divisional field ambulances.

By May 4, 23 (Ind.) Fd. Amb. had taken over from 1 (Bur.) C.C.S. in Pyingaing and had opened its M.D.S. The C.C.S. had occupied an abandoned farm but these premises were found to be so very unsuitable by the field ambulance—they were filthy and the surrounding ground was strewn with the reeking corpses of farm animals—that this unit at once moved into a nearby *phongyi kyaung*. On May 5 and 6, 37 (Ind.) Fd. Amb. passed through Pyingaing on its way to Shwegyin, carrying a large number of patients with it. It opened a light A.D.S. in Shwegyin and another on the jetty at Kalewa, across the river, at which the steamers from Shwegyin were unloaded. On the 8th the M.D.S. of 37 (Ind.) Fd. Amb. took over from 1 (Bur.) Fd. Amb. in Kalewa and that evening 23 (Ind.) Fd. Amb. arrived at Shwegyin from Pyingaing, bringing its patients with it. On the 9th, 23 (Ind.) Fd. Amb. crossed to Kalewa, taking with it one 3-tonner and two ambulance cars and leaving a light A.D.S. behind in Shwegyin. In Kalewa the unit took over from 37 (Ind.) Fd. Amb., which thereupon moved on to Inbaung there to open its M.D.S. on May 11, replacing 1 (Bur.) C.C.S. The field ambulance admitted some 108 patients almost at once, including two Indian refugee women in labour. 23 (Ind.) Fd. Amb. followed and joined 37 in Inbaung before moving on. 13 Lt. Fd. Amb., abandoning its transport, crossed the Chindwin at Shwegyin. When on May 10 the Japanese attacked the basin at Shwegyin, the A.D.S. of 23 (Ind.) Fd. Amb. came under fire and moved nearer the ferry. It marched out of the basin with the rearguard to Kaing and thence crossed the river to Kalewa.

On May 12 and 13, 37 (Ind.) Fd. Amb., having evacuated 208 patients by lorry to the north, admitted another 139, packed up and moved on to Khampat there to replace 4 (Ind.) C.C.S. The unit remained here for twenty-four hours during which time it dealt with 85 admissions and then moved on to Tamu there to take over from 2 (Bur.) C.C.S. and to admit 85 serious cases and several hundreds of minor ones. The unit then moved on to Lokchao. On May 12 the final withdrawal from Kalewa began and all the casualties in 23 (Ind.) Fd. Amb. were evacuated and one company of the unit set out for Tamu. Early on the following morning, as the transport conveying the casualties had not returned and as 63rd Bde. was moving off, A.D.M.S. Indian 17th Division ordered the remainder of the field ambulance to depart, leaving the equipment it had been guarding behind but carrying two casualties that had been discovered in a broken-down and abandoned ambulance car. On the march

WITHDRAWAL FROM BURMA

the unit met the returning lorries and these were sent back to Kalewa to collect the equipment. But this had vanished and all in the space of an hour. 23 (Ind.) Fd. Amb. moved through Inbaung, where 37 was functioning to Yazagyo where it took over from 2 Bur.G.H. It stayed there for two days and then moved on to a point 35 miles south of Tamu where it opened its M.D.S. It moved thence first into Tamu and then on to Lokchao where it joined up with 37 on May 17.

Lokchao was indeed a most desolate place. It lay in a valley with steep rock-strewn sides which were thinly covered with bamboo. Through this valley had passed a swollen stream of refugees; here they had halted and here very many had died. The whole area was a cesspit in which flies had multiplied to constitute a veritable plague. The monsoon rain fell continuously. All the cover the troops had consisted of two groundsheets per man and a quantity of parachute silk, salvaged from the air-drop at Tamu. The nursing of patients in such conditions left everything to be desired. Here the two field ambulances stayed awaiting transport and as they waited the rain made their rescue less and less possible. On the morning of the 20th the units set out for Palel on foot, leaving behind small parties to guard the equipment and two ambulance cars which were to follow as soon as the track was dry enough. On May 22, 2nd Burma Bde. left Lokchao and with this rearguard of Burcorps travelled the last parties of these two field ambulances, carrying their patients some of whom travelled in the brigade transport. Among the girders of the brigade's bridging material the officer commanding 37 (Ind.) Fd. Amb. attended the birth of yet another Indian baby. On the 23rd the field ambulance parties were picked up by M.T. and conveyed to Palel whence they made their way to Imphal where 23 (Ind.) Fd. Amb. was accommodated in the Police Barracks and 37 took over the regimental hospital of the Assam Rifles.

Soon 37 was holding over 1,000 patients and 23 (Ind.) Fd. Amb. had admitted over 500. In the C.C.S. in Gauhati there were some 2,000 and the medical units in Dimapur were equally grossly overcrowded. Sickness reached epidemic proportions and malaria was exceedingly rife. In retrospect it would seem that many of those whose illness was diagnosed as malaria were in fact suffering from scrub typhus. For these troops who had endured so much there was to be no rest; for their reception no adequate arrangements had been made, for them there was no change of clothes, no shelter from the rain and no protection from the mosquito. They, together with Indian 23rd Division from India, were required to prevent the further advance of the Japanese; for them there was no leave (only 5 per cent. of them were to be allowed to be away from their units on leave at a time). The division was transformed into an Indian light division of two brigades and a reconnaissance battalion, half on A.T. and half on M.T. The transport of the division was drastically reduced.

63rd Bde. with 37 (Ind.) Fd. Amb. went to Kohima while 48th Bde. and 23 (Ind.) Fd. Amb. remained in Imphal, and training was at once begun. Later the division was sent to the Bishenpur area of the Imphal Plain, an intensely malarious area, and there its medical services staged a 'medical week' during which intensive courses of instruction in hygiene and disease-prevention and control were given to as many officers below the rank of major-general as possible. For the 1943 monsoon season the division was sent to Shillong.

In Myitkyina the situation became difficult by the first week in May. On the 5th all the patients and about three-quarters of the staff of 4 Bur.G.H. were evacuated by air to India. On May 6, 6 Bur.G.H. with some 60 patients, including six who were seriously ill, reached Myitkyina. Patients and staff were taken direct from the station to the airfield for immediate evacuation. When the first of the planes to be loaded was taking off, Japanese aircraft suddenly appeared and fired upon it. Some of the patients on the airfield were hit and had to be taken back to the civil hospital in the town. Two British planes reached the airfield in the evening but only one landed. As soon as it had become stationary, the walking wounded rushed towards and into it and before the stretcher cases could be loaded into it, the plane took off.

At about 0100 hours on the morning of May 7, the officer commanding 4 Bur.G.H. and the remaining personnel set off on foot for India, each man carrying one blanket. One car and one ambulance car accompanied the column. Thirteen patients, too ill to be moved, were left in the civil hospital in Myitkyina. The party in charge of the rations got separated from the main body and the rations were looted, the column being left with only enough for two or three days. The two vehicles were used to ferry the men forward on the road towards Sumprabum. There the road, such as it was, ended and a track through the jungle began.

The small column now began its march through the dreaded Hukawng Valley towards Ledo over jungle-covered hills, 4,000–8,000 ft. high in places, highly malarious and infested with leeches. The track was marked by the rotting corpses of the refugees who had died. When the rains came the track gave way to a morass. Yet, these men, ably led, reached their goal, exhausted and ill but alive. They passed into the care of the organisation that had been created by the tea-planters of Assam for the reception of the Indian refugees.*

In Indian 17th Division, during its passage through the Kabaw Valley, not less than 50 per cent. of the troops contracted malaria.

---

*see *Forgotten Frontier* by Geoffrey Tyson, 1945, published by W. H. Targett & Co. Ltd., Calcutta.

Large numbers of these were also suffering from diarrhoea and skin sores were exceedingly common. During the first few days in Imphal, 8 (Ind.) C.C.S. tried, without much success, to cope with a sick parade of about 1,000 a day. (*see* Appendix V.) About 400 of these were sent on each day to Dimapur. It became necessary to require R.M.Os. to hold and treat their sick in unit lines. The field ambulances opened A.D.Ss. to serve the brigades and 37 (Ind.) Fd. Amb. opened to admit sick officers and 23 (Ind.) Fd. Amb. did likewise to provide care for sick B.O.Rs.

The circumstances were such as to make accurate accounting impossible but it was reasonably estimated that about 6,000 sick were brought out of Burma by the medical units of the Army Medical Services, the majority by road and river, the fortunate minority by air. Inevitably there were immobiles who had to be left behind but fortunately they were relatively few. There were the 13 left in the civil hospital in Myitkyina. The records suggest that about 30 were left in the care of villagers during the withdrawal. D.D.M.S. makes reference to some 15-30 who were left behind in Mohnyin in the care of two medical officers who volunteered to stay with them; these medical officers having families in Burma. A number of wounded lying in Ye-U very nearly got left behind when Burcorps began its withdrawal to Shwegyin. They had been overlooked but it happened that A.D.M.S., having a last look round before joining divisional H.Q. for the withdrawal, found them just in time.

MEDICAL ARRANGEMENTS

Burma Army was withdrawing into a sparsely populated region of the country where there were very few buildings of a size sufficient to accommodate a general hospital. There was no possibility of building new accommodation for these before the monsoon broke. The Army was moving into a highly malarious zone. It is not surprising therefore to learn that the Major-General in charge of Administration at Army H.Q. should express the view in his *Administrative Review* of April 19 that the medical situation was a gloomy one. It became even more so when it was learnt that the transport planes which had been doing such invaluable work in evacuating casualties from Shwebo were to move to Myitkyina in order to reduce the length of their flight and so increase their lift. It would be more difficult for the Medical Services to congregate the cases for evacuation in Myitkyina than it had been in Shwebo.

The movement of the general hospitals began. Those in Mandalay closed. Those in Maymyo were holding some 1,600 patients; 1 Bur.G.H. in Shwebo and 6 Bur.G.H. in Sagaing were both full. The hospital river steamers were packed with patients and it was understood that a further 900 were on their way up-stream. One of the ambulance trains was in Shwebo and the second was known to be derailed near Meiktila.

The Chinese in Burma Army area had over 2,000 wounded and had no place to send them to and no means of moving them. The Army-in-Burma and the Chinese armies serving in Burma were so very different in so many different ways that it was inevitable that to render mutual aid was sometimes made difficult by misunderstanding. The Chinese armies had no supply, no administrative services. They had been fighting for many years in their own country and had supplied themselves by means of local purchase. In early 1942 the Chinese in Burma were about 20,000 strong. Burma Army supplied and maintained them. With them were four surgeons and about thirty trained orderlies together with a Friends' Ambulance Unit and the staff of a Mission Hospital, the Harper Memorial Medical Unit at Namhkam. The latter was headed by Dr. Seagrave and included one or two medically qualified young men and some 40 Karen nurses whom he himself had trained. (*See* Appendix VI). The Friends' Ambulance Unit, raised and equipped in the United States for service with the Chinese army in the war against Japan, remained in Burma to serve the Chinese there. These two units did magnificent work. The Army Medical Services had lent the Chinese 1 (Bur.) C.C.S., 2 (Bur.) S.S., part of 4 Bur.G.H. in Taunggyi and a 100-bed section of 41 I.G.H. The Chinese were also given all the medical supplies they asked for. The medical units, of course, admitted Chinese military patients equally with those of the Army-in-Burma. For evacuation purposes the Chinese were lent an ambulance train and a 'hospital' steamer, the *Siam*. The attitude of the Chinese in Burma towards casualties and trains and the like was so peculiar—to the occidental—that it was regarded as strange when the train was broken down into small bits and used for purposes very different indeed from those for which it was lent. There was one unforgettable scene on the platform of Maymyo railway station when a Chinese general, after a most heated argument, at pistol point attempted to force the D.D.M.S. himself to hand over an ambulance train for use for non-medical purposes.

By a stroke of good fortune there appeared an officer serving with the R.A.M.C. who was a Chinese, had escaped from Shanghai and then from Hong Kong. D.D.M.S. promptly made him a medical liaison officer. Later he served as medical representative with the chief liaison officer to the Chinese armies.

D.D.M.S. personally took control of the evacuation. He despatched patients in the Maymyo hospitals by any available train to 2 Bur.G.H. in Monywa, 1 Bur.G.H. in Shwebo and 4 Bur.G.H. in Myitkyina. He sent off by train advance parties of 3, 7 and 8 Bur.G.Hs. and 41 I.G.H.

to Mohnyin and Katha. He made A.D.M.S. L. of C., whom he sent off to Myitkyina, responsible for the supervision of medical arrangements in the distant north. He recalled the ambulance train from Shwebo and the one from Meiktila, when this had been got on to the rails again, to Maymyo and used them to clear the hospitals there to Shwebo. 60 I.G.H. in Mandalay was loaded on to five river 'flats' and with its remaining patients set out by river to Kyaukmyaung on the Irrawaddy, 17 miles east of Shwebo, where it continued to function, partly on the 'flats' and partly in huts. 2 Ambulance Train, with five coaches added, took aboard 438 patients, 73 nursing staff, the medical personnel of 2 Bur.G.H. from Monywa, the staff of the District Laboratory and of the Dental Centre, a detachment of R.A.M.C. orderlies and the essential equipment of the general hospital and, being divided into two parts, set off for Shwebo and Myitkyina. At the first stop outside Mandalay the engine crews disappeared. Volunteers were obtained from Mandalay and again the train set off. It took five days to reach its destination and from Myitkyina all the patients and all the nurses were evacuated by air to India.

When the hospital population in Maymyo had been reduced to about 50 with about 200 medical personnel, all these were sent to Shwebo by road in a convoy of ambulance cars and lorries which D.D.M.S. had obtained. 6 Bur.G.H. in Sagaing got away *en route* for Myitkyina by rail and river with all its 600 patients, its equipment and even its tentage.

Most of the hospital population was moved by ambulance train and hospital river steamer from the hospital area at Maymyo and Mandalay to Myitkyina. From Myitkyina further evacuation by road, rail and river was impossible and only evacuation by air remained. In ten days in April, ten Dakotas evacuated 1,900 soldiers and civilians across the mountain barrier that separates Burma from the valley of the Brahmaputra.

D.D.M.S. happened to discover that L. of C. had made no arrangements for the movement of the Burma Hospital Corps Depot in Sagaing. He helped the officer commanding the unit to get the families, some 450 women and children, away by river in the last convoy for Katha. The 250 men, taking one lorry to carry rations and the like, marched the 270 miles to Tamu, where with the approval of higher authority the Burmese members of the party turned back and re-entered Burma. The R.A.M.C. Depot in Maymyo got away safely, thanks to the initiative and qualities of leadership displayed by its commanding officer. He acquired seven derelict vehicles from the M.T. Dump, repaired them, loaded them with his records and his cash and set off for Mandalay and Shwebo. In Shwebo the party boarded a train and coaling it and watering it themselves, and operating the signals and the switches, set off for

Naba. Reaching this town the party then marched to Tamu *en route* for Imphal.

Before 2 Bur.G.H. got away from Monywa it was involved in an air raid while waiting in the train in the station. Two blazing coaches of this train were uncoupled by the officer commanding and a party of volunteers and pushed away from the vicinity of a second train that was full of ammunition. It was impossible to move the hospital train for several hours while the ammunition was exploding. However, there were no casualties though the commanding officer had his shorts burnt off him.

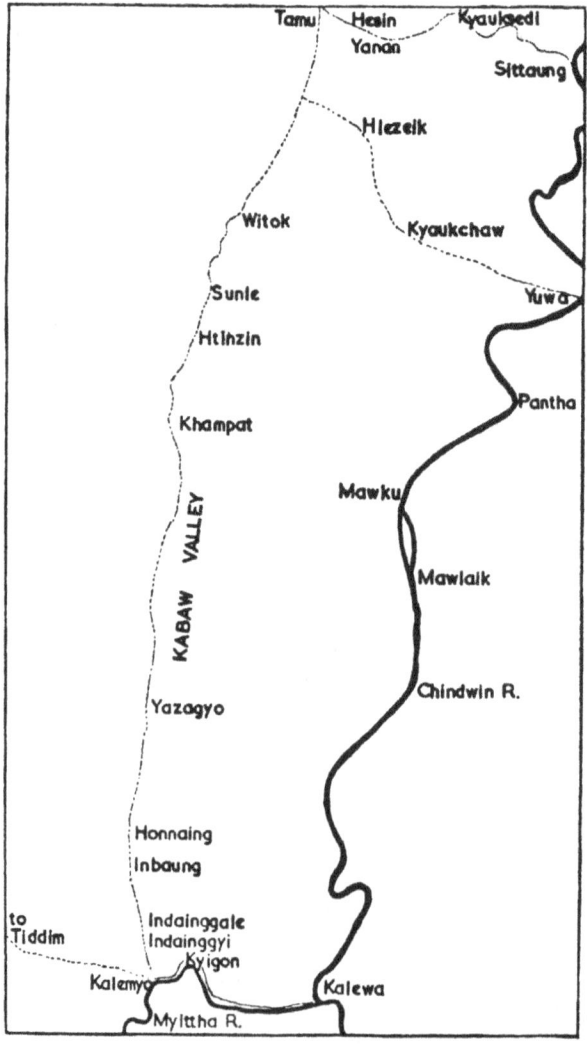

FIG. 12. The Kabaw Valley

WITHDRAWAL FROM BURMA

When Maymyo was clear of casualties, D.D.M.S. went to Shwebo where he made his plans for the final stage of this phase of the campaign. In addition to the main route to the Indo-Burma frontier, from Ye-U through Kaduma, Pyingaing, Kalewa, and the Kabaw Valley to Tamu, there were two subsidiary routes. The northern one ran from Katha along the railway to Mogaung and thence through the Hukawng Valley and the Pangsau Pass to the Ledo road. The southern subsidiary route was by paddle steamer up the Chindwin to Kalewa and thence by the Tamu route. For this there were only a few steamers available and so the numbers that could travel this way were very limited.

In general outline D.D.M.S's. plan was to place a series of medical units along the route, each of these evacuating into the one immediately behind it (to the west of it). When the foremost (the furthest away from the frontier) was no longer admitting patients and was empty, it was to close and move rearwards (towards the frontier) and take its place at the tail of the series and open again. On the main route the undermentioned units were employed. Their movements illustrate the manner in which they leap-frogged over each other. In front of this series were the divisional field ambulances which replaced the members of the series as this moved India-wards. At the Indian end of the route medical units from India took their places in the series.

It had been assumed that India would take over from the Army-in-Burma at Tamu, finding all the medical units required to continue the chain of medical installations between Tamu and Imphal. But no such arrangements had been made and so the Burma Army chain had to be extended onwards to Imphal.

Shwebo	1 Bur.G.H.	Later used as an auxiliary unit at Kalewa
Ye-U	2 Bur.G.H.	From Monywa
Kaduma	1 (Bur.) C.C.S.	From Meiktila and Shwebo. Later to Inbaung
Pyingaing	2 (Br.) S.S.	From Mandalay *via* Sagaing and Kin-U
22-mile stage	8 (Ind.) C.C.S.	For a short time only
Shwegyin	4 (Ind.) C.C.S.	Later replaced by an extemporised ambulance party from Army H.Q.
Kalewa	2 Bur.G.H. 2 (Bur.) C.C.S. F.A.U.	From Ye-U This unit was here for 48 hours and then went on to Khampat and across the frontier.

These units were relieved by 1 (Bur.) Fd. Amb. when the retreating columns had passed them and this unit in its turn was replaced by

23 (Ind.) Fd. Amb. The larger medical units were then distributed as follows:

Inbaung	1 (Bur.) C.C.S.	The C.C.S. functioned here for 6 days and then being relieved by 37 (Ind.) Fd. Amb. moved on to Imphal and opened there.
Yazagyo	2 Bur.G.H.	Until relieved by 23 (Ind.) Fd. Amb.
Khampat	4 (Ind.) C.C.S.	Until relieved by 37 (Ind.) Fd. Amb.
Witok	8 (Ind.) C.C.S.	Until relieved by 23 (Ind.) Fd. Amb.
Tamu	2 (Bur.) C.C.S.	Functioned for 10 days in an evacuation camp established by the Burma Oil Company for the reception of their employees. It treated over 2,300 individuals.
Lokchao	16 (Ind.) S.S. 1 (Bur.) Fd. Amb.	Until relieved by 23 (Ind.) Fd. Amb.
The Saddle above Palel	An improvised staging section	Personnel from the staffs of the hospital river steamers. Until relieved by 37 (Ind.) Fd. Amb.
Palel	40 (Ind.) S.S. A C.M.H. (50 beds) A C.M.H.	From India From India From India
Imphal	1 (Bur.) C.C.S. 8 (Ind.) C.C.S. 13 (Ind.) C.C.S.	From India.

1 (Bur.) C.C.S., carrying its equipment in one ambulance car, marched 27 miles from Kalewa to Inbaung where it opened to admit 50 patients within the first hour. Five major operations were performed during the night and by the morning of the following day the unit had settled down to the routine disposal of some 150–200 casualties a day. 2 (Bur.) C.C.S., without transport of any kind, set out from Kalewa for Tamu. Such equipment as was taken with the unit was carried by the personnel of the unit, the commanding officer and another carrying the surgical equipment in a canvas bag slung on a bamboo pole. In Tamu the unit functioned for ten days before it moved on and during this period no less than 2,300 sick and wounded were admitted.

The inclusion of 4 and 8 (Ind.) C.C.Ss. in this series will have been noted. D.D.M.S. replaced these units on the hospital steamers *Assam* and *Mysore* by detachments from 60 I.G.H. The C.C.Ss. were then instructed to make themselves mobile once more by purchasing bullock carts or in any other way that seemed reasonable.

The 'long walk' will surely never be forgotten by those who took part in it. The medical units found it very difficult to decide what equipment to take and what to leave behind. They found it imperative to maintain strict march discipline and to do everything possible to maintain morale. 8 (Ind.) C.C.S. acquired an abandoned Austin Seven and used it to ferry forward the faint-hearted and the sore-footed. In this unit it was forbidden to drink save from the water bottle and this was filled with tea each morning. It was insisted that latrines should be dug at each halt.

Once the Chindwin was crossed the feeling that the Japanese were close behind and drawing nearer died down but the road ahead still seemed as interminable as ever until the mechanical transport columns from India were encountered. But anxiety reappeared when it was clearly demonstrated that the Indian drivers were by no means well acquainted with the gears of their machines and when it was revealed that the road, with its innumerable hair-pin bends was truly fearsome. However, 8 (Ind.) C.C.S. reached Imphal intact.

In Imphal the unit took over from a small C.M.H. which had been accommodated in *bashas* next to the civil hospital. When the rains came the field in which the *bashas* stood became a bog and it was fortunate that the C.C.S. was able to move into the civil hospital itself. Within a very short period the unit found cause to increase the number of its beds progressively until it was holding some 1,100 patients. Special smallpox and cholera wards had to be provided. A nearby school and a Jain temple were brought into use.

Malaria and dysentery, contracted during the 'long walk', quickly swelled the numbers of the sick. The malaria was B.T. and M.T. and manifested itself in every conceivable form, dysenteric, choleraic and cerebral. Many patients displayed bronchial, nephritic and even dental symptoms and three of the cases admitted had been sent in as instances of acute appendicitis.

Over 70 per cent. of the O.Rs. of the unit and 90 per cent. of its officers suffered from one or the other or both of these complaints.

By August, when the unit was relieved, it had mastered its difficulties and was functioning efficiently and smoothly.

3 Bur.G.H. in Mohnyin was instructed to march out by way of the Hukawng Valley but its commanding officer was strongly advised by the local commissioner to travel by the Hopin–Uyu River route. On the 4th the unit set out for Hopin marching past Indawgyi Lake and through the jungle to the Uyu River some twenty-five miles away. This was reached on the 9th and the gear was then transferred to country dug-out canoes from the bullock carts that had carried it thus far. The unit

travelled by day down stream to reach the Chindwin on the 15th. Thus far the journey had been pleasant and enjoyable and the villagers had been most friendly and hospitable. On the 17th the unit set out from Tonhe for Imphal along a track that had been much used by refugees. The rains had started and the track had been churned into a stream of mud. The camp sites that had to be used had become much fouled. Imphal was reached on the 23rd.

The northern route through the Hukawng Valley was greatly crowded with refugees and abounded in disease hazards. Along it travelled 60 I.G.H. which left Mogaung on May 4, travelling at first by lorry and later on foot accompanied by bullock transport to Shingbwiyang. Beyond this place there was no road, no transport and no food for six marches. Drenched by the rain the personnel of this unit struggled along the treacherous track knee-deep in mud. At night, after a scanty meal of rice and salt, they tried to sleep wherever they could in the wet jungle. The diary of the unit tells how these men, with their legs pock-marked with the bites of leeches and with their feet all sodden and blistered, ran short of rations after four days for the reasons that some of the men did not carry sufficient and that others threw theirs away. On the 17th the leading elements of the unit reached Nampong and a few days later the rest, less those who had died on the way, caught up with them and moved on to Margherita.

Along the northern subsidiary route D.D.M.S. placed in series 3, 7 and 8 Bur.G.Hs. and 59 and 60 I.G.Hs. This route was of considerable use so long as Myitkyina was the air evacuation centre. The time came, however, when it could no longer be used for the reason that the railway line north of Shwebo became blocked with wrecked trains.

D.D.M.S. collected all the river steamers that were available and formed a flotilla out of them. This was sent when fully loaded from Mandalay to Katha on the Irrawaddy, the patients sent on by train to Myitkyina, the vessels sunk and the crews, medical staffs and others who could march sent off *en route* for Ledo by the northern subsidiary route.

MEDICAL ARRANGEMENTS IN INDIA

In that part of India into which Burma Army had entered there were but few military medical installations. At Dimapur, railhead, there was a small general hospital, 66 C.G.H., which remained in this site until the very end of the campaign. At Gauhati on the Brahmaputra, riverhead, was a C.C.S. soon to be replaced by 52 C.G.H. In the Assam Plain there were five small military and civil hospitals. There were two military hospitals in Shillong and a 1,000-bed general hospital in Tezpur across the river.

Evacuation from Dimapur to Gauhati was by improvised ambulance train (metre gauge), and from Gauhati by river steamer down the Brahmaputra to Sirajganj, a 36-hour journey, where 75 (Ind.) C.C.S., soon to be transformed into a general hospital, functioned amid the desolate marshes of that region. From Sirajganj broad gauge trains, ambulance trains and improvised ambulance trains, conveyed the patients for distribution among the hospitals in Calcutta, Ranchi and those of Central Command. So great was the traffic during the autumn months of 1942 that train loads of patients reached places as far away from the eastern front as Sialkot and Poona. In Calcutta there were two general hospitals, in Ranchi a combination of four but these were by no means sufficient and the hospitals in every military station in Eastern and Central Commands were required to take their quota of patients. Every one of these hospitals underwent a 25 per cent. expansion.

A distribution scheme was devised that seemed to meet the needs of the situation but it was partially wrecked by infuriating delays in the running of the trains and by misunderstandings between those who ran the trains and those who fed the patients on the trains; all too frequently a train failed to stop at the halt where the food was waiting and did stop at stations where there was neither food nor water. The arrangements that were made were not facilitated by the general atmosphere of political unrest in this part of India, unrest which, on occasion, took very ugly forms.

THE WITHDRAWAL FROM ARAKAN

Up to March 18, 1942 the garrison of Akyab, a place of considerable importance as an air base, consisted solely of 14/7th Rajput Regt. It was then strengthened by the addition of H.Q. Ind. 109th Bde., 6/9th Jat Regt., 9/7th Rajput Regt., and two anti-aircraft units from India. On March 23 the Japanese occupied the Andaman and Nicobar Islands, from which the small garrison, a battalion of Gurkhas and a company of 1st W. Yorks, had been withdrawn on the 12th. On that day and again on March 24 Akyab was heavily bombed from the air and the garrison, with the exception of 14/7th Rajput Regt., one section of 67th H.A.A. Regt. and two troops of Ind. 1st Lt. A.A. Regt., was promptly withdrawn. After this the town was constantly raided and morale suffered and the incidence of sickness among the garrison mounted. By May 4 the situation had become critical for Japanese troops were approaching the port. Having demolished the port installations the garrison left for Chittagong by sea.

With the battalions were the regimental medical officers. Use was made of the civil hospital in the town and evacuation was by sea to Chittagong and Calcutta.

REFLECTIONS UPON THE WORK OF THE ARMY MEDICAL
SERVICES DURING THIS PHASE OF THE CAMPAIGN

The work of the Army Medical Services is done in a setting that is created by the general military situation and the quality of that work is very largely determined by the conditions in which it is performed. The circumstances that attend an enforced, hurried withdrawal lasting for a considerable period of time and being more or less continuous are such as to diminish the ability of these Services to give of their best. There was much about this phase that was very unsatisfactory. For the very simple reason that they were not available and could not be made available at the time, the Army-in-Burma remained very deficient in respect of medical units throughout the whole of this phase. General Hutton, in his report (which is included in General Wavell's *Despatch* of May 14, 1942, published March 11, 1946) has much to say concerning the various disabilities from which the Army Medical Services suffered. He points out that conscription failed to make good the deficiencies; that the Burma Hospital Corps was not reliable and failed badly owing to mass desertions, and that after the bombing of Rangoon it became increasingly difficult to obtain labour. Units arrived without their equipment; two M.A.Ss. without their cars, field ambulances without their transport. General Hutton states that in his opinion the wounded suffered very considerable hardship and with this opinion all who served in this theatre at this time will agree. The breakdown of the civil medical services and the arrival of the Chinese armies with practically no medical services of their own imposed heavy additional burdens upon the Army Medical Services.

General Alexander, in his report (also included in the *Despatch* cited above) states that the problem of evacuating to India the sick and the wounded was a source of constant anxiety. 'When the withdrawal north of Mandalay commenced, I decided that the sick and wounded must be evacuated at all costs. Consequently, hospital equipment and medical stores were abandoned in order to save the patients. At the end of April when the Japanese captured Lashio a considerable number of sick and wounded were on the Irrawaddy *en route* to Myitkyina. It was impossible to make any change in this plan but I understand that the majority of these men reached India safely. The remainder of the sick and wounded were evacuated to India by motor transport. There can be no doubt that many of the wounded travelling in lorries over the bumpy road to Shwegyin and Tamu endured great suffering. It was better, however, that they should endure this rather than be left behind and the fact that 2,300 men were evacuated in this way, with very little transport available, is evidence of the efficiency and tireless devotion of the Medical Directorate.' In this connexion it is of interest to note that careful observation revealed that badly wounded men travelled better when transported in open lorries on thick beds of straw than when evacuated in the standard ambulance car which sucked in its own dust through the openings at the back.

The withdrawal to Dunkirk, the evacuation of Norway and of Greece and the stampedes along the North African shore all demonstrate clearly the difficulties that the too rapid movement of an army creates for its medical services. But the conditions that attended the retreat in Burma were surely far more purgatorial than those which characterised these others. It was through the sweltering heat and the choking dust of the waterless oilfields, through the Death Valley that ran from Kalewa to Tamu, through the wilderness of the Hukawng Valley to Ledo, through one of the most intensely malarious areas in the world and through areas that had been fouled and poisoned by the pitiful refugees who, in seeking the aid of the retreating army, offered in return the threat of deadly contagion.

What surely is remarkable is that so large a proportion of the Army in Burma did live to cross the frontier.

D.D.M.S., summing up his impressions of this phase of the campaign, comments upon the need for physical fitness and mental fitness among all ranks of the medical services. He noted time and time again that elderly officers and other ranks cracked up at awkward times and refers to no less than nine senior medical officers who collapsed at critical periods and had to be replaced. He also remarks that it has now become necessary for all medical officers and senior N.C.Os. to be able to drive a motor vehicle and to undertake running repairs. (It is to be expected that in the future it will be observed that it is desirable that every medical officer shall be able to manage a helicopter or a light plane.)

It is unfortunate that the outstanding feature of this phase of the campaign in Burma was the insufficiency of the arrangements made in India for the hospitalisation of the sick of Burma Army. The incidence of sickness was far higher than had been expected and consequently the hospital provision was utterly inadequate in respect of beds, of staff and of equipment. The few existing hospitals were multiplied by improvisation and hurriedly raised medical units were drafted into the areas of Assam and Eastern Bengal. The sick often arrived before the hospital was ready to receive them and so they had to lie around until accommodation for them could be prepared. The hospitals of Eastern Bengal were overwhelmed by the vast torrent of sick that flowed into them. Only by the great exertions of the grossly overtaxed medical and nursing staffs and by the devoted voluntary service rendered by members of the local civilian communities was a breakdown of the medical arrangements and its consequences avoided.

In the beginning of this campaign the medical services in Burma were totally unprepared for war; at the end of this phase of the campaign the medical services of India were unprepared for the consequences of defeat. Months filled with feverish activity had to pass before the staffs of the hospitals accommodating the sick and the wounded of Burma Army were working in conditions that enabled them to give to those in their care the skilled attention they so badly needed.

APPENDIX V

TOTAL SICK WASTAGE OF INDIAN 17TH DIVISION FROM MAY 24, 1942 TO JUNE 1, 1942 (INCLUSIVE)

16th Bde. Strength 1,504

*Cases sent to 8 (Ind.) C.C.S.	177
Cases detained in A.D.S. and R.A.Ps.	127
Cases attending M.I. Rooms for treatment	228
Total sick wastage	532
Sick wastage percentage	35·3

48th Bde. Strength 3,142

*Cases sent to 8 (Ind.) C.C.S.	126
Cases detained in A.D.S. and R.A.Ps.	170
Cases attending M.I. Rooms for treatment	194
Total sick wastage	490
Sick wastage percentage	15·6

63rd Bde. Strength 1,696

*Cases sent to 8 (Ind.) C.C.S.	163
Cases detained in A.D.S. and R.A.Ps.	132
Cases attending M.I. Rooms for treatment	152
Total sick wastage	447
Sick wastage percentage	26·3

Div. Troops. Strength 3,566

*Cases sent to 8 (Ind.) C.C.S.	740
Cases detained in A.D.S. and R.A.Ps.	100
Cases attending M.I. Rooms for treatment	534
Total sick wastage	1,374
Sick wastage percentage	38·5
Total Div. Strength	9,908
Total Div. Sick Wastage	2,843
Total Div. Sick Wastage percentage	28·7

* Most of the cases sent to 8 (Ind.) C.C.S. had been evacuated up the line; about 250, however, were retained to be returned to the division on discharge from the C.C.S.

N.B. Most of the cases were Malaria, about 20 per cent. showing dysenteric symptoms in addition.

APPENDIX VI

NOTES ON CERTAIN INDIAN AND OTHER MEDICAL UNITS

The Field Ambulance

(Animal and Mechanical Transport) or (Animal Transport).

The basic composition of the unit was a headquarters and two companies. The headquarters could provide an administrative section and the personnel for a light or a heavy M.D.S. Each of the companies could form an A.D.S. or could be divided into a headquarters section and two platoons, each of which could form a light A.D.S.

The Indian Bearer Units

These were reorganised in 1942 and renamed bearer companies. The company was divisible into two bearer sections and was capable of carrying 25 patients at a time allowing eight men, working in relays of four at a time, for the carriage of each patient. These units were used for the transport of patients unfit to be carried on mules.

The Casualty Clearing Station

This was organised into a light section of 50 beds, a heavy section of 150 beds and an administrative headquarters. The light section had an operating team attached to it. The heavy section was divisible into two half sections of 75 beds each and could be ferried forward in two lifts.

The Staging Section

These most useful multi-purpose units were of two kinds originally, the Indian and the British variety. Later these were replaced by the combined staging section designed to hold 20 Indian and 5 British beds and capable of expansion to 40 Indian and 10 British beds.

The Malaria Forward Treatment Unit

This was organised to hold and to treat 600 patients. Two such units were allotted to each division operating in a highly malarious terrain. They were equipped and staffed for the diagnosis of the disease as well as for its treatment.

The General Hospital

Developments affecting the general hospital led to the creation in 1942 of the Indian General Hospital (Combined) (I.G.H.(C.)). It consisted of a headquarters so constituted that it mattered not at all how many of its component sections were British or Indian; an Indian wing of 1–5 sections and a British wing of 1–5 sections, provision being made for further expansion either of Indian or British beds or both.

The Ambulance Transport

This was a ship used for the transport of the sick and wounded but carried no distinguishing marks. Only one such vessel was commissioned during the war. It was used for the conveyance of troops on the outward voyage from

India but brought 300–350 casualties back on its return journey. The facilities for the care of the casualties on such transport were not equal to those on a hospital ship.

The Mobile Surgical Unit

The establishment of this unit was 1 surgeon, 1 anaesthetist, 1 nursing sister, 1 corporal and 1 private, operating room attendants of the R.A.M.C., 1 subedar I.M.D., 2 nursing section sepoys, 4 ambulance section sepoys, and N.Cs. (E). of the I.M.C. Later, as a result of the experience gained, the subedar was replaced by a medical officer, the nursing sister was deleted from the establishment and two more B.O.Rs. were added to it.

The Friends Ambulance Unit

The full story of the F.A.U. is given in *Friends Ambulance Unit* by A. Tegla Davies. 1947. Allen and Unwin. It is indeed a remarkable story of the service given by these members of the Society of Friends, pacifists all, who insisted on retaining the identity of the unit in which they served, who picked and chose what tasks they would and would not undertake and who claimed the final authority over the members of the unit. Teams of these Quakers worked in India and in China where they transported medical supplies and helped the Seagrave Unit and provided medical teams for service with the Chinese armies.

The American Field Service

A brief account of this voluntary American organisation was given in the second of these campaign volumes. It will suffice here to report that 538 members of this organisation served in the Indo-Burmese theatre. An ambulance company 300 strong was provided for service on the Burma front and the advance party reached India in June 1943. A number of British W.Os., of Indian General Service Corps personnel and mess servants, water-carriers and the like were added to the company. There were four sections, three of them equipped with Chevrolet heavy ambulances, twenty-five in all and the fourth with twenty-four (later thirty-six) jeeps. Later the organisation was changed to two platoons, each platoon being subdivided into three sections each with its heavy and its jeep ambulances. In all they provided 50 jeep ambulances, 40 large motor ambulances, 30 load carriers and a number of miscellaneous vehicles. The members of this unit served everywhere in Burma where the fighting was furious. In practically every divisional medical unit war diary there is to be found the entry 'Evacuation by A.F.S.' Nine of the members of this unit lost their lives in Burma and four others were wounded.

The Seagrave Hospital Unit

In 1922 Dr. Seagrave, an American citizen, was sent by the American Baptist Mission to the hospital this organisation had founded in Namhkam in the Shan States. Here he developed a very extensive surgical practice among the Kachins. Dr. Seagrave trained as many nurses and midwives as possible for service in the Shan, Kachin and Karenni States of Burma.

WITHDRAWAL FROM BURMA

The Burma Road, then being constructed, passed within four to five air miles of Namhkam. The first 300 miles of this road were through highly malarious country and the labourers suffered severely from this disease. The members of the staff of the American Mission Hospital were invited by British officials to extend their medical care to cover those labourers. Near the hospital was an aircraft manufacturing company's plant where many thousands of Chinese were employed. The staff of the hospital was also asked to look after them. As a result its members learnt Chinese.

When the Japanese invaded Burma Dr. Seagrave offered the services of himself and his staff to the Government of Burma as a mobile hospital. General Alexander gratefully accepted this gracious offer and six large trucks and much equipment were provided out of the lend-lease stores in Rangoon docks. Dr. Seagrave became an honorary lieutenant-colonel and the unit was assigned to the Chinese Army, setting up its headquarters in Loilem. The staff of the hospital at this time consisted of two medical men besides Dr. Seagrave, an administrative officer, six American and Burmese missionaries acting as drivers and thirty-four Burmese nurses. Twelve Burmese men who had volunteered to serve with the unit without pay were posted to the area east of Salween and to the area in the central portion of the Shan States respectively.

Six small 'clearing stations' in charge of nurses from the hospital were opened near to the front and these were visited at regular intervals by the medical staff.

When in March 1942 General Stilwell arrived to assume command of the Chinese in Burma Dr. Seagrave asked to be allowed to transfer from the British to the American Army. This request was immediately granted and so the remainder of the story of the Seagrave Unit belongs not to this volume but to the Official U.S. Medical History of the War.

NOTE *The Burma Regiment* (*see* pages 79 and 253)

After the retreat from Burma the Gurkhas and Kumaoris, of the 7th Burma Rifles and the Punjabis and Sikhs of the 8th Burma Rifles, were formed into the 1st Battalion Burma Regiment, while the Karens and other Burma classes were drafted into the 2nd Burma Rifles which operated with the Chindits. The Burma Regiment consisted at first of six battalions, a Reconnaissance Regiment (7th) and Training Battalion (10th) based on Hoshiarpur, but of the active battalions only 1st, 2nd and 4th remained in existence, the others being used as drafts for them. A Company of one of these latter battalions— 5th Buregt.— assisted the Garrison of Kohima and remained there during the siege, as did a Garrison Company of Burma Regiment after its withdrawal into Kohima from Phekakedzumi.

CHAPTER 4

THE ABORTIVE OFFENSIVE IN ARAKAN. SEPTEMBER 1942

As has been related, during the last days of the retreat from Burma there was a small garrison in Akyab. A Japanese force embarking in Taungup sailed up the coast to Minbya, east of Akyab, and thence sent parties to the north and to the west. On May 4 the Akyab garrison was withdrawn by sea and later in the day the Japanese occupied the island and the port.

The Japanese were now in possession of the whole of Burma and it was reasonably expected that when the rains ceased they would attempt to invade India either by land or by sea. In India itself there was much political unrest and the time soon came when the leaders of the Congress Party had to be interned.

In February 1942 Indian 14th Division was sent from Ranchi to Eastern Bengal to guard the Indo-Burma frontier in that region and to prevent any Japanese incursion into India from Arakan. The division then consisted of Indian 47th and 49th Infantry Brigades. H.Q. Division was first in Comilla and later in Maynamati, about five miles to the west of this town. 47th Bde. moved into the Fenny area and 49th Bde. into the area of Noakhali–Laksam–Chandpur. 41 (Ind.) Fd. Amb. joined the division on March 31 and opened its M.D.S. in a school in Fenny to serve 47th Bde. Its 'A' and 'B' Coys. established their A.D.Ss. in Fazilpur and Farhadnagar respectively. They were in *basha* huts and each could hold 150 patients. The M.D.S. could accommodate 300. Early in April 47 (Ind.) Fd. Amb. arrived in Maynamati and its 'A' and 'B' Coys. moved into Noakhali–Laksam–Chandpur area to provide three A.D.Ss. for the three defended localities. H.Q. 47 (Ind.)Fd. Amb. remained in Maynamati to tend the sick among the divisional troops. On May 5 part of the M.D.S. of 41 (Ind.) Fd. Amb. moved from Fenny to the defended locality of Govindpur. It was followed by the rest of the M.D.S. later.

During these days the field ambulances were kept very busy with malaria and gonorrhoea cases. 47 (Ind.) Fd. Amb. was also responsible for the provision of medical detachments for three mobile columns, each detachment consisting of a medical officer, a B.O.R., 3 stretcher squads, 80 riding mules for the conveyance of casualties and 6 mules for the transport of equipment.

THE OFFENSIVE IN THE ARAKAN, 1942

In May, 49th Bde. and 47 (Ind.) Fd. Amb. left the area for Imphal. to join Indian 23rd Division. The A.D.S. of 'A' Coy. of 41 (Ind.) Fd. Amb. moved from Fazilpur to Daulatganj to replace an A.D.S. of 47 (Ind.) Fd. Amb.

Eastern Army, with its headquarters in Ranchi in Bihar, was responsible to G.H.Q. India for the internal security and external defence of Eastern India and therefore for the conduct of operations against the Japanese forces in Burma. In its forward zone Eastern Army had two corps deployed to guard the frontier. IV Corps, with its headquarters in Imphal, in Assam, and with Indian 23rd Division (Ind. 37th and 49th Bdes.) and the remains of Indian 17th Division (Ind. 48th and 63rd Bdes.) under command, was in the north. In the south was XV Corps with its headquarters in Calcutta first and in Barrackpore later and with Indian 14th Division (Ind. 47th Bde.) around Comilla, with detachments in Chittagong and Indian 26th Division (Ind. 4th, 36th and 71st Bdes.) under command. 26th Division was engaged almost exclusively on internal security duties. Between the right flank of IV Corps and the left flank of XV Corps there was a gap of about a hundred miles, completely unguarded at first but later actively patrolled by the small vessels of a flotilla, 3 I.W.T. (Sunderbans) Flotilla, that had been created out of the Army Inland Water Transport Service.

In August 1942 Eastern Army H.Q. took over from H.Q. IV Corps which thereupon returned to Ranchi to build around itself a new set of formations, including 70th Division and Indian 50th Tank Bde. Nearby, in Ramgarh, was General Stilwell with the Chinese Divisions, 22nd and 38th, that he had brought out of Burma and for which some 13,000 reinforcements had been flown by American airmen over 'the Hump'. In the vicinity of Saugor in the Central Provinces was Brigadier Wingate training Indian 77th Bde. in preparation for its employment as a long range penetration group.

Field Marshal Viscount Wavell, C. in C. India, had decided to keep the Japanese forces in Burma engaged in order to disrupt any plans they might be making for the invasion of India. He therefore instructed his commanders to make ready for the capture of Akyab and for the reoccupation of northern Arakan, for the strengthening of the position in the Chin Hills and for the occupation of the line of the Chindwin between Kalewa and Sittaung. These were to be the tasks for the campaigning months of 1942–43. He decided further that of these tasks the capture of Akyab should be the first to be launched. Shortage of landing craft and of troops adequately trained in amphibious warfare made it necessary to be content with a methodical thrust straight down the Mayu Peninsula with a final hop by ferry across the estuary of the Mayu River to Akyab island.

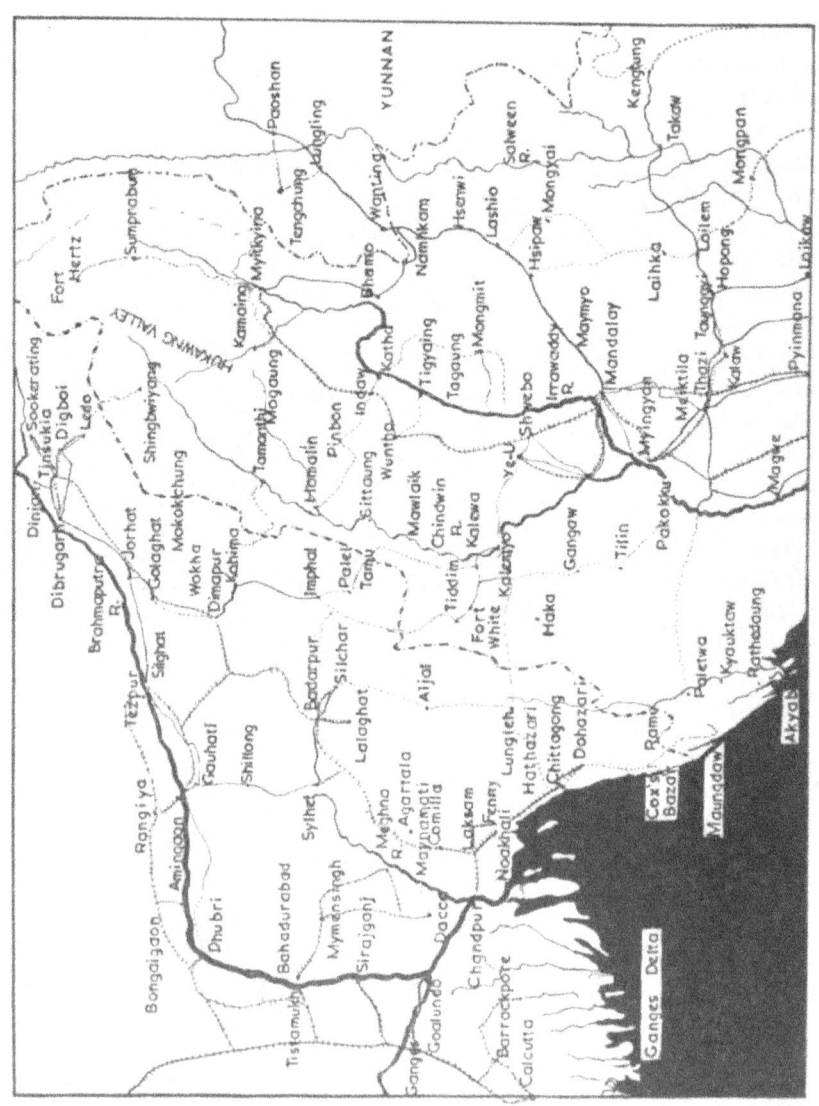

FIG. 13. The Indo-Burma Frontier

Indian 14th Division and 6th Bde. of 2nd Division (which was in the Bombay area training for combined operations against Akyab) were chosen as the formations to take part in this operation. On July 7, 123rd Bde. (10th L.F.; 8/10th Baluch; 1/15th Punjab) from Imphal joined Indian 14th Division in Chittagong. It had suffered much from sickness in the north and was not in fighting trim. With this brigade came 45 (Ind.) Fd. Amb. which established itself in the Railway Hospital building in Maynamati. Its 'A' Coy, was split up into a number of detachments which accompanied mobile columns engaged in active patrolling to the south of Chittagong. Early in September its 'B' Coy. moved from Maynamati to relieve the M.D.S. of 41 (Ind.) Fd. Amb. in Govindpur.

In September Indian 14th Division was ordered to move southwards and establish contact with the Japanese. This it did with Ind. 123rd Bde. in the lead. Ind. 55th Bde. of Indian 7th Division now joined Indian 14th Division and took 123rd Bde's. place in Chittagong. In October detachments of 1/15th Punjab entered Maungdaw and Buthidaung without encountering any opposition. But on October 24 strong Japanese forces attacked both these places and expelled the Punjabis therefrom forcing them to withdraw *via* Teknaf to the vicinity of Bawli Bazar. Thereafter, until the middle of December, there was no further contact with the Japanese.

The Mayu Peninsula is about ninety miles long; its width varies from about twenty miles in the north to a few hundred yards below the village of Donbaik near the tip at Foul Point. Running down its length are two features, the Mayu Range of hills 1,500 ft. in height and covered with a jungle of bamboo and having in most places very precipitous sides, and the Mayu River, running more or less parallel to the Range and to the east of it. There are four sectors of the peninsula therefore, running from north to south; (i) the coastal strip between the Bay of Bengal on the west and the Mayu Range on the east; (ii) the Mayu Range running like a spine down the peninsula; (iii) the Valley of the Mayu River between the foothills of the Mayu Range on the west and the hills which separate this valley from that of the River Kaladan; and (iv) the Valley of the Kaladan. It is to be noted that north of Buthidaung the River Mayu is known as the Kalapanzin. The main link between the coastal strip and the Valley of the Mayu across the Mayu Range was the Maungdaw–Buthidaung road with its two tunnels. There were also several mule tracks over the range, one over the Goppe Pass linking Goppe Bazar and Bawli Bazar, another over the Ngakyedauk Pass linking Wabyin and Sinzweya, and a track joining Indin and Sinoh.

To the eye at certain times of the year this is a beautiful countryside with its sandy beaches, its blue-green jumbles of hills, its bright green

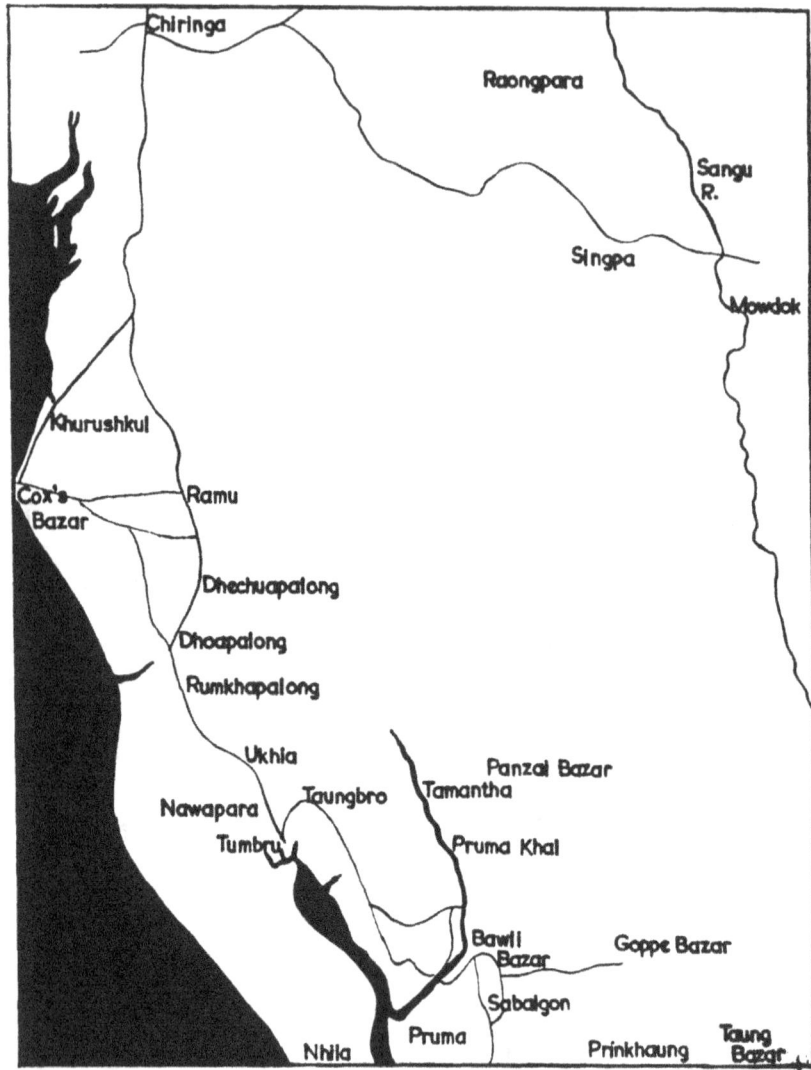

Fig. 14. Arakan. Chiringa–Nhila

valleys and its expanses of paddy-lands. Every valley has its river snaking its way to the sea. But with the coming of the monsoon it becomes a rain-drenched, inhospitable land and in it the mosquito, the tick and the leech lie in wait. It certainly is not a terrain in which to wage war.

The conditions in Arakan presented two major problems to the medical services. The first and the greater was that of the maintenance of the health of the troops and the second that of the evacuation of casualties. During the next two years practically every conceivable form of transport was tried in attempts to overcome the difficulties created by mountain, jungle, chaung and swamp. Over the long distances that had to be travelled there could be no single method and to transport a casualty through the dense bamboo covering the razor-edged ridges required both fortitude and great endurance. To get a casualty from the front line in the vicinity of Donbaik, for example, to the hospital in Chittagong took at least two and a half days with no less than sixteen changes of transport; to get one stretcher case and two walking wounded from the R.A.P. in the Point 551 area to the A.D.S., a distance of less than three miles, took one N.C.O. and five stretcher-bearers seventeen and a half hours. At the end of this journey bearers and casualties were utterly exhausted.

It is of interest to note that of the many contraptions and methods that were tried—the standard stretcher, metal and wire mesh stretchers, bamboo and blanket, single pole and sling, wheeled stretchers, single wheeled, two-wheeled, three-wheeled and rickshaw pattern, mule, pony and man pack-saddles and carrying chairs, single pack and double, mule pony and man travois,-the best of the lot was the standard field stretcher carried on the shoulder by experienced bearers.

For evacuation by road motor ambulance cars, improvised lorries, jeeps adapted to take one, two or three stretchers, country carts and

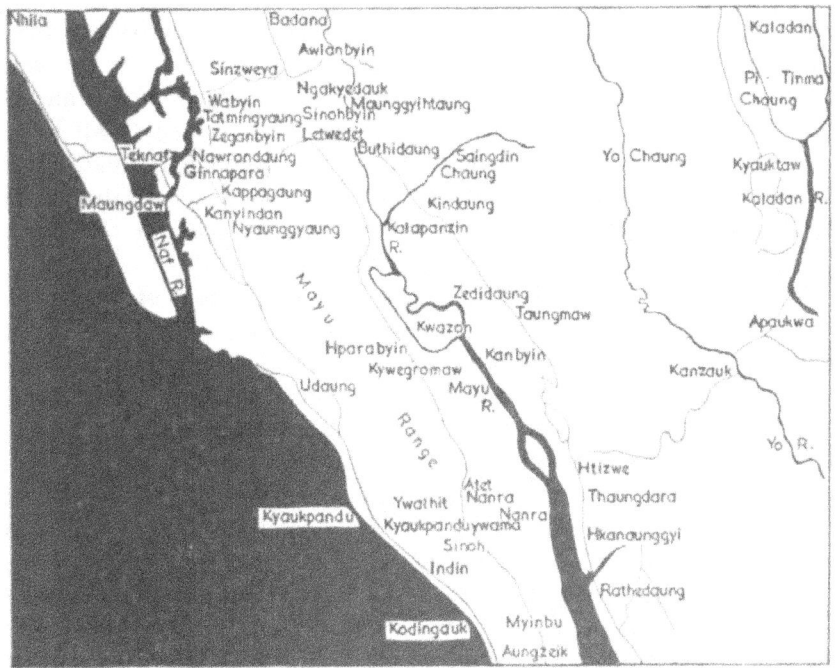

FIG. 15. Arakan. Nhila-Rathedaung

pony tongas were used at different times in different circumstances. For evacuation by river sampans taking one to five patients, larger local river craft, rafts, 'flats,' dhows, coastal steamers and two ocean-going vessels were employed. For evacuation by rail everything from the crudest improvisation to the specially equipped ambulance train were used at one time or another. Evacuation by air became the usual method of casualty evacuation in later years, transport planes conveying casualties on their return journeys.

Communications between Arakan and East Bengal were very few and very undeveloped. A broad gauge railway line from Calcutta to Goalundo Ghat linked up with river steamers for Chandpur across the River Meghna. From Chandpur a metre gauge line ran *via* Laksam and Chittagong to Dohazari, about fifty miles north of the Bengal–Arakan border. Another route from Calcutta was by broad gauge to Santahar, by metre gauge to Tistamukh Ghat, by ferry to Bahadurabad and by metre gauge to Dohazari *via* Comilla and Chittagong. From Dohazari a metalled road ran for about ten miles to the south. In ordinary times coastal steamers plied between Chittagong, Cox's Bazar and Maungdaw and in the River Naf between Tumbru Ghat and Maungdaw. But after the outbreak of war there had been no service beyond Cox's Bazar. When Indian 14th Division moved into Arakan it was transported by coastal steamer from Chittagong to Cox's Bazar and then proceeded, partly by road and partly by river transport, to Bawli Bazar. Its sappers began the construction of a fair-weather road running southwards from the end of the metalled road that began in Dohazari. At first the only channel of intercommunication between the troops on the two sides of the Mayu Range was over the Goppe Pass which linked Bawli Bazar with Goppe Bazar. On the east of the range the River Mayu provided the best means of intercommunication. There was no road leading out of Arakan into Burma proper. There were tracks, like the one from Taungup over the Arakan Yomas to Prome.

On December 16, 1/15th Punjab, the leading battalion of 123rd Bde. to which 1/7th Rajput Regt. had been added, once again entered Maungdaw and, on the following day, Buthidaung and once again without meeting any opposition. Indian 14th Division, on a two brigade front, with 47th Bde. down the coastal strip on the west of the Mayu Range and 123rd Bde. down the Mayu Valley on the east of Mayu River, moved forward towards Rathedaung. By December 27, 47th Bde. had reached Indin and Sinoh and a patrol had actually rounded Foul Point to enter Magyichaung. 123rd Bde., entering Rathedaung, ran into heavy fire. On the 31st, 1/7th Rajput of 47th Bde. in Sinoh were repeatedly attacked but held their ground. The Japanese then withdrew and on the first day of 1943 5/8th Punjab of the same brigade made a reconnaissance down the west side of the Mayu Peninsula to reach Foul Point. No

THE OFFENSIVE IN THE ARAKAN, 1942   107

Japanese troops were encountered. The front line now ran from north of Laung Chaung to north of Rathedaung.

In order to protect the flank of the division as it moved southwards two small forces were sent into the valley of the Kaladan River. 'Tripforce', built around the Tripura State Force, was sent into the upper Kaladan Valley and occupied both Paletwa and Kaladan without opposition. 'Soutcol', built around 8/10th Baluch, marched to the Kaladan Valley from Taung Bazar, building a pack-track L. of C. for itself. Kyauktaw was occupied.

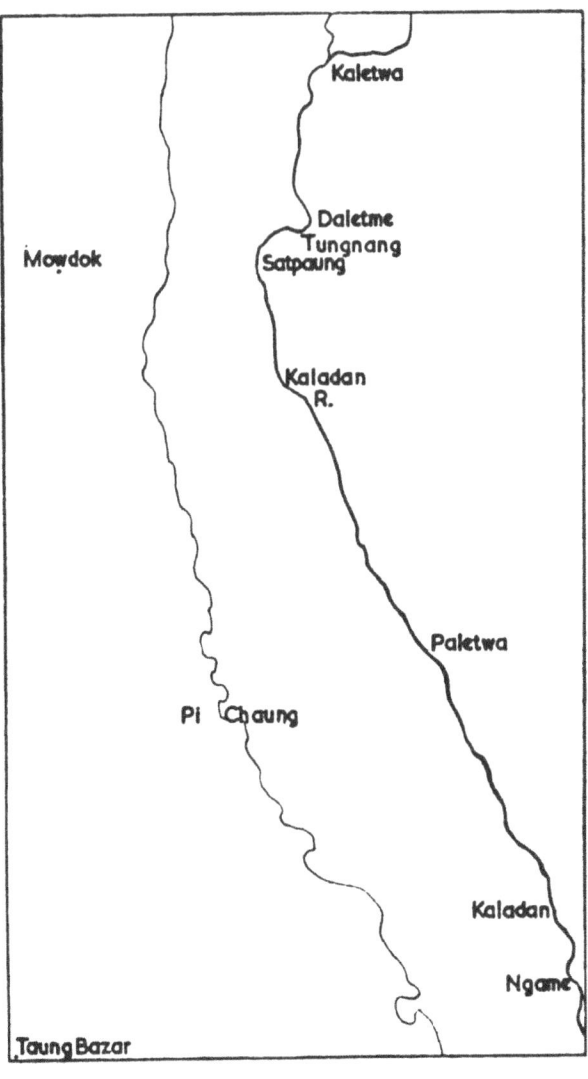

FIG. 16. Arakan. The Valley of the Kaladan

MEDICAL COVER

When Indian 14th Division moved into Arakan in October 1942 its medical units were distributed as follows:

45 (Ind.) Fd. Amb. (123rd Bde.)	H.Q. (closed) in Chittagong.
	'A' Coy. A.D.S. in Cox's Bazar.
	Detachment with 1/15th Punjab moving on Maungdaw.
	Detachment with a company of this battalion in Ramu.
	'B' Coy. in Dohazari.
41 (Ind.) Fd. Amb. (47th Bde.)	With 47th Bde. in the area of Fenny, preparing to move to Chittagong.
28 (Ind.) Fd. Hyg. Sec.	H.Q. and one sub-sec. in Maynamati preparing to move to Chittagong.
	Sub-section with 41 (Ind.) Fd. Amb.
	Sub-section with 'A' Coy. 45 (Ind.) Fd. Amb.
15 (Ind.) C.C.S.	Light section in Chittagong (open).
	Heavy section in Comilla (open).

The detachments of 'A' Coy. of 45 (Ind.) Fd. Amb. with the Punjabis consisted of an assistant surgeon and a stretcher-squad. The one moving on Maungdaw marched with the battalion to Tumbru and travelled therefrom by sampan down the Naf River. When these detachments had been provided, the A.D.S. itself in Cox's Bazar was so very depleted that it was decided to move it to Ramu and bring the H.Q. of the unit to Cox's Bazar. There it opened its M.D.S. on October 17. The handling of patients was far from easy for the casualty had to be brought by sampan alongside a steep slippery slope. The construction of a landing stage was begun.

When Maungdaw and Buthidaung were occupied, the detachment moving with the battalion opened its A.D.S. in Maungdaw. The officer commanding the field ambulance, visiting this detachment, found the village full of acute medical problems. Its conservancy system had broken down. In it were some 12,000 refugees and among these there was much sickness of a serious kind, the number of deaths averaging about fifteen a day. The divisional hygiene section was ordered forward but before it could reach Maungdaw the Japanese had attacked and driven the Punjabis out of the place. On November 10, 'B' Coy. 45 (Ind.) Fd. Amb., then in Dohazari, moved forward to Ukhia to open an additional A.D.S. because torrential rain was making evacuation exceedingly difficult. 60 and 63 (Ind.) Fd. Ambs. now joined Indian 14th Division. They were both on A.T. and M.T. scales of transport. 63 relieved H.Q. 45 (Ind.) Fd. Amb. in Cox's Bazar and a company of

60 took over the A.D.S. in Ukhia. H.Q. 45 (Ind.) Fd. Amb., being thus relieved, moved forward to Bawli Bazar and took over the A.D.S. that its 'A' Coy. had established there.

Much needed medical reinforcements had been reaching the front, bearer units, an A.M.U., a mobile surgical unit and three staging sections. After the occupation of Maungdaw and Buthidaung in mid-December the distribution of the medical units was as follows:

45 (Ind.) Fd. Amb. (with 123rd Bde.)	H.Q. and 1 (Ind.) Bearer Unit, M.D.S. in Buthidaung.
	'A' Coy. with Soutcol. detach. in Taung Bazar.
	'B' Coy. and S.Bs. of 1 (Ind.) Bearer Unit with 10th L.F. of 123rd Bde. south of Buthidaung moving on Taungmaw.
41 (Ind.) Fd. Amb. (with 47th Bde.)	Less a light section and with 2 (Ind.) Bearer Unit less one company moving south of Maungdaw by A.T.
	Light sec. 'B' Coy. and one company 2 (Ind.) Bearer Unit moving with 1/7th. Rajput of 47th Bde. east of the Mayu range.
60 (Ind.) Fd. Amb.	H.Q. and 6 (Ind.) M.S.U., M.D.S. in Kanyindan nr. Maungdaw.
	'A' and 'B' Coys. in Kanyindan. Personnel helping in M.D.S.
63 (Ind.) Fd. Amb.	H.Q., M.D.S. in Cox's Bazar.
	'A' Coy., S.S. in Bawli Bazar.
	'B' Coy., S.S. in Nawapara nr. Tumbru at the head of the Naf Estuary.
15 (Ind.) C.C.S.	16 (Ind.) M.S.U. attached (closed) in Chittagong ready to move forward to Maungdaw.
18 (Ind.) A.M.U.	28 (Ind.) Fd. Hyg. Sec.
	Detachments at key points on the L. of C.
43, 44 and 46 (Ind.) S.Ss.	Moving south of Chittagong to Dohazari, Maungdaw and Buthidaung.

As the division advanced southwards 45 (Ind.) Fd. Amb. moved with 123rd Bde. along the east bank of the Mayu Estuary. It had to leave a small detachment of one medical officer and 20 O.Rs. in Buthidaung to function as a staging section until the arrival there of 46 (Ind.) S.S. By December 31, H.Q. 45 (Ind.) Fd. Amb. had opened its M.D.S. in

Zedidaung and 'B' Coy. its A.D.S. in Htizwe. On the first day of 1943 'B' Coy. moved its A.D.S. forward to Thaungdara. Evacuation from 123rd Bde. was by sampan up river to Buthidaung and thence by road to 15 (Ind.) C.C.S. in Maungdaw.

At the end of the advance into the Mayu Peninsula, the distribution of the forward medical units east of the Mayu Range was as follows:

46 (Ind.) S.S.	In Buthidaung.
60 (Ind.) Fd. Amb.	Half-company in Zedidaung.
45 (Ind.) Fd. Amb. with 6 (Ind.) M.S.U. attached	M.D.S. in Thaungdara.
45 (Ind.) Fd. Amb.	A.D.S. in Kanbyin.
45 (Ind.) Fd. Amb.	Relay Post in Hkanaunggyi.
1 (Ind.) Bearer Unit	Detachments between M.D.S., A.D.S., and Relay Post, the remainder in Ywathit between Kyaukpandu and Atet Nanra.

The time taken by a casualty to reach the C.C.S. in Maungdaw could be as long as 19 hours, 6 hours to reach Zedidaung, 6 hours waiting for the next tide, 6 hours to reach Buthidaung and 1 hour to get to Maungdaw.

41 (Ind.) Fd. Amb. was moving with 47th Bde. down the coastal strip on the west. The unit was on A.T. and had with it 2 (Ind.) Bearer Unit. By December 30 its M.D.S. was open in Kyaukpandu, a light A.D.S. of 'A' Coy. in Kodingauk and a heavy section A.D.S. of 'B' Coy. in Atet Nanra. Later the heavy section of the M.D.S., moved to Atet Nanra and thus enabled the heavy section A.D.S. of 'B' Coy. to join its light section in Kyaukpanduywama. When the A.D.S. of 'B' Coy. moved to Sinoh, a detachment of an assistant surgeon, six O.Rs. and fifty S.Bs. was left in Atet Nanra to serve as a staging post for casualties being evacuated from Sinoh to the M.D.S. Evacuation in 47th Bde. at this time was from the R.A.Ps. by S.B. squad or by mule; from the A.D.S., to the M.D.S. of 45 (Ind.) Fd. Amb. in Buthidaung by sampan and from the M.D.S. to the C.C.S. in Maungdaw by ambulance car.

THE ASSAULTS UPON THE JAPANESE POSITIONS AT DONBAIK AND RATHEDAUNG AND THE JAPANESE COUNTER-OFFENSIVE

It had become clear that the Japanese were holding strong defensive positions about Donbaik and Rathedaung which they had reoccupied. On January 18 and 19, 47th Bde. attacked the Donbaik position

THE OFFENSIVE IN THE ARAKAN, 1942

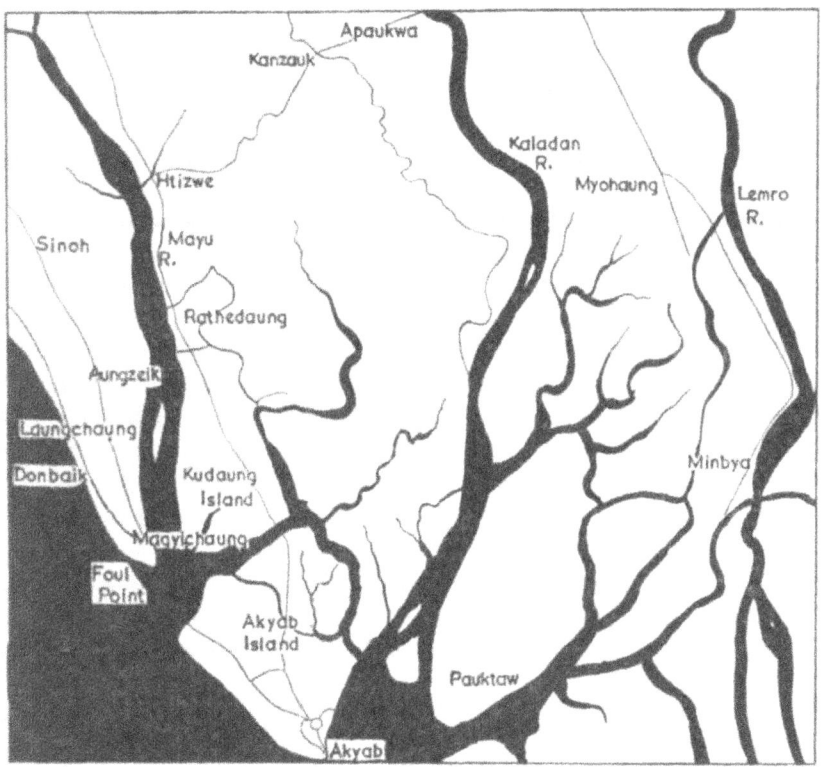

FIG. 17. Arakan. Rathedaung-Akyab

unsuccessfully and was thereafter relieved by Ind. 55th Bde. (of Indian 26th Division) which, on February 1, again attacked the position but without success. On February 3, 123rd Bde. attacked the Japanese positions at Rathedaung to gain a certain success initially but ultimately to fail. On February 17, 55th Bde. once more attacked the Donbaik position but again without success. This brigade was then relieved by Ind. 71st Bde. of Indian 26th Division and withdrew to Ukhia. Field Marshal Viscount Wavell was very unwilling to give up the attempt to clear the Mayu Peninsula and instructed G.O.C. Eastern Army to use 6th Bde. of 2nd Division, which had been waiting to play its part in the final assault upon Akyab Island, to reinforce 71st Bde. in yet another assault upon the Japanese positions at Donbaik. On March 18, 6th Bde. made a very gallant and desperate effort to break through the Japanese defences. Advancing over open ground strewn with the dead of the earlier assaults, the brigade got among and even on top of the 'bunkers' but was then caught in a merciless artillery barrage and forced to retire. All hopes of taking Donbaik were now relinquished.

Meanwhile the Japanese had launched a counter-attack. Two strong columns, one of which had marched from Central Burma and the other which had moved into the Kaladan Valley from Akyab, now threatened 'Tripforce' and 'Soutcol' and obliged them to withdraw to the north. The Japanese then broke into the valley of the Mayu River and struck behind 55th Bde. opposite Rathedaung. The brigade was forced to withdraw up the Mayu Valley to Buthidaung. The Japanese next crossed the Mayu River and fell upon the flank of 47th Bde. and rolled it up. 47th Bde. disintegrated and, losing practically all its equipment, struggled in small parties over the hills. Without pause the Japanese marauding column crossed the Mayu Range through the jungle and scrambling down the precipitous sides of the hills, debouched into the coastal strip there to strike the rear of 6th Bde. as it was withdrawing from its attack upon Donbaik. The brigade headquarters in Indin was overrun and the brigadier and most of his staff killed or captured.

Ind. 4th Bde. of Indian 26th Division, which had been concentrating in the Maungdaw area during these most disturbing events, was used to open up a new L. of C. for 47th Bde. south of Buthidaung. On April 14 Indian 26th Division took over the operational control of troops in Arakan and General Slim of XV Corps assumed general control of troops in the Arakan area and Chittagong. The general situation was serious. The Japanese were intensifying their attacks in all sectors. Ind. 4th Bde. of Indian 26th Division and 6th Bde. of 2nd Division were concentrated south of the Maungdaw–Buthidaung road and 71st Bde. of Indian 26th Division was ordered to move to the north and south of the 'Tunnels' area where this road passed through the two tunnels.

On May 4 the Japanese occupied Point 551 on the Mayu Range, immediately to the south of the Maungdaw–Buthidaung lateral road and dominating it. Ind. 36th Bde. of Indian 26th Division was ordered to dislodge them but was unable to do so. On the following day the Japanese cut the road so that Buthidaung had to be evacuated hurriedly and much transport east of the cut was lost. 23rd Bde. of 70th Division, which had reached Bawli Bazar on May 7 passed under command of Indian 26th Division and was assigned the task of protecting the left flank of the divisional L. of C. between the Maungdaw–Buthidaung road and Dohazari. All troops east of the Mayu Range were ordered to cross to the west. By May 8 they had done so by way of the Ngakyedauk Pass, south of Bawli Bazar.

Field Marshal Viscount Wavell now issued instructions to the effect that positions to cover the Maungdaw–Buthidaung road, the Maungdaw airfield and the mouth of the Naf were to be held during the monsoon season in as great a depth as possible and that offensive action on both sides of the Mayu River was to be undertaken. But General Slim was

THE OFFENSIVE IN THE ARAKAN, 1942

forced to conclude that it was beyond the power of the forces that were available to hold on to the Tunnels area and the western part of the Maungdaw–Buthidaung road and that Maungdaw must be given up, so that a new position in open country could be occupied. The Army Commander reluctantly agreed with this conclusion and so on May 11, Indian 26th Division withdrew from Maungdaw and took up a position that ran from Taung Bazar–Goppe Bazar–Bawli Bazar–Pruma Chaung–Nhila–Mathabhanga. The Japanese did not follow up.

Indian 26th Division (Ind. 4th, 36th, 71st Bdes., 6th Bde. of 2nd Division and 23rd Bde. of 70th Division) was back more or less in the positions from which Indian 14th Division had set out on its southwards advance five months before.

MEDICAL COVER

For the attack on the Japanese positions about Donbaik by 47th Bde. eight to sixteen stretcher-bearers of 2 (Ind.) Bearer Unit were attached to each R.A.P. 'A' Coy. 41 (Ind.) Fd. Amb. provided an A.D.S. for the brigade. During the first week of February this A.D.S. evacuated 173 casualties. When 123rd Bde. attacked Rathedaung 45 (Ind.) Fd. Amb. provided the medical cover and during the engagement dealt with over 200 casualties. When on February 18, 55th Bde. attacked, 41 (Ind.) Fd. Amb. established a car post within a hundred yards of one of the R.A.Ps. This field ambulance evacuated 148 casualties during the battle. Towards the end of the month it was decided to evacuate casualties by way of the Mayu River to the M.D.S. of 45 (Ind.) Fd. Amb. in Thaungdara instead of *via* Atet Nanra to the M.D.S. of 41 (Ind.) Fd. Amb. So, 44 (Ind.) S.S. was sent to Sinoh to stage casualties from 47th Bde. despatching them to Thaungdara by sampan. 'B' Coy. 41 (Ind.) Fd. Amb. had moved to Myinbu and when the staging section established itself in Sinoh the detachment of 41 in Sinoh rejoined its company in Myinbu.

The distribution of the medical units at this time was as follows:

Donbaik Sector

41 (Ind.) Fd. Amb. and 2 (Ind.) Bearer Unit	'A' Coy. Light section A.D.S. in Kodingauk.
	'A' Coy. Heavy section A.D.S. in Indin.
	'B' Coy. A.D.S. in Myinbu.
	44 (Ind.) S.S. in Sinoh.
	Detach. 41 (Ind.) Fd. Amb. Staging Post in Atet Nanra.
	M.D.S. 41 (Ind.) Fd. Amb. in Kyaukpanduywama.

Rathedaung Sector

45 (Ind.) Fd. Amb. and 1 (Ind.) Bearer Unit	'B' Coy. A.D.S. in Kanbyin. Relay Post in Hkanaunggyi. M.D.S. and 6 (Ind.) M.S.U. in Thaungdara.
60 (Ind.) Fd. Amb. Half-company	In Buthidaung.
46 (Ind.) S.S.	In Buthidaung.
15 (Ind.) C.C.S.	In Maungdaw.

On February 28 the M.D.S. of 45 (Ind.) Fd. Amb. and 6 (Ind.) M.S.U. moved from Thaungdara to Htizwe. The A.D.S. of 'B' Coy. moved from Kanbyin to Thaungdara, leaving a light section A.D.S. and one-third section of the Bearer Unit in Kanbyin. On March 4 this light section A.D.S. also moved to Thaungdara. At this time casualties were being evacuated by sampan *via* Lainggwingyi Chaung. On March 9 the A.D.S. in Thaungdara withdrew to Htizwe and the M.D.S. with its attached M.S.U. from Htizwe to Kyaukbyinzeik there to open on a light scale, its heavy equipment being sent back by river to Buthidaung. To assist 45 (Ind.) Fd. Amb. the H.Q. and a half company of 60 (Ind.) Fd. Amb. were sent forward to Buthidaung. The other half company of 'B' Coy. of 60 (Ind.) Fd. Amb. was running a staging section in Zedidaung and 'A' Coy. was in Taung Bazar. Motor ambulances were running on a fair-weather road between Htizwe and Buthidaung which the Sappers had constructed. On March 12 the M.D.S. of 45 (Ind.) Fd. Amb. and 6 (Ind.) M.S.U. moved from Kyaukbyinzeik to Remyet Chaung and a detachment was sent to reinforce the A.D.S. in Htizwe.

On March 9 'B' Coy. of 41 (Ind.) Fd. Amb. moved from Myinbu to Aungzeik, the A.D.S. of 'A' Coy. remaining in Indin. The M.D.S. in Kyaukpanduywama was reinforced with a detachment of 6 Fd. Amb. which was with 6th Bde. of 2nd Division, and 7 (Ind.) M.S.U. on March 11. On the 14th the A.D.S. of 'B' Coy. in Aungzeik was shelled and was therefore moved back to Myinbu. Evacuation was by the Mayu River to the M.D.S. of 45 (Ind.) M.D.S. in Kyaukbyinzeik but because this route was now in full view of the Japanese it was decided to make use of the route *via* Atet Nanra to the M.D.S. of 41 (Ind.) Fd. Amb. in Kyaukpanduywama.

For the last desperate assault upon the Donbaik position 'A' Coy. 41 (Ind.) Fd. Amb., the A.D.S. of 6 Fd. Amb. and 2 (Ind.) Bearer Unit provided the immediate cover. Evacuation was to the M.D.S. of 6 Fd. Amb. in Kyaukpanduywama.

During the course of the confused fighting when the Japanese thrust from the Kaladan Valley across Mayu River and Range into the coastal plain in the region of Indin, all the equipment of 'A' and 'B' Coys. of

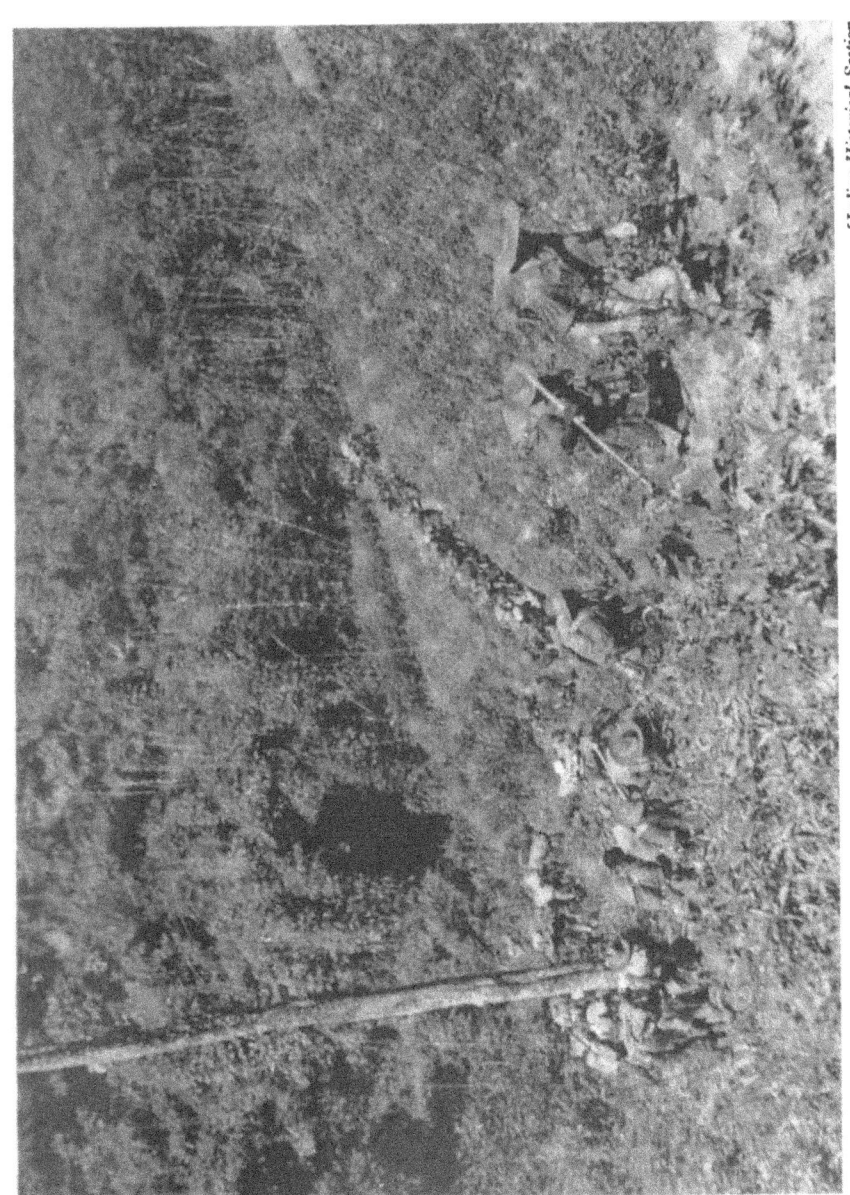

PLATE I. Jungle.

PLATE II. A track newly hewn through virgin country. March 1943.

45 (Ind.) Fd. Amb. was lost. The company that was the 'Soutcol' lost one medical officer, one assistant surgeon and several O.Rs. and its transport animals.

On March 28, H.Q. and 'A' Coy. of 41 (Ind.) Fd. Amb. were withdrawn to Maungdaw. 45 (Ind.) Fd. Amb., being relieved by 60 (Ind.) Fd. Amb., left the divisional area. 60 (Ind.) Fd. Amb. opened its M.D.S. in Kindaung and A.D.Ss. in Kyaukbyinzeik and about a mile north of Taungmaw. 'A' Coy. of this unit remained in Taung Bazar, evacuating its casualties to 46 (Ind.) S.S. in Buthidaung *en route* for the C.C.S. in Maungdaw.

When, at the beginning of April, Indian 26th Division relieved Indian 14th Division, its divisional medical units were:

1 (Ind.) Fd. Amb. serving Ind. 4th and Ind. 55th Bdes.
60 (Ind.) Fd. Amb. serving Ind. 71st Bde.
6 Fd. Amb. with 6th Bde. of 2nd Division.
28 (Ind.) Fd. Hyg. Sec.

Non-divisional medical units associated with the division at this time were:

1 (Ind.) Bearer Company	8 F.T.U.
20 and 35 M.A.Ss.	63 (Ind.) Fd. Amb. (L. of C. unit)
15 (Ind.) C.C.S.	44, 46 and 50 (Ind.) S.Ss.
16 (Ind.) Mob. X-ray Unit	11 and 16 Fd. Amb. Tps. R.I.A.S.C.
6 and 7 (Ind.) M.S.Us.	Hospital 'flat' *Pennar*, sloops and sampans.

During the active patrolling that filled the rest of the month, 1 (Ind.) Fd. Amb. and 6 Fd. Amb. provided cover for Ind. 4th and 6th Bdes. operating on the west side of the Mayu Range. Evacuation from these brigades was by road to 15 (Ind.) C.C.S. in Maungdaw and thence by hospital 'flat' up the Naf River to Tumbru Ghat and from there by M.A.S. to Dohazari. There the casualties were transferred to hospital trains which conveyed them to the hospitals of Eastern Command, staging at Ramu—the M.D.S. of 63 (Ind.) Fd. Amb.—and at Chiringa— 50 (Ind.) S.S.

It had been decided that G.O.C. Indian 14th Division should be given a subordinate commander to control operations east of a line inclusive Buthidaung–Taung Bazar–Panzai Bazar to protect the left flank of the division. 'Mayforce' had taken over control east of the Mayu River. Ind. 55th Bde. of 'Mayforce' in the vicinity of Hparabyin evacuated its casualties by regimental stretcher-bearers, bearer unit personnel and by mule to the sampan-head on the Mayu River whence they were conveyed by launch or sampan to Buthidaung where 46 (Ind.) S.S. provided a staging halt. From Buthidaung evacuation was by road to Maungdaw. Immobiles were held by H.Q. 60 (Ind.) Fd. Amb.

Towards the end of April Ind. 36th Bde. with 48 (Ind.) Fd. Amb. joined the division and 23rd Bde. of 70th Division with 189 Fd. Amb. moved up to Cox's Bazar to form a strategic reserve. 15 (Ind.) C.C.S. moved from Maungdaw to Tumbru Ghat and in its place in North Island, Maungdaw 1 (Ind.) and 6 Fd. Ambs. established a combined M.D.S. to which 7 (Ind.) M.S.U. and 8 F.T.U. were attached. Evacuation to this M.D.S. was by regimental stretcher-bearers, bearer unit personnel, field ambulance troop mules and by ambulance cars working from car posts. From the M.D.S. evacuation to the C.C.S. in Tumbru was by hospital 'flat' *Pennar* with 44 (Ind.) S.S. aboard.

When the Maungdaw–Buthidaung road was cut by the Japanese early in May, 'Mayforce' moved northwards through Letwedet towards Taung Bazar. Before leaving Letwedet as many casualties as possible were evacuated through the Ngakyedauk Pass as far as Wabyin where 48 (Ind.) Fd. Amb. with 6 (Ind.) M.S.U. had established a light M.D.S. 60 (Ind.) Fd. Amb. moved with 'Mayforce' and opened its M.D.S. in Goppe Bazar. Evacuation therefrom was by bearer unit personnel and mules over the Goppe Pass as far as Bawli Bazar South.

When the division moved back into the 'monsoon' line the brigade group on the right—from Nhila to Mathabhanga, north of Nhila, on the coast—was served by 46 (Ind.) Fd. Amb. with its H.Q. and one company in Tumbru where its M.D.S. was established and its A.D.S. in Nhila. The brigade group on the left—Pruma Chaung to Taung Bazar—was covered by 48 (Ind.) Fd. Amb. with its M.D.S. on the north bank of the chaung and its A.D.S. on the south bank and with detachments in Goppe Bazar and Taung Bazar.

When the position had become stabilised the following medical arrangements came into force within the division:

1 (Ind.) Fd. Amb.	M.D.S. in North Island, Maungdaw.
	One company with Ind. 4th Bde.
	One company with Ind. 71st Bde.
6 Fd. Amb.	One company with 6th Bde.
	The rest of the unit looking after British casualties passing through the M.D.S. of 1 (Ind.) Fd. Amb.
48 (Ind.) Fd. Amb.	M.D.S. at the sampan-head in the vicinity of Ponnazeik.
	The two companies with Ind. 36th Bde.
46 (Ind.) Fd. Amb.	M.D.S. near the sampan-head in the Bawli Bazar area.
	The two companies concerned with the evacuation of casualties from Goppe Bazar to Bawli Bazar by means of stretcher-bearers and the riding mules of 11 Fd. Amb. Tp.

THE OFFENSIVE IN THE ARAKAN, 1942

189 Fd. Amb.	One company working along with H.Q. 46 (Ind.) Fd. Amb. looking after British casualties in the area held by 23rd Bde. around Bawli Bazar.
60 (Ind.) Fd. Amb.	M.D.S. in Goppe Bazar. The two companies concerned with the evacuation of casualties from Taung Bazar to Goppe Bazar by means of stretcher-bearers and sampans.
6 (Ind.) M.S.U.	With H.Q. 46 (Ind.) Fd. Amb. forming an advanced operating centre.
7 (Ind.) M.S.U.	With the M.D.S. of 1 (Ind.) Fd. Amb. North Island.
8 F.T.U.	With the M.D.S. in North Island.
27 (Ind.) Fd. Hyg. Sec.	In the area of Rumkhapalong.
18 (Ind.) A.M.U.	In Ukhia.
1 (Ind.) Bearer Unit	In North Island.
11 Fd. Amb. Tp.	With 46 (Ind.) Fd. Amb.
35 M.A.S.	Responsible for evacuation by road, when this was feasible, between Bawli and Tumbru.

Hospital 'flats', *Pennar* and *Folkestone*, and creek steamers, plied between Maungdaw and Tumbru Ghat.

Evacuation

Ind. 4th and 6th Bdes.	Pre-monsoon. By ambulance car to the M.D.S. in North Island. Monsoon. By stretcher-bearer or mule to car post in Kanyindan and thence by ambulance car to the M.D.S.
Ind. 55th and Ind. 71st Bdes.	Pre-monsoon. By ambulance car to the M.D.S. Monsoon. By ambulance car to the M.D.S.
Ind. 36th Bde.	Pre-monsoon. By ambulance car to the M.D.S. Monsoon. By stretcher-bearer to sampan-head in the vicinity of Ponnazeik and thence by sampan to the M.D.S.
23rd Bde.	From Taung Bazar to Goppe Bazar by sampan and thence by S.B. and mule to Bawli Bazar.
From M.D.S. to C.C.S.	By hospital 'flat' or creek steamer from North Island, Maungdaw to Tumbru Ghat.
From Bawli Bazar to Tumbru	Pre-monsoon. By ambulance car. Monsoon. By stretcher-bearer to sampan-head at Bawli Bazar and thence by sampan to Tumbru.

During May, 23rd Bde. was relieved by 14th Bde., also of 70th Division, in Cox's Bazar, and six weeks later this brigade in its turn was relieved by Ind. 36th Bde., with 48 (Ind.) Fd. Amb. of Indian 26th Division. Early in June, 72 I.G.H. (600 beds), 36 (Ind.) Mob. Fd. Lab. and 15 (Ind.) Mob. X-ray Unit, together with a sub-depot of 21 (Ind.) Depot of Medical Stores, moved into Cox's Bazar to be accommodated in Khurushkul on the north bank of the River Baghkhali.

On August 1, H.Q. 354 L. of C. Sub-area assumed command of all medical units as far south as Tumbru Ghat inclusive. About this time Indian 26th Division organised a jungle warfare school for its medical officers, an enterprise that attracted much favourable comment. In September 1943 this division was relieved by Indian 7th Division and moved back to Chittagong and Maynamati.

During this period of active service in Arakan much was learnt by the divisional medical services, much that set the pattern of medical policy for the future. The following were the main lessons that were learnt and remembered:

(i) Medical organisation must be adapted to the requirements of casualties and not *vice versa*.

(ii) In a terrain that shows great variation, the location of medical units must be considered in terms of the time taken to get the casualty back and not in terms of distance.

(iii) In conditions such as obtained in Arakan at this time all medical tactical considerations must be based on I.W.T. and A.T. and not on M.T.

(iv) In such conditions it is imperative to cut down the amount of equipment to be carried to the absolute minimum. Under jungle conditions there is no place for more than the minimum of tentage, service stretchers and volatile anaesthetics.

(v) The employment of bearer unit personnel, field ambulance troops, sampans, launches and creek steamers for evacuation proved to be eminently satisfactory.

(vi) The attachment of mobile surgical units to the M.D.S. was amply justified.

(vii) The appointment of a divisional resuscitation officer who toured all the medical units did much to ensure the maintenance of stocks of transfusion materials.

(viii) The issue to all fighting patrols of instructions concerning diet, anti-malaria precautions and the treatment and evacuation of casualties proved to be very successful.

(ix) The attachment of a detachment of the field hygiene section to each brigade proved to be very successful.

(x) It was demonstrated that the health of the troops could be maintained at a high level even in the conditions that existed by the observance of strict anti-malaria unit discipline, by the routine drill of taking suppressive mepacrine daily together with intensive anti-adult (mosquito) spraying measures. Heat stroke and heat exhaustion did not constitute problems of any magnitude.

(xi) It was amply demonstrated also that by the cultivation of a high standard of 'water discipline' and by taking all possible steps to ensure that pure drinking water was available to the troops, it was possible, even in such circumstances, to hold the water-borne diseases in check.

MEDICAL ARRANGEMENTS

In February 1942, when Indian 14th Division moved from Ranchi into Eastern Bengal the only military hospitals in the area were a C.M.H. of 50 beds in Chittagong, a detention hospital in Patenga, an I.M.H. in Comilla and another in Dacca, each of about 20 beds. No arrangements had been made for evacuation from Indian 14th Division into these and A.D.M.S. 14th Division had to discover for himself what system of evacuation out of the divisional area could best be adopted. On March 22, 15 (Ind.) C.C.S. was warned to be ready to move to Comilla. The I.M.H. there had been expanded to 100 beds and additional buildings had been taken over to permit a further expansion up to 300 beds. Requests for metre gauge ambulance coaches and for an advanced depot of medical stores had been submitted to higher authority.

In April the decision was reached to withdraw from Chittagong should the Japanese invade East Bengal. The C.M.H. in Chittagong and the detention hospital in Patenga were closed down and a small hospital of 16 beds, 6 British and 10 Indian, in Chittagong with the medical officer i/c R.A.F. personnel in the area, one I.M.S. officer and a subedar of the Tripura State Medical Service, replaced them. Evacuation from this hospital was by rail to Calcutta until 15 (Ind.) C.C.S. had established itself in Comilla. Cases in need of immediate surgical intervention were transferred to the civil hospital in Chittagong. Surplus stores of this civil hospital were sent back to Comilla. 15 (Ind.) C.C.S. reached Comilla on April 18 and absorbed the I.M.H. and the staff and stores sent to Comilla from Chittagong. As there was no scheme for the evacuation of casualties from Comilla, the C.C.S. applied for additional equipment and the construction of *basha* wards to accommodate an additional 300 patients was begun. These *bashas* were neat-looking buildings, well ventilated and cool but they had bamboo floors, walls and roofs which creaked ceaselessly and swayed in the wind. In the monsoon everything in them became damp or sodden. By the middle of May the C.C.S. was grossly overcrowded with afebrile cases of malaria. Since all attempts to obtain an Indian convalescent depot had been entirely fruitless, a rest camp was improvised in Comilla. Such patients as were fit to travel in them were despatched by ordinary passenger trains to Calcutta, to Lucknow, to Dinapore on the Ganges, even to Lebong near Darjeeling. Eventually arrangements were made for the evacuation of patients *via* Daudkandi, on the Meghna, south-east of Dacca, to Dinapore and Sirajganj by river steamer.

In September the C.C.S. was warned to be prepared to move forward as an I.G.H. was being sent to Comilla. On October 1 a light section of the C.C.S. moved into the railway buildings in Chittagong. The C.C.S. was now functioning as a general hospital in duplicate. By the end of November both portions of it were overcrowded; in Comilla there were about 1,000 patients, in Chittagong about 300. The staff of the unit had become depleted through sickness and no reinforcements had reached it. On December 17 the light section in Chittagong was relieved by 68 I.G.H. and the main body in Comilla by 92 I.G.H. on the 21st. The C.C.S., after a brief rest, moved across the Bengal–Arakan border to open in Maungdaw with 540 beds and to continue to function as a general hospital. It was joined by a British and an Indian dental unit and by 16 (Ind.) Mob. X-ray Unit. Three metre gauge ambulance coaches had now become available for evacuation between Chittagong and Comilla. One medical officer and four B.O.Rs. were sent to staff these on August 8.

In January 1943 there were in Eastern Army Area 316,000 Indian and 111,200 British troops. For them the authorised scale of hospital beds was:

	Indian Troops per cent.	British Troops per cent.
Sick		
All troops in IV Corps Area	10	10
,, ,, in Indian 14th Division Area	4	6
Indian State labour units in IV Corps Area	8	
,, ,, ,, ,, in 14th Div. Area	3	
Air Casualties. All Troops	0·5	0·5
Battle Casualties		
(Calculated on 26,000 Indian and 4,000 British troops in IV Corps Area and 13,000 Indian and 2,000 British troops in Indian 14th Division area)	4	4
Number of beds required		
Indian		25,298
British		8,244
Number when 70th Division became added to Eastern Army		
Indian		25,298
British		8,600

	Indian	British
Total number of beds available	10,333	4,665
Authorised expansions	1,115	491
Provisional arrangements made for	4,911	1,900
	16,359	7,056
Deficiencies	14,965	3,935
Expected deficiencies at the end of 1943	8,931	1,544

Owing to the continuing shortages in respect of personnel, the garrison and field hospitals in Eastern Army Area could not be expanded and so it became necessary to evacuate from the area considerable numbers of casualties who normally would have been retained therein. In April 1943 arrangements were made for the provision of 2,800 beds for Indian troops in Lucknow and for another 2,600 beds in the hospitals then forming in Bareilly and Moradabad.

Following the withdrawal to the Taung Bazar–Mathabhanga line on May 10 and when the situation had become stabilised, 8 (Ind.) and 9 (Br.) C.C.Ss. were moved to Dhoapalong where in addition to dealing with the ordinary run of medical and surgical cases they took over from 63 (Ind.) Fd. Amb. a malaria forward treatment centre. Evacuation was now as follows:

Nawapara to Cox's Bazar by road *via* Ramu and Rumkhapalong (the Rumkhapalong link road became unusuable when the rains began).

Cox's Bazar to Chittagong by steamer or by road *via* Ramu to Dohazari and thence by rail to Chittagong. The steamer could take 100 patients and was available four days a week. In Cox's Bazar there were 1,000 beds, 600 in 72 I.G.H., 200 in 8 (Ind.) C.C.S. and 200 in 9 C.C.S. *Ex* Chittagong by hospital ship to Calcutta or by rail to Comilla and Dacca. The hospital ship took away 1,250 patients every tenth day. Fifty patients were sent away by train each day. There were 1,600 beds in Chittagong, 700 in 68 I.G.H., 500 in 56 I.G.H. and 400 in the advanced malaria treatment centre.

Since no aircraft were available for evacuation purposes it was inevitable that there should be much that was unsatisfactory about evacuation. In most parts of the region there were no roads and where there were roads these were, with very few exceptions, unmetalled. Evacuation by river, though slow, was of all methods the most comfortable but the number of suitable vessels was very small indeed in relation to the number of those to be carried. A small fleet of Akyab sloops was built up and as many sampans as possible collected. The sloops were later replaced by three creek steamers and later still a number of large metal 'flats' was made available, each of them capable of carrying

200 men. The most unsatisfactory feature of these 'flats' was that they got so very hot in the sun.

For 47th Bde. when it was moving down the coastal strip on the west, evacuation by water transport was always practicable. Casualties were 'nested' by large and small river craft at the head of the Naf Estuary and from there they were taken by ambulance car to the rear, in the later stages of the operation to the medical installations in Dhoapalong.

For 123rd Bde. moving on the east of the Mayu River the only possible method of evacuation was by hand-carriage or mule over the Goppe Pass and from the foot of this by ambulance car to the rear.

For 'Tripforce' and 'Soutcol' evacuation had to be by local river craft on the Kaladan River when this was possible. But for the most part the casualties had to be hand-carried. The local Mugs were expert in making bamboo stretchers and in carrying them over long distances. At Kyauktaw and Apaukwa two small airstrips were constructed and from these two Lysander aircraft evacuated a number of casualties to Cox's Bazar before the Japanese drove the columns back. From Kyauktaw, by mule, to Taung Bazar took four days and from Taung Bazar to the foot of the Goppe Pass another two days.

The time taken to get a casualty back to a C.C.S. or hospital was such that it was necessary to form a chain of staging units along the route of evacuation. Such a unit might be a staging section, a field ambulance or even a hospital. It was also necessary to hold as many cases as possible in the forward hospitals. Many a casualty ultimately found himself in a hospital in the far north or in the far south of India, having spent short periods of time in four or more staging units, having travelled in five or more different forms of transport and having covered as many as 1,000 miles in two to four weeks on the way. Parts of this journey for many must have been a hideous nightmare of suffering.

Losses in killed, wounded and missing in these operations were about 2,500. But the battle casualties were greatly over-topped by those caused by disease, particularly by malaria.

'The medical situation continued to require constant enlargement of the hospitals in the operational area and strained India's inadequate resources to the utmost. Malaria remained the chief problem. During the Arakan operations casualties from malaria were extremely heavy and the sick rate in Assam was also high. Weekly admissions to hospital in Eastern Command reached 10,000 in June (1943), of which over half were due to malaria'. Field Marshal Viscount Wavell's *Despatch*. London Gazette Supplement. 20th April, 1948.

In the Arakan operations of 1942–43 the Army Medical Services encountered problems of great magnitude and complexity; the means of solving them or for reducing their military importance were not yet readily available. But much was observed and much was learnt. In

THE OFFENSIVE IN THE ARAKAN, 1942

retrospect it is possible to recognise in what was done at this time the beginnings of the systems of disease prevention that later in this campaign were to be acknowledged as important contributions to victory.

THE HEALTH OF THE TROOPS

The sick-rate at its worst was no less than 8 per 1,000 per day (2,900 per 1,000 per annum) with the peak of 15 per 1,000 per day (5,475 per 1,000 per annum). Only by strong reinforcement could the formations retain their efficiency as instruments of war.

In Indian 14th Division during the period April–December 1942 the total admissions to 15 (Ind.) C.C.S. on account of malaria were about 7,500 in a force whose average strength during the period was around 15,000.

TABLE 2

Indian 14th Division. Admissions to 15 (Ind.) C.C.S. on account of Malaria. April–December 1942

Month	Br. Officers	B.O.Rs.	I.O.Rs. and Non-combatants
April	1	1	28
May	3	63	433
June	7	76	541
July	12	143	436
August	2	93	450
September	7	86	402
October	10	130	678
November	33	556	1,931
December	13	268	1,114
	88	1,416	6,013

Total 7,517

The treatment of these cases was not always satisfactory. All too frequently the patient had to be evacuated solely for the reason that all who could be moved out of the divisional area were so moved in order to release beds; treatment tended to be interrupted therefore. At times there was a local shortage of anti-malarial drugs. Not all the medical officers were familiar with the technique of administering intravenous quinine.

The control of the mosquito was impossible at this time. During the monsoon season the greater part of the countryside was under water. An anti-malaria unit was with the division but it could not possibly cope with the conditions that existed. The breeding of the mosquito had to be accepted as something beyond the control of the division and all attempts to reduce the mosquito population had to be focused upon the destruction of the adult insect by pyrethrum spray and upon measures of self-protection on the part of the troops by the use of repellent creams and veils. Spraying could not be very effective since no degree of concentration could be attained in the typical bamboo hut. The pumps that were then available were far from efficient. The repellent cream was greasy and unpleasant in the humid heat of Arakan and was universally unpopular.

The creation of the malaria forward treatment unit is an excellent example of the manner in which an urgent and serious problem caused by the exceptionally high incidence of a particular disease resulting in a very considerable man-power loss is met by the provision of a new medical unit specially designed to cope with it. The creation of the venereal diseases treatment centre or unit is another. In the early summer of 1943 malaria was so rife that the evacuation of malaria cases into the wide spaces of India meant that the fighting formations were losing trained and experienced men for as long as three to six months on account of an attack of this disease. It came to be recognised that there was an urgent need for some kind of medical unit in the forward area that could hold and treat these cases. So, all the hospitals in the forward area were instructed to split off one, two or even three sections to form special malaria sections, these to be housed separately in *bashas* and to be equipped to feed and to hold malaria patients during their convalescence. The time away from the unit was, in this way, reduced to three to five weeks. These sections soon claimed official recognition and so evolved into the malaria forward treatment units which did such truly magnificent work in preventing man-power loss and in maintaining the fighting efficiency of the formations.

Dysentery in its incidence never assumed the proportions of a problem. The maximum number of admissions in one week during these nine months was twelve.

One fatal case of enteric occurred in an officer who had evaded inoculation.

An outbreak of cholera in Bawli Bazar occurred in December. Undoubtedly it spread to the troops from the refugees. There were 20 cases among the troops with 15 deaths. Only two of the fatal cases had documentary evidence of having been inoculated.

Surprisingly enough, when the sparseness of the population in Arakan is considered, the incidence of venereal diseases was high. The C.C.S. was obliged to reserve some 70 beds for these cases. In one week no less than 30 cases were admitted. The techniques of treatment then in vogue were relatively inefficient when contrasted with those that were rapidly evolving elsewhere, as were also the techniques of diagnosis.

Skin diseases here, as everywhere else and at all times, ranked high in the list of the causes of man-power wastage. Boils and fungus infections of the feet were exceedingly prevalent. *Tinea pedis* was quite a problem. Among British personnel some 65–70 per cent. were affected. Routine foot inspection, the provision of spare pairs of socks and of water for washing did much to keep this serious nuisance in check.

In the field of hygiene the standards attained in the division were on the whole surprisingly good. The standard latrine was the deep trench with fly-proof cover but this could not be constructed in the water-logged ground. Attempts were made to construct this type of latrine on ground that had been raised artificially but the fly larvae climbed up the bamboo revetment and the maggots had to be destroyed by the periodic burning of rags soaked in paraffin. No satisfactory type of fly-trap was discovered. One difficulty of peculiar interest presented itself. The I.O.R. objected to handling latrine lid covers and so these were almost invariably left behind when the unit moved on.

No systematic arrangements for ablution seem to have been made. There was an over-abundance of water everywhere and so no trouble developed.

There occurred the apparently inevitable misunderstanding concerning the function of the field hygiene section. All too frequently unit commanders assumed that the personnel of the section were hewers of wood and drawers of water and expected them to do the jobs that required to be done. The paucity of well-trained and thoroughly competent N.C.Os. in these sections certainly contributed largely to this misunderstanding.

Medical supplies were the cause of anxiety on occasion. The poor, overloaded lines of communication were the cause of much delay in the delivery of supplies to the forward units. The sulpha drugs had to be used very sparingly and sulphaguanidine had not yet reached this front.

It has to be remembered that a large proportion of the members of the Army Medical Services with Indian 14th Division were inexperienced and were learning the ways in which their knowledge and skill could best be exercised in the field.

APPENDIX VII

EASTERN ARMY. ORDER OF BATTLE. JANUARY 1943
(*Abbreviated*)

Indian 14th Division
  Ind. 47th Bde.
    1st Innisks.
    1/7th Rajput
    5/8th Punjab

Ind. 55th Bde.
   2/1st Punjab
   8/6th Raj.Rif.
   1/17th Dogra.

Ind. 88th Bde. (Comilla–Chittagong area)
   5/9th Jat.
   14/13th F.F.Rif.
   1/16th Punjab

Ind. 123rd Bde.
   10th L.F.
   8/10th Baluch
   1/15th Punjab

Indian 26th Division

Ind. 4th Bde.
   6/11th Sikh
   8/8th Punjab
   3/9th G.R.

Ind. 36th Bde.
   1st N. Staffs.
   8/13th F.F.Rif.
   5/16th Punjab

Ind. 71st Bde.
   1st Lincolns
   7/15th Punjab
   9/15th Punjab

6th Bde. of 2nd Division
   1st R.S.
   1st R.W.F.
   1st R. Berks.
   2nd D.L.I.

23rd Bde. of 70th Division
   1st Essex
   2nd D.W.R.
   4th Border

IV Corps

Indian 17th Lt. Division

Ind. 48th Bde.
   1/4th G.R.
   2/5th R.G.R.
   1/7th G.R.

Ind. 63rd Bde.
  1st Glosters
  1/3rd G.R.
  1/10th G.R.

Divisional troops

Infantry
  1st W. Yorks
  4/12th F.F.R.
  7/10th Baluch

Indian 23rd Division

Ind. 1st Bde.
  1st Seaforth
  1st Assam Regt.
  1st Patiala Inf.

Ind. 37th Bde.
  3/3rd G.R.
  3/5th R.G.R.
  3/10th G.R.

Ind. 49th Bde.
  4/5th Mahratta L.I.
  5/6th Raj.Rif.
  6/5th Mahratta L.I.

Ind. 77th Bde. (Independent)
  13th Kings
  3/2nd G.R.
  2nd Burif.

APPENDIX VIII

INDIAN 26TH DIVISION. MEDICAL ORDER OF BATTLE. APRIL 1943

Divisional Units
  1 (Ind.) Fd. Amb.
  60 (Ind.) Fd. Amb.
  6 Fd. Amb. (6th Bde. of 2nd Division)
  27 (Ind.) Fd. Hyg. Sec.
  48 (Ind.) Fd. Amb., with Ind. 36th Bde. joined in May

Non-divisional Units

    15 (Ind.) C.C.S.
    6 and 7 (Ind.) M.S.Us.
    16 (Ind.) Mob. X-ray Unit
    63 (Ind.) Fd. Amb. (L. of C.)
    44, 46 and 50 (Ind.) S.S. (Comb.)
    11 and 16 (Ind.) Fd. Amb. Tps. R.I.A.S.C.
    20 and 35 M.A.Ss.
    28 (Ind.) Fd. Hyg. Sec.
    1 (Ind.) Bearer Coy.
    Hospital 'Flat' *Pennar*; sloops and sampans
    18 and 23 (Ind.) A.M.Us.
    8 F.T.U.

APPENDIX IX

INDIAN 14TH DIVISION. MEDICAL ORDER OF BATTLE. APRIL 1943

Divisional Units

    41, 45 and 60 (Ind.) Fd. Ambs.
    6 Fd. Amb. (6th Bde. of 2nd Division)
    28 (Ind.) Fd. Hyg. Sec.

Non-divisional Army and G.H.Q. Units

    15 (Ind.) C.C.S.
    6 and 7 (Ind.) M.S.Us.
    8 F.T.U.
    16 (Ind.) Mob. X-ray Unit
    44, 46 and 50 (Ind.) S.Ss.
    18 and 23 (Ind.) A.M.Us.
    74 I.G.H. 5 secs.
    20 and 35 M.A.Ss. less one sub-sec. of 35
    63 (Ind.) Fd. Amb.
    1 and 2 (Ind.) Bearer Coys.
    Hospital ships, sampans.

CHAPTER 5
THE FIRST 'CHINDIT' EXPEDITION. FEBRUARY 1943

IT HAD been decided in October 1942 between General Wavell, as he was then, and Marshal Chiang Kai-shek that there should be launched as soon as possible a seaborne expedition against Lower Burma and an advance by land forces into Upper Burma. An account of the much modified offensive in Arakan has been given. The land advance it was agreed, would take the form of (i) an advance by the Chinese Corps (22nd and 38th Divisions) then being assembled in the area of Ramgarh in Bihar, from Ledo to Myitkyina, (ii) a complementary advance by a Chinese force from Yunnan to link up with the Chinese Corps and (iii) an advance by IV Corps of Eastern Army from Manipur towards Mandalay. In December General Wavell discussed the details of this operation with General Stilwell who was very anxious, in spite of all the administrative difficulties that were being encountered, to secure as much of northern Burma as possible in order to provide cover for the construction of a road by U.S. engineers from Ledo through Myitkyina to Paoshan where it would join up with the old 'Burma Road'. It was agreed that D-day should be March 1, if the administrative situation permitted.

On IV Corps' front Indian 23rd Division had advanced two brigades into the Tamu area and Indian 17th Division had moved forward towards the Chin Hills down a new road that was being constructed in the direction of Tiddim. There was much active patrolling in the Kabaw Valley and also in the valley of the Chindwin and Kachin Levies, based on Sumprabum, to the north of Myitkyina, were harassing such Japanese troops as were in this area.

Early in 1942, during the early stages of the retreat from Burma, General Wavell had asked for the services of Lieut.-Colonel Wingate, an artillery officer, who had served under him in Palestine and East Africa and who had led patriot forces successfully into Abyssinia, intending to employ him in organising similar guerilla activities in Burma. But by the time Colonel Wingate reached India *en route* for Burma the military situation in Burma was such as to make the initiation of such activities pointless. However, Colonel Wingate visited the Bush Warfare School in Maymyo and elaborated his ideas concerning the type of guerilla operations that would be suitable to the circumstances and conditions in Burma. He then placed before General Wavell a proposal to train a brigade for long range penetration behind the Japanese lines. This proposal met with approval and Indian 77th Brigade was formed and placed under Brigadier Wingate. The brigade came to consist of 13th The King's Regiment (Liverpool); 3/2nd Gurkha Rifles; 142nd Commando Company (composed of volunteers from infantry battalions, commandos, and a few regular sappers and intended to provide each of the columns with a squad of saboteurs); eight R.A.F. sections (to maintain wireless contact with Agartala and to organise the supply drops); 2nd Burma Rifles, mainly Kachins and Karens, the reconnaissance unit of the L.R.P. Gp.; a mule transport company and later a bullock transport company. It is to be noted that these were not specially selected units; they were such as happened to be available at the time. The brigade began its training in July 1942 in the neighbourhood of Saugor in the Central Provinces (now Madhya Pradesh).

General Wavell intended that this brigade should penetrate into Central Burma when the two operations to which reference has been made were launched. When it was reluctantly decided that the resources available were such as to preclude anything more than a limited advance into Upper Burma, the question arose as to whether 77th Bde. should be used at all during the winter of 1942–43. However, in order to give the greatest possible support to the Chinese advance it was decided that the brigade should be used in Upper Burma to cut the Japanese lines of communication to Myitkyina, Bhamo and Lashio. The brigade thereupon entrained for Manipur Road (Dimapur) whence it marched the 133 miles to Imphal. As the plan involved the supply of the brigade by air, an air-base was constructed at Agartala, north of Comilla where three months' supplies of every kind for the brigade were accumulated.

Then it was learnt that the Chinese in Yunnan were not to advance into Burma and so once more it seemed that no useful purpose could be served by the proposed incursion by 77th Bde. General Wavell discussed the situation with Brigadier Wingate and finally it was decided that the operation should be undertaken. The directions given to Brigadier Wingate were:

(i) to enter Burma through the front held by IV Corps;
(ii) to cut the main north-south railway between Mandalay and Myitkyina;
(iii) to harass the Japanese in the Shwebo area; and
(iv) if circumstances were favourable, to cross the Irrawaddy and cut the railway between Maymyo and Lashio.

The men of Indian 77th Bde. 'the Chindits' (from Chinthe, the brave one, the leogryph, the griffon-like creature that guards the entrance to a Buddhist temple) were organised into a number of columns, each 400 strong, large enough to deliver effective blows yet small enough to

THE FIRST 'CHINDIT' EXPEDITION

elude the enemy. Each column consisted of an infantry company and a support group from which battle groups could be formed, together with signals, medical, sabotage, reconnaissance and R.A.F. sections. Each column had 15 horses and 100 mules to carry its equipment, weapons, ammunition, wireless set and the supplies that were picked up at the dropping points. A column was sub-divided into a number of 'dispersal groups', each 40 strong. If a column encountered opposition too strong to be overcome, it fragmented into dispersal groups and these separated to make their own ways to a pre-arranged assembly point. If a dispersal group ran into serious trouble it fragmented into parties of twos and threes which separated and made their ways to a pre-arranged rendezvous.

The Chindits were to set out with everything they needed either on their persons or on pack-animals. One blanket and one ground-sheet per man were carried on the mules. Each man was to carry about 70 lbs. on his person. Replenishment was to be by air-drop and by local purchase. Having no vulnerable land-link with their base they were free to move in any direction at any time for they were not road-bound by their transport. Road-blocks could not trouble them. The columns were connected with each other and the brigade with base by a wireless net.

Though it was hoped that the Chindits would disrupt the military activities of the Japanese it was recognised that the major benefits that would stem from the expedition would be the fruits of experience in this long range penetration work, the raising of the morale of the troops who were preparing to meet the Japanese in battle, the proof that the Britisher, the Indian, Gurkha and the Kachin were as good jungle fighters as the Japanese and the encouragement given to the Kachins and others by the presence of the Chindits to play their parts in the ejection of the Japanese from Burma.

On February 8, 1943, the brigade, in seven columns, each self-contained with pack transport, with machine-guns and mortars but with no artillery, set off from Imphal on an adventure that was expected to last about three months. The immediate problem was that of getting 3,000 men and about 1,000 animals over the Chindwin and then across some 150 miles of Japanese-occupied territory without interception. To attract the attention of the Japanese away from the main body of the Chindits, two of the Gurkha columns were sent to cross the river at Auktaung, 35 miles south of Tonhe and Indian 23rd Division staged a simulation of an attack upon Kalewa. These two columns were to cross the river some time before the main body of the brigade and after moving to the south to force the Japanese to notice them, they were then to move quickly to the east, cross the Irrawaddy at Tagaung, south of Katha, and make their way to the mountainous area around

Mong Mit, east of Lashio, and there await the coming of the rest of the brigade which was to cross the Chindwin near Tonhe, between Sittaung and Homalin.

One of the Gurkha diversionary columns whose incursions were made obvious by the day-time dropping of supplies and by undisguised movement, was ambushed and forced to disperse. Most of the men eventually recrossed the Chindwin; some joined up with the other column which reached and crossed the Irrawaddy at Tagaung according to plan on March 10. The columns of the main body crossed the Chindwin unmolested and reached the railway which was duly cut in many places. The widely separated columns then crossed the Irrawaddy between March 9 and 18. But difficulties then began to multiply. The weather was very hot; water was hard to find; the Japanese were much more numerous than had been expected so that it was by no means easy to arrange for the dropping of supplies; many of the dropped supplies could not be collected; rations were short and the incidence of sickness was mounting among the troops and also among the pack animals (anthrax?). Eventually Brigadier Wingate was compelled to agree that it had become necessary to be content with what had been accomplished and to return to India.

Turning about the Chindits attempted to cross the Irrawaddy at Inywa, south of Katha, but were prevented doing so by the Japanese. Certain of the columns promptly broke up into dispersal groups which crossed the river at widely separated points and headed for the Indo-Burma frontier. Most of the groups reached the Chindwin in the vicinity of Sittaung, east of Tamu; one column crossed the river as far north as Tamanthi and proceeded to Kohima; one marched due north to reach Fort Hertz while another trekked due east to reach Paoshan whence it was flown to India by the U.S.A.A.F. The bulk of those who got back reached India during the first week in June, having spent four months in Japanese occupied territory and having marched about 1,000 miles.

Of the 3,000 who set out about 2,182 returned. Of those who did not, some 400 were battle casualties, about the same number fell into Japanese hands and about 100 of the Burma Rifles were permitted to stay behind in order to protect their families. The transport animals were either lost through enemy action or else were eaten. Much equipment and considerable quantities of stores were destroyed during the return journey.

The enterprise had no strategic value. It is to be looked upon as an experiment designed to test Brigadier Wingate's hypothesis, an expensive experiment maybe but one that was held to be necessary. Certainly much that was learnt from it was incorporated into the plans and tactics of subsequent and more ambitious undertakings of the same kind. It demonstrated that a force of this kind could penetrate as far as it liked into Japanese-held territory and that it could be supplied solely by air-drop.

MEDICAL ASPECTS

Before leaving Imphal it was explained to every officer and man by Brigadier Wingate personally that if for any reason anyone could not move with the column at the pace that tactical considerations imposed on the brigade, he would be left behind in a village or transported to an emergency airstrip, if such could be made available. Everything possible would be done to ensure the provision of all available care. The seriously wounded would be put in charge of an officer specially detailed for this purpose at the tail of the column. During the march they would be left in a village previously selected by the commander of the column. A printed proclamation would be given to the villagers looking after such casualties telling them that if they took care of these they would be rewarded and that if they did not they would be punished and their villages destroyed by the air force.

There was one instance of evacuation by air during this expedition. A Dakota transport aircraft was sent to pick up 17 casualties from one of the columns near Bhamo. The clearing in a teak forest was only 800 yards long; nevertheless the aircraft landed and got away again safely. Save for this there was no air evacuation. Such wounded and sick as could not keep up with the column were carried forward and left in villages, some of them being recovered when Burma was re-occupied. Since this had to be the accepted policy, the position of the medical officer in this brigade came to be an unusual one. The official attitude to sickness in the brigade was likewise unusual; it had to be because of the strangeness of the circumstances that characterised the expedition.

> 'Another great difficulty (encountered during training) was the tendency of troops to go sick. For the slightest ache or pain or abrasion troops went on sick parade. 'Hypochondria is a prevailing malady of Englishmen and civilised nations. Everybody is taught to be doctor-minded' said Wingate in a talk to the troops. 'This may be all right in normal civil life, where ample medical facilities are available, but when men are about to step into the jungle for an unknown period of time, they have to become used to diagnosing their own complaints and as far as possible curing themselves.
>
> 'Within three weeks of the commencement of training 30 per cent. of the troops were either in hospital or trying to get there. A month later the figures had gone up to 70 per cent. The time had come to put a stop to this. Wingate came to the conclusion that most of the troubles were more imaginary than real and in any case most of the ailments were insufficient to put a man out of action. Men were warned that if they went sick on the

expedition it would be just too bad. The lives of the rest could not be jeopardised by waiting for the stragglers. They had to be toughened. Attending sick parade without good cause was made a punishable offence. Platoon and column commanders were instructed sufficiently to treat all normal slight sicknesses. The doctors only attended really ill or seriously injured patients. By the end of the training period sick parades had been reduced from around 70 per cent. to less than 3 per cent. Men learned the value of quinine and atebrin for malaria, sulfaguanidine for dysentery and the other sulfa drugs for all wounds liable to infection.'*

This is the extreme form of the teaching of what came to be known during the war years as the 'tough school'. Among army officers there were those who held the view that the regimental medical officer was a source of great help; there were others who looked upon him as an impediment to the achievement of efficiency and a godsend to the malingerer. According to the first the morale of a unit is raised when it is known that should a man go sick or get hurt, skilled medical attention is available. According to the second, the doctor is himself an invitation to such as wish to avoid the uncongenial or the dangerous by reporting sick with some kind of vague and ill-defined ache or pain or anxiety. The doctor himself is a 'cause' of sickness in the sense that were he not available to provide excuses for the inadequate and the inefficient, such sickness would not occur.

Much can be said in support of both these points of view for the reason that in any large unselected group there are likely to be two kinds of individuals, those who readily make use of sickness of a generalised kind as a respectable excuse for avoiding that which they find unpleasant or unattractive and those who look upon such sickness as something that is unbecoming in a man with any claim to dignity. It is to be acknowledged that all regimental medical officers are not of equal worth, some are more easily and more readily deceived than others by the complaints of those who, not being sick, seek an escape from responsibility into the shelter of sickness. Some have learnt the techniques of reassuring the hesitant and the faint-hearted and of comforting those who are quite reasonably afraid.

If the medical officers attached to this brigade were good specimens of their kind, and they seem to have been, then it is possible to maintain that proper use was not made of them. It is disappointing to encounter evidence that suggests that senior combatant officers could yet be found whose actions were guided by completely false conceptions concerning the rôle of the R.M.O. in the cultivation of unit efficiency. The practice of military medicine does not consist either wholly or primarily in the diagnosis and treatment of sickness and injury; it consists essentially in

---

* Extract from *Wingate's Phantom Army* by W. G. Burchett, published by Frederick Muller, 1946.

giving assistance of a highly specialised kind to those whose job it is to maintain the health and efficiency of the unit and of the individuals who comprise it. Health is a prerequisite to all else; there can be no efficiency, no morale in its absence. During the period of training these medical officers could have done much to help Brigadier Wingate to train his men to appreciate health, to avoid preventable disease and to cultivate self-reliance and self-care.

In the excerpt quoted above there are two points that demand comment. The first is the implied suggestion that the fall in the sick-rate during training supports the contention that the sick-parade is abused. That it is commonly abused is beyond all doubt but the figures given do not prove that this was so in 77th Bde. Some of the fall must have been due to continuous elimination from the brigade of such as could not, or as did not wish to, stand up to the rigours of training or could not endure the thought of spending so long a time in conditions of danger and discomfort. 'Back at the training centre he put his columns through the stiffest exercises they had yet undergone. Those that were considered unfit were weeded out. About 20 per cent. of both British and Gurkha troops were rejected and the columns reduced to seven'. Part of the fall must have been due to improvement in the general condition of those who ultimately came to enjoy the training. 'Pale flabby flesh turned brown and hard. Chests began to fill out. Muscles developed where there had been soft outlines before. After a time they began to like it . . . they began to glory in a new feeling of self-reliance'. Part of the fall may have been due to the fact that training started in June and ended in January and in that part of the world these two months are very different in so far as the incidence of disease is concerned.

The other point is the implied suggestion that nothing is easier than to distinguish between what are termed 'normal slight illnesses' and 'really serious' ones. This is by no means always so for many a serious illness in its beginnings seems to be very mild and slight. The aim of medicine in such cases is to identify the nature of the disease as early as possible so that it may be brought under control before it becomes serious. The policy adopted in this brigade was a dangerous one; it demanded that the platoon and column commander should attempt to do that which the R.M.O. had been trained to do infinitely better and in doing it run the risk of making a completely erroneous diagnosis to the grave danger of the patient.

It is reported that Brigadier Wingate was of the opinion, or that he expressed the opinion, that 'if a man is sufficiently tough, he could avoid sickness even in the jungle'. There is truth in this point of view so long as the sickness that is being considered is the kind that is developed, not necessarily consciously, to cover a desire to get out of conditions of discomfort and danger. It is also true that 'toughness' of this kind can postpone the point in the development of an illness when the individual concerned is compelled to acknowledge that all is not well. But it is extremely doubtful that such an attitude can affect in any significant way the occurrence and severity of a large number of diseases which in their course quickly overwhelm all resistance, physiological and psychological. As will be recorded, practically every man in this brigade needed hospitalisation on his return to India and quite a large proportion of them had so drained their capital of vitality that for long periods of time they were unable to resume their former (army) occupations.

In retrospect, it is very difficult indeed to suggest that any discernible difference in the kind or amount of sickness in this brigade would have resulted from any greater or any different employment of medical knowledge and skill. The conditions were such that no matter how 'tough', how fit a man might be, his breaking-point was reached before the expedition was ended. Only the very exceptional individual, the exceptionally fortunate individual, was able to postpone the expression of the consequences of his exposure to so many and so potent disease evoking agencies until he had reached India again. Since there was no evacuation any surgical intervention was hazardous for there could be no postoperative care of those who had to be left behind. The R.M.O. could not do much more than the platoon officer could do or than the man could do himself in the matter of prescribing medicines for malaria or diarrhoea or for the dusting of abrasions and wounds.

All ranks had been vaccinated and inoculated (with the exception of the brigadier it would appear), and thus protected against smallpox, the enteric group of fevers, tetanus and cholera.

With the brigade was a senior medical officer and with each column:

	British Column	Gurkha Column
Medical officer	1	1
B.O.Rs.	2	—
G.O.Rs.	2	4

Two mules were allotted to each column for the transport of medical stores. This limited the amount to be carried to about 300 lbs. Orderlies were trained to find any particular item in a pannier in the minimum of time. The medical officer was allowed a certain degree of freedom in the choice of the contents of the panniers and of the methods of packing these. Since the medical officer could not be everywhere along the length of a strung-out column, first-aid haversacks were issued, containing such things as elastoplast, bandages, sulphonamide powder and morphia. These haversacks were carried by the dispersal groups and patrols and instructions in the use of their contents was given. There was no special transport for the conveyance of casualties. Stretchers and litters were constructed out of bamboo.

Each dispersal group was responsible for the digging of its own shallow trench latrines. The group commander was responsible for the choice of the sites for bivouacs and latrines. All drinking water was sterilised either by the individual himself or else by the water-point orderly.

The rations consisted of:

Shakapara biscuits	12 ozs.
Cheese	2 ozs.
Milk Powder	1 oz.
Raisins and almonds	9 ozs.
Tea	$\frac{3}{4}$ oz.
Sugar	4 ozs.
Salt	$\frac{1}{2}$ oz.
Chocolate or Acid drops	1 oz.
Cigarettes	20
Matches	1 box
Total weight of one day's rations	2 lbs.

The chocolate and the cheese were sometimes replaced with dates. Some of the tins of cheese were blown and the biscuits were commonly badly deteriorated. When the columns were widely dispersed it was impossible to supply them by air-drop. It is to be noted that the ration included nothing that required cooking. It was expected that the meal halt would never exceed twenty minutes. In this time water for the making of tea could be boiled. The ration was deficient in fats and in bulk and it was intended that it sould be supplemented by local purchase. On occasion it was augmented by the dropping of such items as tins of corned beef or of baked beans. It was thought that on this ration the men could remain fit for about three months. The nature of the operation, however, did not permit the different columns to organise a supply drop as and when required and none of them received the full scale. The average number of rations received by the troops was forty in eighty days and so, since it was commonly impossible to purchase foodstuffs locally, inevitably the men became mal-nourished.

Once again it was learnt that morale must be built upon sound foundations of food and water, a ration adequate in quantity and in quality and one that appealed to the appetite.

The clothing and equipment of the Chindit consisted of:

Hat. Felt (Australian type).
Shirt. Tuck-in type (flannel).
Trousers. Khaki-drill or battledress.
Boots. Standard British, Australian or South African pattern.
Anklets. Standard web pattern.
Equipment. Standard Mills type.

Carried in the pack were:
- Spare pair socks.
- Toggle rope.
- Water-wings.
- Jersey, pullover (optional).
- Mosquito veil.
- Cap comforter.
- 6 days' rations.
- 2 grenades.

The initial issue of equipment was the same for all the columns but column commanders were given a fairly free hand as to what they jettisoned and replaced. Thus, in one of the columns the men had neither toggle ropes nor water-wings. In place of toggle ropes they used parachute cords and for river crossings they improvised 'floats' by wrapping equipment in groundsheets. Some of the larger men preferred the Everest Man Pack Carrier to the Mills equipment. The water-wings were replaced by inflatable rubber belts. The Indian pattern ammunition boot lasted about a fortnight in the jungle. Brigadier Wingate suggested that for the dry weather rubber boots should be provided and that the sole should leave the impression of a naked foot. The mosquito veil preferred was a tubular affair that could be slipped over the hat and with a tape through the top which could be tightened over the brim. The bottom of the veil was tucked into the neck of the shirt. Pashmina Kashmir blankets were preferred to the regulation issue for the reason that they were lighter and could be folded into a smaller bundle.

The health of the troops, excellent in the beginning, slowly and progressively deteriorated. Sore feet were universal, diarrhoea common, epidermophytosis and infestation with body louse and scabies fairly frequent. Laryngitis and bronchitis tended to be troublesome. On their return to India it was found that beri-beri was exceedingly prevalent among the Chindits and that many of them had contracted malaria after re-crossing the Chindwin. All those who passed through the front held by IV Corps were sent to 19 (Ind.) C.C.S. in Imphal. All save a few were in need of hospitalisation. The average loss of weight among them was two stones. However, rest, good food, good nursing and good doctoring, combined with a warm welcome, soon repaired the ills of the majority but for a sizeable minority a long period of time was required to bring them back to the condition they were in when first they set out upon what was certainly a great adventure.

CHAPTER 6

THE OVERLAND ADVANCE OF XV CORPS IN ARAKAN. NOVEMBER 1943

AS HAS been stated, Indian 26th Division, at the beginning of the monsoon season in 1943 was holding the line Taung Bazar–Sabaigon–Nhila in Arakan. H.Q. XV Corps moved back from Chittagong to Ranchi and began to prepare for the offensive that was to be launched when the rains ended. It was arranged by Eastern Army that Indian 5th and 7th Divisions would replace Indian 26th Division which would then pass into corps reserve. General Slim asked for an additional formation to send down the Kaladan Valley to give protection to the left flank and 81st (West African) Division, less one brigade, which had been training in the Bombay area and which was of peculiar interest for the reason that it was on a man-pack basis, having no transport animals and no vehicles, was allotted to XV Corps for this purpose.

As the monsoon drew to its close Indian 5th and 7th Divisions began to replace Indian 26th Division and H.Q. XV Corps moved to a site near Bawli. No sooner had this happened than General Slim was called to take over the command of Fourteenth Army. His place in XV Corps was taken by General Christison. These changes were the direct outcome of the creation of the South-East Asia Command (S.E.A.C.) with its headquarters in Delhi. This assumed responsibility for all forces and all operational activities in Burma, Ceylon, Malaya and the Netherlands East Indies. The part of India east of the Brahmaputra, hitherto under G.H.Q. India, also passed to S.E.A.C. The forces of this new command were to be based on India and supplied and maintained by India. Under S.E.A.C. was 11 Army group with three corps, IV, XV and XXXIII. Of these the first two passed u/c Fourteenth Army. This organisation was brought into being to direct operations in all the countries mentioned above when, at some time in the future, Allied Forces re-entered them.

On November 1, 1943 XV Corps assumed operational control of the Arakan area south of Chittagong. It had under command Indian 5th and 7th and 81st (W.A.) Divisions.

In the northern sector of Fourteenth Army Area was IV Corps with Indian 17th Light Division (48th and 63rd Bdes.) holding the Fort White–Tiddim area and with Indian 23rd Division in the Imphal Plain. This division was about to be relieved by Indian 20th Division and at this time one brigade of 20th Division, 80th Bde., was under command

23rd Division. In the far north (Northern Combat Area Command, N.C.A.C.) were Chinese 22nd and 38th Divisions under General Stilwell, in the area between Ledo and Maingkwan and moving on Maingkwan.

At the Quebec Conference the Supreme Allied Commander, S.E.A.C., Vice-Admiral Lord Louis Mountbatten, had been instructed to undertake operations in Burma having for their objects the development of air communications and the establishment of land communications with China and the prevention of any possible reinforcement from Burma of Japanese forces in the Pacific theatre in which United States forces were about to launch an offensive. The plans approved at Quebec were:

(i) The capture by Fourteenth Army of the Katha-Indaw area, this then to be held by a division either flown in or else moved in overland.
(ii) The capture of Mogaung and Myitkyina by Chinese–American forces from Ledo.
(iii) An advance on Bhamo and Lashio by Chinese forces from Yunnan.

By the end of November 1943 these plans had become translated into a number of inter-connected offensives.

(i) The capture of the Andaman islands by Indian XXXIII Corps in an amphibious operation.
(ii) The occupation of the Mayu Peninsula in Arakan by Indian XV Corps, followed by an amphibious assault on Akyab.
(iii) An advance across the Chindwin by Indian IV Corps on the central front with the object of drawing off the Japanese main forces from (iv).
(iv) An advance by Chinese 22nd and 38th Divisions from Ledo to Myitkyina to cover the construction of a road to Paoshan where it would link up with the old 'Burma Road'.
(v) A long range penetration operation by 'Special Force'.
(vi) An air-borne operation by the Indian parachute brigade with an Indian division to seize the Rail Indaw area, first to co-operate with (iv) and later with (vii).
(vii) An offensive by the Chinese Yunnan armies into the Lashio-Bhamo area.

A variety of complications intervened, however, so that it finally became necessary to reduce this list to four projects for the coming campaigning season. These were:

(i) The overland advance of XV Corps in Arakan.
(ii) The advance of Chinese 22nd and 38th Divisions from Ledo.
(iii) The long range penetration operation by 'Special Force'.
(iv) An advance on the main front in Assam by IV Corps to the Chindwin.

Late in September 1943 Indian 7th Division made a series of local advances in Arakan. Its 114th Bde. was operating on the east side of the Mayu Range and its 89th Bde. in the coastal strip in the west.

XV CORPS IN ARAKAN. NOVEMBER 1943

During the next few weeks the division maintained a steady pressure against the Japanese forward positions. In November Indian 5th Division assumed responsibility for the coastal plain, the western slopes of the Mayu Range and for the crest of this range, and Indian 7th Division was concentrated on the east of the Mayu Range. A road through the Ngakyedauk Pass was constructed to connect the two sides of the range; bridges and airstrips were built. Early in December 81st (W.A.) Division began to concentrate in the area of Chiringa.

On the night of November 30/December 1, Indian 7th Division began a two-pronged advance southwards on the east side of the Mayu Range. Its 33rd Bde. crossed the Ngakyedauk Chaung just to the north of Ngakyedauk village, and occupied the area extending from this village to the ridge about a mile and a half to the north-west of Sinohbyin village. By December 3 it had extended its area to the hills overlooking Maunggyihtaung and Sinohbyin. At the same time 89th Bde. had pushed forward down the Tatmin Chaung and established forward positions on the hills south of the chaung, one mile west of Tatmingyaung. The division was now close up to the main Japanese positions which ran from the crest of the Mayu Range to the foothills of the Arakan Yomas on the general line Maungdaw–Razabil–Letwedet–Kalapanzin River. On December 20, Indian 5th Division advanced to push back the Japanese outposts and to enter the Maungdaw plain in front of Razabil.

About half-way between Maungdaw and Buthidaung, the metalled road that joined them, some sixteen miles in total length, ran through two tunnels, an east and a west tunnel. Formerly a light railway had connected Maungdaw with the paddy lands of the Kalapanzin Valley. The line was no longer there but the road followed its track. The Japanese main positions in the hills covered this road from end to end and in three places had been developed into veritable fortresses, the tunnel area, at Letwedet and at Razabil.

MEDICAL COVER

When Indian 7th Division moved into Arakan two of its field ambulances, 44 and 54, relieved two of the field ambulances of Indian 26th Division (46 and 48) in Tumbru and Bawli. When its third field ambulance, 66, arrived it was sent to Bawli and 54 (Ind.) Fd. Amb., thereupon moved over the Goppe Pass with 114th Bde. 7 (Ind.) M.S.U., already in Bawli, became attached to 66 (Ind.) Fd. Amb. while 8 (Ind.) M.S.U., arriving, was placed on an 'all pack' basis and sent to Goppe there to join 54 (Ind.) Fd. Amb. 1 (Ind.) Bearer Coy., which had been active throughout the monsoon season, was responsible for evacuation from Taung Bazar over the Goppe Pass to Bawli Bazar. Its work was so arduous that in October it became necessary to relieve it with 2 Bearer

Coy. 51 (Ind.) A.M.U. and 32 (Ind.) Fd. Hyg. Sec. remained in the vicinity of divisional H.Q. but had detachments out with the brigades. In Goppe, Bawli and Tumbru the field ambulances of the division were occupying sites prepared and elaborated by those of Indian 26th Division and had accommodation for 50, 200 and 100 cases respectively.

As 114th Bde. pushed down the valley of the Kalapanzin on either side of the river it was accompanied by an A.D.S. of 54 (Ind.) Fd. Amb. which opened in *bashas* in Taung Bazar. Evacuation to the A.D.S. was by stretcher-bearer and sampan up the Kalapanzin. With the brigade was also Ind. 13 Fd. Amb. Tp. R.I.A.S.C. The A.D.S. could hold 50 patients so that this number could be accommodated overnight as was often necessary as the distances were so great. From Taung Bazar to Goppe Bazar the patients were transported in local river craft, a journey of about eight hours. A staging post was established at Prinkhaung, about half-way between the two places, where a medical officer and some 20 O.Rs. were stationed. Later the sampans were replaced by assault boats with outboard motors, supplied by the I.W.T. But as the river was tidal in these parts these boats could travel northwards of Prinkhaung only on certain tides. After the end of the monsoon the level of the water in the river fell very considerably and these boats could no longer be used. Since it was found unsatisfactory to place a patient in charge of the Arakanese boatmen for the four hour journey by river from Prinkhaung to Goppe, evacuation was by stretcher-bearer and mule.

It took two days for the casualty to reach the surgeon and to reduce this interval 44 (Ind.) Fd. Amb. moved to Goppe Bazar in November and 54 (Ind.) Fd. Amb., with 8 (Ind.) M.S.U. attached, took over the A.D.S. which had moved from Taung Bazar to the vicinity of Linbabi. The M.D.Ss. at Taung Bazar and Goppe Bazar expanded until each was almost the size of a C.C.S. so that evacuation over the Mayu Range might be reduced to the absolute minimum. They were accommodated in *bashas* constructed by local labour. It had become usual for the field ambulances to move by river, using bamboo rafts; 54 (Ind.) Fd. Amb. even designed a collapsible operating theatre made of bamboo which, being dismantled, could be packed upon such a raft. The whole medical L. of C. in the valley of the Kalapanzin was the river and R.A.Ps. and A.D.Ss. were sited, if possible, on the river bank and had their own landing stages. At night it was usual for them to withdraw into the perimeter of the unit or formation to which they were attached. Evacuation by river was comfortable and peaceful, if somewhat slow. At night there was always the danger of being torpedoed by a floating log.

The evacuation from Goppe Bazar to Bawli Bazar over the Mayu Range was by mule-track through dense jungle and across a dozen wide streams to the foot of the range and then up a gradient of 1 in 5 to reach the top. From the foot of the track on the western side of the range the path ran for about four miles through paddy fields to reach Bawli Bazar. The divisional engineers later made a single-track motorable road from Bawli South so that evacuation by ambulance car became possible from the west end of the track to the south jetty on the bank of the River Naf. The journey from Goppe to Bawli over the range took a stretcher party of eight as long as sixteen hours. A small medical detachment was therefore stationed at the top of the pass so that a medical officer could give help if this were required. At the western end of the pass H.Q. 2 (Ind.) Bearer Coy. was stationed to organise the loading of the patients into the ambulance cars. To help the walking wounded over the pass there were two field ambulance troops, R.I.A.S.C. Each of these could make one trip every two days. To carry the men's kits extra mules were needed. On reaching the jetty the patients were sent across the Naf by sampan to the Bawli M.D.S., a most palatial affair consisting of some twenty large *bashas* with inter-connecting corridors and with accommodation for 318. This M.D.S. was run by 66 (Ind.) Fd. Amb. until mid-December when this unit was relieved by 15 (Ind.) C.C.S. For about a month this field ambulance had functioned very much as a C.C.S., serving Indian 5th and 7th Divisions, for Indian 5th Division had now taken over the west side of the range. It had been admitting and evacuating about 100 casualties a day. Evacuation was mainly by river steamer for the reason that the road between Bawli and Tumbru became impassable during the rains. On board the river steamer was a staging section. The steamer could take about 300 patients and the journey took about three hours. In Tumbru 44 (Ind.) Fd. Amb. had been relieved by 75 (Ind.) Fd. Amb. of Indian 5th Division in October. The field ambulance in Tumbru was responsible for collecting the patients from the steamer at the jetty, for staging them for the night and for conveying them to 8 (Ind.) C.C.S. in Rumkhapalong, 15 miles to the north.

Up to the middle of December, therefore, the journey of the casualty being evacuated would be:

Date of receipt of wound	By S.B. and sampan to the A.D.S. in Taung Bazar.
Plus 1	By sampan or assault boat to the A.D.S. in Prinkhaung and thence by S.B. to Goppe Bazar M.D.S.
Plus 2	By S.B. over the Goppe Pass, by car to the jetty on the Naf, by sampan to the M.D.S. of 66 (Ind.) Fd. Amb. in Bawli.
Plus 3	By river steamer to Tumbru and by car to the M.D.S. of 44 (Ind.) Fd. Amb. and on by car to 8 (Ind.) C.C.S. in Rumkhapalong.

Plus 4	. . .	By M.A.S. to Cox's Bazar and by motor launch across to Khuruskhul Island to 72 I.G.H.
Plus 5	. . .	By lighter to Chittagong and by car from quay to 56, 77 or 68 I.G.H.
Plus 6	. . .	By car to quay and by ship to Calcutta.
Plus 7	. . .	At sea.
Plus 8	. . .	Arrive Calcutta. Admitted to hospital or entrained for a hospital elsewhere in India.

In early December the Ngakyedauk Pass was opened to jeeps and 66 (Ind.) Fd. Amb., being relieved by 15 (Ind.) C.C.S., in Bawli, was ferried over the pass to open its M.D.S. at the eastern end where it was joined by 12 (Ind.) M.S.U. It was provided with twelve jeeps from the divisional anti-tank regiment but since these had not been adapted for taking stretchers each of them could only take one stretcher at a time. A small A.D.S. was left at the west end of the pass to supervise the transfer of patients from jeep to ambulance car. By the middle of January the pass could accept the standard ambulance car and so for the first time evacuation was possible from a divisional M.D.S. to a corps M.D.S. by means of corps transport (a M.A.S.).

When in early December 114th Bde. moved completely over to the east bank of the Kalapanzin it was, of course, on the left of the line. 33rd Bde. was in the centre and 89th Bde. on the right. 54 (Ind.) Fd. Amb. was moved to the junction of the Ngakyedauk Chaung and the Kalapanzin River where it opened on the south bank of the river and received the casualties of 114th Bde. and also of the left flank battalion of 33rd Bde. Whenever possible the casualties were brought by water to the M.D.S. and sent on therefrom by sampan up the Ngakyedauk Chaung to an A.D.S. of 44 (Ind.) Fd. Amb. that was with 33rd Bde. Later a road following the line of the chaung to the river was constructed and evacuation by ambulance car then became possible.

As 89th Bde. pressed down the eastern foothills of the Mayu Range it built roads as it went along and an A.D.S. followed it, placing itself at the end of the road as it became elongated and transferring patients from jeep to car.

As soon as Goppe Bazar was clear of Indian 7th Division troops, 44 (Ind.) Fd. Amb. moved its M.D.S. into divisional reserve near the site of 54 (Ind.) Fd. Amb.

In November the R.A.F. had selected a site near Taung Bazar for a landing-strip. This was ready for use in January and it was expected that air evacuation would then become the rule. But from the point of view of the medical services this airstrip was badly sited for it was well to the flank and the journey to it from the nearest M.D.S. was a very long one.

42 (Ind.) S.S. was posted to Taung Bazar in February to act as an air evacuation centre but on the very next day the Japanese counter-offensive engulfed Taung Bazar and the staging section.

By the third week of December the distribution of the medical units of XV Corps was as follows:

Ind. 36th Bde. Gp. (Indian 26th Division)
    16 (Ind.) Fd. Amb. Tp. R.I.A.S.C. — In Cox's Bazar
    1 (Ind.) Fd. Amb. — In Cox's Bazar

Indian 5th Division
    10 (Ind.) Fd. Amb. — In Maunghnama
    45 (Ind.) Fd. Amb. — In Nawapara
    75 (Ind.) Fd. Amb. — In Sabaigon South (south of Bawli)
    7 (Ind.) Fd. Hyg. Sec. — In Maunghnama

Indian 7th Division
    44 (Ind.) Fd. Amb. — In Goppe Bazar
    54 (Ind.) Fd. Amb. — In Badana (sampan-head)
    66 (Ind.) Fd. Amb. — At west end of Ngakyedauk Pass
    32 (Ind.) Fd. Hyg. Sec. — Laung Chaung

XV Corps
    H.Q. Medical — In Dhechuapalong
    15 (Ind.) C.C.S. — In Bawli North
    7 (Ind.) M.S.U. — ,,
    81 (Ind.) Mob. X-ray Unit — ,,
    43 (Ind.) Sub-depot Medical Stores — ,,
    1 (Ind.) Bearer Unit — In Cox's Bazar
    37 (Ind.) S.S. (Comb.) — ,,
    15 (Ind.) Mob. X-ray Unit — ,,
    18 (Ind.) Dental Mech. Unit — ,,
    50 (Ind.) S.S. (Comb.) — In Chiringa
    51 (Ind.) A.M.U. — In Laung Chaung
    8 (Ind.) C.C.S. — In Dhoapalong
    25 (Ind.) C.C.S. — ,,
    12 (Ind.) M.S.U. — ,,
    28 F.T.U. — ,,
    16 and 80 (Ind.) Mob. X-ray Units — ,,
    55 (Ind.) Fd. Hyg. Sec. — ,,
    42 (Ind.) Sub-depot Medical Stores — ,,
    2 (Ind.) Bearer Coy. — In Garrett's Garden
    42 (Ind.) S.S. (Comb.) and 46 (Ind.) S.S. (Comb.) — In Tumbru
    38 (Ind.) A.M.U. — ,,
    Hospital 'flat' *Pennar* and 6 hospital creek vessels — ,,
    8 (Ind.) M.S.U. — In Badana (sampan-head)

XV CORPS' ASSAULT UPON THE MAUNGDAW-BUTHIDAUNG LINE

The tactical plan, briefly stated, was as follows:

A methodical advance up to the main Japanese defensive positions; a mopping up of the Japanese in front of these; the capture of the two buttresses and finally the isolation and reduction of the tunnels fortress. Indian 5th Division was to attack and take Razabil while Indian 7th Division moved round behind Letwedet to take Buthidaung in the rear and then Letwedet also in the rear. Meanwhile 81st (W.A.) Division would move down the Kaladan Valley, capture Kyauktaw and cut the Kanzauk–Htizwe road which was the Japanese lateral line of communication. The engineers of Indian 7th Division constructed a road that would take tanks and medium guns out of a track which wound its way across the Mayu Range about five miles north of the Maungdaw–Buthidaung road. This was to be used for the provision of stores and equipment to Indian 7th Division during the coming battle.

On the night of December 30/31 Indian 5th Division opened the attack. Its 161st Bde. moved to the high ground to the north-west of Bakkagonna, about five miles north of Razabil and early in the morning of the 31st, attacked the Japanese positions which, in this area, consisted of a series of low hillocks grouped around a larger hill, known as the 'Tortoise' (Point 124). A whole week was required to reduce the outlying positions and then the troops slipped past the 'Tortoise' and 2nd W. Yorks took Maungdaw on January 9, 1944. Then the division turned its attention to the 'Tortoise' itself. This was a very elaborately prepared position with the typical Japanese 'bunkers'. The attack was preceded by a very heavy bombardment from the air and by the artillery and when this ceased the tanks and 4/7th Rajput moved forward, shortly to be checked. Meanwhile the area between the Razabil–Bawli road and Point 731 was being swept by 2nd Suffolk and 1/17th Dogra. By a process of slow attrition the Japanese positions were taken bit by bit until only the core remained as stubbornly defended as ever.

At this point General Christison unleashed Indian 7th Division on the east side of the Mayu Range. 2nd K.O.S.B. had seized a hillock —the Taungdaungwa Feature—that overlooked the Maungdaw-Buthidaung road between the tunnels and Buthidaung and had held on to it as did 4/8th G.R. who relieved the Scots. 9th Bde. of Indian 5th Division had crossed the range to relieve 89th Bde. of Indian 7th Division so that it could be used in the attack upon Buthidaung preparatory to the assault upon the Letwedet buttress. Where the Ngakyedauk Pass road debouched into the valley, a maintenance area for the troops in the valley of the Kalapanzin was laid out with supply depots, ammunition dumps, vehicle parks, dressing stations, etc. This was to become known

XV CORPS IN ARAKAN. NOVEMBER 1943

as Indian 7th Division's 'administrative box'. But before Indian 7th Division struck, the Japanese opened a counter-offensive which was meant to be the beginning of an invasion of India.

INDIAN 5TH DIVISION. MEDICAL COVER

This division had moved from Lohardaga *via* Chittagong and Ukhia to Bawli South between October 3 and 9, 1943. 75 (Ind.) Fd. Amb. at once established its M.D.S. in Tumbru and its A.D.S. in Nhila. For the attack on the outer works of the Razabil position 45 (Ind.) Fd. Amb. on December 30 opened a light A.D.S. at the west foot of the Ngakyedauk Pass and one company of 75 (Ind.) Fd. Amb. opened an A.D.S. in the area of Ponnaz, evacuating to the M.D.S. of 45. Casualties were numerous, 83 being brought into the R.A.P. in Kwela-binga by S.B. squads by 1030 hours. From the vicinity of Kayugyaung casualties were brought by sampan to a car post established in Zeganbyin by 75 (Ind.) Fd. Amb. and transported thence by ambulance car to the A.D.S. of 75 in Ponnaz. The light section of 15 (Ind.) C.C.S. was working at the M.D.S. of 45 (Ind.) Fd. Amb. Evacuation remained difficult throughout this action because of the activities of numerous snipers and of machine-gunners and so casualties had to be held in the R.A.Ps. until nightfall. Extra blankets, dressings and stretchers were carried forward to the R.A.P. of 4/7th Rajput. By January 4, a jeep track from Zeganbyin to Nawrondaung had been constructed and along this casualty evacuation was rapid. By January 10 the A.D.S. of 10 (Ind.) Fd. Amb. had moved forward to the vicinity of Bakkagonna and to this casualties were brought from the R.A.Ps. either by sampan or S.B. squad. From this A.D.S. evacuation was to the M.D.S. of 10 (Ind.) Fd. Amb. in Chota Maunghnama.

When the division entered Maungdaw a detachment of 'B' Coy 10 (Ind.) Fd. Amb. relieved 45 (Ind.) Fd. Amb. in the light A.D.S. at the foot of the Ngakyedauk Pass and the rest of the unit moved on to Maungdaw there to open an A.D.S. Evacuation therefrom was by sampan to the A.D.S. of 75 (Ind.) Fd. Amb. in Ponnaz and by launch to the M.D.S. of 10 (Ind.) Fd. Amb. in Chota Maunghnama. This M.D.S. remained in this site until January 26 when it moved to Milestone 25 on the Razabil–Bawli road. Evacuation from this M.D.S. had been by water up the estuary of the Naf. At the medical nodal point near Chota Maunghnama was 23 (Ind.) C.C.S. to which was attached 28 F.T.U. 7 (Ind.) M.S.U. had joined the division and was attached to 45 (Ind.) Fd. Amb. With the field ambulances were 5, 22 and 23 Fd. Amb. Tps. R.I.A.S.C. and 1 (Ind.) Bearer Coy. 20 and 45 M.A.Ss. were available for evacuation purposes. Two river steamers were used for evacuation from Maungdaw to Tumbru Ghat and one launch linked up with a car post at Aminpara. Late in January, 7 (Ind.) M.S.U., 15 (Ind.) M.S.U. and 8 F.T.U. joined the division.

During the assault on the 'Tortoise' 'A' Coy. of 75 (Ind.) Fd. Amb. opened its A.D.S. to the south of Bakkagonna and was made responsible for evacuating all casualties from the R.A.Ps. to the west of the Razabil–Bawli road. A car post and a W.W.C.P. were established about a mile to the south of this A.D.S. as soon as the preliminary bombardment ceased. 'B' Coy. of 75 (Ind.) Fd. Amb. opened its A.D.S. to the northwest of Bakkagonna and was made responsible for the evacuation of casualties from the R.A.Ps. to the east of the Razabil–Bawli road. The headquarters of this unit also opened an A.D.S. on this site. Evacuation from the A.D.S. of 'A' Company was to the M.D.S. of 45 (Ind.) Fd. Amb. on a site just to the east of Zeganbyin and thence to 23 (Ind.) C.C.S. in the vicinity of Chota Maunghnama by ambulance car. From the A.D.S. of 'B' Company and from that of the H.Q. Company evacuation was by creek steamer to Tumbru Ghat where 42 and 46 (Ind.) S.Ss. were functioning.

The preliminary bombardment of the Razabil position caused a number of civilian casualties and 'A' Coy. of 75 (Ind.) Fd. Amb. was occupied a whole day in attending to them.

To provide medical cover for 2nd Suffolk and 1/17th Dogra during the operation between the Razabil–Bawli road and the Mayu Range, the surgical elements of the two companies of 45 (Ind.) Fd. Amb. moved forward with them to establish themselves at car posts which had been opened in the rear of the two R.A.Ps. To each R.A.P. 20 S.Bs. were attached to carry the casualties to the car posts whence evacuation was by ambulance car to the M.D.S. of 45 (Ind.) Fd. Amb. near Zeganbyin and from there to 23 (Ind.) C.C.S. near Chota Maunghnama.

THE JAPANESE COUNTER-OFFENSIVE

It had become known that the Japanese forces in Burma were being strongly reinforced, that a new Japanese Army H.Q. had been formed to control operations in Arakan and that a formation of the Indian National Army had been moved close up to the front in Arakan. The indications were that the Japanese were preparing to launch a counter-offensive not only in Arakan but also in the north. Indian 26th Division in the Chittagong area was warned to be prepared to move to the south and arrangements were made that when it did so its place in the Chittagong area would be taken by 36th Division which was in Calcutta. General Slim had decided that should the Japanese attack isolate Indian 5th and 7th Divisions or parts thereof, the formations concerned would hold fast to their positions, dig in and defend them. They would be supplied by air-drop. Arrangements to this end were made.

On February 4 the Japanese counter-offensive opened with the sudden appearance of a strong Japanese force at Taung Bazar well to the rear of Indian 7th Division. This force had passed partly round the east flank of the division through the jungle and partly through the positions held by 114th Bde. Almost simultaneously strong frontal attacks were made by Japanese forces in the area north and north-west of Buthidaung.

The Japanese operational plan was captured early in the battle. Its avowed purpose was the destruction of XV Corps and the capture of Chittagong. The reinforced 55th Division had been divided into three parts. The first of these—'Tanahashi' Force—about 7,000 strong, was to move secretly through the jungle between the left of Indian 7th Division and the right of 81st (W.A.) Division and seize Taung Bazar from the east. It was then to turn south, overrun the 'administrative box' near Sinzweya and cut the Ngakyedauk Pass, thus isolating Indian 7th Division to the east of the Mayu Range. The second part—'Kubo' Force—about a battalion strong, was to make an even wider sweep to cut the track leading south from Goppe Bazar and then, turning west, was to cross the Mayu Range and cut the Bawli–Maungdaw road near Maunghnama, thus isolating Indian 5th Division. The third part—'Doi' Force—was to put in holding attacks on both the Indian divisions from the south. It was expected that when thus isolated the divisions would concentrate their energies upon attempts to reopen their communications. In characteristic Japanese fashion the operation was planned according to a fixed time-table; it was to last exactly ten days. Underlying the plan was the assumption that victory would attend every step of Japanese advance and that supplies, transport and guns would be captured in quantity and become available to the Japanese troops who carried five days' rations, no more.

89th Bde. of Indian 7th Division, which had been freed by the coming of 9th Bde. of Indian 5th Division, was sent north to check the Japanese movements to the south from Taung Bazar. It partially succeeded in doing so near Ingyaung but some of the Japanese managed to outflank the brigade and to fall upon the headquarters of Indian 7th Division in the area of Laung Chaung. The staff dispersed and most of them made their way into the divisional and corps troops' administrative box at Sinzweya. This defended locality was in a cupped area of dried-up paddy fields; it was about a mile square and encircled by low hills. Within the area were several small hillocks, one of them known as M.D.S. Hill for the reason that on it one of the field ambulances had established its dressing station. Within the box there was a collection of administrative troops, some 8,000 altogether, men of labour units, sappers, ordnance units, mule companies and the like. There were two battalions of infantry, to begin with, 2nd W. Yorks and 4/8th Gurkha Rifles. Two other battalions were later added, 2nd K.O.S.B.

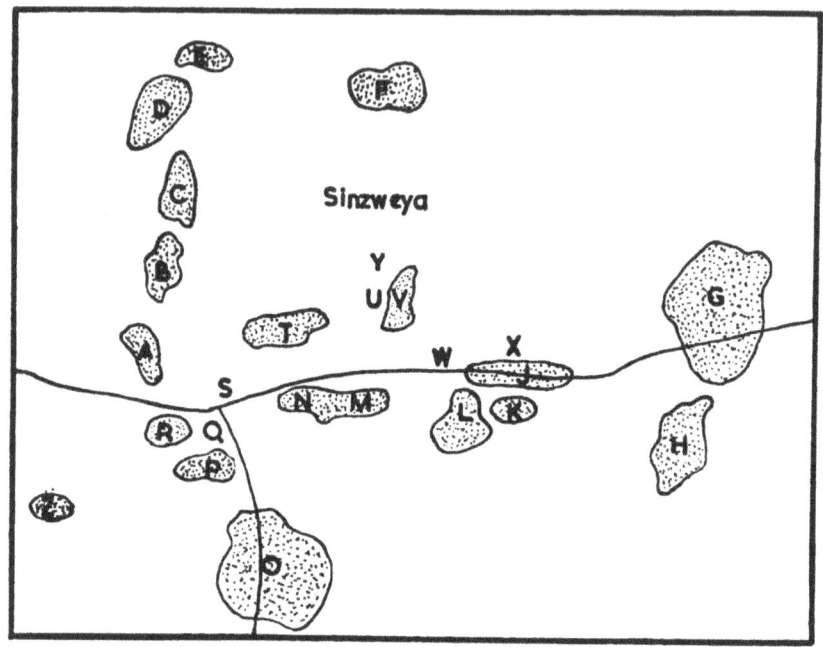

Fig. 18. Indian 7th Division's Administrative Box, Sinzweya.
(after the arrival of 89th Brigade)

A. One coy. 2nd W. Yorks.
B. Supply Depot
C. Two supply issue sections
D. One mule company
E. 89th Bde. 'B' Echelon
F. 33rd Bde. 'B' Echelon
G. 4/8th G.R. of 89th Bde.
H. 89th Bde. H.Q.; 2nd K.O.S.B.
J. Divisional Signals; one section M.T.
K. 136th Fd. Regt. 'B' Echelon
L. One battery 24th Lt. A.A. Regt.; later one company 7/2nd Punjab of 89th Bde.
M. H.Q. Indian 7th Division; H.Q. 9th Bde.; Two guns of 24th Mountain Regt.
N. Garrison H.Q.
O. 9th Bde. 'B' Echelon; one battery of 24th Mountain Regt.
P. Reinforcements, 1st Queen's, 1st Lincolns and 2nd K.O.S.B.
Q. M.D.S.
R. Rear H.Q. 7th Division
S. Two heavy A.A. guns
T. Mobile reserve of two companies of 2nd W. Yorks.; later of two companies 2nd K.O.S.B.
U. One squadron 25th Dragoons
V. Half battery 24th Lt. A.A. Regt.
W. One squadron 25th Dragoons
X. One battery 6th Medium Regt. R.A.
Y. Ammunition Dump
Z. Part of 'V' Force.

and 7/2nd Punjab. There were about a dozen batteries of guns of different calibre and two squadrons of 25th Dragoons. The tanks of the Dragoons and the guns guarded the soft-skinned vehicles, the dressing stations and H.Q. Every part of the box was vulnerable and every part was searched by the Japanese guns and mortars. But the Japanese did not retain the mastery of the sky over the battle area for the R.A.F. and the U.S.A.A.F. swept them from it and the planes of Troop Carrier

FIG. 19. The Boxes of Indian 5th and 7th Divisions

Command delivered the goods, some 1,626 tons of supplies of all kinds in some 900 sorties.

The brigades of the two Indian divisions were all dug in for all-round defence and beat off all attacks. On February 7 patrols of Indian 7th Division, moving up the Ngakyedauk Pass from the east encountered strong opposition as did patrols of Indian 5th Division on the following day approaching the pass from the west. The Japanese forces attacking frontally ('Doi' Force) and around the flank ('Tanahashi' Force) had succeeded in joining up according to plan and Indian 7th Division had been isolated. 'Kubo' Force had also succeeded in crossing the Mayu Range through the jungle and had cut the Razabil–Bawli Bazar road near Maunghnama, also according to plan, and had isolated Indian 5th

Division. But neither of these encircled divisions behaved as the Japanese expected them to; they did not frantically attempt to reopen the cut roads and retreat along them, they stayed in their boxes sending out fighting patrols to cut the Japanese communications while Indian 26th Division moved southwards through the Goppe Pass from Bawli Bazar into the valley of the Kalapanzin to re-occupy Taung Bazar and to press upon the rear of the Japanese columns and 36th Division moved down the Bawli–Razabil road towards the road-block at Maunghnama.

The Japanese assaults upon the entrenched brigades grew in intensity as their achievements lagged behind their time-table. A party of about six officers and sixty O.Rs. burst into the area of M.D.S. Hill during the moonless night of February 7/8 and were not ejected therefrom until the morning of the 9th. Supply dropping began on the 11th. On the 12th, the initiative was no longer possessed by the Japanese. Strong detachments were sent out from the brigade boxes of Indian 7th Division to ambush and destroy the mule and porter supply columns of the Japanese. The advance of 81st (W.A.) Division down the valley of the Kaladan was now threatening Kyauktaw and would soon be menacing the Japanese right rear. An airstrip was completed near Taung Bazar and from it air evacuation commenced. Indian 26th Division and 36th Division moving south would shortly begin to compress the Japanese forces between themselves and the rock-like Indian 5th and 7th Divisions. The end of the battle was in sight.

Accepting defeat, the Japanese endeavoured to escape. By February 20 the growing shortage of food and of ammunition, the lack of success and the very considerable losses they had endured had exerted their full effects upon the Japanese troops. The Ngakyedauk Pass was reopened by Indian 5th Division on the 24th. 'Kubo' Force was destroyed amid the crags and caves of the Mayu Range and the rest disintegrated. Over 4,500 Japanese lost their lives in this operation; their bodies were buried. Hundreds more must have perished and remained undiscovered in the jungle.

XV Corps now resumed its advance on March 5. It met fierce opposition but Buthidaung was taken by Indian 7th Division on the 11th and the assault upon the Letwedet buttress began. By the end of March the whole of the Buthidaung–Letwedet area was clear of Japanese. Meanwhile Indian 5th Division had begun its assault upon the Razabil buttress which was captured on March 12 after exceedingly bitter fighting. Then 36th Division attacked the 'tunnels fortress' itself. The western tunnel was rushed on March 27 but on April 1, 1st Glosters were repulsed in an attack upon the eastern tunnel. Attacking again on the 4th the tunnel was taken and finally cleared on the 6th.

At the end of March Indian 5th Division was relieved by **Indian 25th Division** and was transported to IV Corps' sector by air.

XV CORPS IN ARAKAN. NOVEMBER 1943

Of the Japanese positions along the Maungdaw–Buthidaung road there now remained only Point 551. This was under attack throughout April. Indian 26th Division assaulted it unsuccessfully on three occasions during this month. However, on May 3, at the fourth attempt, this dominating hill was taken.

In the valley of the Kaladan success had not been complete. 81st (W.A.) Division reached Apaukwa early in March but was then violently attacked and forced to withdraw hurriedly to the north-west of Kyauktaw. Collecting in the area of Kaladan village, the division moved across to the valley of the Kalapanzin and to the vicinity of Taung Bazar. A detachment covering the divisional transport withdrew more slowly up the valley of the Kaladan. It was overtaken by the pursuing Japanese and driven into the valley of the Sangu which runs northwards to the west of, and parallel to, the valley of the Kaladan.

General Slim now began to prepare for the expected Japanese onslaught on the main front. In order to reduce as far as possible demands for air-supply in Arakan and to avoid sickness among the troops in this sector, it was agreed that XV Corps should take up a line that could be safely held by relatively few troops, that lay in a healthy area and that could be supplied by land. So a firm hold was maintained on Taung Bazar, on the high ground west of Buthidaung, on the tunnels area, on Maungdaw and on the mouth of the Naf River.

36th Division was withdrawn to Shillong. Indian 7th Division followed Indian 5th Division to the northern sector. By the end of May XV Corps was holding the line in Arakan with Indian 25th and 26th Divisions and 81st (W.A.) Division. 25th Division was in the tunnels area covering the Maungdaw–Buthidaung road; 26th Division had one brigade in the Bawli–Goppe–Taung Bazar area, one brigade about Taungbro at the head of the Naf Estuary and its third brigade in Cox's Bazar. 81st (W.A.) Division was around Chiringa.

MEDICAL COVER DURING THESE EVENTS

INDIAN 7TH DIVISION

When the Japanese counter-offensive started on February 4, the medical units of Indian 7th Division were distributed as follows:

East of the Ngakyedauk Pass	M.D.S. of 66 (Ind.) Fd. Amb.
	12 (Ind.) M.S.U.
	48 (Ind.) Dental Unit
	28 F.T.U.
South of the junction of the Ngakyedauk Chaung and the Kalapanzin River	M.D.S. of 54 (Ind.) Fd. Amb.
	9 (Ind.) M.S.U.
	H.Q. 44 (Ind.) Fd. Amb. (closed)

In Ind. 33rd Bde's. area	A.D.S. of 44 (Ind.) Fd. Amb.
	2 (Ind.) Bearer Coy. one platoon
	15 (Ind.) Fd. Amb. Tp. R.I.A.S.C.
In Ind. 114th Bde's. area	A.D.S. 54 (Ind.) Fd. Amb. in Kwazon
	A.D.S. 54 (Ind.) Fd. Amb. in Oktaung
	Detach. 54 (Ind.) Fd. Amb. at the sampan-head
	13 (Ind.) Fd. Amb. Tp. R.I.A.S.C.
	2 (Ind.) Bearer Coy. one platoon
In Taung Bazar	42 (Ind.) S.S.
In Laung Chaung	A.D.M.S.
	H.Q. 33 (Ind.) Fd. Hyg. Sec.
	H.Q. 51 (Ind.) A.M.U.
	H.Q. 2 (Ind.) Bearer Coy.

Each of the M.D.Ss. was capable of holding 300 patients and each was running a forward malaria treatment centre. Casualties were brought to the M.D.S. of 54 (Ind.) Fd. Amb. by S.Bs., by jeep, by ambulance car or by sampan. From this M.D.S. they were taken by sampan to Taung Bazar and by air from Taung Bazar to Comilla or by road to the M.D.S. of 66 (Ind.) Fd. Amb. whence they were taken by road to 15 (Ind.) C.C.S. in Bawli.

42 (Ind.) S.S. in Taung Bazar was the first of the medical units to be disturbed by the Japanese counter-offensive. It got its walking wounded away to the M.D.S. of 66 (Ind.) Fd. Amb. but two of its I.O.Rs. were killed and its commanding officer wounded. With 89th Bde., sent northwards to oppose the Japanese movement to the south, went a company of 66 (Ind.) Fd. Amb. and extra stretcher-bearers of 2 (Ind.) Bearer Coy. The M.D.Ss. of 54 and 66 Fd. Ambs. were instructed to evacuate all their lying cases at once to 15 (Ind.) C.C.S. in Bawli and to return all afebrile malaria cases to their units. 54 was told to send enough men and material to the A.D.S. in Kwazon to enable it to hold and treat cases. 44 and 54 (Ind.) Fd. Ambs. were told to move at once into the administrative box of Indian 7th Division at the foot of the Ngakyedauk Pass. All walking wounded were to make their way to 66 (Ind.) Fd. Amb. All unit transport was to be pooled and 44 Fd. Amb. would be the first to move. 54 sent its equipment by sampan up the Ngakyedauk Chaung *en route* for the administrative box. 44 got into the box safely but when it was 54's turn to move the road between its site and the box had been cut. However, the personnel managed to filter into the box next morning but the equipment in the sampans fell into Japanese hands. A.D.M.S. Indian 7th Division was involved in the disruption of the divisional

XV CORPS IN ARAKAN. NOVEMBER 1943

headquarters but was among those who ultimately made their way into the box.

In the administrative box on the evening of February 7 there were all three of the divisional field ambulances. 66 (Ind.) Fd. Amb. had its M.D.S. on the wooded slope of a hillock that was given the name of M.D.S. Hill. Across the Ngakyedauk Chaung, which ran through this box into that of 89th Bde., were the M.D.Ss. of 44 and 54 (Ind.) Fd. Ambs. under canvas, previously a canteen, about two hundred yards away from the M.D.S. of 66 (Ind.) Fd. Amb. and to the north of it. This M.D.S. occupied three dry nullahs which had been deepened and widened, so that the operating theatre and wards were all below ground level. The whole of this area was screened by thick jungle but the southern end of one of the nullahs passed through the perimeter of the box to enter the jungle. Attached to this M.D.S. were 12 (Ind.) M.S.U., 28 F.T.U. and 48 (Ind.) Dental Unit. It is recorded that the work of the O.R.A. of the M.S.U. was seriously disrupted and the O.R.A. himself distinctly startled when a young and inquisitive elephant ambled through the operating theatre. Guarding this area were a company of 2nd W. Yorks. of Ind. 9th Bde., a small party from 2 (Ind.) Bearer Coy. and small parties of 1st Queen's, 1st Lincolns and 2nd K.O.S.B. Divisional Rear H.Q. was nearby. All convalescent malaria B.O.Rs. were armed and a roving patrol was maintained. All those patients who could walk were moved from the M.D.S. to the nullah to the north of M.D.S. Hill so that on the 7th only about 30 patients remained in the unit. A.D.M.S. Indian 7th Division occupied a slit trench quite near the M.D.S. of 66 (Ind.) Fd. Amb.

As has been stated, a party of Japanese troops broke into the box in the area of the M.D.S. Hill during the darkness of the night of February 7/8. The officer commanding 66 (Ind.) Fd. Amb. and one of his colleagues managed to avoid the Japanese and made their way to the Command Post to give the alarm. A party of 2nd W. Yorks was sent to eject the Japanese but could not do so. It was impossible at this time to collect troops in sufficient numbers for this particular job and since there were patients in the medical unit it was impossible to eject the Japanese by means of gun or mortar fire. In the M.D.S. the Japanese rounded up about 30 members of the staff and patients for interrogation. After this they were forced to help their captors to pack medical stores and equipment and afterwards were taken to a nullah and kept there under guard. On the morning of the 8th a counter-attack was launched to clear the M.D.S. area. The Japanese used their prisoners as a screen. By the evening it had become obvious that the Japanese would be forced to withdraw from the M.D.S. area as the pressure upon them grew increasingly stronger. They first shot all their B.O.R. prisoners, next the I.O.Rs. and finally the turn of the six medical officers came. They were shot through the ear. One of them, miraculously, was not killed but only stunned. Coming to, he shammed dead and chose his time to roll into a trench. He came out of his trench next day when the M.D.S. area had been finally cleared of Japanese.

By midday on February 8 a steady stream of casualties was flowing into the other medical units from the fighting around M.D.S. Hill. An improvised M.D.S. was established by 66 (Ind.) Fd. Amb. in the nullah where the walking wounded had been sheltered since the previous evening. But equipment was very deficient and key personnel had been lost by all of the three field ambulances. A.D.M.S. Indian 7th Division therefore instructed these medical units to pool their resources and set up a combined main dressing station to the north of M.D.S. Hill. The officer commanding 66 (Ind.) Fd. Amb. was appointed S.M.O. of the administrative box and the officer commanding 54 (Ind.) Fd. Amb. took over the command of the combined M.D.S. A surgical centre was organised by two of the surgeons who had survived, in a *basha* close to this combined M.D.S.

More than 1,000 battle casualties were admitted to the medical units within the box during the period February 8–23, 724 to the combined M.D.S. Of these 724, 42 died, 189 were returned to their units and 493 were evacuated over the Ngakyedauk Pass. Of the remaining 280 who were treated in medical units other than the combined M.D.S., 240 were evacuated by air and the others were returned to their units. This evacuation by air was possible because an airstrip had been constructed in the box of 114th Bde. Twenty-five wounded Japanese were admitted to these medical units.

The casualties among medical personnel were:

TABLE 3

Indian 7th Division. Administrative Box. Sinzweya. Casualties among Medical Personnel

	Killed	Wounded	Missing	
Officers . .	6	5	5	(4 rejoined their units later)
B.O.Rs. . .	5	1	1	(plus another who escaped)
I.O.Rs. . .	12	16	126	(97 rejoined their units later)

As can readily be imagined the resources of these medical units were stretched to the utmost. Operations had to be carried out a few hundred yards away from the perimeter and snipers were busy. Yet 242 operations were performed on 169 patients. These included:

Head and Face . . 22	Compound fracture arm	
Chest 13	and hand . . . 16	
Thoraco-abdominal . . 2	Compound fracture leg	
Abdomen . . . 10	and foot . . . 41	

To perform blood transfusion under such circumstances must have been a most difficult proceeding yet no less than 120 patients were transfused. As day succeeded day it became increasingly difficult to maintain high standards of sanitation within the box and flies multiplied to become a plague. On February 14 the troops were put on suppressive mepacrine and repellent cream and pyrethrum powder were distributed. At no time did a shortage of medical supplies develop, save very locally. Everything that was needed dropped in abundance from the skies, though sometimes not quite in the right place, the bulk of the mepacrine for example was dropped in the Goppe area.

The medical services of Indian 7th Division had good reason for being satisfied with the quality of the work they did during this siege of the administrative box. Perhaps the most significant feature of this work was the evacuation by air of so many casualties from the defended locality of 114th Bde. while this was in the very midst of a battle.

INDIAN 5TH DIVISION

On February 1 'B' Coy. of 10 (Ind.) Fd. Amb. accompanied Ind. 9th Bde. over the Mayu Range to join Indian 7th Division. On the following day the field ambulance with 123rd and 161st Bdes., 45 (Ind.) Fd. Amb. with 123rd Bde. and 75 (Ind.) Fd. Amb. with 161st Bde., moved into the brigade boxes because of reported Japanese infiltration. Heavy rain made evacuation rearwards to the C.C.S. in Chota Maunghnama impossible for the next three days. On February 7 the A.D.S. of 10 (Ind.) Fd. Amb. at the foot of the Ngakyedauk Pass withdrew to rejoin its parent unit in the divisional box and the medical nodal point with 23 and 25 (Ind.) C.C.Ss. and 71 (Ind.) Fd. Amb. moved back to Bawli, where 71 (Ind.) Fd. Amb. assumed responsibility for evacuation through the Goppe Pass. A detachment of 72 (Ind.) Fd. Amb. was attached to 71 to help in this work. On the 5th the company of 10 (Ind.) Fd. Amb. with 9th Bde. had been ordered to move into this brigade's box, but was unable to do so for the reason that its transport had become immobilised by the effects of the heavy rain. The company dug itself in just outside the perimeter of Indian 7th Division's box and managed to slip into the box on the 9th. While outside the box the unit had become involved in two of the Japanese assaults but had come to no harm. 71 (Ind.) Fd. Amb. in Bawli was bombed but there were no casualties. Evacuation from the east of Ngakyedauk Pass ceased on this day for the Japanese succeeded in blocking the pass. Vehicles on the Briasco–Bawli road were mortared and machine-gunned but it has to be reported that the ambulance cars using this road were not molested.

On the 9th, 8 F.T.U. and 7 and 15 (Ind.) M.S.Us. were moved back to Bawli to become attached to the C.C.Ss. there. On February 12 new arrangements were made. 45 (Ind.) Fd. Amb. with 123rd Bde. was to evacuate casualties from the hills about the Ngakyedauk Pass; 75 (Ind.) Fd. Amb. was to serve the divisional front in the south astride the Wabyin–Razabil–Maungdaw road, evacuating to the M.D.S. of 45 (Ind.) Fd. Amb. and 10 (Ind.) Fd. Amb. was made responsible for the evacuation of casualties from the divisional headquarters area. From the M.D.S. evacuation was to be by the cars of 20 M.A.S. On the 16th and 17th 22 Fd. Amb. Tp., attached to 75 (Ind.) Fd. Amb., was loaned to 71 (Ind.) Fd. Amb. to help in evacuating casualties over the Goppe Pass and ten squads of 1 (Ind.) Bearer Coy. were lent to 1 (Ind.) Fd. Amb. of Indian 26th Division to help in evacuation on the Mayu Range north of Briasco Bridge.

On February 24 the Ngakyedauk Pass was reopened and a convoy of ambulance cars with an escort of armoured cars went through it from west to east until 1230 hours. This and a second convoy cleared 296 casualties from the M.D.S. of 66 (Ind.) Fd. Amb. in Indian 7th Division's administrative box, conveying them to the M.D.S. of 45 (Ind.) Fd. Amb. whence they were sent on to the C.C.Ss. in Bawli. On the following day another 130 casualties were evacuated from Indian 7th Division's area.

On March 2/3, Ind. 9th Bde. crossed the Mayu Range from east to west to rejoin Indian 5th Division and with it came the company of 10 (Ind.) Fd. Amb. 22 Fd. Amb. Tp. and the detachment of 1 Bearer Coy. rejoined their parent units.

On the 5th, 10 (Ind.) Fd. Amb. with 15 (Ind.) M.S.U. and 1 (Ind.) Bearer Coy. moved to North Island, Maungdaw, the field ambulance going to Ginnapara. On the following day 45 (Ind.) Fd. Amb. with 7 (Ind.) M.S.U. and 18 (Ind.) A.M.U. moved to Yemyettaung. Evacuation from Yemyettaung was to the Kappagaung jetty by R.C.Ls. and thence to Bawli North by creek steamer. On the 8th, 75 (Ind.) Fd. Amb. was despatched to Kanyindan to provide cover for 9th and 161st Bdes. Evacuation from 10 (Ind.) Fd. Amb. was, for serious cases, by air from a landing strip to Ramu and beyond.

On March 19 the relief of Indian 5th by Indian 25th Division began and preparations were made for the transfer of Indian 5th Division to the Imphal sector.

36TH DIVISION

This division had an exceptional composition. It consisted of two infantry brigades and all its battalions were British. Many of the divisional troops and service units were Indian. Attached to 29th Independent Bde. Gp. (1st R.S.F., 2nd R.W.F., 2nd E.Lan.R. and 2nd S.Lan.R.), last encountered in Madagascar, was 154 (Br.) Fd. Amb.; to 72nd Bde. (6th S.W.B., 10th Glosters and 9th R.Sussex), 69 (Ind.) Fd. Amb. Attached to the division were 22 (Br.) C.C.S. with an Indian increment, 27 (Br.) F.T.U., 13 (Ind.) M.S.U. and 5 (Ind.) Bearer Coy.

It was the practice in 69 (Ind.) Fd. Amb. to subdivide each of the two companies into four sections, each of one officer and twenty-three O.Rs. and to attach a section to each of the three battalions in action and to retain the fourth section as a reserve. With the battalions the equipment of the section was carried by man-pack. The section followed the trail of the R.M.O. and evacuated casualties to the axis of advance of the battalion along which the cars of the field ambulance collected them. When necessary the fourth section opened an A.D.S. in the area of brigade headquarters. The headquarters company of the field ambulance was subdivided into three sections concerned respectively with reception, treatment and holding and evacuation.

In the fighting in which 36th Division was about to become involved it was customary for the battalions to be widely separated and it was found that this system of attaching a section of this size to a battalion was satisfactory. Should the battalion become isolated, a not uncommon happening, the section could establish an adequate A.D.S. in the battalion box. The section became an accepted part of the battalion and was protected by the battalion. But on occasions the field ambulance personnel were used by the battalion to replace its own S.Bs. for the collection of casualties in front of the R.A.P.

In 29th Independent Bde. Gp. it was the custom for 154 (Br.) Fd. Amb. to attach a section of one officer and eighteen O.Rs. to each of the four battalions.

The division had been trained for employment in amphibious operations and had been waiting in India until such time as suitable employment presented itself. In early 1944 the division was earmarked for the projected assault upon Akyab but the Japanese counter-offensive led to the postponement of this enterprise.

29th Bde. reached Chittagong on February 7 and on the following day the field ambulance moved forward to Chiringa where a C.R.S. was opened on the 9th. On February 13 a M.D.S. was established in Bawli Bazar. One medical orderly, two drivers and one ambulance car were attached to each of the battalions. On the 17th an A.D.S. was established in the battalion box of 2nd E.Lan.R. in the Ngakyedauk Pass by a section of one officer and twenty-six O.Rs. with one ambulance car. On March 2 the M.D.S. moved from Bawli Bazar to Zeganbyin inside the brigade H.Q. box near the western end of the Ngakyedauk Pass and on the following day 13 (Ind.) M.S.U., 27 F.T.U. and a platoon of 5 (Ind.) Bearer Coy. were placed under command of the brigade. Six D.U.K.Ws. were placed at the disposal of the brigade for evacuation to 22 C.C.S. in Bawli Bazar. On March 6 when the Japanese attacked the brigade H.Q. box there was no interruption of evacuation. On March 13 the M.D.S. moved to Wabyin at the western end of the Ngakyedauk Pass. On the 21st an A.D.S. was opened in the divisional H.Q. box at Chota Maunghnama. On the 23rd the mobile surgical unit, the field transfusion unit and the platoon of the bearer company moved from 154 (Br.) to 69 (Ind.) Fd. Amb. While with 154 (Br.) Fd. Amb., 13 (Ind.) M.S.U. had performed forty major operations on battle casualties. Four of the patients died in the M.D.S. Fifteen minor operations on non-battle casualties were also undertaken. 27 F.T.U. transfused 19 patients, using 87 pints of plasma and 8 pints of blood. Among these 19 there were 4 deaths. It was concluded by the officer commanding this field ambulance that his unit alone could not have provided the service demanded and that under such conditions as those that existed in Arakan at this time the addition of a mobile surgical unit, a field transfusion unit and additional S.Bs. should be considered as essential.

The A.D.S. in the box of 2nd E.Lan.R. between February 17 and April 15, when it was closed and joined the M.D.S., treated 477 battle casualties and sick. The A.D.S. in the divisional box at Chota Maunghnama, between March 23 and April 26, had dealt with 228 battle casualties and sick. The M.D.S. during the period February 11–March 9 had admitted 1,459 casualties and sick. Of this grand total of 2,154, 101 were battle casualties, 536 were cases of malaria, 404 of N.Y.D.(F.) and 309 were cases of dysentery and diarrhoea. 635 were returned to their units after treatment. On May 10, 154 (Br.) Fd. Amb. moved with the division to Shillong.

On February 23, 69 (Ind.) Fd. Amb. moved forward from Chittagong to Cox's Bazar to take over the site vacated by 1 (Ind.) Fd. Amb. of Indian 26th Division. On the 28th the site of the M.D.S. in Bawli Bazar was taken over from 48 (Ind.) Fd. Amb. of Indian 26th Division. On March 3, when the division moved to Chota Maunghnama the M.D.S. moved from Bawli Bazar into the divisional H.Q. box. Sections were with the battalions guarding the passes over the Mayu Range in this area.

On March 21, 72nd Bde. took over from 161st Bde. of Indian 5th Division the positions in the vicinity of the West Tunnel on the Maungdaw–Buthidaung road and the M.D.S. moved to Yemyettaung. Evacuation was now to the M.D.S. and thence by L.C.M. *via* the

River Naf to Bawli. Forty S.Bs. from 5 (Ind.) Bearer Coy were divided among the battalions. The M.D.S. in Yemyettaung was within a box and was quite near the loading pier at Kayugyaung.

For the attack by 72nd Bde. on the Tunnels, A.D.M.S. 36th Division placed 7 (Ind.) and 13 (Ind.) M.S.Us. and 27 (Br.) F.T.U. with 69 (Ind.) Fd. Amb. so that should evacuation become interrupted by roadblocks and the like surgical facilities would still remain available. The attack on the Tunnels opened on the 26th and that on the 'Hambone' feature on the 29th. An A.D.S. and a car post of four cars were established by two of the sections of the field ambulance and evacuation was by the Naf River to Bawli. Casualties were not numerous but they included a high proportion of 'exhaustion' cases. These were dealt with by the psychiatrist of 36th Division who attached himself to 69 (Ind.) Fd. Amb. In this action 13 (Ind.) M.S.U. worked as far forward as the A.D.S.

On April 6, when 2nd R.W.F. of 29th Bde. Gp., u/c 72nd Bde. Gp., attacked the East Tunnel and occupied it without encountering resistance a section of 154 (Br.) Fd. Amb. accompanied the battalion as did also 25 S.Bs. of 5 (Ind.) Bearer Coy.

On April 9, 72nd Bde. was relieved by Indian 53rd Bde. of Indian 25th Division and moved back to the vicinity of Chota Maunghnama. On May 10, 69 (Ind.) Fd. Amb. moved with 36th Division to Shillong.

22 C.C.S. reached Chittagong on February 28, 1944 and on March 8 took over the site occupied by 15 (Ind.) C.C.S. in Bawli Bazar. There it remained until April 23 when it transferred its immovable patients (13) to 25 (Ind.) C.C.S. which replaced it and moved to Dimapur where it was to take over the British section of 66 I.G.H. (C).

81ST (WEST AFRICAN) DIVISION

This division came into being on March 1, 1943 in Nigeria. It was built out of three already existing independent brigades to which were added the requisite number and variety of divisional troops. The brigades and their field ambulances were:

    3rd (W.A.) Brigade (Nigeria); 3 (W.A.) Fd. Amb.
    5th (W.A.) Bde. (Gold Coast); 5 (W.A.) Fd. Amb.
    6th (W.A.) Bde. (Nigeria, Sierra Leone and Gambia); 6 (W.A.) Fd. Amb.

The divisional troops included men from all four West African Colonies. Attached to the three brigades and composed almost entirely of Nigerians were 3, 5 and 6 (W.A.) Fd. Hyg. Secs. In support of each brigade was a casualty clearing station; 27 (W.A.) C.C.S. (a Nigerian unit) was with 3rd Bde., 31 (a Gold Coast unit) with 5th Bde. and 29 (a Sierra Leone unit) was with 6th Bde.

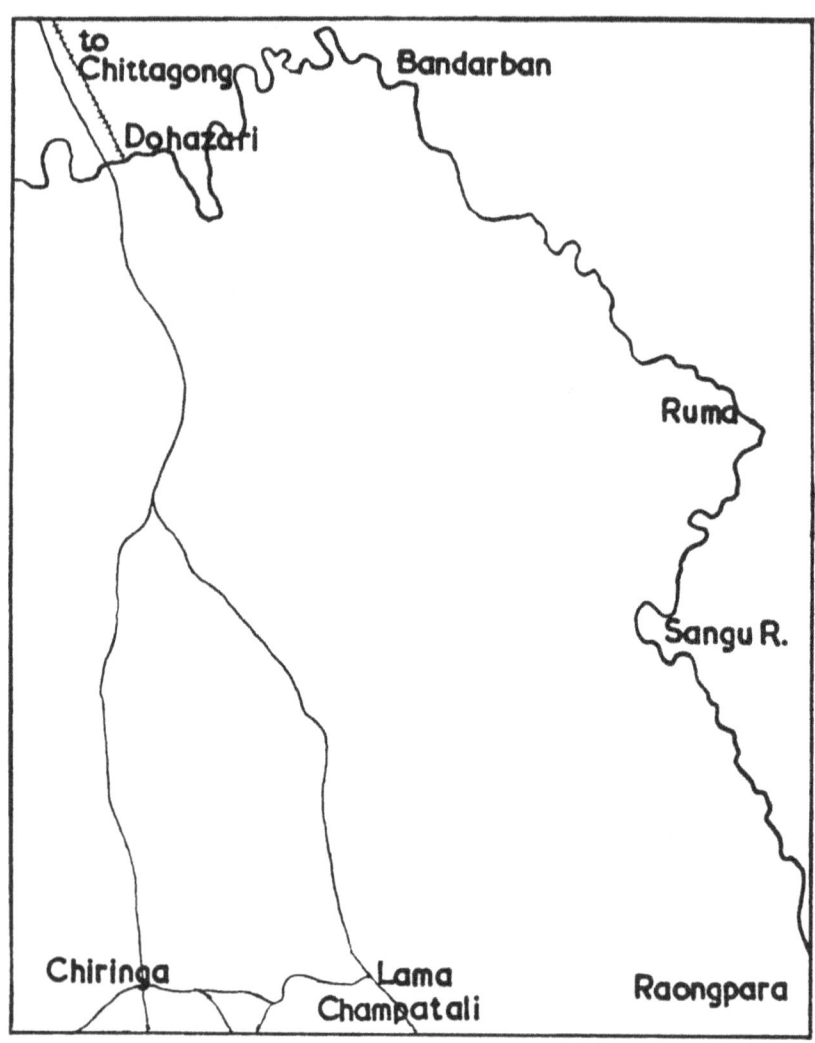

Fig. 20. Dohazari–Chiringa and Ruma

The division reached India *en route* for the Burma theatre between July and October 1943. Its 3rd Bde. was at once detached and sent to join 'Special Force' together with its field ambulance, its field hygiene section and 27 (W.A.) C.C.S. The rest of the division carried out training exercises in the Nasik area until in November the division moved to Arakan, by train to Calcutta, by sea to Chittagong, by train to Dohazari and then by road to Chiringa. On arrival there 6th (W.A.) Bde. set off immediately for Satpaung, accompanied by its field ambulance, *en route* for the valley of the Kaladan. The rest of the division soon followed. From Chiringa to Satpaung there was only a single

PLATE III. Typical Arakan hill country.

PLATE IV. A Patrol wading through a jungle stream.

Imperial War Museum

PLATE V. Casualties being evacuated on mules.

PLATE VI. A stretcher case being carried aboard a special hospital sampan on the way to a Casualty Clearing Station on the Arakan Front.

[*Imperial War Museum*]

PLATE VII. Arakan. Ambulance raft on a chaung.

[*Imperial War Museum*

PLATE VIII. Jeep evacuating casualty to Medical Staging Point. Arakan Front.

[*Imperial War Museum*

PLATE IX. Arakan. Ambulance convoy bringing wounded from 7th Division after its relief.

[Imperial War Museum

PLATE X. Evacuation of wounded by aircraft to Base Hospital from the Arakan Front.

[Imperial War Museum

footpath that for half of the 80 miles ran across the grain of the north-south mountain mass. It was decided to convert this path into a jeep-track. Covered by one of the brigades, the divisional engineers together with the second brigade and local labour carved this track across some of the very worst country in Burma, hindered by unexpected heavy rain and by an outbreak of cholera. While this 'West African Way' was being constructed, the divisional gunners made themselves an alternative route, 'Gunner Way', some 25 miles long. By the middle of December the division was concentrated in the Daletme–Satpaung area in the upper reaches of the River Kaladan. The division was then reinforced by 7/16th Punjab and 11th (E.A.) Scout Battalion. The Indian battalion was to protect the rear of the division as it moved southwards while the East African battalion was to operate on its left flank. The division was expected to reach Kyauktaw by about the middle of January 1944 but its progress was delayed through the loss at sea of the ship carrying its anti-aircraft and anti-tank guns. The division was to be supplied entirely by air. For the evacuation of its casualties the division was to construct a series of airstrips, both for the Moth and for the Dakota. For river transport rafts were to be much used.

The division reached the outskirts of the village of Kaladan early in February and on the 10th and 11th attacked strong-points in its vicinity but without success. The division was then ordered to by-pass such opposition and head for the Kanzauk Pass with all speed in order to play its part in the defeat of the expected Japanese counter-offensive by threatening to cut their L. of C. and by threatening their right flank. When Kaladan was by-passed the Japanese garrison abandoned the village and withdrew southwards. The division then crossed the Pi Chaung near its confluence with the Kaladan River and occupied Kyauktaw and Apaukwa and thereafter advanced towards the Kanzauk Pass.

The Japanese then counter-attacked 81st (W.A.) Division and mauled it so severely that for a time it could not be used for strenuous fighting. However, in April, the division cleared the Japanese from the area of Kaladan village. At this time Indian 7th Division had left the Arakan front for the north and the West African division, less 7/16th Punjab and 1st Gambia Battalion, was withdrawn from the Kaladan Valley to replace this Indian division. It marched right through the Japanese lines along a single-file track out of the Kaladan Valley over the Mayu Range into the valley of the Kalapanzin just south of Taung Bazar and then proceeded to Chiringa.

It is to be noted that the West African field ambulance consisted of a H.Q. company and three bearer companies. In the headquarters company was a surgical team consisting of a graded surgeon, an O.R.A., a British N.C.O. and four African N.Os. This team could be attached to one or other of the bearer companies as required. With the H.Q. company also was a dental team consisting of a dental officer, a clerk-orderly and an A.O.R. The bearer company was divisible into a headquarters and two bearer sections, each with an officer in charge. Each section consisted of four stretcher-squads, two African N.Os. and an African N.C.O. Clerks, cooks, sanitary and water-duty men formed part of the H.Q. of each company. Stores and equipment were carried on the head of auxiliary personnel and also by the unit personnel. Thirty-four auxiliary personnel were allotted to each of the bearer companies and each of them carried a load of 40 lbs. Of these 34 porters, 7 were used for the carrying of one day's rations for the unit. No definite number of porters was allotted to the headquarters company since its loads varied so greatly. When it was about to move it applied to brigade H.Q. for the auxiliary personnel it needed.

As the division moved from Chiringa across the ninety miles of

FIG. 21. Ruma–Mowdok and Satpaung

mountain and jungle *via* the valley of the Sangu into the valley of the Kalapanzin, casualties had to be left in a series of staging posts formed by the field ambulances and often consisting of a British N.C.O., a N.O. and one or two A.O.Rs. Portions of the route were too difficult for a stretcher party carrying a casualty. All casualties occurring west of Raongpara were therefore carried back to Champatali, 30 miles away and thence by porters to Chiringa where 50 (Ind.) S.S. was stationed. Casualties occurring to the east of Raongpara were carried forward to Singpa, 20 miles on and thence by porters to an A.D.S. in Mowdok. From here they were conveyed by porters down the River Sangu, a five days' journey, to Bandarban and thence by ambulance car to Patia and to a West African C.C.S.

As the division moved forward from Mowdok to Satpaung on the Kaladan River an A.D.S. was opened in Tungnang close to the river to hold casualties since evacuation for the time being was impossible; the track was too rough. An outbreak of cholera now occurred to add to the very great difficulties of the situation. Between December 20 and January 2 there were 72 cases and 44 deaths.

When the division reached Milawa, near Paletwa, a M.D.S. was opened there. It moved on to Pi Chaung two miles further south shortly afterwards. Evacuation was now by river to Tungnang and thence over the mountains to Mowdok and then again by river, the Sangu, to Bandarban and on, by M.A.S., to the rear. At Khonwei a landing strip 300 yards long was constructed, a mile from the M.D.S. and air evacuation by Moth aircraft to the rear hospitals became possible.

As the advance southwards continued large landing strips (1,700 yards long) capable of accepting Dakotas (D.C.3.) which could take up to 30 casualties, were constructed. A company of a field ambulance was usually sited near the airstrip to act as an air evacuation centre. As far as possible these airstrips were sited near to the River Kaladan so that the casualties could be brought to them by river.

Then came the Japanese counter-attack which pushed the West African division back to Kyauktaw and beyond. Two battalions, one the Gambian and the other the 7/16th Punjab, remained behind to hold the Japanese in check and to cover the withdrawal of the divisional transport up the valley of the Kaladan. The Japanese pressed hard upon this detachment and forced it out of the Kaladan Valley into that of the Sangu. The division itself left Kyingri on March 28 to return to Kaladan. All kit was drastically reduced. D.A.D.M.S., the chief clerk, the A.D.M.S'. office equipment, the headquarters company of each of the two field ambulances and the two hygiene sections were all classified among the non-essentials and were included in the transport column. The division now depended upon the mobile surgical teams of the field ambulances and upon bearer company personnel.

Reaching the Kaladan River, 6th Bde. crossed along with two companies of 6 (W.A.) Fd. Amb. From March 29 to April 10, when the division left Kaladan, it was involved in small engagements every day and every day there were casualties. An airstrip was constructed at Ngame but only four casualties were evacuated from it before its use was denied by the advance of the Japanese. Sixty casualties were evacuated from the airstrip at Kaladan. Between 150 and 200 casualties were sent along with the transport column in the care of a company of 6 (W.A.) Fd. Amb. An officer of 5 (W.A.) Fd. Amb. with surgical experience was attached to this company.

By April 10 the division had begun to move out of the Kaladan Valley towards that of the Kalapanzin. About halfway along this most difficult route the division rested for ten days at Saingdin Chaung. An airstrip at Pyinhla was used whenever possible and 41 casualties were evacuated from it. Many casualties were carried forward with the division. On May 13 Taung Bazar with its Dakota airstrip was reached. The division crossed the River Kalapanzin here, leaving 5th (W.A.) Bde. on the right bank. On June 11 the division began its move to its monsoon quarters at Chiringa.

Altogether 1,592 casualties were evacuated to Cox's Bazar and to Comilla during the course of these events. The method of evacuation by air was completely successful.

INDIAN 26TH DIVISION

Indian 26th Division consisting of 4th, 36th and 71st Brigades was served by 1, 46 and 48 (Ind.) Fd. Ambs. and 27 (Ind.) Fd. Hyg. Sec. At different times 6, 7, 10 and 11 (Ind.) M.S.Us., and 28 F.T.U. were attached to the division as were also 11 (Ind.) Fd. Amb. Tp. and 2 (Ind.) Bearer Coy. In February 1944, 1 (Ind.) Fd. Amb., serving with 36th Bde., was in Cox's Bazar; 46 (Ind.) Fd. Amb., with 4th Bde. had its H.Q. in Goppe Bazar and companies in Prinkhaung and Badana and 48 (Ind.) Fd. Amb., with 71st Bde., was in Bawli Bazar North.

On March 4, 46 (Ind.) Fd. Amb. established its M.D.S. at the east end of the Ngakyedauk Pass. To the M.D.S. 11 (Ind.) M.S.U. was attached. Wards were constructed of split bamboo and were roofed with reeds. 'B' Coy. of this unit was running an A.D.S. that was located near brigade H.Q. Evacuation was from A.D.S. to M.D.S. by ambulance cars of the unit and from the M.D.S. to 23 (Ind.) C.C.S. by 53 M.A.S. On March 19 it was considered necessary to distribute Sten guns among unit personnel. It was arranged that all medical cases should be sent to 1 (Ind.) Fd. Amb's. 'A' and 'B' Coys. which were in Buthidaung and that 46 (Ind.) Fd. Amb. should admit all the surgical cases. On April 13, 28 F.T.U. joined the division and was attached to the M.D.S. of 46 (Ind.) Fd. Amb., taking over resuscitation duties. On the 15th, 60 battle casualties were admitted. Difficulty was caused by the cessation of evacuation by night. The roads were very bad, lights were prohibited and Japanese patrols were active. So it was that the time interval between wounding and surgical intervention tended to become undesirably prolonged.

On April 16 it was possible to shorten the evacuation route by sending casualties through 46 (Ind.) S.S. at Kayugyaung. On the 20th casualties from 81st (W.A.) Division were admitted to the M.D.S. and as it was reported that there were smallpox contacts among them they had to be segregated and sent back to 23 (Ind.) C.C.S. by special convoy. At the beginning of May both A.D.S. and M.D.S. were working under pressure for no less than 460 casualties passed through them in two days. The M.D.Ss. of 1 and 48 (Ind.) Fd. Ambs. had been closed, preparing for a move and so could not help. The stress was felt most by those concerned with maintaining records and with the labelling of the patients' kit but the mobile surgical unit was forced to restrict its keenest attention to those with abdominal wounds and with fractured femurs.

On May 8/9, 4th Bde. and 'B' Coy's. A.D.S. moved back to Wabyin and thence by M.T. to Tumbru Ghat. 10 (Ind.) M.S.U., which had been with this A.D.S., returned to 25 (Ind.) C.C.S. in Bawli Bazar. 'A' Coy. soon followed and the M.D.S. at the east end of the Ngakyedauk Pass then closed, and, leaving a small section with 69 (Ind.) Fd. Amb. (XV Corps) likewise moved to Tumbru Ghat, 11 (Ind.) M.S.U. and 28 F.T.U. returning to 23 (Ind.) C.C.S. Evacuation from Tumbru Ghat was by way of 81 (Ind.) S.S. in Tumbru Ghat to 125 I.G.H. Malaria was rife in certain units of the division, especially in 1st Wilts. During the monsoon period while the countryside was often flooded the unit engaged in training for jungle warfare. On September 8 the unit relieved 48 (Ind.) Fd. Amb. in Bawli, 16 (Ind.) Fd. Amb. Tp. remaining with 46. Evacuation was by personnel of 2 (Ind.) Bearer Coy. from the top of Goppe Pass to the junction of the Bawli–Maungdaw and the Bawli roads; by ambulance car to the M.D.S. in Bawli and thence to the jetty; to the C.C.S. by launch. About 60 casualties a day were being evacuated at this time.

48 (Ind.) Fd. Amb., like 46 had moved with the division from Maynamati Camp to Fenua near Chittagong in January 1944. By February 8 the unit had moved *via* Dohazari to Bawli North there to be accommodated partly in *bashas*. On January 12 'A' Coy. moved to Goppe Bazar, its equipment being carried on twenty-two mules, and there opened an A.D.S., and on the 15th moved on to Taung Bazar. With this company were ten riding mules of 11 (Ind.) Fd. Amb. Tp. On the 17th 'B' Coy. moved to Grikegyaung *via* Garrett's Garden to open its A.D.S. in *bashas*. This A.D.S. functioned as a staging post. Some 250 casualties, mainly sick, passed through it, during the period

February 18–28. On the 29th H.Q. and the M.D.S. of this field ambulance moved from Bawli Bazar to Wabyin and the A.D.S. of 'B' Coy. to Badana West.

On March 2, H.Q. 48 (Ind.) Fd. Amb. was occupying a position just outside the administrative box of Indian 7th Division and was informed that it was to move within the perimeter of 1/18th R.Garh.Rif. of 71st Bde. It found itself in the vicinity of a burial-area remarkable for a pungent smell of putrefaction before it moved within the Garhwali's perimeter. There was much firing in the area of the M.D.S. but the only casualties received were two Japanese, one of them dead on arrival. 1 Section of 'A' Coy. left 'A' Coy. H.Q. in Taung Bazar on March 1 to open a light A.D.S. in support of 5/1st Punjab in Paledaung East, the equipment being carried on seven pack-mules borrowed from 8/13th F.F.Rif. Five riding mules were attached for evacuation purposes. The headquarters of 'A' Coy. and 2 Section proceeded to Awlanbyin East in support of 71st Bde., the equipment being carried on sixteen mules. Men and mules swam across the Kalapanzin River, the equipment being transported on bamboo rafts. An A.D.S. was opened in Awlanbyin and almost immediately 30 casualties were received from 54 (Ind.) Fd. Amb. of Indian 7th Division.

Meanwhile 1 Section of 'A' Coy. had encountered difficulty of an unusual kind. The stretcher-bearer squads of the field ambulance had been ordered by an officer of 5/1st Punjab to carry ammunition forward. The field ambulance officer in charge of the squads refused to allow the men to carry out this order. A subedar of 5/1st Punjab at pistol point, ordered field ambulance personnel to remove ordnance stores from a dump that was under enemy fire. One of the field ambulance sepoys was wounded while so engaged. The officer commanding the field ambulance, being informed of these events, saw the officer commanding the Punjabis who promptly took steps to demonstrate to his unit that field ambulance personnel, claiming the protection of the Red Cross, could not be so employed.

On March 6 an arrangement was made whereby the casualties admitted to the light A.D.S. in Paledaung East would be evacuated through the A.D.S. of 54 (Ind.) Fd. Amb. (Indian 7th Division) east of the Kalapanzin River and then by motor sampan through ferry-head to the M.D.S. of 48 (Ind.) Fd. Amb. 'B' Coy. 48 (Ind.) Fd. Amb. built a jetty in the Ngakyedauk Chaung and on the 7th the first batch of casualties from the light A.D.S. evacuated by this route arrived. On March 13 the light A.D.S. of 'A' Coy. moved to the vicinity of Sinohbyin.

There was considerable Japanese activity in the vicinity of the M.D.S. of 48 (Ind.) Fd. Amb. about this time and an occasional air raid but casualties were few. On the 25th about 80 Japanese entrenched themselves near to the box of 1/18th R.Garh.Rif. and during the fighting that followed evacuation from the M.D.S. was impossible. Precautionary preparations for a sudden move to a firm base were made. The field ambulance was to be protected by the rearguard of the Garhwalis. The officer commanding the field ambulance made contact with 1 (Ind.) Fd. Amb. south of the Maungdaw–Buthidaung road in 36th Bde's. area and discussed arrangements for the evacuation of casualties in the event of 71st Bde. operating in that area. R.I.A.S.C. personnel manned a section of the perimeter allotted to the field ambulance; the reception ward of the M.D.S. was converted into a strong point and Sten guns were distributed to the officers and men of the medical unit and to such patients as were capable of handling them. Eleven casualties from the 1/18th R.Garh.Rif. were admitted during the night of March 25/26 and on the following day sixteen tanks harboured in the vicinity of the M.D.S. and it became possible to stand-down. The field ambulance personnel at once began to dig-in the M.D.S. to a depth of 5 ft.

On April 7 the brigade was involved in heavy fighting and the M.D.S. of 48 (Ind.) Fd. Amb. was accordingly busy. On May 1 the M.D.S. closed and on the 5th proceeded to Ukhia *via* the Ngakyedauk Pass and Wabyin. 'A' Coy. went to Taung Bazar and 'B' Coy. to Goppe Bazar. 'B' Coy. opened an A.D.S. in a nullah. This was shelled and one of the unit's R.I.A.S.C. personnel was wounded. The A.D.S. treated 147 battle casualties between May 3–6. Leaving a light section behind the company withdrew to Sinzweya under brigade orders. The light section soon followed but had to leave its equipment behind. Thence it moved to Goppe Bazar and established its A.D.S. During May some 900 casualties were evacuated through 'B' Coy.

During the month of June the M.D.S. of 48 (Ind.) Fd. Amb. was in Ukhia, 'A' Coy. in Taung and Goppe Bazars and 'B' Coy. in Bawli Bazar. A case of cholera had occurred in 1st Lincolns and so all ranks of the field ambulance were inoculated. Evacuation was to 1 (Ind.) M.F.T.U. in Redwinbyin. Activity was much reduced at this time for the monsoon rains were exceedingly heavy. In July the rains continued. 1 (Ind.) Fd. Amb. staged a jungle warfare course which was attended by personnel of the other divisional medical units. In Goppe Bazar floods disrupted the work of 'A' Coy.; the wards were all under water and three of the *bashas* collapsed. Evacuation to Bawli was impossible for a time. On the 25th it became possible to send 35 patients back to Bawli on riding mules and 5 more on stretchers.

In August the M.D.S. moved from Ukhia to Bawli Bazar and took over from the A.D.S. In September 'B' and 'A' Coys. changed over in Goppe and Taung Bazars. On October 6 the Japanese attacked the Goppe stronghold. A platoon of the Green Howards was detailed to guard the medical unit. Rifles were distributed among the unit personnel and such patients as could use them. On the 7th the Japanese withdrew.

On the 10th the field ambulance began to move to Tumbru Ghat with 71st Bde., being relieved in Goppe Bazar by 1 (Ind.) Fd. Amb. From Tumbru Ghat the unit moved back to Dohazari *en route* for Chittagong, Calcutta, Alipore and Cocanada where training in combined operations was begun in preparation for the assault landing on Akyab Island.

These operations in Arakan had witnessed a number of significant developments in the provision of medical cover and in the system of evacuation. Evacuation from the divisions in the valley of the Kalapanzin and west of the Mayu Range was greatly facilitated by the use of the stretcher-fitted jeep. This was made possible by the construction by the engineers of jeep tracks over the passes of the Mayu Range and to the forward areas. This method constituted a great advance on the mule or stretcher-bearer method of 1942-43.

It became the policy to group a number of medical units, relatively close to the front line, for the holding and treatment of cases of uncomplicated malaria and of other light sick. The geography of the Naf Peninsula made this possible for this area could not easily be involved in the characteristic Japanese movement round the flank to the rear of a position. The Naf River was much used for the smooth if slow transport of casualties to the grouped medical units on the Peninsula. There were three C.C.Ss. and three M.F.T.Us. in this medical area and their use greatly reduced the amount of movement of the sick and also reduced the time these spent away from their units. Two of the C.C.Ss. admitted the general run of cases, each taking 50 in rotation. The third C.C.S. received the specialist type of case, the psychiatric and the V.D. This system ensured that the staffs of all three units had adequate rest intervals. It was usual for an Indian staging section to be placed in charge of reception. Evacuation from this medical area was by river to Tumbru Ghat, then by road to 125 I.G.H. in Dhoapalong and by river and road to Cox's Bazar where 1,700 Indian, 300 British and 1,000 West African beds were available. From Cox's Bazar evacuation was by sea to Chittagong. Dacca was being developed as a large hospital centre.

The evacuation chain still involved a very considerable number of stages and changes of transport. The incidence of sickness, and especially of malaria, was so high that in spite of the development of the forward holding units, the M.F.T.Us., and of the increase in the number of hospital beds in the forward zone, it was still necessary to send large numbers of relatively light sick patients to the base hospitals in India, some of them over 1,000 miles away. As far as possible such patients were saved the long journeys by road, rail or river by being despatched from the airstrips at Bawli Bazar and Ramu to Comilla.

MEDICAL ARRANGEMENTS

By the middle of 1943 much that had been unsatisfactory in the arrangements made to provide hospital cover for the formations fighting in Burma had been removed. In the north, in the Imphal area the provision of C.C.Ss. and small general hospitals had continued to improve throughout the year and it was becoming possible to retain a considerable proportion of the patients in this forward zone. Convalescent depots had been improvised and thereafter regularised and at the end of the year there were two of these units in Imphal and five in Kohima. Vast improvements had been effected in the roads and casualties could now be evacuated by ambulance car in fair comfort. Staging sections were available and were distributed to give the greatest service. In Manipur Road two general hospitals were to be opened and the place developed as a satisfactory railhead. A pool of small hospitals in the Assam Plain was receiving a proportion of the casualties that were evacuated from the forward zone. Ambulance trains, becoming available, were brought forward for use on both the broad and metre gauge lines and contributed much to the raising of the morale of the troops. Gauhati was developed so that 52 I.G.H. could receive and distribute patients (i) up the hills to the Shillong hospital and convalescent depot group; (ii) up river to Tezpur and the hospitals in its vicinity which dealt with the less severe cases and returned them to their units, and (iii) down river by a well organised hospital river steamer service to Sirajganj and the base hospitals in Calcutta and in Ranchi. Medical stores and Red Cross stores were now well developed.

The greatest development during the past twelve months had occurred in the Central zone. An advanced medical base was forming in Dacca and its satellites, Comilla and Agartala. This development was part of the general scheme to remove the necessity of sending casualties too far away from the front. Distances are so vast in India that if men had to be sent as far back as Ranchi, for example, months elapsed before their units saw them again. Dacca was ideally situated for such a development. It was a university town, pleasant and well built. It was on the river and railway and had an airfield. University buildings, schools and the new Government House offered really excellent accommodation. It was ultimately to have no less than five general hospitals and four convalescent depots capable of accommodating no less than 10,000 patients.*

In the southern zone 68 I.G.H. in Chittagong remained the key unit in the evacuation system. To it was added 56 I.G.H. Embarkation

---

* Up to 1942 the Army was responsible for providing hospital accommodation for R.A.F. personnel in India. This arrangement was found to be unsatisfactory and so the R.A.F. began to satisfy its own needs in respect of hospital beds. (*see R.A.F. Medical Services*, Vol. III. Campaigns. p. 702.)

medical staffs and units were organised and a system of reception and evacuation by sea and by rail was evolved. The interval between Chittagong and the front line was outfitted with a series of medical units, C.C.Ss. and M.F.T.Us. at Dhoapalong and general hospitals in Khurushkul Island near Cox's Bazar. The lighter cases could now be held in the forward zone.

Eight hospital river steamers were now available in addition to the rightly famous veteran Chinese river steamer *Wu Sueh*, converted into the one and only hospital ship and one with a very proud record.

It was in this fashion that the Army Medical Services pursued their development during this period. A location statement of the C.C.Ss. and the general hospitals in Eastern India as in October 1943 is given in Appendix XII.

APPENDIX X

XV CORPS. ORDER OF BATTLE AS AT DECEMBER 17, 1943

(much abbreviated)

H.Q. XV Corps

5/9th Jat.	Mowdok u/c 81st W.A. Div.
M.G. Bn. F.F.R.	Maynamati
1st Bihar	Lungleh

Medical

42 Sub-depot Medical Stores	Dhoapalong
43 ,, ,, ,,	Bawli North
1 (Ind.) Bearer Coy.	Cox's Bazar
2 (Ind.) ,, ,,	Garrett's Garden
37 (Ind.) S.S. (C.)	Cox's Bazar
42 ,, ,,	Tumbru
46 ,, ,,	,,
50 ,, ,,	Chiringa
52 (Ind.) Fd. Hyg. Sec.	Dhoapalong
38 (Ind.) A.M.U.	Tumbru
51 ,, ,,	Laung Chaung
15 (Ind.) Mob. X-ray Unit	Cox's Bazar
16 ,, ,,	Dhoapalong
80 ,, ,,	,,
81 ,, ,,	Bawli North
7 (Ind.) M.S.U.	,, ,,
8 ,, ,,	Badana, sampan-head

12 (Ind.) M.S.U.	Dhoapalong
28 F.T.U.	,,
18 (Ind.) Dent. Mech. Unit	Cox's Bazar
8 (Ind.) C.C.S.	Dhoapalong
15 ,, ,,	Bawli North
25 ,, ,,	Dhoapalong
Hospital 'flat' *Pennar* and six Creek vessels	Tumbru Ghat

Ind. 36th Bde. of Indian
    26th Division   Cox's Bazar
    14/12th F.F.R.   ,, ,,
    8/13th ,, Rif.   ,, ,,
    5/16th Punjab   ,, ,,

Medical
    1 (Ind.) Fd. Amb.   ,, ,,
    16 (Ind.) Fd. Amb. Tp. R.I.A.S.C. ,, ,,

Indian 5th Division   Chota Maunghnama
  Ind. 9th Bde.   Bawli North
    2nd W. Yorks   ,, ,,
    3/9th Jat.   ,, ,,
    3/14th Punjab   ,, ,,
    3/2nd Punjab, one coy.   ,, ,,

  Ind. 123rd Bde.   Ngakyedauk Pass
    2nd Suffolk   Wabyin
    2/1st Punjab   Zeganbyin
    1/17th Dogra   ,,
    3/2nd Punjab, one coy.   Ngakyedauk Pass

  Ind. 161st Bde.   Balukhali
    4th R.W.K.   Maunghnama
    1/1st Punjab   Bawli North
    4/7th Rajput Regt.   Nhila
    3/2nd Punjab, one coy.   Balukhali

Medical
    10 (Ind.) Fd. Amb.   Maughnama
    45 ,, ,,   Nawapara
    75 ,, ,,   Sabaigon South
    7 (Ind.) Fd. Hyg. Sec.   Maunghnama

Indian 7th Division   Laung Chaung
  Ind. 33rd Bde.   Awlanbyin
    1st Queens   ,,
    4/15th Punjab   ,,
    4/1st G.R.   ,,
    1/11th Sikh, one coy.   ,,

Ind. 89th Bde.   Ngakyedauk Pass, eastern end
    2nd K.O.S.B.   ,,   ,,
    7/2nd Punjab   ,,   ,,
    4/8th G.R.   ,,   ,,
    1/11th Sikh, one coy.   ,,   ,,

Ind. 114th Bde.   Bogyigyaung
    1st Som. L.I.   Taung Bazar
    4/14th Punjab   Bogyigyaung
    4/5th R.G.R.   ,,
    1/11th Sikh, one coy.   Letpanywa

Medical
    44 (Ind.) Fd. Amb.   Goppe Bazar
    54   ,,   ,,   Badana sampan-head
    66   ,,   ,,   Ngakyedauk Pass, western end
    32 (Ind.) Fd. Hyg. Sec.   Laung Chaung

APPENDIX XI

81ST WEST AFRICAN DIVISION. ORDER OF BATTLE

(much abbreviated)

81 W.A. Division

    H.Q. 5th W.A. Bde.

        5th Gold Coast Regt.
        7th ,,   ,,   ,,
        8th ,,   ,,   ,,

    Medical
        5 (W.A.) Fd. Amb.
        5 (W.A.) Fd. Hyg. Sec.
        31 (W.A.) C.C.S.

    H.Q. 6th W.A. Bde.

        4th Nigeria Regt.
        1st Sierra Leone Regt.
        1st Gambia Regt.

    Medical
        6 (W.A.) Fd. Amb.
        6 (W.A.) Fd. Hyg. Sec.
        29 (W.A.) C.C.S.

        (3rd W.A. Bde. had been detached from the division for service with Indian 3rd Division ('Special Force').)

APPENDIX XII

EASTERN COMMAND AND FOURTEENTH ARMY. LOCATION OF GENERAL HOSPITALS AND CASUALTY CLEARING STATIONS IN EASTERN INDIA.

OCTOBER 1943

East of the Brahmaputra

Tiddim	16 (Ind.) C.C.S.
Palel	14 (Ind.) C.C.S.
Thoubal	24 (Ind.) C.C.S.
Imphal	19 (Ind.) C.C.S.
	41 I.G.H. (H.Q., 3 Br. and 7 Ind. secs.)
Kohima	49 I.G.H. (H.Q. and 10 secs.)
	53 I.G.H. (H.Q., 2 Br. and 5 Ind. secs.)
Kigwema	59 I.G.H. (H.Q. and 10 secs.)
Silchar	23 (Ind.) C.C.S.
	25 (Ind.) C.C.S.
Manipur Road	66 I.G.H. (H.Q., 3 Br. and 7 Ind. secs.)
Jorhat	45 I.G.H. (H.Q., 3 Br. and 7 Ind. secs.)
Sibsargar	51 I.G.H. (H.Q., 2 Br. and 5 Ind. secs.)
Margherita	13 (Ind.) C.C.S.
Dibrugarh	44 I.G.H. (H.Q., 2 Br. and 5 Ind. secs.)
Amarabari	43 I.G.H. (H.Q., 3 Br. and 7 Ind. secs.)
Gauhati	52 I.G.H. (H.Q., 3 Br. and 7 Ind. secs.)
Shillong	124 I.G.H. (H.Q., 2 Br. and 5 Ind. secs.)
Agartala	18 (Ind.) C.C.S.
Maynamati	74 I.G.H. (H.Q., 3 Br. and 7 Ind. secs.)
Dacca	62 I.G.H. (H.Q., 2 Br. and 5 Ind. secs.)
	63 I.G.H. (H.Q. and 10 secs.)
Comilla	92 I.G.H. (H.Q., 2 Br. and 5 Ind. secs.)
Chittagong	68 I.G.H. (H.Q., 3 Br. and 7 Ind. secs.)
	56 I.G.H. (H.Q., 3 Br. and 5 Ind. secs.)
	77 I.G.H. (2 secs.)
Dohazari	82 I.G.H. (H.Q., 3 Br. and 7 Ind. secs.)
Khurushkul Island (Cox's Bazar)	72 I.G.H. (H.Q., 2 Br. and 5 Ind. secs.)
Dhoapalong	8 (Ind.) C.C.S.
	9 (Br.) C.C.S.

West of the Brahmaputra

Sirajganj	75 I.G.H. (H.Q., 3 Br. and 7 Ind. secs.)
Calcutta	47 B.G.H. (1,200 beds)
Midnapore	39 I.G.H. (H.Q., 2 Br. and 5 Ind. secs.)
Dinapore	67 I.G.H. (H.Q., 2 Br. and 5 Ind. secs.)

West of the Brahmaputra—contd.

Ranchi	15 (Ind.) C.C.S.
	125 I.G.H. (H.Q., 3 Br. and 7 Ind. secs.)
	119 I.G.H. (H.Q., 2 Br. and 5 Ind. secs.)
	83 I.G.H. (H.Q., 1 Br. and 3 Ind. secs.)
	84 I.G.H. (H.Q., 1 Br. and 3 Ind. secs.)
	76 I.G.H. (H.Q. and 10 secs.)
Lohardaga . . .	80 B.G.H. (200 beds)
	77 I.G.H. (4 secs.)
Chas	77 I.G.H. (H.Q. and 4 secs.)
Namkum . . .	69 I.G.H. (H.Q., 2 Br. and 5 Ind. secs.)

C.C.Ss.	I.G.Hs.	B.G.Hs.
8 (Ind.) Dhoapalong	39 Midnapore	47 Calcutta
13 (Ind.) Margherita	41 Imphal	80 Lohardaga
14 (Ind.) Palel	43 Amarabari	
15 (Ind.) Ranchi	44 Dibrugarh	
16 (Ind.) Tiddim	45 Jorhat	
18 (Ind.) Agartala	49 Kohima	
19 (Ind.) Imphal	51 Sibsargar	
23 (Ind.) Silchar	52 Gauhati	
24 (Ind.) Thoubal	53 Kohima	
25 (Ind.) Silchar	56 Chittagong	
	59 Kigwema	
9 (Br.) Dhoapalong	62 Dacca	
	63 Dacca	
	66 Manipur Road	
	67 Dinapore	
	68 Chittagong	
	69 Namkum	
	72 Khurushkul Island (Cox's Bazar)	
	74 Maynamati	
	75 Sirajganj	
	76 Ranchi	
	77 Chittagong, Lohardaga and Chas	
	82 Dohazari	
	83 Ranchi	
	84 Ranchi	
	92 Comilla	
	119 Ranchi	
	124 Shillong	
	125 Ranchi	

CHAPTER 7

SPECIAL FORCE. (INDIAN 3rd DIVISION) OPERATION 'THURSDAY' FEBRUARY 1944

AS HAS already been stated, among the operations to be undertaken in 1944 were:

(i) the advance of Chinese 22nd and 38th Divisions under General Stilwell from Ledo to occupy Northern Burma up to the Mogaung-Myitkyina area in order to provide cover for the building of the road from Ledo to Paoshan;

(ii) the long range penetration by 'Special Force' to cut the communications of the Japanese northern front.

It was hoped that it would be found possible for the Chinese forces in Yunnan to co-operate by advancing towards Lashio.

By October 1943 the two Chinese divisions had moved from Ramgarh to Ledo. Chinese 30th Division and a U.S. regiment of three battalions —5307 Provisional Regiment, Merrill's Marauders—which had trained with 'Special Force' in long range penetration work and which was intended to be included in 'Special Force' but which had been transferred to General Stilwell's command, made ready to follow. With this force was a Chinese tank group and also a force of Kachin irregulars under U.S. officers. At Fort Hertz were Kachin Levies under British officers and a battalion of Burma Rifles, guarding an airstrip which was used as an emergency landing ground by the aircraft plying over the 'Hump'. This garrison was placed by General Slim under General Stilwell's command.

This force met little opposition to begin with as it moved forward from Ledo in the direction of Shingbwiyang but in November its advance was checked. General Stilwell had been away at the Cairo Conference. Returning, he resumed personal charge of the operation and moved forward on December 24. Whenever the Japanese in front of him attempted to stand he attacked and by the end of the month reached Shingbwiyang in the Hukawng Valley and had set out for Shaduzup at the head of the Mogaung Valley. While Chinese 22nd Division moved on Taro (January 30) and Pumsin (March 29), Chinese 38th Division and the U.S. L.R.P.Gp. moved on Maingkwan and Walawbum. These places were strongly defended but the Japanese were driven out of the

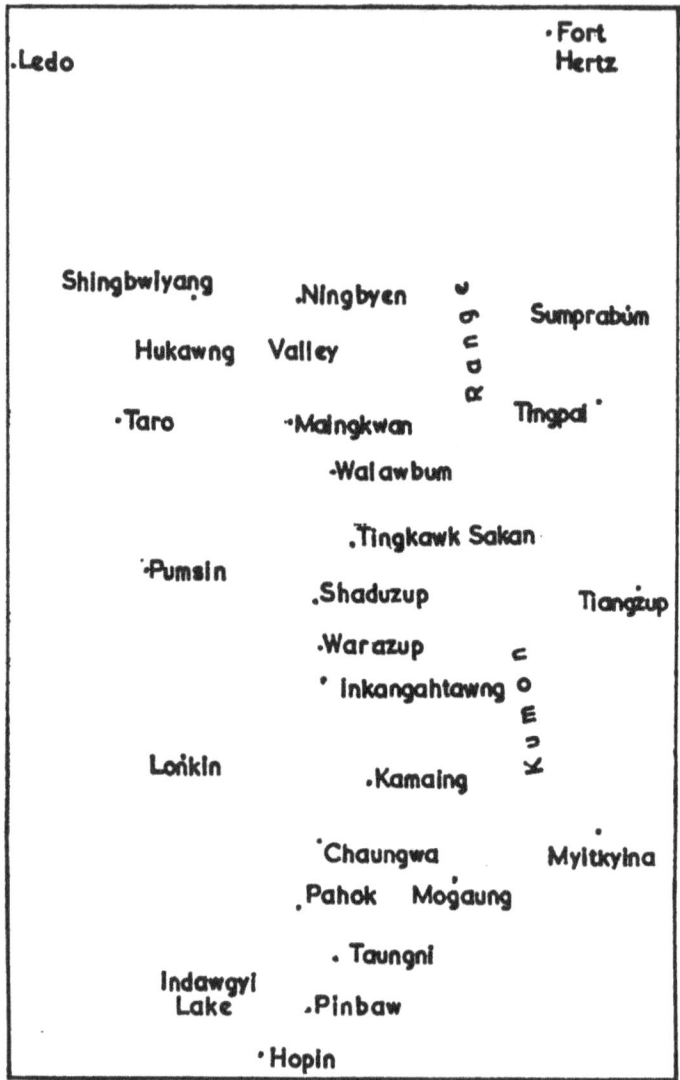

Fig. 22. Ledo–Indawgyi Lake

first on March 5 and of the second on March 7. A large part of the Hukawng Valley was now clear of Japanese.

The time had come for the intervention of 'Special Force'.

While the first Chindit expedition was still in Burma, General Wavell had decided to have a second brigade trained in this particular kind of warfare. Accordingly Indian 111th Bde. was formed (1st Cameronians, 2nd King's Own, 3/4th G.R. and 4/9th G.R.) and began its training in the jungles of the United Provinces between Jhansi and Jubbulpore.

SPECIAL FORCE. OPERATION 'THURSDAY'

Brigadier Wingate had returned from the Quebec Conference with authority to raise a force of six brigades each of four battalions. ('Special Force'). For purposes of deception it was designated Indian 3rd Division although in composition it was British, Gurkha and West African. (Indian troops could not be included because of their peculiar food needs.) With it there were some U.S. airfield engineers. To 111th Bde. was added Indian 77th Bde. (1st Kings; 1st L.F.; 1st S.Staffords.; 3/6th G.R.). Then 70th Division, which had fought in Syria (as 6th Div.) and had formed the garrison of Tobruk, was added, its three brigades 14th, 16th and 23rd being provided with an additional battalion apiece through the transformation of the divisional reconnaissance regiment and the division artillery into infantrymen. Finally 3rd West African Brigade (6th, 7th and 12th Nigeria Regts.) was allotted to the force to bring its strength up to that of two standard infantry divisions. It came to have an elaborate staff and administrative set-up. The force was placed under the command of Major-General Wingate. It was concentrated in the area Gwalior–Jhansi–Nowgong–Jubbulpore–Saugor for training. The force was organised into 'Special Force' H.Q. and six brigades. Of these brigades 23rd was later transferred to the Kohima front and the West African brigade was broken down into its component battalions which were used for airstrip defence. During the training period the brigades worked independently and were widely separated from each other. The training and especially the exercises were arduous and realistic; they tested the resources of the troops to the utmost.

A column was comprised of an infantry company of four platoons each of four sections; a support group of two medium machine-guns and two 3-in. mortars; a demolition group of sappers; and a reconnaissance platoon, of which a quarter consisted of hill tribesmen. The strength of a column was close on 400 men and 60 animals, mostly mules but including a few chargers. It is of interest to note that 2nd B.W. of 14th. Bde. of 70th Division, on becoming part of 'Special Force', became divided into two columns which took their numbers from the old numbers of this regiment, the senior of the columns calling itself 73 and the junior 42.

In February 1944 a joint directive by the U.S. Commander of the Eastern Air Command and General Slim, commanding Fourteenth Army, was given to the Commander of U.S. No. I Air Commando and to Major-General Wingate, ordering 'Special Force' to march and fly in to the Rail Indaw area. This Indaw is on the Mandalay–Myitkyina railway; there is another Indaw—Oil Indaw—to the south-west of it. The objectives named in this instruction were:

(i) to help the advance of General Stilwell's force on Myitkyina by cutting the communications of the Japanese troops in this area, harassing their rear and preventing their reinforcement;

(ii) to create a favourable situation for the Yunnan Chinese forces to cross the Salween and enter Burma;
(iii) to inflict the greatest possible damage and confusion on the Japanese in Burma.

General Wingate had learnt much from the first expedition. He had concluded that about two months was as long as the average Chindit could be expected to stand up to the rigours of life in the jungle. He therefore divided his force into two and planned to use half of it at a time. Half of it would enter Burma and after two or three months would be relieved by the other half and this in its turn would be replaced by the first half after 2-3 months. It was assumed that by October or thereabouts the task of the Chindits would be finished and that General Stilwell's Chinese, the Yunnan Chinese and IV Corps would have linked up and that Northern Burma would be clear of all Japanese troops.

In early January 1944, 16th, 77th and 111th Bdes. were selected to form the first wave of the force to enter Burma and proceeded to their concentration areas, 16th Bde. to the vicinity of Ledo, 77th Bde. to that of Lalaghat in the valley of the Brahmaputra and 111th Bde. to that of Imphal. Each of these brigades left its brigade depot staff in Orchha near Jhansi. The air base of the Force was in Sylhet. The rear headquarters of the brigades and Force Tactical H.Q. were in Imphal until the Japanese offensive, which began shortly after 'Special Force' had set out for Burma, made it necessary for them to move back to Sylhet.

General Wingate had been persuaded by the experience of the first expedition that the only possible method of supply and of evacuation was by air. At the Quebec Conference he had been assured that the U.S.A.A.F. would provide the necessary men and machines. U.S. No. 1 Air Commando undertook to fly the Chindits in and Troop Carrier Command to supply them thereafter. The importance of the rôle that these two organisations played in this expedition cannot be overemphasised.

The first plan involved the transport by air of 77th Bde. to a Chinese airfield in Yunnan whence the brigade would march into Burma to make contact with the other brigades which were to march in from the west. To each of the three brigades a squadron of light planes was to be allotted for casualty evacuation, the aircraft being based on airfields to the west of the Chindwin and behind IV Corps' front. But it was quickly realised that these planes were unable to fly to the vicinity of Indaw and back again without refuelling. It was also discovered that the Japanese were holding the east bank of the Chindwin in fair strength and that if 16th and 111th Bdes. had to fight their way across the river between Tamanthi and Kalewa they could endure crippling losses at the very outset of the operation. Then it was learnt that the Chinese could not make an airfield in Yunnan available.

SPECIAL FORCE. OPERATION 'THURSDAY'

It so happened, however, that about this time, after the brigades had moved from Gwalior to the area of Imphal, successful trials had been carried out with the gliders of U.S. No. I Air Commando so that it became possible to think of flying the brigades into Burma. General Wingate now formulated his 'stronghold' plan whereby each brigade would construct a Dakota landing strip for itself somewhere within 50 miles of Rail Indaw in an area as inaccessible as possible. This would be the core of a defended locality which would be guarded by a battalion of infantry with A.A. and field artillery and which would form a firm base for the brigade's light plane squadron. These planes would fly out to temporary airstrips, collect the casualties and fly them back to the stronghold and the Dakota strip.

The final tactical plan was as follows: 16th Bde. (2nd Queen's, 2nd Leicesters, 51/69th Fd. Regt., R.A., 45th Recce. Regt.) would march into Burma, setting out a month or so before the other brigades were flown in. This brigade would make for an area, selected on the map, some 27 miles to the north-west of Rail Indaw and given the name of 'Aberdeen'. The other two brigades, conveyed in gliders, would land in two areas, selected on the map, named 'Piccadilly' (which had been used in the first expedition), 40 miles to the north-east of Rail Indaw, and 'Broadway', 35 miles east-north-east of Indaw. The troops would at once, with the help of the U.S. airfield engineers, using bulldozers, also conveyed by glider, proceed to clear the area and to construct a landing strip fit for Dakotas. Reinforcements would then be flown in and casualties would be flown out. On the second night of the operation more gliders with more troops would land in another area, 'Chowringhee',* about 35 miles to the east of Indaw. Two of these areas would be transformed into 'strongholds', each serving as a base for a brigade. It would be garrisoned by a battalion of infantry supported by A.A. and field guns. Each stronghold was far removed from roads, in an unpopulated area, near water and was a natural clearing in the jungle; within it or nearby there was sufficient flat land to make the construction of an airstrip easy. From its stronghold a brigade would sally forth on its various tasks, it would construct a temporary airstrip whenever necessary and this would be used by light aircraft plying between it and the stronghold.

It was not intended to convert 'Chowringhee' into a stronghold for the reason that it was too accessible. It was intended that either 'Piccadilly' or 'Broadway' should be abandoned. When the brigades were established

---

*'Piccadilly', 'Broadway' and 'Chowringhee' were chosen as a compliment to the men of Britain, the United States of America and of India who were taking part in the adventure; they are the names of famous thoroughfares in London, New York and Calcutta respectively. 'Aberdeen' was chosen for a different reason—it was the birthplace of the wife of the commander of 'Special Force'.

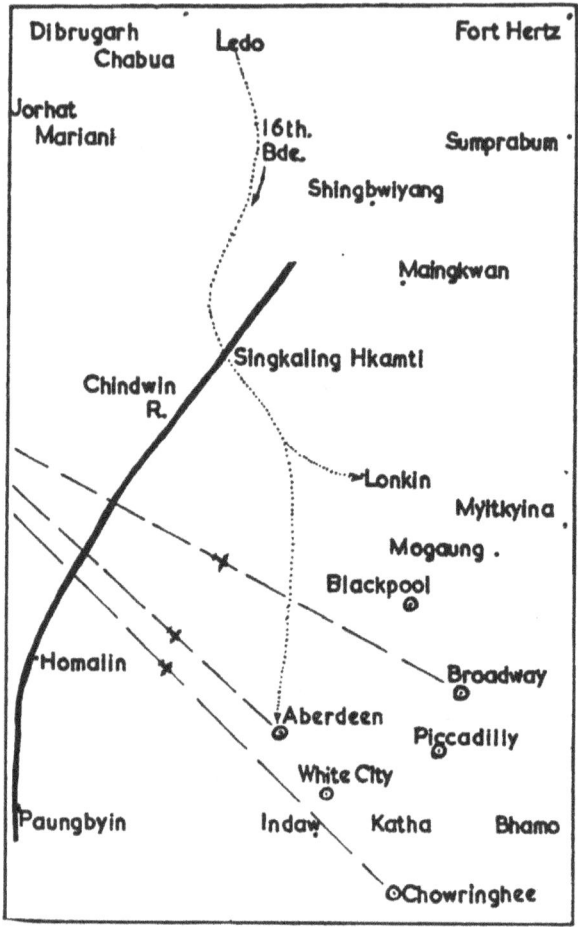

Fig. 23. Operation 'Thursday'

they would proceed to capture the airfield at Indaw which would then be garrisoned by an infantry battalion to be supplied by Fourteenth Army. This being done, the Chindits would then mill round north Central Burma cutting the railway line, blocking the road, destroying Japanese dumps and generally making complete nuisances of themselves.

On February 8, 16th Bde. set out from Ledo. It reached the Chindwin at Singkaling Hkamti, and using inflatable boats, rubber dinghies and, brought in by glider, assault boats with outboard motors, crossed the river to raid Lonkin, 50 miles to the south of Maingkwan at General Stilwell's request. By the end of March the brigade, supplied by air-drop, had passed the great Indawgyi Lake and had established itself in 'Aberdeen' about 25 miles from the Mandalay–Myitkyina railway line. In just over six weeks the brigade had covered 450 miles of exceedingly difficult country.

On the evening of March 5 the Lalaghat airfield was crowded with gliders, their tow-craft and the troops who were to act as the spearhead for the Chindits on 'Piccadilly' and 'Broadway'. Gliders were loaded with jeeps, bulldozers and the like. Just as Operation 'Thursday' was about to begin recent photographs of the two landing zones arrived. 'Piccadilly' was seen to be covered with huge tree trunks. Though at the time it was thought that this could mean that the Japanese had become aware of the proposed fly-in, it was learnt later that Burmese lumbermen were using the clearing for drying timber. General Slim decided that the operation should proceed and so the troops who should have gone to 'Piccadilly' were diverted to 'Broadway'.

At this time 77th Bde. had the following composition:

Striking Force
  H.Q. 77th Bde.
    Hong Kong Volunteers, one pln.*
    1st L.F.
    1st S.Staffords
    3/6th G.R.

Stronghold Garrison Force
  1st Kings
  Indian 53rd Observation Unit
  One troop, R.A.
  One troop Light A.A.
    attached
      U.S. Light Plane Force
      U.S. Engineers
      U.S. Ground Control personnel

u/c 77th Bde.
  3/9th G.R.
  'Dahforce'

The composition of 111th Bde. was as follows:

Adv. Bde. H.Q.
  4/9th G.R.   (49 and 94 Columns)
  3/4th G.R.   (30 ,, 40 ,,)
  2nd King's Own (41 ,, 46 ,,)
  1st Cameronians (26 ,, 90 ,,)
  6th Nigeria Regt.

---

* A party of officers and men of the Hong Kong Volunteer Defence Corps and of the Hong Kong and Singapore Royal Artillery had been sent to the Bush Warfare School at Maymyo before the Japanese entered the war. The fall of Hong Kong meant, of course, that they could not hope to return to Hong Kong until the end of the war. So, they were incorporated into the Chindits.

Of the 61 gliders that took off, 35 landed at 'Broadway'; 8 crashed in friendly territory; 9 landed in Japanese occupied areas; 2 crashed on the airstrip when taking off and 7 were recalled because of heavy congestion at 'Broadway'. At 'Broadway' the first six crash-landed. Three of them were so badly damaged that they could not be moved before the next wave of gliders came in. Some of these crashed into the stationary gliders and in the darkness it seemed that the adventure had finished almost before it had begun. In fact a signal was sent back to H.Q. Force that the attempt to land had failed. However, with the coming of the morning when the U.S. engineers began to clear up the wreckage it became evident that the crash-landings had been successful. Thirty-one men had been killed and thirty injured but there were 350 who were safe. Much of the equipment that was urgently needed had not reached 'Broadway' or reaching it had been smashed. Nevertheless, within twenty-two hours 'Broadway' was ready to receive the next lot of gliders. Next night 62 Dakotas landed at 'Broadway' and the assault glider part of 111th Bde. reached 'Chowringhee' unopposed. By March 11 the whole of 77th Bde. and half of 111th Bde. (the Cameronians and the King's Own) were at 'Broadway' and the other half of 111th Bde., with Brigade H.Q. and 'Dahforce'—Kachins with British officers for use in raising the local tribes—were safely at 'Chowringhee'. Between March 5 and 10 nearly six hundred Dakota and a hundred glider sorties had massed some 9,000 troops and 1,100 animals exactly where they were intended to be. 16th Bde. was at 'Aberdeen'.

The Japanese reactions to these events were distinctly tardy. They were just about to launch a major offensive against IV Corps' front and their troops were moving into position. The incursion of the Chindits was not permitted to interfere with their plans and so some time was required before they could collect and organise a number of units to deal with the Chindits. By the time the Japanese air force paid any attention to the Chindits the strongholds had the protection of A.A. guns and of the R.A.F.

On March 16, 77th Bde., which had marched west from 'Broadway', eliminated a small Japanese garrison near Mawlu on the Mandalay–Myitkyina railway and established a new stronghold and airstrip at 'White City'* nearby. The rail and road communications of the Japanese facing General Stilwell were now cut. The Japanese were therefore obliged to take notice of the Chindits and a force about 6,000 strong was sent against 'White City'. 77th Bde. withstood a number of fierce assaults and then the Japanese withdrew.

From 'Chowringhee' 'Morrisforce'—4/9th G.R. (49 and 94 Cols.)

---

*The name 'White City' refers to the appearance given to the area by the large numbers of parachutes that festooned everything.

and 40 Column of 3/4th G.R.—marched eastwards to the Burma-China frontier and thence northward towards Myitkyina to cut the Bhamo–Myitkyina road. H.Q. 111th Bde. and 30 Column of 3/4th G.R. moved well to the west of Indaw towards a rendezvous point about 130 miles away, there to join up with the Cameronians and The King's Own from 'Broadway'.

The Japanese offensive against IV Corps was now in full swing and the tactical situation about Imphal and Kohima was giving rise to a certain anxiety. Nevertheless, General Slim decided to reinforce the Chindits. 14th Bde. was flown in to 'Aberdeen' during the period March 22–April 4 and by April 12, 3rd W.A. Bde. had been distributed in battalions to the different strongholds.

General Wingate, flying by night from 'Broadway' to Lalaghat was killed when the bomber carrying him crashed in the hills near Bishenpur.

Indaw proved to be too well guarded and the assault upon it by 16th Bde. aided by part of 14th Bde. was repulsed. Chindit columns were now roaming about the area north of Indaw on both sides of the railway, fighting many minor engagements and completely blocking the railway as well as seriously interrupting the flow of traffic on the road. The Japanese were obliged to send more and more troops to oppose the Chindits who, evacuating 'White City' marched 80 miles over the mountains to establish another stronghold at 'Blackpool' to the north of Hopin. 16th Bde. was so exhausted by its march into Burma and by the abortive attack on Indaw that it was found necessary to have it flown out in returning transport aircraft.

Meanwhile General Stilwell had broken into the Mogaung Valley, driving the Japanese southwards. Two more Chinese divisions were on their way to join him so that his prospects for inflicting serious defeat upon his antagonists were very bright.

But in the second week of March, as will be told later, the Japanese were besieging Kohima and had isolated Imphal. It began to look as though General Stilwell's only line of communication in the valley of the Brahmaputra was about to be cut. General Stilwell offered to halt his advance and to send Chinese divisions to the aid of IV Corps. But General Slim, being confident of the outcome of the Kohima battle, decided that General Stilwell should not be deprived of his victory. He therefore retained Chinese 38th Division and was promised that if his communications were cut they would not remain so for more than ten days.

On April 28 three battalions of 'Merrill's Marauders'—the U.S. equivalent of the L.R.P. units—and six battalions of Chinese troops set out for Myitkyina across the mountains. Having made their way for nearly one hundred miles over the most difficult country, they rushed the airfield at Myitkyina and drove the Japanese guarding it into the town.

An attack upon the town on May 19 was unsuccessful and after this the Chinese, reinforced until they numbered some 30,000, settled down to besiege the place. It was not until August 3 that it was taken.

While the investment of Myitkyina was proceeding the Chindits were fighting desperately to hold 'Blackpool'. 'Morrisforce'—part of 111th Bde. plus 'Dahforce'—was moving north up the Bhamo road towards Myitkyina. General Slim now placed the Chindits under General Stilwell's command.

On May 10/11, 40,000 Chinese troops in Yunnan crossed the Salween and within a few days 32,000 more had joined them and began to force their way into the mountains north of Mengta, in the vicinity of Lameng and at Pingka. The Japanese facing them slowly withdrew converging on Lungling. In August a fierce Japanese counter-attack abruptly halted the Chinese advance for a time and thereafter slowed it down. The Japanese position in North Burma was fast becoming perilous. This huge mass of the Yunnan Chinese was pressing heavily upon the Japanese forces facing it; General Stilwell's main force was closing in on Kamaing; the Fort Hertz garrison was moving southwards from Sumprabum and 'Morrisforce' was advancing on Myitkyina from the east of the Irrawaddy.

The Cameronians and the King's Own of 111th Brigade reinforced by the King's and 3/9th G.R. who arrived from 'Broadway' held 'Blackpool' against constant attack for three whole weeks and in so doing cut the Japanese lines of communication at a most critical time. The stronghold was very closely invested and was bombarded with both field and medium artillery. To interfere with the system of supply by air the Japanese made use of A.A. guns and so air evacuation had to be given up. Then the weather broke and air supply necessarily ceased. On May 25 the Chindits, carrying their wounded, broke through the encircling ring and set off for the vicinity of Indawgyi Lake there to make contact with other Chindit columns.

On June 16, Chinese 22nd Division took Kamaing and on the 20th, 77th Bde. stormed into Mogaung, just ahead of Chinese 38th Division. By this time it had become apparent that the Japanese offensive against IV Corps had ended in failure and that the Japanese must shortly begin to pull out of northern Burma. It had become apparent also that the Chindits had shot their bolt, as had also the U.S. Marauders.

The Commander of 111th Bde., less 'Morrisforce', urged that his men should have a medical examination and that all men not fit for action should be evacuated at once. When higher authority refused his request he asked to be relieved of his command, protesting that the men were being given tasks that they could not carry out in their present physical condition. They had had a dietary deficiency of about 800 Calories a day for 110 days and the average weight loss per man was between

30 and 40 pounds. After a particularly bitter series of signals he learnt that his request had at last been granted.

General Lentaigne had informed the Supreme Commander, S.E.A.C. that 'the whole force is now worn out, both physically and mentally and to keep them in close contact with the enemy indefinitely until a particular objective is made good is really not practical politics.' It was agreed that the two brigades of 'Special Force' that had been longest in the field should be medically examined and that all unfit men should be evacuated to India and that the rest of the Chindits should be relieved just as soon as 36th Division, then in Shillong, could reach the front and pass under General Stilwell's command.

In 111th Bde. 'At nameless spots in the jungle, over the next three days, every man was examined by medical boards consisting of two or three doctors. The strength of my four and a half battalions then totalled about 2,200 men. Those adjudged fit for any kind of action, in any theatre of operations, numbered 118, being 7 British officers, a score of British soldiers, and 90 Gurkhas'.

'Without waiting for further instructions I ordered all the unfit to move out to the road in their battalion formations, and march toward Kamaing, where Force H.Q. staff would take over.'*

An interesting observation concerning the state of health of the men of one of the brigades at the end of the operation is offered in W. F. Jeffrey's *Sunbeams like Swords*,† pages 167–8. 'It took us about a week to walk from Mogaung to the all-weather airfield at Shaduzup.... We went by easy stages, halting for long periods in the heat of the day and bivouacking early in the evening. There was no need to reconnoitre our paths or stop to cut our way through jungle with our blunt *kukris*. We kept to the road, and there were no Japanese to worry us ... and our watch on the bivouac perimeter was a perfunctory affair. To be sure, we still had mud and water and mosquitoes; but what were a few bites or a fever if we were going home, to clean clothes, hot baths, fresh vegetables, and unbroken sleep night after night? After "White City" and the Lohinche hills, the journey to Shaduzup should have been a pleasant enough stroll, when we could ruminate peacefully upon lucky escapes and pleasures to come.

'And yet it was not so; the march home tried us considerably, and it remained in most of our minds as a grim episode with its own problems and perplexities. Once or twice it seemed even tragic. We had, I suppose, few reserves of strength to draw upon. Weeks of living and sleeping in rain, on hard rations, had taken an inevitable toll, and sleep no longer had the deep and invigorating effect upon us that it had before. The

---

* *The Road past Mandalay* by John Masters, published by Michael Joseph, 1961.
† Published by Hodder and Stoughton, 1950.

tension of battle had disappeared suddenly. We were no longer keyed up to fight continually with only brief respites, and our nerves, which had been stretched taut for so long, now began to sag dangerously. We were suffering from the dark and complex aftermath of fear, with its associations of uneasiness and self-examination. We began to think and to remember.

'Before we left Mogaung, the most ill men had been taken to the light plane strip and evacuated by air, so that, when we began to march, we were ostensibly fit men. But, after a day, many men who were chronic sufferers of malaria began to burn and tremble; old jungle sores broke down afresh and diarrhoea literally ran through the column. Men fell out on the march, and, after a rest, straggled on in pairs or in groups. . . . Some of them were beyond caring and were content to be left lying in a wet ditch'.

MEDICAL COVER

Shortly after its creation an A.D.M.S. (later to become a D.D.M.S.) was appointed to 'Special Force'. On his recommendation a D.A.D.M.S., a D.A.D.H., a D.A.D.M., a medical officer i/c Force H.Q. staff and five clerks, R.A.M.C. were posted to it. With the force at the time when it was formed were the medical units of 70th Division, 173, 189 and 215 Fd. Ambs. and 3 (W.A.) Fd. Amb. of 81st West African Division. The field ambulances of 70th Division were disbanded and out of them a number of a new-type medical unit, the brigade medical unit (3 Officers and 32 O.Rs. and 8 O.Rs. R.A.S.C.), was formed. Its equipment was that of a headquarters company of a standard field ambulance with certain slight modifications in respect of ordnance stores and tentage. The brigade medical unit was designed to serve the following functions:

(i) to provide a 30-bed hospital in the brigade area during training and non-operational periods and at brigade H.Q. or in any other firm base during operations;
(ii) to supply reinforcements to the columns as required;
(iii) to supply medical stores to columns of its own brigade in a training area and in an operational area for a period of approximately three months.

There was considerable discussion between Major-General Wingate and his D.D.M.S. concerning the size and composition of the medical element of a column. The latter recommended that it should consist of one medical officer and eleven O.Rs., R.A.M.C. for a British column or I.A.M.C. for an Indian column. This recommendation was not accepted for the reason that in General Wingate's opinion the size of this element would increase the total size of the column to the point when it became unwieldy. He maintained that one medical officer and two O.Rs. would be quite sufficient as they would be called upon to deal only with severe illnesses or injuries. He suggested that the chaplain should be employed as a medical orderly. Ultimately a compromise was reached and each column, it was agreed, should have a medical officer, a sergeant and two O.Rs., R.A.M.C. or three O.Rs. in an Indian column which lacked a chaplain.

Each brigade was supposed to have six ambulance cars on its establishment but since these were unobtainable 3-ton lorries fitted with Berridge equipment were issued instead and these were later replaced by 15-cwt. trucks to carry four patients. The officer commanding the brigade medical unit indented on the Medical Stores, Jhansi, for stores in bulk and issued these to the columns as and when required.

During the period of training all casualties requiring hospitalisation were evacuated by 'Special Force' vehicles to the hospitals in Jhansi and its satellites.

Jhansi	a B.M.H.; an I.M.H.
	21 B.G.H, (600 beds), later replaced by 80 B.G.H. (200)
	40 W.A.G.H. detachment
	41 Ind. Con. Depot (B.T.)
	46 Ind. Con. Depot (I.T.)
Chattarpur	9 (Br.) C.C.S. (opened at the end of January 1944)
Talbahat	27 (W.A.) C.C.S. (75 West African beds; 25 British)

To begin with an ambulance train stabled near Jhansi was available for the conveyance of casualties but this was later replaced by two ambulance coaches which were coupled to an ordinary passenger train. But since there was only one such train a day and since this passed through the brigade area around Mahoba at midnight this arrangement proved to be unsatisfactory. It required that a small loading party should remain permanently at the station and travel each night with the coaches to Jhansi. When 9 C.C.S. opened in Chattarpur the problem was solved for a patient requiring hospitalisation urgently could now be sent to this unit. Evacuation from 77th and 111th Bdes. presented no difficulty for their training areas were not far from Jhansi. The West African brigade had its own C.C.S. in Talbahat and its field ambulance had retained its normal establishment of eleven ambulance cars. From the West African C.C.S. further evacuation was to 40 W.A.G.H. in Jhansi.

When in early January 16th, 77th and 111th Bdes. moved to their concentration areas around Ledo, Lalaghat and Imphal respectively, the brigade medical units of 16th and 77th Bdes. accompanied them. In 111th Bde. there was no such unit and the sick needing hospitalisation were sent to the military hospital at Milestone 16 on the Tiddim road. At this time it had been decided that Agartala was to be Force air base and that when brigades went into Burma these brigade medical units would move there. However, it was later found that Agartala could accommodate the air base of one brigade only and so Sylhet was used instead, Agartala being used as the air base of 14th Bde. of the second wave. At the brigade depots at Orchha near Jhansi there was no medical staff. A medical officer was appointed by Central Command to the combined depots of 16th, 77th and 111th Bdes. The depots of 14th, 23rd and 3 (W.A.) Bdes. were in the Lalitpur area and a medical officer of 27 (W.A.) C.C.S. was detailed to serve as medical officer in charge of this area. Later the brigade depots of 14th, 16th and 23rd Bdes. moved to Bangalore, the medical officer at Orchha going with them. The depots of 77th and 111th Bdes. moved to Dehra Dun where the medical officer with the Burma Rifles battalion there took over the medical charge of the two depots.

General Wingate issued instructions to the effect that only the A.D.M.S. (appointed when the Force moved forward in January 1944 and became divided into an operational wing and the base in Gwalior) was to function in the operational area where he would be attached to Tactical Headquarters in the capacity of medical adviser. The rest of the D.D.M.S's. staff would remain with the Main Headquarters in Gwalior. A later instruction forbade D.D.M.S. to visit the operational area or to make contact with his A.D.M.S.

The newly appointed A.D.M.S. joined General Wingate and a small planning echelon of Force Tactical H.Q. in Sylhet. He was instructed to make whatever arrangements he considered necessary for the reception of casualties evacuated by air to the air bases at Sylhet and Agartala and to the airfields and airstrips used by light planes evacuating casualties from the columns. He was to make these arrangements after consultation with D.D.M.S. Fourteenth Army. A few days later A.D.M.S. learnt that Operation 'Thursday' was to make its beginning on the following evening.

This was the first time the medical services of 'Special Force' were permitted to consider the design of arrangements for dealing with casualties rearwards of the point at which the casualty was loaded into an aircraft by a column medical staff. No arrangements whatsoever had been made for the hospitalisation of casualties occurring during the initial landings or during the subsequent operations. A.D.M.S. had to make hurried and improvised arrangements with the help of D.D.M.S., Fourteenth Army who at this particular time was very much absorbed in the making of preparations for the reception and distribution of the many casualties that were expected to result from the impending Japanese offensive. He had had no previous warning of this new and heavy commitment. Fortunately there was in Sylhet a small hospital that was being used for the accommodation of the sick and injured in the labour units engaged on aerodrome sites and this was made available for the reception of 'Special Force' casualties. It was equally fortunate that the matron and nursing sisters of 91 I.G.H. in Imphal had been sent back to Sylhet and were therefore available for posting to this hospital which, deficient as it was in respect of everything, staff, technical staff, equipment, functioned as a C.C.S. Evacuation therefrom was by ambulance train to hospitals in Eastern India. In 'Special Force' this hospital came to be regarded, quite mistakenly, as belonging exclusively to 'Special Force'. Gradually this small improvised hospital was built up into an I.G.H.

The bulk of the casualties evacuated by air arrived at Sylhet. Transport aircraft landed there at all times of the day and night, no prior notice that they were carrying casualties having been received. Frequently and for a variety of reasons they were routed to other airfields as far apart as Dinjan and Imphal. With the available resources it was impossible to cater for all eventualities but medical detachments were on duty at Sylhet, Hailakandi, Lalaghat and Agartala. Because of the uncertainty concerning the arrangements for evacuation that prevailed at the beginning of the operation, column medical officers were instructed to carry their casualties with them by means of stretcher parties or on ponies and do everything possible to treat and cure them without evacuation. It was accepted that under certain circumstances it might be necessary to leave casualties in the care of friendly villagers or even hidden in some place near water, with food, ammunition and money so that they could hope to survive until help arrived or until they were sufficiently recovered to make their own way to safety. But in this second Chindit expedition the accepted policy was to make every possible effort to get every casualty flown out. Casualty evacuation was part of the accepted responsibilities of the Air Commando and to this end this was supplied with light communication aircraft which were known as the 'Blood Chariots'. It had been recognised that the prospect, if seriously wounded or ill, of having to be left behind in some jungle hut to face a lonely, lingering and painful end, or, if captured by the Japanese, to endure hideous torture before dying was one that strained the fortitude of the bravest of men too greatly.

Whenever possible the columns constructed light plane airstrips in the area in which they were operating and their casualties were evacuated therefrom to the nearest Dakota airstrip. The light planes used were of two types, the obsolescent L.1 and the L.5 'the flying mess tin'. It had been intended that each brigade would have its own allotment of light planes but this arrangement proved to be impracticable and so the squadrons were pooled and from the pool the whole force was supplied.

The casualties were carried to the light plane airstrip by the local villagers or by their own comrades in the column acting as stretcher-bearers. They were invariably escorted by an armed guard.

It was expected that with the coming of the monsoon the Dakotas would find it impossible to land on the strips in the strongholds. For this reason among others, the Chindits tended to move their area of operations northwards so that the light plane strips would come within easier range of the permanent airstrips on the airfields at Myitkyina, Wazarup and Tingkawk Sakan, in the rear of General Stilwell's front. This change in the axis of evacuation presented a number of new and complex problems. The area was one of high hills and deep valleys, the valleys being marshy and flooded as a rule. The monsoon clouds piled up against the mountain ranges so that the light planes would be required to fly blind though they were not equipped for doing so. The new evacuation axis led right into the U.S. lines of communication and the airstrips that would have to be used were also in use by the Americans. When this axis was used a detachment of a brigade medical unit was stationed at Ledo and another at Dinjan airfield. The Americans had their base hospitals in Ledo and Shingbwiyang. Forward of these they had field hospitals on the airstrips at Myitkyina, Wazarup and Tingkawk Sakan to which their ambulance cars brought casualties from the forward areas. The U.S. and Chinese casualties, collected at Myitkyina, Wazarup and Tingkawk Sakan, were transported back to Ledo and Shingbwiyang by Dakota aircraft of the air evacuation unit at Chabua. This same unit evacuated 'Special Force' casualties from the same three forward airfields to Ledo where they were staged by the detachment of the brigade medical unit stationed there. In the evening the aircraft, returning to their base at Chabua, collected these casualties and conveyed them to Dinjan where the other detachment of the brigade medical unit loaded them into ambulance cars and despatched them to the C.M.H. in Panitola. Serious cases requiring immediate hospitalisation were retained in Ledo and admitted to 44 I.G.H. which had been established there to serve the Indian labour units working on the Ledo–Myitkyina road. From the combined military hospital in Panitola, which functioned as a C.C.S., further evacuation was to the hospitals in Digboi and Dibrugarh. To these two hospitals and to that in Panitola M.F.T.Us. were attached.

When in early June the Chindits had moved north from 'White City' and 'Blackpool' and were operating against the Japanese lines of communication from their new base near Indawgyi Lake and when 77th Bde. was developing its attack upon Mogaung and 'Morrisforce' was nearing Myitkyina, the brigades had accumulated a considerable number of casualties. At one time 1,200 were awaiting evacuation. The monsoon at its height made airstrips unusable and flying impossible. That this would happen had been foreseen and arrangements had been made for two Sunderland flying-boats from Ceylon to come to the rescue by making use of Indawgyi Lake. These Sunderlands had been engaged on submarine patrol work; however they jettisoned their guns and skimming the trees to creep under the Japanese fighter net they landed safely. 'Gert' and 'Daisy' as they were called, took safely to India nearly 600 casualties. Yet for them there were no maintenance facilities, their anchorages in the Brahmaputra at Dibrugarh were exposed to a 15-knot current bearing large uprooted trees and similar débris. They were required to climb to 10,000 ft., virtually their maximum ceiling, to get over the Patkai Range and then through dense monsoon clouds to descend to the surface of the lake which itself was 1,200 ft. above sea level. They had to fly by day and they were unarmed. It was inevitable that evacuation by Sunderland could not continue for long; one of the boats was sunk at her moorings by a floating tree trunk and the wing-floats of the other were badly damaged.

However, General Stilwell's force was now at Kamaing on the Kamaing River. The Sunderlands had been bringing on their outward journeys assault boats and outboard engines. With these and country craft the Royal Engineers assembled a fleet for casualty evacuation from Indawgyi Lake to Kamaing and up the Kamaing River to Wazarup, a journey of some twelve hours altogether. Arrangements were made for the provision of two additional brigade medical units one for Wazarup and the other for the establishment of two staging posts on the route so that the journey could be divided into three four-hour spells. An advance party consisting of an officer and eight O.Rs. with 400 lbs. of equipment was flown in to Wazarup from Sylhet. The remainder proceeded by rail to Dinjan for onward despatch by air. Until the staging post parties arrived, improvised staging sections were established at the Lake and along the route by the medical staffs of the columns and a skeleton brigade medical unit was flown in by the U.S. Air Evacuation Unit to Wazarup. Arrangements were also made for the transfer of such as were awaiting evacuation at Lake Indawgyi to Kamaing, staging at Chaungwa and Manwe *en route* where medical parties had been stationed. At Kamaing all serious cases were admitted to the U.S. field hospital where they remained until they were fit to be sent on to Wazarup. The journey down the Indaw Chaung to Kamaing was not without its dangers. The sluggish stream was heavily laden with masses of water hyacinth; Japanese stragglers were occasionally to be encountered and the Chinese soldiery were inclined to shoot first and enquire about the nationality of the target afterwards.

From Kamaing evacuation was by a shuttle service provided by British manned U.S. assault craft to Wazarup, a journey against the current which took twelve hours and which was most uncomfortable. Head cover could not be provided and so the casualties were exposed to the sun and the drenching rain. No medical attention could be provided during the actual journey; there were far more boats than medical orderlies. Though many hundreds of casualties were evacuated along this route, with the exception of one fatal accident, all journeyed safely.

From Wazarup, where a brigade medical unit was eventually established, evacuation was by Troop Carrier Command aircraft to Dinjan, north-west of Tinsukia. When flying was impossible for any reason the casualties were sent by road to Shaduzup to the U.S. evacuation hospital there. This was an uncomfortable journey involving no less than three transfers from ambulance car to ferry over the meandering Kamaing River. From Shaduzup evacuation was by light plane to the all-weather Dakota strip at Tingkawk Sakan and thence by Dakota to Dinjan.

When at the end of June the three brigades to the west of the railway had established a firm base at Lakhren, a light plane strip was constructed and as long as this continued to be usable casualties were evacuated therefrom by light planes to Tingkawk Sakan. When it became unusable evacuation was by river to Kamaing and Wazarup. A few captured elephants were used for the transport of the more serious cases from the areas in which the columns were fighting to the airstrip at Lakhren along muddy mountain paths.

When 77th Bde. was investing Mogaung after its withdrawal from 'White City' it had some 250 casualties awaiting evacuation. The railway was in the hands of the Japanese; the countryside was for the most part under water. A plan to use a light plane fitted with floats was found to be impracticable. By mid-June the number of casualties awaiting evacuation had risen to over 300 seriously wounded. A light plane airstrip was made by placing layers of branches of trees and coconut mats upon a base of sand bags and from this the casualties were transported to the airfield at Myitkyina whence they were evacuated by returning transport aircraft to Dinjan.

Following the capture of Mogaung a detachment of 80 (Ind.) Para. Fd. Amb. of Indian 50th Parachute Brigade was dropped at the Pahok crossroads to establish a staging post there. Evacuation was now through Pahok by road to Kamaing, thence by river to Wazarup. When the area around Pahok had been cleared of Japanese a light plane airstrip was constructed at the Pahok crossroads and thereafter evacuation was direct to the airfield at Myitkyina. When the Myitkyina–Mogaung railway line was freed, it became the main route of evacuation. Rolling stock was plentiful but engines were practically non-existent. Jeeps were converted for use on rails by a change of wheels. Each jeep could draw one 20-ton 'flat'. Three such 'ambulance trains' were used. Later it became possible to replace the jeeps by six petrol motor-driven trucks, which were flown in. By these means the accumulated casualties were evacuated.

In mid-August, as the Japanese withdrew southwards, the medical unit in Wazarup was moved to Milestone 15 on the Pahok–Taungni road. At this point the remaining brigades of 'Special Force' were

PLATE XI. Chindit casualties awaiting evacuation by air.

PLATE XII. A casualty being emplaned into a Stinson Light Aircraft. Mayu Range.

[Indian Historical Section

PLATE XIII. The Interior of a Dakota equipped for casualty evacuation. Four rows of stretchers on each side, three stretchers in each row.

[*Indian Historical Section*]

relieved by 36th Division. Reaching India, the brigades, less 16th and 23rd, went to a reception camp at Tinsukia. There they got their first hot bath for months and were completely reclothed and equipped. D.D.M.S. formed the opinion that at least 30 per cent. of the men reaching this camp would not be fit for front line service for at least a year. He expressed the view that three months was about the maximum period for service in operations of this kind, a view which agreed with General Wingate's own policy of changing brigades every two or three months and one which finds full support in the figures which tell of the incidence of disease in the different months of the expedition. D.D.M.S. also observed that much sickness and diarrhoea was caused by putting these newly returned men on to a full normal ration immediately. He recommended that they should be introduced to this ration gradually and that in an operation of this kind advantage should be taken of any period of stationary fighting, in a stronghold for example, and a change of ration dropped by air.

THE HEALTH OF THE TROOPS

TABLE 4.

Special Force. Operation 'Thursday'. Casualties.

Brigade	Killed and Died of wounds		Wounded		Missing	
	Offrs.	O.Rs.	Offrs.	O.Rs.	Offrs.	O.Rs.
14th	14	227	23	191	2	32
16th	13	85	14	164	5	74
77th	46	346	84	1,156	11	168
111th	17	107	24	465	6	130
3rd W.A.	11	78	23	290	1	23
	101	843	168	2,266	25	427

Total Officers	294
Other Ranks	3,536
	3,830

Japanese known to have been killed, wounded or captured . . 5,311

THE PRINCIPAL DISEASES AFFECTING THE TROOPS

The total number of admissions to the base hospitals on account of disease and injury (enemy action) during the course of this operation was 7,217, an admission rate of 40 per cent. of the total numbers at risk (18,000). Of these, 5,422 or 75·1 per cent. of the whole were admitted on account of disease and 1,795 or 24·9 per cent. on account of wounds.

30 per cent. of the whole force were evacuated on account of disease; only 9·9 per cent. of the force were evacuated on account of wounds.

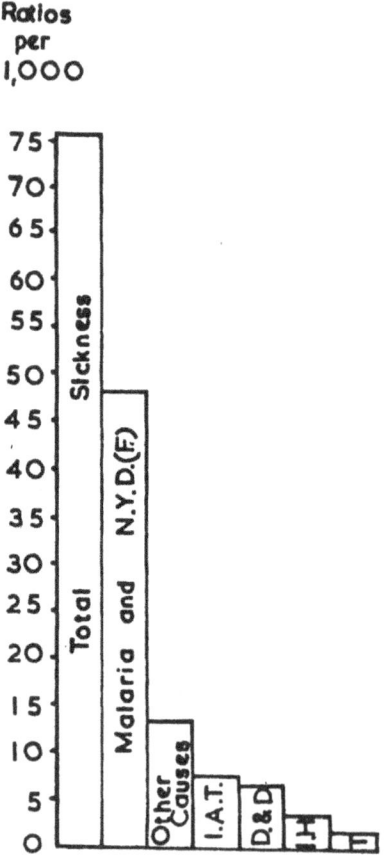

Fig. 24. 'Special Force'. Principal Diseases affecting the Troops. Average Monthly Incidence.

N.Y.D.(F.)	Not yet diagnosed. Fever
I.A.T.	Inflammation of the Areolar Tissue
D. & D.	Dysentery and Diarrhoea
I.H.	Infective Hepatitis
T.	Typhus

MALARIA

Of the 5,422 who were evacuated from the columns on account of disease, 3,108 or 57·3 per cent. were diagnosed as malaria or N.Y.D.(F.) Counting the N.Y.D.(F.) as malaria, which is reasonable, then malaria affected at least 17·3 per cent. of the total force. But since it is known that only the seriously ill patients were evacuated it is quite certain that this figure of 17·3 per cent. is far below the real one.

Benign tertian was more common than the malignant form. It is probable that almost every individual in the brigades in Burma contracted this disease. Certainly it was the greatest impediment to success that was encountered. Malaria affected fighting efficiency and morale. Affecting the general condition of the individual deleteriously, it lowered his powers of resistance to other diseases which became added to malaria. It led directly to progressive exhaustion, anaemia and general debility.

Green battledress was worn, mosquito repellent cream, head veil and cotton gauntlets were issued. Every officer and man carried his container with mepacrine tablets. But in the conditions that existed it was well-nigh impossible for the individual to observe all the rules of self-care. The actual distribution of mepacrine tablets was uncertain; supplies reached brigade rear H.Q. but forward of this it was never quite certain that they would reach the columns. At times it was necessary for a column to restrict the use of this drug to the cure of the disease and not to employ it in routine suppressive treatment. It was often impossible and always difficult to hold 'mepacrine parades' and thus ensure that everybody was taking his dose. It is certain that the cream, the veil and the gauntlets were not regularly used by all. There was no enforcement of anti-malaria measures; self-protection against the mosquito was not made a matter of discipline. On men who had died of cerebral malaria the containers were found to be full of untouched mepacrine tablets. The jungle hammock which would have protected the man was heavy and suffocating. It became obvious to all concerned that the strictest discipline was essential during the period required for the cultivation of that automatic behaviour pattern which ensures that as a matter of course and without any exercise of conscious thought the individual does all those things that safeguard him against the bite of a mosquito. In the column it was found that it was feasible to give a sick man a shot of intravenous quinine and that he could then keep up with the column and be treated as he travelled, so long as his equipment was carried for him (on a mule was the rule) and as long as he had lots of water to drink.

The column medical officers came to the conclusion that with the third attack evacuation should be the rule. But since this would have resulted in such depletion of the total numbers in the column such a policy could not be adopted. On admission to base hospital almost all the B.O.Rs. gave a history of repeated attacks, a few had had as many as 16, the average was 4 to 5. In 5 per cent. of these patients a complete course of treatment still left the man with a positive blood slide, so that it had to be repeated. There was much down-grading to categories B and C of those admitted to hospital as was to be expected when

40 per cent. of those who were admitted had been evacuated as being unfit for active service for at least three months owing to anaemia and debility. The case-fatality-rate is not known but it seems unlikely that more than 3 per cent. of those who contracted the disease died of it.

The effect of an outbreak of malaria upon the men of one of the brigades is depicted in *Sunbeams like Swords* (page 70).

'A large force moved by parties out of "White City", picking their way cautiously through the minefields which guarded the approaches, and marched northwards towards the bridge we had blown a week ago. No. 50 Column formed part of the force and went ahead of the remainder. We bivouacked near the blown bridge and reconnoitred up the railway line for three or four miles; there was nothing to report. But by the second evening the column had the look of a force which had suffered great loss. About thirty men were lying near the R.A.P. shivering in their blankets, and at intervals more men reeled through the bamboo trees towards the doctor and his orderlies who were working furiously beside their open medical panniers. Malaria had hit us badly and was doing the Japanese's work for them. The effect of such an epidemic, violent and sudden, was bound to be unhappy; it was easy to imagine that fever was beginning when you had a headache or were tired; and the comforts available to us in the jungle were hardly inviting . . .

'At stand-to next morning we could see in the faint light that the circle of blankets round the R.A.P. was wider. Altogether fifty men had malaria in varying degrees of severity . . . Towards evening a platoon from 2nd L.F. column which had now joined the "White City" garrison from the south, reached our bivouac and took charge of the worst fever cases. They would be a hopeless handicap to us in our attack on Mohnyin but in "White City" they would have a chance to do light duties until they had recovered. By next day ten more men were down with fever and were unable to march; and we had no choice but to take them to the blown bridge, which was now becoming a permanent rendezvous, and make them as comfortable as possible in the undergrowth. They would be safe, we thought, for a day or two until a relief party from "White City" reached them. Luck, however, was against them, for on the next evening when we were marching on Mohnyin, a Japanese patrol came to look at our handiwork and found them in the bushes. The soldiers had five minutes bayonet practice before their supper. Only one man escaped and when he staggered into the Namaan observation post, his reason had nearly gone. Somehow he had hidden from sight under a comrade's dead body and had managed to lie still for a night and the best part of a day while the Japanese soldiers had laughed round their fires and their sentries had strolled among the dead.'

DYSENTERY AND DIARRHOEA

483 were admitted on account of these complaints, 9 per cent. of the total number of those evacuated on account of disease. It is indeed most difficult to observe the rule that only water known to be safe must be drunk when living in such conditions as existed in the world of the Chindit. It was frequently impossible for water to be sterilised; the sterilising tablets disintegrated, the powder that was issued in lieu of the tablets was not easy to handle, it was issued in 7lb. tins and these were difficult to carry and when they were opened frequently the free chlorine content of the powder quickly diminished. In one column the use of toilet paper was prohibited for the reason that having been used and left lying about it marked the path of the column. Far too often it was assumed that no other troops would occupy the ground that a particular column was using so that no care was taken to keep or to make it clean. There were no sanitary orderlies as such, sanitary jobs were fatigues. In the stronghold the latrines that were constructed conformed to no known pattern, they were too shallow to be classified as deep trench latrines and too deep to be accepted as shallow ones. Seldom did they have any kind of superstructure. The bore-hole type, enlarged by the skilful use of gelignite, was found to be satisfactory so long as it was provided with a lid and was kept closed when not in use. But, granting that it must have been exceedingly difficult to follow the teaching of the sanitarian in these matters, it is impossible to avoid the conclusion that it was the accepted teaching in 'Special Force' concerning the relative unimportance of these matters that was partly if not largely responsible for the incidence of these intestinal diseases.

The bacillary form was the commoner type. It was not usually necessary to evacuate cases of dysentery uncomplicated by malaria. Sulphaguanidine was not always available, unfortunately.

INFECTIVE HEPATITIS

220 cases of this disease were evacuated, 4 per cent. of all those evacuated on account of disease. 111th Bde. with 145 cases was the main source. The severity of the symptoms increased as month succeeded month. The disease was present in this brigade before it entered Burma.

INFLAMMATION OF THE AREOLAR TISSUE

531 men were evacuated and admitted to hospital on account of this condition, 10 per cent. of those evacuated on account of disease. Of this number no less than 350 were evacuated during the last month of the operation. It seemed that this condition developed in men whose general healthiness had progressively become diminished by exposure to hardship, monotonous diet, fatigue and the like. During the earlier

months of the operation the incidence of this condition was negligible whereas during the last month it mounted with alarming speed.

It would be expected that skin diseases would behave in the same way. Jungle sores, septic prickly heat, tinea of the feet and groin, impetiginous lesions around the flexures, burst bullae leaving raw surfaces that became infected, boils and carbuncles were all common complaints the incidence of which became higher as the operation neared its end. Personal cleanliness was a state not easily attained or maintained. Hands and nails were dirty; clothes were wet and foul; the general condition of the troops slowly degenerated. In this operation the Chindits did not fragment into dispersal groups and enter villages to leave their casualties and to purchase food. Since they did not so commonly come into contact with the local people they did not suffer much from louse infection.

TYPHUS (SCRUB)

There were 116 cases of this dreadful disease admitted to the base hospitals, 2·1 per cent. of the total admitted on account of sickness. Another 40 cases are known to have died or to have recovered before they could be evacuated. It seemed that infection was associated with passage through open country covered with elephant grass and with water. Rats were very rarely seen and it was thought that possibly the local field mouse was involved. The most distressing feature of the disease was, perhaps, the extreme apathy that overcame the patient. It is recorded that in the Black Watch (14th Bde.) attempts were made to counteract this apathy by the playing of the bagpipes!

It seems probable that when General Wingate was proclaiming his views concerning the nature of sickness and was shaping his policy concerning the attitude to be adopted to it in 'Special Force' he had not expected to encounter such a disease as this. To make sure of avoiding the possibility of contracting the disease by the exercise of intelligent self-care was not possible. Nor was it possible, under the conditions that existed, to secure protection through the use of insecticides and repellents. (D.B.P. impregnated clothing was not available in the early part of 1944). The causal agent did not discriminate between the careful and the careless, between the staunch and the irresolute. The onset of the disease was sudden and the prostration extreme. In the warm moist climate the fever was intolerable. Adequate facilities for nursing the patient did not and could not exist; no cool drinks could be given; no sick diet but only the same ration that had been issued for months on end. 29·7 per cent. of those who contracted the disease died of it. It is impossible to maintain that the essential difference between those who died and those who recovered was a reflection of differences in respect of attitudes to sickness in general. Typhus is a disease that overrides all such differences between individuals.

MALNUTRITION

A month after the force had returned to India 34 cases of frank avitaminosis were admitted to hospital, 7 of them from 14th Bde., 27 from 77th and 111th Bdes. They were all B.O.Rs. Of the 7 from 14th Bde. all had multiple neuritis, 6 of them had had malaria and 3 had had jungle sores. In the 27 the following complaints were encountered:

lassitude and muscular weakness	24	diarrhoea	9
heartburn	10	pain in legs . . .	24
flatulence	20	muscle cramps . . .	14
vomiting	19	paresis in limbs . .	10
anorexia	22	impairment of memory and loss of concentration . .	3
atrophic glossitis . . .	19		

The extreme degree of depression among these patients was very noticeable. There can be no doubt that they had been suffering from avitaminosis in a sub-clinical form for some considerable time before admission. Once more it was learnt that the nutritionist can design and provide the perfect ration but that this does not mean the troops will eat it. These men had been throwing the biscuits of their 'K' ration away because they did not like the taste.

MEDICAL EXAMINATION OF A SAMPLE OF RETURNING CHINDITS

In a series of 401 Chindits admitted to a base hospital subsequent to their return from Burma conditions shown below were encountered.* It is to be noted that the actually ill among the party had been retained in the more forward hospitals and that the frank malaria cases had been removed and sent on to a M.F.T.U. The following list is therefore not a true indication of the incidence of morbidity among an unselected and representative group. The medical officer who examined these men observed that they formed a remarkably homogeneous group in respect of many attributes shared in common, that there was a stereotype and a 'Chindit syndrome'—superior intelligence and morale, good manners, long hair and dirty nails, emaciation and pallor, showing the symptoms of fatigue and hunger and suffering from malaria, dysentery and skin sepsis.

---

*Morris, Lt.-Col. J. N. *Report on the Health of 401 Chindits*. Journ. R.A.M.C. June 15, 1945.

	Number	As percentage of the total sample
Disturbances of Nutrition		
Loss of weight, 10 lb, and more	171	90
	(of 191 men)	(of this sample)
Glossitis—diarrhoea	86	21
Angular stomatitis	5	1·2
Oedema of legs	7	1·7
Alimentary Infections		
(155 or 38 per cent.)		
Dysentery	80	20
E.H. Cysts	18	4·5
Worms	43	10
Flagellates	14	3·5
Simple diarrhoea without glossitis or evident infection	35	8·7
Infective hepatitis	87	22
Malaria	127	32
Anaemia	108	27
Skin sepsis	217	54
Polyneuritis	14	3·5
Scrub typhus	6	1·5
Weil's disease	3	0·7
Psychoneurosis	3	0·7
Injuries including E.A.	21	5·2
Miscellaneous	40	10
	1,085	

PSYCHIATRIC EXAMINATION OF A SAMPLE OF RETURNING CHINDITS

The psychiatrist attached to 'Special Force' was able to examine a cross-section of three of the brigades as these passed through the reception camp at Tinsukia immediately after their return from Burma. He examined a total of 833 men—372 of 14th Bde. (126 B.W.; 88 Leicesters; 84 Bedfs. Herts. and 74 Y. and L.), 189 of 77th Bde. (about equal numbers of L.F. and of S.Staffords), and 272 of 111th Bde. (97 Cameronians and the rest from the King's Own and the R.A.). None of the men examined showed any sign of mental illness and no man was referred to the psychiatrist by the column medical officers, by members of the staffs of the local hospitals or by the camp medical officer. Considering the severity of the hardships to which these men had been exposed morale was surprisingly good. It was the unanimous opinion of the men of 14th Bde. that they would be ready for another 'go' in six months' time. The men of 77th Bde., though critical of many things, offered their comments in a constructive and co-operative manner in an attempt to ensure that next time things would be much better. In the 111th Bde. group the attitude was very different indeed. Not one of them expressed his willingness to take part in another expedition; indeed no less than 184 of the 272 declared that they would rather do detention than face another expedition under the same conditions as the one just ended. It became obvious that the view expressed depended very largely indeed on the record of the brigade while in Burma. If the brigade had finished with a resounding success, morale was high; if a reverse had led to acute disappointment, it was low.

Interrogation revealed that the factors which affected morale profoundly were:

PROMISES

14th Bde. Men of the B.W. and Y. and L. complained bitterly of broken promises. They had been led to believe that each task that was undertaken was to be the last before returning to India. Every time this promise was not kept morale slumped. The men of the Leicesters and of the Bedfs. Herts., on the other hand, had no such complaint for no such promises were given to them.

77th Bde. The troops were told that they were to return to India before the monsoon and also after the 'White City' enterprise was completed. Their hopes, thus raised, were dashed and their morale sank.

111th Bde. The troops had been told that they would be returning to India before the monsoon broke. Then they were told that the 'Blackpool' enterprise was to be the very last commitment. Chaplains and column medical officers confirmed the men's assertion that when these promises were broken the morale of the brigade was greatly and adversely affected.

THE DURATION OF THE OPERATION

14th Bde. All the men were of the firm opinion that the expedition lasted too long and maintained that it should have been terminated before the coming of the monsoon.

77th Bde. All the men examined were of the same opinion. They thought that three months was the limit in such a project.

RATIONS

The men of 14th and 77th Bdes. were unanimous in complaining of the monotony that soon became quite intolerable.

CLASS DISTINCTION

14th Bde. There was a general opinion that there was far too much distinction between officers and men, the former being favoured in respect of equipment and also of evacuation.

77th Bde. Apart from a few isolated instances, the officers of this brigade commanded the complete confidence of their men; in the case of certain of the officers this admiration had become enlarged into frank hero-worship.

111th Bde. In this brigade there had been a complete change in the atmosphere following the 'Blackpool' affair. After this the men became exceedingly critical of their officers, maintaining that their leadership had become very faulty and the administration of the brigade quite chaotic.

MEDICAL INSPECTION AND MEDICAL TREATMENT

14th Bde. Every man without exception complained that he had not been thoroughly examined medically before the brigade left for Burma and that since his return his own medical officer had completely neglected him. They also presented the view that despite the admirable efforts made by the column medical officers—with two exceptions—the medical care and medical treatment they received while in Burma had been utterly inadequate. They stated that it was by no means uncommon for a man reporting sick to be turned away by the medical officer with the remark that he had nothing to give them. The Bedfs. Herts. men stated that one of their columns was without a medical officer for six weeks and that during that time a regimental lance-corporal deputised for him, giving intravenous quinine and pentothal and undertaking a variety of minor surgical operations.

77th Bde. The men complained that the medical attention they received was extremely inadequate. The majority of them stated that they did not care to report sick even when feeling exceedingly ill lest they should be accused of malingering. They bemoaned the lack of stretcher-bearers. They were firmly of the opinion that the medical establishment of the force was inadequate. The men who had suffered from surgical conditions were invariably loud in their praises of the medical officers and orderlies.

111th Bde. All the medical officers, save one, were very highly regarded. The exception was one who found satisfaction in behaving after the manner of the caricatured sergeant-major of the music-hall.

MEDICAL STANDARDS

14th Bde. It was the general opinion that it had been a profound mistake to include in the columns men of 38 or 39 years of age, men of little more than 8 stones in weight and men who wore glasses.

Among men of all the three brigades there was a general complaint that when men were examined for re-grading before the brigades left for Burma, medical boards disregarded the opinions and observations of the medical officers who knew the men. It was felt that specialists on the staffs of hospitals and serving on these boards were not knowledgeable concerning the conditions that obtain in the field and it was thought that much less importance should be attached to their decisions and much more should be given to the observations of the R.M.Os. It was observed that a very large proportion of those who had been recommended for re-grading and who had not been re-graded by these boards, later had to be evacuated from the columns on medical grounds during the expedition.

MEDICAL ADMINISTRATION

The medical officers of 111th Bde. were of the opinion that the provision of medical supplies during the 'Blackpool' episode was so faulty that the morale of the brigade was profoundly affected. A medical officer of 3rd (W.A.) Fd. Amb. expressed the view that medical arrangements were faulty because those in the rear areas had no knowledge of the conditions that existed in a stronghold. This contrast between the front and the rear has always been stressed; it always will be stressed. Criticism of senior administrative medical officers by the regimental officers is to be expected and up to a point encouraged, for it gives satisfaction to the latter and often in no way affects the manner in which the former discharge their duties.

MEDICAL EVACUATION

14th Bde. Every one of the men who were interviewed stated that he had had no confidence whatsoever in the arrangements for evacuation from the column and that he had been fearful lest, going sick, he would have to be carried along with the column.

77th Bde. All the men were loud in their praises of the pilots of the planes that were used for evacuation and everyone of them had been confident of getting out safely if wounded.

SCRUB TYPHUS

14th Bde. Without exception the men had all been greatly disturbed by this disease. They had seen their friends 'dying like flies' and had been afraid to visit them lest they should contract the fever.

PUBLIC FLOGGING OF BRITISH OTHER RANKS

111th Brigade. This was greatly resented by all. It was first ordered in a Chindit Column in the case of a sentry who fell asleep on duty.

REPATRIATION

77th Bde. This was a very sore point among those concerned, those with five years' service overseas before the start of the expedition.

These were strongly of the opinion that they should not have been sent in.

111th Bde. This complaint was widespread in this brigade. Many of these men due for repatriation lost their lives during the operation.

AN ANALYSIS OF CHINDIT ADMISSIONS. PANITOLA MILITARY HOSPITAL

Between June 6 and August 15, 1944, 706 battle casualties were admitted to the military hospital, Panitola, having been evacuated from Burma by air and some of them reaching hospital on the day during which they received their wounds. The interval was usually 2–3 days; occasionally it was a week. The condition of the patients on arrival was surprisingly good; they were emaciated and many were suffering from malaria as well as from their wounds. The condition of the wounded man was usually better than that of the sick man. The contrast between the general condition of the British and of the West African patient was very marked; the former, typically, was haggard and much affected by the hazards of the expedition, the latter was relatively well-looking and did not commonly suffer from jungle sores and tinea infestation. The Gurkha came midway between the two, his general condition was usually good but he suffered from boils, ulcers and other skin conditions.

Shell wounds were very rare and grenade wounds outnumbered gunshot wounds by as many as 2:1. The majority of the wounded had wounds of the extremities including many compound fractures. The next largest categories were wounds of the thorax and wounds of the head and neck. Penetrating or perforating wounds of the abdomen constituted a very small proportion of the whole for the reason that the majority of those with them had died in Burma. There was one fatal case of tetanus among those admitted to hospital. Most of the casualties showed signs of dehydration on arrival. Stocks of plasma were more than ample but the lack of whole blood was felt.

Because of the unusual policy of retaining all but the dangerously ill in the column, the figures for hospital admissions cannot be compared with those that relate to a force in which the moderately sick and injured are also sent into a medical unit to receive the treatment that will ensure that they can be returned to duty in the minimum time. The number of admissions gives no indication whatsoever of the incidence of disease or of the number of battle casualties in the column.

The fluctuations of this ratio can be very misleading unless it is remembered that what is being recorded is the number of admissions to the base hospitals and not the number whose condition required that they should be admitted thereto. Only those who were evacuated

TABLE 5

'Special Force'. Fortnightly Incidence of the Principal Diseases affecting the troops during the Operation. (Ratios per 1,000.) (The evacuation-rate and also the hospital admission-rate.)

Fortnight Ending	March 18	April 1	April 15	April 29	May 13	May 27	June 10	June 24	July 8	July 22	Aug. 5	Aug. 19
Malaria and N.Y.D.(F)	1·12	3·23	11·14	26·24	22·45	4·30	13·52	12·16	33·67	43·71	98·4	60·06
Diarrhoea and Dysentery	0·16	1·61	1·60	2·06	6·00	0·23	2·08	1·04	3·12	6·24	16·48	14·18
Inf. Hepatitis	0·16	—	—	0·30	1·33	0·30	1·12	1·12	1·29	4·88	11·84	4·65
Typhus	—	—	—	0·18	1·04	0·15	4·08	0·43	0·64	0·69	3·36	1·40
I.A.T.	—	—	—	—	1·49	0·38	2·96	1·64	7·80	8·96	27·68	21·1
Other Causes	3·59	4·20	5·38	6·30	10·81	1·90	4·00	2·85	6·60	7·02	25·76	20·5
	5·03	9·04	18·12	35·08	43·12	7·26	27·76	19·24	53·12	71·50	183·52	121·89

could be admitted and the *tempo* of evacuation varied greatly. At times it ceased temporarily. The figure for May 27 in the above table is a reflection of the effects of the withdrawal from 'Aberdeen' and 'Broadway' with their Dakota airstrips. Only from these was large scale evacuation possible. Thereafter, evacuation was by light plane and was therefore very liable to interruption by the weather. The figure of May 27 merely indicates that far fewer were being flown out at this time; it does not mean that there were fewer casualties. The fall in the incidence around

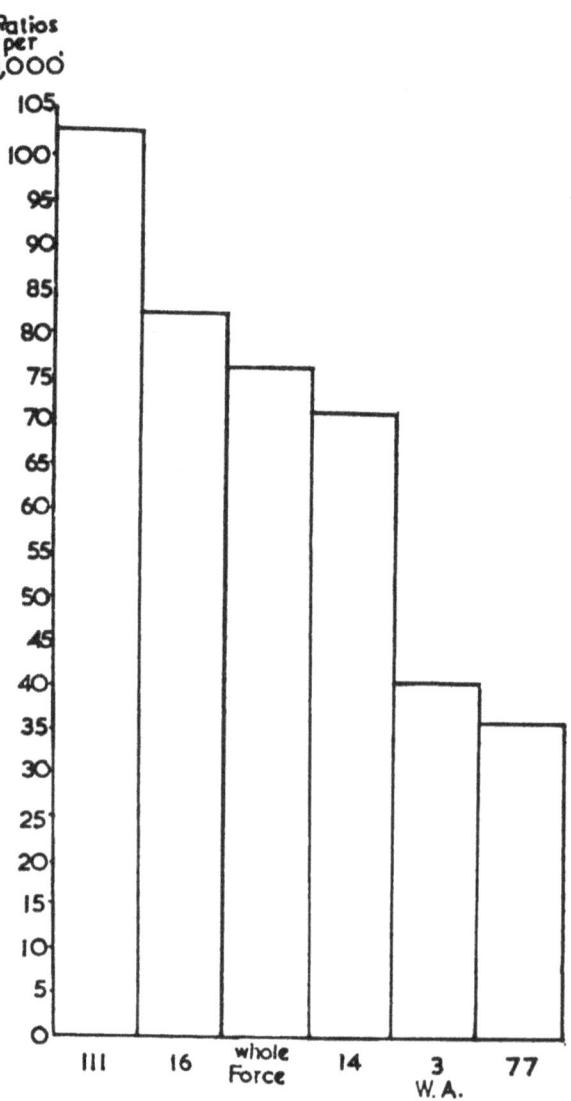

FIG. 25. 'Special Force'. Average Monthly Sickness. All Causes. By Brigades

June 24 is a reflection of the fact that about this time the operation that resulted in the capture of Mogaung on June 20 had been associated with the tightening up of evacuation, for every man was needed and every man that could be retained in the column was not evacuated. After this the numbers evacuated increased rapidly and so the hospital admission-rate rose from 53·1 for the week ending July 8 to 183·5 for that ending August 5.

When allowance is made for the fluctuations in respect of evacuation due to the weather or to changes in the tactical situation, it is seen that sickness due to the incidence of the principal diseases affecting the troops, as evidenced by the movement of the hospital admission-rate, increased rapidly as month succeeded month.

TABLE 6

'Special Force'. Total Admissions to Hospital on account of Sickness and of Wounds. By Brigades. (Ratios per 1,000 per month.)

Brigade	Approx. Strength	Total Admissions		Total Sick		Total Battle Casualties		Ratio Sick to B.Cs.
		Number	Ratio	Number	Ratio	Number	Ratio	
14th	3,600	1,433	79·61	1,271	70·61	162	9·00	7·8:1
16th	3,600	1,038	96·11	888	82·22	150	13·90	5·9:1
77th	5,100	1,759	65·69	940	35·11	819	30·59	1·2:1
111th	2,900	2,033	127·46	1,650	103·45	383	24·01	4·3:1
3rd W.A.	2,800	954	56·79	673	40·06	281	16·73	2·4:1
	18,000	7,217	100·23	5,422	75·30	1,795	24·92	3·0:1

Because the strength of the brigades varied considerably as did also the exposure of the different brigades to the risk of going sick or of being wounded, the analysis is per 1,000 per month. The brigades were operating in different areas and at different times; some were continuously on the march, others were stationary for different periods. 14th Bde. spent much of its time in the region of Indawgyi Lake, a most insalubrious area. 16th Bde. marched into Burma and arrived at 'Aberdeen' fairly exhausted. 77th Bde. spent some of its time in the healthy hills to the south of Mogaung. 111th Bde. spent more time than the others in the operational area and like 14th Bde. spent part of that time in the region of Indawgyi Lake. 3rd W.A. Bde. was in hilly country for most of its time.

111th Bde. had the highest admission-rate because so many casualties were admitted on account of sickness. 'Morrisforce', the 1,500 strong column that operated on the east bank of the Irrawaddy and moved northwards towards Myitkyina, is included in 111th Bde. in the above table. Following the withdrawal from 'Blackpool', with its forced marches through swamp and jungle, admissions on account of sickness and battle casualties increased. 68 per cent. of the admissions on account of malaria and 60 per cent. of those on account of dysentery belong to the period subsequent to the withdrawal from 'Blackpool'. These are diseases in which a display of intelligent self-care is demanded if they are to be avoided.

16th Bde. ranks second in the table. Here again it is the figure for the admissions on account of sickness that accounts for the position of the brigade in the list. This brigade was in the operational area for three months as contrasted with the others which were there for five. It was not exposed to the monsoon. But it marched in, no less than 360 miles in single file, and in so doing had become exhausted and more prone to disease. This exhaustion was worsened by the failure of the attack on Indaw airfield. 14th Bde. had a remarkable ratio of sick to battle casualties, nearly 8:1. It took part in no pitched battle. It was continuously on the march and was involved in much skirmishing. Several small outbreaks of typhus occurred in this brigade and this seriously affected the morale of the troops for it was a hideous and seemingly mysterious disease.

77th Bde. was the one that interpreted the non-evacuation policy most rigorously. Some of the men in it had as many as twelve attacks of malaria before being evacuated. Admission to hospital on account of sickness was much less frequent in this brigade than in any other. Admission on account of wounds was more frequent. It was involved in more engagements than any of the other brigades.

3rd W.A. Bde. had by far the lowest admission rate. Its employment was different from that of the other brigades. It was composed, in the main, of representatives of a different ethnic group.

Table 7

'Special Force'. Average Monthly Admissions to Hospital on account of the Principal Diseases. By Brigades. (Ratios per 1,000.)

Brigade	Total Sick	Malaria N.Y.D. (F.)	Dysentery, Diarrhoea	Infective hepatitis	Typhus	I.A.T.	Other Causes
14th Bde.	70·61	40·94	5·61	1·78	4·33	8·28	9·67
16th Bde.	82·22	52·31	11·30	—	—	1·39	17·22
77th Bde.	35·11	20·47	2·39	1·01	0·15	3·92	7·17
111th Bde.	103·45	64·01	6·14	9·09	1·00	10·84	12·04
3rd W.A. Bde.	40·06	14·11	5·57	0·95	1·05	5·30	13·10
Whole Force	75·30	43·20	6·70	3·10	1·60	7·40	13·40

14th Bde. suffered more than the others from typhus which first made its appearance at the beginning of May. The cases gradually increased in number until about 40 had been evacuated and a further 12 had either died or had recovered before they could be evacuated. Cases continued to occur sporadically until August when a fresh outbreak occurred confined almost entirely to one battalion of the brigade. There were about 60 cases altogether and of these more than 30 per cent. ended in death.

But it was malaria that accounted for 68 per cent. of the admissions to hospital from this brigade. During the last few weeks of the operation almost 250 cases of I.A.T. were evacuated. 16th Bde. had no infective hepatitis and no typhus. I.A.T. was not responsible for much evacuation and in this connexion it is to be noted that this brigade served three months only in 'Special Force' in Burma and was withdrawn before the monsoon broke. 75 per cent. of its admissions to hospital were on account of malaria and intestinal diseases.

In 77th Bde. the policy of evacuating only those beyond repair in the column was rigorously observed. The extent of evacuation on account of sickness from this brigade can therefore be regarded as a critical comment upon the contention that the really tough individual, the resolute, the determined, the proud, can escape sickness even in the jungle. Evacuation from this brigade on account of malaria and dysentery was about 50 per cent. of that in 14th Bde. and a third of that in 111th Bde. Its cases of malaria admitted to hospital were notable for the reason that they had had several attacks and were extremely debilitated. In so far as dysentery is concerned it is to be remembered that this brigade was almost continuously on the move; it may be therefore that it managed to avoid fouled ground.

The Commander of 77th Bde. provides the following figures and makes the following remarks:*

Strength of 77th Bde

1st Kings	48 Offrs.	900 O.Rs.
1st L.F.	42	791
1st S.Staffords	55	854
3/6th G.R.	34 (Br. only)	967
Bde. H.Q.	27	389
267/69th L.A.A. Regt.	2	63
'R' Troop 160th Fd. Regt.	3	45
	211	4,009

Bde. H.Q. includes among O.Rs. a defence company, and Chinese, Burma Rifles, R.A.C. and R.A.F. personnel.

---

* *Prisoners of Hope* by Michael Calvert, published by Jonathan Cape, 1952.

TABLE 8

'Special Force'. 77th Bde. Casualties, March 5–August 1, 1944

	Killed Died of Wounds		Died of Disease		Wounded and Evacuated		Wounded and not evacuated		Sick Evacuated		Missing	
	Offrs.	O.Rs.	Offrs.	O.Rs.	Offrs.	O.Rs.	Offrs.	O.Rs.	Offrs.	O.Rs.	Offrs.	O.Rs.
1st Kings . . .	3	42	—	4	6	120	3	15	3*	55*	3	128
1st L.F. . . .	4	77	—	8	8	117	—	18	4	196	1	14
1st S.Staffords . .	13	140	—	—	14	193	7	38	3	175	—	2
3/6th G.R. . . .	16	101	—	—	11	241	8	68	5	14	—	—
Bde. H.Q. . . .	11	43	1	5	11	76	4	13	8	49	2	7
	47	403	1	17	50	747	22	152	23	489	6	151

* figures for March 5 to May 17 only.
Offrs. includes V.C.Os. and G.C.Os.
Bde. H.Q. includes all the rest with the exception of the R.A.

SPECIAL FORCE. OPERATION 'THURSDAY'

1,309 out of a total of 4,220 were evacuated, 31 per cent. of the force.
2,108 out of a total of 4,220 became casualties, 49·9 per cent.
About 25 per cent. of those who returned to India had to be admitted to hospital on account of malaria, jungle sores, dysentery and other diseases.

111th Bde's. record is relatively bad. Its admissions to hospital on account of sickness was the highest in 'Special Force'. Yet its experience differed in no particular way from that of the other brigades. Its morale was relatively low after the withdrawal from 'Blackpool' and there was an increase in the incidence of sickness following this withdrawal. The Commander of 111th Bde. less 'Morrisforce', in his book *The Road past Mandalay* refers to this matter.

'While we waited for orders ... the brigade began to suffer a fearful falling off in general health. The malaria rate remained comparatively low, though double what it had been. What horrified me, as the days passed, was the absolute lack of reserve strength in the men's bodies. Beginning about June 1, a man with a cut finger would probably show anaemia; then the cut would go bad; then his whole body would droop and in a day or two, he would die. Men died from a cold, from a chill, from the exertion of a patrol to the nearest village four miles away. Mild malaria cases became helpless, men with jungle sores or dysentery collapsed. Certainly a few of these men were taking the easy way out, but when I called all the medicos together for a conference, they assured me that a high proportion of the British troops, officers and men, were in fact on the threshold of death from exhaustion, undernourishment, exposure, and strain. It needed only a small push to send such men over'.

A minor epidemic of infective hepatitis occurred in this brigade; of the 145 cases 90 were evacuated during the last month of the operation.

3rd W.A. Bde. had the best record of all in so far as admissions to hospital was concerned.

TABLE 9

'Special Force'. Admissions to Hospital on account of Sickness and of Wounds. By Officers and Other Ranks and by Ethnic Group (Gurkhas include Indian, Burmese, Chinese, Chins and Karens of whom there were relatively very few). (Ratios per 1,000.)

	Strength	Total Admissions		Total Sick		Total Battle Casualties	
		Number	Ratio per 1,000	Number	Ratio	Number	Ratio
Officers	1,050	259	246·7	201	191·4	58	55·2
B.O.Rs.	10,800	4,770	441·6	3,760	348·2	1,010	93·5
G.O.Rs.	3,450	1,391	403·2	902	261·5	489	141·7
W.A.O.Rs.	2,700	797	295·1	559	207·0	238	88·1
	18,000	7,217	401·0	5,422	301·2	1,795	99·0

The high admission on account of wounds among the Gurkhas is noteworthy. Gurkha battalions were engaged in more than one major clash with the Japanese. The relatively low sickness-rate among officers is not surprising; they tend to look after themselves more and are more able to do so than are O.Rs.; they are aided by their responsibilities for since they are in charge of others they have good reason to endeavour to preserve their health and to avoid sickness. Such endeavour is in itself health-promotive. The West African stood up to the conditions exceedingly well. He had been exposed to malaria, dysentery and many another disease as an infant and child and had managed to survive. In surviving he had developed resistances and immunities of a general and of a specific kind. He could live in a state of relative harmony with the pathogenic organisms which struck down those who were the products of a very different experience. The conditions of the country in which Operation 'Thursday' took place were, in many important respects, not unlike those of that which had cradled them.

It is to be noted that in the case of infective hepatitis, typhus and I.A.T. there is no great difference between officers and other ranks in respect of incidence and that in the case of malaria and dysentery the difference is marked. The explanation of this would seem to be that differences in personal habits relating to self-care and self-protection against infective hepatitis, typhus and I.A.T. do not make much, if any, difference to the possibility of encountering these diseases whereas in the case of malaria and dysentery they do. As a general rule other ranks are not so meticulous in matters of personal hygiene as are their officers and as a general rule other ranks are not so easily able to give attention to such matters as are their officers. Even in the conditions in which 'Special Force' lived these differences were probably to be noted.

In Table 10 it is revealed in the most striking way that of all the British other ranks who were evacuated and admitted to hospital one in every five was evacuated on account of malaria.

The Gurkhas were not evacuated in such numbers on account of malaria and of dysentery as were B.O.Rs. Having been exposed to these diseases in infancy and childhood and having survived they possessed a resistance similar to that of the West African. Possibly as a result of selection and of their way of life generally they were physically tougher than the product of Britain's cities. That no case of typhus occurred among them is to be explained, probably, by the suggestion that they did not happen to come into contact with its causal organism. It is probable that I.A.T. was just as common among the Gurkhas as among other groups but that the Gurkha was not much troubled by it and was not so frequently evacuated on account of this condition.

The West Africans were splendid specimens of physical humanity. Their admissions on account of sickness were relatively few because

TABLE 10

'Special Force.' Admissions to Hospital on account of the Principal Diseases. By Officers and Other Ranks and by Ethnic Group. (Ratios per 1,000.)

	Total Admissions		Officers		B.O.Rs.		G.O.Rs.		W.A.O.Rs.	
	Number	Ratio per 1,000	Number	Ratio	Number	Ratio	Number	Ratio	Number	Ratio
Malaria and N.Y.D.(F.) .	3,108	172·6	78	74·3	2,262	209·7	609	176·5	156	57·8
Dysentery and Diarrhoea	483	26·8	27	25·7	349	32·3	30	8·7	77	28·5
Infective Hepatitis .	220	12·2	10	9·5	139	12·9	55	13·0	16	5·9
Typhus .	116	6·4	10	9·5	89	8·2	—	—	17	6·2
I.A.T. .	531	29·5	28	26·7	332	30·7	67	19·4	104	38·5
Other Causes.	964	53·6	48	45·6	586	54·3	141	43·8	189	70·0
	5,422	301·1	201	191·4	3,757	348·2	902	261·5	559	207·0

their admissions on account of malaria were relatively few. Admissions on account of dysentery on the other hand were numerous and with the coming of the monsoon disability resulting from I.A.T. became the major cause of evacuation from the column.

When the war ended it was learnt that Japanese 53rd Division, which was involved in the fighting at 'White City' and 'Blackpool', suffered grievously from malaria. The officers who were interrogated were unable to give actual figures but they stated that the division's record in respect of the incidence was probably the worst in Burma and that a high proportion of the cases were fatal. The Japanese anti-malarial drugs were in a dump that was captured by one of the Chindit columns.

It was learnt too that Japanese 24th Independent Mixed Brigade which was involved in the attack on Mawlu near 'White City', lost by death from disease and wounds some 3,000 men.

Japanese Fifteenth Army officers when interrogated stated that 'Among the many things for which we envied the British forces were their medical services and their facilities for the evacuation of sick and wounded by air. Many of our casualties, who, with similar facilities, would have recovered, had to be left to die'.

OBSERVATIONS BY THE SENIOR MEDICAL OFFICER, 111TH BRIGADE

From a report by S.M.O. 111th Bde., written at the end of the Long Range Penetration operations, it is possible to gain an understanding of the peculiar difficulties that complicated the work of the medical personnel serving with the Chindit brigades. This report covers the period March–July 1944 inclusive and deals with the medical aspects of the operations carried out by twelve columns, 6 British, 3 Gurkha, 1 mixed (Bde. H.Q.) and for part of the time, 2 West African.

In April 1943, 111th Bde., when first formed, consisted of 2 British, 4 Gurkha and 1 mixed columns. It was warned that it was to enter Burma before the end of the year and therefore underwent intensive training throughout the hot weather and the rains of 1943 without a break on the plains of Central India. The decision to remain in the plains throughout the monsoon, against medical advice, and to undertake the most strenuous forms of field training, drinking water being withheld for long periods during the day, eventually led to a complete breakdown in the health of the troops. In October it was necessary to stop all training in order that the troops might rest and recuperate. They had suffered badly from malaria, dysentery, infective jaundice and sepsis and had become anaemic. Fourteen days' rest and the issue of the 'rehabilitation' scale of rations worked wonders but the recovery was not complete, the general health of the troops was adversely affected by this mistaken method of training, the effects of which lasted throughout the operations in Burma. The experience of this brigade showed quite clearly that men cannot be made 'tough' by pushing them to the limit of human endurance over a period of months during training.

It came to be the practice to take lots of saline before setting off for the day's work, to provide plentiful liquid during the course of the day, under supervision, and to reach the evening bivouac with filled water-bottles.

It was not until the second week in January 1944 that the medical orderlies were up to strength and when they did arrive they were quite untried and untrained in the kind of work in which they were going to play so vital a rôle. There was the same delay, seemingly quite unnecessary, with the medical stores and panniers. So it was that the last weeks before the brigade moved into the Imphal Plain at the end of the month were overcrowded with activities of all kinds and filled with confusion. When the brigade marched across the hills from Silchar to Bishenpur each of the columns had a medical establishment of 1 M.O., 1 sergeant and 3 privates R.A.M.C. plus 1 'medical' mule. (It was quickly discovered that all the essential gear of the column M.O. could not be loaded on to one mule.) A column had ten ponies, two of which were fitted with saddles specially designed for the carrying of casualties.

Every M.O. and every medical orderly (when posted to the brigade in time) received instruction in map-reading, in the use of the compass, rifle, Bren-gun, revolver and grenade and in the art of digging-in. They could not expect to be treated as protected personnel by the Japanese and it was necessary to prevent the sick and wounded falling into the enemy's hands. On several occasions during the operation a M.O. and his few orderlies were called upon to provide protection to a large party of non-mobile casualties.

Every officer and man in the brigade was encouraged to 'be his own doctor'. The M.Os. of the columns offered courses of instruction and encouraged them to attend the sick parades in order to learn how to do such things as apply dressings, take temperatures, administer morphia. Many of the platoon commanders studied these matters seriously in order to improve their ability to look after their own men. They were amply rewarded when later in the jungle they were able to tend the sick and the wounded with considerable skill.

In Bishenpur training was continued in a camp in the jungle and it quickly became apparent that much of the sickness among the troops was a sequel to or a continuance of the sickness that had been contracted during the earlier training period. There was much malaria and dysentery. The state of health of the reinforcements that were now reaching the brigade was most unsatisfactory. For example, forty-eight hours before 41 Column was due to leave by air for Burma, 91 reinforcements reported for permanent duty. They were examined by the column M.O. who found that:

- 2 had to be rejected immediately. Of these one was definitely insane while the other had defective vision, less than 6/60 both eyes;
- 60 were rejects from other L.R.P. columns and were physically and/or psychologically unfit for service with this brigade;
- 25 were either 'unsalted' (several of these had been in the East for less than 14 days) or else suffered from some physical disability;
- 3 were fit.

Though this batch was not typical of all those that joined the brigade the standard of physical and mental fitness of the reinforcements throughout the whole period was appallingly low.

Up to this time the brigade had been unable to obtain mepacrine and had therefore not been able to start suppressive treatment against malaria. But at the end of February A.D.M.S. of what had now become Indian 3rd Division visited the camp and arrangements were then made for sufficient mepacrine to be available at 'air base' and for suppressive treatment to start. At this time S.M.O. Bde. could obtain no information concerning arrangements for the reception of casualties being evacuated by air.

The fly-in on the nights of March 8 and 9 was entirely successful, there being no casualties. During the first week of operations the brigade carried out a number of tasks with the aid of direct air support, crossed a major river, ambushed parties of the enemy, constructed road blocks and blew up bridges and the like. In these early days the main medical problem was diarrhoea of a non-specific type. The treatment adopted was as follows:

Diarrhoea with epigastric symptoms. Chlorodyne m.XV morning and evening.
If not quiescent after 48 hours, a full course of sulphaguanidine, gm. 1 per stone weight stat., plus half this dosage every 4 hours up to 200 tablets. (The sulphaguanidine was dropped in 5 gm. tablets in waxed paper strips.)

Diarrhoea with abdominal symptoms. Tabs. Cret. et Opio. grns. IV stat. followed by tabs. II after 4 hours and a further tabs. II after 8 hours from the beginning of the treatment.
If not quiescent after 24 hours, the full course of sulphaguanidine, as above.
Where this failed Carbason tabs. I three times a day (t.d.s.) until quiescent or until treatment was manifestly useless.

This treatment proved to be exceedingly satisfactory and very few cases had to be evacuated on account of intestinal trouble until near the end of the operations when the resistance of the troops had become greatly diminished. Treatment by means of purges and emetin is quite

SPECIAL FORCE. OPERATION 'THURSDAY'

impossible when the patient must carry a 65 lb. load for 8–9 hours every day over exceedingly difficult country and be ready at all times, day and night, to spring into action.

It was learnt that it was unwise to permit anyone to take part in an enterprise of this sort who had had a full course of treatment for amoebic dysentery during the previous twelve months.

During training much attention had been paid to water discipline and all ranks were fully acquainted with the importance of chlorinating their drinking water. But after a few weeks in Burma the supply of water-sterilising tablets ceased and powder was dropped instead. This was completely unsuitable for the circumstances and the authorities were repeatedly informed that the supply of sterilising powder to highly mobile troops was merely a waste of valuable aircraft space. Because of its mobility the brigade was never in a position to employ the 'Master' water bottle or to use canvas tanks. Throughout the rest of the operation it remained impossible to ensure that the drinking water was sterilised and the troops were therefore exposed to the threat of an epidemic.

Malaria began to be troublesome 2–3 weeks after the beginning of the operations. Suppressive treatment was carried out with the utmost thoroughness, the whole-hearted co-operation of column commanders and column medical officers in this matter being a feature of the operation. The S.M.O. formed the opinion that had it not been for this suppressive treatment the brigade would have been operationally ineffective at the end of 5 to 6 weeks. At the end of the 6th week fresh malaria became the major cause of sickness.

The whole brigade was given mepacrine tabs. I t.d.s. for 5 days after which the normal dose tabs. I per day was resumed. The effect of this massive treatment was dramatic in the extreme. But with the passing of time the response of fever to quinine became progressively less and it became obvious that individual resistance was dropping. Several of the columns went on tabs. II per day as a routine, as did the S.M.O. himself, with no observable ill-effects. In this extraordinary form of warfare the soldier was expected to go into action although he had a temperature of 105 degrees. Under these circumstances the usual forms of treatment could not be employed. In the brigade the following procedure was adopted in all cases of malaria and suspected malaria.

(i) The man's pack was carried on a mule.
(ii) The man himself marched, fully armed.
(iii) On the first day of the illness he was given quinine grns. 6 intravenously.
(iv) After 6 hours a further 6 grns. were given intravenously.
(v) After a further 6 hours a further 3 grns. were given intravenously. (Quinine grns. 15 were thus given during the first 12 hours.) The quinine ampoule grns. 6 was the source of the drug.

(vi) On the 2nd, 3rd and 4th days quinine grns. 10 were administered t.d.s. orally.

(vii) From the 5th to the 14th day mepacrine tabs. I were given t.d.s.

At no time during the operations was pamaquin used. No serious effects of the administration of these large amounts of quinine intravenously were observed and the treatment proved to be most effective. Since at this time the troops did not approach within four miles of any inhabited area and carefully avoided all well-defined bullock-cart tracks the high incidence of fresh malaria is not easily explained. It was suggested that maybe the mosquito had a range of flight longer than was usually commonly thought.

By the end of the fourth week 39 wounded and 18 sick had been evacuated from the brigade by air. At this stage of the operation the daily routine of the M.O. of a column was as follows: A cup of hot tea, attention given to the seriously ill, packs shouldered and the medical party moved off at the rear of the column. If this party included any seriously ill or wounded men the M.O. was busy during all of the 10 minute halts. The midday halt lasted from $1\frac{1}{2}$ to 2 hours. During this the M.O. attended the sick in the medical party and held a sick parade. It was not usual for fires to be permitted during this midday halt; they were allowed for an hour at dawn and at dusk. It was found that a small but effective smokeless fire could be made at the bottom of a 2-ft. trench with the waxed cartons of the American 'K' ration. Hot tea was the great morale reviver and was taken at the beginning of the day and at the end of the day's march. The medical party often reached the night-harbour 2 hours later than the head of the column. Here, when bamboo was available, improvised shelters for the sick and wounded were erected, and a sick parade was held half an hour after arrival. Then, and only then, could the M.O. begin to look after himself.

As the days passed the numbers of the sick and wounded that had to be included in the medical party grew and the time soon came when these had to be disposed of in order that the mobility of the column should not be too greatly impaired. They were (i) flown out from hastily improvised landing strips, (ii) unloaded on to the S.M.O. if he was in contact, or (iii) left in a nearby village in the care of the local inhabitants.

The column M.O. was required to be a man of many parts, ready at any time of the day or night to attend to casualties, capable of organising his medical party to beat off an enemy attack, adept in the management of mules, cheerful and optimistic at all times in the company of others, even when tired and haunted by the dreadful thought that it would be impossible to get his patients flown out. Upon his attitude and his behaviour a great deal depended.

Another vital factor in the maintenance of morale was the light plane. The pilots never failed to come when requested and throughout the whole of the operation S.M.O. 111th Bde. saw only two accidents, one plane crashed when landing and another when taking off and in neither case was there any loss of life. The light plane was the brigade's only visible link with the outside world.

By the end of April the majority of the officers and men were showing unmistakable signs of fatigue. They were disinclined to engage in any form of physical activity beyond that required to get them from one harbour to the next and among them the sick-rate was rising in an ominous fashion. But two days of rest at 'Aberdeen' did them all a power of good and the brigade was ready for the arduous climb across the mountains to the east. On May 8 it occupied the 'Blackpool' stronghold to the west of Pinbaw on the main road and railway line from Mandalay to Mogaung in the north.

Within twenty-four hours the Japanese attacked and within thirty-six hours began to shell the stronghold. The brigade, already tired, dug in, put up wire and constructed a Dakota strip with all possible speed and under fire. Each column M.O. established his own dug-in R.A.P. while the S.M.O. with his medical orderlies set up a M.D.S. D.D.M.S. 'Special Force' visited 'Blackpool' and stayed at the M.D.S. for twenty-four hours, discussing with the S.M.O. such matters as the air-drop of medical supplies and telling him of the many and serious difficulties that existed in the rear areas. This visit did much to clear up a number of misunderstandings and to reassure the brigade that those in the rear were doing their utmost to help.

A staging section was established on the airstrip and each evening at 1900 hours, when the shelling had died down, casualties were taken to the staging section to be flown out before dawn. When for any reason there were casualties with the staging section at dawn these were taken back to the M.D.S., which was forced by the shelling to change its site. The shelling, to which the brigade had no effective reply, adversely affected the general well-being of the troops. During a single morning's shelling, lasting one and a half hours, over 300 shells landed in the stronghold to inflict 74 casualties, 38 of them fatal. Every morning and evening the Japanese 105 mms. regularly shelled the brigade positions. On two occasions these were bombed from the air and on two others 15 Japanese aircraft machine-gunned them.

By May 20 the assault had increased in intensity and casualties became increasingly numerous. On the 23rd the Japanese captured the airstrip and so brought evacuation by air to an end. The M.D.S. became overcrowded and to make matters worse, the rains were beginning. The replenishment of such articles as groundsheets, hand torches and lime, so essential for good hygiene, by air had not been satisfactory and shortages were developing. A splinter-proof operating theatre was being constructed but it was proving difficult to provide cover for the patients against missiles and against the weather. There were now about 100 men to be nursed and only 4 nursing orderlies to attend them; it was impossible to provide adequate cooking facilities and rations were running short. The water supply was a mile distant. The sanitary arrangements were crude in the extreme. 'K' ration boxes were used for bedpans. A surgical team had been flown in but the conditions were such that it could not exercise its skill and excision, débridement, the application of sulphonamide and immobilisation with plaster-of-Paris, where practicable, were all that could be done with safety.

May 24 saw very heavy fighting with many casualties and on the following day the stronghold was abandoned. The M.D.S. at this time was accommodating some 150 severely wounded men together with a very large number of sick and slightly wounded. Only twenty-four hours' medical supplies remained. After about five hours of exposure to sniping, mortaring and shelling the medical party set out on a march of four days up a 2,000 ft. slope and along a river bed, pulling, dragging or carrying its immobiles and with nothing but a little tough mule-flesh to offer them. Yet not a single man among them died.

When Mokso Sakan was reached at the end of May most of those who had taken part in the fighting at 'Blackpool' were completely exhausted and in urgent need of rest. Higher Command was informed to the effect (*see on*). The light plane airstrip at Mokso was functioning intermittently and it seemed probable that evacuation by flying boat from 'Dawlish' on Lake Indawgyi, 6 miles away, would be arranged. It was decided therefore to avoid all unnecessary movement of the seriously wounded and to fly them out as light planes became available. A staging section was stationed at the airstrip. All the seriously wounded were eventually flown out in this way.

At this time the numbers of the seriously sick were rapidly increasing, malaria heading the list of causes. Infective hepatitis was arousing anxiety but typhus did not occur in this brigade while in Burma though several of the men did develop clinical symptoms of this disease after they had been flown out. The S.M.O., the column M.O. and the combatant officer concerned reviewed all the worst cases in each group and those who were considered unfit to carry on were sent to 'Dawlish' where the Sunderland flying boats were now operating.

On June 8 the S.M.O. was informed verbally by the M.O. at 'Dawlish' that a proportion of the men who had been flown out were being considered for further immediate active employment. The brigade M.Os. were unanimously of the opinion that these men were quite unfit for any form of active service for the time being. They knew the men and knew their medical histories; they also knew what fighting in the jungle meant.

When it became evident that the evacuation resources could not possibly cope with the numbers of those who were awaiting evacuation,

170 of these were returned to their columns and proceeded north to take part in more fighting. As was expected they acted as a brake upon the activities of the brigade and it became abundantly clear that they should not have been retained but evacuated. By the end of June the health of the troops, and particularly of the British among them, was at its lowest. Many of the men were walking skeletons, were quite ineffective as soldiers and were even incapable of looking after themselves. At Padigahtawng 419 men passed through the M.D.S. in 16 days and about one-third of these, mainly British, were sent back to Lakhren for evacuation. Of those evacuated it was considered that some 20 per cent. would not recover their health and strength for a period of from one year to the end of their lives, while the other 80 per cent. would remain permanently unfit for any further L.R.P. work.

The M.D.S. at Padigahtawng was constructed by Gurkhas from bamboo leaves and parachute cloth. The cooking and eating utensils were also made of bamboo and bedclothes and clothing from parachute cloth. A clinic was held for the local hill people. The rain fell day and night almost without ceasing.

On July 4, three columns were detailed to proceed to Waring and attempt to push eastwards to the main Japanese line of communications. On the 8th and 9th the columns were involved in heavy fighting and many casualties were incurred including 3 fractured femora, one of which was treated by means of a hip spica plaster-of-Paris and the other two by Thomas' splint.

When the Padigahtawng position was abandoned the M.D.S. closed and the medical party had 79 wounded men in its care as it moved across difficult country in the rains. During the first three days there were Japanese parties to be eluded but on the fifth day Mla was reached and the casualties were put on the main Mogaung–Kamaing road on the following day. During this journey one of the casualties (G.S.W. through-and-through chest) died.

Reviewing the experiences of these operations the S.M.O. of 111th Bde. offers the following observations:

Selection for L.R.P. work. Exceptional degrees of 'toughness' are not required. Any young man who is physically fit, free from locomotory defects and psychologically well adjusted can be regarded as suitable. The physical strain is much greater than that in the more usual forms of warfare and one tour of duty will render the majority of men unfit for a second tour for a period of several months. The psychological element in a man's make-up is of immense importance; it certainly accounts for more than 50 per cent. of the qualities that fit a man for L.R.P. work. It was noticeable that the younger members of the column showed signs of exhaustion sooner than did their somewhat older companions. The oldest category, almost without exception, broke down physically as the operations neared their end. In the opinion of the S.M.O. age is an all-important factor in determining an individual's suitability for this kind of service. In his view the following limits should be observed:

B.O.R. and Br. officers up to and including the rank of captain	20–30 years
Br. officers of field rank, including C.Os.	20–35 years
Gurkhas	20–35 years
Brigade commanders	individual cases to be judged on merit

MEDICAL CONDITIONS AND THEIR TREATMENT

This was limited by the following factors:

(i) lack of specialised equipment;
(ii) lack of trained personnel;
(iii) lack of protection against the elements, mud and rain;
(iv) lack of regular evacuation;
(v) constant movement.

The principles of therapy are the same wherever medicine is practised. The dramatic aspects of surgical intervention tend to convey the impression that the surgeon overtops the physician in usefulness in this type of warfare, as in others. Actually this is not so for progressive exhaustion is the greatest of all the problems and the most troublesome of the conditions, far greater than wounds caused by enemy action. The main medical problems which presented themselves during the operation were, in order of importance,

(i) mental ill-health, battle neurosis, anxiety neurosis, lowered morale;
(ii) malaria;
(iii) dysentery;
(iv) infective hepatitis;
(v) secondary anaemia and associated lassitude.

Sepsis and jungle sores usually played a predisposing part in the production of more serious sickness.

The S.M.O. formed the firm opinion that mental ill-health would not have figured so prominently had rigorous selection and 'weeding out' been practised in the beginning. Its incidence among normal people is intimately associated with the general well-being of the individual which in turn depends on his make-up, upon the morale of the group of which he is a member and upon the harshness of the conditions to which he is exposed. In the case of the British soldier it is of the greatest importance to 'put him in the picture', to inform him of what is afoot and what is intended. Nothing so quickly destroys a man's will to go on fighting as the conviction that he is being 'thrown about' for no reason. Column medical officers were agreed that one of their main tasks was that of maintaining the morale of the group by being cheerful and confident, no matter how wretched the conditions might be, and by allowing their colleagues to unload their worries and anxieties upon them when these had become too heavy to be borne alone. The platoon subaltern especially was in need of such help for his task in L.R.P. is in many ways the hardest of all.

A condition that came to be known as 'L.R.P. strain' manifested itself in a complete unwillingness to think and in some cases in a lack of desire to continue living. The patient became incapable of doing the simplest thing for himself and seemed to have the mind of a child. One such patient actually fell asleep during an action when machine-guns were firing in his direction from a distance of some 300 yards. Recovery from this condition followed a short rest from all physical exertion.

When the conditions were such as to make evacuation impossible for the time being, the morale of even the most stout-hearted among the troops tended to fall. When this happens it is imperative that the M.O. shall do something for the seriously wounded in his care who are awaiting evacuation, even though it be nothing more than the injection of sterile water or the giving of an unnecessary intravenous drip. These men must feel that they are being cared for and since they look to the M.O. he must not fail them.

The treatment of infective hepatitis was not very successful and most of the cases did very badly towards the end of the operation. The man's pack was carried on the mule while the man himself, carrying his arms, marched with the medical party until such time as he could face the 'K' ration again.

A condition similar to Trench-foot of 1914–18, with oedema of the ankles and chronic sepsis of the feet was common. It was due to a combination of factors. The feet were wet for long periods of time; the soldier was seldom in a position to take care of his feet and sand and clay gained access into the boots; the general physical condition of the men was progressively deteriorating and most of them were suffering from a degree of malnutrition.

Large yellow-nosed, blood-sucking flies that could bite through jacket and pants caused much distress among the sick and wounded who could not defend themselves and much annoyance to the hale. Transport animals when attacked by these flies often stampeded and when this involved animals carrying casualties the suffering of these men was greatly aggravated.

SURGICAL CONDITIONS AND TREATMENT

In so far as surgery was concerned the column M.O. had to be prepared to deal with any surgical emergency as it arose and to jockey serious surgical cases over a period that might extend to several weeks in the worst possible conditions—wet clothing, wet dressings, short rations, lack of accommodation and hot drinks—in which only the most primitive attempts to avoid sepsis were possible. The rule was that no surgical intervention other than the absolutely necessary should ever be considered. The aim was immediate débridement under sodium pentothal where applicable, shock being dealt with where necessary. This was followed at the next stage by sulphonamide occlusion. Usually limb and thoracic wounds were immobilised in plaster-of-Paris. Drainage was allowed for by the construction of anterior and posterior casts, or by windows. Generally speaking, head wounds, in the absence of intra-cranial haemorrhage, did well though the porterage of these cases over long distances in very difficult terrain, presented its own problems. These wounds were treated by conservative débridement and sulphonamide occlusion. Wounds of the eye did amazingly well; sulphonamide was mainly responsible for this. Because sucking wounds of the chest were seen early and closed immediately by suturing, not a single case died. Penetrating wounds of the abdomen did badly, even when seen early. Surgical intervention was usually on a very limited scale. Only one case survived sufficiently long to be flown out. Wounds of the limbs did surprisingly well following débridement, sulphonamide occlusion and immobilisation. In several hundreds of such cases, some of them with badly shattered bones, the circulation remained such that conservative surgery was possible and not a single amputation was performed in the field. As far as could be ascertained only few amputations were subsequently found to be necessary. Foreign bodies were left *in situ* unless readily accessible. Except in the case of a tiny wound, haemorrhage or a sucking wound of the chest, primary suturing was avoided. The S.M.O. saw one case in which it had been performed, a subaltern whose radial artery had been torn by a mortar splinter. This had been dealt with by a through-and-through suture, the only possible method under the circumstances.

Running fights on the march usually yielded few casualties and the majority of the wounds were of the abdomen and the proximal ends of the lower limbs. 'Dug-in' fighting on the other hand yielded a high proportion of head and chest wounds.

Sodium pentothal was the only anaesthetic used and it proved to be of the greatest value in every form of surgery from oral to abdominal. Where prolonged doping was required, e.g. when flying out certain types of wounded, hyoscine and morphia were used.

The threat of gas gangrene was ever present for penetrating wounds of the lower limbs tended to become heavily contaminated. These cases had to be retained for a period of weeks. They responded satisfactorily to complete opening-up, hydrogen peroxide applied locally and massive doses of sulphonamide given orally.

EVACUATION

In air evacuation of casualties the following points have to be considered.

(i) The availability of sufficient and suitable light planes.
(ii) Through wireless communication at the time of requirement.
(iii) Availability of personnel to construct airstrips, the existence of sites for such airstrips and the ability of the pilots to locate them.
(iv) Suitable behaviour on the part of the enemy.

The service rendered to this brigade by the pilots of these light planes was such that not a single living casualty was abandoned during the whole of the operation.

For the carriage of a casualty on the march the standard stretcher was seldom used for hand carriage was far too exhausting. The pony, with its modified casualty saddle, was used to transport unconscious patients and undoubtedly saved many lives. The pony, however, did not stand up at all well to the conditions of jungle warfare and it was concluded that all spare animals, other than the three chargers for recce. purposes, should have been riding mules, since these can be used as pack animals by altering the saddlery. Mule side stretchers could not be used in such difficult country. The S.M.O. improvised a bamboo frame to carry stretcher cases on a mule.

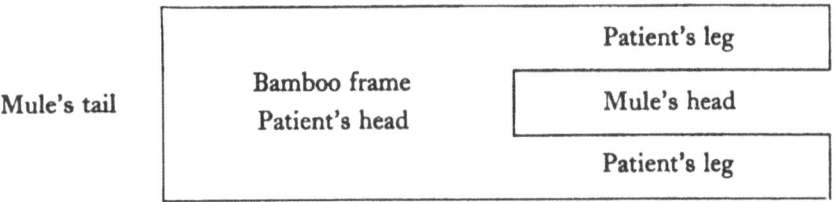

This method of porterage had its uses but demanded very careful watching because of the see-saw motion of the frame. Later a form of travois was constructed. It consisted of a double framed bamboo stretcher, the front handles of which were suspended by triple parachute cords from either side of the mule's saddle while the rear handles rested on the ground. Around each of these rear handles a rope was tied. Two men, one on either side of the mule, held these ropes and guided the base of the stretcher around rocks and across roots. The stretcher consisted of a cord 'charpoy' mattress suspended from the bamboo frame. On the underside of the mattress it was necessary to fix a groundsheet to protect it against roots and bushes. The patient was tied to the stretcher by means of bandages running from his padded axillae to the top of the stretcher on either side. On one occasion an unconscious man with head injuries was transported in this fashion for no less than six days and over very difficult country, steep rocky slopes, river beds and a main road crossing in an area abounding in Japanese parties. The man survived and was eventually flown out. He was given water, sugar and rum by way of the nose and his bladder was emptied by catheter periodically.

During the last few weeks of the operation thick mud and floods made many areas impassable for mules and ponies and elephants had to be used. An elephant could carry two sitting or one stretcher case 10 miles a day.

ARMS AND EQUIPMENT

The weight carried by the individual in these operations was 60–65 lbs., half the body weight of some of them. This task in itself sets a limit to the time the individual can be expected to carry on even when the conditions are of the best.

CLOTHING

The bush hat proved to be most satisfactory. Shirts were far more satisfactory than battledress blouses. The long jungle battledress trousers were reasonably satisfactory though they tended to chafe the skin badly when wet. The gas cape, because it was so light, was very useful but neither it nor anything else could keep the wearer dry when on the march in heavy rain. To begin with the quality of the socks that were issued was very poor. They became hard and shrank, to give rise to much foot trouble and avoidable disability. In operations of this kind an adequate supply of suitable socks is of prime importance. On one occasion during the height of the monsoon a request for an air-drop of socks was made. The reply was to the effect that there were none available. On another after the troops had been more or less continuously soaked by rain for about five weeks the brigade was advised by wireless to wear dry socks !

The webbing equipment and pack were totally unsuitable, the material was heavy, absorbed water, restricted movement and placed the entire weight on the shoulders. The need for a light frame to fit between the shoulders and the lumbar region was keenly felt.

The face net for protection against the mosquito was useless because of its tendency to cling to the skin when wet. The repellent used in this brigade was 'Skat' and this was satisfactory up to two hours after application.

MEDICAL EQUIPMENT

Every medical officer carried in each of his trouser pockets by day and by night, phials of morphine (tubunic morphine gr. $\frac{1}{4}$ sterile, with needle and ready for immediate use). The mule panniers which accompanied each column were excellent in design; it was possible to find every important drug, dressing or instrument in the dark without unloading the mule. But they had certain disadvantages, being heavy, vulnerable to damage and subject to warping. A light metal pannier with all its joints waterproofed would have been better.

Every platoon had two men trained as stretcher-bearers and each platoon carried a medical haversack. These were made under brigade arrangements. The standard medical haversack was not suitable, it is not waterproof, it tears too easily and it admits rain through the top. A water-tight container is required.

There was no room on the medical mule for such items as plaster-of Paris, tea, sugar, tinned milk and spare waterproof covers and when conditions were difficult the M.Os. had to manage without them. At other times they were distributed among other mules and it says much for human nature that these precious items usually turned up intact at the end of the day. Certain of the contents of the panniers were jettisoned, e.g. paraldehyde and the fish liver oil. Of all the drugs not included, the most sought after was gentian violet, very popular with both M.Os. and patients. The lack of a small heating stove for the preparation of hot dressings, etc. was acutely felt.

RATIONS

The U.S. Army 'K' ration was used throughout the operation interrupted all too infrequently by the arrival of such luxury items as bread, margarine, tinned fruit and tinned stew. At the end of two months' campaigning the state of health of the troops indicated that this 'K' ration contained a sufficiency of protein, minerals and vitamins and had a satisfactory calorie value. But it did become very monotonous. After a fortnight individuals began to discard different items, finding them unappetising and later even nauseating; dextrose tablets, bouillon powder, corn pork loaf, cheese were the first to go in most cases but some individuals began to reject the fruit or chocolate bar. After four weeks most individuals were discarding a proportion of each day's ration so that its balance was disturbed. The luxury items partly restored the balance and developing ingenuity in discovering new ways of cooking and serving the 'K' ration helped greatly. No instance of avitaminosis was seen by the S.M.O. until the closing stage of the operations.

The L.R.P. ration should have the following properties:

(i) the package should be light in weight;
(ii) it should be waterproof;
(iii) it should be easily opened;

(iv) it should contain the day's 3 meals in 3 separate packs;

(v) the contents should yield 4,000 calories, 120 gms. protein and an adequacy of minerals and vitamins;

(vi) the contents should require no cooking but should be such as can be heated when circumstances permit;

(vii) the contents should not invariably be the same.

It cannot be too often reiterated that the same ration opened day after day with the foreknowledge that today's will be the same as yesterday's and tomorrow's the same as today's, has a most depressing effect upon the best of soldiers and lowers the morale of a formation to a marked degree. Time comes when the individual approaches his food with mixed feelings of desire and distaste, a desire for something different and a loathing of that which he expects.

Salt was important under the conditions that existed. It was dropped from the air in crystal form in flimsy paper wrappings which were promptly thrown away by everybody. Salt tablets would have been far more useful. Ascorbic acid tablets were dropped in the early days of the operation on the scale of one per man per day. But as time passed they grew less and less in number and finally ceased altogether.

SUPPLY BY AIR-DROP

The receipt of medical supplies was sporadic due to:

(i) non-availability of the items demanded;

(ii) errors in cipher;

(iii) paucity of aircraft;

(iv) inability of aircraft to get through to the dropping zone;

(v) inability of pilots to find the dropping zone;

(vi) loss of supplies during the drop;

(vii) tampering with supplies on the part of personnel concerned with their despatch.

The non-arrival of urgently needed medical supplies created many difficulties and on two occasions caused a real crisis. It was felt in the brigade that N.A.—not available—relating to ordinary items should never be found on the packing slip when, as in this case, the details of the approximate requirements were known beforehand. The general shortage of supplies in India was responsible for the development of the habit of cutting down the demands of the brigade. For example the suppressive treatment of malaria was in constant danger of being interrupted by the non-arrival of the required quantities of mepacrine. It had been agreed at the outset that mepacrine would be dropped along with the rations. But this was not done and the columns were continually being faced with the prospect of exhausting their stocks.

It had been estimated at the beginning that about 90 per cent. of the dropped supplies would be found by the brigade. This proved to be far too optimistic an estimate particularly when the columns were on the move. Undoubtedly many medical packages were lost in this way. It was usual for medical supplies to be distributed among a fairly large number of parachute containers. The result of this was that many of the items went astray. It was concluded that the loss of the whole of a drop of the usual run of medical supplies in one container marked with the Red Cross would have been less serious than the wide dispersal of the items packed in several containers. On the other hand, precious drugs such as quinine or sulphaguanidine should always be broken down into several packages and dropped in different containers each of them clearly marked.

RETURNS

The weekly medical return was regularly compiled and despatched by air whenever this was possible. The S.M.O. formed the opinion that the following details, transmitted by wireless and in code where possible, would have sufficed:

(i) strength of column;
(ii) No. of cases of malaria;
(iii) No. of cases of dysentery;
(iv) No. of cases of jaundice;
(v) No. of cases of typhus;
(vi) incidence of any other troublesome disease;
(vii) any other news of importance medically.

The report ends with the observation that throughout the entire operation the lack of a medical organisation with an appropriate establishment was acutely felt.

MEDICAL SUPPLIES

To begin with each brigade had its own store which was replenished from 16 (Ind.) Depot Medical Stores. The medical officers with the columns submitted their indents every five days. These were sent to the brigade store for decoding and supply. The brigade store was warned when the packages were to be at the Air Supply Section for delivery. In general, medical supplies had a low priority and could remain with the Air Supply Section for long periods of time. Later it was arranged that in order to save time and transport, quartermasters in charge of column supplies should collect the medical stores along with the ordnance and other stores for their respective columns. 18 (Ind.) Depot Medical Stores replaced 16 (Ind.) Depot as the source of supply. Items that were asked for and that were not included in the code list were usually provided by the local hospitals. Two standard types of 'bricks' of supplies were developed, the 'ten-day' drop and the 'before and after engagement' drop. This system proved to be useful but it certainly was wasteful. Inevitably there were temporary shortages of certain much used and much needed drugs. Difficulty was encountered in obtaining a sufficient number of suitable wooden or metal containers for tablets. Mepacrine tablets for 500 men required only a small container, but a small container could easily be lost. If supplied in larger quantities they deteriorated. In the end mepacrine tablets were included in the package containing the ration.

Medical comforts were in very great demand. It can be assumed that they were much used to supplement the ration. The ration was the U.S. 'K' Ration, excellent but, in spite of its excellence, monotonous if no variation is ever encountered. It was modified to suit the taste of the Chindits, a variety of biscuits replacing the one kind; tea, milk powder and sugar being added. Commonly the tins of meat, milk and jam were of such a size that their contents could not be used at one meal so that the remainder was thrown away. It is to be noted that the man might be carrying as much as 70 to 145 lbs. on his person, far more than the optimum and that he could not possibly add another 7 lbs. or so to his load.

THE TACTICAL POLICY AS THIS AFFECTED THE WORK OF THE MEDICAL SERVICES OF 'SPECIAL FORCE'

'Special Force' cut the railway and road from Mandalay to Myitkyina and the road from Bhamo to Myitkyina and kept them cut for a long time. The Japanese efforts to clear their communications were both unsuccessful and costly. But the activities of 'Special Force' did not compel the Japanese division facing General Stilwell to withdraw. It is for others to decide whether or not this operation was successful and to what extent it contributed to the ultimate defeat of the Japanese in northern Burma. It is for others also to decide whether or not the cost of the expedition, in terms of man-power loss, was justified by the consequences of this military enterprise. All that can properly be considered here is the question as to whether or not, had General Wingate's policy been different, the Army Medical Services could have given him greater help and could have mitigated or eliminated much of the suffering due to preventable disease among the troops. General Wingate acted on the assumption that preventive measures could not be effective under jungle conditions and that even if they were effective it was not worth while employing them. It is understood and accepted that in certain circumstances tactical considerations must completely overwhelm all solicitude for the sick and hurt. The representatives of the medical services, having made it perfectly clear that it will remain impossible for them to discharge their functions in any adequate measure, place the responsibility for the consequences of the tactical plan upon the General Staff. In war this difficult situation is not infrequently encountered. The General Staff accepts the responsibility for the decision that for tactical reasons medical intervention must be restricted. This is a point that has to be remembered when General Wingate's decisions concerning the employment of the medical services of 'Special Force' are being considered. These decisions must be examined apart from the manner in which they were announced and in which they were translated into action. The soundness of a policy is not destroyed by the idiosyncrasies of its advocate.

Undoubtedly the main consideration that weighed with General Wingate was the overriding need to eliminate everything that was inessential, that could be dispensed with, from the column. He wanted the column to be all 'teeth' and without 'tail'. He therefore insisted that the medical element of the column should be reduced to the absolute minimum. His D.D.M.S. and also the Medical Directorate G.H.Q. (I.) expressed the opinion that the medical cover that was to be permitted was utterly inadequate. This opinion was registered but was overwhelmed by General Wingate's tactical conceptions. His military superiors did not override his decisions. The situation had to be accepted, therefore, by the medical services.

General Wingate's policy relating to the evacuation of casualties was distinctly unusual. But because it was unusual it was not necessarily mistaken, having regard to the conditions in which the troops were to live and fight. The novel almost invariably evokes reactions that tend to condemn it. The policy and its consequences have to be examined quietly and critically. Evacuation by air was to be the rule. No other method could be adopted. The machinery of air evacuation was provided. The weather and the Japanese were the main agencies which could make air evacuation hazardous or impossible. A man was retained in the column until disease had so lowered his efficiency that he was of no further use to the column. In this way an attempt was made to maintain the strength of the column. The officers and men had been carefully selected and the highest standards of fitness had been demanded, the morale among them was high and so it was that though a man might be retained with the column until he dropped in his tracks, his resilience was such that no permanent harm was done to him. The resolution and powers of endurance among the Chindits were exceptional; they carried on when other men elsewhere would have been sent into a medical installation. This, at least, was the teaching in 'Special Force'. Any sick or wounded man who could keep up with the column or who could become convalescent within a short period of time was retained in the column and either kept on his feet or put back on his feet as quickly as possible. The very strictest selection was practised in determining which of the sick or wounded should be evacuated.

This policy of non-evacuation necessarily meant that the medical personnel with the column had to do many things that usually are done in the M.D.S. of a field ambulance, in a C.C.S., even in a general hospital. They had to nurse men gravely ill with malaria, dysentery or infective hepatitis, as well as cases of typhus awaiting evacuation and in addition do all the fatigues for themselves and for their patients. Such a policy may work well for a time if the medical element is sufficiently numerous and the patients sufficiently few. In 'Special Force' it worked well for the first few weeks of the expedition but completely failed to do so thereafter as the sick-rate rose steeply and as the climatic and physical conditions became progressively worse. Then it became abundantly evident that the medical element of a column was far too small in relation to the numbers of the sick and wounded and the facilities for the treatment of patients utterly inadequate. No system of harmonising the numbers of the casualties in a column and the number of medical personnel to look after them had been designed. It had been intended that the brigade medical unit would be flown in to a stronghold there to function as a field hospital but air-lift space was too limited and so the arrangement fell to the ground. The column medical personnel did set up an improvised field hospital but the necessary equipment was lacking. The failure to fly-in a unit that could have established a field hospital within a stronghold e.g. the M.D.S. of a field ambulance with an attached M.S.U., is perhaps one of the regrettable features of this expedition.

A graphic description of such a 'hospital' at the time of the attack on Mogaung is given in *Sunbeams like Swords* (page 151). 'The hospital was in a dip in the ground. It consisted of parachute cloths stretched across bamboo poles which kept out most of the rain. Inside, the men were lying in two long rows, some on improvised beds of bamboo, others on ground sheets. Blankets and parachute cloth covered them up and absorbed some of the moisture that seeped through the roof. At the end of the hut, a sort of cubicle served as a surgery, equipped with rations boxes and the ubiquitous parachute cloth. . . . Both our battalion doctors were on duty in the hospital. . . . They looked tired and drawn after working all through the previous night . . . the planes were finding it increasingly difficult to land and take off on the wet ground, but there was one American sergeant who said that he would keep coming until the last wounded man had gone. He was as good as his word'.

General Wingate decided to permit only his A.D.M.S., appointed only just before the operation began, to enter the forward zone. Only at

SPECIAL FORCE. OPERATION 'THURSDAY'

the very last moment did he permit any medical tactical planning to be undertaken. His D.D.M.S. and staff were not permitted to discharge their appointed functions with the force. No system of inter-communication between D.D.M.S., A.D.M.S., S.M.Os. brigades and medical officers with the columns was developed. Medical messages from the columns were incorporated in the body of the routine signal messages for Rear H.Q. These were seldom extracted and passed on to D.D.M.S. Attempts to institute a system of medical situation reports was unsuccessful and in those instances in which the S.M.O. did compile a 'sitrep', as in 14th Bde. for example, it never reached the medical branch of Force H.Q.

This situation is by no means unique. If for overwhelming reasons the commander of a force decides to disregard the medical element in his staff he is at liberty to do so. There are circumstances when he is obliged to do so. But at a time when there was such a shortage of medically qualified men it surely was a waste to have this staff and yet make no use of it. To appoint a D.D.M.S. under such conditions was to expose a man to the certainty of frustration.

Even during the period of training it became clear that the medical element of a brigade could not cope with the numbers and varieties of the sick. The troops of a brigade were so widely dispersed during training that the medical element could not provide adequate cover because of the paucity of its numbers. There were no sanitary orderlies; they were absorbed completely into the fighting strength of the brigade and so sanitary jobs became fatigues and the general level of sanitation in the brigade distinctly low. In General Wingate's training pamphlet dealing with 'Comfort in Bivouac' it was taught that 'Except when the bivouac is occupied and evacuated within the same night strict orders must be issued regarding the use of latrines. The object of this will be to prevent flies and other annoyances. It will, however, be a waste of labour to dig latrines unless the bivouac is to be occupied for more than a week. Men should carry out their functions at distances not less than 100 yards from the perimeter'. Such teaching is to be condemned utterly for it completely disregards the possibility that other troops will pass that way later. In any military force this lack of consideration for others can lead to catastrophe.

Towards the end of the training period the health of the troops had deteriorated to a marked degree. Large numbers were suffering from malaria. In one of the brigades during a period of six weeks during the training no less than 70 per cent. of its total strength had been hospitalised on account of malaria. During this training no anti-malaria precautions were observed. It was possible, however, to put them on anti-malaria treatment and to give them rest, recreation and good food before Operation 'Thursday' began and they were soon in excellent condition again. During this period there was much elimination from the force of both officers and O.Rs. Some of the medical officers were replaced because they were discovered to be physically below standard. It had been observed that it was not necessarily the most robust, the strongest physically that made the best Chindit, it was the individual who, by virtue of his character, was able to give his complete loyalty to the idea which had given birth to the Chindit.

In retrospect it seems regrettable that the brigade medical unit, living with the brigade during its period of training, was not encouraged to take part in this training. It served merely as a collecting post to which the column medical officers sent their casualties for disposal. This was surely a most extravagant waste of medical man-power.

The medical services of the force could not function in any helpful way during the emplaning of the brigades. The troops were too widely scattered and in any case only the A.D.M.S. and the medical officers with the columns were allowed in the forward area.

The medical work performed in the columns was, judged by the condition of those patients who were evacuated and were admitted to the base hospital, surprisingly good. It was carried out in the most unpropitious circumstances, inadequate equipment, lack of cover, inclement weather and, when air evacuation became impossible for any reason, far too few medical personnel to tend the patients. As the months passed the medical officers became increasingly overworked, losses of mules had resulted in loss of equipment. Case notes could not be maintained and sent out with the patient for paper disintegrated and writing became illegible. So it was that the hospitals at the base could never be sure of what the patient had been given, anti-tetanus serum, sulphonamides and the like. If the medical element of a column—one medical officer, one sergeant and two O.Rs. R.A.M.C. or three O.Rs. I.A.M.C.—was sufficient while air evacuation proceeded without interruption and while the weather was fine, it most certainly was not after the monsoon had broken and when air evacuation was halted. It might have been enough in the case of a brigade that had been flown in and that stayed in for three months and no more; it most emphatically was not enough for a brigade that marched in or that stayed in for five months.

Evacuation was successful. The aeroplane as a vehicle used for the transport of casualties came to be looked upon as something no more remarkable than a motor ambulance car. At the Quebec Conference it had been agreed that all casualties would be flown out. To this end the Air Commando was provided with aircraft equipped for this purpose—L.1 (Vultee Vigilant), L.5 (Stinson Reliant), C.64 (Norseman) and C.47 (Dakota). During the 26 days preceding the actual start of the expedition about 700 casualties were evacuated by air from troops advancing towards the Chindwin. They were picked up from

SPECIAL FORCE. OPERATION 'THURSDAY'

improvised airstrips mainly by L.1s. called forward by wireless. A number of casualties in a commando unit that had landed on the banks of the Chindwin to the south of the main crossing were evacuated by glider. The gliders were snatched up and towed to Imphal by Dakotas. At one time at 'White City' aircraft with casualties were taking off at one end of the airstrip while fighting was proceeding at the other. The aircraft were actually under fire as they took off and landed. During the period from the end of May to the beginning of July over 500 sick and wounded were evacuated from Indawgyi Lake, among them cases of scrub typhus. The casualties were taken out to the Sunderland flying boat by inflatable dinghies. It seemed that there was no situation that could defeat the men who flew the machines that rescued the wounded and gravely sick from the Chindit columns. Only the worst of weather could interfere with their tackling of the truly tremendous tasks they so resolutely undertook.

It has to be recorded that a small number of casualties had to be abandoned during the withdrawal from 'Blackpool'. The seriously wounded could not be collected because of the ferocity of the fighting. On a few occasions when speed of movement was all important and stretcher-bearers had failed to find them, a number of grievously wounded were left behind; they were so ill that their chances of recovery were minimal.

The brigade major of 111th Bde. who, following the appointment of General Lentaigne as General Wingate's successor, had been placed in command of the portion of the brigade operating to the west of the Irrawaddy gives, in his book *The Road past Mandalay*,* a most vivid description of the conditions that attended this withdrawal from 'Blackpool' and, in so doing, depicts the essential difference between this theatre of war and all the rest, in so far as the seriously wounded man and the medical officer were concerned:

> 'A doctor spoke to me—"Will you come with me, sir?" I followed him down the path. It was clear of moving men. The whole block was clear except for a part of 26 Column. A little way down the path we came to forty or fifty ragged men, many slightly wounded, who had carried stretchers and improvised blanket litters from the Main Dressing Station as far as this. Here they had set down their burdens, and now waited, huddled in the streaming bamboo, above and below the path. I noticed at once that none of them looked at me as I stopped among them with the doctor.
>
> 'The stretchers lay in the path itself, and in each stretcher lay a soldier of 111 Brigade. The first man was quite naked and a shell had removed the entire contents of his stomach. Between his chest and pelvis there was a bloody hollow, behind it his spine. Another had no legs and no

---

* John Masters, 1961, published by Michael Joseph.

hips, his trunk ending just below the waist. A third had no left arm, shoulder, or breast, all torn away in one piece. A fourth had no face and whitish liquid was trickling out of his head into the mud. A fifth seemed to have been torn in pieces by a mad giant, and his lips bubbled gently.

'Nineteen men lay there. A few conscious. At least, their eyes moved but without light in them.

'The doctor said, "I've got another thirty on ahead, who can be saved, if we can carry them". The rain clattered so loud on the bamboo that I could hardly hear what he said. "These men have no chance. They're full of morphia. Most of them have bullet and splinter wounds beside what you can see. Not a chance at all, sir, I give you my word of honour. Look, this man's died already, and that one. None can last another two hours, at the outside".

'Very well. I have two thousand lives in my hand, beside these. One small mistake, one little moment of hesitation and I will kill five times these nineteen.

'I said aloud, "Very well. I don't want them to see any Japanese". I was trying to smile down into the flat white face below me, that had no belly but there was no sign of recognition, or hearing, or feeling. Shells and bombs burst on the slope above and bullets clattered and whined overhead.

"Do you think I want to do it?" the doctor cried in helpless anger. "We've been fighting to save that man for twenty-four hours and then just now, in the M.D.S. he was hit in the same place". His voice changed.

"We can't spare any more morphia".

"Give it to those whose eyes are open", I said. "Get the stretcher-bearers on at once. Five minutes".

He nodded and I went back up the ridge, for the last time. One by one, carbine shots exploded curtly behind me. I put my hands to my ear but nothing could shut out the sound.

. . . I walked down the path, looking, but the bodies had been well hidden in the bamboo and the path was quite empty. I muttered "I'm sorry" and "Forgive me" and hurried on . . .'.

The attitude of the Japanese towards the wounded prisoner-of-war was not influenced in any way by considerations such as those that are enshrined in the Geneva Convention. Experience left no doubt that these doomed and dying men would, when discovered, be mutilated and slaughtered. In circumstances such as these it was ethically correct for the medical officer to ensure that they should not regain consciousness and thus endure further suffering. His action in the medical field stemmed from compassion as did also that of the combatant officer who gave the order that these men should be shot. In both cases the motive was the same.

APPENDIX XIII

The Commander of 16th Brigade offers the following observations and opinions which clearly indicate that he accepted and acted on the view that disease prevention was part of an officer's job and not the sole and special responsibility of the medical officer.

Excerpt from *The Wild Green Earth*
by Bernard Fergusson*

'There is no doubt that in 1943, when a sick man had to go on walking or be left behind, the standard of resistance shown was higher than in 1944, when he had a good chance of being evacuated; and this despite the fact that the standard of troops in 1944 was higher than in the previous year. In 1943 men went stumbling on when they were far gone in delirium; their instinct kept them going, until they were recovered, while in 1944 it sufficed to keep them going only as far as a light plane strip.

'Malaria was the serious enemy. The first year, by virtue of the surreptitious and tiptoe nature of the trip, we avoided villages, and thus went far to avoid malaria; the second year we were much in villages and suffered thereby, while those who sojourned near the Indaw Lake had a high percentage of fever. Mosquito nets and cream were impracticable in our type of warfare, and the wonderful boon of D.D.T. had not yet reached us; we were therefore obliged to rely entirely on suppressive tablets of atebrin (1943) and mepacrine (1944).

'A comparison of my observations over two years shows that in the first we were comparatively free of malaria, although the precautions we took were fewer; which would seem to confirm that the matter of avoidance or non-avoidance of villages really was the deciding factor. In 1943 we were on the go from the 25th of January until the 25th of April, a period of 93 days. Up to the 28th of March when my column dispersed in the Shweli Valley we had taken no malarial precautions of any sort, and yet we had only six cases, all of which were relapses. Not until the 8th of April did we start taking atebrin, and by then I only had enough to issue three a week instead of the statutory one a day, calculating that we should reach the British lines more or less when we did. Suppressive tablets do not prevent you from getting malaria; they only keep it under until you can get proper treatment and only until the infection becomes so powerful that it bursts through. To this point, which some doctors dispute, I will return later.

'From the 10th of April onwards, I had only thirty men to observe, since I was forced to split up into small parties. Of these thirty, not one got malaria until we crossed the Chindwin on the 25th of April. Thereafter twenty-nine out of the thirty got it and all these cases developed, as was to be expected, ten days after we stopped atebrin, and nine days after we left the notorious Kabaw Valley, where the risks of infection were high. One case was cerebral, and proved fatal. Other parties had similar figures, except those which chose

---

* 1946, published by Collins.

longer routes, and ran out of atebrin earlier in consequence; they developed malaria on the march.

'In 1944 we started on mepacrine six weeks earlier, on the 1st of March, at a tablet a day, and a crash course, as we called it, of three a day for five days once in every three weeks. We began getting primary cases, as opposed to relapses, during the last week in March. Then one column, through missing supply drops, was without mepacrine for three days, and speedily reached a figure of 30 per cent. malaria. After that all columns, even those which had been taking their mepacrine regularly, began developing cases; and the only plausible explanation is that the infection had once more become too strong for the protection.

'There was a school of thought among the doctors that if you religiously took your tablet a day, you could not get malaria; they claimed that reports from Australia had proved this; they went so far as to say that if you got malaria, it was proof that you had been dodging your mepacrine; and I have had many a row with the doctors over this. However the contention of the doctors that mepacrine was a certain bulwark against malaria lost a great deal of ground when two of my medical officers themselves contracted the disease in the middle of a crash course. By the time we came out four out of nine doctors had caught it. It was most enjoyable to see them trying to persuade their own superiors (who had been loud in their quotations from Australian statistics) that they had honestly not been dodging their mepacrine.

'In one respect we had the wrong attitude to malaria; we looked upon it as inevitable; we believed that we were all bound to get it every so often. Good work and propaganda by commanders, doctors and men elsewhere had shown that this is by no means true. Some divisions, like the 17th early decided that it was nonsense and demonstrated by results that malarial figures could be cut by thousands if enough trouble was taken—though admittedly they were able to take measures impossible in our way of living. But in one respect we had the right attitude, in that we never treated malaria as a disease meriting evacuation. Unless, of course, it was cerebral, the man would get over it and be fit for work again in a week. Even in 1944, when evacuation was possible, we only applied it in a bad case, or when a man had had it so often that all the marrow (I speak figuratively; I don't want the doctors to mock me) had gone out of his bones. Men whose attacks had run into double figures were not likely to be of much use; they were always relapsing.

'Dysentery was fairly scarce, and a man would often claim to have had dysentery when his trouble was the humbler and less romantic diarrhoea. The worst disease of the lot was a form of scrub typhus which I first heard of from the Americans, and which was to be found chiefly in the Mogaung and Hukawng Valleys. There were no cases in my column and I never heard of any in my brigade.

'Health in the jungle is not only the business of the doctor or the commander; it is the job of every officer and of every individual. Minor ailments easily developed into major ones, with the danger of being overwhelmed by them not far off; they were like jackals snapping at you to try to get a hold.

One such danger was prickly heat . . . any scratch might start a sore and any sore might spread all over your body. The best preventative of prickly heat is the frequent exposure of the body to the sun; it took a war to get this truth recognised; and whereas of old sunbathing was forbidden, it is now compulsory.

'Prickly heat develops where there is tightness of clothing; round the waistband of your trousers, where the weight of your pack rests upon your back, where your rolled-up sleeve chafes the inside of your arm at the elbow.

'All jungle sores are potentially dangerous unless carefully tended.

'Foot-rot was another serious problem. Splashing through chaungs twenty times a day, your feet were never dry; and although we carried three spare pairs of socks one could not always be changing them. Whenever possible we let the air get at our feet; and indeed at the midday halt a general strip would take place; shirts were off for sunbathing, socks were off for air. Cleanliness was prized; the British soldier is by nature cleanly and seldom has to be urged towards his ablutions.

'Where foot-rot developed, the doctors usually applied gentian violet; but so far as I am concerned, the miracle drug is sulphanilamide, of which a little sprinkled in a wound seems to put the risk of infection beyond doubt.

'Another medical rule which was strictly enforced was the order forbidding men to remove ticks from themselves, instead of reporting to a M.O. or medical orderly. Any fool can pull a tick out of himself; but the brute's head usually comes off and stays under the skin. We had so many cases of this happening, risking not only bad sores but an outbreak of typhus as well, that it had to be forbidden, and the medical orderly would do the trick with methylated spirit and tweezers. Leeches in moderation do no harm; palaungs are a bore to everybody, but to some more than others.

'A personal medical kit, in my view, should have six items, a good disinfectant (we all have our favourite and I have mine); gentian violet; sulphanilamide; adhesive plaster; suppressive tablets; and morphia. The last we carried both in tablet form and as an ampoule for purposes of injection. Other items can be added to taste.

'After the first expedition, few officers and men were fit to go again; many ended the war still in a low medical category. Even Wingate, indomitable though he was, confessed before his second thrust went in that he thought no Chindit should operate for more than three months on end. I believe this to be sound. I believe also that nobody under twenty-two or over thirty-eight, should be allowed to come'.

The S.M.O. of 111th Bde. agrees with the observation that the continuous administration of mepacrine to suppress malaria was not invariably successful. In many an instance malaria 'broke through' in spite of crash treatment. It seemed that when the individual's resistance had fallen below a certain critical level efforts to suppress the disease became unavailing. He disagrees with the opinion that leeches in moderation do no harm for the simple reason that these creatures never restrained their numbers or their appetites.

APPENDIX XIV

INDIAN 3RD DIVISION ('SPECIAL FORCE'). ORDER OF BATTLE. MARCH 1, 1944

Adv. H.Q. Indian 3rd Division
  14th Inf. Bde. Adv. H.Q.
    1st Bedfs. Herts.
    7th Leicesters
    2nd B.W.
    2nd Y. and L.

  16th Inf. Bde. Adv. H.Q.
    2nd Queen's
    2nd Leicesters
    45th Recce. Regt.
    51st/69th Fd. Regt. R.A.

  77th Inf. Bde.
    1st Kings
    1st L.F.
    1st S.Staffords
    3/6th G.R.

      u/c
    3/9th G.R.
    'Dahforce'

  111th Inf. Bde. Adv. H.Q.
    2nd King's Own
    1st Cameronians
    3/4th G.R. ⎫
    4/9th G.R. ⎬ 'Morrisforce'

  3rd W.A. Inf. Bde. Adv. H.Q.
    6th Nigeria Regt.
    7th Nigeria Regt.
    12th Nigeria Regt.

Medical
  173, 189, 215 Fd. Ambs.
  3 (W.A.) Fd. Amb.
  33 Fd. Hyg. Sec.
  3 (W.A.) Fd. Hyg. Sec.
  27 (W.A.) C.C.S.

CHAPTER 8

THE JAPANESE INCURSION INTO INDIA, MARCH 1944

IT HAS been told how, in the early months of 1942, in spite of constant harassment by the pursuing Japanese, the Army-in-Burma, fighting many rearguard actions, managed to get across the Chindwin and into India in fair order. It had to reach Assam before the monsoon broke and it just managed to do so. The Japanese halted on the line of the River Chindwin.

To cover this withdrawal of Indian 17th and 1st Burma Divisions, Indian 23rd Division was ordered on April 25, 1942 to move from the vicinity of Ranchi to the Indo-Burma border in the north. By May 6 its 1st Bde. (7/14th Punjab; 1st Assam Regt.; 1st Patiala Infantry; 1st Seaforth) was in Tamu with two of its battalions on their way to Kohima. This brigade was to occupy and hold Shenam. The other two brigades of this division, on reaching the front, were to proceed to the vicinity of Imphal there to constitute a mobile reserve.

In June 1942 the situation was still an anxious one. Eastern Army with its headquarters in Ranchi in Bihar and with 70th Division and Indian 50th Armd. Bde. in reserve, had two weak corps forward, IV Corps in the north with its headquarters in Imphal and XV Corps in Arakan. IV Corps consisted of Indian 17th and 23rd Divisions. Later Indian 20th Division joined IV Corps.

During June the Japanese began to withdraw from their positions along the Chindwin between Homalin and Kalewa. They announced their intention of attacking the Chin Hills area around Kalemyo and reports were received to the effect that they were preparing to move against Fort White and Falam. But nothing came of these threats and patrols of Indian 23rd Division failed to meet any Japanese troops in this area.

Between February and July 1942 some 148,000 refugees made their desperate way through Tamu *en route* for Imphal and beyond. The largest number of them arrived during May just when the Army-in-Burma was using the very same route and when Indian 23rd Division was moving in the opposite direction into Assam. By the end of July the refugee problem had been brought under control and the military authorities were at last able to devote their attention to their own affairs, to increasing the numbers of troops in the forward area, to the training of these troops, to the improvement of communications and to the cultivation of the support of the local Nagas, Chins and other hill peoples in this region.

Ind. 1st Bde. was now holding the Shenam area. On May 11, 49th Bde. (5/6th Raj.Rif.; 2/19th Hyderabad Regt.; with u/c the Kalibahadur and Shere Regts.) took up positions in the Palel and Shuganu area and in mid-June the third brigade of Indian 23rd Division, Ind. 37th Bde. (3/3rd G.R.; 3/5th R.G.R.; 3/10th G.R.) occupied the line Ukhrul–Litan–Yaingangpokpi–Imphal. 63rd Bde. of Indian 17th Division was now in Kohima watching the tracks leading through the Naga Hills. In addition to these regular units there were men of 'V' Force and of the Assam Rifles, semi-military units, under command of IV Corps.*

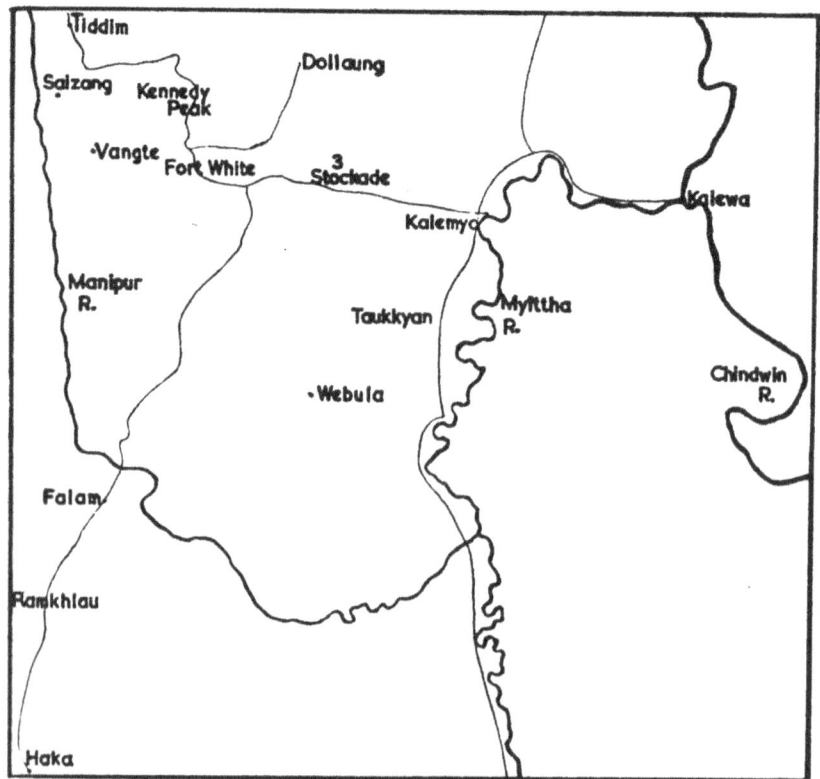

FIG. 26. The Tiddim–Kalewa–Falam–Haka Area

---

* 'V' Force was raised for the purpose of organising the hill tribes of the Assam–Burma border for the collection of information concerning the Japanese and for harassing them should they cross the frontier. The Assam Rifles' peace-time job had been to aid the civil police in the control of the more inaccessible hill areas. In 1942 they were brought entirely under army control and thereafter were primarily employed in support of 'V' Force and in maintaining order in the areas in which they were operating.

JAPANESE INCURSION INTO INDIA

In October and November 1942 a detachment of 2/5th R.G.R. of Ind. 48th Bde. of Indian 17th Division was sent to operate on the main Kalewa–Tiddim–Falam road to support the Chin Levies and at once came into contact with bodies of Japanese troops. This aggressive patrolling was continued for the next three months. By March 1943 the Imphal–Tiddim road had been completed so that the battalion in Tiddim could now be supplied by jeep. From Tiddim a jeep track to Fort White was under construction. Towards the end of April the Japanese made an exploratory raid and in order to prevent any repetition of this type of incursion 2/5th R.G.R. was distributed in Tiddim and at No. 3 Stockade.

Between Fort White and the 9,000 ft. high Kennedy Peak and No. 3 Stockade there ran a ridge, 9 miles long, with its upper half clothed in dense leech-infested jungle. The lower half was covered with scrub which, east of No. 3 Stockade, melted into the vast teak forests of the Kalemyo Plain. To the west of No. 3 Stockade was a knife-edged hill—'Basha Hill'—which dominated the Stockade.

Late in May the Japanese attacked No. 3 Stockade and forced its garrison to withdraw. As a consequence of this Fort White had to be abandoned. But since the Japanese did not exploit their success, Fort White was reoccupied on May 25. H.Q. 48th Bde. moved up to Tiddim and 'Basha Hill' was attacked though without success. H.Q. Indian 17th Division had now moved forward from Shillong and its 63rd Bde. relieved 48th Bde. In October the Japanese thrust toward Haka, Webula and along the Falam–Fort White road and against Dollaung. They captured Falam on November 4 and Haka on the 11th. The whole of the south-eastern area of the Chin Hills was now in Japanese possession and they were in a position to attack the Tiddim–Fort White area both from the south and from the east. The attack on the outposts of Fort White opened on November 12/13. The forward elements of 63rd Bde. were forced to retreat and on the 14th it became necessary for the garrison of Fort White to withdraw to Tiddim. The Japanese did not follow up their success.

On December 14, 63rd Bde., served by a company of 37 (Ind.) Fd. Amb., attempted to dislodge the Japanese from their positions at Milestone 22 between Kennedy Peak and Fort White but the attempt proved to be both unsuccessful and costly. Thereafter both sides contented themselves with intensive patrolling and with minor local actions. In the Tamu area the opposing forces held their outpost lines lightly. In November 1943 Indian 20th Division began to move forward, its H.Q. establishing itself in Shenam. During December the build-up of the division continued steadily and in January 1944 it prepared to move forward into the Kabaw Valley. On January 18 the division entered Kyaukchaw with the very considerable help of the R.A.F. and U.S.A.A.F.

During February and March evidence of various kinds accumulated which clearly showed that the Japanese army in Burma was being strongly reinforced and that it was the Japanese intention to attack on IV Corps' front in the near future. In IV Corps there were now Indian 17th, 20th and 23rd Divisions, together with Ind. 50th Para. Bde. and Ind. 254th Tk. Bde. The distribution of these formations was as follows:

H.Q. IV Corps and Corps Tps.	Imphal
Ind. 254th Tk. Bde.	Milestone 109, Dimapur–Imphal road
Kalibahadur Regt. two coys.	Imphal
H.Q. Indian 17th Division	Tiddim
H.Q. Ind. 48th Bde.	Vital Corner–Kennedy Peak
H.Q. Ind. 63rd Bde.	Tiddim
H.Q. Indian 20th Division	Tamu
H.Q. Ind. 32nd Bde.	Hlezeik on the Tamu–Kyaukchaw road
H.Q. Ind. 80th Bde.	Milestone 16 on the Tamu–Sittaung road
H.Q. Ind. 100th Bde.	Nanmunta Chaung
H.Q. Indian 23rd Division	Milestone 6 on the Imphal–Palel road
H.Q. Ind. 1st Bde.	Kuntaung
H.Q. Ind. 37th Bde.	Milestone 109 on the Dimapur–Imphal road
H.Q. Ind. 49th Bde.	Milestone 36 on the Imphal–Ukhrul road
H.Q. Ind. 50th Para. Bde.	Milestone 10 on the Kohima–Jessami road

Indian 17th Division was based on Tiddim in the Chin Hills and was thus at the end of the 165-mile road that ran from Imphal where H.Q. IV Corps was established. The division had outposts as far forward as Kennedy Peak. Indian 20th Division was in the Tamu area. Between these two divisions was an 80-mile gap of jungle-covered mountain. Indian 23rd Division was in the vicinity of Imphal. Ind. 50th Para. Bde. was in Ukhrul. Ind. 254th Tk. Bde. consisted of two regiments, one Indian and the other British. In Imphal was 221st Group R.A.F. which was part of the 3rd Tactical Air Force which in turn was part of the Eastern Air Command, a composite U.S. and British organisation.

One of the operations to be undertaken during the campaigning season of 1943–44, it will be remembered, was the advance of IV Corps beyond the Chindwin. The overriding consideration that profoundly influenced all planning in S.E.A.C. at this time was that of recovering northern Burma so that the communications with China might be developed and made secure. It was because of this that 'Special Force' had been despatched into Burma and that IV Corps had seized positions that dominated the Kabaw Valley and the Chin Hills. Behind this screen the vast Imphal Plain had been transformed into a huge forward base for Fourteenth Army and Dimapur (Manipur Road) into a great railhead. Dimapur, as late as 1942, had the reputation of being a pestilential place. Yet it quickly became transformed into an area in which many thousands of men were employed. This transformation was made possible by the success of the anti-malaria measures that were taken on medical advice. Some 800 miles of drains were constructed to deny the mosquito its breeding places. The Imphal Plain, 3,000 ft. above sea level, is about 600 sq. miles in extent and is the only considerable area of relatively flat land in the whole region. It is surrounded by a great mass of jungle-covered mountains and lies about half-way between the valley of the Brahmaputra and the Central Plain of Burma. On it had been constructed many *basha* camps, hutted hospitals, dumps, depots and parks of all kinds, mainly around the small, pleasant township of Imphal, the capital of Manipur State, and Palel. On the Imphal Plain too had been constructed a number of airfields and airstrips. From Dimapur a metalled road ran through Kohima, 40 miles away, to Imphal, another 86 miles farther on, where it forked, one limb running down the Kabaw Valley to Tamu and the other down the valley of the Manipur River to Tiddim and so leading to the Kalewa Gap and the Central Plain of Burma. All the roads in this area ran north-south and were therefore parallel to the front line which was the line of the Chindwin. They were not very far removed from this and so, should the Japanese attack successfully in this area there was always the danger that these roads would be cut.

The Imphal Plain was the only possible forward base in this region and so long as it remained the base of a force that was advancing into the Central Plain of Burma it was satisfactory. But as a base of a force that was fighting a defensive action it was not without fault for leading back from it into India there was but one road and one that ran parallel to the front. If the Japanese gained possession of the Imphal Plain they would be greatly advantaged; they could then cut the Assam–Bengal railway which was General Stilwell's supply line; they could overrun the Assam airfields and so disrupt the air-borne traffic over the 'Hump' to China; they could thus isolate China and the path into Bengal would be open.

All ideas of an immediate offensive on the part of IV Corps had to be jettisoned when on March 6/7 the Japanese launched their offensive which was meant to make an end of the forces facing them and to open the way to Delhi. Three Japanese divisions of their Fifteenth Army, 15th, 31st and 33rd, with supporting troops, a force of nearly 100,000 men in all, moved in three different directions on three linked but separate tasks that, according to the time-table, were to be concluded in ten days.

General Slim had decided that should the Japanese attack with the intention of fighting a battle that should decide the course of the campaign in Burma he would accept the challenge, but would fight the battle on ground of his own choosing. He would fight it on the Imphal Plain. Here his own supply difficulties would be eased whereas those of his antagonist would become magnified should the Japanese fall behind their fixed time-table. Since he was to depend so much on the ability of the

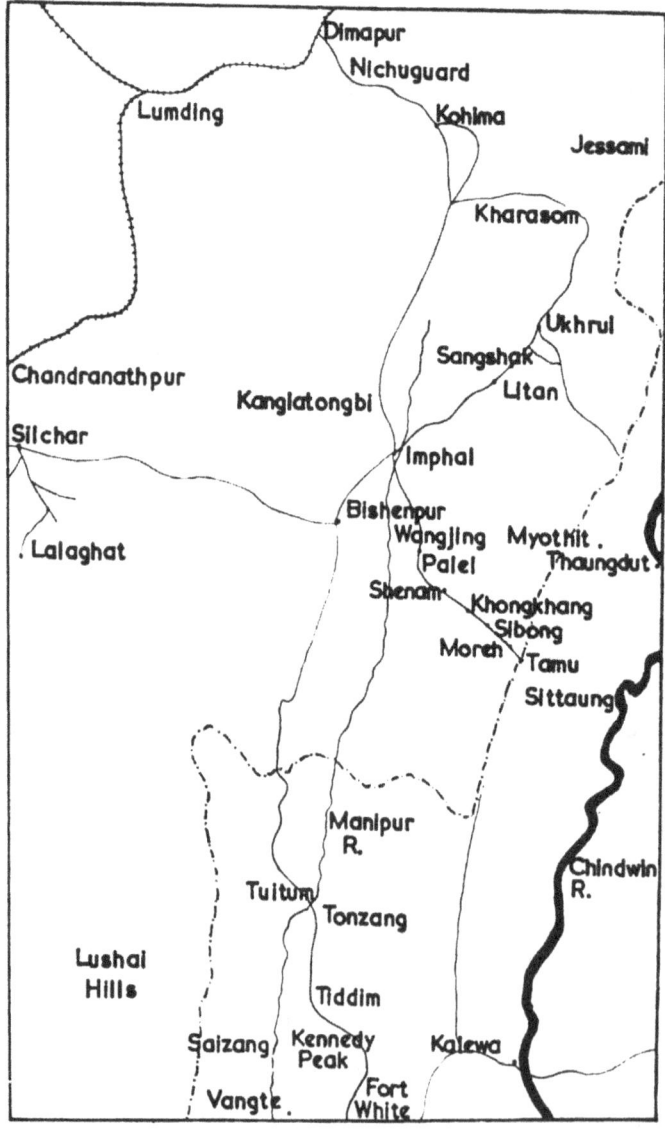

FIG. 27. The Imphal Plain

JAPANESE INCURSION INTO INDIA

Air Force to provide cover and to supply by air-drop, he decided to make the two all-weather airfields at Imphal and Palel the core of the defensive scheme. These two areas would be transformed into strong-points with garrisons created out of the very many administrative units in the Plain. All the non-combatants that could be spared would be sent out. He made tentative arrangements for the transfer to IV Corps' front of Indian 5th Division from Arakan and of 2nd Division from the Bombay area.

The tactical plan that was adopted was for Indian 17th Division to fall back rapidly from the Tiddim area to Imphal, when ordered to do so, leaving one brigade group about 40 miles south of Imphal to guard the southern approaches. The division would pass into corps reserve and would be used in counter-offensive action. Indian 20th Division, on

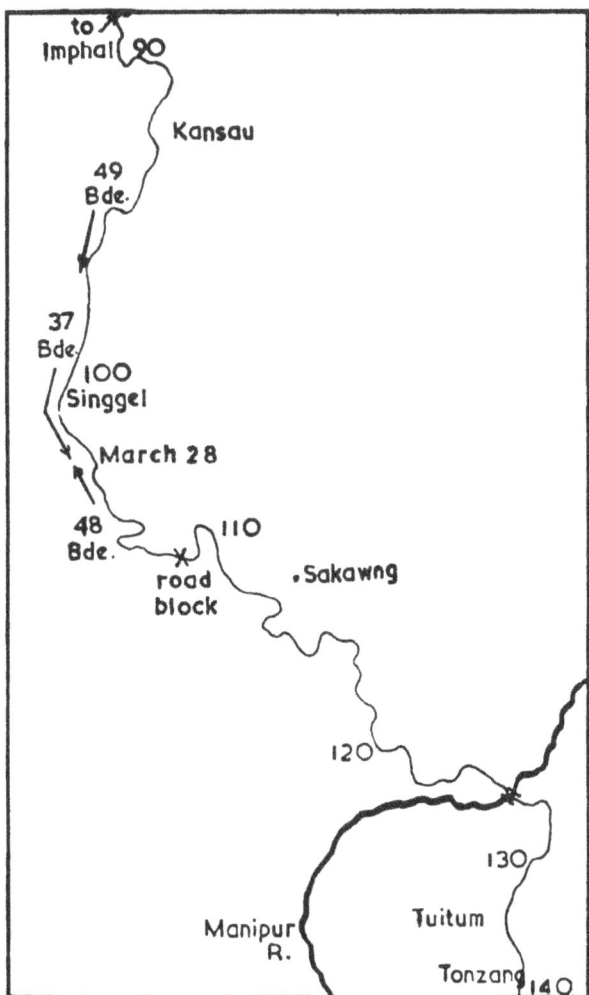

FIG. 28. The Withdrawal of Indian 17th Division from the Tiddim area to Imphal

the other hand, would fall back slowly from the Tamu area and concentrate in the vicinity of Moreh. When all the administrative and suchlike units on the divisional L. of C. had got back safely to Imphal, the division would fall back to the vicinity of Shenam and there stand to guard the south-east approaches to Imphal. Indian 23rd Division, leaving one brigade group in Ukhrul, would join Indian 17th Division, Ind. 50th Para. Bde. and Ind. 254th Tk. Bde. in corps reserve.

Japanese 33rd Division, crossing the Chindwin in the vicinity of Kalewa, advanced in two columns, one of which attacked Indian 17th Division's positions along the line of the Manipur River near the hill village of Tonzang, 20 miles to the north of Tiddim, while the other column moved over the hills to the north through thick jungle to the west of the Tiddim–Imphal road. On March 13 it was reported that strong Japanese forces were moving in the hills about 60 miles north of Tiddim and to the west of the road. Indian 17th Division was therefore ordered to withdraw at once. It set out on its 167-mile journey on the 14th with its 2,500 vehicles, its 3,500 animals and its casualties. But the road was cut at Tonzang and also further to the north at Milestone 109 where a supply camp was located. On March 18, 37th and 49th Bdes., of Indian 23rd Division were despatched down the Imphal–Tiddim road to give aid to Indian 17th Division.

On March 13, 63rd Bde. of Indian 17th Division moved from Tiddim to Tonzang to help the small garrison of 1st W. Yorks there. The Japanese got round behind Tonzang and established a road-block at Milestone 132 near Tuitum village, just north of Tonzang. After very bitter fighting the brigade cleared this. On the 18th, 48th Bde. of Indian 17th Division crossed the Manipur River and moved northwards. Between the 20th and 26th, this brigade cleared the road between Milestones 110 and 100 and when this had been done, 63rd Bde. destroyed the bridge over the river and withdrew from the Tonzang area. 48th Bde., continuing its northward march, cleared the road up to Milestone 98. At the same time, 37th Bde. of Indian 23rd Division, followed by 49th Bde. of the same division, was fighting its way down the road and attacking a Japanese strong-point at Milestone 96. The two divisions quickly joined up and cleared the rest of the road. On April 5 Indian 17th Division, with the bulk of its transport and all its casualties reached Imphal. During this eventful march the division had been supplied by air-drop. The two brigades of Indian 23rd Division remained in the vicinity of Milestone 38 to block the road to Imphal from the south.

Meanwhile, Japanese 15th Division had crossed the Chindwin on improvised bamboo rafts in the vicinity of Thaungdut and was moving towards Imphal on the axis Myothit–Sangshak–Litan. Further to the north Japanese 31st Division had crossed the Chindwin in eight columns between Homalin and Tamanthi and was advancing with a speed that

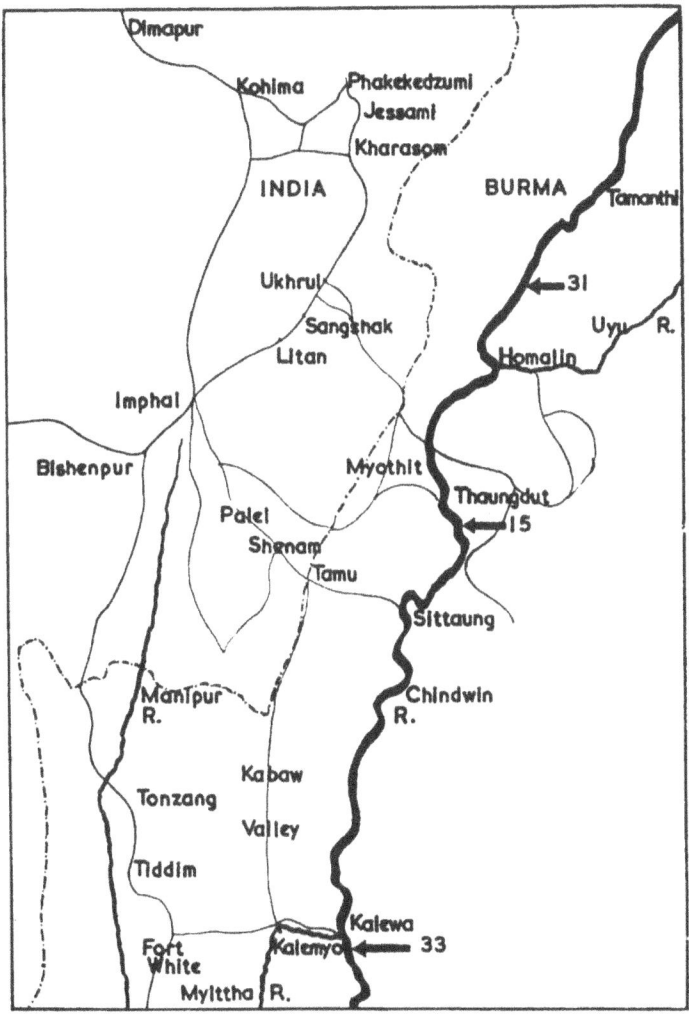

FIG. 29. The Japanese Incursion into India

was surprising in the direction of Kohima and Dimapur. Crossing the Chindwin on March 15, by the 27th the Japanese had reached Kharasom, about 28 miles south-east of Kohima and on the following day attacked 1st Assam Regt. in its prepared positions in the vicinity of Jessami, forcing it to withdraw to Kohima. A Burma Garrison Company was in Phakekedzumi and Kohima, at this time, was garrisoned by 2nd W. Yorks., 3rd Assam Rifles and the Nepalese Shere Regt. On March 28 the W. Yorks moved to Imphal, their place in Kohima being taken by 1/1st Punjab.

In the path of Japanese 31st Division at Ukhrul was Ind. 50th Para.

Bde. of two battalions (152nd and 153rd Para. Bns.) with u/c two companies of the Kalibahadur Regt. and 4/5th Mahratta of Indian 23rd Division. On March 19 an advancing Japanese column surged against the defensive positions of this small force and after two days of strenuous fighting forced it to withdraw to Sangshak, about 9 miles to the south of Ukhrul and about 28 miles north-east of Imphal. Here a most bitter engagement was fought during the next four days. On the 26th one of the water points was lost and since the area occupied by the brigade was too small to permit the R.A.F. to provide water by airdrop, its defenders were obliged to disengage and make their way back to Imphal.

An equally bitter action was being fought at Litan about 18 miles to the north-east of Imphal where elements of Ind. 49th Bde., a detachment of Ind. 50th Para. Bde. and 2/1st Punjab of Indian 5th Division, newly arrived, were attacked on the night of March 25/26 and pushed back from their forward positions. Next day the rest of 123rd Bde. of Indian 5th Division arrived on the scene and the Japanese advance was halted. The position was successfully evacuated on March 27. Parties of Japanese, however, succeeded in reaching the Imphal–Kohima road and on the 30th, a bridge 30 miles to the north of Imphal was blown and a strong road-block established. Imphal was isolated save for the track that ran through Bishenpur to Silchar.

Indian 20th Division had concentrated in the vicinity of Moreh according to plan. On March 12 two Japanese columns had thrust up the Kabaw Valley, screened by Burmese and I.N.A. troops. Indian 20th Division fell back slowly to Tamu and, when on the 16th, a Japanese column, which had crossed the Chindwin at Thaungdut, began to threaten its flank, to Moreh. There it was attacked on the 22nd, but held its ground. The division was then instructed to withdraw to Shenam and Tengnoupal, some 9 miles from Palel, in order that its 32nd Bde. might pass into corps reserve. The other two brigades guarded the south-eastern approaches to the Imphal Plain.

The Japanese tactical plan had by this time become revealed. It was clear that they were closing rapidly and in considerable strength on Kohima. It had been assumed that Imphal would be their main objective and so Dimapur and Kohima were only lightly garrisoned. Steps were taken at once to reinforce the troops in these two places. General Slim detached 161st Bde. from Indian 5th Division *en route* for Imphal and sent it to Dimapur; he arranged for 3rd Special Service Brigade to be sent to Silchar and for 23rd Bde. of 70th Division ('Special Force') to go to Jorhat to cover the railway to Ledo. He warned XV Corps that Indian 7th Division might be wanted on the northern front and he asked that H.Q. XXXIII Corps and 2nd Division should be sent from the Bombay–Poona area to the Dimapur–Kohima area. The evacuation of non-combatants from the threatened areas by air, road and rail was speeded up.

The garrison at Kohima at this time, numbering some 3,500 altogether and including a large proportion of non-combatants was as follows:

Artillery	One 25 pdr. gun with a crew from 24th Reinforcement Camp
Engineers	C.R.E. 112 and staff; G.E. Kohima and staff.
Infantry	1st Assam Regt. Burma Regt. One Garrison Coy.* 5th Buregt. One coy.* 27/5th Mahratta L.I. Two plns. 3rd Assam Rifles, less detachs. 'V' Force, detachs. Shere Regt., Nepalese Contingent.
Signals	221st Line Construction Sec., less detach. Burma P. and T. Sigs. detach. IV Corps 'R' Sigs. detach. 'T' L. of C. Sigs. detach.
Medical	80 (Ind.) Para. Fd. Amb. 53 I.G.H., detach. 19 Fd. Hyg. Sec.
R.I.A.S.C.	46th G.P.T., less two secs. 36th Cattle Conducting Sec. Ind. 87th Fd. Bakery. Ind. 622nd Supply Sec.
Labour	1432nd Coy. I.P.C. less detach.
Miscellaneous	24th Reinforcement Camp. Adm. Comd. Kohima and staff.

Some 500 men in the convalescent depot in Kohima were issued with arms. Trenches were dug, dressing stations prepared and the defences manned. 161st Bde. was sent to Kohima from Dimapur to hold the Kohima Ridge and to transform it into a firm barrier athwart the Kohima–Dimapur road.

MEDICAL COVER

INDIAN 17TH DIVISION

23 and 37 (Ind.) Fd. Ambs. constructed a M.D.S. in Tiddim to serve the troops of Indian 17th Division operating in the Fort White area. It had cleansing and delousing centres and to it a mobile surgical unit was attached. This M.D.S. was taken over by 19 (Ind.) C.C.S.

---

* *See* page 99.

The system of evacuation adopted is well illustrated by the evacuation chain as it was on March 1.

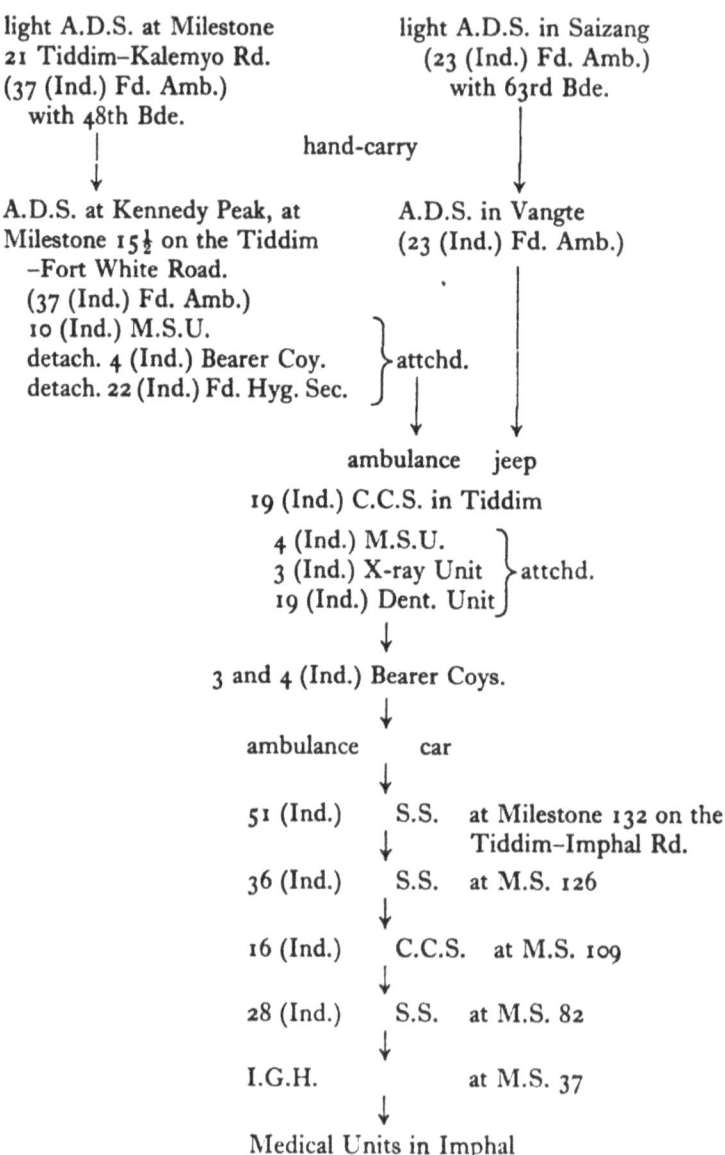

Evacuation from the forward light A.D.Ss. to the A.D.Ss. was by S.B. squad and from the A.D.S. by ambulance jeep to the C.C.S. in Tiddim. During these winter months the main difficulty encountered by the divisional medical services was that of getting the casualty back to the M.D.S. in good time and condition. Hand-carries were very long and exceedingly arduous in this wild and mountainous country; the longest was over eight miles. Much praise was given to the men of the Indian bearer companies for the truly magnificent work they did. It was found advisable to place the mobile surgical unit at the A.D.S. so that such casualties that needed surgical attention urgently and that would be disadvantaged by being sent on by jeep to the M.D.S., might receive it. The A.D.Ss. of 37 (Ind.) Fd. Amb. were subjected to much shelling during the first week in March. The sterilising room of 10 (Ind.) M.S.U. received a direct hit and was destroyed. The work of these units was so greatly interrupted by this shelling that it was decided to withdraw the light A.D.S. to Tiddim and the A.D.S. to a position known as 'Vital Corner' south of Tiddim. Stretcher-bearer squads were left with the R.A.Ps.

When the Japanese threat to Tonzang developed, a battalion of 63rd. Bde. was sent there to take over command of all troops in the vicinity ('Tonforce'). 36 (Ind.) S.S., at the bridge over the Manipur River, provided medical cover for 'Tonforce' and to this staging section 23 (Ind.) Fd. Amb. attached an additional medical officer and a small party of O.Rs. On March 10 the A.D.S. of 23 (Ind.) Fd. Amb. in Vangte was closed and withdrawn to Tiddim. On this day orders were received to the effect that all non-essential medical units were to move back forthwith to Imphal. 19 (Ind.) C.C.S. handed over the small civil hospital building that it had been occupying in Tiddim to 37 (Ind.) Fd. Amb. and on March 11, taking with it some 200 patients and the attached medical and dental units, set off for Imphal which was reached safely. Expecting to be attacked on its way back to Imphal the division was prepared to establish itself in a number of defended localities—'boxes'. The two field ambulances were prepared so to fragment themselves that each box would be provided with an adequate medical element. 37 (Ind.) Fd. Amb. would establish its M.D.S. in the box that sheltered divisional headquarters and would have 10 (Ind.) M.S.U. attached to it. To this box would be transferred from the other boxes only such cases as were in urgent need of expert surgical intervention. Rations and water for 10 days were to be provided in each box.

When the division was ordered to withdraw, only such equipment as was regarded as essential was taken along, the rest being destroyed. It was intended that the A.D.S. of 37 (Ind.) Fd. Amb. at 'Vital Corner' serving 48th Bde., which was to be the rearguard of the division, should move back with this brigade but as no transport for it could be provided by the brigade, the A.D.S., destroying its non-essential equipment, moved back to Tiddim apart from the brigade. It renewed its equipment from the M.D.S. of 37 (Ind.) Fd. Amb. there.

On the march the field ambulances carried their patients with them along the Tiddim–Imphal road. There was no evacuation. Emergency surgery was performed by 10 (Ind.) M.S.U. *en route*. There was much fighting and many casualties and so the numbers to be carried forward steadily increased from day to day. On March 18 the divisional medical units reached the Manipur River bridge in the vicinity of Milestone 126 on the Tiddim–Imphal road. There 23 (Ind.) Fd. Amb. took over from 36 (Ind.) S.S. and prepared to admit up to 300 patients. To this unit 10 (Ind.) M.S.U. was attached. 51 (Ind.) S.S. then joined these two units and the area became the divisional medical area for a short while. Cover for the patients was provided by 40 × 40 ft. tarpaulins on wooden frames, each of these sheltered up to 40 men. On March 20, 37 (Ind.) Fd. Amb. opened its M.D.S. in this medical area with accommodation for another 300 patients and on the following day medical supplies arrived by air-drop.

During 48th Bde's. bitter struggle to clear the road in the vicinity of Milestone 109, medical cover was provided by 37 (Ind.) Fd. Amb. which placed a light A.D.S. on mule-pack with Adv. H.Q. of the brigade in Sakawng and a second light A.D.S. with divisional Main H.Q. at Milestone 116. At Milestone 114 a jeep loading post was established. To each of the light A.D.Ss. 20 stretcher-bearer squads were attached to carry casualties back to the jeep loading post where 20 ambulance jeeps were stationed to transport them back to the medical area at Milestone 126. This medical cover proved to be more than adequate.

On March 23 the medical units were ordered to move forward to Milestone 109. They moved in convoy, 60 5-ton lorries being provided for the transport of the patients and 20 15-cwt. trucks for the conveyance of stores and equipment. In the lorries the patients were to be bedded-down on parachutes, which were laid on the floor of the lorry to a depth of two feet and then covered with blankets. The side tarpaulins were rolled up and the back tarpaulin rolled down to keep the dust out. Each lorry could take 5 stretcher cases slung across the superstructure and 12 semi-lying on the parachutes. One nursing sepoy supplied with water tins and rations was posted to each truck. As was to be expected it was not long before a detachment of the A.F.S. joined the column. As the column moved forward the field ambulances provided mobile A.D.Ss. on mule-pack for their brigades. The head of the medical convoy reached Milestone 109 at 1930 hours on March 25. The convoy had been shelled on the way and there were casualties among the patients. In the camp area at Milestone 109 the site allotted to the medical units was so filthy and untidy that it was decided that the patients must stay in the transport for the night while the area was cleaned up. The medical units were now carrying 668 patients.

At Milestone 109 news was received that the road ahead was blocked between Milestones 104–100 and that fighting was in progress. A.D.M.S. Indian 17th Division therefore required the divisional medical units to be prepared to deal with as many as 1,000 casualties, each field ambulance taking 400 and each staging section 100. In the supply camp at Milestone 109 there was a certain quantity of medical supplies and parties of the medical units were detailed to salvage this. Additional vehicles were also obtained from this source.

On March 28 orders were received for the medical units to move forward to Milestone 86 on the following day. In order that they might set out at first light the patients were loaded into the transport on the evening of the 28th. On the march each brigade had a company of the field ambulance and a detachment of a bearer company attached to it together with a number of mules. The rest of the medical units moved, as before, in convoy, carrying 740 patients. Again the convoy was shelled and again a number of patients were wounded.

When Indian 17th and Indian 23rd Divisions joined up, the medical units of the latter division with 37th and 49th Bdes. came under command of Indian 17th Division. They were 49 (Ind.) Fd. Amb., 4 (Ind.) M.S.U. and 28 (Ind.) S.S. and they were carrying 146 casualties. The M.D.S. of this field ambulance was at Milestone 100. At Milestone 86 an airstrip had been completed and the first light plane landed on it on March 30 after which date cases in urgent need of hospitalisation could be flown back to Imphal.

When on March 31, 48th Bde. went forward to clear yet another road-block at Milestone 72, a company of 37 (Ind.) Fd. Amb., with two platoons of 2 (Ind.) Bearer Coy., accompanied it. Evacuation was by ambulance jeep to the M.D.S. of 37 (Ind.) Fd. Amb. at Milestone 82. It was not until April 1 that this road-block was finally cleared. The casualties in this M.D.S. were loaded on to the transport for the night of April 1/2 and set off for Imphal at 0900 hours on the 2nd. This convoy was joined by 49 (Ind.) Fd. Amb. with its patients.

Casualties occurring in the rearguard, 48th Bde., were brought to the convoy as it moved along or alternatively were taken to the M.D.S. of 37 (Ind.) Fd. Amb. at Milestone 82. When the medical convoy reached Imphal at 2200 hours on April 2 it was carrying 1,102 patients; 57 more were collected on the last stage. These were immediately examined by a team of medical officers provided by the medical units in Imphal and distributed according to their needs among the medical installations in the town. During this withdrawal, with the complete support of the divisional commander, the hygiene measures were strengthened and the divisional hygiene section reinforced by the addition of three medical officers and two N.C.Os. At the end of the withdrawal it was to be noted that the incidence of the preventable diseases of military importance had been remarkably low. There were only four deaths in the medical units during the withdrawal. By April 4 the divisional medical units of Indian 17th Division were congregated at Milestone 41 on the Tiddim–Imphal road and moved into Imphal on the following day.

They went into a number of boxes (defended localities) there.

48th Bde. Box	'A' Coy 37 (Ind.) Fd. Amb.
	4 (Ind.) Bearer Coy. 2 Pln.
	22 (Ind.) Fd. Hyg. Sec.
63rd Bde. Box	'A' Coy. 23 (Ind.) Fd. Amb.
	3 (Ind.) Bearer Coy. 1 pln.
Indian 17th Divisional Box—'Catfish' Box	the remainder of the divisional medical units.
	10 (Ind.) M.S.U. was attached to 37 (Ind.) Fd. Amb.

INDIAN 20TH DIVISION

The medical units of Indian 20th Division at this time were distributed as follows:

42 (Ind.) Fd. Amb.	M.D.S. in Tamu
55 (Ind.) Fd. Amb.	M.D.S. In Tamu, for minor sick and such as seemed likely to require a ten-days' stay.
59 (Ind.) Fd. Amb.	M.D.S. in Moreh, closed but ready to open.
9 (Ind.) M.S.U. and 10 (Ind.) Mob. X-ray Unit	attached to the M.D.S. of 42 (Ind.) Fd. Amb.
26 (Ind.) Fd. Hyg. Sec.	

In front of the M.D.Ss. were companies of the field ambulances providing A.D.Ss., car posts and the like. Evacuation from the M.D.Ss. was by road to 14 (Ind.) C.C.S. at Milestone 69·5 on the Tamu–Palel road. Air evacuation to Imphal from the airstrip at Tamu was available for such as needed hospitalisation.

When the division began its withdrawal to Moreh according to plan, the M.D.S. of 42 (Ind.) Fd. Amb. in Tamu closed on March 17 and that of 59 (Ind.) Fd. Amb. opened in Moreh. During this withdrawal there was much fighting and several of the regimental medical officers were killed. On March 18, H.Q. 42 (Ind.) Fd. Amb. moved back to the vicinity of Shenam. At this time there were many casualties but evacuation by road back to Palel was possible. In Palel 89 I.G.H. was about to be relieved by 14 (Ind.) C.C.S. which had moved back from its site on the Tamu–Palel road. 55 (Ind.) Fd. Amb. moved back into the Moreh perimeter. Since most of the positions occupied by Indian 20th Division were now overlooked by the Japanese, evacuation from the R.A.Ps. had become a hazardous undertaking. On the 29th, when it was decided to

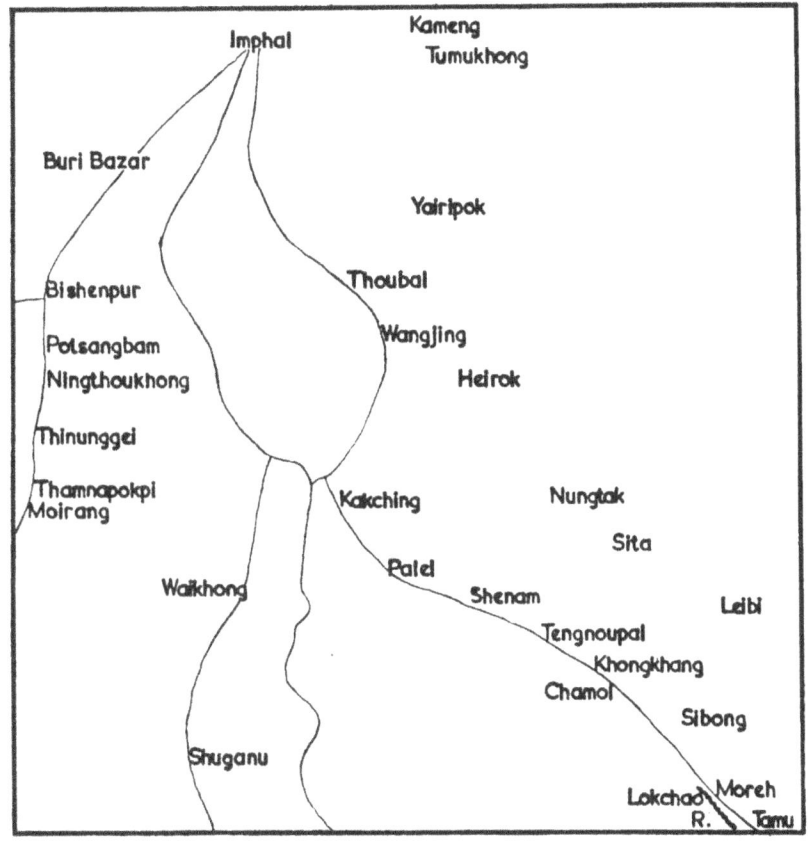

FIG. 30. Imphal–Tamu

withdraw from Moreh, a company of 59 (Ind.) Fd. Amb. moved to Milestone 21 on the Imphal–Palel road. On March 31, 59 (Ind.) Fd. Amb. closed in Moreh and moved back to join this company at Milestone 21. 55 (Ind.) Fd. Amb. withdrew from Moreh to Khongkhang, to the north-west of Sibong, on March 30, and opened its M.D.S. there. During the withdrawal from Moreh to Shenam the light sick and wounded were evacuated to the M.D.S. of 55 (Ind.) Fd. Amb. at Khongkhang and the more seriously ill to the M.D.S. of 42 (Ind.) Fd. Amb. in Shenam. The mobile surgical and X-ray units were transferred from the M.D.S. of 59 to that of 42. On April 4 the M.D.S. of 55 (Ind.) Fd. Amb. in Khongkhang moved into the 'Peacehaven' box in the vicinity of Milestone 21 and to the north of Palel. The only field ambulance now remaining in the forward area was 42 (Ind.) Fd. Amb., with 9 (Ind.) M.S.U. and a company of 55 (Ind.) Fd. Amb. attached, in Shenam.

55 (Ind.) Fd. Amb. then relieved 59 (Ind.) Fd. Amb. in the 'Peacehaven' box and opened its M.D.S. therein while 59 moved back to Wangjing on April 6 to open its M.D.S. to serve the units in the vicinity of the roadhead.

There were now two brigades in the Shenam-Tengnoupal-Sita area and these were being served by an A.D.S. of 55 (Ind.) Fd. Amb. in Shenam. H.Q. 42 (Ind.) Fd. Amb. opened a divisional M.D.S. whence evacuation was to 14 (Ind.) C.C.S. in Palel. The other medical units were able to rest for a while.

INDIAN 23RD DIVISION

When in June 1942 this division took up its position in the Imphal Plain, its medical units were 24, 47 and 49 (Ind.) Fd. Ambs. and 23 (Ind.) Fd. Hyg. Sec. Attached to the division were 7 and 10 (Ind.) Fd. Amb. Tps.

With Ind. 1st Bde. in the Shenam area was 24 (Ind.) Fd. Amb. Since at this time there seemed to be a distinct possibility that this brigade might become isolated if the Japanese advance continued, this field ambulance, establishing its M.D.S. at the Saddle on the Palel-Shenam-Tamu road, provided for accommodation of up to 600 patients. This M.D.S. was and remained short of tentage and equipment of every kind and there was no likelihood that these deficiences could be made good from India. An A.D.S. was established in Shenam in the small hospital there. Evacuation was to 8 (Ind.) C.C.S. in Imphal.

With Ind. 49th Bde. in the Shuganu area was 47 (Ind.) Fd. Amb. which established its M.D.S. in Thoubal and its A.D.S. in the vicinity of brigade headquarters. To this field ambulance 7 (Ind.) Fd. Amb. Tp. was attached. Evacuation to the M.D.S. was by riding mule and improvised *dhoolies** and from the M.D.S. to 8 (Ind.) C.C.S. in Imphal by ambulance car.

With Ind. 37th Bde. in the Ukhrul area was 49 (Ind.) Fd. Amb. which opened its M.D.S. in Litan and distributed four light sections along the road Litan-Ukhrul. To this unit 10 (Ind.) Fd. Amb. Tp. was attached. Evacuation back to the M.D.S. was by riding mule; between Litan and Yaingangpokpi it was by ambulance car; between this place and Sawombung it was by bullock cart and from Sawombung to Imphal it was by ambulance car. A small detachment of 49 (Ind.) Fd. Amb. had been despatched to Fort Hertz.

23 (Ind.) Fd. Hyg. Sec. was in Dimapur. With 123rd Bde. of Indian 5th Division, when it was placed u/c Indian 23rd Division and was in Imphal in reserve, was 45 (Ind.) Fd. Amb.

As has been related elsewhere, at this time 8 (Ind.) C.C.S. in Imphal and 66 I.G.H. in Dimapur were in danger of being overwhelmed by the great numbers of the sick coming out of Burma. The C.C.S. was

---
*Litters for carrying casualties.

evacuating about 600 patients a day. Any temporary blockage of the road from Imphal through Kohima to Dimapur caused by landslides due to rain at once created a most serious situation by damming the stream of evacuated sick. Such road-blocks were to be very common during the monsoon months. Whenever evacuation ceased the field ambulances were called upon to hold their patients. To this end in July, 47 (Ind.) Fd. Amb. established a light section in Shuganu, a small hospital in Palel holding some 150 patients and a second light section on the Palel–Wangjing road, near brigade headquarters. At this time this unit was very seriously handicapped by lack of transport. Some of its vehicles were still in Calcutta, some in Comilla and still others in Dimapur. Only by borrowing a few from 29 M.A.S. did it manage to discharge its functions. 49 (Ind.) Fd. Amb. opened a small hospital in Yaingangpokpi, capable of accommodating 120 patients, and placed a light section in Ukhrul.

By the middle of July the need for more holding accommodation in the Imphal area had become so acute that A.D.M.S. Indian 23rd Division decided to open a camp hospital in Imphal capable of holding up to 700 patients. 47 (Ind.) Fd. Amb. was given the task of organising and running this and the second-in-command of the unit was placed in charge. The old law courts and a girls' school were taken over. It was intended that when 37 (Ind.) Fd. Amb. of Indian 17th Division vacated the regimental hospital in the lines of the Assam Rifles, this building together with certain of the barrack blocks would be incorporated in the hospital.

Early in August, 8 (Ind.) C.C.S. in Imphal was relieved by 19 (Ind.) C.C.S. 36 (Ind.) C.C.S., another IV Corps' unit, was open in Palel. On August 14 the evacuation route was blocked once more and remained so for ten days. During this time the field ambulances had to hold their patients. 24 (Ind.) Fd. Amb. was holding 24, the camp hospital run by 47 (Ind.) Fd. Amb., 268, 47 (Ind.) Fd. Amb., 238 and 49 (Ind.) Fd. Amb., 190. The medical situation should have been eased when, on September 1, 41 I.G.H. moved up to Imphal from Kangpokpi but unfortunately this unit was without medical and ordnance stores. It was accommodated in the camp hospital. It was not until towards the end of the year that the equipment and stores of this hospital could be ferried forward from Dimapur.

At the beginning of October the situation was such that both Indian 17th and 23rd Divisions informed IV Corps that the medical arrangements in their areas had broken down. Admissions to medical units over-topped evacuations to such an extent that the whole medical machinery was slowly but inevitably grinding to a stoppage. Malaria was the cause of the crisis. Corps at once issued instructions to the effect that 500 patients were to be evacuated from the forward medical units rearwards every day. But since the rearward hospitals could not possibly cope with so many, the number was reduced to 150. Admissions at this time totalled some 200 a day and so quite inevitably the situation grew rapidly worse. To render the problem practically insoluble there now reached the forward area large numbers of pioneer units, without any medical officers, it goes without saying, composed of Madrassis, for the most part, unselected, riddled with malaria as a result of their sojourn of a fortnight or so in Dimapur *en route*, and in every way unsuited for the task assigned to them. 19 (Ind.) C.C.S. had to expand rapidly in order to cater for their needs. 9 (Ind.) Depot of Medical Stores was receiving no replenishments at this time and so could not meet the demands of the divisions. It was clear to all concerned that the major task to be undertaken by Indian 23rd Division, and by other divisions also, was that of leaving nothing undone to reduce the incidence of malaria.

On October 8, 49 (Ind.) Fd. Amb. moved from Yaingangpokpi into Imphal to pass into reserve. 36 (Ind.) C.C.S. moved from Palel to the Bishenpur area to open in the Dak bungalow* to serve the troops in this area and also to provide cover for the 6,000 Pioneers working on the Imphal–Tiddim road. On October 17, 47 (Ind.) Fd. Amb. opened an A.D.S. in Wangjing to function as a staging post between Shenam and Imphal. 19 (Ind.) Dent. Unit and 11 (Ind.) Mob. X-ray Unit arrived in Imphal and were attached to 19 (Ind.) C.C.S. 16 (Ind.) C.C.S. was moved up to Imphal preparatory to opening in the Bishenpur area.

Late in November, at long last, 47 (Ind.) Fd. Amb. was able to hand over the camp hospital to 41 I.G.H. and thereafter it became possible to reduce the numbers of those evacuated rearwards of Imphal to 450 a week for the malaria season was drawing to its close. At the end of the year the divisional medical units were distributed as follows:

24 (Ind.) Fd. Amb. M.D.S. and one and a half companies in Shenam, a light section in Khongkhang.

47 (Ind.) Fd. Amb. A.D.S. in Moreh. Rest of unit in Wangjing with an A.D.S. open.

49 (Ind.) Fd. Amb. A.D.S. in Litan. Remainder of unit in reserve in Wangjing.

23 (Ind.) Fd. Hyg. Sec. H.Q. in Thoubal. Sub-sections in Shenam, Moreh and Litan.

Early in 1943 smallpox appeared in the division; it was endemic in the area. A large-scale vaccination campaign was launched. To provide cover for the Pioneers working on the Palel–Tamu road and for a battalion of Ind. 37th Bde. in the area, a light section of 49 (Ind.) Fd.

---

* The Dak is a post for the conveyance of letters or transport by relays of men or horses; the Dak bungalow, a house for travellers at the dak station.

Amb. moved to Milestone 49·3 on this road. On January 19 a detachment of 47 (Ind.) Fd. Amb. opened a main dressing station in Moreh and a company of 24 (Ind.) Fd. Amb. moved to Palel.

From Tamu the division began to probe towards Sittaung and down the Kabaw Valley. 24 (Ind.) Fd. Amb. established an A.D.S. at Milestone 19 on the Tamu–Sittaung road late in March and 47 (Ind.) Fd. Amb., its A.D.S. in Sunle. 24 (Ind.) Fd. Amb. had an A.D.S. first in Hesin in the Kabaw Valley and later in Myothit. To the A.D.S of 24 (Ind.) Fd. Amb. on the Sittaung road 7 (Ind.) Fd. Amb. Tp. was attached. At the beginning of April strong patrols of Ind. 1st Bde. were operating to the east of the Chindwin and encountering Japanese patrols opposite Tonhe, Sittaung, Auktaung and Yuwa. At the same time patrols of 49th Bde. were clashing with Japanese patrols about Yazagyo in the Kabaw Valley. Medical cover for these operations was as follows:

24 (Ind.) Fd. Amb.	M.D.S. in Palel. Light section at Milestone 19 on the Sittaung road, serving 1st Bde. 7 (Ind.) Fd. Amb. Tp. attached. Light section in Sadaw.
	Evacuation east of the Chindwin by bullock cart; west of the river by riding mule and stretcher-bearer squad to Myothit or to the A.D.S. at Milestone 19. Thence by ambulance car to Moreh.
47 (Ind.) Fd. Amb.	Light section in Sunle to serve 49th Bde. Later this section moved back to Moreh. Light section in Kyaukchaw.
	Evacuation by boat to Maw and thence by ambulance car to Moreh where the M.D.S. of 47 (Ind.) Fd. Amb. was open and capable of holding up to 500 patients.
49 (Ind.) Fd. Amb.	Light section at Khongkhang to serve 37th Bde. Rest of unit in reserve at Lokchao. Later this unit moved back to Shenam.
23 (Ind.) Fd. Hyg. Sec.	H.Q. in Moreh. Sub-sections in Lokchao and Sunle. Later H.Q. moved to Langthoubal and the sub-sections to Wangjing and Waithou.

On April 8, 4 (Ind.) M.S.U. and 2 F.T.U. joined Indian 23rd Division and were attached to the M.D.S. of 47 (Ind.) Fd. Amb. in Moreh. As 25 M.A.S. could not produce more than ten runners among the cars the unit was relieved by 22 M.A.S. on the Moreh–Imphal run. 20 (Ind.) A.M.U. attached to Indian 23rd Division functioned from Wangjing.

From June 5–19, 47 (Ind.) Fd. Amb. had an A.D.S. in Chakpi Karong; after the 19th it rejoined the main body of the unit in Wangjing. In September 77 (Bur.) Fd. Amb. took over from 47 (Ind.) Fd. Amb. the hospital in Wangjing in order to free the Indian unit for further training. On November 1, Indian 23rd Division was relieved by Indian 20th Division.

INDIAN 50TH PARACHUTE BRIGADE

With this brigade was 80 (Ind.) Fd. Amb. consisting of H.Q. and four sections. On March 12 one of the sections moved with a battalion of the brigade to Ukhrul and another section with another battalion to Jessami. The rest of the unit left Imphal for Sangshak *via* Litan, leaving its heavy equipment behind. Reaching Sangshak the unit constructed dug-outs for its M.D.S. When Ukhrul was abandoned the section there joined the main body in Sangshak. As the road to Imphal had been cut, the M.D.S. in Sangshak was quickly filled. Medical supplies arrived by air-drop just in time to allay mounting anxiety. On March 24 heavy rain flooded the M.D.S. and great difficulty was encountered in attempts to keep the casualties warm. On the 26th the perimeter of the defended locality was breached near the M.D.S. so that this, its patients and its operating theatre had to be moved hurriedly to a safer site near brigade H.Q. On this day a radio message from Indian 23rd Division was received instructing the brigade to fight its way back. The units each sent parties of not less than fifty men to help the field ambulance to get its casualties away. A number of the more seriously wounded died on the way to Imphal.

Being warned that it would be necessary to withdraw from the Sangshak position very shortly, the medical units decided to get the walking wounded away together with as many stretcher cases as possible. The party set off with a Gurkha escort and split up into a number of small groups to avoid detection. Imphal was reached safely. Later the medical units withdrew to Imphal *via* Litan and by the 30th of the month had reassembled in Imphal and all the casualties had been admitted to the hospitals there. During these events 80 (Ind.) Para. Fd. Amb., lost one officer and ten O.Rs. It also lost a considerable proportion of its equipment. On April 1 the unit passed under command of Indian 5th Division and began to reorganise and re-equip.

THE SIEGE OF KOHIMA

On April 3 General Stopford, commanding XXXIII Corps, established his H.Q. in Jorhat, 65 miles north-north-east of Dimapur and on the following day took over the command of all the troops in the Dimapur-

Kohima area from Major-General Ranking, commanding 202 L. of C. Area. He was given the following directive by General Slim:
   (i) to cover the concentration of his corps as far forward as practicable;
   (ii) to secure the Dimapur base;
   (iii) to reinforce and hold Kohima;
   (iv) to protect, as far as possible without jeopardising (i) and (iii), the Assam railway and the China route airfields in the Brahmaputra Valley.

It was estimated that the Japanese could reach Kohima by April 3, Dimapur by April 11 and the Lushai Hills considerably later. It was accepted that the safety of Dimapur and Kohima depended on the outcome of a race between the speed of the Japanese advance on the one hand and the rate at which the build-up of XXXIII Corps proceeded.

The following reinforcements were due to arrive:

H.Q. 2nd Division and 5th Bde., by air, due to arrive April 2–5
4th Bde. by air   ,, ,, ,, April 10–15
6th Bde. by rail   ,, ,, ,, about April 15–18
33rd Bde. of Indian 7th Division by air from Arakan about April 15–18
11th Cavalry and a squadron of 45th Cavalry   uncertain
23rd L.R.P. Bde. by train from Jhansi   about April 12

XXXIII Corps' tactical plan took the following form:
   (i) 161st Bde. and 1st Assam Regt. would secure the Nichuguard Defile operating u/c 202 L. of C. area.
   (ii) When 5th Bde. arrived it would replace 161st Bde. which would then reinforce the Kohima garrison.
   (iii) 2nd Division would concentrate in the Dhansiri Valley and so would be in a well-roaded area and able to counter-attack at Dimapur if necessary.
   (iv) 33rd Bde., on arrival, would be left with 1st Assam Regt. to hold Dimapur. (This brigade had been involved in much fighting in Arakan; the Assam Regt. had been engaged in violent actions in its withdrawal from Jessami.)
   (v) 2nd Division, with the squadron of 45th Cavalry u/c, would be directed on Kohima and thence on Imphal. 11th Cavalry would patrol the road to Jorhat.
   (vi) 23rd Bde. would concentrate in the area Jamuguri–Nazira and thence operate in two columns, one from Golaghat towards Kohima and the other from Mariani towards Mokokchung with the object of cutting the Japanese L. of C.
   (vii) To the south in the area of the Bishenpur–Silchar track the Nepalese Mahindra Dal Regt. with one company of 25th G.R.,* operating u/c 257 Sub-area, would delay any Japanese advance by that route. Later 33rd Bde. would be employed on this same task.
   (viii) The newly-formed Lushai Bde. would prevent any Japanese advance into the Lushai Hills.

---

*25th G.R., the garrison battalion formed for protection duties at 14th Army H.Q.

The leading elements of 2nd Division arrived in Dimapur on April 2. Two of its brigades and divisional H.Q. were on their way by air and the remaining brigade by rail. Its 5th Bde. arrived on April 4. 161st Bde. of Indian 5th Division, having reached Dimapur by air from Arakan on March 26, had been sent forward to hold the Kohima Ridge. But no sooner had it taken up its positions there than it was hurriedly recalled to oppose the advance on Dimapur of a Japanese force that was reported to be in the area of Nichuguard Pass. This report proved to be unfounded and the brigade was ordered to return to Kohima. This it did on April 5 when its leading battalion, 4th R.W.K., accompanied by a section of 75 (Ind.) Fd. Amb., joined the garrison just after the first night attack by the Japanese had overrun some of the more forward positions. The rest of the brigade had halted for the night in the area of Jotsoma, about 3 miles out of Kohima. Early on the morning of April 7, a company of 4/7th Rajput of 161st Bde. moved into Kohima and a platoon of this company left again almost at once as an escort for some 200 walking wounded and non-combatants who were evacuated from the town. Shortly afterwards the Japanese closed round the town and also got between the rest of 161st Bde. at Jotsoma and Dimapur to establish a road-block at Milestone 32.

Dimapur lies in the low plain of the Brahmaputra Valley. The road from Dimapur to Kohima, about ten miles out of Dimapur, enters the narrow gorge of the Jharnapani stream. From this gorge the road climbs through the Nichuguard Pass to reach a height of 1,000 ft. Thereafter

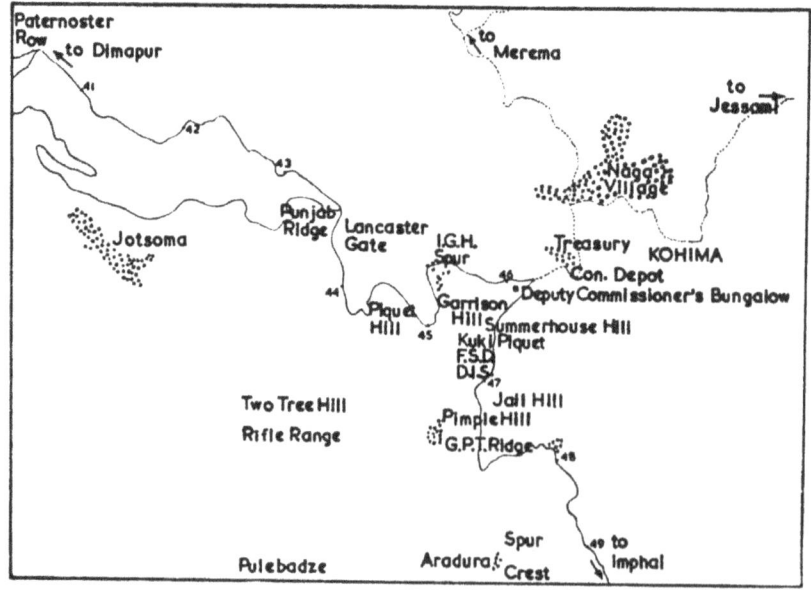

FIG. 31. The Dimapur–Kohima Road

it continues to climb steadily until at Priphema, about 28 miles from Dimapur, it has reached 4,000 ft. After reaching Zubza, eight miles on, it climbs again to reach the crest of the 5,000 ft. Kohima Ridge and the hill town of Kohima itself.

Kohima was a small township resting on a hill top in the midst of wild country. Its central point lay on the junction of the Dimapur–Kohima–Imphal road with the track that ran from Kohima eastwards to Jessami. To the north of this junction was a small wooden fort and from this, along a spur that ran to the south east, was a large convalescent depot of huts with tin roofs. To the north of the fort and overlooking it was a plateau, about a mile by half a mile in extent, on which a Naga village sprawled. Just to the south-west of the junction was the compound of the Deputy Commissioner, I.C.S., on a terraced hillside with its bungalow, its tennis court and its lovely gardens. To the west of the D.C's. compound, on another terraced hillside was the hospital area. There had been two Indian general hospitals on this site but when it was known that strong Japanese forces were approaching the Kohima–Dimapur area these were withdrawn and only a section of 53 I.G.H. left behind (four medical officers). The spur on which this hospital site was, was known as I.G.H. Spur. Running south from the D.C's. compound was Kohima Ridge with a series of knolls, of which Summerhouse Hill was the most northerly and Jail Hill the most southerly. Between the Ridge and the Naga village was the Saddle, about a mile long. The Ridge and the plateau on which the village stood sloped violently downwards with a gradient that in places was about 1 in 1½. To the south-west, Kohima is dominated by the towering masses of Pulebadze and of the Aradura feature, clothed in dense

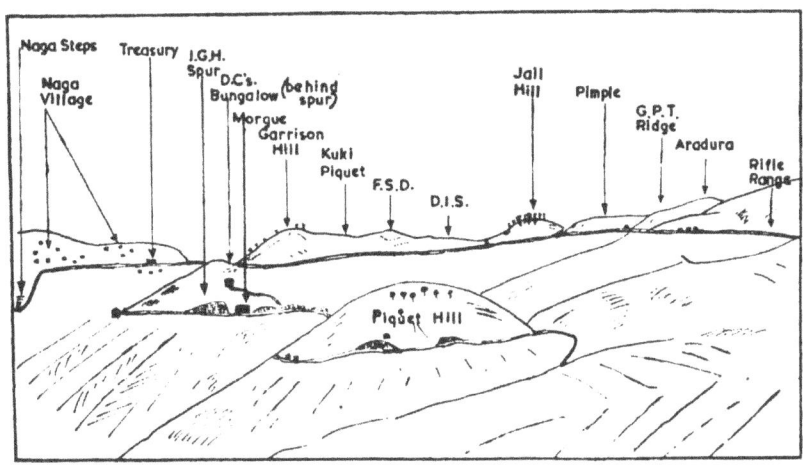

FIG. 32. Kohima. Panorama from Punjab Ridge looking eastwards

jungle that hid great clefts and chasms with sides far too steep to climb and often as deep as 300 ft.

The relative positions of the features to which reference is made in the text are shown in Figure 32. F.S.D. Hill was the site of a field supply depot; D.I.S. Hill the site of a detail issue store; G.P.T. Ridge that of a general purpose transport park.

The extent of the area held by the garrison at the beginning of the siege was shaped somewhat like a triangle with its base uppermost and measuring about 700 yds; the side on the east was about 1,100 yds. long and that on the west about 900 yds. Within this small area were about 3,500 troops, about a third of whom were fighting men and fit to fight. Food and ammunition were plentiful but the water supply was precarious and it was to be expected that its source would quickly pass into the possession of the Japanese. As the Japanese pressure increased through the long days and endless nights of the siege, which was to last a fortnight, the area of the ground held by the garrison progressively shrank. In the end it was a square with sides about 500 yds. long. This shrinkage can best be illustrated by the following table which lists the features held by the garrison on April 6, April 10 and April 18 respectively:*

April 6	April 10	April 18
D.Cs. compound and the ground up to the Dimapur – Kohima road.	southern one-third of the compound	southern one-third of the compound
I.G.H. Spur	eastern one-third of spur	north-eastern half of I.G.H. Spur
Summerhouse Hill	Summerhouse Hill	Summerhouse Hill
Kuki Piquet	Kuki Piquet	—
F.S.D. Hill	northern quarter of F.S.D Hill	—
D.I.S. Hill	—	—

On the night of April 6/7 the Japanese infiltrated into the D.I.S. area and were expelled with considerable loss. On the 7th the troops of the Assam Regt. withdrew from their positions in the area of the I.G.H. Spur and moved to other positions in Summerhouse Hill area. During this move they came under heavy fire and lost heavily. The Japanese occupied a ridge opposite the I.G.H. Spur and gained possession of the waterpoint. On April 9 they attacked the D.C's. compound but were held. On the following day D.I.S. Hill was no longer tenable and was evacuated after nightfall. During the next three days the fighting was less general

---

* Arthur Campbell. *The Siege. A Story from Kohima.* 1956, published by Allen and Unwin Ltd.

but it flared up again on the 13th during which there was much shelling but no large-scale infantry attack. The air-dropping of water and supplies was only partially successful for many of the parachutes fell in Japanese held areas. Fortunately a small spring was discovered just outside the perimeter and this was used at night. The water ration was down to less than a pint a day for the rest of the siege.

During the night of April 13/14 a detachment of 4th R.W.K. moved to the D.I.S. area to prevent any further infiltration by the Japanese. The fighting now grew increasingly fierce and the pressure upon the perimeter increasingly heavier. During the night of April 17/18, following persistent attacks, most of F.S.D. Hill and Kuki Piquet* had to be abandoned. On the 15th a patrol of 4/7th Rajput from the Jotsoma box had succeeded in getting through the Japanese lines into Kohima to bring the news that relief was on its way. It returned to 161st Bde. with the information that the garrison was rapidly reaching a state of utter exhaustion and that unless relief arrived within the next 48 hours Kohima would surely fall On the 16th the garrison could see 161st Bde. battling its way forward along the line of the road. On the 17th it had reached the foot of I.G.H. Spur. At 0830 hours on the 18th, 161st Bde. resumed the attack and two companies of 1/1st Punjab entered Kohima and at once took over a sector of the perimeter. Very shortly after this ambulances arrived and soon a slow procession of torment was winding its way back to Dimapur.

MEDICAL ASPECTS OF THE SIEGE OF KOHIMA

In Kohima at the beginning of the siege were:

53 I.G.H. one section.
75 (Ind.) Fd. Amb. section (with 4th R.W.K.) (and four ambulance cars).
80 (Ind.) Para. Fd. Amb. (Ind. 50th Para. Bde.)
3 R.M.Os.
19 (Ind.) Fd. Hyg. Sec.

A total of 14 medical officers; 9 B.O.Rs., R.A.M.C.; 64 I.O.Rs., I.A.M.C.

When first the Japanese closed upon Kohima the medical situation within the perimeter was far from satisfactory. The garrison was not ready for a siege, each combatant unit with a R.M.O. was dealing with its own casualties and with their evacuation and no adequate cover for the wounded had yet been constructed. The section of 53 I.G.H. on I.G.H. Spur was in an exposed position and so, on April 2, it found new accommodation in a box near the D.C's. bungalow. During the next few days the R.A.Ps. filled to overflowing and numbers of

---

* The Kukis are a hill people whose territory is in the high hills that border the Imphal Plain on the south and east.

wounded were lying in the open. It is to be remembered that the R.M.Os. of the units that had held the forward positions along the western bank of the Chindwin and that had fought a stubborn rearguard action were themselves nearing the point of utter exhaustion, for during the past six days and nights they had never had more than two hours' sleep a night while the battalions withdrew through dense jungle to Kohima.

In the afternoon of April 6 the officer commanding 75 (Ind.) Fd. Amb., who had remained with the rest of his unit at Jotsoma when the section moved with 4th R.W.K. into Kohima, made his way into the town over the hills and along the valleys. He at once took charge of the medical arrangements within the perimeter and acted as S.M.O. to the garrison. He established a central dressing station just to the north of Summerhouse Hill and had trenches dug to accommodate up to 200 stretcher cases. The available medical personnel were distributed among the section of 53 I.G.H., the dressing station and the R.A.Ps. The personnel of the dressing station were divided into three groups, a nursing group which included the followers, sweepers and the like, an evacuation group of sepoys for the carriage of casualties from R.A.P. to the dressing station and an entrenching and supply group. Medical equipment and stores were salvaged from the buildings formerly occupied by the I.G.Hs. and distributed among the R.A.Ps. and the dressing station.

A description of the operating theatre in the dressing station near Summerhouse Hill is given in *The Siege** (page 113). 'It was just five feet deep and was circular, with a diameter of ten feet. The medical stores were piled in three little trenches running off from the main theatre; there was a ramp leading into the centre down which to bring the wounded'. And on page 142, 'In the middle of the theatre was the operating table, a stretcher resting on two trestles, with under it two empty jam tins where the rubbish was thrown. Off to one side were two primus stoves on an old biscuit box with a tray of boiling water on them; in the water were lying a few instruments. Nearby was an enamel basin, also on a primus, and half full of water. An orderly was squeezed up against the box keeping the primuses burning. The theatre was lit by a hurricane lamp hanging from a pole across the centre of the circle, and over this pole were drawn two canvas covers to shield the light. There had not been time to build a timber and earth head-cover'.

By April 9 the medical arrangements were working smoothly and it became possible to create a fourth group out of the dressing station personnel, a resuscitation group. There were some 200 patients in the

---

* *The Siege. A Story from Kohima* by Arthur Campbell, 1956, published by Allen and Unwin Ltd.

D.S. by this time and it became a matter of great emergency to clear it before it got completely choked. It so happened that two platoons of 4/7th Rajput had received orders to rejoin their unit and so it was decided to send a party of walking wounded and sick with them on their return journey to Jotsoma. The route that had to be taken was so difficult that of the casualties only 98 could be selected for evacuation. Three control points were established, one in the dressing station itself, one near the original site of 53 I.G.H. on I.G.H. Spur and the third at the entrance to the nullah just to the north-west of this which led down into the valley that ran below the road to Dimapur. At Milestone 42 on this road a patrol was to meet the parties and set them on their way. Just before they moved off the walking wounded who were to leave were examined to make sure that they were fit enough to stand the journey and at 2045 hours on April 9 the first party of 20 was clear of the control point near I.G.H. Spur. It was led by a Naga guide and by the officer commanding 75 (Ind.) Fd. Amb. and an officer of 4th R.W.K. By 2230 hours the last of the parties had reached the nullah. By midnight news was received that all the parties had reached Milestone 42 safely. They were admitted to the A.D.S. of 75 (Ind.) Fd. Amb., pending evacuation to Dimapur. The officer commanding this unit, his companion, the officer of the Royal West Kents and the Naga guide then turned about and made their way back to Kohima which they reached shortly before daybreak. This march in the dark over extremely uneven ground by these enfeebled, wounded men was for many of them a continuous anguish. There could be no halt though men stumbled and reopened their wounds, for had they stopped many would not have been able to start again.

In the dressing station following this evacuation there remained 104 lying cases of which 32 were seriously ill. The R.A.Ps. were all cleared by the morning of April 10. On this day the Japanese attacked D.I.S. Hill and shelled and mortared the dressing station. Eventually D.I.S. Hill had to be abandoned as had also part of F.S.D. Hill. Before the troops left these positions the casualties were brought back to the D.S. in which a considerable number of the casualties were re-wounded. On April 13 heavy shelling of the D.S. area resulted in 21 deaths and the re-wounding of 30 of the casualties. Two of the medical officers in the D.S. were killed and another was wounded. Owing to this persistent bombardment of this area the nursing of the patients became exceedingly difficult as did also their feeding. The Indians among the patients were fed from the D.S. kitchen, the British with rations obtained from the kitchen of one of the R.W.K. companies. In the evening of this day, the 13th, the bombardment of the D.S. area was renewed and another medical officer was killed together with two of the orderlies. It became necessary to move the dressing station. A part of the adjoining area, where the Shere Regiment had constructed good trenches, was taken over and work upon splinter-proof dug-outs for patients and staff was begun. The D.S. moved into its new accommodation on the following day. A few days earlier a scarcity of blankets in the D.S. had developed. Knowing that there were plenty in a number of lorries abandoned on the road about 500 yards beyond the D.C's. bungalow, the dauntless officer commanding 75 (Ind.) Fd. Amb., with the help of 12 volunteers from among the I.O.Rs. of his unit, made his way through the Japanese lines while fighting was in progress and then crept upon the sentry guarding the lorries. Disposing of him, the party loaded itself with blankets and, after two hours spent in avoiding Japanese soldiery, got back safely to the dressing station.

It is very difficult indeed to find the right words to describe at all adequately the scenes in the dressing station as day succeeded day. For the medical and nursing staff there was no respite. With every temporary lull in the bombardment there were always patients to be tended; the supplies of dressings and drugs were visibly dwindling; replenishment by air-drop was not always successful; the collection of water at night became increasingly dangerous; as the area shrunk and became more and more open as trees and buildings were destroyed, the shelling and mortaring searched every yard within the perimeter and the collection of casualties became more and more difficult. In the dressing station, for the same reasons, the nursing of the patients became less and less satisfactory; in it there were men who had lain upon their stretchers in their shallow holes in the ground for as long as thirteen days and nights. Empty food tins were in use as urinals, of bedpans there were none. There the wounded lay in small groups with the sweet, sickly stench of blood, of rotting wounds and of death and the sound of anguish everywhere around them. Heroic and stubborn as the defence of Kohima had been, to it there must surely come an ending. To endurance there is a limit. The forward troops of 161st Bde. arrived just in time.

Because their need was so great and so urgent it was decided to evacuate the casualties from Kohima immediately, although the Japanese were still holding positions that dominated the road to Dimapur, and in daylight, along a track that was under direct observation by the Japanese. Three control points were established as before, one at the D.S., one in the I.G.H. area and the third where the road and the track met. These were linked by wireless. At the most forward of the three control points, a detachment from the D.S. was stationed to supervise the loading of the ambulances and to ensure that the casualties were fit to make the journey. The convoy was to pass through the perimeter in the sector held by the Assam Rifles at a point where a N.C.O. and six men formed yet another control post. 600 I.O.Rs. were provided by the garrison for stretcher-bearer duties. The walking wounded were to move in parties of 25 at five minute intervals and were to be followed by five groups of stretcher cases with six men to each stretcher. Each group was in charge of an officer.

The evacuation began at 0740 hours on April 18 and proceeded smoothly without any interference by the Japanese. Between 1200 and 1400 hours there was a certain amount of desultory shelling of the I.G.H. Spur area and one officer and three O.Rs. were wounded. Evacuation was halted during the shelling but by 1640 hours all the (300 plus) casualties had been evacuated and were on their way towards Dimapur and the care and comfort of the rearward hospitals.

THE ADVANCE OF 2ND DIVISION FROM DIMAPUR TO KOHIMA

Though 161st Bde. had succeeded in entering Kohima and in relieving its garrison—the West Kents could not muster more than about 250 men when they were relieved—the Japanese still held all the positions around the town and being on the Ridge barred the way south to Imphal. It was to be the task of 2nd Division, Indian 7th Division and 23rd Bde. to complete the work so well begun by the Kohima garrison and by 161st Bde., by driving the Japanese right out of the area and by joining up with the Imphal garrison.

2nd Division had arrived in India in 1942 to form a reserve for use in emergency in any part of the Middle or Far East. It had been trained in combined operations and in jungle warfare. It moved from the Belgaum-Bombay area by road, rail and air. Its leading elements reached Dimapur on March 31; its rearmost element did not arrive until the middle of May. On April 9 XXXIII Corps assigned to 2nd Division the task of opening the Dimapur-Kohima road and relieving the Kohima garrison. By the 11th, H.Q. and two brigades of the division had reached Dimapur. On the 12th, 23rd Bde. of 70th Division ('Special Force') arrived in Jorhat. On the 10th, 5th Bde. of 2nd Division was ferried up the Dimapur-Kohima road as far as Zubza. Fighting its way forward this brigade made contact with 161st Bde. in the Jotsoma box on April 15. 6th Bde. of 2nd Division was then brought forward so that 161st Bde. might be freed to advance towards Kohima. On the 18th, 161st Bde., with air, tank and artillery support, fought its way towards Kohima and finally broke through to join up with the garrison.

On April 19, 161st Bde. attacked the Japanese positions on Kuki Piquet but was repulsed. 2nd Division kept the Dimapur-Kohima road open and along this came the convoys to replenish Kohima. On the 21st, 1st R. Berks. of 6th Bde. moved into Kohima and took over the positions on Summerhouse Hill.

33rd Bde. of Indian 7th Division, newly arrived in the area of XXXIII Corps from Arakan, and 23rd Bde. were now moving eastwards.

The tactical plan was for one brigade of 2nd Division to press against the centre of the Japanese positions about Kohima while the other two brigades of the division, one on either flank, carried out turning movements to seize high ground to the rear of the Japanese line. 161st Bde. was to be held in reserve at Jotsoma and 33rd Bde. (corps reserve) was to cover Dimapur. 23rd Bde. was to continue its thrust towards Jessami to cut the Japanese supply line. When the two flank brigades had reached their objectives, the brigade in the centre would then attack.

On April 21 the leading battalion of the brigade on the left flank, 5th Bde., crossed the valley to the east of the Dimapur–Kohima road and climbed some 2,000 ft. to reach the Bokajan track that runs due north from Kohima. The battalion discovered prepared but unoccupied Japanese positions on the Merema Ridge. During the next few days the rest of the brigade moved forward to join the battalion and on the 28th attacked Japanese positions further to the north but without success. Meanwhile, 4th Bde. on the right flank, crossed the Pulebadze Ridge to attack the Aradura feature from the south-west. Little opposition was encountered but owing to the rain and the exceedingly great difficulties presented by the nature of the ground, the brigade did not travel as fast as had been hoped. Over 300 Naga porters were employed to help the brigade for in places the track that was followed had a gradient of 1 in 1 and every officer and man was carrying about 60 lb. on his person. In the centre, 6th Bde. was fiercely attacked during the night of April 22/23 but held its ground. For the next two days it was under continual pressure. However, on the night of the 27/28th it passed to the offensive and attacked the positions about the D.C's. bungalow to gain ground and to hold on to its gains.

The plan was now changed. The wider turning movements were abandoned and the three brigades prepared to deliver a concentrated attack upon the Japanese positions with the support of the tanks and of the divisional and corps artillery. 4th Bde. was to capture G.P.T. Ridge, advance to Jail Hill and link up with 6th Bde. in the centre which was to capture Kuki Piquet and F.S.D. Ridge. 5th Bde. was to occupy the Naga village and gain control over the Treasury area. The attack began in the early morning of May 4. 4th Bde. reached G.P.T. Ridge but was unable to secure the whole of it and therefore could not advance to Jail Hill. 6th Bde. was not successful in its attempt to take Kuki Piquet and had to give up most of its gains on F.S.D. Ridge because of the intensity of the Japanese fire. 5th Bde. got into the Naga village but was thrust back to its edge. On the 5th efforts were made to consolidate the gains. On May 7, 33rd Bde. was brought into the line and placed u/c 2nd Division to reinforce the attack in the centre. Jail Hill was taken but could not be held in the face of intense and accurate shelling.

During the night of May 10/11 the attack was resumed, much use

JAPANESE INCURSION INTO INDIA

being made of smoke-screens. 33rd Bde. was set the task of capturing Jail and D.I.S. Hills after 4th and 6th Bdes. had cleared G.P.T. Ridge and F.S.D. Hill. The attacks on G.P.T. Ridge and D.I.S. Hill were not completely successful but 33rd Bde. found Pimple Hill unoccupied, took possession of it and went on to gain most of Jail Hill. Under cover of smoke the brigade dug in. During the 11th a minefield between D.I.S. and Jail Hills was cleared and early on the 12th the attack was resumed. Very stubborn opposition was encountered but on the 13th the Japanese fell back and Jail, D.I.S. and F.S.D. Hills, G.P.T. Ridge and Kuki Piquet were all occupied by 2nd Division. While these actions were proceeding, tanks were dealing with the bunkers in the D.C's. compound area. A tank would approach a bunker and fire its 75mm. gun at a distance of 30 yards or alternatively a charge of explosive at the end of a long pole would be thrust through the loophole of the bunker. One by one the bunkers were destroyed. 33rd Bde. was about to launch an attack upon Treasury Hill when it was discovered that the Japanese were withdrawing from it.

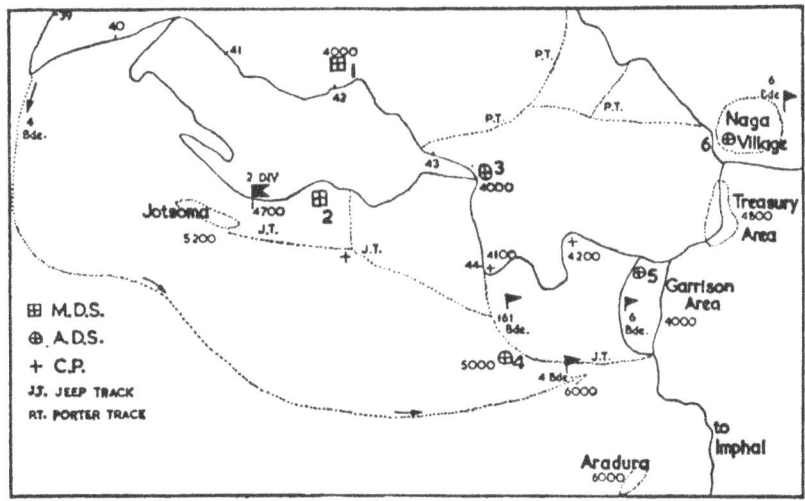

FIG. 33. 2nd Division's Advance on Kohima. Medical Cover

1. Combined M.D.S. of 4 and 75 (Ind.) Fd. Ambs.
2. M.D.S. of 6 Fd. Amb.
3. W.W.C.P. and Medical Control Post
4. A.D.S. of 75 (Ind.) Fd. Amb.
5. A.D.S. of 6 Fd. Amb.
6. A.D.S. of 5 Fd. Amb.

Figures 39–44 are Milestones on the Dimapur–Kohima Road.
4,000 etc. refers to height above sea-level in feet

Kohima was thus reoccupied and the first phase of the battle of Kohima brought to a successful conclusion. But the road to Imphal was still blocked for the Japanese were holding commanding positions in the Naga village area and on the Aradura Spur.

Indian 7th Division, with its 114th Bde., had arrived in XXXIII Corps' area from Arakan, had absorbed its own 33rd Bde. and 161st Bde. of Indian 5th Division and had taken over the left sector of the Kohima front. Indian 268th Motorised Brigade (Lorried Infantry) of Indian 21st Division had arrived on May 16 and relieved 6th Bde. of 2nd Division in the sector just to the south of the D.C's. bungalow. 2nd Division was left with the main Kohima-Imphal road sector and all the ground to the right of this.

Between May 24 and June 2, 33rd Bde. and then 114th Bde. tried hard to overcome the stubborn resistance of the Japanese in the Naga village area but without complete success. However, on June 2 the Japanese broke contact and withdrew towards the east. Meanwhile, 2nd Division had been attempting to dislodge the Japanese from the formidable Aradura Ridge, but the slippery slopes of this 3,000 ft. feature combined with the dour defence of the Japanese garrison to bring the attack to a halt. It was then switched from the western and northern slopes of the Ridge to the eastern. After much fighting 5th Bde. managed to cut the Japanese supply line and following this the Japanese withdrew. The battle of Kohima was over; it had lasted two months; it had ended in the complete defeat of Japanese 31st Division.

MEDICAL COVER. 2ND DIVISION

Under command of 2nd Division for this operation were:

4, 5 and 6 Fd. Ambs.
75 (Ind.) Fd. Amb. (with 161st Bde. of Indian 5th Division)
2 Fd. Hyg. Sec.
14 (Ind.) M.S.U.
44 (Ind.) A.M.U.
A platoon of 5 (Ind.) Bearer Coy. (u/c 75 (Ind.) Fd. Amb.)

For the advance of the division on Kohima M.D.Ss. were strung along the Dimapur-Kohima road. Near Jotsoma on the Dimapur-Kohima road, was the M.D.S. of 6 Fd. Amb. with a surgical team of 13 (Ind.) C.C.S. attached. Near Milestone 42, was the combined M.D.S. of 4 and 75 (Ind.) Fd. Ambs. to which 14 (Ind.) M.S.U. was attached. 4 Fd. Amb. was relieved by 9 (Ind.) Lt. Fd. Amb. which was attached to Ind. 268th Lorried Infantry Bde.

Near Milestone 36 (Zubza), the M.D.S. of 5 Fd. Amb. A.D.Ss. were established as follows:

In the vicinity of Garrison Hill (between Kuki Piquet and Piquet Hill), the A.D.S. of 6th Fd. Amb.
Below I.G.H. Spur, the A.D.S. of 75 (Ind.) Fd. Amb.
To the north of the Naga village, the A.D.S. of 5th Bde.
Four sections of 4 Fd. Amb. moved with 4th Bde.

Car Posts were established at 'Lancaster Gate' to the south of the road in the vicinity of Milestone 44 and between Milestones 45 and 46. At 'Lancaster Gate', a W.W.C.P. was established.

These arrangements proved to be quite satisfactory. The two M.D.Ss. with the attached surgical teams were well protected and could accommodate post-operative patients for 48 hours. Life-saving surgery only was practised in them. The M.D.S. of 5 Fd. Amb. at Zubza functioned as a staging post for casualties being sent back from the two more forward M.D.Ss. to Dimapur.

The weather by this time had greatly deteriorated and the 'jeep-tracks' which were the only means, other than hand-carriage, of getting casualties away from the A.D.Ss., were becoming increasingly difficult. Five armoured ambulance cars were used along the main Kohima road. One of them was hit and wrecked and its crew killed. As the ridges on the right of the main road—G.P.T., Jail, F.S.D., D.I.S. and Kuki Piquet—were cleared it became possible to push the M.D.S. of 6 Fd. Amb. forward to the site of 75 (Ind.) Fd. Amb's. A.D.S. at the bottom of I.G.H. Spur where it developed into a small hospital holding some 170 patients. Its surgical theatre was the kitchen of 53 I.G.H., the only hospital building still standing and under the lee of a very steep bank.

When Indian 7th Division came into the line to clear the Naga village, its 44 (Ind.) Fd. Amb. established its M.D.S. close to that of 6 Fd. Amb. and the two units developed a medical centre that was used during the remainder of the battle, including the clearance of the Aradura feature, until 13 (Ind.) C.C.S. and 8 M.F.T.U. had been moved forward to Kohima.

The A.D.S. of 5 Fd. Amb. accompanied 5th Bde. in the left hook to the north of the Naga village. Evacuation was by Naga porters to the A.D.S. and thence to the M.D.S. at Milestone 42.

When the siege was ended the casualties remaining in Kohima were evacuated by 59 and 61 M.A.Ss. under the command of the second-in-command of 75 (Ind.) Fd. Amb.

THE ADVANCE FROM KOHIMA AND THE LINK-UP WITH IV CORPS

XXXIII Corps' plan now was for 2nd Division, with tank and artillery support, to thrust down the Kohima–Imphal road while Indian 7th Division, on pack transport, moved across country on the left of, and parallel to, the road, keeping pace with 2nd Division and while 23rd Bde., supplied by air-drop, intensified its efforts to reach Ukhrul.

On June 6, 2nd Division began its advance and though there were several brisk encounters with Japanese rearguards, it was not until Viswema was reached at Milestone 60 that the pace of the advance was checked. When this opposition was overcome on the 14th by 4th and 5th Bdes. at a cost of 13 killed and 48 wounded, the advance was resumed. It was checked again in front of Mao Songsang where a high ridge ran at right angles to the road. While the division was preparing to assault this position the Japanese withdrew. The advance down the road was then continued until it was halted a few miles in front of Maram. Here the division destroyed the Japanese rearguard opposing it and thereafter moved on to Milestone 109 where its tanks met the leading elements of 1/17th Dogra of Indian 5th Division moving up the road from Imphal on June 22. XXXIII and IV Corps had thus become joined up and it became possible for a convoy that had left Dimapur loaded with supplies to proceed down the road to Imphal.

Indian 7th Division began its southward advance on June 3. On this day 114th Bde. occupied the village of Chedema, north-east of Kohima. While 161st Bde. protected its left flank, 114th Bde. then moved on to occupy Chakhabama, encountering no opposition. When Kezoma was entered it was found that Japanese rearguards were holding Kidima and Kekrima in strength. 114th Bde's attack on Kidima was not successful but 161st Bde., advancing along the Kohima–Jessami track, attacked and captured Kekrima on the 8th. On June 13, 114th Bde., by-passing

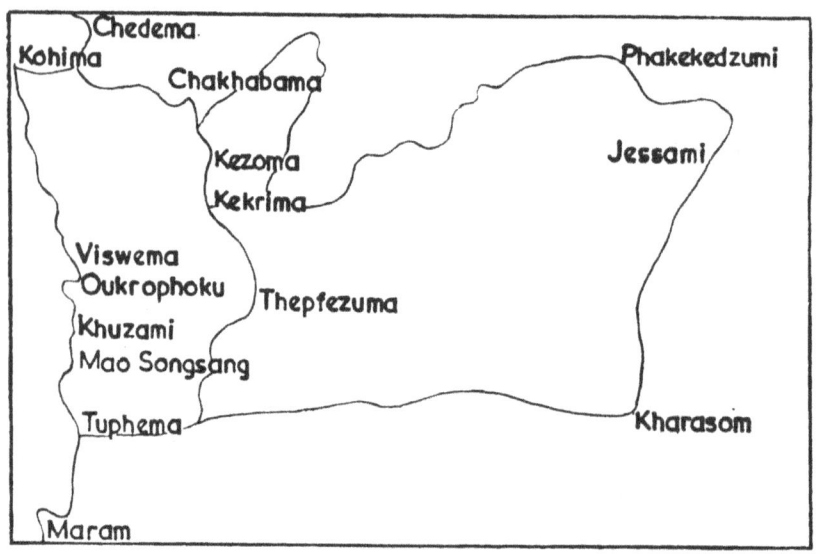

Fig. 34. Kohima–Jessami

JAPANESE INCURSION INTO INDIA

Kidima, thrust southwards, while 161st Bde., cleared the Jessami track as far as Milestone 24. During the night of June 13/14, the Japanese withdrew from Kidima. 161st Bde. proceeded to occupy Thepfezuma to the south-east of Kekrima. 114th Bde. next occupied Oukrophoku which stood athwart the Japanese line of withdrawal from the Mao Songsang position. By June 16, 161st Bde. had reached Milestone 28

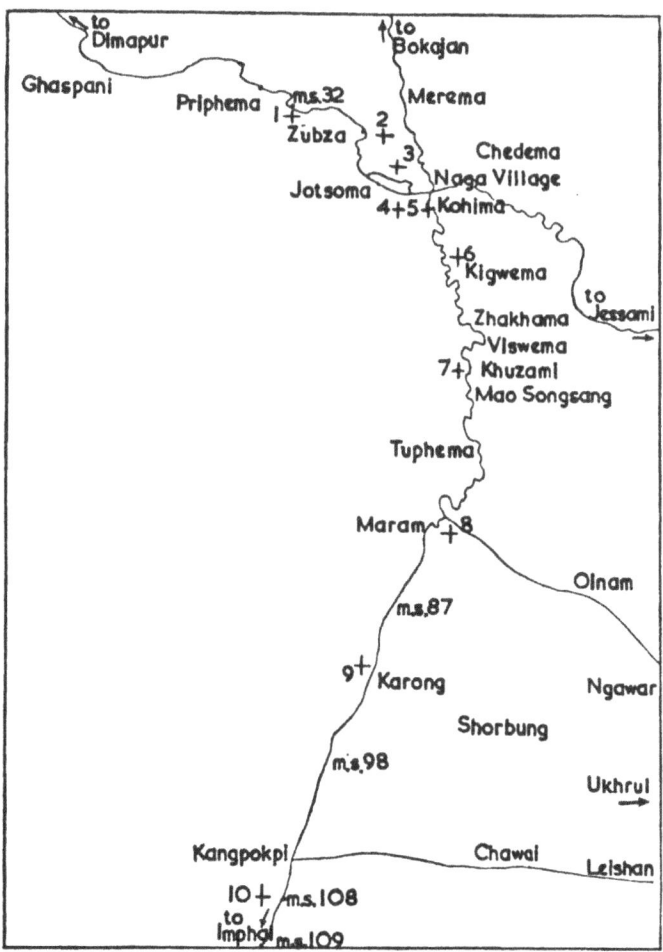

FIG. 35. The Movements of the Main Dressing Stations of 2nd Division during the Battle of Kohima and the Advance down the Kohima–Imphal Road

1. 5 Fd. Amb. April 11–16
   4 Fd. Amb. April 17–22
2. 5 Fd. Amb. April 17—June 7
3. 4 Fd. Amb. May 1–June 8
4. 6 Fd. Amb. April 25–May 18
5. 6 Fd. Amb. May 19–June 20
6. 5 Fd. Amb. June 8–21
7. 4 Fd. Amb. June 15–20
8. 4 Fd. Amb. June 20
9. 6 Fd. Amb. June 22
10. 5 Fd. Amb. June 22

on the Jessami track and 114th Bde. had cut the Tuphema–Kharasom track in the vicinity of Milestone 70. By the 18th, 161st Bde. was also astride this track. These events had much to do with the weakness of the opposition offered by the Japanese to the advance of 2nd Division down the road. The task of Indian 7th Division having been completed, 114th Bde. concentrated in the Mao Songsang area and 161st Bde. moved to the vicinity of Tuphema, leaving two battalions to guard the Jessami and Kharasom tracks.

23rd Bde. pushed eastwards towards Jessami, ambushing Japanese supply columns and dislocating their line of communication.

MEDICAL COVER DURING THE ADVANCE DOWN THE KOHIMA–IMPHAL ROAD

2ND DIVISION AND INDIAN 7TH DIVISION

The axis of the 2nd Division's advance was the road itself and from this the battalions were never more than 500 yards distant. Save when the advance was checked and the troops were deployed to attack some point of opposition, movement was rapid for the troops were ferried by M.T. A number of mobile A.D.Ss. were provided by the field ambulances, each consisting of a medical officer and six N.Os., with a second medical officer in reserve, and either a 3-ton lorry and a penthouse or an ambulance car and a penthouse. Evacuation from R.A.P. to A.D.S. was by armoured ambulance car and from A.D.S. to M.D.S. by M.A.S. or A.F.S. The A.D.Ss. leap-frogged over each other.

Of the M.D.Ss., that of 5 Fd. Amb. was the first to move. It opened in Kigwema on a site where, before the battle, there had been an I.G.H. The building which it occupied had been badly shattered but the M.D.S., with two attached surgical teams, began to function within 24 hours of its arrival. As the incidence of dysentery was beginning to cause a certain anxiety, a special ward of 70 beds was opened. It was decided that a M.D.S. should be established in Chakhabama where 54 (Ind.) Fd. Amb. had an A.D.S., to serve Indian 7th Division. Here only tented accommodation was available. To this A.D.S. a surgical team from 26 (Ind.) C.C.S. was attached. But as Indian 7th Division had not yet caught up with the Japanese rearguards, there had been few casualties and the need for this M.D.S. had not yet arisen. Evacuation from Chakhabama was to Kohima.

The track running from Kohima to Jessami had been regarded as a fair-weather track, motor vehicles being able to use it only during the dry season. It was now necessary to maintain Indian 7th Division along it during a rapid advance in early monsoon conditions. All available jeeps and jeep trailers in XXXIII Corps were collected and a jeep company formed. Chakhabama was developed as an administrative base. In front of Chakhabama reliance was placed on animal transport. The track from Chakhabama to Kohima was but 12 miles long yet the trip along it commonly took as long as four hours. The heavy rains quickly turned the mountain track into a twisting ribbon of mud and after the first few days of use a one-way traffic system had to be introduced. Jeeps, including jeep ambulances driven by A.F.S. personnel, using chains, slithered and skidded along the track to be held up quite frequently by fresh landslides. The Sappers and the Pioneers worked feverishly to keep the track open and as a result of their untiring efforts the troops were never short of ammunition and supplies and the casualties were evacuated.

After Viswema had been captured, since the M.D.S. of 5 Fd. Amb. was too heavily burdened with patients to move forward immediately, the A.D.S. of 4 Fd. Amb. and 14 (Ind.) M.S.U. were stationed in Khuzami, at Milestone 62 on the Imphal road, to stage casualties on their way to Kigwema. By June 12 the M.D.S. of 54 (Ind.) Fd. Amb. had replaced the A.D.S. and this had moved forward to Kekrima, to the north-east of Mao Songsang, leaving the attached surgical team with the M.D.S.

After Mao Songsang and Tuphema had been captured, 2nd Division and Indian 7th Division converged and so evacuation from the latter division was switched along the axis of the former. The M.D.S. in Chakhabama, being superfluous, closed.

On June 19, 44 (Ind.) Fd. Amb. opened its M.D.S. in Tuphema to serve Indian 7th Division. On June 20 the distribution of the medical units of the two divisions was as follows:

Tuphema	M.D.S. 44 (Ind.) Fd. Amb.	dealing with casualties of Indian 7th Division now operating on the Tuphema–Kharasom track.
Kigwema	M.D.S. 5 Fd. Amb.	about to be relieved.
Milestone 64 on the Kohima–Imphal road	M.D.S. 4 and 6 Fd. Ambs. with Surgical Team attached	
Mao Songsang	A.D.S. 6 Fd. Amb.	
Milestone 77	A.D.S. 5 Fd. Amb.	
Maram	H.Q. 4 Fd. Amb.	about to establish its M.D.S.

These arrangements remained in force until the 22nd when XXXIII and IV Corps linked up and the road to Imphal was opened.

23RD L.R.P. BRIGADE

This was a 'Chindit' formation and was divided into a number of columns, six in all. The brigade as a whole had its brigade medical unit and each column its medical element (*see* 'Special Force' Chapter 7).

The columns (33 and 76, 2nd D.W.R.; 34 and 55, 4th Border; 44 and 56, 1st Essex) struck out into the wilderness of the northern Naga Hills on April 12 from their jumping off positions between Jamuguri and Nazira in Assam. On April 15, 33 Column encountered a party of Japanese soldiery as did also 44 Column on the following day near Phekerkrima. On the 26th, in conjunction with 2nd Division, Columns 44 and 56 attacked this place but without success. However, next day, with the help of an air-strike 44 Column succeeded in capturing it. By May 26 the brigade H.Q. had been established in Khuzami. The columns succeeded in cutting the Japanese L. of C. from Kohima to Jessami and eastwards. By June 4 the brigade had captured Phakekedzumi and had blocked the Jessami–Somra track. Airstrips were constructed at Wokha, Mokokchung and Khuzami.

To begin with 23rd L.R.P. Bde. was able to evacuate its casualties by light aircraft which also brought medical supplies forward. Later the aircraft were withdrawn and casualties had to be conveyed to Kohima *via* the Jessami track along which staging posts had been established by 9 (Ind.) Lt. Fd. Amb. of Ind. 268th Lorried Bde. of Indian 7th Division at Chakhabama and at Milestone 28. Malaria had been rife in 23rd Bde. and signs of avitaminosis were making their appearance. As the brigade proceeded southwards and eastwards through Kharasom and along the hill tracks in the Somra Hills towards Ukhrul direct evacuation became impossible and it was necessary to carry the many casualties forward to Ukhrul and thence to Imphal by the Ukhrul–Imphal track. At Ukhrul contact was made with the columns of 89th and 33rd Bdes. of Indian 7th Division each of which was accompanied by a reinforced field ambulance company with surgical team, bearers and porters. One of the surgical teams was 14 (Ind.) M.S.U. with minimum equipment, mule-borne. While on its way from Kharasom to Ukhrul 23rd Bde. suffered a severe outbreak of scrub typhus with an unusually high case-fatality-rate.

MEDICAL ARRANGEMENTS. XXXIII CORPS

It was planned that early treatment and evacuation should be carried out in the forward areas by the R.A.Ps. and divisional field ambulances in the orthodox manner. The M.D.Ss. were to be reinforced by the attachment to them of surgical teams, M.S.Us., or surgical teams from C.C.Ss. and general hospitals. 13(Ind.) C.C.S. and the two M.F.T.Us. were to be sited well forward and the practice of keeping one M.F.T.U. open and the other closed was to be observed. Evacuation was to be by road as a rule for in the area to be traversed there were very few airfields.

During the first phase of the operation, the relief of Kohima, the forward medical cover was to be provided by divisional units. A mobile surgical unit was to be attached to the receiving M.D.S. and a staging section was to be located between Dimapur and Kohima. 13 (Ind.) C.C.S. was to be in Dimapur where 7 (Ind.) M.F.T.U. was to open and 8 was to remain closed and ready to move forward. When a second C.C.S. became available, it would remain closed. Evacuation from Dimapur was to be to Golaghat and Jorhat by ambulance train.

During the second phase, the advance from Kohima down the Kohima–Imphal road, one C.C.S. was to move to Kohima and the other at Dimapur was to close and be prepared to move forward. 8 (Ind.) M.F.T.U. was also to move to Kohima and 7 (Ind.) M.F.T.U. in Dimapur was also to close. Additional staging sections were to be provided for the Kohima–Dimapur L. of C. Evacuation was to be from the C.C.S. in Kohima to Dimapur and thence by ambulance train, as before, to Golaghat and Jorhat.

Following the link-up with IV Corps, both C.C.Ss. were to be opened in Kohima for the reason that this hill town was the only possible medical centre in the area. When the Kohima–Imphal road was open, evacuation might possibly be forward into Imphal for serious cases.

In connexion with the operations to be undertaken by Indian 7th Division and 23rd Bde. jeep evacuation routes were to be developed to the utmost as this was the only possible effective method in such terrain. The A.D.S. or M.D.S. was to be sited at the jeep-head. As far as possible and without detriment to the patient, 23rd Bde's. casualties would not be evacuated out of the corps' area lest they should be lost to their units.

In the Jorhat–Ledo–Dimapur–Kohima area before XXXIII Corps came north were plentiful medical installations, Kohima and Dimapur having been developed as small medical centres on the evacuation route and holding considerable numbers of casualties. (At Kigwema a 1,000-bed I.G.H. (C.); at Kohima a 700-bed I.G.H. (C.), a 1,000-bed I.G.H. (C.) and two convalescent depots; at Dimapur a 1,000-bed I.G.H. (C.), a 1,000-bed I.G.H. (I.T.) and sections of a third I.G.H. plus all the ancillary units that go to make up a hospital base.) But when the Japanese invasion of India began and when it became clear that they were advancing on Kohima and Dimapur in considerable strength, these forward medical units were hurriedly emptied and withdrawn.

In Kohima only a section of 53 I.G.H. (C.) was left and in Dimapur only 66 I.G.H. and a section of 59 I.G.H. This undoubtedly was the correct reaction to the Japanese threat but the very great reduction in the number of hospital beds in the area became associated almost at once with a very great increase in the numbers of troops, especially of British troops, in the area. 2nd Division, 23rd Bde., the British battalions of 161st and 33rd Bdes., and the ever increasing number of corps troops presented a problem of considerable difficulty. There were only 900 British beds in the whole of XXXIII Corps Area (Dimapur, Gauhati and Jorhat, 300 apiece.) 14 B.G.H. was in Dimapur *en route* for Comilla but Fourteenth Army was unwilling to allow this unit to remain and function there. As things turned out, however, this shortage of British beds did not give rise to great difficulty, but only for the reason that there were three ambulance trains stabled in Dimapur so that evacuation out of XXXIII Corps Area was made possible. There can be no doubt that in the beginning the surgical cover was quite inadequate. It was fortunate that 2 M.N.S.U. was attached to 66 I.G.H. for this gave the hospital a second surgeon at a time when, following the relief of the Kohima garrison, the operating theatre of the hospital was required to work right round the clock. Still with XXXIII Corps but in the Bombay Area were three surgeons, two belonging to the medical unit of an Indian beach group and the third to a mobile surgical unit. These were now called forward and two of them were attached to 66 I.G.H. for a period of the emergency and the other to 23rd Bde. in Mokokchung. G.H.Q. (India), hearing of this arrangement, duly protested but agreed to allow these officers to remain with the units until the crisis had passed. 13 (Ind.) C.C.S. and 14 (Ind.) M.S.U. reached Dimapur on April 19.

On April 29, 22 (Br.) C.C.S. reached Dimapur and opened on a site alongside 66 I.G.H. It took over from this hospital its British section and began to function on May 4. On May 1, 26 (Ind.) C.C.S. reached Jorhat and was posted to Golaghat to open there to admit light sick and to act as a convalescent centre for the corps. This C.C.S. opened on May 17 and admitted (i) such as were discharged from hospital and C.C.S. and did not require a prolonged convalescence, (ii) casualties held in corps or divisional medical units and not requiring full hospitalisation, (iii) psychiatric casualties requiring longer treatment than could be given in the psychiatric centre of 78 (Ind.) S.S. at Priphema, (iv) men who in the opinion of the R.M.O. were in need of simple treatment and rest and (v) patients discharged from hospital to reinforcement camps but requiring a further short period of convalescence. On May 2 it was decided to post 38 B.G.H., which had just arrived in Jorhat, to Golaghat and to move 53 I.G.H. (C). to Dimapur. This suggestion was not accepted by General Stopford who thought that Dimapur at this time was no place for a hospital. So 38 B.G.H. opened alongside 53 I.G.H. in Golaghat. By May 18 Dimapur was fairly secure and so 13 (Ind.) C.C.S. and 76 (Ind.) S.S. were moved up the Kohima road to Milestone 31 and a site for them was hacked out of the jungle. Lt. Sec. 13 (Ind.) C.C.S. was to run a 50-bed hospital there until Kohima was relieved. It was intended to move the psychiatric centre to this site. Of the M.F.T.Us., 6 was functioning in Golaghat, 5 in Dimapur and 7, closed in Dimapur, opened there on May 18.

The evacuation policy that was adopted was that the longest holding period in XXXIII Corps Area should be one month either in Jorhat or in Golaghat. Cases requiring longer periods of treatment were to be evacuated from the corps area as early as possible.

As soon as the threat to Kohima and Dimapur had been finally removed, it was decided to restore Kohima to its former rôle of forward medical base, even though this meant that a very great deal of restoration would need to be undertaken. Repairs were effected so quickly that by the time the Imphal road had been opened 13 (Ind.) C.C.S., 8 (Ind.) M.F.T.U., 44 (Ind.) A.M.U., 19 (Ind.) Fd. Hyg. Sec. and 3 A.F.S. had moved into Kohima.

On June 18, Indian 21st Division took over the L. of C. area to the north and east of Kohima. By the 20th, 13 (Ind.) C.C.S. and one surgical team had begun to function in Kohima, evacuating as many of its patients as possible to Dimapur. During the battle there had been a tendency for divisions to attempt to prevent the evacuation of their own casualties out of the divisional areas. They wished to make sure of retaining their own men. Because of the difficulties of evacuation there had been much forward surgery during the battle and much holding of casualties. But now it was decided that the casualties should not be held in the forward medical units for more than seventy-two hours.

Rearwards of Kohima evacuation was organised as follows:

Milestone 31	67 (Ind.) S.S. had replaced 13 (Ind.) C.C.S. here when the latter unit moved forward to Kohima. 4 A.F.S.
Milestone 28	(Priphema) 78 (Ind.) S.S., running a psychiatric centre with the psychiatrist of 2nd Division in charge and with 30 beds. This unit had proved its worth during the battle and was now retained.
Milestone 18	(Ghaspani) 76 (Ind.) S.S. and a M.A.S.

XXXIII CORPS. MEDICAL ORDER OF BATTLE.
APRIL 1944

Corps Troops

13 (Ind.) C.C.S.	33, 44 and 45 (Ind.) A.M.Us.
7 and 8 (Ind.) M.F.T.Us.	67 and 76 (Ind.) S.Ss.
67 (Ind.) Fd. Amb.	75 (Ind.) S.S. and a Pioneer company to form an improvised bearer company
19 (Ind.) Fd. Hyg. Sec.	
82 (Ind.) Mob. X-ray Unit	
14 (Ind.) M.S.U.	
5 (Ind.) Bearer Coy. less one platoon.*	
61 M.A.S.	
5 F.T.U.	

*Still in the Bombay Area. Fourteenth Army asked to call it forward.

The hospitals u/c 202 L. of C. Area were available to XXXIII Corps, as were also the M.A.Ss., and 5 and 6 (Ind.) M.F.T.Us.

XXXIII Corps asked for an additional C.C.S., an additional staging section, another mobile surgical unit and a second mobile X-ray unit.

XXXIII CORPS. CASUALTIES. THE BATTLE OF KOHIMA

'G' Estimate.

Strength. 40,000.

Sick-rate. 3 per 1,000 per diem (120) assuming that all possible steps to control the incidence of malaria were taken.

Battle Casualties. 10 per cent. of the force, 4,000, of which 66⅔ per cent. or 2,700 would require to be evacuated to the rear medical units. It was known that the Japanese were travelling light and were lightly armed. It was expected that not more than 20–30 per cent. of the troops of XXXIII Corps would come into actual contact with the Japanese.

Actual admissions to hospital April–June 1944—10,733, British 6,317, Indian 4,416.

Sick		*Battle Casualties*	
British	3,492	British	2,825
Indian	3,203	Indian	1,213
	6,695		4,038

Average sick-rate per 1,000 per diem 3·48.

TABLE 11

The Battle of Kohima. XXXIII Corps. Casualties.

Battle Casualties	British	Indian	Totals
Gunshot wounds	681	313	994
Shell	648	323	971
Bomb	358	265	623
Grenade	339	112	451
From the air and others	308	91	399
Mortar	149	76	225
'Shrapnel'	92	11	103
Cordite burns	17	8	25
Phosphorus burns	17	4	21
Sten	12	8	20
Blast	13	—	13
Bayonet	4	2	6
Pistol	6	—	6
Psychiatric cases	181	—	181
	2,825	1,213	4,038

During the period April 15–May 21 a total of 1,827 battle casualties were admitted to the medical units of XXXIII Corps the strength of which increased greatly during the period from 16,565 in mid-April to 36,999 in mid-May. The rate was highest in the third week of April, 4·46 per 1,000 and lowest, 1·62 per 1,000 in the third week in May.

TABLE 12

XXXIII Corps. Principal Causes of Sickness. April–June 1944

	British	Indian	Totals	
Malaria and N.Y.D.(F.)	1,649	1,783	3,432	(1,713 proven cases of malaria)
Dysentery and Diarrhoea	1,117	746	1,863	(42 per cent. proved cases of dysentery, amoebic : bacillary ratio, 42 : 100)
Venereal Diseases	109	91	200	
	2,875	2,620	5,495	
Minor Causes	617	583	1,200	
	3,492	3,203	6,695	

The sick-rate was rather high at the beginning of this operation, 7·06/1,000/diem towards the end of April but thereafter it declined to become 4·30 in the early part of May. Thereafter there was a slight but unmistakable rise to 4·65 in the last week of May. The proportion of British to Indian troops was around 2 : 3. In April the sick-rate was 6·83/1,000/diem for British and 7·64 for Indian troops. By the middle of May the figure for Indian troops had fallen to 4·21 whereas that for the British had gone up to 8·72.

XXXIII CORPS.
THE PRINCIPAL DISEASES AFFECTING THE TROOPS
MALARIA

TABLE 13

XXXIII Corps. Incidence of Malaria. By Formation. May 1944

Formation or Unit	Strength	Number of diagnosed Cases of Malaria	Rate per 1,000
2nd Division	14,200	223	16
Indian 7th Division	10,300	406	39
23rd Bde.	3,800	13	3
Indian 21st Division	798	4	5
268th Bde.	1,920	21	6
Corps Tps.	8,700	79	9
	39,718	746	

In April the rate was 0·59 per 1,000; by May 20 it had risen to 1·21 per 1,000. By the end of the month the troops had reached relatively safer areas after having passed through intensely malarious areas on the way.

Malaria was still the greatest hazard to the health of the troops but it was no longer a hazard that could not be controlled. This fact is not to be forgotten when the causes of success during the rest of this campaign are being sought. XXXIII Corps could plan on the assumption that its plans would not be disturbed by the high incidence or morbidity due to malaria. This would not have been possible in 1942. Now the olive-green cotton battledress had been issued; mosquito nets were used whenever possible, gloves and face veils were worn by troops in the rear areas; every unit had a month's supply of mepacrine tablets and very great attention was paid to the drill of taking them regularly. The troops now co-operated intelligently in the matter of self protection against malaria. Three A.M.Us. were allotted to XXXIII Corps and of these one was attached to 2nd Division and the other two to the L. of C. and rear areas. Four M.F.T.Us. were available, two u/c corps and two u/c H.Q. L. of C. Area.

2nd Division could not possibly be unaware of the effects of malaria upon the efficiency of a formation. Its 6th Bde., it will be remembered, served in Arakan for five months at the beginning of 1943. Almost 100 per cent. of the troops were infected and on its return to Ahmednagar in June 1943 the whole brigade underwent the standard 'blanket' treatment consisting of 0·1 gm. mepacrine thrice daily for five days, followed, after an interval of two days, by 0·03 gm. pamaquin daily for three days. Almost immediately following this treatment relapses occurred in such numbers that it became doubtful that the brigade could retain its place in the division. However, 6 Fd. Amb. ran a convalescent camp for the brigade and another 'blanket' course consisting of 30 grs. quinine daily for eight days brought down the relapse-rate to reasonable proportions. On its departure for the north the division was put on suppressive mepacrine, 0·1 gm. daily. In this division, as in others, it was quickly discovered that the mosquito repellent D.M.P. (di-methyl-phthalate), when a wick was used, made an excellent night-light.

DYSENTERY AND DIARRHOEA

About the time when the Kohima–Imphal road was re-opened there was a severe outbreak of dysentery, mainly bacillary. But since certain of the divisions retained many of their cases in unit lines and in the divisional medical units the figure based on hospital admissions can be very misleading. It was noted at this time that malnutrition was not uncommon and on the advice of the Consulting Physician the rations were improved. Five large cases of anti-dysenteric serum, obtained from Melbourne, were flown up to the Kohima front where large numbers of the troops were inoculated. It is not improbable that these measures helped to abort a threatened epidemic. In April the rate was 0·36 per 1,000 and in May it rose to 0·66 but this rise was of short duration.

VENEREAL DISEASES

The incidence of these diseases varied from 0·3 to 0·8 per 1,000.

It can be concluded therefore that, all things being considered, the incidence of preventable morbidity in XXXIII Corps was never high enough to suggest that something was radically wrong in the matter of health education, of co-operation on the part of the troops, of man-management on the part of their officers and N.C.Os., and of intelligent interest in health matters on the part of the officers commanding formations and units.

In Indian 7th Division it was discovered that in certain units the troops were suffering from quite a serious degree of malnutrition. It seemed certain that these units had been improperly fed for quite a long period of time during their stay in Arakan.

2ND DIVISION. CASUALTIES

TABLE 14

2nd Division. Total Admissions to the Field Ambulances. April–July 1944.

Month	Unit	Battle Casualties			Sick			Totals
		2nd Div.	Other Formations		2nd Div.	Other Formations		
			Br. Tps.	Ind. Tps.		Br. Tps.	Ind. Tps.	
April	4 Fd. Amb.	35	4	2	87	6	2	136
	5 ,,	204	4	21	201	3	6	439
	6 ,,	381	13	29	342	5	110	880
May	4 ,,	417	97	1	522	69	3	1,109
	5 ,,	166	25	11	441	77	39	759
	6 ,,	413	45	214	511	55	179	1,417
June	5 ,,	41	1	—	341	39	18	440
	5 ,,	294	—	4	607	58	90	1,053
	6 ,,	130	10	61	613	83	107	1,004
July	4 ,,	—	—	—	519	10	2	531
	5 ,,	—	—	—	255	270	—	525
	6 ,,	2	—	—	273	5	54	334
	Totals	2,083	199	343	4,712	680	610	8,627

1,832 of the 8,627 admissions were in respect of troops of units and formations other than 2nd Division. The battle casualties of 2nd Division do not include 233 psychiatric battle casualties. These figures do not include admissions by the Indian component of the joint M.D.Ss. established by 75 (Ind.) Fd. Amb. and a field ambulance of 2nd Division.

TABLE 15
2nd Division. Battle Casualties. April–June 1944

	Killed	Wounded	Missing	Totals	Per cent.	Ratio Offrs.:O.Rs.
Officers	54	133	8	195	7·2	1
O.Rs.	658	1,889	151	2,698	92·8	12·8
Totals	712	2,022	159	2,893	100·0	—
Per cent.	24·6	70·0	5·4	—	100·0	—

Ratio Killed : Wounded 1 : 2·84

The killed include 65 who died in the M.D.Ss. or *en route* thereto. The figure does not include those who died after they had been evacuated from the M.D.S. The ratio of killed to wounded is unusually high.

TABLE 16
2nd Division. Ratio of Battle Casualties to Sick

	Battle Casualties				Percentages		Ratio
Month	Wounded	Psychiatric	Totals	Sick	B.Cs.	Sick	B.Cs.:Sick
April	620	54	674	630	51·6	48·4	1·07 : 1
May	996	108	1,104	1,474	42·8	57·2	1 : 1·33
June	465	68	533	1,561	25·4	74·6	1 : 2·93
Totals	2,081	230	2,311	3,665	38·6	61·4	1 : 1·58

The figure for the wounded includes those who died in or *en route* to the M.D.S.

TABLE 17
2nd Division. Wounds by Missile. April–June 1944

Month	Shell Wounds	G.S.W. Rifle or M.G.	Bomb	Totals
April	138	333	222	693
May	429	657	303	1,389
June	99	333	109	541
	666	1,323	634	2,623

TABLE 18

2nd Division. Admissions on account of Sickness to M.D.Ss.
April–July 1944

Month		Malaria	Diarrhoea	Dysentery	Infective Hepatitis	N.Y.D.(F.)	Scabies	Other Skin Diseases	Venereal Diseases	Miscellaneous	Totals
April 12,100	Number of Cases Ratio per 1,000	66 5·45	35 2·8	50 4·1	8 0·66	177 14·6	9 0·74	11 0·90	19 1·5	255 21·4	630 52·0
May 11,500	Number of Cases Ratio per 1,000	159 13·8	185 16·0	174 15·1	8 0·69	267 23·2	19 1·65	29 2·5	33 2·8	599 52·0	1,473 127·0
June 11,000	Number of Cases Ratio per 1,000	238 21·8	277 20·6	182 16·5	23 2·09	295 26·8	19 1·7	6 0·54	13 1·18	508 50·7	1,561 141·9
July 12,346	Number of Cases Ratio per 1,000	256 20·7	76 6·15	78 6·31	20 1·62	257 20·7	12 1·0	17 1·38	10 0·81	321 26·0	1,047 84·77
Total Cases April–July		719	573	484	59	996	59	63	75	1,683	4,712

In Table 17 the G.S.W. group includes 10 bayonet wounds, 7 in April, 2 in May and 1 in June. The total includes 542 casualties belonging to other units and formations.

It was noted that during the early part of the operation such wounded Japanese as were brought into the field medical units of 2nd Division attempted, usually successfully, to destroy themselves. As soon as they were conscious they would rip off their bandages and open their wounds. Later, as a consequence of the privation and starvation which they had endured, they accepted medical aid and food eagerly.

The low incidence of malaria in Table 18 is to be noted. It was concluded that practically all the diarrhoea was bacillary dysentery.

It is of interest to compare certain of these figures with those for the year 1943, and with those of the British Army in India 1941.

Ratio per 1,000 per annum:

Malaria	
Average whole division 1943	220·7
British Army in India 1941	144·4
Dysentery and Diarrhoea	
Average whole division 1943	67·6
British Army in India 1941	92·3
Venereal Diseases	
Average whole division 1943	80·1
British Army in India 1941	56·3

These figures do not include 6th Bde. until June; had the 6th Bde. figures been added the ratios would have been considerably higher for this brigade was in Arakan and was riddled with malaria.

TABLE 19

14 (Ind.) Mobile Surgical Unit. Operations performed during the Period May 1–June 7, 1944

Type of Injury	Numbers	Died in M.D.S.
Abdominal	10	4
Thoraco-abdominal	2	2
Chest	4	1
Flesh Wounds	20	2
Compound Fractures	23	—
Major amputations	6	1
Minor amputations	5	—
	70	10

Average time between wounding and operation 8–12 hours.

This M.S.U. was attached for short periods in succession to the combined M.D.S. of 4 and 75 (Ind.) Fd. Ambs. at Milestone 42, to the M.D.S. of 5 Fd. Amb. in Kigwema, to that of 4 Fd. Amb. in Maram and to that of 6 Fd. Amb. in Karong.

TABLE 20

14 (Ind.) M.S.U. Operations performed during the Advance from Kohima to Imphal.

Type of Injury	Numbers	Died in M.D.S.
Chest	2	—
Abdominal	9	4
Compound fractures	13	—
Flesh wounds	25	—
Minor amputations	4	—
Burns	4	—
	57	4

It was learnt that mobile surgical units should preferably be employed in pairs, one leap-frogging over the other. It was concluded that forward surgery of this kind was fully justified if the cases could be held for at least seven days after operation, if adequate nursing facilities were available and if whole blood in considerable quantities was at hand.

TABLE 21

2nd Division. Wounds classified by Missile Treated in 6 Fd. Amb. during the period April 26–June 16, 1944

G.S.W.	73	Undetermined missile		19
Grenade	18	Fall of parachute		1
Mortar	9	Unclassified		15
H.E.	19	Bayonet		1
	Total	155		

TABLE 22

2nd Division. Time between Wounding and Operation. 6 Fd. Amb. April 26–June 16, 1944

6 hours or less	44 per cent.	19–24 hours	9 per cent.
7–12 hours	21 ,, ,,	24 hours plus	4 ,, ,,
13–18 hours	22 ,, ,,	less than 24 hours	94 ,, ,,

Average 10·5 hours

TABLE 23

*2nd Division. Distribution of Wounds by Site. 6 Fd. Amb.
April 26–June 16, 1944*

Type of Case	Number	Evacuated	Died	Known to have died later
Abdominal . . .	20	12	8	3
Chest	1	1	—	—
Maxillo-facial . .	6	4	2	—
Fractures . . .	70	67	3	—
Amputations . .	7	7	—	—
Flesh wounds . .	40	38	2	—
Burns . . .	10	10	—	—
Eye wounds . . .	1	1	—	—
	155	140	15	3

2ND DIVISION. THE ARMY TRANSFUSION SERVICE

Normally the field ambulances obtained and replenished their transfusion stocks from 5 F.T.U. in Dimapur but a field ambulance operating in front of a C.C.S. could, if such an arrangement was productive of more satisfactory results, replenish its stocks from the forward C.C.S.

Each field ambulance held one transfusion box and a minimum of three infusion supply boxes, preferably at the M.D.S. Each infusion box contained 4 bottles of glucose-saline, 8 of dried plasma, 2 of isotonic-saline, 8 of distilled water and 4 plasma giving sets. As soon as a box was finished it was exchanged at the F.T.U. Rearward C.C.Ss. held a minimum of three boxes plus extra stocks of glucose- and isotonic-saline for issue to field ambulances and mobile surgical units. C.C.Ss.' replenishment arrangements were the same as those for the field ambulance. When one C.C.S. leap-frogged over another it took over from the one it was passing its reserves of transfusion materials. Citrated whole blood was flown from Calcutta to Dimapur. A.D.M.S. 2nd Division held a reserve of 96 bottles of dried plasma. The depots of medical stores held dried plasma but did not issue it to any unit which could be served by the F.T.U. M.S.Us. replenished their supplies through the parent unit to which they were attached. Only in special circumstances were transfusion materials issued to staging sections. The hospitals in 202 L. of C. Area obtained their crystalloid solutions from the nearest base depot of medical stores and their plasma from 2 (Ind.) Adv. B.T.U. Fresh blood was obtained as required from volunteer donors among the troops.

TABLE 24

2nd Division. Quantities of Transfusion Fluids used during the Battle of Kohima

	Plasma	Whole blood	Glucose-saline	Total pints
4 Fd. Amb.	264	40	50	354
5 ,, ,,	227	16	18	261
6 ,, ,,	150	52	20	222
	641	108	88	837

Average case received three pints of fluid intravenously. Out of 3,223 battle casualties treated in the divisional field ambulances, 9 per cent. were transfused/infused.

2ND DIVISION. THE ARMY PSYCHIATRIC SERVICE

In 2nd Division it was accepted that the psychiatrist had a rôle to play in the treatment of certain types of battle casualties—the exhausted man, the man who for the time being had reached the limit of his endurance and who required a little time and a little skilled help in order to regain his resilience. Though this division had not been involved in battle since May–June of 1940 during the withdrawal to Dunkirk, its medical services apparently had been profiting from the experience of others. For the reception and treatment of the psychiatric casualty the division established a centre at Priphema, at Milestone 28 on the Dimapur-Kohima road, far enough away from the battle to permit the patient to recover his grip on himself but not so far removed from the battle as to permit him to cultivate the idea that for him the battle was over and done with. Here the psychiatrist of the division and 78 (Ind.) S.S. created a small hospital of 30 beds. Nearly 50 per cent. of those who were admitted to it, and they included all kinds of case from the acute terror state to that of simple exhaustion, were back on full duty after 4–5 days.

Psychiatric cases on the mend but not yet quite fit for return to their units could be sent to the improvised corps light sick and convalescent centre run by 22 (Ind.) C.C.S.

TABLE 25

2nd Division. Disposal of Psychiatric Casualties.

Total number admitted to Centre		181 B.O.Rs.
Disposal R.T.U.		104
Hospital		26
Recategorisation		23
Rear Details		10
Complicated cases		18
		181

Of the complicated cases 13 were regarded as fit for R.T.U. from the psychiatrist's point of view; 4 were thought to need recategorisation and the remaining one was looked upon as one with a bad immediate prognosis.

Analysis of these 181 cases by diagnosis:

Exhaustion	62	Acute anxiety reaction		51
Anxiety neurosis	38	Hysteria		15
N.Y.D. (P.)	12	Reactive depression		3
	Total	181		

TABLE 26

2nd Division. Distribution of Psychiatric Casualties within the Division.

Unit	Number dealt with at Psychiatric Centre April 24–June 27	Total Divisional Psychiatric Casualties	Percentage of Psychiatric Casualties to Total Battle Casualties
1st R.S.	10	37	16·37
2nd Norfolk	14	15	6·52
1st/8th L.F.	14	21	10·5
1st Camerons	4	5	2·8
2nd Dorset	27	27	14·0
7th Worc. R.	2	2	1·6
1st R.W.F.	37	60	23·1
1st R. Berks.	26	26	8·45
2nd D.L.I.	19	22	7·91
2nd Recce. Regt.	3	3	6·3
	156	218	9·8

The remaining 25 cases occurred among R.A.S.C., R.A.M.C., Bde. H.Q. and such like units. The cause of the high figure for 1st R.W.F. was related in the opinion of the psychiatrist, to a low morale caused partly by a series of unsuccessful actions and partly by a complete lack of confidence in a senior officer.

2ND DIVISION. THE ARMY DENTAL SERVICE

TABLE 27

2nd Division. Dental Work performed during the period April–July 1944

Month	Number Attending for Treatment	Treatment completed	Teeth extracted	Teeth conserved	Scalings completed	Dentures supplied, repaired, remodelled	Number awaiting dentures
April and May	655	152	408	135	32	26	268
June	749	157	437	254	72	40	257
July	1,125	228	498	417	196	19	297
	2,529	537	1,343	806	300	85	—

2ND DIVISION. THE ARMY HYGIENE SERVICE

It is possible to touch upon only a very few aspects of soldiering that this service encompasses. In 2nd Division, as in all others, it was learnt anew that it is during and immediately after a battle that unit sanitation tends to slacken off and that stimulation is required. 2 Fd. Hyg. Sec. had its H.Q. usually with rear divisional H.Q. and small sub-sections with the field ambulances to supervise the sanitation activities in the battalions of the brigade to which the field ambulance was attached. The field hygiene section, consisting of a hygiene specialist and 28 O.Rs. including 14 sanitary assistants and a small workshop staff together with 5 R.A.S.C. drivers, was very busy at all times assisting in the correction of faulty hygiene, the provision of sanitary appliances, supervision of water points, disinfestation of clothing and blankets, and helping in the choice of camp sites.

The occupation by 2nd Division of ground previously used by the Japanese troops was inevitably followed by a rise in the incidence of the excremental diseases. In such circumstances hygienic indiscretions are always punished. Summerhouse Hill in Kohima was the foulest of the areas that were occupied; indeed it is doubtful whether it could have been held without the aid of sulphaguanidine liberally administered at the R.A.Ps. Flies were everywhere in their hundreds.

In XXXIII Corps generally, shallow trench latrines were permitted when the camp was to be occupied for less than three days, otherwise deep trench latrines 12–14 ft. deep, were constructed. Bore-hole latrines were used wherever the ground was suitable. Dry refuse was burnt and when this was impossible it was buried deeply. All supplies of drinking water were purified under medical supervision. The daily ration was a gallon per man for cooking and drinking. Fifteen gallons a day for all other purposes was considered ample.

REFLECTIONS UPON THE WORK OF THE MEDICAL SERVICES DURING THE OPERATIONS AROUND KOHIMA

The reinforcement of the troops that were standing in the way of the Japanese 31st Division's advance upon Kohima and Dimapur was hurried and the time available to XXXIII Corps for the making of careful preparation exceedingly brief. The reinforcements arrived in driblets and at the beginning of the operation information concerning the strength and intentions of the Japanese was scanty. The corps was engaged during the period April–June 1944 in an operation against a most redoubtable antagonist, fought in a region that was remarkable for its harshness and inhospitable wildness, for its vast distances and for its climate. XXXIII Corps was fortunate in that it was able to move quickly through a most intensely malarious tract south of Kohima that began in the vicinity of Milestone 82.

In such terrain the evacuation of casualties was far from easy. XXXIII Corps was fortunate in that it could call upon the Nagas. These merry, gentle, courageous and apparently tireless porters carried more smoothly at about thrice the speed of the British stretcher-bearer party. They could carry across country that was quite impossible for British or Indian bearers. Frequently they declined to accept any recompense other than a cup of tea and a cigarette. Their good nature and their prowess attracted the admiration of all who came into contact with them.

The jeep ambulance proved to be the most useful form of transport for evacuation purposes. It could reach A.D.Ss. and even R.A.Ps. along tracks that were impossible for any other vehicle. 2nd Division had four armoured ambulances which were of the very greatest usefulness in conditions when no reliance whatsoever could be placed on Japanese respect for the Red Cross symbol. Mules were not successful; all too frequently the track was not only steep but was also very slippery. They were extensively used by the medical services for 'pack' purposes.

The conditions were such that rapid evacuation of casualties rearwards to a sheltered medical centre rich in surgical and other facilities was impossible. It was necessary to arrange for forward surgery and for the holding of post-operatives. The M.D.S. tended to develop into a field dressing station and to the M.D.S. and exceptionally to the A.D.S. a surgical team or unit was attached. It was not until June 18 that there was a C.C.S. and surgical facilities within less than 6–8 hours motor ambulance journey from the front line. At the beginning of the operation no C.C.S. was available and so 66 I.G.H. in Dimapur had to assume the functions of one. Then when 22 C.C.S. reached Dimapur it was not possible to place it further forward and at the same time protect it from Japanese infiltration. Moreover, the area up to Milestone 42 was highly malarious. So the C.C.S. was opened in Dimapur. When Kohima had been relieved and when the area around Milestone 31 had been dealt with by the A.M.U., the C.C.S. was moved forward.

In XXXIII Corps at the end of this phase of the campaign it was generally held that in conditions and circumstances such as those that had characterised the operations, when terrain, weather, distance and the general military situation all combine to make the work of the medical services difficult, forward treatment saves lives and evacuating kills.

The battle started before 2nd Division's ambulances had arrived and so the two M.A.Ss. had to clear in front of the M.D.S. as well as to the rearward of it. This arrangement proved to be unsatisfactory and was dropped when the divisional ambulance cars and also a platoon of the A.F.S. arrived.

The improvised psychiatric centre at Priphema formed by 78 (Ind.) S.S. was very successful as was also the use of a C.C.S., 22 C.C.S., as a corps light sick and convalescent centre. Improvisation of this kind was necessary and fortunately the Army Medical Services are inclined to be good at it.

It will have been noted that in the beginning of this campaign it was accepted by all that campaigning necessarily stopped when the monsoon broke. But the Supreme Commander decided that this rule should be broken. His Medical Advisory Division at his headquarters, consisting of experts in tropical medicine and hygiene from each of the Services and from the U.S. Army, had given considerable attention to this matter and had advised him concerning the ways in which the troops could be provided with bucklers and shields fabricated out of medical knowledge that would protect them and give them the advantage over their antagonists. When visiting the formations of Fourteenth Army the Supreme Commander shared his views with the troops. 'We are not going to quit fighting when the monsoon comes, like drawing stumps at a cricket match when it rains. The Jap won't expect us to fight on; he will be surprised. We shall fight in places like the Kabaw Valley. We have got anti-malaria devices and we shall have the finest hospitalisation and air evacuation scheme the Far East has ever seen. The Japs who have nothing like ours, will have to fight Nature as well as us.' As the story unfolds it will be seen that, beyond all reasonable doubt, this application by the Allies of medical knowledge to tactical problems did, in the long run, make a very great difference between the fighting efficiency of the Allies and the Japanese respectively.

CHAPTER 9

THE SIEGE OF IMPHAL

THE Dimapur–Imphal road was cut on March 30 and was not reopened until June 22. Between these dates Imphal was besieged though not isolated since there remained one route into and out of it—the sky-route, for as the Allies enjoyed complete superiority in the air, the movement of men and supplies into Imphal and out of it continued almost without interruption by the Japanese though it was of course subject to temporary checks by the weather.

The garrison of the Imphal Plain consisted of Indian IV Corps with Indian 5th Division (9th and 123rd Bdes. and 89th Bde. of Indian 7th Division in place of 161st Bde. in the Dimapur–Kohima sector); Indian 17th Division (48th and 63rd Bdes.); Indian 20th Division (32nd, 80th and 100th Bdes.); Indian 23rd Division (1st, 37th and 49th Bdes.); Indian 50th Para. Bde., less one battalion and Indian 254th Tank Bde. together with corps troops.

IV Corps' plan for meeting the Japanese offensive was to pull back all outlying troops into the Imphal Plain and then to oppose the oncoming Japanese on its perimeter. The main defended locality in the vicinity of Imphal was known as the 'keep' and this was encircled by a number of strong-points, boxes, which were given names such as 'Lobster', 'Shark', 'Shrimp' and 'Catfish', each of them being self-contained in respect of supplies and all of them mutually supporting. A mobile general reserve was concentrated in the keep. Similar arrangements were in force around Palel.

In a country as wild and mountainous as that which surrounded the Imphal Plain, such roads and tracks as there are assume an extraordinary importance. Leading to Imphal through the mountains were six routes; from the north, the road from Kohima and the track that followed the course of the River Iril; from the north-east, the road from Ukhrul; from the south-east, the road from Tamu through Palel; from the south, the road from Tiddim and from the west the track from Silchar through Bishenpur. It was along these that the Japanese tried to break into the Imphal Plain.

When the Japanese columns thrust down the Ukhrul–Imphal road at the beginning of April they were opposed by Indian 23rd Division and Indian 5th Division and halted in the vicinity of Litan. But soon Japanese columns which had made their way to the north of Imphal began to threaten the rear of the troops on the Ukhrul road. A Japanese force attacked Nungshigum, a great hill that dominated the Imphal Plain, on

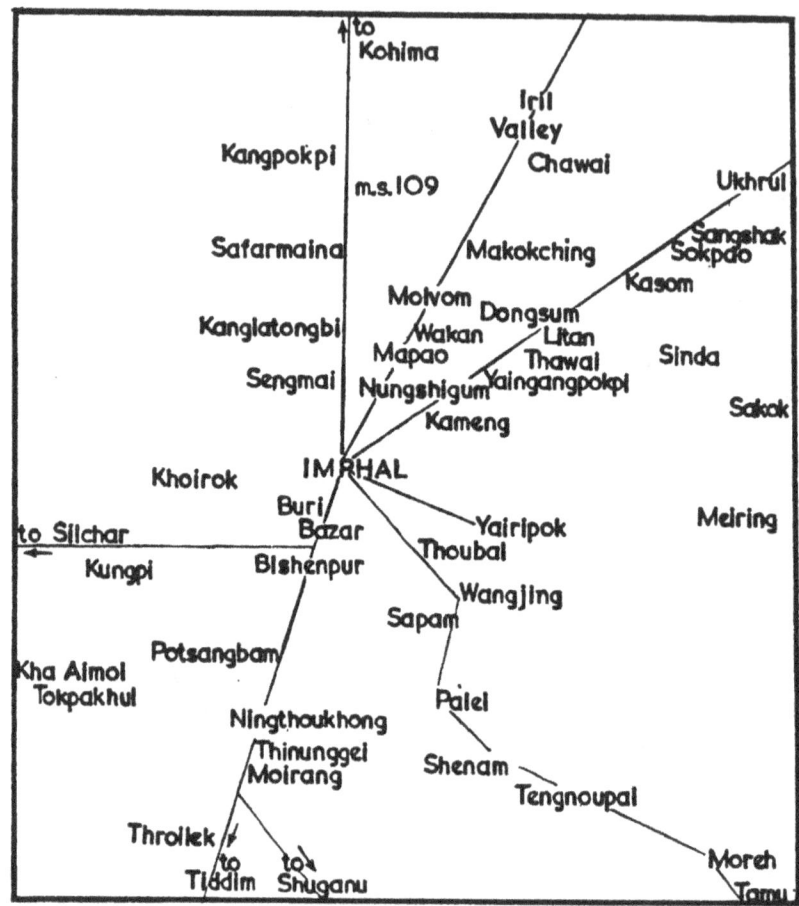

FIG. 36. The Roads to Imphal

April 6. The struggle for this hill continued until the 13th when finally Indian 5th Division, supported by the Air Force and by tanks, gained possession of its twin peaks and held them.

Indian 23rd Division now assumed sole responsibility for the Ukhrul road and Indian 5th Division proceeded to clear the Iril Valley. Between April 16 and May 7 the Japanese were driven from parts of the Mapao Spur which separates the valley of the Iril from the Kohima–Imphal road. 1st Bde. of 23rd Division meanwhile moved through the jungle to reach within 15 miles of Ukhrul itself. Then 1st and 32nd Bdes. maintained a steady pressure on the Japanese in the whole of this sector and it became possible for General Scoones, commanding IV Corps, to regard the situation on this part of the perimeter as being fairly satisfactory.

THE SIEGE OF IMPHAL 303

Indian 20th Division less 32nd Bde. in corps reserve, had 80th and 100th Bdes. holding a 25 mile front running from Tengnoupal, 10 miles south-east of Palel, through Shenam to Shuganu, 15 miles south-west of Palel. The terrain consisted of steep-sided ridges and equally steep-sided nullahs all jungle covered. The line was not a continuous one, the troops were blocking the main Tamu–Palel–Imphal road and all the usable tracks and were occupying the dominating heights and the passes. Active aggressive patrolling enabled them to cover the rest of the front.

On this sector the Japanese made most strenuous efforts to break through to the Plain. Between April 4 and 11 their assaults were almost continuous and made some progress. Between the 15th and the 20th the attacks grew in intensity and on the 22nd parts of the position were overrun. However, the Japanese must have been as exhausted as were their opponents for their success was not exploited and the attacks died down.

Towards the end of April there was much infiltration towards Palel and on the night of April 29/30 a small party actually attacked Palel Keep only to be driven off. On this sector considerable numbers of Indians belonging to the I.N.A. were wandering about the country and were surrendering whenever the opportunity to do so presented itself. 48th Bde. of Indian 17th Division was sent to the Palel sector to comb out Japanese patrols whose activities might interfere with the use of the nearby airfield. This the brigade did between May 6–8 after which it was replaced by 1st Bde. of Indian 23rd Division.

On May 6/7 and 7/8 the Japanese made their final attempts to crash through to Imphal down the main road. Several fierce attacks on Tengnoupal were repulsed but on May 8 the Japanese succeeded in breaking into the positions held by Indian 20th Division. Further attacks on May 9/10 and 10/11 by the Japanese resulted in the loss of more ground. On the 12th, however, Indian 20th Division counter-attacked and regained some of the lost ground. Indian 20th Division was then relieved by Indian 23rd Division and soon the situation in this sector could be regarded as stabilised.

It will be remembered that when Indian 17th Division reached Imphal from Tiddim, two brigades of Indian 23rd Division, 37th and 49th, which had been sent down the Imphal–Tiddim road to help Indian 17th Division, were left to the south of Imphal to check any advance on the part of the Japanese up this road. 37th Bde. was soon called to join its division but 49th Bde. remained. On April 9 it was attacked in its position to the south of Bishenpur at Milestone 30–35 on the Tiddim road. The attack was sternly repulsed. Thereafter 49th Bde. was pulled out to rejoin its division and its place on the Tiddim road was taken by 32nd Bde. of Indian 20th Division from corps reserve.

This brigade took up a new position at Bishenpur where it could command both the Tiddim road and the Silchar–Bishenpur track. On April 14/15 the Japanese attacked towards Bishenpur but were repulsed. They did succeed, however, in blowing up the bridge at Milestone 51 on the Bishenpur–Silchar track and also moved round the flank of the position held by 32nd Bde. Heavy fighting lasting several days resulted.

General Scoones decided to move Indian 17th Division, which had been operating north of Imphal, to block the approaches to Imphal from the west where a threat was rapidly developing. 32nd Bde. was placed u/c Indian 17th Division. On the 19th the division reached the Bishenpur area and went straight into action to the north-east of the village. The Japanese had occupied the village of Ningthoukhong in force and an attempt by 32nd Bde. on April 23 to eject them was unsuccessful as was also a second attempt by Indian 17th Division on the 25th. Though the Japanese advance had been halted, they retained their grip on this village so that the threat to Imphal from the west remained. 32nd Bde. was under constant pressure and casualties on both sides were very heavy. There was much infiltration and stern and sustained fighting by 32nd and 63rd Bdes., with abundant air support, was required before the Japanese were ejected from the village of Potsangbam, two miles south of Bishenpur. On this sector the situation remained decidedly fluid.

63rd Bde. of Indian 17th Division, newly arrived in Imphal, was rushed up to the north to check the Japanese advance down the Kohima–Imphal road after this had been cut on March 30. The Japanese had reached Kanglatongbi, where there was a large supply depot. 63rd Bde., in a series of attacks between April 11 and 15, succeeded in driving the Japanese back towards Kanglatongbi and on May 7 was relieved by Indian 5th Division and rejoined its own division to take part in the fighting about Bishenpur. Leaving 9th Bde. to hold Mapao Spur, 89th Bde. advanced by a series of short hooks while 123rd Bde. thrust up the main road. The supply depot was finally retaken on May 21 and thereafter the division pressed steadily up the road.

By the middle of May the general military situation had become fairly satisfactory. Indeed, IV Corps could expect to take the offensive in the not too remote future and General Slim could begin seriously to plan the complete destruction of Japanese Fifteenth Army. Since large scale offensives on all sectors of the Imphal perimeter could not be nourished at one and the same time it was decided to restrict the coming offensive to an advance by Indian 5th and 20th Divisions to the north and north-east, while on the Palel and Bishenpur sectors Indian 17th and 23rd Divisions kept up a steady pressure against the Japanese forces opposing them.

THE SIEGE OF IMPHAL

The relief of Indian 20th Division by Indian 23rd Division in the Palel sector began on May 13. From the 16th to the 20th the Japanese attacked the Shenam Pass. Ground was lost and retaken. The attacks were resumed between June 9 and 12 and were repulsed. At Shuganu there was much bitter fighting and the advantage in the end remained with Indian 23rd Division. 1st Bde. combed the hills to the east of Palel in attempts to deal with Japanese guns that shelled the Palel airfield and succeeded in putting an end to this nuisance. It also disposed of the remnants of the Gandhi Brigade of the I.N.A.

In mid-May in the Bishenpur sector Indian 17th Division was involved in heavy fighting. On May 15, 48th Bde., moving across country, reached the Tiddim–Imphal road at Milestone 33 and dug in. During the 17th, the Japanese twice attacked this road-block but suffered heavily and were repulsed. On the evening of the 19th they attacked again and again were repulsed. Then, according to plan, 48th Bde. moved north up the road to Moirang, near Milestone 27, which it attacked and captured after two days' fighting. Here another road-block was established. But Indian 17th Division's plan to crush the Japanese in front of it between 48th Bde. at this road-block and the other two brigades moving southwards, failed. So 48th Bde. was ordered to move north and fighting its way from village to village it reached Potsangbam on May 30 and so rejoined the division.

The reason why the plan failed was that the Japanese had attacked the Bishenpur position on May 20/21 and had seized a small hill only a few hundred yards from H.Q. Indian 17th Division. Troops which should have been co-operating with 48th Bde. had to be used to pin down the Japanese on this hill and thereafter to destroy them which was done after five days of bitter hand-to-hand fighting. Other parties of Japanese caused confusion by infiltrating into the mule-lines of 63rd Bde. in Bishenpur and by suicidal attacks upon the guns to the north of the village.

In the second half of May the relief of 23rd Division in the Ukhrul and Iril Valley sector by 20th Division from the Palel sector was completed and the front was taken over by 80th and 100th Bdes. 32nd Bde. of 20th Division was still with Indian 17th Division in the Bishenpur sector. No sooner had Indian 20th Division taken up its positions covering Kameng and Nungshigum than it was discovered that the Japanese were massing troops in the Sangshak area. On June 3, as part of IV Corps' offensive, Indian 20th Division was ordered to advance with the object of destroying the Japanese east of the Iril River and of establishing a brigade group in Ukhrul. When the division did advance it was at once attacked and for a while the outcome remained uncertain. However, by the 13th of June, Indian 20th Division had gained the mastery and the Japanese were pushed back.

On June 7, 80th Bde. had thrust north from Nungshigum up the Iril Valley to reach a point twenty miles north of Imphal. From there it raided the main east-west lateral communications of the Japanese. By the 20th the brigade had moved further to the north and was astride the Japanese L. of C. It was becoming very evident that the Japanese were suffering severely from shortages of all kinds, including food and that their medical services had ceased to function effectively.

On the Imphal–Kohima road Indian 5th Division, after the retaking of Kanglatongbi on May 21, had pressed north. On June 3 the division was ordered to intensify its efforts and to open the Kohima road as far as Karong, about thirty-five miles to the north of Imphal. In spite of torrential rain which was impeding all operations in this region, Indian 5th Division steadily made its way towards Kangpokpi. General Slim, fearing that further attacks might be made on Imphal, instructed General Scoones to limit 5th Division's advance to Kangpokpi. On June 18 the spearheads of Indian 5th Division and of 2nd Division moving south, were only about forty-nine miles apart. On the 22nd they met at Milestone 109 and the siege of Imphal was over.

MEDICAL COVER

INDIAN 5TH DIVISION

This division was employed on the Imphal–Kohima road sector. Its leading elements reached Imphal on March 18 and the move of the division was completed nine days later. Its 161st Bde. was sent to Dimapur and in its place 89th Bde. of Indian 7th Division joined 5th Division. With 89th Bde. came 66 (Ind.) Fd. Amb. 45 (Ind.) Fd. Amb., reaching Imphal on March 20, was attached to 123rd Bde. and on March 25 opened its M.D.S. in the outskirts of Imphal on the Imphal–Ukhrul road along which the brigade was operating. Casualties from the brigade and also from Ind. 50th Para. Bde., which was withdrawing along this road, were admitted to the M.D.S. and evacuated therefrom to the hospitals in Imphal. On March 26, 10 (Ind.) Fd. Amb. reached Imphal and was kept in reserve. On the following day a company of 45 (Ind.) Fd. Amb. moved to Milestone 8 on the Ukhrul road and opened an A.D.S. which was reinforced by the attachment of a surgical team.

The Japanese advancing down the Kohima–Imphal road occupied Kanglatongbi. On April 6, Indian 5th Division was ordered to thrust north against the positions occupied by the Japanese south of Milestone 104. The Iril Valley was to be the boundary between Indian 5th and 23rd Divisions. Indian 17th Division was in reserve and was to give limited support. When 9th Bde. was holding Mapao Spur and 123rd was thrusting up the Kohima road, 10 (Ind.) Fd. Amb. detached a company to serve 9th Bde. 123rd Bde. was working its way up the Iril Valley from Kameng where H.Q. 45 (Ind.) Fd. Amb. had established its M.D.S. on April 3. The brigade was advancing on the Mapao–Molvom area from the east. By the 23rd, 9th Bde. was operating in conjunction with 123rd Bde. from the west and Mapao was finally occupied on April 24. To serve 123rd Bde. H.Q. 10 (Ind.) Fd. Amb. from reserve, opened its M.D.S. just to the north of Wakan and three car posts, one for each battalion, were established. It was now decided to clear the Iril Valley before attempting to attack the strong Japanese position about Molvom from the north-east. Heavy fighting yielded no decisive result and so the plan was changed. Molvom was to be attacked from the west. 123rd Bde. moved secretly to Sengmai. 66 (Ind.) Fd. Amb. opened its A.D.S. on the Kohima road a mile to the south of Sengmai to serve 89th Bde. which was to defend Sengmai and 45 (Ind.) Fd. Amb. closed in Kameng and moved to Sengmai to serve 123rd Bde. as this brigade outflanked the Japanese positions at Kanglatongbi from the west and cut the Kohima road at Milestone 117 behind the Japanese positions. 9th Bde. was to help by aggressive patrolling in the Iril Valley. To serve 9th Bde. 10 (Ind.) Fd. Amb. opened its M.D.S. about ten miles to the north of Imphal on a non-metalled road. This operation began on May 15 and continued until the 21st. Little progress was made. A company of 45 (Ind.) Fd. Amb. accompanied 123rd Bde. and a company of 10 (Ind.) Fd. Amb. was brigaded with 9th Bde. for the final thrust up the Kohima road. On June 12 Molvom was occupied and the advance swept past Safarmaina only to be slowed down by heavy rain and stiffening opposition. H.Q. 10 (Ind.) Fd. Amb. moved forward from reserve to Kanglatongbi to open its M.D.S. there on the 17th. No further move of the divisional medical units took place until the Kohima–Imphal road was opened on June 22. 55 (Ind.) A.M.U. had joined the division on May 13.

INDIAN 17TH DIVISION

When Indian 17th Division reached Imphal from Tiddim its H.Q., divisional troops and divisional medical units were first concentrated in the 'Catfish' box in the Imphal Plain. 48th Bde. moved to the vicinity of Milestone 124 on the Imphal–Kohima road and 63rd Bde. to Sengmai. H.Q. 23 (Ind.) Fd. Amb. established its M.D.S. in the 'Catfish' box. This was well protected and had accommodation for 50 patients. With 48th Bde. went a company of 37 (Ind.) Fd. Amb., a platoon of 4 (Ind.) Bearer Company and a detachment of 22 (Ind.) Fd. Hyg. Sec. With 63rd Bde. were a company of 23 (Ind.) Fd. Amb. and a detachment of 3 (Ind.) Bearer Coy. Evacuation from the medical units of the division was to 41 I.G.H. in Imphal.

On April 19, Indian 17th Division was placed in charge of the

Bishenpur sector and 32nd Bde. of Indian 20th Division, already in this sector, passed under command. With 32nd Bde. were a reinforced company of 59 (Ind.) Fd. Amb., a surgical team from 80 (Ind.) Para. Fd. Amb., (Indian 50th Para. Bde.) and a platoon of 4 (Ind.) Bearer Coy. These combined to form a M.D.S. in the Bishenpur box evacuation from which was by two ambulance cars, three jeeps and, where these vehicles could not pass, by S.Bs. As the volume of work in this M.D.S. increased, a second company of the field ambulance joined it and the officer commanding 59 (Ind.) Fd. Amb. took command of the M.D.S. Evacuation from this M.D.S. was to 24 (Ind.) C.C.S. and 41 I.G.H. in Imphal by A.F.S.

On April 22 one of the companies in this M.D.S. in the Bishenpur box moved to Milestone 22 on the Bishenpur–Silchar track to open an A.D.S. to serve the troops in this area. The Japanese pressure in this sector was particularly heavy and during the persistent shelling several of the personnel of this A.D.S. were wounded. The M.D.S. in the Bishenpur box was also frequently shelled but it was well protected and suffered no great harm, though its vehicles were badly damaged and some of its mules were killed. Evacuation from the A.D.S. was made difficult by the frequent cutting of the track by parties of Japanese troops. Even when the track was open the journey along it was a hazardous one for Japanese snipers were constantly active. On April 30 when the track was opened after a period of closure a large convoy of casualties was evacuated from the A.D.S. to the M.D.S. The patients were in a sorry state, for cotton wool stocks had given out in the A.D.S., leaves were being used for the padding of splints and many of the wounds were septic. During the space of a fortnight the company running this M.D.S. had dealt with over 700 casualties.

On May 11 Indian 17th Division moved to the Bishenpur sector from the 'Catfish' box. Its 63rd Bde. took over the defence of the Bishenpur area from 32nd Bde. which assumed responsibility for operations north and south of the Silchar track. 48th Bde. moved to Waikhong, south-east of Bishenpur. The tactical plan was for 63rd Bde. to advance to Ningthoukhong and thence to Moirang and Throilok while 48th Bde. struck westwards from Waikhong and cut the Tiddim road at Milestone 32.

48th Bde. cut the Tiddim road according to plan and repulsed several fierce Japanese attacks upon the road-blocks it had constructed. But 63rd Bde. could not make much progress and by May 24, 48th Bde. was in danger of being encircled. It therefore withdrew to Moirang near Milestone 27. On the 26th, it was ordered to move north to Ningthoukhong which was reached on the morning of the 29th. The brigade occupied and held on to the northern part of the village against numerous attacks. Heavy rain then brought the fighting to a standstill.

THE SIEGE OF IMPHAL

Medical cover for 48th Bde. during these events was provided by one company of 37 (Ind.) Fd. Amb. which opened an A.D.S. just to the east of the Tiddim road. Evacuation therefrom was by S.Bs. and mules to a boat-point on the Manipur River near the village of Ithai and thence by boat to Shuganu where a light M.D.S. and car post were established by the same field ambulance. From the light M.D.S. further evacuation was to the light M.D.S. of 47 (Ind.) Fd. Amb. in Palel. Evacuation from the boat-point to the light M.D.S. at Shuganu was by pontoon towed by assault craft. Each pontoon could take 4–6 stretcher cases or 16 sitting cases and an assault boat could take 4 sitting cases. Tarpaulins on bamboo frames provided shelter on the pontoon and water was thrown over the tarpaulins periodically to cool the interior. A medical officer travelled with each convoy and each convoy had its armed escort. In the light M.D.S. in Shuganu there was accommodation for 100 patients and here the patients were held over-night because the road to Palel was not safe.

When 48th Bde. moved northwards towards Ningthoukhong the A.D.S. conformed, moving on May 27 to Thamnapokpi, about a mile to the north of Moirang and on the following day to Thinunggei, south of Ningthoukhong. The boat-point and the light M.D.S. were withdrawn to Imphal and the evacuation route *via* Shuganu was closed. Near the A.D.S. in Thinunggei an airstrip was constructed and urgent cases were flown direct to Imphal. To the A.D.S. four medical officers, 40 S.B. squads and 38 riding mules were attached. By May 30 the brigade, accompanied by the A.D.S., reached Ningthoukhong. The A.D.S. was carrying some 120 patients and these were now evacuated, being staged by the A.D.S. of 23 (Ind.) Fd. Amb. at Potsangbam *en route* for Imphal. On the 31st the A.D.S. opened in Potsangbam where it remained until the siege was over.

The rest of 37 (Ind.) Fd. Amb. moved to a new divisional area in the south-west suburb of Imphal on June 3. There it ran an improvised hospital of 100 beds for staging and sorting casualties on their way to the Imphal hospitals. It took over three houses and two huts for this 'rear M.D.S.' H.Q. Indian 17th Division moved to this new area on June 5. At this time heavy rain was making the evacuation of casualties from the forward areas very difficult and cases of 'immersion foot' were occurring among the troops.

63rd Bde. was operating in an area that abounded in well-prepared Japanese positions. The brigade captured Tokpakhul near Kha Aimol south-west of Bishenpur, on May 19 and was repeatedly counter-attacked by the Japanese. On June 7 the brigade was instructed to move back to Bishenpur. It sent a battalion to Potsangbam which had already been occupied by 48th Bde. In these operations 63rd Bde. was served by a company of 23 (Ind.) Fd. Amb. H.Q. of this medical unit remained in the 'Catfish' box in Imphal. The A.D.S. was opened by this company in Oinam near Milestone 12 on the Bishenpur–Silchar track and on the 10th near Milestone 18. There it suffered much from heavy shelling and on the following day withdrew to the shelter of the box of 32nd Bde. Evacuation was exceedingly difficult; the ground was very rough and Japanese snipers very numerous. Evacuation had to be carried out under heavy escort and only during the hours of daylight. Casualties among the stretcher-bearers were numerous.

On May 17, 63rd Bde. began its advance towards Kha Aimol and a detachment of 23 (Ind.) Fd. Amb. moved with the brigade. It established an A.D.S. in the vicinity of Milestone 18 but was forced by shelling to move to a nullah just north of Kha Aimol. When the road was blocked just to the north of Bishenpur on May 20, evacuation to Imphal necessarily ceased and the A.D.S. sent its casualties to the light M.D.S. of 59 (Ind.) Fd. Amb. in Bishenpur. When this became full to overflowing a number of casualties were carried round the road-block into Imphal. On June 6 the A.D.S. in the nullah near Kha Aimol received a direct hit, one medical officer and three O.Rs. being killed and one medical officer and four O.Rs. wounded. On June 7 the A.D.S. moved into Bishenpur and took over the M.D.S. of 59 (Ind.) Fd. Amb. The terrain and nature of the fighting demanded much improvisation from the medical services and this was forthcoming. There was much shelling, communications were continually being interrupted, the military situation remained exceedingly fluid and the rain made its own peculiar contribution to the difficulties. The pattern of evacuation varied greatly but essentially it consisted of hand-carries to the A.D.S. and thence to a boat-point or to a car post where boats or ambulance cars conveyed the patients to a M.D.S.

32nd Bde. was engaged in confused fighting on the Silchar track between May 9–12. On the 13th the brigade positions to the west of Bishenpur were overrun and counter-attacks were only partially successful and had to be abandoned because of the heavy losses endured. On the night of May 20/21 the Japanese attacked a hill to the north of the divisional box but on the 23rd broke contact and moved to the east. On June 10, 32nd Bde. occupied Kungpi.

The M.D.S. of 59 (Ind.) Fd. Amb. in the Bishenpur box continued to serve 32nd Bde. during these operations on the Silchar track. The fighting was of a very confused nature and during the night of May 20/21 the M.D.S. in the Bishenpur box was cut off by the Japanese troops who were attacking the area of Indian 17th Division's H.Q. box near Milestone 11. On the following day there was a steady flow of casualties into the M.D.S. which soon was holding 137 patients. By May 23 fortunately the Japanese had broken contact and evacuation became possible again. As the road to Imphal was still under fire, evacuation by jeep was the method adopted to begin with. By the 29th the M.D.S. was clear. It had dealt with some 2,000 casualties during the previous six weeks. To it had been attached, in addition to the platoon of the bearer company and the surgical team already mentioned, detachments of a field hygiene section and of an anti-malaria unit, a detachment of jeeps and another of the A.F.S. Though this company of 59 (Ind.) Fd. Amb. was primarily intended to serve 32nd Bde. it had admitted casualties from no less than twelve different battalions during the course of the fighting.

On June 7 orders were received for the company to move with 32nd Bde. to the roadhead, Milestone 22½ on the Silchar track. It handed over to 23 (Ind.) Fd. Amb. and on June 9 opened at the roadhead, evacuating to the M.D.S. of 23 (Ind.) Fd. Amb. in Bishenpur by jeep; it had to be by jeep for the rain had made the road impassable for any other form of vehicle. For the brigade's attack on Kungpi a car post was established about a mile in front of the A.D.S. These arrangements continued until the Kohima–Imphal road was opened on the 22nd.

INDIAN 20TH DIVISION

32nd Bde., relieving 49th Bde. of Indian 23rd Division on the Tiddim–Imphal road, decided to pull back from the position held by 49th Bde. about Milestones 30–35 to Bishenpur itself where it could watch not only this Tiddim road but also the track to Silchar. On April 16, 32nd Bde. attacked the village of Kungpi which provided the Japanese with an excellent observation point overlooking the Silchar track. The village was taken but lost again. On April 14, 32nd Bde. passed u/c Indian 17th Division which replaced Indian 23rd Division in this sector.

At the beginning of April the forward elements of 20th Division were holding positions near Tengnoupal. The Japanese attempted to capture Palel by a pincer movement. In the north Sita was attacked on the night of April 4/5 and during the following days. These attacks were unsuccessful and so the Japanese reverted to their infiltration tactics and by April 29 had got to within a few miles north-east of Palel. The Keep was attacked that night from the east and the south. The attack was repeated during the following days but by the end of the first week in May these attacks degenerated into very minor actions and finally ceased altogether.

In the area of Tengnoupal 80th Bde. was being heavily attacked during this period. On May 11, Indian 20th Division was relieved by Indian 23rd Division in this sector. The relief was completed by May 25.

Early in June Indian 20th Division was in the Kameng–Litan sector and was instructed to make a deep penetration towards Ukhrul. 80th Bde. was to advance up the valley of the Iril and 100th Bde. was to advance to the north-west. By June 22, 80th Bde. had reached the Khunthak area in the valley of the River Iril against very weak opposition for the Japanese in this sector were literally starving. 100th Bde. met sterner resistance but when the rains came sustained operations were impossible.

By the first week of April the medical units of this division, which had withdrawn from the Tamu area to Shenam, were distributed as follows:

In Shenam
: the M.D.S. of 42 (Ind.) Fd. Amb.
9 (Ind.) M.S.U.
26 (Ind.) Fd. Hyg. Sec. detachment
55 (Ind.) Fd. Amb. one company

In the 'Peacehaven' box south of Wangjing
: 55 (Ind.) Fd. Amb. less one company
26 (Ind.) Fd. Hyg. Sec. less detachment

near Wangjing 59 (Ind.) Fd. Amb.

Evacuation from the division was to 14 (Ind.) C.C.S. in Palel and thence to the hospitals in Imphal. On April 12 one company of 59 (Ind.) Fd. Amb. left the division with 32nd Bde. which was to pass under command Indian 17th Division while in the Bishenpur sector. 59 (Ind.) Fd. Amb. itself moved to Kakching four miles to the north-west of Palel on April 12. Until the middle of May while this division remained in this sector the medical cover remained unchanged. H.Q. 42 (Ind.) Fd. Amb. served as the divisional M.D.S. and had 9 (Ind.) M.S.U. attached to it. This M.D.S. was well dug-in and its wards could hold up to 250 patients. Only one A.D.S. was maintained in the forward area and this was manned by companies of 42 and 55 (Ind.) Fd. Ambs. in rotation. Evacuation was relatively simple and straightforward as contrasted with the same process in other sectors; ambulance cars could reach several of the R.A.Ps. During April the M.D.S. admitted 315 casualties.

Shell and grenade wounds	75·2 per cent. of the B.Cs.
Rifle and L.M.G. wounds	21·3 ,, ,, ,, ,, ,,
Mortar wounds	3·5 ,, ,, ,, ,, ,,
Wounds of extremities	75·6 ,, ,, ,, ,, ,,
Wounds of head and neck	10·8 ,, ,, ,, ,, ,,

In the first week of May, 14 (Ind.) C.C.S. had to move from the 'Bull' box in Palel to Imphal on account of the persistence of Japanese sniping and so 55 (Ind.) Fd. Amb. was required to open a rear M.D.S. in the 'Peacehaven' box to admit local casualties and also to receive casualties from the M.D.S. of 42 (Ind.) Fd. Amb. in the forward area. 9 (Ind.) M.S.U. joined the rear M.D.S. One company of 55 (Ind.) Fd. Amb. opened an A.D.S. in the 'Bull' box in Palel to stage patients and to cater for local casualties. These arrangements continued in force until Indian 20th Division was relieved by Indian 23rd Division on May 15. 49 (Ind.) Fd. Amb. of 23rd Division took over the M.D.S. in Shenam on May 17. 42 (Ind.) Fd. Amb. thereupon moved with Indian 20th Division and opened its M.D.S. in Waithou, relieving 24 (Ind.) Fd. Amb. of Indian 23rd Division. To this M.D.S. a detachment of 20 (Ind.) A.M.U. and a sub-section of a field hygiene section were attached. 55 (Ind.) Fd. Amb. and H.Q. 59 (Ind.) Fd. Amb. and one company moved with the brigades to the north where operations were to be undertaken by 80th and 100th Bdes. With 80th Bde. was 55 (Ind.) Fd. Amb. and this unit reached Kameng on May 17. On the following day it moved to Milestone 2 on the Imphal–Ukhrul road and on the 19th to Milestone $7\frac{1}{2}$ where the brigade H.Q. was located and where for the first time a suitable site for a M.D.S. was found. 59 (Ind.) Fd. Amb. closed in Kakching and moved with 100th Bde. to the Ukhrul sector on May 14. This medical unit provided a forward A.D.S. moving with the brigade and a stationary A.D.S. at Milestone $10\frac{1}{2}$ to stage casualties on their way to Imphal.

The forward A.D.S. of 59 (Ind.) Fd. Amb. developed into a M.D.S. with operating theatre and wards well dug-in and well protected. The M.D.S. of 55 (Ind.) Fd. Amb., at Milestone $7\frac{1}{2}$ on the Imphal–Ukhrul road, received casualties from both brigades. In June when 80th Bde. was pushing up the Iril Valley it was arranged that one and and a half companies of 55 (Ind.) Fd. Amb., 22 mules and a surgeon with equipment should accompany it. Arrangements were made for evacuation from this brigade by river and by air if the need arose. H.Q. 55 (Ind.) Fd. Amb. was to establish its M.D.S. at Milestone 2. On June 8 the division moved to Sawombung where 42 (Ind.) Fd. Amb. established its M.D.S. to which 10 (Ind.) M.S.U. was attached on June 13. The A.D.S. site of 55 (Ind.) Fd. Amb. was taken over by one and a half companies of 42 (Ind.) Fd. Amb. This site became untenable as the *tempo* of the fighting increased and the A.D.S. was moved back a mile to a site that provided better protection. Between June 8 and 21, 203 casualties were admitted to this A.D.S. of 42 (Ind.) Fd. Amb. Evacuation in this sector was difficult for roads and tracks were few and far between. It was usually by S.B. and mule to Wakan to the north of Kameng and thence by jeep ambulance to the M.D.S. Evacuation from Wakan by boat was also possible.

INDIAN 23RD DIVISION

Indian 23rd Division was concentrated in the area Langthoubal–Waithou–Thoubal. 24 and 47 (Ind.) Fd. Ambs. were in Waithou and 49 was at Milestone 29 on the Imphal–Tiddim road. When 1st Bde. was advancing up the Thoubal Valley one company of 47 (Ind.) Fd. Amb. and 10 (Ind.) M.S.U. accompanied it. The medical units travelled by M.T. to Tumukhong, south-east of Kameng, and thereafter on a mule pack basis marched with the brigade. A car post was established in Tumukhong by 47 (Ind.) Fd. Amb. On April 15, 49 (Ind.) Fd. Amb. opened a light A.D.S. in Yairipok to stage casualties on their way to the Imphal hospitals. On April 18, 49 (Ind.) Fd. Amb. took over the C.P. in Tumukhong from 24 (Ind.) Fd. Amb. 37th Bde., which had been concentrated in the Yairipok area, moved to Kameng on April 12 and to this brigade the second company of 47 (Ind.) Fd. Amb. was attached. The company established its A.D.S. in Kansag. H.Q. 47 (Ind.) Fd. Amb. remained in Waithou.

By April 22, 1st and 37th Bdes. had established contact and so it became possible to close down the southern evacuation route. The A.D.S. of 47 (Ind.) Fd. Amb. therefore moved to Yaingangpokpi about half-way between Litan and Kameng and later to a site about two miles to the west of Litan. 1st Bde. was now in the Kasom area and one company of 47 (Ind.) Fd. Amb. was functioning in Sinda to serve the brigade. On April 22 evacuation from both 1st and 37th Bdes. was along the axis of the Litan–Imphal road. H.Qs. 47 and 49 (Ind.) Fd. Ambs. were moved up to the Kameng area by April 25 but since there was no heavy fighting at this time no M.D.S. was opened; casualties could easily be sent straight back to Imphal. A company of 49 (Ind.) Fd. Amb. opened an A.D.S. in Pungdongbam to cater for the local sick. The A.D.S. of 47 (Ind.) Fd. Amb. serving 37th Bde. and 10 (Ind.) M.S.U. moved to Kasom on April 26 and on the 29th closed and joined 47 (Ind.) Fd. Amb. in the Kameng area.

49th Brigade, it will be remembered, was left at Milestone 30 on the Imphal–Tiddim road after Indian 17th Division had successfully made its way back along the Tiddim–Imphal road, to check any attempted Japanese advance up this road. This position about Milestones 30–35 was fiercely attacked on April 9 but 49th Bde. held its ground. The Japanese then began to infiltrate round the flanks of the position and on April 10 it was decided that 32nd Bde. of the Indian 20th Division should replace 49th Bde. in this sector. 49th Bde. withdrew through 32nd Bde. on April 15 and concentrated in the vicinity of Yairipok.

In the Litan sector 32nd Bde. of Indian 20th Division was u/c Indian 23rd Division for a period. This brigade was operating in the area of Litan moving towards Kasom and seeking out Japanese supply columns. None were discovered and 32nd Bde. was needed in the Bishenpur sector. So 1st Bde. of Indian 23rd Division took over and made a deep thrust into the hills towards Kasom which was occupied without any opposition being encountered. The Japanese attempted to recapture the village on the night of April 15/16 but were repulsed. On the 19th 1st Bde. moved out to capture Sokpao to the north-east. After heavy fighting the village was captured on the 20th. 32nd Bde.

had its H.Q. in Wangjing. 59 (Ind.) Fd. Amb., from the 'Peacehaven' box, accompanied the brigade the task of which was that of disrupting the Japanese L. of C. and so battalion columns moved in various directions. With each battalion went a medical officer with two S.B. squads and six mules. The M.D.S. of 59 (Ind.) Fd. Amb. was established in Wangjing and a car post about two miles to the east of Yairipok where two ambulance jeeps were stationed. On April 10, 32nd Bde. handed over to 1st Bde. of 23rd Division and 59 (Ind.) Fd. Amb. moved to the 'Bull' box in Palel.

On May 11, Indian 23rd Division relieved Indian 20th Division in the Palel sector. 37th Bde., with a battalion from each of 1st and 49th Bdes., was given the task of holding the Tengnoupal area. 1st Bde., less one battalion, was to strike eastwards while 49th Bde. was to take over the defence of the Palel–Shuganu–Kakching sector. There was much fighting with intervals of comparative quiet. The Japanese made one final despairing attempt to take Palel on June 17 which ended in failure. 1st Bde., which had been without rest for a considerable period, was relieved by 49th Bde. Battle casualties and sickness had been the causes of much wastage. The road to Imphal remained blocked and the enfeebled Japanese were now facing the terrible prospect of a dangerous withdrawal through most inhospitable country at the height of the monsoon.

24 (Ind.) Fd. Amb. was in Thoubal and 49 (Ind.) Fd. Amb. moved to Shenam and took over from 55 (Ind.) Fd. Amb. of 20th Division. A.D.Ss. were provided by 24 and 49 (Ind.) Fd. Ambs., that of 24 being sited at 'Hamborie' between Sita and Litan and that of the latter being to the north of the Imphal–Tamu road, some miles in front of the M.D.S. The rear M.D.S. in the Palel box was expanded to hold 150 patients and to it 10 (Ind.) M.S.U. was attached. Ambulance cars of a M.A.S. and of the A.F.S. cleared the M.D.S.

This M.D.S. was functioning as a C.C.S. now that 14 (Ind.) C.C.S. had been withdrawn to Imphal. It admitted 1,297 casualties during the second fortnight of May and of these 618 were battle casualties.

MEDICAL ARRANGEMENTS. IV CORPS

The following medical units were under command or under the administrative control of IV Corps at the time of the opening of the Japanese offensive:

41, 53, 59, 79, 87, 88 and 89 I.G.Hs.
14, 19 and 24 (Ind.) C.C.Ss.
64 and 65 (Ind.) Fd. Ambs.; 77 (Bur.) Fd. Amb.
56 (Ind.) Fd. Hyg. Sec.
3 (Ind.) S.S. (B.T.); 28 (Ind.) S.S. (I.T.); 36 (Ind.) S.S. (Combined)

4, 5 and 10 (Ind.) M.S.Us.
2 and 32 F.T.Us.
7, 10, 20, 21, 22, 32, 45 (Ind.) A.M.Us.
3, 10, 11 and 14 (Ind.) Mob. X-ray Units.
7 (Ind.) Surg. Unit, E.N.T.
19 (Ind.) Dent. Unit (I.T.); 41 (Ind.) Dent. Unit (B.T.).
9 (Ind.) Dent. Mech. Unit.
5 (Ind.) Ophthal. Unit.
30 (Ind.) Fd. Lab.
15, 16 and 17 (Ind.) Con. Depots (I.T.); 27 (Ind.) Con. Depot (B.T.)
45 and 46 (Ind.) Sub-depots Med. Stores.
1, 2, 3, 4, 5, 6, 7, 8 (Ind.) Staging Camps.

The field medical units with the divisions serving in IV Corps at this time were:

	Fd. Ambs.	Fd. Hyg. Secs.	Bearer Coys.
Indian 17th Division	23 and 37 (Ind.)	22 (Ind.)	3 and 4 (Ind.)
,, 20th ,,	42, 55 and 59 (Ind.)	26 (Ind.)	
,, 23rd ,,	24, 47 and 49 (Ind.)	23 (Ind.)	

The locations of certain of these in the first week of April were:

64 (Ind.) Fd. Amb.	Imphal airstrip
65 ,,	Imphal–Tamu road
14 (Ind.) C.C.S.	in 'Bull' box, Palel
19 (Ind.) ,,	Imphal
3 (Ind.) S.S.	Kanglatongbi
28 (Ind.) S.S.	,,
36 (Ind.) S.S.	Imphal
51 (Ind.) S.S.	,,
3 (Ind.) Mob. X-ray Unit	,,
10 (Ind.) ,,	Milestone 21 on the Imphal–Palel road
11 (Ind.) ,,	Imphal–Tiddim road
17 (Ind.) Dental Unit	Imphal
19 (Ind.) ,,	Imphal–Tiddim road
41 (Ind.) ,,	attached 41 I.G.H. Imphal
9 (Ind.) Dent. Mech. Unit	Imphal
4 (Ind.) M.S.U.	Imphal
5 (Ind.) ,,	in 'Bull' box, Palel
9 (Ind.) ,,	Imphal–Tamu road
10 (Ind.) ,,	Imphal
2 F.T.U.	,,
5 ,,	,,
45 (Ind.) Sub-depot Medical Stores	,,
46 (Ind.) ,, ,,	,,
1 A.F.S.	,,
2 A.F.S.	,,

By the first week of April the hospitals, casualty clearing stations and the corps field ambulance and the beds they provided were as follows:

	Indian	British
87 I.G.H. (C.)	300	100
88 I.G.H. (C.)	300	100
89 I.G.H. (C.)	300	100
41 I.G.H.	400	200
79 I.G.H.	600	
14 (Ind.) C.C.S.	200	100
19 (Ind.) C.C.S.	300	100
24 (Ind.) C.C.S.	350	100
64 (Ind.) Fd. Amb.	200	
	2,950 Indian	800 British

Total 3,750

Strength of IV Corps (approximate)	120,000
Beds required at 6 per cent.	10,440
Beds available	3,750
Deficit	6,690

In May sanction was received for the expansion of the bed number up to a total of 7,000, this total being distributed among the units as follows:

41 I.G.H.	from 600 to	1,000
87 I.G.H.	„ 400 „	600
88 I.G.H.	„ 400 „	600
89 I.G.H.	„ 400 „	600
14 (Ind.) C.C.S.	„ 300 „	1,000
19 (Ind.) C.C.S.	„ 400 „	1,000
24 (Ind.) C.C.S.	„ 450 „	1,000
(Ind.) S.Ss.		200
Fd. Ambs.		1,000
		7,000

For this expansion it was decided to use stretchers and bamboo charpoys instead of the ordinary beds and to reduce the space between the beds.

It will be noted that certain units which appear in the first list do not do so in the second. This is because the policy was to retain the minimum number of units in the Imphal Plain having regard to the needs of the corps. Such medical units as were grossly deficient in respect of personnel or equipment were among those which were flown out. In May, 10 (Ind.) A.M.U., 36 and 51 (Ind.) S.Ss., 45 and 46 (Ind.) Sub-depots of Medical Stores and 37, 44, 48 and 67 M.A.Ss. were also flown out. Some of the deficient medical units were amalgamated; the equipment of those that were evacuated was distributed among those that remained.

In the first week of June two staging sections were combined to form a corps convalescent depot capable of holding 850 Indian patients. This expansion, this withdrawal of non-essential units and this improvisation, together with the fact that casualties were fewer than had been expected, went far to repair the deficiency in respect of bed number and also eased the strain on evacuation, which was evacuation by air since there was no other possible way out of the Plain. During the siege, shortages in establishment in respect of both officers and other ranks became increasingly greater and the monsoon caused much dislocation in the hospital service for flooding wrecked sanitary systems and often made it necessary to move patients to other parts of the unit's ground. In 89 I.G.H. the medical staff and the sisters were obliged to do their ward rounds by boat!

Before the Kohima–Imphal road was cut on March 30, a total of 274 lying and 1,547 sitting cases had been evacuated by air from Imphal. With the beginning of the actual siege large-scale evacuation by air began. The patients were transported usually to the airfield at Sapam, about twenty miles distant from the hospital area where aircraft were expected. In the beginning there was no time-table for the arrival and departure of aircraft and consequently some of the batches of patients were caused much hardship; on one occasion the same batch of 400 patients had to be taken to and from the airfield on three consecutive days before they finally got away. No less than six airstrips were being used. It was not possible to move any of the hospitals to sites nearer to these airstrips for the reason that these were outside the defended localities. The corps field ambulance, 64 (Ind.) Fd. Amb., was detailed to act as an improvised air evacuation centre. It provided the parties for the loading of the aircraft and made arrangements to feed the patients if long delays occurred. It is of interest to note that in this theatre there was no development by the land forces of the special air evacuation centre unit as there was in the Middle East and elsewhere although nowhere was air-evacuation conducted on such a grand scale as in Burma. The loading parties became very expert, a plane could be loaded with 12 lying and 30 sitting cases and all their kit in about nine minutes. It is to be noted that the medical authorities had no control whatsoever of the routing of the planes and that any sudden change in the times or destinations of flights had to be accepted by them even though it caused inconvenience and at times even confusion. It came to be the unanimous opinion of the senior administrative medical officers that in any further development of the system of air evacuation it would become necessary to place aircraft exclusively at the disposal of the medical services.

It was inevitable that the stretchers that left Imphal with the patients should not come back; these aircraft in their journeys to Imphal were loaded to maximum capacity with supplies of prime importance to the conduct of the operations. This is quite understandable but the fact remains that during the first fortnight of May the loss of stretchers was already becoming felt and thereafter very strenuous methods had to be adopted to ensure that at least a fairly high proportion of the stretchers were replaced. The problem of stretcher wastage was never solved.

The struggles at Kohima and Imphal were productive of much improvisation in the sphere of evacuation. So many extraordinary difficulties of various kinds interfered with the orthodox procedures that in order to overcome them much ingenuity was evoked and exercised. The armoured ambulances that were used on the Dimapur–Kohima and Kohima–Imphal roads were standard ambulances which had been fitted by I.E.M.E. with $\frac{1}{2}$ inch steel plates to protect the patients and the driver. They were vulnerable from above and from below. They were very heavy and distinctly top-heavy and could only take 2 or 3 stretchers and had to be restricted to the roads. About 50 of these armoured ambulances were in use and were greatly appreciated by those who had need to ride in them.

The jeep ambulance attracted the attention of many medical personnel of ingenious mind. Many contraptions were devised that would allow three or even four stretcher cases to be transported. They did most excellent work. On the Tiddim road where only the jeep could be used, it must have been exceedingly difficult for the driver of such a loaded vehicle to keep it on the slippery, twisted road in blinding rain and axle-deep mud. Two or three of the variants were widely adopted and very soon the jeep ambulance became a normal feature of the forward evacuation scene.

For use on narrow, twisting tracks snaking their tortuous ways through the jungle several forms of wheeled stretchers were produced; a single bicycle wheel, two bicycle wheels, a single motor-cycle wheel, two motor-cycle wheels and an aircraft wheel, fitted with a gear that firmly gripped a standard stretcher, all had their advocates. In one field ambulance a wheeled stretcher built almost completely of bamboo, including the wheel itself, was proudly produced. The form that was built around a single motor-cycle wheel was probably the best of the lot. (Plates XVI–XIX show some of the novelties produced in 2nd Division.)

There was much invention devoted to the production of makeshift beds and ward furniture. Beds, bedside tables, chairs, dressing tables, lampstands, towel rails of bamboo and even bamboo flooring were all much used. The standard 22lb. stretcher was converted into a springy bed by the use of two U-shaped pieces of the steel rods that were used for the reinforcing of concrete. These were fixed into holes bored halfway through the stretcher shafts to form legs. Many hundreds of this type of improvised bed were brought into use in staging sections and the like.

2 F.T.U. remained in Imphal until the end of the siege and was then withdrawn to Calcutta for re-equipping. It thereafter returned to Imphal first to serve in XXXIII Corps and later in IV Corps. In June 1944 it was relieved by 5 F.T.U. During the siege it had functioned as a distributing unit. Its records for the period March 17–June 23 give some idea of the magnitude of the services it rendered.

TABLE 28

2 Field Transfusion Unit. Record of Work performed during the Siege of Imphal.

Total number of casualties admitted to the field medical units	8,044
Total number of casualties dying after admission	464
Total amount of plasma used	2,289 bottles
,, ,, ,, whole blood flown into Imphal from the Ind. Adv. B.T.U.	498 ,,
Total amount of isotonic glucose-saline used	2,217 ,,
,, ,, ,, sodium chloride used	818 ,,
,, number of giving sets utilised	1,095
Estimated number of casualties treated with plasma	843
Average number of bottles of plasma used per case	3
Percentage of casualties resuscitated with plasma	10·4
Percentage of casualties dying after admission	5·7
Estimated number of casualties who recovered after resuscitation	379
Percentage of cases who recovered after resuscitation	44·7

THE HEALTH OF THE TROOPS

Until towards the end of the siege the health of the troops remained remarkably good. During April the sick-rate was 2·3 per 1,000. Thereafter it slowly and progressively increased. By the end of May it had become 2·4 and by the middle of June 3·58. At the end of June the sick-rate was 6·69 per 1,000; this was the monsoon and the peak of the malaria season, the troops were heavily engaged and rations had been cut.

THE PRINCIPAL DISEASES AFFECTING THE TROOPS

MALARIA

By the third week of April the troops operating in areas designated as malarious were placed on suppressive mepacrine treatment. Drainage schemes in the malarious areas were started. Fortunately the pre-monsoon rains were very light; during the whole of April the total rainfall was only 1·9 inches as compared with the 3·5 inches of April 1943. This slight rainfall helped materially in keeping relatively large areas of the Plain free from the mosquito during the greater part of May. Unfortunately the drainage schemes had to be considerably curtailed as the labourers employed on them were evacuated in accordance with the policy of retaining only essential personnel in Imphal. By the middle of May, some of the anti-malaria units had been evacuated, and those that remained were distributed among the 'boxes' situated in malarious areas. It is easier to institute anti-malaria measures in a 'closed society' such as a battalion with its hierarchy of responsibility than it is in a relatively loosely knit body such as a group of corps or area or sub-area troops. In the Imphal Plain these groups were all in 'boxes' which were either in non-malarious areas or else had A.M.Us. in them.

The incidence of malaria in the last week of April was as follows:

TABLE 29

IV Corps. The Incidence of Malaria. By Formation.

Formation	Number	Rate per 1,000 per diem
IV Corps Troops	208	0·73
Indian 5th Division	37	0·61
Indian 17th Division	58	0·39
Indian 20th Division, less one brigade	101	0·84
Indian 23rd Division	25	0·17
Indian 50th Para. Brigade	8	0·65
Indian 254th Tank Brigade	13	0·39

During the early part of May when the fighting was at its height the incidence of malaria remained very low. The anti-malaria units amply proved their worth. Some of the officers commanding these units were encouraged to engage in limited advisory duties in the forward areas and a pamphlet on anti-malaria measures was issued by H.Q. Corps in order to acquaint all ranks with the dangers of this disease and with the methods to be adopted to avoid it.

But with the onset of the monsoon the mosquito flourished and by the end of May the numbers admitted to hospital on account of malaria abruptly increased to 0·9 per 1,000 per diem. Those admitted came mainly from the units fighting in the foothills on the periphery of the Imphal Plain and the incidence of malaria in the Imphal 'Keep' itself did not show any significant rise. Among the fighting troops the only possible anti-malaria measure that could be enforced was the administration of suppressive mepacrine. Nets, spray-guns and anti-mosquito cream were not easily used and tactical necessity often took the troops into the villages. Shortage of petrol limited the movements of the mobile sections of the A.M.Us.

In the first week in June the rate rose to 1·2 per 1,000 per day but fell to 0·9 by the middle of the month. 9·8 inches of rain had fallen in the first half of June and so there was much mosquito breeding. There were severe epidemics in certain formations. In Indian 17th Division two battalions, 2/5th Royal Gurkha and 9th Border were particularly affected. These battalions had been carrying out some fairly long range penetrations in the foothills south of Bishenpur under very difficult conditions. Owing to supply difficulties mepacrine was not available to detached sections and platoons. For the week ending June 24 the incidence of malaria was at the rate of 3·0 per 1,000 per day. The units were at once put on a course of 0·3 gm. of mepacrine a day for five days and by July 1 the rate had fallen to 1·7/1,000/diem. The rate for the corps as a whole likewise fell as the formations moved out of the most malarious areas with the end of the siege. It became possible to tighten up anti-malaria measures and the administration of mepacrine for suppressive purposes and to undertake the treatment of those who were actually suffering from this disease.

DYSENTERY AND DIARRHOEA

After malaria, this disease group accounted for the highest number of admissions to hospital. By the beginning of May the rate had risen from the 0·41/1,000/diem of April to 0·5. The policy at this time was to evacuate from Imphal all cases not likely to be fit to return to duty within a 'reasonable' time. By the end of May the figure had risen further to reach 0·70 and by the middle of June still further to become 0·9 per 1,000. The standard of sanitation in the forward areas left much to be desired. Water supplies were distinctly primitive in these areas. Flies abounded.

It is to be noted that 399 out of the 538 cases were cases of dysentery, that there was a sharp drop from the beginning to the end of the month, that 24 per cent. of the cases of dysentery were of the protozoal type and that there was a marked drop in the number of cases of protozoal dysentery during the course of the month.

PLATE XIV. Nagas clearing a road.

[*Indian Historical Section*

PLATE XV. A convoy of jeep-ambulances on the Imphal-Kohima road, carrying casualties to the Kohima Hospitals.

PLATE XVI. 2nd Division. Motor cycle stretcher attachment.

PLATE XVII. 2nd Division. Motor cycle stretcher attachment.

PLATE XVIII. 2nd Division. One wheeled folding stretcher-carrier.

PLATE XIX. 2nd Division. One wheeled folding stretcher-carrier.

TABLE 30

41 I.G.H. (C.) Imphal. Admissions on account of Dysentery and Diarrhoea during the month of May 1944. (Examinations carried out by 25 Field Laboratory attached to the Hospital.)

Category of Patient	Numbers			
	1st–10th	11th–20th	21st–31st	Totals
Officers	12	7	15	34
B.O.Rs.	85	60	48	193
I.O.Rs.	83	76	91	250
Non-combatants	13	8	13	34
Labourers	18	4	5	27
	211	155	172	538
Protozoal form	64	25	7	96
Bacillary	68	26	30	124
Bacillary exudate	—	11	5	16
Clinical; indefinite exudate	34	75	54	163
	166	137	96	399
Protozoal Dysentery:				
Officers	3	—	—	3
B.O.Rs.	26	8	4	38
I.O.Rs. (includes non-combatants and labourers)	35	17	3	55
	64	25	7	96

VENEREAL DISEASES

During April and May these diseases showed a fairly high incidence. Indeed during the course of a period of thirty days no less than 250 cases of these diseases were evacuated out of the Imphal Plain, about 5 per cent. of the total cases evacuated during this period. The loss of man-power due to this cause was such that towards the end of May it was decided to reduce the evacuation of these cases to the minimum. 100 beds, 70 Indian and 30 British, were set aside in 41 I.G.H. (C.) for the reception and treatment of venereal cases. The increased interest within IV Corps in these diseases and in their control probably had something to do with the decline in the numbers reporting sick with them; in the last fortnight of May there had been 82 cases, in the first fortnight of June there were only 8.

TYPHUS

There were 14 cases of this disease during the siege, 6 in the Bishenpur area and 4 in the area of Palel, the other 4 being widely spread elsewhere in the Plain.

MALNUTRITION

The progressive reduction of the ration during the period when the weather was interfering seriously with the system of air-supply gave rise to a certain anxiety concerning the possibility that malnutrition would render the troops more prone to disease. The supply of fresh vegetables from local sources quickly gave out. By the middle of May the ration yielded approximately 3,500 Calories. By the beginning of June its caloric value was further reduced by 10 per cent., the ration for British troops being 2,864 Calories, that for Indian troops 2,994. It was recognised that this scale was much too low for troops involved in fighting during the monsoon season. But the rations had to be reduced even further about the middle of June when the calorie value fell to 2,750 per day. There was no possibility of any improvement until the siege was lifted. All those who were being evacuated from Imphal were placed on half rations. Vitamin tablets were liberally distributed. Such malnutrition as occurred did not reach the stage when it became the main or a major contributory cause of recognisable disease.

When the Kohima–Imphal road was opened on June 22 the effect upon the quantity and quality of the ration was immediate. Fresh meat and fresh vegetables were issued within a few days and the full scale ration made its welcome appearance early in July.

The supply of medical stores was adequate at all times during the siege. 17 (Ind.) Depot Med. Stores remained to serve as a base depot.

FOURTEENTH ARMY. MEDICAL PLANNING

Fourteenth Army was planning and preparing for a major offensive that would end in the destruction of the Japanese forces in Burma and in the reoccupation of that country. The Imphal base was to be the forward base of Fourteenth Army as this moved deep into Burma. Hospitals therefore were largely concentrated in the north and on the L. of C. from Imphal through Dimapur to the territory of Eastern Command in India. A network of medical units sufficient to satisfy all local needs had been constructed and this was capable of local or general expansion should the occasion arise. In the Ledo Road section the Americans had established their medical installations from which evacuation by air was to their base hospitals in Calcutta, Agra and Gaya. In Digboi, Dibrugarh, Panitola and Margherita there was a series of hospitals concerned primarily with the needs of the vast labour forces that were engaged in this area. Evacuation therefrom was by train to Gauhati and Tezpur. In the area were convalescent depots so that evacuation out of the area could be controlled.

In the Imphal–Dimapur area there were hospitals, convalescent depots, medical and Red Cross stores, hygiene and anti-malaria units in numbers sufficient to satisfy all reasonable local needs. In the Imphal Plain there were five general and four smaller hospitals and four convalescent depots. Along the Tamu, Tiddim and Ukhrul roads C.C.Ss. had been sited and in the pleasant little hill town of Kohima there were three general hospitals and five convalescent depots. Evacuation was by Manipur Road to Gauhati and on to Shillong, Sirajganj and to the other hospital centres in Eastern Bengal.

The advanced medical base, Dacca–Agartala–Comilla, was pursuing a very rapid expansion and Sylhet and Agartala were much used in connexion with Operation 'Thursday'.

The southern sector was considered to be of relatively minor importance. A chain of medical installations had been established from Bawli and the Naf River, through Dhoapalong, Ramu, Chiringa, the West African divisional base, Dohazari and Cox's Bazar where Khurushkul Island, 'Mercy Island', was in process of development into a medical enclave with jetties, roads, hospitals, laboratories, Y.M.C.A. and Y.W.C.A. establishments and convalescent depots. In Chittagong the two expanded hospitals were adequately housed and were capable of further expansion.

The advance of XV Corps in Arakan and the subsequent counter-offensive by the Japanese did not strain the medical services for there was no overwhelming torrent of sick as there had been in the previous years. The developments which especially affected the medical services during these operations were the great expansion of the system of air-supply and of the system of air-evacuation by light plane from improvised airstrips. Another development of significance was the arming of the medical units.

The Japanese offensive in the northern sector had a very definite and a very profound effect upon the medical services and their plans. There was a hurried transfer of considerable numbers of troops from Arakan to the Imphal Plain; there was an exodus of many tens of thousands of non-combatants from the area and therefore the withdrawal of many medical units from this area which suddenly had become the front line. The policy of holding as many patients as possible in the forward hospitals was replaced by one of evacuating as many as possible to the rear. Since there was need for hurry there was much evacuation by air and so there developed the practice of air evacuation on a grand scale which dealt with about 2,000 a month to begin with and with as many as 8,000–12,000 a month before the end of the campaign.

The withdrawal of about 25 per cent. of hospital cover meant, of course, that there were some 11,000 beds fewer when beds in greater numbers were in demand. The hospitals that remained in the area were grossly overcrowded and their staffs over-strained. Field hospitals cannot easily be moved and they required to be accommodated in buildings during the monsoon. The use of the aeroplane for evacuation purposes involved the siting of hospitals near airfields.

It was decided therefore that the main medical centres should be at Shillong, Sylhet, Agartala and Comilla. Agartala and Comilla were selected because it was from these places with their aerodromes that Imphal was to be supplied. Sylhet was chosen for the reason that it was already in use, receiving casualties by air from Operation 'Thursday'. These four centres already possessed good intercommunications which could easily be further improved and both Agartala and Comilla were connected by rail with Dacca. The following moves were therefore ordered:

To Shillong	53 I.G.H. from Kohima
	25 (Ind.) Con. Depot (B.T.)
To Sylhet	14 B.G.H., 200 beds, from the Kohima–Imphal road
	9 (Ind.) M.F.T.U.
To Agartala	51 C.G.H.
	11 and 12 (Ind.) M.F.T.Us.
	17 (Ind.) Con. Depot (I.T.)
To Comilla	19 I.G.H. from Imphal
	14 B.G.H. less 200 beds
	10 (Ind.) M.F.T.U.
	21 (Ind.) Con. Depot

Fourteenth Army. Strength

new additions	
XXXIII Corps H.Q. and corps troops	23,000
36th Division	13,500
2nd Division	18,700
Indian 23rd Division	23,400
Indian 5th Division	19,300
Ind. 50th Para. Bde.	2,100
	100,000
previous strength	518,000
	618,000

Distribution of Formations

Zone I	IV Corps and troops in the Imphal Plain including Indian 5th, 17th, 20th and 23rd Divisions, Ind. 50th Para. Bde., 256 Sub-Area	150,000
Zone II	XXXIII Corps and troops including 2nd Division, 23rd, 33rd, 161st and Lushai Bdes., 202 L. of C. Area, with 251, 252 and 253 Sub-Areas, Fort Hertz and labour	223,000
Zone III	H.Q. 404 Area with 452 and 257 Sub-Areas. Indian 19 Division less one brigade	102,000
Zone IV	XV Corps and troops including Indian 7th, 25th, 26th, 36th and 81st (W.A.) Divisions less one brigade of Indian 7th Division. 451 Sub-Area	143,000
		618,000

Hospital Beds

Zone I	Open and working	1,800
	Closed but available for opening when sites are found	1,400
		3,200
Zone II	Open and working	9,800
	Four M.F.T.Us. moving in	2,400
		12,200
Zone III	Open and working	3,600
	Moving in	1,200
		4,800
Zone IV	Open and working, including four M.F.T.Us.	8,500
	Total Fourteenth Army	28,700
Dacca	Open and working	5,900
	Due from India. 38 B.G.H., 42 I.G.H. and 8 (Ind.) M.F.T.U.	6,400
	Total Cover	41,000

Daily Admission Rates at 6·5 per 1,000

Zone I	980
II	1,450
III	660
IV	930
Total Army	4,020

The hospital bed cover showed a deficit of 16,800 in the first week of April. It was intended to meet this by crisis expansion of medical units, by evacuation of cases out of the Army Area and by the importation of additional hospitals from India.

Number of beds expected from India	6,400
25 per cent. expansion (25,000 beds available in Zones II–IV)	8,000
	14,400
Deficit 16,800–14,400	2,400
To meet this, a daily evacuation of	170
Total maximum absorption capacity of India	538
Evacuated to India, daily *via* Calcutta	200
via Sirajganj	225
	425
Surplus capacity of India	113
Surplus capacity of Dacca	100
Total surplus capacity ex-Army	213

It was intended to make use of this surplus capacity by increasing the numbers evacuated from Fourteenth Army Area by rail, river and air by 170 a day to offset the deficiency in the Army Area. One Indian general hospital was released by Fourteenth Army to India to function in Ranchi. This raised the absorption capacity of India to 573 patients per day. This meant that about a 1,000 casualties a day could be evacuated to India (including the hospital centre at Dacca), should ever the need arise and assuming that the transport facilities were augmented and that the medical administrative authorities in India agreed to accept so large a number.

Evacuation was to be by air, by rail and by river.

By air. It was assumed that returning transport aircraft would be used for casualty evacuation. In addition, five or six Anson aircraft, fitted to take four or five stretcher cases each, were expected to reach India from the United Kingdom for attachment to the transport squadrons specifically for use in casualty evacuation. A number of L.5

communication aircraft was also expected from the United Kingdom and these, it was assumed, would be available occasionally for the same purpose. The airfields to be used in the air evacuation were to be Comilla, Agartala and Sylhet.

By rail and river. From Manipur Road casualties could be routed north-east by rail to the hospitals in the vicinity of Dibrugarh whence they could travel down the Brahmaputra to Gauhati or Tezpur. Or, they could be routed from Jorhat by rail direct to Gauhati. From Gauhati evacuation was mainly by river to Sirajganj for distribution by rail among the hospitals further to the west and south. Alternatively they could be sent by rail to Shillong and thence *via* Sylhet and *via* Chittagong they could be distributed among the hospitals further to the west and south. From Arakan evacuation was mainly *via* Chittagong to Dacca.

Early in 1943 H.Q. Eastern Army had arranged for a hospital river-steamer service to cover the river L. of C. (the Brahmaputra) and the coast between Chittagong and Cox's Bazar. Based on Gauhati were the steamers *Mallard*, *Swift*, *Kite* and *Lark*. Four others, based on Daudkandi, served the lower part of this river L. of C. Based on Chittagong were three coastal ships, *Aila*, *Mekla* and *Bevra* and to these were added later two considerably larger ships, *Nalchera* and *Badora*, which could take about 30 lying and 60 sitting cases each. Eventually Eastern Army had twelve such steamers functioning as hospital river or coastal steamers. In addition to these there were in the Naf Estuary a large hospital 'flat', several small tugs, a number of fast launches and a fleet of 16 dhows and on the chaungs of Arakan there were numbers of sampans of all varieties fitted out for the transport of casualties. Finally, definite establishments were obtained for these somewhat unusual instruments of evacuation and a service was organised.

The hospital river steamers ran occasionally from Dibrugarh to Gauhati and Tezpur. This section of the line of evacuation was a difficult one for the river was inclined to change its course during and after the floods and sandbanks were numerous.

They plied
   (i) between Gauhati and Tezpur to carry patients who were likely to be back with their units within six weeks;
   (ii) between Gauhati and Sirajganj, carrying those patients who were to be sent on by rail to the base hospitals. The river at Sirajganj was very liable to change its course. After the floods in one year the river channel was seven miles distant from the rail terminus and reception station that had been built upon its bank;
   (iii) between Comilla and Daudkandi and Goalundo to serve the Comilla-Dacca hospital centres;
   (iv) between Chittagong and Calcutta; and
   (v) between Maungdaw and Cox's Bazar.

The bottle-necks were Gauhati, Daudkandi and Chittagong and 52 I.G.H. in Gauhati, 74 I.G.H. at Comilla and 68 I.G.H. in Chittagong were usually holding patients far in excess of their authorised capacity.

The steamers were stern-wheelers or paddle steamers and the accommodation was very limited. Initially the patients were accommodated on mattresses placed directly on the deck. Then wooden trestle beds were provided and later still iron piping beds and naval pattern double-tiered bunks were made available. Side screens were used to protect the decks against rain. Cooking arrangements, facilities for minor surgery and accommodation for the medical and nursing staff— one or two M.Os., two Q.A.I.M.N.S. personnel, a variable number of N.Os. (R.A.M.C. or I.A.M.C.), cooks and the like—had to be improvised.

Evacuation by river was liable to interruption. D.D.M.S. Eastern Army, on the *Lark*, when inspecting the evacuation system found himself marooned with some 150 patients for 48 hours high and dry upon a sandbank.

Ships below 500 tons were not included by the Admiralty in the category of hospital ships which could claim the protection of the Red Cross. Invariably difficulty was encountered by the medical services when attempts were made to reserve the river-steamer kind of ship exclusively for medical purposes; they were always urgently needed for the transport of reinforcements and stores on the outward journey. Such an arrangement cannot possibly be satisfactory from the point of view of the medical services and there can be no doubt whatsoever that in most circumstances the Red Cross symbol does provide protection to these small vessels. From the biased point of view of the medical services it seemed imperative that these ships used for evacuation purposes should be used solely for medical purposes, carrying medical reinforcements and supplies only on the outward trip.

The medical units that were withdrawn from the Imphal Plain were sent either to the Comilla–Agartala area, where the aerodromes being used for the air-supply of IV Corps were sited, or else to the valley of the Brahmaputra in north-east Assam to provide cover for XXXIII Corps.

The medical branch of Fourteenth Army issued a directive concerning evacuation. In it the policy was defined in the following terms:

(i) the retention of all sick and wounded who could be expected to recover within a period of three weeks in forward hospitals and M.F.T.Us.;

(ii) the efficient and rapid evacuation of all longer term cases to Comilla, Agartala or Dacca, where all patients who could be expected to recover within two months were to be retained;

(iii) the rapid evacuation of all patients who would require longer hospital treatment than two months to the base hospitals in India Command;

(iv) the early selection of certain special types of serious and urgent cases, such as gunshot wounds of the head, maxillo-facial injuries, penetrating eye wounds, severe burns, fractures of the femur, etc., and their rapid selective evacuation to the specialist units where they could be treated most efficiently.

The distribution of hospitals in March and in July 1944 is given in Appendix XV. The pattern of grouping hospitals centrally and of placing transit hospitals peripherally was considered to be the most economical in respect of the provision of specialist facilities and of transport and it also eliminated the disadvantages that were associated with the frequent moves of hospitals in response to changes in the tactical situation. This pattern of distribution certainly covered all sectors of the front.

Dacca was the base hospital centre and Comilla was being developed as a medical centre. But the constructional work both at Dacca and at Comilla could not keep pace with the demands for beds. Furthermore Dacca could not be used to the full for the reason that there was an acute shortage of aircraft. The medical services had no ambulance aircraft which could be moved by the medical authorities in accordance with medical needs. Throughout the battle of Imphal one squadron of Dakota ambulance planes could have covered the evacuation of all the sick and wounded to Dacca and could have brought back supplies on their outward trip. Peak periods of evacuation could have been covered by small-scale evacuation in supply aircraft to Comilla and Chittagong where there were hospitals with empty beds.

In the second week of May it was learnt that Comilla was no longer to function as the air-supply base. Agartala, Sylhet and Fenny were to become the main bases. One C.C.S., one S.S., and a depot of medical stores were moved to Fenny and evacuation to Comilla from Fenny by rail was arranged.

Systems of supply by air, transport by air and evacuation by air had developed so quickly and had become so unremarkable that it was difficult at the time to realise that something of very considerable historical importance was happening. The need for this development was urgent. Land communications in this theatre were so bad that some method of supplementing them was essential. India, the base, was itself so vast that an internal air communication system was very necessary.

In this theatre supremacy in the air was a major factor in determining the issue of the fighting on the ground. By the end of 1943 the Japanese airforce had virtually ceased to exist for it was no longer able to influence the course of the military operations.

During the siege of Imphal 150,000 men, 138 miles from railhead, had to be supplied. They needed some 400 tons every day and these had to be delivered into an area ringed about by Japanese guns. Some 22,000 tons of supplies and over 20,000 troops were flown into the Plain and from it some 35,000 non-combatants and many thousands of sick and wounded were withdrawn.

Those in the Plain came to depend upon the Allied Air Forces as much as did the brigades of 'Special Force'. Medical tactical planning came to be as profoundly affected by the newer responsibilities of the Air Force as were the tactical plans of the General Staff.

Air evacuation on this scale reduces very considerably the need for the provision in the forward zone of those units which are concerned with the accommodation, the feeding, the treatment and the transportation of casualties. The number of the medical units can be reduced as can also the number of ambulance cars, since one aeroplane is the equivalent of very many cars in respect of its capacity. The need for the provision in the forward zone of special facilities such as highly specialised mobile surgical, neuro-surgical and the maxillo-facial units is removed. Usually such air evacuation reduces very considerably the interval between wounding and exposure to skilled surgical intervention. To the casualties themselves the contrast between the forward field units, no matter how good they are, with their lack of comfort and security and the advanced base or base hospitals is indeed great. The contrast between the speedy comfort of air-evacuation and the tardy, uncomfortable or even exceedingly painful journey by track, road, rail or river is even greater.

APPENDIX XV

LOCATION STATEMENT OF HOSPITALS AND MALARIA FORWARD TREATMENT UNITS. FOURTEENTH ARMY. MARCH AND JULY 1944

March			July		
Sookerating	C.M.H.		Sookerating	C.M.H.	not yet opened
Panitola	C.M.H.		Panitola	C.M.H.	100 Br.; 200 Ind. Beds
Digboi	C.M.H.		Digboi	C.M.H.	100 Br.; 200 Ind.
Ledo	44 I.G.H.		Ledo	44 I.G.H.	200 Br.; 500 Ind.
Dibrugarh	C.M.H.		Dibrugarh	C.M.H.	not yet opened
				49 I.G.H.	300 Br.; 700 Ind.
				45 I.G.H.	3 secs.
Jorhat	45 I.G.H.		Jorhat	45 I.G.H.	300 Br.; 700 Ind.
Neamati	C.M.H.		Neamati	C.M.H.	16 Br.; 84 Ind.
Golaghat	—		Golaghat	38 B.G.H.	600 Br.
Manipur Rd.	43 I.G.H.		Manipur Rd.	43 I.G.H.	– Br.; 1,000 Ind.
	66 I.G.H.			66 I.G.H.	300 Br.; 700 Ind.
Kohima	48 I.G.H.		Kohima	—	300 Br.; 700 Ind.
	53 I.G.H.			—	200 Br.; 500 Ind.
M.S. 116 on the Kohima–Imphal Rd.	59 I.G.H.		M.S. 116	—	– Br.; 1,000 Ind.
	14 B.G.H.				1,200 Br.
	79 I.G.H.				– Br.; 1,000 Ind.
Kanglatongbi	41 I.G.H.		Kanglatongbi	—	300 Br.; 700 Ind.

March		July		
Imphal	87 I.G.H.	Imphal	87 I.G.H.	100 Br.; 300 Ind.
			41 I.G.H.	from Kanglatongbi
			89 I.G.H.	100 Br.; 300 Ind. from Palel
Palel	89 I.G.H.	Palel	—	
On the Imphal–Tiddim Rd.	88 I.G.H.	On the Imphal–Tiddim Rd.	—	100 Br.; 300 Ind.
Silchar	124 I.G.H.	Silchar	124 I.G.H.	200 Br.; 500 Ind.
Tezpur	C.M.H.	Tezpur	C.M.H.	not yet opened
			43 I.G.H.	from Manipur Rd.
Gauhati	52 I.G.H.	Gauhati	52 I.G.H.	300 Br.; 700 Ind.
Shillong	B.M.H.	Shillong	B.M.H.	500 Br.
			I.M.H.	– Br.; 1,300 Ind.
			59 I.G.H.	5 secs. from the Kohima–Kanglatongbi Rd.
Sylhet	91 I.G.H.	Sylhet	91 I.G.H.	100 Br.; 300 Ind.
Agartala	74 I.G.H.	Agartala		300 Br.; 700 Ind.
	92 I.G.H.			200 Br.; 500 Ind.
			79 I.G.H.	from the Kohima–Kanglatongbi Rd.
			86 I.G.H.	100 Br.; 300 Ind.
Comilla	—	Comilla	14 B.G.H.	from the Kohima–Kanglatongbi Rd.
			74 I.G.H.	from Agartala
			92 I.G.H.	from Agartala

THE SIEGE OF IMPHAL

March			*July*	
Dacca	62 I.G.H.		Dacca	62 I.G.H.	300 Br.; 700 Ind.
	63 I.G.H.			63 I.G.H.	1,000 Ind.
	76 I.G.H.			76 I.G.H.	1,000 Ind.
	77 I.G.H.			77 I.G.H.	1,000 Ind.
	17 B.G.H.			17 B.G.H.	1,200 Br.
	46 W.A.G.H.			46 W.A.G.H.	1,000 W.A.
Chittagong	56 I.G.H.		Chittagong	56 I.G.H.	200 Br.; 500 Ind.
	68 I.G.H.			68 I.G.H.	300 Br.; 700 Ind.
				105 E.A.G.H.	1,000 E.A.
Chiringa	49 W.A.G.H.		Chiringa	49 W.A.G.H.	1,000 W.A.
Dohazari	82 I.G.H.		Dohazari	82 I.G.H.	100 Br.; 300 Ind.
Cox's Bazar	58 I.G.H.		Cox's Bazar	58 I.G.H.	1,000 Ind.
	72 I.G.H.			72 I.G.H.	200 Br.; 500 Ind.
Dhoapalong	125 I.G.H.		Dhoapalong	125 I.G.H.	300 Br.; 700 Ind.

Total Hospitals 40

Total Hospital Beds 8,416 British
 20,384 Indian
 2,000 West African
 1,000 East African
 ―――――
 31,800

Malaria Forward Treatment Units, each with 600 beds, British and Indian:

1 (Ind.) M.F.T.U.	in Buthidaung	9 (Ind.) M.F.T.U.	in Silchar
2 "	"	10 "	Comilla
3 "	Maungdaw	11 "	Agartala
4 "	"	12 "	Chittagong
5 "	Manipur Rd.	13 "	Dibrugarh
6 "	Golaghat	14 "	Tinsukia
7 "	Manipur Rd.	15 "	Shillong
8 "	Kohima	16 "	Ledo
	Total Beds 9,600		
	Grand Total 41,400 Beds		

APPENDIX XVI

THE ARMING OF THE PERSONNEL OF MEDICAL UNITS

Article 8 of the Geneva Convention expressly permits the arming of medical units.

'The following conditions are not considered to be of such a nature as to deprive a medical formation or establishment of the protection guaranteed in Article 6;

(i) That the personnel of the formation or establishment is armed and that they use the arms in their own defence or in that of the sick and wounded in charge, etc.'

In September 1942 the following scale of arms was decided upon for medical units:

Field Ambulance	a pool of 50 rifles and 6 machine carbines
Field Hygiene Section	15 rifles
Bearer Unit	9 rifles

Because of the flagrant disregard for the Red Cross emblem on the part of the Japanese and because of the deliberate killing of patients in medical units and of the medical personnel of these units, it was decided in 1944 that medical unit personnel should be armed:

with pistols	officers, V.C.Os., Br. W.Os.
with rifles	O.Rs. attached R.I.A.S.C., etc.

The units where a departure from this rule was made were:

Unit	Armed with Pistols	Armed with Rifles	Armed with Stens
Fd. Amb.	Offrs., V.C.Os., motor cyclists	Attached personnel other than those with Stens	Attached V.C.Os. First drivers of vehicles
	(50 rifles and 6 Stens were provided in addition in field ambulances where necessary)		
Lt. Fd. Hyg. Sec.	Officer and V.C.O.	Attached personnel	—
Fd. Hyg. Sec.	Officer	Combatants other than those with Stens	W.O., V.C.O., Drivers of 'B' vehicles
Fd. Amb. Parachute	Offrs., V.C.Os., and O.Rs.	Attached R.I.A.S.C. and ambulance section I.H.C. personnel in H.Q.	Two batmen in H.Q. and one per section
C.C.S.	Offrs., V.C.Os., motor cyclists	Attached ranks other than those with Stens	Attached V.C.Os., clerks and first drivers of vehicles
A.M.U.	Officer	—	V.C.O. and drivers

Unit	Armed with Pistols	Armed with Rifles	Armed with Stens
Bearer Coy.	Officer	Havildars, naiks, lance-naiks, ambulance section I.H.C., batmen and spare drivers	V.C.Os. and 5 attached drivers
Field Hospitals	Offrs. and V.C.Os.	Attached personnel other than those with Stens	First drivers
Con. Depots	Officers	—	O.Rs. excluding medical
B.T.Us.	Officers	—	Drivers
Medical stores transit depot	Officer and V.C.O.	—	Drivers
Reserve base depot medical stores	Officers	Drivers other than those with Stens	W.O., V.C.Os. First drivers
Staging Section	Officer and V.C.O.		

APPENDIX XVII

Excerpt from the Despatch of General Sir George J. Giffard, G.C.B., D.S.O., A.D.C., Commander in Chief, 11 Army Group, South-East Asia Command. *Operations in Burma and North-East India from 16th November, 1943 to 22nd June, 1944.*

Supplement to the London Gazette, 13th March, 1951.

The Medical Aspect. A. Organisation

The medical organisation in Fourteenth Army was originally based on the assumption that the main operations would be forward of Imphal. Hospitals were consequently largely concentrated in the north and, in order to avoid evacuation down a long line of communication, they were sited well forward. The Japanese thrust against Imphal, however, necessitated their removal, and a situation arose in which about 25 per cent. of our hospitals became temporarily non-effective. This would have been serious had it not been for two saving factors; firstly, air transport provided a link between our northern and southern lines of communication, enabling casualties to be rapidly cleared to hospitals serving the Arakan Front; and secondly, the sick rate on both fronts fell far short of the estimate for which provision had been made.

In the south, where extensive operations had not been originally contemplated, and where the forces engaged were smaller, our hospitals had not been concentrated so far forward.

Considerable discussion took place early in the year between 11 Army Group and General Headquarters, India, regarding the adequacy or otherwise of the hospitals.

The decisions then taken proved to be sound on the whole, in spite of our forecasts being wrong and of radical alterations in the lines of evacuation. Although there is still a decided shortage of medical officers, and a serious shortage of nurses and nursing personnel, there has been no general shortage of hospital accommodation, but anxiety is always present in an unhealthy tropical theatre of war.

At the beginning of the year, facilities for evacuation were reviewed, and as a result of representations made by me to the Supreme Allied Commander, six hospital ships were allotted to Fourteenth Army.

Further, a co-ordinating committee, invested with executive authority, which includes representatives of 11 Army Group and General Headquarters, India, and of the many services affected, has been set up to deal in detail with the complicated problem of medical evacuation. Its measures have so far proved effective, notwithstanding the many problems which have arisen.

One interesting feature of the recent fighting is that the medical personnel have found themselves on occasions called upon to undertake part of the responsibility for their own defence. That medical personnel had to fight proved to be a necessity—it was not a question as to whether they should defend themselves, but how best they could do so.

The complicated problem of medical evacuation from Arakan involved the use of almost every conceivable form of transport. Hand carriages, mules, jeeps, ambulances, D.U.K.Ws., sampans, flats, paddle steamers, hospital ships, ambulance trains, and light and heavy aircraft have all had to be employed over one stage or another of the journey.

To and from 81 (West African) Division operating in the Kaladan Valley, medical supply and evacuation has had to be entirely by air. That the arrangements worked smoothly is due both to the medical officers concerned and to the skilful co-operation of the R.A.F.

I have already mentioned how the evacuation of casualties by air from Imphal Front prevented a serious situation developing when certain hospitals had to be closed down. This air evacuation continued throughout the operations about Imphal and was instrumental in saving many lives. In addition to casualties, two large General Hospitals were flown out with all their valuable equipment.

The total number of casualties evacuated by air during the first half of 1944, from all fronts, was over 24,000. Rapid and adequate air transport facilities abolish at one stroke the unsatisfactory and difficult clearance of casualties down long surface lines of communication, with all their attendant disadvantages. This method of moving the wounded has a most beneficial effect on the morale of the fighting soldier.

The Medical Aspect. B. Sick Rate

The most satisfactory feature on the medical side has been the surprisingly low sick rate during the first six months of the year. The expected rise to 5 or 6 per 1,000 per diem has not happened and the rate in May was as low as $3 \cdot 1$ per 1,000, including battle casualties. This is an almost incredibly low figure compared with that for 1943, which was 6 per 1,000 per diem; and, in spite of the seasonal increase of malaria, it has since dropped to $2 \cdot 9$.

Since November 1943 food supply greatly improved, and more fresh meat, fruit and vegetables became available. It is probable that this improvement in rations has been a major cause in keeping down the sick rate.

The most serious menace we have to face, where disease is concerned, is of course malaria, and this can only be overcome by unremitting effort and vigilance. The malaria rate, up till the end of June, has remained consistently low compared with last year. This is remarkable, since operations have been carried out on a greatly extended scale, and many more troops have been exposed to the risk of infection. If the same rate had obtained in Arakan and at Imphal from March to June as in the same months of 1943, the effect on operations would have been serious.

I attribute this satisfactory state of affairs to four factors—firstly, better anti-malarial discipline; secondly, the improved anti-malarial organisation which, under medical control and aided by the engineers, has freed certain areas from the mosquito; thirdly, the ample flow of anti-malarial supplies of all kinds; and last, but not least, improved morale, since troops in good fettle look after themselves better in every way than when they are depressed.

The efficacy of D.D.T. as an anti-mosquito spray is shortly being tested in the Kabaw Valley.

The Medical Aspect. C. Miscellaneous Medical Points

There has been no noticeable change in the physical standard of British reinforcements, which can only be classed as average.

The physical standard of young soldiers in the Indian Army had improved during the period under review, particularly in combatant units.

The Army Pathological Service suffers, in this Theatre, from the lack of laboratories. The importance of accurate laboratory diagnosis requires no stressing.

Dental facilities are altogether inadequate. The accepted ratio of dental officers to troops is one per 1,000 for the British and one per 10,000 for Indian. The present ratio is one per 7,000 and 30,000 respectively.

The present standard of training of medical personnel in this Theatre does not compare altogether favourably with that in others, but, taking into consideration the expansion which the Medical Services have undergone, and the acute shortage of medical officers in India, it is, I am sure, as good as can be expected. Training is, I know, continuous and intensive in the India Command and the situation is improving.

The supply of medical stores, including drugs, has been most satisfactory. The consumption of mepacrine in Fourteenth Army as a malaria suppressive has reached twelve million tablets a month.

The problem of providing adequate medical supervision for the large amount of civilian labour employed in the Fourteenth Army area is being met at present, but it may become more difficult when civilian labour forces have to be moved into re-conquered territory as our troops advance.

The thirteen convalescent depots in 11 Army Group have proved their value as an essential link between hospital and reinforcement camp.

CHAPTER 10

THE RETURN TO BURMA

FOURTEENTH Army had been set three tasks; to re-establish communications between Kohima and Imphal; to clear the Dimapur–Imphal Plain–Yuwa–Tamanthi area of Japanese and to advance across the Chindwin between Yuwa and Tamanthi. The first of these had been successfully completed and attention could now be paid to the remaining two. General Slim allotted to XXXIII Corps the task of clearing the area north of the line Kangpokpi–Ukhrul and to IV Corps that of clearing the area to the south and west of this.

At Kohima and Imphal the efforts of Japanese Fifteenth Army to break through to Dimapur and beyond had ended in complete and disastrous failure, in spite of the very remarkable resolution, endurance and valour displayed by the rank and file. They had been beaten by men as brave as themselves, by men above them in skill and perception, by men much better led and far better serviced. The immoderate over-confidence of their higher command which had led them to assume that their armies must inevitably be victorious, that they could safely depend upon captured supplies for their maintenance and so could dispense very largely with lines of communication, had clearly and conclusively been shown to be unjustified. Their 31st Division, so badly mauled at Kohima, was withdrawing along the Kohima–Jessami and the Tuphema–Kharasom tracks while its rearguard opposed the advance of 2nd and Indian 7th Divisions towards Imphal. This rearguard had melted into the hills on either side of the Kohima–Imphal road as this advance continued. Japanese 15th Division was stretched in a wide arc with its northern tip on the Imphal–Ukhrul road and its southern tip on the Imphal–Tamu road. It was divided into three groups. The first of these, which had been facing Indian 5th Division as this thrust up the Kohima road from Imphal, had now taken to the hills to the east of the Kohima–Imphal road. The second group, which had been sternly checked by Indian 20th Division in the vicinity of Milestone 18 on the Imphal–Ukhrul track when it was attempting to thrust into Imphal along the Litan–Imphal road and along the Iril Valley, was now firmly entrenched in the hills in front of Ukhrul. The third, along with units of Japanese 33rd Division, was engaged in vain efforts to press along the Tamu–Palel road towards Imphal. The main body of Japanese 33rd Division, in better shape than the other two, was involved in strenuous attempts to break through the positions of Indian 17th Division about Bishenpur and so reach Imphal from the south.

Japanese 31st and 15th Divisions were withdrawing into most inhospitable country, into the mountainous area that marks the boundary between Assam and Burma. Moreover, the monsoon had broken and the rain had turned the roads, tracks and bridle-paths into bogs and rivulets of dirty, yellow mud. Landslides continually blocked them. The hillsides were commonly so steep that steps had to be cut into them before laden mules could climb them. The jungle was so dense in places that paths literally had to be hacked through it while from the dripping vegetation thread-like leeches, scarcely visible, dropped on man and beast to gorge themselves with blood. The supply and medical services of Japanese Fifteenth Army had broken down with the result that it was not only a dispirited army, it was a starving and a disease-riddled one. It could hope to escape complete disaster only if the monsoon brought all large-scale fighting to an end for the time being. But there was to be no respite for the Supreme Allied Commander had decided that the full *tempo* of war should be maintained right through the monsoon period so that no opportunity should be given to the Japanese to reorganise and re-form and so that the destruction of Japanese 31st and 15th Divisions might be completed.

Immediately after the reopening of the Kohima–Imphal road the commanders of XXXIII and IV Corps met in Imphal and made their plans for the clearing of the hills on either side of the Kohima–Imphal road and for the reoccupation of Ukhrul, the supply base for the Japanese formations in this area. In the most northerly section of this road, between Kohima and Maram, Indian 20th Division methodically sought out the bands of Japanese troops that were hurriedly making their way back to Ukhrul as did also Ind. 268th Lorried Bde. along the Jessami and Kharasom tracks. But from these parts the Japanese had gone. South of Maram, the brigades of 2nd Division, 4th, 5th and 6th in this order from north to south, were engaged upon the same task and they encountered considerable opposition. Indeed, it was only with the aid of strong air support that they were able to dislodge bodies of Japanese troops from certain of the villages and prepared entrenched positions. However, by the end of the first week of July this area was clear and 2nd Division moved back to the vicinity of Maram, its 4th Bde. to Kigwema and its 5th to Imphal.

THE CAPTURE OF UKHRUL

XXXIII Corps' plan to secure Ukhrul and to complete the destruction of Japanese 15th and 31st Divisions was, briefly, as follows:

THE RETURN TO BURMA

2nd Division would be responsible for the security of the road L. of C., excluding the Maram–Imphal section.

Indian 7th Division would advance across country with two brigade groups on a pack basis and on air supply and attack Ukhrul from the north and from the east in conjunction with Indian 20th Division of IV Corps which would attack from the south. (Later Indian 20th Division was placed u/c XXXIII Corps in order that the attack might be directed by one corps H.Q.)

23rd L.R.P. Bde. would send out columns on three axes that eventually converged upon Ukhrul from the north, east and south-east to cut the Japanese L. of C. and escape routes to the east.

Indian 21st Division (consisting at this time of Ind. 268th Lorried Bde. and Ind. 45th Cavalry) would maintain patrol bases on the Jessami and Kharasom tracks.

To begin with H.Q. XXXIII Corps would be in Kigwema and on July 1 in Imphal.

At dawn on June 27, Ind. 33rd Bde. of Indian 7th Division set out from Maram along the track that ran to the south-east through Oinam, Ngawar and Tallui. At the same time 89th Bde., also of Indian 7th Division, left Kangpokpi along a track that ran due east through Chawai, Mollen, Leishan and Luinem. No opposition was encountered until the brigades were within a few miles of Ukhrul. Near Tallui elements of 33rd Bde. met units of 23rd Bde. and at Luinem 89th Bde. and Indian 20th Division made contact. 23rd Bde. had moved on

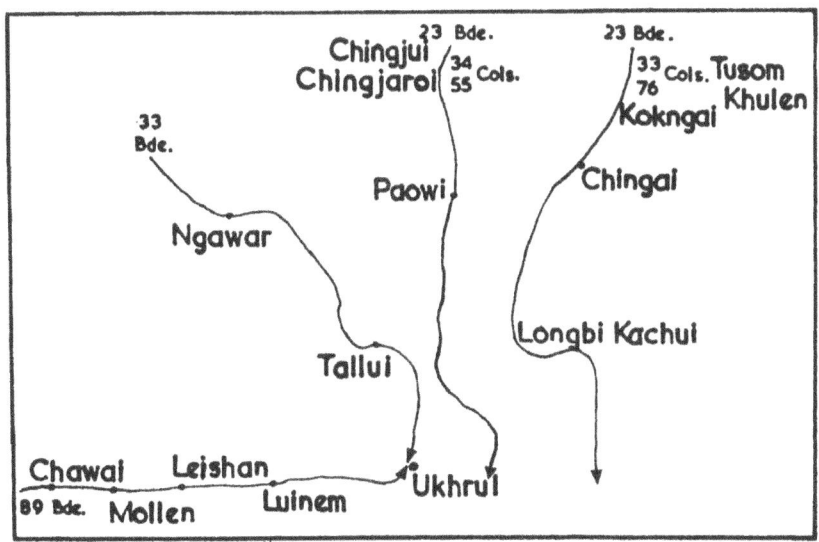

FIG. 37. Indian 7th Division's Advance on Ukhrul. June 27–July 8, 1944

Ukhrul from the north and was to attack it from the east. The three axes along which its columns had moved were *via* Chingjui, Chingjaroi and Paowi, *via* Kokngai and Longbi Kachui and further to the east, *via* Somra and Saiyapaw. By July 1 the columns had taken up positions which completely blocked the Japanese escape routes towards Homalin and to the north.

On July 3 the advanced elements of 89th Bde. unexpectedly burst into the southern outskirts of Ukhrul before they were checked. During the following days, as the pressure exerted by the encircling force gained in strength, the Japanese troops in the fort and in the northern and south-eastern parts of the town gradually slipped away and during the night of July 8/9 it was discovered that the last of them had departed. Ukhrul, which had been in Japanese hands for more than three months, was reoccupied.

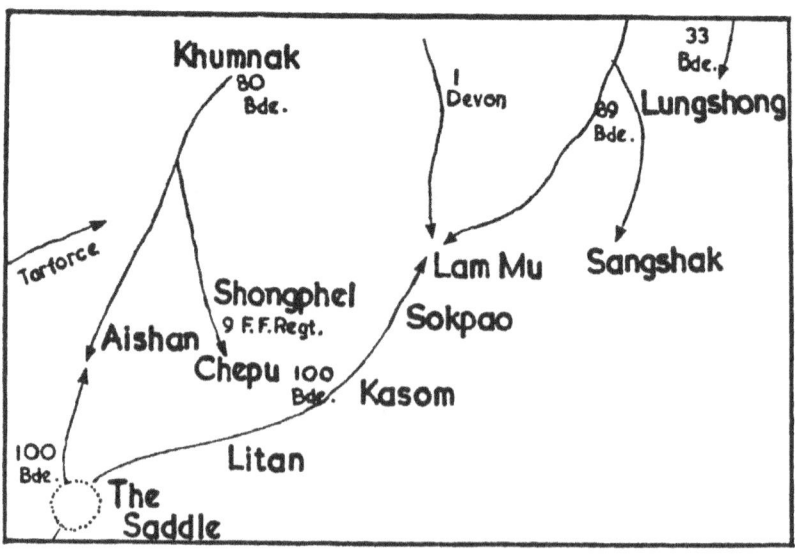

Fig. 38. Indian 20th Division. The reopening of the Imphal–Ukhrul Road. July 1–16, 1944

The next task was that of reopening the Ukhrul–Imphal road. By June 22, Ind. 100th Bde. of Indian 20th Division had reached, and had then been checked at, the 'Saddle', a feature to the south-west of Litan on the Imphal–Ukhrul road. At this time 80th Bde. of the same division had reached the vicinity of Chawai and Mollen. On June 23, Ind. 80th Bde. was instructed to move to the area of Khunthak and thence advance in a southerly direction as soon as 89th Bde. of Indian 7th Division had reached Khunthak so as to threaten the rear of the Japanese opposing 100th Bde. 80th Bde. reached the vicinity of Khunthak on June 26 and the place was occupied on the following day when 33rd and 89th Bdes. set out from Maram and Kangpokpi. Meanwhile 100th Bde. had been attacked and had been obliged to vacate certain of its positions. The fighting continued for several days and it was not until July 10 that Japanese resistance was finally overcome and the road reopened.

Even then there were still many scattered strong parties of Japanese troops in what were now rear areas, about Shorbung, facing 2nd Division, in the bend of the Iril River around Pashong and Dongsum and in the vicinity of the Saddle, of Aishan and of Thawai. Operations directed to the elimination of these bands were started even before Ukhrul had fallen. 2nd and Indian 20th Divisions moved against them in such a way that they were driven against 23rd and 33rd Bdes. which stood athwart the escape routes to the east. On July 2 and 3, XXXIII Corps had issued instructions that defined the operations to be undertaken after the fall of Ukhrul. 23rd Bde. was to send two columns to the Ukhrul area there to co-operate with 89th Bde. in blocking the escape route from the Shorbung area while the rest of the brigade swung in a wide arc to cut the route at Chattrik and Ongshim. 33rd Bde. was to march round Ukhrul to block the routes *via* Lungshong and Kamjong and *via* Sakok and Meiring. Improvised formations were to be sent to block the Kasom route and those to the south between Kamjong and Humine. These operations were carried out in the most wretched of conditions; mist and low cloud perpetually blanketed the hills so that supply by air-drop was impossible; the mud was so thick and so deep that even the jeep could not be used. Surra broke out among the mules. And so it happened that the net could not be drawn sufficiently around the retreating Japanese and most of them got away to reach the Chindwin and safety. When it had become clear that success could not attend these efforts it was decided to discontinue them. Indian 7th Division began to move back to Kohima on July 22 and by the 26th, 23rd Bde. had begun its withdrawal to Zubza. 4th Bde. of 2nd Division assumed responsibility for the defence of the Ukhrul area.

When Indian 20th Division had completed its task of mopping up in the area between Aishan and Sangshak and of blocking the routes to the south from Sangshak, it began to move back to Thoubal, its 80th Bde. going to Wangjing and its 100th Bde. to Waithou. Ind. 50th Para. Bde. assumed control of the area thus vacated by Indian 20th Division for the time being. This brigade was itself relieved shortly afterwards by 100th Bde.

In this manner the large area of hill and forest between the Kohima–Imphal road in the west and the Chindwin River in the east, with the exception of a salient across the river in the vicinity of Palel, was cleared and the remnants of Japanese 15th and 31st Divisions were forced back beyond the river. Very considerable success, if not complete, had attended the efforts of the formations serving in this sector at this time. Such success in such conditions was necessarily dependent upon many factors, upon the determination and the ability of all ranks to overcome the many obstacles presented by the terrain and by the weather, by the quality of the work of the administrative, engineer and medical services, and by the magnitude of the aid given to the troops on the ground by the U.S.A.A.F. and the R.A.F. For movement, for supply, for close support in battle since artillery

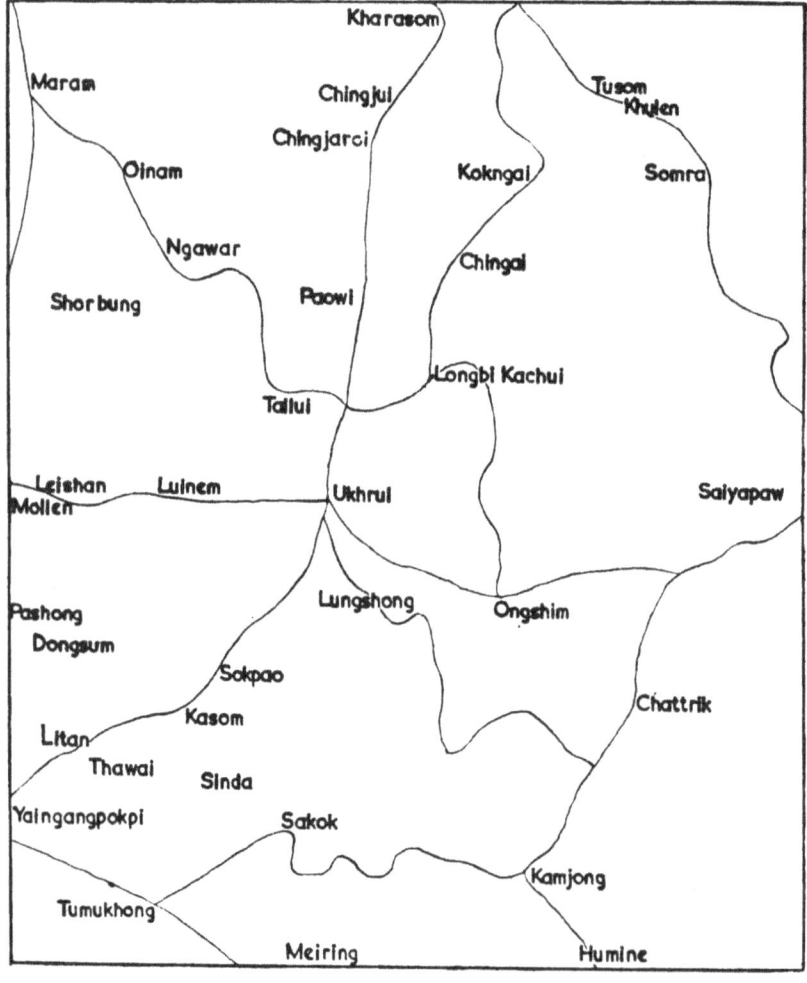

FIG. 39. Maram–Humine

could not effectively co-operate with infantry columns operating over wide areas of jungle-clad hills, and for the evacuation of its casualties, the Army was obliged to turn to the Air Forces, as had been the case in the recent past and as was to be the case so very often in the immediate future.

MEDICAL COVER

With 33rd Bde. on its advance against Ukhrul *via* Maram, Oinam, Ngawar and Tallui went an A.D.S. of 44 (Ind.) Fd. Amb. to which was attached an improvised surgical team and a squad of stretcher-bearers from 5 (Ind.) Bearer Company. The M.D.S. of this unit was open in Kohima. The equipment of the A.D.S. was carried on twenty mules, that of the surgical team on another five. The quantity of personal kit and equipment carried by the man was strictly limited. It was accepted that the evacuation of casualties rearwards would be impracticable because of the nature and condition of the ground and that they would therefore have to be carried forward to Ukhrul.

The brigade moved in three columns each of which was provided with a detachment of the A.D.S.; the surgical team moved with the rearmost of these detachments. During the first day's long march, such as fell sick were evacuated to the M.D.S. of 54 (Ind.) Fd. Amb. in Maram. As the advance continued Naga porters were engaged in each village as it was reached to help carry the casualties forward. The weather worsened and the rain fell continually. On July 4 the brigade opened its assault upon Ukhrul and the A.D.S. remained a few miles distant from the town until this had been captured. By July 8 the A.D.S. was holding some 100 patients, most of them suffering from one or other form of mild illness. The surgical team opened up near the A.D.S. and was kept busy.

With 89th Bde. on its advance from Kangpokpi went an A.D.S. of 66 (Ind.) Fd. Amb. to which was attached 14 (Ind.) M.S.U. Naga porters were engaged as stretcher-bearers. The M.D.S. of this unit was open in Kangpokpi. Such casualties as occurred during the advance were carried forward until Ukhrul was reached.

On July 3, H.Q. Indian 7th Division moved to Milestone 10 on the Imphal–Ukhrul road. With it went a light M.D.S. of 66 (Ind.) Fd. Amb. which opened at this site.

When Ukhrul had been occupied 33rd Bde. pressed on to the southeast while 89th Bde. turned south to join up with Indian 20th Division on the main Imphal–Ukhrul road. The A.D.S. of 54 (Ind.) Fd. Amb. handed over its patients to the A.D.S. of 66 (Ind.) Fd. Amb. in Ukhrul and moved with 33rd Bde. but the unit found it impossible to proceed beyond Lungshong because of the continuous rain and the mud.

Evacuation from the brigade to the A.D.S. was by Naga porter, a journey that came to take as long as two days.

With 23rd Bde. went an A.D.S. of 9 (Ind.) Lt. Fd. Amb. which opened at Milestone 30 on the Kohima–Jessami track to function as a staging post. A total of 77 casualties passed through this A.D.S. but of these only a very few were battle casualties, the great majority being cases of fever, exhaustion or avitaminosis. From this A.D.S. evacuation at first was by light aircraft of the U.S.A.A.F. but as the advance continued to the south it became necessary to carry the casualties forward to Ukhrul. As had been the case with the brigades of 'Special Force', so it was in this 'Chindit' brigade; after a time the sick-rate began to rise sharply as the troops began to suffer from malnutrition and weariness. A severe epidemic of typhus with an unusually high case-fatality-rate occurred.

When at the end of July, 33rd and 89th Bdes. of Indian 7th Division were withdrawn to Kohima for rest, the medical detachments rejoined their parent units. 4 Fd. Amb. serving 4th Bde. of 2nd Division, opened its M.D.S. in Maram.

THE CAPTURE OF TAMU

At the time of the reopening of the Kohima–Imphal road the Japanese force, consisting of units of Japanese 15th and 33rd Divisions, and attempting to reach Imphal along the Tamu–Palel road, had been checked in the vicinity of Tengnoupal by Indian 23rd Division. Its 37th Bde. with its H.Q. in Shenam, had been bearing the brunt of the Japanese attacks. 1st Bde. was in the area of Kakching guarding the road from Tengnoupal to Imphal in the area of Thoubal. The third brigade of the division, Ind. 49th Bde. had its H.Q. in Heirok and its task was that of preventing any Japanese infiltration between the positions held by Indian 23rd Division and those of Indian 20th Division on the Ukhrul road. The Japanese were actively probing the positions held by Indian 23rd Division and had succeeded in seizing a prominent hill feature about three miles away from Palel itself. Several days of fierce fighting with much artillery and air support were required before the Japanese could be thrust off this hill and from others nearby. Small parties of Japanese actually managed to reach the bridge and the airfield at Palel before the area was finally cleared.

Early in July the active patrolling by Indian 23rd Division was intensified since it seemed probable that the Japanese would shortly be forced to withdraw eastwards and preparations were made for the pursuit and destruction of the Japanese should they withdraw. 23rd Division was strengthened by the addition of 5th Bde. of 2nd Division, Ind. 268th Lorried Bde., less one battalion, and a number of armoured, artillery, engineer, machine-gun and pioneer units. Should the Japanese begin to withdraw it was intended to destroy the bridges over the Lokchao Stream near Tamu so as to prevent them getting away and then by a frontal assault, to annihilate them. Two squadrons of R.A.F. Hurribombers were to provide air support. Ind. 268th Bde's. task would be to protect the L. of C. of 49th Bde., to maintain the Nungtak track in a state of good repair and so to engage the Japanese in the Khudei Khulen area that they would be unable to withdraw and escape. Ind. 37th Bde., in the centre and supported by all the corps artillery and a number of tanks, was to assault the Japanese positions at Lokchao. Ind. 1st Bde. was to advance north-eastwards along a jeep track leading to Chamol, attack the Japanese right flank, roll it up and get behind the Japanese position. 49th Bde. was to make a wide turning movement through the hills to cut the main Tamu–Imphal road about ten miles behind the Japanese positions. 5th Bde. was to be placed immediately behind Ind. 37th Bde. on the main road and was either to support this brigade or else was to exploit any success that might be gained. If it turned out to be impossible to destroy the Lokchao bridges, a strong road-block covering them was to be constructed.

The Japanese did begin to pull back and so Ind. 49th Bde. set out on July 20 on its march through the hills to reach Sita on the following day, Leibi on the 22nd and Sibong on the 23rd. During the night of July 22/23 the rest of the division advanced to find the bridges very strongly defended. In torrential rain fierce fighting took place while attempts to construct the road-block were made. By the 27th, 1st Bde. had completed its turning movement and had reached Lokchao. But the Japanese were not to be trapped, they withdrew across the Lokchao Stream and blew the bridges. They then occupied fresh positions and as these were located they were systematically attacked, with air support and finally overrun. The Japanese were soon in headlong retreat and the road to Tamu and the Chindwin was open. Tamu was entered by 5th Bde. on August 4. It was found to be a veritable charnel house. Abandoned transport and smashed equipment choked the streets. The very numerous dead, dead of starvation and of disease, were to be encountered everywhere and among them a few still living but very near to death were found. The moisture-laden air was heavy with the stench of decomposition and flies in their countless hordes covered everything. There was but one way of cleansing this small border town, by purging it with fire.

During this advance of Indian 23rd Division it became possible to appreciate the magnitude of the defeat which the Japanese in this sector had suffered. Several small military field hospitals were uncovered and in them, lying on their stretchers, were the Japanese wounded and sick, shot through the head so that they might be spared the indignity of surrender. Considerable numbers of I.N.A. sick were also encountered and these were evacuated into Palel.

Indian 23rd Division was by now very weary, it had been fighting continuously for more than six months and needed a rest. It was relieved by 11th East African Division and moved back to the Shillong area.

MEDICAL COVER

With Indian 23rd Division at this time were serving:

24, 47 and 49 (Ind.) Fd. Ambs.	68 (Ind.) A.M.U.
9 (Ind.) M.S.U.	7 and 10 Fd. Ambs. Tps. R.I.A.S.C.
17 (Ind.) Dent. Unit	One section, A.F.S.
23 (Ind.) Fd. Hyg. Sec.	

On July 1 the distribution of these units was as follows:

M.D.S. 24 (Ind.) Fd. Amb.	in Wangjing
M.D.S. 47 (Ind.) Fd. Amb.	Palel
M.D.S. 49 (Ind.) Fd. Amb.	Shenam
9 (Ind.) M.S.U.	Shenam
23 (Ind.) Fd. Hyg. Sec.	Palel
68 (Ind.) A.M.U.	Palel
17 (Ind.) Dent. Unit	Palel

When 5th Bde. of 2nd Division joined Indian 23rd Division it was accompanied by an A.D.S. of 5 Fd. Amb. When Ind. 268th Bde. came under command of the division it was accompanied by 9 (Ind.) Lt. Fd. Amb.

When on July 19, 49th Bde. set out on its outflanking march *via* Nungtak–Sita–Sibong, it was accompanied by an A.D.S. of 24 (Ind.) Fd. Amb. and by about 100 Nepalese porters. 9 (Ind.) Lt. Fd. Amb. reached the Palel area on July 24 and established its A.D.S. in Heirok. A detachment of this A.D.S. moved to Nungtak when 49th Bde. was about to set out on its outflanking operation thus relieving the A.D.S. of 24 (Ind.) Fd. Amb. which was therefore freed to accompany the brigade. Evacuation from the Sita–Nungtak area was by hand-carriage to Sengmai Turel and thence to Palel by jeep ambulance. When the division passed through 49th Bde. in its positions at Sibong, a light M.D.S. of 9 (Ind.) Fd. Amb. moved from Heirok on July 27 and opened in Tengnoupal at Milestone 44 on the Imphal–Tamu road. The A.D.S. of 24 (Ind.) Fd. Amb. with 49th Bde. was for most of the time holding as many as a hundred patients, including many critically ill battle casualties. A surgical team from 26 (Ind.) C.C.S. was attached to this M.D.S. The A.D.S. of 5 Fd. Amb. was established in Moreh to serve the forward elements of 49th Bde. After the capture of Tamu and the relief of Indian 23rd Division by 11th E.A. Division, the M.D.S. of

THE RETURN TO BURMA

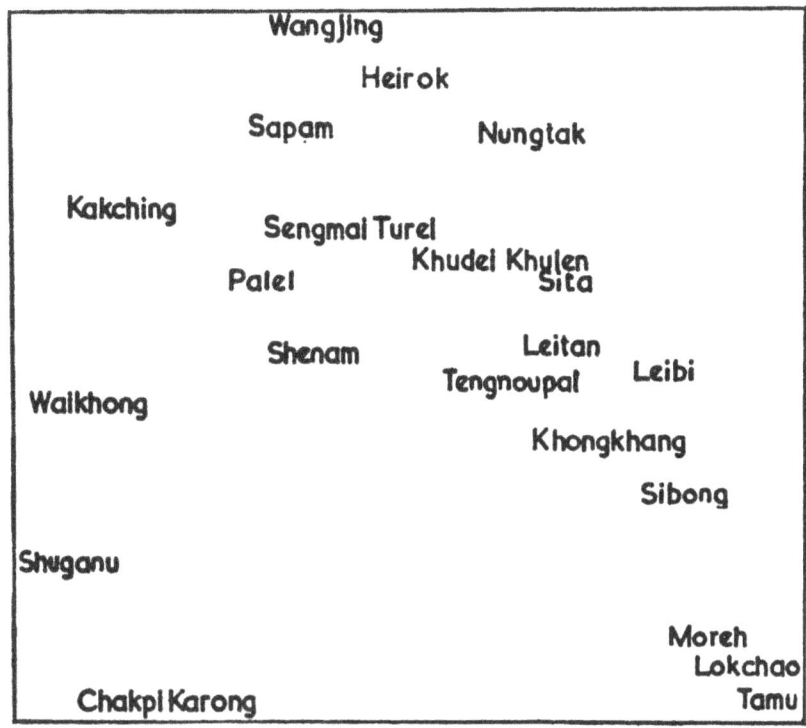

FIG. 40. Wangjing–Tamu

9 (Ind.) Lt. Fd. Amb. at Milestone 44 rejoined its parent unit in Heirok. 26 (Ind.) C.C.S. was moved from Imphal to Palel to provide additional cover for Indian 23rd Division; it took over the site of the M.D.S. of 47 (Ind.) Fd. Amb.

THE ADVANCE TO TIDDIM AND KALEMYO

By June 22 the fighting in the Bishenpur sector, which had been bitter and confused, had diminished somewhat in intensity. It had yielded no decisive result. The Japanese had been withdrawing from the hills to the north of the Bishenpur–Silchar track into which they had infiltrated but were holding in considerable strength their positions in the Thinunggei–Ningthoukhong area, at Ingourek and near Milestone 20 on the Silchar track. After its junction with 2nd Division on the Kohima–Imphal road on June 22 Indian 5th Division had been sent to help Indian 17th Division in the Bishenpur area.

Indian 17th Division had, in addition to its own 48th and 63rd Bdes., 32nd Bde. of Indian 20th Division under command. This brigade was engaged in eliminating Japanese positions along the track. 63rd Bde.

was operating in the hills to the north of the track and around Khoirok while 48th Bde. was holding a position on the main Bishenpur–Imphal road covering Bishenpur and with its forward elements in Potsangbam and Ningthoukhong. But torrential rain had turned the area of these villages into a swamp, the road was a foot under water and the defensive positions that had been prepared were flooded. 48th Bde. was pulled back nearer Bishenpur, therefore, but left a battalion in Potsangbam with a company in Ningthoukhong. On June 25, 48th Bde. was relieved by 63rd Bde. and moved to the track area to help 32nd Bde. 63rd Bde. did not place a garrison in Ningthoukhong.

Indian 5th Division now relieved Indian 7th Division so that the latter might prepare for the proposed major thrust to the south. 32nd Bde. rejoined its own division. While these events were taking place 48th Bde. was instructed to push down the Tiddim road from Potsangbam and capture the villages of Ningthoukhong and Kha Khunou near Milestone 21, and thereafter press on to Thinunggei village, a mile or so farther to the south. At the same time 63rd Bde. was ordered to move southwards from the track area. After much very heavy fighting, beginning on July 11, Ningthoukhong and Kha Khunou were finally captured and held against several fierce counter-attacks. Kha Khunou was not firmly held until the 16th when the Japanese withdrew, leaving behind tanks, guns and equipment in considerable quantity. 63rd Bde. then took up the pursuit and by July 18 had reached Milestone 25 on the Imphal–Tiddim road. On this day Indian 5th Division assumed control of operations in this sector. Nevertheless, 63rd Bde. was instructed to continue its advance under command of this division. It did so until the 22nd when it reverted to the command of Indian 17th Division and 161st Bde. of Indian 5th Division went into the lead.

On July 18, H.Q. Indian 5th Division had moved to Buri Bazar where its 9th Bde. was concentrated. Its 123rd Bde. moved on to the Imphal–Tiddim road to pass through 161st Bde. and to capture Moirang on July 19. Then Ind. 9th Bde. passed through and advanced to capture Churachandpur and to push its patrols as far down the road as Milestone 41 which was reached on the last day of the month.

XXXIII Corps took over operational control from IV Corps on this date, H.Q. IV Corps going back to India for a brief rest. To the command of XXXIII Corps passed Indian 5th and 17th Divisions and, a fortnight later, the Lushai Brigade. The corps now included no less than five divisions, two infantry brigades and one tank brigade. At this time:

2nd Division was resting in the Maram area with its 4th Bde. near Ukhrul and its 5th Bde. near Sibong.

Indian 5th Division had begun its advance down the Tiddim road and its forward elements had reached Milestone 41 on July 31.

Indian 7th Division was resting in the Kohima area.

11th East African Division, newly arrived from the Chittagong area, was moving forward to take over from Indian 23rd Division and to continue the advance to Kalemyo through the Kabaw Valley.

Indian 20th Division was in the Wangjing–Thoubal area.

Indian 23rd Division, which had been advancing down the Tamu road, was approaching Tamu.

Lushai Bde. was operating from bases in the Lungleh–Champai area against the Imphal–Tiddim road, the L. of C. of Japanese 33rd Division.

XXXIII Corps was now instructed to:
  (i) pursue the Japanese with not less than one brigade group on each of the following axes:
    (a) Imphal–Tiddim–Kalemyo–Kalewa
    (b) Tamu–Indainggyi–Kalewa
    (c) Tamu–Sittaung;
  (ii) occupy Sittaung and deny the use of the Chindwin River to the Japanese;
  (iii) seize Kalewa, if a favourable opportunity presented itself, so that a bridgehead across the river might be established later on.

The operation instructions for this new offensive were issued on August 7. The intention was to eliminate all Japanese troops still on the west bank of the Chindwin from Tamanthi to Kalewa and to secure crossings over the Rivers Myittha and Chindwin at Kalemyo and Kalewa respectively. Indian 5th Division was instructed to speed up

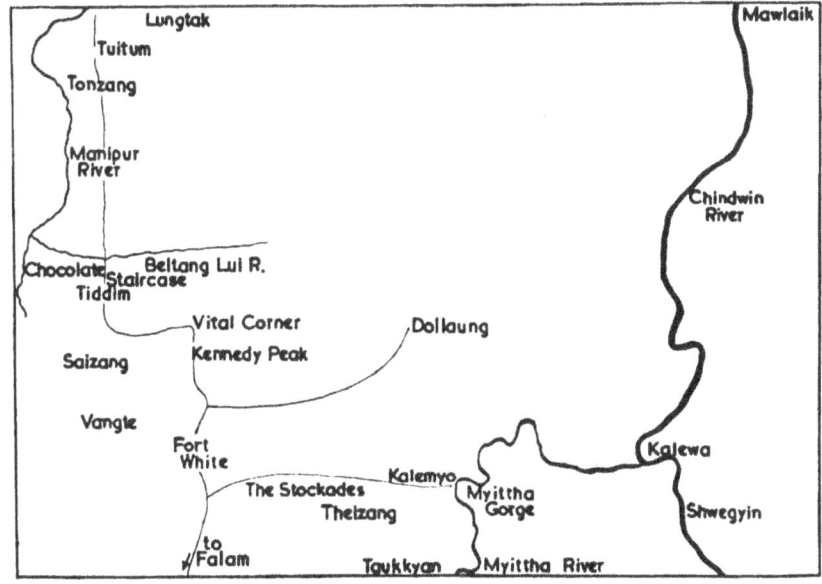

Fig. 41. The Advance to Tiddim and Kalemyo

its advance down the Tiddim road, pressing on to join up with 11th E.A. Division as these two formations neared Kalemyo. 11th E.A. Division was instructed to secure Sittaung with one brigade group, to establish a company of infantry in Kuntaung and in Mintha to protect the northern flank of the Tamu-Sittaung road and then to send one brigade group through the Kabaw Valley on Kalemyo. This division was instructed to keep 3rd E.A. Bde. on the Palel-Tamu road for the time being until further instructions were received from corps. Indian 7th, 17th and 20th Divisions were instructed to engage in aggressive patrolling and to destroy all bodies of Japanese troops found in their divisional areas.

THE ADVANCE OF INDIAN 5TH DIVISION

Japanese 33rd Division was withdrawing down the Tiddim road, covered by the stubborn resistance of resolute rearguards. The advance of Indian 5th Division therefore took the form of a continuous steady pressure down the road itself combined with a number of hooks round the flanks of the positions taken up by the rearguard. By August 4 the division had reached Milestone 50 and Ind. 9th Bde. went into the lead. By the 8th this brigade had reached Milestone $55\frac{1}{2}$, by the 15th, Milestone 67, by the 21st, Milestone 75, just inside Burma, and by the 23rd, Milestone 84. The brigade had averaged two miles a day in the very worst kind of weather and against really tough opposition. It had received incredibly efficient air support. During the last twenty-six days of its advance 9th Bde. had had 9 killed and 85 wounded. No fewer than 507 had been lost to the brigade during the same period on account of sickness. This battle casualty : sick ratio of 1 : 5·4 depicts in the clearest manner how severely was the endurance of these men tested by the conditions that existed. Success is itself a factor that tends to keep the sick-rate low but at this time in this brigade the rain and the mud and the bitterness of the fighting combined to offset the effects of success. 161st Bde. now went into the lead, a detachment moving into the hills to the east of the road in an attempt to get behind the positions in which the Japanese were standing. The road was cut but the Japanese held on to their positions between Milestones 86 and 90. These were then heavily bombed and during the night of August 27/28 the Japanese withdrew and 161st Bde. moved forward to join up with the detachment at the road-block. By August 31 the leading elements of 161st Bde. had reached a series of defended positions extending from Milestone 100 to Milestone 109. It was noted that the resistance now being encountered was not nearly so resolute as it had been. By September 4, Milestone 105 had been reached, by the 9th, Milestone 117 and by the 13th, Milestone 121 and from here the Manipur River could be seen. On the following day the river was reached and found to be in full flood. The bridge

PLATE XX. A transport plane drops supplies, including Medical Supplies. Tiddim road.

Indian Historical Section

PLATE XXI. Tiddim Front. Chin Hills. A Forward Psychiatric Unit.

(Imperial War Museum)

PLATE XXII. Jungle. Lushai Brigade in Action. November 1944.

PLATE XXIII. Loyal Chin tribesmen bringing in wounded of Lushai Brigade. November 1944.

[Imperial War Museum

PLATE XXIV. A Lushai Brigade casualty being carried by Chin tribesmen on an improvised stretcher. [Imperial War Museum]

PLATE XXV. Chin tribesmen have carried this casualty of the Lushai Brigade over 20 miles, through terrible country and jarring tracks.

PLATE XXVI. This Medical Officer has travelled some 200 miles on foot to tend the wounded of the Lushai Brigade.

[*Imperial War Museum*]

PLATE XXVII. Evacuation of wounded from front line by glider.

across it had been destroyed during the withdrawal of Indian 17th Division from Tiddim to Imphal at the beginning of the Japanese assault upon the Imphal Plain. Because the river constituted so formidable an obstacle it was decided to make a wide outflanking movement, using 123rd Bde. This brigade was pulled out of the line and sent by lorry back along the road through Bishenpur to Imphal when it turned south again and travelling by the Imphal–Shuganu road along the east bank of the Manipur River, got behind the Japanese positions before which the division was checked. The brigade was on a pack basis and was supplied by air. By September 14 it had seized the high ground south-east of Tonzang and opposite the point at which the rest of the division would strike the river at Milestone 126. The Japanese promptly withdrew from the river line.

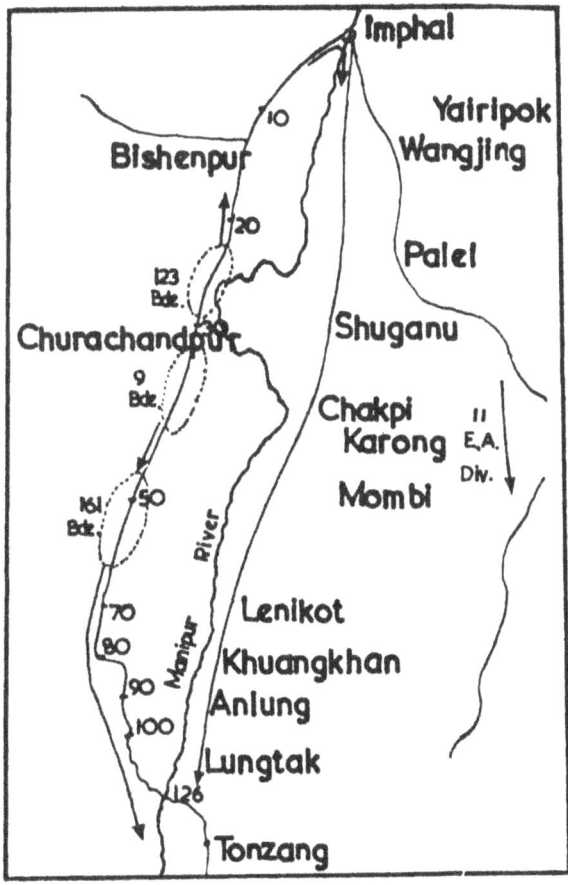

FIG. 42. The Outflanking March of 123rd Brigade
via Imphal and Shuganu
August 30–September 14, 1944

With the very greatest difficulty a ferry was constructed and the troops began to cross the raging torrent on September 16. Tonzang was found to be strongly held. Attacks upon it were unsuccessful but during the night of September 20/21 the Japanese evacuated the place and it was occupied next day. It was now decided that 123rd Bde. should advance on a wide front to clear the road between Tiddim and 'Vital Corner' while the other two brigades maintained a firm base for the division in the area between the river crossing and Tonzang.

The engineering resources of Fourteenth Army were too limited to maintain both the Imphal–Tiddim and the Imphal–Tamu roads and so it was decided to abandon the Tiddim road as a line of communication and to allow it to deteriorate after Indian 5th Division had passed. Since there were no landing strips along this road the division had to be supplied by air-drop. Since the road was to be allowed to deteriorate evacuation along it would become impossible and casualties would have to be carried forward or else 'nested' in villages. General Slim asked for a few nurses to accompany this division on its march down the Tiddim road. Very many volunteered and a few were chosen. Their presence made a very great contribution to the maintenance of the morale of the division.

By the evening of September 23, 123rd Bde. had reached Milestone 143 without meeting any opposition. Indeed the advance continued to be unopposed until the brigade reached the area of Milestones 146 and 147. The Japanese positions there were duly outflanked and their defenders eliminated. The brigade then crossed the Beltang Lui River on the 29th to approach 'Chocolate Staircase', so named because viewed from below the short-terraced lengths of the road as they climbed upwards appeared as a series of golden steps carved out of the purple jungle. This remarkable hillside road had been built by Chin labourers in 1942; it rose over 3,000 ft. in 7 miles and the average gradient was 1 in 2. It was not a metalled road and so at this time it was ankle-deep in mud. The Japanese positions in this area were outflanked as was the custom and the advance continued. On October 17 Tiddim was entered, the Japanese having withdrawn from it.

Without pause the advance towards Kalemyo was continued. On October 18, 123rd Bde. was 2 miles to the south of Tiddim and was nearing Kennedy Peak which had been fortified by the Japanese. 123rd Bde. was instructed to complete the occupation of 'Vital Corner' area while Ind. 9th Bde. continued to advance along the main road. To overcome the expected resistance at Kennedy Peak, Indian 5th Division made two wide turning movements; 161st Bde. on the right, aimed at the road junction 2 miles to the south of Fort White while a battalion made for the road in the vicinity of 'the Stockades' some 10 miles east of Fort White. 9th Bde. was to make a close left hook to cut the road just south of the Peak. The remainder of the division was to continue to thrust down the road. The attack was to be supported by a number of air-strikes. On October 25 the defensive positions covering 'Vital Corner' were located and were then subjected to severe aerial bombardment. But when 123rd Bde. attacked it was sternly repulsed. Meanwhile 9th Bde. had reached Milestone 4 on the Tamu-Kalemyo road. There was much fierce fighting in the vicinity of 'Vital Corner' on November 2 and 3 but eventually the entire area was cleared. 9th Bde., following up the retreating Japanese, prepared to assault Kennedy Peak but patrols of 123rd Bde. discovered that this height had been abandoned. A road-block was established at Milestone 19 by this brigade so that the defenders of Kennedy Peak found themselves trapped. The road to Kalemyo was now open and on the evening of November 13 the leading elements of Indian 5th Division and of 11th E.A. Division entered the town. The casualties of Indian 5th Division during this remarkable operation totalled 88 killed, 293 wounded and 22 missing. Of the 53 P.o.W. the division had collected, most were moribund with beri-beri. Indian 5th Division was flown out to the Imphal Plain to rest and refit.

MEDICAL COVER

INDIAN 17TH DIVISION

While Indian 17th Division was serving in the Bishenpur sector before being relieved by Indian 5th Division, 23 (Ind.) Fd. Amb. and 59 (Ind.) Fd. Amb. (with 32nd Bde. of Indian 20th Division) provided medical cover. They were distributed as follows:

A.D.S. 23 (Ind.) Fd. Amb.	in Khoirok
Lt. M.D.S. ,,	Bishenpur
M.D.S. ,,	Imphal
A.D.S. 59 (Ind.) Fd. Amb.	at Milestone 23 on the Bishenpur-Silchar track
Lt. A.D.S. ,,	at Milestone 21 on the Bishenpur-Silchar track
M.D.S. ,,	in Imphal functioning as a small hospital for the divisional minor sick

Evacuation from the A.D.S. of 59 (Ind.) Fd. Amb. was by jeep ambulance to the Lt. A.D.S. at Milestone 21. From this point the jeep ambulances could not operate for the reason that the track was in full view of Japanese positions in the hills overlooking the track. The casualties were carried by stretcher-bearers along mule tracks for a distance of about two miles to a point where a relay post was established.

From here they were carried to a car post whence ambulance cars conveyed them to the light M.D.S. of 23 (Ind.) Fd. Amb. in Bishenpur. From there they were sent on to one or other of the hospitals in Imphal. The second field ambulance (37 (Ind.) Fd. Amb.) of Indian 17th Division was closed.

INDIAN 5TH DIVISION

10, 45 and 75 (Ind.) Fd. Ambs. were with 9th, 123rd and 161st Bdes. respectively. The other divisional medical units were 7 (Ind.) Fd. Hyg. Sec., 55 (Ind.) A.M.U. and 5 (Ind.) M.S.U. On July 26 a company of 45 (Ind.) Fd. Amb. moved with 123rd Bde. to the southern part of the sector. On July 4, 161st Bde. moved to Buri Bazar and to serve it 75 (Ind.) Fd. Amb. opened an A.D.S. therein. To it 5 (Ind.) M.S.U. was attached. On July 11 this brigade moved by mule track north of the Silchar track to the west of the Imphal–Tiddim road and with it went the A.D.S. of 75 (Ind.) Fd. Amb. to which were posted several stretcher-bearer squads that were attached to 32nd Bde. On July 15, 161st Bde. relieved 32nd Bde. and the A.D.S. of 75 (Ind.) Fd. Amb. took over the A.D.S. site of 59 (Ind.) Fd. Amb. The evacuation chain remained as before.

45 (Ind.) Fd. Amb. had its A.D.S. in Bishenpur and from it evacuation was to 41 I.G.H. in Imphal and for minor cases to the M.D.S. of 75 (Ind.) Fd. Amb. also in Imphal. On July 19, following the fighting at Ningthoukhong, 9th Bde. went into the lead and H.Q. 45 (Ind.) Fd. Amb., which had been functioning in Imphal, moved to a site near Potsangbam and opened its M.D.S. there. The A.D.S. of this medical unit moved from Bishenpur to join the M.D.S. to which the mobile surgical unit was attached. By the 20th the area south of the Silchar track had been cleared and it could therefore be used by the jeep ambulances. The stretcher-bearers were returned to their respective units.

With 9th Bde., as it moved rapidly to the south, went an A.D.S. of 10 (Ind.) Fd. Amb. which opened at Milestone 35 on the Imphal–Tamu road on August 1. Following upon the heels of 9th Bde. came 123rd Bde. On July 20, 45 (Ind.) Fd. Amb. had opened an A.D.S. at Milestone 31 to serve this brigade. On August 5 the M.D.S. of 10 (Ind.) Fd. Amb. was established at Milestone 37 and the A.D.S. at Milestone 48.

Evacuation was now through the M.D.S. of 45 (Ind.) Fd. Amb. at Milestone 19. By the 15th this M.D.S. had moved up to Milestone 37 to function as a divisional M.D.S. capable of holding up to 100 patients. As the advance continued, the M.D.S. of 75 (Ind.) Fd. Amb. moved up from Imphal to Milestone 54. 5 (Ind.) M.S.U. which had been attached to the M.D.S. of 45 (Ind.) Fd. Amb. at Milestone 37 was now moved up to join the M.D.S. of 75 (Ind.) Fd. Amb. at Milestone 54. The line of evacuation had now become considerably extended and ambulance cars were provided. A section of the A.F.S. also arrived to take part in this work.

As the advance of 9th Bde. continued with undiminished speed the A.D.S. of 10 (Ind.) Fd. Amb. moved to Milestone 64 and the M.D.S. of 45 (Ind.) Fd. Amb. at Milestone 37 closed and prepared to move forward. The corps medical units were now moved forward to relieve the rearward divisional ones. By August 21, 13 (Ind.) C.C.S. from Kohima had taken over from the M.D.S. of 45 (Ind.) Fd. Amb. at Milestone 37. It had been intended to place this C.C.S. at Milestone 82 where an airstrip was available but transportation difficulties and the weather combined to make this impossible and so the unit opened, partially, at Milestone 37. By August 26 it had about 90 beds available and these were being used mainly for the accommodation of scrub-typhus patients.

10 (Ind.) Fd. Amb. opened its M.D.S. at Milestone 74 on August 21. The intention had been for 123rd Bde. to pass into the lead at Milestone 42 but the advance of 9th Bde. had been so swift that this had not happened. By August 22, 9th Bde. had reached Milestone 83 and 161st Bde. was concentrated in the vicinity of Milestone 54, ready to pass into the lead when 9th Bde. reached Milestone 83. The A.D.S. of 75 (Ind.) Fd. Amb. with 161st Bde. joined the M.D.S. of the same unit at Milestone 54. It was assumed that 161st Bde. would become involved in a series of outflanking movements each lasting about three or four days and that during these operations casualties would have to be carried forward. The R.A.Ps. of the battalions were therefore reinforced with one medical officer and eight to twelve stretcher-bearers provided from the field ambulance personnel. The equipment that was taken consisted of medical and surgical panniers, transfusion supplies and two or three tarpaulins. It was carried on mules and several riding mules were allotted to the unit for the transport of the casualties. This arrangement proved to be quite satisfactory.

On August 23, 161st Bde. passed through 9th Bde. at Milestone 83 and went into the lead. A company of 75 (Ind.) Fd. Amb. accompanied the brigade and opened its A.D.S. at Milestone 80, its M.D.S. still being at Milestone 54. On August 24 the M.D.S. of 10 (Ind.) Fd. Amb. moved on to Milestone 80 and two days later to Milestone 82. 5 (Ind.) M.S.U. from 75 (Ind.) Fd. Amb. joined this M.D.S. as did also the A.D.S. which had been accompanying 9th Bde. in its advance. The M.D.S. was shelled and a few casualties resulted before its reception room and wards had been deeply dug in. From this M.D.S. evacuation was to 13 (Ind.) C.C.S. The road between the M.D.S. at Milestone 82 and the M.D.S. at Milestone 54 where the ambulance cars were stabled became so bad as the result of the incessant rain that the journey between them took five to six hours. When 161st went into the lead the A.D.S. of 75 (Ind.) Fd. Amb. moved on to Milestone 89 on August 29 and to Milestone 96 on September 2. Jeeps were used to evacuate casualties from the A.D.S. along the steep and exceedingly muddy road to the M.D.S. of 10 (Ind.) Fd. Amb. which, on September 6, was at Milestone 109. The length of the evacuation chain had now become such that it was necessary to place 67 (Ind.) Fd. Amb. u/c Indian 5th Division. It was used to provide a staging post at Milestone 62 on September 9. The M.D.S. of 75 (Ind.) Fd. Amb. had by this time moved on to Milestone 99 where it was joined by 5 (Ind.) M.S.U. from 10 (Ind.) Fd. Amb. at Milestone 82. By September 15 the A.D.S. of 75 (Ind.) Fd. Amb. had opened at Milestone 109 and on the following day this unit moved to the bank of the Manipur River. As the evacuation chain lengthened 7 (Ind.) M.F.T.U. was moved from Dimapur to Milestone 80 on the Imphal–Tiddim road on September 12 in order to provide the means whereby patients could be held for fairly lengthy courses of treatment in the forward area. The staging post at Milestone 62 continued to function there and 67 (Ind.) Fd. Amb. was instructed to establish a second post at Milestone 97 on September 18. As the evacuation line continued to grow longer this second staging post was moved forward to Milestone 109 and a third one took its place at Milestone 97. 67 (Ind.) Fd. Amb. opened its A.D.S. at Milestone 125 on September 24 and accepted responsibility for the evacuation of casualties from this A.D.S. to the M.F.T.U. at Milestone 80.

16 (Ind.) C.C.S. now arrived in the forward zone and was sited at Milestone 37 where it took over from 13 (Ind.) C.C.S. which then moved on to Milestone 82. 16 (Ind.) C.C.S. opened on September 19. Evacuation from 13 (Ind.) C.C.S. was to 7 (Ind.) M.F.T.U. at Milestone 80 and thence to 16 (Ind.) C.C.S. at Milestone 37. Battle casualties were very few in number and most of those who had to be evacuated were suffering from one form of disease or another. The rapid deterioration of the Imphal–Tiddim road meant that casualties had to be either held or else carried forward until Tiddim was reached. It was intended to move both of the C.C.Ss. and the M.F.T.U. into Tiddim as soon as possible, there to form a divisional medical centre. In preparation for this the M.F.T.U. and 16 (Ind.) C.C.S. were moved forward to Milestone 126 on September 30.

On September 20, 45 (Ind.) Fd. Amb. had established its M.D.S. in Tuitum village near Milestone 132 and there it was joined by 5 (Ind.) M.S.U. The M.D.Ss. of 10 and 75 (Ind.) Fd. Ambs. were closed and moved forward to Milestone 126, ready to cross the Manipur River. 75 (Ind.) Fd. Amb. crossed on September 29 and moved past the M.D.S. of 45 (Ind.) Fd. Amb. to reach Milestone 139. An Indian dental unit and 82 (Ind.) Mob. X-ray Unit now joined Indian 5th Division and were ear-marked for the Tiddim divisional medical centre. After October 6, casualties were carried forward by all medical units and R.A.Ps. and two of the staging posts were closed down and the personnel returned to

Imphal. 13 (Ind.) C.C.S. remained at Milestone 82 for it was holding many scrub-typhus patients who needed very careful nursing and who could not be moved without considerable risk. Nursing sisters were sent forward from Imphal to this C.C.S. which on October 7 had well over a hundred of these serious cases.

A corps field maintenance area was established at Milestone 82 to administer the units in the area. It continued to function until all evacuation had been completed. Evacuation from Milestone 82 to Imphal was by road through a staging post at Milestone 37. The jeep ambulances of 61 M.A.S. and of 67 (Ind.) Fd. Amb. and the four-wheel drive cars of the A.F.S. section were used for this purpose. There was no possible alternative method that could be adopted. Three Tiger Moth aircraft that had attempted to land on the airstrip at Milestone 82 had crashed one after the other, so bad had the strip become, and after this all ideas of evacuation of casualties by air had to be abandoned. At the end of October, 13 (Ind.) C.C.S. was able to close down. Together with the staging post at Milestone 37 it then moved back to Imphal.

For the wide outflanking movement by 123rd Bde. towards Tonzang *via* Imphal and Shuganu on the eastern side of the Manipur River, the brigade group was to march *via* Chakpi Karong–Mombi–Khuangkhan and form a base at Anlung. It set out from Churachandpur on September 1 to concentrate at Shuganu. Accompanying it were 45 (Ind.) Fd. Amb. and a company of 67 (Ind.) Fd. Amb., a detachment of 67 (Ind.) S.S., a detachment of 7 (Ind.) Fd. Hyg. Sec. and a surgical unit. The staging section established a staging post in Shuganu and a second one in Chakpi Karong. For its approach march the brigade was divided into a number of columns and to each of these a detachment of a field ambulance was attached. As the column moved forward the detachment established a series of staging posts, each of which closed after the column had passed beyond it when it moved forward to open again. No direct line of evacuation from the columns to Imphal had been organised. Until the columns reached Khuangkhan evacuation rearwards was through the staging posts to 19 (Ind.) C.C.S. on the Palel road. The road from Palel to Waikhong was suitable for motor ambulances. On September 3, a car post was established in Waikhong. From Waikhong to Chakpi Karong the road was passable by jeeps only and so fifteen jeep ambulances were placed at the disposal of 67 (Ind.) Fd. Amb's. staging post in Chakpi Karong for use in evacuation rearwards of the car post in Waikhong. Forward of Chakpi Karong evacuation was possible only by mule and by stretcher-squad. On September 17, 67 (Ind.) Fd. Amb's. staging section returned to Imphal, its task having been completed.

On September 12, a company of 45 (Ind.) Fd. Amb., with a surgical team attached, moved forward to Anlung and two days later to Lungtak.

The mules were now beginning to show signs of exhaustion and the field ambulance company was encountering much difficulty in getting patients and equipment transported. It became necessary to move forward piecemeal in sections.

It was on September 14 that the brigade first came into contact with the Japanese. By the 16th a light M.D.S. had been opened in Lungtak. Accompanying the column moving north-west to reach the Imphal-Tiddim road went a detachment of the M.D.S. and the surgical team. No opposition was encountered. The main body of the M.D.S. moved forward with its casualties on October 19, leaving behind one medical officer and six O.Rs. to tend the immobiles. By this time a detachment of 75 (Ind.) Fd. Amb. with 161st Bde. was functioning on the west bank of the Manipur River. When the detachment of 45 (Ind.) Fd. Amb. reached the east bank of the river all of its patients were ferried across to the detachment of 75 (Ind.) Fd. Amb. on the east bank for evacuation along the main road to Imphal. The personnel and patients of 45 (Ind.) Fd. Amb. left behind in Lungtak were now brought forward and ferried across the river to join 75 (Ind.) Fd. Amb. H.Q. 45 (Ind.) Fd. Amb., reaching Tuitum village, opened its M.D.S. in the vicinity. 123rd Bde. had encountered very little opposition indeed, its battle casualties totalled 6 and its sick 118 during the course of the operation.

By October 5 the following medical units were on the east bank of the Manipur River:

10, 45 and 75 (Ind.) Fd. Ambs.	82 (Ind.) Mob. X-ray Unit
16 (Ind.) C.C.S.	69 (Ind.) Dental Unit
7 (Ind.) M.F.T.U.	7 (Ind.) Fd. Hyg. Sec.
5 (Ind.) M.S.U.	8 (Ind.) Bearer Company

45 (Ind.) Fd. Amb. moved forward to Tonzang and 5 (Ind.) M.S.U. arrived to relieve the surgical team from 19 (Ind.) C.C.S. which then crossed the river and rejoined its parent unit in Palel. The M.D.S. of 10 (Ind.) Fd. Amb. was opened on the east bank at the point of the crossing. 7 (Ind.) M.F.T.U. was split into two section, 'A' and 'B' each with bed strength of about 250.

On October 5, 'A' section of the M.F.T.U. reached Milestone 135 near the M.D.S. of 45 (Ind.) Fd. Amb. and opened to receive patients. On the same day H.Q. 75 (Ind.) Fd. Amb. moved on to Milestone 145 and opened there to accommodate 100 patients. To this M.D.S. the surgical team of 16 (Ind.) C.C.S. was attached. 'B' section of the M.F.T.U. also moved to Milestone 145, remaining closed until October 13 when it formed a small hospital of 100 beds and later of 200 beds. Casualties were now held and treated in the forward area.

After Tiddim had been occupied the advance was continued along the Tiddim–Kalemyo road. On October 19, H.Q. 10 (Ind.) Fd. Amb. moved forward to Milestone 156 and there opened its M.D.S. 16 (Ind.) C.C.S. was now brought forward to Tiddim on October 23 to open on the following day. 82 (Ind.) Mob. X-ray Unit and 69 (Ind.) Dental Unit which had been functioning at Milestone 135 were brought forward on October 25 and together with a section of 7 (Ind.) M.F.T.U. moved into Tiddim. The second section of the M.F.T.U. then followed and joined up with the first section. The divisional field ambulances, having evacuated their patients into the M.F.T.U. moved to the vicinity of Tiddim and remained closed. The officer commanding 75 (Ind.) Fd. Amb. was attached to 7 (Ind.) M.F.T.U. to supervise the care of the scrub-typhus cases which numbered about 200 at this time. By the end of the month the divisional medical centre in Tiddim had taken shape. It consisted of 16 (Ind.) C.C.S. and 7 (Ind.) M.F.T.U. and these together with a number of ancillary units provided about 800 beds altogether. Since at this time there was no possibility of getting patients back to the hospitals in Imphal a great deal of treatment of a hospital kind had to be undertaken. An airstrip was constructed at Saizang, about 9 miles to the south of Tiddim and the first light aircraft landed on it on November 4. A detachment of 75 (Ind.) Fd. Amb. was stationed at the airstrip to act as an air evacuation unit. Evacuation was by L.5s. of the U.S.A.A.F. based on Yazagyo in the Kabaw Valley. At the airstrip there the casualties thus evacuated were received by 10 (B.C.) C.C.S. which was serving with 11th E.A. Division. By November 19, 421 casualties had been evacuated by air from the divisional medical centre at Tiddim. The scrub-typhus patients in 16 (Ind.) C.C.S. were not evacuated, even when evacuation by air had become possible, until they had been afebrile for about four weeks. The mortality among them was only 7 per cent. One reason for this low case-fatality-rate was the presence in 16 (Ind.) C.C.S. of seven nursing sisters who gave particular care to these patients during the early critical phase of the illness.

When 161st Bde. set out on its outflanking movement towards Fort White in connexion with the attack upon Kennedy Peak, a company of 75 (Ind.) Fd. Amb. went with it. Casualties had to be carried forward until the hook was complete and the brigade joined up with the rest of the division in the Fort White area. Arrangements were made for the air-dropping of medical supplies should it be found that these were needed. The brigade marched for three successive nights through the jungle and rested by day to avoid detection. It reached Fort White on November 8 by which date 9th Bde. had also reached this area, having advanced down the main road. The patients being carried by 75 (Ind.) Fd. Amb. were then evacuated to the divisional medical centre in Tiddim. On November 9 instructions were issued to the effect that the H.Qs. of 10 and 45 (Ind.) Fd. Ambs. were to move to Fort White there to establish a divisional M.D.S. capable of accommodating 300 patients. Casualties were few, however, and so 10 (Ind.) Fd. Amb. did not open in Fort White until November 26. 75 (Ind.) Fd. Amb. opened there to admit medical cases and 45 (Ind.) Fd. Amb. accepted all surgical cases. Then as the numbers admitted dwindled 7 (Ind.) M.F.T.U. in Tiddim was able to close and move up to Fort White, having evacuated its remaining patients by air from the Saizang airstrip. 16 (Ind.) C.C.S. continued to function in Tiddim until December 1.

When Kalemyo was occupied, 7 (Ind.) M.F.T.U. was moved forward to Taukkyan, about six miles south of Kalemyo and near to an airstrip on November 21. Evacuation by Dakota was now possible. On November 26, 45 and 75 (Ind.) Fd. Ambs. in Fort White closed and moved into Kalemyo, remaining closed. 10 (Ind.) Fd. Amb. remaining in Fort White, also closed on November 30 and moved forward into Kalemyo. 5 (Ind.) M.S.U. joined 7 (Ind.) M.F.T.U. in Taukkyan. On December 2, 16 (Ind.) C.C.S. closed in Tiddim and moved up to Kalemyo where a XXXIII Corps' medical centre was formed around it. The centre included 7 (Ind.) M.F.T.U., 82 (Ind.) Mob. X-ray Unit and 69 (Ind.) Dent. Unit.

Indian 5th Division, its tasks being completed, now moved back by air and by road to rest and refit.

THE OPERATIONS OF LUSHAI BRIGADE

The composition of this brigade, like that of the great majority of formations, varied considerably from time to time. When first it came under XXXIII Corps it consisted of four Indian infantry battalions (1st Bihar, 1 R./9th Jat, 6/9th Jat and 6/19th Hybad.) together with units of Lushai and Chin Levies and 'V' Force elements. Then 7/14th Punjab became part of it. Its order of battle as on October 10 is given in Appendix XVIII. Its base was in Aijal, about 100 miles to the south-west of Imphal. Its responsibility had been to prevent Japanese infiltration into the Lushai Hills. When the advance down the Imphal-Tiddim road was taking place, General Slim ordered this brigade to dislocate Japanese traffic on the road from Tiddim northwards and to render this useless as a line of communication. It was placed u/c Indian 5th Division on August 15. Three of its battalions were spread along the west of the road from Milestone 44 to Tiddim. The rest of the brigade was launched on a drive into the Chin Hills to capture Falam and Haka and to rouse the Chins. The brigade did all that was required of it and more. Traffic on the Tiddim road behind the Japanese was completely disrupted. Falam was captured on October 17 and Haka two days later. By the end of November the brigade was on the Chindwin 20 miles south of Kalewa and was raiding the east bank of

THE RETURN TO BURMA

the river. It then pushed south along the valley of the River Myittha towards Gangaw and cleared the whole of the area west of the Myittha. The brigade operated for six months on pack transport, supplemented very occasionally by air-drop. It had moved across a roadless country, over jungle-covered mountains and had caused a very considerable amount of material damage and no little anxiety to the Japanese.

MEDICAL COVER

The field ambulance serving the Lushai Brigade was 77 (Bur.) Fd. Amb. This unit was the lineal heir of 1 (Bur.) Fd. Amb. which was last encountered as it made its way to Tamu during the retreat from Burma in 1942. Reaching India the unit had been disbanded, its officers being attached to 1 Bur. G.H. and its O.Rs. to H.Q. Burma Hospital Corps, both in Hoshiarpur in the Punjab. When the time came for the return to Burma in March 1943 these officers and men were reassembled to form the nuclei of two Burma field ambulances, numbers 77 and 78. The first of these was appointed to provide medical cover for Lushai Brigade, the second to participate in the relief work undertaken in an area which had been stricken by famine.

The establishment of 77 (Bur.) Fd. Amb. was less than that of the standard Indian unit and when it moved forward with the brigade the strength of a company was not more than 40 all told and that of the M.D.S. being about 80. Among the I.O.Rs. were certain tradesmen and a number of ambulance sepoys. All the unit's vehicles were left behind at the rear depot as soon as it moved into the hills. Mules, each carrying 120 lbs., and Lushai, Chin or Nepalese porters, each carrying 50 lbs., were provided. A company of the field ambulance required 40 mules or 100 porters and the M.D.S. 75 mules or 230 porters for the transport of equipment, kits and rations. The men were allowed to take 20 lbs. of kit, carried partly on the person and partly by mule or porter.

Blanket	1	Socks, worsted	2 prs.
Mosquito net	1	Vest, cotton	2
Ground sheet	1	Jersey, pull-over	1
Shirts	2	Hat	1
Trousers	2 prs.	Web equipment	1 set
Boots	1 pr.	Dah or Kukhri	1
Shoes, canvas	1 pr.	Lines, bedding	1
Boot laces	1 pr.	Cape, anti-gas	1

Everybody was encouraged to acquire and carry parachute cords for these made excellent lashing material.

The terrain that was to be dominated by the brigade included the Lushai Hills, the Chin Hills, the valley of the River Myittha and part of the range of hills that stretched eastwards to the Chindwin. The average height of these hills is 4,000–6,000 ft. The vegetation that covers them varies from dense bamboo jungle to pine forest. On the eastern slopes of the Chin Hills mixed forest predominates. In this whole area there were no roads; bridle tracks meandered through the hills to connect the widely separated villages.

It is convenient to consider the activities of 77 (Bur.) Fd. Amb. in three phases of the brigade's advance; (i) in the Lushai Hills, (ii) in the Chin Hills and (iii) in the valley of the Myittha River, it being understood that when the bulk of the brigade was in one of these areas, its forward elements were in another. The first phase consisted in the main in establishing firm bases near the eastern edge of the Lushai Hills area.

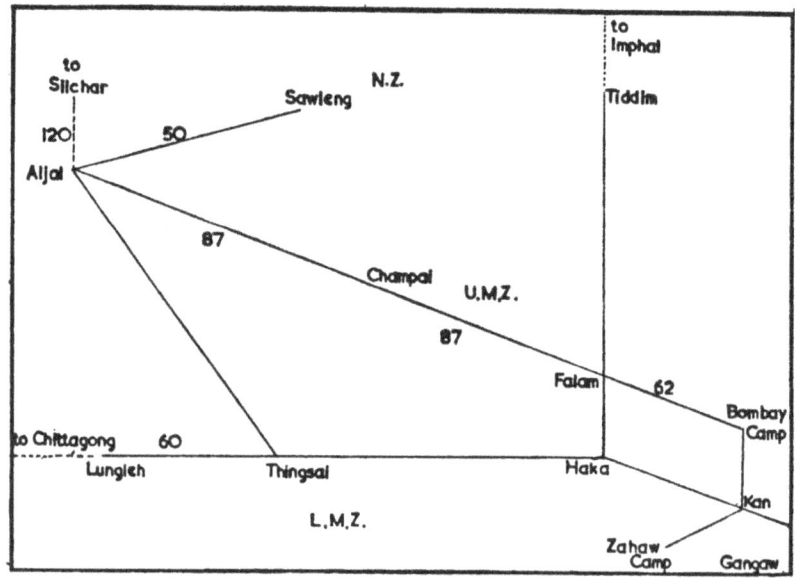

Fig. 43. The Lushai Brigade. Medical Cover
(N.Z. Northern Zone; U.M.Z. Upper Middle Zone;
L.M.Z. Lower Middle Zone. The figures are the distances in miles)

During this semi-static phase the Lushai Hills area was divided into four zones, northern, upper middle and lower middle and southern, the headquarters of the brigade being in Aijal. To provide the troops in these different zones with medical cover, one company of the field ambulance was sent to the lower middle zone (L.M.Z.) and a half-company to each of the northern (N.Z.) and upper middle (U.M.Z.) zones. The headquarters of the unit remained in Aijal, establishing its M.D.S. and retaining a light section of the M.D.S. in reserve. When a fourth battalion joined the brigade this light M.D.S. went with it to an area between the northern and the upper middle zones. The distances between the M.D.S. in Aijal and the forward detachments of the unit ranged between 50 and 120 miles. It was considered that the southern zone was sufficiently well served by the R.M.Os. of the battalions. The troops in this zone were more mobile that those in the others and were in touch with the company of the field ambulance in the lower middle zone. Intercommunication between the forward detachments and the M.D.S. had to be through H.Qs. battalions and H.Q. Bde.

The policy was for the forward detachment to hold and treat its patients, evacuating to the M.D.S. only such as were considered to be unlikely to return to duty for a month or more or who were such as should be sent before a medical board. Each of the detachments constructed a 'hospital' capable of accommodating 50 patients. At the M.D.S. there was accommodation for 150. The R.M.O. could hold about 10 to 14 in his dressing station. Each detachment held a two months' supply of drugs and dressings, one month's working stock and one month's reserve, and each was issued with extra surgical instruments. Indents were submitted through the brigade 'Q' branch. The forward detachments were supplied by air-drop so that their medical supplies arrived with their rations. The M.D.S., while in Aijal, was supplied by land route. In the later phases of the operation supply was entirely by air. The system of air supply was amazingly efficient; on one occasion, for example, 36 hours after an urgent request for two dental syringes had been sent off, they arrived. Only on one occasion did a parachute fail to open and then, as luck would have it, the container landed on soft ground. The wooden panniers proved to be unsatisfactory for the reason that they got broken rather easily. Three-inch mortar bomb containers were substituted for them whenever possible. *Yakdans** were far too bulky and quickly became damaged when the mules carrying them had to move along a narrow track on the side of a steep hill, as was often the case.

Such casualties as were sent back to the M.D.S. were, if walking or sitting cases, conveyed on riding ponies or, if stretcher-cases, by porters on improvised stretchers made out of bamboo and gunny. On the Champai–Aijal route, 87 miles, a staging post, manned by a sergeant, R.A.M.C. and four ambulance sepoys, was established about mid-way and was well stocked with rations and essential drugs and dressings. A nursing sepoy always accompanied any patient evacuated from the forward areas. From Thingsai in the lower middle zone, where the full company of the field ambulance was stationed and where it was running a modified M.D.S., evacuation was not to Aijal, 120 miles away, but along another L. of C., Lungleh–Chittagong. Casualties were carried by porters to Lungleh where an Indian staging section received them. Such as needed hospitalisation were thence transferred along jungle

---

*Mule panniers usually of leather, fitted in pairs on a pack saddle. Normally just boxes, but specially fitted out for medical units. Carried up to 80 lbs. weight.

tracks, down river in country craft and finally by steam launch to Chittagong.

From the M.D.S. in Aijal, further evacuation was to Silchar either by road or else by river. The road journey, 120 miles, was by motor ambulance or by 15-cwt. truck along rough tracks that wound their way through the hills. The journey by water was by country boat down a river that ran through deep gorges; along its course were several stretches of shallow rapids where the water ran exceedingly swiftly. The journey by road and that by river took two days and these were not free from discomfort. Such surgical operations as had to be performed before evacuation by air became possible had to be undertaken by the medical officers of the field ambulance. Four abdominal operations were performed, two splenectomies, one resection of a portion of a ruptured small intestine and one for a ruptured sigmoid colon. Only one of these survived, one of the splenectomies. The M.D.S. in sites other than in Aijal and the forward detachments constructed operating theatres, usually of wood or bamboo with a tarpaulin roof and with gunny walls lined with parachute cloth. The earth floor was covered with a tarpaulin. A portable steam steriliser and dressing drums were supplied by air. A theatre lighting set was improvised as was also an operating table. In Aijal the M.D.S. was allowed the use of the operating theatre and one of the wards of the Station Military Hospital.

When the brigade moved into the Chin Hills its units became much more mobile. The Japanese had begun to withdraw from the Imphal Plain. In the northern zone some of the troops advanced so far from their base at Sawleng that the medical detachment together with the troops left behind at this base were withdrawn to Aijal and two nursing orderlies from the field ambulance were attached to the R.M.O. of the battalion. Casualties were thenceforward evacuated northward to Tiddim until the column turned southwards and then they could more conveniently be sent to the light M.D.S. located between the northern and upper middle zones.

From now onwards it was the rule that the detachment of the field ambulance moved with the column to which it was attached. Temporary *bashas*, constructed by field ambulance personnel, were used to provide 'hospital' accommodation. Time came when Aijal had receded too far to the rear and so the M.D.S. moved forward to Falam, 174 miles away, soon after its capture in October. Owing to transport difficulties the detachment that had joined the M.D.S. from Sawleng was obliged to stay in Champai for the time being. The troops that had been operating in the northern and upper middle zones now joined up at Falam. Those in the lower middle and the southern zones moved east, then south-east through Haka and then south. The brigade was now ordered to move into the Myittha Valley. The M.D.S. remained in Falam, in the civil hospital there. There was very little evacuation during this phase. Casualties were few and were carried forward with the columns, riding ponies being used. An L.5 airstrip was constructed at Ramkhlau and to this 13 casualties were sent from Falam, 13 miles away.

The entry of the brigade into the Myittha Valley was hurried for the Japanese were now retreating very rapidly. The M.D.S., having stayed in Falam for three weeks, moved forward to 'Bombay Camp' along with the brigade's main H.Q. The detachments moved with the battalions, of which at this time there were only three. From 'Bombay Camp' air evacuation was the rule and so the field ambulance was at long last able to evacuate rather than to hold. The detachments with the battalions now provided A.D.Ss. from which casualties were evacuated to the M.D.S. by porter, bullock cart, country boat or jeep. When the river was used the journey stretched to about 60 miles so that it was necessary to provide two staging posts along the route. Each of these was staffed by a sergeant, R.A.M.C. and four ambulance sepoys. Then the M.D.S. moved forward to Zahaw Camp, on the way to Gangaw and evacuation continued to be by air for there was an airstrip near the M.D.S. site.

CASUALTIES

Malaria was the chief cause of morbidity in the brigade. The benign, malignant and quartan forms were all encountered. The incidence reached its peak during the last week of June 1944 and thereafter declined to reach its lowest point during the last week of October. The subsequent rise was just about half of that of the previous June. Relapses were about two and a half times as frequent as were fresh cases. Strict anti-malaria precautions were enforced throughout the whole operation and suppressive mepacrine was taken regularly.

Diarrhoea, it was noticed, occurred relatively frequently among such as were of poor physique, who were anaemic or had suffered from malaria. As is always the case in such circumstances the men with venereal disease had contracted it in the plains before entering the hills or had recently been on leave.

Typhus appeared in epidemic form in late November when the brigade was concentrating in the foothills in the Myittha Valley. It was typically scrub-typhus country with much tall elephant grass. A member of the Typhus Research Team who visited the brigade expressed the opinion that the disease was undoubtedly scrub-typhus. In retrospect it seemed that at this particular time the medical officers were inclined to make the diagnosis of scrub-typhus in instances of malaria, not a bad fault for it meant that the patient did receive special care. There were only three deaths ascribed to the disease among those who were not evacuated beyond the field ambulance. In an attempt to control the incidence of the

TABLE 31

Lushai Brigade. 77 (Bur.) Fd. Amb. Admissions, Discharges, Transfers and Deaths

	M.D.S. H.Q.	A.D.S. 'A' Company	A.D.S. 'B' Company	Totals
Admissions	2,169	469	549	3,187
Discharges	1,087	322	483	1,892
Transfers	1,062	143	64	1,269
Deaths	18	4	2	24

Of the transfers from the M.D.S. 499 were transported by air, 175 by road, 334 by water and 54 were handed over to the unit that relieved the M.D.S.

TABLE 32

Lushai Brigade. 77 (Bur.) Fd. Amb. Principal Causes of Admission

Cause of Admission	M.D.S. H.Q.	A.D.S. 'A' Company	A.D.S. 'B' Company	Totals
Battle Casualty	3	9	—	12
Battle Accident	21	13	7	41
Malaria B.T.	99	59	8	166
„ M.T.	464	4	8	476
„ Q.	2	—	—	2
„ Clinical	263	217	259	739
„ Cachexia	91	4	—	95
Malaria totals	919	284	275	1,478
Typhus	204	39	7	250
Dysentery amoebic	31	8	2	41
„ bacillary	27	6	13	46
Diarrhoea	115	11	10	136
V.D. Syphilis	2	—	—	2
„ Gonorrhoea	15	—	1	16
„ venereal sore N.Y.D.	6	1	1	8
Scabies	79	1	47	127
Pneumonia	8	2	14	24
Bronchitis	15	5	10	30

disease 'Skat' (Dimethyl-phthalate) was used liberally for the spraying of clothing and for the smearing of the skin of all exposed parts of the body.

When the effects of the activities of the brigade are considered it is of considerable interest to note that these were achieved at a cost of only a dozen battle casualties. The number of the killed was not known to the

THE RETURN TO BURMA

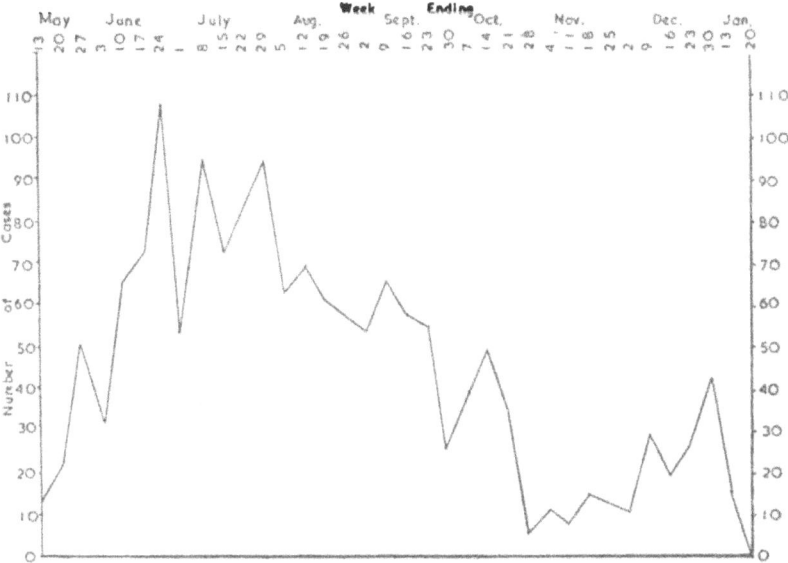

FIG. 44. 77 (Bur.) Fd. Amb. Admissions on account of Malaria, Lushai Brigade. May 1944–January 1945

field ambulance. None of the wounded who were admitted died while in the care of the field ambulance. From the purely medical point of view an interesting aspect of the activities of 77 (Bur.) Fd. Amb. is that which relates to the difficulty of evacuating casualties during the early part of the operation. During this period it would have been reasonable to have attached a mobile surgical unit with mule and porter transport to the field ambulance. But as things turned out, such a unit would have been called upon to do very little indeed. When the light airstrip became available all difficulties connected with evacuation disappeared. Here, as elsewhere at this time, the U.S. light aircraft pilots rendered service of immense value. The lack of a dentist was felt at times; it was only late in the operation that a dental officer visited the brigade. The riding ponies that were used for casualty evacuation were not ideal for this purpose. It would have been far better to have attached a field ambulance troop with its mules to the field ambulance.

THE ADVANCE OF 11TH EAST AFRICAN DIVISION

This division, consisting of 21st, 25th and 26th Brigades, had been serving in Ceylon Army Command before sailing for Chittagong in May 1944. It then passed u/c Fourteenth Army and was under 404 Area for local administration. At the end of July it moved to Imphal by air and by rail and its Main H.Q. opened in Palel on August 6. It then began to move towards Tamu and thence down the Kabaw Valley for Kalemyo. As Indian 5th Division moved down the axis Fort White–Kalemyo, the

East African division came down from the north with the ultimate object of capturing Kalewa.

On August 16 its 26th Bde. crossed the Yu River and having overcome the resistance of a series of Japanese rearguards entered Sittaung on September 4. The conditions in this small riverside town were as hideous as were those that had appalled Indian 23rd Division when entering Tamu. By September 10 a small bridgehead had been established on the east bank of the Chindwin. The rest of the division entered the Kabaw Valley and swept such opposition as was encountered before it. At Yazagyo the advance was checked for a while but was later continued until on November 2 the division was only 12 miles away from Kalemyo.

Meanwhile a battalion had been working its way through the hills to the east in an attempt to capture the small but useful river port of Mawlaik on the Chindwin. The place was found to be strongly held. On October 20 an assault upon it was launched by 21st E.A. Bde. but without success. It was not until November 10, after a series of fierce and long sustained attacks that the Japanese defenders were finally driven out. Immediately the place had been captured 1st Assam Regt., on loan to 11th E.A. Division, crossed the river, established a small bridgehead on the eastern bank and turned south to move on Kalewa.

By November 12 the main body of the division had reached a point only 5 miles away from Kalemyo. 21st Bde., moving down both sides of the Chindwin, now began to constitute a serious threat to the Japanese opposing the main body of the division. The Japanese withdrew and 21st and 25th Bdes. entered Kalemyo on November 13.

26th Bde. occupied Indainggyi while 25th Bde. moved down the axis of the road towards Kalewa. Until Hurribombers had blasted their positions before Kalewa the Japanese resistance was most resolute. They withdrew in an orderly fashion, taking with them the bulk of the stores from the numerous dumps in the vicinity. It was not until December 2 that Kalewa was entered. During the night of December 3/4, 25th E.A. Bde. crossed the Chindwin at Kalewa and was followed by 26th E.A. Bde. The Japanese violently opposed the establishment of the bridgehead and again the aid of the Air Force had to be enlisted. It was not until the 8th that the Japanese ceased their attempts to prevent the enlargement of the bridgehead and began to withdraw towards Shwegyin. On the 10th the Chindwin was bridged. The spans of a Bailey bridge, 1,154 ft. long, were assembled on the Myittha, towed into the Chindwin, and fitted together all in the brief space of thirty-six hours by the Indian Sappers and Miners. Japanese aircraft unsuccessfully attempted to destroy the bridge soon after its erection. It was not damaged and the bridgehead on the eastern bank was speedily enlarged. By December 13 the Japanese having withdrawn further to the east, Shwegyin was occupied.

This event marked the end of 11th East African Division's contribution to Fourteenth Army's reoccupation of Burma. Towards the end of the year the division moved back to Bokajan near Golaghat in Assam to rest and refit. In April 1945 it moved again, to Chas near Ranchi in Bihar and there it remained until the war ended.

MEDICAL COVER

The divisional medical units that accompanied the division to Ceylon were 2 (Zanzibar), 6 (Uganda) and 10 (East African) Field Ambulances, 71 (East African) Field Hygiene Section and 21 (East African) Mobile Malaria Section. While serving in Ceylon Army Command in March 1944 a reorganisation of the divisional medical services was effected and out of the three field ambulances were created 2 (Z), 6 (U) and 10 (E.A.) Fd. Ambs. and 60 (E.A.) and 61 (Z.) Field Dressing Stations. From 5th Group East African Auxiliary Pioneer Corps was formed a stretcher-bearer company. In May, 150 E.A.G.H., 11 (E.A.) Con. Depot and 10 (Belgian Congo) C.C.S. became attached to the division and for the transport of its casualties 2 (E.A.) M.A.C. was provided.

When the division reached Chittagong its medical units were sited either in Chittagong itself or else in Dohazari. It was arranged that 10 (B.C.) C.C.S. should replace 81 (West African) C.C.S. in Patia. The division's sick were admitted to 56 I.G.H. in Chittagong (Africans) and to 68 I.G.H. in Chittagong and 82 I.G.H. (C.) in Dohazari (British). Serving the needs of the division were 27 (Ind.) Fd. Lab. attached to 56 I.G.H. and 32 (Ind.) Depot of Medical Stores which was situated on the Chittagong–Hathazari road. E.A. Hospital Sections 111, 112 and 113, which had been attached to 56 I.G.H. were replaced by 150 E.A.G.H.

When the division moved to Imphal, Calcutta was designated as the divisional base. The division took over from Indian 23rd Division in the Palel area and to it were attached 14 (Ind.) M.S.U., 27 F.T.U. and a detachment of the A.F.S. 61 (Z.) F.D.S., 27 F.T.U. and 14 (Ind.) M.S.U. moved at once to a site just to the north of Moreh there to set up an advanced surgical centre. Evacuation therefrom was by way of a casualty clearing post established by 6 (U.) Fd. Amb. at Milestone 71 on the Imphal–Tamu road, to 10 (B.C.) C.C.S. in Palel. A detachment of this C.C.S. was attached to 89 I.G.H. in Imphal to look after African patients. 10 (E.A.) Fd. Amb. moved to Milestone 69 and sent a half-company to Hesin, east of Tamu along the Tamu–Sittaung road, and detachments with the patrols of 36th K.A.R. which were probing along this road towards Sittaung and to the south of Sittaung in the direction of Kundaung. On August 12, H.Qs. 71 (E.A.) Fd. Hyg. Sec. and 21 (E.A.) Mob. Mal. Sec. moved forward to Milestone 69 and a surgical team from 10 (B.C.) C.C.S. was attached to 61 (Z.) F.D.S. and 14 (Ind.)

M.S.U. to 6 (U.) Fd. Amb. On the 14th the half-company of 10 (E.A.) Fd. Amb. in Hesin was relieved by a company of 6 (U.) Fd. Amb. and rejoined its parent unit at Milestone 69. 76 (Ind.) S.S. now joined the division and was posted to Milestone 54. 10 (E.A.) Fd. Amb. moved forward to Kyauksedi, farther along the Tamu–Sittaung road and sent a detachment with 36th K.A.R. to Sunle on the Myittha River and on the Tamu–Kalemyo road. 2 (Z.) Fd. Amb. was moved from Palel to Yanan, on the Tamu–Sittaung road about midway between Hesin and Kyauksedi.

By August 24 the evacuation chain had become lengthened and the distribution of the medical units was as follows:

Palel ———————————— Tamu ———————————Sittaung

Strung along the Palel–Tamu Road	Strung along the Tamu–Sittaung Road
Palel 10 (B.C.) C.C.S. 112 E.A. Hosp. Sec. H.Q. 2 (E.A.) M.A.C.	At the Ferry over the Yu River Detach. 10 (E.A.) Fd. Amb. and two A.F.S. cars
M.S. 54 76 (Ind.) S.S. and one car of 2 (E.A.) M.A.C.	Kyauksedi Detach. 6 (U.) Fd. Amb.
M.S. 60 H.Q.A.F.S.	M.S. 18 Two A.F.S. cars and two jeeps
M.S. 69 61 (Z.) F.D.S. 27 F.T.U. H.Q.5 (Ind.) Bearer Coy. Surgeon *ex* 60 (E.A.) F.D.S.	M.S. 30 Coy. 6 (U.) Fd. Amb. and two A.F.S. jeeps
M.S. 70 2004 (E.A.) Stretcher Bearer Coy.	Strung along the Kabaw Valley from Tamu M.S. 2 Car-post. Two amb. cars M.S. 9½ R.M.O. 13th K.A.R. One squad Stretcher-bearers Two A.F.S. jeeps Witok Detach. 10 (E.A.) Fd. Amb. and one jeep Sunle A.D.S. 10 (E.A.) Fd. Amb. and four jeeps 4 miles beyond Sunle Detach. 10 (E.A.) Fd. Amb. and one jeep

To Kalemyo

Early in September, 10 (B.C.) C.C.S. moved forward to Milestone 69 and 61 (Z.) F.D.S. closed and moved on to Htinzin, beyond Sunle in the Kabaw Valley. On the same evacuation route 6 (U.) Fd. Amb. opened at

Milestone 9½, it being no longer required on the Tamu–Sittaung evacuation route. 40 (E.A.) F.S.U. was now with the division and was posted to Htinzin there to join 61 (Z.) F.D.S. 10 (E.A.) Fd. Amb. then moved to the head of the evacuation chain along the Kabaw Valley to open in Khampat. Evacuation along the Kabaw Valley became impossible for a time because of the effects of the rain. The track was ankle-deep in mud and the frail bridges over the swollen streams were quickly washed away. The casualties had to be held in the divisional units for the time being. D.U.K.Ws. were used for casualty evacuation between Khampat and Hesin and across the Yu River at Sunle. At one time elephants were used for the same purpose.

XXXIII Corps now moved 88 I.G.H.(C.) with 111, 112 and 113 E.A. Hosp. Secs. attached, forward from Imphal to Milestone 30 on the Palel–Tamu road. 10 (B.C.) C.C.S., thus being freed, moved on to Moreh where it was joined by 26 (Ind.) C.C.S. from Palel. 10 (B.C.) C.C.S. then moved forward to Milestone 32½ between Htinzin and Khampat and shortly afterwards into Khampat itself. To 26 (Ind.) C.C.S. an East African hospital section, improvised out of divisional resources was attached to look after African patients.

In the second week of October, 165th Liaison Squadron of No. 1 Commando Gp. U.S.A.A.F. arrived in Tamu. It had some thirty L.5s. and three Norseman C.64s. as well as a number of gliders and a few Tiger Moths, adapted to take stretchers and with R.A.F. pilots. These began at once to transport to Tamu between 80 and 100 casualties daily from the forward airstrip which was about 30 miles to the south of Tamu. The journey took a quarter of an hour or so.

As the division continued to move down the Kabaw Valley the medical units, leap-frogging, moved on to Yazagyo, 10 (E.A.) Fd. Amb. reaching there first, soon to be followed by the field transfusion unit, the mobile malaria section, the field hygiene section and 6 (U.) Fd. Amb.

Serving 21st E.A. Bde. as this moved down the line of the Chindwin towards Mawlaik was 2 (Z.) Fd. Amb. which opened in Mawku, evacuation being by air to Yazagyo. In the Kabaw Valley 61 (Z.) F.D.S., 6 (U.) Fd. Amb., 27 F.T.U. and a little later 60 (E.A.) F.D.S. moved forward to Honnaing, just to the north of Inbaung. Next 61 (Z.) F.D.S. with 40 (E.A.) F.S.U. and 10 (E.A.) Fd. Amb. moved on to a site south of Indainggyi and evacuated their casualties to the airstrip at Honnaing. Corps then moved 13 (Ind.) C.C.S. to Honnaing, the airstrip at Kyigon being used for evacuation.

When Kalewa was occupied 40 (E.A.) F.S.U., 27 F.T.U. and 6 (U.) Fd. Amb. moved into the village and one company of the field ambulance went into the ferry-head on the west bank of the Chindwin just to the north of Kalewa together with four sections of the stretcher-bearer company. By December 12, 61 (Z.) F.D.S., 40 (E.A.) F.S.U. and 27

F.T.U. were functioning in the bridgehead on the east bank. Evacuation was across the river and then by jeep to an airstrip in north Kalewa or by ambulance car to 13 (Ind.) C.C.S. in Honnaing.

When the division moved to the Golaghat area to rest 15 (E.A.) M.F.T.U. joined it. In the Sittaung bridgehead at the beginning of October, Ind. 268th Bde. had taken over from 11th East African Division. With this brigade was 9 (Ind.) Lt. Fd. Amb. which relieved 6 (U.) Fd. Amb.

MEDICAL ARRANGEMENTS

On July 1, H.Q. XXXIII Corps moved into Imphal so that until H.Q. IV Corps left for India there were medical branches of two corps H.Qs. functioning side by side. When XXXIII Corps took over it came to include Indian 5th, Indian 7th, 11th East African, Indian 19th and Indian 20th Divisions, Ind. 268th Bde. and Ind. 254th and 255th Tk. Bdes. and no less than fifty medical units of different kinds. An additional A.D.M.S. Sub-area post was sanctioned in July but was not filled until September. When H.Q. IV Corps left, the territory administered by XXXIII Corps extended from north of Imphal to Tamu and Tiddim and as the advance towards the Chindwin proceeded the extent of this territory continuously enlarged. The medical cover that could be provided by corps was adequate in the circumstances but Fourteenth Army was faced with the very difficult problem of reorganising the hospital system in its area. The prevailing policy was still to evacuate as many as possible from the forward areas to the rear *via* Comilla and Dacca. In retrospect it is clear that this policy resulted in the retention in the forward area of the relatively severe cases with a long duration-of-stay, on purely medical grounds, and the evacuation to the rear areas of the relatively light cases, for the reason that these could be moved without risk, so that these were lost to their units for a considerable, and medically unnecessary, period of time.

This policy was inevitably associated with the provision of specialist surgical facilities in the forward area for the reason that speedy and safe evacuation was so often impossible. Undoubtedly this arrangement was justified but it was learnt once more that the surgical unit or team that is to function in the M.D.S. or even in the A.D.S. of a field ambulance must be a really mobile unit with a regularised establishment and equipment and the like of its own; it should not be an improvisation. In the conditions that characterised these operations, it was agreed, the mobile surgical unit should take with it only a light scale of equipment suitable for mule transport.

The prevalence of scrub-typhus and the immobility of patients suffering from this disease created problems that were solved by the provision of 'holding centres' and staging posts or in the case of the East African division by the use of the field dressing station.

During the advance of Indian 5th Division along the Imphal–Tiddim road and on through Fort White to Kalemyo two C.C.Ss. and one M.F.T.U. were used to provide medical cover. At the beginning of the advance 13 (Ind.) C.C.S. was in Churachandpur at Milestone 38 and evacuation was to Imphal direct. As the advance proceeded rapidly to Milestone 82 and beyond, the C.C.S. was moved forward in two portions to the corps F.M.A. at Milestone 82 while 7 (Ind.) M.F.T.U. was sited in the vicinity of Milestone 80. Both of these corps units were opened under command of the division. The corps field ambulance (67) was also placed at the disposal of the division and did exceedingly useful work in staging and evacuating up to the crossing of the Manipur River at Milestone 126. Evacuation from Milestone 82 to Imphal was entirely by road with staging at Churachandpur. Between Milestones 126 and 82 the condition of the road was exceedingly bad and cars of 61 M.A.S., of the A.F.S. and of 67 (Ind.) Fd. Amb. were used. An attempt to provide the means for evacuation by air was made but, as has been related, all three of the Tiger Moths that tried to make use of the airstrip at Milestone 82 crashed, one after the other, and so the project was abandoned. 16 (Ind.) C.C.S. was brought up to Churachandpur where it remained closed but provided a staging post where patients could rest over-night.

When the Manipur River was crossed by the division at the level of Milestone 126, because the road back could not be maintained in a state that would allow the division to be supplied and casualties to be evacuated by road, it was decided to place the whole force on air-supply. All casualties that could be moved were at once evacuated to 13 (Ind.) C.C.S. at Milestone 82 with the result that for the next three weeks this unit spent all its time in treating battle casualties and sick, the latter including many scrub-typhus cases who had suffered severely from the journey back to the C.C.S. from the forward area.

16 (Ind.) C.C.S. and 7 (Ind.) M.F.T.U. were now placed by corps under the command of the division and these units, together with the mobile surgical, dental and X-ray units, crossed the Manipur River. Owing to the speed of the advance, however, they did not open fully until Tiddim was reached. Sections did function in Tizaung and at Milestone 144. In Tiddim a medical centre capable of holding 800 patients was established by these units which were on light scales. This centre did a great deal of very effective work during the period when no evacuation was possible. The construction of an airstrip some nine miles south of Tiddim on the only possible site in this mountainous countryside took a long time. D.D.M.S. XXXIII Corps decided that since the casualties, a large proportion of them being scrub-typhus cases

could not be evacuated, it was essential to bring nursing officers forward. The divisional commander accepted this proposal and so four nursing officers accompanied 16 (Ind.) C.C.S. when it moved forward and a further three were flown up in Austers from Palel.

This policy of D.D.M.S. Corps evoked much serious discussion between corps and Fourteenth Army. Criticism ceased, however, when the records of these forward units which, perforce, were holding and nursing cases manifestly in need of hospitalisation, revealed in the clearest possible manner that the policy had resulted directly in a significant lowering of the case-fatality-rate and the relatively speedy return to their units of about two-thirds of those admitted. It was to be observed that the case-fatality-rate among those suffering from scrub-typhus in 16 (Ind.) C.C.S. was significantly lower than that among those who had been evacuated to 13 (Ind.) C.C.S. at Milestone 82. It seemed to be proven beyond all question that these patients, in the febrile stage of their disease, could not endure the rigours that attended evacuation by road.

When Tiddim was left behind, a section of 16 (Ind.) C.C.S. was moved to Fort White and the divisional medical centre in Tiddim gradually closed down as its patients were evacuated by air. By the time Indian 5th Division had joined up with 11th East African Division at Kalemyo, it was possible to bring 16 (Ind.) C.C.S. and 7 (Ind.) M.F.T.U. to Taukkyan, some seven miles south of Kalemyo and adjacent to a large airstrip which had been constructed by the Japanese and which was quickly taken into use. From this medical centre evacuation by both light aircraft and by C45s. was possible to Imphal and to Comilla and also to the corps medical units still in the Kabaw Valley. The M.F.T.U. opened with some 200 beds while the C.C.S. closed down to refit. The rear details of both of these units here rejoined their parent units from Imphal. Corps H.Q. was established in Yazagyo at this time and now that air evacuation had become the rule and as an outcome of the experience gained at Tiddim, a corps medical centre was opened at Inbaung at Milestone 73 on the Tamu-Kalemyo road where a light airstrip was already in existence. This centre consisted of 13 (Ind.) C.C.S., 26 (Ind.) C.C.S. from Moreh where it had been relieved by a unit of IV Corps and 8 (Ind.) M.F.T.U. This was the first occasion when the bulk of the corps medical units had been grouped in this way and it was recognised at once that the arrangement had many advantages. The combined resources of the units ensured a high standard of medical attention and a discernible reduction in the duration-of-stay. An airstrip capable of receiving aircraft up to the C.46 standard, i.e. with a runway 750 yds. long, was constructed and at the same time the airstrip at Indainggale, two miles to the south, a full sized double runway capable of accepting all varieties of aircraft, was under construction and was being joined up with the Inbaung centre by means of a good fair-weather road.

The Inbaung centre was developed in attractive wooded surroundings on either side of the Neyinzaya Chaung which was suitably bridged by the Engineers. 13 (Ind.) C.C.S. which had been resting in Palel after leaving Milestone 82 was the first of the units to reach Inbaung. It was closely followed by 8 (Ind.) M.F.T.U. from Milestone 60 on the Palel–Tamu road and lastly came 26 (Ind.) C.C.S. The centre received its first patient on November 27 and by December 8 was fully extended. In addition to these major units the centre included:

The corps psychiatric centre.
A dental centre with one Indian M.D.U. (B.T.), one M.D.U. (I.T.) and a dental mech. unit.
Two mobile X-ray units.
A sub-depot of medical stores.
A section of a mobile laundry (I.A.O.C.).
A bath unit (I.A.O.C.).
A staging section.
An anti-malaria unit.
A sub-section of the corps field hygiene section.
A M.A.S. and for a time a section of the A.F.S.
A platoon of an Indian bearer company.
The corps field ambulance (67) providing a staging area.

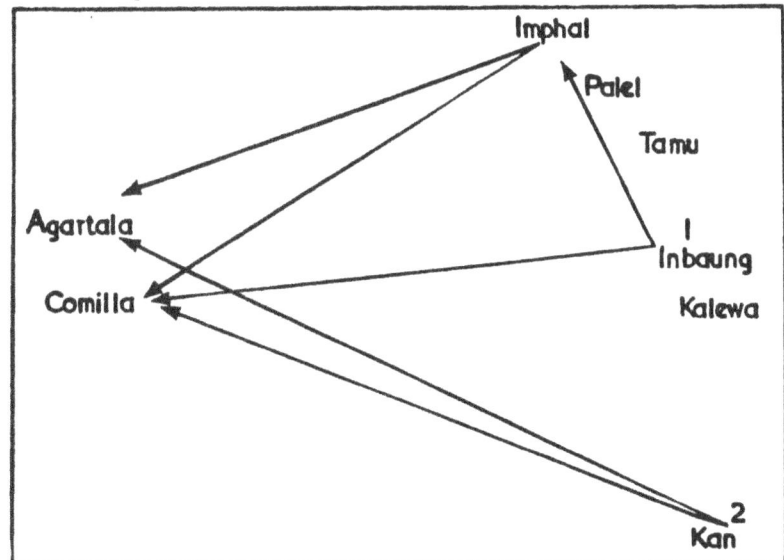

FIG. 45. Fourteenth Army. Air Evacuation Arrangements. December 1944–February 1945.
1. XXXIII Corps Medical Centre. (13 and 26 (Ind.) C.C.Ss and 8 (Ind.) M.F.T.U.)
2. IV Corps Medical Centre. (14(Ind.) C.C.S. and 4(Ind.) M.F.T.U.)

The two C.C.Ss. opened alternately, one receiving one day, the other the next. The M.F.T.U. admitted the medical cases, not, it is to be noted, only malaria cases. The senior of the two C.C.S. commanding officers was appointed as S.E.M.O. of the centre and in addition to running his own unit he co-ordinated the activities of all the units in the centre.

The casualties arrived from forward airstrips in light aircraft of U.S. 164 and 166 Squadrons on the light airstrip. They came from 11th E.A. Division from the vicinity of Kalewa and the east bank of the Chindwin and from the Lushai Bde. operating in the Gangaw Valley. Evacuation from the centre was by C.46s. and C.47s. from the Indainggale airstrip where a detachment of the medical section of Indian 45th Beach Group was functioning as an air evacuation unit.

TABLE 33

XXXIII Corps. Casualties. June 22–December 16, 1944

Average Weekly Strength of XXXIII Corps	Total Admissions to Medical Units All Causes	Average Daily Rate Per 1,000
88,578	49,966	3·10
Principal Causes of Admission	Number of Admissions	Average Daily Rate per 1,000
Malaria and N.Y.D.(F.)	20,430	1·26
Dysentery and Diarrhoea	6,849	0·42
Typhus	2,245	0·13
Battle Casualties	2,868	0·18

Approximate number evacuated by light aircraft 4,600

It is to be noted that typhus accounted for about as many casualties as did enemy action. The case-fatality-rate among those suffering from typhus was 10 per cent. Malaria constituted a constant drain but its incidence was far lower than had been expected. D.D.T. was introduced into the corps in September and was used extensively thereafter. This insecticide, together with the repellents, D.M.P. and D.B.P. and also with penicillin did much to yield a low sick-rate during the extremely trying monsoon period and also while the troops were traversing the Kabaw Valley.

It cannot be denied that during these operations in mountainous country, with exceedingly few roads and these impassable for long periods of time, the casualties suffered much hardship in spite of the provision of medical care in the forward areas.

TABLE 34

XXXIII Corps. Battle Casualties, June 22–December 16, 1944

Formation	Killed Offrs.	Killed O.Rs.	Wounded Offrs.	Wounded O.Rs.	Missing Offrs.	Missing O.Rs.
2nd Div.		10 (Br.)	4 (Br.)	44 (Br.)		
Ind. 5th Div.	5 (Br.) 4 (V.C.Os.)	9 (B.O.Rs.) 65 (I.O.Rs.)	13 (Br.) 6 (V.C.Os.)	44 (B.O.Rs.) 17 (I.O.Rs.)	1 (Br.)	1 (B.O.R.) 6 (I.O.Rs.)
Ind. 7th Div.		13 (B.O.Rs.) 19 (I.O.Rs.)	3 (Br.) 2 (V.C.Os.)	44 (B.O.Rs.) 116 (I.O.Rs.)		
11th E.A. Div.	14 (Br.)	8 (Br.) 153 (A.O.Rs.)	40 (Br.)	22 (B.O.Rs.) 697 (A.O.Rs.)	4 (Br.)	3 (B.O.Rs.) 24 (A.O.Rs.)
Ind. 20th Div.	5 (Br.) 2 (V.C.Os.)	5 (B.O.Rs.) 45 (I.O.Rs.)	3 (Br.) 7 (V.C.Os.)	17 (B.O.Rs.) 192 (I.O.Rs.) 1 (I.O.R.)		2 (I.O.Rs.)
Ind. 21st Div.						
23rd Bde.		3 (B.O.Rs.) 1 (I.O.R.)	3 (Br.)	10 (B.O.Rs.) 4 (B.O.Rs.) 4 (I.O.Rs.)		
Ind. 254th Tk. Bde.			1 (Br.)	3 (I.O.Rs.)		
Ind. 268th Bde.		4 (I.O.Rs.)				
Corps Tps.	2 (Br.)	5 (I.O.Rs.)	3 (Br.)	9 (B.O.Rs.) 21 (I.O.Rs.)		8 (I.O.Rs.)
	32 (26 Br. 6 V.C.Os.)	340 (48 Br. 139 I.O.Rs. 153 A.O.Rs.)	85 (70 Br. 15 V.C.Os.)	1,396 (194 B.O.Rs. 505 I.O.Rs. 697 A.O.Rs.)	5 (5 Br.)	44 (4 B.O.Rs. 16 I.O.Rs. 24 A.O.Rs.)

APPENDIX XVIII

XXXIII CORPS. ORDER OF BATTLE. JULY 10, 1944

H.Q. XXXIII Corps
    149th R.A.C.
    11th and 45th Cavalry
    1st Medium Regt.
    Ind. 80th Inf. Coy (14th Punjab)

2nd Division
    2nd Recce. Regt.
    2nd Manch. M.G. Bn.
    10th, 16th and 99th Fd. Regts. R.A.
    100th Light A.A./A-Tk. Regt. R.A.

  4th Bde.
    1st R.S.
    2nd Norfolk
    1/8th L.F.

  5th Bde.
    7th Worc. R.
    2nd Dorset
    1st Camerons

  6th Bde.
    1st R.W.F.
    1st R. Berks.
    2nd D.L.I.

Indian 7th Division
    Ind. 24th and 25th Mtn. Regts.

  33rd Bde.
    1st Queens
    4/1st G.R.
    1st Buregt.

  89th Bde.
    2nd K.O.S.B.
    1/11th Sikh
    4/8th G.R.

  114th Bde.
    2nd S. Lan. R.
    4/14th Punjab
    4/10th G.R.

Indian 20th Division
    9th Field Artillery Regt., R.A.
    114th Jungle Field Regt., R.A.
    Ind. 23rd Mtn. Regt.

32nd Bde.
  1st Northamptons
  9/14th Punjab
  3/8th G.R.

80th Bde.
  1st Devon
  9/12th F.F.R.
  3/1st G.R.

100th Bde.
  2nd Border
  14/13th F.F. Rif.
  4/10th G.R.

Ind. 50th Para. Bde.
  152nd Indian Para. Bn.
  153rd Gurkha Para. Bn.
  50th Indian Para. M.G. Coy.

Indian 21st Division

Ind. 268th Bde.
  2/4th Bombay Grenadiers
  5/4th Bombay Grs.
  17/7th Rajput
  1st Chamar
  27/5th Mahratta L.I.

Indian 23rd Division

Jat M.G. Bn.
2/19th Hybad.
158th Jungle Fd. Regt., R.A.
Ind. 3rd Fd. Regt.
Ind. 28th Mtn. Regt.
Ind. 2nd L.A.A./A.Tk. Regt.

Ind. 1st Bde.
  1st Seaforth
  1/16th Punjab
  1st Patiala Inf.

Ind. 37th Bde.
  3/3rd G.R.
  3/5th R.G.R.
  3/10th G.R.

Ind. 49th Bde.
  4/5th Mahratta L.I.
  6/5th Mahratta L.I.
  5/6th Raj. Rif.

Ind. 254th Tk. Bde.
> 3rd D.G.
> 7th Cavalry
> 3/4th Bombay Grs.

23rd L.R.P. Bde.
> 60th Fd. Regt. (60th and 88th Columns)
> 2nd D.W.R. (33rd and 76th Columns)
> 4th Border (34th and 55th Columns)
> 1st Essex (44th and 56th Columns)

XXXIII CORPS. ORDER OF BATTLE. OCTOBER 10, 1944

H.Q. XXXIII Corps
> 11th Cavalry
> 1st and 8th Medium Regts., R.A.
> 101st H.A.A. Regt.
> 44th L.A.A. Regt.
> Ind. 1st Survey Regt.
> Ind. 2nd Fd. Regt.
> Ind. 80th Inf. Coy. (14th Punjab)

2nd Division (as above)

Indian 5th Division
> 4th Fd. Regt. R.A.
> 28th Jungle Field Regt. R.A.
> 56th Lt. A.A/A.T. Regt. R.A.
> Ind. 24th Mtn. Regt.

> Ind. 9th Bde.
>> 2nd W. Yorks.
>> 3/9th Jat.
>> 4th J. and K. Inf.

> Ind. 123rd Bde.
>> 2/1st Punjab
>> 3/2nd Punjab
>> 1/17th Dogra

> Ind. 161st Bde.
>> 4th R.W.K.
>> 1/1st Punjab
>> 4/7th Rajput

Lushai Bde.
  1 R./9th Jat.
  8/13th F.F. Rif.
  7/14th Punjab
  1st Bihar
  2nd Assam Rifles, eight plns.
  Western (Chin) Levies

11th East African Division
  5th K.A.R. (Recce. Bn.)
  13th K.A.R. (Div. H.Q. Bn.)
  302nd, 303rd and 306th Fd. Regts.
  304th A/Tk. Regt.

  21st E.A. Bde.
    2nd (Nyasaland) K.A.R.
    4th (Uganda) K.A.R.
    1st Northern Rhodesia Regt.

  25th E.A. Bde.
    11th (Kenya) K.A.R.
    26th (Tanganyika Territory) K.A.R.
    34th (Uganda) K.A.R.

  26th E.A. Bde.
    22nd (Nyasaland) K.A.R.
    36th (Tanganyika Territory) K.A.R.
    44th (Uganda) K.A.R.

Indian 20th Division
  Jat M.G. Bn.
  4/17th Dogra (Divisional H.Q. Bn.)
  9th Field Artillery Regt. R.A.
  114th Jungle Field Regt. R.A.
  111th A/Tk. Regt.
  Ind. 23rd Mtn. Regt.

  Ind. 32nd Bde. (as on page 383)
  Ind. 80th Bde. (as on page 383)
  Ind. 100th Bde. (as on page 383)

  Ind. 254th Tk. Bde. (as on page 384)

  Ind. 268th Bde.
    4/3rd Madras
    1st Chamar
    1st Assam Regt.
    Mahindra Dal Regt.
    Kalibahadur Regt.

APPENDIX XIX

LOCATION STATEMENT. GENERAL HOSPITALS, CASUALTY CLEARING STATIONS, MALARIA FORWARD TREATMENT UNITS, FIELD HOSPITALS, EASTERN COMMAND AND FOURTEENTH ARMY. OCTOBER 1944

Panitola	14 (Ind.) M.F.T.U.	
Dibrugarh	13 (Ind.) M.F.T.U.	
	49 I.G.H. (C.)	H.Q. and 3 British and 7 Indian Sections
	45 I.G.H. (C.)	3 secs.
Digboi	16 (Ind.) M.F.T.U.	
Ledo	44 I.G.H. (C.)	H.Q. 2 Br.; 5 Ind.
Jorhat	45 I.G.H. (C.)	H.Q. 3 Br.; 7 Ind.
Golaghat	6 (Ind.) M.F.T.U.	
Manipur Road	59 I.G.H. (I.T.)	H.Q. and 10 secs.
	66 I.G.H. (C.)	H.Q. 3 Br.; 7 Ind.
	38 B.G.H. (600 beds)	
	5 (Ind.) M.F.T.U.	
Kohima	53 I.G.H. (C.)	H.Q. 2 Br.; 5 Ind.
Imphal	14 (Ind.) C.C.S.	
	19 (Ind.) C.C.S.	
	24 (Ind.) C.C.S.	
	7 (Ind.) M.F.T.U.	
	10 (Ind.) M.F.T.U.	
	41 I.G.H. (C.)	H.Q. 3 Br.; 7 Ind.
	87 I.G.H. (C.)	H.Q. 1 Br.; 3 Ind.
	89 I.G.H. (C.)	H.Q. 1 Br.; 3 Ind.
Palel	88 I.G.H. (C.)	H.Q. 1 Br.; 3 Ind.
Imphal–Tamu road		
Milestone 28	13 (Ind.) C.C.S.	
Milestone 63	8 (Ind.) M.F.T.U.	
Moreh	26 (Ind.) C.C.S.	
Tiddim	16 (Ind.) C.C.S.	
Sahmaw near Myitkyina	22 (Br.) C.C.S.	
Nhila	15 (Ind.) C.C.S.	
	3 (Ind.) M.F.T.U.	
Bawli	25 (Ind.) C.C.S.	
Maunghnama	2 (Ind.) M.F.T.U.	

Redwinbyin near Maungdaw	23 (Ind.) C.C.S.	
	1 (Ind.) M.F.T.U.	
Dhoapalong	125 I.G.H. (C.)	H.Q. 3 Br.; 7 Ind.
Cox's Bazar	49 W.A.G.H. (900 beds)	
	58 I.G.H. (I.T.)	H.Q. and 10 secs.
	72 I.G.H. (C.)	H.Q. 2 Br.; 5 Ind.
Chiringa	29 (W.A.) C.C.S.	
	8 (Ind.) C.C.S.	
Dohazari	82 I.G.H. (C.)	H.Q. 2 Br.; 5 Ind.
Chittagong	12 (Ind.) M.F.T.U.	
	56 I.G.H. (C.)	H.Q. 2 Br.; 5 Ind.
	68 I.G.H. (C.)	H.Q. 3 Br.; 7 Ind.
Fenny	18 (Ind.) C.C.S.	
Comilla	150 E.A.G.H. (1,000 beds)	
	71 I.G.H. (C.)	H.Q. 3 Br.; 7 Ind.
Maynamati	92 I.G.H. (C.)	H.Q. 2 Br.; 5 Ind.
	14 B.G.H. (1,200 beds)	
Agartala	4 (Ind.) M.F.T.U.	
	11 (Ind.) M.F.T.U.	
	86 I.G.H. (C.)	H.Q. 1 Br.; 3 Ind.
	51 I.G.H. (C.)	H.Q. 2 Br.; 5 Ind.
	79 I.G.H. (I.T.)	H.Q. and 10
Sylhet	91 I.G.H. (C.)	H.G. 1 Br.; 3 Ind.
Silchar	9 (Ind.) M.F.T.U.	
	124 I.G.H. (C.)	H.Q. 2 Br.; 5 Ind.
Gauhati	52 I.G.H. (C.)	H.Q. 3 Br.; 7 Ind.
	15 (Ind.) M.F.T.U.	
Tezpur	43 I.G.H. (I.T.)	H.Q. and 10
Dacca	62 I.G.H. (C.)	H.Q. 2 Br.; 5 Ind.
	63 I.G.H. (I.T.)	H.Q. and 10
	76 I.G.H. (I.T.)	H.Q. and 10
	77 I.G.H. (I.T.)	H.Q. and 10
	17 B.G.H. (1,200 beds)	
	46 W.A.G.H. (800 beds)	(Section at Chas)
Sirajganj	67 I.G.H. (C.)	H.Q. 2 Br.; 5 Ind.
Jhingergacha	28 (Ind.) C.C.S.	
Calcutta	47 B.G.H. (1,200 beds)	
Midnapore	39 I.G.H. (C.)	H.Q. 2 Br.; 5 Ind.

Chas	46 W.A.G.H. (200 beds)	
	49 W.A.G.H. (100 beds)	
	152 W.A.G.H.	
	25 (W.A.) C.C.S.	
	28 (W.A.) C.C.S.	
	30 (W.A.) C.C.S.	
	37 I.G.H. (C.)	H.Q. 2 Br.; 5 Ind.
	84 I.G.H. (C.)	H.Q. 1 Br.; 3 Ind.
Namkum	42 I.G.H. (I.T.)	H.Q. and 10
Bermo	4 (Ind.) Fd. Hospital	
Ranchi	75 I.G.H. (C.)	H.Q. 3 Br.; 7 Ind.
	139 I.B.G.H. (1,000 beds)	
	86 I.G.H. (I.T.)	H.Q. and 10
Lohardaga	69 I.G.H. (C.)	H.Q. 2 Br.; 5 Ind.
	83 I.G.H. (C.)	H.Q. 1 Br.; 3 Ind.
Dinapore	21 B.G.H. (600 beds)	
	138 I.B.G.H. (1,000 beds)	

CHAPTER 11

FROM THE CHINDWIN TO THE IRRAWADDY

IN June 1944 the Chiefs of Staff had issued a directive relating to Burma. It laid down that the objectives of the proposed offensive were 'to develop, broaden and protect the air-link to China, in order to provide maximum and timely flow of petrol, oil and lubricants and of stores to China in support of Pacific operations. So far as is consistent with the above, to press against the enemy by exerting maximum effort, ground and air, particularly during the monsoon season, and in pressing such advantages, to be prepared to exploit the development of overland communications to China. All the operations must be dictated by the forces at present available or firmly allotted to S.E.A.C.'

In H.Q. S.E.A.C. three alternative plans were being prepared:

Plan X. The Northern Combat Area Command (N.C.A.C.) (General Stilwell), reinforced by more British and Indian divisions from Fourteenth Army, to be the main striking force and to secure up to the line Katha–Lashio, while the Chinese Yunnan armies advanced to join up in the vicinity of Lashio. The much diminished Fourteenth Army to conduct a limited offensive across the Chindwin.

Plan Y. (Operation 'Capital'). Fourteenth Army to be the main striking force and to secure the Mandalay area. N.C.A.C. and the Yunnan Chinese armies to stage an offensive from the north and to join up with Fourteenth Army in the vicinity of Maymyo.

Plan Z. (Operation 'Dracula'). Rangoon to be captured by an amphibious and airborne operation followed by a drive northwards to link up with Fourteenth Army thrusting south.

Ultimately it was decided to adopt a combination of Plans Y and Z, this to take the following form:

(i) An advance across the Chindwin by Fourteenth Army supported by 221st Group, R.A.F. to occupy the area between the Chindwin and the Irrawaddy. Success to be exploited to include the capture of Mandalay.

(ii) A complementary advance by N.C.A.C. and the Chinese Yunnan force, supported by 10th and 14th U.S.A.A.Fs., to the line Thabeikkyin–Mogok–Lashio.

(iii) A limited advance in Arakan by XV Corps, supported by 224th Group, R.A.F. to secure the forward positions and prevent interference with the airfields.

(iv) As these operations progressed, a sea and airborne assault to seize Rangoon sometime before the 1945 monsoon (about March).

General Giffard, commanding 11 Army Group, instructed General Slim, commanding Fourteenth Army, to prepare for his part in Operation 'Capital' which, as far as Fourteenth Army was concerned, would consist of three phases:

Phase 1   An overland and airborne advance to secure the Kalewa–Kalemyo area.
Phase 2   An overland and airborne advance to secure the Shwebo Plain.
Phase 3   The liberation of Burma as far south as the line Pakokku–Mandalay, where Fourteenth Army could expect to join up with N.C.A.C. about Maymyo.

General Slim, in drawing up his plans, was intending to rely upon the Air Force to supply Fourteenth Army in this operation. This meant that casualty evacuation would be by air. He planned to fight a decisive battle in the Shwebo Plain, north-west of Mandalay and to the west of the Irrawaddy, whereby Fourteenth Army's superiority in respect of air cover and of armour would confer very great advantages upon it. General Slim was freed of the responsibility for XV Corps, for N.C.A.C. and for the huge L. of C. Command in his rear, so that he could give the whole of his attention to the affairs of this vital central front.

In mid-October General Stilwell had returned to the United States to take over the post of Commanding General, Army Ground Forces in the United States. In the China–Burma theatre he had been succeeded by three officers, by General Sultan as Commander N.C.A.C., by General Wedemeyer as Commander United States Forces in the China Theatre and as Chief of Staff to Marshal Chiang Kai-shek and by General Wheeler as Deputy Supreme Commander, S.E.A.C.

Early in November an integrated Anglo-American headquarters, Allied Land Forces South-East Asia (A.L.F.S.E.A.) had replaced 11 Army Group. Under its command were placed Fourteenth Army, XV Corps, L. of C. Command, 36th Division and Ceylon Army Command. Assigned to it also were 'Special Force', Ind. 50th Para. Bde., two tank regiments and a number of other small units of different kinds. It exercised operational control over the Allied Forces in N.C.A.C. through General Sultan. To command A.L.F.S.E.A. General Leese was appointed.

The tasks assigned to the major components of A.L.F.S.E.A. were as follows:

XV Corps
  (i) by a limited offensive to clear Arakan down to the line Akyab–Minbya, thus freeing a number of units for employment elsewhere;
  (ii) to secure a base for mounting Operation 'Dracula'.

N.C.A.C.
  (i) to capture and secure the line of the old Burma Road and its junction with the new road from Ledo;
  (ii) to hold the airbase at Myitkyina;
  (iii) to conform with Fourteenth Army in its advance on Lashio.

Fourteenth Army
  (i) to seize Kalewa and Kalemyo while N.C.A.C. forces advanced to a line Hopin–Nalong;
  (ii) to assault the Ye-U area by an overland and airborne operation and to secure Burma down to a line Kalewa—Ye-U–Shwebo by mid-March while the N.C.A.C. forces made a complementary advance to a line Thabeikkyin–Mogok–Mongmit–Lashio;
  (iii) to secure Burma down to a line Mandalay–Pakokku while the N.C.A.C. forces advanced to a line Maymyo–Lashio.

At this time, November 1944, the general military situation was as follows:

In Arakan 81st W.A. Division had reached the outskirts of Paletwa in its advance down the Kaladan Valley and the leading brigade of 82nd W.A. Division had arrived.

On the central front in the Tiddim–Kalemyo area a brigade of Indian 5th Division of XXXIII Corps had captured Kennedy Peak (November 5). The Stockades had been taken (November 10 and 12). 11th E.A. Division, advancing down the Kabaw Valley was about to link up with Indian 5th Division and to enter Kalemyo. A brigade of this division had taken Sittaung and had moved down both banks of the Chindwin towards Kalewa.

In N.C.A.C. 36th Division was nearing Pinwe and Chinese 38th Division had occupied Myothit and Lungling. The reopening of land communications with China was imminent.

On October 1, H.Q. Fourteenth Army had moved from Comilla to Imphal. On November 1, H.Q. IV Corps had returned from Ranchi to Imphal with General Messervy in command. To IV Corps were allotted Indian 7th and 19th Divisions together with Ind. 255th Tk. Bde.; to XXXIII Corps were assigned 2nd and Indian 20th Divisions, Ind. 268th Bde., and Ind. 254th Tk. Bde. Indian 19th Division was a newcomer to this theatre; it had been raised in 1941 in India and had spent the intervening years in training.

IV Corps was instructed to break through to the Shwebo Plain from Sittaung and to seize, by an airborne operation if necessary, the airfields in the Shwebo–Ye-U area and XXXIII Corps was ordered to advance through the Kalewa bridgehead on the same area. As soon as the two corps made contact Ind. 255th Tk. Bde. of IV Corps was to be sent through XXXIII Corps' front to join IV Corps while the Lushai Bde.

and the newly arrived 28th E.A. Bde. were to push down the west bank of the Chindwin towards Gangaw to protect the right flank of XXXIII Corps and the main L. of C. to the bridgeheads. As soon as XXXIII Corps crossed the Chindwin at Kalewa 11th E.A. Division was to be flown out to India to rest and refit.

As has already been told, 11th E.A. Division, between December 6 and 16, had succeeded in establishing a firm bridgehead at Kalewa. Into this 2nd Division had begun to pass on December 12 having moved from its concentration area in the vicinity of Yazagyo.

A second bridgehead across the Chindwin was established by Indian 20th Division of XXXIII Corps. On November 10 this division was instructed to provide one brigade group on animal transport to operate eastwards from Mawlaik, where a bridgehead would be established, towards Pyingaing *via* Chingyaung. A second brigade was to be prepared to move into the Kalewa area to relieve Indian 5th Division, and the rest of the division was to pass into corps reserve in the Htinzin area. Its 32nd Bde. moved to Sunle in readiness for the crossing of the Chindwin at Mawlaik and its 80th Bde. prepared to move to Kalewa.

On November 22, 32nd Bde. set out and by December 3 was concentrated at Mawlaik. The Chindwin was crossed without any opposition being encountered. Over 5,000 men, 1,450 mules and 30 tons of equipment crossed on rafts within the space of 100 hours. The brigade then set out for Pyingaing which was reached on December 16. On December 19 the rest of the division crossed the Chindwin through the Kalewa bridgehead and moved on Pyingaing.

IV Corps had been ordered to seize Pinlebu with at least one brigade group and to reconnoitre routes from the Chindwin east to the railway corridor down which 36th Division was operating with a view to moving a larger force on this axis. For this task Indian 19th Division, the 'Dagger Division', was selected. The idea of sending this force to Pinlebu and then on to Indaw was that it might release 36th Division to help the Chinese and the U.S. 'Mars' Task Force to clear the Burma Road by taking over the task of securing the main railway line. 62nd Bde. of Indian 19th Division was ordered to cross the Chindwin at Sittaung, as an independent task force on a long range penetration assignment, and to capture Pinlebu. The brigade crossed the river on rafts on November 18/19. Reconnaissance reports were so favourable that on November 20 the plan was changed and it was decided that the whole division should take part in this advance. Several clashes with small parties of Japanese occurred, casualties being evacuated from the light airstrip that was quickly constructed at Nanbon on November 26. Pinbon was entered on December 15 and contact with Chinese units was made as the advance towards Indaw proceeded. On this date Ind. 62nd Bde. set out for Pinlebu. The Mu River was crossed at Pintha and Ingon and Pinlebu was entered on the 13th. The Japanese had abandoned the place the day before. 36th Division at this time was on the line Pinwe–Naba–Katha–Rail Indaw. Its 72nd Bde. was crossing the Irrawaddy at Katha prior to moving south-eastwards while the rest of the division was to move from Indaw to Tigyaing to cross the river there.

The advance of 62nd Bde. continued without incident. Wuntho was occupied on December 19 and Kawlin on the following day. Ind. 64th Bde. of 19th Division entered Banmauk unopposed and its patrols pressed on to Rail Indaw where they met troops of 36th Division on December 16. The third brigade of the division, 98th, was following close on the heels of 64th Bde. Nankan was entered by 64th Bde. on December 19 after slight opposition had been overcome while 98th Bde. reached Kawlin on December 21. By the 23rd Kyaikthin had been entered and by the 26th, when the division passed to the command of XXXIII Corps along with Ind. 268th Bde., the leading elements of the division were on the line Kanbalu–Sadwingyi–Baw.

Indian 19th Division had advanced nearly 250 miles in five weeks over some of the most difficult country imaginable. The opposition encountered was very intermittent and for the most part negligible. The *élan* of the division was quite remarkable.

Because the opposition encountered by 36th, Indian 19th and 20th and 11 East African Divisions in their crossing of the Chindwin and in the subsequent eastwards advance had been so slight, it was concluded that the Japanese commander was not intending to dispute the advance to the Irrawaddy but was withdrawing beyond this river to take up a defensive line on its eastern bank. He had created the impression that he had decided to make his stand on the Shwebo Plain deliberately and it was only in mid-December that it became evident that considerable Japanese forces had already withdrawn behind the Irrawaddy. Since the tactical planning of Fourteenth Army thus far had been based on the reasonable assumption that the Japanese would decide to stand and fight in the Shwebo Plain, this deliberate withdrawal behind the Irrawaddy called urgently for a new tactical plan.

One of the several alternative plans that had been considered along with the one that had been finally adopted, was now revised. This had for its purpose the destruction of the main Japanese forces in the area Mandalay–Thazi–Chauk–Myingyan. According to it XXXIII Corps, with Indian 17th Division added to it, was to force crossings of the Irrawaddy north and west of Mandalay, thus drawing to itself the bulk of the Japanese divisions in the region, while IV Corps, moving secretly south in the Gangaw Valley, was to appear suddenly at Pakokku, seize a crossing over the river and strike with armoured and airborne forces at Meiktila, the main administrative centre of the Japanese forces and the site of their main supply bases, dumps, depots and airfields. In this

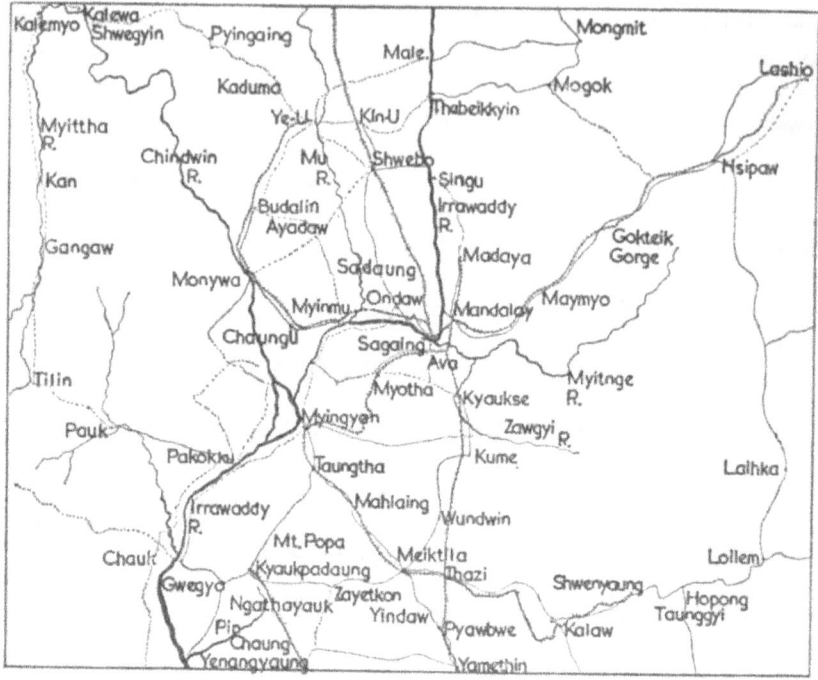

Fig. 46. Kalewa–Yenangyaung

manner it was hoped to crush the Japanese between the two corps, XXXIII Corps coming down from the north and IV Corps standing firm in the south. If the battle ended in victory it was intended that Fourteenth Army should rush southwards with all possible speed to take Rangoon before the monsoon broke.

This was indeed a bold plan and one full of administrative risks. However, as there was no preferable alternative it was adopted. It is to be noted that time was very short for the monsoon would break in March and that IV Corps had to move in secrecy some 320 miles down the Gangaw Valley, making its own road as it moved, and at the end make a sudden and surprise assault upon a town of such importance to the Japanese that it could be taken for granted that they would fight most resolutely to hold on to it. The risks became intensified when on December 10 three squadrons of Dakotas that had been engaged in the maintenance of Fourteenth Army were ordered to leave immediately for China where the Japanese had begun to overrun the forward U.S. airfields. S.A.C.S.E.A. and A.L.F.S.E.A. managed to obtain other aircraft from one source or another to replace those that had been taken away but not before a very serious retardation in the preparations for the new offensive had occurred. Delay at this particular time was exceptionally serious because of the imminence of the monsoon.

General Slim's intentions were made explicit in his operation instruction of December 19.

(i) In conjunction with N.C.A.C. to destroy the enemy forces in Burma;

(ii) to advance to the line Henzada–Nyaunglebin;

(iii) to seize any opportunity to advance from that line and capture a south Burma port.

There was a redistribution of formations between the two corps:

IV Corps	XXXIII Corps
Indian 7th Division	2nd Division
Indian 17th Division	Indian 19th Division
Ind. 255th Tk. Bde.	Indian 20th Division
Lushai Bde.	Ind. 254th Tk. Bde.
28th East African Brigade Group	Ind. 268th Bde.

Army Reserve

Indian 5th Division

Preparations for the offensive proceeded apace. Numerous airstrips were constructed; preparations were made for the repair and maintenance of the railway line whenever this could be secured and boats were collected or assembled on the Chindwin and others were mass-produced by I.W.T. companies from India and local labour out of the teak logs that were provided by Fourteenth Army's elephant companies.

The line of communication, apart from direct air-supply, would be:

(i) by the all-weather road from Dimapur, railhead, to Tamu, 206 miles;

(ii) by the fair-weather road from Tamu to Kalewa, 112 miles. On this section the novel expedient of covering the earth surface of the road with Hessian cloth dipped in bitumen was adopted;

(iii) across the Chindwin by Bailey bridge and by a fair-weather road to Shwebo and thence by an all-weather but very rough road to Mandalay, 190 miles, serving XXXIII Corps;

(iv) by boat from Kalewa to Myingyan, 200 miles, serving IV Corps;

(v) by an all-weather road and, it was hoped, by rail from Myingyan to Meiktila, 59 miles.

It being necessary to persuade the Japanese Command that IV Corps was still moving into the Shwebo Plain on the left of XXXIII Corps and that any movement in the Gangaw Valley was merely an attempt to distract attention away from the imminent attack on Mandalay from the north, a dummy IV Corps H.Q. was to be left behind at Tamu when the real H.Q. moved out and the real H.Q. was to maintain wireless silence until the very last moment.

XXXIII CORPS

XXXIII Corps' tactical plan was as follows:

(i) to capture and construct airfields in the Ye-U–Shwebo area;
(ii) to capture Monywa and construct airfields there;
(iii) to cross the Irrawaddy, capture Mandalay and be prepared for a further advance southwards.

The tasks assigned to the component formations were as follows:

2nd Division was to continue its advance and capture the area Ye-U–Shwebo as rapidly as possible, preparatory to a southward advance on Mandalay.

Indian 19th Division was to continue to advance on its existing axis, Kawlin–Kanbalu–Shwebo, capture Shwebo and thereafter cross the Irrawaddy near Thabeikkyin and operate against Mandalay.

Indian 20th Division was to advance south-east on the axis Chindwin River–Pyingaing track–Palusawa–Songon–Budalin, capture Monywa and then cross the Irrawaddy and operate against Mandalay from the south-west.

Ind. 268th Bde. was to move down the Mu River *via* Kyunhla, maintaining contact by means of patrols with 2nd and Indian 19th Divisions.

Since it was very necessary to capture intact the irrigation works at the Kabo weir, upon which a vast rice growing area depended, and the airstrips in the Shwebo Plain, so that these could immediately be used for the maintenance of the corps and for the provision of air cover, a rapid advance was called for. Without these airfields the rear services could not hope to maintain a corps of three and a half divisions and an armoured brigade along a line of communications that either ran through mountains or else, for the most part, lacked a metalled surface.

2ND DIVISION (XXXIII CORPS)

2nd Division passed through 11th East African Division's positions in the Kalewa bridgehead on December 19 and advanced rapidly on Pyingaing which was reached on the 23rd. The Japanese withdrawal in this area was speeded by the approach of elements of Indian 20th Division which had crossed the Chindwin at Mawlaik. Contact with 100th Bde. of this division was made on the following day. 6th Bde. then moved on Wainggyo and Kaduma, having to fight for the possession of both of these places. Kaduma was entered on the last day of 1944. 6th Bde. then set out for Kabo Weir which was captured intact. Meanwhile 5th Bde. had moved against Ye-U. The Japanese rearguard in this town fought a skilful delaying action and it was not until January 3 that the town was cleared. By January 5 the brigade had established a bridgehead across the Mu River and the division began its advance on Shwebo.

4th Bde. was now brought forward from the Kabaw Valley. Shortage of transport had been so acute that this brigade had to wait there until the transport of the other brigades could be sent back to ferry it forward.

4th Bde. moved along the axis of the Ye-U–Shwebo road, 5th Bde. on the axis of the Shwebo Canal. Opposition was encountered by 4th Bde. at Payan and was quickly brushed aside. Nevertheless delays of this kind enabled Indian 19th Division to get to Shwebo first. The two divisions then proceeded to clear the remaining Japanese out of the town and thereafter 2nd Division continued its advance towards the Irrawaddy on the axis of the Shwebo–Mandalay road and on that of the Shwebo–Sagaing railway. On January 6, 6th Bde. was in Taganan and on the following day 4th Bde. entered Sadaung and 5th Bde. Wetlet. During the next ten days the division carried out wide mobile patrols. By the 15th the leading elements of the division had reached to within a thousand yards of Padu which was found to be strongly held. 4th Bde. reached Wetthabok by the 20th and having rounded up and liquidated numerous parties of Japanese stragglers advanced on Ondaw. A small mobile column secured the high ground between Sadaung and Ondaw on January 17. On the 18th the division resumed its advance. Nyaungbinwun was entered and Legyi found to be clear. On the 28th an attack

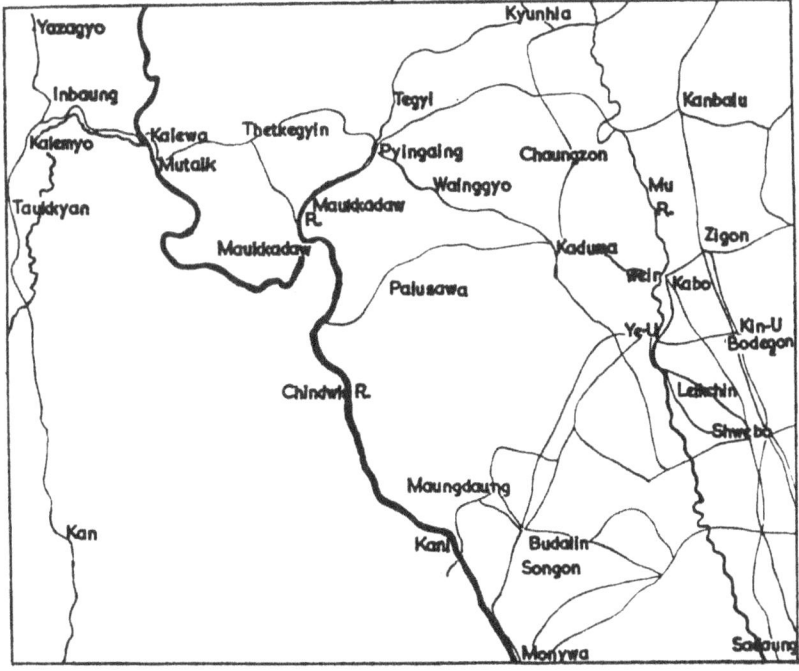

Fig. 47. 2nd Division. Yazagyo–Sadaung

was launched against Kyaukse on the Sagaing road but was not completely successful. On the last day of the month, after a heavy air-strike and bombardment the division attacked and finally occupied the village of Ywathitgyi and on February 4 Kyaukse, on the Sadaung–Sagaing road, was captured.

The Japanese positions in this area were very strong, running from the village of Ywathitgyi to the tip of the Sagaing Hills. Against them the division now began to press.

MEDICAL COVER

At the beginning of this operation the divisional medical units of 2nd Division were all in Yazagyo in the Kabaw Valley, near to divisional headquarters. On December 18, 6 Fd. Amb. moved forward to the vicinity of Mutaik to open its M.D.S. there. To this M.D.S. 9 (Ind.) M.S.U. and 27 F.T.U. were attached. On the 20th, 5 Fd. Amb. left Yazagyo to accompany 6th Bde. on its advance towards Pyingaing. This unit was the first of the field ambulances to cross the Chindwin. On December 22 the unit reached Thetkegyin where it established a car post and where it became involved in an air raid which caused many casualties. The field ambulance opened its M.D.S. to deal with these near the airstrip from which evacuation was by light aircraft to the corps medical centre at Inbaung. On the following day 4 Fd. Amb. moved forward from Yazagyo to Pyingaing, 6 Fd. Amb. in Mutaik closed and 9 (Ind.) M.S.U. and 27 F.T.U. were transferred from 6 Fd. Amb. to the M.D.S. of 5 Fd. Amb. in Thetkegyin. By the 27th, the airstrip near Pyingaing was ready for use and 4 Fd. Amb. provided a section to act as an improvised C.A.E.U. On the 28th, 4 Fd. Amb. opened its M.D.S. in Pyingaing. On December 29, 6 Fd. Amb. moved from Mutaik to Tawgyin, remaining closed until the next day when its M.D.S. was opened. On the last day of the year 5 Fd. Amb. left Thetkegyin for Wainggyo, remaining closed.

On January 1, 5 Fd. Amb. moved on to Kaduma and opened its M.D.S. on the 3rd. On the 4th, 4 Fd. Amb. moved forward from Pyingaing to the airstrip in the vicinity of Ye-U and there established its M.D.S. in which, by the 8th, there were some 200 patients. 6 Fd. Amb. closed in Tawgyin on January 6 and moved on to Tebaunggwe to open its M.D.S. on the following day. On the 8th, 5 Fd. Amb. in Kaduma closed and moved on to Leikchin on the Ye-U–Shwebo road, opening its M.D.S. there on the 12th. This unit next moved on to a point just to the south of Shwebo where its M.D.S., to which 5 (Ind.) M.S.U. and 27 F.T.U. were attached, was opened. On the 17th, 4 Fd. Amb. from Ye-U opened its M.D.S. in Sadaung and to this 9 (Ind.) M.S.U. was attached. In Ye-U this field ambulance had been replaced by 16 (Ind.) C.C.S. and

THE CHINDWIN TO THE IRRAWADDY 399

76 (Ind.) S.S. On the 29th, 6 Fd. Amb. from Tebaunggwe reached Ondaw there to open its M.D.S. to which 9 (Ind.) M.S.U. was transferred from the M.D.S. of 4 Fd. Amb. in Sadaung. To this M.D.S. also, the corps psychiatric team was attached.

On the 4th of February, 5 Fd. Amb. moved from Shwebo into Legyi close to the north bank of the Irrawaddy, remaining closed. On the 10th, 4 Fd. Amb. moved up from Sadaung to Kinywa where it established its M.D.S. to which 5 (Ind.) M.S.U. was attached. Preparations for the assault crossing of the river proceeded apace. Each of the field ambulances had equipped itself with 120 beds made by the unit carpenters out of timber salvaged from bomb-damaged buildings. The bed consisted of a frame made of 2 in. × 2 in. timber over which a ground sheet could be

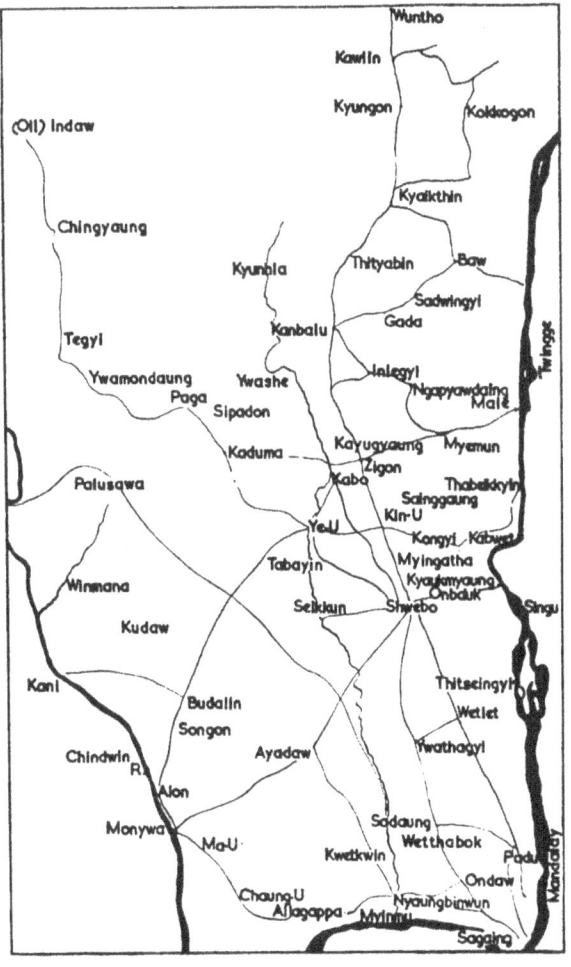

FIG. 48. Wuntho–Mandalay

stretched. It could easily and quickly be assembled and just as easily and quickly dismantled. It was considerably lighter than the standard stretcher and could be packed neatly.

About this time there was difficulty in obtaining medical stores and comforts; as long as three weeks could elapse between demand and receipt. The division was living amid a civilian population among which smallpox was common and plague not unknown. 44 (Ind.) A.M.U. was divided into four sections, each supplied with a power sprayer and a section was allotted to divisional H.Q. and to each of the three brigades. Whenever the tactical situation permitted D.D.T. solution was extensively used. The dental state of the division left much to be desired as for a month and more there had been only one dental officer with the division and so the numbers of those awaiting dental treatment had been steadily enlarging. A second dental officer joined the division on February 10.

INDIAN 19TH DIVISION (XXXIII CORPS)

As has been related, before its transfer to XXXIII Corps this division had already taken Pinlebu and had linked up with 36th Division at Rail Indaw thus establishing a continuous line that ran from India to the border of China. When it passed to XXXIII Corps the division was in the area of Kokkogon, about 25 miles south-east of Wuntho. For its advance on Shwebo its 98th Bde. was moving on Kanbalu, its 64th Bde. on Baw and its 62nd Bde. on Sadwingyi. Numerous Japanese strongpoints had to be overwhelmed, at times with the aid of air-strikes, but by January 2 Kanbalu was entered and the gateway to the plains had been opened. 62nd Bde. entered Inlegyi and 64th Bde. moved on Myemun, sending patrols to Male and Thabeikkyin on the Irrawaddy. At Myothit this brigade ran into strong opposition but this was finally overcome during the morning of January 7 and patrols at once probed their way into Shwebo. 62nd Bde. following up swiftly, relieved the detachments of 64th Bde. in the riverside villages of Male, Thabeikkyin and Kabwet. 98th Bde. advancing from Sainggaung reached Kin-U on January 6 and the outskirts of Shwebo on the following day. The division now concentrated its attention upon clearing the west bank of the Irrawaddy between Thabeikkyin and Singu, preparatory to crossing the river.

MEDICAL COVER

When Indian 19th Division, then under command of IV Corps, moved to its concentration area on the Tamu-Sittaung road, 51, 52 and 53 (Ind.) Fd. Ambs. moved with it. During the crossing of the Chindwin A.D.Ss. were attached to the brigades by the field ambulances. A divisional M.D.S. was established in Thanan by 51 (Ind.) Fd. Amb.

which also opened an A.D.S. at Milestone 6 on the Thanan–Tonhe road. Evacuation from the M.D.S. was by M.A.S. car to 24 (Ind.) C.C.S. in Tamu. On December 4, 53 (Ind.) Fd. Amb. opened in Tonhe to serve 98th Bde. Evacuation from this medical unit was through the M.D.S. of 51. Evacuation across the Chindwin was not without its difficulties for at this point the river is about 300 yards across and there was no bridge. The casualties had to be ferried across by boat. The journey back to Tamu took about eight hours. On December 11, 52 (Ind.) Fd. Amb. opened its M.D.S. in Leu on the Tamu–Pinlebu road. Casualties had to be held in this unit until arrangements for their evacuation could be made.

On December 14 the M.D.S. of 52 (Ind.) Fd. Amb. moved to Sinlamaung after it had been relieved in Leu by 51 (Ind.) Fd. Amb. 53 (Ind.) Fd. Amb. followed to reach Sinlamaung on the 21st. As the rapid advance of the division continued 51 (Ind.) Fd. Amb. moved into Pinlebu and on the 19th on to Wuntho where it opened its M.D.S. which was joined by 4 (Ind.) M.S.U. There was an airstrip near Kawlin, about 6 miles from the M.D.S., and on it 53 (Ind.) Fd. Amb. provided an improvised air evacuation centre. So that it might hope to keep up with the division 53 (Ind.) Fd. Amb., less one company, was now mechanised, issued with extra equipment and attached to 64th Bde. On December 26, 51 (Ind.) Fd. Amb. moved from Wuntho *via* Kawlin to Tinhmaw to join 62nd Bde. which was then involved in heavy fighting and was suffering severe losses. The field ambulance opened its M.D.S. to admit the casualties and later moved on to the railway station at Kyaikthin where very satisfactory accommodation was available. A very comprehensive medical installation with medical and surgical wards and a ward for dysentery cases was developed. Evacuation from the front line back to this M.D.S. was far from easy, however. Casualties had to be hand-carried along narrow, steep tracks which were overlooked by the Japanese. Evacuation rearwards from the M.D.S. was, on the other hand, most satisfactory both by road and from a light aircraft airstrip quite close to the M.D.S. The journey from this M.D.S. of 51 (Ind.) Fd. Amb. back to the A.E.C. of 53 (Ind.) Fd. Amb. near Kawlin, by road took from three to four hours, by air, ten minutes. At Kawlin further evacuation was by Dakota.

53 (Ind.) Fd. Amb., less the detachment at the Kawlin airstrip, accompanied 64th Bde. throughout the advance. 52 (Ind.) Fd. Amb. moved from Sinlamaung to Pinbon on December 29 and then on to Kyaikthin, alongside the M.D.S. of 51. It next moved on to Thityabin to open its M.D.S. in dug-outs. It was followed by 51 (Ind.) Fd. Amb. on January 4 and on the following day this unit moved on to Kin-U where it opened its M.D.S. to serve 98th Bde. then involved in heavy fighting. As this brigade advanced the field ambulance opened in Bodegon, 10 miles to the south of Kin-U, one company being attached

to the brigade to provide an A.D.S. if necessary. The M.D.S. of 52 (Ind.) Fd. Amb. in Thityabin now became the main divisional M.D.S. To it 4 (Ind.) M.S.U. was attached and near to it an airstrip was constructed. On January 8 this M.D.S. closed and moved on to Zigon where it remained closed as the M.D.S. of 51 (Ind.) Fd. Amb. was providing all the service that was required at this time.

53 (Ind.) Fd. Amb. was now in Zin where it remained until January 5 when it moved into Myemun and later to a point 2 miles east of Shwebo with 64th Bde. The detachment on the airstrip at Kawlin now rejoined its parent unit which moved on to Ta-on on the west bank of the Irrawaddy, 5 miles east of Shwebo. The M.D.S. of 51 (Ind.) Fd. Amb. together with H.Q. 52 (Ind.) Fd. Amb. remained in Zigon. The M.D.S. was functioning as the main divisional M.D.S. and had 4 (Ind.) M.S.U. attached to it. An airstrip was constructed within 200 yards of it. Casualties were now numerous; on January 9, for example, 87 were evacuated by air from this M.D.S. When Shwebo had been captured there was a lull in the fighting and the medical units were given time to rest and refit.

INDIAN 20TH DIVISION (XXXIII CORPS)

When this division passed to the command of XXXIII Corps its 80th Bde. moved to Kalemyo there to relieve 9th Bde. of Indian 5th Division. 32nd Bde. crossed the Chindwin at Mawlaik with the intention of clearing the jungle-covered area on the flank of 2nd Division as this moved towards Kalewa. But when the advance of 2nd Division was virtually unopposed, 32nd Bde. was instructed to help this advance by constructing road-blocks and preparing ambushes to the east of Pyingaing. This being done the brigade concentrated in Pyingaing and moved

---

Key to Fig. 49

1. XXXIII Corps' Medical Centre
2. 59 (Ind.) Fd. Amb. M.D.S. December 15–22
3. 55 (Ind.) Fd. Amb. A.D.S. January 4–14
4. XXXIII Corps' Medical Centre
5. 42 (Ind.) Fd. Amb. M.D.S. January 14–February 1
6. 59 (Ind.) Fd. Amb. A.D.S. January 5–12
7. 59 (Ind.) Fd. Amb. M.D.S. January 22–February 9
8. 55 (Ind.) Fd. Amb. M.D.S. February 1–12
9. 42 (Ind.) Fd. Amb. A.D.S. February 1–12
10. 42 (Ind.) Fd. Amb. M.D.S. February 10–March 12
11. 55 (Ind.) Fd. Amb. M.D.S. February 13–March 6
12. XXXIII Corps' Medical Centre
13. 59 (Ind.) Fd. Amb. M.D.S. March 8–18
14. 55 (Ind.) Fd. Amb. M.D.S. March 12–24
15. 42 (Ind.) Fd. Amb. M.D.S. March 15–23
16. 55 (Ind.) Fd. Amb. M.D.S. March 22–April 10
17. 59 (Ind.) Fd. Amb. April 3–12
18. 42 (Ind.) Fd. Amb. M.D.S. March 30–April 12
19. IV Corps' Medical Centre

south to join its division in its advance on Maukkadaw. This advance was uneventful and the division moved on Budalin. Leading elements of 32nd Bde. reached Kudaw, north-west of Budalin on January 5, and by the 7th Budalin itself was surrounded. For the next three days 32nd Bde. could make but little headway for the Japanese were skilfully disposed and well dug in, with extensive bunkers in and on the edge of the town. They fought with a ferocity that was reminiscent of the earlier

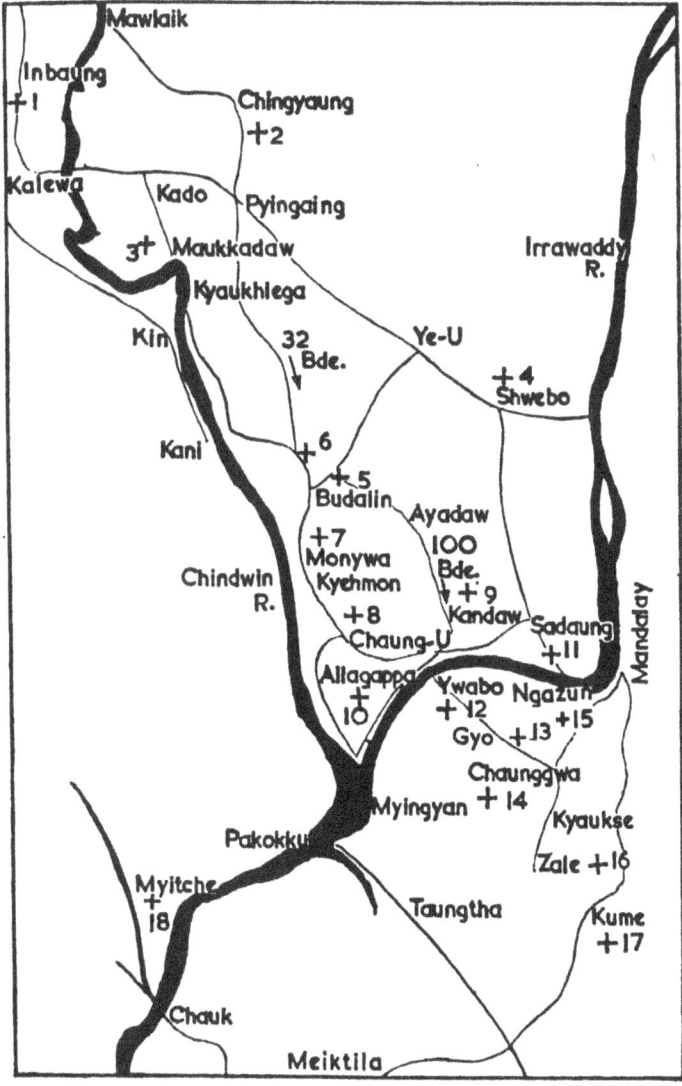

FIG. 49. Indian 20th Division. The Movements of the Field Ambulances during the Advance into Burma. Inbaung–Kume

years of the war and it was not until most of them had been killed or disabled that the remaining few were overwhelmed.

On January 3, 80th Bde., in the rear of the division, reached Maukkadaw. 32nd Bde. was directed on Monywa and 100th Bde. on Ayadaw. 32nd Bde. reached Alon on January 13 and sent out patrols to discover the strength of the Japanese in Monywa. 80th Bde. moving along the east bank of the Chindwin reached Winmana on the 12th. To the east of Alon 32nd Bde. encountered some opposition but was able to continue its advance with one battalion moving along the main road to the completely wrecked town of Monywa, and with the other two battalions making detours to the north and to the south of the town so as to get behind it. The fighting for Monywa was fairly severe but the town was completely encircled and after a series of air-strikes was taken on January 22. Tactical H.Q. and Main H.Q. Fourteenth Army moved into Monywa on February 6.

With the help of air-strikes 100th Bde. took Ayadaw on January 16. The Japanese facing Indian 20th Division now withdrew hastily towards Myinmu on the northern bank of the Irrawaddy closely followed by 100th Bde. which reached Kwetkwin on January 18. Resistance in the vicinity of Tizaung was brushed aside and the advance to Myinmu and Allagappa continued while patrols made contact with 2nd Division on the line of the Mu River. On January 20 Myinmu fell to 100th Bde. which was now on the line of the Irrawaddy between Allagappa to the confluence of the Mu and Irrawaddy. Allagappa was occupied on the 24th and three days later Chaung-U was entered. The Japanese still held a small triangle of ground to the south of the road between Monywa and Myinmu and were still in the area between Chaung-U and Allagappa. 80th Bde. gradually cleared the latter area and when Chaung-U was captured 32nd Bde. was instructed to clear the triangle. 100th Bde. had already cleared the eastern part of it and now 80th Bde. cleared most of the rest, but not all for the Japanese could not be dispossessed of a small bridgehead to the west of Sameikkon. 100th Bde. entered Letkapin on February 1 and by the 4th had driven all Japanese troops from the area around this village. By the 12th the whole area occupied by Indian 20th Division had been cleared.

MEDICAL COVER

The divisional medical units were 42, 55 and 59 (Ind.) Fd. Ambs. and 26 (Ind.) Fd. Hyg. Sec. During the four months' rest that had followed the battles about Imphal, the medically unfit had been weeded out of the division, the I.O.Rs. had been dewormed and all the officers and men had been intensively trained in the observance of anti-malaria and anti-typhus precautions. Such medical officers as had served as R.M.Os. for eighteen months or more were cross-posted to field ambulances.

With 32nd Bde., when it crossed the Chindwin at Mawlaik, was 59 (Ind.) Fd. Amb. providing a pack-borne A.D.S. to which 10 (Ind.) M.S.U. was attached. Prior to this move the M.D.S. of this field ambulance had been in Htinzin whence evacuation was either to Moreh or else to the airstrip at Tamu. The A.D.S. had Lushai men among its personnel and these were peculiarly adept at making all kinds of useful things out of bamboo—beds and ward furniture, for example. Parachute cloth from the supply drops provided bed linen. The single fly sheets of the 180 lb. tent were used to give shelter. The operating tent was a 180 lb. tent raised on bamboos, and without the centre pole, to 6 ft. above ground and completed with the walls of an E.P.I.P. tent. The theatre could be carried on one mule. The allotment of mules was:

A.D.S. Stores and equipment	17 mules
10 (Ind.) M.S.U. „ . . .	16 „
Rations	4 „
Bedding of personnel	7 „
	44 „

When 32nd Bde. had crossed the Chindwin airstrips were constructed on the eastern bank and at Chingyaung where 59 (Ind.) Fd. Amb. established its M.D.S. Evacuation was to the corps medical centre at Inbaung. On January 10 evacuation from the airstrip at Budalin became possible and here on the 14th, 42 (Ind.) Fd. Amb. opened its M.D.S. Attached to this were 10 (Ind.) M.S.U. and a surgical team from 5 (Ind.) B.M.U. While functioning in Budalin 42 (Ind.) Fd. Amb. learnt, as many other medical units had done in other theatres, that when among a civilian population it is necessary for a military medical unit to open a civilian wing. This was done in Budalin and in this civilian wing of its M.D.S. 42 (Ind.) Fd. Amb. dealt, successfully it is credibly reported, with its first obstetrical case. Some score of advanced leprosy cases which had been collected during the fighting about Monywa were also admitted. The M.D.S. of 59 (Ind.) Fd. Amb. moved from Htinzin to the vicinity of Kyigon on January 1, a company of the field ambulance being attached to 32nd Bde.

On January 20, 59 (Ind.) Fd. Amb. moved to Budalin, remaining closed. Evacuation from Budalin was to Shwebo where the corps medical centre was now established. On January 22, 59 (Ind.) Fd. Amb. moved on to Monywa there to open its M.D.S. Evacuation from Monywa was to Budalin by road. The divisional armoured ambulance car was used for this purpose but because of its weight in relation to its engine power it proved to be very unreliable. (Eventually it was given as a present to Indian 5th Division at Meiktila.) Evacuation to base of such casualties as required long hospitalisation was possible from the airstrips at Alon and Monywa.

42 (Ind.) Fd. Amb. was attached to 100th Bde. Its M.D.S. had been established in the vicinity of Khampat in September. On the last day of December 1944 it moved with its brigade on its left hook that captured Ayadaw, and Myinmu. It established its A.D.S. in Kandaw whence evacuation was direct to the corps medical centre. At the end of December the M.D.S. moved to Kyigon. On January 14 it moved forward into Budalin where it opened its M.D.S. and where later it was joined by 55 and 59 (Ind.) Fd. Ambs., both of which remained closed. At the end of January the M.D.S. of 42 (Ind.) Fd. Amb. closed in Budalin and moved forward to Allagappa there to prepare a well protected M.D.S. for use during the assault crossing of the Irrawaddy. It found suitable accommodation in a *phongyi kyaung* and with the help of bulldozers provided by the Engineers and of civilian labour, constructed a series of wards and two operating theatres below ground level. The roofs were of canvas which was drenched with water at intervals to bring the temperature down.

55 (Ind.) Fd. Amb. was attached to 80th Bde. Throughout December its M.D.S. was open in a small village named Thazi, near Kalewa. When the brigade moved forward to Maukkadaw an A.D.S. of the field ambulance accompanied it. The next move of the field ambulance was to Budalin where it remained closed. On February 1, 55 (Ind.) Fd. Amb. moved into Chaung-U where it opened its M.D.S. to serve 80th Bde. which was then clearing the triangle south of the Monywa–Myinmu road between the Chindwin and the Irrawaddy. There was plague in Chaung-U but fortunately it did not spread to the troops. The M.D.S. moved into Allagappa to open on February 13.

XXXIII CORPS. MEDICAL ARRANGEMENTS

As was foreseen evacuation of casualties had presented a number of intractable problems. For part of the time evacuation by light aircraft was impracticable and the old methods of hand-carriage, mule-carriage and jeep ambulance had to be used. The unmetalled roads were quickly churned into mud during the monsoon and whole stretches became impassable to vehicles of any kind. The rains caused frequent landslides along the hill sections of the roads. In the Kabaw Valley the wheels of the ambulances, jeep as well as standard, would sink to the axle in the deep sticky, black clay. Even the four-wheel drive of the jeep could not conquer the mud and the vehicles had to be man-handled over the worst of the stretches. It could take an ambulance two days and nights to cover the distance between Sittaung and Tamu. Between Pantha and Tamu, a distance of about 8 miles, the stretchers had to be hand-carried. On the Chindwin, as has already been stated, D.U.K.Ws. were used for the transport of casualties.

As the monsoon drew to its close it became possible to construct light aircraft strips along the Kabaw Valley road though not along the more mountainous Tiddim road. The troops moving down this Tiddim line of advance passed through one of the worst scrub-typhus belts in the region and as a consequence of this the forward medical units tended to become very congested. In the Kabaw Valley the airstrips were constructed at intervals of about 50 miles. Evacuation by glider was also carried out, the absence of trees making it possible for the Dakotas to snatch up the nylon ropes of the gliders from the ground. The gliders used could take 15 sitting or 4 lying plus 5 or 6 sitting cases.

After Shwebo had been captured it was intended to establish the corps medical centre in the Ye-U–Shwebo area but considerable difficulty was encountered in moving medical units forward for stretches of the road east of Kalewa were almost impassable. There was now no certainty that the Dakotas could take casualties since Comilla was not being used as a supply centre and they were flying from airfields further to the north. Yet it was quite impossible to adopt the policy of holding patients in the forward medical units since this would throw an additional burden on the supply service which was already stretched to the utmost by the demands of the fighting formations. A corps medical centre was built up, though very slowly, in the vicinity of Ye-U. Using the first line transport of the divisional medical units the light section of 16 (Ind.) C.C.S. was ferried forward to Ye-U north airfield where it took over from the M.D.S. of 4 Fd. Amb. which had been functioning as the air evacuation unit in this area. Then 76 (Ind.) S.S. was flown in from Kawlin and continued to control the light aircraft evacuation arrangements.

Indian 20th Division developed a divisional medical centre in Budalin consisting of the surgical element of the medical unit of Ind. 5th Beach Group, 10 (Ind.) M.S.U. and the M.D.Ss. of the divisional field ambulances. Evacuation from this centre was by light aircraft to the corps medical centre at Inbaung. Evacuation was now switched to the corps medical centre at Ye-U whence further evacuation was by Dakota to Imphal and Comilla. Indian 19th Division's casualties were similarly evacuated to Ye-U.

In January it was decided that Shwebo should be developed as a corps maintenance area and a site was chosen to the north-east of the town for the corps medical centre. To it the main body of 16 (Ind.) C.C.S. was sent. This unit opened at once to provide 200 beds. After a few days its light section joined it and then a further 200 beds were opened. Under Army arrangements 10 (Ind.) M.F.T.U. and 8 (Ind.) C.C.S. were flown in from Imphal to Ye-U, because the airfield at Shwebo was not quite ready, and moved on from there to Shwebo by bullock carts,

150 of them altogether. Around these units, 8 and 16 C.C.Ss. (600 beds) and 10 M.F.T.U. (850) the following units became aggregated:

> the corps psychiatric centre (75 beds);
> 27 F.T.U.;
> the V.D. wing of 41 I.G.H. (attached to 16 C.C.S.);
> one M.N.S.U. attached to 16 C.C.S.;
> two mobile X-ray units;
> one field laboratory;
> 48 (Ind.) Sub-depot Med. Stores;
> an ophthalmic unit (spectacle supply);
> one M.A.S.;
> two Indian staging sections;
> one East African M.A.C.;
> three sections of the A.F.S. (jeeps);
> a dental centre consisting of:
> > one Ind. dental unit (B.T.);
> > one Ind. dental unit (I.T.);
> > one Ind. Dent. Mech. unit.

Shwebo was an excellent site for a medical centre of this kind. To it there was easy access from Indian 20th Division's area, Chaung-U-Myinmu, from 2nd Division's area in the Sagaing hills and from Indian 19th Division's area about Kyaukmyaung. 2nd Division's casualties could be brought by light aircraft from the M.D.Ss. in Sadaung and Ondaw in about 20–30 minutes. Those of Indian 20th Division could reach the corps medical centre within 40–50 minutes. But because the site was surrounded by all kinds of military installations, as is almost invariably the case, it was decided that the centre could not rightly claim the protection of the Red Cross flag. Steps were taken to camouflage it. The lack of a senior officer commanding the centre led to certain difficulties in the co-ordination of the activities of the various component units. A light aircraft squadron of the U.S.A.A.F. was allotted to the centre solely for casualty evacuation. The use of transport aircraft for evacuation purposes led to much confusion for there was no means of knowing where the casualties would find themselves, at Comilla or Imphal or Chittagong and so the distribution plans of Fourteenth Army and of L. of C. Command could not be observed. Quite often casualties who had been evacuated by air had to be returned to the centre for the reason that they could not be conveyed to a base where a medical unit could accept them, or to which they were addressed. An improvised A.E.C. with 50 beds and with facilities for feeding patients had to be developed at the Shwebo airfield. The situation improved at once when R.A.F. 7 Casualty Air Evacuation Unit arrived.

Medical supplies were brought forward to the main airfield mixed, of necessity, with engineer stores, ordnance equipment, rations and the like and much sorting had to be done to separate them from the rest. This arrangement led to difficulty in respect of transfusion supplies which, not infrequently, were taken to the wrong destination. For the distribution of these transfusion supplies to the forward units, light aircraft were employed. These light aircraft were used to return cured patients to their units on discharge. To use the most suitable mechanical tool to do the particular job that has to be done, in the most efficient and the easiest way is known to be a characteristic of the American male. It was very instructive to witness this habit exercised in this way. To the American airman the use of a light plane for such purposes was the obvious, in fact the only possible method.

Towards the end of February it had become apparent that another corps medical centre was needed if gross overcrowding of the Shwebo centre was to be avoided. A subsidiary centre was therefore opened in Sadaung, south of Shwebo. The primary purpose of this subsidiary corps medical centre was to serve 2nd Division; Indian 19th and 20th Divisions were to remain dependent upon the main centre at Shwebo. At first the only medical unit that could be sent to Sadaung was 7 (Ind.) M.F.T.U. which moved up from Taukkyan near Kalemyo by road to open on February 12. To it were attached 9 (Ind.) M.S.U. and a mobile X-ray unit so that it could deal with surgical cases. Later this centre was augmented by the arrival of 13 (Ind.) C.C.S. from Inbaung, of the M.D.S. of the corps field ambulance and of certain of the ancillary units from Shwebo. Eventually it came to include one C.C.S., one M.F.T.U., one M.D.S., a field laboratory, a field transfusion unit, an ophthalmic unit, a V.D. wing, a dental centre and a sub-depot of medical stores. There was a light aircraft airstrip at Sadaung as well as one capable of accepting Dakotas. To the latter were now coming all the supply aircraft.

IV CORPS

IV Corps' tactical plan was, briefly, as follows:

Lushai Bde. was to thrust far and fast towards Pauk; 28th E.A. Bde. was to move south with all speed to support Lushai Bde. and to relieve it in the lead, if necessary. (It was hoped that the Japanese would mistake this brigade for 11th E.A. Division which was known to belong to XXXIII Corps.) Indian 7th Division's engineers were to make the road down which IV Corps was to march fit for transporting guns to Lushai Bde. This road to Gangaw was very much of a mixture. The first 90 miles from Tamu took the form of a road of average quality for this part of the world; the next 60 were 'jeepable' and the last 30 only 'muleable'.

The main operation was given the code name 'Multivite' and was divisible into four phases.

Vitamin A   The capture of Pakokku by Indian 7th Division which thereafter was to advance towards Seikpyu and Yenangyaung.

Vitamin B	The establishment by Indian 7th Division of a corps bridgehead across the Irrawaddy in the Pakokku–Pagan area.
Vitamin C	The concentration of the corps, including Indian 17th Division, Ind. 255th Tk. Bde. and the corps artillery on the east bank of the Irrawaddy.
Vitamin D	A lightning overland thrust assisted by an airborne operation if possible, to seize the Meiktila–Thazi area, this to be followed by the liquidation of any Japanese forces that still might be to the south and south-west of Mandalay.

For the execution of this daring plan, which for its success depended very largely indeed upon a combination of speed and deception, it was arranged that Indian 17th Division should be enabled to depend entirely upon mechanical and air transport.

While Indian 7th Division and 28th E.A. Bde. were concentrating in the area of Tamu, the division moving thereto from Kohima, the Lushai Bde. was in contact with the Japanese near Myaukkon, to the north of Gangaw and the engineers were busy mending the road. This had been cut up very badly by the heavy mechanical transport and in places the dust was over 2 ft. deep. Along its sides were hundreds of abandoned Japanese vehicles. It was arranged that the left flank of Indian 7th Division during its southward march should be protected by the Falam Levies and the Lushai Scouts. 7/2nd Punjab was detailed to protect the extreme left flank advancing southwards along the west bank of the Chindwin towards Pakokku.

The Japanese positions at Myaukkon were naturally very strong though their garrisons were numerically weak. The attack by Lushai Bde. upon them opened on December 8 but it was not until January 10, following an 'earthquake minor' air-strike* that the Japanese abandoned them. That night the Japanese also withdrew from Gangaw and the whole area was cleared.

In the meantime 28th E.A. Bde., followed by 114th Bde. of Indian 7th Division, had been moving down the Gangaw Valley. Myintha was reached on January 4 and the Gangaw airstrip, 30 miles further south, on January 8. Indian 7th Division, setting out from its concentration area on December 28, reached Kan on January 4. The Lushai Bde. was then withdrawn to Kan and then flown out to India. By January 17, 114th Bde. was in the Gangaw area and the rest of the division in Kan. Periodic rains seriously hampered movement for it turned the deep dust into cloying mud. 28th E.A. Bde. quickly cleared the Gangaw area and went into the lead again followed by 114th Bde. Brushing aside the

---

* An 'earthquake strike' consisted of a planned heavy attack by a large number of medium or heavy bombers, followed immediately by a heavy artillery bombardment and an infantry assault.

THE CHINDWIN TO THE IRRAWADDY

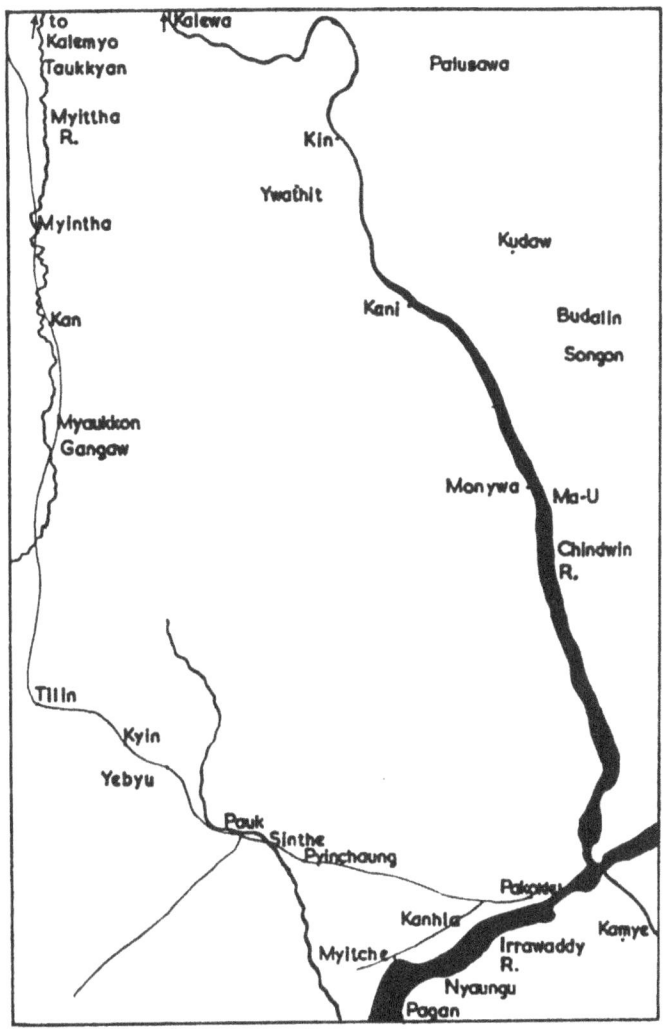

FIG. 50. The Advance of IV Corps to the Irrawaddy at Pakokku by way of the Kalemyo–Gangaw–Tilin–Pauk Road

resistance of small but determined rearguards and removing the many obstructions the Japanese had placed across the tracks, the East Africans reached Tilin on January 23 and Yebyu on the 26th. In Yebyu they made contact with 89th Bde. of Indian 7th Division which had been carrying out a wide encircling movement of some 180 miles cross country, being supplied by air. The brigade had reached Yebyu two days earlier than the appointed day but nevertheless was just too late to cut off the Japanese who had been holding the place. 89th Bde. now went into the lead and entered Pauk on the 28th and reached Pyinchaung on the following day.

33rd Bde., which had been rehearsing the techniques of river crossing in Gangaw, was now moved up to Pauk and 114th Bde., passing through 89th Bde., set out for Pakokku. Meanwhile the East African brigade advanced southward to attack Seikpyu which was stoutly defended by a small but resolute garrison. The attack opened on February 8 but it was not until the 12th that the whole of Seikpyu was occupied. The attack on Pakokku by 114th Bde. opened on February 5 when the Japanese positions at Kanhla were assaulted. Indecisive fighting continued throughout the following days but slowly the area between Kanhla and Pakokku was cleared and Pakokku taken. 89th Bde. entered Myitche on February 10 and reached the Irrawaddy opposite Pagan.

7/2nd Punjab, the reconnaissance battalion of Indian 7th Division, had marched some 250 miles cross country, carrying everything on the man or on mule-back, and being supplied by air. As it marched the battalion built temporary airstrips which could take light aircraft. From these the casualties were evacuated. It never fought a pitched battle but its patrols had many encounters with scattered parties of Japanese.

Ind. 255th Tk. Bde. moved from Imphal to Tamu to follow Indian 7th Division to Pakokku. The 400 mile journey took the brigade eight weeks. The road was so bad that tank transporters could only be used on parts of it.

Indian 17th Division reached Imphal from Ranchi during January and was then reorganised. Its 99th Bde. was transformed into an airportable brigade and was concentrated at Palel ready to be flown to Meiktila. Ind. 48th and 63rd Bdes. and the rest of the division gave up their mules, pooled their mechanical transport along with that taken away from Indian 5th Division and 11th East African Division, and made themselves completely motorised. The division then moved south to concentrate in the Pauk area by February 18.

MEDICAL COVER

INDIAN 7TH DIVISION (IV CORPS)

When this division concentrated in the Tamu area prior to its southward move two of the divisional field ambulances, 44 and 54 (Ind.) Fd. Ambs., opened a combined M.D.S. in Tamu itself. When the division was in Kan on January 17, 54 (Ind.) Fd. Amb. opened there and remained there until the end of the month. A company of this field ambulance moved with Ind. 114th Bde. towards Gangaw and beyond. Another company was attached to 33rd Bde. during the southward move. The M.D.S. of 54 first moved on to Pauk and then, on February 10, to Kanhla. 44 (Ind.) Fd. Amb. opened its M.D.S. in Kan as it passed through and then moved on to Pauk. 66 (Ind.) Fd. Amb. was attached to 89th Bde. It reached Kan on January 16 and remained there, open, until it moved on to Kyin on January 28. On February 10 it moved on to Myitche.

Evacuation from 33rd and 114th Bdes. was by air by light aircraft from the airstrips that were constructed as the advance continued. But from 89th Bde. on its 180-mile encircling move it was exceedingly difficult to get the casualties back for the brigade was moving through thick jungle. Mules were used to get them back to Kyin.

INDIAN 17TH DIVISION (IV CORPS)

During its move to the south behind Indian 7th Division the divisional field ambulances, 23 and 37 (Ind.) Fd. Ambs. were attached to the two brigades, 48th and 63rd. The divisional casualties were treated by these medical units and evacuated from the airstrips by light plane. The third divisional field ambulance, 50 (Ind.) Fd. Amb., was with Ind. 99th Bde. in Palel.

IV CORPS. MEDICAL ARRANGEMENTS

In early December H.Q. IV Corps, newly returned to Burma and situated in the Tamu area had 24 (Ind.) C.C.S. and 16 (Ind.) M.F.T.U. Evacuation from these units was carried out partly by air from a nearby Dakota strip and partly by road to 88 I.G.H. on the Tamu–Imphal road and thence by road to Imphal. On Christmas Day Corps H.Q. moved to Taukkyan on the Myittha River, a few miles south of Kalemyo where a regrouping of medical units took place and by January 12 those allotted to IV Corps, 14 and 19 (Ind.) C.C.Ss. and 4 and 9 (Ind.) M.F.T.Us. had arrived in this area. 19 (Ind.) C.C.S. and 9 (Ind.) M.F.T.U. had opened in Taukkyan by mid-January but as only Lushai Bde. was in action and as its casualties were being taken direct to XXXIII Corps' medical centre at Inbaung on which the light plane squadron was based, the work of these medical units was exceedingly light.

From Taukkyan IV Corps' medical centre moved to Kan where the first fully developed IV Corps' air-head was developed. The light section of 14 (Ind.) C.C.S. moved there on January 11 and by the 14th it, together with 4 (Ind.) M.F.T.U. was admitting patients. The one mobile surgical unit at the disposal of IV Corps had been attached to 66 (Ind.) Fd. Amb. which was serving 89th Bde. of Indian 7th Division. Casualties were few in number, however, and the surgical facilities of the C.C.S. were sufficient to deal adequately with them. To deal with African casualties and to overcome the language barrier 111 E.A. Hospital Section was included in this centre. Admissions averaged 30–40 a day at this time and they arrived by light plane. Evacuation from this centre was by air to Comilla. 19 (Ind.) C.C.S. and 9 (Ind.) M.F.T.U. were brought forward to this centre from Taukkyan but remained closed.

The next air-head was at Sinthe, 10 miles beyond Pauk and as soon as this area had been cleared and the airfield repaired the light section of 19 (Ind.) C.C.S. was flown there and within twenty-four hours was admitting patients. One by one the other components of IV Corps' medical centre at Kan were flown forward the last of them reaching Sinthe on February 15.

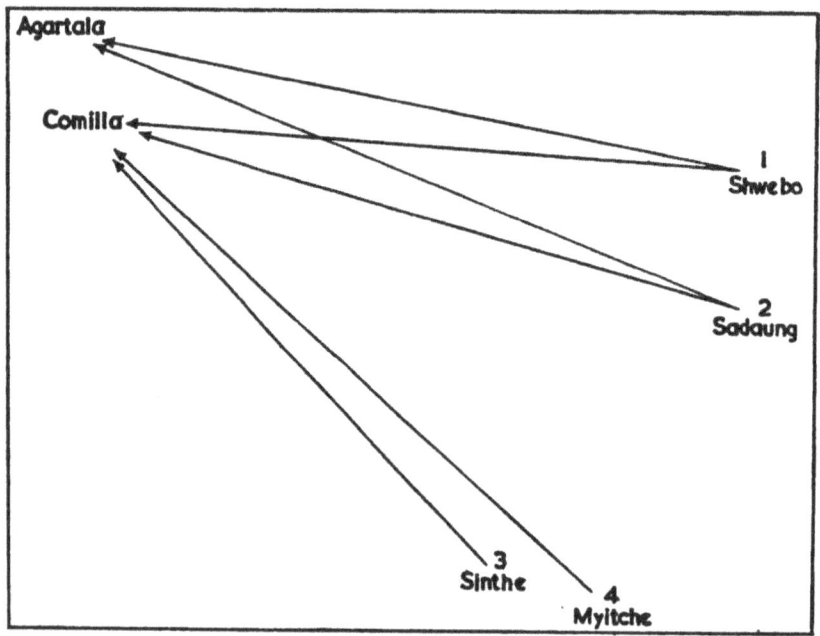

FIG. 51. Fourteenth Army. Air Evacuation Arrangements. February–March 1945.

1. XXXIII Corps' Medical Centre.   8 and 16 (Ind.) C.C.Ss., 10 (Ind.) M.F.T.U.
2.   ,,   ,,   ,,   ,,   13 (Ind.) C.C.S., 7 (Ind.) M.F.T.U.
3. IV Corps' Medical Centre.   19 (Ind.) C.C.S., 9 (Ind.) M.F.T.U. until 22.3.45
4.   ,,   ,,   ,,   ,,   14 (Ind.) C.C.S., 4 (Ind.) M.F.T.U. from 16.3.45

L. OF C. COMMAND. MEDICAL ARRANGEMENTS

The hospitals in the central group at Comilla, Agartala and Dacca were designated advanced base hospitals. They provided approximately 12,000 beds. A directive on the evacuation and distribution of casualties was issued by D.D.M.S., L. of C. Command by instruction of D.M.S., A.L.F.S.E.A.

THE CHINDWIN TO THE IRRAWADDY

(i) R.A.P.
(ii) Field Ambulance
       (A.D.Ss. sometimes split off and then formed additional links in the evacuation chain.)
  Function First aid and emergency treatment.
(iii) Corps Medical Centre
       (Usually two C.C.Ss. and two M.F.T.Us. with certain specialist units, e.g., ophthalmic unit, head injury unit.)
  Function Major emergency treatment, holding all cases expected to be fit within three weeks.
(iv) Advanced Base Hospitals
  Function Definitive treatment of all except long-term cases and treatment of special injuries, severe eye injuries, psychiatric cases, severe burns, holding of all cases expected to be fit for discharge within two (later three) months.
(v) Base Hospitals
  Function Long-term treatment of all kinds. Receiving all patients not expected to recover within two (later three) months.

Out of this directive evolved a standard medical lay-out which, with certain local modifications, was adopted for the rest of the campaign.

With the Fighting Division

  Divisional field ambulances with the possible reinforcement of a mobile surgical unit.

  Hygiene and anti-malaria units. Divisional psychiatric centre.

  Evacuation by light plane or by road to the divisional medical centre and rest centre.

  Thence by air or by road to the corps medical centre.

With Corps

  Corps field ambulance as the nucleus of the corps medical centre. Possibly, mobile surgical units and the light section of a C.C.S.

  Corps hygiene and anti-malaria units.

  Triage carried out. Light cases retained in the 'holding' pair of units (C.C.S. and M.F.T.U.). More serious cases evacuated in returning Dakotas to the Army medical centre.

With Army

  Army medical centre with a staging section or air casualty reception unit to receive, sort and distribute the casualties. A holding pair or pairs of C.C.Ss. and M.F.T.Us. for surgical (C.C.S.) and medical (M.F.T.U.) cases respectively.

  A psychiatric wing.

  Evacuation to Advanced Hospital Base by aircraft returning thereto.

In Advanced Base
> General hospitals with all facilities, laboratories and special departments.
> Convalescent depots and reinforcement camps.
> Special sections or specialist hospitals, e.g. eye injuries, psychiatric.
> Air reception and air evacuation units.
> A distribution staff.
> Evacuation by rail or river to the Base Hospital Centres.

About 60 per cent. of the casualties were held and treated in the corps medical centre; the remaining 40 per cent. (10 per cent. of the total) passed through the advanced base hospital to the base hospital.

Though distances lengthened no modification of these arrangements became necessary so long as the medical centre still remained within Dakota range and so long as reinforcements were sent in by air. So long as reinforcements were flown in, casualties could be flown out. At every airfield in the advanced hospital base to which returning aircraft might come, reception units had to be maintained because of the uncertainty of the time and the place of the arrival of returning aircraft.

THE MEDICAL ADVISORY DIVISION. S.A.C.S.E.A.

At the headquarters of the Supreme Allied Commander, South-East Asia (S.A.C.S.E.A.), in Paradenya, Kandy, Ceylon, a medical advisory division consisting of four senior medical officers, one from each of the Services, Navy, Army, Air Force, and one from the U.S. Forces, had been created with the concurrence of the Prime Minister. This group of advisers was called a division because the organisation of this headquarters was on the Navy model. Its responsibility was to advise the Supreme Commander on all matters medical; to keep constant watch on medical affairs throughout the command and for this purpose to maintain a statistical section; to keep in constant touch with medical research, particularly with that in the field of tropical medicine in all Allied countries; to advise on and devise methods for the application of the techniques of scientific research to the particular problems of S.E.A.C. and to act as general liaison of officers with the Medical Directorates and Branches of the component parts of S.E.A.C.

The records show that this M.A.D. was involved in the provision of adequate stocks of anti-malarial drugs and in the development of methods of distribution that ensured that they were available to all in need of them; in the provision of adequate stocks of D.D.T.; in the experimental investigation of the advantages of the spraying of insecticides from the air; and in the development of fish-netting impregnated with D.D.T. in place of mosquito netting. It played a part in the administrative aspects of the development of scrub-typhus vaccine and in helping the Consulting Physician of 11 Army Group to get from Australia by air a supply of sulphaguanidine when a severe epidemic of dysentery broke out in Kohima. It also played a prominent part in the formation and organisation of the S.E.A.C. branch of the Red Cross Society.

In his *Report to the Combined Chiefs of Staff*, the Supreme Allied Commander, when discussing the affairs of this Medical Advisory Division, observes that it was found necessary to appoint a chairman, later a director, on whom rested the responsibility of initiative, evaluation of investigations and direct liaison with principal medical officers of Services and medical departments elsewhere and recommends that in any future supreme allied command a division of this type should be created.

This is a matter that commands very careful consideration. It has to be remembered that the Supreme Allied Commander had, earlier, been at the head of the Combined Operations organisation and had then collected around himself a strong group of scientific advisers which included a number of outstanding biologists and physicists. In this group he placed much confidence. The Navy, the Army and the Air Force each had its own group of scientific advisers and of scientists engaged in actual research but Combined Operations found it necessary to create its own machinery. S.E.A.C. was likewise compounded out of Naval, Army and Air Force elements, furthermore it was an Anglo-American confederation. For these reasons it was deemed necessary to invent this novel medical body. Its constitution indicated clearly the composite nature of the organisation it was intended to serve. The Supreme Commander was undoubtedly wise when he decided to ask for the creation of a mechanism which could discharge the functions outlined above; there can be no two opinions concerning this. The question to be considered is whether or not the M.A.D. as constituted, was the best form this mechanism could take, the purely political aspects of the matter being disregarded.

That eventually it was found to be desirable to appoint a chairman or director of this division is best interpreted as meaning that experience had shown that at the apex of an organisation of this kind there should be one person and not four. In the Army it is the senior administrative medical officer of the formation that is the adviser of its commander.

No matter how large and how comprehensive his staff may be, all the information and all the advice that is placed before, or proffered to, the commander ultimately flows along the single channel of the senior administrative medical officer. It is required of him that he shall be able to understand what scientists in the medical field are doing and saying and to know enough about the Army and of soldiering generally to be able to judge whether or not that which is done or said can be applied within the Army and to its advantage. In a composite force, if the medical problems of the different Services differ significantly, it could be necessary to have them examined and also to have suggested solutions examined by such as are intimately acquainted with the factors that are responsible for the differences that distinguish the Services. Maybe it is desirable to have the equivalent of a senior administrative medical officer in triplicate or as in this case in quadruplicate. But as far as the records show the advice that was offered and the problems that were studied were not such as were affected in any way by the colour of the uniform or by the nationality of the wearer. The only reason why one senior administrative medical officer with the appropriate qualifications could not have proffered advice, have interpreted the results of scientific enquiry carried out by others and have maintained contacts just as well as did the chairman or director of this group, would seem to be that no one person could be acceptable to all three Services. A supreme commander can be given honorary rank of high degree in the two Services other than his own; however, it is impossible to imagine a surgeon rear-admiral being also a lieutenant-general and an air vice-marshal.

The trend undoubtedly was and is towards an integration of the Services; S.A.C.S.E.A., like Combined Operations H.Q. before it, was a development that indicated the shape of things to come. With an ever increasing degree of integration it is most unlikely that the medical advisory mechanism at the headquarters of the commander will include a representative of the medical services of each of the component Services. It seems much more likely that the best and most economical set-up would be found to be a serving officer, Navy, Army or Air Force, as senior administrative medical officer, selected on account of his qualifications for the post, and a scientific adviser, a scientist of repute working in the field of one or other of the medical sciences.

Had there been such a senior administrative medical officer in S.A.C.S.E.A., he could have called upon the Medical Research Council for help, through the appropriate service medical directorate. A scientific adviser could have been made available without any difficulty whatsoever. There would have been no difficulty in the way of getting an establishment for a pool of research workers and of getting this filled with men with the appropriate qualifications.

The creation and development of this unusual type of mechanism did not appear to result in the facilitation of the flow of medical intelligence into S.E.A.C. for the reason that it was not part of the very large machinery that was concerned with the collection and distribution of scientific knowledge likely to be of value to the medical services of the Armed Forces. This mechanism was very complete and very efficient. The flow of medical intelligence between the United States and Britain through the medium of the Medical Research Council and its American

PLATE XXVIII. Kalewa. A forward airstrip.

PLATE XXIX. Kalewa. L.5 taking off wounded from a forward airstrip. One L.5 has crashed.

[*Imperial War Museum*]

PLATE XXX. In range of enemy gunfire, L.5s. landing at a forward airstrip to meet wounded coming in on foot, by mule and by stretcher, December 1944.

[*Imperial War Museum*

PLATE XXXI. Ywathitgyi. Battle casualty receiving treatment in a hurriedly constructed first-aid post.

PLATE XXXII. 'A Field Hospital' near Ondaw, 1½ miles from the front line. General view showing, left, part of the hospital kitchen; centre, officers ward; right, a ward.

[*Imperial War Museum*]

PLATE XXXIII. A jungle Casualty Clearing Station.

[*Indian Historical Section*]

equivalent was exceptionally rapid. Had the advisory mechanism in S.A.C.S.E.A. been part of the advisory and investigational machinery that had been developed in Britain and in the African and European theatres, it is possible that its value would have been much increased.

The creation of the Medical Advisory Division was an important event in military medical history. It was asked for by the commander of very large forces in a theatre where medical problems loomed larger than in most others. Its creation earned the complete approval of the Prime Minister himself. It can safely be assumed that he too was of the opinion that medical knowledge and medical recommendation in a military setting had their important contributions to make to the successful waging of the war. The Medical Services, Navy, Army and Air Force, do not ask for more than this for it is this faith that begets the opportunities they seek to demonstrate that it is not misplaced.

APPENDIX XX

ALLIED LAND FORCES, SOUTH-EAST ASIA. ORDER OF BATTLE. MID-NOVEMBER 1944

(abbreviated)

Northern Combat Area Command

    (*a*) 36th Division (flown in to relieve 'Special Force')

    (*b*) Chinese First Army
        Chinese 30th Division
            „   38th   „
            „   50th   „

    (*c*) Chinese Sixth Army
        Chinese 14th Division
            „   22nd   „

    (*d*) 'Mars' Force
        U.S. 475th Infantry Regt.
        U.S. 124th Cavalry Regt. (dismounted)
        One Chinese regiment

    (*e*) A Chinese Tank Brigade

Fourteenth Army

    (*a*) IV Corps
        Indian 7th Division
            „   19th   „
            „   268th Lorried Brigade
            „   255th Tank Bde.

(b) XXXIII Corps
    2nd Division
    Indian 5th Division
        ,,   17th   ,,
        ,,   20th   ,,

    11th East African Division
    28th E.A. Bde.
    Lushai Bde.
    Indian 254th Tk. Bde.

XV Corps
    Indian 25th Division
        ,,   26th   ,,
    81st West African Division
    82nd ,,   ,,   ,,
    Indian 50th Tk. Bde.
    3rd Commando Brigade (Army and Marines)
    22nd E.A. Bde.

Lines of Communication Command
    202 L. of C. Area
    404   ,,   ,,
    and a large number and variety of base units

Ceylon Army Command
    Three locally enlisted battalions.
    A number and variety of base units.
    The garrisons in Addu Atoll and Diego Garcia.

APPENDIX XXI

MEDICAL BUILD-UP 1943–1944

Strength, Number of Beds provided and Beds as a Percentage of Strength. Fourteenth Army. 1943–1944

Strengths

Date	Formation	British	Indian	West African	Totals
Jan. 1 1943	Eastern Army	54,605	218,807	—	273,412
July 1, 1943	Fourteenth Army	30,353	209,913	—	240,266
Jan. 1, 1944	,,	47,744	332,637	26,590	406,971
May 1, 1944	,,	115,493	421,548	33,643	570,684
Oct. 1, 1944	,,	84,760	434,416	65,601	584,777

(These figures do not include those of the labour force which increased to number about 124,000)

Bed-cover provided

Date	Formation	British	Indian	West African	Totals
July 1943	Eastern Army	2,600	13,100	—	15,700
Feb. 1944	Fourteenth Army	7,700	20,100	2,000	29,800
July 1944	,,	10,536	27,564	2,000	40,100
Oct. 1944	,,	11,100	26,700	2,300	40,100

(These figures include beds in M.F.T.Us. and Con. Depots)

Beds as percentage of Strength

Date	Formation	British	Indian	West African	Totals
July 1943	East of the Brahmaputra (Fourteenth Army Area)	8·5	6·25	—	6·55
Feb. 1944	Fourteenth Army	16·2	6·06	7·5	7·3
July 1944	,,	9·1	6·5	5·95	7·0

(The target was 10 per cent. for British and over 7 per cent. for the others)

APPENDIX XXI—continued

11 Army Group. Increase in the Numbers of Field Medical Units. 1943–1944

Units	Increase
Indian Bearer Companies	from 2 to 5
C.C.Ss.	,, 9 ,, 14
M.F.T.Us.	,, 0 ,, 16
Staging Sections	,, 26 ,, 46
Fd. Hyg. Secs.	,, 5 ,, 23
A.M.Us.	,, 14 ,, 33
Con. Depots	,, 6 ,, 7

APPENDIX XXI—continued

Numbers of Medical Personnel in Eastern/Fourteenth Army 1943-1944

Categories	January 1943 Authorised	January 1943 Actual	Per cent.	July 1943 Authorised	July 1943 Actual	Per cent.	January 1944 Authorised	January 1944 Actual	Per cent.
Officers	1,455	1,256	87	1,871	1,601	86	2,788	2,430	87
Br. Nurses	1,022	356	35	1,002	229	30	1,230	528	43
Ind. Nurses	788	214	27	1,524	491	32	1,770	640	36
B.O.Rs.	1,971	2,013	102	3,331	2,672	80	4,577	3,628	79
I.O.Rs.	15,959	14,069	92	20,159	17,615	67	31,474	26,318	84
Non-Combatants enrolled	15,551	13,144	85	22,102	17,385	85	30,156	24,261	80

Categories	July 1944 Authorised	July 1944 Actual	Per cent.	July 1944 Actuals including those on 'X' list*	Percentage including those on 'X' list
Officers	1,929	1,814	94	2,011	105
Br. Nurses	519	435	—	—	82
Ind. Nurses	662	238	—	—	37
B.O.Rs.	3,490	3,253	93	3,832	113
I.O.Rs.	12,935	12,477	96	14,247	111
Non-Combatants enrolled	13,938	12,449	90	14,544	105
V.C.Os.	872	394	45	410	47

(These figures are for all field medical units including the Indian General Hospitals. Approximately two-thirds of them were in what became Fourteenth Army. The shortage of nurses was to some slight extent made good by the arrival in India from the United Kingdom of 250 V.A.Ds. in October 1944. Of these 200 were posted to 11 Army Group.)

*List of promised reinforcements.

APPENDIX XXII

FROM THE CROSSING OF THE CHINDWIN TO RANGOON. FOURTEENTH ARMY. CALCULATION OF BED-COVER REQUIRED

Strength

Fourteenth Army was to be built up to a maximum of two British and five Indian divisions, two Indian tank brigades, one independent brigade, two independent battalions together with Army, IV Corps and XXXIII Corps troops and, for two-thirds of the operation, one East African brigade. 36th and Indian 5th and 17th Divisions were employed only for the last one-third of the period.

Total strengths to be covered were:

	B.T.	I.T.	A.O.Rs.
For two-thirds of the period	48,093	89,667	5,500
with additional for one-third of the period	9,100	34,000	—
	57,193	123,667	5,500

Grand Total 186,360

(These figures take into account the decrease caused by the fly-out of formations. Only Army units are considered.)

Medical Cover

The medical cover initially considered necessary, excluding corps and divisional field ambulances, beach group medical units and staging sections was:

one I.G.H. (B.T.) (600 beds)	eight Ind. C.C.Ss.
one I.G.H. (C.) (1 Br. Sec.; 3 Ind. Secs.)	nine Ind. M.F.T.Us.
three I.G.Hs. (3 Br. Secs.; 5 Ind. Secs.)	one E.A. Hosp. Sec.

together with one convalescent depot (B.T.) (500 beds) and two convalescent depots (I.T.) (500 beds each).

Reckoning a C.C.S. as 50 B.T. and 150 I.T. beds and an Ind. M.F.T.U. as 200 B.T. and 400 I.T. beds, the maximum potential number of beds was thus composed of:

B.T.	3,500
I.T.	6,600
A.O.Rs.	100
	10,200

This would have represented a maximum potential percentage bed-cover of:

	B.T.	I.T.	A.O.Rs.
For the first two-thirds of the period	7·27	7·4	1·8
last third	6·14	5·3	1·8

Since the A.O.Rs. could be, and were, treated in British and Indian medical units the relatively small African cover was not regarded as a serious matter.

In actual fact, however, on account of transport difficulties and of the rapidity of the advance, it was possible to deploy only:

seven C.C.Ss.
eight M.F.T.Us.
one E.A. Hosp. Sec.

88 I.G.H. (C.) (one Br.; three Ind. secs.) was established in Kalewa but worked under the aegis of, and for, 505 District and had little concern with Fourteenth Army troops. The maximum potential number of beds available was thus:

B.T. 1,900; I.T. 4,250; A.O.Rs. 100: Total 6,250, or, a maximum potential percentage bed-cover of:

	B.T.	I.T.	A.O.Rs.
For the first two-thirds of the period	3·9	4·7	1·8
last third	3·28	3·4	1·8

It was appreciated at the beginning that 33 per cent. of the beds would be idle at any one time, owing to the closure of units and their forward movement. The actual number of beds available was thus reduced to:

B.T. 1,300; I.T. 3,833; A.O.Rs. 100: Total 5,233, which reduced the actual percentage bed-cover to:

	B.T.	I.T.	A.O.Rs.
For the first two-thirds of the period	2·7	4·2	1·8
last third	2·05	3·1	1·8

The necessity to provide beds in 505 District, its areas and sub-areas, as these came into being in the rear of Fourteenth Army and the impossibility of moving all the available medical units within the Army area during the final race down the river and railway axes, reduced the number of beds still further. For a force consisting of B.T. 37,700; I.T. 135,870; A.O.Rs. 2,000, a total of 175,570, there were only seven C.C.Ss., six M.F.T.Us. and the one E.A. hospital section, producing a potential maximum bed number of:

B.T. 1,500; I.T. 3,450; A.O.Rs. 100: Total 5,050
and an actual maximum number of:

B.T. 1,033; I.T. 2,350; A.O.Rs. 100: Total 3,483
and an actual percentage bed-cover of:

B.T. 2·74; I.T. 1·73; A.O.Rs. 5·0.

This cover, though exceedingly light, proved to be adequate for the reasons that the sick-rate remained very low during the period and evacuation out of Army area was sufficient to prevent the filling of the medical units in Army area.

CHAPTER 12

THE CROSSING OF THE IRRAWADDY. THE CAPTURE OF MEIKTILA BY IV CORPS. THE CAPTURE OF MANDALAY BY XXXIII CORPS.

FOURTEENTH ARMY now stood along a two hundred mile stretch of the Irrawaddy from Male in the north to Pakokku in the south. The fighting that had occurred during its advance from the Chindwin had not been on a large scale for the Japanese were deliberately withdrawing behind the Irrawaddy and only rearguards opposed XXXIII Corps as it thrust eastwards towards Shwebo and the river, and the spearhead of IV Corps as this pushed southwards through Gangaw and then south-eastwards to Pauk and Pakokku. These rearguards had fought with great determination and had clung to their positions with remarkable tenacity. The nature of the fighting during these events was such that casualties were not numerous; it was their evacuation that had constituted the major problem of the medical services.

In both Corps preparations for the assault crossing of the Irrawaddy were proceeding. Indeed Indian 19th Division had already secured two bridgeheads across it during the second week of January. An account of this event was withheld until this point in the narrative so that it might be presented along with those of the other crossings since all of them were inter-connected enterprises deriving from one and the same plan. The Irrawaddy was a more formidable water obstacle than any of the rivers of Italy or Germany. To force the crossing of such a river in the face of the kind of opposition that the Japanese could offer required the most careful planning and preparation after very thorough reconnaissance. It demanded the wisest of judgements in the choice of the crossing places and for its successful execution much deception, much surprise and great swiftness of action were essential. From Twinnge, seventy miles north of Mandalay, the river flows through an area of thick forest and jungle for some forty miles. Along twenty-four miles of this stretch, between Thabeikkyin and Kyaukmyaung, it runs through a gorge, about 500 yards wide. Then the countryside becomes flat and the river widens to about 2,000 yards. At its confluence with the Chindwin its width has become about 4,000 yards. The current varies with the season. With the rains it runs at five to six miles an hour; in the dry season at about two miles in the wider stretches but in these

THE CROSSING OF THE IRRAWADDY

navigation is made difficult by the numerous islets and sand-banks which shift their positions with each monsoon. At Mandalay the difference between high and low water level is thirty-one feet. In March and April the river is subject to sudden rises. In general the eastern and southern bank dominates the approaches to the river on the opposite bank save in the loop at Sagaing where the hills on the north bank dominate the whole countryside.

INDIAN 19TH DIVISION (XXXIII CORPS)

Following the fall of Shwebo and Kin-U Indian 19th Division closed on the line of the Irrawaddy. On January 7 its 64th Bde. was instructed to secure Kabwet but so tenaciously did the Japanese hold on to this bridgehead that it was not until the last day of the month that it was eliminated and then only after a series of quite heavy air-strikes. On the 10th, 62nd Bde. sent patrols across the Irrawaddy at Thabeikkyin and proceeded to probe the line of the river from Male to Makauk, entering Kyaukmyaung and sending patrols across the river at this point. Ind. 98th Bde. was now in the vicinity of Thabeikkyin and on January 19 got a whole company across. During the next three days three more companies crossed and the small bridgehead was enlarged. During the night of January 14/15 the divisional reconnaissance battalion, 1/15th Punjab, crossed the river at Kyaukmyaung, to be followed during the next four days by the whole of 64th Bde.

By this time it appeared that the Japanese had decided that these events were much more than the mere probings of patrols for they began to reinforce their troops in the areas of the two bridgeheads and to launch a series of attacks upon the perimeters. These attacks were all beaten off and in the Kyaukmyaung bridgehead 64th Bde. was able to seize a ridge of scrub-covered rock that ran parallel to the river and about three miles from its eastern bank and also a small bare peak, called Pear Hill, that rose sharply about three miles from the original crossing. These successes deprived the Japanese of all direct observation over the bridgehead. When the Japanese decided that the real threat was to come through the Kyaukmyaung bridgehead they tried their utmost to liquidate this. Some of the bitterest fighting of the whole campaign occurred around Pear Hill. But it so happened that the Japanese reinforcements reached the area of the bridgehead in small driblets and that as they arrived were at once flung in to the continuous battle. By the end of the month it seemed that they acknowledged that they could not hope to eliminate the bridgehead and that they had decided to be content to contain and neutralise it.

In the Thabeikkyin bridgehead 98th Bde. was called upon to withstand several sporadic attacks but these were all held and the brigade continued to consolidate its positions.

The great value of this feat of arms on the part of Indian 19th Division lay in the fact that it persuaded the Japanese Command that it was the intention of Fourteenth Army to make its main crossing of the Irrawaddy in this area. The attention of the Japanese was therefore attracted away from the Pakokku area. They reacted in a way that suggested that they had decided that Indian 19th Division's crossing was part of a plan by which this division was to link up with 36th Division which was already on the east bank of the Irrawaddy about forty miles to the north of Thabeikkyin, preparatory to a drive on Mandalay from the north by IV Corps.

Having withstood the Japanese assaults so successfully, Indian 19th Division now went over to the offensive and prepared to resume its advance. 62nd Bde. began to enlarge the area of the Kyaukmyaung bridgehead and was joined on February 7 by 64th Bde. By the 13th, 64th Bde., with the aid of air-strikes, had gained the mastery in Singu and 62nd Bde. was exploiting eastwards. All this while 98th Bde. in the Thabeikkyin bridgehead had been actively patrolling and consolidating. The fighting in this area was not nearly so fierce and so sustained as it was in the Kyaukmyaung bridgehead.

INDIAN 20TH DIVISION (XXXIII CORPS)

By the second week of February Indian 20th Division was poised for the crossing of the river. The area selected for the crossing was at the bend of the river, south of the village of Allagappa. At this point the Irrawaddy is 1,500 yards wide and its banks are steep. The current flows at the rate of three knots. However, this particular stretch of the river was only lightly defended and moreover it was at this point that the inter-divisional boundary of Japanese 31st and 33rd Divisions reached the river. The crossing had to be made in ranger boats towed in a train and powered by outboard motors known to be unreliable.

The remote objective of Indian 20th Division was the Mandalay–Meiktila road in the Myittha and Kyaukse areas. The immediate one was the establishment of a bridgehead on the south bank of the Irrawaddy from which the thrust towards the Mandalay–Meiktila road could be made. The plan was for 100th Bde. to cross at Satpangon and establish a bridgehead with a perimeter running through Ywathit, Talingon, Gaungbo and Alethaung, and for 32nd Bde. to make a subsidiary crossing with not more than two battalions opposite Letkapin and thereafter to link up with the right of 100th Bde. in the Kanlan–Ywathit area. The third battalion of this brigade was to cross when the bridgehead was of sufficient depth. 80th Bde. was to be prepared to move into the bridgehead and to break out from it.

On February 12 the R.A.F. thoroughly pounded the Japanese gun positions in the area of the crossing points and then, during the night of February 12/13, 100th and 32nd Bdes. began to cross. Both of the first flights had serious trouble with the outboard motors so that some disorganisation resulted. The second flights were more fortunate. In the 100th Bde. bridgehead the build-up was fairly rapid and by the

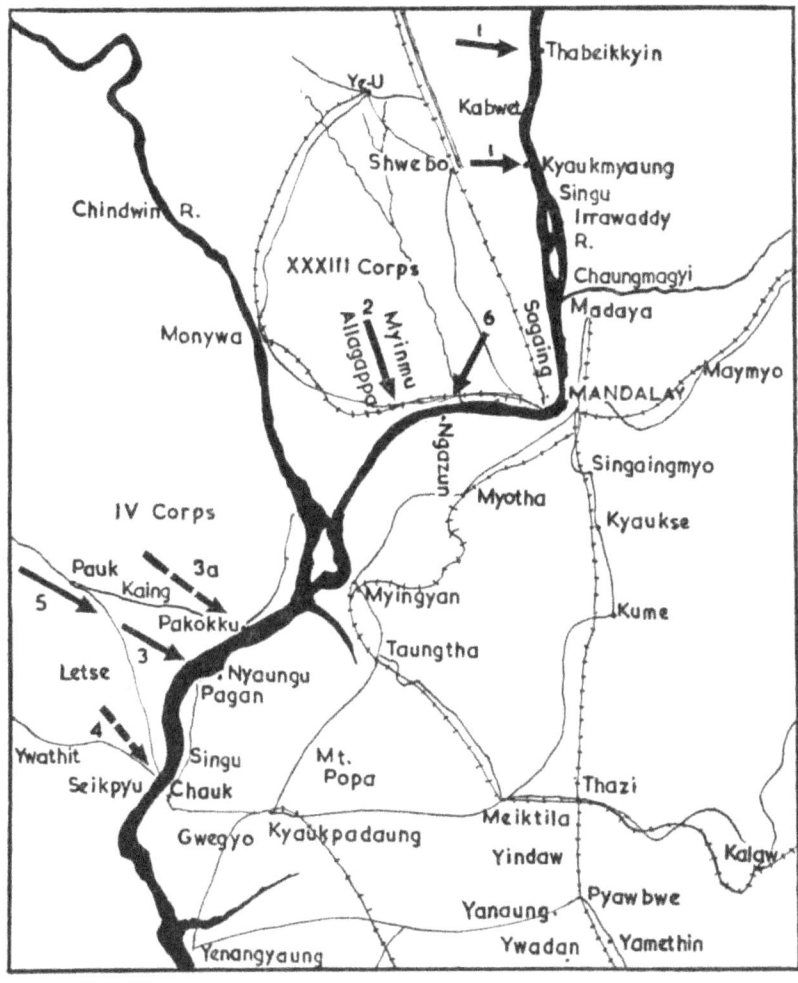

FIG. 52. The Assault Crossings of the Irrawaddy.

1. Indian 19th Division
   January 14
2. Indian 20th Division
   February 12
3. Indian 7th Division
   February 13
3a. 114th Brigade of Indian 7th Division. Feint
   February 13
4. 28th East African Brigade. Feint
   February 13
5. Indian 17th Division
   February 18
6. 2nd Division
   February 24

morning of the 15th the brigade was well established and a ferry service was working smoothly. The bridgehead was subjected to much mortaring but its area was slowly enlarged.

The opposition encountered by 32nd Bde. was much more determined. The Japanese guns raked the area and there were very frequent attacks by relatively small parties of Japanese troops. The battalion in the bridgehead could be reinforced by no more than a company of another battalion and so could not do more than hold on to the ground it occupied.

On February 21 80th Bde. began to cross into the bridgehead of 100th Bde. charged with the task of linking up this with that of 32nd Bde. The Japanese pressure was so strong and so continuous, however, that the brigade was unable to do this. The task was then given to 32nd Bde. It was completed by March 6 by which time the Japanese were withdrawing troops from the bridgehead area and were sending them eastwards to oppose IV Corps in the Meiktila area.

Indian 20th Division now linked up with 2nd Division on its left and prepared for the thrust to the east.

INDIAN 7TH DIVISION (IV CORPS)

The third crossing of the Irrawaddy was made by Indian 7th Division on February 14, far to the south-west of the crossings so far described, in the vicinity of Pakokku. The task of this division was that of establishing a bridgehead through which Indian 17th Division could pass on its way to the Meiktila area. It has already been recorded that Indian 7th Division had reached the Kan–Gangaw area by January 17, that 89th Bde. making a wide encircling sweep had reached Yebyu on the 25th and thereafter had proceeded to Myitche, which was reached on February 5, and that 114th and 33rd Bdes. had closed up to the line of the Irrawaddy. The site of the crossing was to be at Nyaungu, half-way between Chauk and Pakokku where the river is at its narrowest in this area, being less than three-quarters of a mile across. A sand-bank, some 800 yards long, made a straight crossing impossible. The far bank of the river, save along the frontage of Nyaungu town, consisted of high cliffs, intersected with dry chaungs every few hundred yards whereas the near bank was flat and low-lying.

It was decided that the crossing should be in four phases:
  (i) a battalion of 33rd Bde. would cross on the night of February 13/14 and would capture four beaches and the cliffs one mile north-east of Nyaungu;
  (ii) the remainder of 33rd Bde., with some armour, would then reinforce this bridgehead;
  (iii) a rapid advance from the bridgehead would be made to capture Nyaungu and a beach at the point of the narrowest part of the river;

(iv) the bridgehead would then be expanded to take the whole of IV Corps which would cross by the direct Nyaungu route as soon as possible.

To confuse the Japanese it was planned to make two feint crossings opposite Chauk by 28th E.A. Bde. and opposite Pakokku by 114th Bde. of Indian 7th Division. In addition to these 1/11th Sikh was to make a subsidiary crossing about six miles south of the main crossing.

33rd Bde. began to cross at 0345 hours on February 14. The first flight, a company of 2nd S.Lan.R., landed on the southern shore about an hour later, climbed to the top of the cliffs and dug-in. On the west bank the rest of the battalion began to cross just as dawn was breaking. Everything went wrong, outboard motors refused to start, boats leaked, the different companies got thoroughly intermixed, the strong current and the wind proved to be too much for the feeble engines and the boats began to drift downstream. The occupants of other boats, confused by what was happening, steered after them, and to crown all the Japanese on the far bank opened fire with rifles and machine-guns. Several of the boats were sunk and casualties mounted. Though an air-strike quickly silenced the Japanese on the eastern bank, the attempted crossing had ended in failure and the company of 2nd S.Lan.R. was in considerable peril. The tanks and the guns on the near side opened up and the R.A.F. bombed the Japanese positions on the far side and so enabled such boats as were still afloat to make a covered withdrawal. It was then decided to put 4/15th Punjab across a little further upstream, under air, artillery and tank cover. By 1140 hours the whole of the battalion was across and in an hour or so all the beaches on the far bank had been cleared of Japanese and fighting patrols were well forward. Before dark practically the whole brigade had crossed over.

1/11th Sikh of 89th Bde. had also encountered misfortune. The Sikhs had to make use of country craft and local boatmen, for all the assault craft had been allotted to 33rd Bde. On February 11 patrols crossed the river to find the southern end of Pagan unoccupied. On the following day the Sikhs moved on to an island in mid-river and by dawn on the 13th the battalion was safely hidden. At 0400 hours on the 14th the leading company set off in the large unwieldy boats and as these neared the far shore they came under a hail of machine-gun fire. The Burmese boatmen, not unnaturally, panicked. The boats, out of control, drifted downstream. At length the boatmen were persuaded to row again and to take the boats back to their island starting point. Though only one man had been wounded it had been made perfectly clear that without some form of assault craft which could be handled by the troops themselves it would remain impossible to land on the opposite shore.

However, on the 15th a small boat, flying a white flag, put off from the eastern shore and approached the island in mid-stream. It contained two I.N.A. sepoys who brought the welcome news that the Japanese had evacuated Pagan, leaving behind as its garrison members of the I.N.A. who wished to surrender. A platoon of 1/11th Sikh quickly crossed the river, entered Pagan and accepted the surrender of its garrison. By the end of the day the Sikh battalion was in the outskirts of Pagan, the ancient capital of Burma with its 1,200 temples, long since disused and in ruins.

Early on February 15, 89th Bde. began to cross over into the main bridgehead and by the following day this was 6,000 yards wide and 4,000 yards deep. On the 17th, Indian 17th Division began to move into the bridgehead and to concentrate on the road to Ngathayauk. The expected Japanese attack did not come until this day. As 33rd Bde. extended its territory Japanese troops retreating from Pakokku attacked it but were driven off. On the 18th, 89th Bde., south of Pagan, met Japanese troops coming north from Chauk and withstood their attack. During the next few weeks these attacks became a common occurrence but they failed completely to disrupt the plans of Fourteenth Army.

2ND DIVISION (XXXIII CORPS)

The fourth and last crossing of the Irrawaddy was that of 2nd Division of XXXIII Corps at the village of Ngazun between Mandalay and Indian 20th Division's bridgehead at Allagappa. It has already been recorded that after the capture of Ywathitgyi on February 2, 5th and 6th Bdes. had concentrated in this area preparatory to crossing the Irrawaddy, while 4th Bde. had moved to contain the Japanese in their positions in the Sagaing hills. On February 13 orders were issued for the assault crossing. 5th Bde. was to establish itself in a bridgehead in the general area Ngazun–Ngalun–Thabyetha, 10 miles to the east of the bridgehead of Indian 20th Division, prior to its advance eastwards on Mandalay. Between the 14th and 24th there was much active patrolling and offensive operations against the Japanese positions in the Sagaing area were continued. On the 23rd, Ind. 268th Bde. relieved 4th Bde. in the Sagaing area and 4th Bde. then moved to 6th Bde's. area so as to free this brigade to make the crossing along with 5th Bde. The site selected was Ngazun. Here the river was between 1,000 and 1,500 yards wide with many sand-banks and shoals. The current ran at about $2\frac{1}{2}$ knots.

Three battalions were to make the initial crossing and were to land on 'A', 'B' and 'C' beaches respectively. The battalion heading for 'C' beach was fired on while crossing during the moonlit night of February 24/25 but one company managed to get ashore. The battalion aiming for 'A' beach met heavy automatic and mortar fire, seventeen of its boats were sunk and the battalion had to return to the northern shore.

But the battalion directed on 'B' beach succeeded in getting across in the face of opposition and this beach was reinforced under cover of smoke all through the following day. By nightfall of the 25th two battalions of 5th Bde. were established on the south bank. On the 26th the bridgehead was further expanded and 5th and 6th Bdes. were on the south bank as well as twenty tanks of 3rd D.G. Ngazun village was attacked by 6th Bde. on the 27th and 4th Bde. crossed the river. By March 6 2nd Division had made contact with Indian 20th Division to the west.

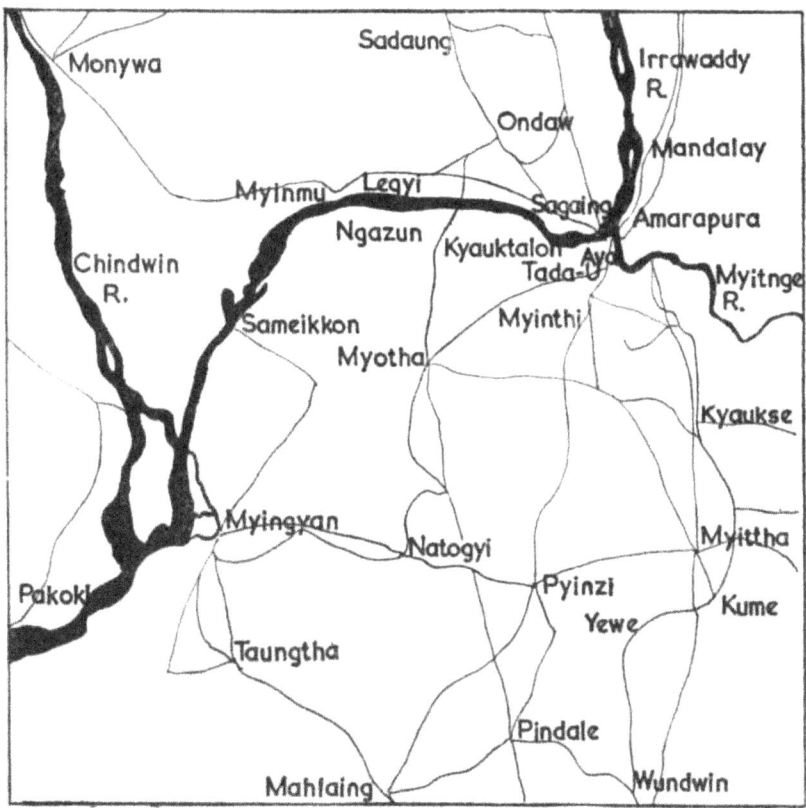

FIG. 53. 2nd Division. The Assault Crossing of the Irrawaddy. February 24, 1945

The scene was set for a breakout from the bridgeheads towards Meiktila and Mandalay. The decisive battle was imminent.

The crossing of the Irrawaddy had been accomplished with astonishing ease. The Japanese appeared to be completely puzzled by the inter-relationships of the different crossings and had apparently reached quite erroneous conclusions concerning their significance. The feint opposite Chauk by 28th E.A. Bde., for example, had evoked particularly strong reactions. The Japanese had considerable numbers of troops on the west bank of the river in this area and these were used with vigour to drive the East African brigade some miles back from the river. It was decided to withdraw the East African brigade to a safer area now that the task it had been set, to divert the attention of the Japanese away from the Nyaungu area, had been successfully accomplished. The brigade was withdrawn to Letse. The Japanese followed to besiege the brigade in its 'box'. It became necessary to send 4/14th Punjab of 114th Bde. to help the East Africans. For a month or more fighting in this area continued. When it died down 28th E.A. Bde. was flown out to Dohazari and took no further part in the campaign.

Indian 7th Division at this time was occupying a position that ran in an arc from Letse on the west bank of the Irrawaddy, held by 28th E.A. Bde., across the river south of Pagan, through the bridgehead, now ten miles deep, to a point twelve miles upstream of Nyaungu. Facing the division and 28th E.A. Bde. were Japanese troops that had been collected from far and wide and that were occupying the hills round Taungtha which dominated the road from Myingyan to Meiktila. It was imperative for IV Corps to secure that liberty of action which the capture of the small but important river port of Myingyan and the permanent opening of the Myingyan-Meiktila road would give. Columns from Indian 7th Division, supplied by air, were pushed out from the Nyaungu bridgehead towards Myingyan. Leaving a detachment to mask the town 33rd Bde. pushed on towards Taungtha, where on high ground that ran across the road to Meiktila were entrenched considerable numbers of Japanese troops. Until this area had been cleared the administrative base party of Indian 17th Division, about to move from Nyaungu, could not reach Meiktila. The forward move of H.Q. IV Corps and of Indian 5th Division, about to assemble in the bridgehead area, would also be greatly impeded unless this obstruction were removed. Taungtha itself was captured without much difficulty on March 6 but the Japanese held firmly on to a hill feature a mile southeast of the village. This was not finally cleared until the 14th. There remained one more hill feature to be taken. This was to the north-west of Taungtha and had been occupied on March 7 but had been lost again. Several attempts were made to eject the Japanese from it but all were unsuccessful. 161st Bde. of Indian 5th Division had reached the area and now relieved 33rd Bde. and took over the task of capturing the hill feature which dominated the countryside in all directions. For several days the fighting continued but the outcome remained indecisive until during the night of March 29/30 the Japanese withdrew.

THE CROSSING OF THE IRRAWADDY 435

Being thus relieved, 33rd Bde. turned its attention to the capture of Myingyan. The attack was opened on March 16 but it was not until the 22nd that the town was finally cleared. The building of wharfs began immediately and soon the boats that had been built in the Kalewa shipyards were berthed and unloading in them. Equally strenuous efforts were made to get the Myingyan–Meiktila railway line in working order. The road to Meiktila was open and Indian 5th Division and H.Qs. IV Corps and Indian 17th Division began to move forward.

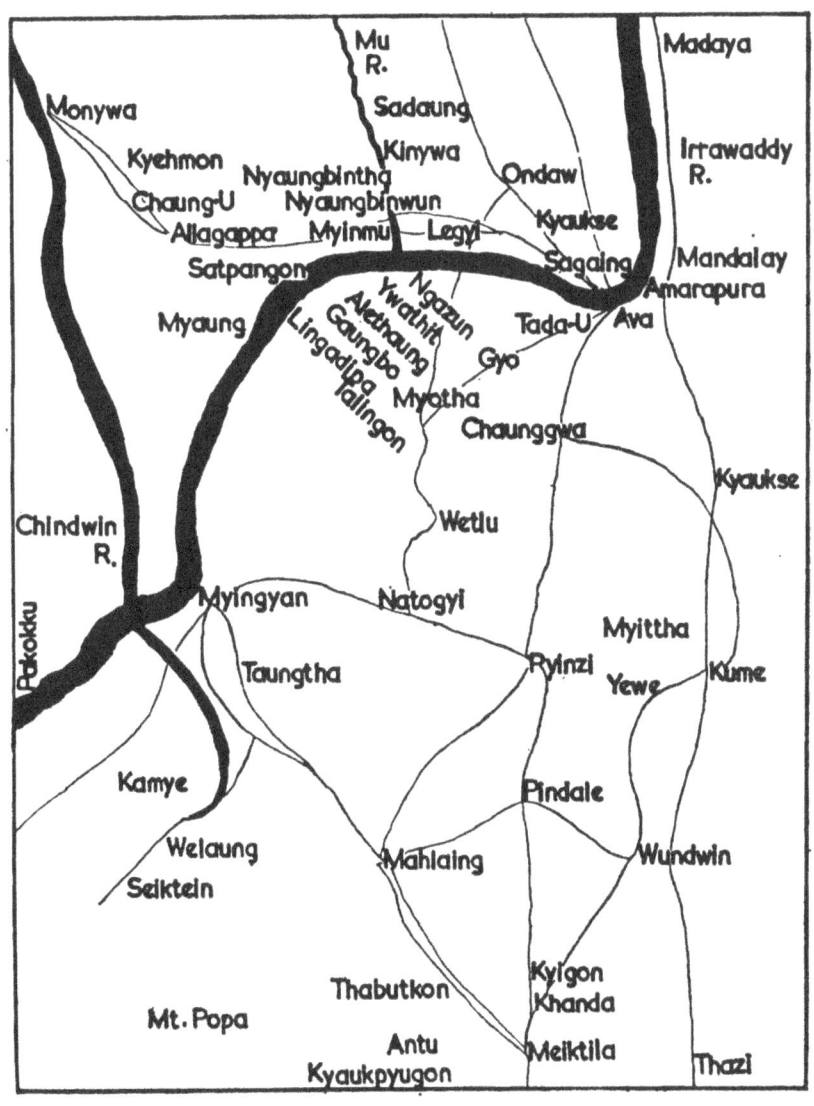

FIG. 54. The Mandalay–Meiktila Area

THE CAPTURE OF MEIKTILA BY IV CORPS

Between February 18 and 21, Indian 17th Division and Ind. 255th Tk. Bde. crossed the Irrawaddy into the bridgehead of Indian 7th Division and expanded this into an assembly area. On the 21st, before the whole of the division was across, a mechanised and armoured column consisting of 48th Bde. and tanks of 255th Tk. Bde. burst out of the Nyaungu bridgehead, 48th Bde. leading on the axis of the road to Ngathayauk and the tanks on an axis south of the road through Wetlu. The rest of the division followed, armoured cars in front, then tanks and infantry, more infantry, then the 3,000 vehicles of the column and finally a rearguard of infantry and tanks. As it proceeded the division sealed off its rear and subsisted on supplies dropped from the air. Every night the division was to harbour behind a perimeter bristling with weapons.

Opposition was first met at Seywa, a mile west of Ngathayauk. This was overcome and Ngathayauk found to be empty. From Hnawdwin three roads ran to the east, the most southerly of them to Seiktein, the middle one to Welaung and the northern one to Kamye. The Welaung one was not suitable for vehicular traffic and so while 63rd Bde. took the Seiktein route the rest of the division followed the other. The southern column reached Seiktein without incident on February 23 and then turned northwards towards Welaung which was found to be empty. The rest of the division moving on Kamye met fanatical resistance at Oyin, four miles south-east of Ngathayauk but this was finally broken. The advance on Taungtha was then resumed. On the 24th, 48th Bde. attacked the town and took it without much difficulty. When 63rd Bde. reached Taungtha late that afternoon the whole division moved on towards Mingan, three miles beyond Taungtha to harbour for the night. The whole area between the Mahlaing and the Welaung roads was found to be infested with Japanese snipers and over a hundred of them had to be flushed and destroyed before harbouring was complete.

On the 25th while 48th Bde. remained behind to collect the supply drop, the rest of the force pushed on to Mahlaing which was entered on the 26th without interference. A column making a wide left hook had captured the Thabutkon airstrip, 13 miles to the north-east of Meiktila. This made it possible for Ind. 99th Bde., the air-transportable brigade of Indian 17th Division, to be flown in, beginning at midday on the 27th. While H.Q. Indian 17th Division and 48th Bde. remained at Sedaw, 16 miles from Meiktila, 63rd Bde. preceded by armoured cars, pressed along the road towards the town. At Milestone 8 the armoured cars found the bridge down and the road mined. 63rd Bde. by-passed the road-block at Milestone 8 but encountered another at Milestone 6. Tanks broke through both of them and a defended nullah was then cleared. The force harboured for the night at Milestone 6. The 85 mile advance

THE CROSSING OF THE IRRAWADDY

from Nyaungu to Meiktila had been completed in about as many hours.

Meiktila stands on the edge of a large artificial lake which is practically divided into two large sheets of water, the north and the south lakes, by a causeway that bridges a narrow neck of water that joins the two lakes. Over this causeway ran the railway and the road bridges. In the Meiktila area the ground is cross-patched with irrigation channels and ditches. It was learnt later that the Japanese garrison had consisted of four airfield defence units, some 2,000 men altogether, a miscellaneous collection of administrative and L. of C. troops totalling some 2,500 and about 400–500 hospital patients.

Indian 17th Division's plan for the capture of Meiktila provided for a three-pronged attack. All the roads leading to the town were to be blocked. Ind. 255th Tk. Bde. was to carry out an outflanking movement to the north and east of the town and then to attack it from the east. Ind. 48th Bde. was to attack from the north along the axis of the road from Mahlaing. Ind. 63rd Bde. was to attack from the west.

On February 28, 63rd Bde., leaving almost all its transport at Thabutkon, moved forward towards Kyaukpyugon on foot. A divisional artillery harbour was formed at Antu from which the guns could support an attack on Meiktila from any direction. 48th Bde., closing in from the north, had moved to Milestone 3 on the Mahlaing–Meiktila Road. 255th Tk. Bde. moved round the north of Meiktila and then north-east and then east of Meiktila by bounds to block the road from Meiktila to Thazi and then to Pyawbwe and finally to regroup and move on the town. The tanks and accompanying infantry were met by very heavy fire from heavy guns, anti-tank guns and machine-guns firing from bunkers and fortified houses. Snipers were abundant, resistance was fanatical. The task could not possibly be completed that night and so the brigade withdrew to harbour for the night about two miles out of the town, leaving only strong patrols therein. Japanese troops infiltrated back into the areas from which they had been driven and in the darkness many sharp encounters occurred.

March 1 saw some of the bitterest of all the fighting. As 48th and 63rd Bdes. moved forward they encountered mounting opposition. 48th Bde. set out to clear the area to the north of the lakes. The area between the Dak bungalow and the railway line was heavily mined and large numbers of machine-gun posts had been sited in houses. After a heavy day's fighting the brigade withdrew to Kyigon for the night. 63rd Bde. attacked Kanna, west of Meiktila, with the support of armour and an air-strike. The latter set the local hospital on fire while attacking the many bunkers in its compound and some 50 to 60 patients perished in the flames.

On March 2, 48th Bde. with artillery, tank and air support, resumed the attack and slowly drove the Japanese from house to house and from street to street until they were cooped up in the southern sector with their backs to the south lake. 63rd Bde. in similar fashion cleared the west of the town. On the 3rd the east sector of the town was cleared after exceedingly bitter fighting. When only fifty or so Japanese soldiers were all that were left in this area, these leapt into the lake, preferring death to the ignominy of surrender. During the next two days the town had to be swept systematically to get rid of the many snipers lurking in the drains, ditches and broken ground and in the numerous outlying hamlets west of Khanda. The Japanese asked for no quarter and every one of them had to be killed or completely disabled before resistance ended.

Following its capture Meiktila was divided into sectors and each of these was made ready to withstand a siege, for it was expected that the Japanese would shortly make every effort to retake the town. Columns, usually of brigade strength, were sent out to carry out sweeps. H.Q. Indian 17th Division and 48th Bde. moved into the cantonment area, 63rd Bde. remained in Meiktila town area and 99th Bde. took over the Kyigon area. The Thabutkon airstrip was given up and the larger one to the east of Meiktila brought into use as air-head.

From the north, the north-west and the south Japanese troops moved towards Meiktila and quickly came to outnumber its defenders who adopted the policy of sallying forth to meet the Japanese as these arrived piecemeal and to destroy them before they could become absorbed into an organised and overwhelming force. These bodies of Japanese troops were to be encountered on all the roads that converged upon Meiktila, information concerning them was received from a variety of sources and by various means, and columns of infantry and armour and air-strikes were unleashed against them. Though these Japanese reinforcements were greatly harassed and suffered much loss both of men and transport, they did succeed in congregating around Meiktila in considerable numbers and in interfering with the use of the airfield, about two miles out of the town. There were not enough troops to spare for the complete perimeter defence of the airfield and the Japanese managed to get quite close to it. Their guns were brought near enough to prevent the airfield being used and for a time the dropping of supplies became the rule. Indian 5th Division's 9th Bde. (air-transportable) was flown in while the strip was under direct artillery fire. The fly-in was completed by March 17.

Soon after the arrival of this brigade, the Japanese succeeded in reaching the very edge of the airfield and so all landings ceased, petrol supplies became dangerously low, casualties could not be flown out except by the occasional light aircraft from a small strip inside the town itself and stocks of supplies became progressively smaller. However, the Japanese were gradually pushed back from the vicinity of the airfield

THE CROSSING OF THE IRRAWADDY

and the situation became easier although it was not until the end of March that the broken ground to the north of the airfield with its many nullahs, in which the Japanese guns were concealed, had been cleared by 63rd Bde. from the west and north and 99th Bde. from the south and south-east.

THE CAPTURE OF MANDALAY BY XXXIII CORPS

While IV Corps was engaged in the capture and defence of Meiktila, XXXIII Corps was preparing for the moment when its divisions would break out of their bridgeheads and race for Mandalay. Indian 19th Division had repulsed all attempts on the part of the Japanese to liquidate its bridgeheads at Thabeikkyin and Kyaukmyaung. Indian 20th Division waited in its bridgehead between Myinmu and Allagappa, 40 miles from Mandalay. 2nd Division was completing its concentration in its bridgehead at Ngazun about 25 miles to the west of Mandalay. 268th Bde. was guarding the open flank between Indian 19th Division and 2nd Division and was in constant contact with the Japanese forces in the Sagaing hills.

On February 26, 64th Bde. of Indian 19th Division, supported by armour, suddenly emerged from the Kyaukmyaung bridgehead and moved into the foothills to the east. On the following day 62nd Bde. joined 64th Bde. and together the two drove southwards, literally engulfing such Japanese troops as got in their way. Any considerable pocket of resistance was by-passed, being left for 98th Bde. to deal with as it thrust from the Thabeikkyin bridgehead in the wake of the other two brigades. By March 3 the division was out of the hills and the pace of its advance quickened. On March 5 it crossed the Chaungmagyi Chaung, eighteen miles to the north of Mandalay and the last natural obstacle before the city. Strong defensive positions at Madaya were stormed by 98th Bde. before they could be manned. As the division neared Mandalay the resistance stiffened but it remained unco-ordinated for by this time the Japanese 15th Division, which had been severely punished at Imphal and equally badly mauled during its attacks upon Indian 19th Division's bridgeheads, was completely destroyed as a fighting formation. On March 8, Indian 19th Division reached the northern outskirts of the city in which resistance was well organised in two areas, on Mandalay Hill and in Fort Dufferin.

Mandalay Hill is a striking tapering rock that rises quite abruptly from the plain to nearly 800 feet to dominate the whole countryside and the whole of the city. Its steep sides, especially the south, east and west, are covered with buildings of one kind and another, temples, stairways and the like, and on the northern side the Japanese had constructed many strong-points and machine-gun posts. It stands like a sentinel on the northern edge of the city and separated therefrom by Fort Dufferin. Fort Dufferin is a vast rectangular walled enclosure situated at the north-east edge of the city about a mile south-west of Mandalay Hill and also about a mile to the east of the Irrawaddy. It enclosed about one and a quarter square miles of flat parkland dotted with buildings of various kinds, Government House, club, hospital, barracks, gaol and, upon a large raised area, the teak Royal Palace of Thibaw, the last of the Burmese kings, the Queen's Palace, lesser queens' palaces, audience hall, as well as a number of stone buildings. The fort has a crenelated 23 ft. high wall, faced with thick brickwork and backed by earth embankments 30 ft. wide at ground level and 12 ft. near the top. All round the fort is a moat about 75 yds. wide. Each side of the fort has a main gate in the centre with a bridge leading to it.

Early on March 9, 98th Bde. stormed up the northern slope of Mandalay Hill, bombing and tommy-gunning its way past the machine-gun posts and caves. The fighting continued until the 11th when the last of the Japanese on the hill were destroyed by rolling petrol drums down into the cellars into which they had withdrawn and then setting these alight by means of Very lights or tracer bullets.

For the next three days Indian 19th Division fought its way into the city and around the fort until on the 15th Fort Dufferin was completely surrounded. An attempt to storm the fort by 98th Bde. was unsuccessful mainly because the attackers were so impeded by the lotus that grows so luxuriantly in the moat. Old fashioned siege methods, reminiscent of the Indian Mutiny, were then revived, medium guns were brought up to within 500 yds. of the wall in an attempt to breach it; scaling ladders were prepared and storming parties detailed. After several costly attempts to get across the moat had failed, the Air Force took over, using 500 lb. and then 2,000 lb. bombs. On the 13th the Air Force bombed the interior of the fort and all the teak buildings of the Royal Palace and most of the others were destroyed. The artillery blasted more than fifty holes in the north, east and west walls, some of the breaches being 12 yds. wide. The bombing of the walls from the air caused no appreciable damage.

Just when it began to seem that it would be sensible to mask the fort and get on with the southward advance a great deal of activity of an unusual kind in and around the fort was noticed during the night of March 19/20 and in the early morning, after an air-strike, a group of Anglo-Burmans, carrying a white flag and a Union Jack, appeared at the North Gate to bring the news that the Japanese garrison had departed during the night. Some of them were intercepted, some were hunted down during the next few days as they hid in deserted houses in the city, some got clean away.

THE CROSSING OF THE IRRAWADDY

62nd Bde. had taken no part in this amazing operation. On March 6 it had set out along smugglers' tracks over the mountains south-eastwards for Maymyo, the summer capital of pre-war Burma. After a four days' trek the brigade suddenly burst into this quiet hill station to surprise and overwhelm the Japanese garrison of administrative and base troops. This being done the brigade left one battalion (2nd Welch) behind in the place and marched back to Mandalay to rejoin the division.

INDIAN 20TH DIVISION (XXXIII CORPS)

By the beginning of March Japanese pressure upon the perimeters of Indian 20th Division's bridgeheads slackened as troops were taken away for use in attempts to oppose the advance of IV Corps towards Meiktila. The morale of the Japanese that remained to face Indian 20th Division was low and the capture of Taungtha by IV Corps had cut off their food supplies. Thus it was that when the time came for the Indian division to issue forth from its bridgeheads it met a dispirited enemy some of whom quickly withdrew into the hills south of Myotha while the rest retreated towards the area of Kyaukse. On March 2 the division began to fight its way out of the bridgeheads and by the 5th all three of its brigades were ready to advance eastwards on Mandalay. By the 10th, 80th Bde. overcoming strong resistance had captured Gyo to the southeast while 32nd Bde. had advanced three miles. By the 12th 100th Bde. had captured the road junction at Myotha. During the following week the division occupied a number of villages, some of them without fighting, destroyed many parties of Japanese troops and with air support reached to within two miles of Kyaukse by March 23. Here 80th Bde. was checked and so 32nd Bde. began an encircling movement southwest of the town. After a week's hard fighting Kyaukse was entered and much booty captured. Meanwhile 100th Bde., less one battalion and with two armoured car regiments, raided the Japanese communications to the south. Pyinzi was captured on March 20 by a column that was intending to link up with Indian 17th Division of IV Corps. On the following day, the day when Mandalay was finally cleared by Indian 19th Division, 100th Bde. captured Pindale and took Wundwin after a sharp fight in which the majority of the two hundred Japanese L. of C. troops in the town were killed. The brigade then turned northwards to Kume which was captured on the 23rd. This daring raid caused great havoc for it completely disrupted the system of Japanese command over a wide area at a very critical moment. Very large quantities of stores and technical equipment were captured, including two complete trains loaded with arms and ordnance stores. Many hundreds of Japanese were killed and fifty-three emaciated prisoners were taken; they were patients in a field hospital and remained alive because the staff was given no time in which to destroy them. The division thereafter continued to send out mobile columns in all directions to surprise, to harass and to destroy. On March 29 patrols of 100th Bde. operating south of Wundwin made contact with Indian 17th Division.

2ND DIVISION (XXXIII CORPS)

2nd Division began to emerge from its bridgehead at Ngazun on March 7. On March 11 its 5th Bde. captured Kyauktalon and pressed on eastwards to reach a point within two miles of the Myitnge River by the 15th. 6th Bde., operating to the south of 5th Bde. and facing very stubborn opposition, reached to within two miles of Tada-U by this date. On March 17, 5th Bde. captured the old Ava Fort near to the Ava Bridge and secured the southern half of this bridge and by the 21st the Ava-Mandalay road had been opened and 2nd Division had joined up with Indian 19th Division. 6th Bde. by this time had reached the Myitnge and had inflicted heavy losses on the Japanese units that were retreating before Indian 19th Division. 4th Bde. now passed through 6th Bde. on March 18 to advance on Sado where considerable opposition was encountered. On the 20th, 5th Bde. was firmly established in the Amarapura area and its patrols were probing northwards towards Mandalay to make contact with patrols of Indian 19th Division moving southwards. On the 28th, 5th Bde. moved to Myingyan and 4th Bde., having moved to Pyinzi, started to advance westwards towards Natogyi, 17 miles to the west of Myingyan, linking up with 268th Bde. there. From Pyinzi patrols entered Mahlaing and 4th Bde. continued to advance along this axis.

INDIAN 268TH BRIGADE (XXXIII CORPS)

Having cleared Sagaing, this brigade moved to the south-west on March 20 to Myotha clearing the north end of the Ava Bridge on the way. Its leading elements reached Myingyan on the 26th.

It was on this date that the Burma Defence Army, serving with the Japanese, openly rebelled to cause considerable confusion. Later, changing sides, this force was to become the Burma National Army.

MEDICAL COVER

INDIAN 7TH DIVISION (IV CORPS)

For the crossing of the Irrawaddy by 33rd Bde., 44 (Ind.) Fd. Amb. opened a light M.D.S. at Milestone 8 on the Pauk-Pakokku road. One company of the field ambulance was attached to the brigade and this opened an A.D.S. near the river when it became clear that the crossing was not going to be successful. Additional cars, stretchers and blankets were sent to this A.D.S. When the second attempt to cross had been successful this A.D.S., having evacuated all its patients, moved up to the river's edge on its western bank and a detachment of 54 (Ind.) Fd. Amb. formed a car post there. On February 14 a company of 54 (Ind.) Fd. Amb. with a number of ambulance cars and jeep ambulances crossed the river to open an A.D.S. in the bridgehead. Evacuation was from R.A.P. to the A.D.S. of 54 (Ind.) Fd. Amb. whence the casualties were ferried across the river in returning river craft to the car post of 54 (Ind.) Fd. Amb. on the west bank and thence to the M.D.S. of 44 (Ind.) Fd. Amb. at Milestone 8.

When the division had got across, 44 and the rest of 54 (Ind.) Fd. Ambs. moved into the bridgehead to open in Nyaungu. Evacuation was by light aircraft to IV Corps medical centre in Sinthe.

INDIAN 17TH DIVISION (IV CORPS)

23 (Ind.) Fd. Amb. crossed the river into the Nyaungu bridgehead on February 21. To it 8 (Ind.) M.S.U. was attached. It moved with 63rd Bde. through Ngathayauk on the 22nd to open its M.D.S. in the vicinity of Pyinbin. When the brigade turned north to move on Taungtha its casualties were carried forward.

With 48th Bde. was 37 (Ind.) Fd. Amb. The field ambulance opened its M.D.S. in Kamye on February 22. A light airstrip was constructed nearby and evacuation was by light aircraft. On the 24th, 23 (Ind.) Fd. Amb., with 8 (Ind.) M.S.U. attached, opened its M.D.S. in Taungtha. Casualties were evacuated from this M.D.S. to the airstrip at Kamye and thence to the corps medical centre at Sinthe. When 63rd Bde. went into the lead to reach Mahlaing on the evening of February 26, it was accompanied by 23 (Ind.) Fd. Amb. The casualties were carried forward and evacuated from Mahlaing by light aircraft. This field ambulance next moved to the airstrip at Thabutkon there to open its A.D.S., to which 8 (Ind.) M.S.U. was attached, to provide cover for 99th Bde. which was flown in from Palel on February 27. Its M.D.S. was established at Milestone $11\frac{1}{2}$ on the Thabutkon–Meiktila road to serve 63rd Bde. and when this brigade made its wide out-flanking movement to the south of Meiktila the field ambulance went with it and on February 29 opened an A.D.S. in Antu. It also sent a light A.D.S. with the column that established the road-block on the Meiktila–Kyaukpadaung road.

On March 1, 63rd Bde. moved into Meiktila West and 23 (Ind.) Fd. Amb. opened its M.D.S. in Kanna to serve it. Evacuation from this M.D.S. was to a car post in Antu and thence to an airstrip for evacuation to the corps medical centre. During the clearing of Meiktila casualties were numerous. On March 2, for example, 23 (Ind.) Fd. Amb. admitted 75. 99th Bde. in the airfield area was served by 50 (Ind.) Fd. Amb. which was sited nearby. The casualties in the dressing station of 23 (Ind.) Fd. Amb. in Kanna were transferred to the M.D.S. of 50 (Ind.) Fd. Amb.

for evacuation by medium aircraft from the Meiktila airfield. 23 (Ind.) Fd. Amb. then established its M.D.S. near a light airstrip in the western part of the town. Evacuation from this M.D.S. was to that of 50 (Ind.) Fd. Amb.

When the division sent out columns along all the roads leading to Meiktila the field ambulances provided detachments and ambulance cars for attachment to them. When the main airfield could not be used, because it was under artillery and mortar fire, casualties were taken to the M.D.S. of 23 (Ind.) Fd. Amb. on the light airstrip and to this the mobile surgical unit was attached. At one time during this period of non-evacuation some 300 casualties accumulated in the M.D.S. of 50 (Ind.) Fd. Amb. To get them from this M.D.S. to that of 23 (Ind.) Fd. Amb. was a distinctly hazardous business. When evacuation became possible again no less than 637 casualties were transported by light aircraft in five days. During the month of March a total of 2,033 casualties were evacuated by air from Meiktila. On March 25 the M.D.S. of 50 (Ind.) Fd. Amb. closed and two surgeons were flown in to reinforce the staff of 23 (Ind.) Fd. Amb.

INDIAN 19TH DIVISION (XXXIII CORPS)

63 (Ind.) Fd. Amb. was the first of the divisional medical units to cross the Irrawaddy. It did so on February 12 and opened its M.D.S. in Singu, due east of Shwebo and on the east bank of the river. On the 18th, 52 (Ind.) Fd. Amb. followed and also opened its M.D.S. in Singu. 51 (Ind.) Fd. Amb. remained on the west bank in Kyaukmyaung to receive the casualties that were sent back across the river by the other two field ambulances and to despatch them to the corps medical centre in Shwebo. The field ambulances attached A.D.Ss. to the brigades. The A.D.S. in the Thabeikkyin bridgehead was soon able to evacuate casualties by light aircraft direct to the corps medical centre in Shwebo. In the Kyaukmyaung bridgehead about a hundred a day were being evacuated through the M.D.S. of 51 (Ind.) Fd. Amb. This M.D.S. closed on February 21 and moved to Shwedaik, still on the western bank, to open there to cater for the minor sick of the division. On February 27 this M.D.S. closed, handed its immobiles to 67 (Ind.) S.S. and, crossing the river, moved forward into Singu.

When the division began its advance on Mandalay, 53 (Ind.) Fd. Amb. moved to Taungbetywa and opened its M.D.S. Evacuation therefrom was to the M.D.S. of 52 in Singu. On March 10 the M.D.S. of 53 moved forward to Madaya. A light airstrip was completed at Singu just in time to prevent the M.D.S. of 52 (Ind.) Fd. Amb. becoming overwhelmed by the flow of casualties. 53 (Ind.) Fd. Amb. next moved from Madaya with 98th Bde. and in its place in Madaya came the M.D.S. of 52 (Ind.) Fd. Amb., with 8 (Ind.) M.S.U. attached. 51 (Ind.)

THE CROSSING OF THE IRRAWADDY

Fd. Amb., leaving a detachment at the airstrip in Singu, moved forward to provide cover for the crossing of the Chaungmagyi Chaung just to the north of Madaya. H.Q. 51 (Ind.) Fd. Amb. reached Madaya on March 6 and the two companies of the unit with 98th Bde. reached the

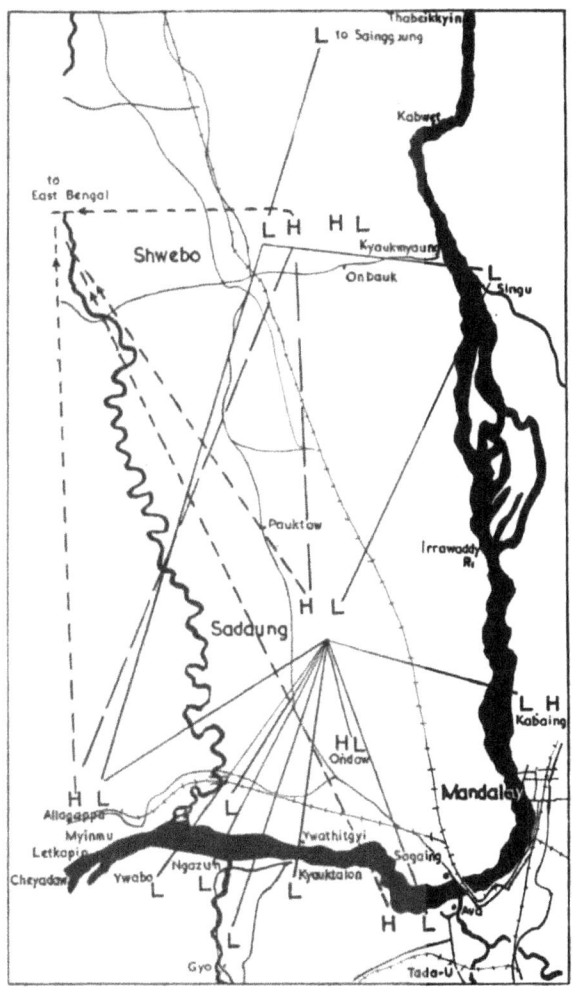

FIG. 55. XXXIII Corps. Casualty Air Evacuation at the Time of the Capture of Mandalay

```
H = Heavy strip
L = Light strip
——————————— L.5. Route
——  ——  ——  C.64. Route
— — — — — — C.47. Route.
```

northern outskirts of Mandalay by March 8. On the 10th the headquarters of the unit moved to Kabaing and opened its M.D.S., casualties being evacuated therefrom to the M.D.S. of 52 (Ind.) Fd. Amb. in Madaya. As soon as an airstrip had been constructed at Kabaing casualties were evacuated by light aircraft to the corps subsidiary medical centre in Sadaung. On March 16 the M.D.S. of 52 joined that of 51 in Kabaing and began to admit the minor sick and also considerable numbers of civilians from Mandalay. 53 was with 98th Bde. and was evacuating its casualties direct to the corps medical centre in Sadaung. This pattern of medical cover remained unchanged until Mandalay had been captured and cleared.

INDIAN 20TH DIVISION (XXXIII CORPS)

When 100th Bde. of Indian 20th Division crossed the Irrawaddy the R.A.Ps. were sited on the southern bank of the river as was also the A.D.S. of 42 (Ind.) Fd. Amb. which tucked itself into the face of the high steep south bank. From the A.D.S. casualties were sent back across the river in returning folding-boat rafts and pontoon rafts and in motor-driven boats to a car post in Myaung village south of Allagappa on the north bank. A road had been constructed from this village to join the main Monywa–Sagaing road which ran through Allagappa, a thirty minutes' drive away. The divisional medical centre in Allagappa consisted of the M.D.Ss. of 42 and 55 (Ind.) Fd. Ambs., 10 (Ind.) M.S.U., a surgical team from 5 (Ind.) Beach Medical Unit, a surgeon from 13 (Ind.) C.C.S., an anaesthetist who happened to be available, 2 F.T.U. and some B.O.Rs. collected from the divisional medical units. A number of visitors from Fourteenth Army—liaison officers—were put to work in this centre. Four nursing officers were sent forward to join it and, as is always the case, raised the level of post-operative care very considerably. The Consulting Surgeon, Fourteenth Army, visiting the division, attached himself to the centre and did his share of the operating.

The bridgehead of 32nd Bde. was under such heavy fire that 59 (Ind.) Fd. Amb. was not able to get across the river and establish itself in it. The field ambulance stayed on the northern bank until 100th Bde's. bridgehead had become well defined and then crossed into this and made its way thence into the subsidiary bridgehead of 32nd Bde.

In the divisional medical centre in Allagappa, 42 (Ind.) Fd. Amb. admitted the surgical cases, 55 (Ind.) Fd. Amb. the medical. The first of these units dealt with more than 1,000 casualties during its stay in Allagappa. The minor sick were evacuated by road to Monywa where a group of Fourteenth Army medical units was open. Light aircraft flew casualties to the corps medical centre at Sadaung. Returning Dakotas took surgical cases, fit to travel, to Comilla and Chittagong. Since most casualties reached the divisional medical centre late in the day or during the night, about eight hours after the receipt of their wounds, and since the light aircraft did not fly by night, forward surgery had to be undertaken in the divisional medical centre.

When on March 2 the division began its advance out of the bridgehead, the M.D.S. of 59 (Ind.) Fd. Amb. opened in Lingadipa to serve the whole division, evacuating its casualties to the M.D.S. of 55 (Ind.) Fd. Amb. in Allagappa. On March 8 the M.D.S. of 59 moved on to Ywabo and that of 55 to Gyo to open there on the 12th. 10 (Ind.) M.S.U. was attached to the M.D.S. of 55. Evacuation of the more serious medical cases was now to Monywa and that of surgical cases to Sadaung. On March 17, 59 (Ind.) Fd. Amb. moved from Ywabo to Chaunggwa there to cater for the divisional minor medical and for civilian cases. On March 20, 55 (Ind.) Fd. Amb. closed in Gyo and moved to Ngazun there to open its M.D.S. with 10 (Ind.) M.S.U. attached. To this M.D.S. were also attached a surgical team from 8 (Ind.) C.C.S. in Tada-U, 2 F.T.U. and a dental unit. The nursing officers from the divisional medical centre in Allagappa moved forward to join this M.D.S.

It was at this point that cholera made its appearance in the division. By March 27 there had been 40 cases and 9 deaths. The nursing officers were largely responsible for saving the lives of those who survived. When the epidemic died out the nursing officers were recalled by their own unit and as a token of the division's respect and admiration a captured Japanese staff car was presented to them on their departure.

When Kyaukse had been captured 42 (Ind.) Fd. Amb. moved forward to Kume where its A.D.S. combined with the M.D.S. of 59 (Ind.) Fd. Amb. in Zale, whither it had moved on April 4, to provide cover for 100th Bde.

The three British battalions serving with Indian 20th Division were now transferred to 36th Division, being replaced by two Indian and one Gurkha battalions.

2ND DIVISION (XXXIII CORPS)

For the crossing of the Irrawaddy the following arrangements were made:

S.M.O. 5th Bde. (officer commanding 5 Fd. Amb.) would establish an aid post in each assembly area on the north bank. To these aid posts all returning river craft carrying casualties would be directed. They would be unloaded by personnel of 5 Fd. Amb. manning the aid posts and loaded on to ambulance cars which would convey them to the M.D.S. of 4 Fd. Amb. in Kinywa. One bearer officer and a detachment R.A.M.C. would accompany each leading battalion and the bearer officer would be responsible for the evacuation of casualties from the R.A.Ps. to the beach and for the loading of the casualties on to the craft returning to the north bank. A car post would be established by

5 Fd. Amb. in the vicinity of the aid posts on the north bank and from this pool cars leaving the aid posts would be replaced.

The A.D.S. of 5 Fd. Amb. would cross into the bridgehead under arrangements to be made by H.Q. 5th Bde. as soon as the situation permitted. When the division broke out of the bridgehead 5 Fd. Amb. would establish its M.D.S. in the bridgehead area and become responsible for the evacuation of casualties from 5th and 6th Bdes. and for all medical arrangements in the bridgehead area. A.D.M.S. would then assume responsibility for the arrangements on the north bank. When 5 Fd. Amb's. M.D.S. was established 4 Fd. Amb. in Kinywa would close. From the M.D.S. of 4 Fd. Amb. in Kinywa the most serious cases would be flown by light aircraft to the corps medical centre at Sadaung. The rest would be conveyed by road to Sadaung. 4 Fd. Amb. would be responsible for the loading of the light aircraft on the Kinywa airstrip. This unit would retain all sick likely to be fit to return to their units within seven days. As soon as possible a light airstrip would be constructed in the bridgehead area and casualties would then be flown direct to the corps medical centre. I.O.R. casualties from corps R.A. units would be sent to 67 (Ind.) Fd. Amb. in Kinywa through 4 Fd. Amb. B.O.Rs. would be treated in 4 Fd. Amb.

5 (Ind.) M.S.U. would be attached to the M.D.S. of 5 Fd. Amb. in the bridgehead and when 4 Fd. Amb. closed 9 (Ind.) M.S.U. would revert to command D.D.M.S. XXXIII Corps.

Casualties from 4th Bde. would be evacuated to 6 Fd. Amb. in Ondaw. D.D.M.S. Corps would post a surgeon to 6 Fd. Amb. Evacuation from 6 Fd. Amb. would be by light aircraft to the corps medical centre at Sadaung.

These arrangements worked smoothly. The total number of casualties evacuated to the M.D.S. of 4 Fd. Amb. during the first 24 hours of the operation was 75 of whom 43 were evacuated by light plane on D-day+1 to Sadaung. The average interval between the time of the receipt of the wound and admission to the M.D.S. was $3\frac{1}{2}$ hours.

It was on March 1 that 5 Fd. Amb. established its M.D.S. in Ngazun and to it 5 (Ind.) M.S.U. was attached. On the following day 6 Fd. Amb. closed in Ondaw and moved up to Maungdaung, remaining closed. This unit moved across the Irrawaddy to Ngazun on the 5th still remaining closed. On the 13th, 4 Fd. Amb. crossed the river and moved to Kyauktalon, remaining closed. On the following day 6 Fd. Amb. established its M.D.S. in Myinthi and to this M.D.S. 5 (Ind.) M.S.U. was attached. On the 16th, 4 Fd. Amb. joined 6 Fd. Amb. in Myinthi but remained closed. On March 19, 4 Fd. Amb. established its M.D.S., to which 5 (Ind.) M.S.U. was attached, in Sizon. Evacuation was by rail from Tada-U to Sizon. Jeeps were modified so as to run on the railway line. On March 25, 5 Fd. Amb. moved to Myotha, remaining closed and on the 28th this unit moved to Shwegu, together with 5 (Ind.) M.S.U. On the following day 4 Fd. Amb. moved into Pyinzi. These frequent and long moves of the divisional field ambulances were associated with considerable difficulty for additional transport was not easily obtained.

On April 3 the division began to leave Myingyan by air for Kanchrapara near Calcutta, there to begin its preparations for Operation 'Dracula'. These preparations included an examination of the men of all units by the R.M.Os. and by the divisional psychiatrist in an attempt to eliminate all those who were unfit.

MEDICAL ARRANGEMENTS. IV CORPS

On February 14, Indian 7th Division crossed the Irrawaddy. At first there was no light airstrip on the east bank of the river and so a mobile surgical unit was sent into the bridgehead to attach itself to a field ambulance while a second M.S.U. was held in reserve at 19 (Ind.) C.C.S. Shortly before the crossing of the river the average number of casualties reaching the corps' medical centre each day was between 60 and 70, mostly battle casualties; after the crossing the number rose to 100 or more on many days.

The intention had been to site the next corps medical centre in or near Meiktila, when that in Sinthe had become too remote from the front. The fighting in the Meiktila area was so fierce and so long sustained, however, that the idea had to be given up. On March 1, H.Q. IV Corps moved up to Myitche on the Irrawaddy opposite Pagan. Sinthe was now 40 miles back and Indian 17th Division in the Meiktila area, 80 miles to the east, had nothing but its divisional medical units and a mobile surgical unit to provide it with medical cover during some of the fiercest fighting of the whole campaign. Indian 7th Division was in action about Taungtha and near Chauk while 28th E.A. Bde. was being heavily attacked in its box at Letse. Indian 5th Division was about to arrive in the forward area. The medical centre at Sinthe had become badly sited for it was in one corner of the very large area that it served. It contained 19 (Ind.) C.C.S. and 9 (Ind.) M.F.T.U. together with a number of subsidiary units. Evacuation to it from the Meiktila area was by medium aircraft, from Indian 7th Division and the East African brigade by light aircraft.

It was decided to establish a corps medical centre in Myitche which had both light and heavy airstrips. The first of the units to arrive was 14 (Ind.) C.C.S. from Kan which began to admit patients on the 16th. A mobile surgical unit—14 (Ind.) M.S.U.—which had been with Indian 7th Division was withdrawn and posted to this corps medical centre. An improvised surgical team from 19 (Ind.) C.C.S. in Sinthe was flown in to Meiktila on March 19 to help the field ambulances.

By March 20 evacuation by medium aircraft from the Meiktila airfield had become impossible for the reason that the airfield was under fire. On March 23 such a plane, loaded with casualties, and about to take off, was hit and disabled, fortunately without loss of life. After this, evacuation was by light aircraft only for a time. These aircraft could not reach Sinthe without refuelling and so evacuation had to be to Myitche. So, 19 (Ind.) C.C.S. was brought forward from Sinthe to Myitche to open alongside 14 (Ind.) C.C.S. on March 25. Two more mobile surgical units reached Myitche, one of them, with equipment, was attached to 19 (Ind.) C.C.S., the other, without equipment, was flown into Meiktila to reinforce the hard-pressed surgical staffs. There were now two theatres and three surgical teams in Meiktila and four theatres and four teams in Myitche. Casualties piled up in Meiktila as a consequence of the interruption of evacuation but 165th Liaison Squadron redoubled its efforts and for a whole week worked to capacity and even beyond for the L.5s. often carried two casualties at a time. On March 26, for example, 226 casualties were brought to Myitche by light plane, 171 from Meiktila, 157 of these being battle casualties. Evacuation from Meiktila by light aircraft was so well organised and so well performed that the pilots gained the admiration of all.

MEDICAL ARRANGEMENTS. XXXIII CORPS

The corps medical centre at Sadaung had grown until it included one C.C.S., one M.F.T.U., one M.D.S. a field laboratory, a field transfusion unit, an ophthalmic unit, a venereal diseases treatment centre and a dental centre. The Sadaung site was not really suitable for a corps medical centre and when Sadaung gave place to Ondaw as the supply centre from which the transport planes set out and to which they returned carrying casualties, its unsuitability became more obvious. All medical stores now had to be brought from Ondaw to Sadaung and special arrangements had to be made, when this was possible, for the returning planes to call at Sadaung. As the divisions moved further and further away from Shwebo and Sadaung the light aircraft began to encounter difficulty in getting casualties back to these centres from the airstrips in the divisional areas. Indian 20th Division found it necessary to develop a divisional medical centre in Allagappa around the M.D.Ss. of 42 and 55 (Ind.) Fd. Ambs.

It was to the M.D.S. of 42 (Ind.) Fd. Amb. that Consulting Surgeon Fourteenth Army attached himself during the fortnight in which this unit was called upon to deal with over 900 battle casualties. At this time the corps medical centre in Sadaung was working to capacity and it became necessary from time to time to organise mass evacuation by road and air to Shwebo in order to bring some slight and temporary relief to Sadaung. When 2nd Division was across the Irrawaddy and as casualties were so few it was possible to close 8 (Ind.) C.C.S. in Shwebo and bring it forward to Kinywa in readiness for the formation of a new corps medical centre south of the Irrawaddy after Mandalay had fallen.

In XXXIII Corps during these operations the proportion of 'medical' cases, as contrasted with 'surgical', returned to duty from the corps medical centres varied considerably but generally was in the region of 75 per cent. There were remarkably few deaths from 'medical' causes. In a series of 9,734 'medical' admissions to eight M.F.T.Us. the fatality-rate was only 0·35 per cent. and in another series of 1,924 'medical' admissions to three C.C.Ss. it was only 0·31 per cent.

The total number of casualties evacuated by light aircraft in IV and XXXIII Corps areas during March was 8,309; the total number carried by transport aircraft being 6,608.

D.D.M.S. Fourteenth Army records that in one Japanese military hospital in Mandalay the case-fatality-rate for malaria was of the order of 80 per cent. and remarks that had the figure of 8 per cent. been reached in a British or Indian hospital its commanding officer, the A.D.M.S. and the D.D.M.S. concerned would certainly have quickly changed their addresses and their posts. This fatality-rate can quite reasonably be used as a yardstick wherewith to measure the efficiency of the Japanese medical services as compared with that of the medical services of Fourteenth Army, it being remembered that at this time the Japanese services had more or less completely broken down. This does not necessarily mean that the Japanese medical services were inherently faulty, though there is plentiful evidence which goes to show that in fact they were; no medical service can function efficiently, no matter how potentially good it is, in a setting in which chaos has corroded organisation and in which despair has destroyed all sense of responsibility.

TABLE 35

XXXIII Corps. Casualties. February 20–March 31, 1945.

Average Weekly Strength of XXXIII Corps 76,813	Total Admissions (Total number evacuated beyond the R.A.P.) 14,652	Average Daily Rate per 1,000 1·95
Principal Diseases	Admissions	Average Daily Rate per 1,000
Malaria and N.Y.D. (F.)	3,175	0·42
Dysentery and Diarrhoea	1,048	0·14
Typhus	154	0·02
Battle Casualties	4,556	0·60

TABLE 36

XXXIII Corps. Number of Casualties evacuated and Amounts of Medical Supplies and Ordnance Stores delivered by 164th Liaison Squadron. February 20–March 31, 1945.

Casualties Evacuated	By L.5	5,053
	By C.64	1,114
		6,167
Medical Supplies Ordnance Stores	By L.5	294,165 lbs.
	By C.64	125,405 ,,
		419,570 ,,

CHAPTER 13

THE COMPLEMENTARY OPERATIONS IN NORTHERN COMBAT AREA COMMAND AND IN ARAKAN

THOUGH to do so is to disturb the chronological order of events somewhat, it is convenient at this point to turn away from the affairs of Fourteenth Army, victorious at Meiktila and at Mandalay, and to follow the fortunes of 36th Division in N.C.A.C. and of XV Corps in Arakan. It will be remembered that the operations about to be described were intended to be part of Operation 'Capital' and to be complementary to those undertaken by Fourteenth Army.

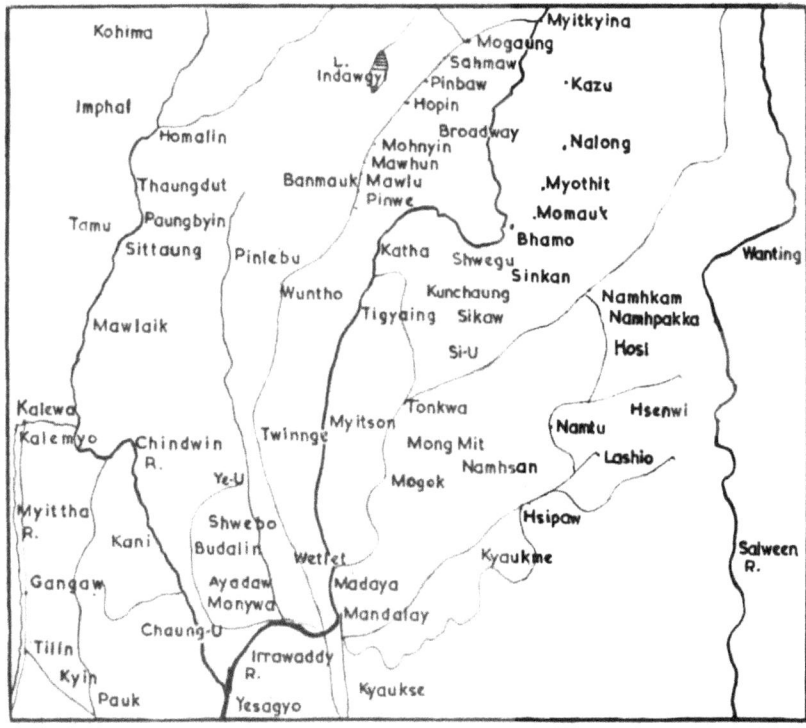

FIG. 56. Northern Combat Area Command. The Southward Advance of 36th Division, 'Mars' Brigade and of Chinese First and Sixth Armies. August 1944–March 1945.

I. The Southward Advance of 36th Division, 'Mars' Brigade and Chinese First and Sixth Armies

While Fourteenth Army was advancing towards the Irrawaddy, much had been happening in N.C.A.C. When General Sultan took over command his force was well south of Myitkyina. Early in August 1944, 36th Division, then consisting of 29th and 72nd Bdes., had begun its march down the 'railway corridor' on the main line from Mogaung to Naba, near Katha. On the division's left Chinese Sixth Army (22nd and 50th Divisions) had advanced on a parallel axis and further to the east Chinese First Army (30th and 38th Divisions) with 'Mars' Bde., and Kachin Levies, was advancing on Lashio.

The routes taken by these formations were, briefly, as follows:

36th Division: Mogaung, Sahmaw (Aug. 6), Pinbaw, Hopin, Mohnyin (Oct. 19), Mawhun, Mawlu (Nov. 1), Pinwe (Nov. 30), Katha (Dec. 11).
   Right Column: Katha, Tigyaing (Dec. 23), Twinnge (Jan. 24), Mong Mit (Mar. 9).
   Left Column: Katha, Kunchaung, Myitson (Feb. 11), Mong Mit.
   Whole Division: Mong Mit (Mar. 9), Mogok (Mar. 19), Kyaukme (Mar. 30).

Chinese Sixth Army: Mogaung, Hopin.
   Right Column (50th Div.): Mawlu, Shwegu (Nov. 6).
   Left Column (22nd Div.): Hopin, Broadway (Oct. 26), Shwegu (Nov. 6).
   Whole Army: Shwegu, Sikaw, Tonkwa (Dec. 8).
   50th Div.: Tonkwa, Namhsan, Hsipaw, Kyaukme and Namtu, Hsipaw, Kyaukme (Mar. 16).

Chinese First Army: Myitkyina (Aug. 3), Kazu, Nalong, Myothit (Oct. 27), Momauk (Nov. 14), Bhamo (Dec. 15), Namhkam (Jan. 15), Wanting (Jan. 21), Namhpakka, Hosi (Jan. 18), Hsenwi (Feb. 19), Lashio (Mar. 7), Hsipaw.

U.S. 'Mars' Brigade: Myitkyina (Aug. 3), Kazu, Nalong, Momauk, Sikaw, Tonkwa, Hosi, Hsenwi, Lashio.

As 36th Division debouched from Naba Junction at the southern end of the railway corridor, it made contact with Indian 19th Division on December 16. It then crossed the Irrawaddy at Katha by raft and sampan from west to east and continued its advance down both banks of the river, through Tigyaing and Twinnge on the west bank and through Kunchaung and Myitson on the east. Contact with 'Mars' Force was made. On December 19, Ind. 26th Bde. joined 36th Division and moved to Indaw.

The Chinese Yunnan Force, U.S. trained and equipped, had crossed the Salween in May of 1944 and for many long months had fought grim battles between the Salween and the Shweli Rivers. In December, at a cost of some 19,000 dead, it succeeded in linking up with Chinese First Army which had captured Bhamo. On January 27 the road route from India through Burma to China was open and on the very next day the first convoy set out from Ledo for Chungking. Then suddenly Marshal Chiang Kai-shek ordered all Chinese forces in N.C.A.C. to return to China without delay. Pending this move they were not to go further south than the line Lashio–Hsipaw–Kyaukme. It was agreed, however, that the bulk of the transport squadrons should not be used for the purpose of returning the Chinese troops to China until Rangoon had fallen or until the first of June, whichever was the earlier.

On February 27 General Leese of A.L.F.S.E.A. ordered General Sultan to advance to the Lashio–Kyaukme line, to co-operate with Fourteenth Army in the battle for Mandalay and then to exploit southwards towards Loilem.

36th Division had forced the passage of the Shweli River at Myitson on February 9 and with the very considerable help of the U.S.A.A.F. had held on to the bridgehead so gained against repeated assaults which persisted for a whole month. The Japanese then withdrew southwards and 36th Division followed to clear up the Mong Mit area, to capture Mogok with its ruby mines and to link up with 'Mars' Force in Kyaukme on March 30.

In view of the impending dissolution of N.C.A.C. General Slim asked for the return to Fourteenth Army of 36th Division. This request was granted, but as will be seen, the division did not serve in Fourteenth Army for very long.

On March 7 Chinese First Army captured Lashio and on the 16th Hsipaw was occupied. The Chinese then halted and the Japanese, leaving only a few detachments behind, moved southwards to join their compatriots opposing Fourteenth Army. 'Mars' Brigade was flown out to China and N.C.A.C. came to an end. The Chinese took no further part in the campaign in Burma.

36TH DIVISION

After its participation in the operations in Arakan, this division had moved to Margherita to pass under command of N.C.A.C. and to be employed in an advance southwards from Myitkyina. The camp at Margherita was as unsatisfactory as any camp could possibly be; it was knee-deep in mud and the whole area around it was highly malarious. All the time the division remained there it rained. The division was flown to Myitkyina; the airfield had been captured by 'Mars' Bde. but the town of Myitkyina was still in Japanese possession. The divisional artillery was Chinese; attached to the division was a U.S. portable hospital, packed on mules. Air cover was supplied by U.S. 10th Airforce. The division was to be supplied by air.

From Myitkyina the division moved cross country to the west of Mogaung, preparatory to advancing down the railway corridor from Mogaung to Katha. The universal mud made progress slow and even the jeep was defeated. On August 6, 72nd Bde. attacked and gained a feature known as Hill 60, 10 miles south of Mogaung, at a cost of 31 killed and 63 wounded. Divisional H.Q. was established in Sahmaw where it remained throughout the monsoon. Most of the 60 jeeps which constituted the divisional transport were used in lieu of railway engines on the line, U.S. engineers having adapted them for the purpose, while the rest plied between Mogaung and Sahmaw, ferrying forward stores and equipment. The road surface was soon destroyed by the traffic and so the road-using jeeps had to operate in pairs, one always being prepared to tow the other. The jeeps were expected to do the 28-mile round trip three times a day during the monsoon period and so it is not surprising

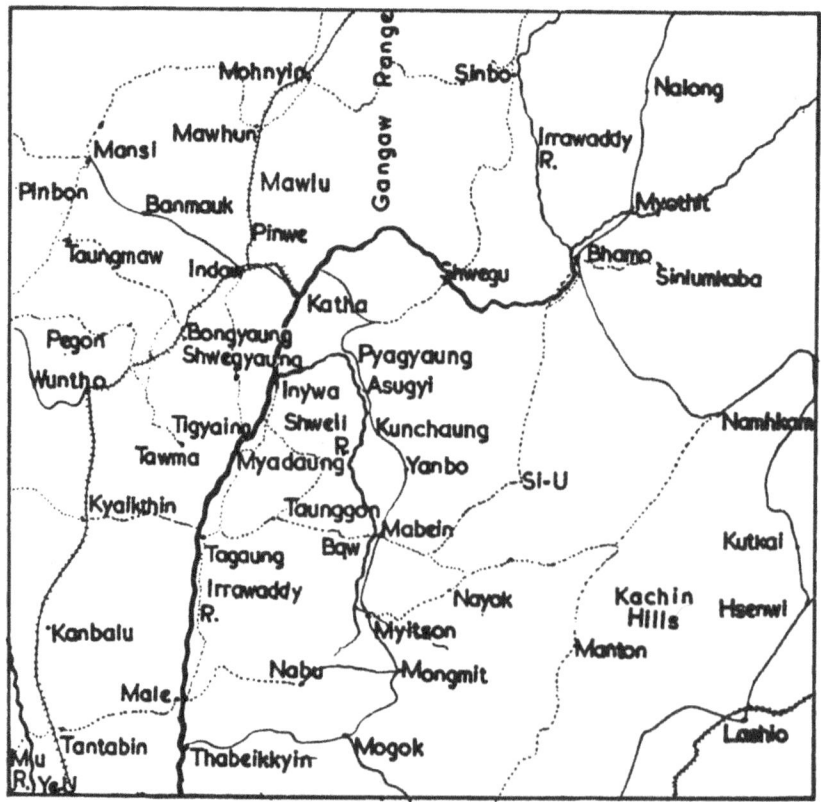

FIG. 57. 36th Division. Mohnyin–Mogok

to learn that the drivers became exhausted and that the vehicles remained unserviced. Later, two railway engines, built out of odds and ends and bits and pieces, made their useful contributions to the advance of the division.

Until Thaikwagon was captured by 9th R. Sussex on August 17, 72nd Bde. remained in the lead. Then 29th took the lead and Pinbaw was taken by 2nd R.S.F. on August 27. Thereafter the advance continued through Bilumyo, Mohnyin, Kadu and Mawhun, the last of these places being captured on October 31 by 1st R.S.F. 72nd Bde. now went into the lead again and after capturing Tonlon met very stubborn resistance at Pinwe. Supported by the divisional artillery and by the Airforce, the brigade battled for this place from November 10 to November 24 but with very little success. 29th Bde. then relieved 72nd Bde. and continued the attack. The Japanese withdrew and on the last day of November, 1st R.S.F., the pipers in the van, marched into the town. In this action the division's losses were 57 killed, 202 wounded and 5 missing.

On December 11, patrols of 29th Bde. entered Katha and Rail Indaw and the journey down the railway corridor was ended. The division's

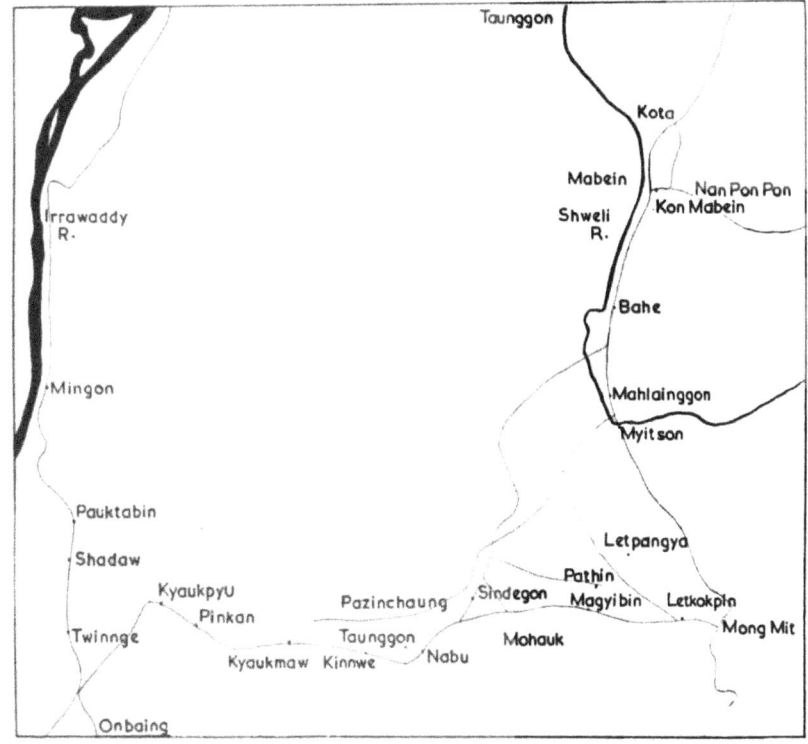

Fig. 58. 36th Division. Taunggon–Mong Mit

next task was that of taking Mong Mit, 150 miles further to the south. The tactical plan adopted for this operation was as follows: 29th Bde. would cross the Irrawaddy at Tigyaing and move southwards along the eastern bank of the river as far as Twinnge and then turn eastwards and head for Mong Mit. Meanwhile 72nd Bde. would cross the Irrawaddy at Katha and follow the road through Yanbo, Mabein, Bahe and Myitson so as to move on Mong Mit from the north and from the west. As has been told Indian 26th Brigade (2nd Buffs, 2/8th Punjab, 1/19th Hybad, 1/1st G.R.) joined the division on December 19, landing at 'Broadway' and moving to Indaw.

Mabein was occupied according to plan by 9th R. Sussex on January 15, 1945 and on the 18th far to the east, Twinnge was entered by 1st R.S.F. of 29th Bde. Bahe was occupied by 6th S.W.B. on January 25.

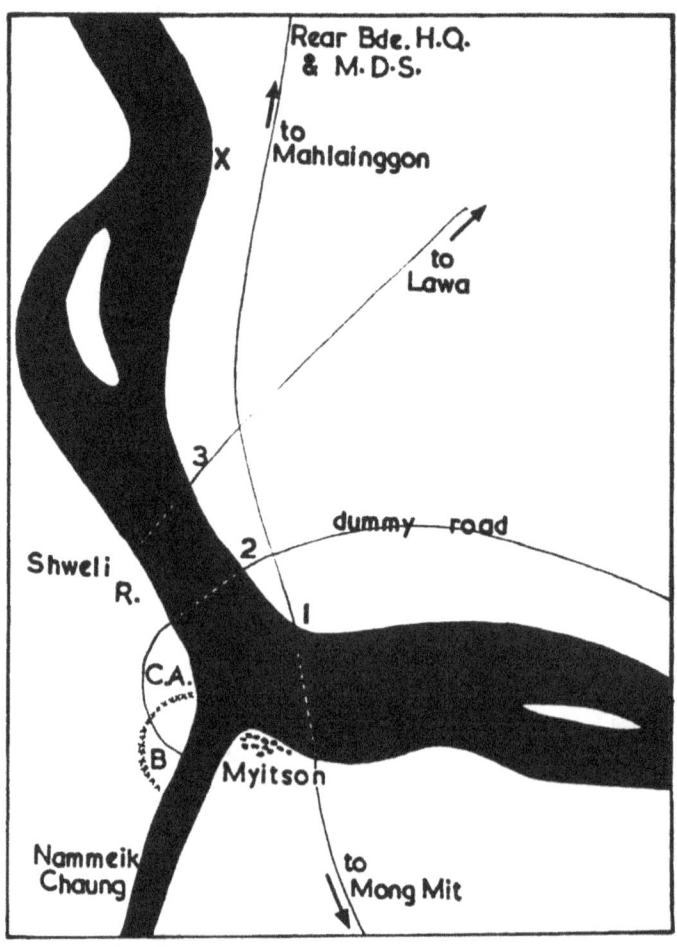

FIG. 59. 36th Division. The Action at Myitson

The Japanese were found to be holding Myitson in considerable strength and Ind. 26th Bde. was given the task of ejecting them. The ensuing action proved to be the fiercest ever fought by the division.

It was decided to cross the Shweli River opposite the village of Myitson and to establish a bridgehead. On February 1, under cover of darkness, a patrol of the Buffs got across and found the Japanese positions unoccupied. Next morning, under cover of a smoke screen, a company of the Buffs began to cross but at once ran into a hail of machine-gun, mortar and artillery fire. Nevertheless the crossing was made and the company established a small bridgehead which was held against repeated attacks during the afternoon and the following night. During the night of February 2/3 the rest of the battalion attempted to make the crossing but only about 130 officers and men succeeded in reaching the bridgehead. Only five of the forty assault boats remained undamaged. Since to reinforce the bridgehead was proving to be so difficult the troops in it were withdrawn and a different plan adopted. Under cover of a heavy artillery screen the withdrawal was completed. The division's losses in this action were 28 killed, 55 wounded and 31 missing.

In order to persuade the Japanese that it was intended to cross the river by making use of the island to the east of the Mahlainggon–Mong Mit road, a road towards this island was built and dummy food and ammunition dumps were constructed along it in places where the Japanese were bound to see them. The actual crossing was made at the point marked X in Fig. 59, well to the north of the bend of the river at Myitson. 1/19th Hybad. got across successfully, as did 2/8th Punjab at the crossing marked 3 in the figure. These two battalions then proceeded to the concentration area (C.A. in the figure) on February 8. They were seen and were shelled but got across the Nammeik Chaung on the morning of the 9th without much difficulty and moved on the village of Myitson to meet the most determined resistance. The bridgehead was expanded between February 9 and 12. On the 13th Japanese troops, making their way through the tall, thick elephant grass, cut the connexion between the concentration area and No. 2 crossing but were quickly thrust back.

It was now decided to withdraw the advanced brigade H.Q. *via* No.2 crossing to rear brigade H.Q. since it seemed that the Japanese were determined to hold on to the block they had inserted between the concentration area and advanced brigade H.Q. This was done during the night of February 14/15. At the same time the brigade commander crossed the river by No.1 crossing and joined the two battalions isolated in the vicinity of Myitson. The Japanese continued to assault the bridgehead and on February 17 made an especially fierce onslaught.

This was sternly repulsed by the Punjabis and thereafter the Japanese withdrew from Myitson.

In the meantime 29th Bde. Gp. had been moving eastwards from Twinnge towards Mong Mit and on March 2 its leading elements met a patrol of 9th R. Sussex of 72nd Bde. The two brigades had been separated for about three months. The way to Mong Mit was now open and 26th and 72nd Bdes. raced towards it. 2/8th Punjab of 26th Bde. got there first to be warmly welcomed by the inhabitants. On March 19, 1/19th Hybad. of the same brigade entered Mogok.

The division was now informed that it was to pass to Fourteenth Army and that it was to be sent to the Mandalay area there to relieve Indian 19th Division so that the Indian division could take part in the

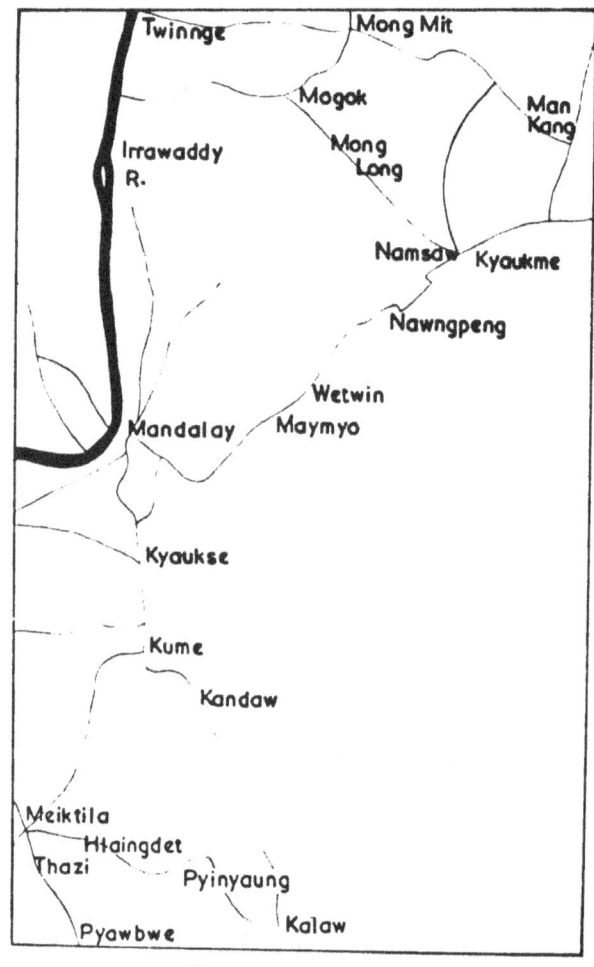

Fig. 60. 36th Division.
Mong Mit–Mandalay–Kalaw Area

impending thrust southwards to Rangoon. Thereafter the division was to be sent back to India to rest. 72nd Bde. was flown from the C.47 airstrip at Mong Long into Mandalay whence 9th R. Sussex proceeded to Maymyo. Then suddenly the plans for the division were changed; it was ordered to take over the Meiktila area from Indian 20th Division.

On April 14, H.Q. 36th Division was in Kume to the south-east of Mandalay and 29th and 72nd Bdes. were moving towards Kalaw while Ind. 26th Bde. was getting ready to be flown out to India. By the 27th, 29th and 72nd Bdes. were concentrated in the vicinity of Pyinyaung and on the following day 72nd Bde. launched an unsuccessful attack upon the Myittha defile. The intention was that when this defile had been cleared 29th Bde. would pass through and capture Kalaw. But the Japanese were holding a naturally very strong position and offered very stubborn resistance, defying all the attempts that were made to dislodge them. During the action the divisional losses were 520 killed, 1,466 wounded and 58 missing, a total of 2,044. Thus it was that the last action to be fought by the division was not to be included among its many successes. By April 8 the division had been relieved by Indian 19th Division, and was being flown to India. 29th Bde. was the last to go, on May 10.

MEDICAL COVER

The medical units that served with 36th Division were:

22 C.C.S.	46 (Ind.) Fd. Amb.
13 and 15 (Ind.) M.S.Us.	and with the brigades
15 (Ind.) M.F.T.U.	34 (Ind.) Fd. Amb. with 26th Bde.
75 and 87 (Ind.) S.Ss.	69 (Ind.) Fd. Amb. with 72nd Bde.
71 (Ind.) M.C.U.	154 Fd. Amb. with 29th Bde.
44 (Ind.) Fd. Hyg. Sec.	

With the division there were seven ambulance cars until one of them struck a mine and then there were six. Jeeps and 30-cwt. trucks could be obtained on demand from the divisional pool. For evacuation purposes mules, bullock carts and, on occasion, elephants were used. The two-tier stretcher-attachment for use with the jeep was discarded for the reason that when a jeep so equipped was driven over the very rough primitive tracks through deep mud, great discomfort was caused to the casualty in the upper berth. 34 (Ind.) Fd. Amb. designed a simple apparatus which enabled the jeep to take two stretcher cases side by side as well as one sitting case alongside the driver in the front seat. During the worst of the weather it was necessary to borrow 6-wheeled vehicles from a U.S. ambulance section. Two aircraft, fitted to take stretchers, accompanied the division as did also a U.S. engineer company whose task it was to build the airstrips.

For much of the time 13 (Ind.) M.S.U. was the only surgical unit with the division and it was fortunate therefore that it was possible to call upon the services of a U.S. surgical team that was with the Chinese artillery group attached to the division. This U.S. team was always sited in the vicinity of the forward divisional M.D.S. and an arrangement developed whereby the Americans did the surgery while the M.D.S. personnel provided the post-operative care. So long as the division moved on a single axis it became the rule for the mobile surgical unit to deal with the minor surgical cases only, the more serious being left for the U.S. surgical team. But to this very satisfactory system there came an end for in December 1944 the Chinese artillery group and so also the U.S. surgical team, left the division. A second mobile surgical unit was at once asked for. As things turned out, however, this second mobile surgical unit was not needed until Katha was reached when the division split into two widely separated parts, one brigade moving along the axis Tigyaing–Twinnge and the other along the axis Katha–Yanbo–Mabein and Myitson.

When Katha was reached, 22 C.C.S. and 15 (Ind.) M.F.T.U. in Sahmaw were 122 miles to the rear. The surgical team of the C.C.S. had been brought forward to make good the loss of the U.S. surgical team and so the C.C.S. itself could not function as a C.C.S. Casualties were being flown past it direct to the base. At Christmas the C.C.S. and the M.F.T.U. were ferried forward to Katha and 15 (Ind.) M.S.U., joining the division, was attached to the C.C.S. Because evacuation by air was proceeding without hindrance there was no need for surgical intervention within range of the Japanese guns.

It was the practice in the division for the field ambulance serving a particular brigade to attach to each of the battalions in the brigade a detachment of adequate but of no specified size. The detachment was intended to serve as a reinforcement of the regimental medical personnel. It was necessary, of course, for the officer commanding the field ambulance to ensure that the battalion commander did not use these men as regimental stretcher-beareres in place of battalion personnel. A.D.M.S. 36th Division attracted criticism to himself on account of this policy but he was satisfied that in the circumstances that obtained at the time it was amply justified. A battalion commonly was operating far removed from all others; it could find itself isolated for days at a time and forced to rely upon its own resources within its box. Rations, ammunition and the like could be and were dropped to battalions cut off in this way but medical personnel could not be dropped and the medical resources of the battalion were not enough to provide adequate care for the battalion's casualties which could not be evacuated for the time being. The attachment of a detachment of a light section of a field ambulance, if the period of isolation were not too prolonged, could and did enable the R.M.O. to provide adequate care.

During the long advance the routine method of casualty evacuation was by hand-carriage to the R.A.P. by the regimental stretcher-bearers; from the R.A.P. by jeep to the A.D.S. or M.D.S. where primary surgery was undertaken and where the casualty was held until fit to travel; by ambulance car or light aircraft from the A.D.S. or M.D.S. to the nearest C.47 airstrip and thence by Dakota to the C.C.S. or straight on to the base. The only difference between A.D.S. and M.D.S. was in respect of size and this was determined by the number of casualties that were expected in any given action. There were times and places when vehicles could not be used in evacuation and then hand-carriage by parties of 6 to 8 S.Bs. to a stretcher had to be employed, in getting casualties away, for example, across paddy lands knee-deep in mud.

The evacuation of the wounded man was satisfactory; that of the sick was not. Malaria was rife, the general sick-rate was high. When the engineers, who worked day and night in the perpetual rain and in the mud, had repaired the railway line, this was used for the evacuation of the sick as far as Mogaung. But the road from Sahmaw to Mogaung, 14 miles away, was unbelievably bad, so bad that only the American 6-wheelers could use it and even these could get no further along it than Namyin Chaung for the bridge across this had been blown. The sick had to cross over a very temporary contraption or had to be carried over it; they then were conveyed by jeep to the Mogaung River, a mile away, and ferried across this to reach Mogaung. From here they travelled by jeep train to Myitkyina whence Dakotas took them to base. In September 1944 an airstrip was constructed at Sahmaw and this made the terrible journey by road unnecessary.

As the advance continued the length of the line of evacuation progressively increased. The 70 mile journey from Mawlu back to Sahmaw, for example, took as long as 36–48 hours. Two railway coaches had been converted so as to carry twelve stretcher cases; sitting cases had to be content with the ordinary open truck with awnings. In Mohnyin the staging section held patients overnight and serious cases were flown out from the light airstrip nearby. Until Dakota airstrips had been constructed in succession at Yanbo, Katha, Bahe, Mong Long and Namsaw, the evacuation of the sick continued to be unsatisfactory.

From the time when the first of the airstrips had been constructed at Sahmaw, the division depended entirely upon the U.S. squadron of light aircraft (one L.1, one L.5 and nine L.5Bs.) for the evacuation of its casualties. Although it was used for other purposes as well, casualty evacuation was at all times regarded by the squadron as the first priority. A Dakota ambulance aircraft equipped to carry twenty-four stretcher cases, made daily journeys to the forward D.C. strip. On each C.47

airstrip a medical party was stationed for staging purposes. The Americans were prepared to evacuate as many as 1,500 a day in an emergency, using returning empty cargo aircraft. The general policy was to have such patients as were likely to be fit to return to their units in three weeks or less taken to the C.C.S. or to the M.F.T.U.; the others being taken on to base.

The paucity of ground transport in this division meant that everybody had to develop an appreciation of the difference between the desirable and the essential. The division and its medical units had to travel with the minimum loads. Tentage and tarpaulins were reduced to the absolute minimum and in their place parachutes were used to provide shelter. In the rear areas tentage was dropped in fairly liberal quantities. Bamboo was used extensively for a multitude of purposes. Medical supplies, like everything else, came in by air, being dropped until D.C. airstrips were constructed. To begin with a consolidated indent on behalf of all the medical units was submitted each month by A.D.M.S., but when the C.C.S. had settled in at Sahmaw, it dealt with this matter. As the L. of C. lengthened it became necessary for this responsibility to be shared, A.D.M.S. indenting for the forward units while the C.C.S. and the M.F.T.U. submitted their own demands. For supplies additional to those included in the monthly indent, a special demand could be submitted and the materials asked for would be delivered in four days or less according to the urgency of the demand. The U.S. pilots were very unwilling to drop the British standard stretcher fearing that damage to the aircraft would be caused.

The advance was so lengthy and the halts so frequent that soon every man in a medical unit had become expert in the packing and in the unpacking of some particular piece of equipment. Every man knew exactly what he had to do and did it expeditiously; the sanitary orderlies closed the old latrines on the site being left, and dug new ones on the new site; the staff of the admission tent struck the tent and repitched it; the cooks loaded their own trucks and unloaded them at the end of the journey. The regular order of departure and arrival was (i) cooks; (ii) admission and resuscitation tents and teams, ward tents and orderlies; (iii) heavy stores and equipment. The cooks prepared a hot meal *en route* and this was eaten either on the march if this was long, or at the journey's end.

34 (Ind.) Fd. Amb. served Ind. 26th Bde., moving with it from India to Burma at the end of 1944 and reaching Katha on December 30. On January 4, 1945, the unit moved to Asugyi, its 'A' Coy. accompanying brigade H.Q. to Kunchaung where it opened its A.D.S. to replace the M.D.S. of 69 (Ind.) Fd. Amb. that was with 72nd Bde. Later in the day the M.D.S. of 34 reached Kunchaung and there relieved the A.D.S. Evacuation was to 22 C.C.S. which was open in

Katha. On January 15, H.Q. and 'B' Coy. of the field ambulance moved forward to Yanbo, evacuation being from Yanbo to Katha by air. On the 21st the whole medical unit moved on to Nan Pon Pon where for the first time it admitted battle casualties from 2/8th Punjab. These were evacuated to the M.D.S. of 69 (Ind.) Fd. Amb., to which 13 (Ind.) M.S.U. was attached, in Kota. On January 22 the A.D.S. in Nan Pon Pon closed but the M.D.S. remained open to admit the sick of 26th and 72nd Bdes. On the 28th, 34 (Ind.) Fd. Amb. moved on to Bahe there to open its M.D.S. with accommodation for 100 patients. To this M.D.S. the surgical team of 22 C.C.S. was attached. To this M.D.S. came the casualties from the action at Myitson; there were 30 of them on February 1, 34 on the 2nd and the same number on the 3rd. They were sent back by ambulance jeep and lorry to the airstrip at Mahlainggon.

On February 8 the medical plans for the renewed attack on Myitson were completed. A strong A.D.S. was to be sited near the brigade Tac. H.Q. in the concentration area and light sections were to be attached to the battalions of the brigade. On the west bank of the Shweli at crossing No.2 a staging section would be posted to get the casualties across the river on rafts and in boats while on the east bank two ambulance cars would be stationed to transport the casualties to the M.D.S. which would be opened near brigade Rear H.Q.

On February 9 the A.D.S. was established in the concentration area and to it two jeep ambulances were attached to transport casualties from the Nammeik Chaung to the A.D.S. and thence to the staging section at Crossing No. 2. 1/19th Hybad. had 54 casualties when crossing the chaung and approaching the village of Myitson. The M.D.S. admitted 62 casualties on February 10, 65 on the 11th and 35 on the 12th. On February 13 when the Japanese got between the battalions in the concentration area and advanced brigade H.Q., evacuation from the light sections of the field ambulance with these battalions had to be direct to the M.D.S. On the 14th the A.D.S. was pulled back to join the M.D.S. which on this day admitted 51 casualties. On February 15 supplies were ferried across the river at crossing No. 1 and 73 casualties were brought back on the return journeys during the hours of darkness and in silence because the outboard motors, if used, attracted the attention of the Japanese. Casualties on the 16th numbered 38, on the 17th, 68 and on the 18th, 92.

On February 28 the M.D.S. moved back to the airstrip at Mahlainggon. During the month of February it had admitted a total of 829 casualties and the surgical team of 22 C.C.S. had carried out some 350 operations. In the M.D.S. during this period there had been 50 deaths. During the crossing of the Nammeik Chaung some equipment had been lost; it was replaced by air-drop.

On March 7 'A' Coy and the light section with 1/1st G.R. moved into Myitson to relieve the M.D.S. of 69 (Ind.) Fd. Amb. by opening an A.D.S. On March 16 this A.D.S. moved forward to Milestone 16 on the Mogok Road and, when Mogok had fallen, into the town itself. The M.D.S. of 34 (Ind.) Fd. Amb. at this time was in Mong Mit. On March 22 the A.D.S moved into Mong Long, transferring its few immobiles to the M.D.S. of 69 (Ind.) Fd. Amb. which had reached and had opened in Mogok. The M.D.S. of 34 (Ind.) Fd. Amb. followed and on April 7 the whole field ambulance moved into Wetwin and on the following day into Maymyo along with 22 C.C.S.

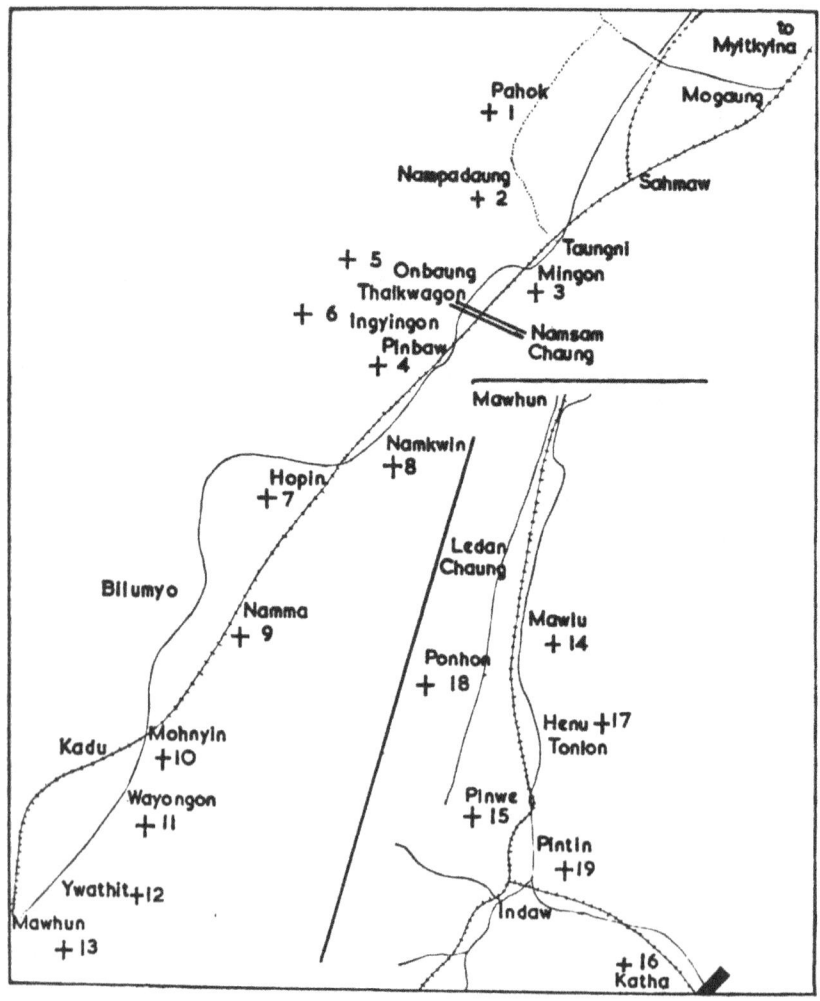

FIG. 61. 36th Division. The Movements of the Divisional Field Ambulances during the Advance down the Railway Corridor

On April 10, 34 (Ind.) Fd. Amb. moved forward to a point about ten miles to the south of Kyaukse on the Mandalay-Rangoon trunk road. Its A.D.S. was opened in Ingon, about six miles south of Kyaukse, on April 23 and its M.D.S. moved into Meiktila, remaining closed.

Early in May this field ambulance was flown out to Poona.

69 (Ind.) Fd. Amb. with 72nd Bde. moved from Shillong to Margherita on July 2, 1944 and between this date and the end of the month was flown to the airfield at Myitkyina. The unit marched from there to Mogaung and Pahok, reaching this small village on the last day of the month. Here it opened its M.D.S. and admitted its first patients on August 1. An A.D.S. was established at Milestone 12 on the Pahok-Taungni track. Evacuation was by air. On August 17 the A.D.S. moved forward to Sahmaw Chaung. Light sections of the field ambulance were with the battalions of the brigade which was in control of the Pahok-Taungni area. The A.D.S. next moved to Nampadaung where it admitted many malaria and infective hepatitis cases. The tracks were so bad in this area that only the U.S. 6-wheelers could be used. On the 18th the A.D.S. moved forward to Mingon on the railway line and evacuation by rail became possible from Mingon to Sahmaw, it being necessary to carry the patients across the numerous breaks in the line. On the 22nd, half of the M.D.S. joined the A.D.S. in Mingon.

Key to Fig. 61

1.	69 (Ind.) Fd. Amb.	M.D.S.	August 1
2.	,, ,,	A.D.S.	,, 7
3.	,, ,,	A.D.S.	,, 18
4.	,, ,,	M.D.S. and A.D.S.	September 17
5.	154 Fd. Amb.	M.D.S.	August 24
6.	,, ,,	A.D.S.	,, 25
7.	,, ,,	A.D.S.	,, 27
	69 (Ind.) Fd. Amb.	M.D.S.	October 17
8.	154 Fd. Amb.	M.D.S.	August 28
9.	69 (Ind.) Fd. Amb.	M.D.S. (closed)	October 22
10.	154 Fd. Amb.	A.D.S.	,, 20
	,, ,,	M.D.S.	,, 21
11.	,, ,,	A.D.S.	,, 21
12.	,, ,,	A.D.S.	,, 23
13.	,, ,,	A.D.S.	,, 27
	,, ,,	M.D.S.	,, 30
		Indian Staging Section	
14.	69 (Ind.) Fd. Amb.	A.D.S.	November 5
	,, ,,	M.D.S.	,, 8
15.	,, ,,	A.D.S.	December 8
	,, ,,	M.D.S.	,, 13
16.	,, ,,	A.D.S.	,, 14
	,, ,,	M.D.S.	,, 17
17.	154 Fd. Amb.	A.D.S.	November 2
	,, ,,	M.D.S.	,, 13
18.	,, ,,	A.D.S.	,, 13
19.	,, ,,	A.D.S.	December 8

When on August 25, 29th Bde. went into the lead for the attack on Pinbaw, 154 Fd. Amb., with 29th Bde., combined with 69 (Ind.) Fd. Amb. to provide medical cover. Up to this point 69 alone had been serving both the brigades and had admitted no less than 1,875 sick since the division reached Burma. Of these 1,085 had been cases of malaria.

On September 17 the A.D.S. of 69 (Ind.) Fd. Amb. moved from Mingon to Pinbaw where it opened and where the M.D.S. joined it. On October 17 the M.D.S. moved forward to Hopin and on the 22nd to Namma, remaining closed for one of the staging sections was functioning here at this time. On November 5 the A.D.S. opened near Mawlu station and three days later the M.D.S. established itself in Mawlu itself. U.S.A.A.F. 60 Mobile Surgical Unit, serving with the Chinese artillery attached to the division, co-operated with the M.D.S. of 69 (Ind.) Fd. Amb. to the great advantage of the casualties. Evacuation was by air from 'White City', the Chindit stronghold, and by rail by jeep train. As the evacuation chain lengthened staging parties were placed at Mawlu and Henu. During the period November 6–27, 13 (Ind.) M.S.U. remained attached to the M.D.S. of 69 (Ind.) Fd. Amb. and performed 101 operations on battle casualties.

On December 8 the A.D.S. opened in Pinwe there to be joined by the M.D.S. on the 13th. The M.D.S. did not open until the following day when the A.D.S. moved on to Katha. On the 17th the M.D.S. took over from the A.D.S. in Katha whence evacuation was either by rail or else by light aircraft to Sahmaw. At the end of the month the field ambulance crossed the Irrawaddy and reached Pyagyaung. On January 1, 1945 first the A.D.S. and later the M.D.S. opened in Kunchaung. On January 4 the A.D.S. opened in Yanbo and closed on the 5th when the M.D.S. took its place. Heavy rain made evacuation impossible for a time and so the M.D.S. had to hold its patients. On January 11 the A.D.S. moved on to Kota near a light airstrip and on the following day the M.D.S., with the surgical team of 22 C.C.S. attached, took over from the A.D.S. which moved on to Kon-mabein and on the 25th to Konkha. Next the M.D.S. moved to Mahlainggon where it was joined by the A.D.S. on February 2.

Casualties incurred by 26th Bde. during the attack on Myitson were staged through the M.D.S. of 69 (Ind.) Fd. Amb. During this action both the A.D.S. and the M.D.S. of 69 were moved to new sites on several occasions because of the shelling. On March 7 the A.D.S. moved to Letpangya as did the M.D.S. on the following day. To the M.D.S. the surgical team of 22 C.C.S. was attached. On the 10th the A.D.S. moved to Letkokpin and on the following day to Magyibin there to be joined by the M.D.S. on the 12th. On the 20th the A.D.S. opened at Milestone 16 on the Mong Mit–Mogok road and on the 21st the M.D.S. moved into Mogok there to open on the following day.

OPERATIONS IN N.C.A.C. AND ARAKAN

On the last day of March the M.D.S. moved on to Mong Long and was flown in to Mandalay where it opened in Fort Dufferin. On April 20 the A.D.S. of 69 (Ind.) Fd. Amb. was in Kandaw. On the 23rd the M.D.S. reached Kandaw and the A.D.S. moved on to Nyaunggyat and later to Patchaung. Many cholera cases were now being admitted to the M.D.S.; there were 27 altogether during March (8 B.O.Rs.; 19 I.O.Rs.) and of these 4 died. The field ambulance then moved into Meiktila and was flown to Imphal during the first week of May *en route* for Poona.

154 Fd. Amb. with 29th Bde. moved with the division to Margherita transit camp and then proceeded to Myitkyina on August 14. It then went on to Mogaung by jeep train and thence by road to Sahmaw. On August 24 the unit moved by jeep train to Onbaung where the M.D.S. was opened. Prior to this casualties had been sent to the M.D.S. of 69 (Ind.) Fd. Amb. in Pahok. 154's A.D.S. was established in Ingyingon on the 25th.

On August 27 the A.D.S. moved forward to Hopin and the M.D.S. to Namkwin on the following day. During the month of September, 154 Fd. Amb. admitted 737 patients (119 malaria, 404 N.Y.D. (F.), 65 diarrhoea and dysentery, 70 minor septic conditions, 4 battle casualties, 75 other causes); of these 88 were evacuated by air. On the last day of the month the number of patients held was 115 sick.

On October 16 all patients in the M.D.S. were transferred to 22 C.C.S. and the field ambulance moved to Namma. On the 20th the A.D.S. opened in Mohnyin and on the following day in Wayongon, the M.D.S. moving into Mohnyin. As the brigade advanced the A.D.S. opened in succession in Ywathit, Mawhun and Ledan Chaung while the M.D.S. moved up to Mawhun. During this month the field ambulance admitted 602 patients (43 battle casualties, 84 malaria, 180 N.Y.D. (F.), 81 minor septic conditions, 23 infective hepatitis, 191 other causes.) During the advance from Hopin to Mawhun hand-carries were particularly long and arduous, being over very rough ground and across paddy-lands. In Ledan Chaung with the A.D.S. were the field ambulance orderly room and the dental centre. The advantage of this arrangement was that it greatly facilitated the administrative work for the reason that the A.D.S. was always sited in close proximity to brigade H.Q.

On November 2 the A.D.S. moved forward to Henu. U.S. 60 Mobile Surgical Unit, veritably a portable hospital, was co-operating with the field ambulance and this arrangement enabled 13 (Ind.) M.S.U. to devote itself to the casualties of 72nd Bde. On November 13 the A.D.S. moved on to Ponhon and the M.D.S. took its place in Henu. During the month of November the field ambulance admitted 23 officers, 837 B.O.Rs. and 119 I.O.Rs. These were classified as 354 malaria, 165 N.Y.D. (F.), 62 dysentery, 27 diarrhoea, 19 infective hepatitis, 58 battle casualties, 68 minor septic conditions and 266 other causes.

On December 6 the A.D.S. moved forward to Pinwe, on the 8th to Pintin and on the 12th to Kya-In where it was joined by the M.D.S. On the 18th the A.D.S. moved on to Kunchaung and on the 24th to Tigyaing. The field ambulance crossed the Irrawaddy on the last day of the year and the M.D.S. opened in Myadaung.

During January 1945 the moves of the A.D.S. were Tagaung (January 2), Pauktabin (12th), Shadaw (21st) and Twinnge (24th) while those of the M.D.S. were Mingon (6th), Pauktabin (10th), Shadaw (22nd) and Twinnge (24th). During the month evacuation was by light plane, 117 being the total number of those so evacuated. Admissions were 12 officers, 228 B.O.Rs. and 16 I.O.Rs. These were classified as 49 malaria, 6 N.Y.D. (F.), 12 diarrhoea, 13 non-amoebic dysentery, 1 venereal disease, 33 battle casualties, 3 typhus fever, 16 minor septic conditions and 133 other causes.

During February the moves of the A.D.S. were Kyaukpyu (February 2), Pinkan (7th), Kyaukmaw (9th), Kinnwe (14th), Milestone 25 on the Kinnwe–Nabu road (18th), and Pazinchaung (27th) and those of the M.D.S. Pinkan (5th), Kinnwe (11th), Milestone 25 on the Kinnwe–Nabu road (20th), Taunggon (24th) and Pazinchaung (28th). On each of these moves the unit carried forward with it about 90 patients, the A.D.S. unloading them on to the M.D.S. or *vice versa*. The number of admissions during February were 314 (101 malaria, 57 N.Y.D. (F.), 18 dysentery and diarrhoea, 51 battle casualties and 87 other causes). Seventy-two of these were evacuated by light aircraft from the airstrips at Twinnge, Kyaukmaw and Kinnwe.

During March the A.D.S. moved in succession to Sindegon, with 13 (Ind.) M.S.U. attached, (March 4), Mohauk (7th), Pathin (9th), Mong Mit, where a few days rest were enjoyed (12th), Mogok (22nd), Man Kang (29th) and the M.D.S. to Sindegon (3rd), Mohauk (8th), Pathin (9th), Mong Mit (12th) and Mogok (22nd) where it relieved 69 (Ind.) Fd. Amb. on the 29th. The month's admissions were 326, including 53 malaria, 4 diarrhoea, 12 dysentery, 5 minor septic conditions, 9 battle casualties, 38 other causes. From the airstrip at Sindegon 35 battle casualties and 97 sick were evacuated. From the D.C. strip at Mong Mit 72 sick were flown out.

During April the moves of the A.D.S. were to Pyawnghkawng (April 4), Maymyo (9th), Hlaingdet (11th) for the attack on Kalaw, Kywedatson (27th), Milestone 43 on the Meiktila-Kalaw road and those of the M.D.S. from Mogok to Namsaw (3rd), Maymyo (11th) and Meiktila (25th). In this month 386 admissions included 90 malaria, 33 N.Y.D. (F.) and P.U.O., 44 dysentery, 23 diarrhoea, 3 heat exhaustion, 11 minor septic conditions, 40 local injuries, 100 other causes. Those evacuated numbered 214. D.C. strips were constructed at Mong Long, Namsaw,

Maymyo and Meiktila. A light airstrip was available at Thazi. Early in May 154 Fd. Amb. left Meiktila for Poona *via* Imphal.

Between August 19, 1944 and May 12, 1945, 154 Fd. Amb. had admitted:

Officers	126
B.O.Rs.	4,236
I.O.Rs.	375
Chinese	4
	4,741

The diagnoses made included:

Malaria and N.Y.D. (F.)	2,438
Dysentery and diarrhoea	484
Venereal diseases	13
Special Cases:	
Appendicitis	
Psychiatric	133
Infective hepatitis	
Typhus	23
Battle casualties	305

Deaths:	Offrs.	1
	B.O.Rs.	19
	I.O.Rs.	2
		22

13 (Ind.) M.S.U., while with the division performed 315 operations on 304 patients, 266 being battle casualties or accidents. (Table 37.)

The case-fatality-rate among the gas gangrene and the anaerobic cellulitis cases was high. The reason for this was probably a multiple one, the long and difficult line of evacuation, the delay in operating because the surgeon was working alone, the lack of the best nursing skill at field ambulance level and the lack of F.T.U. facilities at this level. In this M.S.U. the routine surgical procedure consisted in enlarging the wound, in removing dead and damaged tissue, and in incising fascia followed by immobilisation with a splint, padded plaster or a Tobruk splint. M. & B. 693 was given to all; if vomiting was troublesome sulphathiazole was substituted. Penicillin, when it had become available, was administered to twenty-two of the patients.

At the time of the action at Pinwe blood transfusion supplies were brought forward from the C.C.S. by light aircraft. A donor panel was maintained in the C.C.S. then in Sahmaw and only about forty minutes run away. But for most of the time blood had to be obtained from donors on the spot. From July to December 1944 it was estimated that 300 pints

TABLE 37

13 (Indian) Mobile Surgical Unit. Operations performed while with 36th Division.

Condition	Number of Cases	Number of Deaths
Compound fractures	60	—
„ „ with nerve injury	6	—
„ „ with injury to main blood vessels	7	—
Flesh wounds, uncomplicated	110	1
„ „ with nerve injury	5	—
„ „ with injury to main blood vessels	9	1
Head and maxillo-facial injuries	7	—
Gas-Gangrene of limb	6	5
Anaerobic cellulitis and myositis	2	—
Amputations other than for gas gangrene	11	1 (Japanese P.o.W.)
Thoraco-abdominal wounds	3	2
Abdominal wounds	16	8
Chest wounds	5	—
Eye wounds	2	—
Fractures and dislocations, simple	4	—
Burns, thermal	13	—
„ phosphorus	9	1 (a Burmese boy who played with a bomb)
Minor sepsis	21	—
Appendicectomies	7	—
Circumcision and meatotomy	1	—
	304	19

Mortality: Injury due to enemy action . . 7·1 per cent.
All cases . . . . . 6·0 „ „

of plasma, 70 pints of blood and 170 pints of glucose-saline were used in 13 (Ind.) M.S.U. and that between January and the time when active operations ended in so far as 36th Division was concerned, when 13 (Ind.) M.S.U. was attached to 29th Bde. operating independently, 169 pints of plasma, 50 pints of blood and 58 pints of glucose-saline were used.

44 (Ind.) Fd. Hyg. Sec. attached a sub-section to each of the brigades in the division. Each sub-section consisted of 2 British N.C.Os., 1 naik,

1 sepoy, 2 R.I.A.S.C. sepoys and 9 N.C. (Es.). Each sub-section and its stores could be moved in one 30-cwt. truck. One of the more disagreeable jobs the unit had to undertake was that of burying the Japanese dead. When Katha was reached D.D.T. became available and immediately a motor-sprayer was issued to each sub-section. Twenty gallons of D.D.T. in solution were issued to each major unit in the division for local anti-malaria and general sanitary measures. Aerial spraying was used on two occasions but it was difficult to make appropriate arrangements for it to be carried out for the reason that the brigades were usually on the move and in close contact with the Japanese. The Japanese defensive positions, when captured, were invariably found to be in a most filthy state and heavily booby-trapped. In one of the sub-sections five casualties were caused by these booby-traps, when cleaning up the Pinwe area. The sub-section attached to 29th Bde. had the misfortune to fall into an ambush at Twinnge and had one killed and three wounded.

At Kume drinking water had to be obtained from the river; it was heavy with sediment. The field hygiene section had to construct, with the help of the sappers, rough sand and brick filters out of 50-gallon oil drums. There was a paucity of tarpaulins and canvas tanks.

The hygiene section rightly claimed some of the credit for the fall in the incidence of dysentery and diarrhoea from 21/1,000/week to 0·8/1,000/week.

71 (Ind.) M.C.U. worked in the closest co-operation with the field hygiene section and like it had its sub-sections with the brigades. Routine malaria surveys were made by the officer commanding the unit and these were acknowledged to be of great value in those areas in which the divisional units remained for any appreciable length of time, at Sahmaw, for example.

II. XV Corps' Limited Advance in Arakan

In Arakan were four divisions, Indian 25th and 26th, 81st and 82nd West African. In addition there were 3rd Commando Brigade and Indian 50th Tank Brigade. Opposing this force was a much smaller Japanese one. The plan adopted was that of pushing the Japanese back and then containing them with one division, the rest becoming free for employment elsewhere; Akyab was to be taken, the mouth of the Kaladan River secured and the area to the east of this as far south as the Myebon Peninsula was to be held. XV Corps had the support of 224th Gp. R.A.F. and also that of a naval task force. Most of the naval craft that were available were those that had been left in Burma waters for the reason that they were too decrepit to be transferred to Europe for employment in Operation 'Overlord'. As has been recorded already, in

November 1944 XV Corps ceased to belong to Fourteenth Army and became an independent corps operating directly under command of A.L.F.S.E.A.

The tasks assigned to the component formations of XV Corps were as follows:

> 81st W.A. Division was to continue its advance down the Kaladan Valley from Paletwa to Myohaung.
>
> 82nd W.A. Division was to capture Buthidaung, cross the Kaladan River and move southwards on Htizwe. Thereafter it would move eastwards over the Kanzauk Pass into the Kaladan Valley and there relieve 81st W.A. Division which, when Myohaung had been taken, would pass into XV Corps reserve at Chiringa for eventual shipment to India. 82nd W.A. Division would continue the southward advance from Myohaung to Myebon.
>
> Indian 25th Division was to clear the Mayu Peninsula and the Mayu Valley, with 82nd W.A. Division acting as a left flank-guard, along the general axis of the Mayu River as far as Htizwe, with the object of seizing Foul Point and Kudaung Island as soon as possible.
>
> Indian 26th Division, with 3rd Commando Bde., under command, was to make a seaborne assault to capture Akyab and was then to consolidate the whole of Akyab Island. The division would then move north-east cross country and exploit to the line Minbya–Myebon where it would link up with 82nd W.A. Division.
>
> 22nd East African Brigade, when it arrived, was to pass u/c XV Corps and join the corps reserve in Chiringa, being prepared to secure any part of the L. of C. against Japanese attack.

It will be remembered that in May 1944 the 'monsoon line' in Arakan was being held by Indian 25th and 26th and 81st West African Divisions. Indian 25th Division was in the Tunnels area covering the Maungdaw–Buthidaung road, Indian 26th Division had one brigade in the Bawli–Taung Bazar area, one brigade about Taungbro at the head of the Naf Estuary and its third brigade in Cox's Bazar. The West African division, following its withdrawal from the valley of the Kaladan was concentrated in the Chiringa area. Throughout the monsoon months there was much aggressive patrolling on the part of Indian 25th and 26th Divisions interspersed with a few minor operations usually for the possession of some dominating hill feature. When the rains ceased the divisions began to prepare themselves for the coming offensive.

INDIAN 25TH DIVISION

This division, with the ace of spades as the divisional sign, was formed in South India at the beginning of August 1942. It first saw service in February 1944 when it was rushed to Arakan to protect the right flank of XV Corps from the coastal plain of the Naf River to the spine of the Mayu Range. In the 'monsoon line' Indian 25th Division's sector

OPERATIONS IN N.C.A.C. AND ARAKAN

included the Maungdaw keep and the Maungdaw–Buthidaung road as far to the east as Point 551. Through the seven rain-filled months the division continually harassed the Japanese facing it by patrol and ambush, the troops being supplied and supported by the Navy, using barge, sampan and creek steamer. In September the division fought for and gained possession of a number of peaks and hill features in order to facilitate the advance that was to take place when the clear months of late autumn arrived.

In mid-December the division began its advance to the south, one of its brigades travelling down the Mayu River by boat, another down the coastal plain to the west of the Mayu Range and the third following up along the ridge itself. The division was supplied from the sea and, encountering negligible opposition, reached the tip of the Mayu Peninsula at Foul Point on December 26. Kudaung Island, which is separated from Akyab Island only by a narrow channel, was occupied. Preparations for a set-piece assault landing of Akyab Island were then made but it was discovered that the Japanese garrison of the island had left on the last day of 1944 and so the division, poised for the assault, was ferried across the Mayu Estuary to land on the north beach without encountering any opposition.

In an attempt to cut the coast road that ran between Myohaung and Taungup through Kangaw, Tamandu and An, ahead of the retreating Japanese, 3rd Commando Bde. followed by 74th Bde. of Indian 25th Division landed on January 12, under cover of naval and air bombardment, on the Myebon Peninsula and established a firm bridgehead in this strange terrain, half land, half water, consisting of vast mangrove swamps intersected by an intricate network of creeks and chaungs containing small hump-backed tree-crowded islets. The Japanese opposed the expansion of the bridgehead and before the Myebon Peninsula was finally cleared there was much fierce fighting.

On January 22 the commando brigade carried out a second landing near Kangaw again under cover of a naval and air bombardment. This obscure village, some miles up a narrow creek, was surrounded by a series of low hills that rose abruptly from the plain. The Kangaw beachhead was nothing but a mud-bank, an opening in the mangroves about as wide as two of the landing craft. During the fourteen hours when Ind. 51st Bde., an all Indian brigade with Indian officers, was landing on this tiny beach, it was under heavy gun-fire directed from the Japanese observation posts on the hills. Then came the task of driving the Japanese off these hills tunnelled through and through with intricate systems of trenches and deep bunkers. The commandos and Indian 51st Bde., supported by the tanks of 19th Lancers, having withstood Japanese assaults for six days, on January 29 turned to the attack to take Kangaw and to establish a road-block to the south of it.

On February 2, Ind. 74th Bde. of Indian 25th Division attacked the Japanese positions two miles north-east of Kangaw. By February 8 the leading brigade of 82nd W.A. Division was in contact with the Japanese 9 miles north of Kangaw. On the 9th, 2nd W.A. Bde., passed u/c Indian 25th Division and a series of co-ordinated attacks were made on the successive Japanese positions. After nine days of strenuous fighting the whole area was finally cleared.

The Japanese forces in Arakan were congregated into two groups, one about An, blocking the road over the pass and the other at Taungup, covering the road to Prome. XV Corps formations were distributed as

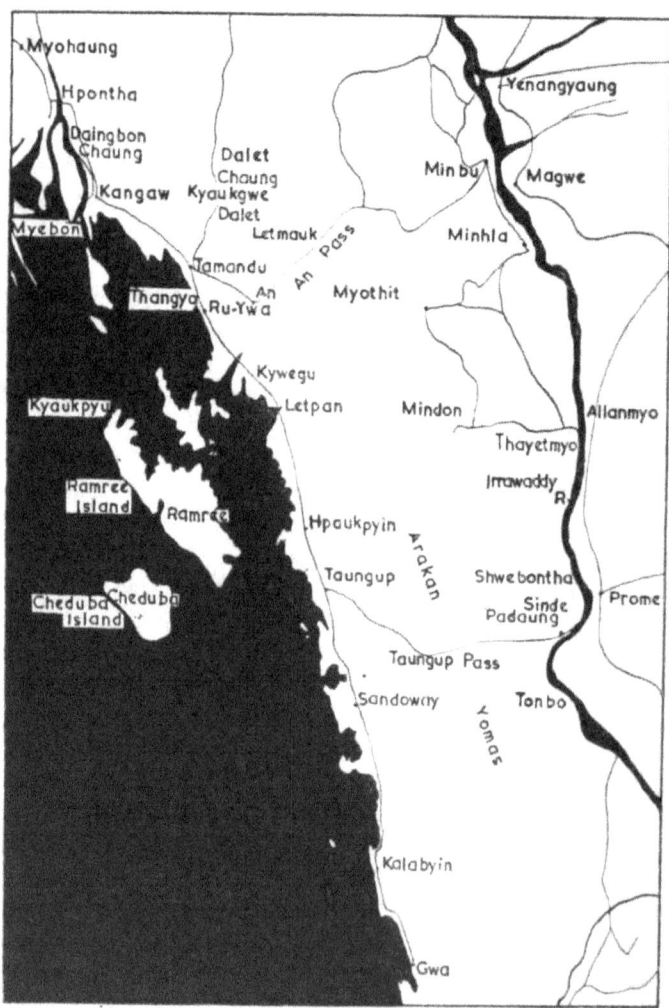

Fig. 62. Arakan. Myohaung–Gwa

follows: Indian 25th Division was on the general line Kangaw–Myebon; 82nd W.A. Division was driving the Japanese southwards against this line; 3rd Commando Bde. was concentrated in Myebon and Indian 26th Division, with 22nd E.A. Bde., was clearing Ramree Island, and raiding the Japanese communications between the An Chaung and Taungup. Because of the demands of Fourteenth Army it had been becoming increasingly difficult to maintain XV Corps and so 81st W.A. Division and part of Ind. 50th Tk. Bde. had been withdrawn from it. The intention of XV Corps was to prevent the Japanese crossing the Arakan Yomas and interfering with the southward advance of Fourteenth Army. XV Corps was now instructed by General Leese (i) to develop Akyab and Ramree as air-supply bases for Fourteenth Army, (ii) to clear north and central Arakan, (iii) seize a bridgehead at Taungup and (iv) to open the Taungup–Prome road if possible before the monsoon. The first of these tasks was to have precedence over the others. It is to be noted that Taungup was not a port but merely a village on a narrow winding creek and that the road from Taungup to Prome was only a fair-weather track running for most of its length through thick bamboo jungle.

On February 16, Ind. 53rd Bde. of Indian 25th Division landed at Ru-Ywa, a village on the coast about fourteen miles due west of An. A medium battery was secretly landed on a small unoccupied island 4 miles from the proposed bridgehead. The village of Ru-Ywa was quickly taken and 17/5th Mahratta L.I. then proceeded to occupy the 1,000 ft. hill that rose almost perpendicularly behind it. It was not until the 19th that the Japanese began to attack the bridgehead. These attacks were repulsed but not without difficulty. 2nd W.A. and 74th Bdes. were now added to 53rd Bde. in the bridgehead and preparations were made to encircle the Japanese force at An.

It was at this point that it was decided that 82nd W.A. Division should continue to advance towards An, being supplied entirely by air until such time as supply by road from Tamandu became feasible. It was also decided that Indian 26th Division, operating from Kyaukpyu should establish a brigade group on the mainland at Letpan, 35 miles south-east of Ru-Ywa, with a view to driving down the coast to Taungup. But the success of Fourteenth Army in Central Burma and the need to exploit this success without delay called for all available air resources. It was not possible, therefore, to maintain 82nd Division by air and so this division was obliged to change its axis of advance so that its brigades could be supplied by road and water. Its 4th Bde. was ordered to cross the Dalet Chaung and to make for Tamandu by the Tamandu–An road, linking up with 2nd W.A. Bde. which was approaching this road from the south. The whole division was then to attack An frontally. It became imperative that Tamandu should be captured with all possible speed. The crossing of the Dalet Chaung proved to be more difficult than had been expected and so 4th W.A. Bde. was brought down to Tamandu along the northern bank of the river where the opposition was much slighter.

From Ru-Ywa one brigade of Indian 25th Division pushed south along the coast road while the other thrust northward towards the coastal village of Tamandu. With the support of air-strikes and of a bombardment from the naval sloops, the infantry and armour forced the Japanese out of the village on March 13 into the jungle-covered hills through which their escape route to Letmauk and An ran. By March 15, Ind. 74th Bde. was no longer in touch with the retreating Japanese who were being pursued towards An by 4th W.A. Bde. Indian 25th Division was then withdrawn to Ru-Ywa and Akyab *en route* for India.

MEDICAL COVER

Some of the fiercest fighting in this operation of XV Corps occurred during the assault landings at Myebon and Kangaw. Evacuation from the beaches was planned to take place in three stages. Casualties were collected in a beach dressing station, established by a beach medical unit and in it first-aid surgery was carried out. The casualties were then conveyed in L.C.M. and L.C.T. to a L.C.I.(D.) (a landing craft infantry, serving as a depot ship). On this vessel was a mobile surgical unit with a hundred beds. The third stage was to a hospital ship which at best could come to within about two miles of the shore.

The divisional medical units accompanying Indian 25th Division to Arakan in March 1944 were 56, 58 and 61 (Ind.) Fd. Ambs. and 30 (Ind.) Fd. Hyg. Sec. Attached to the division was 1 (Ind.) Bearer Company and 18 (Ind.) A.M.U. When it relieved Indian 5th Division its 58 (Ind.) Fd. Amb. took over from 45 (Ind.) Fd. Amb. in Yemyettaung on March 17. On the 20th the M.D.S. of this medical unit opened in Ginnapara, taking over from 10 (Ind.) Fd. Amb. of Indian 5th Division. To serve Ind. 51st Bde. a company of the field ambulance opened an A.D.S. in Nyaunggyaung. On the 25th, 58 (Ind.) Fd. Amb. opened an A.D.S. in Kanyindan where it was shelled and had one of its ambulance cars hit.

On March 24, 61 (Ind.) Fd. Amb. reached Tumbru and on the following day proceeded to Maungdaw. On the 28th it moved to Ginnapara and on the last day of the month opened its M.D.S. in Kanyindan.

On April 1, 56 (Ind.) Fd. Amb. reached Bawli and on the following day opened its M.D.S. in Kanyindan and established an A.D.S. in the vicinity of the West Tunnel to serve Ind. 53rd Bde. Evacuation from the M.D.S. was by D.U.K.W. to the M.D.S. of 61 (Ind.) Fd. Amb. in Kanyindan. On the 7th the M.D.S. of 58 (Ind.) Fd. Amb. in Ginnapara closed. Between April 1–7 it had admitted, treated and evacuated some 240 patients. On the 8th, 58 casualties, 11 of them battle casualties, were admitted to the M.D.S. of 61 (Ind.) Fd. Amb. in Kanyindan. On the 10th this M.D.S. was joined by 15 (Ind.) M.S.U. and 1 (Ind.) Bearer Coy. and 18 (Ind.) A.M.U. were in its vicinity.

On April 12, 8 (Ind.) M.S.U. joined the A.D.S of 56 (Ind.) Fd. Amb. in the Tunnels area. On the following day the M.D.S. of 58 (Ind.) Fd. Amb. moved from Ginnapara to Nawrondaung to function there as a staging section. The M.D.S. of 61 (Ind.) Fd. Amb. was being provided with *basha* huts and the Engineers were constructing an operating theatre in Kanyindan in preparation for the monsoon. On April 24, 'A' Coy. of 58 (Ind.) Fd. Amb. opened an A.D.S. in Wabyin. During the latter part of April the average daily admissions to the M.D.S. of 61 (Ind.) Fd. Amb. in Kanyindan numbered about 70 of which 50 were sick and 20 battle casualties.

There was no change in the distribution of the divisional medical units or in the divisional plans for dealing with casualties until October. There were moves of the mobile surgical units during this period; on May 11, 8 (Ind.) M.S.U. left the A.D.S. of 56 (Ind.) Fd. Amb. in the Tunnels area to join the M.D.S. of 61 (Ind.) Fd. Amb. and 15 (Ind.) M.S.U. from 61 joined the A.D.S of 56. On the 12th, 6 (Ind.) M.S.U. also joined the M.D.S. of 61 in Kanyindan. On June 17, 15 (Ind.) M.S.U. moved from the A.D.S. to the M.D.S. of 56 (Ind.) Fd. Amb. In August, 15 (Ind.) M.S.U. left 56 (Ind.) Fd. Amb. for 25 (Ind.) C.C.S. and was replaced by 12 (Ind.) M.S.U. from 8 (Ind.) C.C.S. On August 22, 6 M.S.U. left 56 (Ind.) Fd. Amb. for 25 (Ind.) C.C.S.

On October 11, 61 (Ind.) Fd. Amb. moved from Kanyindan to Maungdaw. On the 21st the A.D.S. of 'B' Coy. 58 (Ind.) Fd. Amb. began to move from Nawrondaung to the Tunnels area to take over from the A.D.S. of 56 (Ind.) Fd. Amb. on the 24th. Following this relief the A.D.S. of 56 moved to Wabyin there to take over from 'A' Coy. of 58. On the 26th the M.D.S. of 56 was established in Kayugyaung and the M.D.S. of 58 moved from Nawrondaung to Maungdaw. At the end of October divisional H.Q. moved from Maungdaw to Razabil.

During November the only change was the arrival of 8 F.T.U. and its attachment to the M.D.S. of 56 (Ind.) Fd. Amb. in Kayugyaung. On December 11 this transfusion unit together with 12 (Ind.) M.S.U. were transferred to 61 (Ind.) Fd. Amb. which had moved from Maungdaw to Razabil on November 24. The M.D.S. of 58 in Maungdaw was closed on December 9 and began to prepare itself for the advance to Akyab in which it was to serve Ind. 53rd Bde. On December 12, the A.D.S. of 56 joined the M.D.S. in Kayugyaung.

On December 20, 56 (Ind.) Fd. Amb. opened its M.D.S. in Razabil and on Christmas Day 61 (Ind.) Fd. Amb. moved to the Tunnels area from Razabil. Meanwhile 58 (Ind.) Fd. Amb. was moving with 53rd Bde. On December 22 it was transported by boat and raft to Seinnyinbya, its A.D.S. on a raft being open during the journey. On the 24th its M.D.S. was open in Seinnyinbya and its A.D.S., ready to replace the M.D.S. when this moved forward, about 500 yards to the north of the M.D.S. site. On the 25th the M.D.S. moved to Thonzaungywa and the A.D.S. to the site vacated by the M.D.S. in Seinnyinbya. Evacuation was by river to Buthidaung. On the 27th the M.D.S. moved on by river to Kwazon there to open. A C.C.P. to serve 17/5th Mahrattas was established in Kywegromaw. Until an airstrip had been constructed the M.D.S. was obliged to hold its patients. On the 30th 'A' Coy. attached a light A.D.S. to 9th Y. and L. which was setting out for an assault on Kudaung Island. On December 28, the A.D.S. of 56 (Ind.) Fd. Amb. moved from Kayugyaung to Udaung.

On January 1st, 61 (Ind.) Fd. Amb. was at Foul Point and H.Q.

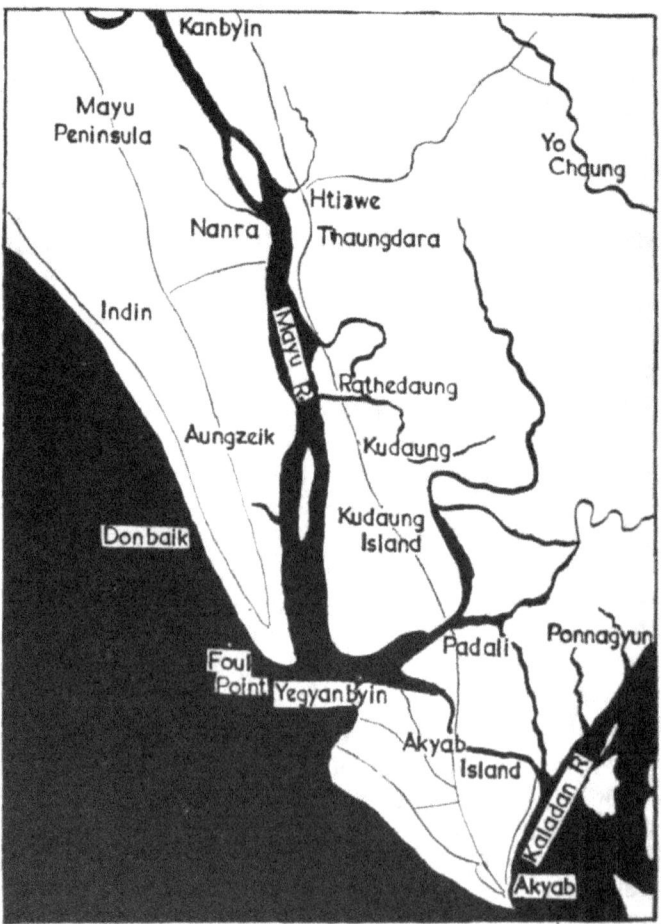

Fig. 63. Arakan. Akyab Island

and the M.D.S. of 58 (Ind.) Fd. Amb. moved by raft from Kwazon to Rathedaung, the M.D.S. being open during the journey. On the 2nd a light A.D.S. of 58 (Ind.) Fd. Amb. was attached to 4/5th R.G.R. for the assault landing on Akyab Island. Casualties were evacuated by the Navy to Nhila, 20 altogether. On January 6, 58 (Ind.) Fd. Amb. less two light sections left Rathedaung for Padali on Akyab Island and there the M.D.S. was established. On this day 61 (Ind.) Fd. Amb. moved from Foul Point to Akyab Island.

On January 7, 59 (Ind.) Fd. Amb. moved by boat from Padali to Yegyanbyin, carrying casualties forward. On the 9th the unit passed into reserve clearing its patients into 61 (Ind.) Fd. Amb. in Akyab. 6 (Ind.) M.S.U. which had been serving with the field ambulance now reverted to division.

Preparations for the assault landing at Myebon were now begun. The M.D.S. of 56 (Ind.) Fd. Amb. in Razabil was closed when relieved by 71 (Ind.) Fd. Amb.; 58 (Ind.) Fd. Amb. and 12 (Ind.) M.S.U. moved from Yegyanbyin to Akyab and attached a light A.D.S. to 3rd S.S. Bde.; 61 (Ind.) Fd. Amb. was already in Akyab. On January 12, 56 (Ind.) Fd. Amb. moved from Razabil to Foul Point.

The assault landing at Akyab was unopposed. The R.I.N. established an advanced landing craft base north of the town and opened a 50-bed sick bay there. To it R.N., R.I.N. and R.M. casualties were admitted. Evacuation was by road to Chittagong or by sea or air to Calcutta.

For the assault landing on January 12 at Myebon the R.I.N. medical assault party arranged to take casualties on the troop decks of the L.C.I. The more serious cases were diverted to H.M.I.S. *Narbada* in which the M.S.U. was functioning. The L.C.Ms. transported the casualties from the shore to the L.C.Is. and also to the *Narbada*. A hospital ship was anchored in Hunter's Bay. On January 15 the M.S.U. went ashore to join the M.D.S. of a field ambulance.

For the assault landing at Kangaw the medical arrangements were similar. A naval M.O. went ashore with the brigade.

The assault landing on the Myebon Peninsula was mounted in the brief space of two days. The plan was for 3rd Commando Bde. to land at 0900 hours on January 12 and to be followed on D-day+1 by 74th Bde. of Indian 25th Division. The medical tactical plan was as follows: one company of 58 (Ind.) Fd. Amb., with 6 (Ind.) M.S.U. attached, was placed u/c 3rd Commando Bde. and 58 (Ind.) Fd. Amb., less one company and with one company of 61 (Ind.) Fd. Amb. and 12 (Ind.) M.S.U. attached, was placed u/c Ind. 74th Bde. The company with the commando brigade would establish its A.D.S. in the beachhead as soon as possible and would evacuate casualties by returning landing craft to H.M.I.S. *Narbada* on which 6 (Ind.) M.S.U. was to function in the early stages of the operation. The hospital ship *Karapara* would lie at anchor 14 miles out to sea from D-day onwards. On D-day+1, 58 (Ind.) Fd. Amb. less one company and with 12 (Ind.) M.S.U. attached would land with Ind. 74th Bde. and open its M.D.S. in some convenient site near the beach. The company of 61 (Ind.) Fd. Amb. would accompany 74th Bde. as this passed through the commando brigade. At this point 6 (Ind.) M.S.U. would land and join the M.D.S. of 58 (Ind.) Fd. Amb. so that there would be two surgical units ashore.

In the event the A.D.S. with the commando brigade was divided into two half companies and landed at H-hour+3 minutes. Since the beach was composed of mud it was impossible to carry much equipment ashore. Evacuation by returning landing craft was satisfactory save that all casualties were taken first of all to a L.C.I.(D.) for triage, under naval medical arrangements. Light cases were retained there for treatment and for subsequent evacuation to H.S. *Karapara* while the serious cases were taken on to H.M.I.S. *Narbada*. In retrospect it seemed that it would have been a much better arrangement to have sorted out the serious cases ashore and to have had them sent direct to H.M.I.S. *Narbada*.

The L.C.M. on which the main body of 58 (Ind.) Fd. Amb. and 12 (Ind.) M.S.U. were being brought ashore broke down and did not reach the beachhead until D-day+3. The result of this delay was that the company of 61 (Ind.) Fd. Amb. did not accompany Ind. 74th Bde. As things turned out this caused no great inconvenience for the reason that the commando brigade, and not 74th Bde. was involved in the fighting. 6 (Ind.) M.S.U. remained aboard H.M.I.S. *Narbada* until D-day+4 by which time 12 (Ind.) M.S.U. had begun to function in association with the M.D.S. of 58 (Ind.) Fd. Amb. on 'Easy' Beach.

From this point onwards the arrangements worked smoothly. Evacuation from 3rd Commando and 74th Bdes. was by S.B. and M.T. to the M.D.S. of 58 (Ind.) Fd. Amb. where the two surgical units were functioning and from the M.D.S. to the hospital ship by landing craft. An airstrip was constructed and a few casualties were evacuated by air.

58 (Ind.) Fd. Amb.	Total Casualties Admitted	Number receiving life- or limb-saving surgery in 6 M.S.U. aboard H.M.I.S. Narbada
January 12 (D-day)	11	6
13	10	4
14	8	7
15	1	—
16	13	—
17	17	—
	60	17

For the assault landing at Kangaw it was planned that 3rd Commando Bde. should land at 1300 hours on D-day (January 22) to the west of Kangaw and that when a beachhead had been secured 51st Bde. of Indian 25th Division would follow, the commando brigade then being withdrawn. The medical tactical plan was as follows:

(1) 16 S.Bs. from 1 (Ind.) Bearer Coy. would be allotted to each commando, a total of 64.

(2) 61 (Ind.) Fd. Amb., less one coy. and together with 12 (Ind.) M.S.U. would be u/c 3rd Commando Bde.

(3) 50 S.Bs. from 1 (Ind.) Bearer Coy. would be attached to 61 (Ind.) Fd. Amb.

(4) The company of 58 (Ind.) Fd. Amb., which had served 51st Bde. during the landing on the Myebon Peninsula, would remain with this brigade and land with it.

(5) Evacuation from the beachhead would be by minesweeper to a hospital ship anchored off Frederick Island in Hunter's Bay.

(6) S.M.O. Commando Bde. would land with one of the Cdo. R.A.Ps. at H-hour+60 and select a site for the A.D.S.

(7) A skeleton A.D.S. of 61 (Ind.) Fd. Amb. would land at H-hour+60.

(8) The M.D.S. of 61 (Ind.) Fd. Amb. would land at H-hour+3 hours.

(9) 12 (Ind.) M.S.U. would function on H.M.I.S. *Narbada* until the M.D.S. had established itself ashore.

(10) When 51st Bde. landed 61 (Ind.) Fd. Amb. would be withdrawn from the commando brigade and placed u/c 51st Bde.

(11) Evacuation would be by bearer company S.Bs. to the A.D.S. or to the M.D.S. and thence to the beach by S.Bs. of the field ambulance or of the bearer company. Landing craft would convey the casualties needing surgical intervention urgently to H.M.I.S. *Narbada* while minesweepers would take the rest either to H.S. *Wu Sueh* in Hunter's Bay off Frederick Island, 15 miles south of Myebon, or else to Myebon where 6 M.S.U. was functioning on Easy Beach.

In the event these plans did not materialise. A new A.D.M.S. joined the division on D-day+1 and the D.A.D.M.S. had been appointed only six days before the operation was launched. No landing craft were specially set aside for evacuation work and there were so many of them that it was impossible for all their commanders to be briefed at all adequately by the embarkation medical officer on the beach. The M.D.S. landed on time but its equipment did not arrive until D-day+1 and when it did it was unloaded on to a different beach. However, by midday on D-day+1 the M.D.S. and its equipment had joined up and the M.D.S. opened on the reverse slope of Hill 170. The A.D.S. which had been established on the original beach was then closed and joined the M.D.S. An E.M.O. was left on the beach to supervise evacuation.

The M.D.S. was about ¾ mile from the beach which was now being used. Between the two a jeep track was constructed and two stretcher jeeps arrived on D-day+5. The track was then extended for another ¾ mile eastwards and four more jeep ambulances arrived. The casualties were embarked on any available landing craft and taken to H.M.I.S. *Narbada* where the M.S.U. itself undertook triage until the M.D.S. ashore was properly established. Patients requiring life-saving surgery were retained on the *Narbada* and the rest sent on by minesweeper to the hospital ship or to Myebon Beach. There was much shelling in the vicinity of Hill 170 and though the M.D.S. itself was protected by being on the reverse slope the commotion of the shelling was very disturbing.

51st Bde., with one company of 58 (Ind.) Fd. Amb., landed on D-day+4. An A.D.S. was opened at once on 'Fox' Beach. On the following day, the 27th, the A.D.S. moved further inland to a feature known as 'Pinner'. There it split itself into two, one light A.D.S. remaining in this site and the other moving inland to a feature called 'Berwick', 450 yds. to the east of 'Pinner' to open there on January 30. The light A.D.S. at 'Pinner' received a direct hit on February 3, 2 I.O.Rs. being killed and a V.C.O. and 2 I.O.Rs. wounded.

12 (Ind.) M.S.U. on the *Narbada* closed at 1500 hours on D-day+3 for the reason that the sloop was leaving the area. It had been intended to transfer the M.S.U. to H.M.I.S. *Jumna* but it was found possible to site it alongside the M.D.S. of 61 (Ind.) Fd. Amb. There it opened at midday on D-day+4. During this move urgent cases were taken to 6 M.S.U. on Easy Beach, Myebon. 12 (Ind.) M.S.U. was unable to retain its post-operatives on account of the very limited space available. At times, also, far too many casualties were sent to it from the M.D.S. so that after resuscitation many had to be sent on to 6 M.S.U. at Myebon, 3–4 hours away, by landing craft.

On February 1 (D-day+11), 58 (Ind.) Fd. Amb., less the one company already u/c 51st Bde., was brought to Kangaw and relieved 61 (Ind.) Fd. Amb., less one company, which then returned to Myebon on February 2. On the 3rd, 12 (Ind.) M.S.U. was relieved in Kangaw by 6 (Ind.) M.S.U. from Myebon and returned to Myebon. During this relief 56 (Ind.) Fd. Amb., which had arrived at Myebon with 53rd Bde., took over the M.D.S. on Easy Beach. Three days later 61 (Ind.) Fd. Amb., a company of which was already u/c 74th Bde. at Myebon, took over the M.D.S. from 56 (Ind.) Fd. Amb. which then began to prepare for a further operation by 53rd Bde.

In the Kangaw area fierce fighting continued and casualties were numerous. On February 2 the Lt. A.D.S. in 'Pinner' was moved forward to 'Berwick', joining up with the other platoon to form a complete company A.D.S. The evacuation of casualties during the action on February 11 when 7/16th Punjab attacked the 'West Finger', a feature due north of Hill 170, was unusually difficult. The R.A.P. was sited on the northern end of Hill 170 and between this and the A.D.S. were a chaung, about 100 yds. of water-logged ground and some 200 yds. of paddy land, the whole area being swept intermittently by small arms fire. Field ambulance stretcher-bearers and regimental stretcher-bearers combined to get some 30 casualties back. On the 12th the whole area was flooded by spring tides so that the hills became islands and jeep ambulances could no longer be used. All available S.Bs. were pooled to form bearer relay posts. Hand-carries ranged from 2–3 miles from R.A.P. to M.D.S. through water, or at low tide, through mud. The embarkation party on the beach was obliged to withdraw to the M.D.S. because of the flooding. After the 17th the floods subsided and evacuation by jeep ambulance was resumed.

On the 17th a pursuit column set out from Kangaw down the road to Yet Chaung. A light section of the A.D.S. was moved forward to Obin Taung to provide cover for the column and the remaining platoon of the A.D.S. returned to the M.D.S. at Hill 170. On the 21st the medical units, beginning with 6 (Ind.) M.S.U. began to move back to Myebon, the move being completed by the 25th.

61 (Ind.) Fd. Amb.	Total Casualties	Number receiving life- or limb-saving surgery	
		by 12 (Ind.) M.S.U. aboard Narbada	by 6 (Ind.) M.S.U. at Myebon
January 22	13	2	—
23	42	6	—
24	74	9	—
25	11	1	—
26	77	3	—
27	33	3	—
28	131	8	20
29	79	8	—
30	67	6	—
31	142	10	10
February 1	27	4	—
	696	60	30

Of these 583 or 84 per cent. were battle casualties; 106 or 15 per cent. were sick and 7 or 1 per cent. were accidental injuries. 28 patients died in the M.D.S., a mortality-rate of 4 per cent. The chief causes of death were sucking wounds of the chest and penetrating wounds of the abdomen. 15 patients, mostly with chest injuries, received preliminary resuscitation in the M.D.S. and were evacuated without surgical intervention. Three cases of gangrene were seen in the M.D.S., two of the leg, one of the chest wall.

Of the cases dealt with by the mobile surgical units there were:

		per cent. of the whole
Abdominal wounds, penetrating	19 or	21·1
Compound fractures of the femur	14 ,,	15·6
Major amputations	10 ,,	11·1
Major flesh wounds	8 ,,	8·9
Main arterial damage	4 ,,	4·4
Other compound fractures	19 ,,	21·1
Abdominal, non-penetrating	2 ,,	2·2
Enucleation, eye	1 ,,	1·1
Head wounds, penetrating	3 ,,	3·3
Knee joint, penetrating	6 ,,	6·7
Chest wounds, penetrating	4 ,,	4·4
	90 ,,	100

58 (Ind.) Fd. Amb.	Total Casualties Admitted	Numbers receiving life- or limb-saving surgery in 6 (Ind.) M.S.U.
February 2 (D-day+11)	19	—
3	14	6
4	36	2
5	24	5
6	17	5
7	19 (incl. 1 P.o.W.)	4
8	9	—
9	3	—
10	5	1
11	35	9 (incl. 1 P.o.W.)
12	16	1
13	5	1
14	19	4
15	17	6
	238	44

Of these 179 or 78 per cent. were battle casualties; there were 8 deaths in the M.D.S.

Of those dealt with by the M.S.U. there were:

	per cent. of the total
Abdominal wounds, penetrating	1 or 2·3
Compound femurs	3 ,, 6·8
	(all with gross main arterial damage)
Major amputations	2 or 4·5
Major flesh wounds	6 ,, 13·7
	(incl. 3 with gross main arterial damage)
Other compound fractures	14 or 31·8
	(incl. 2 with gross main arterial damage)
Head wounds, penetrating	6 or 13·7
Head, non-penetrating	2 ,, 4·5
Chest, penetrating	5 ,, 11·4
Severe phosphorus burns	1 ,, 2·3
Knee joint, penetrating	2 ,, 4·5
Maxillo-facial wounds	2 ,, 4·5
	44 ,, 100

On February 21 and 23, 3 civilian battle casualties were admitted to the M.D.S. and on the 24th, 7 West African and 3 civilian battle casualties were received.

A.D.M.S. Indian 25th Division found reason to express his dissatisfaction, as many others involved in combined operations had done previously, with the arrangements for the clearing of the M.D.Ss. Intercommunication between himself and the naval authorities was grossly imperfect, from his point of view. At the beginning of the operation the *Wu-Sueh* was standing off Frederick Island in Hunter's Bay, 15 miles to the south of Myebon. On D-day+1 it was suddenly learnt from the Director of Movement and Transportation that this hospital ship was about to depart and that a hospital carrier was expected in her place. The carrier would remain for two days only for the reason that she needed to be re-coaled and watered every 5–6 days and this could only be carried out at Akyab. The carrier duly arrived on D-day+2 and stood 4 miles off Easy Beach, Myebon. A L.C.I., evacuating casualties from Kangaw at night on D-day+2 passed her and proceeded to Hunter's Bay in search of the hospital ship which could not be found. The L.C.I. then made contact with the carrier and trans-shipped its patients. On D-day+3 the *Wu-Sueh* was sighted at anchorage about 3 miles off Easy Beach. When contact was made on the following morning she was found to be holding some 100 patients and to have received none during the last 24 hours. She was prepared to stay until full or for a week. It was then decided to use the *Wu-Sueh* as a floating hospital and to ferry cases from her to Akyab by means of hospital carriers. This arrangement broke down almost at once for H.Q. XV Corps ordered the ship to return to Akyab. She sailed on the morning of D-day+4. Carriers were then used to clear the M.D.Ss. the casualties from Kangaw being landed at Easy Beach, Myebon, whenever a shortage of carriers occurred. On D-day+7 the M.D.S. on Easy Beach was required to hold 187 cases for the reason that no carrier had arrived there. An empty L.C.I., returning to Akyab, was staffed with a small medical party and used to clear the M.D.S.

On D-day+8 it was decided to send a carrier up the Daingbon Chaung to clear the Kangaw M.D.S., the vessel calling at Myebon on its way to Akyab and picking up other cases there. The vessel in the Daingbon Chaung was supplied with a wireless set by the divisional Signals and thus the difficulties of inter-communication were overcome. Later two small creek steamers were used in the Daingbon Chaung on a shuttle service and the larger carriers plied between Myebon and Akyab. The creek steamers were coaled and watered from the carriers when they met at Myebon. Thus it was that it was not until D-day+9 that casualty evacuation from the M.D.Ss. could be regarded as satisfactory and that A.D.M.S. was in a position to control the means of keeping the M.D.Ss. clear.

A.D.M.S. noted that casualties among medical personnel were numerous during these operations, particularly among the bearer company personnel attached to the commandos. These specially trained and employed troops had no regimental stretcher-bearers of their own and so the bearer company personnel had to serve as such. The medical officers attached to the commandos were unaccustomed to dealing with Indian troops and so their control over the bearer company personnel remained imperfect. Bearer company personnel did not carry arms or entrenching tools and thus were unable to protect themselves. One R.M.O. and 10 I.O.Rs. were killed and 1 M.O., 1 V.C.O. and 33 I.O.Rs. wounded. Eight of the killed and 24 of the wounded belonged to the bearer company.

Evacuation by air involved complicated arrangements. The number of patients and their diagnoses had to be notified to corps H.Q. by 1900 hours on the day before the evacuation was to take place. There was no airstrip at Kangaw so that casualties for evacuation by air had to be conveyed to the M.D.S. on Easy Beach, Myebon which was near a light airstrip. This meant a hand-carry and a trip by landing craft to the M.D.S., and a journey by jeep over a poor road to the airstrip, where a small improvised air evacuation unit was stationed, connected by telephone with the M.D.S. Casualties frequently arrived at Myebon late in the afternoon so that quite commonly corps could not be notified by 1900 hours. Signals from corps notifying the time of arrival of the aircraft at Myebon were usually received long after the aircraft had arrived. Other formations which had to rely solely on evacuation by air had the first call on such aircraft as were available and so Indian 25th Division occasionally had to do without. The road between the M.D.S. and the airstrip was so bad that casualties for evacuation were not sent to the airstrip until the aircraft had actually arrived so as not to be exposed to the possibility of having to be brought back to the M.D.S. In the end the most satisfactory arrangement was found to be to send back a message each morning by the first returning pilot to the officer controlling the aircraft used for evacuation purposes indicating the day's requirements.

When a Dakota strip had been constructed at Myebon it was arranged that as from February 12 one Dakota should be sent each day to Myebon to clear the M.D.S. This arrangement, satisfactory in so far as Indian 25th Division was concerned, was disrupted when, without any warning, L.5s. carrying casualties from 4th W.A. Bde. began to land at Myebon. Fifty were disemplaned within a few hours on the 12th. They were kept on the Dakota strip awaiting emplaning but since the Dakota did not arrive they had to be taken to the M.D.S. which by this time had moved from Easy Beach to Myebon Jetty, about a mile from the Dakota strip Later in the evening both light and heavy aircraft arrived and the casualties were hurriedly returned to the airstrip and by nightfall 25 lying and 7 sitting cases had been got away. On February 13, some 120 casualties, Indian 25th Division and 4th W.A. Bde., were being held in the M.D.S. until the 14th when one Dakota arrived. There was no evacuation by air on the 15th. On the following day, in response to an urgent request, the corps evacuation officer visited Myebon, sized up the situation and promptly arranged for 5 Dakotas to clear the M.D.S. 138 casualties were evacuated and thenceforward frequent visits by this officer ensured that Kangaw and Myebon were kept clear.

The divisional bids on corps resources for the assault landing at Ru-Ywa were for a hospital ship until the conclusion of the initial phase of the operation; one L.C.I.(D.) on which a M.S.U. could function until a second M.S.U. attached to a M.D.S. ashore, was ready; a third M.S.U., to be landed as soon as was possible; two hospital carriers for ferrying casualties to the hospital ship; one company of the corps field ambulance to serve the commandos, should these be employed in the operation, and four L.C.As. for evacuation from the beach to the L.C.I.(D.). All these bids could not be met. In the event the following facilities were available:

(1) H.Cs. *Badora* and *Nalchera*.

(2) One L.C.I.(D.) with a Naval M.O. and the transfusion officer of 8 F.T.U.

(3) Four L.C.As. detailed by the Navy after landing the first flight of troops.

(4) One company of the corps field ambulance.

(5) 56 (Ind.) Fd. Amb. with 12 (Ind.) M.S.U. attached.

(6) Detachments of 1 (Ind.) Bearer Coy. and 30 (Ind.) Fd. Hyg. Sec.

(7) 2 (W.A.) Fd. Amb., with 2nd W.A. Bde., providing cover for that brigade.

(8) A reserve of medical supplies built up in Myebon; a further 12 tons of medical stores to be loaded at Chittagong on a coaster to provide maintenance for the operation from D-day+3 onwards.

Later, with 74th Bde. and H.Q. Indian 25th Division, there moved into the area of the operation 61 (Ind.) Fd. Amb., 30 (Ind.) A.M.U. and the main bodies of the bearer company and field hygiene section. During the planning conferences it was found necessary to object to the shipment of medical personnel and of medical unit equipment in different landing craft and to point out that medical units could accept responsibility for the burying only of those who died while in their care. As 56 (Ind.) Fd. Amb., less one company, and the detachments of the bearer company and field hygiene section had to be transported from Myebon in a hospital carrier, no other shipping space being available, it had to be accepted that evacuation could not begin until these medical units had been trans-shipped into landing craft.

The 'G' estimate of casualties during the first three days of the operation was 200, a figure which proved to be greatly in excess of the actual number.

The medical tactical plan was as follows:

During the first phase when, on the night of D-day−1/D-day, the commandos secured gun positions on 'Charterhouse Island' to cover the actual landing, a reinforced platoon of the corps field ambulance (71 (Ind.) Fd. Amb.) would be placed u/c of the commando party and would function on a L.C.I.(L). This light A.D.S. would not land unless it was absolutely essential for it to do so in order to provide medical cover. Casualties would be retained in the A.D.S. until this phase of the operation had been completed and the party returned to Myebon, but urgent surgical cases would be evacuated to Myebon by means of a motor launch provided by the Navy. The rest of the corps field ambulance would remain at Myebon.

For phase two, the assault landing by 53rd Bde. north of Ru-Ywa and the establishment of a beachhead, one company of 56 (Ind.) Fd. Amb. would be placed u/c 53rd Bde. A.D.M.S. would be aboard the hospital carrier anchored near the creek steamer which carried the divisional tactical H.Q.

(1) The company commander would land with the R.A.P. of the leading battalion and select a site for his A.D.S.

(2) A non-medical officer of the field ambulance would act as embarkation medical officer and would land at H-hour+30 and establish an embarkation post on the beach. He would carry with him four small Red Cross flags which he would fix to the four L.C.As. detailed by the beach master for casualty evacuation after the landing of the first flight.

(3) One company of 56 (Ind.) Fd. Amb., plus 13 stretcher-bearers of the bearer company, would land with the second battalion to go ashore and would establish an A.D.S. With this company the field ambulance commander himself would land and select a site for the M.D.S.

(4) The field ambulance, less one company and reinforced by 36 S.Bs. of the bearer company, would land with the second flight at H-hour+3 or 4 hours and establish the M.D.S.

(5) The M.S.U. would function aboard the L.C.I.(D.) which would be moored alongside the hospital carrier *Badora* at the ferry control point until it was feasible for it to go ashore and join the M.D.S. To the M.S.U. would be attached 9 S.Bs. of the bearer company to assist in the hand carriage of patients aboard the carrier and in their trans-shipment.

(6) A wireless set would connect Main Div. H.Q., the carrier and the creek steamers operating up the Daingbon Chaung (the Kangaw operation was still continuing).

(7) Evacuation would be by hand-carriage from A.D.S. and M.D.S. to the embarkation point on the beach, until jeep ambulances were forthcoming. From the beach to the hospital carrier it would be by landing craft. Sorting and resuscitation would be undertaken on the carrier. Cases requiring surgical intervention would be transferred to the M.S.U. aboard the L.C.I.(D.) alongside the carrier. When the M.D.S. ashore was fully functioning, sorting and resuscitation on the carrier would be necessary only when the M.D.S. was overwhelmed with a rush of casualties. H.C. *Badora* (70 lying cases) would remain at the ferry control point during D-day and D-day+1 and would then return to Akyab, being replaced by H.C. *Nalchera* (40 cases). These two carriers would then provide a shuttle service, each of them remaining at the ferry control point for two days. Aboard each of them were two medical officers and two nursing officers. In view of the 'G' estimate of casualties this arrangement could not be regarded as satisfactory,

but to it there was no possible alternative. No hospital ship was available. Evacuation by air would commence just as soon as a strip could be constructed.

For phase three when 2nd W.A. Bde. was to be ferried on D-day+2 from Kangaw to the beachhead whence it would advance on An by the Ru-Ywa–An track, casualties from this brigade would be dealt with by 2 (W.A.) Fd. Amb. and evacuated through the M.D.S. of 56 (Ind.) Fd. Amb. so long as the brigade could maintain contact with the Ru-Ywa beachhead. Thereafter evacuation would be solely by air from light airstrips constructed by the brigade. Should it remain impossible to construct airstrips the brigade would carry its casualties forward until an L. of C. could be opened.

In the event these plans had to be modified. 74th Bde. had to be employed and in its preparations only slight attention was given to the problem of casualty evacuation. The company commander landed with the R.A.P. on 'Oboe Red' Beach as planned and decided to utilise the site of the R.A.P. of the leading battalion when this moved forward as the site for the A.D.S. The non-medical officer landed on Oboe Red Beach as planned and established his embarkation point. But as the beach-master had received no instructions concerning the allotment of landing craft for casualty evacuation purposes difficulty at once arose. Eventually two L.C.As. were assigned for casualty evacuation but the officers in charge of them declined to have the Red Cross emblem affixed to their craft. During the course of this operation the difficulty of obtaining landing craft for casualty evacuation increased in magnitude. On many an occasion casualties had to lie about on the beach for two hours and more while arrangements for their evacuation were being made. Stretchers and blankets were lost to the medical units in considerable numbers. The field ambulance company with the second battalion landed as planned and established an A.D.S. with one platoon in a wood about 1,500 yds. from the beach while the second platoon joined the embarkation officer's party on the beach. The field ambulance trans-shipped from the carrier into landing craft and went ashore as planned. The carrier was then prepared for the reception of casualties. The field ambulance remained on the beach, closed, for the night. As casualties were very few in number at this time A.D.M.S. went ashore to enquire as to the possibility of getting the M.S.U. ashore at first light on D-day+1 while things were relatively quiet. But as the M.D.S. had not yet opened the M.S.U. could not be accepted until D-day+2.

On D-day+1 the M.D.S. equipment was man-handled 1,500 yds. across swamp and paddy land to the wood where the M.D.S. opened in a nullah near brigade H.Q. The site chosen was not very satisfactory for there was considerable movement in the area and an airstrip was being constructed nearby. On D-day+2 the M.S.U. came ashore and joined the M.D.S. An A.D.S. was established in Ru-Ywa village and the platoon helping the embarkation party on the beach was withdrawn to the M.D.S. During the evening of D-day+3 and during D-day+4 the Japanese shelled the beach area consistently and evacuation from the beach was halted. As the casualties on the beach awaiting evacuation grew in numbers it was necessary to load them on to a L.C.M. under heavy shell fire and get them away. The beach was then closed in so far as casualty evacuation was concerned and a new beach at Ru-Ywa village was opened. The hand-carry from the M.D.S. to this new beach was some 3,000 yds., jeep ambulances were not yet available. The beach itself was not suitable for the landing craft had to sail up a very narrow and shallow chaung to reach it and this could be done only for an hour on either side of high tide. The journey from beach to carrier now took two hours. Later another new beach further to the south-east in the same chaung was opened and in this the craft could operate for two to three hours on either side of high tide. But only one landing craft could use the beach at any one time and so, since the beach was being used for all purposes, casualty evacuation was commonly greatly delayed.

At this point it was decided to bring in 74th Bde. Gp. from Myebon to move north from Ru-Ywa to Tamandu, forming a beachhead for the crossing of the Dalet Chaung by 4th W.A. Bde. of 82nd W.A. Division moving south from Dalet and forming a F.M.A. in the Tamandu area for the maintenance of the West African Division, less one brigade, in its march down the Tamandu-An road to link up with 3rd W.A. Bde. already proceeding to the An area from Ru-Ywa. 51st Bde. was to return to Akyab after the completion of the Kangaw operation but until this happened arrangements were to be made at Myebon for the evacuation of casualties from Kangaw and Myebon. Evacuation from 82nd W.A. Division at this time was by air from north of Dalet to Myebon. The following medical cover was arranged: One company of 58 (Ind.) Fd. Amb. and 6 (Ind.) M.S.U. were to move from Kangaw to Myebon; 61 (Ind.) Fd. Amb. and 6 (Ind.) M.S.U. were to move to Ru-Ywa with 74th Bde. Gp. One company of 61 (Ind.) Fd. Amb. was to remain u/c 74th Bde.; 58 (Ind.) Fd. Amb. less one company was to remain at Kangaw and move with 51st Bde.; one company of 58 (Ind.) Fd. Amb. together with one company of 71 (Ind.) Fd. Amb. (XV Corps), the light section of which had already returned to Myebon with the commando party, were to remain at Myebon to deal with the local sick and with evacuation by sea and by air. When joined by 58 (Ind.) Fd. Amb., less one company, the whole was to move from Myebon to Akyab with 51st Bde.; the remainder of 1 (Ind.) Bearer Coy, less a detachment of 20 S.Bs. u/c 58 (Ind.) Fd. Amb., was to proceed to Ru-Ywa; 6 (Ind.) M.S.U., on arrival in the Ru-Ywa area was to function aboard the L.C.I.(D.) until the forward movement of 74th Bde. made it necessary for the unit to go ashore in support.

Save that 6 (Ind.) M.S.U. had to be landed on February 26 for the reason that the Navy required the immediate release of the L.C.I.(D.) and went into reserve with 61 (Ind.) Fd. Amb. at Ru-Ywa, the arrangements unfolded very much according to plan. During the night of February 22/23 the M.D.S. in the woods received a direct hit and 1 I.O.R. was killed and 2 medical officers and 6 I.O.Rs. wounded. During the same night the R.M.O. of 17/5th Mahrattas was wounded in his R.A.P. in the hills away to the east. On the 23rd a new site was prepared for the M.D.S. about 700 yds. to the south-east of its previous site and to this the M.D.S. moved on the 24th.

A company of 61 (Ind.) Fd. Amb. accompanied 74th Bde. along the Ru-Ywa–Tamandu track. Evacuation was to the M.D.S. of 56 (Ind.) Fd. Amb. The A.D.S. established by this company was in Dokekan on March 3. From this place the brigade was to cross the Me Chaung but no arrangements for the evacuation of casualties across the chaung had been considered by the brigade in its planning for this operation. Fortunately A.D.M.S. was able to arrange with the Navy for one L.C.A. with a medical party aboard, to proceed to the Me Chaung to evacuate casualties. The L.C.A. was able to make only one trip each day for the reason that it was required to report daily at the Ferry Control Point. Casualties were also evacuated on a second L.C.A. which brought supplies to the brigade each day.

61 (Ind.) Fd. Amb. opened its A.D.S. just across the Me Chaung on March 4 and a light A.D.S. went forward to Tamandu with brigade H.Q. Since brigade H.Q. decided that it was impossible to provide protection for more than one company of the field ambulance it was arranged that a staging post should be left on the north side of the Me Chaung crossing where the A.D.S. had been and that the remainder of the field ambulance company should establish its A.D.S. in Tamandu. Later, on instructions of brigade H.Q., the staging post joined the A.D.S.

At 1900 hours on March 5 a message was received that 3/2nd G.R. of 74th Bde. had suffered heavy casualties and that for their evacuation three L.C.As. were required at Tamandu. The Navy was unwilling to send L.C.As. there at night. In view of the facts that the A.D.S. with 74th Bde. was required to hold these 80 casualties and that to obtain L.C.As. wherewith to evacuate them had been shown to be impossible, the brigade commander was again advised by A.D.M.S. that his medical cover was insufficient. He was offered a light M.D.S. and a M.S.U. but these were declined. However, A.D.M.S. arranged for the despatch to

Tamandu of the officer commanding 61 (Ind.) Fd. Amb. and a small party of N.Os. and S.Bs. with stores and tentage on the 6th. Visiting the A.D.S. on this day A.D.M.S. found that it was holding 92 casualties, that no L.C.As. had arrived or were expected and that no facilities for evacuation across the Me Chaung existed. Arrangements were immediately made for the evacuation of 22 lying and 16 sitting cases by road to the Me Chaung for embarkation on the daily maintenance L.C.A. that was expected. A small medical party was posted on the bank of the Me Chaung with tents to stage these casualties. No landing craft were to be discovered in the Dalet Chaung and 3 jeeps and 2 ambulance cars were called forward from Ru-Ywa to the south bank of the Me Chaung to evacuate cases when the ferry bridge then under construction was finished. Divisional H.Q. was asked to take steps to have landing craft sent to the jetty at Tamandu.

The maintenance L.C.A. failed to arrive for the reason that it had been diverted to the jetty at Tamandu and did not proceed up the Me Chaung. The casualties waiting there were therefore sent on by road, after crossing over the ferry bridge. The rest of the casualties in the A.D.S. in Tamandu were evacuated by three L.C.Ms. which eventually made their appearance. Two of these vessels trans-shipped their patients to the hospital carrier at the ferry control point, the third went on to the beach where the M.D.S. was functioning. By 1530 hours the A.D.S had been cleared, 105 cases in all being evacuated.

On March 7 the A.D.S. of 4 (W.A.) Fd. Amb. crossed the Dalet Chaung and the surgeon and anaesthetist of this unit were loaned to 61 (Ind.) Fd. Amb. The West African field ambulance remained closed and so casualties from the West African brigade were admitted to the Indian field ambulance. Two L.C.As. were now assigned solely for evacuation purposes and despite protests from their commanders the Red Cross flag was affixed to them. All evacuation from the Ru-Ywa area was by way of Oboe Red Beach and the A.D.S. in Ru-Ywa was closed and moved to this beach.

On March 8 in accordance with orders issued by the divisional commander 61 (Ind.) Fd. Amb., less a detachment and with additional S.Bs. and 6 (Ind.) M.S.U. attached, was moved into Tamandu where a full M.D.S. with facilities for surgery was established. From this M.D.S. evacuation was direct to the hospital carrier which was lying off Tamandu. No airstrip had been constructed at Tamandu and cases for evacuation by air had to be taken to Ru-Ywa until March 16 when the medical units were withdrawn from the Ru-Ywa area. 74th Bde. passed u/c 82nd W.A. Division on March 11. The rest of Indian 25th Division withdrew from Ru-Ywa to Akyab, the move being completed on March 18.

56 (Ind.) Fd. Amb.	Total Casualties	Number receiving life- or limb-saving surgery in 12 (Ind.) M.S.U.
February 16 (D-day)	4	—
17	8	4
18	4	—
19	15	1
20	14	2
21	20	2
22	61	3
23	30	11
24	16	2
25	30	3
26	17	2
27	20	1
28	24	2
March 1	35	1
2	35	5
3	31	1
4	23	6
5	70	9
6	54	2
7	17	3
8	14	1
9	4	—
10	3	—
11	5	—
	554	61

Of the 554, 326 were battle casualties (59 per cent.) and 228 were sick or accidental injuries (41 per cent.). The figures include 43 casualties from 82nd W.A. Division, 23 of them battle casualties. There were 11 deaths in the M.D.S.; 3 cases were dead on arrival and 1 died on the carrier after evacuation from the M.D.S.

Of the 61 requiring surgical intervention the classification was as follows:

Abdomen, penetrating	12 (2 deaths)
Head, penetrating	2 (1 death)
G.S.W. Spine	2
Maxillo-facial wounds	2
Compound fracture of femur	6
Other compound fractures	9 (1 death)
Knee joint, penetrating	8
Major amputations	4
Major flesh wounds	16 (1 death)
	61

61 (Ind.) Fd. Amb.	Total Casualties Received	
	Indian 25th Division and Others	82nd W.A. Division
March 3 (D-day+15)	23	—
4	16	—
5	57	—
6	78	—
7	25	11
8	8	67
9	17	67
10	3	58
11	7	3
	234	206

Of these 78 per cent. were battle casualties, 11·29 per cent. were sick and 10·8 per cent. were accidental injuries. There were 4 deaths in the M.D.S., 1 of Indian 25th Division, 3 of 82nd W.A. Division. 6 (Ind.) M.S.U. carried out life-saving surgery on 25 cases, 23 of the West African Division, 2 of Indian 25th Division.

Evacuation by Air

March 2	4
3	1
4	2
5	—
6	—
7	8
8	10 (incl. 1 W.A.O.R.)
9	6
10	7 (incl. 1 W.A.O.R.)
11	3
15	2 (both W.A.O.Rs.)
	43

(Penetrating wound eye/eyes 6; G.S.W. Head 3; compound fractures and amputations 7; G.S.W. abdomen 3; G.S.W. chest 5; penetrating knee-joint 3; G.S.W. spine 1; major flesh wounds 1; miscellaneous G.S.W. 13; sick 1.) The miscellaneous G.S.W. cases would not normally have been sent by air but there was no other means available at the time.

TABLE 38

Indian 25th Division. Admissions to Medical Units. By Cause. January–March, 1945.

Week ending	Strength	Admissions to Medical Units	Admission-rate per 1,000 per diem	Malaria N.Y.D.(F.)	Dysentery, Diarrhoea	Venereal Disease	Mumps	Infective Hepatitis	Battle Casualties
13. 1.45	17,456	101	0·83	28	3	1	—	1	10
20. 1.45	19,909	310	2·22	61	2	4	—	—	89
27. 1.45	13,997	315	3·22	42	9	2	—	1	172
3. 2.45	11,747	518	6·32	24	2	2	—	—	434
10. 2.45	12,714	234	2·63	25	8	5	—	1	101
17. 2.45	20,543	272	1·86	32	3	5	—	—	129
24. 2.45	18,476	275	2·26	34	9	—	—	—	115
3. 3.45	18,316	189	1·48	47	2	3	1	2	66
10. 3.45	10,007	345	4·92	26	4	—	—	—	221
17. 3.45	12,039	21	0·25	6	—	1	—	—	1
24. 3.45	12,144	38	0·42	6	1	3	—	—	—
31. 3.45	17,456	54	0·44	14	—	—	—	—	—

[Imperial War Museum

PLATE XXXIV. Wading through a chaung.

PLATE XLIII. Buthidaung Embarkation Point, January 1945. Native sampans used both for carrying wounded and supplies.

[Imperial War Museum

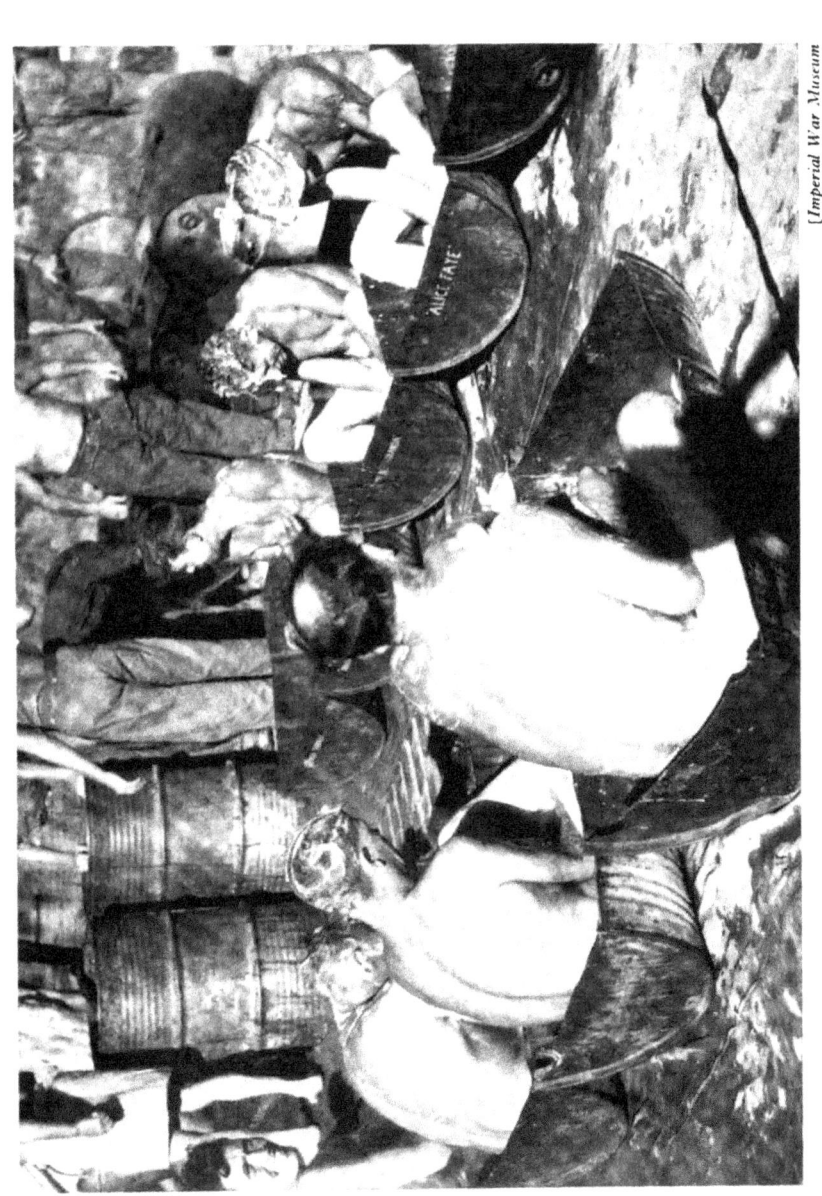

PLATE XXXVI. Typical Mobile Bath Unit for forward troops.

[Imperial War Museum]

PLATE XXXVII. Hopin to Mawlu. November 1944.

PLATE XXXVIII. A Regimental Aid Post. February 1945.

[Imperial War Museum]

PLATE XXXIX. Myitson. February 1945. A front line Regimental Aid Post. *[Imperial War Museum*

PLATE XL. Myitson, February 1945. Stretcher bearers of the Buffs make their way through tangled scrub.

[*Imperial War Museum*]

PLATE XLI. Kumi ration carriers in the Arakan. November 1944.

[Imperial War Museum]

PLATE XLII. Supplies, including medical supplies, dropped to 81st West African Division in the Kaladan Valley.

PLATE XLIII. Buthidaung Embarkation Point. January 1945. Native sampans used both for carrying wounded and supplies.

[Imperial War Museum]

[*Imperial War Museum*

PLATE XLIV. Arakan, November 1944. West African wounded being evacuated by Kumis on native raft.

PLATE XLV. R.I.N. Landing Craft, Mechanised at the Zani Chaung Supply Head, south of Sabyin, 18 miles from Taungup with supplies. On their return trip they will carry casualties.

PLATE XLVI. Evacuating casualties by D.U.K.W. Kyaukpyu.

PLATE XLVII. Ru-Ywa. An Indian Dental Mechanic Unit in the Beachhead.

PLATE XLVIII. A Main Dressing Station, Kangaw.

[Indian Historical Section]

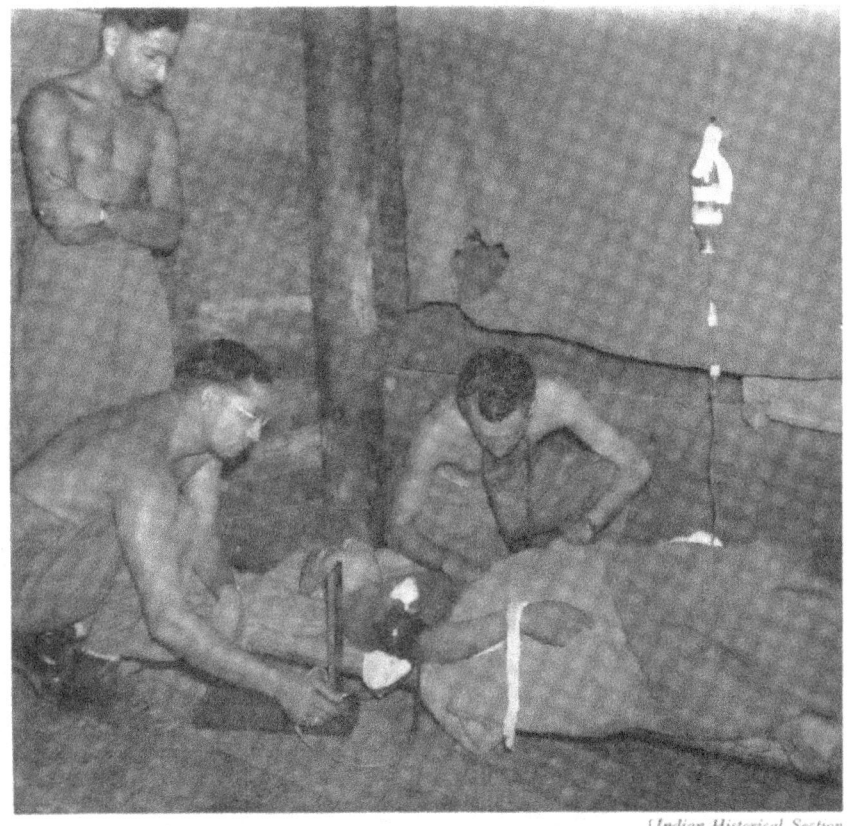
PLATE XLIX. A Field Transfusion Unit in the Arakan.

PLATE L. A post-operative unit of 'a Field Hospital' in a forward area in Burma.

Imperial War Museum

INDIAN 26TH DIVISION

The 'Tiger-head' division had held the 'monsoon line' in Arakan for two seasons and twice had been used to stabilise a situation that threatened danger. In 1944 it assumed responsibility for the two bastions of the line at Taung and Goppe Bazars, the third brigade being in Cox's Bazar in reserve. No sooner had the monsoon ended than a Japanese force, a battalion strong, attempted to get astride the Goppe Pass in early October. This force lost about a quarter of its strength in engagements with 1 R./9th Jat and with the Green Howards and disintegrated.

On January 21, under cover of a heavy naval and air bombardment, 71st and 4th Bdes. of Indian 26th Division assaulted Kyaukpyu at the northern tip of Ramree Island, this operation following upon the landing of 3rd Commando and Indian 25th Division on Akyab nine days previously. After two brief skirmishes with Japanese patrols, Kyaukpyu was taken. The naval bombardment and the air-strike had reduced the opposition to negligible proportions. By the end of the first week about two hundred square miles of the island had been cleared, roughly the northern half. In eighteen working days the divisional sappers built 50 miles of road, repaired 40 bridges and a number of airstrips. Ramree town was entered and the Japanese faded away into the maze of swamp and chaung that fills the north-east corner of Ramree Island. The Navy lay in wait for those who tried to escape by sampan.

On January 26 a force of five hundred Royal Marines landed on Cheduba Island to meet with no opposition. Indian 26th Division took over from the Marines shortly afterwards.

On March 13, Ind. 4th Bde. of Indian 26th Division made another assault landing, this time at Letpan, 35 miles north of Taungup. Once again the Japanese were taken by surprise and by noon on March 13 a firm beachhead had been established. By the 23rd the brigade, closely followed by 22nd E.A. Bde., had reached to within eleven miles of Taungup. Japanese resistance now began to stiffen and counter-attacks were launched. It was not until the night of April 13/14 that the Taungup Chaung was forded and the coastal village of Taungup entered. The sole inhabitant was the caretaker of the Government bungalow who, being awakened at 0400 hours by a patrol, promptly produced the guest book from its hiding place and asked the officer in charge of the party to sign! The last entry had been made by a British officer in 1942.

Indian 26th Division now handed over to 4th W.A. Bde. of 82nd W.A. Division, and returned with all possible speed to Ramree Island to prepare for Operation 'Dracula'.

H.Q. XV Corps and Indian 26th Division remained in Ramree; all the other formations sooner or later returned to India. In Arakan airfields were constructed and stocks of supplies of all kinds were built up against the time when Fourteenth Army, advancing southwards, would need them.

4TH AND 71ST BRIGADES. THE ASSAULT LANDING AT KYAUKPYU, RAMREE ISLAND

MEDICAL COVER

For this operation 46 and 48 (Ind.) Fd. Ambs., served 4th and 71st Bdes. respectively, each consisting of 11 officers, 16 B.O.Rs., 3 V.C.Os., 175 I.O.Rs. These were distributed as follows:

'A'	Coy.	2 officers;	0 V.C.Os.;	3 B.O.Rs.;	45 I.O.Rs.:	Total	50
'B'	Coy.	2 ,,	0 ,,	2 ,,	46 ,,	,,	50
H.Q.	Coy.	7 ,,	3 ,,	11 ,,	84 ,,	,,	105

In 48 (Ind.) Fd. Amb.

'A' Coy. was divided into two light sections (1 and 2)
'B' Coy. ,, ,, ,, two light sections (3 and 4)
H.Q. Coy. ,, ,, ,, a light M.D.S. (5 Offrs.; 2 V.C.Os.; 10 B.O.Rs.; 28 I.O.Rs. (1 R.I.A.S.C.))
a rear M.D.S. (2 Offrs.; 1 B.O.R.; 48 I.O.Rs. (7 R.I.A.S.C.))

Attached to 48 (Ind.) Fd. Amb. were:

One platoon of 2 (Ind.) Bearer Coy. (75 I.O.Rs.)
(10 with each light section; 25 with the light M.D.S.; 10 with the rear M.D.S.)
11 (Ind.) M.S.U.
25 (Ind.) C.C.S. detachment
27 (Ind.) Fd. Hyg. Sec. detachment
28 F.T.U.

1 Lt. Sec. ('A' Coy.) was attached to 1st Lincolns and 3 Lt. Sec. ('B' Coy.) to 5/1st Punjab. The convoy carrying the first flight of the division, including 48 (Ind.) Fd. Amb., arrived off Ramree Island on January 21, 1945. The Lt. M.D.S. landed from a L.C.M. on 'Fox Red' beach at Kyaukpyu and moved into a derelict barrack building. Detachments were at once sent to evacuate casualties from the Lincolns and Punjabis on the landing beaches. A.D.M.S., coming ashore, selected, in conjunction with the beach master, a site for the C.E.P. quite near the barracks. Rear M.D.S. together with 11 (Ind.) M.S.U., 28 F.T.U., the detachments of 25 (Ind.) C.C.S. and of 27 (Ind.) Fd. Hyg. Sec. landed and moved to the vicinity of the town jail. Evacuation on this first day was from the Lt. M.D.S. to the hospital ship *Vasna*, lying offshore. 3 Lt. Sec. was placed in charge of the C.E.P.

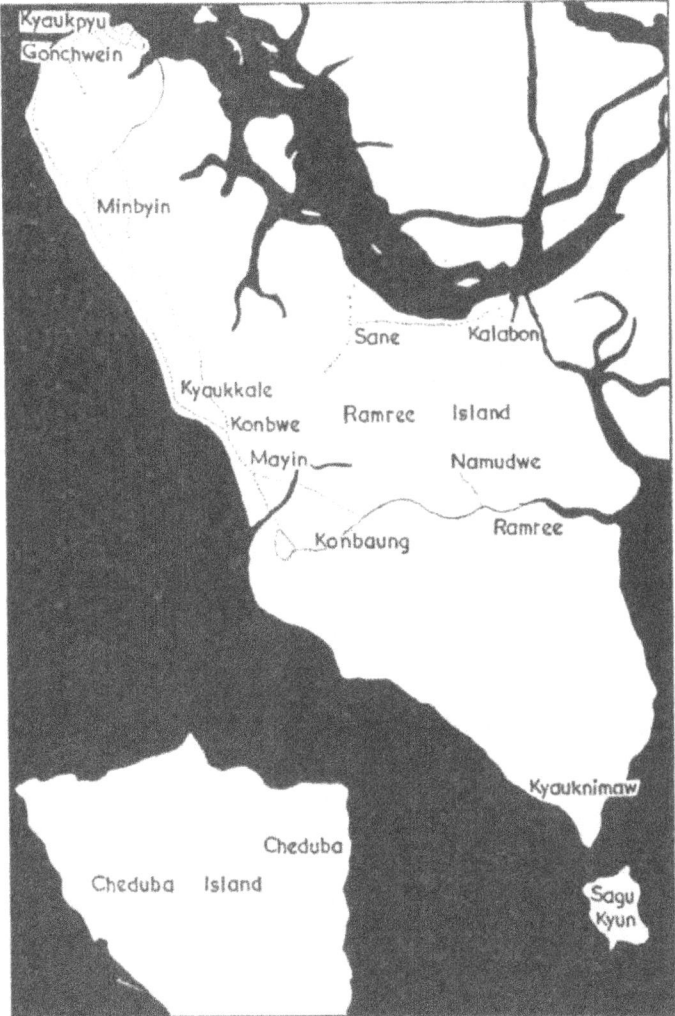

Fig. 64. Arakan. Ramree Island

On January 23 the light M.D.S. of 48 (Ind.) Fd. Amb. moved forward to Minbyin where it opened. 1, 2 and 4 Lt. Secs. all joined the Rear M.D.S. in the jail area. On the 24th the Rear M.D.S. moved to Minbyin and the three light sections to Kyaukkale with 71st Bde. On January 30, 1 Lt. Sec. moved with 1st Lincolns to the vicinity of Konbwe and the Rear M.D.S. moved forward to Mayin.

On January 23, 1 (Ind.) Fd. Amb. proceeded to Kyaukpyu by sea from Chittagong and on the 29th sent a light section to Sagu Kyun Island to serve units of 36th Bde. On January 30, 46 (Ind.) Fd. Amb., with 4th Bde., embarked at Chittagong for Kyaukpyu. The unit discovered that no arrangements for the feeding of the troops aboard the ship had been made and undertook the job of cooking for them all. The field ambulance landed on February 1 when 'B' Coy. opened its A.D.S. in Kyaukpyu. The M.D.S. soon relieved the A.D.S. which moved on February 3 to Mayin.

On February 3, 2 Lt. Sec. of 48 (Ind.) Fd. Amb. joined 1 Lt. Sec. in Konbwe. The Rear M.D.S. which had moved forward to Mayin was relieved by 'B' Coy. of 46 (Ind.) Fd. Amb. 11 (Ind.) M.S.U. remained in Mayin with the A.D.S. of 'B' Coy of 46 (Ind.) Fd. Amb. On the 4th the Lt. M.D.S. moved on to Yebadin where it was joined by 3 Lt. Sec. On February 5 the Rear M.D.S. of 48 (Ind.) Fd. Amb. joined the Lt. M.D.S. in Yebadin. By this time 3 Lt. Sec. in Minbyin was functioning as a staging section. The M.D.S. of 46 (Ind.) Fd. Amb. replaced the A.D.S. of 'B' Coy. of the same medical unit in Mayin. On the 7th, 'B' Coy's. A.D.S. was opened in 'Naga Village'. On the 4th a detachment of 'A' Coy. of 46 (Ind.) Fd. Amb. was sent to Cheduba Island where Indian 26th Division had taken over from the Royal Marines. This detachment returned to Mayin on February 14.

On February 7, 1 Lt. Sec. of 48 (Ind.) Fd. Amb. moved on to Namudwe where it opened an A.D.S. which received casualties from 1st Lincolns and evacuated them to the M.D.S. in Yebadin. On the 9th, 2 Lt. Sec. moved into Ramree Town and was followed almost immediately by the Lt. M.D.S. One I.O.R. was killed and another wounded while the M.D.S. was moving in. On the 10th the Lt. M.D.S. was joined by 7 (Ind.) M.S.U. and on the 12th by the Rear M.D.S. On February 15, 'B' Coy. of 46 (Ind.) Fd. Amb. established its A.D.S. in Sane to serve the Green Howards. A V.C.O. and three stretcher-bearer squads were attached to the battalion to transport casualties back from the R.A.P. to the A.D.S. by river. From the A.D.S. in Sane evacuation was by ambulance car to the M.D.S. in Mayin. On the 19th, 46 (Ind.) Fd. Amb. began to move back to Gonchwein where it was to prepare itself for the landing on the mainland of Burma at Letpan.

On February 25, 1 Lt. Sec. of 48 (Ind.) Fd. Amb. left Namudwe for Kalabon where it opened its A.D.S. to serve the Lincolns. 'B' Coy. of 48 (Ind.) Fd. Amb. had opened an A.D.S. in Konbaung on February 12 and on the 27th moved forward to Namudwe there to take over from 'A' Coy. At this time 1 (Ind.) Fd. Amb. had its M.D.S. in Kyauknimaw in the south of Ramree Island and A.D.Ss. at Kyauknimaw and Sagu Kyun. 7 (Ind.) M.S.U. and a platoon of 2 (Ind.) Bearer Coy. were now attached to 1 (Ind.) Fd. Amb.

On March 16, 48 and 1 (Ind.) Fd. Ambs. moved back to the Gonchwein area, 48 *en route* for Madras and 1 to remain on Ramree Island, but both to prepare for Operation 'Dracula'.

4TH BRIGADE. THE ASSAULT LANDING AT LETPAN

MEDICAL COVER

46 (Ind.) Fd. Amb. began to prepare for this operation when in mid-February it moved from Sane and Mayin to the concentration area at Gonchwein. On March 9 a detachment of the unit was sent into Kyaukpyu to acquaint itself with the arrangements for the embarkation of the unit on the following day. A section of 'A' Coy. was attached to 2/13th F.F.Rif. and a section of 'B' Coy. to 2nd Green Howards. Each of these sections was to open an A.D.S. on the beach upon which the battalion landed. To the third battalion of the brigade, 1/18th R.Garh. Rif. an officer of the field ambulance was attached to help the R.M.O. and another officer of the medical unit was made responsible for the management of a C.E.P. There were three beaches, 'Able', 'Baker' and 'Easy', the C.E.P. was to be established initially on Able beach.

On March 12, 'A' Coy's. section landed on Baker beach and 1/18th R.Garh.Rif. on Easy beach. On the following day 'B' Coy's. section landed on Able beach and established its A.D.S. Two ambulance cars, one 15-cwt. truck and one jeep were available for evacuation. On March 14 the rest of 'A' Coy. landed on Able beach and joined the A.D.S. of 'B' Coy. On the 15th the headquarters of the unit disembarked and the M.D.S. took over from 'B' Coy's. A.D.S. on Able beach.

On the 16th the A.D.S. of 'A' Coy. left 2/13th F.F.Rif. and attached itself to H.Q. 4th Bde. On the 17th the A.D.S. of 'A' Coy. moved into Lamu village with H.Q. 4th Bde. while the A.D.S. of 'B' Coy. left Able beach for Pyinwin village. On the 19th 'A' Coy. moved from Lamu village to Sabyin and on the following day the C.E.P. moved from Able beach to Lamu. On the 21st the M.D.S. took over from 'A' Coy. in Sabyin to which village the C.E.P. moved from Lamu. On March 24, 'A' Coy. moved to Hpaukpyin and on the 27th to Kyaukmaungnama while the M.D.S. opened in Kindaunggyi where it was joined by 'B' Coy. Evacuation by air had become possible by this time.

In so far as this medical unit was concerned the month of April was uneventful and at its end it left the Burmese mainland to return to Ramree Island there to make ready for Operation 'Dracula'.

81ST WEST AFRICAN DIVISION

This division, following its withdrawal from the valley of the Kaladan in the early part of 1944, had returned to it in October. Its first task was that of capturing Singpa and Mowdok, on Indian soil and occupied by the Japanese in the previous June. The division concentrated in the area of Tukpui, three miles to the west of Mowdok. 1st Sierra Leone Regt. captured Mowdok into which the garrison of Singpa had withdrawn. By October 18 the Japanese were beyond the Indian border.

The advance was then continued in three columns, one moving along the Pi Chaung; one along the valley of the Kaladan and the third along an old jeep track that had been constructed in 1943. The Japanese were steadily pushed back to within about three miles of Paletwa. It was then that the division received its orders to continue its advance and to take Myohaung. It was decided to leapfrog two of the brigades, 5th and 6th, down the Kaladan Valley and to leave only a protective detachment on the Pi Chaung axis.

On December 4, 5th and 6th W.A. Bdes., and the divisional troops, crossed the Kaladan at the village of Tinma, just south of Kyingri on the Pi Chaung. Elements of the division left on the west bank patrolled vigorously to create the impression that an advance down both sides of the river was proceeding. The division rested at Tinma and constructed a Dakota airstrip. On the 19th the advance was resumed with 6th Bde. in the lead and by the 22nd Thandada, a village some six miles southeast of Thayettabin, was reached. For three days the Air Force carried out a saturation attack on the Japanese positions in this area with the result that the Japanese ceased to probe the positions held by the West Africans. Meanwhile on the west bank of the river the divisional reconnaissance regiment had moved southward towards Apaukwa and Kanzauk where it made contact with 4th Bde. of 82nd W.A. Division.

The two divisions then combined for the attack on Myohaung and after a sharp engagement the place was taken on January 25. 81st W.A. Division thereupon retraced its steps to Chiringa and took no further part in the campaign.

MEDICAL COVER

Because in 1943 the divisional field ambulances had found it to be exceedingly difficult to overcome the ever increasing difficulties that are invariably associated with a lengthening L. of C., XV Corps attached 71 (Ind.) Fd. Amb. and a number of Indian staging sections to the division for this operation. The field ambulance established its M.D.S. at the head of the L. of C. in the Sangu Valley, then in Singpa on November 11 and then in Mowdok when this place was occupied. Lack of transport prevented the unit proceeding further. Time came when this field ambulance was out of touch with the division as this continued its southward advance and when this happened the unit reverted to XV Corps.

With the division was 15 (Ind.) M.S.U. but paucity of transport prevented the forward movement of this unit and so only a surgeon, an anaesthetist, one O.R.A. and twelve head-loads of equipment accompanied the division, the rest of the unit being returned to XV Corps. The divisional field ambulances, 5 and 6 (W.A.) Fd. Ambs., lightened their loads, the M.D.S., less a small administrative staff, the graded surgeon and the dental officer, was left behind and this much reduced H.Q. attached itself to the A.D.S. that was open. It was found later that it had been a mistake to leave the personnel of the H.Q. company behind for they were needed as reinforcements to the A.D.Ss. when casualties were numerous. For the head-carriage of the R.M.Os.' medical equipment and stores, wicker baskets covered with cloth were used; they were light, 6 lbs. only, and were fairly waterproof. Two hygiene sections went with the division, 5 and 6 (W.A.) Fd. Hyg. Secs. They were merged to form a unit consisting of H.Q. and two sections. The officer commanding one of the units, thus released, became D.A.D.H. to the division.

The division rapidly developed a high degree of dexterity in constructing airstrips, for the Dakota as well as for the Moth and the L.5. But difficulty was encountered when the pilots displayed a firm reluctance to accept as a passenger a patient suffering from an infectious disease. As a rule the light aircraft were used as feeders for the Dakotas. Practically everything connected with this operation was an improvement upon the standards reached the year before. Rations were much better from every point of view; so also was the provision of medical supplies. Yet the records of the two years show that the health of the troops in the 1944–45 operation was not so good as it had been in 1943–44. The reasons for this would seem to be (i) 6th (W.A.) Bde. had been campaigning for a whole year and was stale; (ii) the operation began during the monsoon and (iii) there was a considerable epidemic of infective hepatitis which accounted for no less than 920 of the recorded sick. The incidence of cholera, smallpox, dysentery and diarrhoea and of pneumonia was lower than it had been the year before. The standard of sanitation in the division was certainly much higher than in 1943–44. It still remained impossible to persuade the African soldier that it was desirable to allow an interval of at least thirty minutes to elapse before drinking water that had been chlorinated.

It was observed once again that the African soldier can exist on light Army rations for long periods of time, that he makes himself comfortable in the most difficult of circumstances and that, when fed and watered, he is a most cheerful fellow. He is meticulous in respect of personal cleanliness. In billets he faces what to him is a serious hazard, overcrowding with its consequent pneumonia, a disease to which he is particularly prone. He is an excellent athlete and thoroughly enjoys team games. But, sad to relate, whenever the opportunity to become infected presents itself, he is almost certain to contract venereal disease.

In the early phases of the operation, while a secure base about Frontier Hill (Mowdok Taung), Labawa, Satpaung and Daletme was being secured, evacuation was mainly by river, the division making its own rafts which were manned by locally enlisted labour. The divisional evacuation chain was as follows:

In Singpa	a field ambulance and a field transfusion unit
Kumai	a company of a field ambulance
Thanchi	a field ambulance less one company
Ruma	a staging section
Bandarban	a West African C.C.S.
Dohazari	a West African C.C.S.

Fig. 65. 81st West African Division. Chittagong–Paletwa

From Thanchi to Dohazari the journey on the River Sangu took 3 days; between Kumai and Thanchi it took 2 days by porter; between Singpa and Kumai there were 53 rapids and the journey by river was possible only when the water was low, as in November; when it was possible it took 2 days; between Mowdok and Singpa the journey took 2 hours.

When the Kaladan Valley was reached evacuation by air became possible as airstrips were constructed along the route at Ngasha (Moth)

Bongyo (M.), Teimagyaung (M.), Auklo (M.), Kyingri (Dakota), Tinma East (M.), Tinma (D.), Thandada (M.), Naleik (M. and D.) and Westdown (Point 317) (M. and D.). *See* Fig. 66.

The divisional evacuation chain then became:

In Satpaung	a field ambulance less one company
Leingthan	a company of a field ambulance
Labawa	a company of a field ambulance
Mowdok	a field ambulance less one company
Kumai	a staging section
Thanchi	a West African C.C.S.
Ruma	a staging section
Bandarban	a staging section

From Paletwa to Daletme the journey was by river in outboard boats; from Daletme to Mowdok was a 3 days journey by porter, staging at Leingthan and Labawa, the most difficult part being that over Frontier Hill, the gradient in places being 1 in 2.

During the period October–December 1944, 1,174 casualties were evacuated by air, 710 by water and 23 by land.

A field ambulance was attached to each of the brigades during the southward advance and a West African C.C.S. with a F.T.U. attached, was stationed in the firm base for emplaning duties. A section of jeep ambulances, and a section of the River Casualty Transport were involved in the evacuation.

27 (W.A.) C.C.S. remained in India, being stationed in succession at Talbahat, Lalitpur where it was u/c 'Special Force', Aundh and Sholinghur. 29 (W.A.) C.C.S. combined with 31 (W.A.) C.C.S. and 31 (Ind.) S.S. to run a 250-bed hospital in Chiringa, evacuating to 40 W.A.G.H. and 72 I.G.H. in Cox's Bazar by river-craft. 29 stayed in Chiringa until April 1945 when it moved back to Kalahasti near Madras, opening there and evacuating to 153 W.A.G.H. In July 1945 the unit moved again, this time to Dhond where it provided a wing of 50 beds for the combined military hospital there.

31 (W.A.) C.C.S. first of all ran a 400-bed hospital in 404 L. of C. Area, evacuating to 46 W.A.G.H. and to 68 I.G.H. It then moved by rail to Dohazari and thence in three parties to Mowdok by sampan, using 100 sampans altogether, and thence to Leingthan by track with 6 jeep-loads and 50 head-loads of equipment and stores. The jeeps then ferried the stores on to Satpaung whence they travelled by raft to Paletwa where the C.C.S. joined H.Q. 81st W.A. Division. It was quickly decided, however, that this site was not the place for a C.C.S. And so the unit retraced its steps to Dohazari and Chiringa. A light surgical section was detached from the unit and joined 6 (W.A.) Fd. Amb. in Mowdok but after two days there it moved back to Thanchi

TABLE 39

81st West African Division. Weekly Medical Situation Report. September 1944–January 1945.

Week ending	Strength	Number admitted to Divisional Medical Units	Average Daily Rate per 1,000	Died
30. 9.44	18,511	495	3·68	—
7.10.44	18,988	496	3·74	—
14.10.44	18,903	445	3·36	2
21.10.44	19,027	421	3·16	3
28.10.44	19,366	320	2·36	—
4.11.44	17,929	308	2·45	—
11.11.44	18,217	316	2·49	2
18.11.44	18,149	201	1·58	1
25.11.44	18,214	335	2·68	—
2.12.44	17,986	191	1·51	1
9.12.44	18,862	459	3·48	—
16.12.44	18,866	229	1·73	1
23.12.44	19,234	188	1·39	1
30.12.44	19,278	284	2·10	—
6. 1.45	19,604	331	2·41	—
13. 1.45	19,795	249	1·80	—
20. 1.45	19,559	217	1·58	3
27. 1.45	19,243	249	1·85	5

TABLE 40

81st West African Division. Numbers evacuated by Air Each Week, By Cause. November 1944–January 1945.

Week Ending	B.Cs.	Malaria	N.Y.D. (F.)	Dysentery and Diarrhoea	Infective Hepatitis	Scrub Typhus	Miscellaneous	Totals
4.11.44	7	5	36	11	1	27	43	130
11.11.44	4	11	11	2	—	1	15	44
18.11.44	5	4	4	—	18	6	11	48
25.11.44	36	8	10	4	2	21	50	131
2.12.44	3	1	8	6	3	—	7	28
9.12.44	24	17	19	16	129	8	184	397
16.12.44	30	2	4	1	25	—	82	144
23.12.44	37	8	16	27	46	—	79	213
30.12.44	35	2	7	3	4	—	28	79
6. 1.45	26	4	17	7	67	—	138	259
13. 1.45	18	10	8	6	17	—	78	137
20. 1.45	3	4	14	7	50	—	142	220
27. 1.45	55	9	9	3	18	—	74	168

OPERATIONS IN N.C.A.C. AND ARAKAN 509

there to join 70 (Ind.) S.S. When the condition of the river interrupted evacuation from Mowdok this light surgical section went forward to Mowdok again for a period of five days.

FIG. 66. 81st West African Division. Daletme to Myohaung. Airstrips at Ngasha, Bongyo, Auklo, Kyingri,* Tinma,* Thandada and 'Westdown'*.
*Dakota, the rest, Moth

82ND WEST AFRICAN DIVISION

This division was formed in August 1943. Of its three brigades, 1st and 2nd had taken part in the East African campaign, 1940–41, and its 4th Bde. had a nucleus of battle-tried officers and men. The division reached India in the summer of 1944 and underwent further training in Bihar in preparation for employment in Burma. The first brigade to reach Arakan was 2nd W.A. Bde. which began to concentrate in the vicinity of Taung Bazar on November 8, taking over from Indian 26th

Division and assuming responsibility for the Kalapanzin Valley area. On the 29th, 4th W.A. Bde. arrived along with the divisional H.Q. which established itself in Razabil. 4th Bde. relieved 2nd Bde. in Taung Bazar. By December 8 the third brigade (1st) had reached the front.

It was intended that 1st and 2nd Bdes. should attack the Tunnels area, assisted by Indian 25th Division, while 4th Bde. defended Taung Bazar and the upper Kalapanzin Valley until any threat of a right hook by the Japanese had been dispelled by the advance of 81st W.A. Division down the valley of the Kaladan. The attack upon the Tunnels area was to be opened by Indian 25th Division which was to assault and capture two prominent features in the Japanese positions. Then 2nd Bde. was to advance down the Maungdaw-Buthidaung road to Buthidaung while 1st Bde. moved against Baguna, crossed the river and seized a feature on the opposite bank that dominated the river and so made the use of the river by Indian 25th Division possible. Eventually the division was to cross the hills, descend into the valley of the Kaladan and link up with 81st W.A. Division which it was to relieve.

On December 14, 2nd W.A. Bde. launched its attack upon Buthidaung which was entered without much opposition being encountered. Then the brigade established a bridgehead across the Kalapanzin. 1st W.A. Bde. then crossed into the bridgehead and the seven hundred river craft of various kinds that had been collected in the port of Maungdaw and in the nearby creeks and chaungs were transported along the Maungdaw-Buthidaung road and launched on the Kalapanzin River which was to serve as the L. of C. 1st W.A. Bde. captured the dominating feature—the so-called 'Vital Corner' and the river was opened. These river-craft were to form the first line transport of Ind. 53rd Bde. of Indian 25th Division and also a second line echelon for this brigade and for 82nd W.A. Division.

While Ind. 53rd Bde. made very rapid progress down the axis of the river, 82nd W.A. Division was meeting with determined resistance on the road from Buthidaung into the valley of the Kalapanzin. Its 4th Bde. moved up from Taung Bazar to join the rest of the division which ultimately succeeded in clearing the area. The division then moved southwards into the valley of the Mayu (it will be remembered that south of Buthidaung the Kalapanzin becomes the Mayu) meeting with decreasing opposition and entering Htizwe and Rathedaung. The division then crossed the hills into the Kaladan Valley and its 4th Bde. took part in the action which ended in the capture of Myohaung. Its 1st Bde. pushed on to reach the vicinity of Minbya.

The next task of the division was that of pressing on southwards in order to drive the Japanese facing it against the positions of the troops that had landed at Kangaw. Indian 25th Division, supplied from the sea, had moved down the Mayu Peninsula to reach its tip at Foul Point on December 26, and then to occupy Kudaung Island which is separated from Akyab Island only by a narrow channel. On January 2 it was discovered that the Japanese garrison had left Akyab Island on the last day of 1944 and so Indian 25th Division, which was poised for an assault, occupied it without encountering any opposition. It was apparent that the Japanese were withdrawing to the south. There was but one road they could use, the coast road that ran from Myohaung through Kangaw, Tamandu and An to Taungup. XV Corps promptly decided to cut this road ahead of the retreating Japanese. It possessed the power to do so for 224th Gp. R.A.F. had command of the air and the naval task force command of the sea. It was planned to seize the Myebon Peninsula, 30 miles to the east of Akyab by seaborne assault and also to strike at Kangaw 8 miles further to the east by a second amphibious operation. On January 12 the commando brigade (1st and 5th Army and 42nd and 44th Royal Marine Commandos) landed on the Myebon Peninsula and quickly overcame such opposition as was encountered. It was followed by 74th Bde. of Indian 25th Division, supported by bombardment from sky and sea. A firm bridgehead was established and several fierce attacks by the Japanese were sternly repulsed. The whole of the Myebon Peninsula was then systematically cleared. On January 22 a second landing was carried out by the commando brigade near Kangaw under cover of a naval and air bombardment. The Japanese reacted very quickly and violently and for six days repeatedly attacked the small bridgehead. The commandos, reinforced by Indian 25th Division, hung on and indeed on the 29th turned to the attack to take Kangaw and to establish a road-block to the south of it, thus finally closing the Japanese escape route. Two days later the Japanese, reinforced, attacked again. The struggle lasted for three whole days and at the end the Japanese were driven from the field, leaving over 300 dead behind them. Ind. 51st Bde. had secured a dominating position north of the road and gained touch with 2nd W.A. Bde. of 82nd W.A. Division. Caught between the two the Japanese disintegrated and took to the hills.

While 2nd W.A. Bde. was co-operating with Indian 25th Division in this way the rest of 82nd W.A. Division moved through the hills towards Kyweguseik to cut off the Japanese retreating from Kangaw and to discover a way across the mountains to Dalet with a view to a further advance on An which lay at the western end of the An Pass through the Arakan Yomas, connecting Arakan with Burma proper. Kyweguseik was found to be held in strength and so, leaving a detachment to mask it, the rest of the division pressed on towards An, being maintained by air. 2nd W.A. Bde. was ferried from Kangaw to the bridgehead established by Indian 25th Division at Ru-Ywa so that it might advance on An by way of a winding track that meandered through the forest-covered mountains. The brigade reached the bridgehead between February 18 and 22 and at once began to pass through Indian 53rd Bde. Because it was now found that the rest of the division could not be supplied by air it was decided that it should advance along the same axis as 2nd W.A. Bde. for then it could be supplied by road and by river.

By the beginning of April, 82nd W.A. Division was between Tamandu and An with 22nd East African Brigade under command. Its 1st W.A. Bde. was in contact with the Japanese, its 4th Bde. was in Tamandu, waiting to move to Taungup whenever this became feasible and its 2nd Bde. was moving along the coast road to the south to relieve 4th W.A. Bde. which, being relieved, moved to Taungup on April 17. By the 28th 4th Bde. had cleaned up the Taungup area and had passed u/c A.L.F.S.E.A. The rest of 82nd W.A. Division and 22nd E.A. Bde. pressed hard on the heels of the Japanese as they withdrew from Arakan in attempts to make them turn about and stand. But their efforts were not successful and the Japanese got away in fairly good order and by May 15 Arakan was clear of them.

Through no fault of its own XV Corps had not been able to carry out all the tasks that had been set it. The Japanese, with a strong block on each of the ways out of Arakan over the Arakan Yomas into Burma proper, retained control of both of these roads. They could reduce their numbers in Arakan and send reinforcements to their compatriots facing

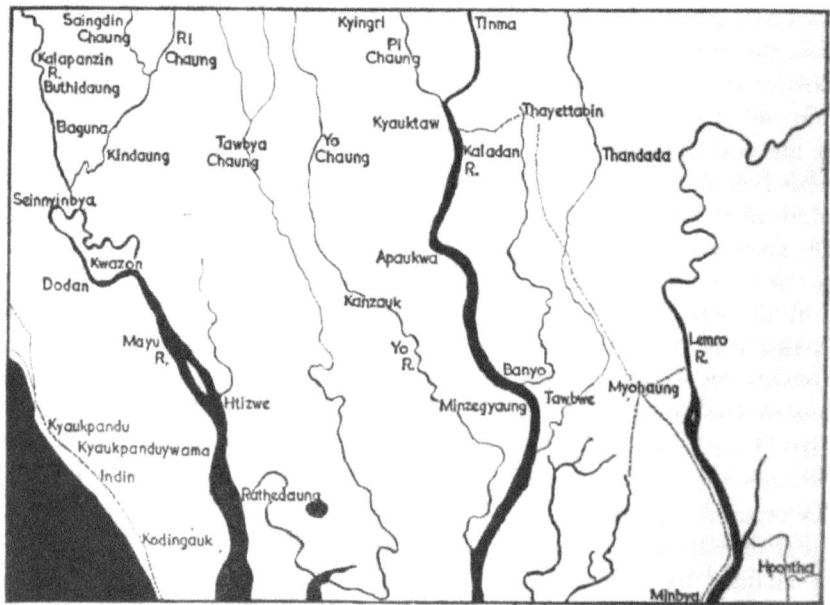

FIG. 67. 82nd West African Division. Buthidaung–Minbya

Fourteenth Army should they choose to do so. XV Corps, however, had succeeded in developing Akyab and Ramree as air-supply bases for Fourteenth Army and this was a contribution of very great value to this army's ultimate victory.

MEDICAL COVER

'A' Coy of 1 (W.A.) Fd. Amb. was attached to 1st W.A. Bde. for its advance to Baguna. It opened its first A.D.S. in a *basha* in Baguna East. Moving to Baguna West it came under fire, constructed a dug-in ward and admitted its first casualty. Evacuation was to the M.D.S. of 1 (W.A.) Fd. Amb. through the C.C.P. of 2 (W.A.) Fd. Amb. on the Maungdaw–Buthidaung road. 1 (W.A.) Fd. Amb. crossed the Kalapanzin without much difficulty and at once opened its M.D.S. to admit some 90 casualties from 2nd Nigeria Regt. which was attacking Japanese positions in the village of Dodan. Evacuation was to a light airstrip constructed nearby for the more serious cases while the light cases were got away by river to Buthidaung. The field ambulance crossed the Saingdin Chaung near Kindaung and, opening, admitted many casualties from 4th W.A. Bde. Evacuation was by river along the Saingdin Chaung and the Kalapanzin.

Three weeks later the field ambulance moved along the Rathedaung–Akyab road and opened its A.D.S. in the box of 3rd Nigeria Regt. at Mehpauk. A light airstrip was constructed nearby and evacuation was to Teknaf, minor cases being sent by road to 25 (Ind.) C.C.S. now in Buthidaung. Then came the heavy rain to make evacuation by any other means than the river impossible. 'A' Coy 1 (W.A.) Fd. Amb. accompanied 1st Nigeria Regt., carrying four days' rations, across the Tawbya Chaung and the Yo Chaung to Kanzauk and Apaukwa. Thereafter the advance continued down the west bank of the Kaladan until Minzegyaung village was reached when the river was crossed and an A.D.S. opened in Banyo. During the action at Myohaung the M.D.S. of 1 (W.A.) Fd. Amb. was in Tawbwe. Evacuation from the R.A.Ps. during this action was by L.C.M. and from the M.D.S. to Apaukwa also by L.C.M. to a nearby Dakota airstrip. A light airstrip was constructed alongside the M.D.S. in Tawbwe.

Serving 2nd W.A. Bde. was 2 (W.A.) Fd. Amb. It had moved out of Chiringa over the Goppe Pass to Goppe Bazar to take over from 1 (Ind.) Fd. Amb. of Indian 26th Division and to establish its M.D.S. On November 7 its 'A' Coy went to Taung Bazar to take over from a company of 1 (Ind.) Fd. Amb. and to open its A.D.S. On November 26, 'A' Coy handed over this site to a company of 4 (W.A.) Fd. Amb. and returned to Goppe Bazar. On the following day 2 (W.A.) Fd. Amb. in Goppe Bazar handed over to 4 (W.A.) Fd. Amb. and moved by M.T. to Razabil to support 2nd W.A. Bde's. attack upon the Tunnels.

On December 11, 2nd W.A. Bde. and 2 (W.A.) Fd. Amb. marched to a concentration area in the foothills about three-and-a-half miles west of Buthidaung. The field ambulance opened its M.D.S. in this area and to this the surgical team of 30 (W.A.) C.C.S. was attached. One officer and a number of stretcher-bearer squads were attached to each of the battalions and a mobile C.C.P. was established on the axis of the Maungdaw-Buthidaung road to receive casualties from these detachments and to pass them rapidly through the forward medical units to the M.D.S.

The casualties from 1st and 4th W.A. Bdes., operating in the hills to the east of the Kalapanzin, were first attended by 1 and 4 (W.A.) Fd. Ambs. respectively and then passed on to the M.D.S. of 2 (W.A.) Fd. Amb. in its site about three-and-a-half miles west of Buthidaung. As soon as Buthidaung had been captured on December 16, 2 (W.A.) Fd. Amb. moved into the town and opened its A.D.S. The casualties from 1st and 4th Bdes. arrived by river and were evacuated from the M.D.S. by M.A.S. to 15 (Ind.) C.C.S. On December 27 a light section of 2 (W.A.) Fd. Amb. was sent to provide cover for 3rd Gold Coast Regt. which was in action at the confluence of the Saingdin and Pi Chaungs. Casualties were evacuated by river to the M.D.S. near Buthidaung *via* the Saingdin Chaung and a C.C.P. at Kindaung ferry. Following this action the M.D.S. moved forward about seven miles.

On January 12, 1945, 'A' Coy, 2 (W.A.) Fd. Amb., together with a section of the Auxiliary Group carriers, set off for Htizwe at the entrance to the Kanzauk Pass. There the company took over from 'A' Coy. of 1 (W.A.) Fd. Amb. and opened its A.D.S. to provide cover for 1st and 2nd Bdes., Main H.Q. 82nd W.A. Division and attached troops during the march through the Kanzauk Pass into the valley of the Kaladan. On the 23rd the field ambulance entered the pass, one company accompanying each of the battalions. Casualties were evacuated by jeep ambulance to the A.D.S. in Htizwe whence they were transported to the Htizwe Chaung and sent off by boat to 30 (W.A.) C.C.S. which was now in Buthidaung, a ten-hour journey. On January 25 the A.D.S. in Htizwe closed and moved with the rearmost column of the brigade through the pass. On the following day 'C' Coy. took over the staging post at the Dakota strip at Apaukwa and evacuated some 140 casualties from 1st and 4th Bdes. between January 26 and February 1. The rest of the field ambulance continued to move with 2nd W.A. Bde., carrying casualties forward by jeep to a Dakota strip three-and-a-half miles north of Myohaung where 'A' Coy. took over the staging duties from a company of 4 (W.A.) Fd. Amb. 'A' Coy. also established a jeep post at Panmyaung ferry on the Lemro River. From the Dakota strip casualties from all three brigades of 82nd W.A. Division, from 5th W.A. Bde. of 81st W.A. Division, from 81st Divisional Recce. Regt. and

OPERATIONS IN N.C.A.C. AND ARAKAN

from 82nd Divisional troops were evacuated. Between January 28 and February 5, 173 were flown out. On February 3, 2 (W.A.) Fd. Amb. crossed the Lemro with 2nd W.A. Bde. by L.C. and concentrated on the south bank of the Hpontha Chaung where 'A' Coy. joined it.

Following the fall of Myohaung the M.D.S. of 1 (W.A.) Fd. Amb. crossed the Lemro and moved to Thalechaung. When 1st W.A. Bde. began its advance to Dalet all the casualties had to be carried forward. Eight mules were made available for this purpose. At Kyaukgwe an airstrip was constructed. The brigade was checked in front of Dalet village but ultimately overcame the opposition and captured the place. The field ambulance established its M.D.S. in the village but found that its work was so impeded by the clouds of dust that it moved to a site outside. Another light airstrip was constructed here and some 250 casualties flown out.

During the advance towards An a small section of the field ambulance was attached to each of the several columns. The main body of 'A' Coy. of 1 (W.A.) Fd. Amb. took over the site of the A.D.S. of 4 (W.A.) Fd. Amb. in Letmauk where an airstrip was constructed. 'A' Coy. was joined by the H.Q. Coy. of the unit on the following day and the M.D.S. was then opened. The airstrip here was shelled and three A.O.Rs. of 'B' Coy. were wounded. Evacuation was now by air to Ramree Island, minor cases being sent by jeep to Tamandu to the M.D.S. of 4 (W.A.)

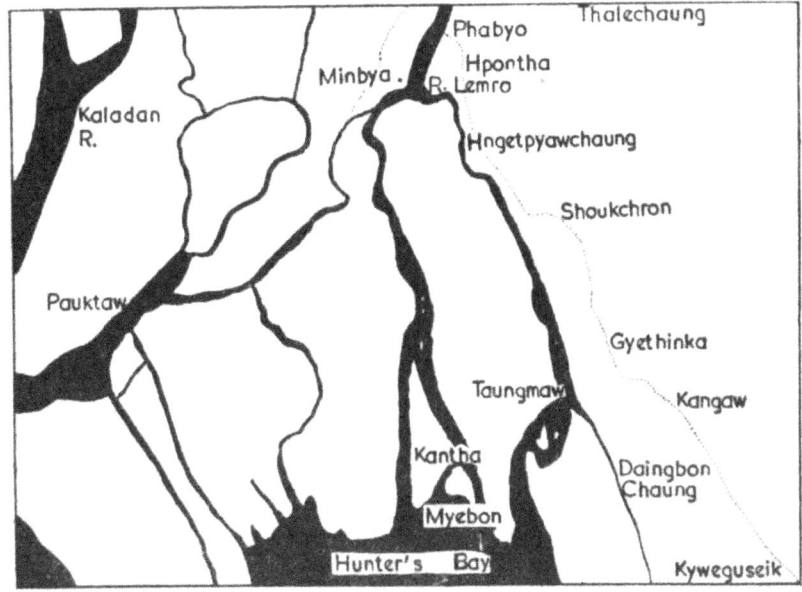

FIG. 68. 82nd West African Division. Hpontha–Taungmaw

Fd. Amb. On April 14, 1 (W.A.) Fd. Amb. moved into Tamandu where it opened its M.D.S., relieving 4 (W.A.) Fd. Amb.

Evacuation from 2nd W.A. Bde. as it drove south from Hpontha Chaung in a three-pronged advance against stiffening opposition was as follows:

> From 1st G.C. Regt. operating along a track due south of Hpontha, by jeep to a staging post established by 1 (W.A.) Fd. Amb. at the Hpontha airstrip.
>
> From 3rd G.C. Regt. operating southwards down a trackless valley to the west of 1st G.C. Regt., by hand-carry to a rendezvous whence relays of stretcher-bearers carried the casualties back to the M.D.S. in Hngetpyawchaung, about six miles away.
>
> From 2nd G.C. Regt., operating to the west of 3rd G.C. Regt. along a track that ran south to Phabyo, by jeep-ambulance to the M.D.S. in Hngetpyawchaung.
>
> From the M.D.S. in Hngetpyawchaung, by light aircraft to the Dakota strip that had been constructed at Hpontha.

By February 8 the high ground south of Phabyo had been cleared and on the following day 2 (W.A.) Fd. Amb. with 2nd W.A. Bde. concentrated near Kanni in preparation for the attack upon Kangaw. During the advance to Kanni 33 casualties were evacuated to the M.D.S. whence they were sent on by light aircraft to an airstrip that had been constructed by 6th Auxiliary Group for 61 (Ind.) Fd. Amb. at Myebon. On February 13, 2 (W.A.) Fd. Amb., less 'B' Coy. and a detachment of 'C' Coy. moved with the brigade administrative column to Shoukchron where it opened its M.D.S. 'B' Coy. established an A.D.S. to serve 2nd G.C. Regt. while a detachment of 'C' Coy. accompanied 3rd G.C. Regt. A C.C.P. was established at Gyethinka to serve 2nd and 3rd G.C. Regts. Casualties from these battalions were transported by a combination of hand-carriage and jeep ambulance to the M.D.S. in Shoukchron and from the M.D.S. to 61 (Ind.) Fd. Amb. in Myebon by light aircraft and by power-boat. On February 18 these battalions, having completed their tasks, rejoined the brigade in Taungmaw. Their casualties during this operation had numbered 3 British and 42 A.O.Rs.

On February 19, 2 (W.A.) Fd. Amb. and 2nd W.A. Bde. moved by L.C. to the beachhead which had been established by Ind. 53rd Bde. of Indian 25th Division at Ru-Ywa. During the landing Japanese artillery caused a small number of casualties which were promptly evacuated to the M.D.S. of 56 (Ind.) Fd. Amb. of Indian 25th Division in Ru-Ywa. On the 22nd 1st G.C. Regt., with 'A' Coy. of 2 (W.A.) Fd. Amb. advanced eastwards to Kyauksalaung on a branch of the

Yo Chaung, the rest of the field ambulance following a few days later. 'A' Coy. with 1st G.C. Regt., next advanced eastwards to reach Sabagyi where a Japanese attack was repulsed. Casualties from this action had to be carried back to the M.D.S., about six miles away across rough, trackless country. On February 28 the battalion formed a firm base in the vicinity of Sabagyi and repulsed further Japanese assaults. The casualties were carried back to the M.D.S. which had moved forward with brigade H.Q. to Kutywa and from here they were taken to Kyauksalaung, six miles away, the journey taking six hours owing to the nature of the country, and then by jeep ambulance to Ru-Ywa.

On March 3, all the troops who had been engaged in protecting the L. of C. back to Ru-Ywa were withdrawn and from this time onwards there was no rearward evacuation, casualties had to be carried forward with the brigade. The country was so wild and so thickly wooded that it was impossible to construct airstrips. The next three weeks were filled with arduous labour for at the end of every day's march, usually in the face of opposition, the field ambulance had to dig itself in to provide protection for the ever increasing number of patients. On March 4, 'A' Coy. moved with the brigade's administrative column up the Kut Chaung and the Myauk Chaung, carrying 16 casualties.

2nd W.A. Bde. was now about to become involved in the capture of An. By March 6 the number of casualties being carried by the field ambulance was 35, too many for the porterage that was available. The axis of advance was now changed from An to Letmauk and two additional sections of the Auxiliary Group were attached to the unit. On March 10 the M.D.S. of 2 (W.A.) Fd. Amb. moved with the brigade's administrative column about two-and-a-half miles to a new site to the north-west where it held 30 lying and 84 walking casualties. One hundred and fifty Aux. Gp. personnel evacuated these along a narrow, steep track, the stretcher being carried by two men, on the head. On March 12 the brigade formed a tight box. As had now become the custom, the field ambulance established its M.D.S. in a dry chaung. Thirteen days elapsed before any of the casualties could be got away and during this period it became increasingly difficult to provide adequate cover for them. Bush beds were made out of bamboo. But at no time was there any shortage of food or water and medical supplies never failed to arrive by air-drop, though often just in the nick of time. On one occasion, in response to an urgent emergency request, penicillin was flown in by light plane. There was much shelling and casualties were numerous. On March 15, 3 A.O.Rs. of the field ambulance and 1 O.R. of the Auxiliary Group were killed and 3 B.O.Rs., 2 A.O.Rs. of the field ambulance and 11 O.Rs. of the Aux. Gp. were wounded. The M.D.S. was soon holding 170 patients.

On March 17 the Japanese succeeded in establishing themselves in the perimeter line of 2nd W.A. Bde's. box. However, on the 24th, 4th W.A. Bde. came to the rescue. Next day the evacuation of the casualties began, 200 extra porters being employed and 50 extra stretchers being provided by the division. Eighty lying and 136 walking wounded were thus evacuated, there being 6 porters to each stretcher. The column was divided into 4 sections and each of these was provided with a strong escort as it set out for Letmauk, 6 miles away, where the other two field ambulances of the division, 1 and 4, were open. From Letmauk evacuation was by light aircraft.

On April 1, 2 (W.A.) Fd. Amb. proceeded with 2nd W.A. Bde. to an area about four miles north of Taungup, a march of about eighty miles. During this march a company of the field ambulance was assigned to each of the battalions of the brigade and such as fell sick *en route* were carried forward by jeep and evacuated from Kywegu and from Letmauk by hospital carrier. The brigade assumed responsibility for the area north of Taungup, relieving 4th W.A. Bde. and began operations against the Japanese withdrawing to the east along the Taungup–Prome track. The field ambulance provided cover as follows: the M.D.S. was open on the Kindaunggyi–Taungup road, 4 miles north of Taungup; a light section was attached to each of the battalions to reinforce the R.A.P. and a C.C.P. was established 4 miles east of the M.D.S. in a F.S.D. area. Evacuation from 1st G.C. Regt. was direct to the M.D.S. by hand-carry and by jeep; from 2nd G.C. Regt. to the C.C.P. by hand-carry by S.Bs. of the light section of the field ambulance attached to the battalion and thence to the M.D.S. by S.Bs. of the C.C.P. Evacuation from the M.D.S. was by jeep ambulance and ambulance cars to 30 (W.A.) C.C.S. now in Kindaunggyi.

For 4th W.A. Bde's. attack on Taungup, 4 (W.A.) Fd. Amb. did not open and the casualties of this brigade and of the Green Howards who were attached to it, were admitted to the M.D.S. of 2 (W.A.) Fd. Amb. On April 30, 4 (W.A.) Fd. Amb. crossed the Taungup Chaung in support of 4th W.A. Bde. which entered Taungup unopposed. A few days later this brigade moved south towards Sandoway.

Meanwhile 2nd W.A. Bde. had been driving the Japanese from the hills to the east of Taungup along the axis of the Taungup–Prome track and 22nd E.A. Bde. was engaging them further to the north-east. On May 8 a detachment consisting of 2 (W.A.) Fd. Amb. and 6th Aux. Gp. personnel marched to Kaname to make contact with 22nd E.A. Bde. and to evacuate 10 lying and 20 walking casualties, mainly sick. On May 10, 'A' Coy. of 2 (W.A.) Fd. Amb. took over from 71 (Ind.) Fd. Amb. which had been serving the East African brigade, the Indian medical unit then proceeding to Taungup *en route* for India. 2 (W.A.) Fd. Amb. thereafter became responsible for the medical support of both 2nd W.A. and 22nd E.A. Bdes. From this time onward the work of the field ambulances of 82nd W.A. Division was very much of the ordinary routine kind.

TABLE 41

82nd W.A. Division, Arakan. 2 (W.A.) Field Ambulance. Admissions to the Main Dressing Station. October 15, 1944–May 17, 1945.

Offrs.	113
B.O.Rs.	191
A.O.Rs.	2,075
I.O.Rs.	159
Civilians	5
P.o.W.	6
	2,549

Of the West African casualty clearing stations attached to this division, 25 (W.A.) C.C.S. first functioned as a M.D.S. in Chittagong in early November 1944. On November 18 it passed u/c XV Corps and moved to Redwinbyin. Lacking stores it could not open until December 3. Thereafter it admitted over 600 patients in 19 days. The patients arrived and left by landing craft for there was no road communication with Redwinbyin. Then on Christmas Eve its light section moved to Buthidaung where it was joined by the rest of the unit on Boxing Day. Evacuation was to Maungdaw and thence by hospital ship. In a period of six weeks over 1,000 patients were admitted. In February the C.C.S. moved into Maungdaw and on March 5 to Dohazari and Chittagong for Akyab by sea. Arriving there the unit went on to Ru-Ywa. But as no proper protection for the unit could be found and as no water supply could be made available, the C.C.S. returned to Akyab. Then it was sent to Ramree Island but as no suitable site for it could be found, it returned once more to Akyab. There it remained for a month, unopened. Then it was sent to Taungup.

28 (W.A.) C.C.S. was moved from Chas to Teknaf to provide cover for the attack on Buthidaung, December 9–31, 1944. Its patients arrived by sea from Maungdaw and were evacuated to Tumbru by sea and thence to Cox's Bazar by ambulance car. The C.C.S. then moved to Kyaukpyu to join 30 (W.A.) C.C.S., 1 (Ind.) M.F.T.U., 23 (Ind.) C.C.S. and was later joined by 125 I.G.H. and part of 152 W.A.G.H. A light aircraft airstrip had been constructed nearby. Patients arrived by D.U.K.W. and by light aircraft and were evacuated to Akyab and Comilla by D.U.K.W. and by Dakota. During March and April 1945,

28 (W.A.) C.C.S. admitted 1,007 patients and of these 342 were battle casualties. The C.C.S. moved to Sandoway as the operation in Arakan drew towards its end. The C.C.Ss. were brought into close contact with the brigades which they were to serve, 28 being with 4th W.A. Bde., 25 with 2nd W.A. Bde. and 30 (W.A.) C.C.S. with 1st W.A. Bde. Evacuation was to 152 W.A.G.H. now on Ramree Island, a twenty-four hour journey.

After the end of hostilities and prior to its repatriation in March 1946, 28 (W.A.) C.C.S. functioned in Taungup and finally in Tharrawaddy. 152 W.A.G.H. ultimately found itself in Rangoon.

30 (W.A.) C.C.S. moved from Chas to Arakan in December 1944. It functioned in Redwinbyin on the Naf alongside 1 (Ind.) M.F.T.U. and 25 (Ind.) C.C.S. On December 13 a light section of the C.C.S. moved to Buthidaung to be followed almost immediately by the rest of the unit. During the next three weeks it admitted well over 1,000 patients. In March 1945 the C.C.S. moved to Akyab then to Ru-Ywa and then to Ramree Island, doing very little in any of these sites. In April it moved to Kindaunggyi where it served 2nd W.A. Bde. and evacuated its patients to 152 W.A.G.H. in Ramree by river steamer. Prior to its repatriation the unit moved to Comilla.

22ND EAST AFRICAN BRIGADE

This brigade reached India from Ceylon in December 1944 and was placed in XV Corps passing into corps reserve at Chiringa. On December 17 the brigade began to take over the defence of the Tunnels area from Ind. 51st Bde. of Indian 25th Division. Later it moved to Akyab and then to Kyaukpyu there to relieve Ind. 4th Bde. of Indian 26th Division. For the final phase in Arakan this brigade was set the task of destroying the Japanese forces in the Kywegu area and then of thrusting towards An. When Indian 25th Division withdrew to Akyab at the end of March, 1945, 22nd E.A. Bde. relieved Ind. 53rd Bde. in Ru-Ywa and assumed control of all operations in this area. It advanced towards An, meeting with negligible opposition and by March 30 its leading elements were in Letpan. The brigade then passed u/c 82nd W.A. Division and was involved in the advance on Taungup.

Medical cover for the brigade was provided by 110 (E.A.) C.R.S. which reached Calcutta from Colombo on December 10, 1944 and thence proceeded to Chittagong. It then moved forward to Wabyin on December 23 and to Razabil on January 1, 1945. There it functioned, evacuating to 31 (W.A.) C.C.S. in Nhila. The unit moved with the brigade to Akyab Island and then to Ramree Island where it opened on February 17. 71 (Ind.) Fd. Amb. was attached to this brigade for a time as was 2 (W.A.) Fd. Amb.

MEDICAL ARRANGEMENTS

XV Corps was well supplied with medical units and these were used with a skill that had been sharpened by much experience. With the divisions were the field ambulances, bearer companies, mobile surgical units, field transfusion units, field hygiene sections, field ambulance troops (R.I.A.S.C.) and anti-malaria units. At the corps medical centre were the C.C.Ss., the M.F.T.Us., the staging sections, the corps psychiatric centre, mobile field laboratories, mobile dental units, X-ray units and sub-depots of medical stores as well as such specialist teams as neuro-surgical, ophthalmic and E.N.T.

Evacuation systems had undergone a continuous improvement. Whereas in 1943 the journey of a wounded man involved as many as sixteen changes of transport and took 5–7 days to complete, evacuation by air, now the rule, involved only three changes and took only 2–3 hours. The average time taken to reach the C.C.S. was well within the prescribed 6–8 hours after wounding.

The mobile surgical unit, here in Burma, as did the field surgical unit in Europe, amply demonstrated its worth. At Kangaw, for example, one of the field ambulances, with a mobile surgical unit attached to it, dealt with 696 battle casualties, 10 per cent. of them requiring emergency surgery. The combination of M.D.S., M.S.U. and F.T.U. undoubtedly saved many lives. In December 1944, 2 F.T.U. was informed that 600 pints of blood would be required for the impending assault on Akyab. Three hundred Group 'O' donors were checked and held in readiness in Calcutta and Dehra Dun and a promise given to the effect that 100 pints of blood from 2 F.T.U. and from 1 (Ind.) Adv. B.T.U. would be forthcoming on forty-eight hours' notice and on three successive days should this be necessary. Arrangements were made for the attachment of an officer of the base transfusion unit to the base depot of medical stores in Chittagong which was to function as the intermediate supply base between the Indian advanced base transfusion unit and the forward medical units. The B.T.U. also undertook to provide an improvised distributing unit from its own personnel and to send this to operate between Chittagong and the forward medical units. To prevent any undesirable speculation in Calcutta concerning this sudden increase in the demand for whole blood, the transfusion railway coach was sent there as though on a routine visit, to collect blood for plasma production. The actual transportation of transfusion supplies was to be the responsibility of H.Q., A.L.F.S.E.A. However, the occupation of Akyab was unopposed and so these arrangements were never tested.

The assault landings demanded a new surgical lay-out. Emergency surgery was carried out aboard the destroyer, the sloop and the larger

TABLE 42

XV Corps. Battle Casualties. Arakan. 1 September, 1944–17 May, 1945

	Killed						Wounded						Missing						Grand Totals
	B.O.	V.C.O.	B.O.R.	I.O.R.	A.O.R.	N.C.E.	B.O.	V.C.O.	B.O.R.	I.O.R.	A.O.R.	N.C.E.	B.O.	V.C.O.	B.O.R.	I.O.R.	A.O.R.	N.C.E.	
Ind. 25 Division	17	7	41	244	—	8	19	25	95	872	—	4	1	—	4	37	—	—	1,374
Ind. 26 Division	14	3	47	82	—	—	21	2	83	277	—	1	2	—	39	35	—	—	606
81 W.A. Division	3	—	5	—	66	—	9	—	20	—	314	—	1	—	—	—	20	—	438
82 W.A. Division	29	—	19	—	428	—	94	—	61	—	1,417	—	2	—	1	—	34	—	2,085
Corps Tps.	4	—	2	11	—	—	1	—	2	40	—	2	—	—	—	1	—	—	63
Ind. 50 Tk. Bde.	3	—	1	16	—	1	6	—	—	23	—	—	—	—	—	1	—	—	51
3 Cdo. Bde.	4	—	62	—	—	—	18	—	164	77	—	—	1	—	14	—	—	—	340
22 E.A. Bde.	1	—	7	—	30	—	4	—	—	—	82	—	—	—	4	—	8	—	136
	75	10	184	353	524	9	172	27	425	1,289	1,813	7	7	—	67	74	62	—	5,093
			1,155						3,733						205				

landing craft until such time as the hospital ship could be brought close in-shore. The coastal ambulance steamers, *Nalchera* and *Badora*, each carrying 175 patients and the creek ambulance steamers *Agni*, *Vanu* and *Lali* (40 lying and 60 sitting) were used. The creek steamers serving 82nd W.A. Division in the creeks and chaungs around Taungup, Gwa and Ramree Island were fitted with wireless so that they could announce the number of patients they were bringing and the expected time of their arrival.

The medical units in Akyab, Kyaukpyu and Ramree Island respectively, as in March 1945, are given in Appendix XXIII. After the beachhead had been secured an attempt was made to evacuate the short-term cases (less than three weeks) by coastal ambulance steamer to the corps medical centre first in Akyab and later at Kyaukpyu on Ramree Island. Light airstrips were constructed and the more serious cases were transported by light aircraft to the corps medical centre. At Kyaukpyu the airstrip was constructed adjacent to one of the C.C.Ss. and so the casualties could easily be hand-carried from the aircraft to the ward. From Kyaukpyu rearward evacuation was by sea by the ocean-going hospital ships *Karoa*, *Karapara*, *Ophir*, *Vasna*, *Melchior Trueb* and *Wu Sueh* to Chittagong, where such as were likely to recover within three months were disembarked and sent by ambulance train to Dacca, Agartala or Comilla. Long-term cases were retained on board and taken on to Calcutta or Madras for distribution among the base hospitals.

XV CORPS. CASUALTY RATES

(excluding battle casualties)

October–December 1944   2·1 per 1,000 per day
January–April 1945   1·1 per 1,000 per day

The proportion of battle casualties to sick was:

    1943   1:130 approx.
    1944   1: 19
    1945   1: 3

In Arakan, as on the central front, full use was made of the newer instruments of disease prevention and control,—discipline, D.D.T. and suppressive mepacrine. It is of importance to note that XV Corps reduced its malaria incidence to minimal figures in eight weeks and this at a time when the corps was operating in areas where the spleen-rate was 100 per cent. The rate which had been well over 12 per 1,000 per day in 1942–43 was reduced to 0·14.

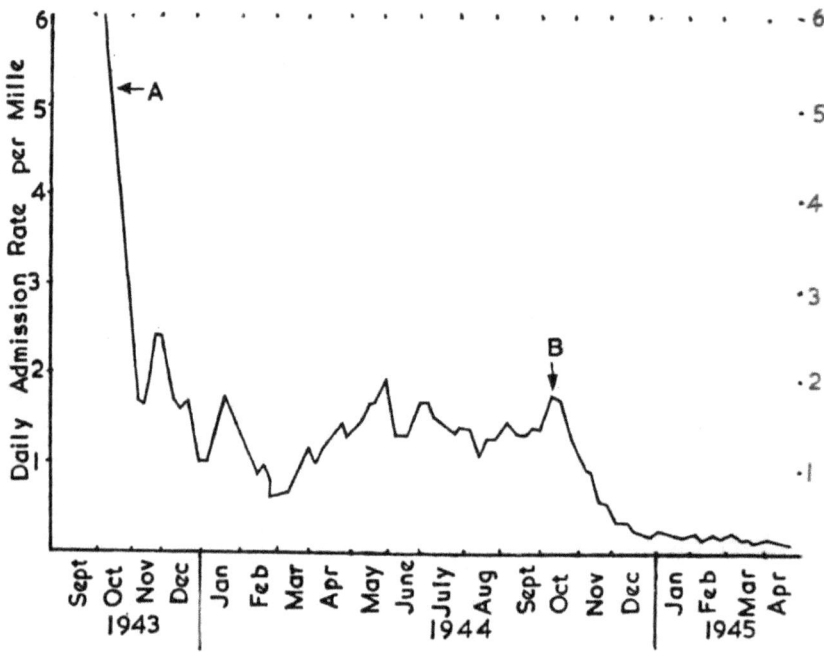

Fig. 69. XV Corps. Arakan. The conquest of Malaria

A. The beginning of the first drive against malaria when XV Corps was about to take over operational control of the Arakan front. At this time there was widespread scepticism throughout the corps concerning the value of suppressive mepacrine. Nevertheless the result was good though not good enough.

B. The beginning of the second and intensified drive which was given full and active support by the corps commander. In order to secure the intelligent co-operation of the troops they were informed of the experimental work that had been carried out at Cairns in Australia with mepacrine. Unit anti-malaria discipline was tightened and D.D.T. much used. The astonishing and dramatic fall in the daily admission-rate on account of malaria enabled the Army Medical Services to demonstrate the efficacy of their anti-malaria armamentarium and the military value of Preventive Medicine.

A.L.F.S.E.A. MEDICAL ARRANGEMENTS

As soon as shipping space became available 28 and 95 I.G.Hs. and a R.A.F. mobile hospital were transported to Akyab to serve XV Corps. 125 I.G.H., 12 (Ind.) M.F.T.U., 110 (E.A.) C.R.S. and a West African hospital section were opened on Ramree Island and dental, X-ray, surgical and pathology units were attached to these units to which the forward medical units of XV Corps evacuated their casualties.

In the central sector it proved to be impossible to send hospitals out of the L. of C. Command into the forward zone. Only 88 I.G.H. was moved forward from Palel to Kalewa. Later 89 I.G.H. was also moved forward but only as far as Moreh. No hospitals actually crossed the Chindwin into the Burma central plain. It was far easier to fly the casualties out than to bring the hospitals into Burma from Assam.

Fourteenth Army, in addition to its army, corps and divisional field medical units had, for its advance across the Irrawaddy and thence to the south,

   8 Indian casualty clearing stations
  10 Indian malaria forward treatment units
   9 Indian mobile surgical units
   5 field transfusion units
  10 Indian anti-malaria units
   3 Indian field laboratories
  23 Indian dental and dental mechanic units
   9 Indian mobile X-ray units.

These were grouped into one army and two corps medical centres at Shwebo, Sinthe and Monywa, having moved forward from the Kalewa-Kalemyo area in January. Patients requiring up to twenty-one days' treatment were retained in these medical centres, the rest being evacuated to the advanced base hospitals within L. of C. Command.

In N.C.A.C. the same policy was adopted, patients requiring no more than twenty-one days' treatment being retained.

Casualties evacuated in A.L.F.S.E.A. during the period January–March 1945 were:

By air	.	.	.	.	.	22,362
By rail	.	.	.	.	.	21,699
By sea	.	.	.	.	.	9,435
By road	.	.	.	.	.	9,010
By river	.	.	.	.	.	3,047

All the road, river and rail evacuation occurred in L. of C. Command in Assam and Bengal and represents the distribution of casualties within the advanced base hospital area. No casualties were evacuated to the advanced bases by rail, road or river by Fourteenth Army, XV Corps or N.C.A.C. The sea evacuations represent the numbers evacuated from XV Corps to Chittagong. The air evacuation figure represents only the number flown into and within L. of C. Command. Light aircraft evacuations within Fourteenth Army, XV Corps and N.C.A.C. numbered 15,214 during the period January–March 1945. The river evacuations were by nine hospital river steamers plying on the Brahmaputra, transporting casualties in the northern L. of C. *via* Gauhati to Sirajganj and from Comilla to Dacca *via* Daudkandi.

The numbers evacuated from the advanced base hospital into India Command during this period were:

By sea	4,419
By river	2,933
By air	2,631
By rail	12

Save for those evacuated by air *ex* A.L.F.S.E.A. most of the patients travelled by more than one form of transport before reaching Calcutta or Madras.

APPENDIX XXIII

LOCATION STATEMENT. GENERAL HOSPITALS, CASUALTY CLEARING STATIONS, MALARIA FORWARD TREATMENT UNITS, FIELD HOSPITALS AND BEACH MEDICAL UNITS. EASTERN COMMAND AND ALLIED LAND FORCES, SOUTH-EAST ASIA. MARCH 1945

Panitola	14 (Ind.) M.F.T.U.	
Dibrugarh	49 I.G.H.(C.)	H.Q., 3 Br. 7 Ind. Secs.
Ledo	44 I.G.H.(C.)	H.Q., 2 Br. 5 Ind.
Patiagaon	6 (Ind.) M.F.T.U.	
Jorhat	45 I.G.H.(C.)	H.Q., 3 Br. 7 Ind.
Golaghat	60 (E.A.) C.C.S.	(at Milestone 48 on the Dimapur–Golaghat road)
	61 F.D.S.	,,
	5 (Ind.) M.F.T.U.	
	15 (E.A.) M.F.T. Centre	
	10 (Belgian Congo) C.C.S.	
Dimapur	59 I.G.H.(I.T.)	H.Q. and 10 secs.
	66 I.G.H.(C.)	H.Q., 3 Br. 7 Ind.
	43 I.G.H.(I.T.)	H.Q. and 10 secs.
Kohima	53 I.G.H.(C.)	H.Q., 2 Br. 5 Ind.
Imphal	1 Bur. G.H. (200 beds)	
	38 B.G.H. (600 beds)	
	93 I.G.H.(C.)	H.Q., 2 Br. 5 Ind.
	87 I.G.H.(C.)	H.Q., 1 Br. 3 Ind.
	41 I.G.H.(C.)	H.Q., 3 Br. 7 Ind.
Imphal–Palel rd., Milestone 16·3	18 (Ind.) C.C.S.	
Palel	88 I.G.H.(C.)	H.Q., 1 Br. 3 Ind.
Moreh	89 I.G.H.(C.)	H.Q., 1 Br. 3 Ind.
	94 I.G.H.(C.)	H.Q., 2 Br. 5 Ind.

Katha	22 C.C.S.	
	15 (Ind.) M.F.T.U.	
Shwebo	16 (Ind.) C.C.S.	
	8 (Ind.) C.C.S.	
	10 (Ind.) M.F.T.U.	
Alon	5 (Ind.) B.M.U.	
	11 (Ind.) M.F.T.U.	
Sadaung	13 (Ind.) C.C.S.	
	7 (Ind.) M.F.T.U.	
Sinthe	9 (Ind.) M.F.T.U.	
Myitche	14 (Ind.) C.C.S.	
	19 (Ind.) C.C.S.	
	4 (Ind.) M.F.T.U.	
Minbyin	1 (Ind.) M.F.T.U.	
Arakan on mainland opposite Ramree Island	1 (Ind.) B.M.U.	
Ramree Island	125 I.G.H.(C.)	H.Q., 3 Br. 7 Ind.
	30 (W.A.) C.C.S.	
	110 (E.A.) C.R.S.	
	12 (Ind.) M.F.T.U.	
Kyaukpyu	28 (W.A.) C.C.S.	
	25 (Ind.) C.C.S.	
	23 (Ind.) C.C.S.	
Akyab	15 (Ind.) C.C.S.	
	95 I.G.H.(C.)	H.Q., 2 Br. 5 Ind.
Maungdaw	25 (W.A.) C.C.S.	
Chiringa	29 (W.A.) C.C.S.	
	31 (W.A.) C.C.S.	
Khurushkul Island	49 W.A.G.H. (1,000 beds)	
	58 I.G.H.(I.T.)	H.Q. and 10 secs.
	72 I.G.H.(C.)	H.Q., 2 Br. 5 Ind.
Dohazari	82 I.G.H.(C.)	H.Q., 1 Br. 3 Ind.
	152 W.A.G.H. (1,000 beds)	
	108 (E.A.) C.R.S.	
Chittagong	28 I.G.H.(C.)	H.Q., 1 Br. 3 Ind.
	56 I.G.H.(C.)	H.Q., 2 Br. 5 Ind.
	68 I.G.H.(C.)	H.Q., 3 Br. 7 Ind.
	115 E.A.G.H. Sec. (100 beds)	
	3 (Ind.) M.F.T.U.	
Comilla	14 B.G.H. (1,200 beds)	
	150 E.A.G.H. (1,000 beds)	

Maynamati	74 I.G.H.(C.)	H.Q., 3 Br. 7 Ind.
	92 I.G.H.(C.)	H.Q., 2 Br. 5 Ind.
	96 I.G.H.(I.T.)	H.Q. and 10 secs.
Agartala	86 I.G.H.(C.)	H.Q., 2 Br. 1 Ind.
	51 I.G.H.(C.)	H.Q., 2 Br. 5 Ind.
	79 I.G.H.(I.T.)	H.Q. and 10 secs.
Sylhet	91 I.G.H.(C.)	H.Q., 1 Br. 3 Ind.
Silchar	124 I.G.H.(C.)	H.Q., 2 Br. 5 Ind.
Gauhati	52 I.G.H.(C.)	H.Q., 3 Br. 7 Ind.
Tezpur	84 I.G.H.(C.)	H.Q., 1 Br. 3 Ind.
Dacca	46 W.A.G.H. (1,000 beds)	
	17 B.G.H. (1,200 beds)	
	62 I.G.H.(C.)	H.Q., 2 Br. 5 Ind.
	76 I.G.H.(I.T.)	H.Q. and 10 secs.
	77 I.G.H.(I.T.)	H.Q. and 10 secs.
	63 I.G.H.(I.T.)	H.Q. and 10 secs.
Sirajganj	67 I.G.H.(C.)	H.Q., 2 Br. 5 Ind.
Jhingergacha	28 (Ind.)C.C.S.	
Calcutta	119 I.G.H.(C.)	H.Q., 3 Br. 7 Ind.
	21 B.G.H. (600 beds)	
Midnapore	39 I.G.H.(C.)	H.Q., 2 Br. 5 Ind.
Chas	75 I.G.H.(C.)	H.Q., 3 Br. 7 Ind.
Namkum	133 I.B.G.H.(B.T.)	
	(1,000 beds)	
Bermo	4 (Ind.) Fd. Hosp.	
Ranchi	9 I.B.G.H.(B.T.)	
	(800 beds)	
	139 I.B.G.H.(B.T.)	
	(1,200 beds)	
	42 I.G.H.(I.T.)	H.Q. and 10 secs.
	47 B.H.G. (1,200 beds)	
Ratu-Piska	69 I.G.H.(C.)	H.Q., 2 Br. 5 Ind.
Lohardaga	83 I.G.H.(C.)	H.Q., 1 Br. 3 Ind.
Dinapore	138 I.B.G.H.(I.T.)	
	(1,000 beds)	
	41 I.B.G.H.(I.T.)	
	(1,000 beds)	
	24 I.G.H.(C.)	H.Q., 2 Br. 5 Ind.

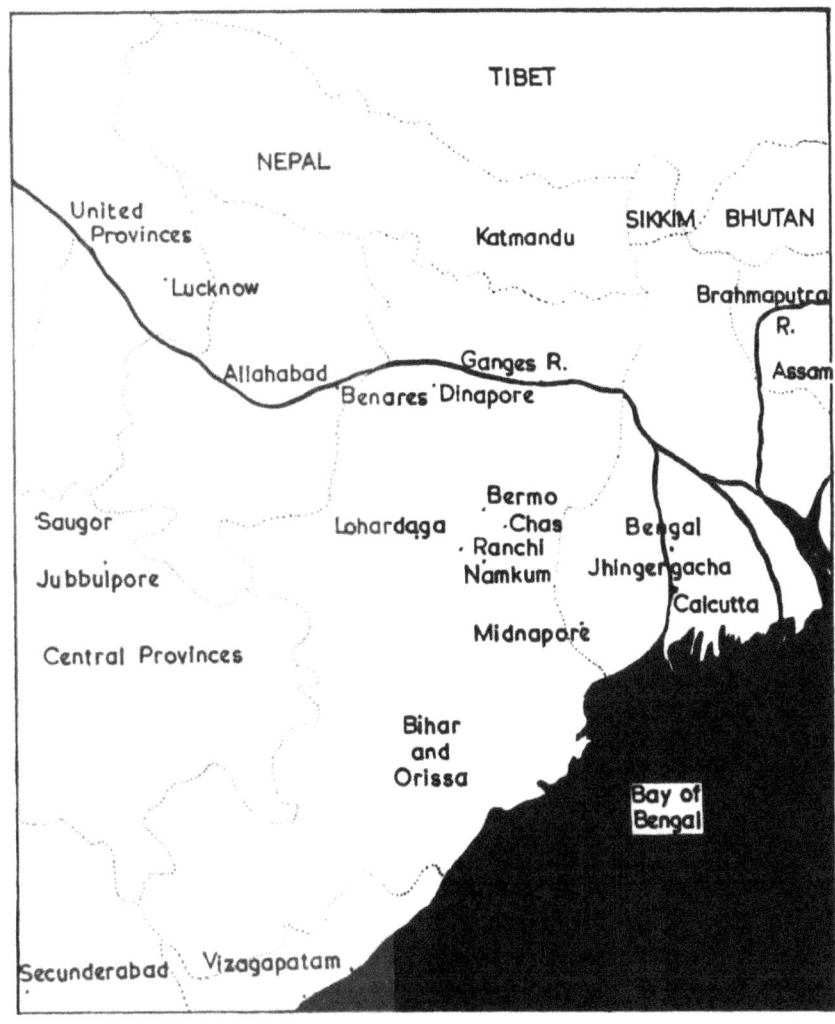

Fig. 70. Eastern India

CHAPTER 14

THE DRIVE TO THE SOUTH.
THE CAPTURE OF RANGOON.
THE CLOSING PHASE.
THE RE-OCCUPATION OF JAPANESE-HELD TERRITORIES.

WITH MANDALAY, the City of the Kings, and Meiktila taken, Rangoon, the Burmese capital, became Fourteenth Army's main objective. But before the march to the south could be begun the large area between IV and XXXIII Corps had to be cleared. On March 18 General Slim had outlined his plans for the capture of Rangoon before the monsoon broke (about the middle of May). He divided the forthcoming operation into three phases, (i) the battle then continuing in the Mandalay Plain, (ii) an interval for regrouping and generally mopping-up and (iii) the advance to the south. In phase (ii) IV Corps, with Indian 5th and 17th Divisions (both mechanised and with an air-transportable brigade) and Indian 255th Tk. Bde. was to strike at the Japanese positions about Pyawbwe while XXXIII Corps, with 2nd and Indian 20th Divisions was to clear the Mandalay–Maymyo–Mahlaing–Myingyan area so as to free all roads and railways for use in phase (iii). Then Indian 7th Division would replace 2nd Division in XXXIII Corps and while IV Corps (Indian 5th and 17th) set out for Rangoon, following the axis of the road and railway, Kyaukse–Thazi–Yamethin–Pyinmana–Toungoo–Pyu–Nyaunglebin–Pegu, XXXIII Corps (Indian 7th and 20th) on the right, following the axis of the Irrawaddy, would seize Seikpyu and Chauk, and thereafter capture in succession Magwe, Yenangyaung, Prome and finally, unless IV Corps got there first, Rangoon. At the beginning of phase (iii) Indian 19th Division, passing to Army control, was to be used for the protection of the left flank and communications of IV Corps in the Meiktila area.

This regrouping involved a delicate logistic manoeuvre for whereas 2nd and Indian 20th Divisions were required to move from north-east to south-west, parts of Indian 5th Division at the same time and in the same area, had to move from north-west to south-east to reach the railway axis. Indian 7th Division was already in the valley of the Irrawaddy and was transferred from IV to XXXIII Corps on March 29.

From Meiktila, where H.Q. IV Corps was established at this time, to Rangoon by rail is 320 miles; from Chauk to Rangoon *via* the valley of

CAPTURE OF RANGOON—CLOSING PHASE 531

the Irrawaddy is 375. The time at the disposal of Fourteenth Army for the taking of Rangoon was at most five weeks. It had to average at least ten miles a day against opposition and in spite of demolitions and mining. If Rangoon had not been taken before the rains came, the operation could end in disaster and Fourteenth Army might be obliged to withdraw to the Mandalay area or even to the line of the Chindwin. The 108 mile stretch of fair-weather road of the 600 mile L. of C. from Dimapur to Meiktila would not stand up to monsoon conditions and supply by air would inevitably become irregular. Few of the airfields between the start and the end of this southward advance were of the

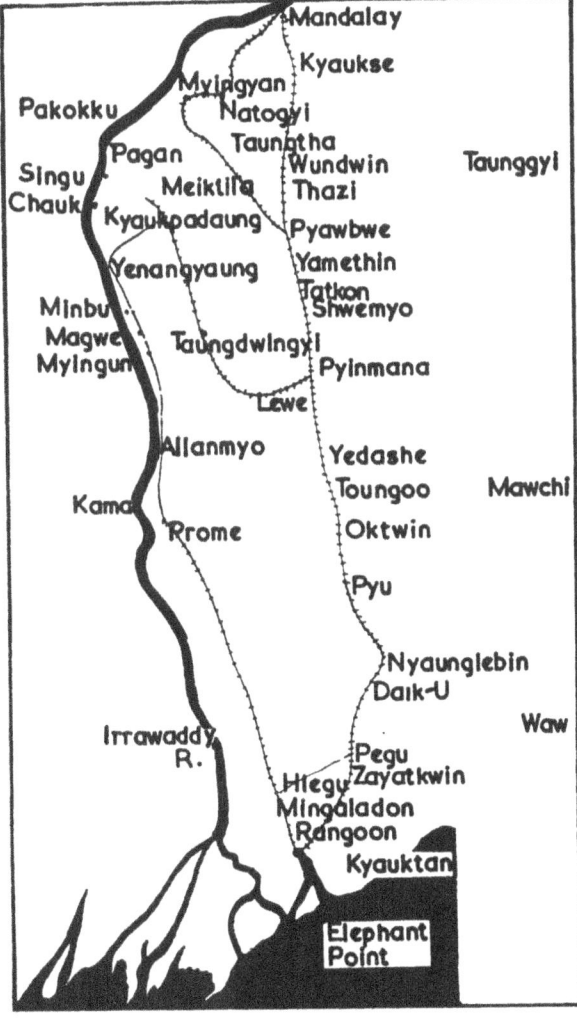

FIG. 71. Mandalay–Rangoon

all-weather variety and most of them would certainly become unusable as far as supply aircraft were concerned with the onset of the monsoon. The withdrawal of the U.S. transport aircraft in June for employment in China would make the problem of supply of the forward formations of Fourteenth Army insuperable. Even when Rangoon had been taken it had to be expected that before the port could be used the 24 mile stretch of the River Hlaing would have to be ridded of mines and its banks cleared of Japanese troops.

To insure against possible failure it was decided to revive the plans for an amphibious and airborne assault upon Rangoon (Operation 'Dracula'). D-day for the amphibious part of the operation was fixed for May 2 and the operation was to be unleashed if Fourteenth Army had not reached the city by that date. XV Corps in Arakan began to prepare for this operation.

The general method of advance to be adopted by IV Corps down the trunk road was to be the seizure of an airstrip, or of a site upon which an airstrip could be constructed, at intervals of 50 miles or thereabouts by a rapid forward bound, followed by the fly-in of one or other of the air-transportable brigades (9th of 5th Div.; 99th of 17th Div.). While the brigade held the strip the rest of the division would make its next bound. The two divisions would leap-frog over each other. Should the resistance in any locality be such as required considerable time for its overcoming, it was to be disregarded by these two divisions racing for Rangoon. Such defended localities were to be by-passed and dealt with after Rangoon had fallen.

It was planned that on the railway axis IV Corps troops should be supplied by air south of Toungoo and by road, and it was hoped, by rail also, north of Toungoo. On the river axis one of the divisions and part of the tank brigade could be supplied by air but the rest would have to rely on road and river transport.

At the end of March the formations of XXXIII Corps were occupied as follows: Indian 20th Division was moving against Kyaukse, an important road and rail junction on the line between Mandalay and Thazi; Indian 19th Division was clearing the area around Mandalay and preparing to move southwards towards Meiktila; 2nd Division, which had been operating in the Ava area, closing the Japanese escape routes to the south, had joined up with Indian 19th Division and was about to hand over that area to this division and to concentrate in the general area Tada-U. The formations of IV Corps were occupied as follows: After the Japanese attempts to retake Meiktila had been thwarted, Myingyan had been taken and the road between this place and Meiktila had been opened. IV Corps formations were now busy mopping up east of Pakokku, Pagan and Chauk and their patrols had penetrated to the vicinity of Mount Popa and of Kyaukpadaung.

CAPTURE OF RANGOON—CLOSING PHASE 533

Kyaukse was captured by 80th Bde. of Indian 20th Division on March 30 and this event marked the end of phase (i). 5th Bde. of 2nd Division and 268th Lorried Infantry Bde. of XXXIII Corps, moving south-west from the Myingyan–Natogyi area and destroying many isolated Japanese detachments on the way, encountered very stubborn opposition from some 600 Japanese entrenched on the steep slopes of Mount Popa, a 500 ft. high extinct volcano that rises abruptly from the plain. Air-strikes and artillery bombardment were required to soften up the position before the Japanese defenders withdrew on April 19/20. 5th Bde. then moved forward to join up with 268th Bde. While 5th Bde. was occupied in this way the rest of 2nd Division was being flown out to India from Myingyan. By April 25, 5th Bde. had followed. This division was to be the follow-up division of the force that was to take Rangoon from the sea.

XXXIII CORPS ON THE RIVER AXIS

Meanwhile, Indian 7th Division had captured Kyaukpadaung on April 12 and Chauk by April 18. This division had been given the tasks of capturing the oilfields area and of clearing the west bank of the Irrawaddy, southwards, at the same time cutting off such Japanese forces as were attempting to withdraw eastwards from Arakan. 33rd Bde. was instructed to capture Kyaukpadaung and Gwegyo and then move on Chauk from the south-east while 89th Bde. attacked the town from the north. By April 11, 33rd Bde. had reached the Pyinma Chaung, some eight miles north-west of Kyaukpadaung and on the morning of the 12th the outskirts of the township were entered. On April 13 the whole of Kyaukpadaung was cleared and much booty captured. 33rd Bde. then moved towards Gwegyo, a small village on the Yenangyaung–Chauk road. It was expected that the Japanese would attempt to hold on to this village in order to permit an orderly withdrawal towards Yenangyaung from Chauk. By first light on the 14th, 33rd Bde. had established a road-block about a mile-and-a-half from Gwegyo on the Yenangyaung–Chauk road and after a sharp encounter the village was captured and its garrison annihilated.

On April 17, 89th Bde. set out for Singu to secure the south end of the Chauk ridge. Singu was quickly cleared and this being done 89th Bde. moved on Chauk from the north. In the south-east corner of the oilfields was a hill feature which dominated the area of Chauk and also the road to Gwegyo. 33rd Bde. closing on Chauk from the south-east captured this dominating hill-feature on April 16. At dawn on the 18th it was discovered that the Japanese had vacated Chauk and the two brigades joined up. 114th Bde. moving down the west bank of the Irrawaddy occupied Seikpyu on the 20th.

33rd and 89th Bdes. then prepared for the attack upon Yenangyaung itself. 33rd Bde. began to work its way into the hills that surrounded the oilfield area while 89th Bde. set off on a wide outflanking movement to cut the main road short of Yenangyaung. By the 21st the oilfield area had been completely encircled save along the Irrawaddy shore. As 33rd Bde. closed in stern opposition was encountered at Twingon and as this was slowly overcome it became clear that the Japanese were pulling out, carrying out demolitions on a large scale as they departed across the river. Two more days were required for the mopping up of stray parties of Japanese hiding in caves and dug-outs but at length the capture of the oilfields was complete and large quantities of equipment, ammunition, guns and vehicles were captured in the town. 33rd Bde., in the thirteen days since it had left the concentration area in Nyaungu, had advanced 110 miles and had fought three major engagements.

In order to exploit this success 89th Bde. crossed the Irrawaddy at Kyaukye and moved on Salin from the south while 114th Bde. moved against this place from the north along the west bank of the river. 33rd Bde. after consolidating its gains, sent strong patrols with tank support towards Magwe.

After Indian 20th Division had captured Kyaukse, 30 miles to the south of Mandalay, it was relieved by 36th Division which had passed from N.C.A.C. to Fourteenth Army. When it had finished clearing the Myittha–Wundwin area it changed two of its brigades from A.T. to M.T., by taking over the transport of 2nd Division when this was being flown out to India. Its British battalions (2nd Border, 1st Devon and 1st Northamptons) were transferred to 36th Division and 2/8th Punjab, 1/19th Hybad and 1/1st G.R. were transferred from 36th Division to Indian 20th Division. Indian 20th Division, on April 10, began to move down the axis of the road westward from Meiktila to Zayetkon and thence south towards Magwe and Allanmyo. Its first objective was Taungdwingyi, 43 miles east-south-east of Magwe, some 65 miles from Meiktila and about half-way between the railway and the river axes of advance. It was a vital road and rail junction in the Japanese system of communications.

32nd Bde. led the advance and reached Zayetkon on April 11. No Japanese troops were encountered but contact was established with elements of the Burma Defence Army, now hostile to the Japanese and from these it was learnt that Natmauk was clear. Taungdwingyi was entered on April 14; its garrison consisted of I.N.A. units. Satthwa was entered on the 17th. Without pause, 32nd Bde. pushed on to learn that on the 18th the Japanese had reoccupied Satthwa. An air-strike hurried their departure on the 24th. 32nd Bde. had started an encircling movement to contain the Japanese in Satthwa but this was not complete before its garrison withdrew.

Meanwhile 80th Bde. had been ferried forward from Kyaukse through

CAPTURE OF RANGOON—CLOSING PHASE

Meiktila to the Natmauk area and began to advance from there down the road to Magwe on April 17. Magwe was captured on the 19th. For the next few days mopping up operations were carried out. South of Magwe a Japanese hospital was uncovered. In it the patients refused to surrender and died resisting. At Myingin another hospital was found; its 53 patients, in the last stages of starvation, were taken prisoner. While XXXIII Corps troops cleared the area 80th Bde. pressed on. The Japanese to the north of Magwe and on the east bank of the Irrawaddy could now escape only by crossing the river. This they did and the considerable force of Japanese moving down the west bank was harried by 89th and 114th Bdes. of Indian 7th Division.

On April 21, XXXIII Corps issued instructions to the effect that Indian 20th Division was to advance on and capture Prome with all possible speed. 100th Bde. passed through 32nd Bde. on the road leading from Satthwa to Allanmyo on April 24 and having overcome Japanese resistance especially at Milestone 224 on the outskirts of Allanmyo on the 27th advanced to capture this town after thirty-six hours' fighting.

Meanwhile 80th Bde. was advancing southward from Magwe, rounding up parties of Japanese as these tried to get across the Irrawaddy and escape to the east. 100th Bde. was in the lead and overcame a Japanese rearguard at Bwetgyi, about twelve miles south of Allanmyo, to get within fifteen miles of Prome by May 1. On the following day the brigades moved on, meeting no opposition and entered the very considerable river port of Prome, now shattered and in ruins. The capture of Prome meant that the Japanese still in Arakan could no longer make use of the Taungup–Prome track.

On May 1 the situation in XXXIII Corps area was as follows: H.Q. Corps was in Magwe; Indian 20th Division was about to capture Prome; Indian 7th Division, less two brigades, was in Magwe, the two brigades were operating on the west bank of the Irrawaddy; 268th Bde. was in Allanmyo preparing for operations on the west bank of the river.

IV CORPS ON THE ROAD AND RAILWAY AXIS

The first stage of the race to Rangoon was an advance to Toungoo with all possible speed. This operation was divided into three phases:

(i) Indian 17th Division was to capture Pyawbwe. Target date, April 7.

(ii) Indian 5th Division, less its 9th air-portable brigade, supported by armour, was to pass through Indian 17th Division and secure an air-head at Pyinmana. Target date, April 15. Indian 17th Division, following up closely was to take over this air-head.

(iii) Indian 5th Division was to capture Toungoo. Its air-transportable brigade would be flown in from Meiktila. Target date, April 25.

Supply would be entirely by air.

Indian 17th Division, leaving a small garrison in Meiktila, set out on March 30 for Pyawbwe, some twenty-four miles to the south-east. It planned to move against the strong Japanese positions in this area from three directions. 99th Bde. was to move east from Meiktila, capture Thazi and then move southwards parallel to the main road and seize the high ground to the north of Pyawbwe. 48th Bde. was to push down the main road towards Pyawbwe followed by 63rd Bde. which would leave the main road south of Yindaw and proceed due south, passing through Yanaung, and attack Pyawbwe from the west. An armoured column was to clear Yanaung before 63rd Bde. got there and then proceed to Ywadan to cut the main road at Milestone 306, whence it would send a detachment to Yamethin at Milestone 300.

99th Bde. moved towards its objective on March 31. In the villages in its path towards Thazi and in Thazi itself strong Japanese parties were encountered. Air-strikes helped greatly to clear several of these villages but precious time was consumed. On April 4 the brigade was instructed to contain Thazi and move south clearing all the villages in its path. The reduction of Thazi was left to a brigade of Indian 19th Division with 21st Mountain Regt. in support. 99th Bde. then moved across country parallel to the main road.

On the main road patrols of 48th Bde. found Kandaung occupied. An air-strike and an artillery bombardment preceded an infantry attack on April 3 when part of the village was cleared and early on the 4th the Japanese withdrew, leaving the village heavily booby-trapped and mined. The brigade then moved on to Yewe where stiff resistance was met. The village was finally cleared in the afternoon of the 4th. For three whole days Yindaw was bombed from the air and shelled from the ground but its Japanese garrison would not budge. It was decided to by-pass the place and 99th Bde. moved past it to the east and the rest of Indian 17th Division moved round it to the west.

48th Bde. reached the main road again south of Yindaw and found that Sadaung was strongly held. It was not until the 8th that Sadaung was finally cleared. Parties of Japanese troops were occupying all the villages in this area and time was consumed in turning them out. Yanaung was captured on April 8 and on the following day the main road south of Pyawbwe was cut and a detachment sent to Yamethin.

Meanwhile 63rd Bde., moving across country, had reached Kyauktaung and by April 9 Pyawbwe was encircled though not completely for there remained a small escape route to the south-east. On the 9th, 99th Bde., supported by tanks, captured the high ground north of Pyawbwe without much trouble. On this day Yindaw fell to 161st Bde. of Indian 5th Division which was following up Indian 17th Division and which had been assigned the task of reducing this village while Indian 17th Division pushed on. 48th and 63rd Bdes. of Indian

CAPTURE OF RANGOON—CLOSING PHASE

17th Division closed in and on the 10th Pyawbwe fell to a concerted attack. The Japanese losses in this battle were such that it seemed that only a break in the weather could now prevent the capture of Rangoon by IV Corps within the appointed time. This was the last occasion when a large Japanese field force was used in a co-ordinated fashion to block the southward march of Fourteenth Army.

Indian 5th Division now went into the lead. Its 123rd Bde., with an armoured spearhead, passed through the 'Black Cat' Division in Pyawbwe on April 11. The brigade was divided into nine columns moving in some 1,200 lorries accompanied by tanks, guns, trucks, jeeps, bridging materials and armoured cars. The columns passed through Yamethin but when darkness fell a Japanese suicide party, 300–400 strong, and with anti-tank guns, made its way back into the town from the east and held up the soft-skinned transport of the division. It was not until April 14 that the last of the Japanese in Yamethin had been eliminated and the road opened again. A large amount of equipment, stores and ammunition was captured.

Meanwhile the engineers had been constructing a by-pass road to the west of Yamethin for the use of 161st Bde. This brigade passed by Yamethin on April 14 and reached Tatkon which was cleared during the morning of the 15th. Moving on, the brigade was checked at the Sinthe Chaung near Shwemyo Bluff, a ridge seven hundred feet high that completely dominated the road. While 161st Bde. pressed against the Japanese position, 123rd Bde. made a forced outflanking march deep through hills and jungle to take it in rear. On April 18 a concerted attack overwhelmed the Japanese defenders. 99th Bde. of Indian 17th Division moved forward to take over the Shwemyo area and 9th Bde. of Indian 5th Division was brought forward to Tatkon by road from Meiktila.

Indian 5th Division, with all its three brigades, set off for Pyinmana on April 18. Demolitions and sniping caused delays but on the 19th the armoured spearhead got to within four miles of the town which was found to be strongly held. Leaving a battalion to carry on operations against the town, the armour by-passed it and seized the airfield at Lewe which was immediately repaired and made ready for the fly-in of gliders of the Forward Airfield Engineers. The reduction of Pyinmana by 63rd Bde. of Indian 17th Division began on April 21. 123rd Bde. of Indian 5th Division and armour of Ind. 255th Tk. Bde., at once set out for Toungoo, 60 miles on and only 187 miles from Rangoon. 161st Bde. concentrated at Thawatti, preparatory to following hard upon the heels of 123rd Bde. On April 22 the armoured spearhead of 123rd Bde., brushing aside feeble opposition on the way, reached Milestone 177, two miles to the north of Toungoo, and occupied the airfield. The armour, followed closely by 7th Y. and L., then swept through Toungoo and its garrison fled. The target date for the capture of this town was April 25; it was taken on the 22nd. Rangoon was now only 166 miles away. In order to prevent the retreating Japanese reaching Toungoo before Indian 5th Division, word had been sent out to the Karens telling them that the day of their rising had come. They did much, as did also the R.A.F., to decide the outcome of this race.

Pushing on, the leading elements of 123rd Bde. reached Oktwin by the evening of the 22nd. On the 24th, 161st Bde. went into the lead to reach Pyu, and its armoured spearhead to reach Penwegon, on April 25. Here Indian 5th Division halted to permit Indian 17th to go into the lead. It should have done this on the previous day but Indian 5th Division was not to be halted in its headlong rush to the south. It was known to Fourteenth Army formations that Operation 'Dracula' was due to be launched and though IV Corps was still some 144 miles away from Rangoon an effort was to be made to cover this distance in six or seven days.

It was intended that Indian 17th Division should move with all possible speed, capture Pegu and the airfield area, develop the airfields and move on towards Zayatkwin and thereafter press on towards Rangoon *via* Hlegu and Taukkyan. Indian 5th Division, following up, was to move on Rangoon *via* Zayatkwin, Sadalin and Ledaunggan, approaching the city from the north-east and east. Its 9th Bde. was to be flown in from Pyinmana to take over the Pegu area. On April 25, Indian 17th Division set out and by the end of the day its armour had advanced about 33 miles. On the 26th, its leading elements reached Kaukkwe, 2 miles north of Nyaunglebin, without meeting opposition. By the evening of this day its armoured spearhead was in Daik-U, only 85 miles from Rangoon. On the 27th Pyinbongyi was reached and here the resistance encountered was stubborn. Fighting continued all through the day. Eventually the numerous Japanese suicide parties were eliminated by the infantry with tank support and the advance resumed. Payagale was reached on April 28. The area was thickly mined and suicide parties were numerous. Slowly the resistance was overcome and the mines cleared and the division pressed on to cut the Payagyi-Waw road, three miles east of Payagyi. This was the road that led to the Sittang River and thence to Moulmein.

Following an air-strike and an artillery bombardment, 63rd Bde. advanced on Payagyi to find that the Japanese had abandoned it. The brigade pressed on towards Pegu, the outskirts of which were reached during the evening of April 29. Pegu is situated on both banks of the Pegu River over which were one road and two railway bridges. The main road bridge was in the western part of the town; one of the railway bridges was three miles to the north of the town and the other was about half a mile from its northern outskirts which began at Milestone 51.

CAPTURE OF RANGOON—CLOSING PHASE

On the evening of April 29 while 63rd Bde. harboured at Milestone 55, a company of 1/10th Gurkha Rifles advanced towards the main bridge at Milestone 29. Stiff opposition was encountered but the company dug itself in at Milestone 51·7 and on the following day its patrols discovered that the bridge had been completely destroyed. The following tactical plan was then adopted. 48th Bde. was to cross the Pegu River, move down its west bank and capture the railway station. 63rd Bde. was to capture the high ground to the north-east of Pegu and advance down the main road as far as the road bridge. 255th Tk. Bde. was to move across country to attack Kamanat and other villages to the south and then move on Pegu from the north-east to join up with 63rd Bde. at the road bridge.

On April 30, when 48th Bde. attacked, the Japanese blew the railway bridges but finding that two girders of the more southerly of the two were still intact, a platoon of 4/12th F.F.R. scrambled across under cover of an artillery barrage, and established itself on the far bank. By nightfall, in spite of violent opposition, a second platoon got across into the bridgehead. Another company of the battalion was successful in crossing the river at the level of the other railway bridge and from these two bridgeheads an attack upon the railway station was launched. This was ultimately successful and the division began to cross the river as the Sappers speedily repaired the railway bridges on May 1. By the 2nd the whole of the Pegu area had been cleared.

IV Corps' advance had been held up for two days, just when it seemed that the race to Rangoon might be won. It had travelled over 300 miles in three weeks and was now only 50 miles from its goal. On the afternoon of April 29 the rains came, a fortnight early. All movement of tanks and wheeled vehicles off the road became impossible and no aircraft could take off or land. The Pegu River rose in full flood. Rations, already reduced, were now reduced still further. It was now quite clear by this time that Indian 17th Division—'God Almighty's Own', as its admirers called it—which had been forced out of Burma three years before, was not to have the honour of being the first to enter the capital.

On April 30, Indian 17th Division encountered a party of some 250 American, British and Indian P.o.W. who were on their way from Rangoon jail by road to Moulmein *via* Waw and whose escort had disappeared. From them it was learnt that in the jail were some 600–700 men too unfit to have accompanied them. These ex-P.o.W., the manner of whose release indicated the state of confusion that existed in Japanese circles at this time, were quickly evacuated to Comilla by air.

OPERATION 'DRACULA'. XV CORPS

It will be remembered that in preparation for operations that would begin with the crossing of the Chindwin, three alternative plans had been considered by S.E.A.C. and that of these plan 'Z' dealt with the capture of Rangoon by a large-scale amphibious and airborne operation ('triphibious' was the term invented by the Prime Minister to describe such collaborative activities of the three Services), followed by a drive northwards to meet Fourteenth Army, moving south. According to this plan the rôle of Fourteenth Army was to be a subsidiary one. The plan was dropped for neither the force nor the equipment required for its execution were available. It will be remembered too that in Operation 'Capital' S.E.A.C. had modified this combined assault upon Rangoon, making it complementary to the southward advance of Fourteenth Army. But at the time when the directive for this operation was issued the equipment required for Operation 'Dracula' was still not available. However, when it became likely that the Japanese would decide to hold on to Rangoon in strength while Fourteenth Army was stretched along a most precarious supply line in monsoon weather, the question of re-vitalising Operation 'Dracula' was considered. General Slim wished that when Fourteenth Army approached within striking distance of Rangoon, a seaborne assault should be unleashed. A number of formations had been freed by Fourteenth Army and by XV Corps because of supply difficulties so that troops were now available and in S.E.A.C. there were landing craft sufficient for a limited operation. Early in April the Supreme Commander issued instructions to the effect that an amphibious assault on Rangoon by one division with a drop by a parachute battalion was to be prepared for not later than May 5. This operation was to be mounted by XV Corps in Arakan.

The final plan for Operation 'Dracula' took the following form: Indian 26th Division was to be the assault division and 2nd Division the follow-up division. A composite battalion provided by 2nd and 3rd Gurkha Para. Battalions would be dropped on D-day−1 to the west of Elephant Point, charged with the task of destroying the defences in this area. Then minesweepers would clear a channel up to the level of Bassein Creek, about twelve miles from the mouth of the Hlaing River. Ind. 36th Bde. of Indian 26th Division would then land above Elephant Point on the west bank of the river on D-day and a battalion of Ind. 71st Bde. of the same division would land on the east bank and move on Kyauktan. The rest of 71st Bde. and Ind. 4th Bde. would then land and follow up, seizing Kyauktan and thrusting on towards Syriam. On D-day+9, 6th Bde. of 2nd Division would take over from 71st and 4th Bdes. and these would then seize Syriam and clear the area while the rest of 2nd Division passed through and advanced on Rangoon.

The assault force was mounted in Akyab and Ramree Islands and set out between April 27 and 30. It had strong air cover and a naval escort. Twelve bomber squadrons were allotted to the operation and a

CAPTURE OF RANGOON—CLOSING PHASE

strong naval covering force with British, Dutch and French warships guarded the convoy from interference. A destroyer force foregathered off Rangoon and on April 30 intercepted eleven ships carrying Japanese troops to Moulmein. Nine of these ships were sunk.

On May 1 heavy air attacks were made upon all known defences on both banks of the Hlaing River and at 0630 hours the paratroops were dropped. Elephant Point was easily captured. Torrential rain now began to fall and continued to fall until the evening of May 3. 71st and 36th Bdes., having been transferred to landing craft early in the morning of May 2, landed according to plan. Kyauktan was entered as was also Syriam. The flooded countryside on both sides of the river prevented the landing of vehicles, guns and stores on the west bank of the river while on the east bank a caterpillar tractor had to be used to pull the guns a few yards from the river's edge. One landing craft carrying key engineer and medical personnel struck a mine. There were very few survivors and all the officers aboard were killed.

An Air Force pilot flying over Rangoon saw on the roof of one of the blocks of Rangoon jail, written in large letters, a message to the effect that the Japanese had departed and that there were P.o.W. in the jail. This pilot, belonging to 221st Group, R.A.F. had then landed on the airfield at Mingaladon to find the cantonment deserted. In landing he had burst a tyre and so could not take off again. He therefore made his way into the city and to the jail. There he met, among others, an officer of the R.A.A.F. and together they concocted a plan. The R.A.A.F. officer with other R.A.F. personnel set off for Mingaladon to prepare the airfield for the aircraft that would soon be arriving. The R.A.F. pilot embarked in a sampan and set forth to meet the oncoming ships. As a result of the information he brought the build-up of the assault force by sea was cancelled. Of 2nd Division only 6th Bde. landed on D-day+8, the remainder of the division staying in Calcutta. The move of H.Q. XV Corps to Rangoon was also cancelled.

It was not until the evening of May 3 that 36th Bde., having struggled for interminable miles across water-logged country, appeared on the Hlaing River immediately south of Rangoon docks, to learn that the Japanese had left the city on April 28. The rest of the division soon followed and took immediate steps to quell the disturbances that had followed upon the departure of the Japanese. The G.O.C. Indian 26th Division acted as the Military Governor of Rangoon and allotted to each of his brigades an area of the city to administer.*

Rangoon was completely under control by May 5 and so elements of

---

* Rangoon is the anglicisation of Ran-kon which in Burmese means 'war ended' or 'end of strife'. It was the name given to the small village on the Hlaing River after the conquest of Lower Burma by King Alaungpaya in 1755.

Indian 26th Division set out along the Rangoon–Pegu and the Rangoon–Prome roads to link up with Indian 17th and 20th Divisions.

When Pegu was finally taken Indian 17th Division had been regrouped for the final dash to Rangoon. The armoured column was split up, the armoured cars and tanks joining 48th and 63rd Bdes. and 1/3rd G.R. reverting to 99th Bde. which was to be left behind to hold the Pegu area. The other two brigades set out on May 2 in torrential rain. 48th Bde. crossed the Pegu River by way of a Bailey bridge but by the time 63rd Bde. was due to cross the rain had rendered the approaches to the bridge impassable and the brigade was marooned. The road to Hlegu was very heavily mined and booby-trapped and road-blocks had to be cleared. The bridge beyond Intagaw had been completely demolished. Most of 1/7th Gurkha Rifles either swam across this chaung or else got over by means of a bamboo foot-bridge on May 4 and pressed on towards Hlegu. The bridge at Hlegu had also been blown and the Japanese were holding the western bank. However they departed hurriedly when elements of Indian 26th Division approached from the south. The two divisions linked up on May 6 at Hlegu, 28 miles from Rangoon. 48th and 63rd Bdes. in Intagaw and in the vicinity of Milestone 41, respectively, carried out extensive patrolling in all directions and thereafter pulled back to Pegu where sufficient cover for the troops during the monsoon could be provided.

100th Bde. of Indian 20th Division had entered Prome on May 2. It was then decided that 100th Bde. should clear the area around Prome and Shwedaung and the east bank of the Irrawaddy while 32nd Bde. captured Paungde and thereafter advanced on Rangoon. But the weather deteriorated and it became imperative to get to Rangoon with all possible speed. Shwedaung was occupied by 100th Bde. on May 3 and on the 6th, 32nd Bde. passed through 100th Bde. and reached Paungde without opposition. The advance was continued and several clashes with small parties of Japanese soldiery occurred. Useful information concerning the Japanese was given to 32nd Bde. by members of the Burma Defence Army. On May 11 a set-piece attack was about to be made on the Japanese positions along the Minhla Chaung when it was discovered that following an air-strike and an artillery bombardment the Japanese had withdrawn after blowing the bridge. Letpadan was reached on May 12 and on the 13th Tharrawaddy. The advance was then checked for the bridge at Thonze was down. On the 14th, 32nd Bde. made its way through Okkan which was found to be clear. On the 15th the advance continued and at Hlegu at Milestone 60, 9/14th Punjab of 32nd Bde. linked up with 1st Lincolns of 71st Bde. of Indian 26th Division and the road to Rangoon was opened. Indian 26th Division now passed u/c XXXIII Corps.

THE CLOSING PHASE

The tactical situation was a most interesting one. Fourteenth Army had cut two exceedingly long and very narrow lanes from north to south, one along the line of the railway, more than 300 miles long and with an average width of less than two miles, and the other along the line of the Irrawaddy, about 200 miles long and somewhat broader than the first. On either side of these lanes and in between them were Japanese troops to the number, it was estimated, of about 77,000 altogether. Their exact locations were difficult to determine at all accurately since at this time everything was in a state of flux. It was thought that there were four main concentrations:

(i) east of the Meiktila–Rangoon road in the Shan and Karen hills about Kalaw, Loilem and Kemapyu;

(ii) around the estuary of the Sittang River and down the Tenasserim coast;

(iii) between the Sittang and the Irrawaddy, mainly in the Pegu Yomas; and

(iv) west of the Irrawaddy and in the Irrawaddy Delta.

The only possible intention that the Japanese could reasonably entertain at this time was to extricate as many of their troops in Burma as possible into Thailand. Since most of their formations had lost their transport, their guns and their bridging material this was bound to be a most difficult enterprise, for there were the Irrawaddy and the Sittang to be crossed and the Pegu Yomas to be traversed in monsoon weather and by jungle tracks. The Japanese were receiving no supplies, no rations, no ammunition, for the air route to them had been closed.

The task of Fourteenth Army, that of preventing as many as possible of these Japanese troops getting away to reorganise beyond the Sittang, was also a very difficult one. Attention and energy were being directed toward the impending assault upon Malaya and away from the ending of the campaign in Burma. Formations were being earmarked for the Malayan adventure and were thus lost to Fourteenth Army. Every mile of the two north-south lanes could not possibly be guarded, all that could be done was to place detachments at intervals along them and to patrol the gaps between these while mobile columns thrust out in all directions to track down and destroy such bodies of Japanese troops as were encountered.

General Slim now issued the following orders:

> IV Corps. To destroy all enemy attempting to cross the Pegu Yomas from west to east; to take Mokpalin and to advance with Indian 19th Division (which now reverted to IV Corps) as far as Thandaung, twenty miles east of Toungoo and thus secure Fourteenth Army's line of communication.

XXXIII Corps. To destroy all enemy in the Irrawaddy Valley; to open the road and railway from Prome to Rangoon and to capture Bassein. (This task was assigned to Indian 20th Division.) Indian 7th Division was to send one brigade to the west of the Irrawaddy to destroy the Japanese forces to the south of the general line connecting Prome and Okshitpin. Another brigade of this division was to operate on the east bank of the river while the third was to move to Dayindabo to pass u/c Indian 20th Division. Ind. 268th Bde. was to cut the escape routes west of Thayetmyo and then concentrate in the Allanmyo area.

36th Division on the Taunggyi–Thazi road was replaced by 64th Bde. of Indian 19th Division, placed u/c IV Corps and instructions were issued to this brigade to seize Kalaw. In the Arakan 82nd W.A. Division was directly u/c A.L.F.S.E.A.

By May 10 the distribution of the formations of IV Corps was as follows; in the extreme south Indian 5th Division covered the area of the main trunk road between Hlegu northwards to Pyinbongyi; in the centre Indian 17th Division stretched from Pyinbongyi to Pyu and in the north was Indian 19th Division from Pyu to Toungoo, with one brigade in the Meiktila area. An intelligence screen composed of Burma National Army personnel was operating on both sides of the road.

Indian 5th Division was assigned the task of securing Kyaikto, after having destroyed the Japanese forces between Waw and the Sittang River. Ind. 9th Bde. opened the Payagyi–Mokpalin road as far as Waw without much difficulty and cleared the area between Pegu and the southern end of the Pegu Yomas. The heavy rainfall made the employment of tanks and the movement of artillery exceedingly difficult as the brigade fought its way into Nyaungkashe. The Japanese were in considerable strength in the area of the Sittang bridge, which had been blown, overlooking the river from the jungle-clad hills on the east bank. The idea of launching an assault against Mokpalin was given up and Indian 5th Division was ordered to remain in readiness to occupy the town should the Japanese withdraw.

123rd and 161st Bdes. of Indian 5th Division, during this time, were engaged in active patrolling in all directions and destroyed many small parties of Japanese. The weather conditions in which these patrols carried out their tasks were exceedingly bad.

In the central sector all three brigades of Indian 17th Division likewise patrolled extensively in their respective areas and occasionally clashes with parties of Japanese occurred. In the northern sector 62nd Bde. of Indian 19th Division advanced along the Mawchi road east of Toungoo against stubborn resistance. 98th Bde. went into the lead and by May 28 the Thandaung road junction at Milestone 13 was captured. So resolute was the opposition that in three weeks Indian 19th Division had advanced only 13 miles eastwards from Toungoo. 64th Bde.,

CAPTURE OF RANGOON—CLOSING PHASE

relieving 36th Division in the Kalaw area on May 10, at once encountered very determined opposition, as 36th Division had done, from the Japanese occupying a very strong natural position on a high hill bounded by steep-sided chaungs which completely dominated the twisting road. This was the 'Staircase' 12 miles north of Kalaw. The bridges on the road were down. Much valuable information concerning the position and its defenders was provided by friendly civilians. On May 29, following an air-strike 64th Bde. captured the 'Staircase' area and thus opened the way to Kalaw which was entered on June 7.

At the end of April, 89th Bde. of Indian 7th Division had been sent across the Irrawaddy to move westwards and south-westwards into the area of the Prome–Taungup road in order to deny this road to such Japanese forces as attempted to escape from Arakan into Burma proper. The brigade operated in a number of columns. Minbu was captured and handed over to 114th Bde. of Indian 7th Division at the beginning of May. 89th Bde. then set out on a long hook towards the south-west passing through Yenanma on May 6 to reach Kaingngegyi where a brisk action was fought on the 9th. The Japanese broke off the action and moved down the line of the Yegyi Chaung. 89th Bde. lay in wait for them near Taungdaw where very severe fighting took place, the brigade having 18 killed and 48 wounded.

Indian 20th Division at this time was stretched for about 135 miles along the line of the river axis and was called upon to dispute two main attempts on the part of the Japanese to get across the Irrawaddy, one in the area of Zalon–Kama which was held by 80th Bde. and the other in 100th Bde's. area south of Shwedaung. 80th Bde. was ordered to proceed to the Allanmyo area and this it did after considerable skirmishing with parties of Japanese in the area of the Yin Chaung. On May 4 the brigade moved on to Tititut to take over the area south of the Bwetgyi Chaung to the Prome–Paukkaung road. Several boats carrying Japanese troops across the river at Kama were destroyed on May 4 and 6. 268th Bde. at Thayetmayo on the east bank of the river sent two of its battalions across to push down towards Kama with the result that the Japanese gave up the idea of crossing at Kama and began to concentrate at Taukma, further to the south. Zalon on the east bank, it seemed, had been selected as the site of the bridgehead. By the 15th there were some 4,000 Japanese troops ready to cross into a small bridgehead that had been established on the 13th. There was much fighting during the following days and though most of the attempts to cross were defeated several small parties of Japanese managed to slip through and make their way into the Pegu Yomas.

80th Bde. was then ordered to move south to relieve 71st Bde. of Indian 26th Division in the Taikkyi area, north of Rangoon, as this division was being withdrawn from Burma. 33rd Bde. of Indian 7th

Division took over from 80th Bde. on May 21. The small Japanese bridgehead at Zalon was cordoned off. A large-scale attempt to break out was made on May 28/29 but only a few small parties got away. By the end of the month the west bank of the Irrawaddy in this area was clear. 268th Bde. was dealing with stragglers whose numbers grew progressively less.

100th Bde. of Indian 20th Division had reached the area of Shwedaung at the beginning of May just in time to forestall a large-scale Japanese crossing of the Irrawaddy. About three hundred did get across on May 5 but were forced to retire to their boats and return whence they came. 4/10th G.R. crossed over to the west bank and engaged parties of Japanese troops and these moved southwards towards Yegin. But here 32nd Bde. of Indian 20th Division was ready to intercept them. Several parties of Japanese troops were able to avoid all ambushes and to make their way into the Pegu Yomas, though the majority of such parties were caught and destroyed.

By the beginning of June the task of preventing the passage of Japanese troops across the Irrawaddy from west to east was finished. Indian 20th Division was now required to maintain law and order between the Irrawaddy and the Pegu Yomas. The troops remained in quarters and came out only when information was brought by Burma National Army men (now known as the Patriot Burmese Forces) that a Japanese party had been located.

6th Bde. of 2nd Division reached Rangoon from Calcutta and entered Bassein unopposed on May 25.

At the end of May there was a complete reorganisation of the Allied Land Forces. This was made necessary by the imminence of the invasion of Malaya. H.Q. Fourteenth Army, which had moved into Judson College, Rangoon, went to India there to prepare for the Malayan adventure. A new army—Twelfth Army—was formed to control all land operations in Burma. Its headquarters was formed very largely out of that of XXXIII Corps which closed down. In Twelfth Army were included Indian 7th and 20th Divisions, 82nd West African Division (operational command only), 6th Bde. of 2nd Division, 268th Bde. u/c Indian 7th Division, IV Corps, consisting of Indian 5th, 17th and 19th Divisions and Ind. 255th Tk. Bde., and 'V' Force and Force 136. 221st Group, R.A.F. provided Twelfth Army with air support. The Patriot Burmese Forces were associated with Twelfth Army. Indian 5th and 26th Divisions and 254th Tk. Bde. were to return to India immediately and Indian 7th and 20th Divisions, with other troops, were to be mounted from Rangoon for the Malayan invasion. I Area and 505 District were established, the first in Rangoon, the second in Meiktila; in them were many administrative units and eighteen infantry battalions. General Slim was about to replace General

PLATE LI. Rangoon Jail. An I.M.S. Officer examines the stump of a patient whose leg he amputated. No anaesthetic was available at the time.

[*Indian Historical Section*]

PLATE LII. Rangoon Jail. A group of Prisoners-of-War at the time of their liberation.

[*Indian Historical Section*]

PLATE LIII. Men wounded in the battle for Pyinbongyi being tended by medical personnel on the battlefield.

[Imperial War Museum

PLATE LIV. A member of the American Field Service tending a wounded Gurkha. Sittang, August 1945.

[*Imperial War Museum*

Leese as commander of the Allied Land Forces and his place with H.Q. Fourteenth Army in India was to be taken by General Dempsey who had commanded Second Army in North-West Europe. General Stopford, from XXXIII Corps, was commanding Twelfth Army.

IV Corps, disposed between the Sittang and the Pegu Yomas, was instructed to:

(i) patrol westwards into the Pegu Yomas to harry the Japanese trying to escape towards the Sittang River;

(ii) to block the main routes and exits from the Pegu Yomas;

(iii) to advance with one brigade group on the axis Meiktila–Kalaw–Taunggyi;

(iv) to advance on the axis Toungoo–Mawchi; and

(v) to maintain one brigade group in an offensive/defensive rôle on the west bank of the Sittang River.

Indian 7th Division with 268th Bde. under command, was ordered to mop up stragglers in the area Allanmyo–Kama–Prome and to operate with offensive patrolling into the Pegu Yomas from the west. Indian 20th Division was to patrol offensively into the Pegu Yomas from the area Paungde in the north to Hmawbi in the south and mop up stragglers in the vicinity of the road–railway axis. 6th Bde. and 255th Tk. Bde. were to be held in reserve in Rangoon. Should the Japanese thrust towards Rangoon they would form a mobile column. In addition 6th Bde. was to maintain garrisons in Syriam and Bassein and operate water-borne patrols in the Irrawaddy Delta in conjunction with the Navy. 82nd W.A. Division was to remain in Arakan until the monsoon was over.

On the Rangoon–Prome axis Indian 7th Division, with 268th Inf. Bde. under command, was covering the sector between Prome and Shwedaung. The sector between Shwedaung and Hmawbi was occupied by Indian 20th Division. Towards the end of June there was so little activity in its area that Indian 7th Division was moved to IV Corps' front there to relieve Indian 5th Division, ear-marked for Malaya. By the first week of July therefore only Indian 20th Division, with 22nd E.A. Bde. under command, was left on the Rangoon–Prome axis.

Between Rangoon and Meiktila the formations of IV Corps were distributed as follows; between Hlegu and Pyinbongyi, Indian 5th Division; between Pyinbongyi and Pegu, Indian 17th Division and between Pyu and Toungoo, with some units on the Mawchi road east of Meiktila, Indian 19th Division. Though there were many encounters with parties of Japanese troops attempting to escape eastwards no major action was fought during June.

It will be remembered that 9th Bde. of Indian 5th Division was waiting in the vicinity of Nyaungkashe, near the western end of the Sittang bridge for an opportunity to take Mokpalin. While clearing the left bank of the river it was discovered that the Japanese forces on the eastern bank were contemplating a local counter-offensive across the Sittang. The whole of the area between Waw and the river had become a huge lake during the monsoon and the only means of communication was either along the railway embankment or else by water transport. On June 19 and 20 Nyaungkashe was shelled by the Japanese who then attacked westwards. This attack coincided with the relief of 9th Bde. of Indian 5th Division by 89th Bde. of Indian 7th Division on June 21. By the 29th when Indian 7th Division had assumed complete command of the whole of the southern sector the Japanese had gained considerable ground and 4/8th G.R. in Nyaungkashe were isolated. All attempts to relieve them were unsuccessful and on July 7 they were instructed to destroy their guns and equipment and withdrew during the night of July 7/8. 33rd Bde. arriving in this area, formed a corridor extending south-west from Satthwagyon along which the Gurkhas could withdraw. Carrying all their wounded and most of their equipment, the Gurkhas formed a hollow square and waded through the water and the mud to safety. The Japanese withdrew at the same time and ultimately the fighting in this area died down.

Operations on the Mawchi road continued throughout June and July and Indian 19th Division made steady if slow progress, despite the resistance that was encountered and in spite of the rain and the mud. On the Taunggyi road the opposition was not so stubborn and Taunggyi itself was entered on July 25. The other formations of IV Corps were all engaged in active patrolling.

Information concerning the intention of the Japanese in the Pegu Yomas to break out towards the east was obtained by patrols of 'V' Force and on July 4 an operation order giving all the details, save only the actual date, was captured. From other sources it was concluded that the date was July 20. This information enabled IV Corps to post its formations to block every one of the proposed lines of escape. Indian 17th Division, based on Penwegon, and Indian 19th Division, in the Pyu Chaung–Toungoo area, were the two divisions that were affected. Four battalions of infantry and a field battery from Indian 20th Division were moved from the west of the Pegu Yomas to strengthen the forces waiting to block the passage of the Japanese to the east.

The Japanese held to their plan to the very last detail. They began to move on July 19, when a party of about a hundred of them attacked a platoon post of 48th Bde. of Indian 17th Division at Pado and was repulsed. From then onwards until August 4 and in the sectors held by both Indian divisions, party followed party at intervals along the same tracks to run into well prepared ambushes and to suffer very heavy casualties. Such as did get across the road were harried by mortar and artillery fire and chased by infantry. Lying in wait for them along the

CAPTURE OF RANGOON—CLOSING PHASE 549

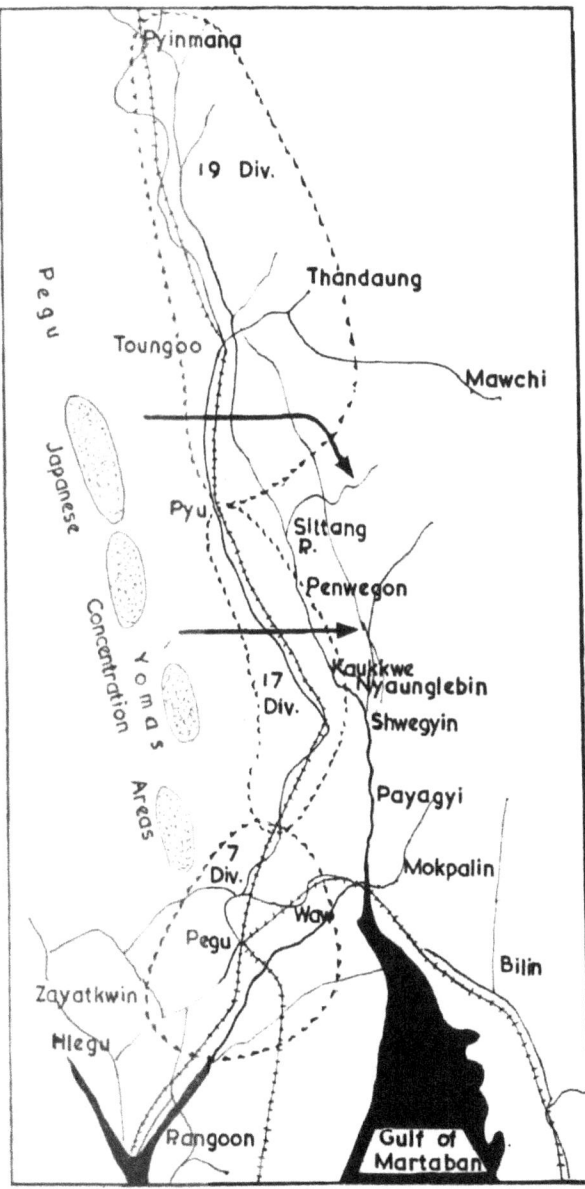

Fig. 72. The Battle of the Breakout

Sittang River was 114th Bde. of Indian 7th Division, which had relieved Indian 5th Division. The Burmese Patriot Forces constituted yet another obstacle. The swift-flowing river was greatly swollen, being at this time about 300 yards across. Of the 16,000–19,000 who set out not more than 4,000–5,000, it was estimated, reached the east bank of the Sittang and escaped to the south.

These were not hale men. Because of the complete disorganisation that had overtaken most of the Japanese formations, they had no transport save a few bullock carts; their supplies were exhausted and they were forced to subsist on what they could find by foraging; the monsoon was in full blast and for them there was no shelter; their sick, and they were very numerous, could be offered nothing and between one and two thousand of them, it was estimated, too weak to march, had been left in the Yomas to die. Yet the question of surrender did not arise. IV Corps' losses during the 'battle of the breakout' were 95 killed and 322 wounded.

On August 6 the first atomic bomb destroyed Hiroshima and on the 9th the second fell on Nagasaki. On August 12 Japan surrendered unconditionally.

MEDICAL COVER

The field ambulances with a division during the swift advance towards Rangoon leap-frogged one over the other and in succession opened to admit casualties. Having got these back to the nearest M.S.U. attached to a field ambulance in the series and sited near a light aircraft airstrip, the field ambulance closed and bounded forward. Since casualties were few the divisional field ambulances encountered no difficulty which they did not quickly overcome. To give a detailed account of the work of the divisional medical units of all the divisions is unnecessary and would be profitless. It will suffice to consider the medical services of two divisions, of Indian 5th Division as this moved down the axis of the railway and road and of Indian 20th Division as this moved southward from Prome.

INDIAN 5TH DIVISION

It was accepted that the advance to the south would be swift, that a number of relatively minor actions would be fought against Japanese rearguards, that casualties would not be numerous and that evacuation by air would at all times be possible, though perhaps with temporary interruptions on account of the weather. The field ambulances were brigaded and travelling as light as possible, were to leap-frog over each other. In the event, the simple arrangements that were made proved to be more than adequate. The collection, treatment and evacuation of casualties proceeded smoothly.

March 12, 1945   10 (Ind.) Fd. Amb. by road from the area of Jorhat to Palel and thence by air to Meiktila.

         20   75 (Ind.) Fd. Amb., attached 161st Bde., from the Jorhat area to Kamye where it opened its M.D.S.
45 (Ind.) Fd. Amb., 123rd Bde., to Kamye.

April   1   75 (Ind.) Fd. Amb. to Meiktila where it opened to admit all IV Corps medical cases.
45 (Ind.) Fd. Amb. to Meiktila, remaining closed.

CAPTURE OF RANGOON—CLOSING PHASE

April	6	45 (Ind.) Fd. Amb. to Kandaung.
	7	A.D.M.S. to Kandaung, with divisional H.Q.
	8	75 (Ind.) Fd. Amb. to Yindaw.
	10	45 (Ind.) Fd. Amb. in Yetlet.
	12	A.D.M.S. in Yindaw.
	13	75 (Ind.) Fd. Amb. at Milestone 305. Evacuation by light aircraft.
	14	45 (Ind.) Fd. Amb. at Milestone 300. Evacuation through 75 at Milestone 305.
	15	A.D.M.S. in Tatkon, Milestone 278.
		75 (Ind.) Fd. Amb. open in Tatkon. Evacuation by light aircraft.
	17	10 (Ind.) Fd. Amb., attached 9th Bde., took over duties at Tatkon airstrip.
	18	75 (Ind.) Fd. Amb. to Shwemyo, Milestone 271.
	19	A.D.M.S. to Milestone 272, with divisional H.Q.
	20	75 (Ind.) Fd. Amb. to Milestone 249. Evacuation from light airstrip.
		45 (Ind.) Fd. Amb. to Milestone 251.
		A.D.M.S. to Milestone 250.
	21	10 (Ind.) Fd. Amb. to Milestone 250.
		45 (Ind.) Fd. Amb. to Milestone 220.
	22	45 (Ind.) Fd. Amb. to Milestone 171. Evacuation by light aircraft from strip at Milestone 171, by Dakota from heavy airstrip at Milestone 173.
		9 (Ind.) M.S.U. joins 45 (Ind.) Fd. Amb.
		75 (Ind.) Fd. Amb. to Milestone 176.
	23	10 (Ind.) Fd. Amb. to Milestone 232 u/c corps.
	24	Medical stores, captured in Toungoo, distributed among medical units.
		Indian 17th Division into the lead.
	26	75 (Ind.) Fd. Amb. to Milestone 143. Evacuation by light aircraft.
	27	45 (Ind.) Fd. Amb. to Milestone 157.
	28	A.D.M.S. to Milestone 144.
	29	45 (Ind.) Fd. Amb. to Milestone 99.
		75 (Ind.) Fd. Amb. to Milestone 96.
May	1	75 (Ind.) Fd. Amb. to Milestone $92\frac{1}{2}$. Evacuation from both light and heavy airstrips.
		45 (Ind.) Fd. Amb. opens at Milestone 99. Evacuation through 75 (Ind.) Fd. Amb.
	2–4	No movement of field ambulances. No evacuation because of heavy rain.
	5	45 (Ind.) Fd. Amb. to Milestone $62\frac{1}{2}$. Evacuation by light aircraft.
	6	75 (Ind.) Fd. Amb. to Milestone $64\frac{1}{2}$.

May	7	75 (Ind.) Fd. Amb. in Waw to serve 9th Bde. Evacuation through 45 (Ind.) Fd. Amb. at Milestone 62½.
	9	5 (Ind.) M.S.U. joined the division and was attached to 75 (Ind.) Fd. Amb. in Waw. 13 (Ind.) C.C.S. to Pegu.
	11	Heavy rain prevented all evacuation. 45 (Ind.) Fd. Amb. at Milestone 62½ was holding over 200 patients.
	12	10 (Ind.) Fd. Amb. which had been held up on Lewe airfield near Pyinmana by the rain, rejoined division.
	13–14	With an improvement in the weather air evacuation was resumed and all patients held by 45 and 75 (Ind.) Fd. Ambs. were got away.
	15	10 (Ind.) Fd. Amb. sent a company into Waw to relieve 75 (Ind.) Fd. Amb. with 9th Bde. 75 (Ind.) Fd. Amb. to Pegu leaving 5 (Ind.) M.S.U. with 10 (Ind.) Fd. Amb.
	16	45 (Ind.) Fd. Amb. with 55 (Ind.) Dent. Unit and 1 (Ind.) Dent. Mech. Unit to Milestone 29, Hlegu, where it opened in the small local hospital. 10 (Ind.) Fd. Amb. to Milestone 62½.
	23	5 (Ind.) M.S.U. from Waw joined 45 (Ind.) Fd. Amb. in Hlegu.
	24	45 (Ind.) Fd. Amb. in Hlegu opened to admit sick among IV Corps troops west of the Pegu River. 13 (Ind.) C.C.S. to take the sick from east of the river.

By the end of June, A.D.M.S. and all the divisional medical units, save 10 (Ind.) Fd. Amb. in Hlegu, were in Mingaladon.

TABLE 43

Indian 5th Division. Admissions to Medical Units. April–June 1945.

Week ending	Rate per 1,000 per diem
April 21	0·77
28	0·54
May 5	0·72
19	0·93
June 2	1·21
9	0·95
16	0·94
23	1·19

CAPTURE OF RANGOON—CLOSING PHASE

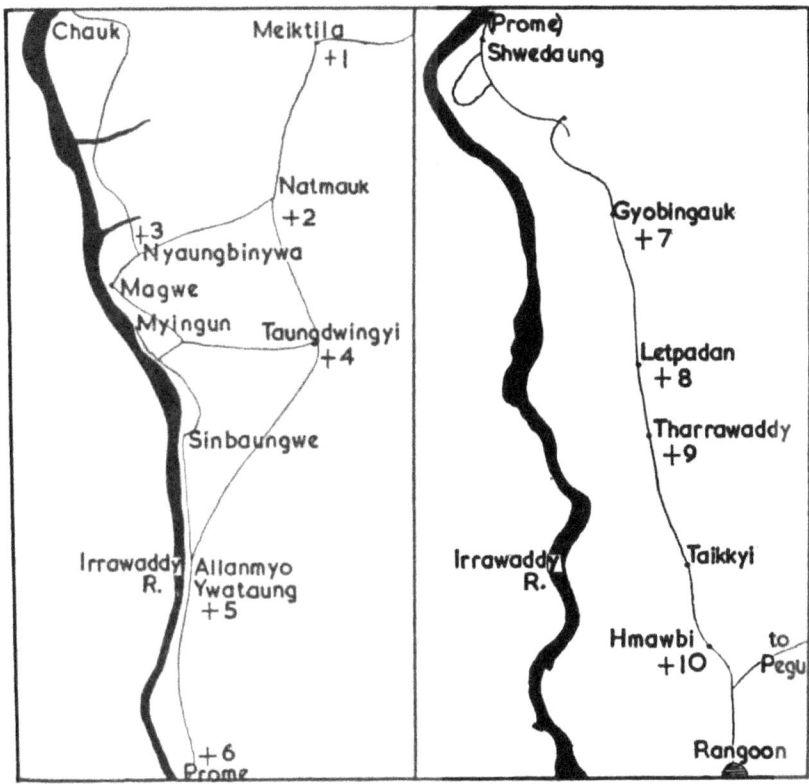

FIG. 73. Indian 20th Division. The Movements of the Divisional Field Ambulances during the Advance into Burma. Meiktila–Hmawbi

1.	55	(Ind.)	Fd.	Amb.	M.D.S.	April	10
2.	59	,,	,,	,,	M.D.S.	,,	12
	55	,,	,,	,,	M.D.S.	,,	14–27
3.	55	,,	,,	,,	A.D.S.		
4.	59	,,	,,	,,	A.D.S.	,,	14–May 4
5.	42	,,	,,	,,	M.D.S.	,,	30–May 5
6.	55	,,	,,	,,	M.D.S.	May	4–29
7.	59	,,	,,	,,	M.D.S.	,,	9–28
8.	42	,,	,,	,,	M.D.S.		
9.	59	,,	,,	,,		,,	28
10.	55	,,	,,	,,		,,	30

INDIAN 20TH DIVISION

The advance of this division from Meiktila southwards took the form of a series of bounds, each of about 50–70 miles. With each of the brigades of the division was a strong A.D.S. 55 (Ind.) Fd. Amb. opened its M.D.S. in the *phongyi kyaung* in Natmauk on April 14 and here it remained until the 27th. This unit dealt with the casualties from the fighting around Magwe. During this action an A.D.S. of 55 (Ind.) Fd.

Amb. served with 80th Bde. Evacuation was to the medical centre at Myitche which XXXIII Corps had taken over from IV Corps.

59 (Ind.) Fd. Amb. was the next to open its M.D.S., in Taungdwingyi, April 14–May 4. Then 42 (Ind.) Fd. Amb. set out with an armoured column for Prome and opened its M.D.S. in Ywataung, a few miles south of Allanmyo on April 30. The light aircraft were operating far beyond their economic range and therefore had to carry petrol for use on their return journey. The rains now came to make flying at all times difficult and sometimes impossible. On May 2, ten aircraft took off from the strip at Ywataung and every one of them was forced to turn back. Later in the day they tried again but only got as far as Magwe. Corps then sent 14 (Ind.) C.C.S. forward to Allanmyo where it opened on May 10. 55 (Ind.) Fd. Amb. had opened its M.D.S. in Prome on May 4. Evacuation was to Allanmyo.

To cover 32nd Bde's. southwards dash 59 (Ind.) Fd. Amb. opened its M.D.S. in the civil hospital in Gyobingauk on the Prome–Rangoon road. On May 15 at Milestone 60 the leading elements of 32nd Bde. met those of 71st Bde. of Indian 26th Division moving north from Rangoon.

Towards the end of May the divisional medical units moved into their monsoon quarters, 55 (Ind.) Fd. Amb. in Hmawbi, 59 (Ind.) Fd. Amb. in Tharrawaddy and 42 (Ind.) Fd. Amb. in Letpadan, all on the Rangoon–Prome road.

In this division it was the custom for each field ambulance to place a strong A.D.S. with its brigade during operational periods. This A.D.S. was not under the command of the brigade but was in support of it. It always had either the officer commanding the field ambulance or else the second-in-command in charge of it, acting as S.M.O. brigade, and at least two other medical officers as well as an officer in charge of the stretcher-bearers of the field ambulance. The rest of the field ambulance —H.Q. and one company—together formed the M.D.S. and the M.D.Ss. leap-frogged forward.

In addition to the three field ambulances the division had with it 10 (Ind.) M.S.U., sometimes 15 (Ind.) M.S.U. as well, a surgical team from one of the C.C.Ss. or from 5 (Ind.) Beach Medical Unit, three Indian dental units, 20 (Ind.) A.M.U., 26 (Ind.) Fd. Hyg. Sec., a platoon of 4 (Ind.) Bearer Coy., detachments of 60 and 61 M.A.Ss., a platoon of the A.F.S.,A.C.C. and during February and March, a field transfusion unit. Sub-sections of the A.M.U. and field hygiene section were attached to the A.D.Ss. with the brigades. The jeep ambulances of the A.F.S. were usually attached either to the R.A.Ps. or else to the A.D.Ss. During the advance from Meiktila each A.D.S. was given transport sufficient to meet its own needs and the rest of the vehicles were pooled. The method of employment of the transport can be illustrated as follows:

CAPTURE OF RANGOON—CLOSING PHASE

13.4.45   M.T. allotted to 59 (Ind.) Fd. Amb.
14.4.45   59 (Ind.) Fd. Amb. moved from Meiktila to Natmauk.
15.4.45   M.T. returned to Meiktila.
16.4.45   M.T. allotted to 55 (Ind.) Fd. Amb. and this unit moved from Meiktila to Natmauk.
17.4.45   M.T. returned to Meiktila.
18.4.45   M.T. moved medical ancillary units from Meiktila to Natmauk.
19.4.45   M.T. returned to Meiktila.
20.4.45   M.T. allotted to 42 (Ind.) Fd. Amb. and this unit moved from Meiktila to Natmauk.
21.4.45   M.T. moved 59 (Ind.) Fd. Amb. from Natmauk to Taungdwingyi, and so on.

Normally the A.D.S. with a brigade leaguered within the brigade's perimeter. On the move the A.D.S. was responsible for its own defence. The M.D.S. that was functioning in the vicinity of divisional H.Q. was protected by the divisional defences and if the division moved off, leaving the M.D.S. behind, a platoon of the divisional defence battalion was left with it. Transfusion supplies were flown from the corps medical centre in returning light aircraft. The division itself provided about 50 per cent. of the blood that was needed. The refrigerator of the F.T.U. was mounted on an antiquated 3-ton lorry which was constantly breaking down. Medical stores were obtained from the sub-depot of medical stores at the corps medical centre. They were brought forward by the light aircraft. In this division the office of the A.D.M.S. was never split between the main and rear divisional headquarters; it remained complete with Main H.Q. and there either the A.D.M.S. or his D.A.D.M.S. was always to be found.

Following the re-entry into Rangoon, Indian 20th Division was relatively free from active operations for some three months. It was stretched from Hmawbi to Letpadan along the Rangoon–Prome road. To the north of it were troops of Indian 7th Division and 22nd E.A. Bde. 14 (Ind.) C.C.S. was open in Paungde and 67 (Ind.) Fd. Amb. (XXXIII Corps) in Prome both under A.D.M.S. 253 Sub-area. 42 (Ind.) Fd. Amb., with sub-sections of the anti-malaria unit and of the field hygiene section, was in Letpadan. It staged patients travelling from 67 (Ind.) Fd. Amb. and 14 (Ind.) C.C.S. on their way to Rangoon. Its officers ran clinics, with the help of Karen nurses, paid as interpreters, to serve the civilian population. 59 (Ind.) Fd. Amb. was in Tharrawaddy and in about the best building in the town. It functioned as a C.C.S. and could accommodate 150 patients. This unit did much to help South Burma District and I Area (Rangoon). Two nursing officers from S.B. District and later three from 19 (Ind.) C.C.S. were attached to this unit. Also attached to it were the three dental units, 10 (Ind.) M.S.U., the A.M.U. and the field hygiene section. 55 (Ind.) Fd. Amb. was in

Hmawbi in the agricultural college buildings and assumed responsibility for all casualties south of Taikkyi.

Towards the end of July, 19 (Ind.) C.C.S. moved from Magwe to Taikkyi. 10 (Ind.) M.S.U. then left the division and returned to IV Corps. Evacuation from this C.C.S. was by road to Rangoon, 180 miles away. The road did not stand up to the heavy military traffic and the railway between Prome and Paungde was used. Between Thonze and Rangoon the railway was not yet suitable for the evacuation of casualties. The Rangoon hospitals, three months after the reoccupation of the capital, were not in a position to hold cases and so a very considerable number of light cases were being evacuated to India and lost to the division. With the coming of 19 (Ind.) C.C.S., Indian 20th Division was able to retain more of its casualties in the divisional area.

Three battalions of this division were involved in the operations in the Pegu Yomas during June. Later four battalions were switched to IV Corps front for the final battle. Much of the fighting took place in heavy rain and in flooded country. Yet there was no rise in the sick-rate; there was a slight rise in the incidence of foot troubles but these quickly cleared up when the fighting finished and when the men could take care of their feet.

INDIAN 26TH DIVISION. OPERATION 'DRACULA'

Late in March 1945 the divisional medical units moved to the concentration area at Gonchwein to prepare for Operation 'Dracula'. 1 and 48 (Ind.) Fd. Ambs. embarked at Kyaukpyu on May 1, 46 (Ind.) Fd. Amb. on the 4th. On May 2, 1 and 48 (Ind.) Fd. Ambs. arrived off Rangoon. The M.D.S. of 1 (Ind.) Fd. Amb. (36th Bde.) landed on the west bank of the Hlaing (Rangoon) River, 18 miles south of the capital, at 0700 hours. No opposition was encountered and there were no casualties. One officer and twelve I.O.Rs. were sent from the beach by L.C.I. to Elephant Point to tend and evacuate about 30 casualties. This party rejoined the M.D.S. in Rangoon, where it had established itself near St. John's Convent School, on the following day. On the 5th, 4 casualties were evacuated from the M.D.S. by means of impressed vehicles and *via* a naval motor launch to a hospital ship lying off 45 miles from Rangoon. 6 (Ind.) M.S.U. arrived and was attached to the M.D.S. Its usefulness was somewhat impaired by lack of equipment; this had been lost on a L.C.T. which had struck a mine as it moved up the river. A.D.M.S. 26th Division lost his life when this craft was sunk. A number of vehicles, having been landed, reached the M.D.S.; they included one ambulance car, one jeep and the transport of 11 (Ind.) M.S.U.

On May 6 the officer commanding 28 F.T.U., which had landed,

CAPTURE OF RANGOON—CLOSING PHASE

made an inspection of hospital facilities in Rangoon. Two more ambulance cars reached the M.D.S. as did also two 15-cwt. trucks. During the next eight days evacuations numbered:

7th	.	26	11th	.	27
8th	.	27	12th	.	26
9th	.	20	13th	.	35
10th	.	24	14th	.	28

Three more vehicles reached the unit on the 7th; its unaccompanied stores and three ambulance cars arrived on the 8th; on the 10th, two Karen nurses and on the 15th one Karen and one Chinese reported to the M.D.S. for duty. On the 12th, 28 F.T.U. was attached to 48 (Ind.) Fd. Amb. and 6 (Ind.) M.S.U. to 15 (Ind.) C.C.S., then functioning in Rangoon. On the 16th the unit began to prepare to leave Burma; its patients were transferred to 1 (Ind.) M.F.T.U. which had opened on the site of the M.D.S. on the 23rd and on the 28th, 1 (Ind.) Fd. Amb. sailed from Rangoon for Madras.

During its brief stay in Rangoon the M.D.S. of 1 (Ind.) Fd. Amb. had admitted and treated 19 officers, 4 A.O.Rs., 200 B.O.Rs., 381 I.O.Rs. and 65 civilians, a total of 669.

46 (Ind.) Fd. Amb. (with 4th Bde.) arrived off Rangoon on May 6. Its commanding officer, 'A' Coy. and a detachment of 2 (Ind.) Bearer Coy. went ashore and proceeded to the staging camp which was in the buildings of the Rangoon General Hospital. On the following day the rest of the unit landed and were billeted in Campbell Road. The M.D.S. was then opened in No. 10, Campbell Road. The unit had very little to do and on the 21st it began to leave Burma by way of the staging camp in the general hospital, embarking on the M.V. *Devonshire* for Madras on the 22nd.

The light M.D.S. of 48 (Ind.) Fd. Amb. (71st Bde.) landed from a L.C.I. on May 2 on one of the chosen beaches in the Hlaing River and moved to Kyauktan by motor launch. On the following day the rest of the unit landed at Kyauktan and moved to Syriam by M.T. on the 4th. On the 5th the M.D.S. moved out to Rawlinson Barracks, Mingaladon where the light M.D.S. opened for the treatment of the minor sick. Evacuation was to 1 (Ind.) Fd. Amb. in Rangoon. The military cantonment at Mingaladon was in a most insanitary state, the buildings had been badly damaged by Allied bombing and had been ransacked by looters. Mosquitoes abounded and since no D.D.T. was available, 'Skat' (D.M.P.) was used in its place. The unit spent most of its time in cleaning up the area. Admissions were very few, which was just as well for the unit's equipment had gone down with the vessel that had struck a mine and was being salvaged.

On May 15, 48 (Ind.) Fd. Amb. moved to Hmawbi to open there in the buildings of the Agricultural College. A light section was sent to Taikkyi as was also the light M.D.S. a little later. Accommodation for these was found in the local hospital. 11 (Ind.) M.S.U., 28 F.T.U. and 2 (Ind.) Bearer Coy. were all attached to 48 (Ind.) Fd. Amb. To serve outlying battalions light sections were sited in Myaungtanga and in Wanetchaung. Evacuation was by road and rail to 15 (Ind.) C.C.S. in Rangoon.

On May 25 the unit moved with 71st Bde. into Rangoon and was accommodated in the Secretariat building. This proving to be most unsatisfactory, permission was obtained for the unit to move into five bomb damaged houses in Windermere Gardens. There the unit remained with very little to do, until it sailed from Rangoon for Madras on June 13.

MEDICAL ARRANGEMENTS

From what has been told of the system of supply that was to be adopted to serve XXXIII and IV Corps in their advance on Rangoon, it will have been reasonably concluded that the system of casualty evacuation that would be developed would conform to the same general plan. The difficulties that stand in the way of bringing forward to it the *matériel* that a fighting formation needs are, in general, the same as those that stand in the way of getting its casualties back from the forward area to the rear. The methods that are adopted to solve the problems of supply are, in general, the same as those which are employed in casualty evacuation. The advance was planned to be swift and no great attention was to be paid during the actual advance to the building up of a secure L. of C. This being so, there could be no place for such large and cumbersome medical units as general hospitals in the exceedingly long and narrow salients that the two corps were intending to carve into Japanese-occupied Burma. Such units could not hope to keep pace with the formations they were intended to serve. It had already been learnt, before the Irrawaddy was crossed, that, granting evacuation by air was possible, it was sufficient to provide the corps with very light medical cover, this taking the form of a C.C.S. and a M.F.T.U., with evacuation thereto by means of light aircraft and evacuation from this corps medical centre by means of heavy transport aircraft returning to the supply airfields. This was the system that was adopted for the advance on Rangoon. It is of interest to note that the M.F.T.U. in Burma came to assume the same functions as did the F.D.S. in Europe; it provided accommodation and medical care and enabled patients to be held in the forward area. In Europe it had been found that the best arrangement was to combine the F.D.S. with one or more F.S.Us. and a F.T.U. to form an A.S.C. In Burma the practice developed of combining a C.C.S. and a M.F.T.U., together with a variety of ancillary units, such as a mobile X-ray Unit, a field laboratory, a dental unit, to form a corps medical centre.

CAPTURE OF RANGOON—CLOSING PHASE

Two C.C.Ss. and two M.F.T.Us. were allotted by Army to each of the corps and around these the corps formed two medical centres. As the advance left one corps medical centre far behind, that is, beyond the range of the light aircraft, another was established out of units provided, if necessary, from Army reserve, the rearward C.C.S., M.F.T.U. and ancillary units then reverting to Army reserve. Usually it was the C.C.S. of the C.C.S.-M.F.T.U. pair that closed first, emptying its remaining patients into the M.F.T.U. to await evacuation. Exceptionally it was necessary to clear the M.F.T.U. by mass evacuation to an advanced base hospital. This procedure was adopted with reluctance for it involved the evacuation from the forward area of relatively light cases. As the advance continued M.F.T.Us. were shed in rear areas to look after the L. of C. personnel, but since they had no surgical facilities they were not adequately equipped to serve as area hospitals.

In Burma the M.F.T.Us. proved their worth over and over again both when they were used in the fight against malaria and later when they were used to provide holding facilities in the forward zone for such sick and injured as did not need high-grade nursing skill.

On April 4, when IV Corps H.Q. opened in Meiktila, the first of the Army units, 24 (Ind.) C.C.S. was flown in from Inbaung. On its heels came 26 (Ind.) C.C.S. Indian 17th Division was heavily engaged about Pyawbwe; Indian 19th Division had passed from the command of XXXIII Corps to Army and had come down from the north of Meiktila and Indian 20th Division was passing through Meiktila on its way to the Irrawaddy axis. The Army medical centre was to provide cover for these formations. Considerable fighting was in progress and the strain upon the centre, while it was forming, was heavy. Fortunately evacuation presented no unusual problems and so the centre was rapidly cleared by air evacuation to Myitche or direct to Comilla. The corps and the divisional field ambulances were all open and were evacuating direct to the airstrip. During the first half of April the average daily admission-rate was between 200–300, with a large proportion of battle casualties. By this time both the C.C.Ss. were well established and all evacuation was direct to Comilla. Because of the large numbers being admitted the C.C.Ss. could not hold cases, other than the immobiles, longer than 48 hours. Inevitably therefore during this period many minor sick were evacuated to Bengal.

The centre was sited on a large promontory projecting into one of the lakes, some 1,000 yds. long and 1,000 yds. deep. The area had been the scene of very bitter fighting and was covered with the litter of battle, fox-holes, bunkers, slit trenches, broken-down tanks and the like. In one section of the area was a British burial ground. There were three damaged houses in the area, the two C.C.Ss. each used one of them as an operation block and the third was converted into a Sister's mess. As time passed the area was cleared and the different units established themselves in regular lines. The centre came to include two C.C.Ss. and three M.F.T.Us. together with a number of ancillary units. A medical staging area in which medical units in transit could be accommodated was developed.

During the advance the airfield at Comilla came to be too far away and so casualties were switched to the Akyab and Ramree staging centre *en route* for Comilla and later to Chittagong whence they were evacuated by ambulance train to the advanced base hospitals. The time spent on the road by casualties was considerably prolonged by this arrangement and it was fortunate that the numbers requiring evacuation became greatly diminished during this phase of the operation.

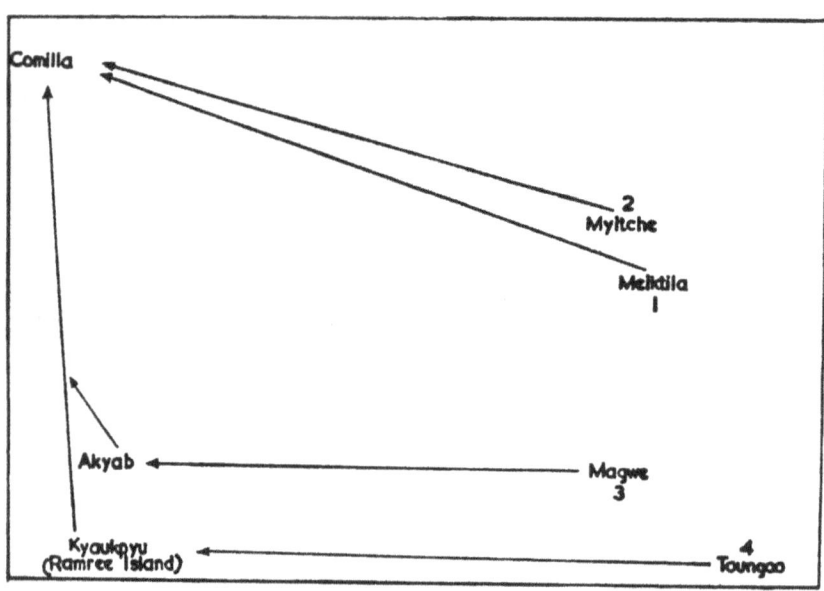

FIG. 74. Fourteenth Army. Air Evacuation Arrangements.
End of March 1945 onwards

1. Army Medical Centre
    24 and 26 (Ind.) C.C.Ss.; 6 and 8 (Ind.) M.F.T.Us.
2. XXXIII Corps' Medical Centre
    14 and 19 (Ind.) C.C.Ss.; 4 (Ind.) M.F.T.U.
3. XXXIII Corps' Medical Centre
    19 (Ind.) C.C.S. and 9 (Ind.) M.F.T.U.
4. IV Corps' Medical Centre
    16 (Ind.) C.C.S. and 11 (Ind.) M.F.T.U.
In Ramree Island
    28 (W.A.) C.C.S., 23 and 25 (Ind.) C.C.Ss. (in Kyaukpyu)
    125 I.G.H.(C.), 30 (W.A.) C.C.S., 12 (Ind.) M.F.T.U., 110 (E.A.) C.R.S.
In Akyab
    95 I.G.H.(C.), 15 (Ind.) C.C.S.
In Comilla
    14 B.G.H., 150 E.A.G.H.

During April the total number of casualties evacuated by light aircraft from IV and XXXIII Corps' areas was 4,950, the total number carried by transport aircraft, 4,720.

It was intended to establish an advanced base hospital centre in Rangoon to consist of 10,000 beds. But because the end of the fighting came so swiftly this number was reached only after the campaign was ended and then only as an emergency measure to cope with the sudden influx of R.A.P.W.I.

The hospital centre in Rangoon was designed to hold such as could be expected to recover within three months and included a number of special units such as a maxillo-facial unit and those dealing with head injuries, severe burns, severe ophthalmic injuries and certain types of psychiatric disorder. The first of the hospitals to reach Rangoon were 38 B.G.H. and 58 I.G.H. Evacuation from Rangoon was:

    by rail to Mandalay and Prome;
    by light aircraft to Prome (and from Magwe to Meiktila);
    by transport aircraft to Meiktila, Myitkyina and Kalewa;
                   to Kyaukpyu and Akyab;
                   to the base hospitals in India;
    by sea to the base hospitals in India.

XXXIII CORPS

When XXXIII Corps was switched to the Irrawaddy axis and IV Corps to the railway axis there was no corresponding switch of the corps medical units; it was decided that the centres already in being should cover the formations moving into their respective spheres. 8 (Ind.) C.C.S. was moved from Shwebo to Tada-U to cover Indian 19th Division operating south of Mandalay and Indian 20th Division in the Kyaukse area. 16 (Ind.) C.C.S. was moved from Shwebo to Kinywa in preparation for a later forward move to Meiktila by road and thence by air to Toungoo. These moves left only 10 (Ind.) M.F.T.U. in the Shwebo centre and this unit was handed over to 505 District (a formation which followed the Army, taking over the administration of rear areas) to cover the comparatively small number of troops in the Shwebo–Mandalay area. Eventually this unit was split between these two places.

The cover for XXXIII Corps now became:

(a) The Meiktila centre which was being built up by Army from the original centre at Inbaung for the diagonal move across; and

(b) The Myitche centre which had been covering the crossing of the Irrawaddy by IV Corps at Pakokku.

As Indian 7th and 20th Divisions advanced down the Irrawaddy axis the Myitche centre was moved forward piecemeal to cover them. First 19 (Ind.) C.C.S. moved by road to Magwe at the end of April and this unit was quickly followed by 9 (Ind.) M.F.T.U. partly by road and

TABLE 44

XXXIII Corps. Casualties. March 17–May 12, 1945

Formation	Week ending March 17 Strength	Casualties	Week ending March 24 Strength	Casualties
2nd Div.	15,877	69	15,682	70
Ind. 7th Div.	—	—	—	—
Ind. 19th Div.	18,272	70	19,222	110
Ind. 20th Div.	18,399	175	17,870	130
Ind. 268th Bde.	3,550	22	2,290	4
Ind. 254th Tk. Bde	6,636	—	6,636	7

Formation	Week ending March 31 Strength	Casualties	Week ending April 7 Strength	Casualties
2nd Div.	15,636	11	15,425	17
Ind. 7th Div.	18,339	31	19,247	53
Ind. 19th Div.	19,235	56	—	—
Ind. 20th Div.	19,165	131	16,628	38
Ind. 268th Bde.	1,829	7	2,541	—
Ind. 254th Tk. Bde.	6,701	8	5,815	5

Formation	Week ending April 14 Strength	Casualties	Week ending April 21 Strength	Casualties
2nd Div.	—	—	—	—
Ind. 7th Div.	19,192	46	18,432	76
Ind. 19th Div.	—	—	—	—
Ind. 20th Div.	18,628	11	19,032	24
Ind. 268th Bde.	2,543	—	2,674	—
Ind. 254th Tk. Bde.	5,765	1	5,873	1

Formation	Week ending April 28 Strength	Casualties	Week ending May 5 Strength	Casualties
2nd Div.	—	—	—	—
Ind. 7th Div.	18,774	19	18,621	26
Ind. 19th Div.	—	—	—	—
Ind. 20th Div.	18,912	75	18,501	74
Ind. 268th Bde.	2,732	—	3,331	—
Ind. 254th Tk. Bde.	5,768	10	5,748	19

Formation	Week ending May 12 Strength	Casualties
2nd Div.	—	—
Ind. 7th Div.	17,424	43
Ind. 19th Div.	—	—
Ind. 20th Div.	18,949	51
Ind. 268th Bde.	—	—
Ind. 254th Tk. Bde.	4,746	9

CAPTURE OF RANGOON—CLOSING PHASE

partly by river. When Allanmyo was occupied 14 (Ind.) C.C.S. leap-frogged through to establish itself there. This was the arrangement that sufficed until Rangoon was entered. The one remaining unit at Myitche, 4 (Ind.) M.F.T.U., moved by road to join the Army centre at Meiktila.

IV CORPS

After the resistance at Shwemyo Bluff had been overcome the speed of IV Corps' advance quickened. 16 (Ind.) C.C.S. was in Meiktila, waiting to fly in to the first suitable airfield that was overrun. It had been intended to place it on the Lewe group of airfields south of Pyinmana which was the limit for satisfactory evacuation to Meiktila by light aircraft. However, the advance of Indian 5th Division was so headlong that it became apparent that Lewe would become out of satisfactory range of the forward troops before the C.C.S. could move in and open and before the light plane squadron could be transferred. When Toungoo fell on April 22 it was decided to put 16 (Ind.) C.C.S. on the airfield there. The C.C.S. with its nursing officers, flew in and began to function on the 25th. Until the light squadron had moved its base from Meiktila to Toungoo evacuation was not smooth. There was a temporary shortage of petrol and the weather was worsening. Fortunately casualties were light.

The C.C.S. was no sooner opened in Toungoo than the forward troops were almost out of range. On April 29, Indian 17th Division had captured Payagyi, the first of the Pegu group of airfields. Indian 17th Division had a M.D.S., with a mobile surgical unit attached, on this airstrip and a limited number of casualties were flown back direct to base but for the most part evacuation was by light plane to Toungoo. The approach of the monsoon made it imperative to find accommodation for 13 (Ind.) C.C.S. and Pegu was the only possible site. On May 2 twenty-four plane loads of 13 (Ind.) C.C.S. were flown to Payagyi, ready to move into Pegu as soon as resistance there had ceased. May 3 was a day of heavy rain and all but two of the remaining sorties of 13 (Ind.) C.C.S. were abortive; indeed elements of the unit were scattered on five different airfields in Burma and East Bengal. On May 5 a suitable site in Pegu was selected and the unit began to move in. The light squadron did not move from Toungoo to Pegu but began to return to India. Evacuation to Pegu therefore had to be by road. The heavy rain temporarily brought evacuation by heavy aircraft to an end but as casualties at this time were light, the reduced C.C.S., the corps and divisional field ambulances were able to deal with all that came in. On May 9 the weather improved and air evacuation to base was resumed. On the 10th the rest of the C.C.S. was flown in. Towards the end of the month weather conditions enforced the abandonment of the Pegu airfield and evacuation by road to Rangoon was instituted.

When the advance of IV Corps to the south ended at Hlegu the corps was strung out along the trunk road from Meiktila to Pegu and medical cover had to be provided all along the route. The light plane squadron that had been so active in casualty evacuation had been withdrawn. The road surface was bad in most parts. The arrangements made by IV Corps were as follows: In the northern sector at Meiktila was an Army medical centre, evacuation from the Kalaw area thereto being by ambulance car. In the central sector there was a IV Corps' medical centre at Toungoo consisting of 16 (Ind.) C.C.S., 11 (Ind.) M.F.T.U. and ancillary units. This centre dealt with casualties from Indian 19th Division operating along the Toungoo–Mawchi road and engaged in intensive jungle fighting. From Toungoo evacuation to the base hospitals was by Dakota. On the airstrip at Toungoo a C.A.E.U. was established. To Toungoo evacuation was by road. There had been considerable difficulty in finding a suitable site for the M.F.T.U. in Toungoo for the area was very badly fouled and had become covered with secondary jungle. It was also very liable to flooding. After much searching a site was selected, cleared and drained. In the southern sector of the corps' area, 13 (Ind.) C.C.S. was sited in Pegu, in a school building on the moat bund. The great disadvantage of this site was that it was restricted so that any

TABLE 45

IV Corps. Total Sick-rates per 1,000 per Diem. May 5–September 15, 1945

Week ending	IV Corps	Corps Tps.	Ind. 5th Div.	Ind. 7th Div.	Ind. 17th Div.	Ind. 19th Div.	22nd E.A. Bde.
5.5.45	1·05	1·03	0·47	—	0·52	2·31	—
12.5.45	1·32	1·10	1·08	—	0·89	2·51	—
19.5.45	1·29	0·69	1·08	—	0·92	2·79	—
26.5.45	1·94	1·20	1·53	—	1·18	2·81	—
2.6.45	1·89	1·00	1·57	—	1·10	3·64	—
9.6.45	2·00	0·65	1·20	—	1·41	4·38	—
16.6.45	1·68	0·99	1·10	—	1·54	2·80	—
23.6.45	1·52	0·81	1·20	—	1·67	2·37	—
30.6.45	1·50	0·84	0·70	—	1·49	2·93	—
7.7.45	1·98	1·02	—	2·41	2·02	2·47	—
14.7.45	1·90	1·38	—	2·19	1·60	2·16	—
21.7.45	1·67	1·19	—	2·09	1·34	2·00	—
28.7.45	1·29	0·96	—	1·31	1·34	1·60	—
4.8.45	1·28	0·82	—	1·45	1·59	1·47	—
11.8.45	1·34	0·90	—	1·29	1·60	1·64	—
18.8.45	1·27	0·95	—	1·72	1·32	1·10	—
25.8.45	1·29	0·86	—	1·24	1·94	1·06	2·05
1.9.45	1·03	0·78	—	—	1·37	1·05	0·55
8.9.45	1·03	0·78	—	—	1·14	1·08	1·51
15.9.45	1·20	1·14	—	—	1·13	1·07	2·62

TABLE 46

IV Corps. Total Sick-rates. Average Daily Admission-rates per 1,000 per Diem. By Cause. May 5–September 15, 1945

Week ending	Total Admissions	Battle Casualties	Sick	Malaria	Dysentery and Diarrhoea	Infective Hepatitis	Venereal Diseases
5.5.45	1·58	0·53	1·05	0·29	0·15	0·03	0·02
12.5.45	1·81	0·49	1·32	0·30	0·13	0·06	0·02
19.5.45	1·65	0·36	1·29	0·36	0·11	0·07	0·01
26.5.45	2·22	0·28	1·94	0·75	0·17	0·09	0·01
2.6.45	2·08	0·19	1·89	0·63	0·13	0·09	0·03
9.6.45	2·34	0·34	2·00	0·90	0·13	0·07	0·03
16.6.45	1·83	0·15	1·68	0·55	0·13	0·07	0·15
23.6.45	1·54	0·02	1·52	0·51	0·12	0·07	0·02
30.6.45	1·43	0·03	1·50	0·48	0·10	0·07	0·03
7.7.45	2·34	0·36	1·98	0·60	0·16	0·08	0·07
14.7.45	1·97	0·07	1·90	0·48	0·17	0·10	0·11
21.7.45	1·80	0·13	1·67	0·34	0·12	0·10	0·08
28.7.45	1·68	0·39	1·29	1·27	0·08	0·07	0·06
4.8.45	1·40	0·12	1·28	0·32	0·10	0·05	0·07
11.8.45	1·42	0·08	1·34	0·23	0·10	0·05	0·06
18.8.45	1·29	0·02	1·27	0·22	0·08	0·05	0·09
25.8.45	1·30	0·007	1·29	0·21	0·11	0·05	0·05
1.9.45	1·14	0·005	1·03	0·15	0·04	0·05	0·07
8.9.45	1·05	0·02	1·03	0·20	0·05	0·04	0·07
15.9.45	1·20	—	1·20	0·19	0·05	0·07	0·14

expansion that had to be made had to be on ground that was commonly under water. No suitable site for the M.F.T.U. could be found within the prescribed perimeter. The corps field ambulance, 65 (Ind.), was housed in a *phongyi kyaung* and was able to provide 200 beds. This medical centre provided cover for the troops operating along the Sittang River and in the Pegu area. Evacuation from Pegu was by road to Rangoon or by air to Mingaladon and thence by road to Rangoon. 44 (Ind.) Sub-depot of Medical Stores was in Pegu and was initially replenished by air-drop as were also the medical units in Toungoo. Later when depots of medical stores were opened in Rangoon, the units in Pegu were supplied by these by road.

At the beginning of September, 9 (Ind.) M.F.T.U. opened in Payagyi, 11 miles to the north of Pegu for the reception of the seriously sick or wounded Japanese P.o.W. To its staff Japanese medical personnel were added. At Penwegon, halfway between Toungoo and Pegu, where H.Q. Indian 19th Division was situated, one of the divisional field ambulances established its M.D.S. and this was reinforced by a mobile surgical unit for the reason that it was expected that the main attempt on the part of the Japanese to break-out would take place in this area. Should Penwegon become isolated and evacuation therefrom temporarily interrupted, this M.D.S. could then deal with local casualties. These medical arrangements proved to be completely satisfactory.

Skin complaints were very common in the corps, especially fungus infections. An adviser in dermatology was posted to the corps and rendered excellent service. D.D.M.S. Corps ascribed the satisfactory state of health of the corps to the excellence of the malaria and hygiene discipline in the divisions, to the regular use of mepacrine, to the extensive use of D.D.T. and to the regular administration by the R.M.Os. of sulphaguanidine in early cases of diarrhoea.

THE RE-OCCUPATION OF JAPANESE-HELD TERRITORIES

It was the intention, as soon as Rangoon had fallen, to proceed with the plans for the invasion of those countries which had been seized by the Japanese during the war. The territory of S.E.A.C. had been extended to include Malaya, Singapore, Thailand, Indo-China, the Netherland East Indies, Hong Kong, Borneo and the Andaman Islands. In all of these areas were intact, unbeaten Japanese forces amounting to about half a million men and it was by no means certain that all of these were prepared to obey the instruction to surrender that had been issued by the Japanese Supreme Headquarters. In Indo-China and in the Netherland East Indies, there were strong nationalist groups, armed by the Japanese, which had seized power and were resisting the restoration of French and Dutch sovereignty. In all these areas there were many thousands of P.o.W., American, Australian, British, Canadian, Dutch, Indian and French, starving, dying from disease and facing the risk of mass murder. Every effort had to be made to get succour to them at the earliest possible moment. Every day's delay meant that more of them would surely die before relief reached them. But a difficulty had been created. The overall control of the Japanese surrender had been given by the Combined Chiefs of Staff to General MacArthur, the Supreme Commander in the Pacific and he had issued instructions to the effect that no landings in or re-entry into Japanese-held territory would be made until he had personally received the formal surrender of the Japanese Empire. This was not to take place until September 2.

Because of the plight of the P.o.W. in the territory of S.E.A.C., the Supreme Commander South East Asia Command decided to disregard this ban on landing. On August 28 pamphlets informing these P.o.W. of the Japanese capitulation were dropped over all known camps (Operation 'Birdcage') and the delivery by air-drop of some 950 tons of supplies and of some 120 relief personnel began (Operation 'Mastiff'). 'Mercy' ships were despatched, loaded with supplies ahead of the various forces that were waiting to set out for their different destinations, the supplies to be distributed under the guardianship of the Japanese.

On September 3, H.Q. Indian 7th Division, 114th Bde. and a number of medical units were flown in to Bangkok airfield, the rest of the division following between this date and September 8. Royal Marines of the East Indies Fleet of the Royal Navy took over Penang from its Japanese garrison on September 3 and Tactical H.Q. XV Corps and Indian 5th Division sailed on to reach Singapore on September 5. Indian 20th Division was flown to Saigon, staging at Bangkok and on the 9th, XXXIV Corps comprising Indian 23rd and 25th Divisions, with Indian 50th Tk. Bde. and British 5th Independent Para. Bde., began to land in the Port Swettenham–Port Dickson area of Malaya unopposed. To Hong Kong went 3rd Commando Bde. on September 10 and the colossal task of disarming and collecting the half million undefeated Japanese began in earnest. Later Indian 26th Division, staging at Singapore, landed in Java.

The kinds and numbers of the medical units ear-marked to accompany these forces are shown in table 47.

Although, as will be seen, adequate medical arrangements were made for these landings, the distribution of medical stores during a rapidly changing operational situation and at a time filled with commotion and uncertainty, left much to be desired and might have proved inadequate if opposition had been met. It is reported that one convoy sailed without medical stores and that in one troopship a naval surgeon found nothing more than one haversack containing first-aid kit. Moreover, owing to lack of shipping space, some medical units were separated from their stores and equipment.

As an example of the methods adopted to rescue Allied P.o.W. and internees and to round up and disarm Japanese soldiery in these countries, the story of Indian 20th Division in French Indo-China, as it was then, is told.

Indian 20th Division was given the tasks of liberating the prisoners-of-war, of disarming the Japanese military personnel and of maintaining law and order south of the 16° parallel. A small advanced party was flown in to Saigon on September 5. It included the officer commanding 59 (Ind.) Fd. Amb. In French Indo-China there were some 2,200 British, 6,500 French, 1,800 Dutch, 70 Australian, 200 American and 100 Indian P.o.W. and also about 750 Chinese and 500 Javanese coolies, held against their will, some 12,120 altogether. They were mostly in two camps, in Saigon and in Phnom Penh. Medical officers had been parachuted into the camps during Operation 'Mastiff'. The general state of health of these R.A.P.W.I. was good; of the British only about 60 were seriously ill and of these only 3 were unfit for immediate evacuation. Those who needed hospitalisation were admitted to the French Hôpital Grall;

TABLE 47

Medical Units allotted to the Task Forces for the Re-occupation of Japanese-held Territories

	Indian XXXIV Corps Malaya	Indian 7th Div. Thailand	Indian 20th Div. Indo-China	Indian 116th Bde. Andamans	2nd Div. Hong Kong	Indian 26th Div. Java	Total
Field ambulances	12	3	3	1	1 coy.	3	23
Fd. Hgy. Sections	7	2	2	1	2	2	16
Base Sanitary Sections	—	1	1	—	2	1	5
Bearer Companies	2	—	—	—	1 pln.	—	3
C.C.Ss.	4	1	1 (a)	—	1	1	8
M.F.T.Us.	1	2	—	—	1	—	4
Gen. Hospitals	3	1 (c)	1 (b)	1 (c)	1 (c)	2 (d)	9
Depots of medical stores	—	1	—	—	—	2 detach.	3
Sub-depots of medical stores	4	—	1	1	1	—	7
Dental Units	8	2	2	2	2	1	17
Dent. Mech. Units	2	1	1	1	—	—	5
X-ray Units	5	—	—	1	—	—	6
Field laboratories	2	1	1	1	1	1	7
A.M.Us.	7	1	1	1	3	2	15
Ophthalmic Units	3	1	1	1	—	1	7
E.N.T. Surgical Units	1	—	1	—	—	1	3
Mobile Surgical Units	5	1	1	—	1	1	9
Field Transfusion Units	5	1	—	—	—	—	6
	71	19	17	11	16	19	153

(a) with X-ray unit; (b) H.Q. and 5 Indian and 2 British sections; (c) H.Q., 3 Indian and 1 British sections; (d) one of them as in (b) the other as in (c).

CAPTURE OF RANGOON—CLOSING PHASE 569

the rest were flown out, the British to Rangoon, the Australians and Americans under arrangements with their own governments and the Dutch by sea early in October.

The first flight of the division—80th Bde.—was sent in by air beginning on September 13. S.A.C.S.E.A. Control Commission No. 1 was also despatched. A.D.M.S. Indian 20th Division went in with this first flight as did also a light M.D.S. of 55 (Ind.) Fd. Amb. with a surgical team from 24 (Ind.) C.C.S., detachments of 26 Fd. Hyg. Sec. and 20 (Ind.) A.M.U. and the divisional psychiatrist.

Until as late as March 9, 1945 the Japanese had not interfered with the French administration of the country but on that date they interned the French and took over the administration. On August 12, when Japan capitulated, they handed over the reins of government not to the French but to Viet Minh, the principal Annamite national party. Viet Minh at once instituted a reign of terror, kidnapping and murdering the French and looting and burning their property. Such was the situation when the first flight of Indian 20th Division arrived on the scene. Two thousand French R.A.P.W.I. were at once armed from a Japanese dump. During the night of September 22/23 the French seized the government offices and police posts and fighting between them and the Annamites flared up. In these clashes troops of Indian 20th Division sometimes became unwillingly involved. There were 60,000 Japanese troops in southern Indo-China. Some of them were employed in the protection of Allied nationals and for the defence of certain vital points.

The main body of Indian 20th Division together with Indian 16th Cavalry, H.Q. 555 Sub-area, 237th Docks Operating Company and numerous ancillary units as well as R.A.F. and R.A.F. Regiment elements arrived by sea on October 7. H.Q. Indian 20th Division assumed the rôle of H.Q. Allied Land Forces, French Indo-China (A.L.F.F.I.C.). The total numbers of Indian and British troops in this command were around 22,000. The medical cover was as follows:

Divisional units
42, 55 and 59 (Ind.) Fd. Ambs.
26 (Ind.) Fd. Hyg. Sec.
20 (Ind.) A.M.U.

Non-divisional units
51 I.G.H. (C.)
24 (Ind.) C.C.S.
9 (Ind.) M.S.U.
26 (Ind.) Fd. Lab.
15 (Ind.) E.N.T. Surg. Unit
16 (Ind.) Ophthal. Unit
38 F.T.U.
46 (Ind.) Sub-depot Med. Stores
56 (Ind.) Dent. Unit (B.T.)
70 (Ind.) Dent. Unit (I.T.)
25 (Ind.) Dent. Mech. Unit
75 (Ind.) Fd. Hyg. Sec.
Detach. Red Cross

80th Bde. was placed in charge of the south of Saigon and the large Cholon area; 32nd Bde. was given charge of an area stretching from the north-east suburbs of the city and including the airfield; the centre of the city was a French responsibility; 100th Bde. was to control an area of about 150 sq. miles north of the city and in this area it was intended to concentrate all the Japanese troops.

55 (Ind.) Fd. Amb. served 80th Bde. In the same building in which this field ambulance was established were 26 (Ind.) Fd. Hyg. Sec., 20 (Ind.) A.M.U., 46 (Ind.) Sub-depot Medical Stores with its 50 tons of stores and the divisional psychiatrist. 59 (Ind.) Fd. Amb. was in a building that the Japanese had used as a hospital. With it were the dental units forming a dental centre. This field ambulance served 32nd Bde. 42 (Ind.) Fd. Amb. with 9 (Ind.) M.S.U. and detachments of the field hygiene section and of the anti-malaria unit were with 100th Bde. It proceeded on October 10 to Thu Duc, 10 miles from Saigon, to open there in a convent. Small detachments of the unit were stationed in Thu Dau Mot and Bien Hoa. Convoys from Thu Duc to Saigon made their way through hostile country every second day. A clinic for the local civilians was organised by 42 (Ind.) Fd. Amb. and 9 (Ind.) M.S.U. 24 (Ind.) C.C.S. was in a nunnery in Cholon. A veneral diseases treatment centre was formed in the C.C.S. When 51 I.G.H. arrived it opened in a building that had been used by the Japanese as a naval hospital, l'Institut Tabard. Its opening was much delayed by the non-arrival of its equipment and stores. With the hospital were 15 (Ind.) E.N.T. Surg. Unit, 16 (Ind.) Ophthal. Unit and to it 38 F.T.U., which thus far had been with 55 (Ind.) Fd. Amb. and then with 24 (Ind.) C.C.S., was transferred. 9 (Ind.) M.S.U. was also brought from Thu Duc to join it. As 66 (Ind.) Mob. X-ray Unit failed to reach Saigon a Japanese X-ray plant was taken over together with its radiographer. 26 (Ind.) Fd. Lab. was housed in the Pasteur Institute, Saigon. Later this unit was absorbed into 51 I.G.H. When 75 (Ind.) Fd. Hyg. Sec. arrived very late, it was grossly deficient in respect of personnel and stores. A base sanitary section was expected but failed to appear. The Red Cross detachment of two women and three men dealt with very large consignments of stores that arrived.

The medical branch of the Control Commission took charge of all Japanese medical arrangements until the formation of A.L.F.F.I.C. when a medical officer was posted to Phnom Penh, the capital of Cambodia, as representative. 555 Sub-area administered all the non-divisional medical units and also the Japanese civilian internee camps. Three medical officers at Sub-area proved to be more than enough and so the staff-captain was posted to 51 I.G.H.

CAPTURE OF RANGOON—CLOSING PHASE

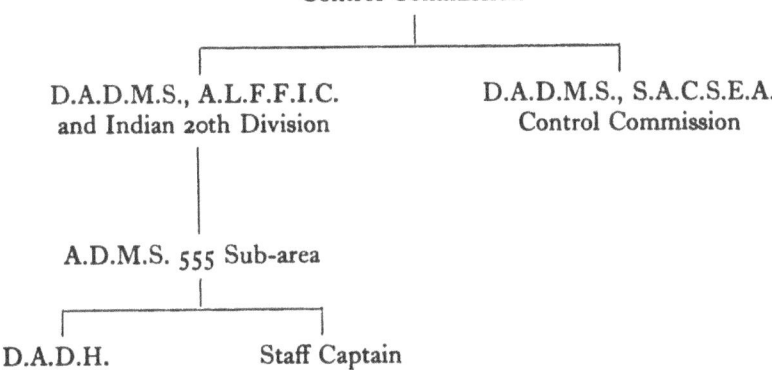

During the time the division was in Saigon the sick-rate ranged from 1·05 to 1·76/1,000/diem. There were 117 battle casualties. There were 11 cases of scrub typhus. There was an outbreak of mumps. Venereal diseases were responsible for a third of all hospital admissions, the rate varying from 0·15 to 0·58/1,000/diem. The average weekly number admitted on account of venereal diseases was 72 and of these 60 belonged to Indian 20th Division. All attempts to reduce the hazards of infection proved to be unsuccessful.

Japanese medical stores were collected into one depot and quantities were sent to Malaya on the instructions of A.L.F.S.E.A. The Japanese hospitals were concentrated in the area of 80th Bde. to serve the Japanese troops in this area. Out of the 60,000 Japanese 5,000 were in hospital. There were some 300 cases of pulmonary tuberculosis and much chronic malaria and dysentery. The French military and civil authorities were given all possible help and to them quantities of medical stores ample for their needs, were issued. In the same way the Chinese and Annamites themselves were assisted.

By December 1945 the French troops in the country had received strong reinforcements and so it became possible for Indian 20th Division to begin to depart. 32 Bde. Gp. with 59 (Ind.) Fd. Amb. and 75 (Ind.) Fd. Hyg. Sec. left for Borneo at Christmas time and in the middle of January 1946, 80th Bde. Gp., with 55 (Ind.) Fd. Amb., 24 (Ind.) C.C.S., 9 (Ind.) M.S.U., 20 (Ind.) A.M.U., 70 (Ind.) Dent. Unit (I.T.) and 16 (Ind.) Ophthal. Unit left for the Celebes. At the end of January the rest of the units departed for India leaving behind an inter-service mission to which was attached 2/8th Punjab, 9/12th F.F.R. and a number of ancillary units, numbering in all some 3,000. A section of 51 I.G.H., 56 (Ind.) Dent. Unit (B.T.) and 25 (Ind.) Dent. Mech. Unit were left to provide medical cover. Rear H.Q. Indian 20th Division, which included its A.D.M.S., left Saigon for India on February 12, 1946.

APPENDIX XXIV

ALLIED LAND FORCES, SOUTH-EAST ASIA. ORDER OF BATTLE. MAY 8, 1945
(*Much abbreviated*)

82nd West African Division
   1st W.A. Bde.
      1st Nigeria Regt.
      2nd ,,   ,,
      3rd ,,   ,,
   2nd W.A. Bde.
      1st Gold Coast Regt.
      2nd ,,   ,,   ,,
      3rd ,,   ,,   ,,
   4th W.A. Bde.
      5th Nigeria Regt.
      9th ,,   ,,
      10th ,,   ,,
   Medical
      1, 2 and 4 (W.A.) Fd. Ambs.
      82nd W.A. Division Field Hygiene Section

22nd East African Brigade
   1st (Nyasaland) King's African Rifles
   3rd Northern Rhodesia Regt.
   1st Rhodesian African Rifles
   Medical
      110 (E.A.) C.R.S.

Indian 41st Beach Group
   Medical
      1 (Ind.) Beach Medical Unit

Indian 45th Beach Group
   Medical
      5 (Ind.) Beach Medical Unit

I Area, S.E.A.C.
   Medical
      14 and 38 B.G.Hs.
      41, 49, 52, 53 and 91 I.G.Hs.(C.), 58 I.G.H.(I.T.)
      18 (Ind.) C.C.S.
      28, 33, 50 and 55 (Ind.) Fd. Labs.
      9 and 16 (Ind.) Ophthal. Units
      7 and 9 (Ind.) E.N.T. Surg. Units
      79 (Ind.) Dent. Unit (B.T.)
      25 and 61 (Ind.) Dent. Units (I.T.)
      29 (Ind.) Dent. Mech. Unit
      51 and 61 (Ind.) S.Ss.(C.)
      48 and 57 (Ind.) X-ray Units

CAPTURE OF RANGOON—CLOSING PHASE

    93 and 94 (Ind.) Mob. X-ray Units
    45 and 54 (Ind.) Fd. Hyg. Secs.
    6 (Ind.) M.F.T.U.
    46 (Ind.) Sub-depot Med. Stores
    30 (Ind.) Depot Med. Stores
    18 (Ind.) Base Depot Med. Stores
    3 (Ind.) Adv. B.T.U.

Fourteenth Army
    1st, 3rd and 4th Assam Rifles
    25th G.R.
    Lushai Scouts (98 Ind. Inf. Coy.)
    Medical

Unit	Location
88 (Ind.) A.M.U.	Imphal
7 (Ind.) Bearer Coy.	Manipur Road (Dimapur)
10 (Belgian Congo) C.C.S.	Golaghat
8 (Ind.) C.C.S.	Teknaf
9 and 17 (Ind.) Depots Med. Stores	Imphal
64 (Ind.) Fd. Amb.	Imphal
19 (Ind.) Fd. Hyg. Sec.	Kohima
9 and 22 (Ind.) Fd. Labs.	Pauk
5 F.T.U.	Imphal
11 (E.A.) Forward Malaria Treatment Centre	Tamu
15 (E.A.) F.M.T.C.	Golaghat
93 I.G.H.(C.)	Imphal
10 (Ind.) M.F.T.U.	Ye-U
11 (Ind.) M.F.T.U.	Kalewa
13 (Ind.) M.F.T.U.	Indainggyi
21 (E.A.) Mob. Mal. Unit, less Detach.	Tamu
15 (Ind.) Mob. X-ray Unit	
79 (Ind.) Mob. X-ray Unit	
15 (Ind.) M.S.U.	
40 (E.A.) F.S.U.	Golaghat
91 (Ind.) Mob. X-ray Servicing Unit	Imphal
5 (Ind.) Ophthal. Unit	u/c XXXIII Corps
11 (Ind.) Ophthal. Unit	u/c IV Corps
14 (Ind.) S.S.(C.)	Sookerating
34 ,, ,,	Palel
43 ,, ,,	Tamu
74 ,, ,,	Agartala
83 ,, ,,	Chittagong
88 ,, ,,	Indainggyi
90 ,, ,,	Golaghat
42 (Ind.) Sub-depot Med. Stores	u/c IV Corps
44 ,, ,, ,, ,,	u/c XXXIII Corps
45 ,, ,, ,, ,,	u/c IV Corps
48 ,, ,, ,, ,,	u/c XXXIII Corps

77 (Bur.) Fd. Amb.	Imphal
78 (Bur.) Fd. Amb.	
9 (Ind.) Dent. Mech. Unit	Shillong
10 ,, ,, ,, ,	Imphal
26 (Ind.) Dent. Unit (I.T.)	Gauhati
41 ,, ,, ,, (B.T.)	Imphal
53 ,, ,, ,, ,,	Imphal
55 ,, ,, ,, ,,	Meiktila

Indian 19th Division
> 1st Assam; 11th Sikh M.G. Bn. and L.A.D., Type I; 1/15th Punjab (Recce. Bn.)
>
> H.Q. Ind. 62nd Bde. and L.A.D. (E.)
>> 2nd Welch
>> 4/6th G.R.
>> 3/6th Raj.Rif.
>
> H.Q. Ind. 64th Bde. and L.A.D. (E.)
>> 2nd Worc. R.
>> 5/10th Baluch
>> 1/6th G.R.
>
> H.Q. Ind. 98th Bde. and L.A.D. (E.)
>> 2nd R. Berks.
>> 8/12th F.F.R.
>> 4/4th G.R.
>
> Medical
>> 51, 52 and 53 (Ind.) Fd. Ambs.
>> 31 (Ind.) Fd. Hyg. Sec.

IV Corps
> Medical
>> 32, 68 and 91 (Ind.) A.M.Us.
>> 14, 19 and 24 (Ind.) C.C.Ss.
>> 65 (Ind.) Fd. Amb.
>> 50 (Ind.) Fd. Hyg. Sec.
>> 32 F.T.U.
>> 4, 9 and 16 (Ind.) M.F.T.Us.
>> 8 and 14 (Ind.) M.S.Us.
>> 3, 8 and 14 (Ind.) Mob. X-ray Units
>> 3 and 89 (Ind.) S.Ss.(C.)
>> 19 and 23 (Ind.) Dent. Mech. Units
>> 17 and 19 (I.T.) and 45 and 49 (B.T.) (Ind.) Dent. Units

Indian 255th Tank Brigade
> (No medical unit in the order of battle)

CAPTURE OF RANGOON—CLOSING PHASE

Indian 5th Division
    17th Dogra M.G. Bn. and L.A.D., Type I; 1st Buregt. (Div. H.Q. Bn.); 3/9th Jat (Recce. Bn.)
    H.Q. Ind. 9th Bde. and L.A.D. (E.)
        4th J. and K. Inf.
        3/2nd Punjab
        2nd W. Yorks.
    H.Q. Ind. 123rd Bde. and L.A.D. (E.)
        1/17th Dogra
        2/1st Punjab
        7th Y. and L.
    H.Q. Ind. 161st Bde. and L.A.D. (E.)
        4th R.W.K.
        1/1st Punjab
        4/7th Rajput
    Medical
        10, 45 and 75 (Ind.) Fd. Ambs.
        7 (Ind.) Fd. Hyg. Sec.

Indian 17th Division
    6/15th Punjab (Div. H.Q. Bn.); 9/13th F.F.Rif. M.G. Bn.; 6/7th Rajput (Recce. Bn.)
    H.Q. Ind. 48th Bde. and L.A.D. (I.)
        4/12th F.F.R.
        1/7th G.R.
        1st W. Yorks.
    H.Q. Ind. 63rd Bde. and L.A.D. (I.)
        7/10th Baluch
        1/10th G.R.
        9th Border
    H.Q. Ind. 99th Bde. and L.A.D. (I.)
        1/3rd G.R.
        1st E. Yorks.
        1st Sikh L.I.
    Medical
        23, 37 and 50 (Ind.) Fd. Ambs.
        22 (Ind.) Fd. Hyg. Sec.

XXXIII Corps
    Medical
        20, 33, 44, 45, 55 and 69 (Ind.) A.M.Us.
        3 and 4 (Ind.) Bearer Coys.
        13, 16 and 26 (Ind.) C.C.Ss.
        67 (Ind.) Fd. Amb.
        56 (Ind.) Fd. Hyg. Sec.
        2 and 27 F.T.Us.
        7 and 8 (Ind.) M.F.T.Us.
        4, 5, 9 and 15 (Ind.) M.S.Us.
        6, 10, 11 and 82 (Ind.) Mob. X-ray Units

        67 and 76 (Ind.) S.Ss.(C.)
        25 (Ind.) Dent. Mech. Unit
        56 (B.T.) and 30, 69 and 70 (I.T.) (Ind.) Dent. Units
Indian 254th Tank Brigade
        14 (Ind.) Lt. Fd. Amb., less one sec.
Indian 7th Division
        2nd Baroda, I.S.F. (Div. H.Q. Bn.); 13th F.F.Rif. M.G. Bn. and L.A.D. (I.); 7/2nd Punjab (Recce. Bn.)
        H.Q. Ind. 33rd Bde. and L.A.D. (E.)
                1st Queens
                4/1st G.R.
                4/15th Punjab
        H.Q. Ind. 89th Bde. and L.A.D. (E.)
                2nd K.O.S.B.
                4/8th G.R.
                1/11th Sikh
        H.Q. Ind. 114th Bde. and L.A.D. (E.)
                2nd S.Lan.R.
                4/14th Punjab
                4/5th R.G.R.
        Medical
                44, 54 and 66 (Ind.) Fd. Ambs.
                32 (Ind.) Fd. Hyg. Sec.
Indian 20th Division
        9th Jat M.G. Bn. and L.A.D. (I.); 4/2nd G.R. (Recce. Bn.); 4/17th Dogra (Div. H.Q. Bn.)
        H.Q. Ind. 32nd Bde. and L.A.D. (I.)
                3/8th G.R.
                9/14th Punjab
                2/8th Punjab
        H.Q. Ind. 80th Bde. and L.A.D. (I.)
                9/12th F.F.R.
                3/1st G.R.
                1/19th Hybad.
        H.Q. Ind. 100th Bde. and L.A.D. (I.)
                14/13th F.F.Rif.
                4/10th G.R.
                1/1st G.R.
        Medical
                42, 55 and 59 (Ind.) Fd. Ambs.
                26 (Ind.) Fd. Hyg. Sec.
Indian 268th Brigade
        1st Chamar
        1/3rd Madras
        4/3rd Madras
        Mahindra Dal Regt.

CAPTURE OF RANGOON—CLOSING PHASE

Chin Hills Bn.
Medical
   9 (Ind.) Lt. Fd. Amb.

XV Corps
  Medical
    105 (Ind.) A.M.U.
      2 and 3 (Ind.) Bearer Coys.
      15 (Ind.) C.C.S.
      37 and 38 (Ind.) Fd. Hyg. Secs.
      28 and 39 F.T.Us.
      1 (Ind.) M.F.T.U.
      6 and 11 (Ind.) M.S.Us.
      16 and 81 (Ind.) Mob. X-ray Units
      37 (Ind.) S.S.(C.)
      50 (Ind.) Sub-depot Med. Stores
      7 (Ind.) Dent. Mech. Unit
      18 (I.T.) and 34 (B.T.) (Ind.) Dent. Units

2nd Division
  2nd Manch. M.G. Bn. and L.A.D. (I.); 2nd Division Recce. Regt. and L.A.D. (II.)
  H.Q. 4th Bde.
    1st R.S.
    1/8th L.F.
    2nd Norfolk
  H.Q. 5th Bde.
    1st Camerons
    2nd Dorset
    7th Worc. R.
  H.Q. 6th Bde.
    2nd D.L.I.
    1st R. Berks.
    1st R.W.F.
  Medical
    4, 5 and 6 Fd. Ambs.
    2 Fd. Hyg. Sec.

Indian 26th Division
  2nd Ajmer (Div. H.Q. Bn.); 12th F.F.R. M.G. Bn.; 6th Raj.Rif. (Recce. Bn.)
  H.Q. Ind. 4th Bde. and L.A.D. (E.)
      1st Warwick.
      2/13th F.F.Rif.
      2/7th Rajput
  H.Q. Ind. 36th Bde. and L.A.D. (E.)
      5/9th Jat
      8/13th F.F.Rif.
      1/8th G.R.

H.Q. Ind. 71st Bde. and L.A.D. (E.)
>1st Lincolns
>5/1st Punjab
>1/18th R.Garh.Rif.

Medical
>1, 46 and 48 (Ind.) Fd. Ambs.
>27 (Ind.) Fd. Hyg. Sec.

APPENDIX XXV

11TH EAST AFRICAN DIVISION. ORDER OF BATTLE. MAY 1945
(Abbreviated)

H.Q. 11th E.A. Division
>5th (K.) King's African Rifles (Div. Recce. Bn.)
>36th (T.T.) K.A.R. (Div. H.Q. Bn.)
>H.Q. 21st E.A. Bde. and Defence Pln. and L.A.D. (S.)
>>2nd (Ny.) K.A.R.
>>4th (U.) K.A.R.
>>1st N.R.R.
>
>H.Q. 25th E.A. Bde. and Defence Pln. and L.A.D. (S.)
>>11th (K.) K.A.R.
>>13th (Ny.) K.A.R.
>>26th (T.T.) K.A.R.
>
>H.Q. 26th E.A. Bde. and Defence Pln. and L.A.D. (S.)
>>22nd (Ny.) K.A.R.
>>44th (U.) K.A.R.
>>46th (T.T.) K.A.R.

Medical
>2 (Z.), 6 (U.) and 10 (E.A.) Fd. Ambs.
>60 (E.A.) and 61 (Z.) F.D.Ss.
>71 (E.A.) Fd. Hyg. Sec.
>2004 S.B. Coy.

28th East African Brigade *(abbreviated)*
>H.Q. 28th E.A. Bde. and Defence Pln.
>>71st (1st Somaliland) K.A.R., at Dohazari

Medical
>108 (E.A.) C.R.S., at Dohazari

(On March 31, 1945 there were included in this brigade 7th (U.) K.A.R. and 46th (T.T.) K.A.R.)

INDIAN 25TH DIVISION. ORDER OF BATTLE. MAY 1945
(Abbreviated)

H.Q. Indian 25th Division
>7/16th Punjab (Div. H.Q. Bn.)
>2/3rd Madras (M.G.) Bn. and L.A.D.

CAPTURE OF RANGOON—CLOSING PHASE

16/6th Raj.Rif. (Div. Recce. Bn.)
H.Q. Ind. 51st Bde. and L.A.D. (E.)
    16/10th Baluch
    8/19th Hybad.
    2/2nd Punjab
H.Q. Ind. 53rd Bde. and L.A.D. (E.)
    17/5th Mahratta L.I.
    4/18th R.Garh.Rif.
    9th Y. and L.
H.Q. Ind. 74th Bde. and L.A.D. (E.)
    14/10th Baluch
    3/2nd G.R.
    6th Oxf. Bucks.
Medical
    56, 58 and 61 (Ind.) Fd. Ambs.
    30 (Ind.) Fd. Hyg. Sec.

36TH DIVISION. ORDER OF BATTLE. MAY 1945
(Abbreviated)

H.Q. 36th Division
    88th Ind. Inf. Coy. (8th G.R.) (Div. H.Q. Coy.)
    2nd Border (Div. Recce. Bn.)
    H.Q. Ind. 26th Bde. and L.A.D.
        2nd Buffs
        1st Devon
        1st Northamptons
    H.Q. 29th Bde. and L.A.D.
        2nd E.Lan.R.
        1st R.S.F.
        2nd R.W.F.
    H.Q. 72nd Bde. and L.A.D.
        10th Glosters
        9th R. Sussex
        6th S.W.B.
Medical
    34 (Ind.), 69 (Ind.) and 154 Fd. Ambs.
    44 (Ind.) Fd. Hyg. Sec.
    22 C.C.S.

INDIAN 23RD DIVISION. ORDER OF BATTLE. MAY 1945
(Abbreviated)

H.Q. Indian 23rd Division
    5/8th Punjab (Div. Recce. Bn.)
    6/8th Punjab M.G. Bn.
    2/19th Hybad. (Div. H.Q. Bn.)

H.Q. Ind. 1st Bde.
    1st Seaforth
    1/16th Punjab
    1st Patiala Inf. (I.S.F.)
H.Q. Ind. 37th Bde.
    3/3rd G.R.
    3/5th R.G.R.
    3/10th G.R.
H.Q. Ind. 49th Bde.
    4/5th Mahratta L.I.
    6/5th Mahratta L.I.
    5/6th Raj.Rif.
Medical
    24, 47 and 49 (Ind.) Fd. Ambs.
    23 (Ind.) Fd. Hyg. Sec.

81ST WEST AFRICAN DIVISION. ORDER OF BATTLE. MAY 1945
(Abbreviated)

H.Q. 81st W.A. Division
    81st (W.A.) Divisional Recce. Bn.
    H.Q. 3rd W.A. Bde.
        6th N.R.
        7th N.R.
        12th N.R.
    H.Q. 5th W.A. Bde.
        5th G.C.R.
        7th G.C.R.
        8th G.C.R.
    H.Q. 6th W.A. Bde.
        1st Gambia
        4th N.R.
        1st Sa.L.R.
Medical
    5 and 6 (W.A.) Fd. Ambs.
    83 (W.A.) Fd. Hyg. Sec.

APPENDIX XXVI

FOURTEENTH ARMY. MEDICAL UNITS. LOCATION STATEMENT. MAY 17, 1945

Army

Surg. Detach. 18 (Ind.) C.C.S.	*en route* Allanmyo–Rangoon
24 (Ind.) C.C.S.	Meiktila
26 (Ind.) C.C.S.	Meiktila

CAPTURE OF RANGOON—CLOSING PHASE

6 (Ind.) M.F.T.U.	Meiktila
8 (Ind.) M.F.T.U.	Meiktila
13 (Ind.) M.F.T.U.	Myingyan—temp. u/c 552 Sub-area of 505 District
16 (Ind.) M.F.T.U.	Meiktila
5 (Ind.) Beach Med. Unit	Myingyan—moving to Toungoo
64 (Ind.) Fd. Amb.	Meiktila—one coy. moving to Tatkon
53 (Ind.) Fd. Amb.	Milestone 27—with 64th Bde. of Indian 19th Div. Thazi-Kalaw road.
19 (Ind.) Fd. Hyg. Sec.	Myingyan—temp. u/c 552 Sub-area
36 (Ind.) Fd. Hyg. Sec.	Meiktila—moving, less detach., to Rangoon
36 (Ind.) Fd. Hyg. Sec. detachment	Rangoon
14, 34 and 83 (Ind.) S.Ss. (C.)	Moving from India but not required by Fourteenth Army
70 (Ind.) S.S.(C.)	Taungtha—temp. u/c 552 Sub-area
75 (Ind.) S.S.(C.)	Meiktila
89 (Ind.) S.S.(C.)	Nyaungu—temp. u/c 552 Sub-area
7 (Ind.) Bearer Coy., less one pln.	Meiktila
7 (Ind.) M.S.U.	Chittagong—u/c XV Corps. Waiting to be flown to Meiktila
13 (Ind.) M.S.U.	Myingyan—attchd. 13 (Ind.) C.C.S. Temp. u/c 552 Sub-area
2 M.N.S.U.	Meiktila
6 (Ind.) E.N.T. Surg. Unit	Comilla—waiting to be flown to Meiktila
38 F.T.U.	Meiktila
8 (Ind.) Mob. X-ray Unit	Myingyan—attchd. 13 (Ind.) C.C.S. Temp. u/c 552 Sub-area
11 (Ind.) Mob. X-ray Unit	Meiktila
15 (Ind.) Mob. X-ray Unit	Meiktila
91 (Ind.) X-ray Servicing Unit	Imphal—lacking technician; awaiting his arrival
5 (Ind.) M.O.U.	Meiktila
11 (Ind.) M.O.U.	Meiktila
6 (Ind.) Subsidiary Spectacle Centre	Meiktila
9 (Ind.) Fd. Lab.	Meiktila
23 (Ind.) Fd. Lab.	Meiktila
V.D. Wing 41 I.G.H.	Meiktila
V.D. Wing 49 I.G.H.	Meiktila
45 (Ind.) Sub-depot Med. Stores	Meiktila
9 (Ind.) Depot Med. Stores	Myingyan—temp. u/c 552 Sub-area
111 E.A. Hospital Section	Myingyan—temp. u/c 552 Sub-area
1 Sec. (Ind.) Mal. Fd. Lab.	Toungoo—an A.L.F.S.E.A. unit, temp. u/c Fourteenth Army
44 (Ind.) A.M.U.	Meiktila—less detach. with 55 (Ind.) Fd. Amb

71 (Ind.) A.M.U.	Myingyan—temp. u/c 552 Sub-area
88 (Ind.) A.M.U.	Meiktila—less detach. moving to Rangoon
88 (Ind.) A.M.U. detach.	Rangoon
53 (Ind.) Dent. Unit (B.T.)	Meiktila
30 (Ind.) Dent. Unit (I.T.)	Meiktila
10 (Ind.) Dent. Mech. Unit	Meiktila
67 (Ind.) Dent. Unit (I.T.)	Temp. u/c 505 District and at Indainggyi pending relief by 'N' (Ind.) Dental Centre, Shillong

IV Corps

8 (Ind.) C.C.S.	Meiktila
13 (Ind.) C.C.S.	Payagyi
16 (Ind.) C.C.S.	Toungoo
7 (Ind.) M.F.T.U.	Myingyan
11 (Ind.) M.F.T.U.	Meiktila—moving to Toungoo
65 (Ind.) Fd. Amb.	Payagyi—temp. u/c XXXIII Corps
65 (Ind.) Fd. Amb. Coy.	Padin—moving to IV Corps
10, 45 and 75 (Ind.) Fd. Ambs.	Area Pegu-Waw—with Indian 5th Div.
23, 37 and 50 (Ind.) Fd. Ambs.	Area Pegu-Nyaunglebin-Mingaladon—with Indian 17th Div.
51 and 52 (Ind.) Fd. Ambs.	Toungoo—with Indian 19th Div.
31 (Ind.) Fd. Hyg. Sec.	Toungoo—Indian 19th Div.
50 (Ind.) Fd. Hyg. Sec.	Pegu
7 (Ind.) Fd. Hyg. Sec.	Area Pegu-Waw—with Indian 5th Div.
22 (Ind.) Fd. Hyg. Sec.	Area Pegu-Nyaunglebin-Mingaladon—with Indian 17th Div.
3 (Ind.) S.S.(C.)	Pegu
7 (Ind.) Bearer Coy.	Pegu
4 (Ind.) M.S.U.	Pegu—attchd. 13 (Ind.) C.C.S.
5 (Ind.) M.S.U.	Area Pegu-Waw—attchd. Indian 5th Div.
9 (Ind.) M.S.U.	Area Pegu-Waw—attchd. Indian 5th Div.
2 F.T.U.	Pegu—attchd. 13 (Ind.) C.C.S.
5 F.T.U.	Toungoo—attchd. 16 (Ind.) C.C.S.
79 (Ind.) Mob. X-ray Unit	Pegu—attchd. 13 (Ind.) C.C.S.
82 (Ind.) Mob. X-ray Unit	Toungoo—attchd. 16 (Ind.) C.C.S.
Corps Psychiatric Centre	Pegu—attchd. 13 (Ind.) C.C.S.
44 (Ind.) Sub-depot Med. Stores	Pegu
45 (Ind.) A.M.U.	Toungoo—attchd. Indian 19th Div.
69 (Ind.) A.M.U.	Pegu
91 (Ind.) A.M.U.	Area Pegu-Nyaunglebin-Mingaladon—attchd. Indian 17th Div.
100 (Ind.) A.M.U.	Area Pegu-Waw—temp. u/c Army
100 (Ind.) A.M.U. detachment	Meiktila
41 (Ind.) Dent. Unit (B.T.)	Toungoo
55 (Ind.) Dent. Unit (B.T.)	Area Pegu-Waw—attchd. Indian 5th Div.

80 (Ind.) Dent. Unit (B.T.)   Pegu
26 (Ind.) Dent. Unit (I.T.)   Area Pegu–Nyaunglebin–Mingaladon—attchd. Indian 17th Div.
68 (Ind.) Dent. Unit (I.T.)   Pegu
69 (Ind.) Dent. Unit (I.T.)   *en route* Sadaung to Meiktila
75 (Ind.) Dent. Unit (I.T.)   Toungoo—attchd. Indian 19th Div.
1 (Ind.) Dent. Mech. Unit   Area Pegu–Waw—attchd. Indian 5th Div.
9 (Ind.) Dent. Mech. Unit   Toungoo
20 (Ind.) Dent. Mech. Unit   Pegu

XXXIII Corps

14 (Ind.) C.C.S.   Allanmyo
19 (Ind.) C.C.S.   Magwe
9 (Ind.) M.F.T.U.   Magwe
67 (Ind.) Fd. Amb.   Magwe
9 (Ind.) Lt. Fd. Amb.   Allanmyo—with Ind. 268th Bde.
44, 54 and 66 (Ind.) Fd. Ambs.   Area Magwe—with Indian 7th Div.
42, 55 and 59 (Ind.) Fd. Ambs.   Area Thayetmyo–Prome—with Indian 20th Div.
56 (Ind.) Fd. Hyg. Sec.   Magwe
32 (Ind.) Fd. Hyg. Sec.   Area Magwe—with Indian 7th Div.
26 (Ind.) Fd. Hyg. Sec.   Area Thayetmyo–Prome—with Indian 20th Div.
67 (Ind.) S.S.(C.)   Magwe
76 (Ind.) S.S.(C.)   Magwe
4 (Ind.) Bearer Coy.   Magwe
10 (Ind.) M.S.U.   Area Tharrawaddy–Prome—with Indian 20th Div.
14 (Ind.) M.S.U.   Area Magwe—with Indian 7th Div.
15 (Ind.) M.S.U.   Allanmyo
19 (Ind.) M.S.U.   Magwe
27 F.T.U.   Magwe—attchd. 19 (Ind.) C.C.S.
32 F.T.U.   Allanmyo—attchd. 14 (Ind.) C.C.S.
3 (Ind.) Mob. X-ray Unit   Allanmyo—attchd. 14 (Ind.) C.C.S.
25 (Ind.) Mob. X-ray Unit   Magwe—attchd. 19 (Ind.) C.C.S.
Corps Psychiatric Centre   Magwe
48 (Ind.) Sub-depot Med. Stores   Magwe
20 (Ind.) A.M.U.   Area Tharrawaddy–Prome—attchd. Indian 20th Div.
32 (Ind.) A.M.U.   Magwe
68 (Ind.) A.M.U.   Area Magwe—attchd. Indian 7th Div.
45 (Ind.) Dent. Unit (B.T.)   Area Magwe—attchd. Indian 7th Div.
49 (Ind.) Dent. Unit (B.T.)   Magwe—attchd. 19 (Ind.) C.C.S.
56 (Ind.) Dent. Unit (B.T.)   Area Tharrawaddy–Prome—attchd. Indian 20th Div.

17 (Ind.) Dent. Unit (I.T.)	Magwe—attchd. 19 (Ind.) C.C.S.
19 (Ind.) Dent. Unit (I.T.)	Area Magwe—attchd. Indian 7th Div.
70 (Ind.) Dent. Unit (I.T.)	Area Tharrawaddy–Prome—attchd. Indian 20th Div.
19 (Ind.) Dent. Mech. Unit	Magwe
23 (Ind.) Dent. Mech. Unit	Area Magwe—attchd. Indian 7th Div.
25 (Ind.) Dent. Mech. Unit	Area Tharrawaddy–Prome—attchd. Indian 20th Div.

APPENDIX XXVII
202 LINES OF COMMUNICATION AREA. MEDICAL ORDER OF BATTLE. MAY 1945

B.M.H.	Shillong
C.M.H.	Dibrugarh
C.M.H.	Digboi
C.M.H.	Silchar
I.M.H.	Shillong
43 I.G.H.(I.T.)	Manipur Road
44 I.G.H.(C.)	Margherita
59 I.G.H.(I.T.)	Manipur Road
66 I.G.H.(C.)	Manipur Road
87 I.G.H.(C.)	Imphal
88 I.G.H.(C.)	Tamu road
89 I.G.H.(C.)	Moreh
94 I.G.H.(C.)	Margherita
8 (Ind.) Con. Depot (B.T.)	Shillong
9 (Ind.) Con. Depot (I.T.)	Shillong
16 (Ind.) Con. Depot (I.T.)	Shillong
17 (Ind.) Con. Depot (I.T.)	Dibrugarh
25 (Ind.) Con. Depot (B.T.)	Shillong
45 (Ind.) Con. Depot (I.T.)	Kohima
District Lab.	Shillong
25 (Ind.) Fd. Lab.	Manipur Road
30 (Ind.) Fd. Lab.	Digboi
31 (Ind.) Fd. Lab.	Imphal
36 (Ind.) Fd. Lab.	Kohima
42 (Ind.) Fd. Lab.	Jorhat
52 (Ind.) Fd. Lab.	Moreh
53 (Ind.) Fd. Lab.	Imphal
57 (Ind.) Fd. Lab.	Imphal
10 (Ind.) M.S.U.	

CAPTURE OF RANGOON—CLOSING PHASE

8 (Ind.) M.O.U.	Manipur Road
11 (Ind.) E.N.T. Surg. Unit	Manipur Road
6 (Ind.) Subsidiary Spectacle Centre	Imphal
28 (Ind.) X-ray Unit	Gauhati
32 (Ind.) X-ray Unit	Imphal
37 (Ind.) X-ray Unit	Shillong
50 (Ind.) X-ray Unit	Manipur Road
61 (Ind.) X-ray Unit	Sylhet
76 (Ind.) X-ray Unit	Imphal
89 (Ind.) X-ray Servicing Unit	Jorhat
24 (Ind.) Base Depot Med. Stores	Ledo
27 (Ind.) Depot Med. Stores	Gauhati
29 (Ind.) Depot Med. Stores	Manipur Road
47 (Ind.) Sub-depot Med. Stores	Ledo
36 (Ind.) Fd. Hyg. Sec.	Manipur Road
46 (Ind.) Fd. Hyg. Sec.	Manipur Road
7 (Ind.) A.M.U.	Palel
9 (Ind.) A.M.U.	Manipur Road
21 (Ind.) A.M.U.	Imphal
22 (Ind.) A.M.U.	Kalewa road
24 (Ind.) A.M.U.	Manipur Road
25 (Ind.) A.M.U.	Silchar
27 (Ind.) A.M.U.	Lumding
28 (Ind.) A.M.U.	Gauhati
31 (Ind.) A.M.U.	Tinsukia
36 (Ind.) A.M.U.	Moreh
61 (Ind.) A.M.U.	Ledo
62 (Ind.) A.M.U.	Kangla
24 (Ind.) S.S.(I.T.)	Dhubri
26 (Ind.) S.S.(I.T.)	Ledo
28 (Ind.) S.S.(C.)	Palel
36 (Ind.) S.S.(C.)	Bongaigaon
40 (Ind.) S.S.(C.)	Sookerating
41 (Ind.) S.S.(C.)	Namrup
57 (Ind.) S.S.(C.)	Nowgong
58 (Ind.) S.S.(C.)	Haflong
60 (Ind.) S.S.(C.)	Mariani
62 (Ind.) S.S.(C.)	Chandranathpur
64 (Ind.) S.S.(C.)	Sylhet
68 (Ind.) S.S.(C.)	Kalewa
69 (Ind.) S.S.(C.)	Taukkyan
70 (Ind.) S.S.(C.)	Shwebo
72 (Ind.) S.S.(C.)	Lumding
73 (Ind.) S.S.(C.)	Sookerating
77 (Ind.) S.S.(C.)	Bhamo
78 (Ind.) S.S.(C.)	Myitkyina
86 (Ind.) S.S.(C.)	Moreh

14 (Ind.) Amb. Train (M.G.)	Dibrugarh
17 (Ind.) Amb. Train (M.G.)	Manipur Road
19 (Ind.) Amb. Train (M.G.)	Manipur Road
68 (Ind.) Army Dent. Centre (I.T.)	Shillong
4 (Ind.) Dent. Mech. Unit	Shillong
26 (Ind.) Dent. Mech. Unit	Manipur Road
27 (Ind.) Dent. Mech. Unit	Gauhati
57 (Ind.) Dent. Unit (B.T.)	Manipur Road
58 (Ind.) Dent. Unit (B.T.)	Gauhati
71 (Ind.) Dent. Unit (I.T.)	Shillong
78 (Ind.) Dent. Unit (I.T.)	Gauhati
'N' Fd. Dent. Centre Class 'B'	Shillong

404 LINES OF COMMUNICATION AREA. MEDICAL ORDER OF BATTLE. MAY 1945

51 I.G.H.(I.T.)	Agartala
56 I.G.H.(C.)	Chittagong
68 I.G.H.(C.)	Chittagong
72 I.G.H.(C.)	Cox's Bazar
74 I.G.H.(C.)	Maynamati
79 I.G.H.(I.T.)	Agartala
82 I.G.H.(C.)	Dohazari
92 I.G.H.(C.)	Maynamati
96 I.G.H.(I.T.)	Maynamati
124 I.G.H.(C.)	Agartala
150 E.A.G.H.	Maynamati
115 Sec. E.A.G.H.	Chittagong
152 W.A.G.H.	Dohazari
11 (E.A.) Con. Depot	Maynamati
15 (Ind.) Con. Depot (I.T.)	Agartala
21 (Ind.) Con. Depot (B.T.)	Comilla
37 (Ind.) Con. Depot (I.T.)	Maynamati
38 (Ind.) Con. Depot (I.T.)	Cox's Bazar
26 (Ind.) Fd. Lab.	Maynamati
27 (Ind.) Fd. Lab.	Chittagong
32 (Ind.) Fd. Lab.	Silchar
41 (Ind.) Fd. Lab.	Agartala
54 (Ind.) Fd. Lab.	Chittagong
4 (Ind.) Ophthal. Unit	Chittagong
10 (Ind.) Ophthal. Unit	Chittagong
15 (Ind.) Ophthal. Unit	Maynamati
8 (Ind.) E.N.T. Surg. Unit	Chittagong
12 (Ind.) E.N.T. Surg. Unit	Comilla
15 (Ind.) E.N.T. Surg. Unit	Agartala
90 (Ind.) X-ray Servicing Unit	Chittagong
85 (Ind.) Mob. X-ray Unit	Maungdaw

39 (Ind.) X-ray Unit	Chittagong
56 (Ind.) X-ray Unit	Maynamati
59 (Ind.) X-ray Unit	Chittagong
72 (Ind.) X-ray Unit	Agartala
77 (Ind.) X-ray Unit	Cox's Bazar
78 (Ind.) X-ray Unit	Maynamati
32 (Ind.) Base Depot Med. Stores	Chittagong
1 (Ind.) Depot Med. Stores	Hathazari
23 (Ind.) Depot Med. Stores	Cox's Bazar
49 (Ind.) Sub-depot Med. Stores	Comilla
51 (Ind.) Sub-depot Med. Stores	Comilla
52 (Ind.) Sub-depot Med. Stores	Chittagong
39 (Ind.) Fd. Hyg. Sec.	Chittagong
10 (Ind.) A.M.U.	Dohazari
23 (Ind.) A.M.U.	Cox's Bazar
59 (Ind.) A.M.U.	Chiringa
66 (Ind.) A.M.U.	Chittagong
67 (Ind.) A.M.U.	Comilla
72 (Ind.) A.M.U.	Chittagong
104 (Ind.) A.M.U.	Dohazari
105 (Ind.) A.M.U.	Dohazari
32 (Ind.) S.S.(C.)	Agartala
55 (Ind.) S.S.(C.)	Chiringa
59 (Ind.) S.S.(C.)	Lungleh
63 (Ind.) S.S.(C.)	Chittagong
71 (Ind.) S.S.(C.)	Comilla
79 (Ind.) S.S.(C.)	Fenny
80 (Ind.) S.S.(C.)	Hathazari
82 (Ind.) S.S.(C.)	Patia
84 (Ind.) S.S.(C.)	Chittagong
66 (Ind.) Amb. Coach	Chittagong
67 (Ind.) Amb. Coach	Chittagong
68 (Ind.) Amb. Coach	Silchar
20 (Ind.) Amb. Train (M.G.)	Chittagong
21 (Ind.) Amb. Train (M.G.)	Chittagong
22 (Ind.) Amb. Train (M.G.)	Chittagong
29 (Ind.) Amb. Train (M.G.)	Chittagong
13 (Ind.) Dent. Mech. Unit	Chittagong
29 (Ind.) Dent. Unit (I.T.)	Maynamati
32 (Ind.) Dent. Unit (I.T.)	Agartala
33 (Ind.) Dent. Unit (I.T.)	Chittagong
38 (Ind.) Dent. Unit (B.T.)	Chittagong
64 (Ind.) Dent. Unit (I.T.)	Sylhet
67 (Ind.) Dent. Unit. (I.T.)	

APPENDIX XXVIII
TWELFTH ARMY. MEDICAL ORDER OF BATTLE
JULY 6, 1945

38 B.G.H.	Rangoon	u/c 1 Area
49 I.G.H.(C.)	Rangoon	u/c 1 Area
58 I.G.H.(I.T.)	Rangoon	u/c 1 Area (Adv. party only)
88 I.G.H.(C.)	Kalewa (Tonnan)	551 Sub-area
91 I.G.H.(C.)	Rangoon	u/c 1 Area
4 (Ind.) M.F.T.U.	Meiktila	Twelfth Army. Temp. u/c 552 Sub-area
6 (Ind.) M.F.T.U.	Rangoon	1 Area
7 (Ind.) M.F.T.U.	Myingyan	Twelfth Army. Temp. u/c 552 Sub-area
8 (Ind.) M.F.T.U.	Meiktila	Twelfth Army. Temp. u/c 552 Sub-area
9 (Ind.) M.F.T.U.	Magwe	Twelfth Army. Temp. u/c 455 Sub-area
10 (Ind.) M.F.T.U.	Mandalay	253 Sub-area
11 (Ind.) M.F.T.U.	Toungoo	IV Corps
13 (Ind.) M.F.T.U.	Myingyan	Twelfth Army. Temp. u/c 552 Sub-area
15 (Ind.) M.F.T.U.	Maymyo	253 Sub-area
16 (Ind.) M.F.T.U.	Meiktila	Twelfth Army. Temp. u/c 552 Sub-area
8 (Ind.) C.C.S.	Rangoon	Twelfth Army. Temp. u/c 1 Area
13 (Ind.) C.C.S.	Pegu	IV Corps
14 (Ind.) C.C.S.	Allanmyo	Twelfth Army. (Moving to Paungde, light section to Prome)
16 (Ind.) C.C.S.	Toungoo	IV Corps
18 (Ind.) C.C.S.	Rangoon	Twelfth Army. Temp. u/c 1 Area
19 (Ind.) C.C.S.	Magwe	Twelfth Army. Temp. u/c 455 Sub-area (moving to Tharrawaddy)
24 (Ind.) C.C.S.	Meiktila	Twelfth Army. Temp. u/c 552 Sub-area
26 (Ind.) C.C.S.	Meiktila	Twelfth Army. Temp. u/c 552 Sub-area
6 Fd. Amb.	Insein	With 6th Bde. of 2nd Division
9 (Ind.) Lt. Fd. Amb.	Prome	With 268th Bde.
10 (Ind.) Fd. Amb.	Rangoon area	With Indian 5th Division
23 (Ind.) Fd. Amb.	Penwegon	With Indian 17th Division

37 (Ind.) Fd. Amb.	Daik-U	With Indian 17th Division
42 (Ind.) Fd. Amb.	Letpadan	With Indian 20th Division
44 (Ind.) Fd. Amb.	Pegu-Waw area	With Indian 7th Division
45 (Ind.) Fd. Amb.	Rangoon area	With Indian 5th Division
50 (Ind.) Fd. Amb.	Kalaw	With Indian 99th Bde.
51 (Ind.) Fd. Amb.	Toungoo area	With Indian 19th Division
52 (Ind.) Fd. Amb.	Toungoo area	With Indian 19th Division
53 (Ind.) Fd. Amb.	Toungoo area	With Indian 19th Division
54 (Ind.) Fd. Amb.	Pegu-Waw area	With Indian 7th Division
55 (Ind.) Fd. Amb.	Hmawbi	With Indian 20th Division
59 (Ind.) Fd. Amb.	Tharrawaddy	With Indian 20th Division
64 (Ind.) Fd. Amb.	Meiktila	Twelfth Army. Temp. u/c 552 Sub-area. Coy. at Tatkon and Kalaw road
65 (Ind.) Fd. Amb.	Pegu	IV Corps
66 (Ind.) Fd. Amb.	Pegu-Waw area	With Indian 7th Division
67 (Ind.) Fd. Amb.	Magwe	Twelfth Army. Temp. u/c 455 Sub-area (moving to Henzada for Lushai Bde., less detachment for Allanmyo)
7 (Ind.) Fd. Hyg. Sec.	Rangoon	With Indian 5th Division
19 (Ind.) Fd. Hyg. Sec.	Meiktila	Twelfth Army. Temp. u/c 552 Sub-area. (Sub-sec. at Myingyan)
22 (Ind.) Fd. Hyg. Sec.	Penwegon	With Indian 17th Division
26 (Ind.) Fd. Hyg. Sec.	Tharrawaddy	With Indian 20th Division
31 (Ind.) Fd. Hyg. Sec.	Toungoo	With Indian 19th Division
32 (Ind.) Fd. Hyg. Sec.	Pegu area	With Indian 7th Division
36 (Ind.) Fd. Hyg. Sec.	Rangoon	Twelfth Army
37 (Ind.) Fd. Hyg. Sec.	Rangoon	Twelfth Army. Temp. u/c 1 Area
44 (Ind.) Fd. Hyg. Sec.	Mandalay	Twelfth Army. Temp. u/c 253 Sub-area *en route* from Imphal
45 (Ind.) Fd. Hyg. Sec.	Rangoon	Twelfth Army. Temp. u/c 1 Area
46 (Ind.) Fd. Hyg. Sec.	Kalewa	Twelfth Army. Temp. u/c 551 Sub-area
50 (Ind.) Fd. Hyg. Sec.	Pegu	IV Corps
56 (Ind.) Fd. Hyg. Sec.	Magwe	Twelfth Army. Temp. u/c 455 Sub-area
4 (Ind.) M.S.U.	Pegu	IV Corps. Attchd. 13 (Ind.) C.C.S.
5 (Ind.) M.S.U.	Rangoon area	With Indian 5th Division

7 (Ind.) M.S.U.	Meiktila	Twelfth Army. Temp. u/c 552 Sub-area
8 (Ind.) M.S.U.	Penwegon	With Indian 17th Division
9 (Ind.) M.S.U.	Kalaw	With Ind. 99th Bde.
10 (Ind.) M.S.U.	Tharrawaddy	With Indian 20th Division
13 (Ind.) M.S.U.	Mandalay	Twelfth Army. Temp. u/c 253 Sub-area
14 (Ind.) M.S.U.	Prome	Twelfth Army. Attchd. Lt. Sec. 14 (Ind.) C.C.S.
15 (Ind.) M.S.U.	Tharrawaddy	With Indian 20th Division
19 (Ind.) M.S.U.	Magwe	With Indian 7th Division. Moving to Pegu
3 (Ind.) M.F.S.U.	Rangoon	Twelfth Army. Temp. u/c 1 Area
2 Neuro-surg. Unit	Meiktila	Twelfth Army. Temp. u/c 552 Sub-area
6 (Ind.) E.N.T. Surg. Unit	Meiktila	Twelfth Army. Temp. u/c 552 Sub-area
9 (Ind.) E.N.T. Surg. Unit	Rangoon	Twelfth Army. Temp. u/c 1 Area
5 (Ind.) Ophthalmic Unit	Meiktila	Twelfth Army. Temp. u/c 552 Sub-area
11 (Ind.) Ophthalmic Unit	Meiktila	Twelfth Army. Temp. u/c 552 Sub-area
16 (Ind.) Ophthalmic Unit	Rangoon	Twelfth Army. Temp. u/c 552 Sub-area
6 (Ind.) Spectacle Sub-centre	Meiktila	Twelfth Army. Temp. u/c 552 Sub-area
9 (Ind.) Fd. Lab.	Meiktila	Twelfth Army. Temp. u/c 552 Sub-area
23 (Ind.) Fd. Lab.	Rangoon	Twelfth Army. Temp. u/c 1 Area
36 (Ind.) Fd. Lab.	Kalewa	Twelfth Army. Temp. u/c 551 Sub-area
46 (Ind.) Fd. Lab.	Mandalay	Twelfth Army. Temp. u/c 253 Sub-area
50 (Ind.) Fd. Lab.	Rangoon	Twelfth Army. Temp. u/c 1 Area
55 (Ind.) Fd. Lab.	Rangoon	Twelfth Army. Temp. u/c 1 Area
3 (Ind.) Mob. X-ray Unit	Allanmyo	Twelfth Army. Attchd. 14 (Ind.) C.C.S.
6 (Ind.) Mob. X-ray Unit	Rangoon	Twelfth Army. Attchd. 8 (Ind.) C.C.S.
8 (Ind.) Mob. X-ray Unit	Myingyan	Twelfth Army. Attchd. 13 (Ind.) M.F.T.U. Temp. u/c 552 Sub-area

CAPTURE OF RANGOON—CLOSING PHASE

10 (Ind.) Mob. X-ray Unit	Kalewa	Twelfth Army. Temp. u/c 551 Sub-area
11 (Ind.) Mob. X-ray Unit	Meiktila	Twelfth Army. Temp. u/c 552 Sub-area
15 (Ind.) Mob. X-ray Unit	Meiktila	Twelfth Army. Temp. u/c 552 Sub-area
48 (Ind.) X-ray Unit	Rangoon	Twelfth Army. Temp. u/c 1 Area
79 (Ind.) Mob. X-ray Unit	Pegu	IV Corps. Attchd. 13 (Ind.) C.C.S.
82 (Ind.) Mob. X-ray Unit	Toungoo	IV Corps. Attchd. 16 (Ind.) C.C.S.
85 (Ind.) Mob. X-ray Unit	Magwe	Twelfth Army. Temp. u/c 455 Sub-area. Moving to Tharrawaddy
93 (Ind.) Mob. X-ray Unit	Rangoon	Twelfth Army. Temp. u/c 1 Area
94 (Ind.) Mob. X-ray Unit	Rangoon	Twelfth Army. Temp. u/c 1 Area
90 (Ind.) Mob. X-ray Servicing Unit	Rangoon	Twelfth Army. Temp. u/c 1 Area
2 F.T.U.	Pegu	IV Corps. Attchd. 13 (Ind.) C.C.S.
5 F.T.U.	Toungoo	IV Corps. Attchd. 16 (Ind.) C.C.S.
27 F.T.U.	Magwe	Twelfth Army. Temp. u/c 455 Sub-area. Moving to Tharrawaddy
32 F.T.U.	Pegu area	With Indian 7th Division
38 F.T.U.	Meiktila	Twelfth Army. Temp. u/c 552 Sub-area
3 (Ind.) Adv. B.T.U.	Rangoon	Twelfth Army
3 (Ind.) S.S.(C.)	Pegu	IV Corps
43 (Ind.) S.S.(C.)	Shwebo	Twelfth Army. Temp. u/c 551 Sub-area
61 (Ind.) S.S.(C.)	Bassein	Twelfth Army. Temp. u/c 1 Area
67 (Ind.) S.S.(C.)	Magwe	Twelfth Army. Temp. u/c 455 Sub-area. Moving to Rangoon
68 (Ind.) S.S.(C.)	Thazi	Twelfth Army. Temp. u/c 552 Sub-area
69 (Ind.) S.S.(C.)	Alon	Twelfth Army. Temp. u/c 551 Sub-area
70 (Ind.) S.S.(C).	Taungtha	Twelfth Army. Temp. u/c 552 Sub-area

74 (Ind.) S.S.(C.)	Tamu-Kalewa rd. M.S. 52	Twelfth Army. Temp. u/c 551 Sub-area
75 (Ind.) S.S.(C.)	Meiktila	Twelfth Army. Temp. u/c 22nd E.A. Bde.
76 (Ind.) S.S.(C.)	Paungde	Twelfth Army. Temp. u/c 551 Sub-area
79 (Ind.) S.S.(C.)	Indainggyi	Twelfth Army. Temp. u/c 551 Sub-area
82 (Ind.) S.S.(C.)	Indainggyi	Twelfth Army. Temp. u/c 551 Sub-area
87 (Ind.) S.S.(C.)	Sagaing	Twelfth Army. Temp. u/c 551 Sub-area
89 (Ind.) S.S.(C.)	Pyawbwe	Twelfth Army. Temp. u/c 552 Sub-area
90 (Ind.) S.S.(C.)	Ye-U	Twelfth Army. Temp. u/c 551 Sub-area
20 (Ind.) A.M.U.	Tharrawaddy	With Indian 20th Division
21 (Ind.) A.M.U.	Indainggyi	Twelfth Army. Temp. u/c 551 Sub-area
22 (Ind.) A.M.U.	Tamu-Kalewa rd. M.S. 52	Twelfth Army. Temp. u/c 551 Sub-area
32 (Ind.) A.M.U.	Rangoon	Twelfth Army. Temp. u/c 1 Area
33 (Ind.) A.M.U.	Kalewa	Twelfth Army. Temp. u/c 551 Sub-area
44 (Ind.) A.M.U.	Magwe	Twelfth Army. Temp. u/c 455 Sub-area
45 (Ind.) A.M.U.	Toungoo	With Indian 19th Division
55 (Ind.) A.M.U.	Indainggyi	Twelfth Army. Moving to Meiktila
68 (Ind.) A.M.U.	Pegu-Waw area	With Indian 7th Division
69 (Ind.) A.M.U.	Pegu	IV Corps
71 (Ind.) A.M.U.	Myingyan	Twelfth Army. Temp. u/c 552 Sub-area
88 (Ind.) A.M.U.	Rangoon	Twelfth Army. Temp. u/c 1 Area
91 (Ind.) A.M.U.	Penwegon	With Indian 17th Division
100 (Ind.) A.M.U.	Rangoon area	With Indian 5th Division
101 (Ind.) A.M.U.	Mandalay	Twelfth Army. Temp. u/c 253 Sub-area
102 (Ind.) A.M.U.	Maymyo	Twelfth Army. Temp. u/c 253 Sub-area
103 (Ind.) A.M.U.	Meiktila	Twelfth Army. Temp. u/c 552 Sub-area
105 (Ind.) A.MU.	Rangoon	Twelfth Army. Temp. u/c 1 Area

1 (Ind.) Mal. Fd. Lab.	Rangoon	Twelfth Army. An A.L.F.S.E.A. unit temp. u/c 1 Area
9 (Ind.) Depot Med. Stores	Myingyan	Twelfth Army. Temp. u/c 552 Sub-area
41 (Ind.) Sub-depot Med. Stores	Mandalay	Twelfth Army. Temp. u/c 253 Sub-area
44 (Ind.) Sub-depot Med. Stores	Pegu	IV Corps
45 (Ind.) Sub-depot Med. Stores	Meiktila	Twelfth Army. Temp. u/c 552 Sub-area
46 (Ind.) Sub-depot Med. Stores	Rangoon	Twelfth Army. Temp. u/c 1 Area
48 (Ind.) Sub-depot Med. Stores	Magwe	Twelfth Army. Temp. u/c 455 Sub-area
49 (Ind.) Sub-depot Med. Stores	Mandalay	Twelfth Army. Temp. u/c 253 Sub-area
50 (Ind.) Sub-depot Med. Stores	Rangoon	Twelfth Army. Temp. u/c 1 Area
1 Psychiatric Centre	Pegu	IV Corps
2 Psychiatric Centre	Magwe	IV Corps
V.D. Wing 41 I.G.H.	Meiktila	Twelfth Army. Temp. u/c 552 Sub-area
V.D. Wing 49 I.G.H.	Meiktila	Twelfth Army. For Rangoon
34 (Ind.) Con. Depot (B.T.)	Maymyo	Twelfth Army. Temp. u/c 253 Sub-area
111 E.A. Hosp. Sec.	Myingyan	Twelfth Army. For Rangoon
7, 8, 9, 10, 11 and 12 San. Secs.	Rangoon	Twelfth Army. Temp. u/c 1 Area
H.Q. 201 M.A.C.	Pegu	IV Corps
H.Q. 202 M.A.C.	Magwe	Twelfth Army. For Rangoon
H.Q. and one pln. A.F.S.	Rangoon	Twelfth Army. For India
A.F.S. one pln.	Prome	Twelfth Army. Moving to Rangoon
A.F.S., two secs.		IV Corps
A.F.S., one pln.	Pegu	IV Corps
A.F.S., one pln.	Meiktila	IV Corps
5 (Ind.) Beach Med. Unit	Syriam	Twelfth Army
4 (Ind.) Bearer Coy.	Magwe	Twelfth Army. One pln. to Paungde for 22nd E.A. Bde.
7 (Ind.) Bearer Coy.	Kalaw	With Ind. 99th Bde.
34 (Ind.) Dent. Unit (B.T.)	Rangoon	Twelfth Army. Temp. u/c 1 Area
41 (Ind.) Dent. Unit (B.T.)	Pyu	With Indian 17th Division
45 (Ind.) Dent. Unit (B.T.)	Prome	With Indian 7th Division

49 (Ind.) Dent. Unit (B.T.)	Toungoo	With Indian 19th Division
53 (Ind.) Dent. Unit (B.T.)	Meiktila	Twelfth Army. Temp. u/c 552 Sub-area
55 (Ind.) Dent. Unit (B.T.)	Rangoon area	With Indian 5th Division
56 (Ind.) Dent. Unit (B.T.)	Tharrawaddy	With Indian 20th Division
79 (Ind.) Dent. Unit (B.T.)	Rangoon	Twelfth Army. Temp. u/c 1 Area
80 (Ind.) Dent. Unit (B.T.)	Pegu	IV Corps. Attchd. 65 (Ind.) Fd. Amb. (Corps)
Br. Dental Centre	Kalewa (Tonnan)	Twelfth Army. Temp. u/c 551 Sub-area. Attchd. 88 I.G.H.
17 (Ind.) Dent. Unit (I.T.)	Magwe	Twelfth Army. Temp. u/c 455 Sub-area. Attchd. 19 (Ind.) C.C.S.
18 (Ind.) Dent. Unit (I.T.)	Rangoon	Twelfth Army. Temp. u/c 1 Area
19 (Ind.) Dent. Unit (I.T.)	Prome	With Indian 7th Division
26 (Ind.) Dent. Unit (I.T.)	Pyu	With Indian 17th Division
30 (Ind.) Dent. Unit (I.T.)	Meiktila	Twelfth Army. Temp. u/c 552 Sub-area
36 (Ind.) Dent. Unit (I.T.)	Myingyan	Twelfth Army. Temp. u/c 552 Sub-area
67 (Ind.) Dent. Unit (I.T.)	Tamu-Kalewa rd. M.S. 52	Twelfth Army. Temp. u/c 551 Sub-area
68 (Ind.) Dent. Unit (I.T.)	Pegu	IV Corps. Attchd. 65 (Ind.) Fd. Amb.
69 (Ind.) Dent. Unit (I.T.)	Rangoon area	With Indian 5th Division
70 (Ind.) Dent. Unit (I.T.)	Tharrawaddy	With Indian 20th Division
74 (Ind.) Dent. Unit (I.T.)	Mandalay	Twelfth Army. Temp. u/c 253 Sub-area. Attchd. 10 (Ind.) M.F.T.U.
75 (Ind.) Dent. Unit (I.T.)	Toungoo	With Indian 19th Division
1 (Ind.) Dent. Mech. Unit	Pegu	IV Corps. Attchd. 65 (Ind.) Fd. Amb.
4 (Ind.) Dent. Mech. Unit	Kalewa (Tonnan)	Twelfth Army. Temp. u/c 551 Sub-area
7 (Ind.) Dent. Mech. Unit	Rangoon	Twelfth Army. Temp. u/c 1 Area
9 (Ind.) Dent. Mech. Unit	Pyu	With Indian 17th Division
10 (Ind.) Dent. Mech. Unit	Meiktila	Twelfth Army. Temp. u/c 552 Sub-area
19 (Ind.) Dent. Mech. Unit	Toungoo	With Indian 19th Division
20 (Ind.) Dent. Mech. Unit	Pegu	IV Corps. Attchd. 65 (Ind.) Fd. Amb.
23 (Ind.) Dent. Mech. Unit	Prome	With Indian 7th Division
25 (Ind.) Dent. Mech. Unit	Tharrawaddy	With Indian 20th Division

CAPTURE OF RANGOON—CLOSING PHASE

APPENDIX XXIX

TWELFTH ARMY. MEDICAL UNITS.
MEDICAL ORDER OF BATTLE. AUGUST 17, 1945

Unit	Location	Command
38 B.G.H.	Rangoon	South Burma District
49 I.G.H.(C.)	Rangoon	S.B. Dist.
52 I.G.H.(C.)	Rangoon	S.B. Dist.
58 I.G.H. (I.T.)	Rangoon	S.B. Dist.
88 I.G.H.(C.)	Kalewa	505 Dist.
91 I.G.H.(C.)	Rangoon	S.B. Dist.
29 (Ind.) Amb. Train	Rangoon	S.B. Dist.
4 (Ind.) M.F.T.U.	Meiktila	Twelfth Army. Temp. u/c 505 Dist.
5 (Ind.) M.F.T.U.	Kalewa	Twelfth Army. Temp. u/c 505 Dist. Moving to Toungoo to join IV Corps
6 (Ind.) M.F.T.U.	Rangoon	Twelfth Army. Temp. u/c S.B. Dist.
7 (Ind.) M.F.T.U.	Myingyan	Twelfth Army. Temp. u/c 505 Dist.
8 (Ind.) M.F.T.U.	Hmawbi	Twelfth Army. Temp. u/c S.B. Dist.
9 (Ind.) M.F.T.U.	Magwe	Twelfth Army. Temp. u/c 505 Dist. Moving to Payagyi to join IV Corps
10 (Ind.) M.F.T.U.	Mandalay	Twelfth Army. Temp. u/c 505 Dist.
10 (Ind.) M.F.T.U. detach.	Maymyo	
11 (Ind.) M.F.T.U.	Toungoo	IV Corps
13 (Ind.) M.F.T.U.	Myingyan	Twelfth Army. Temp. u/c 505 Dist.
15 (Ind.) M.F.T.U.	Meiktila	Twelfth Army. Temp. u/c 505 Dist.
16 (Ind.) M.F.T.U.	Hmawbi	Twelfth Army. Temp. u/c S.B. Dist.
8 (Ind.) C.C.S.	Rangoon	Twelfth Army. Temp. u/c S.B. Dist.
13 (Ind.) C.C.S.	Pegu	IV Corps
14 (Ind.) C.C.S.	Hmawbi	Twelfth Army. Temp. u/c S.B. Dist.
16 (Ind.) C.C.S.	Toungoo	IV Corps
18 (Ind.) C.C.S.	Rangoon	Twelfth Army. Temp. u/c S.B. Dist.
19 (Ind.) C.C.S.	Taikkyi	Twelfth Army. Temp. u/c S.B. Dist.

24 (Ind.) C.C.S.	Meiktila	Twelfth Army. Temp. u/c 505 Dist.
26 (Ind.) C.C.S.	Meiktila	Twelfth Army. Temp. u/c 505 Dist.
65 (Ind.) Fd. Amb.	Pegu	IV Corps
44, 54 and 66 (Ind.) Fd. Ambs.	Area Pegu–Waw	Indian 7th Division
23, 37 and 50 (Ind.) Fd. Ambs.	Area Penwegon–Daik-U–Kalaw	Indian 17th Division
51, 52 and 53 (Ind.) Fd. Ambs.	Area Toungoo	Indian 19th Division
10, 45 and 75 (Ind.) Fd. Ambs.	Area Rangoon	Indian 5th Division
42, 55 and 59 (Ind.) Fd. Ambs.	Area Letpadan–Hmawbi–Tharrawaddy	Indian 20th Division
64 (Ind.) Fd. Amb.	Hmawbi	Twelfth Army. Temp. u/c S.B. Dist.
67 (Ind.) Fd. Amb.	Prome	Twelfth Army. Temp. u/c S.B. Dist.
6 Fd. Amb.	Insein	6th Bde. of 2nd Division. Moving to Rangoon
7 (Ind.) Fd. Hyg. Sec.	Rangoon	Indian 5th Division
19 (Ind.) Fd. Hyg. Sec.	Meiktila	505 Dist.
19 (Ind.) Fd. Hyg. Sub-Sec.	Myingyan	505 Dist.
22 (Ind.) Fd. Hyg. Sec.	Penwegon	Indian 17th Division
26 (Ind.) Fd. Hyg. Sec.	Tharrawaddy	Indian 20th Division
31 (Ind.) Fd. Hyg. Sec.	Toungoo	Indian 19th Division
32 (Ind.) Fd. Hyg. Sec.	Pegu	Indian 7th Division
36 (Ind.) Fd. Hyg. Sec.	Rangoon	Twelfth Army
37 (Ind.) Fd. Hyg. Sec.	Rangoon	S.B. Dist.
45 (Ind.) Fd. Hyg. Sec.	Rangoon	S.B. Dist.
46 (Ind.) Fd. Hyg. Sec.	Kalewa	505 Dist.
50 (Ind.) Fd. Hyg. Sec.	Pegu	IV Corps
56 (Ind.) Fd. Hyg. Sec.	Mandalay	505 Dist.
4 (Ind.) M.S.U.	Hmawbi	Twelfth Army. Temp. u/c S.B. Dist.
5 (Ind.) M.S.U.	Rangoon	Indian 5th Division
7 (Ind.) M.S.U.	Hmawbi	Twelfth Army. Temp. u/c S.B. Dist.
8 (Ind.) M.S.U.	Hmawbi	Indian 5th Division
9 (Ind.) M.S.U.	Hmawbi	Twelfth Army. Temp. u/c S.B. Dist.
10 (Ind.) M.S.U.	Penwegon	IV Corps

CAPTURE OF RANGOON—CLOSING PHASE

13 (Ind.) M.S.U.	Mandalay	Twelfth Army. Temp. u/c 505 Dist.
14 (Ind.) M.S.U.	Rangoon	Twelfth Army. Temp. u/c S.B. Dist.
15 (Ind.) M.S.U.	Kalaw	Ind. 99th Bde. of Indian 17th Div.
19 (Ind.) M.S.U.	Hmawbi	Twelfth Army. Temp. u/c S.B. Dist.
2 M.N.S.U.	Meiktila	Twelfth Army. Temp. u/c 505 Dist.
6 (Ind.) E.N.T. Surg. Unit	Meiktila	505 Dist.
7 (Ind.) E.N.T. Surg. Unit	Rangoon	S.B. Dist. attchd. 49 I.G.H. (I.T.)
9 (Ind.) E.N.T. Surg. Unit	Rangoon	S.B. Dist. attchd. 58 I.G.H. (I.T.)
9 (Ind.) Fd. Lab.	Meiktila	Twelfth Army. Temp. u/c 505 Dist.
23 (Ind.) Fd. Lab.	Rangoon	Twelfth Army. Temp. u/c S.B. Dist.
36 (Ind.) Fd. Lab.	Kalewa	Twelfth Army. Temp. u/c 505 Dist.
46 (Ind.) Fd. Lab.	Mandalay	Twelfth Army. Temp. u/c 505 Dist.
50 (Ind.) Fd. Lab.	Rangoon	Twelfth Army. Temp. u/c S.B. Dist.
55 (Ind.) Fd. Lab.	Rangoon	Twelfth Army. Temp. u/c S.B. Dist.
5 (Ind.) M.O.U.	Meiktila	505 Dist.
11 (Ind.) M.O.U.	Rangoon	S.B. Dist.
16 (Ind.) M.O.U.	Rangoon	S.B. Dist.
2 (Ind.) Spectacle Sub-Centre	Meiktila	505 Dist.
3 (Ind.) Mob. X-ray Unit	Pegu	IV Corps attchd. 13 (Ind.) C.C.S.
6 (Ind.) Mob. X-ray Unit	Rangoon	Twelfth Army. Temp. u/c S.B. Dist. Attchd. 8 (Ind.) C.C.S.
8 (Ind.) Mob. X-ray Unit	Myingyan	Twelfth Army. Temp. u/c 505 Dist. Attchd. 13 (Ind.) M.F.T.U. on arrival Rangoon
10 (Ind.) Mob. X-ray Unit	Kalewa	505 Dist. Attchd. 88 I.G.H.(C.)
11 (Ind.) Mob. X-ray Unit	Meiktila	Twelfth Army. Temp. u/c 505 Dist. Attchd. 26 (Ind.) C.C.S.

48 (Ind.) X-ray Unit	Rangoon	S.B. Dist. Attchd. 91 I.G.H.(C.)
69 (Ind.) X-ray Unit	Mandalay	505 Dist. For absorption by 52 I.G.H.(C.)
79 (Ind.) Mob. X-ray Unit	Hmawbi	Twelfth Army. Temp. u/c S.B. Dist. Attchd. 14 (Ind.) C.C.S.
82 (Ind.) Mob. X-ray Unit	Toungoo	IV Corps. Attchd. 16 (Ind.) C.C.S.
85 (Ind.) Mob. X-ray Unit	Taikkyi	Twelfth Army. Temp. u/c S.B. Dist. Attchd. 19 (Ind.) C.C.S.
93 (Ind.) Mob. X-ray Unit	Rangoon	S.B. Dist. Attchd. 58 I.G.H. (I.T.)
94 (Ind.) Mob. X-ray Unit	Rangoon	S.B. Dist. Attchd. 18 (Ind.) C.C.S. For absorption into 41 I.G.H.
90 (Ind.) Mob. X-ray Servicing Unit	Rangoon	Twelfth Army
2 F.T.U.	Pegu	IV Corps. Attchd. 13 (Ind.) C.C.S.
5 F.T.U.	Toungoo	IV Corps. Attchd. 16 (Ind.) C.C.S.
32 F.T.U.	Rangoon	Twelfth Army. Temp. u/c S.B. Dist.
38 F.T.U.	Meiktila	Twelfth Army. Temp. u/c 505 Dist.
2 (Ind.) Adv. B.T.U.	Rangoon	Twelfth Army
3 (Ind.) S.S.(C.)	Pegu	IV Corps
43 (Ind.) S.S.(C.)	Shwebo	505 Dist.
61 (Ind.) S.S.(C.)	Bassein	S.B. Dist.
67 (Ind.) S.S.(C.)	Rangoon	S.B. Dist.
68 (Ind.) S.S.(C.)	Thazi	505 Dist.
69 (Ind.) S.S.(C.)	Payangazu	505 Dist.
70 (Ind.) S.S.(C.)	Yamethin	505 Dist.
74 (Ind.) S.S.(C.)	Milestone 52 Tamu–Kalewa road	505 Dist.
75 (Ind.) S.S.(C.)	Meiktila	505 Dist.
76 (Ind.) S.S.(C.)	Mawchi road	22nd E.A. Bde.
79 (Ind.) S.S.(C.)	Alon	505 Dist.
79 (Ind.) S.S.(C.) detach.	Milestone 25½ Kalewa–Pyingaing road	505 Dist.

82 (Ind.) S.S.(C.)	Indainggyi	505 Dist.
87 (Ind.) S.S.(C.)	Tatkon	505 Dist.
89 (Ind.) S.S.(C.)	Pyawbwe	505 Dist.
90 (Ind.) S.S.(C.)	Ye-U	505 Dist.
20 (Ind.) A.M.U.	Tharrawaddy	Indian 20th Division
21 (Ind.) A.M.U.	Indainggyi	505 Dist.
22 (Ind.) A.M.U.	Milestone 52 Tamu-Kalewa road	505 Dist.
32 (Ind.) A.M.U.	Rangoon	S.B. Dist.
33 (Ind.) A.M.U.	Monywa	505 Dist.
44 (Ind.) A.M.U.	Magwe	505 Dist. Moving to Prome
45 (Ind.) A.M.U.	Toungoo	Indian 19th Division
55 (Ind.) A.M.U.	Kalewa	505 Dist. Under orders for India
68 (Ind.) A.M.U.	Area Pegu-Waw	Indian 7th Division
69 (Ind.) A.M.U.	Pegu	IV Corps
71 (Ind.) A.M.U.	Myingyan	505 Dist.
88 (Ind.) A.M.U.	Rangoon	S.B. Dist.
91 (Ind.) A.M.U.	Penwegon	Indian 17th Division
100 (Ind.) A.M.U.	Rangoon	Indian 5th Division
101 (Ind.) A.M.U.	Mandalay	505 Dist.
102 (Ind.) A.M.U.	Maymyo	505 Dist. Moving to Thazi
103 (Ind.) A.M.U.	Meiktila	505 Dist.
103 (Ind.) A.M.U. detachs.	Tatkon and Pyawbwe	
105 (Ind.) A.M.U.	Rangoon	S.B. Dist.
1 (Ind.) Mal. Fd. Lab.	Rangoon	Twelfth Army. Temp. u/c S.B. Dist.
10 (Ind.) Base Depot Med. Stores	Myingyan	505 Dist.
3 (Ind.) Depot Med. Stores	Rangoon	S.B. Dist.
41 (Ind.) Depot Med. Stores	Mandalay	505 Dist. Moving to Rangoon to relieve 46 (Ind.) Depot Med. Stores
44 (Ind.) Depot Med. Stores	Pegu	IV Corps
45 (Ind.) Depot Med. Stores	Meiktila	505 Dist.
46 (Ind.) Depot Med. Stores	Rangoon	S.B. Dist.
48 (Ind.) Depot Med. Stores	Tharrawaddy	S.B. Dist.
49 (Ind.) Depot Med. Stores	Mandalay	505 Dist.
50 (Ind.) Depot Med. Stores	Rangoon	S.B. Dist.
V.D. Wing, 41 I.G.H.	Meiktila	505 Dist.
V.D. Wing, 49 I.G.H.	Rangoon	S.B. Dist.

102 (E.A.) Hosp. Sec.	Rangoon	S.B. Dist.
111 (E.A.) Hosp. Sec.	Rangoon	S.B. Dist.
112 (E.A.) Hosp. Sec.	Rangoon	S.B. Dist.
110 (E.A.) C.R.S.	Rangoon	S.B. Dist. Under orders for Toungoo, IV Corps
Corps Exhaustion Centre	Pegu	IV Corps. Attchd. 13 (Ind.) C.C.S.
7 (Ind.) Base San. Sec.	Rangoon	S.B. Dist.
8 (Ind.) Base San. Sec.	Rangoon	S.B. Dist.
9 (Ind.) Base San. Sec.	Rangoon	S.B. Dist.
10 (Ind.) Base San. Sec.	Rangoon	S.B. Dist.
11 (Ind.) Base San. Sec.	Rangoon	S.B. Dist.
12 (Ind.) San. Sec.	Rangoon	S.B. Dist.
H.Q. 202 M.A.C.	Rangoon	S.B. Dist.
H.Q. 202 M.A.C. detach.		Temp. u/c/ 505 Dist.
H.Q. 201 M.A.C.	Pegu	IV Corps
A.F.S., one pln.	Pegu	IV Corps
5 (Ind.) Beach Med. Unit	Syriam	S.B. Dist. Moving to Rangoon
4 (Ind.) Bearer Coy.		One pln. with 22nd E.A. Bde. Rest moving to Rangoon
7 (Ind.) Bearer Coy.	Kalaw	IV Corps. One pln. with Indian 19th Division
1 F.S.U. (Red Cross)	Rangoon	
Sub-depot, Red Cross Stores	Myingyan	
34 (Ind.) Dent. Unit (B.T.)	Rangoon	S.B. Dist.
38 (Ind.) Dent. Unit (B.T.)	Maymyo	505 Dist.
41 (Ind.) Dent. Unit (B.T.)	Daik-U	With Indian 17th Division
45 (Ind.) Dent. Unit (B.T.)	Pegu–Waw area	With Indian 7th Division
49 (Ind.) Dent. Unit (B.T.)	Toungoo	With Indian 19th Division
53 (Ind.) Dent. Unit (B.T.)	Meiktila	505 Dist.
55 (Ind.) Dent. Unit (B.T.)	Rangoon	With Indian 5th Division
56 (Ind.) Dent. Unit (B.T.)	Tharrawaddy	With Indian 20th Division
79 (Ind.) Dent. Unit (B.T.)	Rangoon	S.B. Dist.
80 (Ind.) Dent. Unit (B.T.)	Pegu	IV Corps
Br. Dental Centre	Kalewa	505 Dist.
17 (Ind.) Dent. Unit (I.T.)	Magwe	505 Dist.
18 (Ind.) Dent. Unit (I.T.)	Rangoon	S.B. Dist.
19 (Ind.) Dent. Unit (I.T.)	Pegu–Waw area	With Indian 7th Division
26 (Ind.) Dent. Unit (I.T.)	Daik-U	With Indian 17th Division
30 (Ind.) Dent. Unit (I.T.)	Meiktila	505 Dist.
32 (Ind.) Dent. Unit (I.T.)	Myingyan	505 Dist.
68 (Ind.) Dent. Unit (I.T.)	Pegu	IV Corps

69 (Ind.) Dent. Unit (I.T.)	Rangoon	With Indian 5th Division
70 (Ind.) Dent. Unit (I.T.)	Tharrawaddy	With Indian 20th Division
74 (Ind.) Dent. Unit (I.T.)	Mandalay	505 Dist.
75 (Ind.) Dent. Unit (I.T.)	Toungoo	With Indian 19th Division
1 (Ind.) Dent. Mech. Unit	Rangoon	With Indian 5th Division
4 (Ind.) Dent. Mech. Unit	Kalewa	505 Dist.
7 (Ind.) Dent. Mech. Unit	Rangoon	S.B. Dist.
9 (Ind.) Dent. Mech. Unit	Daik-U	With Indian 17th Division
10 (Ind.) Dent. Mech. Unit	Meiktila	505 Dist.
13 (Ind.) Dent. Mech. Unit	Maymyo	505 Dist.
19 (Ind.) Dent. Mech. Unit	Toungoo	With Indian 19th Division
20 (Ind.) Dent. Mech. Unit	Pegu	IV Corps
23 (Ind.) Dent. Mech. Unit	Pegu–Waw area	With Indian 7th Division
25 (Ind.) Dent. Mech. Unit	Tharrawaddy	With Indian 20th Division

CHAPTER 15

THE HEALTH OF THE TROOPS

FROM THE point of view of the Army Medical Services war appears as a head-on clash between two sets of contrasted forces, the one consisting of such as in their action are destructive, causing disability and death, the other of such as are life-saving, health-promoting and health-restoring. Both sets of forces represent power that derives from scientific knowledge. Of the forces that destroy there are two main kinds. In military records they are classified respectively as battle casualties and sick, the first being due to enemy action, the second being caused by disease. As a source of wastage of man-power the second of these two is far more powerful than the first. Of the forces that are harnessed to the tasks of saving life and limb, of preventing disease and of mitigating the effects of bodily and mental hurt, that which is represented by the Army Medical Services is among the most potent.

The outcome of the interaction of these two sets of forces is clearly revealed by the statistical data that relate to battle casualties, to the sick-rate, to the incidence of disease, and particularly of those diseases which throughout the course of history have always been especially prevalent in armies in the field, or to the case-fatality-rate, to the survival-rate and to the average duration of stay in hospital. The movement of these and of other rates of the same general kind during successive wars, including the Second World War, demonstrates conclusively that the power to save life, to prevent disease and to repair disability had outstripped the power to destroy and to mutilate. But the relationship of these two sets of forces was abruptly and profoundly disturbed when to the forces of destruction was added the atomic bomb. Thereafter the forces of destruction became predominant.

The campaign in Burma is of peculiar interest on account of the remarkable movement of the sick-rate from exceedingly high at its beginning to astonishingly low at its end. The Army Medical Services can with fairness claim that in this dramatic and militarily all important decline in wastage due to disease the value of the contribution which they made to the war effort is faithfully disclosed.

Health is measured by the extent to which it is absent in an individual or in a group, by the extent to which its alternative and contrasted state, ill-health or sickness, far more easily recognised, is present. One of the measures commonly used is the proportion of the population at risk—the army, the corps, the division—that is admitted to hospital in a given period of time. This figure does not represent the total amount of sickness in the population since many forms of sickness do not require for their diagnosis and treatment the special facilities that are to be found only in the larger medical units. Not every individual who is ill seeks the help of his medical officer. Sickness in the present context is to be regarded as *recorded* sickness, as sickness of such a kind and degree that it obliges or persuades the sufferer to report sick. In a general way, however, the admission-rate considered as a proportion of the total population at risk, is a fairly satisfactory and certainly a very useful index of the degree to which health is absent from the population.

Army rates are usually calculated on an annual basis i.e. so many per 1,000 strength per year (the equivalent annual rate, E.A.R.) Sometimes they are given as monthly, weekly or daily rates.

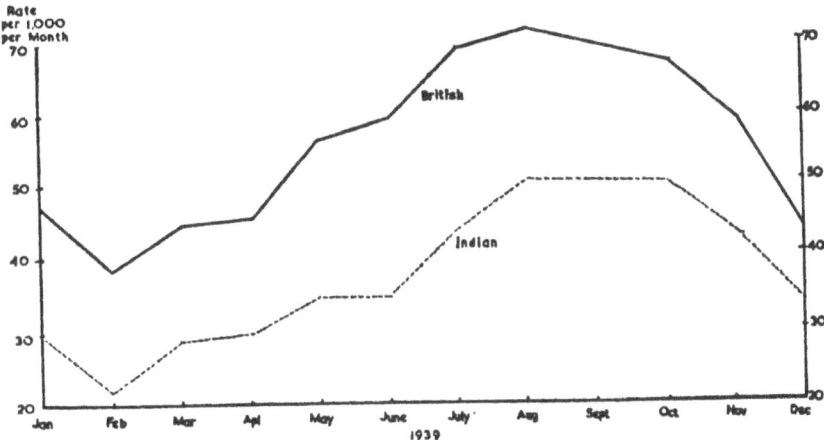

FIG. 75. India 1939. Total Admissions to Hospital. All Causes. Rate per 1,000 Strength per Month.

TABLE 48

India. 1939. Total Admissions to Hospital. All Causes.

Rate per 1,000 per month.

	January	February	March	April	May	June
British Troops	46·4	38·0	44·2	45·4	56·3	58·1
Indian Troops	29·1	21·1	28·1	29·5	34·5	34·4
	July	August	Sept.	Oct.	Nov.	Dec.
British Troops	69·3	71·7	69·8	67·1	59·4	43·5
Indian Troops	43·7	50·1	50·4	50·5	43·1	34·3

Before the Second World War, in the United Kingdom, a sick-rate of 1 or 2 per 1,000 per diem (1 or 2/1,000/diem) was regarded as unexceptional, 3/1,000/diem as disturbing and demanding examination. In a station such as India, where malaria and dysentery were invariably to be encountered, it was usual to find that the sick-rate for British troops was of the order of 40–70/1,000/month while that of Indian troops was about 20–50/1,000/month. The sick-rate fluctuated with the season, the fewest admissions to hospital being in the month of February and the greatest number during the autumn months of August and September. With the coming of the cold weather the rate dropped sharply to rise again in April when the increase in the fly population was associated with an increase in the incidence of dysentery.

INDIA 1941-45

During the war years the graphs showing hospital admissions among troops in India showed the same general features but ran at a higher level. The curve for British troops ranged between 60 and 115/1,000/month while that for Indian troops ranged between 48 and 77/1,000/month.

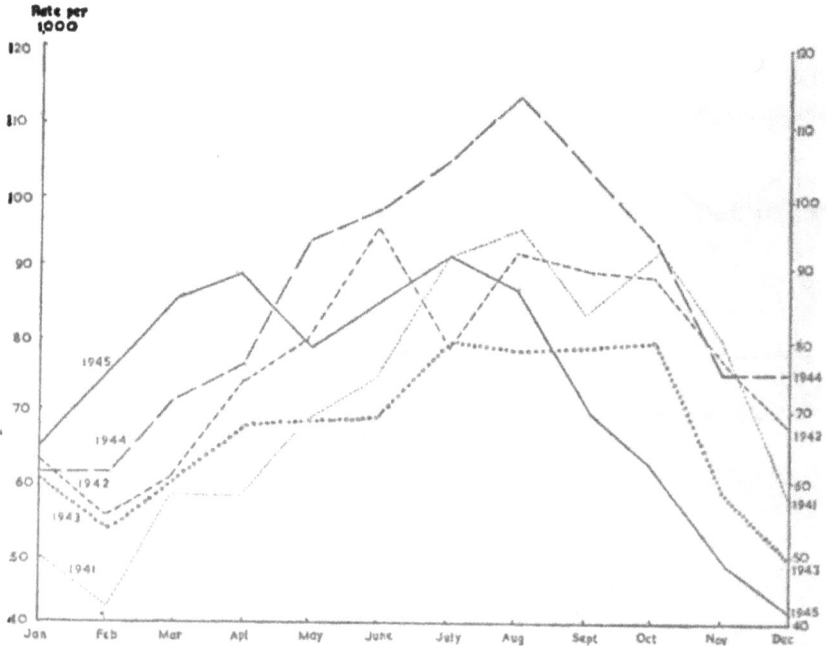

FIG. 76. India 1941–45. Total Admissions to Hospital, British Other Ranks. All Causes. Rate per 1,000 per Month.

The reasons for this war-time worsening of the sick-rate were various. The Army, British and Indian, underwent a vast and rapid expansion, the standards of fitness were lowered and the period of training greatly shortened. The medical services came to include large numbers of medical officers whose knowledge of military medicine was limited and the medical services were not always in a position to help units to protect themselves against the hazards of disease.

In Eastern Army and in the formations that succeeded it the admission-rate was higher than that for India. In IV Corps for example, in 1943 from April to October it was 6/1,000/diem, a rate which means that the number of those going into hospital during the course of a year was equal to three times the number of men in the Corps; it was as though every man in the Corps had been admitted to hospital three times during the course of the year. In 1943, it is to be remembered, there was no D.D.T. and no suppressive mepacrine in IV Corps which was then fighting on the heights and in the valleys around Imphal, Tamu and Tiddim. In Arakan the conditions were such that Indian 26th Division in one week in April 1943 had a rate of 18/1,000/diem which meant that if the rate persisted and if reinforcements in strength did not continually arrive, the division would cease to exist in the space of two months. The periods when the admission-rate was at its highest were the periods when the fighting was most intense for when there is fighting men cannot safeguard themselves at all easily against the hazards of disease. And since at this time the ratio of battle casualties to sick was about 1:100 the shape of the curve showing admissions to hospital was not appreciably affected by the numbers of those admitted on account of wounds.

In Fourteenth Army in 1943 the rate during the months of June to September ranged between about 7 to 8·5 per 1,000 per diem for British troops and round about 5 per 1,000 for Indian troops. In 1944 the rate for British troops reached a peak of just over 5/1,000 diem in June and of just over 4 per 1,000 for Indian troops. The 1944 curve

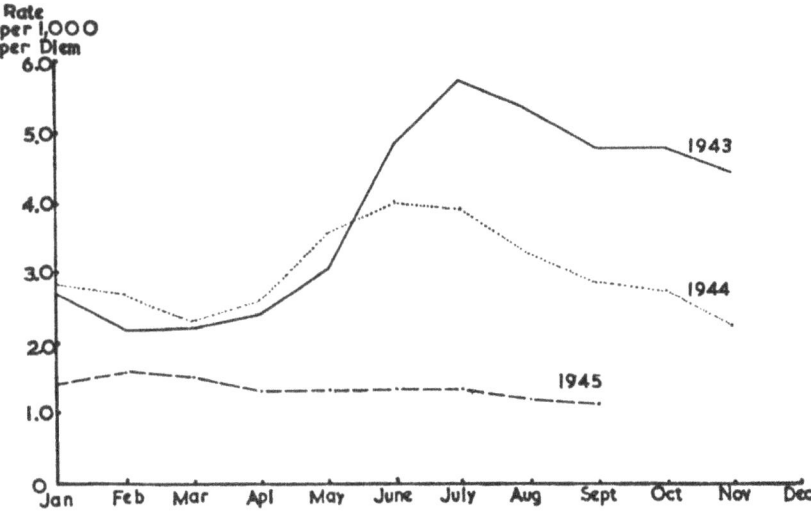

FIG. 77. A.L.F.S.E.A. 1943–45. Admissions to Hospital, All Ethnic Groups. All Causes. Rate per 1,000 per Diem.

for British troops ran at a lower general level than did the 1943 curve. In the case of Indian troops the first part of the curve from January to June was slightly higher in 1944 than in 1943 but in the second half of the year the 1944 curve ran at a much lower level than did that for 1943.

A.L.F.S.E.A. 1943-45

The figures presented by A.L.F.S.E.A., some of them belonging to the period of its predecessors, show in unmistakable fashion the progressive and very impressive improvement in the hospital admission-rate throughout the years 1943-1945. From the last week in June 1944 there was a steady and continuous fall throughout the second half of the year and during the whole of 1945 (January–September). No autumn peak occurred and it is this that indicates that a large measure of control over malaria had been achieved. In 1945 the hospital admission-rate was actually lower than what in peace-time in the United Kingdom would have been regarded as an eminently satisfactory figure. The effect of this demonstrable lowering of the hospital admission-rate upon the man-power problem, upon morale and upon the Army Medical Services themselves must have been very considerable indeed. It is indeed satisfactory when an organisation such as the Army Medical Services can measure the quality of the work it has been doing by the use of such a yardstick as this. It is to be remembered that these figures relate to a population of nearly a million men of different ethnic groups and cultures and scattered widely over a theatre remarkable for the diversity of its geographical and climatic features. The malaria figures are well worthy of careful study. A malaria-rate of 0·2/1,000/diem or

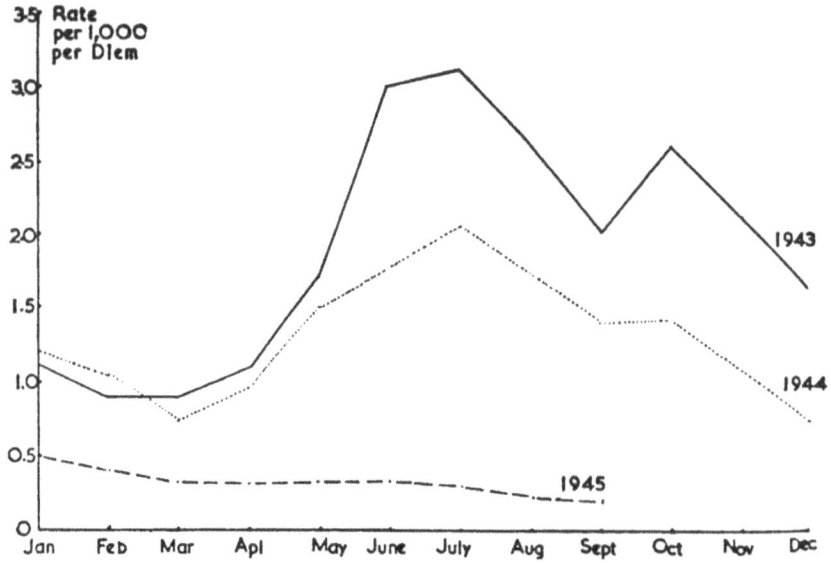

FIG. 78. A.L.F.S.E.A. 1943-45. Admissions to Hospital on account of Malaria and N.Y.D.(F.). All Ethnic Groups. Rate per 1,000 per Diem.

TABLE 49

Allied Land Forces. South-East Asia. 1943, 1944 and 1945. Admissions to Hospital. All Causes and on account of Malaria and N.Y.D.(F.). Rate per 1,000 per Diem.

		Hospital Admission-rate All Causes			Hospital Admission-rate Malaria and N.Y.D.(F.)		
		1943	1944	1945	1943	1944	1945
January	1	—	2·60	—	—	1·25	—
	8	2·55	3·04	1·46	1·30	1·40	0·61
	15	3·15	2·97	1·46	1·20	1·33	0·55
	22	2·70	3·04	1·53	1·10	1·34	0·53
	29	2·40	2·61	1·51	1·09	1·17	0·49
February	5	2·32	2·65	1·64	0·90	1·13	0·49
	12	2·40	2·80	1·48	0·80	1·12	0·43
	19	2·00	2·89	1·64	0·91	1·17	0·51
	26	2·10	2·62	1·52	1·00	0·97	0·42
March	4	2·00	2·64	1·52	0·98	0·91	0·39
	11	2·05	2·37	1·43	0·92	0·79	0·33
	18	2·00	2·14	1·38	0·92	0·66	0·33
	25	2·79	2·40	1·63	0·95	0·75	0·33
April	1	2·40	2·30	1·36	0·93	0·82	0·29
	8	2·20	2·45	1·41	0·88	0·94	0·30
	15	2·10	2·67	1·38	0·94	0·99	0·28
	22	2·60	3·10	1·30	1·30	1·11	0·30
	29	2·80	2·92	1·26	1·70	1·11	0·30
May	6	2·60	3·06	1·28	—	1·06	0·29
	13	2·70	3·87	1·42	1·23	1·43	0·34
	20	2·62	3·51	1·23	1·50	1·79	0·31
	27	4·19	3·75	1·40	2·60	1·84	0·40
June	3	4·95	3·63	1·31	3·30	1·58	0·34
	10	2·83	4·17	1·32	2·20	1·76	0·37
	17	5·70	3·90	1·27	3·49	1·93	0·36
	24	5·70	4·24	1·33	3·30	2·15	0·37
July	1	5·61	4·10	1·37	3·10	2·12	0·39
	8	5·74	3·86	1·44	3·30	2·01	0·36
	15	5·99	3·97	1·41	3·58	2·06	0·31
	22	5·40	3·62	1·33	3·30	2·02	0·30
	29	5·30	3·83	1·32	2·60	2·04	0·28
August	5	5·25	3·48	1·29	2·60	1·95	0·27
	12	5·40	3·54	1·25	2·50	1·68	0·28
	19	5·50	3·15	1·11	2·78	1·73	0·22
	26	5·20	2·90	1·03	2·55	1·56	0·22

TABLE 49—contd.

	1943	1944	1945	1943	1944	1945
September 2	5·65	2·84	1·02	2·68	1·49	0·17
9	4·32	3·02	0·98	1·66	1·34	0·17
16	4·60	4·74	1·10	1·60	1·57	0·22
23	4·41	2·52	1·12	2·10	1·33	0·21
30	—	2·68	1·02	2·25	1·44	0·19
October 7	4·60	2·63	—	2·53	1·45	—
14	4·70	2·83	—	2·60	1·51	—
21	4·80	2·59	—	2·88	1·39	—
28	5·01	2·60	1·09	2·62	1·32	0·19
November 4	5·18	2·16	—	2·65	1·12	—
11	5·57	2·45	—	2·10	1·23	—
18	3·20	2·16	—	1·90	1·08	—
25	3·25	2·09	—	1·90	0·93	—
December 2	3·01	1·75	—	1·95	0·76	—
9	2·80	1·75	—	1·80	0·72	—
16	3·30	1·52	—	1·90	0·70	—
23	2·20	1·50	—	1·15	0·75	—
30	2·70	1·55	—	1·23	0·66	—

less for such a force in such a theatre is one that at the beginning of the war would certainly have been regarded as unattainable.

There is no need to warn members of the Army Medical Services that these figures are not to be accepted as being absolutely accurate or to offer them reasons for any lack of accuracy. Far too many individuals who find the maintenance of records meaningless and boring are involved, when war is being waged, in the collection of statistical data from which other people attempt to extract information of value to the administrator. Under conditions of active service it is never a simple matter to obtain accurate information concerning the strength of a unit. Ration strengths are commonly misleading by as much as 10 to 20 per cent. excess. Nevertheless, these figures, all that were available at the time, do possess a very considerable value in spite of any inaccuracy, for they do yield a reasonably faithful picture of the situation and it is upon them, and not upon others produced later and thoroughly checked for accuracy, that the medical services depended for guidance in respect of policy and action. Policy is shaped by the figures that are available at the time, imperfect though they may be, and not by figures that emerge from careful studies made in the postwar years of all the records that have accumulated from a great variety of sources.

Figure 78 and Table 49 show in the clearest possible manner how complete was the mastery that had been gained over the most potent of the agencies of morbidity in this theatre.

In the table below other figures of the same general kind but from different sources are given:

TABLE 51

Indo-Burma Front and South-East Asia Command (excluding Ceylon) 1942–1945. Admissions to Hospital. British and Indian Troops. By Cause. Rate per 1,000. (Indian Medical History, Medicine, Surgery and Pathology, pages 7 and 8.)

INDIAN TROOPS Diseases	1942 Number	1942 Rate per 1,000	1943 Number	1943 Rate per 1,000	1944 Number	1944 Rate per 1,000	(January–September) 1945 Number	(January–September) 1945 Rate per 1,000
Malaria	60,072	418·33	179,774	478·90	134,688	315·68	18,577	45·63
Dysentery	7,097	49·42	12,729	33·91	15,785	37·00	5,028	12·35
Venereal Disease	6,426	44·75	26,831	71·47	15,647	36·67	12,952	31·81
Minor Septic Diseases	4,044	28·16	13,199	35·16	11,819	27·70	7,639	18·76
Diarrhoea	3,629	25·27	10,499	27·97	14,839	34·78	4,950	12·16
Common Cold	2,091	14·56	12,901	34·37	13,617	31·91	6,687	16·43
Skin Diseases	1,721	11·98	9,012	24·01	10,388	24·35	6,359	15·62
Influenza	1,623	11·30	1,015	2·70	267	0·63	162	0·40
Tuberculosis	303	2·11	573	1·53	506	1·19	507	1·24
Mental Disorders	203	1·41	1,164	3·10	1,827	4·28	2,169	5·33
Other Diseases	34,772	242·14	134,831	359·17	151,037	354·00	63,451	155·86
Injuries (N.E.A.)	5,254	36·59	16,136	42·98	18,494	43·35	15,294	37·57
Total Casualties (N.E.A.)	127,235	886·04	418,664	1,115·27	388,914	911·54	143,775	353·17
G.S.W.	575	4·00	1,416	3·77	6,867	16·09	5,279	12·97
Shell Wounds	58	0·40	452	1·20	3,845	9·01	2,296	5·64
Bomb Wounds	7	0·05	890	2·37	3,809	8·93	2,764	6·79
Blast	—	—	—	—	134	0·31	38	0·09
Total Casualties (E.A.)	640	4·46	2,758	7·35	14,655	34·34	10,377	25·49
Total Admissions	127,875	890·50	421,422	1,122·63	403,569	945·88	154,152	378·66

TABLE 51—continued.

BRITISH TROOPS Diseases	1942		1943		1944		(January–September) 1945	
	Number	Rate per 1,000	Number	Rate per 1,000	Number	Rate per 1,000	Number	Rate per 1,000
Malaria	15,045	334·70	36,201	628·20	32,005	405·58	6,715	96·26
Dysentery	3,946	87·80	7,605	132·00	7,689	97·44	3,392	48·62
Venereal Disease	3,246	72·20	9,101	157·90	5,463	69·23	3,777	54·14
Minor Septic Diseases	2,404	53·50	3,799	65·90	3,841	48·67	2,913	41·76
Diarrhoea	1,872	41·70	4,439	77·00	7,198	91·21	1,822	26·12
Common Cold	525	11·70	1,229	21·30	1,460	18·50	869	12·46
Skin Disease	1,719	38·20	2,881	50·00	2,851	36·13	2,678	38·39
Influenza	171	3·80	311	5·40	79	1·00	18	0·26
Tuberculosis	44	1·00	50	0·90	33	0·42	33	0·48
Mental Disorders	115	2·50	349	6·10	859	10·88	1,216	17·43
Other Diseases	16,779	373·70	34,646	601·30	43,776	554·75	17,357	248·80
Injuries (N.E.A.)	1,491	33·20	3,712	64·40	4,325	54·81	3,180	45·58
Total Casualties (N.E.A.)	47,357	1,053·90	104,323	1,810·40	109,579	1,388·62	43,970	630·29
G.S.W.	178	3·90	509	8·80	4,325	54·81	2,125	30·46
Shell Wounds	6	0·10	156	2·70	1,928	24·43	1,026	14·71
Bomb Wounds	25	0·50	140	2·40	1,724	21·85	660	9·46
Blast	—	—	—	—	65	0·82	22	0·31
Total Casualties (E.A.)	209	4·50	805	13·90	8,042	101·91	3,833	54·94
Total Admissions	47,566	1,058·40	105,128	1,824·30	117,621	1,490·53	47,803	685·24

Throughout the years malaria, dysentery, venereal diseases, minor septic conditions, the common cold and skin diseases were the principal causes of admissions to hospital and therefore of morbidity. During the years 1943 and 1944 injuries due to enemy action increased. In 1942 these seven causes accounted for 70 per cent. of all admissions, for 66 per cent. in 1943, for 59 per cent. in 1944 and for about 49 per cent. in 1945.

TABLE 52

Indo-Burma Front. Burma and South-East Asia Command (excluding Ceylon). Non-Battle and Battle Casualties. British, Indian, African Troops. (Indian Medical History, Medicine, Surgery and Pathology, page 2.)

Year	Non-Battle Casualties			Battle Casualties			Ratio of Battle Casualties to Non-Battle Casualties
	Number	Rate per 1,000		Number	Rate per 1,000		
		Admissions	Deaths		Admissions	Deaths	
1942	178,139	921·14	7·48	872	4·51	—	1 : 204
1943	531,719	1,196·10	4·74	3,735	8·40	0·38	1 : 142
1944	541,575	1,040·91	5·91	24,680	47·43	2·18	1 : 22
1945	213,047	384·13	1·62	16,188	29·19	1·25	1 : 13

TABLE 53

Indo-Burma Front. Burma and South-East Asia Command (excluding Ceylon). The Relationship between Casualties caused by Enemy Action and not so caused. British and Indian Troops compared. (Indian Medical History, Medicine, Surgery and Pathology, page 3.)

Year	British Troops			Indian Troops		
	Casualties (enemy action)	Casualties (non-enemy action)	Ratio of enemy action to non-enemy action	Casualties (enemy action)	Casualties (non-enemy action)	Ratio of enemy action to non-enemy action
1942	209	47,357	1 : 227	640	127,235	1 : 199
1943	805	104,323	1 : 130	2,758	418,664	1 : 152
1944	8,042	109,579	1 : 14	14,655	388,914	1 : 26
1945	3,833	43,970	1 : 11	10,377	143,775	1 : 14

TABLE 54

Indo-Burma Front. Burma and South-East Asia Command (excluding Ceylon). Average Daily Number of Patients under Treatment in Hospitals and Rate per 1,000. Indian Troops. (Indian Medical History, Medicine, Surgery and Pathology, page 6.)

Year	Average Daily Number under Treatment	Rate per 1,000
1943	12,487·92	46·96
1944	10,715·17	33·80
1945	475·97	1·55

In the last three tables the figures for 1945 relate only to the period January–September. The rates and ratios shown in these tables gain greatly in significance when compared with those of other campaigns. The average ratio of wounds to sickness was about 1 : 67. In the Campaign in East Africa, 1940–42, this figure was 1 : 68 in 1940, 1 : 3 in 1941 and 1 : 364 in 1942. The factor most profoundly affecting the ratio is the number of battle casualties; the East African figures indicate that these were very common in 1941 and very rare in 1942. In the Western Desert the daily average number of the constantly sick was 6 per 1,000; in East Africa it was 14 per 1,000.

It is of importance to note that in 1943 and 1944 the number of admissions to hospital exceeded the strength of the force which supplied the admissions. In 1944 of every 1,000 men about 48 were wounded and of these fewer than 3 died of their wounds.

'The general reduction of diseases and the consequent saving in manpower is shown in the following tables. The results in the final year of the campaign can be considered as really satisfactory and are a gratifying record of the work of the medical services, without which it might well have been impossible to carry the campaign to a victorious end.'*

Sickness Rates

1942	1,850 per 1,000 per annum
1943	1,400 ,, ,, ,, ,,
1944	1,000 ,, ,, ,, ,,
1945	500 ,, ,, ,, ,,

Average proportion of Battle Casualties to Sick Admissions

1944	Peak number of casualties for one week	1,668
	Peak number of sick for one week	15,315
1945	Peak number of casualties for one week	2,027
	Peak number of sick for one week	7,893

---

*Excerpt from the Report to the Combined Chiefs of Staff by the Supreme Allied Commander, South-East Asia Command.

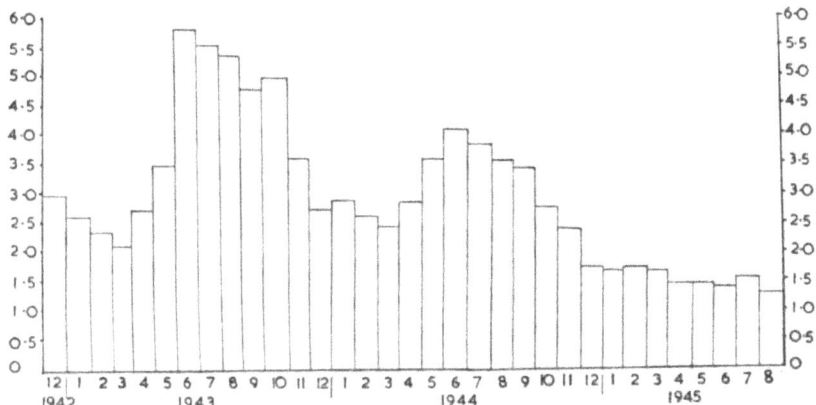

Fig. 79. British, Indian and African Formations in Burma. Hospital Admissions on account of Wounds and Sickness, December 1942–August 1945. Rate per 1,000 per day. (Adapted from the Report to the Combined Chiefs of Staff by the Supreme Allied Commander, South-East Asia Command.)

'From November 1944 to April 1945, both months inclusive, the number of casualties from sickness totalled 69,713 while battle casualties amounted to 17,693. Thus during the period under report, the ratio of medical to battle casualties was 3·93 to 1. Even during the periods of hardest fighting in February and March, the ratio only fell to 2·4 and 1·8 to 1 respectively. Nevertheless, the sick-rate during the same period was surprisingly low. In early March, for example, it was only 0·96 per 1,000 per day; in late April it was 1·42 per 1,000 per day, that is about one-third of the rate in October 1944.

'Such low figures among troops fighting and working in an unhealthy tropical climate, in areas where malaria, dysentery, scrub typhus, smallpox and cholera are endemic are in themselves a great tribute to the medical services. They can be attributed in part to the more extensive use of new drugs, e.g. mepacrine and sulphaguanidine and to the invaluable insecticide, D.D.T. But I would like to lay stress on the important part played by good discipline, particularly in regard to anti-malaria measures and hygiene. Without this discipline, modern medical science and the efforts of the officers of the medical services are largely ineffective.

'There can be few campaigns in history, fought under such adverse conditions, in which the general health of large armies was maintained at such high level. It must not be forgotten that the primary function of the medical services is officially defined as the maintenance of health and the prevention of disease, a function which in popular esteem tends to get lost sight of or overshadowed by the glamour of their other duties in tending the sick and the wounded.'*

---

* Excerpt from the Despatch by Lieutenant-General Sir Oliver Leese, C. in C. Allied Land Forces, South-East Asia Command. *The London Gazette* 6th April, 1951.

FOURTEENTH ARMY

Fourteenth Army had moved through country of the most diverse kinds—mountain, jungle, riverine and plain, much of it notorious for its high incidence of dreadful diseases, and had experienced climatic conditions ranging from the hot and humid jungle of Assam, the cold monsoon rains of Kohima at 7,000 ft., the mists and fogs of Shenam and Tiddim and finally the scorching dry heat of the central Burmese Plain. That outstanding human quality, an ability to adjust and to adapt to a wide range of physico-climatic conditions, was tested to the full.

The average strength of Fourteenth Army during the period November 12, 1944 to May 19, 1945 was 190,151.

Indian Troops	127,299
British Troops	47,142
African Troops	15,710
	190,151

Its greatest size, 250,508, was attained during the week ending March 17, 1945 and its smallest, 140,199, during the week ending December 9, 1944. The numbers of the British troops relative to the total fell considerably towards the end of the campaign, so much so that it became necessary to replace a number of British battalions by Indian. One reason for this drop in the numbers of British troops would seem to have been the lack of transport to bring reinforcements forward from the reinforcement camps in the Comilla area.

TABLE 55

IV, XXXIII Corps and Army Troops. Strengths.
November 12, 1944–May 19, 1945.

Average Strength over the whole period of 188 days	IV Corps	XXXIII Corps	Army Troops
November 12, 1944–May 19, 1945	58,673	73,347	36,033
Greatest Strength	79,193	101,455	60,363
Recorded week ending	2.12.44	31.3.45	17.3.45
Smallest Strength	31,900	59,650	3,608
Recorded week ending	30.12.44	19.5.45	23.12.44

TABLE 56

Fourteenth Army. Numbers evacuated beyond the Regimental Aid Post. November 12, 1944–May 19, 1945.

	Total Number Evacuated	Rate per 1,000 for the period November 12–May 19	Daily Rate per 1,000
British Troops	18,794	398·66	2·11
Indian Troops	36,004	283·62	1·5
African Troops	3,117	198·41	1·05
	57,915	304·57	1·61

THE SICK-RATE

The daily sick-rate (including battle casualties) fell from 2·45/1,000/diem in November 1944 to 1·30/1,000/diem by the end of December. At the same time there was a fall in the malaria sick-rate from 0·85 to 0·49. From December 23, 1944 the battle casualty-rate rose and as a consequence of this the total sick-rate rose to 2·15/1,000/diem in the week ending March 24, 1945. After this the casualty-rate gradually fell and the total sick-rate likewise fell to its lowest point, 1·25/1,000/diem towards the end of April 1945.

The admission-rate for British troops was consistently higher than that for Indian troops. It was below 2/1,000/diem for a short time in December 1944–January 1945 but thereafter rose to vary between 2·0 and 2·7/1,000/diem for the rest of the campaign save for two weeks in April and May. The rate for Indian troops remained below 2·0/1,000/diem for the whole period save for the week ending March 24 when a rate of 2·10 was recorded. Except for the weeks ending March 17 and 24 the admission-rate for African troops was consistently lower than the British and Indian rates.

The admission-rate of IV Corps fell from 2·55/1,000/diem to 0·9 in the week ending February 10 and then rose to a peak of 3·0 (battle casualties 2·75) in the week ending March 24. After this it fell to 1·26 for the week ending April 21 and thereafter rose again. The admission-rate of XXXIII Corps was generally higher than that of IV Corps. It fell from 2·4/1,000/diem on November 18 to 1·15 for the week ending December 16 and thereafter gradually rose to reach 2·55 for the week ending March 3. Thereafter it gradually fell to 1·2 for the week ending May 19.

TABLE 57

Fourteenth Army. Casualties. November 12, 1944–May 19, 1945.

	Number	Rate per 1,000	Rate per 1,000 per Day	Percentage of Totals
Fourteenth Army				
Total Sickness	57,915	304·57	1·62	100
Total Battle Casualties	13,198	69·41	0·39	22·79
Sickness less Battle Casualties	44,717	235·16	1·25	77·22
Malaria and N.Y.D.(F.)	13,952	73·37	0·39	24·09
Dysentery and Diarrhoea	4,398	23·11	0·12	7·61
Venereal Diseases	1,364	7·16	0·03	2·35
Special Diseases	1,904	10·01	0·05	3·29
All Other Causes	23,099	121·51	0·64	39·88
Army Troops				
Total Sickness	5,147	142·84	0·76	100
Total Battle Casualties	101	2·80	0·01	1·96
Sickness less Battle Casualties	5,046	140·04	0·74	98·04
Malaria and N.Y.D.(F.)	1,849	51·31	0·27	35·92
Dysentery and Diarrhoea	434	12·04	0·06	8·43
Venereal Diseases	316	8·77	0·04	6·14
Special Diseases	147	4·08	0·02	2·87
All Other Causes	2,300	63·84	0·34	44·68
IV Corps				
Total Sickness	19,909	339·30	1·80	100
Total Battle Casualties	6,596	112·41	0·59	33·12
Sickness less Battle Casualties	13,313	226·89	1·20	66·88
Malaria and N.Y.D.(F.)	3,837	65·39	0·34	19·27
Dysentery and Diarrhoea	1,247	21·25	0·11	6·26
Venereal Diseases	393	6·69	0·03	1·97
Special Diseases	448	7·63	0·04	2·25
All Other Causes	7,388	125·93	0·68	37·13
XXXIII Corps				
Total Sickness	26,974	368·66	1·95	100
Total Battle Casualties	6,334	86·35	0·46	23·46
Sickness less Battle Casualties	20,640	282·31	1·49	76·54
Malaria and N.Y.D.(F.)	6,533	89·07	0·47	24·23
Dysentery and Diarrhoea	2,182	29·74	0·15	7·72
Venereal Diseases	525	7·15	0·04	1·95
Special Diseases	939	12·80	0·07	3·48
All Other Causes	10,461	143·66	0·75	39·16

THE HEALTH OF THE TROOPS

DEATHS

During this period of 188 days, 1,747 deaths were reported through medical channels: British Troops 566, Indian Troops 1,082 and African Troops 99. Approximately 80 per cent. of these were classified as having been 'killed in action'. The official number of the killed in action from January 1 to May 19, 1945 was: officers 177, other ranks 2,873, a total of 3,050. Part of the difference between these two records was due to the fact that large numbers of the wounded were evacuated out of Army area and not all the deaths were made known to Fourteenth Army.

TOTAL SICKNESS LESS BATTLE CASUALTIES

The total number of casualties due to disease and excluding battle casualties in Fourteenth Army for the period November 1944–May 1945 was 44,717 or 77·22 per cent. of all casualties and an average of 1·25/1,000/diem. The rate reached its highest point of 2·35 in the week ending November 18. Thereafter it fell gradually to range between 1·0 and 1·2. During the weeks ending April 28 and May 5 it was only 0·95, a figure which surely must be regarded as truly remarkable and eminently satisfactory.

IV Corps' rate was generally lower than that of XXXIII Corps, ranging between 2·4/1,000/diem for the week ending November 18 to 0·6 for the week ending February 10, this last figure being the lowest recorded during the whole period for the Army as a whole and for its component corps.

THE PRINCIPAL CAUSES OF MORBIDITY

MALARIA

This was the greatest single cause of morbidity and of man-power loss. In this theatre it was responsible for nearly 50 per cent. of all the recorded sickness during the years 1942–1944 and at times, during the malaria seasons, it accounted for more than 80 per cent. of all admissions to medical units. In three months, from October to December 1942, no less than 18,000 cases were evacuated from Eastern Army alone. It was estimated that in Assam in 1942 there were 76,000 instances of this disease and that in 1943 this figure was doubled. In Eastern Army in 1943 out of half-a-million admissions to medical units over 200,000 were on account of malaria and N.Y.D.(F.). In Arakan one of the brigades lost 69·6 of its strength during the period March–May 1943 through evacuation on account of malaria. The wastage was so great and so rapid that formations were being replaced almost completely every six to eight weeks. In 1944 in Fourteenth Army the numbers of admissions to medical units largely though not exclusively on account of malaria equalled the strength of a standard division each month. The highest rate among Indian troops in Burma and S.E.A.C., excluding Ceylon, was 478·90 per 1,000 in 1943. In the Western Desert, North Africa and Egypt in 1943 the rate was 38·21 per 1,000 and in the East African campaign in 1942, 111·33 per 1,000.

TABLE 58

Fourteenth Army and Component Formations. Admissions to Hospital on account of Malaria. November 12, 1944–May 19, 1945.

	Total Number of Cases	Rate per 1,000	Daily Rate per 1,000
IV Corps	3,837	65·39	0·34
XXXIII Corps	6,533	89·07	0·47
Army Tps.	1,849	51·31	0·27
Indian 5th Division	851	67·21	0·35
11th East African Division	699	31·72	0·16
36th Division	122	7·52	0·04
Indian 19th Division	61	3·25	0·01
	13,952	73·37	0·38

The figure of 13,952 admissions on account of malaria was 24·09 per cent. of all the morbidity leading to admission to a medical unit. It represents an average daily rate of 0·38/1,000/diem or of 73·37/1,000/diem for the whole period of 188 days (Nov. 12–May 19). Together with battle casualties (22·78 per cent.) malaria accounted for 46·87 per cent. of all evacuations from Army area during the period.

The rate fell from 0·94/1,000/diem in November 1944 to 0·23/1,000/diem in the first week of March 1945. Thereafter it rose to become 0·32 by April 21. The use of mepacrine was enforced in Fourteenth Army from November 18, 1944. After this date those who went down with this disease were mostly men recently returned from leave. The disease accounted for six deaths in Fourteenth Army between November 1944 and May 1945.

DYSENTERY AND DIARRHOEA

TABLE 59

Indo-Burma Front. 1942–1945. Admissions (rate per 1,000) to Medical Units on account of Dysentery and Diarrhoea. (Indian Medical History, *Medicine, Surgery and Pathology, page 137.*)

	1942			1943		
	Br.	Ind.	All Troops	Br.	Ind.	All Troops
Dysentery (amoebic)	64·6	2·3	18·07	130·6	33·1	46·98
Dysentery (non-amoebic)	23·2	50·5	41·07	1·4	0·5	0·67
Dysentery (Totals)	87·8	52·8	59·14	132·0	33·6	47·65
Diarrhoea	41·7	27·7	29·14	77·0	27·8	34·56
	1944			1945		
Dysentery (amoebic)	14·84	7·3	8·80	12·08	3·39	4·83
Dysentery (non-amoebic)	82·60	32·7	45·06	36·54	10·49	13·88
Dysentery (Totals)	97·44	40·0	53·86	48·62	13·88	18·71
Diarrhoea	91·21	39·6	46·41	26·12	13·80	13·66

(The distinction between the two forms of Dysentery cannot be regarded as being very reliable.)

TABLE 60

Fourteenth Army and Component Formations. Admissions on account of Dysentery and Diarrhoea. November 1944–May 1945. (Indian Medical History, *Medicine, Surgery and Pathology, page 140.*)

	Total Cases	Rate per 1,000 for the Period	Daily Rate per 1,000	Percentage of Total Admissions from all Causes
IV Corps	1,247	21·25	0·11	6·26
XXXIII Corps	2,182	29·74	0·16	8·09
Army Troops	434	12·04	0·08	8·43
Indian 5th Division	84	6·63	0·05	3·28
11th East African Division	349	15·84	0·15	13·06
36th Division	69	4·25	0·20	15·23
Indian 19th Division	33	1·81	0·26	16·42
	4,398	23·11	0·12	7·59

The overall figures for Fourteenth Army show that the admission-rate on account of dysentery and diarrhoea declined from 0·2/1,000/diem in November 1944 to 0·1/1,000/diem or less during the closing phase of the campaign. In the control of the disease sulphaguanidine played its important part. Every effort was made to treat cases as far forward as possible and most medical officers who were provided with adequate supplies of this drug were encouraged to use it in full doses in every case of diarrhoea. In May, June and July 1944 the number of cases in Fourteenth Army, it was estimated, probably exceeded 100,000. The disease accounted for two deaths.

In the Western Desert and North Africa, 1942, the incidence of this disease among Indian troops was 28·77 per 1,000, in the campaign in East Africa in 1942, 24·82.

VENEREAL DISEASES

TABLE 61

Indo-Burma Front. Incidence (rate per 1,000) of Venereal Diseases. British, Indian and African Troops. (Indian Medical History, Medicine, Surgery and Pathology, page 15.)

	1942	1943	1944	1945 (Jan.–Sept.)
Syphilis	9·54	—	—	5·36
Gonorrhoea	15·23	—	—	10·33
Soft Chancre	4·04	—	—	0·12
Other Venereal Diseases	21·38	—	—	20·44
	50·19	81·17	47·43	36·27

TABLE 62

Fourteenth Army and Component Formations. Incidence of Venereal Diseases. November 12, 1944–May 19, 1945.

	Number of Cases	Rate per 1,000	Daily Rate per 1,000
IV Corps	393	6·69	0·03
XXXIII Corps	525	7·15	0·03
Army Troops	316	8·77	0·04
Indian 5th Division	62	4·89	0·02
11th East African Division	67	3·04	0·01
36th Division	1	—	—
	1,364	7·16	0·04

In Fourteenth Army the rate fell from 0·08/1,000/diem for the week ending November 18, 1944 to 0·02/1,000/diem for the week ending December 16, 1945. Thereafter it remained between 0·02 and 0·04 for the rest of the period.

SPECIAL DISEASES AND CONDITIONS

TABLE 63

Fourteenth Army and Component Formations. Admissions on account of 'Special' Diseases and Conditions. November 12, 1944–May 19, 1945.

	IV Corps	XXXIII Corps	Army Troops	Ind. 5th Div.	11th E.A. Div.	Ind. 19th Div.	36th Div.	Totals
Disease								
Typhus	83	469	29	64	123	—	—	768
Infective Hepatitis	267	235	28	51	25	11	12	629
Smallpox	48	109	39	1	—	1	—	198
Cholera	5	18	20	—	—	—	26	69
Chickenpox	4	44	18	6	1	—	—	73
Diphtheria	1	31	—	—	—	—	—	32
Schistosomiasis	—	—	—	—	39	—	—	39
Mumps	9	6	2	—	2	—	—	19
Enteric Fever	2	6	1	—	—	—	—	9
Cerebro-spinal Fever	5	—	3	1	—	—	—	9
Leprosy	1	1	5	—	—	—	—	7
Tuberculosis	3	3	—	—	—	—	—	6
Paratyphoid Fever	—	—	1	—	1	—	—	2
Acute Ant. Poliomyelitis	4	—	—	—	—	—	—	4
Kala Azar	2	—	—	—	5	—	—	7
Measles	—	4	—	1	—	—	—	5
Leptospirosis	—	4	—	—	—	—	—	4
Scarlet Fever	1	—	—	—	—	—	—	1
Encephalitis lethargica	—	1	—	—	—	—	—	1
Snake bite	2	1	1	—	—	—	—	4
Gangrene	11	7	—	—	—	—	—	18
	448	939	147	124	196	12	38	1,904

	Total Cases	Rate per 1,000	Rate per 1,000 per diem
IV Corps	448	7·63	0·04
XXXIII Corps	939	12·80	0·06
Army Troops	147	4·08	0·02
Indian 5th Division	124	9·87	0·05
11th East African Division	196	8·89	0·04
Indian 19th Division	12	0·64	0·03
36th Division	38	2·34	0·01
	1,904	10·01	0·05

1,904 equals 3·29 per cent. of the total admissions from Fourteenth Army.

TYPHUS

Of typhus fever 768 cases were notified and of these two were classified as murine typhus, the rest being scrub or mite-borne typhus. The peak of the incidence of this disease was reached by December 2, 1944 when 96 cases were notified. From that time onwards the weekly incidence progressively declined until in the week ending February 10, 1945 only two cases were notified and for the week ending May 5, none at all. Up to March 31, 54 deaths (British 18, Indian 23, African 13) had been ascribed to this cause.

These figures refer to Fourteenth Army only and to it only for a brief period of 188 days. They therefore must fail completely to give any true idea of the incidence of this disease in the Indo-Burma theatre. A map showing the distribution of the areas in which this disease was contracted is practically identical with a map showing the route taken by Fourteenth Army from Manipur Road to Kalewa *via* Tiddim and *via* Tamu, through Shwebo and Monywa to Mandalay and thence down the axis of the railway line and down the axis of the Irrawaddy. In almost every area where an action was fought, that is, where troops were deployed and moved across country, there, on the scrub typhus distribution map, is an area to show that the disease was contracted there.

Typhus was the name given by Hippocrates to such fevers as were associated with stupor, the word means mist or smoke. Scrub-typhus was the name by which the disease known to the Japanese as Tsutsugamushi (tsutsuga, disease and akamushi, a small insect) was called. It was known to be transmitted by a trombiculid mite and to have a wide distribution in the Far East. During the first half of 1943 there were but few cases each month but in October and November there were 121 cases in two companies of a British battalion which was patrolling a hill feature known to the troops as Mite Hill, near Tamu. More than 300 cases were admitted into the hospitals of IV Corps during the period September–December 1943. The case-fatality-rate was 6·9 per cent. During the period of the battle in the Imphal Plain, the incidence of the disease was very low. This period coincided with the season with the lowest incidence and moreover the fighting did not take the troops into 'scrub-typhus country'. In June 1944 the incidence rose suddenly. In August there were more than 800 cases recorded and at this time this disease constituted the most serious problem of a medical kind on account of its case-fatality-rate, about 8 per cent. During the next six months the disease assumed an epidemic character and furnished a remarkable example of a disease, usually endemic in habit, suddenly becoming epidemic. The magnitude of this epidemic exceeded that of any previous outbreak of the disease in history. In 1944 there had been over 5,000 cases with some 350 deaths. From captured Japanese documents it was learnt that the Japanese troops stationed along the course of the Chindwin had suffered very severely from this disease.

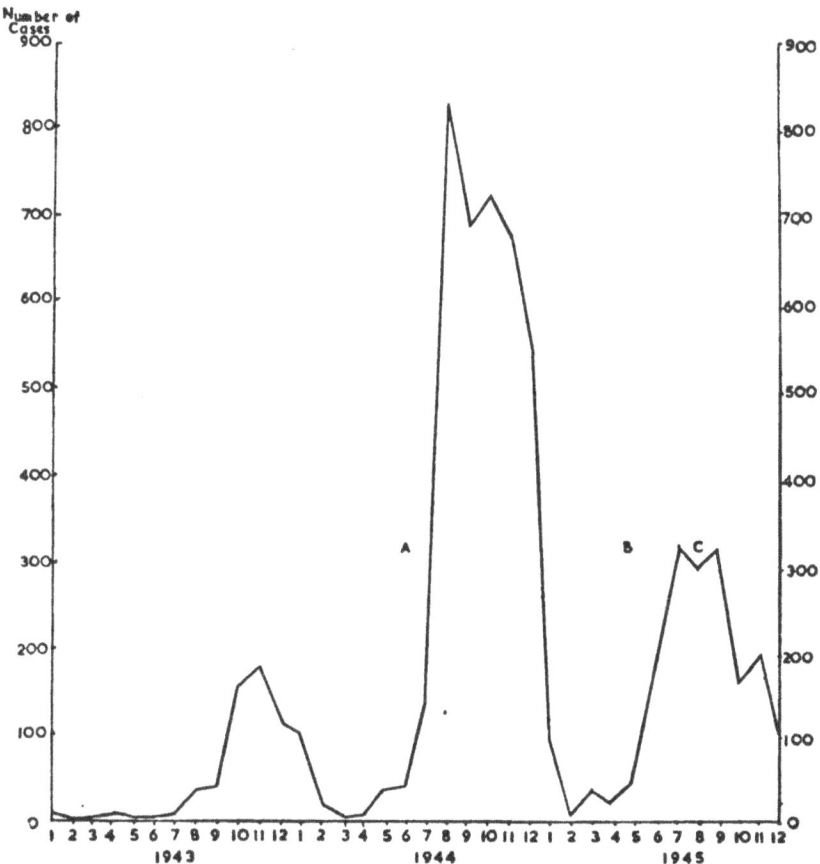

FIG. 80. The Incidence of Tsutsugamushi Fever (Mite Typhus) in Burma and Assam. 1943–45.

After Major P. J. Willcox. *St. Mary's Hospital Gazette*, April–May 1947.

A. The End of the Siege of Imphal and the Beginning of the Advance to the South.
B. The Capture of Rangoon.
C. The End of the War.

The reason for the explosive rise in the incidence of the disease was, undoubtedly, the movement of Fourteenth Army out of the Imphal Plain towards Tiddim and Tamu and beyond through hilly jungle country at a time of the year when the mite is known to be most active and most numerous. The troops commonly bivouacked in areas previously under cultivation and also on sites recently occupied by the Japanese. In these areas a plague of rats was usual. When Kalemyo and Kalewa were reached in December the incidence of the disease promptly fell. The season of highest incidence had passed and the most dangerous areas had been left behind.

During the two months when 2nd W. Yorks were operating along the Tiddim road, no less than 18 per cent. of the battalion went down with the disease and of these 5 per cent. died. In XXXIII Corps between July 1944 and May 1945 there were 2,399 cases with a case-fatality-rate of 10·04 per cent. The disease accounted for 3·3 per cent. of all sickness and for 2·92 per cent. of all admissions to hospital in this Corps. On the average during this period one man in every fifteen went down with the disease. In 11th East African Division, while operating in the Kabaw Valley, some 900 cases occurred. In this division the men very frequently wandered about bare-footed. In Arakan in November 1944 there were about a hundred cases among the West Africans. In 'Special Force' when in the area of Lake Indawgyi between May and September 1944 there were 132 cases. While moving down the railway corridor from Mogaung to Katha 36th Division had 282 cases with a case-fatality-rate of 2·6 per cent.

This foul disease was a very serious one with a sudden onset and a rapid course. The dread of contracting it had a very definite and observable effect on morale. Though its cause was known and though the means for its control were available, its prevention was impossible. Protective clothing can constitute a handicap in battle. It is difficult for front line troops to avoid the mite by keeping clear of the areas where it is most likely to lurk. It cannot be claimed that a mastery over this disease was gained during the war years.

SMALLPOX

This disease was the cause of anxiety towards the end of March 1945 for some 180 cases were reported, 45 of them in one division, Indian 7th. Thirteen deaths occurred, 6 among British troops (49 cases); 4 among Indian (114) and 3 among African (5). As the troops moved southwards through a civilian population in which the disease was fairly common, it was considered advisable to carry out very large scale vaccination schemes.

5,000 and 10,000 doses of vaccine were issued to IV and XXXIII Corps respectively for the vaccination of civilians in their areas.

CHOLERA

No cholera in Fourteenth Army had been reported until the end of March 1945. Between then and May 9 there were three discrete outbreaks. The first began on March 31 in Indian 20th Division of XXXIII Corps. Of 39 cases of acute gastro-enteritis among 17 different units of the division, 16 were notified as cholera. The outbreak occurred in a small triangle between Ngazun, the bridgehead, Singu and Kyaukse. The disease was raging among the civilian population of this area at this time; in Letpan there were 87 cases with 11 deaths. Of the

17 cases among the troops there were 10 deaths, 1 B.O.R. and 9 I.O.Rs. The probable source of infection was water from the river and from canals. In the latter three Japanese corpses had been found. On April 14 and April 28 there were outbreaks in 36th Division and among Army troops. 36th Division at this time was around Kandaw, about 50 miles south-west of Mandalay. The source of the infection was the drinking water. The cases among Army troops occurred in the Myotha–Myingyan area, there being 11 in 244th Line Construction Company of the Corps of Signals, which had not been inoculated before entering Army area. Of these eleven cases one died. Water melons and drinking water were the sources of infection. Five cases occurred in Indian 19th Division when in the Kyaukse area.

There was cholera in Shwebo, Sagaing and Nyaunglebin among the civilian population. A very serious outbreak occurred in the Grand Hotel in Chowringee, Calcutta, much used at the time by officers in transit. The civilian staff numbered about 2,200 and about half of these were food-handlers to a greater or lesser extent. These lived out. The hotel accommodated about 1,000 officers. The sanitary arrangements were not suitable for so large a population in so confined a space but no actual sanitary defect could be detected. It was thought that water in tanks on the roof had been fouled by birds. Between April 20 and 23, 1945 there were 23 cases of cholera among the residents. Among the hotel staff there were 19 individuals who were actually excreting the cholera vibrio, though none of them was ill.

TABLE 64

Burma and South-East Asia Command (excluding Ceylon). Incidence of Cholera. 1942–1945. (*Indian Medical History*, Medicine, Surgery and Pathology, *page 101.*)

	1942		1943	
	Number	Rate per 1,000	Number	Rate per 1,000
British Troops	22	0·44	31	0·45
Indian Troops	75	0·52	265	0·70
West African Troops	—	—	—	—
All forces	97	0·50	296	0·66
	1944		1945	
British Troops	4	0·04	7	0·08
Indian Troops	64	0·15	65	0·16
West African Troops	5	0·13	2	0·05
All forces	73	0·14	74	0·13

For comparison's sake it is of interest to turn to the records for Mesopotamia, 1916–1918.

Admissions on account of Cholera	1916	11·60 per 1,000	
" " "	1917	0·68 " "
" " "	1918	1·09 " "
Deaths	1916	2·09 " "
"	1917	0·23 " "
"	1918	0·47 " "

DIPHTHERIA
Of the 32 cases reported during the period, 26 were among British troops, there being a minor epidemic with 14 cases in a number of R.A. units in May 1945.

ENTERIC
In five of the cases of enteric fever occurring among British troops the individuals were discovered to be unprotected.

SNAKEBITE
Three of the patients died.

GANGRENE
Seven of these patients died.

TABLE 65

Fourteenth Army. Admissions on account of 'All Other Causes'. November 12, 1944–May 19, 1945.

All Other Causes	
Other Local Injuries	3,829
Minor Septic Conditions	2,087
Respiratory Diseases	1,892
Other Skin Diseases	1,459
Common Cold	1,390
Other Digestive Diseases	1,356
Mental Diseases	1,055
Other Eye Conditions	986
Ear, Nose and Throat Diseases	872
Scabies	661
Tonsillitis	524
Pneumonia	196
Circulatory Diseases	186
Influenza	137
Effects of Heat	113
Major Septic Diseases	108
P.U.O.	85
Dengue Fever	53
Trachoma	46
Rheumatic Fever	34
	17,069

THE HEALTH OF THE TROOPS

There were 6,030 more admissions on account of 'All Other Causes' but only small numbers relating to any one of the causes. There were, thus, 23,099 such admissions altogether, 39·9 per cent. of all admissions. In the table the main causes are listed. The ranking of local injuries and of minor septic conditions is worthy of note since theoretically at least, these causes fall into the category of the preventable.

TWELFTH ARMY

TABLE 66

Twelfth Army. Admissions to Medical Units (excluding Battle Casualties) July–August 1945. Rate per 1,000 per Diem.

	July				August		
	7	14	21	28	4	11	18
505 District	1·44	1·62	1·45	1·60	1·67	1·36	1·28
South Burma Dist.	—	—	0·98	1·05	1·29	1·02	0·78
IV Corps	1·98	1·90	1·67	1·27	1·28	1·34	1·26
Ind. 5th Div.	1·33	1·32	1·65	1·11	0·89	—	—
Ind. 20th Div.	1·49	1·50	1·37	1·86	1·81	1·86	2·11
6th Bde.	1·29	2·49	2·62	1·44	1·69	1·74	1·23
Ind. 255th Tk. Bde.	—	0·29	1·33	0·70	—	—	—
Ind. 268th Bde.	0·86	0·90	—	—	—	—	—
82nd W.A. Div.	1·33	1·39	1·26	1·06	—	1·32	0·90
Army Tps.	1·29	1·26	1·13	0·93	0·94	0·91	0·93

TABLE 67

Twelfth Army. Admissions to Medical Units. By Ethnic Group. July–August 1945. Rate per 1,000 per Diem.

	July			August		
	14	21	28	4	11	18
British Officers	2·35	2·20	1·64	1·52	1·55	1·33
V.C.Os. and I.O.Rs.	1·51	1·34	1·40	1·37	1·22	1·07
A.O.Rs.	1·47	1·16	1·10	1·48	1·22	1·04
	1·62	1·45	1·40	1·40	1·26	1·11

TABLE 68

Twelfth Army. Admissions to Medical Units. By Cause. July–August 1945. Rate per 1,000 per Diem.

	July				August		
	1	14	21	28	4	11	18
Malaria and N.Y.D.(F.)	0·40	0·36	0·30	0·29	0·34	0·24	0·21
Dysentery and Diarrhoea	0·15	0·17	0·15	0·11	0·13	0·13	0·09
Syphilis	0·01	0·02	0·02	0·01	0·02	0·02	0·01
Other V.D.	0·06	0·05	0·09	0·08	0·10	0·09	0·09
Scrub Typhus	0·01	0·01	0·01	—	0·01	0·01	0·01
Infective Hepatitis	0·05	0·06	0·05	0·04	0·05	0·03	0·03
Psychiatric Diseases	0·02	0·02	0·02	0·02	0·01	0·02	0·01
Battle Casualties	0·11	0·02	0·04	0·10	0·03	0·02	0·01

Representative of the divisions, the records of 36th and of Indian 20th Divisions are examined in some detail.

36TH DIVISION

No division in this theatre was exposed to greater disease hazards than this; it encountered malaria of a most malignant type, typhus and cholera and these dreaded diseases inevitably exacted their toll. Nevertheless, as was remarked by a number of different observers, the general medical condition of the troops was excellent; they were lean certainly but very fit. Their morale was high. Their feeding was unusually good, frozen meat was a frequent issue, anti-scorbutic and multi-vitamin tablets were regularly taken and fresh vegetables, though not a common issue by any means, did become available when the larger centres of population were entered.

MALARIA

The incidence of this disease in the division, at this time consisting of two brigades and divisional troops, some 12,000–13,000 altogether, can best be illustrated by reference to the records of 15 (Ind.) M.F.T.U. During the period October 1–December 31, 1944 the total admissions to this unit on account of malaria and N.Y.D.(F.) were B.O.Rs. 1,473, I.O.Rs. 793, a total of 2,266. The average number of admissions per month was 755, per week 172·2, per day 24·6. In the latter part of November there were over 600 patients in the unit.

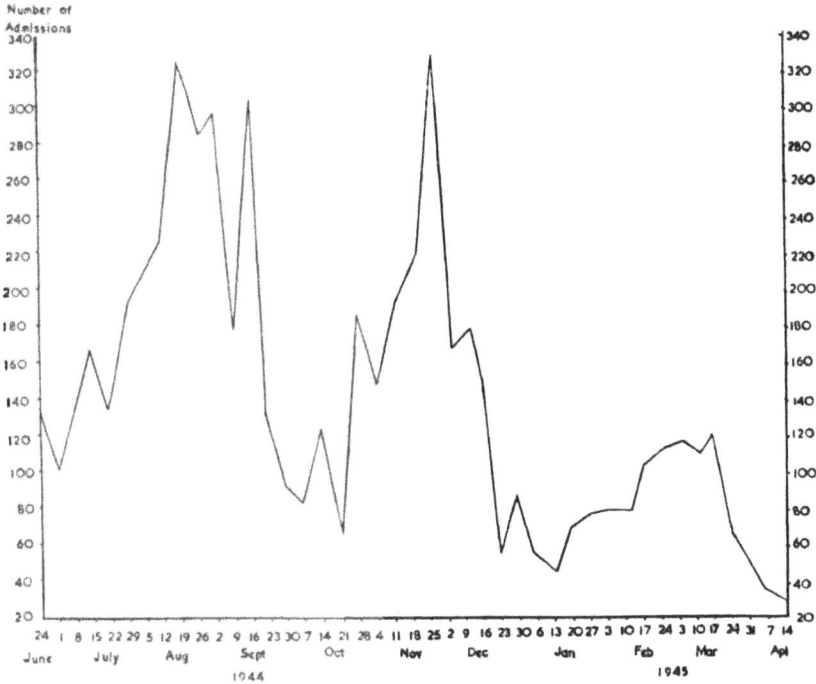

FIG. 81. 36th Division. 15 (Indian) Malaria Forward Treatment Unit. Weekly Admissions on account of Malaria. From Week ending June 24, 1944 to Week ending April 14, 1945.

During the months of October and November the routine treatment was ineffectual in a large number of the cases and several days' treatment with quinine had to be offered additionally. The percentage of instances of cerebral malaria was exceptionally high. In October, 29 out of 100 B.O.R. patients required two or more courses of treatment before the

TABLE 69

36th Division. 15 (Indian) Malaria Forward Treatment Unit. Number of Cases of Benign, Malignant and Cerebral Malaria admitted. October–December, 1944.

Month	B.T.		M.T.		Cerebral Cases		Percentage of Cerebral Cases as compared with M.T.	
	B.O.Rs.	I.O.Rs.	B.O.Rs.	I.O.Rs.	B.O.Rs.	I.O.Rs.	B.O.Rs.	I.O.Rs.
October	191	174	100	66	7	3	7	4·5
November	305	217	179	81	22	5	12·3	6·2
December	123	57	134	14	7	2	5·2	14·3
	619	448	413	161	36	10	8·7	6·2
	1,067		574		46		8 per cent.	

pyrexia subsided and the blood smear became negative. In November 22 out of a consecutive series of 100 needed a second course. Infection was usually heavy and the resistance of the causal organism to therapeutic measures exceptionally high.

During the period January 1–March 31, 1945 the total admissions on account of malaria and N.Y.D.(F.) were B.O.Rs. 415, I.O.Rs. 195, a total of 610. The average number of admissions per month was 203, per week 46·9, per day 6·7.

TABLE 70

36th Division. 15 (Indian) Malaria Forward Treatment Unit. Admissions on account of Malaria. January–March, 1945.

Month	B.O.Rs. B.T.	B.O.Rs. M.T.	I.O.Rs. B.T.	I.O.Rs. M.T.	Total B.T.	Total M.T.
January	49	3	25	3	74	6
February	90	7	43	4	133	11
March	148	25	28	3	176	28
	287	35	96	10	383	45

It is to be noted that whereas in December malignant tertian formed more than half of the cases of malaria in B.O.Rs., it contributed only 12 per cent. to the total in the period January–March.

TABLE 71

36th Division. 15 (Indian) Malaria Forward Treatment Unit. Fresh Cases and Relapses admitted. January–March, 1945. (Fresh, a case with no history of previous attacks during the preceding nine months. Relapse, a positive slide with or without fever.)

	B.O.Rs. Fresh	B.O.Rs. Relapse	I.O.Rs. Fresh	I.O.Rs. Relapse	Totals Fresh	Totals Relapse
January	14	43	13	20	27	63
February	21	82	9	42	30	124
March	46	148	11	25	57	173
	81	273	33	87	114	360

SCRUB TYPHUS

In October 1944 typhus made its sudden and dramatic appearance. During October–December 231 cases occurred, 214 of them in B.O.R.s

THE HEALTH OF THE TROOPS

The peak of the outbreak was in the second half of November and the early part of December. No case occurred in the division thereafter. When the epidemic broke out the division was between Mawlu and Naba. It was not possible to relate the outbreak to any particular type of country or to any association with inhabited localities. Fortunately the disease did not take a very severe form but there were six deaths from it in the M.F.T.U.

CHOLERA

The division had been inoculated. When 72nd Bde. was in the Kandaw area on April 23 and 24, 9 B.O.Rs. and 14 I.O.Rs. went down with the disease. They were treated in the M.D.S. of the field ambulance. Four of the patients died. One of these was a B.O.R. in the R.W.F. who contracted his disease well to the east of Thazi.

DYSENTERY AND DIARRHOEA

The highest incidence was 5/1,000/week and the lowest 0·6/1,000/week, a very satisfactory state of affairs.

INFECTIVE HEPATITIS

195 cases of this debilitating disease occurred within the division.

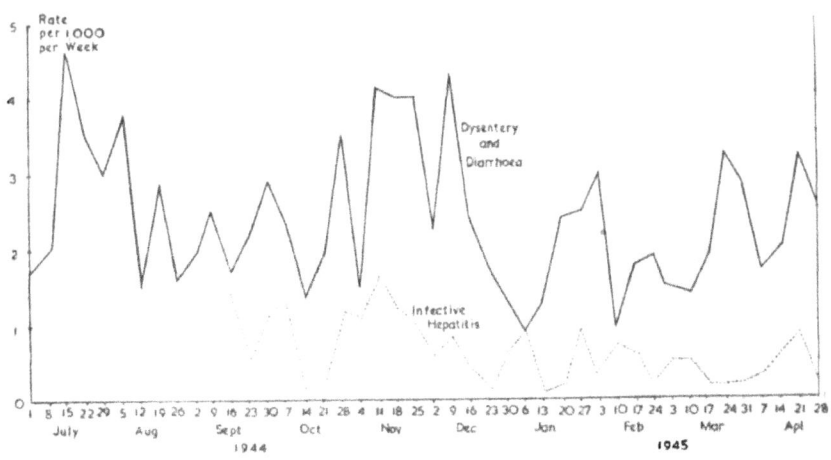

FIG. 82. 36th Division. The Incidence of Dysentery and Diarrhoea and of Infective Hepatitis. July 1, 1944–April 28, 1945. Rates per 1,000 per Week.

INDIAN 20TH DIVISION

TABLE 72

Indian 20th Division. Admissions to Divisional Medical Units and Disposal. December 1–May 31, 1943–1944 and 1944–1945.

Total Admissions	Sick	B.Cs.	Deaths	Evacuation by Road	Evacuation by Air	R.T.U.	Per cent. R.T.U.	Malaria and N.Y.D. (F.)	Malaria and N.Y.D. (F.) as Per cent. of Total
1944–45 7,950	5,605	2,345	170	1,385	4,590	1,785	22·5	1,120	14
1943–44 9,690	7,230	2,460	—	—	—	950	9·9	2,820	29

These figures include neither the Japanese P.o.W. nor the hundreds of civilians who were admitted, treated and evacuated exactly in the same manner as were the division's own men.

The ratio of battle casualties to sick in this division during the period December 1, 1944–May 31, 1945 was 1 : 2·4.

During the period casualties among the medical personnel of the division were 5 killed, an ambulance driver, 2 O.Rs. of the anti-malaria unit and 2 stretcher-bearers of 4 (Ind.) Bearer Company.

The magnitude of the work of the light aircraft squadron on evacuation can be recognised when it is learnt that of the 4,590 casualties evacuated by air, about 4,000 were transported singly.

TABLE 73

Indian 20th Division. Analysis of Admissions to Divisional Medical Units. By Cause. December 1, 1944–May 31, 1945.

	Disease	Admissions	Percentage of Total Admissions on account of Sickness
1.	Diarrhoea and Dysentery, and including Enteritis	697	12·5
2.	Diseases of Digestive System	215	3·8
3.	Infective Hepatitis	210	3·75
4.	Malaria and N.Y.D.(F.)	1,118	20·1
5.	Common Cold	215	3·8
6.	Tonsillitis and Pharyngitis	170	3·0
7.	Respiratory Diseases	180	3·2
8.	Ear, Nose and Throat Diseases	140	2·5
9.	Eye Diseases	160	2·8

THE HEALTH OF THE TROOPS

TABLE 73—contd.

10.	Dental Diseases	105	1·9
11.	Psychiatric Cases	170	3·0
12.	Venereal Diseases	205	3·6
13.	Skin Diseases	210	3·7
14.	Minor Septic conditions	577	10·3
15.	Anaemia	85	1·5
16.	Other causes	577	10·3
17.	**Total Sick**	**5,034**	**89·9**
18.	Battle Accidents	100	1·8
19.	Minor Injuries	321	5·7
20.	Major Injuries (fractures)	70	1·25
21.	Burns and Scalds	80	1·4
22.	**Total Non-sick**	**571**	**10·1**
23.	**Total Admissions N.E.A.**	**5,605**	**100·0**
24.	Battle Casualties	2,345	—
	Total Admissions	**7,950**	—

Notes on table

1. Many of these cases were bacillary dysentery and were returned to their units within a week. The field ambulances admitted such as had not responded to sulphaguanidine within 48 hours; such as were underweight, anaemic or debilitated; such as had a history of previous attacks, and also the chronic type of case.

2. Dyspepsia, gastritis, constipation, N.Y.D. (Abdomen), appendicitis, colic and worms are included in this group.

3. This group accounted for 99 per cent. of all the cases of jaundice.

4. All the R.M.Os. held intra-venous quinine. There were three or four cases of acute mania due to algid malaria.

6. All sore throats are shown. There were less than half a dozen cases of diphtheria all told.

7. This group included pain in the chest, bronchitis, pneumonia and pleurisy.

8. Most cases of otitis were evacuated for the reason that treatment in the field can never be satisfactory.

10. This group included all the men given board and lodging in the field ambulance while waiting for their dentures.

11. This group included exhaustion, a condition which was almost entirely confined to British troops.

13. Mostly ringworm and jungle sores, the latter almost exclusively among British troops.

14. The group included all the boils, the late jungle sores, abcesses, whitlows and such like.

15. This was confined to Indian troops and was due, in the great number of instances, to infestations.

16. In this group were the following: a fatal case of arsenical poisoning by rat-poison from the canteen, a fatal case of snake-bite, a fatal case of smallpox, a few cases of heat exhaustion, a number of haemorrhoids, a prolapsed rectum, cases of renal colic, of orchitis, of epididymitis, of hydrocele, varicocele, two cases of sulphanilamide anuria, accidental poisoning cases, insect bites, dog bites, disorders of the feet and varicose veins; also effort syndrome, chickenpox, mumps, and sciatica contributed to the miscellany.

TABLE 74

Indian 20th Division. Admissions to Divisional Medical Units. By Cause and by Ethnic Group. December 1, 1944–May 31, 1945

Arm of Service	Average Strength	Total Admissions	Rate per 1,000 per Diem	Battle Casualties	Sick	Sick-rate per 1,000	Malaria and N.Y.D. (F.)	Rate per 1,000	Dysentery and Diarrhoea	Rate per 1,000	Venereal Diseases
British Infantry	1,680	1,380	4·5	465	915	2·95	165	0·5	160	0·5	52
Royal Artillery	1,780	730	2·25	70	660	2·03	85	0·25	66	0·2	26
British H.Q. Staffs, Sigs., Pro. and Ord.	240	85	1·95	2	83	1·9	20	0·45	14	0·3	7
British Services—R.E., Medical, R.I.A.S.C., I.E.M.E.	200	45	1·25	3	42	1·15	5	0·15	5	0·15	5
	3,900	2,240	3·15	540	1,700	2·4	275	0·4	245	0·35	90 (0·13)
Indian and Gurkha Infantry	6,570	2,930	2·45	1,450	1,480	1·2	270	0·2	140	0·1	38
Indian Artillery	760	125	0·9	15	110	0·8	15	0·1	7	0·05	2
Indian H.Q. Staffs, Sigs., Pro., Ord., Div. M.T. and Vet.	1,270	250	1·05	6	244	1·05	60	0·25	23	0·1	13
S. and M.I.E.	860	150	0·95	34	116	0·7	16	0·1	9	0·06	6
I.A.M.C.	680	160	1·3	4	156	1·3	25	0·2	12	0·1	2
R.I.A.S.C.	1,920	340	1·0	14	326	0·5	81	0·2	44	0·1	6
I.E.M.E.	540	110	1·1	2	108	1·1	13	0·15	5	0·05	8
	12,600	4,065	1·75	1,525	2,540	1·1	480	0·2	240	0·1	75 (0·03)
Totals	16,500	6,305	2·1	2,065	4,240	1·4	755	0·24	485	0·15	165 (0·05)

This table takes into account only Indian 20th Divisions's own troops. It covers therefore not more than six-sevenths of the total admissions. The difference of the sick-rates for British and for Indian troops respectively is worthy of note. Among the several reasons for the higher British figure is the fact that the British soldier tends to seek medical advice more readily and more often than does the Indian. The British infantryman had the highest admission-rate of the lot, which is not surprising. A sick-rate of 1·4/1,000/diem is indeed remarkable; the target set by the C. in C. was 2·4/1,000/diem.

TABLE 75

Indian 20th Division. Admissions and Disposals. June 1–August 31, 1945

Total Admissions	Sick	Battle Casualties	Deaths	Evacuation by Road	Evacuation by Air	R.T.U.	Percentage of R.T.U. of Total Admissions
(A) 3,596	3,531	65	9	2,429	—	1,130	31·6
(B) 70	38	32	—	—	—	—	—
(C) 7,950	5,605	2,345	170	1,385	4,590	1,785	22·5

(A) For all troops admitted to divisional field medical ambulances.
(B) For divisional troops admitted to IV Corps ambulances.
(C) For troops admitted to the divisional field ambulances during the previous six months, December 1, 1944–May 31, 1945.

The number returned to their units is noteworthy. The holding of minor sick in the R.A.P. was discouraged. It is seen that the monsoon conditions did not affect the sick-rate to any appreciable extent; during this period there were fewer flies, fewer jungle sores and fewer cases of exhaustion. There were fewer British troops with the division at this time and this fact most certainly affected the sick-rate for in these conditions the fewer the British the lower the sick-rate. Skin conditions tended to be commoner during the monsoon months; at one time one Gurkha battalion had as many as 180 cases of 'dhobie itch'. Since during the monsoon period there is more leisure, the incidence of venereal disease, as would be expected, showed a rise, for the division was in the midst of a civilian population.

TABLE 76

Indian 20th Division. Admissions to Divisional Medical Units. June 1–August 31, 1945. By Cause.

Cause	Number Admitted	Percentage of Total Admissions on account of Sickness	Percentage during last six months
Malaria and N.Y.D.(F.)	599	17·0	20·1
Diarrhoea, Dysentery, including Gastro-enteritis	301	8·55	12·5
Minor Septic conditions	245	6·8	10·3
Venereal Diseases	208	5·8	3·6
Respiratory Diseases	191	5·4	3·2
Diseases of Digestive System	171	4·8	3·8
Skin Diseases	164	4·6	3·7
Anaemia	124	3·5	1·5
E.N.T. Diseases	119	3·4	2·5
Infective Hepatitis	116	3·2	3·75
Eye Diseases	115	3·0	2·8
Tonsillitis and Pharyngitis	101	2·9	3·0
Common Cold	76	2·15	3·8
Dental Diseases	50	1·4	1·9
Psychiatric Cases	49	1·4	3·0
Other causes	576	16·2	10·3
	3,205	90·5	89·9
Battle Accidents	35	1·0	1·8
Minor Injuries	206	5·7	5·7
Major Injuries	54	1·5	1·25
Burns and Scalds	31	0·9	1·4
Total Casualties N.E.A.	3,531	100·0	100·0
Battle Casualties	65	—	—
Total Admissions	3,596	—	—

The rise in the incidence of digestive disorders, nutritional anaemia and debility was accepted as evidence of the hardness of the lives the troops had been leading. These conditions occurred almost exclusively among the non-meat-eaters.

During the period (June 1–August 31) there were 12 deaths in the divisional medical units, 2 civilians, 2 suicides, 2 with malaria and 1 with scrub typhus.

TABLE 77

Indian 20th Division. Admissions to Divisional Medical Units. By Cause and by Ethnic Group. June 1–August 31, 1945.

Arm of Service	Average Strength	Total Admissions	Rate per 1,000 per diem	Battle Casualties	Sick-Rate per 1,000	Malaria and N.Y.D. (F.)	Rate per 1,000	Diarrhoea and Dysentery	Rate per 1,000	Venereal Diseases
British Sigs., Division and Bde. H.Qs., B.O.Rs. of Indian Units	515	106	2·20	1	2·20	23	0·58	25	0·52	3
Royal Artillery	970	225	2·50	—	2·50	37	0·41	36	0·40	19
Total British Troops	1,485	331	2·4	1	2·4	60	0·04	61	0·04	22
Gurkha Infantry	3,975	1,185	1·46	86	1·35	179	0·22	130	0·16	66
Indian Infantry	4,815	—	—	—	—	—	—	—	—	—
Indian Sigs., Division and Bde. H.Qs.	1,305	205	1·70	—	1·70	39	0·32	10	0·08	16
Royal Indian Artillery	1,080	114	1·15	—	1·15	6	0·06	5	0·05	2
Indian Engineers	960	97	1·10	—	1·10	10	0·11	6	0·06	12
R.I.A.S.C.	2,110	288	1·47	—	1·47	39	0·20	18	0·09	12
Indian Medical	650	106	1·75	—	1·75	20	0·33	6	0·10	9
I.E.M.E., I.A.O.C.	820	147	1·95	—	1·95	23	0·30	8	0·07	8
Total Indian Troops	15,715	2,142	1·7	86	1·63	316	0·25	183	0·14	125
Totals	17,200	2,473	1·76	87	1·70	376	0·27	244	0·17	147

A sick-rate of 1·7/1,000/diem for a whole division is eminently satisfactory. It will be noted that the venereal disease rate in this period is double what it was for the previous one.

CHAPTER 16

A REVIEW OF THE WORK OF THE ARMY MEDICAL SERVICES

(1) THE ARMY NURSING SERVICE

IN FOURTEENTH Army it was the accepted practice in all units to form a 'dangerously ill' ward in which all those so designated, irrespective of rank or ethnic group, were treated and nursed. In such a ward could be seen a British officer with a Madrassi sweeper on one side of him and an African O.R. on the other. Opposite this group might be found a B.O.R. flanked by a V.C.O. and a Burmese civilian. And in the corner, not uncommonly, there might be a Japanese P.o.W. Different as all these might be in many ways they were all alike in that they urgently needed skilled nursing. Nursing personnel were not plentiful and only in this way could the best and fullest use be made of the very limited resources. Because they were dangerously ill these patients could not be evacuated to the rear hospitals and so nursing officers had to be brought forward and attached to the M.D.Ss. of field ambulances and to M.F.T.Us., to M.S.Us. working in bridgeheads, to units well within range of the Japanese guns and which might conceivably be overrun during a successful Japanese infiltration. The fate that had befallen the members of the Army Nursing Service during the disasters of Hong Kong and Singapore was well known to all. Though it was not accepted by all senior administrative medical officers that it was reasonable and justifiable to employ nursing officers so far forward, in fact they often were. It was the view of those in the best position to know that the low case-fatality-rate among those who were stricken with scrub typhus and who perforce had to be nursed in forward medical units was very largely attributable to the policy of sending nursing officers forward to tend them. That which applies to scrub typhus patients applies also and equally to all patients designated as dangerously ill; the strength of the hope of recovery is determined by the quality of the nursing care that the patient receives.

It is to be remembered that this employment of nursing officers as 'shock troops' sent anywhere where the need for them was greatest, inevitably meant that the members of the Army Nursing Service were overworked, that they were detached for long periods of time from the units to which they 'belonged' and that their mail was received by them very irregularly and after long delays. Yet these disadvantages did not deter them, any more than did the prospect of discomfort and the possibility of danger; the constant, almost universal, plea on the part of the members of the Army Nursing Service was that they should be employed in the forward areas where, in the circumstances which existed, they could hope to render the greatest service. Such an attitude has come to be regarded as being unexceptional, as being characteristic of this Service, demanding no special comment. In Burma as in the other theatres the nursing officer made a contribution to the Army the value of which was exceedingly great, exactly how great it is impossible to estimate.

The devotion to duty and the gallantry of the nursing officers serving with forward medical units were an inspiration to all who came into contact with them and were equalled only by the tenderness and the compassion they displayed towards those placed in their care.

(2) THE ARMY HYGIENE SERVICE

It is always difficult to assess the value of the work of any organisation that is concerned with the prevention of disease. It is to be measured by the non-occurrence or by the low incidence of disease in general or of a particular disease but to ascribe this non-occurrence or low incidence directly to the preventive action taken is somewhat hazardous. So also with advice relating to disease prevention, it is difficult to prove that the non-occurrence of disease is the direct outcome of the advice that was proffered. Nevertheless it would be an offence against common sense to question the statement that the activities of the 'hygiene' officers and of the field hygiene sections contributed very notably indeed to the attainment and maintenance of a truly remarkable low incidence of the diseases of major military importance during the campaign in Burma and to the phenomenal progressive fall in the sick-rate among the troops during the years 1942-1945. For the most part these activities were unspectacular and undramatic but the Army Hygiene Service can claim to have been ultimately responsible for the transformation of Manipur Road from a place to be feared and, if possible, avoided on account of the prevalence of malaria into one in which tens of thousands of men lived healthy lives, playing their essential parts in making the reoccupation of Burma possible.

The field hygiene sections in carrying out their work were called upon to overcome many serious difficulties. There was always a shortage of personnel, especially of B.O.Rs., and of tradesmen. In some units these deficiencies amounted to as much as 25 per cent. There was a shortage of equipment and much difficulty was encountered when attempts were made to obtain such essential materials as wire gauze, timber and nails. In Burma as in other theatres it was not uncommon to encounter the view that the field hygiene section was the proper unit to undertake distasteful and uninteresting sanitary jobs. A section would be called upon to clean up an area that was not the responsibility of any particular unit, or to dispose of dead Japanese and animal carcases. It was necessary at all times to make it abundantly clear that the section was a specialist unit and was not a congregation of unskilled labourers.

The introduction of D.D.T. late in 1944 was followed by a lowering of the standards of personal and public hygiene. To most individuals there is no emotional satisfaction in getting rid of refuse in approved ways. The reputation of D.D.T., a 'wonder drug', was such that to it was ascribed almost miraculous powers. The popular point of view was that because it was available there was no longer any need to take care; sanitary fatigues were no longer necessary. Much effort was required to contradict these opinions and to persuade the soldier, both officer and other rank, that it was still as necessary as ever before to burn or to bury all refuse. Burying was not satisfactory in all places for the Burmese promptly opened all filled-in swill-pits and the like in the search for food.

To protect the troops against the hazards of the water-borne diseases was difficult at all times. Wells were very numerous and as often as not the sentry at a well was unable to enforce strict water discipline. During the rapid advance on Rangoon the supply of water to the troops was made difficult by reason of the fact that the water carts were of an obsolete pattern. Sedimentation tanks were not always available and those used for sterilisation were usually too small.

Though facilities for bathing in a river or canal are widespread in Burma it would have been better had all the divisions been provided with mobile bath units such as those which were in use in 2nd and Indian 20th Divisions.

On the whole rations were satisfactory. Mention has been made of malnutrition in the Chindits due to the monotony of the 'K' ration and of the reduction of the ration by 50 per cent. for a time during the advance on Rangoon in order to allow more ammunition and P.O.L. to be sent forward. But rations in themselves are never enough, the soldier, British, Indian and African, wants his 'canteen' goods with their greater range of variety and of these there was a shortage. Undoubtedly this deficiency had a deleterious effect upon the health and well-being of the troops.

THE PREVENTION OF MALARIA IN THE FIELD

To reinforce the field hygiene laboratory and the field hygiene section in a theatre in which malaria constitutes the major or one of the major problems confronting the Army Medical Services, the mobile malaria laboratory and the anti-malaria unit were created and to them was added the entomological unit more concerned with the search for new knowledge concerning the mosquito than with the application of existing knowledge in the prevention of disease.

1 Malaria Field Laboratory, with its mobile sections, did excellent work during the course of which new knowledge was secured. Malaria surveys revealed the presence of two additional Anopheline vectors of considerable importance, *A. jeyporiensis*, first encountered in the Arakan foothills and prevalent from mid-February until the end of the monsoon, and *A. leucospyrus*, commonly met with in the jungle during and after the rains. The former of these two species was largely responsible for the crippling man-power loss during the operations in Arakan in early 1943. The latter species was responsible for much of the malaria that was contracted in the forests of the Indo-Burma border. In Arakan a field method for the estimation of the concentration of mepacrine in the urine was devised, a fluorimeter being used and the sun's rays being utilised as the source of ultra-violet rays. The employment of this test made it possible for the mobile section of the malaria field laboratory to measure the degree of supervision which commanders exercised over mepacrine consumption by the officers and men of their units. By the use of the test, too, it was possible to demonstrate that poor supervision resulted directly in a rise in the incidence of malaria in the unit. The knowledge that there was such a test had a profound influence upon 'mepacrine discipline' far beyond the range of the units actually tested.

It was found also that wide mesh nets could be mosquito-proofed with dimethyl phthalate and other substances, affording protection even when in contact with the skin. This was a discovery of considerable value but since the trials did not finish until July 1944 mesh-nets of this material could not be produced in sufficient quantities to enable their distribution before the end of the war to be sufficiently wide to include all those who would have benefited by them. Less than 5,000 nets reached Fourteenth Army up to March 1945. This is an excellent illustration of the fact that in circumstances such as those that existed in the latter part of the Second World War, even though the whole resources of a country are geared to serve its Armed Forces, not less than eighteen months are required for a discovery, even of this relatively simple, straightforward kind, to become transmuted into policy and to yield advantageous modification of some aspect of soldiering.

The malaria field laboratory was involved in the experimental application of D.D.T. by aircraft as a spray in kerosene and as a smoke screen dissolved in titanium tetrachloride. The value and limitations of these methods for treating large areas rapidly were defined and it was clearly established for the first time that adult mosquitoes found in an area a few days after spraying came from untreated breeding places within the area and had not entered the area from beyond its boundaries. It was therefore concluded that after effective spraying from the air malaria transmission in the sprayed area would be negligible for as long as three weeks.

PREVENTIVE MEASURES

(a) *Individual Protection*

The teaching in the Burma theatre was the same as that elsewhere. Long trousers were in universal use throughout the day. The battle-dress blouse gave insufficient protection at night for the reason that it left a gap between itself and the trousers and also because of its weave. A change-over from the non-greasy pyrethrum and citronella anti-mosquito cream to dimethyl phthalate and other liquid repellents was completed in 1944. 'Skat', as these new issues were called, met with general approval and were widely used. It was commonly thought that the sentry, waking for his spell of duty during the night often failed to apply the repellent with sufficient care.

Mosquito-net protection was by no means universal, even at the level of Army, corps and divisional H.Qs. where occasionally an individual or several individuals could be found sleeping without a net. The degree to which these nets were used in perimeter camps and the like in which fairly undisturbed nights could frequently be enjoyed was found to vary directly with the confidence the unit had in its guards and with the experience and attitude of the officers concerning malaria casualties. In units in close contact with the Japanese it could not be expected that the men would wear the narrow mesh nets. Some of the new wide mesh nets reached Fourteenth Army just before the advance southwards from Meiktila. First reports from individuals and from formations were unanimous in demanding more. Their superiority over the narrow mesh nets in respect of protection for static sentries, for sleepers and for such as were obliged to travel unencumbered was recognised and a number of modifications were suggested.

(b) *General Protection. The Anti-Malaria Unit*

One anti-malaria unit was attached to each division, to each corps and to Army H.Q. A chain of these units was strung along the L. of C., being located in the main bases where they were under the command of H.Qs. areas and sub-areas. The aim of these units was to reduce as rapidly as possible the number of infective Anophelines in the areas occupied by the troops. Before D.D.T. became available in sufficient quantity in S.E.A.C., it is doubtful that the labours of the A.M.Us. provided any real protection to troops in the forward zone in which there was so much movement. The troops had to rely almost entirely upon methods of self-care. In the rear areas, of course, the A.M.Us. were able to do much with the insecticides then available, e.g. Paris green, and by drainage. The coming of D.D.T. evoked many modifications of the anti-malaria measures. Paris green was no longer used; supplies and apparatus for spraying were issued to C.A.S.(B.) but this organisation had no trained personnel to use them. Malariol was used only occasionally and then as a vehicle for D.D.T. Pyrethrum extract was no longer used in kerosene as an insecticide but in the form of Freon bombs or sparklets; this substance was used on a limited scale. Far fewer drainage schemes were initiated and it came to be accepted that extensive drainage was an engineering responsibility requiring skilled labour.

When the movement to the south quickened its pace the A.M.U. was greatly handicapped by having no transport of its own. Only in one instance, when a large part of 100 A.M.U. moved with Indian 5th Division, was it possible to supply sufficient transport for an A.M.U. without calling upon the divisional pool. All too often the whole or a large part of the A.M.U. had to be left behind when a division moved forward. Risks had to be taken in order to achieve tactical success. Fortunately, as Fourteenth Army moved southwards, it either left behind it the more highly malarious areas or else did not require to enter them.

The magnitude of the contribution to victory made by D.D.T. cannot be computed; it certainly was exceedingly great, possibly overtopping that of all the rest of the purely material things that subscribed in their different ways to the maintenance of the fighting efficiency of the soldier. In this theatre there were two enemies and of the two the infective mosquito was not the less formidable. In a sense the antimalaria unit was a front line combatant unit armed with lethal weapons. With the coming of D.D.T. the importance of these units became greatly enlarged.

Since D.D.T. provided the means for controlling not only the mosquito but also flies and other insect pests, it created a situation in which the relationship of the A.M.U. and the field hygiene section had to be reviewed. Both of them were users of D.D.T. and of sprayers. At first there was an agreement that field hygiene sections should spray messes, cookhouses and latrines while the A.M.U. restricted its spraying activities to out-of-doors. Later it proved to be convenient for the A.M.U. to spray all living accommodation, including messes and cookhouses, leaving only the latrine to the field hygiene section and accept responsibility for all D.D.T. spraying in areas allotted to it, while the field hygiene section only sprayed a limited number of S. and T. establishments such as slaughter-houses, soda water and ice factories or food stores which they had to visit in the ordinary course of their duties.

This development was born of the need to avoid duplication in respect of the demands for supplies and apparatus on the part of two part-time users operating in the same area. The trend was for the A.M.U. to become the sole specialist user of D.D.T. and for all insecticidal work, possibly even including typhus control to become the responsibility of this unit. Such a development, if continued, would create the need for the officers commanding the A.M.Us. to receive a much broadened training to cover other aspects of medical entomology.

Towards the end of the campaign the combatant formations themselves entered into the competition for D.D.T. supplies; more than half of the D.D.T. issued to divisions was being used by the units themselves and not by the field hygiene section or anti-malaria unit attached to the division. Within the division the aim was for each platoon to have its own D.D.T. sprayer and solution.

At first D.D.T. solutions were most commonly used as alternatives to Malariol and pyrethrum solutions and the sprayers then in use were employed for the distribution of the new anti-malarial. Then the extraordinary value of D.D.T. was recognised for it could be used against all kinds of insects not only in a variety of solutions but also as a powder, an emulsion and as a smoke and moreover its action was long-lasting. It was recognised too that new apparatus was required for the application of this material for the sprayers in use even when modified did not prove to be wholly satisfactory. To begin with D.D.T. powder was dissolved in kerosene but kerosene oil grade III was not an S. and T. issue and had to be provided especially for the purpose. Since supply in Burma was so frequently by air this development added to the tasks of the transport system. In IV Corps it was found that diesel oil, an item of regular supply, was a satisfactory substitute for the kerosene.

The publicity given to the spraying of D.D.T. from the air persuaded many that aircraft criss-crossing over an area banished the causal agents of disease from square miles of the jungle and in consequence of this, units and individuals were freed from their responsibilities for preventive measures. It became difficult to persuade those who understandably were looking for an easy solution to the problem of malaria prevention that such spraying did not render the treated area completely safe for troops. It could not be made safe because suitable aircraft were not available in sufficient numbers and repeat spraying was seldom possible without such delay that all the good that had been done was undone. Indainggyi and Mandalay were sprayed from the air but not until the areas had already been occupied for several weeks.

The incorporation of D.D.T. in titanium tetrachloride laid as a smoke screen by aircraft could not be properly tested for the solvent was in short supply and the weather was not always favourable. One such screen, 3,500 yards long, was laid across Army H.Q. in Meiktila but its effects could not be estimated for the reason that there had been much

D.D.T. application on the ground. In Rangoon D.D.T. air-spraying began on D-day+5, the weather on D-day+1 making it impossible to use a smoke screen on that day.

In the Army Medical Services the division of interests between the prevention of disease (health promotion) and the cure of disease (the restoration of health) is sharply demarcated organisationally; the former is the territory of the Directorate of Hygiene and its representatives in the field, the latter the prime responsibility of the consultants and specialists in the clinical branches of medicine. Nevertheless the separation of these interests is not always easily recognised, for example the consultant or adviser in dermatology or in venereology is as much concerned with the prevention of diseases as with their cure. In the case of malaria the relationship of the clinician and the hygiene officer assumed a special interest for the same drug, mepacrine, was used for the prevention (suppression) and for the treatment of the disease. At first a suppressive mepacrine régimen was adopted by only a proportion of the troops; by March 1945 all troops east of the Brahmaputra with negligible exceptions were on it. Before November 1944 the only troops, other than the divisions receiving an issue of mepacrine, were those south of the Pruma Chaung in Arakan and those in the north. Throughout 1944 the issue of mepacrine to formations had been closely controlled by the medical authorities but with the growth of air transport it was found more convenient to let S. and T. handle all routine distribution from F.A.M.Os., while the medical authorities remained responsible for demanding from A.L.F.S.E.A. the correct amount monthly to be handed over through Advanced Echelons North and South to C.A.A.T.O. for distribution to the various F.A.M.Os. Owing to the lack of reserve stocks, S. and T. at A.L.F.S.E.A. were unwilling to take over the entire distribution of mepacrine from that level. The new system worked satisfactorily after a number of initial difficulties had been overcome.

The main difficulties associated with the supply of mepacrine invariably centred around the need, after the original allotments had been planned, for internal redistribution of stocks to meet changes in the tactical disposition of troops. On air supply this was done through C.A.A.T.O. by the medical authorities at advanced echelons and within formations by S. and T. The higher up the scale mepacrine was handed over from the medical authorities to S. and T. the better the distribution achieved. But it was often forgotten that as long as stocks of mepacrine did not permit all supply bases to hold reserves, when a formation changed its method of supply, it had to remain a medical responsibility to initiate the redistribution of bulk mepacrine supplies into positions most suitable for S. and T.

In April 1945 the size of the daily dose of mepacrine was 1·2 tablets per man per day, calculated on actual receipts against the strengths according to the situation reports. The supply was by air and there were no break-downs and no extra doses were ordered. There was no recorded major loss of bulk supplies. The figure of 1·2 tablets took no account of losses of bulk supplies by enemy action nor of extra doses to units and formations with unusually high malaria rates. The supplies given to men going on leave belonged to the following month. It was calculated that the total amount required was 1·5 tablets per man per day of which 1·2 tablets would be supplied for maintenance and restocking unit reserves while 0·3 tablet per man per day would be held by S. and T. as formations reserves. In 1944 the need for every man to carry a small personal reserve became apparent; a ·303 cartridge case with a plug was used as a container.

A comparison of the incidence of malaria in 1944 up to November by 404 Area and by XV Corps respectively, the latter on suppressive mepacrine, the former not, shows clearly that while the rate rose and fell in 404 Area with every rise and fall of malaria transmission, in XV Corps the rate remained steady at a lower rate until October in spite of the fact that the chances of infection were greater in XV Corps than in 404 Area. In October a suppressive mepacrine campaign was launched in Indian 26th Division. The weekly number of malaria casualties which had been between 250–400 fell to below 50 in a period of six weeks, without any diminution in intensity of transmission. In Fourteenth Army the malaria casualty-rate for the first five months of 1945 was about one-fifth of that for the same period of 1944.

Outbreaks of malaria did occur in units and formations on a suppressive régimen. On every occasion the only cause that could be discovered was the failure on the part of the troops to consume the mepacrine tablets regularly. No evidence which stood the test of careful analysis and which suggested that an outbreak of malaria had occurred in spite of regular daily consumption of mepacrine was forthcoming. The reasons for the non-consumption of the mepacrine tablets were found to be various. Not all senior officers in charge of troops accepted the statement that the regular taking of the mepacrine tablet held malaria in check*. This opinion affected the attitude of their junior officers towards 'mepacrine discipline', they did not make certain that every man in their charge did in fact swallow his tablets. Among the troops there was a widespread rumour that mepacrine, like many another drug commonly dispensed in the Army, if taken over long periods, caused impotence. Another notion that was common, was that when malaria is suppressed, it appears with explosive violence when the suppressive treatment ceases

---

* *See* Appendix XIII.

and thereafter persists for the rest of the individual's life. After a period of about eighteen months or so spent overseas with no possibility of visiting his own home and his own people when on leave, the average soldier tends to become 'browned off', apathetic, and when this happens he tends to stop taking care of himself. He is no longer interested in trying to avoid malaria; indeed he may decide that by going sick he will greatly magnify his chances of getting out of a situation that has become most uncongenial. Since in the control of malaria the intelligent co-operation of the individual soldier is necessary, the withdrawal of this co-operation means that the efforts of his officers and of his regimental medical officer are wasted.

A study of stereoscopic air photographs supplied by the Air Force revealed much information of great value concerning the breeding places of the mosquito in areas still in the hands of the Japanese. Such photographs were used in March and April 1945 to determine the state of the perennial streams in the foothills of the Shan States and in the Pegu Yomas, the main breeding places of *A. minimus* before the rains, for it was along the course of these that the Japanese were retreating. In March 1945 orders were issued to the effect that all Japanese P.o.W. should be questioned about the incidence of malaria and about the supplies of quinine. Blood slides were taken from every P.o.W. whenever this was possible. Between the Japanese attack at Meiktila and the fall of Rangoon over 200 slides showed a parasite rate of about 30 per cent., rising in the last weeks of the campaign to 49 per cent. in a group of 41 captured when crossing the Irrawaddy from Arakan.

It is reasonable to conclude that the marked difference in the degree to which malaria was brought and held under control in the Allied and the Japanese land forces respectively during the course of the years 1943-45 was one of the reasons, and indeed one of the most important reasons, why the Japanese were defeated. The diseases of the greatest military importance are neutral in the sense that they are capable of affecting both antagonists and will do so unless ceaseless and strenuous efforts to bring and to keep them under control are made. If effective control is achieved by only one of the antagonists then by that one great advantage is enjoyed, for the control of disease means that large numbers of trained, experienced men, more valuable than raw reinforcements, and who otherwise would be lost, remain in the forward zone. Because the extent of the control over malaria in Fourteenth Army and in XV Corps was so great when compared with that exercised by the Japanese, it was possible for them, and profitable for them, to continue military operations throughout the season of maximum prevalence of malaria, especially of M.T. malaria, for in such circumstances malaria became an ally of the Allies and a formidable and implacable enemy of their opponent. The control of malaria is not easily achieved in a force that has been defeated and is retreating hurriedly through an inhospitable countryside. During the advance from the Chindwin to Rangoon and in Arakan malaria diminished the strength and the power of the Japanese very greatly indeed and made the tasks of Fourteenth Army and of XV Corps appreciably lighter.

(3) THE ARMY DENTAL SERVICE

An A.D.D.S. Eastern Army was appointed in October 1942. An A.D.D.S. 11 Army Group was appointed in February 1944. The post was upgraded to D.D.D.S. in July 1944. An A.D.D.S. Fourteenth Army was appointed in July 1944. An A.D.D.S. L. of C. Command was appointed in September 1944. This command ceased to exist on May 31, 1945. An A.D.D.S. 505 District was appointed when Central Burma had been reoccupied. An A.D.D.S. Twelfth Army was appointed at the end of May 1945. South Burma District and 505 District passed under command of Twelfth Army for administrative purposes. In Ceylon Command (part of 11 Army Group) there was a D.A.D.D.S.

When the A.D.D.S. was first appointed to Eastern Army there were in it three Indian army dental centres, two Indian dental units (B.T.), and one Indian dental unit (I.T.). In Assam there were two Indian dental units (I.T.) but these had become separated from their equipment. One of the two I.A.D.C. officers belonging to one of these units was sent to Bombay to obtain replacements. One of the units opened in Imphal and the other in Dimapur. The only dental laboratory facilities available to the units in Eastern Army were in Calcutta and it was to this laboratory that soldiers in the forward areas requiring dentures were sent until it became possible to have two dental mechanics and the essential equipment sent forward to Dimapur and Imphal.

Dental units were being hurriedly raised in Poona and in January 1943, four Indian dental units (B.T.), four Indian dental units (I.T.) and four Indian dental mechanic units were posted to Eastern Army. Of these three of each kind were sent to the forward areas and the remaining three were posted to Ranchi. Forceps and syringes were distributed among the forward medical units so that medical officers could do emergency extractions; later these items were included in the official standard equipment of the Indian field ambulance and C.C.S.

In 1942 and early 1943 dental stores were exceedingly scarce and units were maintained largely by local purchase in Calcutta of anything that could be obtained, some of it secondhand and much of it of inferior quality. By June 1943 stocks had become larger and better and these were placed in the medical stores in Gauhati, Comilla, Dimapur and Imphal.

For XV Corps in Arakan all that could be provided in 1943 was one Indian dental unit (B.T.) and one Indian dental mechanic unit. These units, 48 (Ind.) Dent. Unit (B.T.) and 18 (Ind.) Dent. Mech. Unit, were involved in the overrunning of the M.D.S. of 66 (Ind.) Fd. Amb. on February 7, 1944. Two of the I.O.Rs. were captured and shot and the officer commanding the dental unit was wounded but managed to get away. When the M.D.S. was liberated the units resumed their work although the box was under almost continuous fire for the next sixteen days.

In March 1944 82nd W.A. Division reached Arakan. Its dental officers were detached from their units whenever possible to care for troops more in need of their services than were their own. When the division trekked into the valley of the Kaladan only the minimum of dental equipment was taken. The dental chair was left behind. When equipment was needed it was delivered by air whenever possible.

In the northern sector the few dental units were very widely separated in space and so it became the custom for the dental unit no matter whether B.T. or I.T., to deal with both British and Indian troops. The dental mechanic units were usually attached to the dental units (B.T.). The suggestion was made to G.H.Q.(I.) that the Indian dental mechanic unit should be abolished, its personnel being added to the establishment of the dental unit (B.T.). The suggestion was not accepted, it being held that the concentration of the mechanics in a special unit had many advantages.

To 2nd Division during its operations about Kohima two dental mechanics from 82nd W.A. Division were attached to help in the overtaking of the very heavy list of those needing dentures.

When Fourteenth Army began its advance into Burma the dental units were required to become mobile. Their equipment and baggage had to be cut down for there was an acute shortage of transport. A request to G.H.Q.(I.) for the addition of a vehicle to the dental unit's W.E.T. had been rejected. However, the units did manage somehow or other to keep up with the fast moving divisions. Exceptionally it was necessary to ferry a unit forward by air. Tents were in use during the advance, the 180 lb. having replaced the much heavier S/Sergt. pattern. The distribution of the dental units was roughly as follows: one dental unit (B.T.) and one dental unit (I.T.) and one dental mechanic unit were attached to each division and to each corps H.Q., those with corps being associated with the most forward corps C.C.S. With the division the units were usually sited well forward, on occasion being attached to the A.D.S. of a field ambulance. The main advantages of this arrangement were that a man requiring dental aid was absent from his unit for only a very short time and that maxillo-facial cases could receive the earliest possible dental attention.

Serving 36th Division were the dental personnel of a C.C.S. and of a field ambulance. During the period November 1944–April 1945 this field ambulance moved its location no less than thirty times and its dental section was open and functioning in eighteen different places in rapid succession. For the most part the dental officer, his clerk orderly and his equipment were transported in a jeep and trailer; occasionally the equipment was taken forward by air.

When Rangoon was reoccupied several of the dental units of Fourteenth Army were established in the capital. With 38 B.G.H. to Rangoon there came its dental department and half of a maxillo-facial unit, the other half having been left in Comilla. A few A.L.F.S.E.A. dental units were strung out along the two corridors along which IV and XXXIII Corps had advanced on Rangoon.

The hurried retreat in 1942, the rapid advance of 1945, the nature of the terrain and of the fighting and the peculiarities of the climate all combined to make the provision of dental care difficult. Nevertheless it was provided.

(4) THE ARMY TRANSFUSION SERVICE*

A transfusion unit (1(Ind.) B.T.U.) was raised in India in March 1942. It went to Iraq and did not return to India until 1944 when it was attached to 3 Base Transfusion Unit in Poona. In April 1942 an instruction was issued to the effect that a resuscitation officer would be appointed in every medical unit.

2 Base Transfusion Unit arrived in India from the United Kingdom in June 1942, accompanied by 8 Field Transfusion Unit. 2 and 5 Field Transfusion Units arrived from the Middle East about the same time. 3 Base Transfusion Unit from the United Kingdom followed closely and arrived in mid-September accompanied by 27 and 28 Field Transfusion Units.

At the time when the first of the base transfusion units arrived there was no transfusion service in India. There had been preliminary discussions between 'civil' and 'military' concerning the formation of such a service. It was proposed that individual medical units should meet their needs for fresh blood by the use of local donor panels while blood collection for serum-plasma processing would be undertaken in military district laboratories and in certain selected civilian hospitals. The establishment of this service had been impeded by lack of the necessary apparatus but a training scheme had been initiated. Some civil centres

---

* The space claimed by a particular service is not to be regarded as an indication of the relative value or importance of that service. Some services, the Nursing and the Hygiene Services, for example, were long established and had attained a very complete organisation and a well-defined function. Others, the Transfusion and the Psychiatric, for example, were relatively new and were developing very rapidly during the war years. The latter kind demanded more space. Furthermore, as was to be expected, far more copious and detailed records of their problems and of their activities were maintained.

had started to bleed donors and to process serum with the apparatus already available in their laboratories. This service was designed to meet both military and civil needs.

The arrival of the first of the specialised transfusion units radically altered the situation. Discussion of the proposed scheme for establishing a transfusion service was reopened and the proposals were reconsidered when it became known that two base transfusion units and several field transfusion units were to be available. As a result of these discussions it was decided that the army would organise a transfusion service on the same lines as in the Middle East, based on the production capacity of the base transfusion units. The district laboratories would be relieved of the additional work of plasma processing, for which they were ill suited by lack of experience, lack of equipment and preoccupation with their proper work. The civil hospital blood banks would continue with processing in certain centres as part of the civil programme and would hold available for the army any surpluses above their requirements for air-raid casualties. Two Desivac drying plants were ordered, the cost being shared between the civil and military budgets. This decision had been reached when the second base transfusion unit and the additional field units arrived in India.

It must be appreciated that India was at this time threatened with a Japanese invasion from the East, and for this reason it was not considered wise to locate the base transfusion units on that side of the country. There was a possibility that the Japanese would invade India from Burma; there was also a grave risk that the invaders would appear on the southern and eastern Indian seaboard. With these factors in mind the responsibility for providing transfusion supplies was divided between the two base transfusion units on a territorial basis. 2 B.T.U. was given the territory of Eastern Army, Central Command and North Western Army (41,738 beds) and the unit was located in the centre of this area in Dehra Dun. From this centre rail communication with all parts of the territory could be maintained; the climate was not unsatisfactory; and the small and very scattered donor panel was not inaccessible. 3 B.T.U. was given the task of looking after the transfusion needs of Southern Army and Ceylon Army Command (18,000 beds). The unit was located in Poona, which appeared to have advantages by reason of proximity to the railways serving the south of India and communicating with Bombay and Calcutta. There was also a large hospital centre in Poona and a relatively large donor potential. Neither of these base units was permitted to move further forward at this time, although their siting in Calcutta and Bangalore respectively was considered. Had this been accepted it would have shortened the long line of communication with the field formations in Eastern Army.

The field transfusion units were disposed at the places where they could be used with the greatest benefit. One field unit was left in reserve at each of the base units; one unit (28 F.T.U.) was sent to Calcutta to forward supplies to Burma and to look after the Calcutta area. Another unit (5 F.T.U.) was sent to Bangalore to be available at any point in the south of India where invasion might come. The remaining unit (2 F.T.U.) was with the field force forward of Calcutta, and acted as distribution centre at Imphal. 22 F.T.U. arrived and was attached to 2 B.T.U. which released 8 F.T.U. at Bareilly for Cox's Bazar in Arakan.

To appreciate fully the difficulties which had to be faced it must be remembered that the two base units had come to India with the totally inadequate establishment of 2 officers, 7 R.A.M.C. orderlies and 4 attached R.A.S.C. and R.E. The equipment which had been brought with them was in accordance with the original base transfusion unit scale which had been designed for a unit working in very close contact with the parent depot at Bristol. In this case the parent depot was some six thousand miles away by sea, at a time when convoys were not frequent and were suffering heavy losses and was deeply committed in supplying the forces engaged in heavy fighting in the Desert. On arriving in India the base unit came under the administration of India with a consequent severance of the direct link through War Office with the parent Army Blood Supply Depot.

Local difficulties were not inconsiderable. Suitable buildings were not immediately available and had to be made ready to house the units. The territory to be covered was huge. The medical units were scattered over a very wide area to correspond with the equally widespread distribution of the troops. Communications were not good, with the railway taxed to the limit and air transport in its infancy. Distances between units, which in England would have been measured in tens of miles, were to be reckoned in hundreds or even thousands. The available donors were very limited in number and were very much dispersed. The civilian population, for political and superstitious reasons, was very reluctant to give any blood to the army and the response from this source was exceedingly small. The Indian troops were not very ready to give blood and did not become available as donors until a considerable amount of slow and insistent propaganda had been used. The British troops were the most obvious source of donors, but the total number of these in the country was relatively small. The potential donors were spread over a vast area of hundreds of thousands of square miles which the base unit, with only one refrigerator truck and a tiny establishment, was unable to cover. In comparison, it may be said that the potential donor panel was equal to that to be found in the medium counties of England but scattered throughout the 1,500,000 sq. miles of India.

The total amount of equipment brought out by the transfusion units was very small even when it had been supplemented by a certain amount of material from transfusion shipments originally destined for Burma and Malaya. Few of the medical units in India possessed any transfusion equipment at all. There was no holding of plasma; only small quantities of saline were available, and little use was made of blood which might have been obtained from local sources.

The transfusion units set about the problem of establishing themselves as rapidly as possible and, after suitable buildings had been allotted and altered, commenced production. During the period before the units could start production the transfusion equipment which had been brought out with the units was issued to medical units on a scale designed to give a minimum of essential equipment to as many of the more important units as possible.

It was evident that there were certain things which had to be done as rapidly as was possible:

(a) Production of transfusion fluids such as salines, wet and dried plasma, grouping serum, and blood had to be set in hand as quickly as possible and on the maximum scale.

(b) Transfusion sets and equipment had to be provided for all the medical units, starting with those most likely to operate in the field or to receive the casualties. These units were always accorded priority over the static or garrison hospitals.

(c) Medical officers had to be trained in the use of transfusion fluids and apparatus and in the techniques of transfusion and resuscitation.

The amount of transfusion equipment which had been brought out by the units was completely inadequate to supply anything but the smallest part of the need. It was essential that additional apparatus should be obtained, either from England or from local sources. As it was evident that apparatus must be obtained as rapidly as possible, and that the greatest possible degree of standardisation of apparatus in all theatres was desirable, it was decided that the original pattern of the excellent United Kingdom sets should be retained. The chief difference made was in the packing of equipment and transfusion fluids. Packings were chosen which were thought to be more suited to the diversity of conditions and transport to be encountered. Experience showed that this was a wise step.

Calculations were made of the scales of equipment necessary to equip all types of units with an initial holding and maintenance supply. As the standard items of transfusion equipment did not exist in the Priced Vocabulary of Medical Stores, a new Section 27 was drawn up to include all items used in transfusion work. Orders were placed on the Supply

Department through the Medical Directorate, G.H.Q.(I.) for the necessary components.

At this time the policy in India was to meet all possible demands from indigenous production rather than to place orders on the already overstrained industrial capacity of the United Kingdom. This necessitated the formulation of detailed specifications of every single piece of transfusion equipment from boxes down to the smallest component; submission to the Controller General of Inspection for approval; and to the Finance Department for sanction.

Once this had been accomplished it was necessary to find firms in India which were able to make the components. India had never developed her production of scientific apparatus but had been dependent on imports to meet her peace-time needs. It was, therefore, difficult to find firms capable of making the items of equipment which were so vitally necessary. As an example, it may be stated that there was only one firm in the whole of India which was able to make neutral glass and therefore capable of making a blood transfusion bottle. The production of neutral glass had only recently been started at the time when the initial orders for these bottles were placed, and the Transfusion Service was allotted only a share of the output of this firm, which was loaded with orders for all other types of laboratory and scientific glassware.

Despite the emphasis which was laid on the urgent necessity for every item of transfusion apparatus to be obtained at the earliest possible moment, the delays which were experienced were very numerous. Supply Departments, though furnished with the names of firms capable of producing various components, insisted on obtaining competitive estimates. Further delays were occasioned by the submission of ridiculously high tenders, submission and inspection of samples and obtaining release of the more rigorously controlled raw materials. Once orders had been placed difficulties were occasioned by the rejection of the entire production of some firms because the quality of the bulk order did not approach that of the sample. Other firms did not fulfil their orders and alternative sources of supply had to be found. In almost every case the output was slow. All these reasons caused further delay in establishing the service.

Some of the more immediate shortages were met by the placing of orders directly by the Medical Directorate. This was made possible by the use of a special financial grant of three lakhs of rupees which had been made to establish the transfusion service, and helped to tide over the interval until the Supply Department started to deliver equipment.

For all these reasons and a host of others, it was not until the later part of 1943 that transfusion apparatus was available on any considerable scale. In the interval the service had been run on a very precarious basis with a very careful husbanding of the available supplies, and meagre issues restricted to the more important units. The fact that all these difficulties were overcome and transfusion equipment produced was due in very large part to the most strenuous personal efforts of the O.C., 2 B.T.U., who discovered many of the firms which eventually produced the equipment and personally supervised most carefully the production of the items.

As soon as the base transfusion units were established in buildings, courses of instruction for officers were commenced. Officers from field units and hospitals were brought to the units and were given a five days' course of concentrated training in the duties of a unit resuscitation officer. An attempt was made to teach the basic facts necessary for the organisation of the transfusion work of a medical unit. The course was based on the lectures given at the Army Blood Supply Depot, Bristol.

Initially this entailed very hard work for the two officers of the base transfusion units for it was additional to all the normal work of the unit. After the personnel of the units was increased, large numbers of officers were taken for training. Courses were also held on similar lines at the units in Calcutta and Bangalore.

At all times the greatest importance was laid on the necessity for the continuation of training, despite extreme preoccupation with the production of transfusion supplies. The transfusion officers trained in this way were sent back to their units with an instruction to form a panel of donors from local sources, unit personnel or civilian donors if possible, and to use this panel for the treatment of casualties and the severe anaemias which were becoming increasingly common among the Indian troops. Courses for orderlies were also held.

No scales of transfusion equipment existed for medical units in India. Scales were drawn up and financial sanction obtained. Hospitals were divided into the following categories for this purpose:— base general hospitals, field general hospitals, garrison hospitals in three divisions of 1–50, 51–350 and over 350 beds. These scales were based on the issues which were authorised in the United Kingdom. I.1248 scales were modified to conform to the extra issues which had been found necessary in the Middle East.

The initial stocks of transfusion apparatus which had been brought to India by the base transfusion units were issued to medical units on a very careful basis of operational priorities. As soon as indigenous production was commenced, these issues were made on an ever increasing scale. This was continued until all units previously raised and all forming units were fully equipped and maintained on this scale.

An additional commitment arose with the need to equip all fighter and bomber squadrons, mobile field hospitals and station hospitals of the R.A.F. The R.I.N. ships and shore establishments proved to be a smaller responsibility.

It was evident that transfusion fluids and equipment had to be packed in distinctive boxes which were easily handled. In view of the difficulties under which many medical units in the field used transfusion equipment, standard packed boxes were developed which contained a fixed proportion of different fluids. This enabled a unit to divide the available stocks very easily between different sections and had the additional advantage that medical officers and orderlies always could rely on finding the same fluids in the same type of box.

These boxes were:—

(a) Box, Infusion Supply Pattern, Stanpack weight 78 lbs.
(b) Box, 14-partitioned, Saline Stanpack weight 56 lbs.
(c) Box, Indian Field Transfusion (1942 Pattern)

These boxes were very different from the standard boxes issued by the Army Blood Supply Depot, Bristol. The box, Infusion Supply Pattern, Stanpack contained 8 dried plasma, 8 distilled water, 4 plasma giving sets, 4 glucose-saline and 2 normal saline. The box, 14-partitioned, Saline Stanpack contained 10 glucose-saline and 4 normal saline. The box, Indian Field Transfusion, was a box issued to field ambulances, ambulance trains, hospital ships, casualty staging sections, light sections of casualty clearing stations, mobile surgical units and other small medical units where it was desirable to have a compact and complete set of transfusion equipment. The box contained sterile bottles, citrate and taking sets, venesection set, blood grouping outfit, splints, collapsible transfusion stands, sphygmomanometer, swabs and other essentials.

These three boxes quickly demonstrated their value and the standardisation proved to be invaluable.

The production of salines was started as soon as the units were able to get their equipment unpacked. At first the production was very small and was limited by the output of stills and the number of bottles which were available. As the supplies increased the output gradually rose month by month. Figures will be given later which will show the output.

Three main crystalloidal fluids were produced; isotonic glucose-saline (2·5 per cent. dextrose and 0·425 per cent. NaCl); isotonic saline; 3 per cent. sodium citrate solution. Other solutions were produced such as 0·5 per cent. sulphanilamide in normal saline, hypertonic 5 per cent. saline, 4·3 per cent. sodium sulphate and 2 per cent. sodium bicarbonate solution, but the issues of these fluids was small compared with those of the three main ones.

Very soon after the base units were established it was realised that it would be possible for them to take over the preparation of all grouping serum for India and Burma. This had been done in the district laboratories previously and it had been observed that there was a great variation in the technique of preparation and titration. Some laboratories were filtering the serum but others had not the Seitz filters to do this. Some of the serum was prepared with the addition of dyes as antiseptics. Great variation in the titre of the serum was observed. For these reasons the preparation of grouping serum was centred on the base transfusion units. All issues of serum to all units in India and the field were made from the stocks prepared at these units.

Standardisation of grouping serum was achieved by the issue in all cases of liquid serum made by the pooling of multiple donors, Seitz filtration and ampouling in small amounts of 0·5c.c. This issue of small amounts ensured a rapid turnover and a reduction of the risk of old stored inert serum being used. The minimum titre was fixed at 1 in 100.

From the very first it was obvious that the great distances, the difficulties of transportation, the scarcity of refrigerators, the lack of suitable ice boxes and similar factors made it impossible to attempt a distribution of blood from the transfusion units, while they were in process of occupying buildings.

Every medical unit was instructed to make the maximum effort to meet it's own needs in respect of blood by the formation of local donor panels and local bleeding. The field transfusion units attempted to meet the needs of surrounding units in this way.

The base transfusion units started a programme to bleed all available donors in order to supply blood to the hospitals in their immediate vicinity and to convert the surplus blood taken to the preparation of wet plasma. All the difficulties mentioned previously were met in the recruitment of sufficient numbers of donors. Details of the numbers of donors bled and the amounts of wet plasma prepared are given later.

In an attempt to overcome the difficulties of the scattered donor panel and the distances which had to be travelled to make contact with and bleed the donors, a railway coach was obtained and fitted up as a combined mobile refrigerator and bleeding coach. It also had sleeping accommodation for a small number of men. The coach was attached to a train and taken to some centre where a donor recruiting campaign had been arranged. On arrival at this centre the team bled for two or three days and stored the blood which had been taken in the refrigerator on the train. This refrigerator had a capacity of approximately 450 pint bottles. When the bleeding was finished, the coach returned by rail to the base transfusion unit and the blood was used for the preparation of plasma.

The bulk of the blood taken by the base transfusion units was used for the preparation of wet plasma. At first the alkali wash method was used but later a change was made to the alkali-002 method. This proved to be moderately successful. Initial difficulties were experienced with the use of seven small 14 cm. Seitz filters and it was not until the beginning of 1943 that it was possible to obtain Pilot filters from the United Kingdom and step up production. With the serum 14 cm. filters the maximum amount which could be prepared in one run was 30 pints, and even with this the later bottles showed a tendency to clot. The use of the Pilot filter made a vast difference to the production. Considerable trouble was experienced with casual contamination during bottling until air conditioning of the plasma rooms at the base units was installed. This made a very considerable difference to the quality of the final product and lowered the rejection rate to a very significant degree.

The keeping properties of wet plasma in the hot weather was a matter which gave rise to some anxiety at first. Although the bottles which travelled by train in the hot weather on their way to the forward units seemed to develop lipoid very readily, these bottles were weeded out at Calcutta. The incidence of this type of wet plasma seemed to be materially reduced with the introduction of new techniques. The demand for wet plasma was such that the stocks had little time to degenerate in storage as they were issued very soon after they had matured for the customary three weeks.

As soon as the magnitude of the supply problem was recognised demands for dried plasma were placed. The Army Blood Supply Depot was unable to accept the full demand at this time because of other commitments and a large portion of the demand was transferred to America. Lyovac Plasma was shipped to meet this demand. While this was an excellent dried plasma, the packing provided was that issued to the civil hospitals in the United States, a type of pack which was unsuitable for the use of field units. This plasma was issued to static and base hospitals and Bristol plasma was reserved for the use of field operational units.

During this first year the main responsibility for the supply of transfusion fluids and apparatus to the front was borne by 2 B.T.U. and the field transfusion units dependent upon this base. 3 B.T.U. was mainly concerned with the supply of the large hospital centres of Southern India and Ceylon. The needs of the Army on the Burma border of India received first priority.

2 F.T.U. was located at Imphal, acting as distributing centre for all units in Assam, including a large L. of C. Area and IV Corps. The resuscitation work of 19 (Ind.) C.C.S. was undertaken by this unit which also prepared small quantities of salines for local use.

8 F.T.U. was stationed in Cox's Bazar, Arakan. Blood was taken from local troops. All plasma and salines issued to the units in Cox's

Bazar and forward of this were distributed by 8 F.T.U. or from 15 C.C.S. Replacement of these stocks was made from a dump held at 68 I.G.H. in Chittagong which was in turn replenished from Calcutta, by sea, rail and air. During the monsoon 8 F.T.U. was withdrawn to Dehra Dun to help 2 B.T.U. to prepare for the next campaigning season.

From the experience gained in Arakan in the first six months of 1943, several lessons were learnt.

(1) field ambulances held cases for several days because of difficult evacuation and therefore salines for the treatment of dehydration were an essential issue as well as stocks of plasma.

(2) field transfusion units were required to a great extent to be self-dependent and at least one 180 lb. tent and additional transport were necessary.

(3) the packing of transfusion fluids in standard boxes was most desirable.

The two base transfusion units were established in permanent buildings and started production and issues to all units. The scale of production was limited by the available equipment and the scarcity of personnel.

The main limiting factor at this time was scarcity of equipment; the units were fully engaged but it was most obvious that an increase in output when further equipment became available could only be achieved by an increase in the number and size of the units.

The length of the lines of communication and the difficulties of ensuring that supplies would reach their destination if entrusted to normal despatch by rail made it imperative that distribution at all stages should be retained in the hands of the Transfusion Service. This added to the strain on the already overtaxed resources of the service.

This policy attracted some severe criticism as it was necessary to keep the field transfusion units, or some of them at least, at a moderately rearward level to act as distribution units. The criticism of this policy was that the units should have been forward doing resuscitation work. It always seemed obvious to the officers of the Transfusion Service that units which made certain that supplies were distributed to forward units were more valuable to the force than when acting as resuscitation teams forward with no certainty that supplies would reach them.

The G.1098 and I.1248 equipment was utterly inadequate. Only one mobile refrigerator vehicle with a total capacity of 80 bottles of blood was supplied to provide refrigerator storage for the unit.

The difficulties in providing adequate accommodation for the base transfusion units were great as the major part of it was supplied by new building at a time when building was slow and materials scarce.

The necessity for air-conditioning plasma processing rooms and providing additional refrigerator space was appreciated early but shortage of materials made their installation a slow business.

According to the records of the Transfusion Service, Eastern Army's admissions to its medical units during the year 1943 on account of wounds totalled about 4,000 whereas admissions on account of dysentery and diarrhoea alone amounted to no less than 36,353. These diseases demand more infusion fluids than any other strictly 'medical' condition; it is for this reason that they are quoted.

In the Arakan operation of this year it was recorded that 8 F.T.U. transfused 87 patients and that the amounts of transfusion fluids per battle casualty were, blood 1·5 pints; plasma 1·7 pints; total protein 3·2 pints and crystalloids 2·1 pints.

The period mid-1943 to mid-1944 was mainly devoted to the gradual development and expansion of the service with a corresponding increase in the production of transfusion equipment and fluids. At the same time there was a considerable increase in the demands made on the service and production never outpaced demand to the extent that a reserve could be accumulated for future operations.

It had not been possible to alter the war establishment of base transfusion units in India until the War Office had taken action. The need for extra personnel was so pressing that it was not practicable to await this action to be taken. A case was submitted for the raising of Indian blood storage units in W.E. VI/88–c/1 for attachment to the base transfusion units. Despite the man-power situation in India, sanction was accorded for these units. These new units afforded extra personnel and equipment to the parent base transfusion unit. This W.E. included 2 medical officers; 2 B.O.Rs., R.A.M.C.; 8 W.A.C.(I.) as transfusion orderlies for assembly, laboratory, clerical and bleeding team work; 1 havildar I.A.M.C.; 2 nursing sepoys; 2 ambulance sepoys; and followers such as dhobies, sweepers, carpenters and cooks etc., who were badly needed and for which no provision had existed previously.

1 Indian Blood Storage Unit was raised at 2 B.T.U. and 2 Indian Blood Storage Unit at 3 B.T.U. in September 1943. The extra men and equipment, once they were made available to the base units, made a great difference to the amount of work which these were able to undertake.

It had become very evident that a new type of unit was essential to act as an intermediate link in the chain of supply between the base transfusion units and the consuming units such as field transfusion units and medical units in the field. The very lengthy lines of communication and the vast area of India made this essential if supplies were to be delivered safely and speedily. This work had been undertaken by field transfusion units in Calcutta and Bangalore but it meant that these two units were thus unable to fulfil their proper rôle.

A case for the raising of units to fill this function was submitted. The formation of two Indian advanced base transfusion units ((Ind.) Adv. B.T.U.), was sanctioned on W.E. VI/88-B/1. These units were raised from 5 and 28 F.T.Us. in Bangalore and Calcutta respectively and the F.T.Us. then reformed with new officers and men.

The war establishment of the (Ind.) Adv. B.T.U. allowed two medical officers; two B.O.Rs., R.A.M.C.; two havildars I.A.M.C.; ambulance sepoys; nursing sepoys, and drivers. The unit was intended to act as a forwarding unit for supplies of transfusion fluid and apparatus manufactured at the base units. In addition the advanced unit bled donors, made small quantities of saline solutions and held training courses. The creation of these units released two field transfusion units for work in the field.

In the forward areas it quickly became evident that the transfusion units needed additional transport. They could not collect their supplies from the airstrip or the dump in their 3-ton refrigerator vehicles nor could they use these for the delivery of supplies to field ambulance M.D.Ss. in many instances for these were often sited in very inaccessible places. Later, in early 1944, all the field transfusion units were provided with a second vehicle, jeep and trailer or 4×15 cwt. truck, the second of these proving to be the better. It was also clearly demonstrated that these units needed more blood-giving and blood-taking sets and a small still. Tentage was also required for the parent unit was often unable to supply this. One 80 lb. and one 180 lb. tent just sufficed and an E.P.I.P. tent was an absolute necessity during the monsoon for the holding of stores.

It was found that the field ambulance A.D.Ss. and M.D.Ss. often required to be supplied with crystalloids as well as with plasma. Often such supplies had to be taken forward by mulepack and when this was so the Infusion Supply Box, weighing 78 lbs. approximately half a mule-load, was a great boon.

Because of the nature of the terrain and of the length of the supply line a pool of N.C.Os. was required for posting along this line at selected points. The introduction of a distributing section into the war establishment of the base transfusion unit removed the need for this pool.

In July 1944 it was considered that a need existed for an officer of the transfusion service on whole-time duty at G.H.Q. (India) to arrange for the provisioning of transfusion apparatus; to co-ordinate the work done by the different units; to distribute the demands made on the service among the units in equitable fashion; and to deal with the increasing administrative work of the service. The appointment of an Assistant Director of Pathology (Transfusion) was created in the

Medical Directorate G.H.Q.(I.) and the officer commanding 3 B.T.U. was appointed to fill this post.

The increase in the size of the base transfusion units and the formation of the Indian advanced base transfusion units made it necessary for the available accommodation to be increased. Although the base units had originally been located in buildings of the permanent type, expansion in most cases had to be in new buildings of the temporary type which were built exceedingly slowly and proved to be very unsuitable for any technical work. The original permanent buildings were used for laboratory work and the temporary buildings as stores. Extra refrigerator space was provided and air-conditioning of the plasma processing laboratories was installed. This proved to be invaluable in the long run but the delays of installation were very trying and at times actually hindered work. Both (Ind.) Adv. B.T.Us. were fortunate in obtaining permanent buildings for their accommodation.

Great difficulty was experienced at all times in securing adequate and reliable water and electrical supplies. Water supplies were insufficient in amount and tended to fail at intervals. This occasioned great difficulties in the operation of distilling plants.

The unreliability of the electrical supplies at both base units made it impossible to use these as sources of heat and primus stoves were required for stills, autoclaves and all other heating. This relatively inefficient and time wasting method was rendered even more ineffective than usual by the poor quality of kerosene and stoves available. It was always the work of at least one man on whole time duty to look after the primus stoves and another to repair them. Even then it was difficult to maintain the necessary output of distilled water.

By this time it had been realised that the productive capacity of India was not able to meet the demands of the Transfusion Service and the majority of orders for 1945 were placed in the United Kingdom. This itself proved to be a great disappointment. Few of the orders placed produced any results during this year. Throughout the year output and issues were restricted by the equipment available and there was at no time any reserve of the more essential items. This was especially so with chemicals, needles, bottles and vital basic equipment such as Pilot filters. In many cases production was delayed until further small stocks of certain components were available.

At this time the limited productive capacity of the United Kingdom was strained by the demands made by A.B.S.D. to satisfy the needs of the Forces in the Mediterranean theatre and to build up the supplies for Operation 'Overlord'. As a result India merely received such supplies as were available against her outstanding orders.

During this year the demands of the field forces steadily increased and as the responsibility for supplying Eastern Army—later to become

Fourteenth Army—was given to 2 B.T.U., this unit found it difficult to maintain the necessary output. 3 B.T.U. had not the same demand placed on it and was much less hard worked.

The formation of the (Ind.) Adv. B.T.Us. in Bangalore and Calcutta released 5 and 28 F.T.Us. for use with the field forces early in 1944. The increase in the size of the base units also freed 27 F.T.U. 32 F.T.U. remained attached to 2 B.T.U. in Dehra Dun.

2 F.T.U. remained at Imphal. This unit collected supplies sent from Calcutta by air and distributed to medical units in the L. of C. Area and IV Corps. Blood was flown from 2 (Ind.) Adv. B.T.U. in Calcutta and was collected from the airstrip and distributed by 2 F.T.U. The unit was attached to a casualty clearing station. A 'dump' or reserve stock of transfusion fluids was held and a subsidiary reserve stock was maintained in the Imphal depot of medical stores for dispersal reasons.

The following system of distribution of transfusion fluids to IV Corps was established, and the following instructions were issued to all units:

Maintenance of Transfusion Fluids—IV Corps.

i. *Field Ambulance*
- (a) Field ambulances in operational areas will hold a minimum of three infusion supply boxes.
- (b) As soon as one box is empty it will be sent by ambulance to the most forward C.C.S. where it will be exchanged for another held in that unit's medical stores.
- (c) Field ambulances situated behind the most forward C.C.S. will exchange their boxes with the nearest field transfusion unit (i.e., 2 F.T.U.). They will not obtain their supplies from a more forward reserve dump, except in very special circumstances.
- (d) Field ambulances wishing to replace individual bottles during quiet periods will under no circumstances obtain these from casualty clearing stations holding reserve supplies but will, if considered necessary, return them to the nearest field transfusion unit irrespective of their position in the field.
- (e) Any field ambulance withdrawn from IV Corps Area will surrender to the nearest transfusion unit all infusion supply boxes with the exception of one which it will always keep to cover any small emergency as stipulated on the W.E.T.

ii. *Casualty Clearing Station*
- (a) All casualty clearing stations will hold a minimum of three infusion supply boxes packed in the standard way together with two 14-partition boxes P.V.27111, which hold glucose-saline and saline.
- (b) Boxes containing empty bottles and used plasma sets will be returned to the nearest field transfusion unit which will issue new boxes in lieu. Individual bottles will not be forwarded except in special circumstances.

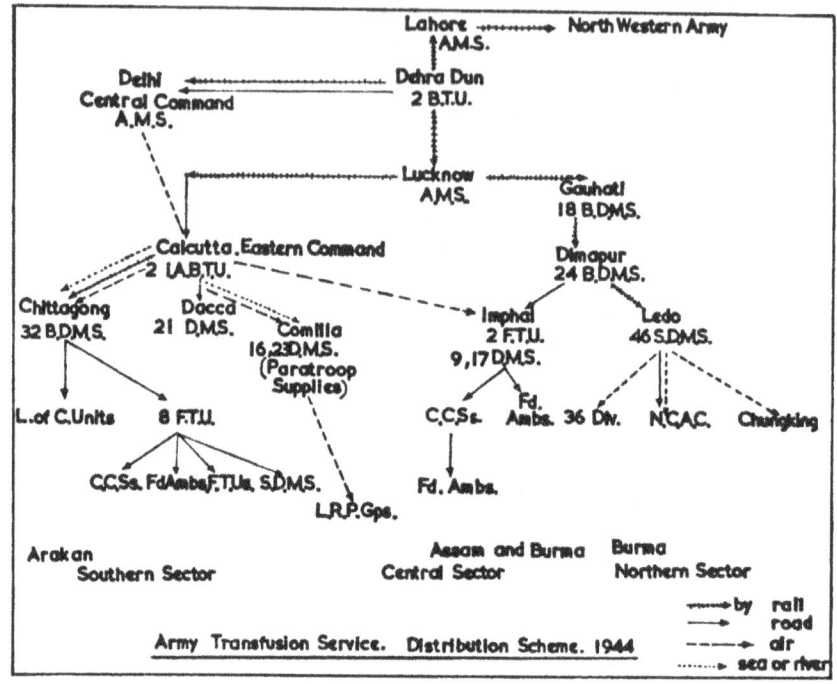

Fig. 83. Army Transfusion Service. Distribution Scheme. 1944.

    A.M.S.   Army Medical Stores
    B.D.M.S.   Base Depot of Medical Stores
    L.R.P. Gps.   Long Range Penetration Groups
    D.M.S.   Depot of Medical Stores
    S.D.M.S.   Sub-depot of Medical Stores
    N.C.A.C.   Northern Combat Area Command

Bulk stores were sent from Dehra Dun to Calcutta, to 28 F.T.U. and later to 2 (Ind.) Adv. B.T.U. From Calcutta supplies were sent forward to Chittagong by road, rail, sea or air or by a combination of two or more of these. By air the journey took about two hours. This method had seldom been available before 1944. By passenger train and river steamer the journey took between 24 and 48 hours. The journey by land and sea was always uncertain and it could not be guaranteed that supplies sent off would reach their destinations east of Calcutta. When they did arrive at Chittagong another 24 hours were required for them to find the units to which they were addressed. For the Northern Sector supplies were sent from Dehra Dun to Imphal by road, rail and river. If sent unescorted they passed along a chain of depots of medical stores and could take as long as three weeks to reach their destinations. By the beginning of 1944 supplies could be sent from Calcutta to Imphal by air and this became the method of choice.

(c) The most forward casualty clearing station, will in addition to its own stock, hold a further ten infusion supply boxes and four 14-partition boxes, in its medical store. These boxes are for issue to field ambulances and mobile surgical units working ahead of the C.C.S. The packing of these boxes will not be altered by the C.C.S. This stock when reduced by a half will be replenished from the nearest transfusion unit to whom all empty bottles and boxes will be returned.

(d) In the event of no member of the Army Transfusion Service being attached to the most forward C.C.S., the resuscitation officer of the latter unit will be held responsible for the maintenance of this divisional reserve, and for ensuring that stocks are not frittered away in an uneconomical manner.

(e) When the forward casualty clearing station is side-stepped by another such unit it will hand over its divisional transfusion reserve stock to this C.C.S. immediately the latter is open to receive casualties.

In Arakan, 8 F.T.U. in Cox's Bazar was responsible for the maintenance of transfusion supplies in that area. It was located at C.C.S. level where it was able to assist with resuscitation in a group of three such units. This F.T.U. and a sub-depot medical stores, located half a mile away from it, both held considerable stocks of transfusion equipment. As in Assam, units obtained their supplies from the field transfusion unit but had been warned to proceed to the sub-depot medical stores should enemy action have rendered the F.T.U. inoperable. Whenever extra casualties were anticipated, the F.T.U. proceeded forward to work with a M.D.S.; on such occasions one man was left behind to supervise the maintenance of the F.T.U. transfusion stock. To ensure effective maintenance of the latter an intermediate dump was established at a base depot medical stores at Chittagong where the F.T.Us. were able to proceed direct by road when occasion demanded. This reserve was split into two blocks; (a) to effect an air-raid precaution and (b) to ensure that supplies intended for forward units were never reduced by those in the rear. The maintenance of the one was the responsibility of the field transfusion units for whom it was specifically reserved, the other that of the Stores which issued it to L. of C. Units.

28 F.T.U. was attached with a mobile surgical unit to the M.D.S. of a field ambulance of Indian 7th Division operating to the east of the Mayu Range, Arakan. In addition to its resuscitation duties it was held responsible for ensuring that the field ambulances in its division were maintained with adequate supplies, replacement being obtained from the Corps' dump held by 8 F.T.U.

The first real test of this organisation came at the beginning of February when Indian 7th Division successfully thwarted the Japanese Arakan thrust. Almost at the beginning of this attack 28 F.T.U. was rendered ineffective, the driver and one R.A.M.C. orderly having been killed, another orderly seriously wounded while the officer suffered an injury to his right arm. The latter subsequently reported that the large 7th Division box had always possessed adequate stocks of transfusion fluids and equipment and demands for plasma by those outside the ring on behalf of those inside it had been in excess of actual requirements; and this in spite of the fact that two-thirds of the plasma supplied had unfortunately fallen among the Japanese. In March personnel of 32 F.T.U. took over from the remnants of 28 F.T.U. and this latter unit was then reformed and re-equipped by 2 B.T.U. in October 1944 prior to its return to Arakan. A visit by O.C., 2 B.T.U. to this part of the front at the end of February disclosed that all units were well satisfied with the supply system, while D.D.M.S. Corps described it as the best of its kind. The Japanese attack had, however, disclosed that there was far too much laxity permitted regarding the issue of transfusion fluids for air-dropping. The store at Comilla received two large demands for parachute supplies in the course of 36 hours which bore no relation to the casualties suffered, and reduced the stock held there to nil. To provide for future eventualities the following organisation was set up.

Parachute Supplies:

(i) Three standard paratroop boxes were introduced, one of which contained wet plasma, a second plasma and sulphanilamide saline and a third crystalloids; all three were complete with giving sets and carried distinguishing letters painted on the outside of their lids.

(ii) The store responsible for parachute supplies was instructed not to issue more than four boxes of each particular pack to any one medical unit at a time, the advanced base transfusion unit to be 'phoned in the event of extenuating circumstances'.

(iii) Initially the stock was fixed at 60 paratroop boxes comprising 180 bottles of plasma, 120 bottles of crystalloids and 60 bottles of sulphanilamide saline, a quantity that was subsequently increased. The store was maintained by rail from Chittagong and by air from Calcutta in emergency.

In this way the following forces were maintained:

General Wingate's Long Range Penetration Groups;
81st West African Division;
Any unit for whom air-dropping became essential.

It was reported that this service worked well. The paratroop boxes which weighed, when packed, 26 lbs. each and fitted into every type of container proved very successful, bottles very seldom being found broken in them.

27 F.T.U. arrived in Arakan in February 1944 with 36th Division, and remained there until shortly before the monsoon. During this period although it was attached to the M.D.S. of a field ambulance it did less resuscitation work than it might have done for the reason that the division considered it so much a part of itself that it would not permit it to be posted to whatever part of the Arakan front most needed the services of such a unit.

The reserve 32 F.T.U. was utilised in the following way: in March, the officer and one B.O.R. proceeded to Arakan where, with two other men loaned by Corps, it substituted for 28 F.T.U. while new personnel were procured and trained for that unit. The driver was sent to the advanced base transfusion unit, where a British driver was urgently needed at the time. The remaining O.R. remained at the base, being unsuitable on medical grounds for work in the field. The unit was reformed at the base in July.

5 F.T.U., which had been in Bangalore, was re-equipped by 2 (Ind.) Adv. B.T.U., at the beginning of April and proceeded to Dimapur, where it did excellent resuscitation work and was responsible for the maintenance of all transfusion fluids for 2nd Division during the battle of Kohima. Subsequently this unit proceeded to Imphal where it took over the forward distribution duties which had been carried out by 2 F.T.U. during the preceding twenty months.

At the end of August 1944 sanction was obtained for the acceptance in India of the new War Establishment for Base Transfusion Units IV/220/1; 2 and 3 B.T.Us. were reorganised on this establishment. The man-power situation only permitted the acceptance of the basic establishment. The sliding scale increase for additional armies and corps, was not sanctioned.

The increase in the size of the units made it possible to increase the output to a considerable extent but the demand had also increased so considerably that the units remained as hard worked as before, especially as no trained personnel were available as replacements. Several months elapsed before the units were brought to their new full strength in respect of men and vehicles.

In August 1944 sanction was obtained for the raising of a third advanced base transfusion unit in Bangalore, and for the reorganising of 1 and 2 Advanced Base Transfusion Units on W.E./VI/88–B/2.

The records of the Transfusion Service indicate that during 1944 the numbers of wounded and of those sick with dysentery and diarrhoea were:

	Central and Southern Fronts		N.C.A.C.
	Wounded	Dysentery and Diarrhoea	Wounded
British, Indian and African troops	26,500	49,000	1,145
U.S. troops	—	—	1,490
Chinese troops	—	—	11,171

Note. 2 B.T.U. provided plasma and grouping serum on demand for N.C.A.C. but the organisation of its transportation service was a responsibility of the U.S. military authorities.

Only four F.T.Us. were with Fourteenth Army and the whole of its L. of C. in 1945.

2 F.T.U. was with XXXIII Corps and was usually included in a corps medical centre.

5 F.T.U. was in Imphal, attached to a British general hospital during January and February and acting as a distributing unit. In March it moved forward to join IV Corps and to be attached to a C.C.S.

27 F.T.U. was with XXXIII Corps and was usually included in a corps medical centre.

22 F.T.U. was with IV Corps and was usually attached to a C.C.S.

In January 1945, 38, 39 and 40 F.T.Us. arrived from England and were sent straight into A.L.F.S.E.A. They were posted to Imphal where they remained with nothing to do until April. It was most regrettable that these units were not given an opportunity to visit one of the base transfusion units in order to gain first-hand information of supply procedure. It would have been very helpful to the units, and their scale of equipment could have been adjusted to that carried by other field transfusion units in the forward areas.

In November 1944 it had appeared probable that the war in Europe would not continue for many more months. It was assumed that when the European war was over South-East Asia would receive reinforcements of men and material and that the Transfusion Service would share in this. The heavy demands made on the United Kingdom to maintain the forces in the West had led to a degree of isolation of the Transfusion Service in India. When the war in the West was terminated it seemed reasonable to expect that India would receive much more consideration.

For these reasons A.D.P.(T.) was sent to the United Kingdom on a liaison visit of five weeks' duration. During this visit he visited the Army Blood Supply Depot in order to collect information on recent technical advances in transfusion work. Information was obtained concerning the units which were likely to come to South-East Asia and discussions were held at the War Office and A.B.S.D. on the scales of apparatus and modifications in equipment which should be sent with these units. Discussions were held with the Consultant in Resuscitation to the Army, the Director of Pathology, the Deputy Director General (Ops.) A.M.S. and others, and from these meetings an estimate of the likely future requirements of transfusion fluids and equipment in the Far East was drawn up. This estimate was based on the figures of issues made by the Transfusion Service in B.L.A., C.M.F. and M.E.F. for forces of corresponding size to those to be deployed in South-East Asia in future operations. In discussions with the Medical Adviser to the Secretary of State for India, provisional action was taken to order further equipment in accordance with this estimate.

In May 1945, Headquarters A.L.F.S.E.A. requested War Office to send an officer on a liaison visit to survey the Transfusion Service. As soon as this was known G.H.Q., India, extended an invitation to this officer to visit India.

O.C. 1 B.T.U., B.L.A. was sent on this liaison visit. All units of the Army Transfusion Service were visited and discussions on the development of the service were held at H.Q., A.L.F.S.E.A. and G.H.Q. India. On his return to the United Kingdom, this officer submitted a report recommending that one of the base transfusion units should be increased in size and placed at the disposal of A.L.F.S.E.A. when Singapore was freed. The provision of addition field transfusion units, equipment, refrigerators and other items was also recommended. Demands were placed on the United Kingdom for personnel, units and equipment. The surrender of the Japanese forces took place before these demands had been met, although action was in hand to supply them.

In January 1945 a problem was encountered concerning the difficulty in forwarding supplies to units in the forward areas. It was suggested to D.M.S., A.L.F.S.E.A. that it seemed advisable that he should have his own adviser in transfusion, who would be able to devote his whole attention to problems of distribution while India would act as a supply base.

The multiplicity of commands and the conflict of their interests in transfusion matters had led to much difficulty and not a little dissatisfaction. During the period January–July 1944, O.C. 2 B.T.U. acted as adviser to A.D.P. in the Medical Directorate, G.H.Q. (India). The unit he commanded was in India Command; the units this supplied were in S.E.A.C. Thus the situation arose in which an officer belonging to one command had dealings with units in another command. In June 1944, D.M.S. 11 Army Group issued instructions to the effect that this officer was to act in his name in transfusion matters affecting Fourteenth Army, XV Corps and L. of C. Command. Then in July, as has been related, O.C. 3 B.T.U. was appointed to the newly created post of A.D.P.(T.) in the Medical Directorate, G.H.Q.(India). As a consequence of this O.C. 2 B.T.U. was no longer permitted to visit the forward field transfusion units supplied by the base transfusion unit which he commanded. The appointment to the post of A.D.P.(T.) was made without 11 Army Group being made aware of it and it created many difficulties which adversely affected the whole of the Transfusion Service. It separated the field transfusion units from the base unit that supplied them; it deprived A.L.F.S.E.A. of the distribution sections that were sanctioned in August. When A.D.P.(T.) left for consultation in the United Kingdom no officer from the Medical Directorate, G.H.Q. (India) visited the forward field transfusion units during November and December 1944. Then in January 1945, O.C. 2 B.T.U. was appointed liaison officer in transfusion matters to A.L.F.S.E.A., retaining the command of his unit. He was forbidden to visit the forward field transfusion units by G.H.Q.(India) and so no senior officer of the Transfusion Service travelled east of the Brahmaputra during a particularly important operational period. In March 1945 O.C. 2 B.T.U. proceeded to H.Q. A.L.F.S.E.A. for a period that was not to exceed three months, to act as adviser. G.H.Q.(India) issued instructions that he was not to communicate with or visit forward units without G.H.Q's. permission and that all special operational demands were to be submitted through H.Q., A.L.F.S.E.A. to the Medical Directorate, G.H.Q.(India). It was difficult for the members of the Transfusion Service in the field to find satisfactory explanations for the seemingly cumbersome nature of the administrative organisation.

In March 1945, Advanced Headquarters, A.L.F.S.E.A. submitted a request through staff channels for the following units:

(a) One base transfusion unit. It was pointed out that to move one of the base transfusion units in this theatre would stop production for approximately three months. It was considered that both of the existing base units were necessary in India to meet the current demands, which were on the increase.

It was stated that a base transfusion unit was understood to be included in the increment force.

(b) Three advanced base transfusion units. It was pointed out that the presence of one of the three existing units was essential in Calcutta for the onward transmission of supplies to A.L.F.S.E.A. The two other units were offered and were moved into A.L.F.S.E.A. territory shortly afterwards.

(c) Nine field transfusion units. All field transfusion units were already in A.L.F.S.E.A. None could be raised in India. It was understood that seven were included in the increment force and that one (36 (E.A.) M.T.U.) was being raised in East Africa.

In July 1945, at a discussion held in Delhi between representatives of H.Q., A.L.F.S.E.A. and the acting adviser in resuscitation, War Office, it was decided that 2 B.T.U. should be expanded and placed at the disposal of A.L.F.S.E.A. when Singapore was freed. The base transfusion unit destined for the increment force would not, therefore, be required and the personnel could be used for the increase in size of the base transfusion unit to be allotted to A.L.F.S.E.A.

From August 1944 to May 1945 the issues of all types of transfusion fluids showed a steady increase each month which mirrored the increasing momentum of the advance of Fourteenth Army and XV Corps. The high level of issue did not fall off until the whole of Burma had been reoccupied. As the forces penetrated deeper into Burma it became necessary to transport an ever increasing proportion of stores by air and eventually this became the only practical method of supply.

Air Transport Command allotted the maximum possible space for this and the forward distribution in many cases was entirely dependent on the availability of aircraft. In all cases the transport of transfusion stores by air was given a relatively high priority but was always competing with the higher priority demands of ammunition and food. The solution would have been the provision of special aircraft for transfusion supplies and this would have made the supply problem much more simple.

The records of the Transfusion Service indicate that the numbers of the wounded and of sick with dysentery and diarrhoea during the three months, January–March 1945 were:

Central and Southern Fronts

	Wounded	Dysentery and Diarrhoea
British, Indian and African troops	8,178	5,993

At this time the two base transfusion units between them were bleeding over 5,000 donors each month. Many of these donors were bled at places which were over two hundred miles from the base unit and the blood had to be brought back in a mobile refrigerator, or in ice boxes by road or by train. Much of this blood had travelled a very considerable distance over very rough tracks and was already twenty-four hours old when it reached the base units. For these reasons it was considered more suitable for the preparation of wet plasma than for forward supply to the field as stored blood. The advanced base transfusion unit in Calcutta had been bleeding six to seven hundred group O donors each month. Blood which was sent forward from Calcutta had to be packed in ice boxes and transported by air. Similarly, blood which was sent from the base transfusion units in Dehra Dun or Poona to Calcutta for onward despatch to the field also required transport by air. The weight of fifteen bottles of blood, packed in an ice box for air despatch, weighed with a full load of ice was 110 lbs. Blood was commonly sent on routine passenger, freight or mail planes. Application for aircraft space had to be submitted to the appropriate Air Priorities Board twenty-four hours in advance. In the case of an airlift from Dehra Dun or Poona to Calcutta the Air Priorities Board was not the same as that which dealt with airlifts forward of Calcutta. On some of the routes forward of Calcutta it was necessary to tranship the blood from one aircraft to another at an intermediate halt, and finally distribute to field transfusion units by L.5.

At first the supplies of whole blood which were sent forward were taken by the advanced base transfusion unit in Calcutta but this unit began to find difficulty in maintaining a sufficient quantity of Kahn negative, group O blood. As a result, it was necessary to fly blood from both base transfusion units for onward despatch to the field. The difficulty of obtaining airlift without submitting an application in advance made it desirable that blood should be sent forward on set days by regular air services.

During this year a change was made to acid-citrate glucose mixture as an anti-coagulant. This increased the time limit within which the blood could be used and reduced the haemolysis caused to the blood by the long distance transportation. Many of the field transfusion units were able to supplement the supply of blood by bleeding local troops.

The blood taken by the base transfusion units was in large part devoted to the preparation of wet plasma. During the first half of 1945 the increase in personnel at these units had permitted an increase in the number of donors bled, to over five thousand a month. From this stock after a certain amount of blood had been used for local transfusion or forward supply, approximately fifteen hundred pints of wet plasma were made. This wet plasma was entirely reserved for use by units in A.L.F.S.E.A.

In mid-1944 the transfusion equipment situation had been unsatisfactory. In the early part of 1945 supplies began to come through from the United Kingdom and by the end of July there were few items in short supply and of these none was significant. A temporary shortage of dried plasma was foreseen in June when monthly consignments had been stopped until all plasma had been enclosed in sealed cans. This danger of dried plasma shortage was averted by the release by the War Office of a shipment of 15,000 bottles uncanned. This was sufficient to tide over the interim period until shipments of the new 'canned' plasma could be recommended. At the start of this year, when the new war establishment for the base transfusion unit was adopted in India, an immediate demand for 32 Type E mobile refrigerators was submitted. None of these refrigerators was shipped until the beginning of July and twelve arrived at the beginning of August. This deficiency of refrigerators very greatly hampered the mounting of Operation 'Zipper' (the reoccupation of Malaya). At this stage the situation with refrigerators was as follows: the refrigerators brought to India with the original units were available plus three most unsatisfactory refrigerators made in India for the advanced base transfusion units. Four type E refrigerators had been received from the United Kingdom. All these units had been worked exceedingly hard in most adverse conditions and required constant servicing by R.E. personnel. The spares held for this purpose were insufficient. The bulk of the trouble was experienced with the J.A.P. petrol engines. It may therefore be said that the mobile blood refrigerator situation was never satisfactory during the period of the war and this was a very great hindrance to the maintaining of supplies of blood forward.

After the capture of Rangoon, the demands for transfusion fluids fell very markedly. Soon after this, the stores build up for Operation

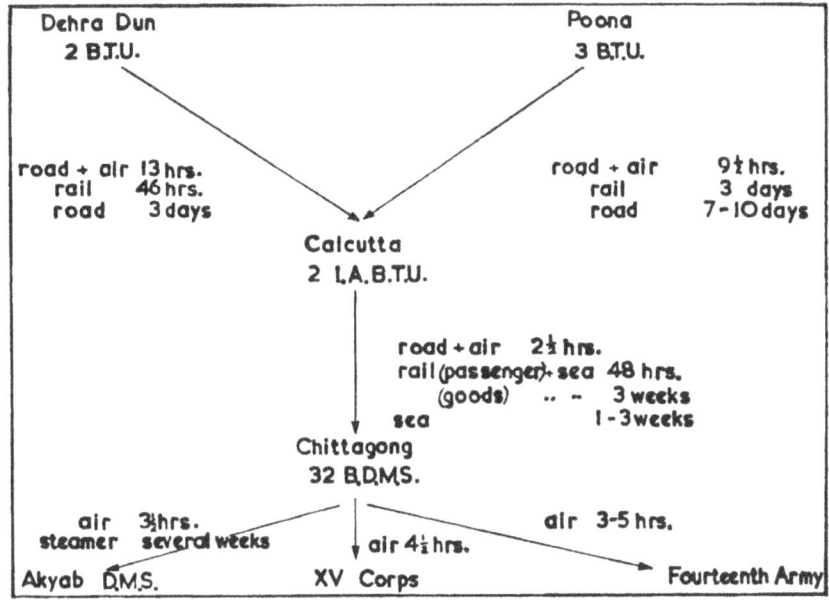

FIG. 84. Army Transfusion Service. Supply Chain 1945.

B.D.M.S.   Base Depot of Medical Stores.
B.T.U.   Base Transfusion Unit.
D.M.S.   Depot of Medical Stores.
I.A.B.T.U. Indian Advanced Base Transfusion Unit.

The road and rail route from Dehra Dun to Calcutta could be reduced by three hours by making use of a nearer airstrip. The rail route between Poona and Calcutta was very unreliable as were the sea routes between Calcutta and Chittagong and between Chittagong and Akyab.

'Zipper' began and kept the base transfusion units busy during July and the earlier part of August. When the Japanese surrender occurred it was still uncertain whether or not Operation 'Zipper' would proceed, and it was necessary to prepare stocks for the recovery of prisoners-of-war and internees in addition to the 'Zipper' stocks.

Arrangements were made to provide all the countries that were to be reoccupied by the Allied land forces with adequate supplies of transfusion materials, of plasma and crystalloids to all of them and of blood to those within air-supply distance of Rangoon. These steps were taken because it was expected that considerable numbers of released P.o.W. and internees would be found to be in need of transfusion therapy. It was arranged that 1 (Ind.) Adv. B.T.U. should proceed to Singapore as early as possible in order that it might act as a supply centre for Malaya, Sumatra and Java, into all of which it would be possible to fly-in whole blood. This unit was also to supply French Indo-China, Hong Kong and Japan by sea. 3 B.T.U. was to be responsible for Burma, Thailand and the Andaman and Nicobar Islands and was to send blood to French Indo-China by air, if required to do so. Inevitably there were many delays. 1 (Ind.) Adv. B.T.U. did not reach Singapore until October and until then 3 (Ind.) Adv. B.T.U. in Rangoon took its place as the supply centre.

2 F.T.U.—minus its refrigerator, lorry and driver, sent by sea—was flown to Bangkok, taking a ton of transfusion stores with it. 5 F.T.U. remained in Burma to provide cover for the troops who, it was expected, would be engaged in guerilla warfare for some considerable time. 8 F.T.U. went to Singapore with the occupying force and there it awaited the coming of 1 (Ind.) Adv. B.T.U. 28 F.T.U. was ear-marked to accompany Indian 26th Division to Java. 32 F.T.U. went with the Marines to Penang, taking with it supplies sufficient to resuscitate 60 casualties. 38 F.T.U. went with Indian 20th Division to Saigon and 39 and 40 F.T.Us. accompanied Indian 5th, 23rd and 25th Divisions to Malaya.

During August and September the base transfusion units in India supplied 2,400 bottles of dry plasma and 5,720 bottles of crystalloids for distribution by sea to all parts of the Far East and also 3,000 bottles of wet plasma for air-dropping on isolated P.o.W. camps. To Colombo there were sent, as an emergency reserve for Java, 600 bottles of wet plasma, 800 of dry plasma, 2,000 bottles of crystalloids and 504 ampoules of dry plasma. Distribution was to be by flying-boat *via* the Cocos Islands.

At the end of September H.Q. A.L.F.S.E.A. placed firm demands upon G.H.Q. (India) for all transfusion stores required by units in S.E.A.C. for the period November 1945–December 1946. It was requested that the stores for Rangoon and for Singapore should be divided into three more or less equal parts and that one-third should be despatched about the middle of November, mid-December and mid-January.

At the end of September 1945 it was expected that all the field transfusion units, save two, would be surplus to requirements by the beginning of November. It was proposed to retain two of the Indian advanced base transfusion units for a further six months and at the end of this period to review the situation.

It was later reported that a considerable portion of the solutions sent to the Far East from India required re-filtering at the Indian advanced base transfusion unit.

BASE TRANSFUSION UNIT PRODUCTION FROM MAY 1943 TO AUGUST 1945

These figures are based on the issues made by the two base transfusion units during 27 months. The figures do not take any note of the production and issues made by the two advanced base transfusion units during this time. 1 (Ind.) Adv. B.T.U. was making issues to 105 and 109 L. of C. Areas and 2 (Ind.) Adv. B.T.U. was satisfying the saline needs of 303 L. of C. Area and at the same time bleeding donors on a large scale for the Calcutta blood bank. 1 (Ind.) Adv. B.T.U. was supplying blood to all the hospitals in Bangalore hospital town.

TABLE 78

The Army Transfusion Service. Base Transfusion Unit Production. May 1943–August 1945.

	Donors bled at the Base Transfusion Units during this period: Monthly figures given	Wet plasma prepared for issue each month. Pint bottles	Army dried plasma issued to field units only. Bottles issued each month	Lyovac dried plasma issued to Base and L. of C. hospitals. Ampoules of 250 c.c.	Glucose-saline issued. Pint bottles	Normal saline issued. Pint bottles
1943						
May	108	9	—	3,120	1,186	289
June	779	203	—	12	265	100
July	1,122	310	5	—	470	160
August	1,678	538	48	—	563	281
September	2,535	614	338	12	741	438
October	1,766	475	188	—	548	194
November	2,670	825	979	—	2,035	811
December	1,531	698	688	536	1,387	582
1944						
January	1,092	333	2,000	778	3,643	1,366
February	2,919	471	1,123	324	1,741	631
March	1,777	641	1,261	382	1,762	792
April	1,601	555	2,176	1,968	3,266	1,546
May	1,540	458	1,814	1,872	3,537	1,316
June	1,982	582	846	678	3,379	1,561
July	1,707	501	22	594	2,652	1,036
August	1,644	588	913	1,314	3,133	1,211
September	1,631	416	431	1,047	2,617	1,049
October	1,794	485	1,152	1,945	4,131	1,499
November	2,290	674	1,630	327	3,833	1,440
December	2,178	659	2,234	1,938	5,694	2,421
1945						
January	2,729	735	2,459	1,603	4,756	2,001
February	4,332	974	4,290	2,060	7,570	3,264
March	4,053	1,152	5,282	2,220	7,865	3,353
April	4,385	1,243	5,747	1,560	13,006	5,663
May	3,773	192	8,833	766	19,863	8,567
June	4,388	300	1,504	1,395	9,176	3,917
July	3,865	2,252	1,900	1,329	7,179	3,184
August	3,332	4,850	4,792	1,853	13,809	5,850
	65,201	21,733	52,655	29,633	129,807	54,522

TABLE 78—contd.

	Fluids for the reconstitution of dried plasma or serum and Lyovac dried plasma. Pint bottles	Sets, plasma giving Overseas pattern	Blood taking sets. Exclusive of all sets used by transfusion unit for bleeding donors	Blood giving sets, issued to medical units	Grouping serum A/2 in ampoules—equivalent numbers of ccs. of B/3 serum issued	Solution of sulphamezathine issued in ampoules and 50 cc. amounts. Figures given in ccs.
1943						
May	438	268	426	465	114	—
June	48	93	4	16	6	—
July	10	29	14	17	—	—
August	48	112	29	29	44	—
September	342	305	62	121	12	—
October	230	164	24	31	118	—
November	1,161	539	276	284	141	—
December	1,871	694	423	447	51	—
1944						
January	1,792	673	441	671	188	1,280
February	1,044	1,417	268	225	49	2,040
March	2,146	1,592	204	205	128	2,100
April	2,731	1,542	289	250	172	11,750
May	3,194	1,067	201	180	178	7,800
June	1,286	865	270	255	234	19,350
July	394	396	317	331	408	8,400
August	1,601	625	60	177	388	600
September	851	261	49	111	156	9,770
October	2,151	787	196	300	568	16,130
November	2,048	1,444	58	169	104	19,620
December	3,171	1,654	607	441	233	9,700
1945						
January	3,377	1,972	345	303	647	12,240
February	6,304	1,209	219	266	338	65,880
March	7,216	3,261	1,734	623	560	90,800
April	7,085	3,759	172	192	219	69,420
May	5,782	5,240	337	227	1,026	58,050
June	2,576	1,606	195	376	354	43,025
July	3,240	3,342	657	810	519	51,050
August	6,500	6,702	516	653	1,005	1,850
	68,637	41,618	8,393	8,175	7,960	500,855

(5) THE ARMY PSYCHIATRIC SERVICE

Before the outbreak of war there were four psychiatric specialist posts in India, one in each of Northern, Eastern and Southern Commands and the other in Western (Independent) District. During the early months of the war there was no officer in India devoting the whole of his time to psychiatric duties. In April 1942 a consultant in psychiatry G.H.Q.(I.) was appointed and under his direction a psychiatric service, modelled on that which had developed in the army in Great Britain, was gradually brought into being. By 1945 there were 42 psychiatric units employing almost 100 whole-time psychiatrists and providing some 1,700 beds for Indian and 1,700 beds for British psychiatric patients. The policy was to link the treatment of these patients with the general hospitals. A standard psychiatric ward of 25 beds was designed and one or more of these units were added to the smaller general hospitals according to local needs. In addition large psychiatric centres were formed in base areas, Comilla, Calcutta, Ranchi, Moradabad, Poona and Secunderabad, with accommodation for several hundred patients. In 1945 it was found necessary to establish a psychiatric hospital of 1,200 beds in Jalahali 'hospital town'. Towards the end of the war there were between 40 and 50 psychiatric centres scattered throughout India, Burma and Ceylon.

In 1944 advisers in psychiatry were appointed to Southern and Eastern Armies and to Central Command, the last of these being responsible also for the supervision of the psychiatric work in North-Western Army. In October 1944 a consultant in psychiatry was appointed to 11 Army Group and later to A.L.F.S.E.A. There was a psychiatrist attached to each corps H.Q. and one to each division in Fourteenth Army. Under D.D.M.S. corps the psychiatrist formed a 50–100-bed exhaustion centre which was attached to one of the corps C.C.Ss. or to a forward hospital. In the division the psychiatrist formed a divisional exhaustion centre attached to a selected M.D.S. of a field ambulance. To these divisional exhaustion centres were sent by the R.M.Os. all patients considered to be suffering from N.Y.D.(P.). As would be expected very few of these men were actually psychiatric cases, for the most part they were suffering from exhaustion. The conditions in this theatre were such as to make unrelenting demands upon a man's powers of endurance and upon his resilience. It was not so much the noise and the power of the weapons of the enemy that constituted the stresses but the silence that engulfed the individual in the jungle, the inability to see and the fear of being seen, the absence of quiet from the night and the completeness of the separation from kith and kin.

Forward psychiatry was gradually developed from 1942 onwards. An account of the work of the psychiatric service in XV Corps traces this development. In XV Corps there were three main ethnic groups, British, Indian and African. Of the Indians some were from the north and others from the south. The corps experienced defeat and ultimate victory. In the early years of the war the Japanese infantryman was regarded, and not without reason, as being invincible. The fighting commonly took place in jungle country in which concealment was easily possible to such as had been adequately trained in this kind of warfare. In the early years, too, malaria and dysentery threatened all and hardly anyone could hope to escape them. The formations and units were understrength and the stretches of duty in the line were over-long. Amenities were unknown to begin with and leave for O.Rs. was exceedingly rare. As time passed the strength of most of these influences became diminished.

The operations in Arakan in 1942-43 ended in defeat and withdrawal. The medical services were overwhelmed with medical cases and the casualties had to be evacuated over very long distances. The Command Psychiatrist, Eastern Command, reporting upon this period stated that no useful purpose would be served by counting psychiatric cases for the whole of Indian 14th Division was for practical purposes a psychiatric casualty. Afterwards, it was used only as a training division.

At this time the psychiatric organisation for dealing with I.O.Rs. was utterly inadequate and so these casualties became distributed all over India. The B.O.Rs. were treated in Calcutta in 47 B.G.H. in which 50 beds were set aside for psychiatric cases. To look after these casualties and others from Assam and from the Royal Navy and the Royal Air Force there were two psychiatrists and a part-time G.D.O. Patients were very commonly not seen by a psychiatrist until a month or more after their symptoms had first appeared. Inevitably, therefore, there was much downgrading. The main symptoms presented by these men were jumpiness, headaches, nightmares, insomnia, restlessness and inability to concentrate. Many of them were very greatly depressed and most of them were seclusive.

In the operations in Arakan in 1943-44, 4 Indian, 1 British and 1 West African divisions were employed. Indian 7th Division was besieged in its boxes and for a time casualties could not be evacuated. 36th Division had been trained for combined operations and had no experience of the jungle. 81st W.A. Division was given a very tough assignment although it was not really ready for operational employment. A psychiatrist was attached to each of these divisions and in addition to the psychiatrist with XV Corps there was another back at Chittagong. The divisional psychiatrist functioned at a divisional M.D.S., his ward being a dug-out covered with tarpaulin or with thatch. The M.D.S., usually near the medium gun positions, was not an ideal site for a psychiatric centre for it could have no amenities and few comforts. The corps psychiatrist functioned at C.C.S. level. His patients were accommodated under canvas, the stretchers being raised on supports. Sheets were available. Washing and latrine facilities were satisfactory and the food was excellent. Medical comforts and Red Cross amenities were plentiful. The guns could be heard but only faintly and air raids were very infrequent. To run a ward of this kind holding both British and Indian it was found that it was necessary to have a nursing staff of 4, 2 British M.N.Os. and 2 British or Indian N.Os. This large staff was required because so many of the Indian patients were psychotics, many of them being toxic-infective psychotics. For these medical as well as psychiatric examination and therapy were necessary and could be undertaken at the C.C.S. level.

All psychiatric casualties requiring prolonged treatment or down-grading were sent back to Chittagong where the psychiatrist was attached to an Indian general hospital.

Indian 7th Division produced relatively few psychiatric casualties. The divisional psychiatrist was killed in the administrative box. Among the psychiatric casualties that did come from this division were several gunners who had been called upon to fight as infantrymen, alongside men unknown to them and using weapons with which they were unfamiliar. In this engagement there was no front line and no rear; the M.D.S. was as much involved in the fighting as was any defended locality. Among the Indian troops of this division there was a considerable number of desertions and of self-inflicted wounds. The officer casualty-rate was high but there were few psychiatric cases among them. This was in striking contract to the psychiatric casualty-rate among the officers of the West African division. These carried exceptionally heavy loads of responsibility because of the unsteadiness of their troops. Of the British psychoneurotics 95 out of the total of 305 were cases of acute breakdown, the rest being slowly developing anxieties commonly with psychosomatic symptoms. The bulk of the Indian psychoneurotics, 263 in all, were hysterias, 26 of them being due to acute and severe strain.

TABLE 80

XV Corps. Psychiatric Casualties. 1943–44. Arakan.

Strength	British 24,000; Indian 45,000
Psychiatric Casualties seen	British 363; Indian 263 (less than 10 per cent. of the total casualties)
Psychoneurosis	British 305; Indian 113 R.T.U. British 176; Indian 66 Evacuated or down-graded British 126; Indian 47
Psychosis	British 23; Indian 86

It was of interest to note that the incidence of psychoneurosis was lower than that reported from other theatres. The corps psychiatrist raised the question as to whether this might mean that men endure the strain of hunting and of being hunted, as in the jungle, better than they do heavy and continuous shelling and bombing. Of the psychoneurotics only about 15 per cent. needed treatment other than that administered in or forward of the corps psychiatric centre. There was difficulty in placing the down-graded I.O.R. and so, unless he made a complete recovery it became necessary to recommend discharge from the army.

During the monsoon season of 1944 there was much offensive patrolling but no large scale action. Indian 25th Division was in the line along with one of the brigades of Indian 26th Division. During this relatively quiet period the psychiatrists examined such as were referred to them and made recommendations concerning their disposal. Quite a number of men were encountered who were developing a mild chronic anxiety state and who, in all probability, would break down and have to be evacuated as soon as the fighting began again.

The cases seen by the corps psychiatrist during the monsoon period, June–October 1944, were distributed as follows:

British . Three-fifths psychoneuroses; one-fifth dull and backward.
Indian . Two-fifth psychosis (one-eighth of all cases being toxic psychoses).
One-third hysterias (with or without associated organic illness).

Disposal
British . One-fifth R.T.U.; one-quarter evacuated; remainder down-graded at corps level.
Indian . Less than one-quarter R.T.U.; three-quarters evacuated.

Psychiatric work in an Indian division was complicated by the presence in the patients of medical conditions such as malaria and infestations. The British troops seen during this period were such as presented long standing anxiety states, with worsening symptoms. Nothing but down-grading could be done with these.

In the operations of 1944–45 Indian 25th and 26th Divisions, 81st and 82nd W.A. Divisions, an East African brigade, a British commando brigade and an Indian tank brigade were involved. Amphibious operations were undertaken but most of the assault landings were unopposed. 81st W.A. Division repeated its long trek of the previous year and was then relieved by 82nd W.A. Division which pushed on to Akyab and beyond. There was not the hard steady slogging that had characterised the fighting of the previous year; engagements were separated by intervals of relative quiet. The troops were now experienced and so endured less strain. But Indian 25th Division had been in the line since March and Indian 26th Division had been in Arakan since 1942 with one break of three months when it was in reserve in cool weather and near the sea. Success had its effects upon the incidence of self-inflicted wounds and desertions, there were very few cases of either, and most of the psychoneurotic reactions that were encountered were due to fatigue that grew steadily greater with the passing of time.

During these operations of 1944-45 in Arakan treatment was not attempted at divisional level. Because the divisions were so widely spread and because there were so many lines of communication psychiatric casualties often by-passed not only the divisional exhaustion centre but the corps one as well. The corps psychiatrist dealt with over 1,000 psychiatric casualties many of them not from front line troops but from L. of C. formations that moved into the corps area as the corps formations moved forward. Again there was a high incidence of psychoneurosis among the British officers and N.C.Os. serving with the West African divisions.

Intercommunication between doctor and patient, when the two are the products of two different and distinct cultures or sub-cultures, is often very imperfect and difficult. The difficulty is magnified when the doctor is a psychiatrist and the patient a man whose system of ideas concerning the nature of illness is totally different from that upon which the theories and practices of the psychiatrist rest. Many of the psychiatrists serving Indian formations were not well acquainted with the cultural backgrounds of the Indian peoples. The I.O.R. typically, differed very markedly indeed from the B.O.R. He was a man who lived in an unsophisticated age of ready belief without a well developed critical faculty. He interpreted religious teachings literally. Rigid taboos, belief in magic and inadequate reality testing according to Western standards were factors that profoundly affected his behaviour and had to be borne in mind when symptoms were being interpreted and methods of treatment considered. As was the case among British troops also, reported or suspected infidelity and desertion on the part of a wife was the potent cause of psychiatric breakdown. The blow to a man's pride, to his Izzat, was so shattering that he could be written off as a soldier. Rough-riding over religious beliefs and practices by thoughtless superiors was occasionally the cause. On the whole the sepoy who did reach the forward area and stayed there remained a well-adjusted person. He accepted the army, its discipline, its customs and its leaders uncritically. He was not interested in ideologies, in the causes of the war; he had a job to do and in the doing of it he took a pride. His standard of living in the army was higher than it had been in civil life. Interest was taken in him and in his welfare. As a rule he got his leave regularly. He did not expect or ask for more. Thus it was that questions of morale and man-management were much simpler in an Indian than in a British division. When uttering judgment upon the members of the I.N.A. it has to be remembered that since the Indian sepoy was not interested in the causes and the purposes of the war as was the British soldier, it was to be expected that in defeat and under pressure many would become inclined to sever their allegiance.

The observations of the psychiatrist who examined the Chindits on their return to India in June 1943, after the first incursion into Burma have been recorded. They derive from the views and attitudes of the men and not of the officers. As the psychiatrist saw them the Chindits came out of Burma as bands of disorganised stragglers, each man attributing his survival entirely to his own efforts. To them it seemed that their officers had failed them and their attitude towards authority was one of fierce hostility. Some of the causes of the low morale were identified as inadequate selection, defects of training, the lack of a sense of purpose, unsatisfactory rations, poor hygiene, defective leadership, and especially, the absence of any means of evacuating the sick and wounded. In the second expedition things were different. There was a pre-arranged and orderly system of evacuation and so the troops retained their confidence in the ability of their leaders to maintain control of the situation and to look after their interests. With better training the troops came to look upon the jungle with less fear. Unless the senior officer of a force, whose views determine policy, acts on the assumption that his senior medical officer has much to offer that will aid him in the attainment of his objective, it is to be expected that the man-power loss from medical causes will be serious. The disastrous losses in effective man-power through illness, mainly malaria and dysentery, which resulted from the policy that stemmed from General Wingate's most peculiar notions concerning the nature of man and of disease, all but wrecked completely the first Chindit incursion.

In the central sector as in Arakan the difficulties in selecting a suitable site for the divisional exhaustion centre were considerable. Rest and quiet could, of course, only be secured at some distance from the line and since they were most desirable the centre was commonly sited a few miles to the rear of the line. When the fighting units went into their boxes (defended perimeter sites) the divisional psychiatrist functioned in one of them, being virtually in the front line. Sometimes the centre was in a dug-out, with a tarpaulin headcover, sometimes it was tented and in one instance it was accommodated in a corrugated iron shed capable of holding some 30–40 charpoys (string beds). Each divisional psychiatrist was provided with two panniers, which could be carried on a mule or in a jeep and which contained a supply of suitable equipment so that if necessary he could work apart from any parent medical unit.

The adviser in psychiatry to Fourteenth Army, against the background of a very extensive experience of the organisation of the psychiatric service in this theatre, expressed the view that the divisional exhaustion centre should remain sufficiently mobile and its organisation sufficiently elastic to enable it to function wherever and whenever the opportunity presented itself. It would be mistaken, in his view, to adhere too strictly to the idea of a linear evacuation chain with A.D.S., M.D.S. and C.C.S. all tidily arranged in series. Evacuation by air was tending to make this arrangement obsolete and the tendency was for the exhaustion centre to become one of several specialist units that functioned right at the front, evacuation being from very near the front to far to the rear, the intermediate medical units thus being rendered superfluous.

The majority of casualties referred to the exhaustion centres, though presenting psychological rather than physical symptoms were not psychiatric cases in the usual sense but were suffering from the effects of a combination of factors of which, as a rule, the most prominent was exhaustion, mental and physical. That this was so was not surprising for the climate, the terrain, the nature of the fighting, the prevalence of malaria and other illnesses, among other factors, all operated to test the resilience of the most stable. It can be stated without fear of contradiction that had there not been a psychiatric service that functioned at divisional level and that prevented unnecessary evacuation, man-power loss due to psychiatric causes would have been crippling.

During the monsoon season in most of the years patrol activity was the main military task. The battle casualty was relatively rare. But in this relatively quiet period the more chronic psychoneurotic conditions became revealed. There was, typically, an increase during these periods of toxic confusional conditions in which the precipitating factors were multiple. Thus malaria and amoebiasis or malaria, hookworm infection and anaemia were frequently found in conjunction with severe psychiatric symptoms. It was possible to treat these chronic cases at the divisional level during these periods and it was clearly demonstrated that a very great deal could be done to retain for further duty men who, untreated, would have been added to the number of chronics in the base hospitals, who would never return to the line. For example, of the British cases treated at XXXIII Corps' psychiatric centre during a period of three months in the monsoon period preceding the 1944 operations, less than 8 per cent. were evacuated to India, some 65 per cent. were returned to their units in their original medical categories and the remainder in a lowered category. The results of this forward psychiatric treatment were uniformly good. On the average, throughout the years about 50 per cent. of British patients and about 36 per cent. of Indian patients referred to the divisional psychiatrist were returned to duty and of these very few broke down again. It is of interest to note that the man-power situation was such that it was considered that if a man returned to duty, fought only for three or four days before going sick again his return was justified. The psychiatrist with XXXIII Corps expressed the view that a rate of 50 per cent. R.T.U. was as good as could be achieved by a divisional psychiatrist in conditions such as obtained in this theatre. From all levels of the psychiatric organisation 72 per cent. of the British and over 60 per cent. of the Indian patients were returned to full duty.

TABLE 81

Examples of Disposal of Psychiatric Casualties. (Indian Medical History. Medicine, Surgery and Pathology, Chapter XX, Appendix G)

2nd Division. On the Kohima–Imphal road. April 24–May 31, 1944

R.T.U.	104
Evacuated	26
Recategorised	23
Posted to rear details	10
Cases complicated by physical disorders	18
	181

Indian 20th Division. Imphal Plain. March 1944

R.T.U.	25
Evacuated	23
Recategorised	3
	51

Indian 26th Division. Arakan. March 15–May 5, 1944

	British Officers	B.O.Rs.	I.O.Rs.
R.T.U.	4	22	34
Evacuated	2	10	24
Referred to corps psychiatrist	2	2	6
	8	34	64

R.T.U. 56 per cent.

36th Division. Arakan. March 5–April 15, 1944

R.T.U.	42 (57 per cent.)
Evacuated	14
Left out of battle	17
	73

The frequent occurrence of medical conditions in association with psychiatric disorders constituted a major problem in this theatre. No less than 50 per cent. of a group of Indian psychiatric casualties examined by the adviser in psychiatry to Fourteenth Army in June 1943 were suffering from medical conditions to which their psychiatric symptoms were secondary. In consequence a hospital order was issued and circulated widely in Eastern Army Area, pointing out that the following organic causes of disease might give rise, as a presenting symptom, to mental disorder: malaria, typhus and heat exhaustion—the most frequent causes—typhoid, meningitis, pneumonia, alcohol (native spirit) and drugs such as opium and hashish (ganja).

The sick-rate due to psychiatric conditions was 1·41 per 1,000 in 1942; 3·10 in 1943; 4·28 in 1944 and 5·33 in 1945. The absolute morbidity-rates for psychosis, psychoneurosis and N.Y.D.(P.) during 1945 were 0·86, 1·20 and 3·26 respectively.

There was no definite establishment for psychiatrists in Fourteenth Army. All psychiatrists in this theatre were held in G.H.Q.(I.)'s pool and were loaned to formation H.Qs. As a result of this, they encountered difficulty in obtaining their ordnance, welfare and Red Cross stores. The need for a psychiatrist for service with Army troops was keenly felt.

(6) THE SUPPLY OF MEDICAL STORES

In general the supply was good and speedy.

METHODS

(a) By air

From Imphal, Comilla, Chittagong or Ramree in this order as the advance progressed. Consolidated demands by formation H.Qs. (Army, Corps or Area) within the allotted tonnages, on C.A.A.T.O. and D.A.D.M.S. Adv. Echelon North (Comilla) or South (Chittagong) who obtained requirements from the nearest base depot or depot of medical stores and arranged their fly-in or air-drop, as demanded, through C.A.A.T.O. and the nearest F.A.M.O. Demands were placed fortnightly in advance, although regular supplies of whole blood and other transfusion requisites, and of calf lymph, were arranged as a definite weekly or bi-weekly automatic supply. Emergency demands could be met at 48 hours' notice at any time.

Air-drops were made to indicated dropping zones, where representatives of the demanding medical units made collection. Air landings were made at F.A.M.Os. of the formation concerned. The F.A.M.O. notified the nearest depot of medical stores or Indian sub-depot of medical stores to collect, usually, through the medical branch of the formation H.Q.

Distribution was made by a combination of corps S. and T. vehicles, the medical units' transport, including ambulance cars, and light ambulance aircraft, direct to the medical unit in accordance with their indents. Fourteen days' reserve stocks of stores in general use were maintained in the depots of medical stores and in the Indian sub-depots.

The defects of the system of supply by air were of two kinds. Aircraft could not fly at all times; they did not invariably go to the airfields where they were expected and occasionally the sortie would be made abortive by one or other form of mechanical mishap. Within the F.A.M.O. there was no medical collecting organisation. The Indian sub-depot of medical stores depended upon the F.A.M.O. for information concerning the arrival of medical stores and upon its own initiative in searching for these among the mass of stores of all kinds on the airfield. The depots of medical stores had no transport of their own. The need was felt for the addition of one sergeant R.A.M.C. or I.A.M.C. with one sepoy clerk, to the establishment of the F.A.M.O. with the specific duty of collecting medical stores. It was considered also that the addition of one lorry 30-cwt. 4 × 4, and one driver, R.I.A.S.C. to the war establishment of the depot of medical stores would have really completed the organisation of this unit.

It was abundantly demonstrated that the system of the supply of medical stores by air possessed many advantages. The supply was very speedy and the need for intermediate depots of medical stores along the supply route was eliminated. There was far less breakage and damage of stores, especially of transfusion fluids.

(b) By road

From 17 Indian Depot of Medical Stores in Imphal. This system of supply was controlled by the same system of demand on Adv. Ech. North. Supply was through L. of C. transport column according to standard procedure, with the only modification that the stores were unloaded into I.W.T. at Kalewa for transport to 9 (Ind.) Depot Med. Stores in Myingyan whence they went on by road or rail to the recipient.

Certain shortages occurred. The rapid replacement of lost field panniers, surgical haversacks and field medical companions was difficult at the beginning of the advance for the reason that supplies had to be obtained from India. Later supplies were placed in the depots of medical stores in A.L.F.S.E.A. The increasing demands for calf lymph and the use of cholera vaccine among the civilian population caused temporary shortages and it was at all times difficult to maintain adequate reserves of anti-gas-gangrene serum.

The distribution of transfusion materials remained difficult until kerosene burning refrigerators had been issued to sub-depots of medical stores, C.C.Ss. and M.F.T.Us. The materials were packed in thermos containers (containers 1 gallon food, portable) with ice at the base depot of medical stores and delivered to the pilots of the aircraft or taken on to the plane by an escort. This part of the distribution system was simple, straightforward and satisfactory. The reception at the airfield at the other end of the journey presented several difficulties. Timely notice of the expected arrival of the aircraft was rarely forthcoming and so much time was wasted by stores personnel and much material was spoilt and wasted. The forward distribution of these materials was unsatisfactory for the reason that there were not enough thermos containers in the forward sub-depot of medical stores. A large proportion of these were necessarily idle at any one time because an empty container on its return journey cannot claim the same priority as can a full one on its passage forward. Moreover, empty containers do not have escorts. It was estimated that there was a shortage of twenty thermos containers in the forward sub-depot of medical stores and of five in the forward C.C.S., M.F.T.U. and F.T.U.

(7) THE ARMY MEDICAL SERVICE

Fourteenth Army had its consultant physician and some 80 per cent. of its complement of medical specialists during the period November 1944–May 1945. It was A.L.F.S.E.A.'s policy to send the best of the younger men to the forward zone. The majority of the medical specialists with Fourteenth Army were graded physicians and quite a number of them had no higher qualification. The work they did was of a good standard in the opinion of the consultant physician.

As was revealed in the previous chapter problems of a 'medical' kind were few and relatively minor ones. The average sick-rate (excluding battle casualties) was $1·25/1,000$/diem and in the last weeks of the campaign often under $1·0/1,000$/diem. The average sick-rate for all causes, except battle casualties, declined from about $2·4/1,000$/diem in November 1944 to just under $1·0/1,000$/diem at the beginning of May 1945. The ratio of medical to all surgical admissions to medical units fell from $21·5 : 1$ in December 1944 to $3·3 : 1$ in April 1945. This decline of the sick-rate occurred during the winter and spring months; it occurred as Fourteenth Army passed from the unhealthy Indo-Burma border region into the healthier Central Burma Plain and into the humid but nevertheless relatively healthy Delta of the Irrawaddy. Undoubtedly these seasonal and topographical factors played their prominent parts in producing the fall in the sick-rate but it is equally beyond doubt that hygiene and medical activities were also concerned. The rates for malaria and dysentery not only declined in the winter months as is the rule but showed no rise in the spring when a rise might have been expected.

The curves for all medical admissions followed fairly closely the curve for admission on account of malaria, this being a clear indication that malaria was the main cause of admission and therefore of serious morbidity. It was noted that, as a direct consequence of the custom of taking mepacrine for suppressive purposes, the pernicious forms of subtertian malaria almost disappeared and that only one case of blackwater fever was encountered in Fourteenth Army during the period.

The consultant physician observed that it was found necessary to avoid the evacuation by air of chest cases with any significant diminution of respiratory reserve and to see that cases of anaemia were not flown out until their haemoglobin was at least 50 per cent. It was also found that cases of 'marasmus' and of scrub typhus travelled badly.

The number of medical cases admitted to C.C.Ss. and M.F.T.Us. varied greatly. At a peak period one M.F.T.U. was holding 853 medical cases and one of the C.C.Ss. 655, the same units having an average of 619 and 440 medical beds occupied during the period January–March 1945. The usual average number of medical cases in M.F.T.Us. was around 200 with a peak of 400–500.

The proportion of medical cases returned to duty from the C.C.Ss. and M.F.T.Us. varied considerably with operational and other circumstances but was generally in the neighbourhood of 75 per cent.

Deaths from medical causes were remarkably few. In 9,734 admissions to eight M.F.T.Us. the fatality-rate was 0·37 per cent. and in a series of 1,924 medical admissions to three C.C.Ss. it was 0·31 per cent. In the latter part of the campaign the principal medical causes of death were smallpox, cerebral malaria, cholera and snakebite, the actual number in each case being small.

The supply of medicaments was generally excellent though there was a shortage of certain anthelmintics and of the newer sulphonamides, sulphathiazole and sulphamethazine.

(8) THE ARMY SURGICAL SERVICE

TABLE 82

A.L.F.S.E.A. Battle Casualties. January–August 1945

Killed	4,869
Wounded	16,517
Missing	555
	21,941

The total number of casualties, due to enemy action, evacuated through the medical channels of Fourteenth Army during the period November 1944–May 1945 was 13,198 or 22·78 per cent. of the total admissions. The rate per thousand per day was 0·36. At the beginning of the period the rate was 0·08/1,000/diem with a small rise on November 18 to 0·11. Thereafter it fell progressively until December 28 and then began to rise again to reach 0·94/1,000/diem on March 24. IV Corps had a much heavier casualty-rate as a consequence of the losses endured during the operations at Meiktila in March and April 1945 when it reached the figure of 2·75/1,000/diem for the week ending March 24.

During the period December 31, 1944–May 19, 1945, a total of 10,900 wounded (officers 391, O.Rs. 10,509) were reported through 'A' channels. During this period the numbers of wounded evacuated through medical channels was 12,505. The difference between the two figures represents the wounded who were not evacuated beyond the M.D.Ss. of the field ambulances; these were not reported to 'A'.

These rates and figures relate to the wounded and those who died of wounds. They do not include those killed in action. The official number of the killed in action from January 1 to May 19 was 3,050, officers 177, O.Rs. 2,873. 1,747 deaths were reported through medical channels during the period November 1944–May 1945, British 566, Indian 1,082, African 99. Approximately 80 per cent. of these were killed in action. Deaths reported through medical channels and taking place in Fourteenth Army Area up to March 31 numbered 1,446 of whom 1,169 were killed in action and 147 died of their wounds.

The surgical cover provided for the formations fighting in Burma was regarded by those responsible for providing it as both deficient and insufficient. The number of surgical teams was strictly limited, provision being on a scale only half that considered necessary in other theatres. The surgical specialists were young and most of them had received their basic training and had been graded in the base hospitals in India.

That the surgical cover was insufficient was inevitable. The total numbers of British and Indian troops to be served were very large. Burma was but one of the several theatres that had to be supplied. The production of medically qualified men and women in the United Kingdom was not geared to the needs of a nation desperately engaged in a global war. In India the production before the war had not even satisfied the needs of the civilian population; those of an army two millions strong could not possibly be met. The pre-war strength of the I.M.S. was 631, 366 of these being in military employ and the rest in civil. There were 261 officers in the Army in India Reserve of Officers (Medical) and 29 in the Indian Reserve of Retired Officers. In the Malayan campaign 242 officers of the I.M.S. and 238 I.M.D. sub-assistant surgeons had been lost. The doctor-patient ratio in a civilian population is far lower than that which is regarded as desirable in the Armed Forces in war. In India at the beginning of the war there was one doctor to every 9,000 of the population and only one nurse to every 60,000. All that could be hoped for was that the Burma theatre should receive its fair share of the medical resources that were available.

There were consultant surgeons with Eastern Command, A.L.F.S.E.A., L. of C. Command and Fourteenth Army. In April 1945 five surgical specialists were posted to A.L.F.S.E.A. and in March of that year it became possible to attach mobile ophthalmic units to the corps medical centres. 2 and 3 M.N.S.Us. came from the United Kingdom, 2 did not find a great deal to do but 3 in Eastern Bengal did much useful work under difficult conditions. A chest surgery team was about to be despatched from the United Kingdom to India when the war ended.

The system of associating a M.S.U. with a C.C.S., a M.D.S. or exceptionally with an A.D.S. developed. In the Indian C.C.S. there was only one surgeon and consequently the attachment of a M.S.U. added greatly to the capacity of the C.C.S. to deal with surgical cases; one surgeon could reinforce the other or could relieve him. But most commonly the M.S.U. was attached to the M.D.S. of a field ambulance and so it was that during busy periods the C.C.S. surgeon and the M.S.U. surgeon were both fully occupied and commonly were overworked.

TABLE 83

Indian 20th Division. Operations performed by 10 (Indian) Mobile Surgical Unit (Five months), 5 (Indian) Beach Medical Unit (Two months), 15 (Indian) Mobile Surgical Unit (One month) and an improvised Surgical Team (Two months). December 1, 1944–May 31, 1945

Nature of Wound	Number of Cases	Deaths
Head (usually toilet only)	29	1
Maxillo-facial (usually toilet only)	36	4
Chest, penetrating	57	7
Thoraco-abdominal	12	7
Abdomen, penetrating and retroperitoneal	68	30
Pelvis and buttock, affecting viscera or bone	18	2
Compound fracture, femur	52	4
Other compound fractures	278	5
Penetrating wounds, knee-joint	31	—
,, ,, other joints	51	—
Major flesh wounds	225	3
Minor flesh wounds	246	—
Anaerobic infection	12	5
Vascular, nerve, burns, simple fractures and the like	118	7
Total Operations	1,233	75

In the Allagappa division medical centre between February 14 and March 6, two of these units worked for eighteen out of the twenty-one nights, the whole night through. On the remaining three nights they worked until past midnight.

During the crossing of the Irrawaddy it became possible to have M.S.Us. with both the C.C.S. and the field ambulance. Four surgical teams were functioning in one and the same advanced surgical centre formed around the M.D.S. of a field ambulance.

This arrangement of having the M.S.U. sometimes with the C.C.S. and at other times with the M.D.S. led to arguments concerning its proper location. There were some who held that unless the surgical facilities the unit represented were placed well forward of the C.C.S. their value was largely wasted. A tendency developed whereby the advanced surgical centre was looked upon as the property of the division, or even of the brigade, which it happened to be serving. This had to be sternly checked. There were others who presented the view that surgical aid should be available in front of the C.C.S. only when circumstances prevent the casualty reaching the C.C.S. within a few hours after wounding and when delay would cause grave deterioration of his general condition. This latter view, quite rightly, prevailed. Surgical intervention implies more than surgery and it is usually far from easy to provide adequate nursing facilities in front of the C.C.S. Towards the end of the campaign both IV and XXXIII Corps had flying squads of nursing officers which could be sent from the C.C.S. forward to the M.D.S. when an A.S.C. was to be established in front of the C.C.S. because of evacuation difficulties.

The convalescent depots could not be used for freeing hospital beds and for conserving man-power for the reasons that their staffs were very inadequate and their facilities far too restricted. They could hold a patient for three weeks, no more, and they could not accept a man still requiring medical attention. Their P.T. instructors had no knowledge of remedial work and there were no masseurs on the staff. There were no specialists in physical medicine in A.L.F.S.E.A. and very few physiotherapists. The M.F.T.U. was on occasion required to function as a convalescent depot at a corps medical centre and was very ill-equipped for such a rôle for it possessed no facilities for rehabilitation.

It was the considered opinion of the surgeons that the field transfusion units abundantly proved their worth but that there were far too few of them to ensure that all who needed their help received it.

In surgical tactical planning the goal that is sought is the provision to the wounded man of the best possible surgical attention in the minimum possible time after wounding. A large and wide variety of factors more or less profoundly affect the possibility of attaining this goal and it is the prime responsibility of the senior administrative medical officer of a force to take all possible steps to remove as many as possible of the factors that tend to prolong the time interval between wounding and surgical intervention, to circumvent them or to mitigate their effects. Only when the wounded man reaches that point in the evacuation chain at which he encounters the surgeon within a certain interval of time after wounding can military surgery proffer its greatest benefits. When for any reason this interval becomes too greatly prolonged, the results of surgical intervention fall short of the best.

Surgery is practised in a setting, tactical, geographical and climatic and since the conditions and circumstances within this setting vary so greatly, it follows that the interval between wounding and surgical intervention must also vary. The optimum from the surgeon's point of view is under six hours in most circumstances.

The conditions in Arakan and Assam were very different indeed from those encountered in the Western Desert of Libya and these differences were reflected in corresponding differences in the tactics employed, in the nature of the fighting and also in the methods that were adopted for the early treatment of the wound and for the evacuation of the wounded man. Military surgery adapts itself to the setting in which it is practised.

The geographical and tactical setting in Burma determined the distribution of the medical units along the evacuation and surgical chain. Because of the scarcity of roads and of the poorness of such roads and tracks as did exist evacuation was greatly impeded. Surgical facilities had to be provided in front of the C.C.S. and the paucity of M.S.Us. was quickly felt. Of C.C.Ss. there was a sufficiency. During the campaign it was not at all unusual for a division or brigade to be broken down into a number of columns operating in isolation. To provide all of these with medical cover was very difficult indeed. *Ad hoc* surgical teams had to be improvised and sent out with minimum equipment. The Indian M.S.U. had far too heavy a load of equipment for employment in the jungle and when such a unit was so employed it had to reduce its load by a ton or so.

In the Western Desert there had developed the system of cleansing the area around the wound, or gently trimming the wound itself and of applying sulphanilamide powder and an occlusive dressing and sending the casualty back without further delay to the nearest C.C.S. by ambulance car along a desert track. The desert was a bacteriologically clean place until fouled by man and to easy and speedy evacuation there was no great impediment. It was thought that the modern missile was sterile owing to its great heat and that its high velocity led to a rending of the clothing so that fragments of material were not usually carried into the depths of the wound. Infection, according to this view, was due to a secondary invasion of the wound by organisms from the skin surrounding the wound or introduced at subsequent inspections and dressings.

In Burma in the early days the surgeons followed the 'Desert' teaching. But after his initial forward treatment, the casualty in this theatre set out on a long and arduous journey by road, rail and water to the base hospital in India. There was no provision for holding and treating in the forward zone and very little *en route*; the casualty passed through one transit hospital after another in the four to six weeks which commonly elapsed between the receipt of the wound and arrival at a centre where serious treatment could be begun. The transit hospitals could do little more than pick out and retain such as were too sick to travel further. By the time the holding hospital was reached many of the wounds were badly infected. The Japanese missile commonly carried into the wound bits of clothing and equipment and also jungle material, leaves and dirt.

By the time of the battles around Kohima and Imphal this 'Desert' method had been given up and delayed primary suture of the wound had to become the established practice. This involved the radical excision of the wound in the forward zone and the provision of holding hospitals in an advanced hospital base. In these hospitals the delayed primary suture of the wound was undertaken. The improvement in the results of surgical intervention quickly demonstrated the advantage of the new method. For example, during the first three months of 1945 of the 8,176 battle casualties admitted to the medical units of Fourteenth Army only 394 died (in these medical units), to yield a survival-rate of 95 per cent., a rate that compared very favourably with those recorded in other theatres. To this improvement certain other factors undoubtedly contributed. Air evacuation was rapidly becoming the main method and it was this that did so much to keep the time interval between wounding, initial surgical treatment and delayed primary suture, to something approaching the optimum. Evacuation from the M.D.S. to the C.C.S. during the hours of daylight was made speedy but casualties received by the field ambulance during the hours of darkness had to be retained therein. The M.S.U. had to be used to overcome the disadvantages of this retention. Together with the M.D.S. of a field ambulance, the M.S.U. was used to provide an advanced surgical centre. Being so used the operating teams were, in rush periods, busy all through the night and had to snatch what sleep they could during the day. Whenever possible sufficient surgical teams were congregated to permit each one of them to function in eight hour shifts. This system not only provided adequate rest periods but it also increased the 'output' of the team.

Another factor contributing to the improvement was the arrival in October–November 1944 in A.L.F.S.E.A. of penicillin, in ample quantities. Another, undoubtedly, was the progressive improvement, born of experience, in the administrative and executive arrangements for ensuring that the casualty and the surgeon met at the earliest possible opportunity in the best possible circumstances.

The policy in Fourteenth Army was to hold in the forward zone abdominal wounds, chest wounds, cases of specific wound infection, e.g. gas-gangrene, tetanus, cases of damage to the main arterial supply to a limb in which there was doubt concerning the efficiency of the collateral circulation, severe burns and injury associated with severe shock, e.g. massive wounds of muscles, until the shock was completely controlled. All other patients were evacuated as a rule on the day following operation and it was rare for them to reach the advanced base later than the third day after wounding.

As has been recorded it became the custom to form a corps medical centre around a C.C.S. and a M.F.T.U. To this centre went the majority of the casualties that had reached the M.D.S. of the field ambulances during the hours of daylight when the light planes could function. To the C.C.S. also were evacuated all the cases which the A.S.C. had been unable to deal with during the night. In order to provide adequate surgical facilities in the corps medical centre the following scheme was evolved. Because the Indian C.C.S. had only one surgeon, as soon as a new centre was formed the surgical team from the closing C.C.S. was brought forward so that two surgeons were available in the most forward and functioning C.C.S. If in a centre there were two C.C.Ss. each of them received casualties by numbers, fifty to a surgeon. It became necessary to control the tendency for the C.C.S. in the corps medical centre to hold its surgical patients. The performance of delayed primary suture in the C.C.S. was sternly discountenanced for the reasons that the theatre and dressing facilities could not guarantee sterility, that the nursing facilities were very limited, that the preparation of penicillin was difficult and time-consuming and that the all important holding period of ten days after suture could not be guaranteed.

When Fourteenth Army debouched from the jungle-clad hills and the fever-haunted valleys beyond the Chindwin and moved into the Irrawaddy Plain, 36th Division was advancing on the right flank of N.C.A.C. down the railway corridor from Mogaung while in Arakan XV Corps was advancing along the valley of the Kalapanzin and Kaladan towards Foul Point and was about to launch its assault upon Akyab. With Fourteenth Army at this time were five M.S.Us. and five Indian C.C.Ss., with 36th Division were one C.C.S. and one M.S.U., and with XV Corps were three C.C.Ss. and five M.S.Us. of which two were about to be transferred to Fourteenth Army. 82nd W.A. Division had its own surgical cover; with it were three graded surgeons, one with each field ambulance, three F.D.Ss. each with a surgeon on its staff and a C.C.S. 2 M.N.S.U. was in Dimapur to serve Fourteenth Army and 36th Division. Later this unit was moved forward and attached to a C.C.S. for the reason that in Dimapur it was largely unemployed. 3 M.N.S.U. was in Comilla with 14 B.G.H. and to it the majority of penetrating head wounds were flown direct from the C.C.Ss. of Fourteenth Army and XV Corps. The ophthalmic department of 14 B.G.H. was working in collaboration with this M.N.S.U.

To begin with there was no maxillo-facial surgical unit in front of Ranchi but later 3 M.F.S.U. was sent to 14 B.G.H. in Comilla so that it, together with the M.N.S.U. and the ophthalmic department of the general hospital might form the 'specialist trinity' that in Italy had so abundantly proved its worth. Comilla developed into the principal surgical centre with 14 B.G.H. and 74 and 92 I.G.Hs. offering a total of 3,000 beds. Transfer from these hospitals was by ambulance train to the group of hospitals in the Agartala-Dacca centre. There was also direct admission to this group of hospitals in which orthopaedic surgeons were congregated to deal with major fractures.

During the final stages of the swift advance on Rangoon life-saving surgery was carried out in the widely scattered M.S.Us. to which casualties were brought by ambulance car. They were evacuated from the M.S.Us. by air to Akyab for onward transmission to Comilla. In Rangoon a C.C.S. was established very shortly after the capital had been entered and from it casualties were evacuated to Chittagong by sea. It was not until 38 B.G.H. and 58 I.G.H. opened in Rangoon early in June that the surgical situation could be regarded as satisfactory.

'Nearly all the British casualties from Fourteenth Army (during its advance across the Chindwin towards Rangoon) were admitted to 14 B.G.H., having been flown direct to Comilla from the airfields of Burma as these were captured with the advance of Fourteenth Army.

'Admissions from Burma only began in earnest in December, and were heaviest in the two months from mid-February to mid-April when the severe fighting took place around Mandalay and Meiktila; as soon as the port of Rangoon was opened admissions from Burma rapidly diminished, but in the five months from December to May, the hospital admitted over eleven thousand casualties. Nearly half of these were surgical cases, the low proportion of medical admissions bearing eloquent witness to the high standard of field hygiene prevailing and the toughness of the Fourteenth Army. The heaviest burden rested on the theatre staff, medical officers, sisters and orderlies, and one recalls their faces, grey with fatigue, as night after night they staggered back to their messes after twelve hours' operating. In the whole period there were twenty-three deaths in hospital—a mortality of two per thousand, truly a remarkable figure when it is recalled that the wards were all, in the early stages, in canvas marquees. The unit must share the credit for this with prompt air evacuation of all casualties and penicillin. As 1945 advanced the marquees were gradually replaced by bamboo *bashas*. The personnel of the unit lived under canvas though *bashas* had been provided for the sisters by the time the rains fell.'*

---

* (*History of the Fourteenth General Hospital, R.A.M.C. 1939-1945*)

In India Command the following hospitals were specially staffed and equipped and constituted specialist centres:

	Base Hospital	Con. Depot	British Beds	Indian Beds	Centre for
Bangalore	One		700	300	Psychiatry
	One		700	300	Ear, nose and throat
					Eye
					Skin
					Plastic surgery
	One		1,200	—	Nerve injury
					Orthopaedic surgery
	One		1,200	—	Nerve injury
					Orthopaedic surgery
		1	2,000	—	
		1	—	1,000	
Dehra Dun	136 I.B.G.H.		—	1,000	Eye
					Orthopaedic surgery
		26	—	500	
Dinapore	138 I.B.G.H.		—	1,000	Eye
		39	—	500	
Karachi	1 I.B.G.H.		800	—	Ear, nose and throat
					Psychiatry
	6 I.B.G.H.		—	1,000	Eye
					Orthopaedic surgery
					Psychiatry
Kirkee	2 I.B.G.H.		—	1,000	Neurology
	7 I.B.G.H.		—	1,000	Ear, nose and throat
					Nerve injury
					Neurosurgery
	8 I.B.G.H.		—	1,000	Artificial limbs
Lucknow	129 I.B.G.H.		—	1,500	Nerve injury
					Neurosurgery
					Plastic surgery
	130 I.B.G.H.		—	1,400	Ear, nose and throat
					Eye
					Orthopaedic surgery
		52	—	1,000	
Moradabad	131 I.B.G.H.		—	1,500	Psychiatry
		45	—	500	

	Base Hospital	Con. Depot	British Beds	Indian Beds	Centre for
Ranchi.	133 I.B.G.H.		1,000	—	Nerve injury Orthopaedic surgery Plastic surgery
	139 I.B.G.H.		1,200	—	Neurology Neurosurgery
	9 I.B.G.H.		800	—	Ear, nose and throat Eye Skin
		32	500	—	
		35	500	—	
Secunderabad	127 I.B.G.H.		1,200	—	Psychiatry
	128 I.B.G.H.		1,200	—	Orthopaedic surgery
	137 I.B.G.H.		100	1,500	Ear, nose and throat Eye Psychiatry
		one	1,000		
		one		500	

EVACUATION POLICY*

Since the evacuation of casualties constituted a problem of great magnitude and complexity during the course of this campaign it is desirable to review the methods that were adopted to overcome the many and serious obstacles that were encountered. During the early weeks of 1942 evacuation was by ambulance car and ambulance train to Prome. Very limited shipping was used for the evacuation of casualties from Rangoon to India by sea. The medical units were withdrawn along the axes of retreat, Pegu–Toungoo–Mandalay by road and rail and to Mandalay up the valley of the Irrawaddy. Hospital river steamers carried casualties to Prome from the south and from Prome and the Yenangyaung area to Mandalay. From Mandalay northwards there was no semblance of an orderly evacuation chain. Formations had to carry their casualties with them. Ambulance trains were used whenever possible. Their crews had to be armed for protection against looters and frequently had to do their own signal and point shifting. The first evacuation by air had been from Magwe. The second was from Shwebo when this area was abandoned. The great majority of the sick and wounded were moved by ambulance train and hospital river steamer from the Mandalay–Maymyo area to Myitkyina. It was fortunate that

---

* The R.A.F. Medical Services. Vol. 1 *Administration* Chap. 10 *Air Evacuation of Casualties* should be consulted.

sufficient aircraft were available to evacuate casualties from Myitkyina to the bases in north-eastern India. In ten days during April ten Dakota C.47s. transported some 1,900 soldiers and civilians to airfields in Assam over the great mountain barrier that separates northern Burma from the valley of the Brahmaputra.

The Army-in-Burma withdrew into India by way of the Kabaw and Hukawng Valleys, assailed by a multitude of disease-evoking agencies. Reaching India some of its very numerous sick were distributed by ambulance train to the hospitals in Dimapur, Shillong and other places in Assam, the rest being despatched by ambulance train to Gauhati, thence by hospital river steamer to Sirajganj and then by ambulance train to hospitals all over India.

From the point of view of the Army Medical Services the evacuation of casualties during the disastrous opening phase of the campaign fell far short of the standard set by these Services. It could not be otherwise. When the circumstances that attended these operations are considered, e.g. the lack of preparedness, the depressing effect of defeat, the confusion of a hurried and seemingly endless retreat, the loss of the base, the potency and variety of the disease hazards that were encountered, the vast length of the evacuation route, the inevitable imperfection of improvisation, it has to be acknowledged that it is indeed remarkable that so many of the casualties got away and remained capable of making a complete recovery. Throughout the whole of the war the Army Medical Services tackled no task of greater difficulty than this. The extent of the success that was achieved was most creditable to all concerned.

During the operations in Arakan in 1942–43 the difficulty attending casualty evacuation was enormous. Roads, where they existed, were exceedingly poor. Evacuation by river and chaung, creek and sea, though comfortable, was extremely slow and therefore, in the view of the surgeon, very unsatisfactory, and the number of suitable craft was quite inadequate. Aircraft were not available. There was much improvisation. A fleet of barge-like Akyab sloops and sampans was collected. Later the sloops were replaced by three creek steamers and later still by large metal 'flats' each capable of carrying up to 200 patients. These 'flats' were not really suitable for the conveyance of sick and wounded men for in the heat of the day they got unbearably hot and stifling. But they had to be used in order to cope with the very large numbers of the sick.

For the brigade advancing down the coastal strip evacuation was by water transport. The casualties were collected at the head of the Naf Estuary and conveyed thence by ambulance car to the forward hospital in Dhoapalong. For the brigade advancing down the valley of the Kalapanzin across the Goppe Pass, evacuation was by the mules of a field ambulance troop and by hand-carriage by Indian bearer company personnel and by local villagers. From the foot of the Goppe Pass it became possible to use ambulance cars to convey the casualties to Dhoapalong.

From the column moving down the valley of the Kaladan evacuation exceptionally was by small local river craft but usually by mule and hand-carriage. The local Mugs were very expert in making stretchers out of bamboo and proved to be tireless and gentle carriers. At Kyauktaw and Apaukwa the column improvised light airstrips and two Lysander aircraft flew out a small number of the most seriously ill among the wounded and sick. From Kyauktaw the bulk of the casualties were transported by mule to Taung Bazar, a journey that took 4 days, and thence to the foot of the Goppe Pass, another 2 days journey. From there ambulance cars conveyed them to Dhoapalong.

Along the evacuation route it became the custom to place whole units or detachments thereof at intervals to stage the casualties, to provide rest, refreshment, medical attention and shelter for the night. It also became the policy to place a number of forward hospitals along this route. As many casualties as possible were held in the forward hospitals in Cox's Bazar, Chittagong and Dacca. Dacca was developed as a hospital centre in order to reduce the length of the evacuation route. It was situated conveniently and centrally for the Assam and Arakan fronts and could offer suitable accommodation. It could be reached by river from the north and from the south. It was connected by a metre gauge railway with Chittagong and with Dimapur. A first class airfield was nearby and was connected with the hospital centre by a good road. Dacca could not claim to have a climate suitable for hospital patients but the only hill station in the East Bengal and Assam region— Shillong—was very inaccessible. The overflow from these forward hospitals was distributed all over India. It was not unusual for a patient to pass through four hospitals and several smaller medical units, to travel in at least five different forms of transport, to cover 1,000 miles and more and to take from two to four weeks to reach his destination at a particular base hospital.

During these operations the incidence of malaria was such that the evacuation system was greatly strained. To begin with staging sections were grouped together to form holding units for short term malaria cases which, because of their numbers, could not be accommodated in the general hospitals and C.C.Ss. From this beginning there developed the malaria forward treatment unit which was used to hold, treat and rehabilitate up to 600 malaria patients likely to become well again within a period of three weeks.

It is to be noted that the title, M.F.T.U., was soon to become a misnomer, for all types of medical cases, including skins and V.D., came to be admitted and treated in these units. Time came when not only 'light' but also 'serious' medical cases were admitted and held. Until the custom of attaching nursing officers to these units, for the specific purpose of tending the seriously ill, developed, it could be maintained that their use for such a purpose was quite wrong.

When the use of the M.F.T.U. became enlarged in this way, because the establishment of the unit was completely bare of surgical facilities, it became the rule to site the unit alongside a C.C.S., the two units working in conjunction. This custom was not without its disadvantages. The two units were not always together; when in an advance the time arrived for the medical units to move forward, for example, it was usual for the C.C.S. to move, leaving the M.F.T.U. behind for the time being, sometimes for considerable periods. When the C.C.S. moved it unloaded its immobiles including post-operatives into the M.F.T.U. As there was no nursing officer on the establishment of the M.F.T.U. this was by no means a good arrangement. Then again, if a seriously ill patient in the M.F.T.U. had to be transferred to the C.C.S. in order that he might receive adequate nursing care, evacuation was often forward. Such transference of seriously ill patients was not in their best interests. Furthermore if the C.C.S. happened to be very busy with battle casualties it was unlikely that a medical case, even if seriously ill, would receive immediate attention.

During the first Chindit incursion in early 1943, arrangements for evacuation were not made. Such casualties as could not keep up with the columns were nested or else were carried forward with the columns. There was one instance of air evacuation. A Dakota transport aircraft was sent to pick up 17 casualties from a clearing near Bhamo and succeeded in doing so.

The operations in Arakan in 1943–44 took the form of a corps attack, instead of a divisional one as in 1942–43, with Akyab as the objective. An assault from the sea had to be cancelled because the landing craft were withdrawn for use in the Italian theatre. The land attack followed the pattern of the operations of the previous year. One division moved down the coastal strip west of the Mayu Range with Maungdaw as its first objective. A second division crossed the Mayu Range at the Goppe and Ngakyedauk Passes and moved down the valley of the Kalapanzin with Buthidaung as its first objective. A third division, 81st W.A. Division, entered the valley of the Kaladan *via* that of the Sangu.

The most significant development in evacuation methods in the case of the two divisions operating in the coastal strip and in the Kalapanzin Valley was the use of the jeep ambulance carrying two stretcher cases. This was made possible by the engineers constructing jeep tracks to the forward areas and through the passes over the Mayu Range. In this way the jeep came to replace the mule. In these operations, notable for the Japanese outflanking attacks on the L. of C., the larger medical units were congregated in the Naf Peninsula where they could not be overrun. The Naf River therefore came to be used as the evacuation route to the grouped three C.C.Ss. and three M.F.T.Us. In general the lines of evacuation were similar to those of the previous year, from R.A.P. to A.D.S. to M.D.S. to C.C.S. or M.F.T.U. Fewer staging sections were needed since the jeep was speedier than the mule. From the Naf Peninsula evacuation was to Tumbru Ghat by river, by road to 125 I.G.H. at Dhoapalong and by river and road to the group of hospitals in Cox's Bazar which offered 1,700 Indian, 1,000 African and 300 British beds. From Cox's Bazar further evacuation was by sea to Chittagong and thence to Dacca. There was a very limited air-lift from Bawli Bazar and Ramu to Comilla.

Evacuation from the West African Division was a much more complicated affair. From the Sangu Valley, where staging sections were spaced at intervals, evacuation was by river in small country craft to Dohazari whence the journey was continued by rail to Chittagong. Once the division entered the valley of the Kaladan it became possible to construct light airstrips (300 yds.) and Dakota strips (1,200 yds.). Evacuation by air was the only possible method. The method proved to be completely successful. Over 1,000 casualties were flown out. Light aircraft and some of the Dakotas took casualties to Cox's Bazar and other Dakotas went direct to Comilla which had been developed as a forward hospital centre for the Arakan front and which had a suitable air base.

The incidence of sickness was again so high that the forward medical units could not accommodate and hold all the light sick that were evacuated into them. So it was that, as in 1942–43, large numbers of these light sick were transported deeper into India to be lost to their units for long periods of time.

For the second Chindit incursion it was arranged that 'Special Force' was to be supplied entirely by air and that its casualties were to be evacuated by an Air Commando Force provided by the U.S.A.A.F. The commando used L.1s. (Vultee Vigilants), L.5s. (Stinson Reliants), C.64s. (Norsemen) and C.47s. (Dakotas) equipped for the purpose of evacuation. Evacuation was from improvised airstrips to the forward hospital area at Imphal. In May 1944, the Air Commando Force was dissolved and the U.S. Air Transport Command took over the task of casualty evacuation from 'Special Force'. The aircraft were based on airfields in north-east Assam and evacuation was to the hospitals in Panitola, Dibrugarh and Ledo from the airfield at Myitkyina. During the monsoon evacuation from the columns operating to the west of Myitkyina became impossible for the reason that the light aircraft could not use the improvised landing grounds in the paddy fields and in the jungle. Sunderland flying boats from the R.A.F. Coastal Command in Ceylon were therefore used for evacuation purposes between Indawgyi Lake, near Myitkyina, and the Brahmaputra at Dibrugarh. The casualties were brought to the flying boat by collapsible dinghy.

When 'Special Force' was replaced by 36th Division in July, 1944 evacuation from this division was by Air Transport Command machines from Myitkyina to north-western Assam.

It was as the Chindit columns were thrusting northwards to harry the Japanese L. of C. in the Myitkyina area that the Japanese invasion of India was launched. Kohima and Imphal were surrounded and the base at Dimapur seriously threatened. Hospitals in Kohima and Imphal were hurriedly withdrawn and deployed. Some went to Comilla and Agartala where the aerodromes from which encircled Imphal was to be supplied were located; others moved northwards to the Brahmaputra valley in north-eastern Assam to cover the troops in the Kohima area and also the Chindit columns evacuation from which was switched to the airfields at Dinjan, Margherita, Chabua and Sylhet. April and May 1944 were critical months. The medical authorities had to relate their plans for evacuation from the Imphal Plain to the locations of the aerodromes that were to be used by the transport aircraft supplying the troops in the forward zone. The evacuation of casualties was to be by returning transport aircraft; these aircraft had to fly to their appointed bases; the forward hospitals therefore had to be sited near these bases. At this time the engineers were overwhelmed with commitments and so in the preparation of these sites there was much improvisation and there was much delay in road construction. Because of the inevitable tardiness in establishing these hospitals in their new locations only a portion of the casualties could be held at Comilla and Agartala and the remainder had to be staged and then sent on to the Dacca centre by ambulance train.

The circumstances that attended the battle for Imphal were such that quite inevitably there developed the system of large scale movement of troops and of casualties by air. There was no other possible method. Two divisions were flown from Arakan to the Imphal front; base installations, including hospitals, were flown out of the Plain; 3 M.N.S.U. *en route* from Imphal to Comilla by air took its patients with it. An average of 1,000 patients a week were flown out. To begin with it was the custom to arrange mass evacuations at intervals and this, as would be expected, sometimes led to overwhelming congestion and chaos at the receiving end; on one occasion a 1,000-bed I.G.H. was accommodating some 4,000 patients. Later a regular, smooth, even flow of casualties was arranged. To begin with the loading of the aircraft had no relation to the destinations of its passengers and the Chittagong group of hospitals became grossly overcrowded with patients from Arakan, Comilla and Dacca, awaiting further evacuation by hospital ship to the base hospitals. This congestion also led to the rearward evacuation of slightly ill patients to make room for the seriously ill. Eventually casualties were evacuated only to Comilla, with an overflow to Agartala when necessary and this system allowed a more careful sorting to be carried out. Long term cases requiring more than two months' hospital treatment were sent by ambulance train to Chittagong to await further evacuation by hospital ship to the base hospitals in India Command. Those requiring less than two months were evacuated by ambulance train to the Dacca group of hospitals. The shorter term sick were held at Comilla and Agartala near to the convalescent depots and reinforcement camps.

The evacuation of casualties by air now became the established practice. But the acute shortage of suitable aircraft and the lack of any control over them by the medical authorities continued to create many difficulties. Henceforth medical planning was based on an all-air evacuation from the forward areas while full use of the other methods of evacuation was to be made in the rear areas.

With the defeat of the Japanese in Arakan and at Kohima and Imphal the initiative passed to A.L.F.S.E.A. XV Corps was placed directly u/c H.Q. A.L.F.S.E.A. as was also 36th Division. A large L. of C. Command was created and Fourteenth Army began to address itself to the task of driving the Japanese right out of Burma. Following the mopping-up operations that followed the battles in the Imphal Plain, the defeated Japanese were pursued, through the monsoon, down the Imphal–Tiddim and Imphal–Tamu roads. All the hospitals were placed in L. of C. Command, those at Comilla, Agartala and Dacca being designated advanced base hospitals, and each corps developed two corps medical centres consisting of C.C.Ss. and M.F.T.Us.

At the beginning of this advance towards the Chindwin evacuation was exceedingly difficult. The country was mountainous and the rains precluded the use of all airstrips other than the rare all-weather ones. Evacuation by light aircraft in front of the C.C.S. was impracticable. Recourse had to be made to the older methods of hand-carriage, mule carriage and jeep ambulance. The roads quickly became bogs of cloying mud and whole lengths of them became impassable to wheeled traffic of any kind. Vehicles had to be unloaded and man-handled and then loaded again at frequent intervals. On the road between Sittaung and Tamu, normally a journey of a few hours, an ambulance frequently spent two days and nights. Stretcher carries were often as long as 10 miles. A section of the river between Tamu and Sunle was found to be navigable and so D.U.K.Ws. were brought up for use in casualty evacuation. These vehicles had previously been used for this purpose in Arakan in the Pruma Chaung and the Naf River. Maintenance difficulties being disregarded, these vehicles proved to be very useful over short distances since their use avoided the need to change transport at river-road junctions.

With the ending of the monsoon it became possible to proceed with the construction of light aircraft strips along the Tamu–Kabaw valley track but not along the more mountainous Imphal–Tiddim–Kalemyo road. It was no longer necessary for the field ambulance or M.S.U. on the Tamu route to carry its seriously ill patients forward or to nest them in care of a detachment; they could now be flown out. On the Tiddim route it was still necessary to hold the seriously ill and unfortunately these troops had to move through one of the worst of the scrub typhus belts.

Along the Kabaw Valley axis of advance light aircraft strips were constructed at intervals of 50 miles or so and evacuation was by L.5s. and Moths. Evacuation by glider also took place, Dakotas snatching Wayco CG4A gliders from the ground by means of nylon ropes. Each glider could take up to 15 sitting cases or 4 stretcher cases in double tier stretcher slings and 5 or 6 sitting. When Yazagyo was reached a light strip was constructed near the village. To it were brought by mule casualties from the troops attacking Mawlaik. Evacuation from Pantha to Tamu by hand carriage, and from Sunle to Tamu by D.U.K.W. was necessary until light airstrips were built.

During the advance on Kalewa XXXIII Corps medical centre was sited near Inbaung. Here all casualties expected to be fit for discharge within three weeks were held and treated. Surgical cases were congregated in the C.C.Ss., medical cases in the M.F.T.U. Casualties were brought by light aircraft from the forward airstrips. Evacuation from the centre was by heavy aircraft to the advanced base hospital centre at Comilla. Approximately 60 per cent. of all the admissions were held in this centre. Of the remaining 40 per cent., evacuated to Comilla, it was found that 25 per cent. (10 per cent. of the total casualties) required further evacuation to the base hospitals in India Command for more than three months' treatment in hospital. To allow for the delayed closure of wounds it was laid down that long-term cases should be evacuated to India as soon as possible after their preliminary treatment. This necessitated a stay of from 10–14 days to 8–12 weeks in the advanced base hospital. Following the establishment of the bridgehead over the Chindwin at Kalewa, Fourteenth Army prepared to advance across the Central Burma Plain to cross the Irrawaddy and to capture Mandalay. In Arakan XV Corps prepared to advance down the Arakan coast in a series of combined operations.

The assault landings in Arakan called for extraordinary methods of evacuation and also for modifications of surgical procedure. Evacuation from the beachhead was planned to take place in three echelons. Casualties were collected in a beach dressing station formed by a beach medical unit and there first-aid surgery was performed. The casualties were then put aboard L.C.Ms. and L.C.Ts. and taken out to a L.C.I.(D.), this phase of the evacuation beginning after the third wave of L.C.Ms. and L.C.Ts. had come inshore and had discharged their cargoes. On the landing craft infantry, depot ship, a mobile surgical unit was stationed with 100 beds. Here life saving surgery could be undertaken. The third step was from L.C.I.(D.) to hospital ship which was able, at best, to come to within two miles of the shore. The hospital ship functioned as a floating C.C.S.

This standard arrangement was not always practicable. Coastal ambulance steamers, *Nalchera* and *Badora* (175 patients) and ambulance creek steamers, *Agni, Vanu, Lali* (40 lying and 60 sitting) were used. The creek steamers operating with 82nd W.A. Division in the chaungs and creeks around Taungup, Gwa and Ramree Island were equipped with wireless and so could send information concerning the number of casualties and the time of arrival.

The surgeons contented themselves with wound excision and immobilisation in plaster-of-Paris, for there was no point in arranging for facilities for the delayed closure of wounds when the patients had to face long journeys after disembarkation from the hospital ship.

When the beachhead was firmly established an attempt was made to sort out the short-term cases (under three weeks) and to get them to the corps medical centre at Akyab, later at Kyaukpyu, by ambulance steamer. Light airstrips were constructed and the more serious cases were flown to the corps medical centre. After treatment there the casualty could be flown by Dakota to Comilla. Evacuation from the corps medical centre was also by sea to Chittagong in the hospital ships *Karoa, Karapara, Amarapoora, Ophir, Vasna, Melchior Trueb* and the *Wu-Sueh*. At Chittagong such as were likely to recover within three months were disembarked for despatch by ambulance train to Dacca, Agartala and Comilla. The rest were taken on by sea to Calcutta and Madras for base hospitals in India Command.

During XXXIII Corps' assault crossings of the Irrawaddy and its advance on Mandalay evacuation was practically entirely by air, taking the form of light aircraft evacuation from the forward airstrips to the corps medical centre and Dakota evacuation from this centre to the advanced base hospitals at Comilla. The pair of corps medical centres leap-frogged as the advance continued. From the surgeon's point of view the further evacuation of patients from Comilla to Agartala and Dacca by ambulance train was not without its hazards. It commonly meant one night in a staging hospital and another in the holding hospital itself before treatment could be continued. Evacuation by aircraft had proved itself to be so satisfactory from the surgeon's point of view that all other methods had been rendered obsolete and undesirable. Because it was by far the best it was the only method that could command the surgeon's unqualified approval. The ambulance car, when good roads are plentiful, undoubtedly has its uses but such roads were very rare in the Burma theatre. In the European theatre air evacuation had developed exceedingly rapidly in competition with ground systems; in the Burma theatre it developed equally rapidly for the reason that it had no competitors. In Burma aircraft had to fly at 9,000 ft. at least to get over the mountainous Indo-Burma border. In the monsoon months the aircraft was liable to be flung about like thistledown in the wind. Flying was by no means always comfortable but had the conditions been far worse than they were it still would have been better to evacuate casualties by air for any deleterious effect the journey might have was certainly far less than that which the casualty would have endured had he been evacuated by road.

During IV Corps' secret advance to Pakokku, its assault crossing of the Irrawaddy and its sudden thrust towards Meiktila evacuation was likewise by light aircraft to the corps medical centre and thence to the advanced base hospitals. The total number of casualties evacuated by light aircraft from both corps during March was 8,309, during April 4,950 and by heavy aircraft during March 6,608, during April 4,720.

To the usefulness of the light aircraft employed in casualty evacuation there was a limit. The L.5, for example, could take only one casualty at a time unless the airstrip was more than 400 yds. long and airstrips of this length were few and far between. During the actual flight there was no possibility of continuing treatment, e.g. by intra-venous drip. The light planes could not fly at night and so the interval between wounding and surgical intervention in many instances became over-long. It was for this reason that whenever possible a mobile surgical unit was posted to airhead. But M.S.Us. were far too few in number and if one was used in this way it meant that a C.C.S. could lack surgical reinforcement during a period of great activity. In so far as the heavy transport aircraft were concerned the casualty was freight, priority freight maybe but still freight accepted after vital supplies of food and ammunition had been discharged. There were no air ambulance orderlies, though occasionally a nursing orderly, R.A.M.C. would be sent along with a special case. As has already been stated the medical services had to match their evacuation arrangements with the arrangements of the supply services. Inevitably therefore there were delays and disappointments; usually it was not possible to get any forewarning of the departure of aircraft from airhead. Tactical changes could suddenly require the use of airfields other than those at which casualties had been collected. An aircraft with casualties aboard would abruptly be directed to a base airfield other than the one near the advanced hospital base. Since there was no control of the movements of aircraft by the medical authorities no system could be developed which considered first and foremost the interests of the sick and the wounded. The time interval between primary and secondary surgery remained incalculable. These transport aircraft were not adapted for evacuation work. They were equipped with racks and slings but that was all. The heating system commonly failed; oxygen was seldom available aboard.

It became the custom for the corps field ambulance, in whole or part, to function as an air evacuation unit; on occasions a staging section took its place. Towards the end of the campaign R.A.F. medical units, specially designed as casualty air evacuation units, came into use and replaced the Army's improvised units. Since these R.A.F. units consisted solely of British personnel (2 M.Os.; 39 B.O.Rs.) it was necessary to attach Indian staging section personnel to them. In Burma, as in other theatres, this development whereby the R.A.F. not only transported casualties but also accepted responsibility for their medical care during transit was one which had to be considered when, after the war had ended, the question of the possibility and desirability of integrating the medical services of the Navy, Army and Air Force was debated. Throughout the greater part of the Second World War the Army Medical Services had been asking that ambulance aircraft, operating under the direct control of the senior administrative medical officer of the land force, should be provided. Such a development did not take place; instead the R.A.F. Medical Services greatly enlarged their sphere of responsibility. It was learnt that any arrangement whereby supply planes are used for evacuation purposes must remain imperfect; that air evacuation can be satisfactory only when aircraft are provided for the sole purpose of casualty evacuation (and the forward transport of medical personnel and supplies) and are placed at the sole disposal of the senior administrative medical officer of a force. Then and only then can the advantages of this form of evacuation be fully conferred upon the casualty. So long as humanitarian considerations play their part in moulding policy, since it was abundantly shown that evacuation by air was the method of choice commanding the unqualified approval of the surgeon, it follows that this is the method that should be adopted rearwards of the main dressing station in the usual kind of setting to the exclusion of all others.

With the passing of time the evacuation of casualties by air became systematised. The medical branches of the formations concerned estimated the probable number of those to be evacuated each day by light aircraft to the corps medical centre and from the corps medical centre to the advanced base hospitals. These estimates were transmitted to the Army Air Transport Organisation at fortnightly intervals and the aircraft allocations were made accordingly. Any operational variation from this planned requirement was signalled to the A.A.T.O. which requested diversion of R.A.F. aircraft accordingly. Estimated times of arrival of the transport ambulance aircraft were signalled to the forward evacuation units on the strips and formations concerned. The light aircraft worked on the direct request from the formation, the division or the brigade, to the squadrons concerned.

To each of the casualty air evacuation units a pool of ambulance cars was attached. As it was approaching the receiving airfield the aircraft informed the control tower by wireless of the number of sitting and lying patients it was bringing. This information was passed on to the casualty evacuation unit on the airfield. The patients were unloaded and attended to before being conveyed to the hospitals of the advanced base group. Documentation was reduced to a minimum compatible with efficiency. The field medical card A.F.W.3118 and the envelope for the field card A.F.W.3118A formed the basis of the recording. On the card and the envelope all that was necessary could be entered. On the forward airstrip the only additional documentation was a record of the total numbers and the names and units of all those evacuated. At the more rearwards strips a nominal roll of the patients in the aircraft load was made out in triplicate. Of this a copy was kept by the despatching unit, one was retained by the pilot of the aircraft and the third was despatched to the receiving unit along with the casualties. At the foot of the nominal roll was entered the numbers of sitting, of lying and of the 'special' cases. At the base airfields returns of all casualties arriving from all the forward airstrips were maintained.

Prior to early 1944 the only aircraft available for light aircraft evacuation were some R.A.F. Tiger and Fox Moths. There were also a few Ansons but these were of little use. Then came three squadrons of the U.S.A.A.F. Air Commandos, 164, 165 and 166 which usually operated with one squadron in reserve. Each squadron had 36 L.5s and 4 or 5 Norsemen. At times a few L.1s were attached. During the advance into Burma a squadron was attached to each of the three corps and an additional flight of 12 L.5s and 3 L.1s was occasionally made available for reinforcement during the peak periods of evacuation. A flight of R.A.F. L.5s of 221st Gp. was made available occasionally for the evacuation of Army casualties as were also a few Auster Tailorcraft.

In many of these aircraft the casualty had to be carried in the sitting position until modifications to the aircraft were made.

Aircraft	Patients carried
L.1	4 lying and 3 sitting, or 8 sitting patients
L.5	1 lying or sitting
C.64 (Norseman)	5 sitting, or 2 or 3 lying
Tiger Moth	1 lying or sitting
Fox Moth	4 sitting, or 1 lying plus attendant
Anson	4 sitting, or 1 lying and 3 sitting
Wayco Glider	15 sitting, or 4 lying and 5 or 6 sitting

The most used of these light aircraft were able to operate from quite small airstrips, 300 to 400 yds. long and 30 yds. wide, which could be constructed by the personnel of the field ambulance when necessary. The strip was marked out in strips of white cloth, with L shaped strips of this material 6 ft. × 1 ft. in size at the corners and other strips along the sides at intervals of 50 ft. A T of the same material was placed to the left of the strip half way along it, with the upright limb of the T pointing towards the aircraft as it came in to land. The Norseman and the L.1 required a strip 600 yds. by 40 yds.; an Anson a strip of 800 yds.

Control of these light aircraft was exercised by the squadron commander who worked in close co-operation with the administration of the corps medical centre. The aircraft were at the sole disposal of the medical services and were available on an as required basis for casualty evacuation from the divisions. The first of the pilots to land on a forward strip was given a written statement by the field ambulance of the numbers, kinds and urgency of the cases awaiting evacuation. On this information the squadron commander back at the airstrip at the corps centre acted.

It was found that on an average a L.5 was able to evacuate five casualties a day. A squadron of 30 such aircraft could evacuate a maximum of 180 cases a day for short peak periods. The aircraft, loaded, could not do more than a 50-mile run and back without refuelling. Allowing for the days when flying was impossible and assuming that 90 per cent. of the aircraft were always in commission it was estimated that a squadron could evacuate about 6,000 patients a month. These light aircraft not only evacuated casualties; they also transported medical personnel, administrative, consultant and reinforcements as well as stores, mail, and transfusion supplies.

For the transport of casualties between the corps medical centre and the advanced base hospital and between the advanced base hospital and the base hospitals, Dakota (C.47) and Commando (C.46) aircraft were used. Occasionally Sunderland and Catalina flying boats were employed. The Dakota could take 18 lying cases and 5 sitting or 30 sitting. The average load was 10 lying and 17 sitting. The Commando could take 24 lying and 8 sitting or 34–40 sitting. At first all returning supply and reinforcement aircraft were used in evacuation between the corps medical centre and the advanced base hospital. Later special squadrons were assigned the primary rôle of flying in reinforcements and evacuating casualties. It was found that these two commitments balanced each other very closely. The rest of the squadrons could be called upon for evacuation duties in an emergency. The airstrip required was approximately 1,200–1,500 yds. long and 50 yds. wide.

The organisation of this air evacuation between the corps medical centre and the base demanded the close co-operation of the formations concerned, the A.A.T.O. and the squadrons to be involved. The evacuation staff of the medical branches notified the A.A.T.O. at fortnightly intervals and a week in advance of the estimated number of casualties to be evacuated as far as the advanced base hospital group. A consolidated demand from Army level had many advantages. When preparing the estimate the 'M' branch conferred in the usual manner with the 'A' and 'G' staffs of the formation. Since this estimate was usually far removed from the actual figure revised estimates were submitted to the A.A.T.O. as new information became available.

During Fourteenth Army's swift advance to the south after the furious fighting around Mandalay and Meiktila a large number of transport planes were withdrawn. As the distance from Comilla lengthened the air supply bases were changed to Akyab and Ramree Islands; and so it became necessary to stage casualties through Akyab and Ramree and later through Chittagong and to send them on to the advanced base hospital centres by ambulance train. It was fortunate that the severe fighting was over and that casualties were relatively few, for this arrangement disturbed the smooth rhythm of evacuation with adverse effects upon the success of delayed primary closure procedures.

During the operations of Twelfth Army in the closing phase of the war there were very few casualties. This was fortunate for the monsoon conditions affected every form of evacuation, roads became unusable, light aircraft could not fly and on the railway the Japanese and Fourteenth Army between them had destroyed almost every bridge and culvert. It had been planned to form an advanced base hospital group of 10,000 beds in Rangoon. The end of the war was so sudden that time for the maturation of this plan had not been available. However the group was formed as an emergency measure to cope with the 16,000 R.A.P.W.Is. who were flown into Rangoon from Thailand and French Indo-China during the last week of August and the month of September 1945. The hospitals in Rangoon were meant to hold patients likely to recover in less than three months and included a number and variety of the specialist units. Hospitals sited in Meiktila and Kalewa were designated garrison hospitals and held their patients up to three months save those requiring the attention of the specialist units.

An advanced base hospital group of hospitals was also built up in Singapore. It was meant to include some 8,000 to 10,000 beds eventually. Evacuation into this group was by air and by hospital ship from garrison hospitals sited in Java, Sumatra, Borneo, Malaya, Thailand, Indo-China, Hong Kong and Japan itself. Four squadrons of Dakotas were employed by the Joint Logistical Planning Committee, S.A.C.S.E.A. to fly in to Bangkok two Indian combined general hospitals. The aircraft then evacuated the sick R.A.P.W.I. in Bangkok to Rangoon and the two hospitals admitted the remaining sick and prepared to provide cover for the division that was being sent to garrison the country. Experience during this mass evacuation of released P.o.W. showed that the best arrangement was to have the combination of the divisional field ambulances, a C.C.S., a M.F.T.U. and a C.A.E.U. in charge of the operation.

Some 9,000 R.A.P.W.Is. were evacuated by air from Saigon to Rangoon *via* Bangkok. From Rangoon further evacuation was by hospital ship to Madras and thence by ambulance train to the Bangalore base hospital area. In Singapore the number of sick awaiting evacuation was of the order of 20,000. Two medical teams and supplies were dropped on the Changi airfield. Other medical personnel were attached to 2 R.A.P.W.I. Control Staff in Singapore. On September 5 additional medical personnel and two general hospitals reached Singapore with the expeditionary force. Among the first ships to reach Singapore were the hospital ships *Karoa*, *Karapara* and *Amarapoora* which took aboard the first convoys of sick R.A.P.W.I. for Madras *en route* for Bangalore. 339 and 352 sick R.A.P.W.Is. were flown out of Malaya in Sunderland flying boats to Madras and Colombo respectively. From the Netherlands East Indies the evacuation of the great majority of the 3,500 British and 1,800 Indian R.A.P.W.Is. was by sea. A few were flown out to Singapore.

'Mastiff' Control S.A.C.S.E.A., the body responsible for the arrangements for the relief and evacuation of the R.A.P.W.I., closed down on September 29 and its duties were assumed by R.A.P.W.I. Main Control A.L.F.S.E.A.

The saving of life and the alleviation of suffering which can be attributed directly to air evacuation during this campaign was, without doubt, very considerable indeed. The time spent by the casualty on the way was cut from weeks in 1942, to days in 1943 and to hours in 1944 and 45. Air evacuation greatly reduced the extent of hospital cover required in the forward zone.

Throughout the campaign, during which some 200,000 wounded and sick were evacuated by air, only one of the aircraft with its casualties is recorded as having been lost. It was a Dakota carrying 24 West Africans from Arakan to Comilla that was caught in a monsoon storm. A second Dakota having taken aboard its passengers and being about to take off from the Meiktila airstrip was fired on by Japanese gunners concealed on the edge of the airfield. Some of the casualties were wounded again and others were killed.

It is to be remembered, when marvelling at the astonishing record of air evacuation in this theatre that in Burma the situation was peculiar. The U.S.A.A.F. and R.A.F. had complete command of the air during the later years of the war. In the absence of such complete mastery the use of aircraft not marked with the Red Cross emblem, or maybe even marked with it, would not have been without very grave risk.

APPENDIX XXX

COMPOSITION OF THE MEDICAL DIRECTORATE G.H.Q. (INDIA) 1945

MEDICAL BRANCHES OF H.Qs. OF COMMANDS, ARMIES, DISTRICTS AND AREAS

In the Medical Directorate G.H.Q. (India) in 1945 there were in D.M.S.5 (Hygiene and Pathology)

    An Assistant Director   (Malaria)
                                        (Nutrition)
                                        (Transfusion)
                                        (Research)
                                        (Malaria. Preventive Research)
                                        (Malaria. Clinical Research)

and in D.M.S.7 (Consultants and Advisers)
                Consultants in Anaesthesia
                                Dermatology
                                Medicine
                                Neurology
                                Ophthalmology
                                Oto-Rhino-Laryngology
                                Psychiatry
                                Radiology
                                Surgery
                                Venereology

        Honorary Consultants in Malariology
                                      Nutrition

    An Adviser in Neurosurgery, and

    Assistants to the consultants in Medicine and Surgery.

In D.M.S.12 was the medical historian.

(*Official Indian Medical History of the War*. Administration, *page 13*)

REVIEW OF THE WORK OF THE A.M.S.

Towards the end of the war on the staffs of Commands, Armies, Districts and Areas were the following posts:

	Commands and Armies	Districts and Areas
D.D.M.S.	5	1
A.D.M.S.	5	18
A.D.H.	5	—
A.D.P.	4	—
A.D.M.	5	—
A.D.D.S.	4	—
D.A.D.M.S. (Stores)	3	—
D.A.D.M.S. (Training)	1	—
D.A.D.M.S.	5	30
D.A.D.H.	3	31
D.A.D.P.	—	2
D.A.D.M.	—	16
S.C.	4	7
(Malariology)	2	—
(Nutrition)	1	—
(Medical)	1	6
Consultant Ophthalmologist	1	—
Physician	3	—
E.N.T.	1	—
Surgeon	3	—
Adviser in Neurology	2	—
Psychiatry	3	—
Anaesthesia	4	—
Venereology	4	—
Ophthalmology	2	—
Radiology	4	—
E.N.T.	4	—
Dermatology	4	—
Nutrition Officer	1	—
Principal Matron	5	—
Staff Matron	4	—
Matron Examiners	7	—
	100	111

(*Official Indian Medical History of the War.* Administration, *page 15*)

The Armies were the North-Western, the Southern, the Eastern which became Eastern Command, Fourteenth Army and Central Command.

APPENDIX XXXI

INDIAN MEDICAL UNITS RAISED 1939-45

(Official Indian Medical History of the War.
Administration, *pages 223-250)*

I.G.Hs.	117 (I.T.37; B.T.9; C.71)
Fd. Hosps.	5
C.C.Ss.	24
Fd. Ambs.	90 (including 15 Lt.; 3 Para.; 3 Armd. Bde.; 1 Motor Bde.; 1 Lt. Div.)
Fd. Hyg. Secs.	84 (including 9 standard divisions; 1 Lt. Div.; 3 Lt.; 1 Armd. Div.)
Beach Medical Units	3
Bearer Coys.	15
Staging Secs.	124 (I.T.30; B.T.16; C.78)
M.F.T.Us.	16
A.M.Us.	122
Ophthalm. Units	29
E.N.T. Surg. Units	20
M.F.S.Us.	2
M.S.Us.	30 (including 6 Para.)
B.T.U.	1
Adv. B.T.Us.	3
Blood Storage Units	2
X-ray Units	97 (including 34 mobile and 3 servicing units)
Fd. Labs.	60
Bact. Lab.	1
Mal. Fd. Lab.	2
Con. Depots	58 (I.T.33; B.T.19; C.6)
Amb. Trains	33
H.Q. Amb. Train	1
Independent Ward Coaches	15
Amb. Coach	1
Hospital Ships	5
Hospital Carriers	3
Hospital River Steamers	12
H.Q. Hospital River Steamer	1
Amb. Transport	1
Trooping Parties	20
Medical Stores	54 (2 Reserve Base; 3 Transit; 10 Base; 25 Depots; 14 Sub-depots)
Malaria Research Unit. Prevention	2
Malaria Research Unit. Clinical	1

Base Typhus Research Team . 1
Field Typhus Research Team . 1
Penicillin Research Team . . 1
Anaemia Investigation Team . 1
Parasitology Research Team . 1
Protozoology Research Team . 1
Neuropathological Research Team 1
Sprue Investigation Team . . 1
Marasmus Research Team . . 1
Biochemical Research Team . 1
Dent. Units 84 (I.T.51; B.T.33)
Dent. Mech. Units . . . 29
Venereal Diseases Centres . . 4
Psychiatric Centre . . . 1
Reception Centres . . . 4

1,186

APPENDIX XXXII

NON-DIVISIONAL MEDICAL UNITS IN AN INDIAN CORPS AS IN AUGUST 1944

Lt. Fd. Amb.	1	As corps field ambulance
C.C.Ss.	4	One corps, one per division
M.F.T.Us.	4	One corps, one per division
M.S.Us.	6	Two per division
F.T.Us.	3	One per division
Mob. X-ray Units . . .	4	One per C.C.S.
A.M.Us.	6	Three corps, one per division
Bearer Coys.	4	One corps, one per division
Dent. Units B.T. . . .	5	Two corps, one per division
„ „ I.T. . . .	4	One corps, one per division
Dent. Mech. Units . . .	5	One per dental unit. British Troops
Fd. Hyg. Secs.	2	Corps
Staging Secs.	6	Three corps, one per division
Sub-depot Med. Stores . .	3	One per division
Mob. Fd. Lab.	1	Corps

(*Official Indian Medical History of the War*. Administration, *page 253*)

In January 1945 a number of modifications were made. One M.S.U. was now attached to each C.C.S. The number of Bearer Coys. was reduced to three. Dental Units I.T. were now increased to two per division and one corps, the total allotment being raised from four to seven.

APPENDIX XXXIII

THE ARMY MEDICAL SERVICES IN INDIA. STRENGTH AS ON DECEMBER 31, 1944

(*Official Indian Medical History of the War. Administration, page 191*)

	Officers		Other Ranks		Others		Totals	
	Actual	Authorised	Actual	Authorised	Actual	Authorised	Actual	Authorised
R.A.M.C.	1,549	Included in I.A.M.C.	8,554	Included in I.A.M.C.	—	Included in I.A.M.C.	10,103	—
R.A.M.C., non-medical	51	Included in I.A.M.C.	—	Included in I.A.M.C.	—	Included in I.A.M.C.	51	—
I.A.M.C.	3,599	5,474	57,414	63,625	59,362	56,940	120,375	126,039
A.D.C.	96	91	193	162	—	—	289	253
I.A.D.C.	104	119	—	—	—	—	104	119
A.B.R.O.(M.)	5	—	—	—	—	—	5	—
A.I.R.O.(M.)	1	—	—	—	—	—	1	—
I.T.F.(M.)	1	—	—	—	—	—	1	—
Nurses (British)	—	—	—	—	2,065	2,678	2,065	2,678
Nurses (Indian)	—	—	—	—	2,068	4,739	2,068	4,739
Unspecified	353	191	5,850	6,758	—	—	6,203	6,949
Totals	5,759	5,875	72,011	70,545	63,495	64,357	141,265	140,777
Overseas	1,079	885	7,869	8,012	7,376	7,134	16,324	16,031
Grand Totals	6,838	6,760	79,880	78,557	70,871	71,491	157,589	156,808

APPENDIX XXXIV

RATIO OF MEDICAL SERVICES, MEDICAL OFFICERS, NURSES AND DENTAL OFFICERS TO TROOPS. 1939–45

(*Official Indian Medical History of the War. Administration, pages 195 and 197*)

	Number of Troops A	Numbers in Medical Services B	Numbers of Medical Officers C	Numbers of Nurses D	Numbers of Dental Officers E	Ratio B to A	Ratio C to A	Ratio D to A	Ratio E to A
December 1939	361,325	13,566	731	287	26	1 : 27	1 : 494	1 : 1,259	1 : 13,897
1940	558,046	28,889	1,326	356	29	1 : 19	1 : 421	1 : 1,567	1 : 19,243
1941	1,020,392	62,527	2,447	494	51	1 : 16	1 : 417	1 : 2,066	1 : 20,008
1942	1,827,417	81,306	4,138	1,724	142	1 : 22	1 : 442	1 : 1,060	1 : 12,869
1943	2,362,156	120,139	4,940	2,804	154	1 : 20	1 : 478	1 : 842	1 : 15,339
1944	2,560,574	157,589	6,234	4,133	200	1 : 16	1 : 411	1 : 620	1 : 12,803
1945	2,644,323	174,740	6,822	4,802	236	1 : 15	1 : 388	1 : 551	1 : 11,205

718 THE ARMY MEDICAL SERVICES

APPENDIX XXXV

THE ESTABLISHMENT OF SPECIALISTS IN INDIAN MEDICAL UNITS

(Official Indian History of the War. Medicine, Surgery and Pathology, page 33)

	Surgeons	Anaesthetists	Physicians	Radiologists	Pathologists	Hygienists	Venereologists	Psychiatrists	Dermatologists	Oto-Rhino-Laryngologists	Ophthalmologists	Malariologists	Gynaecologists	Neurologists
Fd. Hyg. Sec.	—	—	—	—	—	1	—	—	—	—	—	—	—	—
C.C.S.	1	1	1	—	—	—	—	—	—	—	—	—	—	—
I.G.H.(C.) 1 Br.; 3 Ind. Secs.	1	1	1	1	—	—	—	—	—	—	—	—	—	—
" 2 " 5 " "	2	1	2	1	—	—	—	—	—	—	—	—	—	—
" 3 " 7 " "	3	1	2	1	—	—	—	—	—	—	—	—	—	—
I.G.H.(I.T.) 600 beds	2	1	2	1	—	—	—	—	—	—	—	—	—	—
" " 1,000 "	3	1	2	1	—	—	—	—	—	—	—	—	—	—
I.B.G.H.(I.T.) 1,000–1,400 beds	4	2	3	1	—	—	—	—	—	1	1	—	—	—
" (B.T.) 1,500 "	4	2	3	1	—	—	—	—	—	1	1	—	—	—
" " 800–1,200 "	3	2	2	1	1	—	—	—	—	1	1	—	—	—
" " 1,300–2,000 "	4	2	3	1	1	—	—	—	—	1	1	—	—	—
Fd. Hospital	1	1	—	—	—	—	—	—	—	—	—	—	—	—
Beach Medical Unit	1	1	—	—	—	—	—	—	—	—	—	—	—	—
Fd. Laboratory	—	—	—	—	1	—	—	—	—	—	—	—	—	—
Ophthalmological Unit	—	—	—	—	—	—	—	—	—	—	1	—	—	—
Maxillo-facial Surgical Unit	2	1	—	—	—	—	—	—	—	1	—	—	—	—
Mob. Surgical Unit	—	—	—	—	—	—	—	—	—	—	—	—	—	—
E.N.T. Surgical Unit	—	—	—	—	—	—	—	—	—	1	—	—	—	—
Mob. X-ray Unit	—	—	—	1	—	—	—	—	—	—	—	—	—	—
Typhus Research Team	—	—	1	—	1	—	—	—	—	—	—	—	—	—
H.S. *Tairea* and *Karapara*, each	1	1	1	—	—	—	—	—	—	—	—	—	—	—
H.S. *Karoa*	—	—	—	1	—	—	—	—	—	—	—	—	—	—
H.S. *Melchior Treub*	1	1	1	—	—	—	—	—	—	—	—	—	—	—

REVIEW OF THE WORK OF THE A.M.S.

Mal. Forward Treatment Unit														
Hospital Coastal Steamer *Wu-Sueh*		1				1								
Orthopaedic Wing:														
B.T. 500 beds	5				1									
I.T. 1,000 "	10				1									
" 200 "	2				1									
" 300 "	3				1									
" 500 "	5				1									
" 1,000 "	10				1									
V.D. Clinic, Calcutta														
Malaria Research Unit. Prevention							3							1
Central Military Pathology Laboratory														
Malaria Research Unit. Clinical						4								
District Laboratory						1								
Army School of Hygiene														1
P.o.W. Hospital	2		2			2		6						
Serological Laboratory						1								
Dysentery Investigation Team														
Artificial Limb Centre	1				1									
Mass Radiography Centre					1									
Penicillin Research Team														
Base Typhus Research Team														
Anaemia Investigation Team						1								
Biochemical Research Team						1								
Parasitological Research Team						1								
War Wounds Research Team						1								
Inspectorate of Foodstuffs	1							9						
Garrison Hospitals:														
India	102	67	102	67			89							
S.E.A.C.	5	4	5	4									17	
Pool of Specialists														2
Medical Staff Appointments:														
India	6	5	9	4	42	1	14	1	70	39	14	2	21	
S.E.A.C.	8	3	3		21		1		1	1	1	1	19	

At the beginning of the war there were no consultants, no advisers and 87 specialists of various kinds. By the beginning of 1945 there were 1,576 specialists including 261 surgeons, 194 anaesthetists, 259 physicians, 165 radiologists, 164 pathologists, 101 hygienists, 78 venereologists, 86 psychiatrists, 40 dermatologists, 43 oto-rhino-laryngologists, 59 malariologists, 15 gynaecologists and 2 neurologists.

APPENDIX XXXVI

THE CIVIL AFFAIRS SERVICE (BURMA) (C.A.S.(B.))
ORGANISATION

This organisation was intended to work with, and under, Army, to control Civil Affairs and to take over civil administration in the liberated areas until such time as the civil government was re-established. The objects of the medical organisation of C.A.S.(B.) were to provide medical attention to the liberated peoples, to control infectious diseases among the civil population and to care for the battle casualties suffered by it. The organisation was essentially a temporary one which was to give place about September 1945 to a much more ambitious relief scheme.

The two Burma field ambulances and a 100-bed section of a Burmese general hospital were available initially. Expendible medical stores were provided from Army sources but no transport could be allotted to the organisation (the field ambulances had their transport though it was not complete). The equipment of the section of the general hospital was about equal to that of the standard medical inspection room. In the liberated areas many of the staffs of the dispensaries and small local hospitals reported for duty and the medical installations were reopened, the Army supplying such equipment and stores as it could. Obstetrical and gynaecological instruments, though required, could not immediately be supplied. Equipment was sent from India and some was obtained by local purchase in the black market. Instruments that had been buried during the retreat in 1942 were now disinterred.

A moderately satisfactory medical cover gradually came into being in the towns and villages of the rear areas but lack of transport reduced the usefulness of the medical officers. Army placed a section of a motor ambulance convoy at the disposal of C.A.S.(B.). In the forward areas, of course, the responsibility for the evacuation of civilian casualties remained an Army one to the end of the campaign. Hundreds of civilian battle casualties were treated in the mobile surgical units and in the C.C.Ss. and passed along the military evacuation chain. At Comilla adequate C.A.S.(B.) facilities were available and there these casualties were handed over to this organisation to be transferred to local civil hospitals.

APPENDIX XXXVII

EXCERPT FROM FIELD MARSHAL SIR WILLIAM SLIM'S
Defeat into Victory.* PAGES 177-180

(*General Slim, as he then was, had recently assumed command of Fourteenth Army*)

'My second great problem was health (*the first was supply and the third morale*). In 1943, for every man evacuated with wounds we had one hundred and twenty evacuated sick. The annual malaria rate alone was eighty-four per cent. per annum of the total strength of the army and still higher among the forward troops. Next to malaria came a high incidence of dysentery, followed in this gruesome order of precedence by skin diseases and a mounting tale of mite or jungle typhus, a peculiarly fatal disease. At this time, the sick rate of men evacuated from their units rose to over twelve per thousand per day. A simple calculation showed me that in a matter of months at this rate my army would have melted away. Indeed it was doing so under my eyes.

'In anxious consultation with my M.G.A. and my senior medical officers I reviewed our resources. To start with, I discovered that for some reason the medical establishments of the Fourteenth Army were lower than those of other British armies in Africa or Europe, and that actual strengths were gravely below even this reduced establishment. We were short of doctors, nurses and equipment. Our hospitals had been of necessity expanded to take twenty-five per cent. more patients than they were designed to hold. We now had twenty-one thousand hospital beds, all occupied. To nurse these seriously sick or wounded men we had a total of four hundred and fourteen nursing sisters, less than one nurse to fifty beds throughout the twenty-four hours, or in practice one to one hundred beds by day or night.

'Demands for more nurses from home met with the answer that there were none to spare from other fronts and that, anyway, India should provide the nurses for Indian troops who formed the bulk of my army. We might as well have been told that India must provide the aircraft for the air force. Aircraft were not made in India; nor were nurses. The Indian Military Nursing Service, struggling heroically against prejudice and every kind of handicap, was in its infancy and could grow very slowly. In spite of all our efforts, and although General Auchinleck milked the hospitals of India to danger-point to help us, it was clear that any increase in our medical strength would be grievously slow.

'I knew we had to beat Germany first. I was even ready to accept the fact that the Fourteenth Army was the Cinderella of all British armies, and would get only what her richer sisters in Africa and Europe could spare. I would not grumble too much if we came last for men, tanks, guns and the rest, but I would protest, and never cease from protesting, that we should be at the bottom of the list for medical aid. That was not fair, nor, I believe, wise.

'However, as we had long ago discovered, it was no use waiting for other people to come to our help. Nor was it much use trying to increase our hospital accommodation; prevention was better than cure. We had to stop

---

* 1956. Published by Cassell & Co. Ltd.

men going sick, or, if they went sick, from staying sick. We tackled the problem on four main lines:
  (i) The practical application of the latest medical research.
  (ii) The treatment of the sick in forward areas instead of evacuation to India.
  (iii) The air evacuation of serious casualties.
  (iv) The raising of morale.

'The prevention of tropical diseases had advanced immensely within the last few years, and one of the first steps of the new Supreme Commander had been to get to South-East Asia some of the most brilliant research workers in this field. Working closely with medical officers who had experience of practical conditions, they introduced new techniques, drugs, and methods of treatment. (*This refers to the Medical Advisory Division of S.E.A.C.*). Gradually the new remedies became available, although for long we lagged behind in their supply. Sulphonamide compounds, penicillin, mepacrine, and D.D.T. all appeared later than we liked but still in time to save innumerable lives. Without research and its results we could not survive as an army.

'It was, however, forward treatment that brought the first visible results. Up to now, when a man contracted malaria, he had been transported while his disease was at its height, in great discomfort hundreds of miles by road, rail and boat to a hospital in India. Before he reached there he had probably been reinfected several times and while his first bout would be over he was booked for a relapse. In any case he would not return over the congested line of communication for, on the average, at least five months. Often enough he was employed in India and never returned. To avoid all this we organised M.F.T.Us., malaria forward treatment units. They were, in effect, field hospitals, tented or more often in Bashas, a few miles behind the fighting lines. A man reached them within twenty-four hours of his attack of malaria and he remained there for the three weeks or so it took to cure him. He was back fit with his unit in weeks instead of months, the strain on the line of communication was lightened, and he avoided the often terrible discomforts of the long journey. M.F.T.Us. had another advantage. When morale was not high some men welcomed malaria and took no precautions to avoid it, reasoning that a bout of malaria was a cheap price to pay for getting away from the Burma front. If it only took them half a dozen miles from the front and brought them briskly back it was not so attractive.

'For the wounded, forward surgical teams were introduced on an increasing scale. Working almost in the midst of the battle, specially selected surgeons, including some of the leading professors of our medical schools, performed major operations within a few hours of a man being wounded. Their work was brilliant, but it should be remembered that where the surgeon saved the individual life, the physician, less dramatically, saved hundreds by his preventive measures. We also sent nurses—when we had them—further into the battle area than had been usual. There were some diseases, like mite typhus, for which we had then no proved treatment, in which the patient's chance of survival depended more on the nurse than on the doctor. The extra danger and hardship these nurses cheerfully endured were repaid in lives many times over.

'Air evacuation, in the long run, probably made the greatest difference of all to the wounded and sick. Only those who have suffered the interminable anguish of travel over rough ground or tracks by stretcher or ambulance and the long stifling railway journey for days on end, with broken limbs jolting and temperatures soaring, can realise what a difference quick, smooth, cool transport by aircraft can mean. In November 1943 we had for all transport purposes, other than the maintenance of the 81st West African Division in Arakan, only some one hundred and twenty air sorties a month, but the number was rapidly growing and with it our technique of air evacuation. Later, light aeroplanes of the Moth, Auster, or L.5 type picked up the casualties on airstrips hurriedly cut out of jungle or ricefield within a mile or two of the fighting. Each little aircraft carried one lying or two sitting patients and flew them to the supply strip anything from ten to forty miles back. Here the casualties were transferred to Dakotas returning empty from the supply run and flown direct to a general hospital. There were, I remember, heated arguments as to where these hospitals should be situated. Roughly, there was the choice between putting them in such hot sticky places in the plains as at Comilla or in the cool of the hills as at Shillong. I plumped for the plains, because there we could have an airstrip almost alongside the hospital; to reach the hills would have meant long and trying road journeys. So our casualties went almost direct from the battlefield to the hospital and later as convalescents by road from the plains to the hills. There was some shaking of heads among the more orthodox but the results justified it. One such hospital took in during 1944 and 1945 over eleven thousand British casualties straight, in their filthy, blood-soaked battledress, from the front line. The total deaths in that hospital were twenty-three. Air evacuation did more in the Fourteenth Army to save lives than any other agency.

'Good doctors are no use without good discipline. More than half the battle against disease is fought, not by doctors, but by the regimental officers. It is they who see that the daily dose of mepacrine is taken, that shorts are never worn, that shirts are put on and sleeves turned down before sunset, that minor abrasions are treated before, and not after, they go septic, that bodily cleanliness is enforced. When mepacrine was first introduced and turned men a jaundiced yellow, there was the usual whispering campaign among troops that greets every new remedy—the drug would render them impotent—so, often the little tablets are not swallowed. An individual medical test in almost all cases will show whether it has been taken or not, but there are a few exceptions and it is difficult to prove for court-martial purposes. I, therefore, had surprise checks of whole units, every man being examined. If the overall result was less than ninety-five per cent. positive I sacked the commanding officer. I only had to sack three; by then the rest had got my meaning.

'Slowly, but with increasing rapidity, as all of us, commanders, doctors, regimental officers, staff officers and N.C.Os. united in the drive against sickness, results began to appear. On the chart that hung on my wall the curves of admissions to hospitals and malaria forward treatment units sank lower and lower, until in 1945 the sickness rate for the whole Fourteenth Army was one per thousand per day. But at the end of 1943 that was a long way off.'

INDEX

PART I

'Aberdeen', 181, 182, 184, 185, 208, 209 (*Fig. 23*)
Agartala, 130, 171, 175, 176, 189, 190, 191, 326, 334, 336 414, 523, 528, 573, 586, 587, 702, 703, 705 (*Figs. 13, 45, 51*)
Aijal, 364, 366, 367, 368 (*Figs. 13, 43*)
Aishan, 345 (*Fig. 38*)
Akyab, 2, 3, 19, 41, 51, 93, 100, 101, 103, 112, 390, 473 474 477, 478, 479, 481, 487, 488, 493, 495, 499, 511, 513, 519, 520, 521, 523, 524, 527, 561, 705 (*Figs. 1, 13, 17, 63, 74, 84*)
Akyab Island, 111, 170, 474, 475, 481, 511, 520, 540, 710 (*Figs. 17, 63*)
Alethaung, 428 (*Fig. 54*)
Alexander, Field-Marshal Viscount, of Tunis, 38, 47, 51, 53, 60, 94
Allagappa, 72, 404, 406, 428, 432, 439, 446, 447 (*Figs. 48, 49, 52, 54, 55*)
Allanmyo, 1, 18, 52, 53, 54, 55, 61, 62, 63, 534, 535, 544, 545, 547, 554, 580, 583, 588, 589, 590 (*Figs. 6, 9, 62, 71, 73*)
Alon, 18, 19, 74, 404, 405, 527, 591, 598 (*Fig. 48*)
Amarabari (nr. Tezpur), 175, 176
Amarapura, 442 (*Figs. 53, 54*)
Aminpara (nr. Maungdaw), 148
An, 3, 475, 476, 477, 478, 492, 493, 511, 512, 515, 517, 520 (*Fig. 62*)
An Pass, 511 (*Fig. 62*)
Andaman Islands, 93, 140, 568, 673
Anlung, 361 (*Fig. 42*)
Antu, 437, 443 (*Fig. 54*)
Apaukwa, 122, 153, 163, 504 513 514, 699 (*Figs. 15, 17, 66, 67*)
Aradura Spur or Feature, 267, 274, 276 (*Figs. 31, 32, 33*)
Arakan, 1, 2, 3, 16, 18, 24, 93, 100–128, 139–176, 389, 390, 391, 473–524, 527, 533, 535, 540, 544, 545, 547, 652, 660, 665, 666, 698, 702, 703, 704 (*Figs. 9, 14, 15, 16, 17, 62, 63, 64, 65, 67*)
Arakan Yomas, 15, 16, 17, 18, 106, 141, 477, 511 (*Figs. 9, 62*)
Army Air Transport Organisation, 707
Asugyi, 464 (*Fig. 57*)
Atet Nanra, 110, 113, 114 (*Fig. 15*)
Auklo, 507 (*Fig. 66*)
Auktaung, 131, 263 (*Fig. 10*)
Aungzeik, 114 (*Figs. 15, 17, 63*)
Ava, 532 (*Figs. 46, 53, 54, 55*)
Ava Bridge, 18, 19, 61, 64, 72, 74, 442
Ava Fort, 442
Awlanbyin, 168, 173 (*Fig. 15*)
Ayadaw, 404, 406 (*Figs. 46, 48, 49, 56*)

Badana, 145, 166, 168, 172, 174 (*Figs. 15, 19*)
Baguna, 510, 513 (*Fig. 67*)
Bahe, 458, 463, 465 (*Fig. 58*)
Bakkagonna, 146, 147, 148 (*Fig. 19*)
Balukhali, 173 (*Fig. 19*)
Bandarban, 165, 506, 507 (*Figs. 20, 65*)
Bangalore, 190, 651, 652, 655, 661, 663, 667, 696
Bangkok, 567, 674, 710, 711
Banmauk, 393 (*Figs. 56, 57*)
Banyo, 513 (*Fig. 67*)
Bareilly, 121, 652
Basha Hill (nr. No. 3 Stockade, nr. Tiddim), 245
Basin, The, Shwegyin (on the Chindwin), 76, 77
Bassein, 544, 546, 547, 591, 598 (*Fig. 2*)
Baw, 393, 400 (*Figs. 48, 57*)
Bawlake, 19, 59 (*Fig. 9*)
Bawli (Bawli Bazar, Bawli North), 103, 106, 109, 112, 113, 116, 117, 124, 139, 141, 143, 144, 145, 146, 147, 148, 149, 152, 153, 154, 158, 159, 160, 161, 166, 167, 168, 169, 172, 325, 474, 478, 701 (*Figs. 14, 19*)
Bermo, 528 (*Fig. 70*)
Bhamo, 19, 60, 67, 130, 133, 140, 185, 232, 455, 585, 700 (*Figs. 11, 13, 23, 56, 57*)
Bien Hoa (in what was then French Indo-China), 570
Bilin, 33 (*Figs. 3, 72*)
Bilumyo, 457 (*Fig. 61*)
Bishenpur, 84, 185, 217, 252, 262, 303, 304, 305, 308, 310, 311, 312, 314, 342, 352, 355, 357, 358 (*Figs. 2, 29, 30, 36, 42*)
Bishenpur–Silchar Track, 265, 304, 308, 310, 311, 351, 357, 358
'Blackpool', 185, 186, 192, 204, 205, 213, 216, 221, 222, 237 (*Fig. 23*)
Bodegon, 401 (*Fig. 47*)
Bogyigyaung, 174 (*Fig. 19*)
Bokajan (nr. Golaghat), 274, 373
Bombay, 103, 139, 252, 273
Bombay Camp, 369 (*Fig. 43*)
Bongaigaon, 585 (*Fig. 13*)
Bongyo, 507 (*Fig. 66*)
Briasco Bridge (nr. Bawli), 158
'Broadway', 181, 183, 184, 185, 186, 208, 454, 458 (*Figs. 23, 56*)
Budalin, 81, 396, 403, 405, 406 (*Figs. 46, 47, 48, 49, 50, 56*)
Buddha Hill (nr. Sittang Bridge), 35 (*Fig. 4*)
'Bull Box', Palel, 312, 315, 316
Bungalow Hill (nr. Sittang Bridge), 35 (*Fig. 4*)
Burma–China Road (Mandalay–Lashio–nr. Wanting–over the River Salween–Paoshan–Kunming–Chungking), 6, 66, 129, 140, 391, 392
Buthidaung, 103, 106, 108, 109, 110, 112, 113, 114, 115, 116, 146, 149, 152, 153, 160, 166, 169, 474, 475, 480, 510, 513, 514, 519, 520, 700 (*Figs. 15, 19, 67*)

INDEX

Calcutta, 6, 93, 101, 106, 119, 120, 121, 144, 148, 162, 170, 171, 175, 176, 261, 320, 324, 481, 520, 521, 523, 526, 528, 541, 546, 625, 648, 651, 652, 655, 659, 661, 663, 705 (*Figs. 13, 70, 83, 84*)
Casualties
  A.L.F.S.E.A., 605–608 (*Figs. 77, 78*)
  India, 603–604 (*Figs. 75, 76*)
  Indo-Burma Front and S.E.A.C., 609–613, 619 (*Figs. 79, 80*)
  Twelfth Army, 627–628
  Fourteenth Army, 614–627
  Burcorps 79, 85
  IV Corps, 451, 564, 565, 614–625, 627
  XV Corps, 523
  XXXIII Corps, 286, 287, 451, 562, 614–625
  2nd Division, 290–295
  Indian 3rd Division (Special Force), 195–215 (*Fig. 25*)
  Indian 5th Division, 552, 618, 619, 620, 621, 627
  11th East African Division, 618, 619, 620, 621
  Indian 17th Division, 96
  Indian 19th Division, 618, 619, 621
  Indian 20th Division, 627, 632–637
  Indian 25th Division, 485–487, 496–498
  Indian 36th Division, 160, 618, 619, 620, 621, 628–631 (*Figs. 81, 82*)
  81st West African Division, 508
  82nd West African Division, 519, 627
  Lushai Brigade, 370
battle, in,
  A.L.F.S.E.A., 688, 689, 690
  Indo-Burma Front and S.E.A.C., 609, 610, 611, 612, 613
  Twelfth Army, 628
  Fourteenth Army, 616, 617
  Burcorps, 79
  IV Corps, 450, 550, 565, 616, 617
  XV Corps, 522, 523
  XXXIII Corps, 286, 287, 380, 381, 450, 451, 562, 616, 617
  2nd Division, 290, 291, 293–295, 381
  Indian 3rd Division (Special Force), 132, 195, 206, 209, 212, 213, 214, 225, 226
  Indian 5th Division, 354, 357, 362, 381
  Indian 7th Division, 156, 157, 381
  11th East African Division, 381
  Indian 20th Division, 312, 381, 571, 632–637, 690
  Indian 21st Division, 381
  Indian 23rd Division, 315
  Indian 25th Division, 485, 486, 487, 496, 497, 498, 522
  Indian 26th Division, 522
  Indian 36th Division, 160, 459, 461, 470, 471, 472
  81st West African Division, 508, 522
  82nd West African Division, 522
  3rd Commando Brigade, 522
  22nd East African Brigade, 522
  23rd Brigade, 381
  Indian 254th Tank Brigade, 381
  Indian 268th Brigade, 381

Lushai Brigade, 370
evacuation of, 697–711
  A.L.F.S.E.A., 525, 526
  Arakan, 104–106, 170, 698–701, 704, 705
  L. of C. Command, 414–416
  Fourteenth Army, 328–333, 339, 414, 560 (*Figs. 45, 51, 74*)
  IV Corps, 318–320, 450, 451, 561
  XXXIII Corps, 299, 377, 408, 445, 451, 452, 561 (*Fig. 55*)
  Indian 3rd Division (Special Force), 189, 191, 212, 227, 700, 701, 702
  11th East African Division, 374
  Indian 25th Division, 488
  Indian 36th Division, 463, 464
  81st West African Division, 506, 701 (*Figs. 65, 66*)
  Lushai Brigade, 367
psychiatric,
  Indo-Burma Front and S.E.A.C., 609, 610
  Twelfth Army, 628
  XV Corps, 679
  2nd Division, 296–298, 684
  Indian 3rd Division (Special Force), 202–206
  Indian 20th Division, 633, 636, 684
  Indian 26th Division, 684
  Indian 36th Division, 161, 471, 684
'Catfish Box', Imphal, 258, 301, 307, 308, 310
Central Plain of Burma, 247, 525, 704
Chabua, 192, 702 (*Fig. 23*)
Chakhabama, 278, 280, 281, 282 (*Fig. 34*)
Chakpi Karong, 264, 361 (*Figs. 40, 42*)
Chamol, 349 (*Fig. 30*)
Champatali, 165 (*Fig. 20*)
Champai, 353, 367, 368 (*Fig. 43*)
Chandranathpur, 585 (*Fig. 27*)
'Charterhouse' Island (nr. Ru-Ywa), 490
Chas, 176, 373, 519, 520, 528 (*Fig. 70*)
Chattarpur, Bihar, 189
Chattrik, 345 (*Fig. 39*)
Chauk, 17, 56, 61, 64, 393, 430, 431, 432, 434, 449, 530, 532, 533 (*Figs. 6, 8, 46, 49, 52, 71, 73*)
Chaungmagyi Chaung (N. of Mandalay), 439, 445
Chaung-U, 73, 74, 80, 404, 406, 408 (*Figs. 46, 48, 49, 54, 56*)
Chaungwa, 193 (*Fig. 22*)
Chaunggwa, 447 (*Figs. 49, 54*)
Chawai, 343, 344 (*Figs. 35, 36, 37*)
Chedema, 278 (*Figs. 34, 35*)
Cheduba Island, 499, 502 (*Figs. 62, 64*)
Chiang Kai-shek, Marshal, 6, 51, 129, 390, 455
Chindits, 2, 129–138, 177–242, 640
Chinjaroi, 344 (*Figs. 37, 39*)
Chinjui, 344 (*Figs. 37, 39*)
Chin Hills (S. of Tiddim), 15, 16, 129, 243, 246, 247, 364, 366, 368
Chins, 20, 365
Chingyaung (between Mawlaik and Pyingaing), 392, 405

Chiringa, 141, 145, 153, 159, 162, 164, 165, 166, 172, 325, 335, 474, 504, 507, 513, 527, 587 (*Figs. 14, 20, 65*)
Chittagong, 93, 101, 103, 105, 106, 108, 109, 112, 118, 119, 120, 121, 139, 144, 147, 148, 149, 159, 160, 161, 162, 170, 171, 172, 175, 176, 325, 335, 336, 353, 367, 368, 371, 373, 408, 446, 481, 490, 501, 519, 520, 521, 525, 527, 573, 581, 586, 587, 659, 665, 699, 701, 703, 705, 710 (*Figs. 13, 65, 83, 84*)
'Chocolate Staircase' (nr. Tiddim), 356 (*Fig. 41*)
Cholon (in what used to be French Indo-China), 570
Chota Maunghnama, 147, 148, 157, 160, 161, 173 (*Fig. 19*)
'Chowringhee', 181, 184 (*Fig. 23*)
Christison, Lieut.-General Sir Philip, 139, 146
Chungking, 6, 51, 455 (*Fig. 83*)
Churachandpur, 352, 361, 377 (*Fig. 42*)
Comilla, 100, 101, 106, 108, 120, 121, 154, 166, 170, 171, 175, 176, 261, 284, 326, 334, 336, 376, 378, 391, 407, 408, 414, 446, 519, 520, 523, 525, 527, 539, 559, 560, 581, 587, 648, 666, 701, 702, 703, 704, 705, 710 (*Figs. 13, 45, 51, 74, 83*)
Cox's Bazar, 106, 108, 109, 116, 118, 121, 122, 144, 145, 153, 160, 166, 170, 172, 173, 325, 335, 474, 499, 507, 519, 586, 587, 652, 658, 665, 699, 701 (*Figs. 13, 14, 65*)

Dacca, 120, 121, 170, 171, 175, 176, 326, 335, 376, 414, 523, 525, 528, 699, 701, 702, 703, 705 (*Figs. 13, 83*)
Daik-U, 538, 589, 596, 600, 601 (*Figs. 5, 71*)
Daingbon Chaung, 488, 491 (*Figs. 62, 68*)
Dalet, 493, 511, 515 (*Fig. 62*)
Dalet Chaung, 477, 493, 495 (*Fig. 62*)
Daletme, 163, 505, 507 (*Figs. 16, 21, 65, 66*)
Danyingon, 34 (*Fig. 3*)
Daudkandi (on the Brahmaputra), 120, 330, 525
Daulatganj (N.W. of Chittagong), 101
'Dawlish' (on Lake Indawgyi), 222
Dayindabo, 52, 54, 55, 63, 544 (*Figs. 6, 9*)
Dehra Dun, 190, 521, 651, 659, 663, 696 (*Figs. 83, 84*)
Delhi, 139, 247 (*Fig. 83*)
Dempsey, Lieut.-General Sir Miles, 547
Deputy-Commissioner's bungalow, Kohima, 268, 272, 274, 276 (*Figs. 31, 32*)
Dhansiri Valley (nr. Dimapur), 265
Dhechuapalong, 145 (*Fig. 14*)
Dhoapalong, 121, 122, 145, 170, 172, 173, 175, 176, 325, 335, 698, 699, 701 (*Figs. 14, 65*)
Dhond (E. of Poona), 507
Dhubri, 585 (*Fig. 13*)
Dibrugarh, 175, 176, 192, 193, 324, 333, 336, 526, 584, 586, 701, 702 (*Figs. 13, 23*)
Digboi, 66, 192, 324, 333, 584 (*Figs. 11, 13*)
Detail Issue Store (D.I.S.) Hill, Kohima, 268, 269, 271, 275, 277 (*Figs. 31, 32*)

Dimapur (Manipur Road), 2, 73, 81, 83, 85, 92, 93, 129, 130, 161, 171, 175, 176, 247, 251, 252, 253, 260, 261, 262, 264, 265, 266, 269, 271, 272, 273, 278, 283, 284, 285, 306, 325, 333, 341, 360, 395, 526, 531, 573, 584, 585, 586, 622, 648, 667, 698, 699, 702 (*Figs. 11, 13, 27, 29, 83*)
Dimapur–Kohima Road, 253, 266, 273, 274, 276, 285, 319
Dinapore, 120, 175, 176, 388, 528, 696 (*Fig. 70*)
Dinjan, 191, 192, 193, 194, 702 (*Fig. 13*)
Diseases affecting the Troops,
  Beri-beri, 138, 357
  Cerebro-spinal fever, 22, 621
  Cholera, 22, 49, 51, 61, 64, 91, 124, 165, 202, 447, 469, 505, 613, 621, 624, 625, 628, 631
  Diphtheria, 621, 626, 633
  Dysentery and Diarrhoea, 22, 85, 91, 124, 138, 188, 196, 199, 207, 210, 211, 213, 214, 215, 216, 217, 224, 240, 287, 289, 292, 293, 322, 369, 370, 380, 451, 469, 470, 471, 473, 498, 505, 508, 571, 604, 609, 610, 611, 613, 616, 619, 628, 631, 632, 634, 636, 637, 667, 671 (*Figs. 24, 82*)
  Enteric Group, 22, 621, 626
  Infective Hepatitis, 196, 199, 202, 207, 213, 215, 216, 224, 225, 292, 469, 471, 498, 505, 508, 621, 628, 631, 632, 636 (*Fig. 24*)
  Malaria, 20, 21, 30, 83, 91, 122, 123, 124, 138, 188, 196–198, 202, 207, 210, 211, 213, 214, 215, 216, 217, 219, 224, 239, 241, 261, 262, 282, 287, 288, 292, 293, 321, 339, 340, 369, 370, 371, 380, 451, 468, 469, 470, 471, 498, 508, 523, 524, 571, 604, 606, 607, 608, 609, 610, 613, 616, 617, 618, 628–630, 632, 634, 636, 637, 640-648 (*Figs. 1, 24, 44, 69, 78, 81*)
  Plague, 22, 406
  Scrub Typhus, 22, 83, 196, 200, 202, 205, 207, 210, 211, 215, 240, 282, 324, 348, 361, 363, 369, 370, 376, 377, 378, 380, 451, 470, 471, 508, 613, 621, 622, 623, 624, 628, 630, 636 (*Figs. 24, 28, 80*)
  Smallpox, 22, 51, 91, 262, 505, 613, 621, 624, 633
  Venereal, 22, 124, 287, 289, 292, 293, 323, 324, 370, 470, 471, 498, 609, 610, 616, 620, 628, 633, 634, 635, 636, 637
Dodan, 513 (*Fig. 67*)
Dohazari, 106, 108, 109, 112, 115, 121, 162, 167, 170, 175, 176, 325, 335, 434, 506, 507, 519, 527, 586, 587, 701 (*Figs. 13, 20, 65*)
Dokekan (nr. Tamandu), 494
Dollaung, 245 (*Figs. 26, 41*)
Donbaik, 103, 105, 110, 111, 112, 113, 114 (*Figs. 17, 63*)
Dongsum, 345 (*Figs. 36, 39*)
Duyinzeik (on the Thaton–Pa-an Road), 33, 39

INDEX

Elephant Point, 540, 541, 556 (*Fig. 71*)

Falam, 243, 245, 364, 368, 369 (*Figs. 26, 43*)
Farhadnagar (nr. Fenny), 100
Fazilpur (nr. Fenny), 100, 101
Fenny, 100 (*Fig. 13*)
Fenua (nr. Chittagong), 167
Fort Dufferin, Mandalay, 9, 68, 439, 440, 469
Fort Hertz, 16, 132, 177, 186, 260 (*Figs. 11, 13, 22, 23*)
Fort White, 139, 243, 245, 253, 254, 356, 363, 364, 371, 377, 378 (*Figs. 13, 26, 27, 29, 41*)
Foul Point, 103, 106, 474, 475, 480, 481, 510 (*Figs. 17, 63*)
Frederick Island (in Hunter's Bay), 483, 487
Frontier Hill (nr. Mowdok), 505, 507
Field Supply Depot (F.S.D.) Hill, Kohima, 268, 269, 271, 274, 275 (*Figs. 31, 32*)

Gangaw, 74, 365, 369, 392, 409, 410, 412, 426, 430 (*Figs. 13, 43, 46, 50, 56*)
Gangaw Valley, 380, 393, 394, 410
General Purpose Transport (G.P.T. Ridge, Kohima), 268, 274, 275, 277 (*Figs. 31, 32*)
Garrett's Garden (nr. Goppe, Arakan), 145, 167, 172
Garrison Hill, Kohima, 277 (*Figs. 31, 32, 33*)
Gauhati, 83, 92, 93, 171, 175, 176, 284, 325, 334, 525, 528, 574, 585, 586, 648, 698 (*Figs. 13, 83*)
Gaungbo 428 (*Fig. 54*)
Ghaspani 285 (*Fig. 35*)
Giffard, General Sir George 338, 390
Ginnapara 158, 478, 479 (*Fig. 15*)
Goalundo Ghat 106 (*Fig. 13*)
Gokteik Gorge 18 (*Fig. 46*)
Golaghat, 265, 283, 284, 285, 333, 373, 376, 526, 573 (*Fig. 13*)
Gonchwein, 502, 503, 556 (*Fig. 64*)
Goppe Bazar (Goppe), 103, 106, 113, 116, 117, 141, 142, 143, 144, 145, 149, 153, 157, 166, 167, 169, 174, 499, 513 (*Figs. 14, 19*)
Goppe Pass, 103, 106, 122, 141, 143, 158, 167, 499, 513, 698, 699, 700 (*Fig. 19*)
Govindpur (in the Fenny area), 103
Grikegyaung (in Garrett's Garden area), 167
Gwa, 523, 705 (*Fig. 62*)
Gwalior, 179, 181, 190
Gwegyo, 57, 533 (*Figs. 8, 46, 52*)
Gyethinka, 516 (*Fig. 68*)
Gyo, 441, 447 (*Figs. 49, 54, 55*)
Gyobingauk, 554 (*Fig. 73*)
Haflong (N.E. of Silchar), 585
Hailakandi (S.W. of Silchar), 191
Haka, 245, 364, 368 (*Figs. 13, 26, 43*)
'Hambone Feature' (between Litan and Sita), 315
'Hambone Feature' (in the Tunnels area, Maungdaw-Buthidaung Road), 161
Hathazari, 373, 587 (*Fig. 13*)
Heirok, 348, 350, 351 (*Figs. 30, 40*)
Henu, 468, 469 (*Fig. 61*)

Henzada, 18, 51, 395, 589 (*Fig. 6*)
Hesin, 263, 373, 374, 375 (*Fig. 12*)
Hill 60 (nr. Mogaung), 456
Hill 170 (nr. Kangaw), 484, 485
Hkanaunggyi, 110, 114 (*Fig. 15*)
Hlaingdet, 470 (*Fig. 60*)
Hlawga, 38, 40 (*Fig. 5*)
Hlegu, 38, 40, 45, 47, 538, 542, 544, 547, 552, 564 (*Figs. 5, 6, 71, 72*)
Hlezeik, 246 (*Fig. 12*)
Hmawbi, 547, 554, 555, 556, 557, 589, 595, 596, 597, 598 (*Figs. 5, 73*)
Hmawza, 53, 54, 63 (*Figs. 7, 9*)
Hngetpyawchaung, 516 (*Fig. 68*)
Homalin, 1, 77, 132, 243, 250, 344 (*Figs. 10, 11, 13, 23, 29, 56*)
Hong Kong, 4, 5, 566, 567, 568, 638, 673, 710
Honnaing, 375, 376 (*Fig. 12*)
Hopin, 91, 185, 391, 454, 468, 469 (*Figs. 22, 56, 61*)
Hopong, 59, 60 (*Figs. 13, 46*)
Hosi, 454 (*Fig. 56*)
Hparabyin, 115 (*Fig. 15*)
Hpaukpyin, 503 (*Fig. 62*)
Hpontha, 516 (*Figs. 62, 67, 68*)
Hpontha Chaung, 515, 516
Hsenwi, 454 (*Figs. 13, 56, 57*)
Hsipaw, 60, 454, 455 (*Figs. 13, 46, 56*)
Htinzin, 374, 375, 392, 405 (*Fig. 12*)
Htizwe, 110, 114, 146, 474, 510, 514 (*Figs. 15, 17, 63, 66, 67*)
Hukawng Valley, 2, 66, 84, 89, 91, 92, 95, 177, 178, 240, 698 (*Figs. 13, 22*)
Humine, 345 (*Fig. 39*)
Hump, The (the mountain range separating China from Burma and India), 101, 177, 247
Hunter's Bay, 481, 483, 487 (*Fig. 68*)
Hutton, Lieut.-General Sir Thomas, 94

Imphal, 2, 73, 77, 78, 83, 84, 89, 90, 91, 92, 101, 103, 138, 158, 171, 175, 176, 180, 185, 189, 191, 237, 243, 244, 246, 249, 250, 251, 252, 254, 255, 258, 260, 261, 262, 264, 265, 273, 276, 278, 282, 301, 303, 304, 306, 307, 309, 310 312, 313, 314, 315, 316, 318, 319, 320, 341, 342, 343, 348, 351, 355, 357, 361, 371, 373, 375, 376, 377, 378, 391, 407, 408, 412, 413, 439, 469, 526, 573, 574, 581, 584, 585, 589, 648, 652, 658, 668, 686, 702, 704 (*Figs. 10, 11, 13, 27, 28, 29, 30, 36, 42, 45, 56, 83*)
Imphal Keep, 301
Imphal Plain, 2, 84, 139, 217, 247, 248, 249, 252, 301, 303, 307, 317, 318, 321, 341, 355, 357, 368, 622, 702, 703 (*Fig. 27*)
Imphal-Bishenpur Track (or Road), 252, 301, 352
Imphal-Dimapur Road (*via* Kohima), 246, 301
Imphal-Kohima Road, 252, 267, 276, 277, 283, 285, 301, 302, 304, 306, 307, 311, 318, 319, 333, 341, 342, 345, 348, 351
Imphal-Palel Road (part of the Imphal-Tamu Road), 246, 259, 316, 526

Imphal–Tamu Road, 301, 303, 315, 316, 341, 348, 349, 350, 353, 356, 358, 373, 413, 703
Imphal–Tiddim Road, 245, 250, 254, 255, 256, 258, 262, 301, 303, 304, 305, 308, 309, 311, 314, 316, 319, 334, 352, 353, 354, 356, 358, 360, 362, 364, 377, 407, 624, 703
Imphal–Ukhrul Road, 246, 282, 301, 306, 313, 341, 344, 347
Inbaung, 82, 83, 89, 90, 375, 378, 379, 405, 407, 409, 559, 704 (*Figs. 12, 45, 47, 49*)
Indainggale, 378, 380
Indainggyi, 353, 372, 375, 573, 592, 599 (*Fig. 12*)
Indaw (Oil), 179 (*Figs. 10, 48*)
Indaw (Rail), 74, 140, 179, 181, 182, 185, 392, 393, 454, 457, 458 (*Figs. 11, 13, 23, 57, 61*)
Indawgyi Lake, 91, 182, 186, 192, 193, 209, 222, 239, 624, 702 (*Figs. 22, 56*)
Indian General Hospital (I.G.H.) Spur, Kohima, 267, 268, 269 (*Figs. 31, 32*)
Indian Medical Service, 8, 11
Indian refugees (from Burma), 41
Indin, 103, 106, 112, 113, 114 (*Figs. 15, 63, 67*)
Ingon (nr. Pinlebu, on the River Mu), 392
Ingon (S. of Mandalay, nr. Kyaukse), 467
Ingyingon, 469 (*Fig. 61*)
Inland Water Transport Sunderbans Flotilla, 101
Inlegyi, 400 (*Fig. 48*)
Insein, 9, 31, 588, 596 (*Figs. 2, 6*)
Intagaw, 542 (*Fig. 5*)
Inywa, 132 (*Figs. 11, 57*)
Iril Valley, 302, 305, 306, 307, 311, 341 (*Fig. 36*)
Irrawaddy Flotilla Company, 15, 43, 45

Jail Hill, Kohima, 267, 274, 275, 277 (*Figs. 31, 32*)
Jamuguri (nr. Dibrugarh), 265, 282
Java, 567, 674, 710
Jessami, 265, 274 (*Figs. 27, 29, 34*)
Jessami–Somra Track, 282
Jhansi, 178, 179, 180, 189
Jorhat, 175, 176, 252, 264, 273, 283, 284, 285, 333, 526, 550, 584, 585 (*Figs. 13, 23*)
Jotsoma, 266, 269, 270, 271, 273, 274, 276 (*Figs. 31, 33, 35*)
Jubbulpore, 178, 179 (*Fig. 70*)

Kabaing, 446 (*Fig. 55*)
Kabaw Valley (Death Valley), 1, 73, 77, 89, 95, 129, 245, 247, 252, 263, 353, 354, 363, 371, 372, 374, 375, 378, 380, 391, 397, 398, 406, 407, 624, 698, 704 (*Figs. 10, 12, 29*)
Kabo Weir, 396 (*Fig. 47*)
Kabwet, 400, 427 (*Figs. 48, 52, 55*)
Kachin Hills, 15 (*Fig. 57*)
Kachins, 20
Kadu, 457 (*Fig. 61*)
Kaduma, 73, 74, 89, 396, 398 (*Figs. 10, 46, 47, 48*)
Kaing, 77, 82 (*Fig. 52*)

Kaingngegyi (on the Taungup–Prome Track), 545
Kakching, 312, 313, 315, 348 (*Figs. 30, 40*)
Kalabon, 502 (*Fig. 64*)
Kaladan, 107, 153, 163, 165, 166 (*Figs. 15, 16, 66*)
Kaladan Valley, 2, 107, 112, 114, 139, 146, 152, 153, 162, 165, 166, 391, 474, 503, 504, 506, 510, 514, 649, 699, 700, 701
Kalapanzin Valley, 141, 142, 146, 152, 163, 165, 166, 170, 510, 698, 700 (*Figs. 15, 19, 67*)
Kalaw, 66, 67, 461, 470, 543, 544, 545, 547, 564, 581, 589, 590, 593, 596, 597, 600 (*Figs. 13, 46, 52, 60*)
Kalemyo, 74, 77, 243, 245, 351, 353, 354, 356, 357, 364, 371, 372, 374, 377, 378, 390, 391, 402, 413, 525, 623, 704 (*Figs. 10, 11, 12, 13, 26, 29, 41, 47, 56*)
Kalewa, 1, 60, 66, 72, 73, 74, 75, 76, 77, 81, 82, 83, 89, 90, 95, 101, 131, 180, 243, 364, 372, 375, 376, 380, 390, 391, 392, 395, 396, 402, 407, 435, 525, 561, 573, 585, 588, 589, 590, 591, 592, 594, 595, 596, 597, 598, 599, 600, 601, 622, 686, 704 (*Figs. 10, 11, 13, 26, 27, 29, 41, 45, 46, 47, 49, 56*)
Kalewa Gap, 247
Kama, 545, 547 (*Fig. 71*)
Kamaing, 186, 187, 193, 194, 223 (*Figs. 13, 22*)
Kameng, 305, 307, 311, 313, 314 (*Figs. 30, 36*)
Kamjong, 345 (*Fig. 39*)
Kamye, 436, 443, 550 (*Figs. 50, 54*)
Kan, 410, 412, 413, 430, 449 (*Figs. 43, 45, 46, 47, 50*)
Kaname (in the An area), 518
Kanbalu, 393, 396, 400 (*Figs. 47, 48, 57*)
Kanbyin, 110, 114 (*Figs. 15, 63*)
Kandaw 406, 469, 625 (*Figs. 49, 60*)
Kandaung (E. of Meiktila) 536, 551
Kangaw, 475, 476, 477, 478, 481, 483, 484, 485, 487, 488, 492, 493, 510, 511, 516, 521 (*Figs. 62, 68*)
Kangla (N. of Imphal) 585
Kanglatongbi, 81, 304, 306, 307, 316, 333 (*Figs. 27, 36*)
Kangpokpi, 261, 306, 341, 343, 345, 347 (*Figs. 35, 36*)
Kanhla, 412 (*Fig. 50*)
Kani (*Figs. 47, 48, 49, 50, 56*)
Kanlan (nr. Ngazun), 428
Kanna (W. of Meiktila), 437, 443
Kanni (nr. Kangaw), 516
Kansag (in the Kameng area), 314
Kanyindan, 109, 117, 158, 478, 479 (*Fig. 15*)
Kanyutkwin, 50 (*Fig. 9*)
Kanzauk, 146, 504, 513 (*Figs. 15, 17, 66, 67*)
Kanzauk Pass, 163, 474, 514
Kappagaung, 158 (*Fig. 15*)
Karachi, 696
Karen Hills, 543 (*Fig. 9*)
Karens, 20, 538
Karong, 306 (*Fig. 35*)
Kasom, 314 (*Figs. 36, 38, 39*)

Katha, 66, 67, 87, 89, 92, 131, 140, 393, 454, 456, 457, 462, 463, 464, 465, 468, 473, 527, 624 (*Figs. 11, 13, 23, 56, 57, 61*)
Kaukkwe, 538 (*Fig. 72*)
Kawkareik, 13, 14, 19, 29, 30, 31, 39 (*Fig. 2*)
Kawlin, 393, 396, 401, 402,407 (*Fig. 48*)
Kayugyaung, 147, 161, 167, 479 (*Fig. 48*)
Kazu, 454 (*Fig. 56*)
Kekrima, 278, 281 (*Fig. 34*)
Kemapyu, 19, 543 (*Fig. 9*)
Kengtung, 9, 10, 14, 19, 59, 60 (*Figs. 6, 13*)
Kennedy Peak, 245, 246, 254, 356, 357, 363, 391 (*Figs. 26, 27, 41*)
Kezoma, 278 (*Fig. 34*)
Kha Aimol, 309, 310 (*Fig. 36*)
Kha Khunou (on the Imphal-Tiddim Road), 352
Khampat, 82, 89, 90, 375, 406 (*Fig. 12*)
Khanda, 438 (*Fig. 54*)
Kharasom, 280, 281, 282, 343 (*Figs. 27, 29, 34, 39*)
Khongkhang, 259, 262, 263 (*Figs. 27, 30, 40*)
Khonwei, 165 (*Fig. 65*)
Khoirok, 352, 357 (*Fig. 36*)
Khuangkhan, 361 (*Fig. 42*)
Khudei Khulen, 349 (*Fig. 40*)
Khunthak, 312, 344, 345
Khurushkul Island (Mercy Island), 118, 144, 172, 175, 176, 325, 527 (*Fig. 14*)
Khuzami, 281, 282 (*Figs. 34, 35*)
Kidima (S.E. of Kohima and nr. Kekrima), 278, 279
Kigwema, 175, 176, 280, 281, 283, 342, 343 (*Fig. 35*)
Kindaung, 115, 513, 514 (*Figs. 15, 67*)
Kindaunggyi (Letpan area), 503, 518, 520
Kinnwe, 470 (*Fig. 58*)
Kin-U, 19, 89, 400, 401, 427 (*Figs. 46, 47, 48*)
Kinywa, 399, 447, 448, 451, 561 (*Fig. 54*)
Kirkee (nr. Poona), 696
Kodingauk, 110, 113 (*Figs. 15, 67*)
Kohima, 2, 84, 132, 171, 175, 176, 179, 185, 243, 244, 247, 251, 252, 253, 261, 264, 265, 266, 267, 268, 269, 270, 271, 272, 273, 274, 275, 276, 277, 278, 280, 281, 283, 284, 285, 301, 319, 333, 341, 342, 345, 347, 348, 352, 359, 410, 526, 573, 584, 649, 702 (*Figs. 11, 13, 27, 29, 31, 32, 34, 35, 56*)
Kohima Ridge, 253, 266, 267, 273
Kohima-Dimapur Road (*see* Dimapur-Kohima Road)
Kohima-Imphal Road (*see* Imphal-Kohima Road)
Kohima-Jessami Track, 246, 278, 279, 280, 282, 341, 348
Kokkogon, 400 (*Fig. 48*)
Kokkogwa, 56, 62 (*Figs. 8, 9*)
Kokngai, 344 (*Figs. 37, 39*)
Konbaung, 502 (*Fig. 64*)
Konbwe, 501, 502 (*Fig. 64*)
Konkha (nr. Yanbo), 468
Konmabein, 468, (*Fig. 58*)
Kongyi, 77 (*Fig. 48*)
Kota, 465, 468 (*Fig. 58*)
Kudaung Island, 474, 475, 480, 511 (*Figs. 17, 63*)

Kudaw, 403 (*Figs. 48, 50*)
Kuki Piquet, Kohima, 268, 269, 274, 275, 277 (*Figs. 31, 32*)
Kumai, 506, 507 (*Fig. 65*)
Kume, 441, 447, 461, 473 (*Figs. 46, 49, 52, 53, 54, 60*)
Kunchaung, 454, 464, 468, 470 (*Figs. 56, 57*)
Kundaung, 373 (*Fig. 10*)
Kungpi, 310, 311 (*Fig. 36*)
Kunming, (China, on the Mandalay-Chungking Road), 6, 19, 66
Kuntaung (N. of Tamu on the Moreh-Mintha Road), 246, 354
Kut Chaung (in the Ru-Ywa area), 517
Kutywa (in the Ru-Ywa area), 517
Kuzeik (on the Salween River opposite Pa-an), 33, 39
Kwazon, 154, 480, 481 (*Figs. 15, 19, 67*)
Kywedatson (nr. Meiktila), 470
Kwela-binga (E. of Maungdaw), 147
Kwetkwin, 404 (*Fig. 48*)
Kyaikhla, 38 (*Fig. 5*)
Kyaikto, 1, 32, 34, 35, 39, 544 (*Figs. 3, 6*)
Kya-In (in the Kunchaung area), 470
Kyaikthin, 393, 401 (*Figs. 10, 48, 57*)
Kyaukbyinzeik (in the Htizwe area), 114, 115
Kyaukchaw, 245, 263 (*Fig. 12*)
Kyaukgwe, 515 (*Fig. 62*)
Kyaukkale, 501 (*Fig. 64*)
Kyaukmaungnama (in the Letpan area), 503
Kyaukmaw, 470 (*Fig. 58*)
Kyaukme, 454, 455 (*Figs. 56, 60*)
Kyaukmyaung, 87, 408, 426, 427, 428, 439, 444 (*Figs. 48, 52, 55*)
Kyauknimaw, 502 (*Fig. 64*)
Kyaukpadaung (N. of the Yenangyaung and Chauk oilfields), 443, 532, 533 (*Figs. 6, 8, 46, 52, 71*)
Kyaukpadaung (nr. Thayetmyo), 17, 18, 52, 54, 55, 57, 58, 59, 60, 61, 64 (*Fig. 9*)
Kyaukpandu, 110 (*Figs. 15, 67*)
Kyaukpanduywama, 110, 113, 114 (*Figs. 15, 67*)
Kyaukpyu (nr. Twinnge), 470 (*Fig. 58*)
Kyaukpyu, Ramree Island, 3, 477, 499, 500, 501, 502, 503, 519, 520, 523, 527, 556, 561, 705 (*Figs. 62, 64, 74*)
Kyaukpyugon, 437 (*Fig. 54*)
Kyauksalaung (on the Yo Chaung), 516, 517
Kyaukse (N. of Sagaing), 398 (*Fig. 54*)
Kyaukse (S. of Mandalay), 61, 64, 65, 72, 428, 441, 447, 467, 530, 533, 534, 561, 624, 625 (*Figs. 46, 49, 52, 53, 54, 56, 60, 71*)
Kyauksedi, 374 (*Fig. 12*)
Kyauktalon, 442, 448 (*Figs. 53, 55*)
Kyauktan, 540, 541, 557 (*Figs. 5, 71*)
Kyauktaung (nr. Pyawbwe), 536
Kyauktaw, 107, 122, 146, 152, 153, 163, 165, 699 (*Figs. 13, 15, 66, 67*)
Kyaukye, 534 (*Fig. 8*)
Kyehmon, 74 (*Figs. 49, 54*)
Kyigon (nr. Inbaung), 375, 405, 406 (*Fig. 12*)
Kyigon (nr. Meiktila), 437, 438 (*Fig. 54*)
Kyin, 413 (*Figs. 50, 56*)
Kyingri, 165, 504, 507 (*Figs. 66, 67*)

INDEX

Kyondo (E. of Moulmein on the River Gyaing), 19, 29
Kyungyaung (in the Three Pagodas Pass area), 14
Kyunhla, 396 (*Figs. 47, 48*)
Kywegromaw, 480 (*Fig. 15*)
Kyweguseik, 511 (*Fig. 68*)
Kywegu, 518, 520 (*Fig. 62*)

Labawa, 505, 507 (*Figs. 21, 65*)
Lakhren (in the Kamaing area), 194, 223
Lainggwingyi Chaung (nr. Thaungdara), 114
Lalaghat, 180, 183, 185, 189, 191 (*Figs. 13, 27*)
Lalitpur (S. of Orchha), 190, 507
Lamu (nr. Letpan), 503
'Lancaster Gate', Kohima, 277 (*Fig. 31*)
Langthoubal (nr. Wangjing), 263, 313
Lashio, 6, 9, 18, 19, 31, 51, 60, 66, 67, 94, 130, 140, 177, 389, 391, 454 (*Figs. 11, 13, 46, 56, 57*)
Laung Chaung, 107, 145, 149, 154, 172, 173, 174 (*Fig. 19*)
Ledan Chaung, 469 (*Fig. 61*)
Ledaunggan (on the Zayatkin-Rangoon Road), 538
Ledo, 2, 84, 89, 92, 95, 129, 140, 177, 180, 182, 189, 192, 252, 283, 333, 336, 391, 455, 526, 585, 701 (*Figs. 11, 13, 22, 23, 83*)
Leese, Lieut.-General Sir Oliver, 547
Legyi, 397, 399 (*Figs. 53, 54*)
Leibi, 349 (*Figs. 30, 40*)
Leikchin, 398 (*Fig. 47*)
Leikkon, 34 (*Fig. 3*)
Leingthan, 507 (*Fig. 65*)
Leishan, 343 (*Figs. 35, 37, 39*)
Lentaigne, Major-General W. D. A., 187, 237
Letkapin, 404, 428 (*Fig. 55*)
Letkokpin, 468 (*Fig. 58*)
Letmauk, 478, 515, 517, 518 (*Fig. 62*)
Letpadan, 542, 554, 555, 589, 596 (*Figs. 5, 6, 73*)
Letpan, 477, 499, 502, 503, 520, 624 (*Fig. 62*)
Letpangya, 468 (*Fig. 58*)
Letpanywa (Taung Bazar area), 174
Letse, 434, 449 (*Fig. 52*)
Letwedet, 116, 141, 146, 152 (*Figs. 15, 19*)
Leu (on the Tamu-Pinlebu Road), 401
Lewe, 537, 563 (*Figs. 9, 71*)
Linbabi, 142 (*Fig. 19*)
Lingadipa, 447 (*Fig. 54*)
Litan, 244, 250, 252, 260, 262, 264, 301, 311, 314, 315 (*Figs. 27, 29, 36, 38, 39*)
Lohardaga, 147, 176, 528 (*Fig. 70*)
Loikaw, 59 (*Figs. 9, 13*)
Loilem, 10, 13, 19, 31, 44, 59, 60, 455, 543 (*Figs. 6, 13, 46*)
Lokchao, 82, 83, 90, 263, 349 (*Fig. 40*)
Longbi Kachui, 344 (*Figs. 37, 39*)
Lonkin, 182 (*Figs. 22, 23*)
Lucknow, 120, 696 (*Figs. 70, 83*)
Luinem, 343 (*Figs. 37, 39*)
Lumding, 585 (*Figs. 27*)
Lungleh, 172, 353, 367, 587 (*Figs. 13, 43*)
Lungling, 186, 391 (*Fig. 13*)
Lungshong, 345, 347 (*Figs. 38, 39*)
Lungtak, 361, 362 (*Figs. 41, 42*)
Lushai Hills, 265, 364, 366 (*Fig. 27*)

Mabein, 458, 462 (*Figs. 57, 58*)
MacArthur, General Douglas, 566
Madauk, 50 (*Fig. 5*)
Madaya, 18, 439, 444, 445, 446 (*Figs. 6, 11, 46, 52, 54, 56*)
Madras, 502, 523, 526, 557, 558, 705
Magwe, 14, 51, 55, 56, 57, 62, 64, 65, 534, 535, 553, 554, 556, 561, 583, 584, 588, 589, 590, 591, 592, 593, 594, 595, 599, 600 (*Figs. 1, 6, 8, 9, 13, 62, 71, 73, 74*)
Magyibin, 468 (*Fig. 58*)
Magyichaung, 106 (*Fig. 17*)
Mahlaing, 60, 65, 436, 437, 442, 443, 530 (*Figs. 46, 53, 54*)
Mahlainggon, 459, 465, 468 (*Fig. 58*)
Maingkwan, 140, 177, 182 (*Figs. 22, 23*)
Makauk (nr. Male on the Irrawaddy), 427
Male, 400, 426, 427 (*Figs. 46, 48, 57*)
Mandalay, 2, 3, 6, 8, 9, 10, 12, 13, 16, 17, 18, 19, 22, 31, 39, 42, 44, 45, 48, 51, 57, 59, 60, 61, 62, 64, 65, 66, 67, 68, 72, 85, 87, 89, 92, 94, 129, 130, 179, 182, 184, 232, 389, 390, 391, 393, 395, 396, 397, 410, 426, 427, 428, 432, 433, 439, 441, 442, 444, 446, 451, 453, 455, 460, 461, 469, 530, 531, 532, 561, 588, 589, 590, 592, 593, 594, 595, 596, 597, 598, 599, 601, 622, 697, 704, 705, 710 (*Figs. 1, 6, 11, 13, 46, 48, 49, 52, 53, 54, 55, 56, 60, 71*)
Mandalay Hill, 68, 439, 440
Manipur Road (*see* Dimapur) (*Fig. 11*)
Man Kang, 470 (*Fig. 60*)
Manwe (nr. Indawgyi Lake), 193
Mao Songsang, 278, 279, 280, 281 (*Figs. 34, 35*)
Mapao, 307 (*Fig. 36*)
Mapao Spur, 302, 304, 306
Maram, 278, 281, 342, 343, 345, 347, 348, 352 (*Figs. 34, 35, 39*)
Margherita, 92, 175, 176, 324, 467, 469, 584, 702 (*Fig. 11*)
Mariani, 265, 585 (*Fig. 23*)
Martaban, 11, 17, 29, 31, 32, 33, 39, 42 (*Fig. 2*)
Mathabhanga (E. of Nhila), 113, 116, 121
Ma-U, 74 (*Figs. 48, 50*)
Maukkadaw, 403, 404, 406 (*Figs. 47, 49*)
Maungdaw, 103, 106, 108, 109, 110, 112, 113, 114, 115, 116, 117, 120, 141, 146, 147, 149, 153, 158, 160, 167, 169, 474, 475, 478, 479, 510, 513, 514, 519, 527, 586, 700 (*Figs. 13, 15, 19*)
Maunggyihtaung, 141 (*Fig. 15*)
Maunghnama, 145, 149, 152, 173 (*Fig. 19*)
Mawchi, 19, 38, 59, 544, 547, 548, 564, 598 (*Figs. 6, 9, 71, 72*)
Mawhun, 454, 457, 469 (*Figs. 56, 57, 61*)
Mawku, 375 (*Fig. 12*)
Mawlaik, 372, 375, 392, 396, 402, 405, 704 (*Figs. 10, 12, 13, 41, 49, 56*)

Mawlu, 184, 216, 454, 463, 468, 631 (*Figs. 56, 57, 61*)
Mayin, 501, 502, 503 (*Fig. 64*)
Maymyo, 4, 8, 12, 18, 19, 31, 43, 44, 45, 47, 49, 51, 60, 66, 67, 68, 85, 86, 87, 89, 389, 390, 441, 461, 466, 470, 471, 530, 588, 592, 593, 595, 599, 600, 601, 697 (*Figs. 6, 11, 13, 46, 52, 60*)
Maynamati, 100, 103, 108, 118, 167, 172, 175, 176, 528, 586, 587 (*Fig. 13*)
Mayu Peninsula, 2, 101, 103, 110, 111, 140, 474, 475, 510 (*Fig. 63*)
Mayu Range, 103, 106, 109, 110, 112, 114, 115, 141, 142, 143, 144, 146, 148, 149, 151, 152, 157, 158, 160, 163, 170, 475, 665, 700 (*Fig. 15*)
Mayu Valley, 474, 510
Main Dressing Station (M.D.S.) Hill, Sinzweya, 149, 152, 155, 156
Me Chaung (in the Tamandu area), 494, 495
Medical Advisory Division, S.A.C.S.E.A., 416–419
Mehpauk (S. of Buthidaung), 513
Meiktila, 2, 7, 8, 10, 12, 17, 18, 19, 31, 44, 49, 51, 60, 61, 64, 65, 67, 86, 87, 89, 393, 395, 412, 428, 430, 433, 434, 435, 437, 438, 439, 441, 443, 444, 449, 450, 453, 461, 467, 469, 470, 471, 530, 531, 532, 534, 535, 536, 537, 543, 544, 547, 550, 553, 554, 555, 559, 561, 563, 564, 574, 580, 581, 582, 583, 588, 589, 590, 591, 592, 593, 594, 595, 596, 597, 598, 599, 600, 601, 642, 647, 706, 710 (*Figs. 6, 13, 46, 49, 52, 53, 60, 71, 73, 74*)
Meiring, 345 (*Figs. 36, 39*)
Merema Ridge, 274 (*Fig. 35*)
Mergui, 1, 9, 13, 14, 18, 19, 20, 29 (*Fig. 2*)
Messervy, Lieut.-General Sir Frank, 391
Midnapore, 175, 176, 528 (*Fig. 70*)
Migyaungye, 56 (*Fig. 6*)
Milawa (nr. Paletwa on the Kaladan), 165 (*Fig. 66*)
Minbu, 545 (*Figs. 9, 62, 71*)
Minbya, 100, 390, 474, 510 (*Figs. 17, 67, 68*)
Minbyin, 501, 502, 527 (*Fig. 64*)
Mingan (E. of Taungtha), 436
Mingaladon, 8, 12, 19, 31, 48, 541, 552, 557, 565, 582, 583 (*Figs. 5, 71*)
Mingon, 467, 468, 470 (*Figs. 58, 61*)
Minhla, 56 (*Figs. 9, 62*)
Minhla Chaung (nr. Letpadan), 542
Mintha (on the Tamu–Homalin Road), 354
Minzegyaung, 513 (*Fig. 67*)
Mla (in the Mogaung area), 223
Mogaung, 89, 92, 140, 177, 186, 187, 188, 192, 194, 209, 221, 223, 234, 454, 456, 463, 467, 469, 624 (*Figs. 11, 13, 22, 23, 56, 61*)
Mogok, 60, 389, 391, 454, 460, 466, 468, 470 (*Figs. 46, 56, 57, 60*)
Mohauk (in the Mong Mit area), 470
Mohnyin, 67, 87, 91, 198, 454, 457, 469 (*Figs. 11, 56, 57, 61*)
Moirang, 305, 308, 309, 352 (*Figs. 30, 36*)
Mokokchung, 265, 282, 284 (*Fig. 13*)
Mokpalin, 18, 35, 36, 37, 39, 40, 543, 544, 547 (*Figs. 4, 72*)
Mokso Sakan (nr. Lake Indawgyi), 222

Mollen, 343, 344 (*Figs. 37, 39*)
Molvom, 307 (*Fig. 36*)
Momauk, 454 (*Fig. 56*)
Mombi, 361 (*Fig. 42*)
Mong Long, 461, 463, 466, 469 (*Fig. 60*)
Mong Mit, 132, 391, 454, 455, 458, 459, 460, 466, 468, 470 (*Figs. 11, 13, 46, 56, 57, 58, 60*)
Monywa, 18, 19, 64, 66, 67, 72, 74, 80, 81, 86, 87, 88, 404, 405, 406, 446, 447, 599, 622 (*Figs. 11, 46, 47, 48, 49, 50, 52, 53, 54, 56*)
Moradabad, India, 121, 696
Moreh, 250, 252, 258, 259, 262, 263, 350, 373, 375, 378, 405, 525, 526, 584, 585 (*Figs. 27, 30, 36, 40*)
Morris, Lieut.-Colonel J. N., 201
Moulmein, 1, 9, 11, 13, 14, 15, 17, 18, 19, 20, 29, 31, 32, 39, 42, 48, 49, 538, 539, 541 (*Figs. 1, 2*)
Mountbatten, Admiral Lord Louis (Earl), 2, 140, 187, 342, 416–419
Mount Popa, 59, 64, 532, 533 (*Figs. 8, 46, 52, 54*)
Mowdok, 165, 172, 503, 504, 506, 507, 509 (*Figs. 14, 16, 21, 65*)
Mowdok Taung, 505
Mutaik, 398 (*Fig. 47*)
Myadaung, 470 (*Fig. 57*)
Myauk Chaung (in the Ru-Ywa area), 517
Myaukkon, 410 (*Fig. 50*)
Myaung, 446 (*Fig. 54*)
Myaungtanga (in the Hmawbi area), 558
Myawadi, 19, 29 (*Fig. 2*)
Myebon, 474, 477, 478, 481, 483, 484, 485, 487, 488, 489, 490, 493, 516 (*Figs. 62, 68*)
Myebon Peninsula, 473, 475, 481, 483, 511
Myemun, 400, 402 (*Fig. 48*)
Myinbu, 113, 114 (*Fig. 15*)
Myingyan, 17, 49, 64, 65, 66, 67, 393, 395, 434, 435, 442, 449, 530, 532, 533, 581, 582, 588, 589, 590, 592, 593, 594, 595, 596, 597, 599, 600, 625, 686 (*Figs. 6, 13, 46, 49, 52, 53, 54, 71*)
Myinmu, 19, 72, 80, 81, 404, 406, 408, 439 (*Figs. 46, 48, 52, 53, 54, 55*)
Myintha, 410 (*Fig. 50*)
Myinthi, 65, 448 (*Fig. 53*)
Myitche, 412, 413, 430, 449, 450, 527, 554, 559, 561, 563 (*Figs. 49, 50, 51, 74*)
Myitkyina, 2, 18, 19, 60, 62, 66, 67, 68, 77, 78, 84, 85, 86, 87, 92, 94, 129, 140, 177, 179, 182, 184, 185, 186, 192, 194, 209, 232, 391, 454, 455, 456, 463, 467, 469, 561, 585, 697, 698, 701, 702 (*Figs. 11, 13, 22, 23, 56*)
Myitson, 454, 455, 458, 459, 462, 465, 466, 468 (*Figs. 56, 57, 58, 59*)
Myitta, 19 (*Fig. 2*)
Myitta Defile, 461
Myittha, 74, 428, 534 (*Figs. 53, 54*)
Myittha Valley, 72, 77, 366, 368, 369
Myohaung, 474, 475, 504, 510, 511, 514 (*Figs. 17, 62, 66, 67*)
Myotha, 441, 442, 448, 625 (*Figs. 46, 52, 53, 54*)
Myothit (nr. Bhamo), 391, 454 (*Figs. 56, 57*)

INDEX

Myothit (nr. Palel and Sittaung), 250, 263 (*Figs. 27, 29*)
Myothit (nr. Shwebo), 400
Myothit (nr. Taungdwingyi), 64, 65 (*Fig. 8*)
Mugs, 122, 699

Naba, 77, 88, 393, 454, 631 (*Fig. 11*)
Nabu, 470 (*Figs. 57, 58*)
Naf Peninsula, 701
Naga Hills (to the east of the Kohima–Imphal Road), 282
Naga Village, Kohima, 267, 274, 276, 277 (*Figs. 31, 32, 33, 35*)
Naga Village, Ramree Island, 502
Nagas, 20, 271, 274, 277, 299, 347, 348
Naleik (in the Kaladan Valley), 507
Nalong, 391, 454 (*Figs. 56, 57*)
Namaan (nr. Mohnyin), 198
Namhkam, 86, 98, 99, 454 (*Figs. 13, 56, 57*)
Namhpakka, 545 (*Fig. 56*)
Namhsan, 454 (*Fig. 56*)
Namkum, 176, 528 (*Fig. 70*)
Namkwin, 469 (*Fig. 61*)
Namma, 468, 469 (*Fig. 61*)
Nammawngun (nr. Takaw), 10, 13
Nammeik Chaung, 459, 465 (*Fig. 59*)
Nampadaung, 467 (*Fig. 61*)
Namsang (on the Lashio Road, N. of Loilem), 31
Namsaw, 463, 470, 471 (*Fig. 60*)
Namtu, 67, 454 (*Figs. 11, 56*)
Namudwe, 502 (*Fig. 64*)
Namyin Chaung (nr. Mogaung), 463
Nanbon (on the Sittaung–Pinlebu Road), 392
Nankan (on the railway nr. Wuntho), 393
Nanmunta Chaung (in the Imphal area), 246
Nan Pon Pon, 465 (*Fig. 58*)
Natmauk 56, 64, 65, 534, 535, 553, 555 (*Figs. 8, 9, 73*)
Natogyi, 442, 533 (*Figs. 53, 54, 71*)
Nawapara, 109, 121, 145, 173 (*Fig. 14*)
Nawrondaung, 147, 479 (*Fig. 15*)
Nazira (S. of Dibrugarh), 265, 282
Neamati (nr. Jorhat), 333
Neyinzaya Chaung (in Kabaw Valley), 379
Ngakyedauk, 141 (*Figs. 15, 19*)
Ngakyedauk Chaung, 141, 144, 153, 154, 155, 168 (*Fig. 19*)
Ngakyedauk Pass, 103, 112, 116, 141, 144, 145, 146, 147, 149, 151, 153, 154, 156, 157, 158, 159, 160, 166, 167, 169, 173, 174, 700 (*Fig. 19*)
Ngame, 166 (*Fig. 16*)
Ngasha, 506 (*Fig. 66*)
Ngathayauk, 432, 436, 443 (*Figs. 8, 46*)
Ngawar, 343, 347 (*Figs. 35, 37, 39*)
Ngazun, 432, 433, 439, 442, 447, 448, 624 (*Figs. 49, 52, 53, 54, 55*)
Nhila, 113, 116, 139, 147, 173, 481, 520 (*Figs. 14, 15*)
Nichuguard Pass (S.E. of Dimapur), 265, 266
Nicobar Islands, 93, 673
Ningthoukhong, 304, 308, 309, 351, 352, 358 (*Figs. 30, 36*)
North Island, Maungdaw, 116, 117

Nowgong (S. of Tezpur, on the railway), 179, 585
Nungshigum, 301, 305, 306 (*Fig. 36*)
Nungtak, 350 (*Figs. 30, 40*)
Nyaungbinwun, 397 (*Figs. 48, 54*)
Nyaunggyat (nr. Kandaw), 469
Nyaunggyaung (in the Kanyindan area), 478
Nyaungkashe (nr. the western end of the Sittang Bridge), 40, 544, 547, 548
Nyaunglebin, 34, 38, 395, 530, 538, 582, 583, 625 (*Figs. 5, 6, 71, 72*)
Nyaungu, 430, 431, 434, 436, 437, 443, 534, 581 (*Figs. 50, 52*)

Obin Taung (nr. Kangaw), 485
Oinam, 310, 343, 347 (*Figs. 35, 39*)
Okkan, 542 (*Fig. 5*)
Okpo, 53 (*Figs. 6, 9*)
Okshitpin, 544 (*Fig. 9*)
Oktaung, 154 (*Fig. 19*)
Oktwin, 538 (*Figs. 9, 71*)
Onbaung, 469 (*Fig. 61*)
Ondaw, 64, 72, 80, 397, 399, 408, 450 (*Figs. 6, 46, 53, 54, 55*)
Ongshim, 345 (*Fig. 39*)
Operation
    'Birdcage', 566
    'Capital', 389, 390
    'Dracula', 389, 390, 539, 540
    'Mastiff', 566
    'Multivite', 409
    'Overlord', 662
    'Stepsister', 12
    'Thursday', 177–241
    'Zipper', 673
Orchha (nr. Jhansi), 180, 190
Oukrophoku, 279 (*Fig. 34*)
Oyin (E. of Ngathayauk, on the Taungtha Road), 436

Pa-an, 32, 33, 39 (*Fig. 2*)
Padali, 481 (*Fig. 63*)
Padigahtawng (in the Mogaung area), 223
Padin (in the Magwe area), 582
Pado (nr. Penwegon), 548
Padu, 397 (*Fig. 48*)
Pagan, 410, 412, 431, 432, 434, 449, 532 (*Figs. 50, 52, 71*)
Pagoda Hill (nr. the Sittang Bridge), 35 (*Fig. 4*)
Pahok, 194, 467, 469 (*Figs. 22, 61*)
Pakokku, 16, 74, 390, 391, 393, 409, 410, 412, 426, 428, 430, 431, 432, 442, 532, 561, 706 (*Figs. 13, 46, 49, 50, 52, 53, 54, 71*)
Paledaung (nr. Taung Bazar), 168
Palel, 83, 90, 175, 244, 247, 249, 252, 258, 259, 260, 261, 262, 263, 301, 303, 304, 305, 309, 311, 312, 315, 324, 334, 345, 348, 350, 361, 362, 371, 373, 374, 375, 378, 379, 412, 413, 443, 525, 526, 550, 585 (*Figs. 10, 13, 27, 29, 30, 36, 40, 42, 45*)
Palel Keep, 303, 311
Palel–Tamu Road, 262, 374, 375, 379
Palel–Wangjing Road, 261

INDEX 733

Paletwa, 107, 165, 391, 474, 504, 507 (*Figs. 13, 16, 65, 66*)
Palu (S.E. of Myawadi on the River Thaungyin), 29
Palusawa, 396 (*Figs. 47, 48, 50*)
Panghkam (nr. Namhkam), 13
Pangsau Pass (between the Hukawng Valley and the Ledo Road), 89
Panitola (nr. Ledo), 192, 206, 324, 333, 526, 701
Panmyaung, 514 (*Fig. 66*)
Pantha, 75, 406, 704 (*Figs. 10, 11, 12*)
Panzai Bazar, 115 (*Fig. 14*)
Paoshan, 6, 129, 132, 140, 177 (*Figs. 11, 13*)
Paowi, 344 (*Figs. 37, 39*)
Pashong, 345 (*Fig. 39*)
Patchaung (in the Kandaw area), 469
Patiagaon (nr. Jorhat), 526
Patkai Range (to the west of Lake Indawgyi), 193
Pathin, 470 (*Fig. 58*)
Patia, 165, 373, 587 (*Fig. 65*)
Pauk, 72, 409, 412, 414, 426, 442, 573 (*Figs. 46, 50, 52, 56*)
Paukkaung, 54, 545 (*Fig. 7*)
Pauktabin, 470 (*Fig. 58*)
Paungbyin, 78 (*Figs. 10, 11, 23, 56*)
Paungde, 53, 542, 547, 555, 556, 588, 592 (*Figs. 6, 9*)
Paunggwe Chaung, 57 (*Fig. 8*)
Payagale (nr. Payagyi), 538
Payagyi, 38, 538, 544, 563, 565, 582 (*Figs. 5, 72*)
Payan (nr. Shwebo), 397
Payangazu, 598
Pazinchaung, 470 (*Fig. 58*)
'Peacehaven Box' (on the Imphal-Tamu Road), 260, 312, 315
'Pear Hill' (in the vicinity of the Kyaukmyaung bridgehead across the Irrawaddy), 427
Pegu, 1, 3, 17, 18, 33, 35, 38, 39, 40, 49, 65, 530, 538, 539, 542, 544, 547, 552, 563, 564, 565, 582, 583, 588, 589, 591, 592, 593, 594, 595, 596, 597, 598, 599, 600, 601, 697 (*Figs. 5, 6, 71, 72*)
Pegu Yomas, 16, 38, 51, 543, 544, 545, 546, 547, 548, 556, 647 (*Figs. 5, 9, 72*)
Penang, Malaya, 567, 674
Penwegon, 538, 548, 565, 566, 588, 589, 590, 592, 596, 599 (*Fig. 72*)
Phabyo (nr. Kangaw, on the Lemro), 516 (*Fig. 68*)
Phakekedzumi, 251, 282 (*Figs. 29, 34*)
Phekerkrima (W. of Khuzami on the Imphal–Kohima Road), 282
Phom Penh, Indo-China, 567, 570
'Piccadilly', 181, 183 (*Fig. 23*)
Pi-Chaung, 163, 165, 504, 514 (*Figs. 15, 16, 66, 67*)
Piquet Hill, Kohima, 277 (*Figs. 31, 32*)
'Pimple Hill', Kohima, 275 (*Figs. 31, 32*)
Pinbaw, 221, 454, 468 (*Figs. 22, 56, 61*)
Pinbon, 392, 401 (*Figs. 10, 13, 57*)
Pin Chaung, 18, 57, 58, 59, 63, 64 (*Figs. 8, 9, 46*)

Pindale, 441 (*Figs. 53, 54*)
Pinkan, 470 (*Fig. 58*)
Pinlebu, 392, 393, 400, 401 (*Figs. 10, 56*)
Pintha (nr. Pinlebu on the River Mu), 392
Pintin, 470 (*Fig. 61*)
Pinwe, 391, 393, 454, 457, 468, 470, 471, 473 (*Figs. 56, 57, 61*)
'Point' 551, 105, 112, 153, 475 (*Fig. 19*)
Ponhon, 469 (*Fig. 61*)
Ponnaz (in the Maungdaw area), 147
Ponnazeik (in the Maungdaw area), 116, 117
Poona, 93, 467, 469, 648, 651
Port Dickson, Malaya, 567
Port Swettenham, Malaya, 567
Potsangbam, 304, 305, 309, 352, 358 (*Figs. 30, 36*)
Prinkhaung, 142, 143, 166 (*Figs. 14, 19*)
Priphema, 267, 284, 285 (*Fig. 35*)
Prome, 1, 3, 16, 18, 40, 42, 43, 44, 45, 46, 47, 48, 49, 50, 51, 52, 53, 54, 55, 61, 62, 63, 65, 66, 106, 476, 477, 535, 542, 544, 545, 547, 554, 556, 561, 583, 584, 588, 590, 593, 594, 596, 599 (*Figs. 6, 7, 9, 62, 71, 73*)
Pruma Chaung, 113, 116, 645, 703 (*Fig. 14*)
Pulebadze, 267, 274 (*Fig. 31*)
Pumsin, 177, (*Fig. 22*)
Pungdongbam (nr. Litan), 314
Pyagyaung, 468 (*Fig. 57*)
Pyalo, 55 (*Fig. 9*)
Pyawbwe, 7, 530, 535, 536, 537, 559, 592, 599 (*Figs. 46, 52, 60, 71*)
Pyawnghkawng (in the Mandalay-Maymyo area), 470
Pyinbin (nr. Taungtha), 443
Pyinbongyi, 538, 544, 547 (*Fig. 5*)
Pyinchaung, 412 (*Fig. 50*)
Pyingaing, 74, 75, 76, 81, 82, 89, 392, 396, 398, 598 (*Figs. 10, 11, 46, 47, 49*)
Pyinhla (in the Saingdin Chaung area), 166
Pyinma Chaung (N.W. of Kyaukpadaung), 533
Pyinmana, 1, 17, 51, 52, 56, 59, 530, 535, 537, 538, 552, 563 (*Figs. 6, 9, 13, 71, 72*)
Pyinwin (nr. Letpan, Arakan), 503
Pyinyaung, 461 (*Fig. 60*)
Pyinzi, 441, 442, 449 (*Figs. 53, 54*)
Pyu, 38, 50, 530, 538, 544, 593, 594 (*Figs. 6, 9, 71, 72*)
Pyu Chaung, 548

Quebec Conference, 140, 179, 180, 236
Queen Alexandra's Imperial Military Nursing Service (Q.A.I.M.N.S.), 8

Ramgarh, Bihar, 101, 129, 177
Ramree, 477, 499, 502, 520 (*Figs. 62, 64*)
Ramree Island, 477, 499, 500, 502, 515, 519, 520, 523, 524, 527, 540, 705, 710 (*Figs. 6, 62, 64*)
Ramu, 108, 115, 121, 158, 170, 701 (*Figs. 13, 14, 65*)
Ramkhlau, 369 (*Fig. 26*)
Ranchi, 93, 100, 101, 139, 171, 176, 243, 373, 391, 412, 528, 648, 697 (*Fig. 70*)

Rangoon, 1, 2, 3, 4, 5, 9, 10, 11, 12, 13, 14, 19, 20, 31, 32, 33, 37, 38, 39, 40, 41, 42, 43, 46, 48, 50, 51, 59, 65, 73, 94, 389, 394, 455, 461, 520, 530, 531, 537, 538, 539, 540, 541, 542 543, 544, 546, 547, 550, 554, 555, 556, 557, 558, 561, 563, 565, 566, 580, 581, 582, 588, 589, 590, 591, 592, 593, 594, 595, 596, 597, 598, 599, 600, 601, 647, 674, 697, 710, 711 (*Figs. 1, 2, 5, 71, 72, 73*)
Ranking, Major-General R. P. L., 265
Raongpara, 165 (*Figs. 14, 20*)
Rathedaung, 106, 107, 110, 111, 112, 113, 114, 481, 510, 513 (*Figs. 13, 15, 17, 63, 67*)
Ratu Piska (nr. Ranchi), 528
Razabil, 141, 146, 147, 148, 151, 152, 158, 479, 481, 510, 513, 520 (*Fig. 19*)
Recovered Allied Prisoners of War and Internees (R.A.P.W.I.), 561, 567, 569, 710, 711
Red Cross, 570
Redwinbyin (nr. Maungdaw), 169, 519, 520
Reinforcement Camp, Kohima, 253
Remyet Chaung (in the Htizwe area), 114
Ruma, 507 (*Figs. 20, 21, 65*)
Rumkhapalong, 117, 121. 143 (*Figs. 14, 65*)
Ru-Ywa, 477, 478, 489, 490, 492, 493, 494, 495, 511, 516, 519, 520 (*Fig. 62*)

Rivers
  Beltang Lui, 356 (*Fig. 41*)
  Bilin, 18, 33, 34, 35, 39, 42 (*Fig. 3*)
  Brahmaputra, 93, 180, 185, 193, 247, 525, 702 (*Figs. 11, 13, 70*)
  Chindwin, 1, 2, 15, 16 18, 19, 66, 72, 73, 74, 75, 76, 77, 81, 89, 91, 92, 101, 129, 131, 132, 138, 140, 180, 182, 237, 239, 243, 246, 247, 250, 251, 252, 263, 270, 341, 345, 349, 353, 364, 372, 375, 376, 380, 389, 391, 392, 393, 396, 398, 400, 401, 404, 405, 406, 410, 426, 525, 531, 539, 622, 703, 704 (*Figs. 10, 11, 12, 13, 23, 26, 27, 29, 41, 46, 47, 48, 49, 50, 52, 53, 54, 56*)
  Hlaing (Rangoon), 17, 38, 532, 540, 541, 556, 557 (*Fig. 2*)
  Iril (running southwards parallel to the Kohima–Imphal Road), 301, 302, 305, 312, 345
  Irrawaddy, 3, 15, 16, 17, 18, 19, 39, 40, 51, 52, 56, 57, 60, 61, 72, 87, 92, 130, 131, 132, 186, 389, 390, 393, 396, 399, 400, 404, 406, 410, 412, 426, 427, 428, 430, 431, 432, 433, 434, 440, 442, 443, 444, 446, 447, 448, 454, 458, 468, 470, 525, 530, 535, 542, 543, 544, 545, 546, 706 (*Figs. 6, 7, 8, 9, 11, 13, 46, 48, 49, 50, 52, 53, 54, 55, 56, 57, 58, 60, 62, 71, 73*)
  Kaladan, 103, 107, 122, 163, 165, 166, 473, 474, 513 (*Figs. 15, 16, 17, 21, 63, 65, 66, 67, 68*)
  Kalapanzin (the Mayu above Buthidaung), 103, 141, 142, 144, 153, 166, 168, 510, 513, 514 (*Figs. 15, 19, 67*)
  Kamaing (in the far north of Burma), 193, 194
  Lemro, 514, 515 (*Figs. 17, 66, 67, 68*)

Manipur, 77, 247, 250, 256, 309, 354, 355, 356, 360, 361, 362, 377 (*Figs. 26, 27, 28, 29, 41, 42*)
Mayu, 101, 103, 106, 109, 112, 113, 114, 122, 474, 475, 510 (*Figs. 15, 17, 63, 67*)
Mogaung (in the far north of Burma), 185, 240, 463
Mu, 19, 392, 396, 404 (*Figs. 10, 46, 47, 54, 57*)
Myitnge, 18, 72, 442 (*Figs. 46, 53*)
Myittha. 353, 365, 372, 374, 413 (*Figs. 10, 12, 26, 29, 41, 46, 50, 56*)
Naf, 106, 108, 109, 112, 115, 122, 143, 147, 153, 161, 170, 474, 520, 698, 701, 703 (*Fig. 15*)
Pegu (Pegu is on its banks), 538, 539, 542, 552
Salween, 1, 6, 9, 10, 14, 15, 16, 19, 32, 180, 186, 455 (*Figs. 6, 9, 11, 13, 56*)
Sangu, 165, 506 (*Figs. 14, 20, 21, 65*)
Shweli, 239, 455, 459, 465 (*Figs. 57, 58, 59*)
Sittang, 1, 3, 11, 15, 16, 18, 19, 34, 36, 37, 38, 52, 59, 538, 543, 544, 547, 548, 549, 565 (*Figs. 4, 5, 6, 9, 72*)
Uyu, 91 (*Figs. 10, 29*)
Yu, 75, 372, 375 (*Fig. 10*)

Sabagyi (between Ru-Ywa and An), 517
Sabaigon (North & South), 139, 145, 173 (*Fig. 14*)
Sabyin (nr. Letpan), 503
Sadalin (on the Zayatkwin–Rangoon Road), 538
Sadaung (N. of Sagaing), 397, 398, 399. 408 409, 446, 447, 448, 450, 527, 583 (*Figs. 46, 47, 48, 49, 51, 53, 54, 55*)
Sadaung (S. of Yindaw), 536
Sadaw (in the vicinity of Palel), 263
Saddle, The (on the Imphal–Litan Road), 260, 345 (*Fig. 38*)
Saddle, The (between Kohima Ridge and the Naga Village, Kohima), 267
Sado (in the Mandalay area), 442
Sadwingyi, 393, 400 (*Fig. 48*)
Safarmaina, 307 (*Fig. 36*)
Sagaing, 18, 19, 43, 64, 65, 67, 72, 74, 80, 81, 87, 89, 397, 398, 427, 432, 442, 446, 592, 625 (*Figs. 6, 46, 48, 52, 53, 54, 55*)
Sagaing Hills, 398, 408, 432, 439
Sagu Kyun, 501, 502 (*Fig. 64*)
Sahmaw, 386 454, 456, 462, 463, 464, 467, 468, 469, 471 (*Figs. 56, 61*)
Sahmaw Chaung, 467
Saigon, 567, 570, 674, 711
Saingdin Chaung, 166, 513, 514 (*Figs. 15, 67*)
Sainggaung (nr. Kin-U), 400
Saiyapaw, 344 (*Fig. 39*)
Saizang, 254, 363, 364 (*Figs. 26, 27, 41*)
Sakawng, 256 (*Fig. 28*)
Sakok, 345 (*Figs. 36, 39*)
Salin, 534 (*Fig. 8*)
Sameikkon Ferry, 72, 404 (*Fig. 53*)
Sandoway, 518, 520 (*Figs. 9, 62*)
Sane, 502, 503 (*Fig. 64*)
Sangshak, 250. 252, 345 (*Figs. 27, 29, 36, 38*)

INDEX

Sangu Valley, 153, 165, 504, 700, 701
Sapam, 318 (*Figs. 36, 40*)
Satpangon, 428 (*Fig. 54*)
Satpaung, 162, 163, 165, 505, 507 (*Figs. 16, 21, 65, 66*)
Satthwa, 55, 534, 535 (*Fig. 9*)
Satthwagyon (nr. Nyaungkashe), 548
Saugor, 101, 130, 179 (*Fig. 70*)
Sawleng, 368 (*Fig. 43*)
Sawombung (N.E. of Imphal), 260, 313
Scoones, Lieut. General Sir Geoffry, 302, 304, 306
Secunderabad, 697 (*Fig. 70*)
Sedaw (W. of Meiktila), 436
Seikpyu, 61, 409, 412, 530, 533 (*Fig. 52*)
Seiktein, 436 (*Fig. 54*)
Seinnyinbya, 479, 480 (*Fig. 67*)
Sengmai, 307 (*Fig. 36*)
Sengmai Turel, 350 (*Fig. 40*)
Seywa (W. of Ngathayauk on the Ngaungu-Meiktila Road), 436
Shadaw, 470 (*Fig. 58*)
Shaduzup, 177, 187, 194 (*Fig. 22*)
Shan Hills, 543
Shenam, 243, 244, 245, 250, 252, 258, 260, 262, 263, 303, 312, 313, 348, 350 (*Figs. 27, 29, 30, 36, 40*)
Shenam Pass, 305
Shillong, 81, 84, 92, 161, 171, 176, 187, 245, 325, 326, 336, 350, 467, 574, 582, 584, 585, 586, 698, 699 (*Fig. 13*)
Shingbwiyang, 92, 177, 192 (*Figs. 13, 22, 23*)
Shorbung, 345 (*Figs. 35, 39*)
Shoukchron, 516 (*Fig. 68*)
Shuganu, 244, 260, 261, 303, 305, 309, 355, 361 (*Figs. 10, 30, 40, 42*)
Shwebo, 18, 19, 64, 66, 77, 80, 85, 86, 87, 89, 92, 130, 391, 395, 396, 397, 398, 399, 400, 402, 405, 407, 408, 409, 426, 427, 444, 450, 527, 561, 585, 591, 598, 622, 625, 697 (*Figs. 11, 13, 46, 47, 48, 49, 51, 52, 55, 56*)
Shwebo Plain, 390, 393, 395, 396
Shwedaik (in the Shwebo–Singu area), 444
Shwedaung, 52, 53, 62, 542, 545, 546, 547 (*Figs. 6, 7, 9, 73*)
Shwegu, 449, 454 (*Figs. 56, 57*)
Shwegyin, 73, 74, 81, 82, 85, 89, 94, 372 (*Figs. 10, 11, 41, 46*)
Shwegyin (nr. Nyaunglebin), 50 (*Fig. 72*)
Shwemyo, 537 (*Fig. 71*)
Shwemyo Bluff, 537, 563
Shwenyaung, 10, 17 (*Fig. 46*)
Sibong, 259, 349, 350 (*Figs. 27, 30, 40*)
Sibsargar, (N.E. of Jorhat), 175, 176
Sikaw, 454 (*Fig. 56*)
Silchar, 175, 176, 217, 252, 334, 368, 528, 584, 585, 586, 587 (*Figs. 13, 27*)
Sinda, 314 (*Figs. 36, 39*)
Sinde, 52 (*Fig. 62*)
Sindegon (nr. Man Kang), 470
Singapore, 4, 33, 42, 43, 567, 638, 673, 674, 710, 711
Singkaling Hkamti, 182 (*Fig. 23*)
Singpa, 503, 504, 506 (*Figs. 14, 21, 65*)

Singu (nr. Chauk), 533, 624 (*Figs. 52, 71*)
Singu (nr. Kyaukmyaung), 400, 428, 444, 445 (*Figs. 46, 48, 52, 55*)
Sinlamaung, 401 (*Fig. 10*)
Sinobyin, 141, 168 (*Figs. 15, 19*)
Sinoh, 103, 106, 110, 113 (*Figs. 15, 17*)
Sinthe, 414, 449, 450, 527 (*Figs. 50, 51*)
Sinthe Chaung (nr. Shwemyo Bluff), 537
Sinzweya, 103, 149, 169 (*Figs. 15, 18, 19*)
Sirajganj, 93, 120, 171, 175, 176, 325, 525, 528, 698 (*Fig. 13*)
Sita, 260, 311, 315, 349, 350 (*Figs. 30, 40*)
Sittang Bridge, 17, 35, 37, 39, 544, 547 (*Fig. 4*)
Sittaung, 77, 101, 132, 263, 353, 354, 372, 376, 391, 406 (*Figs. 10, 11, 12, 13, 27, 29, 56*)
Sizon (in the Tada–U area), 448
Slim, Field Marshal Sir William (Viscount), 51, 55, 60, 112, 139, 148, 177, 179, 183, 185, 186, 248, 265, 304, 306, 341, 356, 364, 390, 395, 455, 530, 540, 546, 721
Sokpao, 314 (*Figs. 36, 38, 39*)
Somra, 344 (*Fig. 39*)
Somra Hills, 282
Songon, 73, 396 (*Figs. 47, 48, 50*)
Sookerating, 333, 573, 585 (*Fig. 13*)
'Staircase' (nr. Kalaw), 545
Stilwell, General Joseph, 1, 2, 51, 52, 60, 77, 101, 129, 140, 177, 179, 180, 182, 184, 185, 186, 187, 232, 247, 389
Stockades (nr. Tiddim), 245, 356, 391 (*Figs. 26, 41*)
Stopford, Lieut.-General Sir Montague, 264, 285, 547
Sultan, Lieut.-General Dan, 390, 454, 455
Summerhouse Hill, Kohima, 267, 268, 270, 273, 298 (*Fig. 31*)
Sumprabum, 84, 129, 186 (*Figs. 11, 13, 22, 23*)
Sunle, 263, 374, 375, 392, 703, 704 (*Fig. 12*)
Supreme Allied Command, South-East Asia (S.A.C.S.E.A.), Control Commission, 569, 570, 571
Sylhet, 180, 190, 191, 193, 325, 326, 334, 528, 585, 587, 702 (*Fig. 13*)
Syriam, 38, 39, 47, 52, 540, 541, 547, 557, 593, 600 (*Figs. 2, 5*)

Tadagale, Rangoon, 41, 43, 48, 65
Tada-U, 447, 448, 532, 561 (*Figs. 53, 54, 55*)
Tagaung, 131, 132, 470 (*Figs. 11, 13, 57*)
Taikkyi, 48, 545, 556, 558, 595, 598 (*Figs. 5, 73*)
Takaw, 10, 14, 19, (*Figs. 6, 13*)
Talbahat (in the Jhansi area), 189, 507
Talingon, 428 (*Fig. 54*)
Tallui, 343, 347 (*Figs. 37, 39*)
Tamagauk, 52, 54, 63 (*Figs. 7, 9*)
Tamandu, 475, 477, 478, 493, 494, 495, 511, 512, 515 (*Fig. 62*)
Tamanthi, 132, 180, 341, 353 (*Figs. 11, 13, 29*)

Tamu, 1, 12, 41, 66, 73, 75, 77, 81, 82, 83, 87, 88, 89, 90, 95, 129, 132, 243, 245, 246, 247, 250, 252, 258, 263, 348, 349, 350, 353, 365, 372, 374, 375, 376, 401, 405, 406, 410, 412, 573, 584, 592, 594, 598, 599, 622, 703, 704 (*Figs. 10 11, 12, 13, 27, 29, 30, 36, 40, 45, 56*)
Tamu–Kalemyo Road, 357, 374, 378
Tamu–Kyaukchaw Road, 246
Tamu–Palel Road, 258
Tamu–Sittaung Road, 246, 263, 354, 373, 374, 375, 400
Taro, 177 (*Fig. 22*)
Tatkon, 537, 551, 581, 589, 599 (*Fig. 71*)
Tatmin Chaung, 141 (*Fig. 19*)
Tatmingyaung, 141 (*Fig. 15*)
Taukkyan (nr. Kalemyo), 364, 378, 409, 413, 585 (*Figs. 10, 26, 41, 47, 50*)
Taukkyan (N. of Rangoon), 18, 40, 45, 47, 65, 538 (*Fig. 5*)
Taung Bazar, 107, 109, 113, 114, 115, 116, 117, 121, 122, 139, 141, 142, 143, 144, 145, 149, 152, 153, 154, 163, 166, 167, 168, 169, 174, 474, 499, 509, 510, 513, 699 (*Figs. 14, 16, 19*)
Taungbetywa (nr. Madaya), 444
Taungbro, 153, 474 (*Fig. 14*)
Taungdaw (on the Taungup–Prome track), 545
Taungdaungwa Feature (nr. The Tunnels on the Maungdaw–Buthidaung Road), 146
Taungdwingyi, 17, 18, 52, 55, 60, 64, 534, 554, 555 (*Figs. 6, 8, 9, 71, 73*)
Taunggon, 470, (*Fig. 58*)
Taunggyi, 9, 10, 13, 17, 19, 31, 49, 51, 59, 60, 66, 68, 86, 544, 547, 548 (*Figs. 6, 13, 46, 71*)
Taungmaw, 115 (*Fig. 15*)
Taungmaw (N.E. of Myebon), 516 (*Fig. 68*)
Taungni, 194, 467 (*Figs. 22, 61*)
Taungtha, 60, 434, 436, 441, 443, 449, 581, 591 (*Figs. 46, 49, 52, 53, 54, 71*)
Taungup, 18, 51, 100, 106, 475, 476, 477, 499, 511, 512, 518, 519, 520, 523, 705 (*Figs. 6, 9, 62*)
Taungup Chaung, 499, 518
Taungup Pass, 3 (*Fig. 62*)
Taungup–Prome Track, 518, 535, 545
Tavoy, 5, 9, 11, 13, 14, 15, 18, 19, 20 (*Fig. 2*)
Tawbwe, 513 (*Fig. 67*)
Tawbya Chaung, 513 (*Fig. 67*)
Tawgyin (nr. Mutaik), 398
Teaplanters Association, 84
Tebaunggwe (nr. Ondaw), 398, 399
Teimagyaung (in the Kaladan Valley), 507
Teknaf, 103, 513, 519, 573 (*Fig. 15*)
Tenasserim, 1, 5, 11, 16, 18, 543 (*Fig. 2*)
Tengnoupal, 252, 260, 303, 311, 315, 348, 350 (*Figs. 30, 36, 40*)
Tezpur, 92, 171, 325, 528 (*Fig. 13*)
Thabeikkyin, 389, 391, 396, 400, 426, 427, 428 439, 444 (*Figs. 46, 48, 52, 55, 57*)
Thabutkon, 436, 437, 438 (*Fig. 54*)
Thaikwagon, 457 (*Fig. 61*)
Thalechaung, 515 (*Fig. 68*)
Thamnapokpi (nr. Moiring), 309 (*Fig. 30*)
Thanan (nr. Tonhe), 400, 401
Thanchi, 506, 507, (*Fig. 65*)

Thandada, 504, 507 (*Figs. 66, 67*)
Thandaung, 543, 544 (*Fig. 72*)
Thaungdara, 110, 113, 114 (*Figs. 15, 63*)
Tharrawaddy, 18, 47, 48, 50, 53, 520, 542, 554, 555, 583, 584, 588, 589, 590, 591, 592, 594, 596, 599, 600, 601 (*Figs. 5, 6, 73*)
Thaton, 1, 33, 34, 39 (*Figs. 2, 6*)
Thaungdut, 252 (*Figs. 27, 29, 56*)
Thawai, 345 (*Figs. 36, 39*)
Thawatti, 537 (*Fig. 9*)
Thayettabin, 504 (*Fig. 67*)
Thayetmyo, 31, 54, 55, 544, 545, 583 (*Figs. 6, 9, 62*)
Thazi (nr. Meiktila), 10, 17, 22, 51, 59, 60, 393, 410, 437, 471, 530, 532, 536, 544, 581, 591, 598, 599 (*Figs. 6, 13, 46, 52, 54, 60, 71*)
Thazi (nr. Kalewa), 406
Thebyuchaung, 34 (*Fig. 3*)
Thetkegyin, 398 (*Fig. 47*)
Thingsai, 367 (*Fig. 43*)
Thinunggei, 309, 351, 352 (*Figs. 30, 36*)
Thityabin, 401, 402 (*Fig. 48*)
Thityagauk, 56 (*Figs. 8, 9*)
Thonzaungywa (in the vicinity of Kwazon, E. of the Mayu), 480
Thonze, 50, 542, 556 (*Fig. 5*)
Thoubal, 175, 176, 260, 262, 313, 315, 345, 348, 353 (*Figs. 30, 36*)
Three Pagodas Pass, 14, 19 (*Fig. 2*)
Throilok (nr. Moirang), 308
Thu Dau Mot, Indo-China, 570
Thu Duc, Indo-China, 570
Tiddim, 129, 139, 175, 176, 189, 245, 246, 249, 250, 253, 254, 255, 303, 307, 351, 355, 356, 360, 361, 363, 364, 376, 378, 391, 622, 704 (*Figs. 11, 13, 26, 27, 29, 41, 43*)
Tiddim–Fort White Road, 254
Tiddim–Kalemyo Road, 254, 362
Tigyaing, 393, 454, 458, 462, 470 (*Figs. 13, 56, 57*)
Tilin, 72, 411 (*Figs. 13, 46, 50, 56*)
Tinhmaw (nr. Kawlin), 401
Tingkawk Sakan, 192, 194 (*Fig. 22*)
Tinma, 504, 507 (*Figs. 15, 66, 67*)
Tinsukia, 194, 195, 336, 585 (*Fig. 13*)
Tistamukh Ghat, 106 (*Fig. 13*)
Tizaung (between Myinmu and Kwetkwin), 377, 404
Tonbo, 52 (*Fig. 62*)
Tonhe, 2, 92, 131 132, 263, 401 (*Figs. 10, 11*)
Tokpakhul, 309 (*Fig. 36*)
Tonkwa, 454 (*Fig. 56*)
Tonlon, 457 (*Fig. 61*)
Tonnan (nr. Kalewa), 588, 594
Tonzang, 250, 255, 355, 356, 361, 362 (*Figs. 27, 28, 29, 41, 42*)
Tortoise Feature (nr. Razabil), 146, 148
Toungoo, 3, 9, 10, 19, 31, 38, 39, 44, 50, 52, 59, 66, 530, 532, 535, 537, 538, 543, 544, 547, 548, 551, 561, 581, 582, 583, 5 88, 589 591, 592, 594, 595, 596, 598, 599, 600, 601, 697 (*Figs. 6, 9, 71, 72, 74*)
Treasury, Kohima, 274, 275 (*Figs. 31, 32, 33*)
Tuitum, 250, 360, 362 (*Figs. 27, 28, 41*)
Tukpui (nr. Mowdok), 503 (*Fig. 65*)

INDEX

Tumbru, 108, 109, 116, 117, 141, 142, 143, 145, 147, 172, 478, 519 (*Fig. 14*)
Tumbru Ghat, 106, 115, 116, 117, 118, 147, 148, 167, 170, 173, 701
Tumukhong, 314 (*Figs. 30, 39*)
Tungnang, 165 (*Figs. 16, 65*)
Tunnels, The (on the Maungdaw-Buthidaung Road), 112, 113, 141, 146, 153, 161, 474, 478, 479, 510, 513, 520
Tuphema, 280, 281 (*Figs. 34, 35*)
Tuphema-Kharasom Track, 341
Twingon, 57, 58, 59, 64, 534 (*Fig. 8*)
Twinnge, 454, 458, 460, 462, 470, 473 (*Figs. 56, 58, 60*)
Typhus Research Team, 369

Udaung, 480 (*Fig. 15*)
Ukhia, 108, 109, 111, 117, 147, 169 (*Fig. 14*)
Ukhrul, 244, 246, 250, 260, 261, 264, 278, 282, 302, 305, 311, 313, 341, 342, 343, 344, 345, 347, 348 (*Figs. 27, 29, 36, 37, 39*)

Vangte, 254, 255 (*Figs. 26, 27, 41*)
Victoria Point, 1, 5, 18, 29 (*Fig. 2*)
Viswema, 278 (*Figs. 34, 35*)
'Vital Corner' (nr. Tiddim), 246, 255, 356, 357 (*Fig. 41*)
'Vital Corner' (nr. Buthidaung), 510

Wabyin, 103, 116, 158, 160, 167, 168, 169, 173, 479, 520 (*Figs. 15, 19*)
Waikhong, 308, 361 (*Figs. 30, 40*)
Wainggyo, 396, 398 (*Fig. 47*)
Waithou (nr. Wangjing), 263, 313, 314
Wakan, 307, 313 (*Fig. 36*)
Walawbum, 177 (*Fig. 22*)
Wanetchaung (nr. Hmawbi), 558
Wangjing, 260, 262, 263, 264, 315, 350, 353 (*Figs. 27, 30, 36, 40, 42*)
Wanting, 6, 14, 19, 454 (*Figs. 11, 13, 56*)
Warazup, 192, 193, 194 (*Fig. 22*)
'Waring' (in the vicinity of Mogaung), 223
Wavell, Field Marshal, Earl, 6, 53, 94, 101, 111, 112, 122, 129, 130, 178
Waw, 35, 37, 40, 538, 539, 544, 548, 552, 582, 583, 589, 592, 596, 599, 600, 601 (*Figs. 5, 71, 72*)
Wayongon, 469 (*Fig. 61*)
Webula, 245 (*Fig. 26*)
Wedemeyer, General A. C., 390
Welaung, 436 (*Fig. 54*)
'West African Way', 163 (*Fig. 65*)
'Westdown', 507 (*Fig. 66*)
Wetlet, 397 (*Figs. 48, 56*)
Wetlu (nr. Seiktein), 436 (*Fig. 54*)
Wetthabok, 397 (*Fig. 48*)
Wettigan, 52 (*Fig. 9*)
Wetwin, 466 (*Fig. 60*)
Wheeler, General R. A., 390
'White City', 184, 185, 187, 192, 198, 216, 237, 468 (*Fig. 23*)
Willcox, Major P. L., 623.

Wingate, Major-General Orde, 2, 101, 129, 130, 132, 133, 135, 138, 179, 180, 181, 190, 195, 200, 232, 233, 235, 237
Winkwin, 40
Winmana, 404 (*Fig. 48*)
Witok, 90 (*Fig. 12*)
Wokha, 282 (*Fig. 13*)
Wundwin, 61, 441, 442, 534 (*Figs. 46, 53, 54, 71*)
Wuntho, 77, 78, 393, 400, 401 (*Figs. 10, 11, 13, 48, 56, 57*)

Yaingangpokpi, 244, 260, 261, 262, 314 (*Figs. 36, 39*)
Yairipok, 314, 315 (*Figs. 30, 36*)
Yamethin, 530, 536, 537, 598 (*Figs. 9, 46, 52, 71*)
Yanan, 374 (*Fig. 12*)
Yanaung, 536 (*Fig. 52*)
Yanbo, 458, 462, 463, 465, 468 (*Fig. 57*)
Yazagyo, 81, 83, 90, 263, 363, 372, 375, 378, 392, 398, 704 (*Figs. 10, 12, 47*)
Ye, 11, 15, 17, 18, 19, 29 (*Fig. 2*)
Yebadin (Ramree Island), 502
Yebyu, 411, 430 (*Fig. 50*)
Yedashe, 52 (*Figs. 6, 9, 71*)
Yegyanbyin, 481 (*Fig. 63*)
Yegyi Chaung (nr. Taungdaw), 545
Yemyettaung (nr. Ginnapara, N. of Maungdaw), 158, 160, 161, 478
Yenangyaung, 17, 18, 40, 53, 56, 57, 58, 60, 62, 66, 409, 530, 534 (*Figs. 6, 8, 9, 46, 52, 62, 71*)
Yet Chaung (in the vicinity of Kangaw), 485
Yetlet (nr. Yindaw), 551
Ye-U, 18, 19 73, 74, 80, 81, 85, 89, 396, 397, 398, 407, 573, 592, 599 (*Figs. 10, 11, 13, 46, 47, 48, 49, 52, 56, 57*)
Yewe, 536 (*Figs. 53, 54*)
Yin Chaung, 56, 57, 545 (*Figs. 8, 9*)
Yindaw, 536, 551 (*Figs. 46, 52*)
Yinon, 34 (*Fig. 3*)
Yo Chaung, 513, 517 (*Figs. 15, 63, 66, 67*)
Yuwa, 263, 341 (*Figs. 10, 12*)
Ywabo, 447 (*Figs. 49, 55*)
Ywadan, 536 (*Fig. 52*)
Ywathit (nr. Mawhun), 469 (*Fig. 61*)
Ywathit (nr. Seikpyu, W. of the Irrawaddy), 428 (*Fig. 52*)
Ywathitgyi (N. of Sadaung on the Shwebo Road), 398, 432
Ywataung, 55, 554 (*Fig. 73*)

Zahaw Camp, 369 (*Fig. 43*)
Zale, 447 (*Fig. 49*)
Zalon (N.W. of Prome, on the Irrawaddy), 545, 546
Zayatkin, 538 (*Figs. 71, 72*)
Zayetkon, 60, 61, 65, 534 (*Figs. 8, 46*)
Zedidaung, 110 (*Fig. 15*)
Zeganbyin, 147, 148, 160, 173 (*Fig. 15*)
Zigon, 402 (*Figs. 9, 47, 48*)
Zin (nr. Myemun), 402
Zubza, 267, 273, 276, 277 (*Fig. 35*)

PART II

British and Allied Formations

Commands

Allied Land Forces, French Indo-China (A.L.F.F.I.C.), 569, 570, 571
Allied Land Forces, South-East Asia (A.L.F.S.E.A.), 390, 394, 414, 419, 455, 474, 512, 521, 524, 525, 526, 544, 546, 547, 571, 572, 581, 605, 606, 607, 645, 668, 670, 674, 677, 703
Central (India), 190, 651, 677
Ceylon Army, 371, 373, 390, 420, 648, 651
Eastern (India), 115, 175, 324, 329, 330, 526, 676, 678, 713
Eastern Air, 179, 246
Far Eastern, 4
India, 330, 526, 696, 703, 704
Lines of Communication, 390, 408, 414, 420, 525, 648, 703
Northern (India), 676
Northern Combat Area (N.C.A.C.), 140, 389, 390, 391, 395, 419, 453, 454, 455, 525, 534, 667
South-East Asia (S.E.A.C.), 2, 139, 140 187, 246, 389, 390, 416, 417, 418, 540, 566, 609, 611, 612, 613, 618, 625
Southern (India), 676
South-West Pacific (A.B.D.A.), 5
Supreme Allied Command, South-East Asia (S.A.C.S.E.A.), 394, 416–419, 566, 569, 571, 612
Air Transport Command (U.S.), 701, 702
Troop Carrier, 150, 180, 194

Districts, Areas, Sub-areas

Western District (India), 676
South Burma District, 555, 595, 596, 597, 598, 599, 600, 601, 627, 648
505 District, 425, 546, 561, 581, 582, 595, 596, 597, 598, 599, 600, 601, 627, 648
1 Area, 546, 555, 572, 588, 589, 590, 591, 592, 593, 594
105. L. of C. Area, 675
109. L. of C. Area, 675
202. L. of C. Area, 265, 286, 295, 327, 420, 584
303. L. of C. Area, 675
404. L. of C. Area, 327, 371, 420, 507, 584, 646
251. Sub-area, 327
252. Sub-area, 327
253. Sub-area, 327, 555, 588, 589, 590, 592 593 594
256. Sub-area, 327
257. Sub-area, 265, 327
354. L. of C. Sub-area, 118
451. Sub-area, 327
452. Sub-area, 327
455. Sub-area, 588, 589, 591, 592, 593, 594
551. Sub-area, 588, 589, 590, 591, 592, 594
552. Sub-area, 581, 582, 588, 589, 590, 591, 592, 593, 594
555. Sub-area, 569, 570, 571

Army Group

11. 139, 338, 339, 390, 417, 422, 423, 648, 677

Armies

Army-in-Burma (Burma Army), 1, 7, 8, 11, 12, 43, 45, 47, 73, 74, 77, 78, 79, 85, 86, 89, 92, 94, 243, 698
Burma National, Burma Independence, Burma Defence, Burma Patriot Forces, 3, 20, 38, 252, 442, 534, 542, 544, 546, 549
Eastern (India), 101, 111, 120, 121, 129, 243, 421, 423, 605, 617, 648, 651, 662, 677, 713
Fourteenth, 2, 3, 139, 140, 175, 179, 182, 247, 284, 286, 300, 324–340, 341, 356, 371, 373, 376, 378, 389, 390, 391, 393, 394, 404, 408, 414, 419, 421, 423, 424, 425, 426, 428, 432, 446, 451, 453, 454, 455, 460, 474, 477, 500, 513, 525, 530, 531, 532, 537, 538, 540, 543, 546, 547, 560, 573, 580, 581, 605, 614–627, 648, 649, 694, 703, 704, 710, 713, 721, 723
Indian National (I.N.A.), 148, 252, 303, 305, 350, 534
North-Western (India), 651, 677, 713
Southern (India), 651, 677, 713
Twelfth, 3, 546, 547, 588, 589, 590, 591, 592, 593, 594, 595, 596, 597, 598, 627, 628, 648, 710

Corps

I. Burma (Burcorps). 1, 51, 52, 54, 55, 57, 58, 60, 64, 66, 69, 70, 72, 73, 74, 77, 79, 80, 81, 83, 85
IV. 1, 2, 3, 78, 101, 120, 126, 129, 130, 138, 139, 140, 152, 180, 184, 185, 186, 243, 244, 246, 247, 249, 261, 277, 278, 282, 283, 301, 302, 304, 305, 315–320, 321, 323, 325, 327, 330, 341, 342, 343, 352, 376, 391, 392, 393, 394, 395, 400, 409, 411, 412, 413, 414, 419, 424, 426, 428, 430, 431, 434, 435, 436, 439, 441, 442, 443, 449, 451, 530, 532, 535, 537, 538, 539, 543, 544, 546, 547, 548, 550, 554, 556, 558, 559, 561, 563, 564, 565, 574, 582, 588, 589, 591, 592, 593, 594, 595, 596, 597, 598, 599, 600, 601, 605, 614, 615, 616, 617, 618–621, 627, 663, 668, 706
XV. 2, 3, 101, 112, 139, 140, 145, 146, 149, 152, 153, 167, 172, 243, 252, 327

389, 390, 420, 453, 473, 474, 476, 477, 478, 488, 499, 504, 511, 512, 513, 519, 520, 521, 522, 523, 524, 525, 532, 539, 540, 541, 567, 577, 581, 646, 648, 677, 678, 679, 694, 703

XXXIII. 139, 140, 252, 264, 265, 273, 276, 277, 278, 281–289, 298, 299, 320, 326, 330, 341, 342, 343, 345, 352, 353, 364, 375, 376, 377, 379, 380, 381, 382, 384, 391, 392, 393, 394, 395, 396, 400, 402, 406, 409, 410, 413, 420, 424, 426, 427, 428, 432, 439, 441, 442, 444, 445, 446, 447, 448, 450, 451, 452, 530, 532, 533, 535, 542, 543, 544, 546, 547, 554, 555, 558, 559, 561, 562, 567, 575, 582, 583, 614, 615, 616, 617, 618–621, 624, 668, 704, 705

XXXIV. 567, 568

Divisions
  African
    11th East African, 350, 353, 354, 357, 363, 371, 372, 373, 376, 377, 378, 380, 381, 385, 391, 392, 393, 396, 409, 412, 420, 578, 618–621, 624
    81st West African, 139, 141, 146, 149, 152, 153, 161, 163, 164, 165, 166, 167, 174, 188, 327, 339, 391, 420, 473, 474, 477, 503, 504, 506, 507, 508, 509, 510, 514, 522, 580, 666, 678, 680, 700, 723
    82nd West African, 391, 420, 473, 474, 476, 477, 493, 495, 496, 497, 499, 504, 509, 510, 511, 512, 514, 515, 519, 520, 522, 523, 544, 546, 547, 572, 627, 649, 680, 694, 705

  British
    2nd, 103, 111, 112, 113, 114, 115, 126, 127, 128, 249, 252, 265, 266, 273, 274, 275, 276, 277, 278, 280, 281, 282, 284, 285, 288, 289–299, 300, 306, 319, 326, 327, 341, 342, 343, 345, 348, 350, 351, 352, 381, 382, 384, 391, 392, 395, 396, 397, 402, 404, 408, 409, 420, 429, 430, 432, 433, 439, 442, 447, 448, 450, 530, 532, 533, 534, 540, 541, 546, 562, 568, 577, 588, 596, 640, 649, 684
    70th, 101, 112, 113, 116, 118, 120, 126, 179, 188, 243, 252, 273

  Burmese
    1st Burma (Burdiv), 1, 10, 13, 26, 34, 38, 40, 41, 49, 50, 51, 52, 54, 55, 56, 57, 58, 59, 60, 62, 64, 66, 69, 70, 72, 73, 74, 76, 77, 79, 80, 81, 243

  Indian
    3rd (Special Force), 2, 140, 162, 174, 177–242, 246, 332, 390, 624, 666, 682, 701, 702
    5th, 139, 141, 143, 145, 146, 147, 148, 149, 151, 152, 153, 157, 158, 160, 173, 249, 252, 260, 264, 265, 266, 276, 278, 301, 302, 304, 306, 321, 326, 327, 341, 351, 352, 353, 354, 356, 357, 358, 360, 364, 371, 376, 377, 378, 381, 384, 391, 392, 395, 402, 405, 412, 420, 424, 434, 435, 438, 449, 478, 530, 532, 535, 536, 537, 538, 544, 547, 548, 549, 550, 552, 563, 564, 567, 575, 582, 583, 588, 589, 592, 594, 596, 599, 600, 601, 618–621, 627, 674
    7th, 103, 118, 139, 140, 141, 143, 144, 145, 146, 147, 148, 149, 150, 151, 152, 153, 154, 155, 156, 157, 158, 163, 168, 173, 252, 265, 273, 276, 277, 278, 280, 281, 282, 283, 288, 289, 301, 306, 327, 341, 343, 344, 345, 347, 348, 352, 354, 376, 381, 382, 391, 395, 409, 410, 411, 412, 413, 419, 429, 430, 431, 434, 436, 442, 449, 530, 533, 535, 544, 545, 546, 547, 548, 549, 555, 561, 562, 564, 567, 568, 576, 583, 584, 589, 590, 591, 592, 593, 594, 596, 599, 600, 601, 624, 665, 678, 679
    11th (in Malaya), 5
    14th, 100, 101, 103, 106, 108, 113, 115, 119, 120, 123, 125, 128, 678
    17th, 1, 14, 32, 33, 34, 35, 36, 37, 38, 40, 41, 44, 47, 48, 49, 50, 51, 52, 53, 54, 55, 56, 60, 61, 62, 63, 64, 69, 71, 72, 74, 76, 79, 80, 82, 84, 96, 101, 126, 129, 139, 243, 244, 245, 246, 249, 250, 253, 256, 257, 258, 261, 301, 303, 304, 305, 306, 307, 308, 309, 310, 311, 312, 314, 316, 321, 322, 327, 342, 351, 352, 354, 355, 357, 358, 393, 395, 410, 412, 413, 420, 424, 429, 430, 432, 434, 435, 436, 437, 438, 441, 442, 443, 449, 530, 532, 535, 536, 537, 538, 539, 542, 544, 547, 548, 551, 559, 563, 564, 575, 582, 583, 588, 589, 590, 592, 593, 594, 596, 597, 599, 600, 601
    19th, 14, 327, 376, 391, 392, 393, 395, 396, 397, 400, 407, 408, 409, 419, 426, 427, 428, 429, 439, 440, 441, 442, 444, 454, 460, 461, 530, 532, 536, 543, 544, 546, 547, 548, 559, 561, 562, 564, 565, 574, 581, 582, 583, 589, 592, 594, 596, 599, 600, 601, 618–621
    20th, 139, 243, 245, 246, 249, 252, 258, 264, 301, 303, 304, 305, 308, 311, 312, 313, 314, 315, 316, 321, 327, 341, 342, 343, 344, 345, 347, 348, 351, 353, 354, 357, 376, 381, 382, 385, 391, 392, 393, 395, 396, 402, 403, 404, 407, 408, 409, 420, 428, 429, 430, 432, 433, 439, 441, 446, 447, 450, 461, 530, 532, 533, 534, 535, 542, 544, 545, 546, 547, 548, 550, 553, 554, 555, 556, 559, 561, 562, 567, 568, 569, 570, 571, 576, 583, 584, 589, 590, 592, 594, 596, 599, 600, 601, 624, 627, 632–637, 640, 674, 684, 690
    21st, 276, 285, 288, 343, 381, 383
    23rd, 83, 101, 127, 129, 131, 139, 140, 243, 244, 246, 250, 252, 257, 260, 261, 262, 263, 264, 265, 301, 302, 303, 304, 305, 306, 311, 313, 314, 315, 316, 321, 326, 327, 348, 349, 350, 351, 353, 372, 373, 383, 567, 579, 674
    25th, 152, 153, 158, 161, 327, 420, 473, 474, 475, 476, 477, 478, 481, 483, 487, 489, 490, 495, 497, 498, 499, 510, 511, 516, 520, 522, 567, 578, 674, 680

Divisions—*cont.*
  Indian—*cont.*
    26th, 101, 111, 112, 113, 115, 118, 126, 127, 139, 141, 142, 145, 148, 152, 153, 158, 160, 166, 173, 327, 420, 473, 474, 477, 499, 502, 509, 513, 520, 522, 540, 541, 542, 545, 554, 556, 567, 568, 577, 605, 646, 674, 680, 684
    36th, 148, 152, 153, 159, 161, 195, 326, 327, 390, 392, 393, 400, 419, 424, 428, 447, 453, 454, 455, 456, 457, 458, 460, 461, 462, 466, 472, 534, 544, 545, 579, 618–621, 624, 625, 628–631, 649, 666, 678, 684, 694, 703
    39th, 79

Beach Groups (Indian)
  41st, 572
  45th, 380, 572

Brigades
  African
    1st West African (82 Div.), 509, 510, 512, 513, 514, 515, 520, 572
    2nd West African (82 Div.), 476, 477, 490, 492, 509, 510, 511, 512, 513, 514, 515, 516, 517, 518, 519, 520, 572
    3rd East African, 354
    3rd West African (81 Div.), 161, 162, 174, 179, 185, 189, 190, 195, 209, 210, 213, 242, 493, 580
    4th West African (82 Div.), 477, 478, 489, 493, 499, 504, 509, 510, 512, 513, 514, 518, 520, 572
    5th West African (81 Div.), 161, 166, 174, 504, 514, 580
    6th West African (81 Div.), 161, 162, 166, 174, 504, 505, 580
    21st East African (11 Div.), 371, 372, 375, 385, 578
    22nd East African, 420, 474, 477, 499, 512, 518, 519, 520, 522, 547, 555, 564, 572, 592, 593, 598, 600, 680
    25th East African (11 Div.), 371, 372, 385, 578
    26th East African (11 Div.), 371, 372, 385, 578
    28th East African, 392, 395, 409, 410, 411, 412, 420, 429, 431, 434, 449, 578
  British
    3rd Special Service (Commando), 70, 252, 420, 473, 474, 475, 477, 481, 482, 483, 499, 511, 522, 567, 680
    4th (2 Div.), 265, 274, 275, 277, 278, 342, 345, 348, 352, 382, 397, 432, 433, 442, 448, 577
    5th (2 Div.), 265, 266, 273, 274, 277, 278, 342, 348, 349, 350, 352, 382, 396, 397, 432, 433, 442, 448, 533, 577
    5th Independent Para., 567
    6th (2 Div.), 103, 111, 112, 113, 114, 115, 116, 117, 126, 127, 128, 265, 273, 274, 275, 276, 288, 293, 342, 382, 396, 397, 398, 432, 433, 442, 448, 540, 541, 546, 547, 577, 588, 596, 627

7th Armoured, 14, 38, 43, 51, 52, 54, 55, 56, 57, 60, 61, 62, 63, 65, 69, 70, 72, 74, 76
14th (70 Div.) (Chindit), 118, 179, 185, 190, 195, 200, 201, 202, 203, 204, 205, 209, 210, 211, 242, 276
16th (70 Div.) (Chindit), 179, 180, 181, 182, 184, 185, 189, 190, 195, 209, 210, 211, 239, 241, 242
23rd (70 Div.) (Chindit), 112, 113, 116, 117, 118, 126, 179, 190, 195, 252, 265, 273, 274, 278, 280, 282, 283, 284, 288, 327, 343, 345, 348, 381, 384
29th Independent (36 Div.), 159, 161, 454, 457, 458, 460, 461, 468, 469, 472, 473, 579
72nd (36 Div.), 159, 160, 161, 393, 454, 456, 457, 458, 460, 461, 464, 465, 467, 469, 579, 631

Burmese
  1st (Burdiv.), 10, 13, 33, 38, 54, 56, 59, 63, 69, 70, 72, 74, 75
  2nd (Burdiv.), 10, 11, 13, 14, 32, 33, 34, 38, 56, 60, 62, 69, 70, 72, 74, 77, 83
  Maymyo, Rangoon and Tenasserim Bdes., 26

Indian
  1st (23 Div.), 127, 243, 244, 246, 260, 263, 301, 302, 303, 305, 313, 314, 315, 348, 349, 383, 580
  4th (26 Div.), 101, 112, 113, 115, 116, 117, 126, 166, 167, 499, 500, 501, 503, 520, 540, 557, 577
  9th (5 Div.), 146, 149, 150, 155, 157, 158, 173, 301, 304, 306, 307, 352, 354, 356, 357, 358, 359, 363, 384, 402, 438, 532, 535, 537, 538, 544, 547, 548, 551, 552, 575
  13th (1 Burdiv.), 8, 10, 13, 26, 38, 56, 59, 69, 70, 72, 74
  16th (17 Div.), 8, 10, 13, 14, 26, 29, 32, 33, 34, 35, 37, 38, 45, 54, 62, 63, 64, 69, 71, 73, 74, 80, 96
  26th (36 Div.), 454, 458, 459, 460, 461, 464, 465, 468, 579
  32nd (20 Div.), 246, 252, 301, 302, 303, 304, 305, 308, 310, 311, 312, 314, 315, 345, 351, 352, 357, 358, 383, 385, 392, 402, 403, 404, 405, 428, 429, 430, 441, 446, 534, 535, 542, 546, 554, 570, 571, 576
  33rd (7 Div.), 141, 144, 150, 154, 173, 265, 273, 274, 275, 276, 282, 284, 327, 343, 345, 347, 348, 382, 412, 413, 430, 431, 432, 434, 435, 442, 533, 534, 545, 548, 576
  36th (26 Div.), 101, 112, 113, 116, 117, 118, 126, 127, 145, 166, 169, 173, 187, 501, 540, 541, 556, 577
  37th (23 Div.), 101, 127, 244, 246, 250, 257, 260, 262, 263, 301, 303, 314, 315, 348, 349, 383, 580
  44th (17 Div.), 14
  45th (17 Div.), 14
  46th (17 Div.), 14, 32, 33, 34, 35, 37

INDEX

47th (14 Div.), 100, 101, 106, 108, 109, 110, 112, 113, 122, 125
48th (17 Div.), 14, 33, 34, 35, 36, 37, 38, 45, 54, 55, 56, 61, 62, 63, 64, 65, 69, 71, 72, 73, 76, 77, 84, 96, 101, 126, 139, 245, 246, 250, 254, 255, 256, 257, 258, 301, 303, 305, 307, 308, 309, 351, 352, 412, 413, 436, 437, 438, 443, 536, 539, 542, 548, 575
49th (14, 23 Divs.), 100, 101, 127, 244, 246, 250, 252, 257, 260, 263, 301, 303, 311, 314, 315, 348, 349, 350, 383, 580
50th Para., 194, 246, 250, 251, 252, 264, 269, 301, 306, 308, 321, 326, 327, 345, 383, 390
50th Tank, 101, 420, 473, 477, 522, 567
51st (25 Div.), 475, 478, 483, 484, 493, 511, 520, 579
53rd (25 Div.), 161, 477, 478, 479, 484, 490, 510, 512, 516, 520, 579
55th (14 Div.), 103, 111, 112, 113, 115, 117, 126
62nd (19 Div.), 392, 393, 400, 401, 427, 428, 439, 441, 544, 574
63rd (17 Div.), 14, 38, 45, 54, 61, 62, 63, 64, 69, 71, 72, 73, 74, 76, 82, 84, 96, 101, 127, 139, 244, 245, 246, 250, 254, 255, 258, 301, 304, 305, 307, 308, 309, 310, 351, 352, 412, 413, 436, 437, 438, 439, 443, 536, 537, 538, 539, 542, 575
64th (19 Div.), 393, 400, 401, 402, 427, 428, 439, 544, 545, 574, 581
71st (26 Div.), 101, 111, 112, 113, 115, 116, 117, 126, 166, 168, 169, 170, 499, 500, 501, 540, 541, 542, 545, 554, 557, 558, 578
74th (25 Div.), 475, 476, 477, 478, 481, 482, 484, 490, 492, 493, 494, 495, 511, 579
77th (Chindit), 2, 101, 127, 129, 130, 131–138, 179, 180, 183, 184, 186, 189, 190, 192, 194, 195, 201, 202, 203, 204, 205, 209, 210, 211, 212, 242
80th (20 Div.), 139, 246, 301, 303, 305, 306, 311, 312, 313, 344, 345, 383, 385, 392, 402, 404, 406, 428, 430, 441, 533, 534, 545, 546, 554, 569, 570, 571, 576
88th (14 Div.), 126
89th (7 Div.), 140, 141, 144, 146, 149, 150, 154, 155, 174, 282, 301, 304, 306, 307, 343, 344, 345, 347, 348, 382, 411, 412, 413, 430, 431, 432, 533, 534, 535, 545, 548, 576
98th (19 Div.), 393, 400, 401, 427, 428, 439, 440, 444, 445, 446, 544, 574
99th (17 Div.), 412, 413, 436, 438, 439, 443, 532, 536, 537, 542, 575, 589, 590, 593, 597
100th (20 Div.), 246, 301, 303, 305, 311, 312, 313, 344, 345, 383, 385, 396, 404, 406, 428, 429, 430, 441, 442, 446, 447, 535, 542, 545, 546, 570, 576
109th, 93
111th (Chindit), 178, 179, 180, 183, 184, 185, 186, 187, 189, 190, 195, 199, 201, 202, 203, 204, 205, 206, 209, 210, 211, 213, 216, 238, 241, 242
114th (7 Div.), 140, 141, 142, 144, 149, 154, 156, 157, 174, 276, 278, 279, 280, 382, 410, 412, 413, 429, 430, 431, 434, 533, 534, 535, 545, 549, 567, 576
116th, 568
123rd (5 Div.), 103, 106, 108, 109, 110, 111, 113, 122, 126, 157, 158, 173, 252, 260, 301, 304, 306, 307, 352, 355, 356, 357, 358, 359, 361, 362, 384, 537, 538, 544, 550, 575
161st (5 Div.), 146, 157, 158, 160, 173, 252, 253, 265, 266, 269, 272, 273, 274, 276, 278, 279, 280, 284, 301, 306, 327, 352, 354, 356, 358, 359, 362, 363, 384, 434, 536, 537, 538, 544, 550, 575
254th Tank, 246, 250, 301, 321, 376, 381, 384, 385, 391, 395, 420, 546, 562, 576
255th Tank, 376, 391, 395, 410, 412, 419, 436, 437, 530, 537, 539, 546, 547, 574, 627
268th Motorised (Lorried), 276, 282, 288, 342, 343, 348, 349, 350, 376, 381, 383, 385, 391, 393, 395, 396, 419, 432, 439, 442, 533, 535, 544, 545, 546, 547, 562, 576, 583, 588, 627
Lushai, 265, 327, 352, 353, 364–371, 380, 385, 391, 395, 409, 410, 413, 420, 589

Regiments: Battalions

African

East African

The King's African Rifles
    1st Battalion (Nyasaland) (1st (Ny.) K.A.R.), 572
    2nd Battalion (Nyasaland) (2nd (Ny.) K.A.R.), 385, 578
    4th Battalion (Uganda) (4th (U.) K.A.R.), 385, 578
    5th Battalion (Kenya) (5th (K.) K.A.R.), 385, 578
    7th Battalion (Uganda) (7th (U.) K.A.R.), 578
    11th Battalion (Kenya) (11th (K.) K.A.R.), 385, 578
    13th Battalion (Nyasaland) (13th (Ny.) K.A.R.), 374, 385, 578
    22nd Battalion (Nyasaland) (22nd (Ny.) K.A.R.), 385, 578
    26th Battalion (Tanganyika Territory) (26th (T.T.) K.A.R.), 385, 578
    34th Battalion (Uganda) (34th (U.) K.A.R.), 385
    36th Battalion (Tanganyika Territory) (36th (T.T.) K.A.R.), 373, 374, 385, 578
    44th Battalion (Uganda) (44th (U.) K.A.R.), 385, 578
    46th Battalion (Tanganyika Territory) (46th (T.T.) K.A.R.), 578
    71st Battalion (Somaliland) (71st (S.) K.A.R.), 578

INDEX

Regiments : Battalions—*cont.*
African—*cont.*
East African—*cont.*
The Northern Rhodesia Regiment
 1st Battalion (1st N.R.R.) 385, 578
 3rd Battalion (3rd N.R.R.), 572
The Rhodesian African Rifles
 1st Battalion (1st R.A.R.), 572
11th (E.A.) Scout Battalion, 163
East African Auxiliary Pioneer Corps
 5th Group, 373

West African
The Gambia Regiment
 1st Battalion (1st Gambia), 163, 165, 174, 580
The Gold Coast Regiment
 1st Battalion (1st G.C.R.), 516, 517, 518, 572
 2nd Battalion (2nd G.C.R.), 516, 518, 572
 3rd Battalion (3rd G.C.R.), 514, 516, 572
 5th Battalion (5th G.C.R.), 174, 580
 7th Battalion (7th G.C.R.), 174, 580
 8th Battalion (8th G.C.R.), 174, 580
The Nigerian Regiment
 1st Battalion (1st N.R.), 513, 572
 2nd Battalion (2nd N.R.), 513, 572
 3rd Battalion (3rd N.R.), 513, 572
 4th Battalion (4th N.R.), 174, 580
 5th Battalion (5th N.R.), 572
 6th Battalion (6th N.R.), 179, 183, 242, 580
 7th Battalion (7th N.R.), 179, 242, 580
 9th Battalion (9th N.R.), 572
 10th Battalion (10th N.R.), 572
 12th Battalion (12th N.R.), 179, 242, 580
The Sierra Leone Regiment
 1st Battalion (1st Sa.L.R.), 174, 503, 580
81st Recce. Regiment, 514
West African Auxiliary Pioneer Corps
 6th Group, 514, 516, 517, 518

British
149th Regiment Royal Armoured Corps, 382
The 3rd Carabineers (3rd D.G.), 384, 433
The 25th Dragoons (25th DGNS), 150
The 7th Queen's Own Hussars (7th Hussars), 14, 45, 53, 69, 72
The Royal Tank Regiment. 2nd Battalion (2nd R.Tks), 14, 57, 58, 69
The Bedfordshire and Hertfordshire Regiment. 1st Battalion (1st Beds. Herts), 202, 204, 242
The Black Watch. 2nd Battalion (2nd B.W.), 179, 200, 202, 242
The Border Regiment
 2nd Battalion (2nd Border), 383, 534, 579
 4th Battalion (4th Border), 126, 282, 384
 9th Battalion (9th Border), 322, 575
The Buffs. 2nd Battalion (2nd Buffs.), 458, 459, 579
The Cameronians. 1st Battalion (1st Cameronians), 14, 38, 45, 53, 58, 69, 178, 183, 184, 185, 186, 202, 242
The Devonshire Regiment. 1st Battalion (1st Devon), 383, 534, 579
The Dorsetshire Regiment. 2nd Battalion (2nd Dorset), 297, 382, 577
The Duke of Wellington's Regiment. 2nd Battalion (2nd D.W.R.), 14, 35, 37, 53, 69, 126, 282, 384
The Durham Light Infantry. 2nd Battalion (2nd D.L.I.), 126, 297, 382, 577
The East Lancashire Regiment. 2nd Battalion (2nd E.Lan.R.), 159, 160, 579
The East Yorkshire Regiment. 1st Battalion (1st E.Yorks.), 575
The Essex Regiment. 1st Battalion (1st Essex), 126, 282, 384
The Gloucestershire Regiment
 1st Battalion (1st Glosters), 7, 13, 26, 45, 53, 57, 70, 73, 127, 152
 10th Battalion (10th Glosters), 159, 579
The Green Howards. 2nd Battalion (2nd Green Howards), 169, 499, 502, 503, 517
The King's Own Royal Regiment (Lancaster). 2nd Battalion (2nd King's Own), 178, 183, 184, 185, 186, 202, 242
The King's Own Scottish Borderers. 2nd Battalion (2nd K.O.S.B.), 146, 149, 150, 155, 174, 382, 576
The King's Own Yorkshire Light Infantry. 2nd Battalion (2nd K.O.Y.L.I.), 7, 13, 26, 33, 37, 58, 70
The King's Regiment (Liverpool)
 1st Battalion (1st Kings), 179, 183, 186, 211, 212, 242
 13th Battalion (13th Kings), 127, 130
The Lancashire Fusiliers
 1st Battalion (1st L.F.), 179, 183, 202, 211, 212, 242
 1/8th Battalion (1/8th L.F.), 297, 382, 577
 10th Battalion (10th L.F.), 103, 109, 126
The Leicestershire Regiment
 2nd Battalion (2nd Leicesters), 181, 242
 7th Battalion (7th Leicesters), 202, 242
The Lincolnshire Regiment. 1st Battalion (1st Lincolns), 126, 150, 155, 169, 500, 501, 502, 542, 578
The Manchester Regiment. 2nd Battalion (2nd Manch), 382, 577

INDEX

The Northamptonshire Regiment. 1st Battalion (1st Northamptons), 383, 534, 579
The North Staffordshire Regiment. 1st Battalion (1st N. Staffs), 126
The Oxfordshire and Buckinghamshire Light Infantry. 6th Battalion (6th Oxf. Bucks), 579
The Queen's Own Cameron Highlanders. 1st Battalion (1st Camerons), 297, 382, 577
The Queen's Own Royal West Kent Regiment. 4th Battalion (4th R.W.K.), 173, 266, 269, 270, 271, 273, 384, 575
The Queen's Royal Regiment (West Surrey)
   1st Battalion (1st Queens), 150, 155, 173, 382, 576
   2nd Battalion (2nd Queens), 181, 242
The Royal Berkshire Regiment. 1st Battalion (1st R. Berks), 126, 273, 293, 297, 382, 574, 577
The Royal Inniskilling Fusiliers. 1st Battalion (1st Inniks), 14, 69, 125
The Royal Norfolk Regiment. 2nd Battalion (2nd Norfolk), 297, 382, 577
The Royal Scots (The Royal Regiment). 1st Battalion (1st R.S.), 126, 297, 382, 577
The Royal Scots Fusiliers.
   1st Battalion (1st R.S.F.), 159, 457, 458, 579
   2nd Battalion (2nd R.S.F.), 457
The Royal Sussex Regiment. 9th Battalion (9th R. Sussex), 159, 457, 458, 460, 461, 579
The Royal Warwickshire Regiment. 1st Battalion (1st Warwick), 577
The Royal Welch Fusiliers.
   1st Battalion (1st R.W.F.), 126, 297, 298, 382, 577
   2nd Battalion (2nd R.W.F.), 159, 161, 579
The Seaforth Highlanders. 1st Battalion (1st Seaforth), 127, 243, 383, 580
The Somerset Light Infantry. 1st Battalion (1st Som. L.I.), 174
The South Lancashire Regiment. 2nd Battalion (2nd S. Lan. R.), 159, 382, 431, 576
The South Staffordshire Regiment. 1st Battalion (1st S. Staffords), 179, 183, 202, 211, 212, 242
The South Wales Borderers. 6th Battalion (6th S.W.B.), 159, 458, 579
The Suffolk Regiment. 2nd Battalion (2nd Suffolk), 146, 148, 173
The Welch Regiment. 2nd Battalion (2nd Welch), 441, 574
The Wiltshire Regiment 1st Battalion (1st Wilts), 167
The West Yorkshire Regiment
   1st Battalion (1st W. Yorks), 14, 38, 45, 53, 57, 58, 69, 72, 93, 127, 250, 575
   2nd Battalion (2nd W. Yorks), 146, 149, 150, 155, 173, 251, 384, 575, 624
The Worcestershire Regiment
   2nd Battalion (2nd Worc. R), 574
   7th Battalion (7th Worc. R), 297, 382, 577
The York and Lancaster Regiment
   2nd Battalion (2nd Y. & L.), 202, 242
   7th Battalion (7th Y. & L.), 537, 575
   9th Battalion (9th Y. & L.), 480, 579
2nd Recce. Regiment, 297, 382, 577
45th Recce. Regiment, 181, 242
1 Army Commando of 3rd Commando Bde., 511
5 Army Commando of 3rd Commando Bde., 511

Burmese
The Burma Regiment, 99
   5th Battalion, 99, 253
   1st Battalion, 99, 382, 575
The Burma Rifles (Burif.)
   1st Battalion (1st Burif.), 13, 26, 34, 69
   2nd Battalion (2nd Burif.), 13, 14, 26, 69, 127, 130, 132
   3rd Battalion (3rd Burif.), 13, 14, 26, 29, 32, 34, 35, 37, 70
   4th Battalion (4th Burif.), 13, 14, 26, 32, 37, 70
   5th Battalion (5th Burif.), 13, 26, 69,
   6th Battalion (6th Burif.), 13, 14, 26, 29, 70
   7th Battalion (7th Burif.), 13, 15, 26, 32, 34, 69
   8th Battalion (8th Burif.), 7, 13, 26, 32, 33, 37, 70
   9th Battalion (9th Burif.), 27, 70
   10th Battalion (10th Burif.), 27, 70
   11th (Territorial) (11th Burif.), 27, 70
   12th (Territorial) (12th Burif.), 27, 70
   13th (Territorial) (13th Burif.), 27, 70
   14th (Territorial) (14th Burif.), 27, 70
Burma Auxiliary Force (B.A.F.), 7, 27
   Railways Battalion, 27
   Rangoon Battalion, 27
   Tenasserim Battalion, 27
   Upper Burma Battalion, 27
Burma Frontier Force (B.F.F.), 7, 13, 27, 49, 51, 57, 70
   Bhamo Battalion, 27, 70
   Chin Hills Battalion, 27, 70, 577
   Myitkyina Battalion, 27, 70
   North Shan States Battalion, 27, 70
   South Shan States Battalion, 27, 70
   Kokine Battalion, 27, 70
   Reserve Battalion, 27, 70
Burma Military Police, 7, 70
Burma Territorial Force, 7

Regiments: Battalions—*cont.*
Indian
In the pre-war Indian Army there were 10 regiments of Gurkhas, numbered 1 to 10, number 5 being the Royal regiment; 6 regiments of Punjabis, numbered 1, 2, 8, 14, 15 and 16. The numbering of the rest of the regiments was as follows:
- 3rd. The Madras Regiment
- 4th. The Bombay Grenadiers
- 5th. The Mahratta Light Infantry
- 6th. The Rajputana Rifles
- 7th. The Rajput Regiment
- 9th. The Jat Regiment
- 10th. The Baluch Regiment
- 11th. The Sikh Regiment
- 12th. The Frontier Force Regiment
- 13th. The Frontier Force Rifles
- 17th. The Dogra Regiment
- 18th. The Royal Garhwal Rifles
- 19th. The Hyderabad Regiment

There were in addition the armed forces of the independent states (I.S.F.), e.g. Baroda, Bihar and Patiala.
7th Light Cavalry, 384
11th Light Cavalry, 265, 382, 384
16th Light Cavalry, 569
19th King George V's Own Lancers (19th L.), 475
45th Light Cavalry, 265, 343, 382
The Ajmer Regiment. 2nd Battalion (2nd Ajmer), 577
The Assam Regiment. 1st Battalion (1st Assam), 127, 243, 251, 253, 265, 268, 372, 385, 574
The Assam Rifles
  1st Battalion (1st Assam Rif.), 243, 244, 272, 573
  2nd Battalion, 385
  3rd Battalion, 251, 253, 573
  4th Battalion, 573
The Baluch Regiment
  5th Battalion (5/10th Baluch), 574
  7th Battalion (7/10th Baluch), 14, 33, 37, 39, 69, 127, 575
  8th Battalion (8/10th Baluch), 103, 107, 126
  14th Battalion (14/10th Baluch), 579
  16th Battalion (16/10th Baluch), 579
The Baroda Regiment. 2nd Battalion (2nd Baroda), 576
The Bihar Regiment. 1st Battalion (1st Bihar), 172, 364, 385
The Bombay Grenadiers
  2nd Battalion (2/4th Bombay Gren.), 383
  3rd Battalion (3/4th Bombay Gren.), 384
  5th Battalion (5/4th Bombay Gren.), 383
The Chamar Regiment. 1st Battalion (1st Chamar), 383, 385, 576
The Dogra Regiment
  1st Battalion (1/17th Dogra), 126, 146, 148, 173, 278, 384, 575
  4th Battalion (4/17th Dogra), 385, 576
  5th Battalion (5/17th Dogra), 14, 33, 37, 39, 70, 76
The Frontier Force Regiment
  4th Battalion (4/12th F.F.R.), 8, 14, 15, 26, 32, 35, 37, 54, 69, 127, 539, 575
  8th Battalion (8/12th F.F.R.), 574
  9th Battalion (9/12th F.F.R.), 383, 571, 576
  12th Battalion (12/12th F.F.R.), M.G. Battalion, 577
  14th Battalion (14/12th F.F.R.), 173
M.G. Battalion, 172
The Frontier Force Rifles
  2nd Battalion (2/13th F.F. Rif.), 14, 45, 54, 69, 74, 503, 577
  8th Battalion (8/13th F.F. Rif.), 126, 168, 173, 385, 577
  9th Battalion (9/13th F.F.Rif.), 575
  14th Battalion (14/13th F.F. Rif.), 126, 383, 576
M.G. Battalion, 576
The Gurkha Rifles
  1st Regiment
    1st Battalion (1/1st G.R.), 458, 466, 534, 576
    3rd Battalion (3/1st G.R.), 383, 576
    4th Battalion (4/1st G.R.), 173, 382, 576
  2nd Regiment
    3rd Battalion (3/2nd G.R.), 127, 130, 494, 579
    4th Battalion (4/2nd G.R.), 576
  3rd Regiment (Queen Alexandra's Own)
    1st Battalion (1/3rd G.R.), 14, 38, 69, 72, 127, 542, 575
    3rd Battalion (3/3rd G.R.), 127, 244, 383, 580
    5th Battalion (5/3rd G.R.), 38
  4th Regiment (Prince of Wales's Own)
    1st Battalion (1/4th G.R.), 14, 36, 38, 69, 72, 126
    3rd Battalion (3/4th G.R.), 178, 183, 185, 186, 242
    4th Battalion (4/4th G.R.), 574
  5th Royal Regiment
    2nd Battalion (2/5th R.G.R.), 14, 38, 69, 72, 126, 245, 322
    3rd Battalion (3/5th R.G.R.), 127, 244, 383, 580
    4th Battalion (4/5th R.G.R.), 174, 481, 576
  6th Regiment
    1st Battalion (1/6th G.R.), 574
    3rd Battalion (3/6th G.R.), 179, 183, 211, 212, 242
    4th Battalion (4/6th G.R.), 574
  7th Regiment
    1st Battalion (1/7th G.R.), 8, 13, 14, 26, 29, 32, 33, 38, 69, 72, 126, 542, 575
    3rd Battalion (3/7th G.R.), 14, 33, 38, 69, 72
    7th Battalion, 38, 72, 76, 77

INDEX

8th Regiment
  1st Battalion (1/8th G.R.), 577
  3rd Battalion (3/8th G.R.), 383, 576
  4th Battalion (4/8th G.R.), 146, 149, 150, 174, 382, 548, 576
9th Regiment
  3rd Battalion (3/9th G.R.), 126, 183, 186, 242
  4th Battalion (4/9th G.R.), 178, 183, 184, 242
10th Regiment
  1st Battalion (1/10th G.R.), 14, 69, 74, 127, 539, 575
  3rd Battalion (3/10th G.R.), 127, 244, 383, 580
  4th Battalion (4/10th G.R.), 382, 383, 546, 576
2nd Gurkha Para. Battalion, 540, 541
3rd Gurkha Para. Battalion, 540, 541
25th Gurkha Rifles, 265, 573, 576
The Hyderabad Regiment
  1st Battalion (1/19th Hybad), 458, 459, 460, 465, 534, 576
  2nd Battalion (2/19th Hybad), 244, 383, 579
  6th Battalion (6/19th Hybad), 364
  8th Battalion (8/19th Hybad), 579
The Jat Regiment
  1st Royal Battalion (1R/9th Jat), 8, 14, 26, 29, 32, 33, 37, 69, 76, 77, 364, 385, 499
  3rd Battalion (3/9th Jat), 173, 384, 575
  5th Battalion (5/9th Jat), 126, 172, 577
  6th Battalion (6/9th Jat), 93, 364
  M.G. Battalion, 383, 385, 576
The Jammu and Kashmir Infantry, 375, 384
The Kalibahadur Regiment (Nepal), 244, 246, 252, 385
The Madras Regiment
  1st Battalion (1/3rd Madras), 576
  2nd Battalion (2/3rd Madras), 578
  4th Battalion (4/3rd Madras), 385, 576
The Mahindra Dal Regiment (Nepal), 265, 385, 576
The Mahratta Light Infantry
  4th Battalion (4/5th Mahratta L.I.), 127, 252, 383, 580
  6th Battalion (6/5th Mahratta L.I.), 127, 383, 580
  17th Battalion (17/5th Mahratta L.I.), 477, 480, 494, 579
  27th Battalion (27/5th Mahratta L.I.), 253, 383
Paratroops
  2nd Gurkha Para. Battalion, *see* above
  3rd Gurkha Para. Battalion, *see* above
  50th Gurkha Para. M.G. Coy, 383
  152nd Gurkha Para. Battalion, 252, 383
  153rd Gurkha Para. Battalion, 252, 383
The Patiala Infantry. 1st Battalion (1st Patiala Inf.), 127, 243, 383, 580

The Punjab Regiments
  1st Regiment
    1st Battalion (1/1st Punjab), 173, 251, 269, 384, 575
    2nd Battalion (2/1st Punjab), 126, 173, 252, 384, 575
    5th Battalion (5/1st Punjab), 8, 26, 58, 69, 168, 500, 578
  2nd Regiment
    2nd Battalion (2/2nd Punjab), 579
    3rd Battalion (3/2nd Punjab), 173, 384, 575
    7th Battalion (7/2nd Punjab), 150, 174, 410, 412, 576
  8th Regiment
    2nd Battalion (2/8th Punjab), 458, 459, 460, 465, 534, 571, 576
    5th Battalion (5/8th Punjab), 106, 125, 579
    6th Battalion (6/8th Punjab), 579
    8th Battalion (8/8th Punjab), 126
  14th Regiment
    3rd Battalion (3/14th Punjab), 173
    4th Battalion (4/14th Punjab), 174, 382, 434, 576
    7th Battalion (7/14th Punjab), 243, 364, 385
    9th Battalion (9/14th Punjab), 383, 542, 576
    80th Infantry Company (14th Punjab), 382, 383, 384
  15th Regiment
    1st Battalion (1/15th Punjab), 103, 106, 108, 126, 427, 574
    4th Battalion (4/15th Punjab), 173, 431, 576
    6th Battalion (6/15th Punjab), 575
    7th Battalion (7/15th Punjab), 126
    9th Battalion (9/15th Punjab), 126
  16th Regiment
    1st Battalion (1/16th Punjab), 126, 383, 580
    5th Battalion (5/16th Punjab), 126, 173
    7th Battalion (7/16th Punjab), 163, 165, 484, 578
The Rajput Regiment
  1st Battalion (1/7th Rajput), 106, 109, 125
  2nd Battalion (2/7th Rajput), 8, 26, 69, 577
  4th Battalion (4/7th Rajput), 146, 147, 173, 266, 269, 271, 384, 575
  6th Battalion (6/7th Rajput), 575
  9th Battalion (9/7th Rajput), 93
  14th Battalion (14/7th Rajput), 93
  17th Battalion (17/7th Rajput), 383
The Rajputana Rifles
  3rd Battalion (3/6th Raj. Rif.), 574
  5th Battalion (5/6th Raj. Rif.), 127, 244, 383, 580
  8th Battalion (8/6th Raj. Rif.), 126
  16th Battalion (16/6th Raj. Rif.), 579
The Royal Garhwal Rifles
  1st Battalion (1/18th R. Garh. Rif.), 8, 26, 58, 69, 168, 169, 503, 578

Regiments: Battalions—*cont.*
Indian—*cont.*
　The Royal Garhwal Rifles—*cont.*
　　4th Battalion (4/18th R. Garh. Rif.), 579
　The Shere Regiment (Nepal), 244, 251, 253, 272
　The Sikh Regiment (King George V's Own)
　　1st Battalion (1/11th Sikh), 14, 69, 74, 173, 174, 382, 431, 432, 576
　　6th Battalion (6/11th Sikh), 126
　　M.G. Battalion, 574
　The Sikh Light Infantry, 1st Battalion (1st Sikh L.I.), 575
　Indian Auxiliary Force 7
　Indian Territorial Force 7

Levies
　Chin, 245, 364, 385
　Falam, 410
　Kachin, 129, 177, 454
　Karen, 59, 70
　Lushai, 364
　Lushai Scouts, 410, 573
　Hong Kong
　　The Hong Kong Volunteer Defence Corps and the Hong Kong and Singapore Royal Artillery, 181

Forces
　Dahforce, 183, 184, 186, 242
　'Force 136', 546
　Mayforce, 115, 116
　Morrisforce, 184, 186, 192, 209, 242
　Soutcol, 107, 109, 112, 115, 122
　Special Force (Indian 3rd Division) *see* under Divisions
　Tonforce, 255
　Tripura State Force, 107, 119
　Tripforce, 107, 112, 122
　V Force, 150, 244, 253, 364, 546, 548
　Royal Navy, 481, Royal Indian Navy, 481
　Royal Marines (42nd and 44th Commandos of 3rd Commando Brigade), 52, 70, 73, 76, 481, 499, 502, 511, 567
　Royal Air Force, 1, 11, 41, 43, 51, 130, 131, 150, 184, 245, 252, 339, 346, 349, 375, 428, 504, 569, 702, 708, 711
　　221 Group, 246, 389, 541, 546, 708
　　224 Group, 389, 473, 511
　Australian Air Force, 541
　3rd Tactical Air Force, 246

United States of America: Formations and Units
　U.S.A.A.F., 132, 150, 180, 183, 245, 346, 348, 363, 371, 408, 455, 456, 701, 702, 711

　10 U.S.A.A.F., 389
　14 U.S.A.A.F., 389
　164 Liaison Aircraft Squadron, 380, 452, 708
　165 Liaison Aircraft Squadron, 375, 450, 708
　166 Liaison Aircraft Squadron, 380, 708
　The American Volunteer Group, 1, 41, 43
　Mars Task Force, 392, 419, 453, 454, 455
　Merrill's Marauders (5307 Provisional Regt.), 177, 185, 186
　No. 1 Air Commando, U.S.A.A.F., 179, 180, 181, 191, 375, 701

Chinese Formations and Units
　First Army, 419, 453, 454, 455
　Fifth Army, 1, 6, 50, 51, 52, 56, 59, 60, 72, 77, 84
　Sixth Army, 1, 6, 38, 50, 51, 52, 59, 60, 64, 94, 419, 453, 454
　Sixty-sixth Army, 60
　14th Division, 419
　22nd Division, 52, 60, 101, 129, 140, 177, 186, 419, 454
　28th Division, 60
　29th Division, 60
　30th Division, 177, 419, 454
　38th Division, 57, 58, 59, 60, 72, 77, 78, 101, 129, 140, 177, 185, 186, 391, 419, 454
　49th Division, 6, 14, 50, 59
　50th Division, 419, 454
　55th Division, 6, 14, 50, 59
　93rd Division, 6, 14, 59
　96th Division, 52, 60
　98th Division, 50
　200th Division, 50, 51, 52, 60
　Yunnan Force, 129, 177, 180, 186, 389, 455

Japanese Formations and Units
　Fifteenth Army, 216, 247, 304, 341, 342
　15th Division, 247, 250, 341, 342, 346, 348, 439
　31st Division, 247, 250, 251, 276, 299, 341, 342, 346, 428
　33rd Division, 35, 46, 247, 250, 341, 348, 353, 354, 428
　53rd Division, 216
　55th Division, 35, 149
　56th Division, 59
　24th Independent Mixed Brigade, 216
　Doi Force, 149, 151
　Kubo Force, 149, 151, 152
　Tanahashi Force, 149, 151

PART III

Medical and Associated Units

Ambulance Coaches and Trains
Ambulance Coaches, 66, 67 and 68. 587
Ambulance Trains
1 and 2. 11, 32, 71, 87.
3, 42, 71
14, 17, 19. 586
20, 21, 22. 587
29. 587, 595

Anti-malaria units
7 (Ind.) 70, 316, 585
9 (Ind.), 585
10 (Ind.), 316, 318, 587
18 (Ind.), 109, 117, 128, 158, 478, 479
20 (Ind.), 313, 316, 554, 569, 570, 571, 575, 583, 592, 599
21 (Ind.), 316, 585, 592, 599
21 (East African), Mob. Mal. Unit, 373
21 (East African) Mobile Malaria Section, 373, 573
22 (Ind.), 316, 585, 592, 599
23 (Ind.), 128, 587
24 (Ind.), 585
25 (Ind.), 585
27 (Ind.), 585
28 (Ind.), 585
30 (Ind.), 490
31 (Ind.), 585
32 (Ind.), 316, 574, 583, 592, 599
33 (Ind.), 286, 575, 592, 599
36 (Ind.), 585
38 (Ind.), 145, 172
44 (Ind.), 276, 285, 286, 400, 575, 581, 592, 599
45 (Ind.), 286, 316, 575, 582, 592, 599
51 (Ind.), 145, 172
55 (Ind.), 307, 575, 592, 599
59 (Ind.), 587
61 (Ind.), 585
62 (Ind.), 585
66 (Ind.), 587
67 (Ind.), 587
68 (Ind.), 350, 574, 583, 592, 599
69 (Ind.), 575, 582, 592, 599
71 (Ind.), M.C.U. (36 Div.), 461, 473, 582, 592, 599
72 (Ind.), 587
88 (Ind.), 573, 582, 592, 599
91 (Ind.), 574, 582, 592, 599
100 (Ind.), 582, 592, 599
101 (Ind.), 592, 599
102 (Ind.), 592, 599
103 (Ind.), 592, 599
104 (Ind.), 587
105 (Ind.), 577, 587, 592, 599

Base Sanitary Units
7, 8, 9, 10, 11 and 12 (Ind.), 593, 600

Beach Medical Units
1 (Ind.), 527, 572
5 (Ind.), 405, 407, 446, 554, 572, 581, 593, 600, 690

Bearer Companies or Units
1 (Ind.), 109, 110, 114, 115, 117, 128, 141, 145, 158, 172, 478, 479, 483, 490
2 (Ind.), 109, 110, 113, 114, 128, 141, 143, 145, 154, 155, 166, 167, 172, 257, 500, 502, 557, 558, 577
3 (Ind.), 254, 258, 307, 316, 575, 577
4 (Ind.), 254, 258, 307, 308, 316, 554, 575, 583, 593, 600, 632
5 (Ind.), 159, 160, 161, 276, 286, 374
7 (Ind.), 573, 581, 582, 593, 600
8 (Ind.), 362
2004 (East African) S.B. Coy, 374, 578

Brigade Medical Units (Chindits), 188, 189, 282

Burma Hospital Company (later Corps), 8, 12, 42, 43, 44, 67, 71, 87

Camp Reception Stations
108 (East African), 527, 578
110 (East African), 520, 524, 527, 560, 572, 600

Casualty Clearing Stations
1 (Burmese), 13, 28, 31, 33, 39, 44, 49, 71, 82, 86, 89, 90
2 (Burmese), 10, 13, 28, 31, 49, 66, 68, 71, 82, 89, 90
4 (Ind.), 9, 10, 13, 15, 28, 31, 44, 64, 68, 71, 82, 89, 90
8 (Ind.), 43, 48, 61, 62, 71, 85, 89, 90, 91, 96, 121, 143, 173, 175, 176, 260, 261, 387, 407, 408, 414, 447, 451, 479, 527, 561, 573, 582, 588, 590, 595, 597
9 (British), 121, 175, 176, 189
10 (Belgian Congo), 363, 373, 374, 375, 526, 573
13 (Ind.), 90, 175, 176, 277, 283, 284, 285, 286, 359, 360, 361, 375, 376, 377, 378, 379, 380, 386, 409, 414, 446, 527, 552, 563, 564, 575, 582, 588, 589, 591, 595, 597, 598, 600
14 (Ind.), 175, 176, 258, 260, 312, 315, 316, 317, 380, 386, 413, 414, 449, 450, 527, 554, 555, 560, 563, 574, 583, 588, 590, 595, 598
15 (Ind.), 108, 109, 110, 114, 115, 116, 119, 120, 123, 124, 128, 143, 144, 145, 154, 161, 173, 176, 386, 514, 527, 557, 558, 560, 577, 659
16 (Ind.), 175, 176, 254, 262, 360, 362, 363, 364, 377, 378, 386, 398, 407, 408, 414, 527, 560, 561, 563, 564, 575, 582, 588, 591, 595, 598
18 (Ind.), 175, 176, 387, 526, 572, 580, 588, 595, 598

747

Casualty Clearing Stations—*contd.*
  19 (Ind.), 138, 175, 176, 253, 254, 255, 261, 262, 315, 316, 317, 361, 362, 386, 413, 414, 449, 450, 527, 555, 556, 560, 561, 574, 583, 588, 594, 595, 598, 658
  22 (British), 159, 160, 161, 284, 300, 386, 461, 462, 464, 465, 466, 468, 527, 579
  23 (Ind.), 148, 157, 166, 167, 175, 176, 387, 519, 527, 560
  24 (Ind.), 175, 176, 308, 315, 317, 386, 413, 559, 560, 569, 570, 571, 574, 580, 588, 596
  25 (Ind.), 145, 157, 161, 167, 173, 175, 176, 386, 479, 500, 513, 520, 527, 560
  25 (West African), 388, 519, 520, 527
  26 (Ind.), 280, 284, 350, 351, 375, 378, 379, 380, 386, 559, 560, 575, 580, 588, 596, 597
  27 (West African), 161, 162, 189, 190, 242, 507
  28 (Ind.), 387, 528
  28 (West African), 388, 519, 520, 527, 560
  29 (West African), 161, 174, 387, 527
  30 (West African), 388, 514, 519, 520, 527, 560
  31 (West African), 161, 174, 507, 520, 527
  60 (East African), 526
  81 (West African), 373

Convalescent Depots (Indian)
  8 (B.T.), 584
  9 (I.T.), 584
  15 (I.T.), 316, 586
  16 (I.T.), 316, 584
  17 (I.T.), 316, 326, 584
  21 (B.T.), 326, 586
  25 (B.T.), 326, 584
  26 (I.T.), 696
  27 (B.T.), 316
  32 (B.T.), 697
  34 (B.T.), 593
  35 (B.T.), 697
  37 (I.T.), 586
  38 (I.T.), 586
  39 (I.T.), 696
  41 (B.T.), 189
  45 (I.T.), 584, 696
  46 (I.T.), 189
  52 (I.T.), 696

Corps Psychiatric Centres
  IV Corps, 582, 593, 600
  XXXIII Corps, 408, 583, 683

Dental Centres and Units (Indian)
  Dental Centres, 71, 87, 586, 594, 600
  17 (Ind.) Dental Unit (I.T.), 316, 350, 574, 584, 594, 600
  18 (I.T.), 577, 594, 600
  19 (I.T.), 254, 262, 316, 574, 584, 594, 600
  25 (I.T.), 572
  26 (I.T.), 574, 583, 594, 600
  29 (I.T.), 587
  30 (I.T.), 576, 582, 594, 600
  32 (I.T.), 587, 600

  33 (I.T.), 587
  34 (B.T.), 577, 593, 600
  36 (I.T.), 594
  38 (B.T.), 587, 600
  41 (B.T.), 316, 574, 582, 593, 600
  45 (B.T.), 574, 583, 593, 600
  48 (B.T.), 153, 155, 649
  49 (B.T.), 574, 584, 594, 600
  53 (B.T.), 574, 582, 594, 600
  55 (B.T.), 574, 582, 594, 600
  56 (B.T.), 569, 571, 576, 584, 594, 600
  57 (B.T.), 586
  58 (B.T.), 586
  61 (I.T.), 572
  64 (I.T.), 587
  67 (I.T.), 582, 587, 594
  68 (I.T.), 583, 594, 600
  69 (I.T.), 362, 363, 364, 576, 583, 594, 601
  70 (I.T.), 569, 571, 576, 584, 594, 601
  71 (I.T.), 586
  74 (I.T.), 594, 601
  75 (I.T.), 583, 594, 601
  78 (I.T.), 586
  79 (B.T.), 572, 594, 600
  80 (B.T.), 853, 594, 600

Dental Mechanic Units (Indian)
  1. 552, 583, 594, 601
  4. 586, 594, 601
  7. 577, 594, 601
  9. 316, 574, 583, 594, 601
  10. 574, 582, 594, 601
  13. 587, 601
  18. 145, 173, 649
  19. 574, 584, 594, 601
  20. 583, 594, 601
  23. 574, 584, 594, 601
  25. 569, 571, 576, 584, 594, 601
  26. 586
  27. 586
  29. 572

Depots of Medical Stores
  2 Burma, 66, 70
  Base, 71
  Gyogon, 31
  Mandalay, 31
  Myingyan, 600
  Insein, 31, 42
  Rangoon, 8, 12, 31, 42, 65, 67
  1 (Ind.), 587
  3 (Ind.), 599
  9 (Ind.), 262, 573, 581, 593, 686
  10 (Ind.), 599
  13 (Ind.), 66, 71
  16 (Ind.), 231
  17 (Ind.), 324, 573, 686
  18 (Ind.), 231, 573
  21 (Ind.), 118
  23 (Ind.), 587
  24 (Ind.), 585
  27 (Ind.), 585
  29 (Ind.), 585
  30 (Ind.), 573
  32 (Ind.), 373, 587

INDEX

41 (Ind.), 593, 599
42 (Ind.) (Sub-depot), 145, 172, 573
43 (Ind.) (Sub-depot), 145, 172
44 (Ind.) (Sub-depot), 565, 573, 582, 593, 599
45 (Ind.) (Sub-depot), 316, 318, 573, 581, 593, 599
46 (Ind.) (Sub-depot), 316, 318, 569, 570, 573, 593, 599
47 (Ind.) (Sub-depot), 585
48 (Ind.) (Sub-depot), 408, 573, 583, 593, 599
49 (Ind.) (Sub-depot), 587, 593, 599
50 (Ind.) (Sub-depot), 577, 593, 599
51 (Ind.) (Sub-depot), 587
52 (Ind.) (Sub-depot), 587
Red Cross Sub-depot, 600

Ear, Nose and Throat Surgical Units (Indian)
2. 71
6. 581, 590, 597
7. 316, 572, 597
8. 586
9. 572, 590, 597
11. 585
12. 586
15. 569, 570, 586

Field Ambulances
1 (Bur.) (later to be renumbered 77), 9, 10, 11, 13, 30, 40, 47, 48, 49, 61, 62, 64, 70, 81, 82, 89, 90, 264, 315, 365, 370, 371, 574
1 (Ind.), 115, 116, 117, 127, 145, 158, 160, 166, 167, 169, 170, 173, 501, 502, 513, 556, 557, 578
1 (W.A.), 513, 514, 515, 516, 572
2 (Bur.) (later to be renumbered 78), 9, 10, 13, 49, 62, 63, 70, 80, 81, 365, 574
2 (E.A.) (Z), 373, 374, 375, 578
2 (W.A.), 490, 492, 513, 514, 515, 516, 517, 518, 519, 520, 572
3 (W.A.), 161, 188, 205, 242
4 (Br.), 275, 276, 277, 279, 281, 294, 348, 398, 399, 407, 447, 448, 449, 577
4 (W.A.), 495, 513, 514, 515, 516, 518, 572
5 (Br.), 275, 276, 277, 279, 280, 281, 294, 350, 398, 399, 447, 448, 449, 577
5 (W.A.), 161, 166, 174, 504, 580
6 (Br.), 114, 115, 116, 127, 128, 275, 276, 277, 279, 281, 294, 295, 398, 399, 448, 577, 588, 596
6 (E.A.) (U), 373, 374, 375, 376, 578
6 (W.A.), 161, 166, 174, 504, 507, 580
9 Lt. (Ind.), 276, 282, 348, 350, 351, 376, 577, 583, 588
10 (E.A.), 373, 374, 375, 578
10 (Ind.), 145, 147, 157, 158, 173, 306, 307, 358, 359, 360, 362, 363, 364, 478, 550, 551, 552, 575, 582, 588, 596
13 Lt. (Br.), 40, 61, 62, 63, 70, 80, 82
14 Lt. (Ind.), 576
23 (Ind.), 39, 40, 44, 47, 48, 49, 61, 62, 63, 64, 65, 71, 80, 81, 82, 83, 84, 85, 90, 253, 254, 255, 258, 307, 309, 310, 311, 316, 357, 358, 413, 443, 444, 575, 582, 588, 596
24 (Ind.), 260, 261, 262, 263, 313, 314, 315, 316, 350, 580
34 (Ind.), 461, 464, 465, 466, 467, 579
37 (Ind.), 10, 12, 40, 44, 48, 62, 63, 64, 65, 71, 80, 81, 82, 83, 84, 85, 90, 245, 253, 254, 255, 256, 257, 258, 261, 307, 309, 316, 358, 413, 443, 575, 582, 589, 596
39 (Ind.), 39, 40, 44, 49, 71
41 (Ind.), 100, 101, 105, 108, 109, 110, 113, 114, 115, 128
42 (Ind.), 258, 259, 260, 312, 313, 316, 402, 404, 405, 406, 446, 447, 450, 553, 554, 555, 569, 570, 576, 583, 589, 596
44 (Ind.), 141, 142, 143, 144, 145, 153, 154, 155, 174, 277, 281, 347, 412, 442, 443, 576, 583, 589, 596
45 (Ind.), 103, 108, 109, 110, 113, 114, 115, 128, 145, 147, 148, 157, 158, 173, 260, 306, 307, 358, 359, 360, 361, 362, 363, 364, 478, 550, 551, 552, 575, 582, 589, 596
46 (Ind.) 116 117 141 166 167, 461, 500, 501, 502, 503, 556, 557, 578
47 (Ind.), 100, 101, 260, 261, 262, 263, 264, 309, 313, 314, 316, 350, 351, 580
48 (Ind.), 116, 118, 127, 141, 160, 166, 167, 168, 169, 500, 501, 502, 556, 557, 558, 578
49 (Ind.), 257, 260, 261, 262, 263, 313, 314, 315, 316, 350, 580
50 (Ind.), 40, 45, 47, 48, 49, 61, 62, 63, 65, 71, 80, 81, 114, 115, 413, 443, 444, 575, 582, 589, 596
51 (Ind.), 400, 401, 402, 444, 445, 446, 574, 582, 589, 596
52 (Ind.), 400, 401, 402, 444, 446, 574, 582, 589, 596
53 (Ind.), 400, 401, 402, 444, 446, 574, 581, 589, 596
54 (Ind.), 141, 142, 144, 145, 153, 154, 155, 156, 168, 174, 280, 281, 347, 412, 443, 576, 583, 589, 596
55 (Ind.), 258, 259, 260, 312, 313, 315, 316, 402, 404, 406, 446, 447, 450, 553, 554, 555, 569, 570, 571, 576, 581, 583, 589, 596
56 (Ind.), 478, 479, 480, 481, 484, 490, 491, 492, 493, 494, 496, 516, 579
57 (Ind.), 9, 10, 13, 49, 63, 70
58 (Ind.), 478, 479, 481, 482, 483, 484, 486, 493, 579
59 (Ind.), 258, 259, 260, 308, 310, 311, 312, 313, 315, 316, 357, 358, 402, 404, 405, 406, 407, 446, 447, 481, 553, 554, 555, 567, 569, 570, 571, 576, 583, 589, 596
60 (Ind.), 108, 109, 110, 114, 115, 116, 117, 127, 128
61 (Ind.), 478, 479, 480, 481, 482, 483, 484, 485, 490, 493, 494, 495, 497, 516, 579
63 (Ind.), 108, 109, 115, 121, 128, 444
64 (Ind.), 315, 316, 317, 318, 573, 581, 589, 596

Field Ambulances—*cont.*
  65 (Ind.), 315, 316, 565, 574, 582, 589, 594, 596
  66 (Ind.), 141, 143, 144, 145, 153, 154, 155, 156, 158, 174, 306, 307, 347, 412, 413, 576, 583, 589, 596, 649
  67 (Ind.), 286, 360, 361, 377, 379, 448, 555, 575, 583, 589, 596
  69 (Ind.), 159, 160, 161, 167, 461, 464, 465, 466, 467, 468, 469, 470, 579
  71 (Ind.), 157, 158, 481, 490, 493, 504, 518, 520
  72 (Ind.), 157
  75 (Ind.), 143, 145, 147, 148, 157, 158, 173, 266, 269, 270, 271, 272, 275, 276, 277, 294, 358, 359, 360, 362, 363, 364, 550, 551, 552, 575, 582, 596
  77 (Bur.)—*see* 1 (Bur.) Fd. Amb.
  78 (Bur.)—*see* 2 (Bur.) Fd. Amb.
  80 (Ind.) Para., 194, 253, 264, 269, 308
  154 (Br.), 159, 160, 161, 461, 467, 468, 469, 470, 471, 579
  173 (Br.), 188, 242
  189 (Br.), 116, 117, 188, 242
  215 (Br.), 188, 242

Field Ambulance Troops (R.I.A.S.C.)
  1. 13, 70
  3. 12, 71
  4. 70
  5. 71, 147
  7. 260, 263, 350
  10. 260, 350
  11. 115, 116, 117, 128, 166, 167
  13. 142, 154
  15. 154
  16. 115, 128, 145, 167, 173
  22. 147, 158
  23. 147

Field Dressing Stations (East African)
  60 (E.A.), 373, 374, 375, 578
  61 (Z.), 373, 374, 375, 578

Field Hygiene Sections
  1 (Bur.), 13, 70
  2 (Br.), 276, 298, 577
  2 (Bur.), 13, 70
  3 (Ind.), 71
  3 (W.A.), 161, 242
  5 (W.A.), 161, 174, 505
  6 (W.A.), 161, 174, 505
  7 (Ind.), 145, 173, 358, 361, 362, 575, 582, 589, 596
  19 (Ind.), 253, 269, 285, 286, 573, 581, 589, 596
  22 (Ind.), 40, 63, 65, 71, 254, 258, 307, 316, 575, 582, 589, 596
  23 (Ind.), 260, 262, 263, 316, 350, 580
  26 (Ind.), 258, 312, 316, 404, 554, 569, 570, 576, 583, 589, 596
  27 (Ind.), 117, 127, 166, 500, 578
  28 (Ind.), 108, 109, 115, 128
  30 (Ind.), 478, 490, 579
  31 (Ind.), 574, 582, 589, 596
  32 (Ind.), 142, 145, 174, 576, 583, 589, 596
  33 (Br.), 242
  33 (Ind.), 154
  36 (Ind.), 581, 585, 589, 596
  37 (Ind.), 577, 589, 596
  38 (Ind.), 577
  39 (Ind.), 587
  44 (Ind.), 461, 472, 579, 589
  45 (Ind.), 573, 589, 596
  46 (Ind.), 585, 589, 596
  50 (Ind.), 574, 582, 589, 596
  52 (Ind.), 172
  54 (Ind.), 573
  55 (Ind.), 145
  56 (Ind.), 315, 575, 583, 589, 596
  71 (E.A.), 373, 578
  75 (Ind.), 569, 570, 571
  82 (W.A.), 572
  83 (W.A.), 580
  B Sub-section of an Indian Field Hygiene Section, 9, 13
  C Sub-section, 12, 40

Hospitals
  Military
    British (in Burma) (B.M.H.)
      Maymyo, 8, 12, 28, 31
      Mingaladon, 8, 11, 12, 28, 31, 41
      R.A.F. Hospital,
        Lashio, 28, 31
        Namsang, 28, 31
      R.A.F. Sections, 31
    British (in India) (B.M.H.). Shillong, 334, 584
    Burmese (Bur.M.H.)
      Mandalay, 8, 12, 28, 31
      Maymyo, 8, 12, 28, 31
      Meiktila, 8, 12, 28, 31
      Mergui, 13
      Moulmein, 31, 33, 44
      Taunggyi, 10, 13, 28, 31
      Tavoy, 13, 44
      Thayetmyo, 28, 31
    Chinese Military Hospital, Mandalay, 68
    Indian (I.M.H. and C.M.H.)
      Chittagong, 119
      Comilla, 119
      Dacca, 119
      Dibrugarh, 192, 333, 584
      Digboi, 192, 333, 584
      Neamati, 333
      Panitola, 192, 206, 333
      Shillong, 92, 334, 584
      Silchar, 584
      Sookerating, 333
      Tezpur, 92, 334
    Detention Hospitals
      Patenga, 119
      Rangoon, 9, 12, 28, 31, 42
  General Hospitals
    British (B.G.H.)
      14. 284, 326, 333, 334, 387, 527, 560, 572, 694, 695
      17. 335, 387, 528

INDEX

21. 189, 388, 528
38. 284, 285, 327, 333, 386, 526, 561, 572, 588, 595, 650, 695
47. 175, 387, 528, 678
80. 176, 189

Burmese (Bur. G.H.)
1. 12, 28, 31, 66, 67, 71, 85, 86, 89, 365, 526
2. 41, 42, 43, 61, 65, 66, 71, 83, 86, 87, 88, 89, 90
3. 44, 45, 67, 71, 86, 91, 92
4. 49, 66, 68, 71, 84, 86
5. 67, 68, 71
6. 67, 71, 84, 85, 87
7. 69, 71, 86, 92
8. 45, 67, 68, 71, 86, 92

East African (E.A.G.H.)
150. 373, 387, 527, 560, 586

East African Hospital Sections
102. 600
105. 335
111. 373, 375, 413, 581, 593, 600
112. 373, 374, 375, 600
113. 373, 375
115. 527, 586

West African (W.A.G.H.)
40. 189, 507
46. 335, 387, 388, 507, 528
49. 335, 387, 388, 527
152. 388, 519, 520, 526, 586
153. 507

Indian (I.G.H.)
19. 326
24 (C.), 528
28 (C.), 524, 527
37 (C.), 388
39 (C.), 175, 176, 387, 528
41 (C.), 11, 28, 31, 45, 66, 68, 71, 86, 175, 261, 262, 307, 308, 315, 317, 323, 333, 334, 358, 386, 408, 526, 572, 581, 593, 598, 599
42 (I.T.), 327, 388, 528
43 (I.T.), 175, 333, 334, 387, 526, 584
44 (C.), 175, 192, 333, 386, 526, 584
45 (C.), 175, 333, 386, 526
48 (C.), 333
49 (C.), 175, 333, 386, 526, 572, 581, 588, 593, 595, 597, 599
51 (C.), 175, 326, 387, 528, 569, 570, 571, 586
52 (C.), 92, 171, 175, 330, 334, 387, 528, 572, 595, 598
53 (C.), 175, 253, 267, 269, 270, 271, 277, 284, 285, 315, 326, 333, 386, 526, 572
56 (C.), 121, 144, 171, 175, 335, 373, 387, 527, 586
58 (I.T.), 11, 335, 387, 527, 561, 572, 588, 595, 597, 598, 695
59 (I.T.), 11, 28, 44, 67, 71, 92, 175, 284, 315, 333, 334, 386, 526, 584
60 (I.T.), 9, 10, 13, 28, 31, 45, 68, 71, 87, 91, 92
62 (C.), 175, 335, 387, 528
63 (I.T.), 175, 335, 387, 528
66 (C.), 92, 161, 175, 260, 284, 300, 333, 386, 526, 584
67 (C.), 175, 387, 528
68 (C.), 120, 121, 144, 171, 175, 330, 335, 373, 387, 507, 527, 586, 659
69 (C.), 176, 388, 528
71 (C.), 387
72 (C.), 118, 121, 144, 175, 335, 387, 507, 527, 586
74 (C.), 128, 175, 330, 334, 528, 586, 695
75 (C.), 175, 388, 528
76 (I.T.), 176, 335, 387, 528
77 (I.T.), 144, 175, 176, 335, 387, 528
79 (I.T.), 315, 317, 333, 334, 387, 528, 586
82 (C.), 175, 335, 373, 387, 527, 529, 586
83 (C.), 176, 388, 528
84 (C.), 176, 334, 388, 528
86 (C.), 334, 387, 388, 528
87 (I.T. later C.), 315, 317, 334, 386, 388, 526, 528, 584
88 (C.), 315, 317, 334, 375, 386, 413, 425, 524, 526, 584, 588, 594, 595, 597
89 (C.), 258, 315, 317, 318, 334, 373, 386, 525, 526, 584
91 (C.), 191, 334, 387, 528, 572, 588, 595, 598
92 (C.), 120, 175, 334, 387, 528, 586, 695
93 (C.), 526, 573
94 (C.), 526, 584
95 (C.), 524, 527, 560
96 (I.T.), 528, 586
119 (C.), 176, 528
124 (C.), 175, 334, 387, 528, 586
125 (C.), 167, 170, 176, 335, 387, 519, 524, 527, 560

Indian Base General Hospitals (I.B.G.H.)
1 (B.T.), 696
2 (I.T.), 696
6 (I.T.), 696
7 (I.T.), 696
8 (I.T.), 696
9 (B.T.), 528, 697
41 (I.T.), 528
42 (I.T.), 528
127 (B.T.), 697
128 (B.T.), 697
129 (I.T.), 696
130 (I.T.), 696
131 (I.T.), 696
133 (B.T.), 528, 697
136 (I.T.), 696
137 (C.), 697
138 (I.T.), 387, 528, 696
139 (B.T.), 387, 528, 697

Laboratories
Maymyo, 8, 12, 31, 71, 87
Mingaladon, 31
Taunggyi, 31

Laboratories—cont.
  Toungoo, 31
  Vaccine and Sera, Rangoon, 49, 67
  Field, Burmese
    1. 71
    2. 71
    3. 67, 71
  Field, Indian
    3. 71
    9. 573, 581, 590, 597
    22. 573
    23. 581, 590, 597
    25. 323, 584
    26. 569, 570, 586
    27. 373, 586
    28. 572
    30. 316, 584
    31. 584
    32. 586
    33. 572
    36. 118, 584, 590, 597
    41. 586
    42. 584
    46. 590, 597
    50. 572, 590, 597
    52. 584
    53. 584
    54. 586
    55. 572, 590, 597
    57. 584
  Malaria
    1 Mal. Fd. Lab. (Ind.), 581, 593, 599, 641

Malaria Forward Treatment Units (M.F.T.U.) and Centres (M.F.T.C.)
  11 East African M.F.T.C., 573
  15 East African M.F.T.C., 376, 526, 573
  1 (Ind.) M.F.T.U., 336, 387, 519, 520, 527, 557, 577
  2 (Ind.) M.F.T.U., 336, 386
  3 (Ind.) M.F.T.U., 336, 386, 527
  4 (Ind.) M.F.T.U., 336, 380, 387, 413, 414, 527, 560, 563, 574, 588, 595
  5 (Ind.) M.F.T.U., 285, 336, 386, 526, 595
  6 (Ind.) M.F.T.U., 285, 336, 386, 526, 560, 573, 581, 588, 595
  7 (Ind.) M.F.T.U., 283, 285, 286, 336, 360, 362, 363, 364, 377, 378, 386, 409, 414, 527, 575, 582, 588, 595
  8 (Ind.) M.F.T.U., 277, 283, 285, 286, 327, 336, 378, 379, 386, 560, 575, 581, 588, 595
  9 (Ind.) M.F.T.U., 326, 336, 387, 413, 414, 449, 527, 560, 561, 565, 574, 583, 588, 595
  10 (Ind.) M.F.T.U., 326, 336, 386, 407, 408, 414, 527, 561, 573, 588, 594, 595
  11 (Ind.) M.F.T.U., 326, 336, 387, 527, 560, 564, 573, 582, 588, 595
  12 (Ind.) M.F.T.U., 326, 336, 387, 524, 527, 560
  13 (Ind.) M.F.T.U., 336, 386, 573, 581, 588, 590, 595, 597
  14 (Ind.) M.F.T.U., 336, 386, 526
  15 (Ind.) M.F.T.U., 336, 387, 461, 462, 527, 588, 595, 628, 629, 630
  16 (Ind.) M.F.T.U., 336, 386, 413, 574, 581, 588, 595

Maxillo-Facial Surgical Units (M.F.S.U.)
  3 (Ind.), 590, 695

Medical Centres, Army, Corps and Divisional
  Fourteenth Army
    Shwebo, 525
    Meiktila, 559, 560, 561, 563, 564
  IV Corps
    Taukkyan, 413
    Kan, 413
    Myitche, 402, 403, 414, 449, 450
    Sinthe, 414, 443, 449, 450, 561
    Toungoo, 560, 564
  XXXIII Corps
    Kalemyo, 364
    Inbaung, 378, 379, 402, 403, 407, 704
    Shwebo, 402, 403, 405, 407, 414, 444, 561
    Sadaung, 402, 403, 409, 414, 446, 447, 450
    Myitche, 554, 560, 561
    Magwe, 560, 561
  5th Division, Tiddim, 360, 377, 378
  20th Division
    Budalin, 407
    Allagappa, 446, 450, 690

Mobile Neuro-Surgical Units (M.N.S.U.)
  2 (Br.), 284, 581, 590, 597, 690, 694
  3 (Br.), 690, 694, 702

Mobile Surgical Units (M.S.U.) (Indian)
  4. 254, 257, 263, 316, 401, 402, 575, 582, 589, 596
  5. 316, 358, 359, 360, 362, 364, 398, 399, 448, 449, 552, 575, 582, 589, 596
  6. 109, 110, 114, 115, 116, 117, 128, 166, 479, 481, 482, 484, 485, 486, 487, 493, 494, 495, 497, 556, 557, 577
  7. 114, 115, 116, 117, 128, 141, 145, 147, 148, 158, 161, 166, 172, 502, 581, 590, 596
  8. 141, 142, 145, 172, 443, 444, 479, 574, 590, 596
  9. 153, 258, 259, 312, 316, 350, 398, 399, 409, 448, 551, 569, 570, 571, 575, 582, 590, 596
  10. 166, 167, 254, 255, 256, 258, 313, 314, 315, 316, 405, 407, 446, 447, 554, 555, 556, 583, 584, 590, 596, 690
  11. 166, 167, 500, 502, 556, 558, 577,
  12. 144, 145, 153, 155, 173, 479, 481, 482, 483, 484, 485, 490, 491, 492, 496
  13. 159, 160, 161, 461, 462, 465, 468, 469, 471, 472, 581, 590, 597
  14. 276, 281, 282, 284, 286, 293, 294, 347, 373, 374, 449, 574, 583, 590, 597

INDEX

15. 148, 158, 461, 462, 479, 504, 554, 573, 575, 583, 590, 597, 690
16. 109
19. 583, 590, 597

40. (East African Field Surgical Unit (F.S.U.)), 375, 573
Red Cross F.S.U., 600

Mobile Ophthalmic Units (M.O.U.) (Indian)

2. 71
4. 586
5. 316, 573, 581, 590, 597
8. 585
9. 572
10. 586
11. 573, 581, 590, 597
15. 586
16. 569, 570, 571, 572, 590, 597

Mobile X-ray Units (Mob. X-ray Unit) (Indian)

3. 254, 316, 574, 583, 590, 597
6. 575, 590, 597
8. 574, 581, 590, 597
10. 71, 258, 259, 315, 316, 575, 591, 597
11. 262, 316, 575, 581, 591, 597
14. 316, 574
15. 118, 145, 172, 573, 581, 591
16. 115, 120, 128, 145, 172, 577
25. 583
28. 585
32. 585
37. 585
39. 587
48. 572, 591, 598
50. 585
56. 587
57. 572
59. 587
61. 585
66. 570
69. 598
70. 598
72. 587
76. 585
77. 587
78. 587
79. 573, 582, 591, 598
80. 145, 172
81. 145, 172, 577
82. 286, 360, 362, 363, 364, 575, 582, 591, 598
85. 586, 591, 598
93. 573, 591, 598
94. 573, 591, 598

X-ray Servicing Units (Indian)

89. 585
90. 586, 591, 598
91. 573, 581

Motor Ambulance Sections (M.A.S.)

Burmese, 1. 32
East African (2 M.A.C.), 373, 374
Indian
8. 13, 70
20. 115, 128, 147, 158
21. 45, 62, 65, 71
22. 32, 62, 63, 65, 70, 263
29. 261
35. 115, 117, 128
37. 318
44. 318
45. 147
48. 318
53. 166
59. 277
60. 554
61. 277, 286, 361, 377, 554
67. 318
201. 593, 600
202. 593, 600

Psychiatric Centres

1. 593
2. 593

Ships: R.N., R.I.N.; Hospital Ships and Carriers; River Steamers; Creek Steamers; Flats and the Like used for the Evacuation of Casualties.

Agni, 523, 705
Aila, 329
Amarapoora, 705, 711
Assam, 90
Badora, 329, 490, 491, 523, 705
Bevra, 329
Devonshire, 557
Eoro, 71
Fano, 45, 71
Folkestone, 117
Heinrich Jensen, 32
Kalaw, 45, 71
Karapara, 481, 482, 523, 705, 711
Karoa, 523, 705, 711
Kite, 329
Jumna, 484
Lady Innes, 71
Lark, 329, 330
Lali, 523, 705
Mallard, 329
Melchior Trueb, 523, 705
Mekla, 329
Mysore. 43, 44, 49, 61, 62, 71, 91
Nalchera. 329, 490, 491, 523, 705
Narbada, 481, 482, 483, 484
Neuralia, 43
Ophir, 523, 705
Pennar, 115, 116, 117, 128, 145, 173
Siam, 49, 68, 86
Swift, 329
Vanu, 523, 705
Vasna, 500, 523, 705
Wu Such, 172, 483, 487, 488, 523, 705

Staging Camps (Indian)
1-8 inclusive, 316

Staging Sections
Burmese
  1. 28, 32, 71
  2. 28, 32, 49, 71, 86
British
  2. 65, 67, 68, 71, 81, 89
Indian
  3 (C.), 315, 316, 574, 582, 591, 598
  14 (C.), 573, 581
  16. 66, 71, 90, 254
  24 (I.T.), 585
  26 (I.T.), 585
  28 (I.T.), 254, 257, 315, 316, 585
  31. 71, 507
  32 (C.), 587
  34 (C.), 573, 581
  36 (C.), 254, 255, 256, 315, 316, 318, 585
  37 (C.), 145, 172, 577
  40 (C.), 90, 585
  41 (C.), 585
  42 (C.), 145, 148, 154, 172
  43 (C.), 109, 573, 591, 598
  44. 109, 113, 115, 116, 128
  46 (C.), 109, 110, 114, 115, 128, 145, 148, 167, 172
  50 (C.), 115, 128, 145, 165, 172
  51 (C.), 254, 256, 316, 318, 572
  55 (C.), 587
  57 (C.), 585
  58 (C.), 585
  59 (C.), 587
  60 (C.), 585
  61 (C.), 572, 591, 598
  62 (C.), 585
  63 (C.), 587
  64 (C.), 585
  67 (C.), 285, 286, 361, 444, 575, 583, 591, 598
  68 (C.), 585, 591, 598
  69 (C.), 585, 591, 598
  70 (C.), 509, 581, 585, 591, 598
  71 (C.), 587
  72 (C.), 585
  73 (C.), 585
  74 (C.), 573, 592, 598
  75 (C.), 185, 286, 361, 461, 581, 592, 598
  76 (C.), 285, 286, 374, 399, 407, 575, 583, 592, 598
  77 (C.), 585
  78 (C.), 284, 285, 296, 300, 585
  79 (C.), 587, 592, 598
  80 (C.), 587
  81. 167
  82 (C.), 587, 592, 599
  83 (C.), 573, 581
  84 (C.), 587
  86 (C.), 585
  87 (C.), 461, 592, 599
  88 (C.), 573
  89 (C.), 574, 581, 592, 599
  90 (C.), 573, 592, 599

Subsidiary Spectacle Centres (Indian)
  2. 597
  6. 581, 585, 590

Transfusion Units: Base, Field and Storage
Army Blood Supply Depot, Bristol (A.B.S.D.), 652, 655, 658, 662, 668
Base Transfusion Units (B.T.U.)
  1. 650
  2. (Br.), 650, 651, 652, 655, 658, 659, 660, 663, 666, 667, 669, 670
  3. (Br.), 650, 651, 652, 658, 660, 662, 663, 667, 669, 673
Advanced Base Transfusion Units (Indian)
  1. 521, 661, 667, 673, 674, 675
  2. 296, 598, 661, 663, 664, 667, 675
  3. 573, 591, 674
Field Transfusion Units (F.T.U.) (British)
  2. 263, 316, 320, 446, 447, 521, 575, 582, 591, 598, 650, 652, 658, 663, 667, 668, 674
  5. 286, 295, 316, 320, 573, 582, 591, 598, 650, 652, 661, 663, 667, 668, 674
  8. 115, 116, 117, 128, 148, 158, 490, 650, 652, 658, 659, 660, 665, 674
  22. 652, 668
  27. 159, 160, 161, 373, 374, 375, 398, 408, 575, 583, 591, 650, 663, 666, 668
  28. 145, 153, 155, 166, 167, 173, 500, 556, 557, 558, 577, 650, 652, 661, 663, 664, 665, 666, 667, 674
  32. 316, 574, 583, 591, 598, 663, 666, 667, 674
  38. 569, 570, 581, 591, 598, 668, 674
  39. 577, 668, 674
  40. 668, 674
Blood Storage Units (Indian)
  1 and 2. 660
American Field Service Units (A.F.S.), 98, 256, 285, 316, 350, 359, 361, 373, 374, 379, 408, 554, 593, 600
Friends Ambulance Unit (F.A.U.), 86, 89, 98
Red Cross Detachment, 569, 570
R.A.F. No. 7 Casualty Evacuation Unit, 408
R.A.F. Mobile Hospital, 524
Seagrave Hospital Unit, 86, 98
U.S. 60 Mobile Surgical Unit, 456, 468, 469

www.ingramcontent.com/pod-product-compliance
Lightning Source LLC
Chambersburg PA
CBHW050521300426
44113CB00012B/1915